THE WILLIAM H. GASS READER

THE
WILLIAM H. GASS
READER

Alfred A. Knopf · New York · 2018

THIS IS A BORZOI BOOK
PUBLISHED BY ALFRED A. KNOPF

Published in the United States by Alfred A. Knopf,
a division of Penguin Random House LLC, New York, and in Canada
by Random House of Canada, a division of
Penguin Random House Canada Limited, Toronto.
www.aaknopf.com

Knopf, Borzoi Books, and the colophon
are registered trademarks of Penguin Random House LLC.

Owing to limitations of space, acknowledgments for permission to reprint
previously published material can be found following the text.

Library of Congress Cataloging-in-Publication Data
Names: Gass, William H., 1924–2017 author. | Gass, William H., 1924–2017 Tunnel. |
Gass, William H., 1924–2017 Middle C.
Title: The William H. Gass reader.
Other titles: Tunnel. | Middle C.
Description: New York : Alfred A. Knopf, 2018. | "This is a Borzoi Book."
Identifiers: LCCN 2017027717 | ISBN 9781101874745 (hardcover) | ISBN 9781101874752 (ebook)
Classification: LCC PS3557.A845 A6 2018 | DDC 813/.54—dc23
LC record available at https://lccn.loc.gov/2017027717

Jacket photograph by John Clark
Jacket design by Gabriele Wilson

Manufactured in the United States of America
First Edition

to

Mary Henderson Gass

savior

7

Put my eyes out: I can still see;
slam my ears shut: I can still hear,
walk without feet to where you were,
and tongueless, speak you into being.
Snap off my arms: I'll hold you hard
in my heart's longing like a fist;
halt that, my brain will do its beating,
and if you set this mind of mine aflame,
then on my blood I'll carry you away.

—RAINER MARIA RILKE, from the *Book of Pilgrimage*,
which is Book II of *The Book of Hours*, Westerwede, Sept. 18–21, 1901
Translation by William H. Gass

CONTENTS

Acknowledgments

Professor John Upsworth has done a task for me I would never undertake: he attaches an address to every piece of *The Tunnel,* so they appear in the order of their first publication. There were plenty. Some fragments simply repeat themselves, while others are rewritten to appear elsewhere amid alternations. These periodicals desire independence, and can be so read. They also enabled me to feel like a writer during the nearly thirty years of *The Tunnel,* and pertains to as well, *Cartesian Sonata, Middle C,* and, recently, *Eyes.* I also thank *Conjunctions, Harper's, The New York Review of Books, Salmagundi, Partisan Review, TriQuarterly, Esquire, Kenyon Review, Delta, The George Review, Antaeus, The Review of Contemporary Fiction,* and many others.

Some readers have helped by giving me space, subject, idea, love: my wife, daughter Catherine; literary agent Lynn Nesbit, editor Victoria Wilson.

INTRODUCTION

RETROSPECTION

D on't look back," Satchel Paige is supposed to have said; "someone may be gaining on you." Don't look back, Orpheus was advised; you may find your earlier poems better than the ones you will write tomorrow. Lot's wife looked back at Sodom and was so shaken by the sight of the Red Sea swallowing the city she became salt. Look back only if the mess you have made of your life leaves you eager to reach a future that will offer a fairer prospect. Otherwise cover your eyes before blame blinds them the way Oedipus's pin put out his. However, Paul Valéry warns us that no one "can deliberately walk away from any object without casting a backward glance to make sure he is walking away from it."

For anyone who has reached eighty-seven years, as I have, only the past is likely to have much duration; greed and regret will have eaten the present, which is at best a sliver of cake too small for its plate, while the future fears it may cease before having been. I hear it running to get here, its labored breathing like an old man—eighty-seven—on the stairs. Lust and rage, Yeats rightly said, attend one's old age.

So it is in a spirit of disobedience that I look back at what I may have done rather than toward all that remains to be encountered, coped with, perhaps yet accomplished. I say "may have done" because what one has really done is never clear and certainly never comforting. Rarely does one say, "I may have married her but only time will tell."

Your station in the literary world, whatever that might be, does not matter much if you've spent your life chasing words with Nabokov's net. That's still where the results of your life went, into the killing jar, sentenced to a verbal smother, pinned in place, a display that's initially a cause of mild indifference, and then evermore ignored.

Looking back I find it less painful to concentrate on the *kind* of thing that concerned me, rather than on the messes I made or on the few fragile triumphs I may have enjoyed. Looking back I find I fit the epitaph Howard Nemerov once wrote for himself in *Gnomes and Occasions* (1973).

> Of the Great World he knew not much,
> But his Muse let little in language escape her.
> Friends sigh and say of him, poor wretch,
> He was a good writer, on paper.

It turns out that these preoccupations, these bad habits, these quirks number at least seven, though I am sure I am ignoring the ones that really matter. They are: naming, metaphoring, jingling, preaching, theorizing, celebrating, translating.

First: naming.

Critics still write of me as if my interest in words was an aberration. Yet Adam's task has always seemed to me to be, for a writer, the central one: to name, and in that way to know. It wasn't true for Adam, for whom all names were fresher than the daisy, but it is true for us now: a name no longer merely points something out and distinguishes it in that manner from the rest of the world; every name stands for all that has been thought, felt, said, perceived, and imagined about its referent, and represents all that has been discovered during explorations of its indigenous concepts during two thousand years. And since we humans have the deplorable yet entrancing habit of naming things that do not exist, the realm of names is larger than the realm of things as much as the population of China exceeds that of New York State. This passage about naming trees comes from my first novel, *Omensetter's Luck* (New York: New American Library, 1966), and concerns my unfortunate character Henry Pimber, who will end up hanging himself from one of the branches of the trees he sings about.

> The path took Henry Pimber past the slag across the meadow creek, where his only hornbeam hardened slowly in the southern shadow of the ridge and the trees of the separating wood began in rows as the lean road in his dream began, narrowing to nothing in the blank horizon, for train rails narrow behind anybody's journey; and he named them as he passed them: elm, oak, hazel, larch, and chestnut tree, as though he might have been the fallen Adam passing them and calling out their soft familiar names, as though familiar names might make some friends for him by being spoken to the unfamiliar and unfriendly world which

he was told had been his paradise. In God's name, when was that? When had that been? For he had hated every day he'd lived. Ash, birch, maple. Every day he thought would last forever, and the night forever, and the dawn drag eternally another long and empty day to light forever; yet they sped away, the day, the night clicked past as he walked by the creek by the hornbeam tree, the elders, sorrels, cedars, and the fir; for as he named them, sounding their soft names in his lonely skull, the fire of fall was on them, and he named the days he'd lost. It was still sorrowful to die. Eternity, for them, had ended. And he would fall, when it came his time, like an unseen leaf, the bud that was the glory of his birth forgot before remembered. He named the aspen, beech, and willow, and he said aloud the locust when he saw it leafless like a battlefield. In God's name, when was that? When had that been?

I have never been able to break the denominating habit. In a relatively recent piece, "Emma Enters a Sentence of Elizabeth Bishop's," I managed to cram the names of 110 weeds into one paragraph.

Writing has almost always been difficult for me, something I had to do to remain sane, yet never satisfying in any ordinary sense, certainly never exhilarating, and never an activity that might satisfy Socrates's admonition to find a _Logos for my life,_ as I felt it surely had for the authors I admired: even Malcolm Lowry's dissolutely drunken sprees; even Hart Crane's beatings at the hands of sailors, beatings he sought out as he ultimately sought the sea; even Céline's meanness, a bitterness that ate through his heart before it got to his shoes and ate them too; even these malcontents, though nothing justified their wasted ways, their anger, their multiplication of pain, might be, by their works, somewhat saved, their sins hidden under sublime blots of printers' ink.

Number two: whoring and metaphoring.

One aspect of writing was easy, was unstoppable, and that was the flow of imagery that ran through my head like a creek in flood—no—like the babble of voices around a bar at happy hour—no—like a stream of ants toward a source of sugar—oh, no—like carp rise to a dimple of bread—oh, no—oh, no—a cloud of gnats—a giggle when tickled. An attack of bats. I could swat away six and still write eight. It was a curse disguised as a blessing. I was always looking at the world from another word. The wolf spider roams at night from field to field in search of prey, while the mantis sits still as a twig by a flower's sweetened cup until some sucker comes to nose it, and then she, the madam mantis, sups. But these facts interested me mainly because I knew people like that. I was one—a waiter—the sort of waiter who is always looking the other way. So I wanted, when I named a tree, to invoke a plant equal to every phase the plant had seen. I didn't simply want to make a tree with roots, bark, branches, trunk, twigs, nesting birds, needles, and leaves; I wanted to imagine ones that were telly poles too, bore lynch limbs, and had branches to which possums were driven by packs of unpleasant dogs; I wanted trees with doors in them, clothes trees where dress suits were hung; trees that had family histories dangling from their diagrams.

I am not observant of persons, so if I imagine someone whose skin is as smooth and pale as a grocery mushroom, it is the mushroom that did it. Among the thousands of my photographs there may be three (the fairy-tale number) that misinclude people, and even then they look like barely promising piles of rags. Recently, in an essay on François Rabelais, I wrote that while his work looked woolly, its sense was consistent, unified, pure yet iridescent, as though silk had swallowed water. That last image was a simple pun on watered silk that let me gloat a quarter of an hour before its time on the meter was up.

I am an octogenarian now and should know better, but I recently let a sentence reach print so embarrassingly bad its metaphors seemed frightened into scattered flight like quail. I meant to shame myself by reciting it to you, but I find I cannot, sparing myself, not you. Instead I'll quote something that's perhaps passable, from a story called "Order of Insects" in the collection *In the Heart of the Heart of the Country* (New York: Harper & Row, 1968). For this piece I did indeed study cockroaches, and came to admire them immensely (few humans measure up: haven't the humility, the wiles, the longevity or body armor, the moves), but it was as a metaphor made into a symbol that I wanted to use them. A housewife, who narrates the story, has begun finding dead roaches on her downstairs carpet in the morning, apparently killed by her murderously playful cat. As she inspects them she finds a beauty in their construction that imperils her opinion of her own life. She wonders what would happen if we wore our skeletons on the outside, like a costume for Halloween, and concludes this way:

> I suspect that if we were as familiar with our bones as with our skin, we'd never bury dead but shrine them in their rooms, arranged as we might like to find them on a visit; and our enemies, if we could steal their bodies from the battle sites, would be museumed as they died, the steel still eloquent in their sides, their metal hats askew, the protective toes of their shoes unworn, and friend and enemy would be so wondrously historical that in a hundred years we'd find the jaws still hung for the same speech and all the parts we spent our life with tilted as

they always were—rib cage, collar, skull—still repetitious, still defiant, angel light, still worthy of memorial and affection. After all, what does it mean to say that when our cat has bitten through the shell and put confusion in the pulp, the life goes out of them? Alas, for us, I want to cry, our bones are secret, showing last, so we must love what perishes: the muscles and the waters and the fats.

Number three: jingling.

When you are a cowed and confused kid you say to the stupid question grown-ups always ask with such condescension that you want to bruise their shins: I hope to be a fireman when I grow up. But of course you really want to be a poet. Everyone wants to be a poet. It is the beckoning inaccessible peak. How many poets have told us? At twelve I wrote awful Edgar Allan Poe, much as Poe had—jingle all the way; at fourteen I was as interminable as Walt Whitman; I extolled the groceries and made lists of buffalo hunters and Indian scouts. I did patriotism, I'm ashamed to say, and praised mothers. My God, I was even against drink. Most of all, what I wrote was bad. Not just youthful. Not just undisciplined. Bad beyond excuse. After years of futile wondering, I think I now know why. My irreverence, my hatred for authority, my distrust of tradition, my enjoyment of the comforts of middle-class life and my contempt for its philistine values, my habitual "up yours" and "in your eye" attitude, also inhibited my ability to absorb conventional poetic forms. Instead I was attracted to the urchins among them, indecorous lines and unruly stanzas. Ezra Pound, an early hero, too melodious and poetical by half much of the time, would nevertheless burst out, to my delight, with, "Damn it all! all this our South stinks peace," a sestina in praise of bloodshed and war, while at other times condemn such belligerence, as he does in *Hugh Selwyn Mauberley*'s unforgiving anger at the First World War:

> There died a myriad,
>> And of the best, among them,
>> For an old bitch gone in the teeth,
> For a botched civilization. . . .

Or when, in the same poem, he wrote that "his true Penelope was Flaubert," I was immediately moved, because Flaubert has always been my favorite hater, and I was grateful to Pound too, though absurdly, because he was the first poet I knew to use the word *fucking* in a poem. Even if they were panthers that were up to it.

I despised pop tunes, yet I imbibed their forms. When Gertrude Stein wrote: "I am Rose my eyes are blue / I am Rose and who are you? / I am Rose and when I sing / I am Rose like anything," I was perhaps more pleased than was reasonable. I practiced the limerick in secret and dallied with other cheapjack devices. My career as a poet ended in doggerel and japery. Yet I found a use to which I might put them—these dogs. For my novel *The Tunnel* (New York: Alfred A. Knopf, 1995), I invented a historian named Culp, whose subject, I meanly said, was the American Indian, and I claimed that he was energetically engaged in writing a limerickal history of the world, as well as a cycle of such rhymes that shared the same first line: "I once went to bed with a nun." I got good at it—at the limerick, I mean—and began to do to it what I couldn't do to the sonnet—torture its type.

Here are three from the Carthaginian period.

> Over the Alps on an elephant
> went Hannibal out of his element,
> for the elephant's motion
> was so like the ocean,
> he continually punic'd
> upon his best tunics,
> and his slaves had to wash off the elephant.

Earlier:

> Dido wrote to Aeneas,
> Why don't you sail by and see us,
> I'm here all alone
> with my lust and no phone,
> half dead of desire,
> my crotch quite on fire,
> which I've heard you'd put out with your penis.

Later yet:

> Dido said to Aeneas,
> Surely you're not going to leave us?
> you wouldn't flee home
> just to found Rome,
> which will fall anyway,
> so you might as well stay
> to enjoy all my sweet panaceas.

Some nuns:

> I once went to bed with a nun
> by pointing a pistol at one;
> said she, with a quaver,
> that's a good big persuader,
> but what is the point of the gun?

Lastly, my favorite:

> A nun went to bed with the pope,
> who tied her four limbs with a rope.
> It's not that, my dear,
> you have something to fear,
> but I want you quite still
> so nothing will spill
> when your holiness is filled by the pope.

The compulsive doggerel syndrome does not confine itself to dirty verses— otherwise it would not be called "compulsive"—but turns up in almost every line of my prose, in sound patterns that get pushy, even domineering. The narrator of *The Tunnel,* when a child, is caught by his father stealing pennies to play the punchboards so popular in the Depression era, and this is what happens as judgment is made:

> Low, dry, slowly formed, the pronouncement came, my father's voice full of pause and consideration, like maybe a judge's, with a kind of penal finality even in midsentence, midphrase, and unlike the rather pell-mell stridency of his customary dress-me-downs and more commonplace curse-outs, those scornful accounts of my character which always included disclaimers of responsibility for my failures, for my laziness (not a whiff in his family), my shiftiness (in contrast to the stand-up nature of the relatives around me), my myth-making, my downright lying (whose cause could not be anywhere discerned), my obstinacy too, and my prolonged stretches of pout, sulk, and preoccupied silence which I seemed to take an inordinate joy in inflicting upon my undeserving family, who had always done their level best
>
> . . . and all the rest . . .
> fed me, washed me, made sure I was dressed,

repaired what I broke, cleaned what I messed
. . . and all the rest . . .
so I could live like someone blessed,
and bow my head at God's request
. . . and all the rest . . .
but I had fouled my own sweet nest,
and cracked the hearts in their fair chests
. . . and all the rest . . .
so they would treat me, henceforth, as a guest
until such time as I went west
. . . and all the rest . . .
to seek my skuzzy fortune or confessed
my crimes, with remade mind, and soul distressed
. . . and all the rest . . .
whereupon, with sins redressed,
they might—of my presence—make the best:

charges which were rapidly related, as if memorized, and hurled headlong at my head, between my eyes, as I always thought, causing my
knees to bend a bit each time as if to duck, though ritually, a shower
of stones.

Back in the days when there were inner tubes—items none of you now
will remember—air would bubble up in the rubber like a rhyme, just before
it burst.

Number four: preaching.

I have been characterized as—accused of—sentenced to—sentences. Well,
it is easier to study the sentence than the story, and you do have to write a
lot of sentences if you want to pretend to write prose. But I have always been
equally interested in paragraphs. I like, for light reading, texts on rhetoric:
not just those of Aristotle, Cicero, and Quintilian, but also those of George
Campbell, Richard Whately, Joseph Priestley, Hugh Blair, and Thomas De
Quincey. In such works, and only in them, is the question of the form of
the paragraph as well as the shape of the phrase addressed, and the lost art of
eloquence taken seriously.

Any plowboy can become a father, Mencken famously remarked; and
"Every man, as he walks through the streets, may contrive to jot down an
independent thought, a shorthand memorandum of a great truth," De
Quincey says. "Standing on one leg you may accomplish this. The labour of
composition begins when you have to put your separate threads of thought

into a loom; to weave them into a continuous whole; to connect, to introduce them; to blow them out or expand them; to carry them to a close." Just as De Quincey carries his own paragraph to a close by carrying it to the word *close*.

So I have tended, when conceiving characters, to prefer fulminators—preachers and teachers—and allowed them to consider the misfortune, more important to me than any other, apparently: that of missing the opportunities and obligations offered you by the luck of having life. Here is one such preacher, Jethro Furber, speaking to his rural Ohio congregation in *Omensetter's Luck*.

"I ask you now to ask yourselves one simple foolish question—to say: was I born for this?—and I ask you please to face it honestly and answer yea if you can or nay if you must.

"For *this*?

"You rise in the morning, you stretch, you scratch your chest.

"For this?

"All night, while you snored, the moon burned as it burned for Jesus or for Caesar.

"You wash, you dress.

"For this?

"At breakfast there are pancakes with dollops of butter and you drip syrup on your vest.

"So it's for this.

"You lick your lips.

"Ah, then it's this.

"You slide your pants to your knees and you grunt in the jakes.

"It's for this?

"Light's leaving a star while you stare at the weeds; centipedes live in the cracks of the floor; and the sun, the Lord says, shines on good and evil equally.

"So you were meant for this? You've your eyes, your human consciousness, for this?

"Well, you're not entirely easy in your mind. The weather's been poor. There are the crops to get in, payments to make on the farm, ailing calves to tend. Friends have promised to help with the haying, but they haven't, and you've got to keep your eldest son somehow away from that bargeman's daughter—a bitch with cow's teats.

"The mind's for this?

"Wipe yourself now. Hang your pants from your shoulders. There are glaciers growing. But you wish your wife weren't so fat and given to malice, and your thoughts are angry and troubled by this.

"This?

"Very well—you can complain that I've chosen trivialities in order to embarrass you.

"Eat, sleep, love, dress—of course you were born for something better than this."

I carry this refrain on into *The Tunnel,* a novel finished thirty years later, where it turns out that men were made by their alleged creator to murder one another, and to invent the bulldozer in order to dig mass graves.

Along with hundreds of others, I was once asked by a French newspaper to state, in a word, why I wrote. I replied in a sentence suitable for a courtroom. I write to indict mankind. I suppose I could have said: I write to convict mankind, but man has already done that without my help, and, besides, I wanted the use of the pun.

So—on to number five: evidence for a theory. This is my account, the bald facts taken from Holocaust documents, of the death pit at Dubno, and my narrator of *The Tunnel*'s characteristic double-edged use of it.

We read, and therefore see before us a great mound of earth which bulldozers have gouged from the ground. . . . In front of the mound: a mile of naked strangers. In groups of twenty, like smokes, they are directed to the other side by a man with a truncheon and a whip. It will not help to ink in his face. Several men with barrows collect clothes. There are young women still with attractive breasts. There are family groups, many small children crying quietly, tears oozing from their eyes like sweat. In whispers people comfort one another. Soon, they say. Soon. No one wails and no one begs. Arms mingle with other arms like fallen limbs, lie like shawls across bony shoulders. A loose gray calm descends. It will be soon . . . soon. A grandmother coos at the infant she cuddles, her gray hair hiding all but the feet. The baby giggles when it's chucked. A father speaks earnestly to his son and points at the heavens where surely there is an explanation; it is doubtless their true destination. The color of the sky cannot be colored in. So the son is lied to right up to the last. Father does not cup his boy's wet cheeks in his hands and say, You shall die, my son, and never be remembered. The little salamander you were frightened of at first, and grew to love and buried in the garden, the long walk to school your legs learned, what shape our daily life, our short love, gave you, the meaning of your noisy harmless games, every small sensation that went to make your eager and persistent gazing will be gone; not simply the butterflies you fancied, or the bodies you yearned to see uncovered—look, there they are: the inner thighs, the nipples, pubes—or what we all might have finally gained from the toys you treasured, the dreams you peopled, but especially your scarcely budded eyes, and that rich and gentle quality of consciousness which I hoped one day would have been uniquely yours like the most subtle of flavors—the skin, the juice, the sweet pulp of a fine fruit—well, son, your possibilities, as unrealized as the erections of your penis—in a moment—soon—will be ground out like a burnt wet butt beneath a callous boot and disappear in the dirt. Only our numbers will be remembered—not that you or I died, but that there were so many of us. And that we were

. . . —orderly, quiet, dignified, brave. On the other side of the mound, where two young women and the grandmother are going now, the dead have placed themselves in neat rows across an acre-square grave. The next victims clamber awkwardly to the top of the pile where they'll be shot by a young man with a submachine gun and a cigarette. Some of the dead have not yet died. They tremble their heads and elevate their arms, and their pardons are begged as they're stepped on; however, the wounded worry only that the earth will cover their open eyes; they want to be shot again; but the bullets bring down only those above them, and for a few the weight is eventually so great it crushes their chests. . . .

Sometimes a foot slips on the blood-wet bodies, and a fat woman slides face forward down the stack when she is hit. Climbing up, there are quiet words to the wounded, and an occasional caress. From the gunman's end, of course, the mound looks like a field full of false hair. Millions die eventually, in all ways. Millions. What songs, what paintings, poems, arts of playing, were also buried with them, and in what number? who knows what inventions, notions, new discoveries, were interred, burned, drowned? what pleasures for us all bled to death on the ice of a Finnish lake? what fine loaves both baked and eaten, acres of cake; what rich emotions we might later share; how many hours of love were lost, like sand down a glass, through even the tiniest shrapnel puncture?

Of course one must count the loss of a lot of mean and silly carking too. Thousands of thieves, murderers, shylocks, con men, homos, hoboes, wastrels, peevish clerks, loan sharks, drunkards, hopheads, Don Juans, pipsqueaks, debtors, premature ejaculators, epileptics, fibbers, fanatics, friggers, bullies, cripples, fancy ladies, got their just deserts, and were hacked apart or poisoned, driven mad or raped and even sabered, or simply stood in a field and starved like wheat without water; and we shall never know how many callow effusions we were spared by a cut throat; how many slanderous tongues were severed; what sentimental love songs were choked off as though in mid-note by the rope; the number of the statues of Jesus, Mary, or the pope, whose making was prevented by an opportune blindness or the breaking of the right bones; what canvases depicting mill wheels in moonlight, cattle at dawn, children and dogs, lay unexecuted on their easels because of the gas, talent thrown out as if it were the random pissing of paint into a bedpan; so that, over all, and on sober balance, there could have been a decided gain; yet there is always the troublesome, the cowardly, midnight thought that a Milton might have been rendered mute and inglorious by an errant bullet through the womb; that some infant, who, as a precocious young man, might conceive a Sistine ceiling for the world, and humble us all with his genius, as he made us proud of our common humanity . . . well, there is always the fear that this not-yet youth has been halved like a peach; that Vermeer, Calderón, or Baudelaire, Frege or Fourier . . . could conceivably, oh yes, just might possibly . . . have . . . been . . . gently carried to his death between a pair of gray-haired arms, which, otherwise, were no longer even strong enough to disturb a clear soup.

I wrote *The Tunnel* out of the conviction that no race or nation is better than any other, and that no nation or race is worse; that the evil men do every day far outweighs the good—the goods being great art and profound knowledge scientifically obtained.

The poet who has been my unwitting companion in this enterprise, Rainer Maria Rilke, similarly wondered, as his own career grew to a close, whether mankind had justified its reign of terror with some offsetting achievements. He thought about the grandeur of cathedrals. But, really, was it enough? I quote from my translation of the Seventh Elegy:

> Wasn't it miraculous? O marvel, Angel, that we *did* it,
> we, O great one, extol our achievements,
> my breath is too short for such praise.
> Because, after all, we haven't failed to make use
> of our sphere—*ours*—these generous spaces.
> (How frightfully vast they must be,

> not to have overflowed with our feelings
> even after these thousands of years.)
> But one tower was great, wasn't it? O Angel, it was—
> even compared to you? Chartres was great—
> and music rose even higher, flew far beyond us.
> Even a woman in love, alone at night by her window . . .
> didn't she reach your knee?

That *but*—"but one tower was great, wasn't it?"—that plaintive, despairing *but*—as if anything played or painted or built or composed or inscribed—or a little love, honest for a change, and felt by another—could weigh as much as a sigh in the balance against Dubno's pit and its high pile of corpses, or any massacre, even if it is that of fish in a poisoned lake.

I have taught philosophy, in one or other of its many modes, for fifty years—Plato my honey in every one of them—yet many of those years had to pass before I began to realize that evil actually *was* ignorance—ignorance chosen and cultivated—as he and Socrates had so passionately taught; that most beliefs were bunkum, and that the removal of bad belief was as important to a mind as a cancer's excision was to the body it imperiled. To have a head full of nonsense is far worse than having a nose full of flu, and when I see the joggers at their numbing runs I wonder if they ever exercise their heads or understand what the diet of their mind does to their consciousness, their character, to the body they pray to, the salvation they seek.

Yet I had to admit, wondrous as he often was, that D. H. Lawrence was a fascist chowderhead, Eliot an anti-Semitic snob, Yeats fatuous, Blake mad, Frost a pious fake, Rilke—yes, even he—wrong more often than not, and that even Henry James . . . well . . . might have made a misstep once alighting from a carriage. But—there it was again, that *but,* that *yet*—yet Henry was great, surely, if anyone was. How did the artist escape the presumably crippling effects of his intellectual idiocies? Here I had activity number five to help me. It was theorizing. Not about truth. About error. Skepticism was my rod, my staff, my exercise, and from fixes, my escape.

> What is critical to the artist is not the fact that he has many motives (let us hope so), or that their presence should never be felt in his canvases, or found in the narrative nature of his novels, or heard amid the tumult of his dissonances. In the first place, our other aims won't lend their assistance without reward, and they will want, as we say, a piece of the action. No; the question is which of our intentions will be allowed to rule and regulate and direct the others: that is what is critical. It is

a matter of the politics of desire, or, as Plato put it when he asked this question of the moral agent: what faculty of the soul is in control of the will?

I believe [I use this word here with the greatest irony] . . . I believe that the artist's fundamental loyalty must be to form, and his energy employed in the activity of making. Every other diddly desire can find expression; every crackpot idea or local obsession, every bias and graciousness and mark of malice, may have an hour; but it must never be allowed to carry the day. If, of course, one wants to be a publicist for something; if you believe you are a philosopher first and Nietzsche second; if you think the gift of prophecy has been given you; then, by all means, write your bad poems, your insufferable fictions, enjoy the fame that easy ideas often offer, ride the flatulent winds of change, fly like the latest fad to the nearest dead tree; but do not try to count the seasons of your oblivion.

[*Finding a Form,* 1996]

Life may be a grim and grisly business, but the poet's task and challenge remains unchanged. Rilke wrote:

> Tell us, poet, what do you do?
>   —I praise.
> But the dreadful, the monstrous, and their ways,
> how do you stand them, suffer it all?
>   —I praise.
> But anonymous, featureless days,
> how, poet, can you ask them to call?
>   —I praise.
> What chance have you, in so many forms,
> under each mask, to speak a true phrase?
>   —I praise.
> And that the calm as well as the crazed
> know you like star and storm?
>   —because I praise.

["Oh sage, Dichter, was du tust?"]

Celebrating is the sixth preoccupation, then. Because to write well about anything, and it might be mayhem, is to love at least the language that you are attaching to it, and therefore to give it glory. This result can be disconcerting, and there are readers, writers, critics, who feel that such attention as the artist often gives to the awful is itself awful. Even those anonymous, featureless days should be left where they lie, like idle waste, idly discarded—unphrased.

I am sometimes accused of retreating into language, of being a good writer—on paper. It is certainly where I often send my characters—villains or whores, most of them—into a world of words. Is there happiness, fulfillment, to be had from the canvas, the stone, in the score, on the page? Nope, I wrote:

> So even if you hope to find some lasting security inside language, and believe that your powers are at their peak there, if nowhere else, despair and disappointment will dog you still; for neither you nor your weaknesses, nor the world and its villains, will have been vanquished just because now it is in syllables and sentences where they hide; since, oddly enough, while you can confront and denounce a colleague or a spouse, run from an angry dog, or jump bail and flee your country, you can't argue with an image; in as much as a badly made sentence is a judgment pronounced upon its perpetrator, and even one poor paragraph indelibly stains the soul. The unpleasant consequence of every such botch is that your life, as you register your writing, looks back at you as from a dirty mirror, and there you perceive a record of ineptitude, compromise, and failure.
>
> [*Finding a Form*]

Translating (number seven) allowed me to get close to poetry in a way my own feeble efforts would never permit, and—yes—when I had finished a poem of Rilke's I would sometimes imagine I had written it, and that his sounds were mine (as, in English, they had to be), that he was once more alive in me, in all of us who could hear him—say him—be him. I concluded my book *Reading Rilke* (1999) with this paragraph and one poem, as I shall conclude this reading and these remarks.

> The poem is thus a paradox. It is made of air. It vanishes as the things it speaks about vanish. It is made of music, like us, "the most fleeting of all" yet it is also made of meaning that's as immortal as immortal gets on our mortal earth; because the poem will return, will begin again, as spring returns: it can be said again, sung again, is our only answered prayer; the poem can be carried about more easily than a purse, and I don't have to wait, when I want it, for a violinist to get in key, it can come immediately to mind—to my mind because it is my poem as much as it is yours—because, like a song, it can be sung in many places

at once—and danced as well, because the poem becomes a condition of the body, it enlivens our bones, and they dance the orange, they dance the Hardy, the Hopkins, the Valéry, the Yeats; because the poem is a state of the soul, too (the soul we once had), and these states change as all else does, and these states mingle and conflict and grow weak or strong, and even if these verbalized moments of consciousness suggest things which are unjust or untrue when mistaken for statements, when rightly written they are real; they themselves *are* as absolutely as we achieve the Real in this unrealized life—*are*—are with a vengeance; because, oddly enough, though what has been celebrated is over, and one's own life, the life of the celebrant, may be over, the celebration is not over. The celebration goes on.

The Death of the Poet

He lay. His pillow-propped face could only stare
with pale refusal at the quiet coverlet,
now that the world and all his knowledge of it,
stripped from his senses to leave them bare,
had fallen back to an indifferent year.

Those who had seen him living could not know
how completely one he was with all that flowed;
for these: these deep valleys, each meadowed place,
these streaming waters *were* his face.

Oh, his face embraced this vast expanse,
which seeks him still and woos him yet;
now his last mask squeamishly dying there,
tender and open, has no more resistance,
than a fruit's flesh spoiling in the air.

Published in *Life Sentences*, 2012

Fifty Literary Pillars

Texts Influential to My Literary Work

I began to mull over the nature of literary influence (*mull* is not a word indicating any kind of progress) when I was considering opening *A Temple of Texts* (New York: Alfred A. Knopf, 2006) with a pamphlet that the International Writers' Center and the Washington University Library published to celebrate the center's birth in 1990. We arranged an exhibit of books and manuscript materials to accompany a list of fifty works that I was prepared to say had influenced my own work. Our aim was modest: merely to get our endeavor noticed on a busy campus. I dashed my mini-catalogue off in a few days as books called out their authors' names to me, and I could have gone on I don't know how much further. To my dismay, this list was immediately taken to be a roll call of "best books," an activity I have no sympathy for, and certainly did not apply in this case, because not all great achievements are influential, or at least not on everybody. So Proust was not there, or Dante or Goethe or Sophocles, either. Awe often effaces every other effect.

I more fully examine the concept of influence in my essay titled "Influence" in *A Temple of Texts*.

Plato's *Timaeus*

I have been teaching Plato for fifty years. I know I have sometimes bored my students, but Plato has never bored me. His dialogues are among the world's most magical texts. I remember how the *Republic* set fire to my head, and among the other dialogues it is difficult to choose a favorite, but I should say, now, that the *Timaeus* strikes me as his strangest, and perhaps his most profound—at once most mystical and mysterious, hardheaded and mathematical. Beneath the surface of this "likely story" of how the universe was formed, Plato's conception of our world, as the qualitative expression of quantitative law, runs like a river.

Aristotle's *Nicomachean Ethics*

Following my first encounter with Plato, it was hard for me to imagine an equal mind, yet Aristotle showed up shortly after to astonish me. He is, in so many ways, his teacher's opposite: secular and scientific—not soaring—as ripe with common sense as an orchard, and an unrivaled intellectual inventor. Edison's bulbs burn out, but Aristotle's creation of the treatise form, his discovery of the syllogism, his establishment of scientific method remain incandescent. Aristotle's occasional path to a false conclusion is more scenic and exhilarating than a hike in the mountains. Finally, though, it is the commonplace nobility of the *Ethics* that wins me. There is scarcely a badly reasoned or backward line in this book. Plato can sometimes be sourly scary, but Aristotle is solid, forthright, sunny. He may even be right.

Thucydides's *History of the Peloponnesian War*

Here is history seen, endured, and created at the same time. He made many a Greek great by giving them his own thoughts, his own words, by lending them the extraordinary sheen of his mind; and it is there they are reflected like shadows cast by the ghosts of their real selves, for the war need never have taken place. It takes place now, and repeatedly, in this great cool prose, in these half-fictive events passing through an ideal disillusionary mind. Hobbes's mind, Machiavelli's mind, Thucydides's mind, are minds that allow little room for romance, and they became the romantic, unrealized model for mine. If you will believe only that which you know to be true, you will trouble yourself very little with belief.

Thomas Hobbes's *Leviathan, or the Matter, Form, and Power of a Commonwealth*

Hobbes translated—magnificently—Thucydides's *History of the Peloponnesian War.* Moreover, he learned from that work how to look at the world. The first two books of the *Leviathan* are usually the only ones read, but I was equally impressed with the latter half. The book sets the biggest and best intellectual trap I know. In the first part, Hobbes argues that if you are a materialist, and do not believe in any life but this one, you must embrace an absolute sovereignty in order to establish and preserve peace. In the second half, he argues that if you are a Christian, and believe in a life everlasting, then a proper reading of Scripture will convince you to embrace an absolute sovereignty in order to achieve peace and properly obey God. The prose is unequaled in English philosophy.

Immanuel Kant's *Critique of Pure Reason*

It is, of course, a commonplace to admire this book, although it is one panel of a mighty triptych. The *Critique*'s thorny style, its difficult terminology, its original and complex thought drove me crazy when I first tried to cope with it. I wanted to blame Kant for my weakness of intellect, my inadequate background, my flabby character, my toddler's mind-set, and at college I actually threw my copy through a closed schoolroom window. (I attended school at a time when you could commit such childish things if you paid promptly for the labor and the glass. Beer bottles were often pitched out dorm windows. My breakage had to be a cut above.) The three *Critiques,* among many large things, do an important small one: they render the difference between the sort of thought and writing which is inherently and necessarily hard and the kind, like Heidegger's, which forms a soft metaphysical fog around even the easiest and most evident idea.

Ludwig Wittgenstein's *Tractatus Logico-Philosophicus*

A lightning bolt. Philosophy was not dead after all. Philosophical ambitions were not extinguished. Philosophical beauty had not fled prose. I remember that we approached this text (as we did Bertrand Russell's and Alfred North Whitehead's *Principia Mathematica*) with all the reverence due a sacred, arcane work. From the resonant and dark opening lines, *"Die Welt ist Alles, was der Fall ist,"* to its stunning conclusion, we are in the presence of logic delivered as music. How flat the translations are: How unmelodious, unmystical, unmysterious is "The world is everything that is the case." Who would want to consider seriously such a flat-earth remark? Well, a great many, apparently. Wittgenstein's project was akin to Spinoza's (who wrote his own Tractatus), and, as Spinoza's does, it puts us in the presence of the philosophical sublime. The fact that the *Tractatus*'s fundamental assumptions may be quite wrong seems almost beside the point.

Gaston Bachelard's *Poetics of Space*

La favorita. This is writing which gives me a warm feeling, like sunny sand between the toes, or like one of Bachelard's own hearth fires. Bachelard was trained as a positivist; and as an historian of science, he specialized in the alchemists. He wrote an interesting book on relativity, and in *The Philosophy of No,* he laid down a speculative history of the development of intellectual thought which is certainly in the spirit (even if it wildly surpasses it) of Auguste Comte. His interest in the persistent errors which scientists make (alchemists in particular) led him to write, in a psychoanalytic mood, his wonderful books on the four elements. *The Poetics of Space* is his first venture into phenomenology, and what an adventure it is. A famous lecturer, Bachelard was also a very gifted reader, and by "gifted," I mean he knew what a gift a great book is, and responded to each present with witty and intelligent passion. *The Poetics of Space* has the ability to reorganize one's attitude toward reality in an enormously enhancing way.

Samuel Taylor Coleridge's *Biographia Literaria*

I am not the only reader who considers the *Biographia* the greatest work of literary criticism ever—even if Coleridge plagiarizes from the German idealists. I was lucky enough to study it under the gentle and wise guidance of Professor M. H. Abrams. The seminar was built on one directive: we would not only read the *Biographia* but would (by sharing and parceling out the labor) read every book it quotes from, mentions, or alludes to. The result was, in miniature, a university education. In researching my papers for the course, I also learned never to rely on secondary sources, but to trust only primary ones—a teaching that leads directly to this ideal: write so as to become primary.

Paul Valéry's *Eupalinos, ou L'Architecte*

The *Eupalinos* is a dialogue, but it is my favorite essay, and, in the William McCausland Stewart translation, it seems to me to be one of the supreme works of English prose. Valéry had a breathtaking mind, and the quality of his thought was like the quality of his poetry, where nuance was a thing in itself. Culture is a matter of considered and consistent choice, and high culture is concerned with estimations of quality. No writer I know, writing on any subject, demonstrates such a perfect power of discrimination. Here, writing on architecture, Valéry imitates a Platonic dialogue, and without in any way aping the master, he certainly rivals him. Thucydides, writing about the plague in Athens and the revolution in Corcyra, can make your hair stand on end. Valéry, writing about the mysteries of making *anything*, can cause you to lose your breath, or your hair, too, if it has already risen.

Sir Thomas Malory's *Le Morte d'Arthur*

What a debt I think I owe this transcendental fable! Although I had passed out of third grade, I was still a lazy, bored, slow, and inaccurate reader. I disliked school, did sums with all the enthusiasm I would later summon up to clean latrines, and lied a lot to entertain myself. Then at some point in fourth grade, while still floundering in school, I found myself inside some doubtless cleaned-up and dumbed-down version of Malory. Even youthanized, it was faithful enough. And I was lost. The ordinary world was ordinary in a way it had never been before—ordinary to the googolplex power. I knew now what was real, and I would never forget it. I began to eat books like an alien worm. From three a week, I rose to one a day. The page was peace. The page was purity. And, as I would begin to realize, some pages were perfection.

Sir Thomas Browne's *Hydriotaphia: Urne Buriall, or a Discourse of the Sepulchrall Urnes Lately Found in Norfolk*

The full list, the final role of honor, would include all the great Elizabethan and Jacobean prose writers: Traherne, Milton, Donne, Hobbes, Taylor, Burton, the translators of the King James Bible, and, of course, Browne, or "Sir Style," as I call him. I would later find them all splendidly discussed in a single chapter of George Saintsbury's *A History of English Prose Rhythm,* the chapter he called "The Triumph of the Ornate Style." Of course, there are great plain styles. Of course, positivists, puritans, democrats, levelers, Luddites, utilitarians, pragmatists, and pushy progressives have something to say for themselves. There are indeed several musicians after Handel and Bach. And there are other mountains beyond Nanga Parbat. But. But the great outburst of English poetry in Shakespeare, in Jonson, in Marlowe, and so on, was paralleled by an equally great outburst of prose, a prose, moreover, not yet astoop to fictional entertainments, but interested, as Montaigne was, in the drama and the dance of ideas. And they had one great obsession: death, for death came early in those days. First light was so often final glimmer. Sir Style is a skeptic; Sir Style is a stroller; Sir Style takes his time; Sir Style broods, no hen more overworked than he; Sir Style makes literary periods as normal folk make water; Sir Style ascends the language as if it were a staircase of nouns; Sir Style would do a whole lot better than this.

Laurence Sterne's *Tristram Shandy*

I think all my choices are obvious. Only what is left out of the temple is not justifiable. (Why weren't you influenced by Proust? Well, that was probably a good thing.) We always speak of Sterne as ahead of his time, but what was it about Sterne that made him permanently avant-garde? His honesty about artifice? "Leave we then the breeches in the taylor's hands. . . ." Henry James once said, in his snobbiest manner, "I see all round Flaubert." That's what Sterne did. Fiction had scarcely gotten started, and, already, Sterne saw all round it—as well as through. For example, this: "A cow broke in (tomorrow morning) to my Uncle Toby's fortifications. . . ."

Virginia Woolf's Diaries

Pepys, everybody knows about. The lover of diaries, however, is familiar with them all, from André Gide's famous work to Emanuel Carnevali's more obscure entries. Actually, Gide kept a journal, while Cesare Pavese kept a diary, and the difference between a notebook of the sort Henry James tended, which was his workshop, the record of activities that makes up the diary, and the kind of "thought-clock" the journal resembles is an interesting one. Loneliness is the diary keeper's lover. It is not narcissism that takes them to their desk every day. And who "keeps" whom, after all? The diary is demanding; it imposes its routine; it must be "chored" the way one must milk a cow; and it alters your attitude toward life, which is lived, finally, only in order that it may make its way to the private page. It is a pity Virginia's could not have held her head above water a while longer.

Ford Madox Ford's *Parade's End* (the Tietjens tetralogy)

Ford is, for me, a much-maligned, misunderstood, and heroic figure, the author of at least three great works: the *Fifth Queen* trilogy, the masterful epistemological novel *The Good Soldier,* and his Tietjens books. He was a wonderful memoirist, too, a great editor, and a true friend of literature, "a man mad," as he said, "about writing." About fifteen years ago [now nearer thirty], talking to a group of literature students at the University of Leeds, I asked them their opinion of Ford, and fewer than a handful had ever heard of him. No wonder the empire fell into decay. Largely through the efforts of Sondra Stang, Ford's reputation has grown since then, but he is still not accorded the position he deserves. *Some Do Not . . . ,* the first volume of the four, was written in 1924, the year of my birth. I still think it is the most beautiful love story in our language. It is a modern love story, with this astonishing difference: everything is treated with profound irony except the love itself.

William Shakespeare's *Antony and Cleopatra*

There are many famous works, and a few famous writers, who are not among my fifty. It is not just some reasonable limit that has kept them off. My list is supposed to represent works which, I feel, have changed me as a writer in some important way, and while making such a list may be an act of egotism, it does not possess the arrogance of a roll call of Great Books. That is not to suggest that I do not believe in great books, for I believe in very little else—some music, some paintings, a few buildings, perhaps. Great books are great for innumerable reasons, but one of them surely is that they will remain faithful to the values they are made of. And it happens that if an author is too obviously great, the reader can never have the delirious excitement of discovering him or hearing his special note strike, because it has been broadcast in bits and pieces over a whole life. This is so often true concerning Shakespeare. Our society disarms genius. Beethoven is played to death, van Gogh tacked to closet doors, Burns's songs sung by drunks, sublime lines mouthed by movie stars. This play by the Bard, whom immortality has murdered, his texts chewed by actors dressed in business suits, his corpse cut to pieces by directors and the remains dragged by popularity through the street, rose for me in a manner more vibrant than life. The language is yet a cut above the most high, the imagery so flamboyant sometimes as to establish a new style. I became properly fatuous in his presence. I said: "Boy, you sure can write."

Ben Jonson's *The Alchemist*

A man after my own heart. He is capable of the simplest lyrical stroke, as bold and direct as a line by Matisse, but he can be complex in a manner that could cast Nabokov in the shade. Like Rabelais and Joyce, he is a master excrementalist. *The Alchemist* (and the belly is the best one) is no stroll through the park. It is an arduous, even odious, climb. Shakespeare may have been smarter, but he did not know as much. Nowadays, knowing a lot is often thought to be a part of the equipment of a bore, a handicap to the personality, an office impediment. Jonson also makes marvelous lists, and I love lists. His are not as supreme, perhaps, as Rabelais's, but they are quite calorific. The true alchemists do not change lead into gold; they change the world into words.

James Joyce's *Ulysses*

When I was in high school, I tried to smuggle a copy of this once-banned and still "dirty" book past the resolutely puritanical eyes of my hometown librarian. No luck. I'd have placed a curse upon her ovaries had I known where ovaries were. But everything works out for the best, as Dr. Pangloss says. I was then too young for *Ulysses*. When I did read it, I was not struck dumb, as I should have been. Rather, I was flung into a fit of imitation. Like Dante, like Milton, like Proust, like Faulkner, like García Márquez, Joyce is too towering to imitate. It would be years before I could escape his grasp, and I still avoid *Ulysses* when I am working. The only words that dare follow "Stately, plump Buck Mulligan . . ." are Joyce's.

James Joyce's *Finnegans Wake*

. . . Yet no song the sirens sang is as beguiling as the song Anna Livia Plurabelle sings while she rubs her wash clean on a rock by the Liffey. We literary snobs once dressed in *FW* as if it were the latest and most expensive and most extreme of fashion. Like *Tristram Shandy*, it is a permanent member of the avant-garde, and immune to popularization. Graduate students will be forced to corrupt it, of course, and its music will fall into footnotes.

Joyce was recorded reading portions of this work, and his performance is unforgettable and wholly convincing. Passages linger in the memory. The conclusion of the *Wake* is among the most poignant I know, and the idea that it is a cold labor of anal obsessiveness is all-the-way-round wrong. *FW* is the high-water mark of modernism, and not to have been fundamentally influenced by it as a writer is not to have lived in your time. Not to live in your time is a serious moral flaw. Although not to object to our time is an equal lapse in values and perception.

Flann O'Brien's *At Swim-Two-Birds*

My only problem with Brian O'Nolan (two of whose pseudonyms are Flann O'Brien and Myles na Gopaleen) is that he seemed too satisfied to be Irish to be sane. You ought to live in your time, I thought, but try never to be what you have been. Like Joyce and Beckett, O'Brien was an accomplished linguist; like them, too, a darkly comic writer, and a master of pastiche. A cult is all, so far, that he has been able to gather to him, which is too bad, for O'Brien is also an innovator in language. *At Swim-Two-Birds* (the name of an inn, a pub, a puddle of texts) was published in 1939, the year *FW* appeared, and World War II broke out, which makes that date ideal as modernism's triumph and its knell. If you are caught in O'Brien's web of words, you will not be sucked dry and left a hull, but incredibly enriched, filled to the bloat point, ready to pop. There aren't many funnier books. He was also a fine journalist and not a total drunk. He read contemporary literature in five languages, wrote regularly in two, and if he is uneven, he is uneven as a roller coaster is, and not rough as a rough road.

Beckett's *How It Is* and "Ping"

His name is the same as a saint's. He represents perfectly one supreme pole of the art of writing, along with Rilke, Valéry, and Flaubert. His dedication was so total, it regularly threatened his existence. Most of us compromise. That is how one gets on in life, avoids labor disputes, saves a marriage, ducks a war. Even principles get dirtied, and we have to wash them periodically like clothes. Beckett is a minimalist because he is as devoted to his ideals as a Shaker and thinks most things frivolous, or decorative, or vain. And he is no doubt right. He writes equally well in two languages: Nitty and Gritty. He is a minimalist because he compresses, and puts everything in by leaving most of it out. Joyce wished to rescue the world by getting it into his book; Beckett wishes to save our souls by purging us—impossibly—of matter. Only Borges has had a comparable influence. I have only known one other man who bore the brunt and brilliance of his art in his person, who literally "stood for" what he stood for in the best sense, and that was Ludwig Wittgenstein, the only other saint in my modest religion.

The library at Washington University has a wonderful Beckett collection. There you may actually observe (in a manuscript like "Ping" in English, "Bing" in French) the hand of the master at work—with a mind that's mathematical, musical, always skeptical, Cartesian—crossing out, writing in, encircling, fretting in the margins. When I first held "Ping" in my hands, my hands shook, not because of a reverence for relics, but because the pages were pure epiphany.

José Lezama Lima's *Paradiso*

The translation by Gregory Rabassa reads wonderfully, but we know that the jungle has been cleared, the nighttime lit, the tangles, at least some of them, straightened. If *How It Is* is one polar cap of my little literary world, *Paradiso* lies at the other: both forbidding, both formidable, both wholly formed, though so differently achieved. Beckett was as spare in person as his work. Lezama Lima was large, and wore (I believe) a wide white hat, and held forth in cafés, and put his loving fat hands on young men and blessed them with his attention. The Latin American literary boom has heard the firing of many cannons, but none sounds more loudly in my ears than *Paradiso*. Surely, with Carlos Fuentes's *Terra Nostra,* Julio Cortázar's *Hopscotch,* Gabriel García Márquez's *One Hundred Years of Solitude,* and Cabrera Infante's *Three Trapped Tigers,* it forms a fresh Andes. I shall now make a bad joke: if Sir Style is the king of the Baroque, here is the queen. Long may they live and break wind, as Pantagruel would say.

Julio Cortázar's *Hopscotch*

Of the astonishing Latin American writers, I am including only a few in my fifty, simply because only these few jarred my writing hand. But the work of Fuentes, Paz, Neruda, Carpentier, Vallejo, Rulfo, Puig, Donoso, Cabrera Infante, Sarduy, Sábato, García Márquez, Vargas Llosa, and so on, should not be in any sense skimped or neglected. These writers now own the novel. We others, who try our hand at it from time to time, we merely rent. And *Hopscotch* is one reason for the pre-eminence of the Spanish language in contemporary literature. Rich, inventive, sprawling, intelligent . . . I halt on this word, not one I should assign as a special quality to many writers. Joyce, for instance, picks up ideas the way a jackdaw steals buttons off of hanging wash—because they are bright—and he carries them back to his nest, another shiny trophy. But he does not know the inside of any of them. He knows the brutalities of theology, the beauty of its pageantry, the fearfulness of its fanaticism, but not its internal intellectual power. But so many of the great Latins do. They are smart. Many have been diplomats. They are smooth. They have seen their countries ravaged by carpetbaggers and impoverished by homegrown dictators. They are really pissed off.

Jorge Luis Borges's *Labyrinths*

Another amazing mind. Here is the consciousness of a devoted, playful, skeptical intelligence, a man made civilized by the library, as if to prove it can be done. At what a deliciously ironic remove does he observe (through words) the world. What this blind seer sees is just how little we see if fully sighted; how little there is to understand in all we think we know. But Borges is not a man for despair; that, too, is vanity. Nor is there anything new under the sun, not even a new view: that the sun is a hotheaded youth drag-racing the moon to his doom; that it is a hot rock; that it is an idea in God's mind; that it is a bundle of burning perceptions; that it is; that it is not. Borges is a fine poet, too, but he revolutionized our conception of both the story and the essay by blending and bewildering them. He will not be forgiven or forgotten for that.

Thomas Mann's *The Magic Mountain*

Lifetimes don't last long enough for us to have more than two or three vocational revelations. Perhaps I was fifteen when I first read "Disorder and Early Sorrow," but I still remember part of my emotion. I desperately wanted to be "like Mann." It was not just that I wanted to write as powerfully or as profoundly, or even that I wanted to have his art or his mind. I remember trying to understand my desire for that likeness, and it was only later that I decided what my feeling really was: I wanted to be like that story—to have that measured depth, that subtlety, that sense—yes—of its own importance, and even to be its problems, endure its theme. And later I would devour everything he wrote, especially *Death in Venice*. *Doctor Faustus* is an equally admirable novel, I think; but *The Magic Mountain* is a work I have read more often than any other novel, and one I studied carefully when young, and began to see as a complex textual world. I loved the fact that I could read its brief passages of schoolboy French. At St. Louis's yearly Book Fair (the region's most important cultural event), I found a few years back a nice copy of *Joseph in Egypt*. On the flyleaf, in Mann's hand, was a thank-you note to his St. Louis hostess. The book cost me a buck.

Franz Kafka's "A Country Doctor" and Other Stories

Kafka was for me a perfect example of "getting to the party late." By the time I arrived, I had heard of Kafka for several decades; I had read his imitators, and his critics. I had played with his angst as if it were a football. I did not expect to be impressed (something had held me from him), though impressed I was—mightily. But he would not be "an influence." Then, in the middle of Kafka—a Kafka I had begun to teach—I found "A Country Doctor," a mysterious and extraordinary prose lyric, a Kafka in a Kafka. And suddenly, all of Kafka grew more luminous and impenetrable at the same time. Kafka is my next writing project. If I can get to him. [I never did.] I don't play with his angst anymore—the game is no longer a game. He is a great letter writer, a great diarist, too.

Herman Broch's *The Sleepwalkers*

Broch may be the most neglected writer on my list, next to Flann O'Brien (over whom he would tower). I think of Elias Canetti's *Auto-da-Fé,* as well, or Robert Musil's *The Man Without Qualities,* but Canetti is a Nobel laureate now, and Musil is well known, though only from infrequent sightings, like a family ghost. An equally neglected work is Broch's own *Death of Virgil.* Certainly, his books have been translated into many languages, and he has been given the flattery of polite applause. Exiled to the United States, he won awards and received grants. Yet he has been neglected by being insufficiently singled out, his excellence hidden in the hubbub ordinariness predictably receives. *The Sleepwalkers* begins as a psychological narrative, passes through a center made of the "real" world's descriptive surface, and ends as a philosophical lyric. Each phase is masterfully done, but it is the direction of the change that is most significant. If we were to think of the traditional novel as a pane of glass, then *The Sleepwalkers* is a thrown stone, and *The Death of Virgil* its shattered window. We can no longer see out, because there is nothing to see through. Like Mann, he is a "philosophical novelist." Unlike Aldous Huxley, George Orwell, or Anatole France, he is not a novelist of ideas.

Italo Svevo's *Confessions of Zeno* (or *Zeno's Conscience* in William Weaver's marvelous recent translation)

How different German and Italian ironies are. Svevo takes the world seriously by refusing to do so; his touch with everything is light. Mann takes the world seriously in order to make something serious out of what, after all, is rather an absurd affair. His lightest touch leaves a bruise, but not one a bully's blow leaves, one the doctor's inoculation causes. My colleague Naomi Lebowitz has written wonderfully of Svevo, who called himself, on the late occasion of his fame, as she reports, a "*bambino di 64 anni.*" But when he met Joyce, he was a businessman named Ettore Schmitz, and as Ettore Schmitz he lent the impoverished Irishman money. However, when Joyce recommended *Zeno* to Ford Madox Ford and T. S. Eliot (among others of influence), he was the Svevo we know and the author also of an earlier work we didn't know, called *Senilità*—itself quite beautiful. Svevo did not take himself seriously as a literary personage, or romanticize about himself as a pursuer of the great arts. He was in the glassware business. He wrote, sufficiently, not solely, for himself. Svevo is on this list, however, because he opened up Italian literature for me. It was a world to which I had been almost totally oblivious. Dante had been my final stop. And once I had entered the country through Trieste, where one day D'Annunzio would hang his banner, I would make my way slowly and stay in many regions: in Pavese, for example, in Montale, Pratolini, Vittorini, and later in Emilio Gadda's Rome, in the Turin of Primo Levi, in the dreamlands of Italo Calvino.

Gustave Flaubert's Letters

Here I learned—and learned—and learned. My letters. I did not learn how to write. You learn that by writing. After you have read much. I learned what and how to think about writing. I learned what literary ideals were and why they were important. I became only a third-grade fanatic, but every advancement helped. I also got to understand something of my own anger by studying Flaubert's rage. I must say I trust hatred more than love. It is frequently constructive, despite the propaganda to the contrary; it is less frequently practiced by hypocrites; it is more clearly understood; it is painfully purchased and therefore often earned; and its objects sometimes even deserve their hoped-for fate. If you love the good, you have to hate evil. I cannot imagine a love so puerile and thin and weak-kneed it cannot rage. But hate killed Flaubert, I think, and it didn't do Céline many favors. If I had any advice to give a young writer (and I haven't), I would suggest an enraptured reading of these letters. One ought not to feel about women as Flaubert did—he could be coarse and brutal—but he will teach you how to treat a page. Maybe I go too far if I say that every *mot* is *juste*, but certainly every other one is.

Gustave Flaubert's *Bouvard and Pécuchet*

I had read and admired everything else by the master but this late text. I had swallowed the stories, been overwhelmed by *Bovary* and *Education*, admired even Flaubert's Oriental excesses. But I had not gotten to the great "put-down." This book is not for the faintly minded. It is a devastation, a blowup as total as the bomb, of our European pretensions to knowledge. B and P are silent film comics, almost. They Laurel and Hardy their way through wisdom, and leave it a wreck. Their sincere admiration for any subject is equivalent to the announcement of its disgrace. I had thought these things already, thought them all, but I had never found them quite so well expressed. So this work changed me through its confirmation of my prejudices. It made certain that, to this set of attitudes, I should remain not only wed but faithful.

Stendhal's *The Red and the Black*

Boston, 1943. I am about to go down to the submarine base to test out for the school there. I have come into possession of the Liveright Black and Gold edition. (What a wonderful series. I loved them all. There was Jules Romain's *The Body's Rapture*, a kooky, overwrought book, I know now, but it was sex, and it was French. There was Remy de Gourmont's *The Natural Philosophy of Love*, more sex, more French. There was Balzac's *The Physiology of Marriage*, more sex, more French. There was Stendhal's own *On Love*, ditto. There was *The Collected Works of Pierre Loüys*, double dots, double ditto. There was Alexandre Dumas's *The Journal of Madame Giovanni*, which was simply French, a disappointment. And *The Red and the Black*, like checker squares.) Anyway, I am lining up New London in my train table's sights, and scanning the novel I have bought because of the series it is in, thinking that I'm not going to like climbing a rope through all that water, and thinking that the first chapter, a description of a small town, is commonplace, ho-hum, and will I be put in a pressure chamber at sub school like a canned tomato? When, suddenly, I am suckered into Stendhal, and no longer read words (against all the rules of right reading I will later give myself), but barrel along like my own train, a runaway, holding my breath oftener and oftener, aware only of an insistently increasing tension, and it is not because I am underwater; it is because I am inside the magic of this narrative master. *The Charterhouse of Parma* would do exactly the same thing to me, except that I didn't let a sub school come between us, but covered its lengthy length as nearly in one sitting as might be managed, snacking at the edge of it as though it were on a TV tray. That sort of gluttonous read is rare, and never happens to me now, when I read, because I read to write or teach or otherwise to talk, and not because I am a reading madman about to lose his soul to the seductions of a sentence.

Colette's *Break of Day*

Books to go to bed with; books better than most breasts; books that feel like silk sheets someone has spilled crumbs on, for they are not so totally smooth as not to scratch. *Adoration* is the right word if spoken with the right accent. Colette was a heroine, too, who threw off the bribing bangles of her captors, dared to kiss other girls in public, or to appear nude (but so motionless, the tableau might not be living). Works in which the juice runs through your closing teeth. And wise, or, maybe, shrewd. Observant not as a god is, but as an adolescent looking on love, and later like a whore looking on lovelessness and age. Semiautobiographical the way one is semidressed. Never breathless as a schoolgirl, though, or like this prose, disjointed, but long and slow and generous and fine as the line of the leg. *Regarde,* she commanded. And in *Chéri,* she looked at age as it comes to those whose means of life depend on their physical attractions, or, at least, on the promises of the body. *Break of Day* is the classic menopause book. Resilient and resigned, yet rich in resolution, *Break of Day* does not translate *La Naissance du Jour* very well, when what is meant is something like the dawning of the end. American students, I have discovered to my sorrow, do not take kindly to Colette. Is it because, though they exercise their bodies, they never exercise their senses? Or because, though they know a bit about sex, they prefer not to know about sensuality?

John Donne's Poems and Sermons

"Batter my heart," he did. I grew up during the Age of Donne, the era of the New Criticism, when the metaphysical poets were brought, by T. S. Eliot and William Empson, to center stage, where they stood in front of Wordsworth and Shelley and wore outlandish conceits. It was Marvell and Donne, mainly, who set the standard. Crashaw had his thumb on the scale. I learned how admirable oxymorons were, and how to perform catachresis. We hunted ambiguities feverishly, as if they were bedbugs in the blankets. Gotcha. For all their excesses, the New Critics were generally sound about the reading of poetry, and their techniques are still standard. "The circle of bright hair about the bone," we would whisper in one another's ear while dancing, which was probably an improvement on humming along with the band, though no less absurd. Having drunk the poetry, I found the prose. And what prose! He raised rhetoric like a club of war. I must quote. How shall we be when we are angels? "The knowledge which I have by Nature, shall have no Clouds; here it hath: that which I have by Grace, shall have no reluctation, no resistance; here it hath: That which I have by Revelation, shall have no suspition, no jealousie; here it hath: sometimes it is hard to distinguish between a respiration from God, and a suggestion from the Devil. There our curiosity shall have this noble satisfaction, we shall know how the Angels know, by knowing as they know." You have to admire the punctuation. He was another Sir Style, of course, and another deeply doubting believer. Or deeply believing doubter. It depended on the poetic subject. The poet's real loyalty is to the rhyme and to the repetition of that "hath."

Friedrich Hölderlin's Hymns

I like Hölderlin best when his critics say he is mad. Whenever an artist bursts through the limits, he is said to be astigmatic, immoderate, deaf, arthritic, depressed, drunk, insane, syphilitic. Literature has many wonderful poets, each as mad as Blake. However, there are a few poets whose poetry outmodes poetry itself, the way very late Beethoven seems to transcend music and seek another realm. Mallarmé is a prime example. One might include Paul Celan. As if whatever had been done before was no longer enough, as if every old depth had dried up and shown itself shallow, as if every use of language had worn its edge round; the poet at first flutes on his instrument, until, finally, he finds a way to play backward through it, or upside down, or without using any breath, or simply by thinking through the tube, sounding the sense somewhere. The hymns and the late poems of Hölderlin, like the elegies of Rilke and the last lays of Yeats, are no longer poetry. They have eluded her grasp and that of every category. Hölderlin once said this about the death of his wife: that she had borne his children, who were popes and sultans, and that then *"Närret isch se worde, närret, närret, närret!"* ("She went mad, she did, mad, mad, mad!") Near his own end, Hölderlin wrote the poem that passes poetry like an errant bus may run through all its stops. It is the one that begins, in Richard Sieburth's English:

> In lovely blue the steeple blossoms
> With its metal roof. Around which
> Drift swallow cries, around which
> Lies most loving blue . . .

And as I read on, I, who am not a believer, said, my single sincere time, with wonder and devotion, "My God . . ."

Stéphane Mallarmé's *Un Coup de Dés*

Hölderlin had tried to live through a revolution, and felt that in poetry, too, there should be a similar upheaval. Mallarmé made quietness cover his life like a cloth—teaching in a high school, inviting a few friends in of an evening, talking and talking, quietly, in a prose pointed at poetry. In that quiet, gray, low-key, laid-back, nothing life, except for the language devoted to his love of language, he hatched a revolution that has yet to come round to its beginning. A piece of paper, where it became a page, became pure space, a space over which a divinity brooded as though it were the primeval waste. And words were not to be words. When were words in poems ever words? And a book, a book was not to be a book. Open one. Perhaps that opening exposes a great snowfield where a word, now a single dead bird, lay in the snow and sang nothing . . . sang it. I always thought it very exciting to know that there were men who looked on language and its page like that, who lived in a withinness wider than any without, who quietly blew up the Customary (Nietzsche said his books were bombs), so quietly, customers purchased the ruins to furnish their flats. Of course, it is a corrective to remember who came to take tea on Tuesdays at the schoolmaster's: nearly every important literary figure in Paris, or anyone significant who was passing through. Among the *mardistes,* talk was animated and wide open. Manet watched from a wall. Space was made in the dining room for the crowd. The cat, Lilith, sat on the sideboard. Everyone rolled their own. Odilon Redon prepared himself to collaborate on *Un Coup*. Now and then, a flirt would call. Some evenings (at the god-awful hour of 10:00 p.m.) the Pauls Verlaine and Valéry would seat themselves among young men thoroughly cowed and quieter than the furniture.

Ezra Pound's *Personae*

The power of these poems has paled. Pound was the number-one teach in the old days, and T. S. Eliot was number two. Pound told us to "make it new." He cajoled editors to print avant-garde work. He fought for the right and the good and the ideals of art. Maybe I wore Ez out. I certainly wore out Eliot. Some of one's gods grow dim, and perhaps it's because the eyes begin to weaken, or possibly it is because the idols themselves have wearied of their own tainted divinity. It is still beautiful stuff, but I am conscious now of how much pastiche is present, how deep the posturing goes. Perhaps the chaos of the *Cantos,* a work I would once have fought for like a hunting territory, cannot be saved by commentary. Anyway, when I met these poems, they were fresh, their author was brash, and I was young, and still unread.

William Butler Yeats's *The Tower*

Wouldn't we all like to grow old full of lust and rage, as Yeats did? Wouldn't we all like to have a late phase that would unlace the stays, and unwrap everything, and lay it bare for our wise, ripe, appreciative, and lascivious gaze? *The Tower* is not a volume of the late poems. Those I admire even more than the masterpieces here, but this is the book that did its worst and best with me. Poetry has been a beleaguered castle on a cliff for a long time, and my castle had four towers: Yeats, Valéry, Rilke, and Wallace Stevens. Their period produced some of the greatest lyric poetry our European culture has ever seen—perhaps its last gasp. These poets understood that poetry was a calling—and to consciousness a complete one. Yeats wanted to be a seer, and if, as it happened, there was nothing to see, he would invent it, not simply for himself but for everybody else, too. He sets Byzantium down in Sligo. Yeats invested his language with an original richness, as if every word were a suitcase he would open, rummage around in, and carefully repack, slipping a few extras in among the socks. I read him in one gulp—*The Poems of W. B. Yeats*—from end to end, and then in small bites, and finally in ruminative chews. *The Tower* became a tree, and rooted itself in me. Yeats grew old disgracefully. It is the only way to go.

Wallace Stevens's *Harmonium*

I have always believed that genius and originality should be evident almost at once and delivered like a punch—in a paragraph, a stanza, even an image. One should not have to eat the whole roast to determine it once was a cow. That's why I always liked Ford Madox Ford's "page ninety-nine test." (Wyndham Lewis also laid claim to this method.) Open the book to page ninety-nine and read, and the quality of the whole will be revealed to you. (Of course, if you do that to *Harmonium,* you will read from "Anecdote of the Prince of Peacocks," lines stamped with the poet's individuality, but not, I think, genius. Nevertheless, overleaf, you will encounter a poem entitled "A High-Toned Old Christian Woman," and all doubts will be dispelled. Although some individuality is lost, since it might—almost—have been written by Edith Sitwell—"Such tink and tank and tunk-a-tunk-tunk.") With Stevens, you will not be kept long in suspense, if you've begun at page one, as one ought. Shortly you will sense that something extraordinary is happening to the language. By page five, you are reading of "golden quirks and Paphian caricatures," and by page sixteen, you come face-to-face with the first masterpiece, "The Snow Man," which quietly begins "One must have a mind of winter," a line that does true justice to *m* and *n,* and then concludes, so characteristically:

> For the listener, who listens in the snow,
> And, nothing himself, beholds
> Nothing that is not there and the nothing that is.

Listening, our breath taken, we behold it. Later, in that same first work, we shall encounter "Sunday Morning," perhaps the pinnacle of the metapoetical—do I dare to say?

Henry James's *The Golden Bowl*

Here is the late phase, and what the late phase can do. James was born in a late phase and grew phasier all his life, like a jungle vine. By the time he was truly old, he was beyond time, and need not have marked his birthdays. *The*

Golden Bowl, the critics said, was James indulging himself, James parodying James. Critics are a dim lot. It was James being James right enough. I could have listed half a dozen of his novels (from *The Portrait of a Lady* through *The Spoils of Poynton* to *The Wings of the Dove* and *The Ambassadors*) or half a dozen of his tales, and called upon his travel work as well, so that to place only the great *Bowl* here is a bit perverse. I do so because what affected me most about Henry James lay not in some single work itself, but in his style—that wondrously supple, witty, sensuous, sensitive, circumloquatious style—and the *Bowl* is that style brought to its final and most refulgent state. Like Valéry in the realm of the mind, James was a nuancer, and believed in the art of qualification, the art of making finer and finer distinctions (an art that some have said is the special province of philosophy). And Henry James formed the phrase—the slogan—the motto—which I would carve on my coat of arms if I had one: "Try to be someone," he said, "on whom nothing is lost."

He is also supposed to have said, at the moment of his death, "So here it is at last, the distinguished thing." What he actually said, of course, was, "So here it is at last, the extinguishing thing." People will embroider.

Henry James's Notebooks

The workshop of Henry James was the third major classroom of my writer's education. Flaubert's letters were the first course, Gertrude Stein's lectures and stories made up the curriculum of the second, and James's notebooks would constitute the third. What a workshop it was. Transmutations were made there an alchemist might envy. I could see how James's fascination with gossip and social trivia was transformed into his burning moral concerns, and how these, in their turn, were refined in a manner of writing so scrupulous, so delicate, so reflective it became an indictment of the very material it had risen from, as if the odor of the roast were to blame the pig for being pork. Like Proust, James knew how to read and how to write the language of society. Like Proust, too, what he wrote was devastating. To look in this book is like looking into the master's head, into that majestic dome, in order to watch the cogs. Only these cogs don't simply go click.

William Faulkner's *The Sound and the Fury*

American literature, it is often said, has two poles: the conscience-haunted and puritanically repressed novel of "bad" manners, represented by Nathaniel Hawthorne and culminating in James, and the wild and woolly frontier baroque, pioneered by Herman Melville (whose whale ought also to be here), that triumphed in the historical hungers and, far from manifest, destinies we find in Faulkner. His name ought properly to stand here in front of a fistful of titles: *Light in August, As I Lay Dying, The Hamlet,* and so on. *The Sound and the Fury* is a little too Europeanly experimental to be ideal Faulkner. Still, it was just this bridgelike quality to which I initially responded. If he wrote in the world of Joyce, he had to be all right. However, Faulkner wrote in another world as well, in the world of the old-fashioned (as well as the newfangled) epic, and his work has that sort of sweep: it is multitudinously peopled, as foreordained as film, as rhetorical as the circuit rider or the tent-pole reformer. Faulkner's career illustrates another thought for the dark: you can take yourself seriously about only one thing at a time. When Faulkner began to take himself seriously as a thinker, his work as an artist precipitously declined.

Katherine Anne Porter's *Pale Horse, Pale Rider*

What James called "the beautiful and blessed novella" often comes in triads, possibly because a novella is roughly a third of a novel in length, so that it takes three to make a book. There is Flaubert's *Three Tales,* for instance, Stein's *Three Lives,* and Porter's *Pale Horse.* We could compose our own such trios for Chekhov, James, Joyce, Conrad, Faulkner, Colette, too, as well as a number of others. And we would hear no finer music made than here. From her first tale to her last, she was in complete command of her manner—a prose straightforward and shining as a prairie road, yet gently undulating, too. But above all, for me, it was the sharpness of her eye that caught mine, and the quiet reach of her feeling. If *Noon Wine* shook you, *Pale Horse* swooped you, and its lyricism put me to bed with a fever. Its song is matched in our fiction by what? Conrad Aiken's "Silent Snow, Secret Snow" perhaps? Or J. F. Powers's "Lions, Harts, Leaping Does"? A tough lady. She did me the honor of liking my early work. I had the manuscript of my first novel, *Omensetter's Luck,* stolen from me, and the same thief purloined an essay of mine on Katherine Anne, which he changed scarcely at all, and published under his name (Edward Greenfield Schwartz) in the *Southwest Quarterly Review.* He also swiped someone else's essay on Nathanael West. Alas, with her name, I still associate this professional plagiarizer.

Gertrude Stein's *Three Lives*

The circumstances of the blow are so often fortuitous. I read Tolstoy or Proust and say, "Of course." Greatness as advertised, like the beauty of the Alhambra or the Amalfi coast. Cervantes, certainly, no surprise. And have a helping of Dante or Boccaccio. (I tried to seduce a young lady once through the present of the *Decameron,* but that doesn't come under the principle of this collection.) There are texts, and there are times, and sometimes both are right and ring together like Easter changes. (I remember, at Wells Cathedral, the shock of such bells, whose vibrations made me sound.) I didn't read Stein until my first year in graduate school, and I was ready. No prose ever hit me harder. This was the work of the woman they called "the Mother Goose of Montparnasse"? How could you read the central story, "Melanctha," and not take everything she did seriously? I read with an excitement that made me nearly ill, and having finished the book at 1:00 a.m. (having never contemplated reading it in the first place, having been lured, suckered, seduced), I immediately began reading it again from the beginning, singing to myself, and moaning, too, because this tension had caused my stomach to hurt quite fiercely. My head also ached. I was sort of sore-eyed. Was this how it felt to have a revelation? Her prose did produce in me some of the same exhilaration that, say, the description of the Great Frost does in Virginia Woolf's *Orlando,* and some of the terrible tension I have when, in John Hawkes's *The Lime Twig,* Margaret is beaten with the wet rolled-up newspaper; but in addition it produced discovery, amazement, anger (at having been told yet more lies about values by critics and colleagues and teachers). And so, at the end, I was sick, and though hanging over the mouth of the john (where my fears were not confirmed), I knew I had found the woman my work would marry. And I would, in effect, always carry three great faces in my wallet: Virginia Woolf's, Colette's, and Gertrude Stein's. If you ask, like a cinema soldier in a movie foxhole, I will take them out and show them to you.

William Gaddis's *The Recognitions*

It sometimes happens in a writing life that you get lucky, and I have been lucky often. I think that perhaps *JR* is the greater book, but it hardly matters. *The Recognitions* was a thunderclap. It was a dull decade, the fifties, but here was a real sound. [I must have been thinking of American literature too exclusively when I wrote this, because no decade could be dull that saw both William Gaddis and Malcolm Lowry appear with major works. *Under the Volcano* should have been an entry among this fifty. Imagine it as the roof. It took me three starts to get into it; my resistance to it is now inexplicable, though I suspect I knew what I was in for. I have never read a book more personally harrowing. It is also a rare thing in modern literature: a real tragedy, with a no-account protagonist to boot. The Consul is one of the most completely realized characters in all of fiction. However, enough of this effort to make up for a shocking omission.] Okay, it was a dull decade. *The Recognitions* made a real sound. And the sixties would be the novel's best ten years. But here was Mr. Cranky to accompany Sir Style. Here was a man even madder about the general state of things than I was. Here was a man whose business was seeing through—seeing through bodies, minds, dreams, ideals—Superman was Mr. Magoo by comparison. And here was a man who immediately reminded me of another hero (they can't all be present), the Viennese culture critic Karl Kraus, because this man collected mankind's shit, too, and knew where to throw it, and knew where to aim the fan. Then, as affairs would fall out, I had the good fortune to be on the jury that awarded *JR* the National Book Award, and got a little recognition for an author who, till then, had been the idol of a clique. In time, as it also turned out, I met William Gaddis and became his friend. Thus my third rule was realized: In this business, to have the respect of those whom you respect is the only genuine reward. And that reward is quite enough.

John Hawkes's *The Lime Twig*

This novel humbled me in a number of ways. I was reading manuscripts for a magazine called *Accent,* and had in front of my prose-bleary eyes a piece called "A Horse in a London Flat." And I was in a doze. More dreariness. More pretension. When will it all end? How shall I phrase my polite rejection? Something, I don't remember what it was now, but something ten pages along woke me up, as if I had nearly fallen asleep and toppled from my chair. Perhaps it was the startle of an image or the rasp of a line. I went back to the beginning, and soon realized that I had let my eyes slide over paragraphs of astonishing prose without responding to them or recognizing their quality. That was my first humiliation. I then carried the manuscript to my fellow editors, as if I were bringing the original "good news," only to learn that they were perfectly familiar with the work of John Hawkes and admired it extravagantly. Hadn't I read *The Cannibal,* or *The Goose on the Grave?* Where had I been! What a dummy! (Though my humiliation would have been worse if I had written that rejection.)

A number of years had to erode my embarrassment before I could confess that I had not spotted him at once (as I initially pretended). What a dummy indeed. *The Lime Twig* is a beautiful and brutal book, and when it comes to the engravement of the sentence, no one now writing can match him.

Rainer Maria Rilke's *The Notebooks of Malte Laurids Brigge*

There have been books that have struck me like lightning and left me riven, permanently scarred, perhaps burned out, but picturesque; and there have been those that created complete countries with their citizens, their cows, their climate, where I could choose to live for long periods while enduring, defying, enjoying their scenery and seasons; but there have been one or two I came to love with a profounder and more enduring passion, not just because, somehow, they seemed to speak to the most intimate "me" I knew but also because they embodied what I held to be humanly highest, and were therefore made of words which revealed a powerful desire moving with the rhythmic grace of Blake's Tyger; an awareness that was pitilessly unsentimental, yet receptive as sponge; feelings that were free and undeformed and unashamed; thought that looked at all its conclusions and didn't blink; as well as an imagination that could dance on the heads of all those angels dancing on that pin. I thought that the *Notebooks* were full of writing that met that tall order. Of the books I have loved (and there are so many, many more than I could have collected here), from the electrifying alliterations of *Piers Plowman* ("Cold care and cumbrance has come to us all") to the sea-girt singing of Derek Walcott's *Omeros,* there has been none that I would have wished more fervently to have written than this intensely personal poem in prose, this profound meditation on seeing and reading—on reading what one has seen, on seeing what one has read.

Rainer Maria Rilke's *Duino Elegies*

I became a Rilke junkie. I cannot let many days pass without having a fix. The relationship cannot be rationally explained, and I no longer feel the need to. I am not a reader who reads to learn about an author, and I rarely pursue the writer into his or her privacy on account of that person's public utterance; but in Rilke's case, I did: I collected and read every word I could find, whether on or by him, and that is a whole lot of lard. He is the only writer I ever tried seriously to translate, despite his difficulty, and my foreign-language handicaps, for the truth is, I am really a monoglot. Well, I would buy Rilke's kiddie car at auction if it ever came to the block. Who, if I cried, the *Elegies* shout, would hear me among the orders of angels? But I felt I had cried long ago and often, only to be heard now by these poems. They gave me my innermost thoughts, and then they gave those thoughts an expression I could never have imagined possible for them. Furthermore, the poet who thought and wrote these things, for all his shortcomings, actually endeavored to be worthy of his work—and that effort made him, in my eyes, the most romantic of romantics. My passion for this poet was, I thought, a private one, yet I taught his work for thirty years, and even wrote a book, all the while treating his presence in my life as something I kept in a drawer. Strange. These poems also have a remarkable compositional history, and many are the result of the most exemplary inspirational storm our weather-keeping records record.

Rainer Maria Rilke's *Sonnets to Orpheus*

Written in an unheralded and unparalleled burst at the same time that he was furnishing the conclusion of the *Elegies,* these poems are also truly awesome, as my daughters, I'm afraid, would say. It is probably embarrassingly clear by now that works of art are my objects of worship, and that some of these objects are idols at best—rich, wondrous, and made of gold—yet only idols; while others are secondary saints and demons, whose malicious intent is largely playful; while still others are rather sacred, like hunks of the true cross or Biblical texts, and a few are dizzying revelations. Orpheus is the singing god, whose severed head continued its tune as, in addition to its other modes of dying, it drowned.

   And even if one of them suddenly held me against his heart (doesn't the "First Elegy" say?), I would fade in the grip of their completer existence. It is one of Rilke's doctrines, expressed most directly in his poem "The Torso of an Archaic Apollo," that works of art are often more real than we are because they embody human consciousness completely fulfilled, and at a higher pitch of excellence than we, in our skinny, overweight, immature, burned-out souls and bodies, do. Rilke's poems very often seem to me to have been written by someone superhuman.*

* All quotations throughout this book from Rilke's poetry are from William H. Gass, *Reading Rilke* (New York: Alfred A. Knopf, 2000).

I. 1

There rose a tree. O pure uprising!
O Orpheus sings! O tall tree in the ear!
And hushed all things. Yet even in the silence
a new beginning, beckoning, new bent appeared.

Creatures of silence thronged from the clear
released trees, out of their lairs and nests,
and their quiet was not the consequence
of any cunning, any fear,

but was because of listening. Growl, shriek, roar,
shrank to the size of their hearts. And where there'd been
ramshackles to shelter such sounds before—

just dens designed from their darkest desires,
with doorways whose doorposts trembled—
you built a temple in the precincts of their hearing.

Rainer Maria Rilke's Letters

We say that in some letters we see their authors come forth and reveal themselves, often quite plainly and directly, as D. H. Lawrence and Lord Byron do
in their delicious correspondence; sometimes inadvertently, as Proust does,
with his toadying and his flattery, which is as insincere as Pascal's wager; or
deviously, on tiptoe, as Henry James often does. I think in Rilke's letters we
see someone creating a persona, not hiding or revealing one. He (the person)
wishes he had the sentiments, the style, the skills, the virtues, which he (the
poet) exemplifies and champions in his work. Eventually, we can see what
began as pretense becomes truth; the person and the poet coalesce. We tend
to think of Rilke as a poet who also wrote an odd, experimental novel; but
Rilke's prose is not confined to one or a few public prose pieces. He wrote
thousands of letters. In these letters, he made his best friends, had his best
thoughts, made his best love. He is present in his letters, when in his person
he is often waving farewell as he says hello. And his letters, like his poems,
were sent to their recipients in his own calligraphically ornate and careful
hand. One has the sense, reading Rilke, that he is making even the ink.

Postscript

I originally compiled a much longer list, and pared it for the exhibition. After I had made my choices and pell-melled my notes about them, I realized that one book was missing which ought—absolutely—to have been present: Freud's *The Interpretation of Dreams,* a work, among all of his others, that made a convert of me for more than twenty years. This masterpiece I just—well, I just forgot. Let it stand for the Nothing that is not here, and the Nothing that is.

Special Collections, Olin Library, Washington University, 1991

Published in *A Temple of Texts,* 2006

ON READING TO ONESELF

I was never much of an athlete, but I was once a member of a team. Indeed, I was its star, and we were champions. I belonged to a squad of speed readers, although I was never awarded a letter for it. Still, we took on the top teams in our territory, and read as rapidly as possible every time we were challenged to a match, hoping to finish in front of our opponents: that tow-headed punk from Canton, the tomato-cheeked girl from Marietta, or that silent pair of sisters, all spectacles and squints, who looked tough as German script, and who hailed from Shaker Heights, Ohio, a region noted for its swift, mean raveners of text. We called ourselves "The Speeders." Of course. Everybody did. There were the Sharon Speeders, the Steubenville Speeders, the Sperryville Speeders, and the Niles Nouns. The Niles Nouns never won. How could they—with that name. Nouns are always at rest.

I lost a match once to a kid from a forgettable small town, but I do remember he had green teeth. And that's the way, I'm afraid, we always appeared to others: as creeps with squints, bad posture, unclean complexions, unscrubbed teeth, unremediably tousled hair. We never had dates, only memorized them; and when any real team went on the road to represent the school, we carried the socks, the Tootsie Rolls, the towels. My nemesis had a head of thin red hair like rust on a saw; he screwed a suggestive little finger into his large fungiform ears. He was made of rust, moss, and wax, and I had lost to him . . . lost . . . and the shame of that defeat still rushes to my face whenever I remember it. Nevertheless, although our team had no sweaters, we never earned a letter, and though our exploits never made the papers, I still possess a substantial gold-colored medallion on which one sunbeaming eye seems hung above a book like a spider. Both book and eye are open—wide. I take that open, streaming eye to have been a symbol and an omen.

Our reading life has its salad days, its autumnal times. At first, of course, we do it badly, scarcely keeping our balance, toddling along behind our finger, so intent on remembering what each word is supposed to mean that the sentence is no longer a path, and we arrive at its end without having gone anywhere. Thus it is with all the things we learn, for at first they passively oppose us; they lie outside us like mist or the laws of nature; we have to issue orders to our eyes, our limbs, our understanding: lift this, shift that, thumb the space bar, lean more to one side, let up on the clutch—and take it easy, or you'll strip the gears—and don't forget to modify the verb, or remember what an escudo's worth. After a while, though, we find we like standing up, riding a bike, singing *Don Giovanni,* making puff paste or puppy love, building model planes. Then we are indeed like the adolescent in our eager green enthusiasms: they are plentiful as leaves. Every page is a pasture, and we are let out to graze like hungry herds.

Do you remember the magic the word "thigh" could work on you, showing up suddenly in the middle of a passage like a whiff of cologne in a theater? I admit it: the widening of the upper thigh remains a miracle, and, honestly, many of us once read the word "thigh" as if we were exploring Africa, seeking the source of the Nile. No volume was too hefty then, no style too verbal; the weight of a big book was more comforting than Christmas candy; though you have to be lucky, strike the right text at the right time, because the special excitement which Thomas Wolfe provides, for instance, can be felt only in the teens; and when, again, will any of us possess the energy, the patience, the inner sympathy for volcanic bombast, to read—to enjoy—Carlyle?

Rereading—repeating—was automatic. Who needed the lessons taught by Gertrude Stein? I must have rushed through a pleasant little baseball book called *The Crimson Pennant* at least a dozen times, consuming a cake I had already cut into crumbs, yet that big base hit which always came when matters were most crucial was never more satisfying than on the final occasion when its hero and I ran round those bases, and shyly lifted our caps toward the crowd.

I said who needed the lessons taught by Gertrude Stein, but one of the best books for beginners remains her magical *First Reader.* Here are the opening lines of "Lesson One":

A dog said that he was going to learn to read. The other dogs said he could learn to bark but he could not learn to read. They did not know that dog, if he said he was going to learn to read, he would learn to read. He might be drowned dead in water but if he said that he was going to read he was going to learn to read.

He never was drowned in water not dead drowned and he never did learn to read. Are there any children like that. One two three. Are there any children like that. Four five six. Are there any children like that. Seven eight nine are there any children like that.

There turn out to be ten, each with a dog who says he is going to learn to read, and shortly the story gets very exciting.

Back in the days of "once upon a time," no one threatened to warm our behinds if we didn't read another Nancy Drew by Tuesday; no sour-faced virgin browbeat us with *The Blithedale Romance* or held out *The Cloister and the Hearth* like a cold plate of "it's good for you" food. We were on our own. I read Swinburne and the *Adventures of the Shadow.* I read Havelock Ellis and Tom Swift and *The Idylls of the King.* I read whatever came to hand, and what came to hand were a lot of naughty French novels, some by Émile Zola, detective stories, medical adventures, books about bees, biographies of Napoleon, and *Thus Spake Zarathustra* like a bolt of lightning. I read them all, whatever they were, with an ease that defies the goat's digestion, and with an ease which is now so easily forgotten, just as we forget the wild wobble in the wheels, or the humiliating falls we took, when we began our life on spokes. That wind I felt, when I finally stayed upright around the block, continuously reaffirmed the basic joy of cycling. It told me not merely that I was moving, but that I was moving *under my own power;* just as later, when I'd passed my driver's test, I would feel another sort of exhilaration—an intense, addictive, dangerous one—that of command: of my ability to control the energy produced by another thing or person, to direct the life contained in another creature. Yes, in those early word-drunk years, I would down a book or two a day as though they were gins. I read for adventure, excitement, to sample the exotic and the strange, for climax and resolution, to participate in otherwise unknown and forbidden passions. I forgot what it was to be *under my own power, under my own steam.* I knew that Shakespeare came after Sophocles, but I forgot that I went back and forth between them as though they were towns. In my passion for time, I forgot their geography. All books occupy the same space. Dante and Dickens: they are cheek by jowl. And although books begin their life in the world at different times, these dates rarely determine the days they begin in yours and mine. We forget simple things like that: that we are built of books. I forgot the Coke I was drinking, the chair, the chill in the air. I was, like so many adolescents, as eager to leap from my ordinary life as the salmon are to get upstream. I sought a replacement for the world. With a surreptitious lamp lit, I stayed awake to dream. I grew reckless. I read for speed.

When you read for speed you do not read recursively, looping along the line like a sewing machine, stitching something together—say the panel of a bodice to a sleeve—linking a pair of terms, the contents of a clause, closing a seam by following the internal directions of the sentence (not when you read for speed), so that the word "you" is first fastened to the word "read," and then the phrase "for speed" is attached to both in order that the entire expression can be finally fronted by a grandly capitalized "When . . ." (but not when you read for speed), while all of that, in turn, is gathered up to await the completion of the later segment which begins "you do not read recursively" (certainly not when you read for speed). You can hear how long it seems to take—this patient process—and how confusing it can become. Nor do you linger over language, repeating (not when you read for speed) some especially pleasant little passage, in the enjoyment, perhaps, of a modest rhyme (for example, the small clause "when you read for speed"), or a particularly apt turn of phrase (an image, for instance, such as the one which dealt with my difficult opponent's green teeth and thin red hair—like rust on a saw) (none of that, when you read for speed). Nor, naturally, do you move your lips as you read the word "read" or the words "moving your lips," so that the poor fellow next to you in the reading room has to watch intently to see what your lips are saying—are you asking him out? for the loan of his *Plutarch's Lives*?—and of course the poor fellow is flummoxed to find that you are moving your lips to say "moving your lips." What can that mean? The lip mover—oh, such a person is low on our skill scale. We are taught to have scorn for her, for him.

On the other hand, the speeding reader drops diagonally down across the page, on a slant like a skier; cuts across the text the way a butcher prefers to slice sausage, so that a small round can be made to yield a misleadingly larger, oval piece. The speeding reader is after the kernel, the heart, the gist. Paragraphs become a country the eye flies over looking for landmarks, reference points, airports, restrooms, passages of sex. The speeding reader guts a book the way the skillful clean fish. The gills are gone, the tail, the scales, the fins; then the fillet slides away swiftly as though fed to a seal; and only the slow reader, one whom those with green teeth chew through like furious worms; only the reader whose finger falters in front of long words, who moves the lips, who dances the text, will notice the odd crowd of images—flier, skier, butcher, seal—which have gathered to comment on the aims and activities of the speeding reader, perhaps like gossips at a wedding. To the speeding reader, this jostle of images, this crazy collision of ideas—of landing strip, kernel, heart, guts, sex—will not be felt or even recognized, because these readers are after what they regard as the inner core of meaning; it is the gist they want, the heart of the matter; they want what can equally well be said in their own, other, and always fewer words; so that the gist of this passage could be said to be: readers who read rapidly read only for the most general-ized and stereotyped significances. For them, meaning floats over the page like fluffy clouds. Cliché is forever in fashion. They read, as we say, synony-mously, seeking sameness; and, indeed, it is all the same to them if they are said in one moment to be greedy as seals, and in another moment likened to descalers of fish. They . . . you, I . . . we get the idea.

Most writing and most reading proceeds, not in terms of specific words and phrases, although specific ones must be used, but in terms of loose gen-eral sets or gatherings of synonyms. Synonymous writing is relatively easy to read, provided one doesn't drowse, because it lives in the approximate; it survives wide tolerances; its standards of relevance resemble those of a street-walker, and its pleasures are of the same kind.

If any of us read, "When Jack put his hand in the till, he got his fingers burned, so that now he's all washed up at the Bank," we might smile at this silly collision of commonplaces, but we would also "get the drift," the melody, the gist. The gist is that Jack was caught with his hand in the cookie jar and consequently was given a sack he can't put his cookies in. Well, the stupid mother cut his own throat just to get his necktie red. Jack—man—wow!—I mean, he fucked up for sure—and now he's screwed—man—like a wet place—he's been wiped up! Punctuation dissolves into dashes; it contracts, shrinks, disappears entirely. Fred did the CRIME, got CAUGHT, now feels the PAIN. These three general ideas, like cartoon balloons, drift above the surface of the sentence, and are read as easily as Al Capp.

Precise writing becomes difficult, and slow, precisely because it requires that we read it precisely—take it all in. Most of us put words on a page the way kids throw snow at a wall. Only the general white splat matters anyhow.

When I participated in them, speed-reading matches had two halves, like a game of football. The first consisted of the rapid reading itself, through which, of course, I whizzzzed, all the while making the sound of turning pages and closing covers in order to disconcert Green Teeth or the Silent Shaker Heights Sisters, who were to think I had completed my reading already. I didn't wear glasses then, but I carried a case to every match, and always dropped it at a pertinent moment, along with a few coins.

Next we were required to answer questions about what we claimed we'd covered, and quickness, here, was again essential. The questions, however, soon disclosed their biases. They had a structure, their own gist; and it became possible, after some experience, to guess what would be asked about a text almost before it had been begun. Is it "Goldilocks" we're skimming? Then what is the favorite breakfast food of the three bears? How does Goldilocks escape from the house? Why weren't the three bears at home when Goldi-locks came calling? The multiple answers we were offered also had their own tired tilt, and, like the questions, quickly gave themselves away. The favorite breakfast foods, for instance, were: (a) Quaker Oats (who, we can imagine, are paying for the prizes this year, and in this sly fashion get their name in); (b) Just Rite (written like a brand name); (c) porridge (usually misspelled); (d) sugar-coated curds and whey. No one ever wondered whether Goldilocks was suffering from sibling rivalry; why she had become a teenie trasher; or why Mother Bear's bowl of porridge was cold when Baby Bear's smaller bowl was still warm, and Just Rite. There were many other mysteries, but not for these quiz masters, who didn't even want to know the sexual significance of Cinderella's slipper, or why it had to be made of glass (the better to drink from, of course). I won my championship medal by ignoring the text entirely (it was a section from volume II of Oswald Spengler's *The Decline of the West,* the part which begins "Regard the flowers at eventide as, one after the other, they close in the setting sun . . ." but then, of course, you remember that perhaps overfamiliar passage). I skipped the questions as well, and simply encircled the gloomiest alternatives offered. Won in record time. No one's got through Spengler with such dispatch since.

What did these matches, with their quizzes for comprehension, their love of literal learning, tell me? They told me that time was money (a speed reader's dearest idea); they told me what the world wanted me to read when I read, eat when I ate, see when I saw. Like the glutton, I was to get every-thing in and out of the store in a hurry. Turnover was topmost. What the world wanted me to get was the gist, but the gist was nothing but an idea of trade—an idea so drearily uniform and emaciated that it might have mod-eled dresses.

We are expected to get on with our life, to pass over it so swiftly we needn't notice its lack of quality, the mismatch of theory with thing, the gap between program and practice. We must live as we read; listen as we live. Please: only the melody . . . shards of "golden oldies," foreplays of what's "just about out" and "all the rage," of what's "brand new." We've grown accustomed to the slum our consciousness has become. It tastes like the spit in our own mouth, not the spit from the mouth of another.

This trail of clichés, sorry commonplaces, dreary stereotypes, boring slo-gans, loud adverts and brutal simplifications, titles, trademarks, tags, *typ-iques,* our mind leaves behind like the slime of a slug—the sameness we excrete—is democratic: one stool's no better than another to the normally undiscerning eye and impatient bowel. "To be all washed up" is not a kingly expression which "over the hill" or "past his prime" must serve like a slave.

Each cliché is a varlet and a churl, but there's no master. Each one refers us, with a vague wave of its hand, to the entire unkempt class. The meaning we impute to our expressions is never fixed; our thought (and *there* is a self-important term), our thought moves aimlessly from one form of words to another, scarcely touching any, like a bee in God's garden. The fact is that Jack has had it. We all know *that*. He's run the course. And now he's been zapped. Why go on about it?

There are three other ways of reading that I'd like to recommend. They are slow, old-fashioned, not easy either, rarely practiced. They must be learned. Together with the speeder, they describe the proper way to write as well as read, and can serve as a partial emblem for the right life.

That seems unlikely, yet they apply to all our needs, our habits: thinking, seeing, eating, drinking. We can gulp our glass of wine if we please. To get the gist. And the gist is the level of alcohol in the blood, the pixilated breath one blows into the test balloon. It makes appropriate the expression "have a belt." It makes dangerous the expression "one for the road." We can toss down a text, a time of life, a love affair, that walk in the park which gets us from here to there. We can chug-a-lug them. You have, perhaps, had to travel sometime with a person whose passion was that simple: it was *getting there*. You have no doubt encountered people who impatiently wait for the payoff; they urge you to come to the point; at dinner, the early courses merely delay dessert; they don't go to the games, only bet on them; they look solely at the bottom line (that obscene phrase whose further meaning synonymous readers never notice); they are persons consumed by consequences; they want to climax without the bother of buildup or crescendo.

But we can read and walk and write and look in quite a different way. It *is* possible. I was saved from sameness by philosophy and Immanuel Kant, by Gertrude Stein and her seeming repetitions. You can't speed-read *Process and Reality* or *The Critique of Pure Reason*. You can't speed-read Wallace Stevens or Mallarmé. There is no gist, no simple translation, no key concept which will unlock these works; actually, there is no lock, no door, no wall, no room, no house, no world. . . .

One of my favorite sentences is by Gertrude Stein. It goes: "It looked like a garden, but he had hurt himself by accident." Our example is actually two sentences: "It looked like a garden" and "He had hurt himself by accident." Separately, and apart, each is a perfectly ordinary, ignorable element of proletarian prose; but when they are brought together in this unusual way, they force us to consider their real, complete, and peculiar natures. The injury, we may decide, although it looked self-inflicted, planned, kept up, was actually the result of an accident. How much better we feel when we know that Gertrude Stein's sentence has a gloss, because now we can forget it. The fellow was actually *not* trying to defraud his insurance company, although at first it looked like it.

Alas for the security of our comfort, her sentence is not equivalent to its synonymous reading—this consoling interpretation. It cannot be replaced by another. It cannot be translated without a *complete loss of its very special effect*. It was composed—this sentence—with a fine aesthetic feel for "difference," for clean and clear distinctions, for the true weight and full use of the word. If, when we say we understand something someone's said, we mean that we can rephrase the matter, put it in other words (and we frequently do mean this), then Gertrude Stein's critics may be right: you can't *understand* such a sentence; and it has no value *as a medium of exchange.*

We can attempt to understand the sentence in another way. We can point out the elements and relations which, together, produce its special effect. For instance, we can call attention to the juxtaposition of an event which normally happens in a moment (an accident) with a condition which is achieved over a long period of time (a garden); or cite the contrasts between care and carelessness, the desirable and undesirable, between appearance and reality, chance and design, which the two sentences set up; and note the pivotal shift of pronouns ("It looked . . . but he had . . ."). We might furthermore comment on the particular kind of surprise the entire sentence provides, because after reading "It looked like a garden, but . . ." we certainly expect something like "but the plants had all sprung up like weeds."

The isolation of analytical functions in the sentence is accomplished by comparing the actual sentence with its possible variations. What is the force of the phrase "by accident"? We can find out by removing it.

It looked like a garden, but he had hurt himself with a hammer.

We replace "hurt" with "injured" in order to feel the difference a little alliteration makes; what the new meter does; and to understand to what degree, exactly, "hurt" is a more intimate and warmer word, less physical in its implications, yet also benignly general and vague in a way "wounded," for instance, is not.

We can try being more specific:

It looked like a rose garden, but he had hurt himself by slipping on the ice.

We can also see, if we look, how lengthening the second sentence segment spoils the effect of the whole:

It looked like a garden, but he had nevertheless managed to hurt himself quite by accident.

The onset of the surprise must be swift; otherwise everything is ruined. Suppose we extend our example's other arm:

It looked, as well as I could make it out through the early-morning mist, like a garden, but he had hurt himself by accident.

We can make other substitutions, sometimes rather wild ones, in order to measure the distances between resemblances:

It looked like a flower box, but he had hurt himself by accident.
It looked like a Dalí, but he had hurt himself by accident.

It looked like a garden, but he had dug himself up by accident.
It looked like a garden, but he had hurt himself by post.

It is important that we keep our sentence's most "normal" form in front of us, namely: "It looked very intentional, but he had hurt himself by accident." By now, through repetition, and by dint of analysis, the sentence has lost its ability to shock or surprise, and like a religious chant has surrendered whatever meaning it might have had. On the other hand, in a month's time, out of the blue, the sentence will return to consciousness with the force of a revelation.

What we've done, in short, is to re-enact the idealized method of its conscious composition. We have made explicit the nature of its verbal choices by examining some of those which might have been made instead, as if we were translating English into English.

If synonymous reading is to be contrasted with antonymical reading, which stresses untranslatability, difference, and uniqueness; then analytical reading, which looks at the way words are put together to achieve certain effects, should be contrasted with synthetical reading, which concentrates on the quality and character of the effect itself. Synthetical reading integrates every element and *responds*.

Imagine for a moment a consummate Brunswick stew. In such a perfect dish, not only must the carrot contribute its bit, but *this* carrot must contribute *its*. As we sample the stew, we first of all must realize we are eating just that: stew. This knowledge gives our tongue its orientation; it tells us what to look for, what values count, what belongs, and what (like bubble gum) does not; it informs us about the *method* of its preparation. We assure ourselves it is stew we are eating by comparing our present experience with others (or we ask the waitress, who tells us what the chef says). That is, this stew has a general character (look, smell, texture, flavor)—a "gist"—which we then may match with others of its sort. So far we are engaged in synonymous eating (as disgusting as that sounds). One bite of stew, one bowl of chili, one flattened hamburger patty, is like another patty, bowl, or bite. Clearly, for the rapid eater or the speed reader, consciousness will not register much difference, and the difference that does appear will be, of course, in *content*. I've eaten this bowl of porridge, so that bowl must be another one.

But the educated and careful tongue will taste and discriminate this particular stew from every other. Tasting is a dialectical process in which one proceeds from general to specific similarities, but this can be accomplished only through a series of differentiations. Antonymical tasting (which also sounds disgusting) ultimately "identifies" this dish, not only as pure stew, but as Brunswick stew, and knows whether it was done in Creole style or not, and then, finally, it recognizes, in this plate's present version of the recipe, that the squirrels were fat and gray and came from Mississippi where they fed on elderberries and acorns of the swamp oak. One grasps an act, an object, an idea, a sentence, synthetically, simply by feeling or receiving its full effect—in the case of the stew that means its complete, unique taste. I need not be able to name the ingredients; I need not be able to describe how the dish was prepared; but I should be a paragon of appreciation. This quality, because it is the experience of differentiation within a context of comparison, cannot be captured in concepts, cannot be expressed in words. Analytical tasting has a different aim. It desires to discover what went into the dish; it reconstructs the recipe, and re-creates the method of its preparation. It moves from effects to causes.

Reading is a complicated, profound, silent, still, very personal, very private, a very solitary, yet civilizing activity. Nothing is more social than speech—we are bound together by our common sounds more securely than even by our laws—nevertheless, no one is more aware of the isolated self than the reader; for a reader communes with the word heard immaterially in that hollow of the head made only for hearing, a room nowhere in the body in any ordinary sense. On the bus, every one of us may be deep in something different. Sitting next to a priest, I can still enjoy my pornography, although I may keep a thumb discreetly on top of the title: *The Cancan Girls Celebrate Christmas*. It doesn't matter to me that Father McIvie is reading about investments, or that the kid with rusty hair in the seat ahead is devouring a book about handicapping horses. Yet while all of us, in our verbal re-creations, are full of respect for the privacy of our neighbors, the placards advertising perfume or footware invade the public space like a visual smell; Muzak fills every unstoppered ear the way the static of the street does. The movies, radio, TV, theater, orchestra: all run on at their own rate, and the listener or the viewer must attend, keep up, or lose out; but not the reader. The reader is free. The reader is in charge, and pedals the cycle. It is easy for a reader to announce that his present run of Proust has been postponed until the holidays.

Reading, that is, is not a public imposition. Of course, when we read, many of us squirm and fidget. One of the closest friends of my youth would sensuously wind and unwind on his forefinger the long blond strands of his hair. How he read: that is how I remember him. Yes, our postures are often provocative, perverse. Yet these outward movements of the body really testify to the importance of the inner movements of the mind; and even those rapid flickers of the eye, as we shift from word to word, phrase to phrase, and clause to clause, hoping to keep our head afloat on a flood of Faulkner or Proust or Joyce or James, are registers of reason: for reading is reasoning, figuring things out through thoughts, making arrangements out of arrangements until we've understood a text so fully it is nothing but feeling and pure response; until its conceptual turns are like the reversals of mood in a marriage: petty, sad, ecstatic, commonplace, foreseeable, amazing.

In order to have this experience, however, one must learn to perform the text, say, sing, shout the words to oneself, give them, with *our minds, their body;* otherwise the eye skates over every syllable like the speeder. There can be no doubt that often what we read should be skimmed, as what we are frequently asked to drink should be spilled; but the speeding reader is alone in another, less satisfactory way, one quite different from that of the reader who says the words to herself, because as we read we divide into a theater: there is the performer who shapes these silent sounds, moving the muscles of the larynx almost invisibly; and there is the listener who hears them said, and who responds to their passion or their wisdom.

Such a reader sees every text as unique; greets every work as a familiar stranger. Such a reader is willing to allow another's words to become hers, his.

In the next moment, let us read a wine, so as to show how many things may be read which have not been written. We have prepared for the occasion, of course. The bottle has been allowed to breathe. Books need to breathe, too. They should be opened properly, hefted, thumbed. Their covers part like pairs of supplicating palms. The paper, print, layout should be appreciated. But now we decant the text into our wide-open and welcoming eyes. We warm the wine in the bowl of the glass with our hand. We let its bouquet collect above it like the red of red roses seems to stain the air. We wade—shoeless, to be sure—through the color it has liquefied. We roll a bit of it about in our mouths. We sip. We savor. We say some sentences of that great master Sir Thomas Browne: "We tearme sleepe a death, and yet it is waking that kills us, and destroyes those spirits which are the house of life. Tis indeed a part of life that best expresseth death, for every man truely lives so long as hee acts his nature, or someway makes good the faculties of himself. . . ." Are these words not from a fine field, in a splendid year? There is, of course, a sameness in all these words: life/death, man/nature; we get the drift. But the differences! the differences make all the difference, the way nose and eyes and cheekbones form a face; the way a muscle makes emotion pass across it. It is the differences we read. Differences are not only identifiable, distinct; they are epidemic: the wine is light, perhaps, spicy, slow to release its grip upon itself, the upper thigh is widening wonderfully, the night air has hands, words fly out of our mouths like birds: "but who knows the fate of his bones," Browne says, "or how often he is to be buried"; yet as I say his soul out loud, he lives again; he has risen up in me, and I can be, for him, that temporary savior that every real reader is, putting his words in my mouth; not nervously, notice, as though they were pieces of chewed gum, but in that way which is necessary if the heart is to hear them; and though they are his words, and his soul, then, which returns through me, I am in charge; he has asked nothing of me; his words move because I move them. It is like cycling, reading is. Can you feel the air, the pure passage of the spirit past the exposed skin?

So this reading will be like living, then; the living each of you will be off in a moment to be busy with; not always speedily, I hope, or in the continuous anxiety of consequence, the sullenness of inattention, the annoying static of distraction. But it will be only a semblance of living—this living—nevertheless, the way unspoken reading is a semblance, unless, from time to time, you perform the outer world and let it live within; because only in that manner can it deliver itself to us. As Rainer Maria Rilke once commanded: "dance the taste of the fruit you have been tasting. / Dance the orange." I should like to multiply that charge, even past all possibility. Speak the street to yourself sometimes, hear the horns in the forest, read the breeze aloud, and make that inner wind yours, because, whether Nature, Man, or God, has given us the text, we independently possess the ability to read, to read really well, and to move our own mind freely in tune to the moving world.

Washington University in St. Louis commencement address, 1979

Published in *Habitations of the Word,* 1984

Even if, by All the Oxen
in the World

Consciousness comes too easily. We did not learn it like a language. It leaps to its work like a mirror. Yet consciousness can close and open like an eye; its depths are not illusory, and its reflection on itself is not mechanical. It's something won, retrieved, conserved, as love is, and as love should be. It is with regard to consciousness, and the consciousness of consciousness, that I wish to examine popular culture in this country; and I shall simply suppose that cultural objects are created so we can become aware of them, and that those which are popular are so in a double sense: because they are widely approved and widely employed.

Imagine that a mirror, nothing falling into it, began reflecting itself: what a terrifying endlessness and mockery of light—merely to illuminate its own beams. You might think that an empty consciousness, like a vacuum, would immediately fill; that the nerves would pour in their messages like so many spouts from the roof of the skin, but sensing is not so simple as we sometimes suppose. Like falling, descent is easy only once we've jumped. Every consciousness has its rainless lands and polar wastes, its undiscovered and unventured countries. And there are simply boring stretches, like the Western Plains or the dry mouth's taste. Certainly consciousness is capable of subtle, wonderful, and terrifying transformations. After all, it is the dream we live in, and, like the dream, can harbor anything. Although we are alert to changes in our physical and mental health, and have catalogued their causes and conditions, little has been done to describe adequately states of consciousness themselves or evaluate their qualities. Nonetheless, it is the whole of all we are at any time. At any time, if it is thrilling, we are thrilled; if it is filled with beauty, we are beautiful. It is our only evidence we live. Yet nothing seems more obvious to me than the fear, hatred, and contempt men have for it. They find it useful (an electric map of tracks and trains); otherwise it is embarrassing at best, or boring; at worst, it's threatening and horrible. Indeed, it's so much worse than simple black oblivion that only an obstinate, foolish will to live—the simple insistence of the veins which leaves have, cowslips, oxen, ants have just as well—can account for most men's going on, since such a will moves blindly, in roots beneath the ground, in bottle flies and fish, and our feelings are the price we pay for being brained instead of finned. Perception, Plato said, is a form of pain.

The working consciousness, for instance, is narrow, shuttered by utility, its transitions eased by habit past reflection like a thief. Impulses from without or from within must use some strength to reach us, we do not go out to them. Machines are made this way. Alert as lights and aimed like guns, they only see the circle of their barrels. How round the world is; how like a well arranged. Thus, when desire is at an ebb and will is weak, we trail the entertainer like a child his mother, restless, bored, and whining: What can I do? What will amuse me? How shall I live? Then

> L'ennui, fruit de la morne incuriosité,
> Prend les proportions de l'immortalité.

The enjoyment of sensation as sensation, a fully free awareness, is very rare. We keep our noses down like dogs to sniff our signs. Experience must *mean*. The content of an aimless consciousness is weak and colorless; we may be filled up by ourselves instead—even flooded basements, some days, leak the other way—and then it's dread we feel, anxiety.

To tie experience to a task, to seek significance in everything, to take and never to receive, to keep, like the lighter boxer, moving, bob and weave, to fear the appearance of the self and every inwardness: these are such universal characteristics of the average consciousness that I think we can assume that popular culture functions fundamentally with regard to them.

But "before Plato told the great lie of ideals," Lawrence wrote, "/ men slimly went like fishes, and didn't care. . . . They knew it was no use knowing / their own nothingness. . . ." Nothing keeps us back from nothingness but knowing; knowing, now, not necessarily in the sense of squeezing what we know into a set of symbols and understanding those; but knowing in the sense of seeing—seeing clearly, deeply, fully—of being completely aware, and consequently of being perfectly ourselves; for Lawrence lets his pagans speed to their mark as thoughtlessly as arrows.

Must we be drunk or doped or mad, must we be dunced and numb to feed our animal halves? So it appears. The average man does not want to know how he looks when he eats; he defecates in darkness, reading the *Reader's Digest;* his love has an awkward automatic metal brevity, like something sprayed from a can, and any day his present sex may be replaced with plastic; his work is futile, his thought is shallow, his joys ephemeral, his howls helpless and agony incompetent; his hopes are purchased, his voice prerecorded, his play is mechanical, the roles typed, their lines trite, all strengths are sapped, exertion anyhow is useless, to vote or not is futile, futile . . . so in almost every way he is separated from the centers of all power and feeling: futilely he feeds, he voids, he screws, he smokes, he motorboats, he squats before the tube, he spends at least a week each year in touring and a month in memorizing lies—lies moral, religious, and political—he beats the drum or shouts hurray on cue, he wears a neon nightie, swallows pills, and chews his woman's nipples now because a book he's read has told him that he ought to; my God, he jigs, he swigs, he sings the very latest tra-la-las and sends his kids to scouts and all-white schools, he rounds his bottom to a pew, loves pulpitry, and contributes yearly to a cause; with splendid sexlessness he breeds—boards receive their nails with greater sensitivity—he kites the lies he's learned as high as heaven, where they sing like toads in trees, yet he sickens just the same, and without reason, for he's been to bridge and bingo, said his rahs as well as anyone, never borrowed on his insurance, kept his car clean, and put his three sons twice through Yale; but age, which is not real, hangs like a dirty suit inside his freshly pressed tuxedo; thus he fails, assumes another slumber, and dies like merchandise gone out of season.

Imagine for a moment what would happen if the television paled, the radio fell silent, the press did not release. Imagine all the clubs and courses closed, magazines unmailed, guitars unplugged, pools, rinks, gyms, courts, stadia shut up. Suppose that publishers were to issue no more dick, prick, and booby books; movies were banned along with gambling, liquor, and narcotics; and men were suddenly and irrevocably alone with themselves . . . alone only with love to be made, thought, sense, and dreadful life. What would be the state of our nature then, Mr. Hobbes?

It is the principal function of popular culture—though hardly its avowed purpose—to keep men from understanding what is happening to them, for social unrest would surely follow, and who knows what outbursts of revenge and rage. War, work, poverty, disease, religion: these, in the past, have kept men's minds full, small, and careful. Religion gave men hope who otherwise could have none. Even a mechanical rabbit can make the greyhounds run.

People who have seen the same game, heard the same comedians, danced to the same din, read the same detectives, can form a community of enthusiasts whose exchange of feelings not only produces the most important secondary effect of popular culture (the culture hero and his worship services), but also helps persuade people that their experiences were real, reinforces judgments of their values, and confirms their addiction. Popular culture occurs in public; it is as much an event as an experience; and it is reported on in the same spirit. There are therefore both participants and spectators, and in much of popular culture a steady drift toward voyeurism and passivity. As culture rises, it shatters; nothing remains in what were formerly the highest cultural realms but isolated works; isolated now by their character, which repels all but the most devoted and cultivated love, and by the divisive nature of society, which sets them apart in order to destroy them if possible. The objects of popular culture are competitive. They are expected to yield a return. Their effect must be swift and pronounced, therefore they are strident, ballyhooed, and baited with sex; they must be able to create or take part in a fad; and they must die without fuss and leave no corpse. In short, the products of popular culture, by and large, have no more aesthetic quality than a brick in the street. Their authors are anonymous, and tend to dwell in groups and create in committees; they are greatly dependent upon performers and performance; any aesthetic intention is entirely absent, and because it is desired to manipulate consciousness directly, achieve one's effect there, no mind is paid to the intrinsic nature of its objects; they lack finish, complexity, stasis, individuality, coherence, depth, and endurance. But they do possess splash.

It's in a way unfair to popular culture to compare it with the workmanships of artists, since they do perform such different functions; nevertheless, this kind of comparison is not entirely unjust. Both shape a consciousness, but art enlarges consciousness like space in a cathedral, ribboned with light, and though a new work of art may consume our souls completely for a while, almost as a jingle might, if consumption were all that mattered, we are never, afterward, the same; we cannot unconsciously go on in the old way; there is, as in Rilke's poem "Torso of an Archaic Apollo," no place that does not see us, and we must change our life. Even Arnold Bennett noticed that we do not measure classics; they, rather, measure us. For most people it is precisely this that's painful; they do not wish to know their own nothingness—or their own potentialities either, and the pleasures of popular culture are like the pleasures of disease, work, poverty, and religion: they give us something to do, something to suffer, an excuse for failure, and a justification of everything.

If 60 percent of the people of a country are addicts of opium, then we are not rash in inferring there a general sickness of spirit; if alcoholism is epidemic, or suicide, or gambling, still another spiritual malaise can be confirmed; and if a great portion of any population is spending many hours every day driving all life from the mind, in worship of low-cost divinities like the goddess of the golden udder, there's been another plague in spirit, and there are deaths to show for it, and endless deformities. Art does not, I hasten to say, have a hortatory influence; it's not a medicine, and it teaches nothing. It simply shows us what beauty, perfection, sensuality, and meaning are; and we feel as we should feel if we'd compared physiques with Hercules.

None of these complaints is new, and there would be little point in repeating them except that from time to time one senses an effort to Hitlerize the culture of the Folk; make it somehow spring from some deep well of human feeling, as if art were ever the triumph of sincerity over ineptitude, as if passion were a substitute for skill, as if, indeed, its gaucheries were not only charming, but *aesthetically* so . . . this, in order to put out those high and isolated fires, those lonely works of genius which still manage, somehow, amazingly, now and then, to appear. There is no Folk, of course; there are no traditions; fine moral sentiments improve no lyrics, nor beautify their song; the occasional appearance of splendid exceptions does not soften, excuse, or justify anything; popular culture is the product of an industrial machine which makes baubles to amuse the savages while missionaries steal their souls and merchants steal their money.

How romantically he talks about it, you may say; what wretched little dramas he's made up—these wee morality plays from wild exaggerations. "High and isolated fires" indeed. Anything which surrounds us like the air we breathe, with which like wives and husbands we're easy and familiar, can't be so poisonous; we are alive, aren't we? Well, no, if you ask me, we aren't, or only partially. This much cripples consciousness. Therefore, no concessions should be made to it; and those who take their pleasure there should not be permitted to appear to lift those tastes to something higher with scholarly hypocrisy and philosophical pretense. The objects of popular culture are not art; their success or failure should not be judged as art's is; and the pleasures they provide, among goods, come last, even if, as Plato says, they are asserted to be first by all the oxen in the world.

First published in *Frontiers of American Culture,* ed. Ray B. Browne et al.
(West Lafayette, Ind.: Purdue University Press, 1968)
Published in *Fiction and the Figures of Life,* 1970

The Doomed in Their Sinking

Crane went sudden as a springboard. The Gulf gave nothing back. My mother, I remember, took her time. She held the house around her as she held her bathrobe, safely doorpinned down its floorlength, the metal threads glinting like those gay gold loops which close the coat of a grenadier, though there were gaps of course . . . unseemly as sometimes a door is on a chain . . . so that to urinate she had to hoist the whole thing like a skirt, collecting the cloth in fat pleats with her fingers, wads which soon out-oozed her fists and sprang slowly away . . . one consequence . . . so that she felt she had to hover above the hole, the seat (clouds don't care about *their* aim), unsteadily . . . necessarily . . . more and more so as the nighttime days drew on, so that the robe grew damp the way the sweater on a long drink grows, soggy from edge to center, until I found I cared with what success she peed when what she swallowed was herself and what streamed out of her in consequence seemed me.

Though Hart shed his bathrobe frugally before he jumped, my mother, also saving, would have worn hers like the medal on a hussar straight through living room and loony bin, every nursing home and needle house we put her in, if those points hadn't had to come out (they confiscate your pins, belts, buckles, jewelry, teeth, and they'd take the air, too, if it had an edge, because the crazy can garrote themselves with a length of breath, their thoughts are open razors, their eyes go off like guns), though there was naturally no danger in these baubles to herself, for my mother was living the long death, her whole life passing before her as she went, the way those who drown themselves are said to have theirs pass . . . a consequence, yes . . . her own ocean like a message in a bottle, so that she sank slowly somewhere as a stone sill sinks beneath the shoes of pilgrims and tourists, not like Plath with pills, or Crane or Woolf with water, Plath again by gas, or Berryman from a bridge, but, I now believe, in the best way possible, because the long death is much more painful and punishing than even disembowelment or bleach, and it inflicts your dying on those you are blaming for it better than burning or blowing up—during an exquisitely extended stretch—since the same substance which both poisons you, preserves, you both have and eat, enjoy and suffer your revenges together, as well as the illusion that you can always change your mind.

Yet my mother wasn't what we call a suicide, even though she died as though she'd cut her throat when the vessels burst there finally, and my father, who clenched his teeth till neither knees nor elbows would unfist, dying of his own murderous wishes like the scorpion who's supposed to sting itself to death—no—he wasn't one either: both had a terribly tenacious grip on life . . . so that some suicides will survive anything, and many who court death have no desire to wed her. . . . It mixes us up. . . .

Should a suicide be regarded as the last stage of a series of small acts against the self, since the murderer who arsenics his wife little by little is still a murderer though she takes a decade dying; or does this confuse kinds of hostility in a serious way, because harsh words aren't the same as blows or their bruises, desire isn't adultery whatever Jesus preached, not even a degree of it? Cigarettes shorten our life, but the alcoholic's fuddle mimics death (the loss of control, the departure of the soul) in a way the smoker's never does. What can we make of that? We shall manage something.

My mother managed. She was what we call a dedicated passive . . . liquidly acquiescent . . . supinely on the go. Still, she went in her own way—the way, for instance, her robe was fastened.

Socrates acquiesced in his own execution, others demand theirs. The kamikaze pilot intends his death, but does not desire it. Malcolm Lowry, who choked on his vomit, evidently desired his, but did not intend it. Soldiers charging the guns at Verdun neither wished for death nor were bent on it, though death was what they expected. My mother accepted.

I used to think my father was the actively aggressive one because while he sat, temporized, bided and brooded and considered and consolidated, he growled, swore, and made horrible faces.

During the decline of Christian morals, few groups have risen so rapidly in the overall estimation of society. It was dangerous for Donne to suggest that suicide was sometimes not a sin. It was still daring for Hume to reason that it was sometimes not a crime. Later one had to point out that it was sometimes not simply a sickness of the soul. Now it seems necessary to argue that it is sometimes not a virtue.

To paraphrase Freud, what does a suicide want? Not what he gets, surely.

Some simply think of death as the absence of their present state, a state which pursues them like a malignant disease and which cannot be otherwise escaped. Others consider it quite positively, as though to die were to get on in the world. Seventh Heaven, after all, is a most desirable address. Still others spend their life like money, purchasing this or that, but their aim is to buy, not to go broke. Are we to say to them (all and every kind) what we often say to children? No, Freddie, you don't want a pet boa, you wouldn't like the way it swallows mice.

It doesn't follow at all that because it is easy enough to kill yourself, it is easy enough to get, in that case, what you want. Can you really be said to want what you cannot possibly understand? or what you are in abysmal confusion about? or what is provenly contrary to your interests? or is plainly impossible? Is "I'd rather be dead" anything like "I want to be a chewed-up marshmallow"; or "I want 6 and 3 to make 10"; or "I want to be a Fiji princess"; or "I want a foot-long dong"; or "I want that seventh Scotch-on-the-rocks"; or "I would love to make it with Lena Horne"?

It's been said that suicide is a crime of status. Poverty limits it, as it virtuously inhibits so many other vices. It occurs, we are also told, when its victim is not properly folded into the general batter of society, and when external constraints upon one's behavior are weak. (The superego, however, can come down on conscience like a hammer.) So suicide is a disease of singularity and selfhood, because as we are elevated in the social system, and authorities "over" us are removed, as we wobble out on our own, the question of whether it is better to be or not to be arises with real relevance for the first time, since the burden of being is felt most fully by the self-determining self.

In a sense, society has already rejected the prospective suicide, hurled him overboard as Jonah was. His beliefs, all that was beloved, have forsaken him. He is a jinx. Once he is in the water, is it his fault he drowns? Hamlet, of course, has too many motives. Death and adultery have parted him from his family—murder and adultery from his king—imbecility from his love. He's in the firmly impalpable grip of guilt. Above all, he is too fine a spirit for this wormy world. Don't we often think so?

The logic of misery hides its premises to forget its fallacies: Hamlet's a prison; Hamlet's a Dane; Denmark's a prison; then is the world one.

On the other hand, if I were to commit suicide, I am sure it would be from a surfeit of family and society, in a desperate effort to escape its selfish swallowing hug; yet to feel that way may already signify the absence of the necessary melodic relation. To be ruled by Reason, rather than by Father, Nature, King, or God, is an antisocial resolve. The autonomous self listens only to its own voice, unaffected by the grate of force, the lure of bribes, or the temptations of love.

Anyway, men have been killing themselves, we may suppose, as long as life has afforded them the opportunity, but to be sick of life is not the same as having a painful illness or suffering a shame so denobling life is no longer endurable. The presence everywhere of decay, disease, coarseness, brutality, and death—the flow of value into a blank abyss—this death-in-life that made living like the aftertaste of drunken vomit—was the black center of the plague of melancholy which afflicted the Elizabethans.

Hamlet's question, indeed, throws everything in doubt. The doubt becomes a commonplace, and a century later Pope defends the self-slaughter of an unfortunate lady in an elegant poem which takes for granted what continually shocked the Elizabethans—the democracy of death.

> Poets themselves must fall, like those they sung;
> Deaf the prais'd ear, and mute the tuneful tongue.
> Ev'n he, whose soul now melts in mournful lays,
> Shall shortly want the gen'rous tear he pays;
> Then from his closing eyes thy form shall part,
> And the last pang shall tear thee from his heart,
> Life's idle business at one gasp be o'er,
> The Muse forgot, and thou belov'd no more!

Definitions of suicide, like definitions of adultery, are invariably normative, and frequently do little more than reflect the shallowest social attitudes, embody the most parochial perspectives. Above all, these attitudes are for the most part deeply irrational. Failures may be executed, for example, while the corpses of successes are assaulted. Studies of suicide, including those of Alvarez and Choron,* are soon elaborately confused about desire, intention, deed, and consequence, ownership and responsibility (whether we belong to ourselves, society, or God); neglect the difference between act and action, refuse to decide whether to include deaths of soul (Rimbaud?) as well as deaths of body, since holy living may indeed be holy dying, so that physical and metaphysical murders become hopelessly intertwined; and they are content to record, with a tourist's widened eyes, the sweet, sour, wise, or benighted opinions of nearly everyone.

If we are to call suicide every self-taken way out of the world, then even the Platonic pursuit of knowledge, involving as it does the separation of

---

* A. Alvarez, *The Savage God* (New York: Random House, 1972), and Jacques Choron, *Suicide* (New York: Scribner's, 1972).

reason from passion and appetite, is suicidal . . . as are, of course, the search for ecstatic states, and longings for mystical union. It is the habit of such examinations to mess up these matters as if they were so many paints whose purpose was purely to give pleasure to the fingers.

Nowadays the significance of a suicide for the suicide and the significance of that suicide for society are seldom the same. If, according to the social workers' comforting cliché, they are often a cry for help, they're just as frequently a solemn vow of silence. Nevertheless, it is easy to imagine circumstances under which some of our conventional kinds of suicide would be impossible—impossible because we would simply refuse to recognize them. The liver fails. The veins collapse. Sleep seizes the wheel. No suicides there. Suppose that starving yourself were a "going-home-to-God" (no suicide there), while slashing your wrists were a "cowardly-copping-out." In order to speak your piece properly you might have to shoot, hang, or poison yourself. Sprott records the case of "one that hang'd himself, upon his Knees, with a Bible on a Stool open before him, and a Paper to signifie that he had repented."* The liberated woman must do something manly, shotgun herself at the very least, avoid sleeping pills like the devil—that soothing syrup of the oppressed sex. If you don't want the manner of your dying to be a message to mankind, if your aim is just to get the hell out, then you will have to be as clever at disarming symbols as Mallarmé. Alas, the way we think and write about suicides would provide many with still another motive, an additional despair, were they alive again and mercilessly aware.

Breeding is not out of place even here. Petronius, the critics say, had class. Cato has consistently had a good press. And we write cheery loving thank-you notes; we put our affairs in order; we do not leap on top of people, run in front of cars owned by innocent strangers, bleed in public, allow the least hint of indecision, ambiguity, or failure to spoil our aim, and avoid every form of vulgar display. The ledge huggers want to be coaxed, for instance. That's a suicide for shopgirls. On the other hand, if you are, like Mishima, too stylish, your actions risk being thought incomprehensible. My favorites are rather theatrical, though. Choron tells us how Arria, the wife of a Roman senator who'd been caught plotting, in order to stimulate her husband to his duty, plunged a sword into her breast and then handed it to him with the words: *Non dolet* (It does not hurt). Others seek the third rail and interrupt the service; swallow combs, crosses, safety pins, fountain pens, needles, nails; they blow up the planes they are riding in, smother themselves in plastic Baggies, or simply find a wall and dash out their brains. Sprott says that by 1600

* S. E. Sprott, *The English Debate on Suicide from Donne to Hume* (La Salle, Ill.: Open Court, 1961).

> Suicidal types had become traditional: the epicure, the disappointed
> lover, the great spirit, the melancholiac, the jealous man, the fright-
> ened child, the debauched apprentice, the unfortunate merchant, the
> bloody murderer despairing of God's pardon, the desperate zealot, the
> "tender Conscience't Despairer" . . . [p. 36]

Though methods, motives, meanings differ ("Whose head is hanging from
the swollen strap?" asked Crane), most can be expected to mess up their
deaths exactly as they've messed up their lives. Poor folks. Poor ways.

Never mind. If you pay with your life you get a ticket to the tent: martyrs,
daredevils, the accident-prone, those who cheat "justice" as Hannibal did,
or are condemned by it as Seneca was; those who would die rather than surrender, even *en masse,* as the Jews died at Massada; those too poor, too rich,
too proud, too ineffably wicked; all addicts, Cleopatras, all desolate Didos,
mystics, faddists, young sorrowful Werthers; the fundamentally frigid, who
cannot allow life to give them any pleasure; the incurably ill, the mad, the
metaphysically gloomy; widows who go up with the rest of the property, and
all those who from disgust or rage protest this life with emblematic ignitions
and ritual sacrifice . . . it's like cataloguing books according to the color of
their covers . . . the mourners, the divided selves (not just Cartesians, severed
into bum and bicycle as Beckett's men are, but those who are cut up into
competing personalities as vicious as sisters in some *Cinderella*); then the
downright stupid, the inept and careless, the sublimely heroic, the totally
disgraced . . . the color may be significant (the blue cover of *Ulysses* is), but it
is scarcely a mode of classification which carves reality at the joints . . . those
whom guilt feeds on as if they were already carrion; the Virginia Woolfs, too,
who enter their own imagery, and the ones for whom death is a deer park,
a convent, a place in outer space; also the impotent, ugly, acned, lonely; the
inadvertently pregnant; and otherwise those who embrace their assassins, or
who have felt only the hold of their own hand, thus to come and go finally in
the same way . . . from little death to large . . . everyone's welcome.

Lost in lists, in the surveyor's sweepings, borne along on conjecture like
gutter water, the same act can signify anything you like, depending on the
system—even the mood or the line of the eye—which gives it meaning: I
cock my head one way and it appears to me that my mother was murdered;
I cock it another and she seems a specially vindictive suicide; while if I face
firmly forward as one in military ranks she seems to have been overcome
by a rather complex illness, a chronic and progressively worsening disease.
Simply examining "suicides" is like trying to establish a science of—let's
say—*sallescape,* which we can imagine contains the whys and wherefores of

room-leaving. The word confers a fictitious unity upon a rabble of factors, and the ironic thing about suicide itself, intrinsically considered (and what my little litanies have been designed to demonstrate), is that it is a wholly empty act. It is—more than Rigaut, the Dada hero, was—an empty suitcase.

And if the suicide believes his final gesture, like the last line of an obscure poem, will unite, clarify, and give meaning to all that has gone before; or if actual poems have held offhand hints—

> The news from Spain got worse. The President of my Form
> at South Kent turned up at Clare, one of the last let out of Madrid.
> He designed the Chapel the School later built
> & killed himself, I never heard why
> or just how, it was something to do with a bridge.
>
> [John Berryman, "Transit"]

—or seemed like chilling scenarios—

> We have come so far, it is over.
> Each dead child coiled, a white serpent,
> One at each little
> Pitcher of milk, now empty.
>
> [Sylvia Plath, "Edge"]

—so that the line between literature and life appears underdrawn (before she killed herself, Sylvia Plath put out two mugs of milk for her children); or if he has fallen for a romantic comparison like Camus's "An act like this is prepared within the silence of the heart, as is a great work of art," then at least he will suffer no further disappointment dead, because, of course, acts aren't language, and there's no poetry at all in suicide, only in some accounts of it . . . significance, value *in this sense,* belongs solely to sentences. Actions, and other similar events, have meaning only secondarily, as we impute it to them, and so may mean many things to many people. Words are acts only secondarily. They principally exist in the systems which establish and define them (as numbers do in mathematics), so while feasting may mean one thing to a Jew and quite another to a Samoan, the word "*Traum,*" uttered anywhere by anybody, remains irrevocably German.

Death will not fill up an empty life, and in a line of verse it occupies only five letters of space.

Choron's readable little handbook, with its capsule summaries of speculation, its few tables of statistics, brief histories of opinions, merely provokes its questions, instead of asking them, and touches so lightly on all its subjects, they never feel it. Totally porous, the data are simply slowed down a trifle in seeping through. It resembles Choron's earlier *Death and Modern Man* in being a kind of easy introductory text.

Alvarez, observing the immense diversity of his material, wisely offers no solutions. Yet because he does not rigorously differentiate sorts, define terms, regulate interpretations, exclude kinds, but is content to report, reflect, admonish, and look on, his "study" turns out to be gossipy and anecdotal, though sometimes splendidly so, as his account of the suicide of Sylvia Plath is, because Alvarez is sensitive and sympathetic, knows how to handle a text, and writes with conscience and skill about a subject which is close enough to his own personal concerns (he is himself a "failed" suicide) that one could reasonably expect it to shake both skill and conscience as though they were rags in a gale.

It must have seemed like a good idea to sandwich his historical and literary studies of suicide between two kinds of direct acquaintance with it, all the more so when Alvarez's dissatisfaction with most theoretical investigations lies in their natural lack of contact with inner feeling, although much the same might be said of the physical laws for falling bodies, especially when the falling body is your own. The result of this division has not been entirely happy, however. Natural reticence, moral restraint, and simple lack of knowledge make his accounts of suicide from the inside-side seriously deficient in essential data, and therefore reduce them to sensitively told and frequently moving *stories,* although with less excuse Choron manages to make even the expounding of a theory sound like gossip (in effect: "Do you know what Plato said? Well—you won't believe this—but *he* said . . .").

Throughout *The Savage God,* too, again because it has no ruling principle, details fly out like sparks from every point that's struck, to fade without a purpose. The conditions surrounding Chatterton's suicide, for example, are certainly interesting, and Alvarez recites them nicely enough, but which ones really count, and which ones don't, and how do they count if they do, and if they do by how much? Vivid details, picturesque circumstances . . . my mother's copterlike bathroom posture, her gap-pinned robe, miscolored toes . . . well, their relevance isn't clear. Perhaps they have mainly a vaudeville function—to enliven without enlightening. Throughout, my mention of my mother merely mimics the problem.

The value of *The Savage God,* and it is high, lies mainly in the humanity of the mind which composed it, in the literary excellence of its composition, and the suggestiveness of many of its passages—the moment-by-moment thoughtfulness of its author as a reader.

The world of the suicidal is, in a certain sense (for all its familiar elements: pain, grief, confusion, failure, loss . . .), a private and impenetrable one, hence the frustration of those who are trying to help, and whose offers to do so, as raps on the glass disturb fish, often simply insult the suicide immersed in his situation. It is a consciousness trapped, enclosed by a bell jar, in the image which encloses Plath's novel, and Alvarez's book should do a great deal to correct the sentimentalist's happy thought that art is a kind of therapy for the sick, trapped, homeless, and world-weary, and that through it, deep personal problems get worked benignly out.

Poetry is cathartic only for the unserious, for in front of the rush of expressive need stands the barrier of form, and when the hurdler's scissored legs and outstretched arms carry him over the bars, the limp in his life, the headache in his heart, the emptiness he's full of, are as absent as his street shoes, which will pinch and scrape his feet in all the old leathery ways once the race is over and he has to walk through the front door of his future like a brushman with some feckless patter and a chintzy plastic prize.

Rilke sometimes took this therapeutic attitude toward the writing of *Malte Laurids Brigge,* but if writing kept him sane, as he thought, it was one of the chief sources of his misery as well. If life is hard, art is harder. Plath's last poems, considered in this way, are announcements and warnings; they are promises; and their very excellence was a threat to the existence of their author, a woman whom success had always vanquished, and who was certainly defeated without it. Not only does the effort of creation often cultivate our problems at their roots, as Alvarez notes, the rich eloquence of their eventual formulation may give to some "solutions" an allure that is abnormal, one that art confers, not life. And if we have tried often enough, warned, performed, and promised, must we not sometime keep that promise, if only to ensure that our sufferings have not been mockeries and show-offs, and succeed at failure one final time?

Malcolm Lowry, that eminent drunk, perhaps put Plath's particular case best when he wrote:

> When the doomed are most eloquent in their sinking,
> It seems that then we are least strong to save.

Writing. Not writing. Twin terrors. Putting one's mother into words . . . It may have been easier to put her in her grave.

The New York Review of Books, 1972
Published in *The World Within the Word,* 1978

FICTION

THE LOVE AND SORROW OF HENRY PIMBER

I

Brackett Omensetter was a wide and happy man. He could whistle like the cardinal whistles in the deep snow, or whirr like the shy 'white rising from its cover, or be the lark a-chuckle at the sky. He knew the earth. He put his hands in water. He smelled the clean fir smell. He listened to the bees. And he laughed his deep, loud, wide, and happy laugh whenever he could—which was often, long, and joyfully.

He said to his wife when it is spring we'll go to Gilean on the Ohio. That is a fine place for the boy you're making. The air is clear.

Therefore, when the snow sank quietly away into the creeks; therefore, when the rivers had their bellies brown and urgent; when the wind went hungry about the bare-limbed trees and clouds were streamers; then Omensetter said the time is coming and we must be ready.

They washed their wagon. They ironed their Sunday things. They braided the hair of their daughters. They did everything that didn't matter. It made them feel good.

They brushed the dog. They piled the firewood left from winter neatly. They pinched each other a good deal on the behind. Everything that didn't matter and made them feel good, they did.

It rained a week. Then Omensetter said it seems that we are ready, shall we go?

They piled their belongings on the back of the wagon. They heaped them up, one on top of the other: flaming tufted comforts and tattercrossed quilts, plump bags of clothing and sacks of shoes and sewing and a linen tablecloth with stains that were always hidden by the plates; two ladderbacks, a stool and a Boston rocker, a bench of quite hard and eloquent oak, and a drop-leaf table whose top was carved into faces and initials by no one they ever knew; jars, a framed view of the Connecticut River, rubber boots; and in boxes: wooden spoons and pans and stove lids and pot-handle holders and pots, tin silverware and nickel-plated medallions and a toothpick, somewhere, thinly tinted gold with a delicate chain, a mezzotint of St. Francis feeding squirrels, some tools for shaping leather, two pewter goblets and thirteen jelly glasses, seven books (three of which were about birds by the Reverend Stanley Cody); a collection in tobacco tins of toy rings and rice-bead necklaces, amber-colored stones and tiny china figurines and stamped-out metal dogs and cats and horses and two lead hussars in tall hats and bent guns whose red paint had all but worn away; ten- and twenty-penny nails, dolls made from sewn chains of stuffed cloth, small dishes and large crocks, a paper cockade, four flat spiders dead a long time and saved under a stone in the hearth; a saw, a hammer, square, a sledge, other things that were called dolls but were more like pressed grass or pinecones or strangely shaped sticks or queer rocks; any kind of shell whatever—turtle's, robin's, snail's; and not in boxes: a tight bucket and an unassembled plow, a spade, a shovel and an ax, a churn, a wooden tub and washboard, and a great white ironstone basin and a great white ironstone pitcher and a great white enamel pot with a chipped lid that was terribly cold in the morning; a shotgun and some harness and a spinning wheel, a compass in a leather case that always pointed to the west of south, and arrows for the unborn boy to shoot at falling leaves and sparrows in the fall. They piled them up, one on top of the other, until there was a tower in the wagon. On the top they lashed the cradle. The tower teetered when the wagon rolled. They said maybe everything will fall into the road but they really didn't think so, and they didn't trouble to cover anything. Of course the rain would stop, they said, and it did. Omensetter hitched the horse to the wagon. He hopped up with a great flourish and addressed the world with his arms. Everyone enjoyed that. Omensetter's wife swung up too. She rested her arm on his leg and she squeezed his knee. Omensetter's daughters whooped up the back. They snuggled under quilts. They made a house in the tower. Everyone said a prayer for the snowman dead a week. Then Omensetter chucked, the dog barked, and they set out for Gilean on the Ohio, where the air was clear and good for boys. They left behind them, where they'd kissed and talked, water dripping lightly from the eaves of their last and happy home.

There were still a few people in Gilean when Brackett Omensetter came. It had been dry, for a change, all day. George Hatstat's rig was mired down on the South Road even though the South Road drained into the river, and

Curtis Chamlay had turned his wagon back from the western hill that afternoon, being a stubborn man, three hours after he started slipping on its yellow sides. That meant the hill should be impassable since the other slope was generally worse. Consequently everyone was thoroughly amazed to see Omensetter's wagon come sliding down and draw its tilting peak of furniture and tools and clothing into town behind a single wretched horse. They looked at the unprotected quilts, the boxes and the stilting poles, the muddy dog, the high-lashed swaying cradle with bewildered wonder, for all day, in the distance, choked gray clouds had dropped their water in the forests, and even as they watched the wagon coming, away above the western hill, sunshine shining from it, there was a clearly defined acre of rain.

Pausing only to ask directions, Omensetter drove rapidly to the blacksmith's shop, bawling out his name before the wagon had fully stopped and announcing his occupation in an enormous raw voice as he vaulted down, his heels sinking so deeply in the soft ground it held him a moment, lurching, while he rubbed his nose on his upper arm and Matthew Watson emerged from the doorway blinking and shaking his apron. Omensetter rushed to the forge and bent over it eagerly, praising the beauty and the warmth of the fire. He teetered as he pummeled a leg that he said was tingling, his face flushed by the coals and his shadow fluttering. Mat inquired his business. Omensetter groaned and yawned, stretching with an effort that made him tremble. Then with a quiet exclamation he moved by Mat and took a piece of leather from the bench; wound it around his fingers like a coil of hair; let it straighten slowly. He held it gently in his huge brown hands, rubbing it with his thumb as he talked. He spoke in a dreamy monotonous voice whose flow he broke from time to time by peering closely at the edges of the strip he held or by bringing it sharply down against his thigh, smiling at the sound of the crack. He was very good, he said. He would start tomorrow. There was no one in the town brought up on leather, and Mat had far too much to do. That was certainly right, he thought. Mat would see how he was needed. His thumb moved rhythmically. His words were happy and assured, and if Mat's doubts were any obstacle, they calmly flowed around them. I shall work out very well and you can easily afford me. Before Omensetter left, Mat gave him the name and address of his friend Henry Pimber, who had a house which might be rented since it was empty and dissolving and sat like a frog on the edge of the river.

Henry Pimber smiled at Omensetter's muddy clothes, at the girls leaning over the side of the wagon, laughing; at the running, barking dog, the placid, remote wife; though he was conscious mainly of his own wife, quiet in the kitchen now, endeavoring to hear. Sheets of water still glittered in the road;

the sky muttered; yet the wagon stood uncovered, belongings piled into a tower; and Henry felt amazement move his shoulders. Three flies walked brazenly on the screen between them. Omensetter was crosshatched by the wires. To Henry he seemed fat and he spoke with hands which were thick and deeply tanned. His belt was tight though he wore suspenders. His dark hair fell across his face and he'd tracked mud on the porch, but his voice was musical and sweet as water, his moist lips smiled around his words, his eyes glimmered from the surface of his speech. He said he was working for Watson, mending harness and helping out. Henry noticed several squares of screen clogged with paint. There was a tear in the fellow's sleeve, and his nails had yellowed. Clay eased to the porch from his boots. Henry's wife was in the parlor then, tiptoeing. She held her skirts. He said his name was Brackett Omensetter and he came from out near Windham. He was honest, he said. Flies already, Pimber thought, and the swatter in the barn. But they were something to fix his eyes on and momentarily he was grateful. Then his vision slipped beyond the screen and he received the terrible wound of the man's smile. His weakness surprised him and he leaned heavily against the door. He had a horse, Omensetter said. He had a dog, a wagon, a pregnant wife, and little girls. They needed a place to stay. Not large or fancy. A room for the girls. Land enough to vegetable a little and hay the horse. Henry listened for his wife and shook his head. The screen was no protection—futile diagrams of air. He shifted his weight and the clogged squares blotched Omensetter's cheek. There was mud to his thighs. It hung on the wagon's wheels and caked the belly of the dog. His teeth weren't really clean. Henry realized that, heavy-jawed and solemn as Matthew Watson was, as slow and cautious, as full of dreams of geese as he was, continually making the sound of a shotgun in his head, Omensetter had nevertheless instantly overpowered him, set his fears at rest, met his doubts, and replaced his customary suspiciousness with an almost heedless trust; yet to have sent Omensetter to see him this way was strangely out of character too, for Watson knew perfectly well that the ancient Perkins house which Pimber had so recently inherited was very near the river and a yearly casualty of flood. The paint was peeling and the porch would soon be split by weeds. Henry sighed and flicked the screen. He had overpowered even Matthew. Matthew—who listened only to the high honk of the geese and his own hammer, and whose sight had been nearly burned out by the forge.

He had a place, Henry finally said. It was down the South Road near the river, but he hadn't thought of renting it on such notice, at such a time of year. There were difficulties. . . . Omensetter opened out his arms and Pimber, trembling, laughed. There, you see; we'll care for it and keep it well in life. Pimber clenched his fists upon the curious phrase. His wife was in the crook of the door, holding her skirts, breathing carefully. It's down the South Road, though, he said, and near to the river. We all love the water, Omensetter said. Lucy and I are good for houses and we will promptly pay.

Who knew what sort of boots? Five narrow boards between his feet. Three flies regaining the screen. The shadows of clouds on the panes of water. His wife gently rustling. And the stout man is talking, his hands undulating. A button on his shirt is broken. Under his arms there are stains. His stubby fingers clutch the air as though to detain it. Lis-sen. Lis-sen. The dog runs under the wagon. We have wives of the same name, Henry finds himself saying.

There, you see, Omensetter said, as if his words included explanation.

Pimber laughed again. It's down the South Road, I'll get the key. As he moved away he heard her knuckles snap. Behind him she stood stiff and motionless as a stick, he knew. She wouldn't like the mud on her porch either. He said the days of the week. After the habit of his father. He said the months of the year. Then he went the back way for his horse and prepared to hear about his crimes at dinner. Five boards between his boots. Mud on every step. A half a button missing. How many down? His face was broken when he laughed. Sweetly merciful God, Henry wondered, sweetly merciful God, what has struck me?

Omensetter left the wagon out all night, and the next morning he took his horse down the South Road and pulled Hatstat's rig out of the mud where three horses had skidded, kicked, and floundered the day before. Then he went to work as he'd said he would, bringing Hatstat's carriage on to town while his wife, daughters, and the dog moved in the wagon things and cleaned the house. Henry rose at dawn. His wife was scathing. Wrapped in the bedclothes, she confronted him like a ghost. He dawdled along the road to the Perkins house until he heard the children shouting. He tried to help and thus to handle everything he could: he peeked in boxes on the sly and sat in chairs and backed apologetically from room to room ahead of brooms and mops and mop-thrown water, observing and remembering, until, obedient to some overwhelming impulse, astonished and bewildered by it though it filled him with the sweetest pleasure, he secretly thrust one of their tin spoons into his mouth. But this action ultimately frightened him, especially the delight he took in it, and he soon apologized once more for being in the way, and left.

Hatstat thanked Omensetter graciously, and he and Olus Knox, who, with his horse, had helped Hatstat the day before and got mud rubbed through his clothes and lumped up in his crotch, said nice things to people afterward of Omensetter's luck and thought, at the same time, of flood.

Rain fell a week and the river rose, water moving against water, a thin sheet of earth and air between the meeting rise and fall. The rain beat steadily on the river. The South Road drained. Clay banks slid quietly away, pools grew; runnels became streams, streams torrents. Planks laid across the street sank from sight. Everyone wore hip boots who had them. Everyone worried for the south.

You didn't tell him about the river, did you, she would suddenly say. Whenever Henry was at home now, his wife quietly followed him and in a venomous low voice struck with the question. She waited for the middle of an action like filling his pipe or settling himself to read, often when he had no thought that she was near, while shaving or buttoning his pants. You didn't tell him about the water, did you? How are you going to feel when the river's up and you're down there in a boat, getting him out? Or don't you intend to? Is it dangerous there when the river floods? Mightn't you drown?

I might, I might. Would it please you?

I'd have no husband then to shame me. . . . You didn't tell him about the river, did you?

He knows, he said; but his wife would offer him a sweet and gentle smile and sadly turn away. He would try to read or strop his blade—continue whatever it was she'd broken into—but she would suddenly be back again.

Mightn't he?

Before he could direct an answer she'd have passed into another room.

He saw the waterline on the house, you mean? That's how he knows?

Lucy, I told him it was down the South Road.

She laughed.

He knows the South Road, does he? Isn't he from Windham? So you told him it was down the South Road. Did he see the line on the house or the moss on the trees?

Oh, for God's sake, stop.

Those wretched things he had piled in his wagon will be afloat.

No they won't.

He didn't seem to care, though, did he, if they got wet or not. Doesn't strike me as a good sign of a responsible tenant. You'd want to know that kind more than a minute, I should think, what with mud on his boots and clothes and a wagon full of trash wide open to the weather.

Lucy, please.

Them and that baby in her . . . the land so low.

Shut up.

When he rose from his chair or put down his pipe or slammed the strap against the wall, then she would go, but not before she'd asked how much he'd got for it.

The rain stopped but the river rose anyway. It crossed the South Road with a rush. It filled woods. It drowned ponds. It carried away fences. Receding from its mark, it left silt sticking to the sides of trees. It flung skeins of slime over bushes. It took more than it gave. Olus Knox reported that the water came within thirty yards of Omensetter's side yard fence, and it seemed to Henry that more rain had fallen than had in years, yet in the past the Perkins house had always borne the stain of flood high on its peeling sides. Things are running for Omensetter, he said to Curtis Chamlay with what he hoped was a knowing smile. Curtis said apparently, and that was that.

2

Henry Pimber became convinced that Brackett Omensetter was a foolish, dirty, careless man.

First Omensetter ran a splinter in his thumb and with amusement watched it swell. The swelling grew alarmingly and Mat and Henry begged him to see Doc Orcutt about it. Omensetter merely stuffed the thumb in his mouth and puffed his cheeks behind the plug. Then, one morning, with Omensetter holding close, Mat's hammer slipped. Pus flew nearly across the shop. Omensetter measured the distance it shot and smiled with pride, washing the wound in the barrel without a word.

He stored his pay in a sock which hung from his bench, went about oblivious of either time or weather, habitually permitted things which he'd collected like a schoolboy to slip through holes in his trousers. He kept worms under saucers, stones in cans, poked the dirt all the time with twigs, and fed squirrels navy beans and sometimes noodles from his hands. Broken tools bemused him; he often ate lunch with his eyes shut; and, needless to say, he laughed a lot. He let his hair grow; he only intermittently shaved; who knew if he washed; and when he went to pee, he simply let his pants drop.

Then Omensetter bought some chickens from Olus Knox, among them one old hen whose age, as Knox told Henry after, he thought his buyer hadn't noticed. The next morning the hen was gone while the rest ran fearfully and flew in hops. At first they thought she was lost somewhere in the house, but the girls soon found her. They were diving, Omensetter said, hiding under the lifting fog, bending low to see beneath it the supernatural world and one another's bare legs stalking giants. The hen lay dead by the open well and the dog crouched growling at its lip. Henry had come to collect the rent because his wife insisted that he go in person—face to face is safer, she said—and Omensetter showed him the eyes of the fox reflect the moon. The girls swung in graceful turns around the hole, their dresses palely visible. His eyes are like emeralds, they said. They are green emeralds and yellow gold. That's because they're borrowed from the fire at the center of the earth and they see like signals through the dark. Then Omensetter told them of foxes' eyes: how they burn the bark from trees, put spells on dogs, blind hens, and melt the coldest snow. To Henry, kneeling gingerly upon a rotten board, they were dim points of red, and his heart contracted at the sight of their malice.

How do you plan to get him out, he asked, rising in front of Omensetter's chest.

You can see how bad the well wanted him. He'll have to stay where he's been put. That's the way it happened and maybe the well will tire of him and toss him out.

Henry tried to laugh. Kneeling had made him dizzy and a button was missing from Omensetter's coat. Our fox is in our well, our fox is in our well, our well was empty belly, now our fox is in our well, the girls sang, whirling more rapidly.

Be careful there, he said, those boards are rotten and one's missing. The cover should have been repaired.

It was his well really, and he fell silent when he remembered it. Then he tried a cautious, apologetic smile. It might be the fox that had been stealing Knox's chickens, he thought. That would be like Omensetter's luck, certainly—for the fox to seize the bitterest hen, gag on her as he fled, and then fall stupidly through the ground. What an awful thing: to have the earth open to swallow you almost the moment you took the hen in your jaws. And to die in a tube. Henry found he couldn't make a fist. At best, the fox must be badly bruised, terribly cramped, his nose pressed into the damp well wall. By this time his coat would be matted and his tail fouled, and his darkness would extend to the arriving stars. A dog would bloody his paws and break his teeth against the sides and then wear out his body with repeated leaping. By morning—hunger, and the line of the sun dipping along the wall, the fetid smells—bitter exhaustion of spirit. No wonder he burned with malice.

You know what those eyes are? They're a giant's eyes.

The girls squealed.

Sure—that hole goes through to the land of the giants.

Omensetter struck Henry heavily on the back.

As a boy Henry hadn't been able to carry a bucket brimming from the well; he couldn't spade or hoe with strength or plow; he couldn't saw or wield a beaverish ax. He stumbled when he ran; when he jumped, he slipped; and when he balanced on a log, he fell. He hated hunting. His nose bled. He danced, though he could never learn to fish. He didn't ride, disliked to swim; he sulked. He was last up hills, stayed home on hikes, was always "it." His sisters loved to tease, his brothers to bully him. And now he couldn't even make a fist.

Honestly—what are you going to do?

Omensetter swung happily about the well with the girls, their bodies casting a faint shadow on the yellowish grass.

Naa-thing, they sang, naa-thing.

Omensetter must feel the cruelty of his mood, Henry thought, or was he also free of that? Shed of his guilty skin, who wouldn't dance?

Of course you can't do that, he said; you'll have to get him out. He'll starve down there.

He'll have to stay where the hen has put him, Omensetter said firmly. Spring will float him to the top.

That poor animal?—you can't do that. It's dangerous besides.

But Henry thought how he would fare if the earth spoke of his crimes. Suppose the instant you uttered a cutting word, your cheek bled.

Anyway, you'll have to board it up—the girls, he said.

Suppose your tongue split when you lied.

This well, it's in a manner of speaking . . . mine. I totally forgot—the existence of . . .

He sighed. Murder would also be suicide.

I'll help you close it up, he said.

Oh, they enjoy it, Omensetter said. They'd cry if I covered it.

The girls pulled gaily at their father's arms. He began to whirl like a ribboned pole.

How long . . . do you think . . . that giant's eyes . . . will last?

Henry held unsteadily to a sapling.

You could shoot him, I guess. You have a gun.

The well wants him. . . . Maybe he'll get out. . . . Hooh . . . it's getting dark, girls. . . . No . . . whoosh . . . stop.

I'll do it, then, Henry said, and he imagined the shot leaping from the barrels of his gun to rush at the fox.

Lamps lit in the house. Henry measured the walls of his sky while he drifted away to the buggy. It wasn't dippered yet, but soon there'd be nothing to aim by, for darkness would silence the fox's eyes. The grass had begun to glisten. Animals felt pain, he understood, but never sorrow. That seemed right. Henry could crush a finger, still the wound might be a war in a distant country for all the concern he could let it cause him, he lived so fearfully; but such a creature as the fox filled up the edges of its body like a lake the shot would dapple as it entered. You could startle an animal, but never surprise. The buggy's seats were slick, the dew was heavy. He thought he should have a cloth somewhere, a piece of toweling. There were bats overhead. Yes, here's where he had it. Henry began to dry a place for himself. Fluttering like leaves, the bats flew securely. And would the stars be startled, looking up, to find the fox out burning in their early skies?

There you are, you've been reasonably careful, you've kept your butt dry.

Henry spoke crossly and the carriage began to bounce him.

So the well went through to the land of the giants. Why not? Should he turn away from that—that callousness and that romance—to Mrs. Henry Pimber's firm prim mouth? her festive unlatching hands?

Omensetter's a natural-born politician, Olus Knox had said; he's what they call the magnetic kind. How inadequate that image was, Henry thought, when he could draw the heart right out of your side. Jethro Furber had been dramatic, as usual, painfully pinching his hands together. That man, he declared, lives like a cat asleep in a chair. Mat smiled gently: a view full of charity, he said; but Tott was laughing at the sight of Furber actually hold-ing the pieces of himself together while he tried to condemn Omensetter's simple harmony and ease, as Henry guessed, with such a tranquil image. Yet how could Omensetter bear that terrible pair of eyes? Of—of course, Furber stuttered. A cat's a pretty thing, of course. How pretty a man? Is it attractive in a man to sleep away his life? take a cow's care? refuse a sparrow of responsi-bility? Tott shrugged. The cat's an unmitigated egotist, a slothful beast, slave to its pleasure. No need to preach, Tott said, nettled; cats were his idols. I've seen him. Furber swiveled to catch each eye. I've seen him—wading. The memory made Henry grin, slowing the buggy. Wading? He pictured Jethro standing in a puddle, trousers rolled. Tott claimed afterward that Furber filled a chair like a leaky bag of potatoes. No—no—an unsteady stack of packages, a teetery tower, an uncertain clutch—yes—a chair full of perilous parcels—or—in sum: a bunch of unbundling bundles. And sleep? sleep? Sleep is like Siam—he's never been there. It was true, Henry thought, they were utter opposites. Furber's body was a box he lived in; his arms and legs propelled and fended for him like a cripple's crutches and a blind man's cane; while Omensetter's hands, for instance, had the same expression as his face; held out his nature to you like an offering of fruit; and added themselves to what they touched, enlarging them, as rivers meet and magnify their streams. Wading. Amused, Henry formed the word again, and allowed himself to watch the woods fill in. Pasting kites, Furber'd said. Rolling hoops. Holler-ing in the street. Fur-burr (Henry answered now as he should have then), Fur-burr, you're just an old lady . . . yes—a lacy old lady. But the evening had filled in Furber too, and his fierce puritan intensity. For that, Henry was grateful. He knew he'd never get used to the hot dark white-faced little man, always and seldom the same, who claimed one Sunday that the Lord had made him small and had given him his suit of pulpit clothing so he could represent to everyone the hollow inside of their bodies. No, hardly a lacy old lady. We're all niggers here—within, he'd shouted. You have a stomach cramp, he'd said, doubling, knotting his arms about his knees—then I'm its shadow. Once I was eight feet tall, he'd exclaimed, but God made me small for this purpose. What sort of talk was that? . . . Blackened body-hollows. Jesus, Henry thought, like the well's column. Suppose he'd fallen there himself?

> Ding dong bell,
> Pimber's down our well.

Henry tried to urge his horse into a run, but on the badly rutted road, in the poor light, it refused. He cursed a moment, and gave up.

> Who pushed him in?
> Little Henry Pim.

Omensetter was no better than an animal himself. That was right. And Henry wondered what it was he loved, since he thought he knew what he hated.

> Who'll pull him out?
> Nobody's about.

What Omensetter did he did so simply that it seemed a miracle. It eased from him, his life did, like the smooth broad crayon line of the man who drew your cartoon at the fair. He had an ease impossible to imitate, for the moment you were aware, the instant you tried . . .

> What a naughty thing was that,
> To catch our little Pimber at,
> Who never did him any harm,
> But . . .

Or did he move so easily because, despite his size, he wasn't fat inside; he hadn't packed the past around his bones, or put his soul in suet. Henry had seen the engravings—of the skeletons' dance. It was, however, a *dance* . . . and if you had to die to dance . . . ? What were the chances of the fox? The fox, he felt, had never seen his past disposed of like a fall of water. He had never measured off his day in moments: another—another—another. But now, thrown down so deeply in himself, into the darkness of the well, surprised by pain and hunger, might he not revert to an earlier condition, regain capacities which formerly were useless to him, pass from animal to Henry, become human in his prison, X his days, count, wait, listen for another—another—another—another?

When he reached home his wife immediately asked him if he had the rent and how much was it, but he passed through the house in a daze, wild and frantic, and went off again with his gun without answering, so she had to yell after him—what fool thing are you up to now?—but she would see, he thought, bitterly observing that she hadn't thought of him as off to murder or to hunt but only as a fool bent on his foolishness; and in the back of Omensetter's house, not bothering anyone, he shot the fox out with both barrels. The shot screamed on the well sides and one pellet flew up and struck him on the arm so hard through his jacket that it stuck; but he, with great effort, since the cool stars watched, paid no mind to his wound, hearing the fox thrash and go still. Furthermore, I'll board it up tomorrow, he thought.

Driving home slowly, his joy draining away and leaving him fearful and cold, Henry remembered how, as a boy, he had waited at the top of the cellar stairs for his father to emerge, and how, when his father's waist was level with his eyes, without a motive or any kind of feeling that he recognized, he had struck him a terrible blow in the stomach, driving the air from his father's lungs and forcing him to bend abruptly, dropping his startled face near. Henry's mouth had filled with saliva; the base of his tongue had tingled; he had taken breath. Yet thank God he had run, weeping instead. Saliva washed over his teeth as he fled. He remembered too the sound of apples falling slowly on the stairs. His legs had been the first of him to be appalled. They had fallen apart like sticks.

Killing the fox had given him the same fierce heedless kind of joy, and now he leaned back in the buggy, careless of the reins, weak, waiting his punishment. Indeed, he did feel strange. He had sensed his past too vividly. His head rolled with the road. He knew, of course, it was Omensetter he had struck at. He took no care with their life, that man. Luck like his did not come naturally. It had to be deserved. Anger began very faintly to stir in him again, and he was able to steady his head. But the night had blackened, the moon and stars were now under clouds, the world around him had been erased. He sank wearily in his clothes and let his head wag loosely in the circle of his collar.

Upon the beach Henry Pimber rested, passing five white carefully gathered stones from hand to hand. He could not see his face where it had fallen in the water. Omensetter's darkened house stood in his head amid clipped grass. Cold dew struck him and the sound of water in the dusk, soft and distant, like slow steps that reach through sleep, possessed him. The man was more than a model. He was a dream you might enter. From the well, in such a dream, you could easily swing two brimming buckets. In such water an image of the strength of your arms would fly up like the lark to its singing. Such birds, in such a dream, would speed with the speed of your spirit through its body, where, in imitation of the air, flesh has turned itself to meadow. The pebbles fell, one by one, to the sand. Henry struggled with the urge to turn his head. Instead he bent and picked the pebbles up. The moon appeared. The pebbles were the softest pearls—like sweetest teeth. And Lucy's lamp went through his house and climbed the stairs. He flung the stones. They circled out, taking the light. One sank in the water's edge; one clicked on a greater stone; one found the sand; another brushed the marsh weeds. The last lay at his feet like a dead moth. He drove home slowly for a clouding moon.

Henry loved to tell of everything he saw when he passed Omensetter's house, though he was cowardly and quiet about the fox, and neither he nor his listeners ever thought how strange it was they took such interest in the smallest things their newest neighbor did, for Omensetter cast an interest like a shade. It was as though one could, by knowing when his beans went in or when he cut his firewood for washing, hoed, or simply walked a morning in the oak and maple woods like a tree among the trees himself, learn his secret, whatever his secret was, since it must somehow be the sum of these small things all grown together, for as Dr. Orcutt was so fond of pointing out, every measle was a sign of the disease, or as Mat Watson said, every turn of wind or rift of cloud was a parcel of the acreage of weather.

Henry asked him how he knew it was a boy, for girls, he said, were also known to kick, and Edna Hoxie, thin enough, she said, to crawl inside and pull a fat one out, stopped by to offer up her service for the time. But Omensetter said he knew. He said that birthing would be easy for a boy who'd learned to crawl already. Don't be disappointed, Brackett; Olus Knox has three, Henry said. Each time his wife conceived he hoped like you, and he has three. He finds it hard without a boy, with three who'll trade his name away when now she's past her time. It could be just the same with you. I hope not . . . but it could be just the same. You shouldn't count too much on what comes out of her this fall or figure from how hard the baby kicks or from how high it rides. Still Omensetter laughed. He said he knew. He'd read the signs.

At first the wound was merely sore and then the arm was stiff. Get Dr.

Orcutt, for the love of God, Henry said, and slunk to bed. There the stiff-ness spread into the neck. Lucy learned in Gilean that Orcutt was with Decius Clark at the bottom of the county. When Watson and Omensetter arrived, Henry had ceased to speak and his face grew tight as they watched. A shotgun wound? Then slippery elm, I think, Mat said. Lucy wept, run-ning from room to room with balls of cloth in her arms. The lips drew back from the teeth, the eyelids flattened. Opium, I think, Mat said. The body bent. The room should be dark, I think, Mat said. Lucy stumbled up and down the stairs and the jaws at last completely locked. She was drawn in by the wheeze, and when Omensetter asked her suddenly: have you any beets? the rags rolled out of her arms. The Reverend Jethro Furber, his twisted fig-ure like a knotted string, was murmuring, immure him, cure him or immure him—some such thing—if he were really in the corner like a clothes tree, was he? was it Watson where the walls were willowing? Matthew drew off Lucy to another room. How easily he saw them. Godhead hid from him His holy farse. Immure him, Fermy murmuring, cure him or immure him. Through the withering wall he watched her try to kiss him when he helped her on the bed; tear wildly at her clothes. All I lack is a little luck and I'll lick that lock, who said? Mat then tiptoed to the bellowing hall and shut himself in its largest closet. Around him linens, towels, and female things were shelved.

Omensetter made a poultice of mashed raw red beet and bound it to the wound with rags and to the palms of the hands. Henry felt his sight fail as his lips yawned and air strenuously pushed itself between his teeth. Mat observed them from the doorway, apparently calm; but there seemed to be a button broken on his shirt and a tear in his sleeve. Then his body melted. It's up to Henry and the lockjaw now, Omensetter said; it's just between them. I'll stay, Mat said, he needs some company. But Furber hung like a drapery demonstrating him, his hollow—all could see it, billowing thinly, the wall gauze, and God's laws flickering. Omensetter's hands were stained with beet. He doesn't care, he said, his body also dwindling. You loosened her clothing, good, Henry heard Omensetter say as his footsteps faded on the stairs, now she's asleep. Mat held to Henry's hand while Henry whistled steadily like steam.

Orcutt came by evening, tore the poultice off the wound, gave opium and aconite, forced lobelia and capsicum into the mouth, stared at the bandaged palms but did not touch the wrappings, waited for vomiting. Watson said to Henry afterward that in his opinion the jaw had already begun to soften, and he was not surprised when the vomiting began. I'd have sworn it was hopeless, Dr. Orcutt said. The Reverend Jethro Furber came to pray and the jaw was loose by morning. Edna Hoxie, midwife, brazen, asked Omensetter for the recipe and bragged to everyone how easily she'd got it.

3

That Omensetter had a secret no one doubted now. Gossip was continuous, opinion split, the atmosphere political. One would have thought it France. Henry's own salvation was the central thing, and Henry was frequently vexed to the point of tears, weak as he still was, by the constant queries, the noisy quarrels, the wild conjectures of his friends. Nothing escaped them: chance was reperceived as calculation, distant possibilities were carried briskly into likelihood, the flimsiest hypotheses spun into woolens for a tapestry, and each conclusion was communicated to the town like a disease. At first consigned by nearly everyone to God and so to the faith of Reverend Furber, though always by a smaller group to Science and hence to the skill of Dr. Orcutt, the cure—except for a scattered few who insisted upon the will and constitution of Henry himself—was now almost universally awarded to the beet-root poultice and the luck of Brackett Omensetter. But what did this amount to? This credited the cure to . . . what? Edna Hoxie had an increase of trade, though Maggie Scanlon—unwedded, large—scoffed at the question. Don't he always get what he wants, she said. He's happy, ain't he, the sonofabitch. I wish to God I was.

For Henry his illness was a joy and an agony that still went on. Whole days it rained continually and water spilled out of dry containers. He would sit in the sun with a blanket on his knees and feel the rain come down on the stiff summer leaves and fly from the dusty spouts. He begged the fox's pardon constantly, as weak and palsied in his chair, as loose from his will, as he'd been during the first days of his recovery. His arm would dart out, seizing a flood of light in its fist. Well, he'd exclaim in surprise, it still seems to be raining. Lucy would shriek at him, the sun drum on his chest. His eye entered everything like a needle even yet—penetrated, looped, and then emerged—and he hung these pictures on a string like beads around his neck. For hours he fingered the air obscenely, and when he moved, he felt they clicked. He would say to his wife: here's your vulva, it's next to the nose of the beagle; or he'd say: here's your blood, dark as wet bark; or he'd say: here are the stools your bowels are shaping; on and on, until she struck him.

Cruelty brought no relief, as sight did not, and yet he sometimes thought his pain might simply be the pain of his shedding, since it often seemed that he was sloughing like a snake the skins of all his seasons; his white fats and red flesh were lost in a luminous wash. Sunshine lapped at him, rose over him, and soon there were pieces of him drifting off—his head like a hat, legs like logs. Then gently he toweled his bones until they shone. They made a fair tree; they weren't so bad. Henry hadn't been prepared for anyone like Omensetter. He'd been content to believe that he would always live with usual men in a usual world; but he'd lived with himself all these years like a stranger—and with everybody else. So on these shining armatures he fancied that he shaped a fine new unstreaked clay through which life lifted eagerly like moisture warming toward its heat. There was no mistaking Omensetter's likeness; Henry was newborn in that waltzing body now; he had joined it as you join a river swimming; surely Lucy must have seen . . . but he didn't mind if she had. Perceptions no longer pierced his eyes—his needles returning; instead he poured out giddily.

In this mood Henry could remember piling up a mountain in the wagon: the quilts and comforts, the toys, the tools and the utensils—tasting their metals in his mouth. Clouds were living in the river; Gilean was resting by it, the air so clear. There was every house out honest and every barn banked proper to the weather. The trees were beautiful and bare, and the tracks of the wagons glistened. On the way they'd sung "Rose Aylmer." Then sometimes they counted birds. There were rings in the pools of water by the road and the air was clean as it is after rain. He thought it would be healthy for the boy to live by the river, to catch fish and keep frogs, to grow up with good excitement.

But his wife would come and jar him loose. Age had beautifully lined her jaw. Her knuckles were huge. She rattled tins and silverware in drawers.

Where have you got to now? What are you thinking?

Nothing.

Nothing? You should see your face. Nothing!

Nothing.

It's fatty. You should see your face. It's fatty.

No.

What do you go to the shop for? You can scarcely walk yet you're always off down there, and in this weather when it's hot. What do you talk about? Does Tott tell stories? Or is the Furber preaching at you, trying to fish your soul out like the last pickle? Oh, I know what's happened. You've gone to the devil. That's what's happened.

No.

It's fatty.

He would sit so quietly within the shadows behind the forge that visitors scarcely noticed he was there. It was like the effect of his illness, for after a period of pain and confusion he thought his eyes had cleared and he had watched from his bed as if from out of the world. It had been as he imagined it was like to be invisible. Your eyes were open. People looked into them but they didn't think you saw. They were less than a mirror, no more than a painting of eyes. The sickness was nothing. Many times he had struggled to say that he could hear. Being stretched to pieces was nothing. Many times he'd tried to shout I can see, I can see you—hissing instead. Fighting for breath was nothing. Burning was nothing. Locked in a shrinking boot of flesh, hour after hour he remembered Jethro Furber's prayers.

The child of Decius Clark, said Dr. Orcutt through his beard, is very bad. A bee stung him six weeks come Tuesday on the neck. You never saw a bigger swelling.

The doctor's fingers formed an egg.

Clark used to be a potter. Quit. He's farming now—or trying to. Not much account. I won't collect.

Orcutt aimed his spit.

Let's see that finger Matthew smashed.

You're a bastard, Truxton, Watson said.

You took on so, I thought I'd see. Well, Brackett? No charge for curiosity. The nail grow back? Mat told me that he knocked it clean away—is that a fact?

Omensetter held his hand out silently.

Orcutt grinned.

Mat's took up surgery, I see. Might drive me square from business.

He turned the thumb.

A scar of great bravery, the doctor said. What do you charge?

Mat shook his head helplessly.

Well, it always happens, cut like that.

Orcutt dropped the hand. The arm fell muscleless.

A sledge ain't a very thoughtful knife. The next time you get stung like that you see me right straight off and maybe you won't grow up such a swelling.

I hit him accidental, Mat exclaimed.

All round you're mighty lucky, mister, Orcutt said.

Then he asked Hatstat how the fishing was.

Rotten, Hatstat said.

Always is, this time of year, the doctor said.

They should be up.

Ah, George, they never is, you want them to. Ain't that right, Brackett?

It isn't cool enough, said Tott.

Mat rattled through his tools.

It was stifling in the shop, and fiercely hot by the forge.

Well, he's a friendly sort, Clark is, said Dr. Orcutt, spitting. Not much account. I won't collect. But friendly. His wife is taking on about the boy but Clark is calm, I will say that. He's calm. How's your infection, Henry? It all gone? Ain't you out a little early like a winter robin?

It's been weeks, Henry mumbled, backing deeply in the shop.

Home remedy—by God, it's killed an awful lot, Henry. Could have lost that arm, you know. Fix your horseshoe game permanent. Does Brackett play?

We won't let him, said Israbestis Tott.

Too bad, I'd like to see that.

Juice oozed from the doctor's mouth. He spat a running stain.

Everyone fell silent.

The child of Decius Clark is very bad, said Dr. Orcutt once again, but Decius is a friendly sort, and calm.

. . . Then there was Israbestis Tott entertaining him with tunes: jigs, trots, polkas—Henry thought his mind would break. Then there was Matthew Watson, who sat by his bedside with his huge hands in his lap like a pair of frogs; there were endless files of whispering women; there was Jethro Furber in the costume of a witch, threatening the divine with spells; there was Lucy, lovely as a treetop in the door's grain, Furber as a drape, Mat a lamp, Tott a shriek, Furber both frogs, Orcutt their leaps. . . .

A hen's first egg is always female.

Orcutt burned his spit.

Mares who've seen the stallion late have colts. Scientific fact.

Luther Hawkins tested the blade of his knife with his thumb, then sighted along it and winked at the tip.

Ain't it the month, he said. The women get the odd ones.

Orcutt shook his head.

All thought a while in silence. The iron was a pale rose.

I read a Swiss professor . . . hell . . . what was his name? . . . Thury. That's it, Thury. He says the same. Danielson—downstate—has tried it. Works with cows. Works fine. Fact.

Orcutt showed his teeth.

But I couldn't say, you move the problem on from cows to ladies.

Henry giggled against his will.

It's out of my experience, Watson said, and George Hatstat laughed like a whistling train.

Orcutt hitched about and peered at Henry through the dark.

How's Lucy these days, Henry? Bearing up?

Watson put tongs on the iron.

Orcutt rolled his chew. His lips gleamed.

She ought to get out more.

Wars, Watson said.

He began hammering.

Wars, he shouted, more boys . . . replace dead ones.

Sparks flew in arcs and showers to the floor.

Dr. Orcutt wiped his mouth and stared at Henry through the rain of sparks.

The bar—reluctant—bent.

The doctor leaned back, tilting his chair. He gazed solemnly at the ceiling where a spider dropped itself by jerks from a beam.

Omensetter threaded a needle.

There was a lull in the hammering through which Henry's ears sang.

In passing, Lloyd Cate waved.

Each man looked morose and thoughtful.

Tott patted his pockets, hunting his harmonica.

Finally Orcutt said: lucky to be alive by God—in a low but outraged voice.

The hammering began again. The cool iron jumped.

Luther Hawkins moved the blade of his knife with caution, rolling back a sliver like a piece of skin. Hatstat followed him intently, while Omensetter stabbed a piece of leather with his needle.

Orcutt straightened; spat heavily at the dropping spider. The spit bore it off. At this the doctor slapped his knee and stood.

Authorities I've read . . . honest scientific minds, remember, gentle-men . . . claim males are made in special weather . . . they result from special postures . . . or depend upon the testicle that's emptied. Honest scientific minds. It's quite a problem for them. Some screw for science only in the afternoon, while others keep their faith with evening—here Orcutt chuckled—it's a matter of light, I understand, but which makes which I can't remember.

He hefted his bag.

You rest easy, Henry, hey? No lifting. No climbing. No spading. That sort of thing.

Beneath his beard, Orcutt loosened his collar.

Or it's the length of the dick—how far it throws the seed.

The doctor carefully dusted his trousers.

Whew-ee.

Thus he remained a moment.

All that's manure, he said. Manure.

Then he strode away.

Henry watched the forge until it burned his eyes.

Later Curtis Chamlay looked in to ask if anyone intended fishing in the morning, and Luther Hawkins, admiring the point on his stick, carrying on the conversation in his head, chuckled.

Dogs don't care, he said. It's a fact.

George Hatstat said: know what Blenker said that Edna Hoxie told his wife? Douche with milk if you want a girl.

And all she does is douche with the Dutchman.

Hawkins picked dirt from a crack.

That fat Dutchman—how does he get on?

Take it easy, Chamlay said, laughing. Tott's ears are burning.

Why should they, Hawkins said. You listen at that preacher like he does, his ears hears every word there is.

That Dutchman, Chamlay said. I'll bet his cock is curly.

Pig's cock, Hawkins said.

Blenker isn't Dutch, Tott said.

Shit.

Hoxie says boys swell the right teat more.

Ah shit.

No, honest, Curt.

Hatstat clutched his chest.

Girls make special aches in the left side. That's what she said.

She's full of shit.

In the dust Hawkins began a drawing of the Dutchman mounting.

It's meat that does it, Chamlay said. Beef. It's got some chemical.

The bar began to glow again.

Hawkins scratched his drawing out.

I saw one in a bottle at a fair, he said. A little thing, you know. Pink and purply—whatever color. It was pickled . . . wrinkled . . . real pale and upside down in the stuff . . . looked like a pig . . . but dead . . . Jesus.

Mat hefted his hammer impatiently.

Hawkins drew a Mason jar.

It depends on what she eats, Chamlay insisted.

Then Hatstat made a disrespectful noise.

Come on, Omensetter, what do you think? is it going to be a boy?

If she lolls about and stuffs on candy, Chamlay said, she gets a sugar baby—

Naw—shit.

You've got boys, George, right? But Rosa Knox? When Rosa's pregnant all she eats is sugar buns. Ask Splendid Turner if she don't.

Luther Hawkins nodded.

Fact, he said. A scientific fact . . . I wonder what that little Perkins devil filled Maggie Scanlon's belly with.

That Perkins, Chamlay said. I know him. I'll bet it wasn't cock.

You think that belly's growing up from spit, Curt, George said.

What a bitch, said Hawkins. She'll give birth to dogs.

Mat's hammer rang the metal.

Afterward, when Mat had hushed his iron in the rain barrel, they discussed fishing for a long time. Olus Knox had come and he was always eloquent about it. Everyone, that is, but Omensetter did, who sewed on silently, a look of intense bewilderment on his face.

4

I couldn't sleep. Did you notice how restless I was and wound in the sheets? The weather must be changing. I'm always restless then.

She filled her cheeks with air.

Henry ignored his wife's voice; dipped his hand in the wind. The leaves were learning of the cold. He turned his palm, allowing the wind to pass between his fingers. Cool as hill water it seemed to flow from the pale clouds. This is how it feels, he thought, to run through the cup of Omensetter's hands. Time goes coolly through the funnel of his fingers—click, click, click—like water over stones. When he had lately felt the wind he seldom had another feeling; yet there were moments, as if in dream, when he could plunge his hand into the air and feel the stream at the lip of Being, and the hesitating water. There was a bather at the precipice with breasts as great as God's, nippled as the berry bush, bright as frost. Corn-golden hair was gathered to His thighs. Not in my image. Nothing like me. But in the dream that disabled him, he was afloat on the brink, poised above the incredible gulf like a bird, while each minute frightened him by passing over. With his hands on his ears he could feel them falling. Below lay an empty plain where the bright stream dried. It then became a road that thinned to a rail in the cold horizon. He heard the roar of a miracle coming, a long beak looking for snakes.

A soft plop. The air rushed out.

It's going to rain, you can see that.

Henry withdrew his hand.

The rent is due. I'll walk.

Walk. Walk. He'll walk too. You'll pass.

Likely, he said, fetching his coat.

Is walking what the doctor ordered? Whoo. Our room was stuffy as a tomb last night. Didn't you feel it? I don't want him here, heaven knows, that beast. He's like an animal. Breathes like an animal. Awf. Smells like an animal. Heaven knows I don't want him here.

That's why I'm going. He won't come.

Oh no it's not. He'll come. He'll come along. You want to meet him out of sight of me, that's all. You should stay right here and rest. He's just a beast, a beast. And with her big lately he's been a while without her—unless he never paid any mind to her pain.

Lucy, please.

Now they've had that boy it'll be a bit before he'll dare to come at her again, I'd think. Imagine that fat creature sprawled on top of you. I'll bet there's fur on him there like a tom cat's.

For Christ's sake.

Oh pooh, don't be a prude.

She plunged her spoon into a bowl.

I wonder how poor Matthew can afford him, she said in a quieter voice. He can't make as much as his rent, I'm certain of that.

I wish to God—

Salt. Wasn't it last time I left out the salt? You remember. They were flat. You complained all evening and it was wretchedly hot.

Sometimes she made Henry think of steam—of something dangerously vaporous and white—but she stood at the counter now as stiff and metallic as the spoon whose edge she wore around and around in the bowl that she pressed into her stomach.

Well, he works hard and I'm sure he's worth what he's getting. . . . You're down there most of the day since your sickness.

Omensetter saved my life. You hate him for it.

Oh, for sweet sakes, Hen, you know you always denied it. You never said he saved your life before. That sort of magic? You only want to rile me.

She suddenly turned to him with a weak sad face.

I've a lot to complain of myself, Hennie, not just about salt, Hennie—a lot to complain of. You know . . . our . . . and, oh, you oughtn't to do me this way, Hen.

Her face grew hard again.

Well. Wasn't that what you said? It was Dr. Orcutt, I thought, you gave your gratefuls to. Hoosh. My arm tires easy. In this kitchen. You should have seen him in this kitchen—my personal place. Chopping beets. These counters aren't my height. Well, they weren't made for me but for your mother, of course. He stained the wood in them badly, you can see it—there—there—

No, those—

See—over there—and here—and there—there—ah, the dirty beast.

She released the spoon and put her palm on the counter; began patting the wood.

Your mother, now, could stir a day and never sigh more than her usual.

Well, he works. He's handy.

Oh, I'm sure Matthew never regrets him. He *is* handy.

She set the bowl down with a jar.

Though what an easy fool he is to dance the tune for both of you.

Mat pays him properly, and after all, he's grown.

Hoo. He's huge. Takes care of his children on that, does he? And his wife too? She must be mighty saving. What is he owing you?

He pays, he pays.

Lalee. Of course he pays. He's what, if I weren't such a well-raised lady, I would call a poor stupid bastard—a poor stupid bastard.

Well, Lucy, that's one thing—you *are* a lady.

She looked at him sharply.

More than you're a decent man, she said.

Then she began to cry and turned from the counter to blow her nose.

Dr. Orcutt, thought Henry. I hate him. His teeth slide in his beard and his eyes cross.

Come out of the door. Are you hearing me? Henry? When he was here he stared at me like an owl.

You should comb your hair.

It was indecent—how he stared. Stared. He's just an animal. Hairy as a bear. His head turns the whole way around.

I'm going.

Go, then. Go. You'll pass in the woods, the two of you. I know. You'll pass. Must you be walking there? You're catching cold again. I saw you shiver.

No.

Like an old dog going everywhere there is a patch of sun to sit and shiver in. No one ever comes to see us. People used to—Gladys, Rosa, Mat. No one now since you were sick. He always takes the wood path. Why?

It saves time.

Time? Oh dear. Time. The animal. Smell him. There's no time to him. There's only himself. Like a cow whose bowels are moving. Heavens—time. What do you want from him? You'll never get it, whatever it is. He cares for no one, don't you know that? Not even you, Henry. Oh, look what you're doing—letting the wind in. Shut the door.

The path took Henry Pimber past the slag across the meadow creek, where his only hornbeam hardened slowly in the southern shadow of the ridge and the trees of the separating wood began in rows as the lean road in his dream began, narrowing to nothing in the blank horizon, for train rails narrow behind anybody's journey; and he named them as he passed them: elm, oak, hazel, larch, and chestnut tree, as though he might have been the fallen Adam passing them and calling out their soft familiar names, as though familiar names might make some friends for him by being spoken to the unfamiliar and unfriendly world which he was told had been his paradise. In God's name, when was that? When had that been? For he had hated every day he'd lived. Ash, birch, maple. Every day he thought would last forever, and the night forever, and the dawn drag eternally another long and empty day to light forever; yet they sped away, the day, the night clicked past as he walked by the creek by the hornbeam tree, the elders, sorrels, cedars, and the fir; for as he named them, sounding their soft names in his lonely skull, the fire of fall was on them, and he named the days he'd lost. It was still sorrowful to die. Eternity, for them, had ended. And he would fall, when it came his time, like an unseen leaf, the bud that was the glory of his birth forgot before remembered. He named the aspen, beech, and willow, and he said aloud the locust when he saw it leafless like a battlefield. In God's name, when was that? When had that been?

Omensetter was in his large coat today. Pieces appeared between the trees. Then tousled hair. Round hot face: determined, splotched. Pebbly teeth. His arm was lifted in a wave. This disappeared. His hand sprang out of a limb. Henry began to trot. Omensetter crossed a small glade, his feet hidden by bushes. A branch leaped in front of Henry and split his vision at its waist. His pulse grew noisy in his ears. We must take care, he thought, everything is against us.

The elder's pods won't hang through winter, I'm afraid, Omensetter said. The moss is thick and the caterpillar's fur is deep.

I thought I'd walk your way, Henry said, for exercise.

Omensetter laughed. His teeth were bleached.

It wasn't for the rent, I knew you'd be along with that. . . . And how's the boy?

The boy is fine. We have him sleeping south to catch the sun.

What have you named him, I haven't heard.

Amos.

Omensetter lingered on the word.

I've an uncle of that name who's rich.

He chuckled.

Lovely, Henry said. Amos Omensetter. Yes. Lovely. And the girls?

The girls?

How are they?

They're fine, and Lucy's fine. The dog is fine too. So am I.

Good, said Henry. Fine.

The aspen's leaves, he saw, were yellow early. Omensetter held money in his hand. There was a spatter of red in the maples. There the money was and there the end was. It would settle in his hand and be goodbye. Omensetter would present his back and wave. The white oaks, still green, would swallow him, the sound already gone he walked so softly in the forest. Henry bent and picked an acorn up. If there were any other way. He filled his hand with acorns, flipped them all. Omensetter's fist hid the money and Henry was grateful for that, but he saw he had trimmed his nails, and Henry felt terribly wronged. He tried to search Omensetter's face for a deeper sign but they seemed to be standing in a cloud of gnats. Henry waved his hand in front of his eyes.

I'm glad to hear that Amos does so well, he finally said.

It would never do, he thought, to ask if he would live there free.

I want to see how far the turning's gone. Let's climb the hill, it isn't far.

Omensetter held aside a pin oak's limbs and Henry followed him.

A leaf would now and then detach itself and sail into the valley. Henry tried to speak but Omensetter led. The wind flowed around him as around a rock, and Henry didn't feel his voice was strong enough to salmon such a current. He watched a broad leaf break away and dip while the woods sank below them like a receding wave. They stopped for a moment on the bare hillside, and Omensetter pointed to the flare his wife's wash made behind the trees.

Orcutt says she shouldn't do such work, Omensetter shouted, so I've taken to hanging it myself.

He lifted his shoulders expressively.

I can't get the girls to.

Then Henry realized that he could see through that massive green and changing tide as if to bottom.

It was since his sickness. . . . Everything began with—since his sickness. Once, to petrify and die had been his wish; simply to petrify had been his fear; but he had been a stone with eyes and seen as a stone sees: the world as the world is really, without the least prejudice of heart or artifice of mind, and he had come into such truth as only a stone can stand. He yearned to be hard and cold again and have no feeling, for since his sickness he'd been preyed upon by dreams, sleeping and waking, and by sudden rushes of unnaturally sharp, inhuman vision in which all things were dazzling, glorious, and terrifying. He saw then, he thought, as Omensetter saw, except for painful beauty. If there were just a way to frighten off the pain.

The path was steep. His head was nearly level with Omensetter's marching feet—his softly polished shoes. Henry felt abandoned. The blasted fellow understood his luck. He knew. The wind blew strongly and streams of tears protected Henry's eyes.

Perhaps it was the height, perhaps the wind, perhaps he was catching cold after all, but Henry felt his senses blur and merge, then focus again. Something was trying to come up—Omensetter was shouting that the frost was finicky—something was leaping against the sides of his skull. Ah—God—the fox, Henry thought, knuckling his eyes. He'd had the hen in his mouth, life in his teeth, saliva running. Feathers foamed over his nose. And then the earth had groaned. Just a moment ago. He'd never nailed the well shut, though now when he closed his teeth it all latched. Some went early, said Omensetter's shout. The leaves were minnowing. Had he thought they were playing at Adam and Eve? three children and a dog? PARADISE BY RIVERSIDE. Perhaps by Springwater Picturesquely Overrun. Exorbitantly leased from Mr. Henry God, a lesser demon, with insufficient spunk to make a Christ. No. Not Omensetter. He'd always seemed inhuman as a tree. The rest—who visited—were human. They made him sick inside his sickness. There was Mrs. Henry Pimber, her untidy hair, dull eyes, her fallen breasts and shoulders, exclaiming grief and guilt at his demise, while every gesture was a figure in a tableau of desire; there was the Reverend Jethro Furber, a blackening flame, and Mrs. Valient Hatstat, rings spotted on her fingers, a small white scar like an unwiped white of egg lying in the corner of her mouth; there was Dr. Truxton Orcutt of the rotting teeth and juice-stained beard, who looked like a house with a rusting eave; there was Mrs. Rosa Knox, sofa-fleshed and fountain-spoken, with an intermittent titter that shook her breasts, and also Israbestis Tott, together beggar, hurdy-gurdy, cup, chain, monkey; and there was Mrs. Gladys Chamlay, the scratched rod, nose like a jungle bird's, teeth like a beast's; Miss Samantha Tott, so tall she had to stoop in the sun, she thought; and all those others, with their husbands or their brothers, invisible, behind them, making sounds to celebrate the death of tea-weak Henry Pimber; while Mr. Matthew Watson, neither praying, speaking, crying, nor exclaiming, uncomfortable in a corner, surreptitiously scratched a rash through his trousers.

They haven't turned . . . in earnest yet, Omensetter said.

Not Adam but inhuman. Was that why he loved him, Henry wondered. It wasn't for his life—a curse, God knew; it wasn't for the beet-root poultice. It lay somewhere in the chance of being new . . . of living lucky, and of losing Henry Pimber. He had always crammed humanity in everything. Even the air felt guilty. Once he would have seen each tree along this slope boned humanly and branched with feeling like the black bile tree, the locust, despondent even at the summit of the highest summer. How convenient it had been to find his friends and enemies embarked in tame slow trunks, in this or that bent tree, their aspirations safely in high branches and their fires podded into quiet seed. He could pat their bodies with his hands and carve his name and make up animal emotions for them no fruit could contradict. It was always easier to love great trees than people. Such trees were honest. Their deaths showed.

Come on, Henry—what the hell—let's get where we can see.

They were silver in the spring. They were still new green like the river. The sun came to them. The wind turned them. And a dark deep glossy green grew on by the head of summer. It was like the green he sometimes saw, when the sun was right and the wind had died, cover a stone that was lightly underwater. There was hedge green and ivy, slick as slippery elm and cool as myrtle. There was slime green pale with yellow; some that was like moss or grass beneath a rock or the inside of a shuck of corn. There was every shade of green in the world. There was more than the rivers had, more than any meadow.

The wind rushed over the brow of the hill, billowing Henry's coat and flattening Omensetter's hair. Behind them, in the valley, the leaves were quiet as if at the hilltop they had sponged the wind. Here the rush covered their ears. Omensetter shouted something. Henry's toes curled in his shoes to catch the ground. He sidled awkwardly, his coat lashing his legs until his body seemed to sing like wire.

. . . the notch.

Henry ledged after him. His coat ballooned. Somehow, in this mad place, he was losing everything. Omensetter vanished. The ground seemed to fall away. He hadn't known the sea had holes but how else did you drown? Then he saw Omensetter's bushy head and he dropped into the notch, where the wind roared above them like Niagara Falls.

Henry sat on a rock and pulled his coat round him.

You don't like it, Omensetter said.

Oh no, it's fine.

They had to shout.

The cold stone pressed against him.

Lovely view, they said.

It was a terrifying wind.

I come often, Omensetter said. A boat's out. I wonder whose.

Henry shrugged and held on. He thought of the wild beauty of the trees, his own affection for them, his romantic sentiments, his wretched illness with its lying clarity.

Will you climb here in the winter?

Omensetter made a face.

Too cold. Freeze. Don't you love the noise?

No, Henry thought, I don't love the noise; the wind will wash my wits out.

But in the winter, he reflected, when the sun was in the west, the leafless trees would print the snow. Chamlay's snake fence would lace his south fields. Every bush would blossom, each twig sharply thrown, and every paltry post embark for consciousness as huge. The wind might blow here constantly, it would alter nothing; but this was the season of change, Henry's coat billowed out from him, and Omensetter's countenance escaped into the valley. An immense weariness took hold of Henry now, though the sun in the notch was warming. Of course—he'd been a fool—Omensetter lived by *not* observing—by joining himself to what he knew. Necessity flew birds as easily as the wind drove these leaves, and they never felt the curvature which drew the arc of their pursuit. Nor would a fox cry beauty before he chewed.

Remember? . . . Remember coming, Henry shouted finally, pointing to the western hill.

Omensetter put his head up in the stream where the wind blew away his words.

Ah . . . uddy . . . raid it would ray . . .

You were afraid?

. . . ott?

Were you afraid of getting wet?

Ah . . . ur.

You saved my life.

. . . ott?

I said are you happy in Gilean?

. . . ur.

Omensetter left the notch abruptly, and started down. Obedient, Henry followed, and saw between them and the sun a broad-winged hawk like a leaf on the flooding air. The sailor of the wind is loose, he thought; my life is lost down this dead hill. He had raised his arms and now he let them fall. I'm dreadfully sick . . . stupidly sick. A scientific fact. Quiet giggles shook him. And I've scarcely been alive. Henry Winslow Pimber. Now dead of weak will and dishonest weather. Some such disease. How would that look carved on my stone? He stumbled. ". . . for sweet sakes, Hennie, you'll never have a stone . . ." I shall be my own stone, then, my dear, my own dumb memorial, just as all along I've been my death and burial, my own dry well—hole, wall, and darkness. I ought to be exposed upon a mountain where the birds can pick my body, for no one could put himself on purpose in this clay. Besides, anyone who's lived so slow and stupidly as I have ought to spend his death up high. His mouth filled. Poor, foolish, stupid bastard, foolish fellow . . . foolish words . . . But I'd have made a worthier Omensetter—all new fat, wild hair, and furry testicles like a tiger's. Henry spat. A scientific fact. The saliva drifted against his coat. And when I arrived in my wagon like a careless Western hero, clouds would be swimming in the river. Rain would fall beyond us in the forest, the Ohio like a bright hair ribbon . . . Gilean—a dream. Lalee. Naa-thing. Lalee.

I have to sit somewhere.

Oh no, keep up. We'll go on down.

Lucky was he? Was he, Henry wondered—with his polished shoes and all his new concerns.

The river disappeared beneath the trees.

They walked by the creek by the hornbeam tree—Omensetter, his hand in his greatcoat pocket where the rent was, his back indifferent as a wall—by elm and oak and maple, in the bowl that turned by the riverside, toward Henry Pimber's house, where Henry followed, by the aspen, by the suede green sassafras, the beech. The silver morning grass was golden and resilient now. The slate was clean, the sandstones rich as brown sugar, and the red clay, softer after sunshine, moist, kept their feet to the slate, the sugar rocks, and the rough, resilient grass.

I've got to rest, Henry said.

The log was stripped of bark and bleached. It lay by the creek like a prehistoric bone.

Oh say, you've been sick, that's right. That hill is sort of steep. How are you feeling now—good? . . . Fine, that's good.

Omensetter took money from his pocket.

We'll have to move when we can find a place. It's a little wet there for the boy—you understand—it's a little low near the river. Well . . . You've been kind.

The money emptied into Henry's hand.

I'd better see to Lucy now, Omensetter said.

He swayed rhythmically a moment like a bear.

Lucy will be fine.

Sure—still, she must be watched—the boy . . .

Omensetter waved. Limbs divided up his back.

Goodbye.

So, Henry thought, well . . . he's going to leave the fox where he has fallen. Anyway, that's that. Yes. That. Because it was impossible to speak in a wind. And there was only weather in it, after all. Weather. Leaves. Pollen, he'd been told, from infinite plants. Dust too, of course. And the grains that carry cooking, bloom, and pine tree to the nose. Seeds naturally. Flies. Birds' song and the growl of bees. Himself—Pimber—rushing along. Yesterday it was the long night rain that fell, misplaced, through morning. Tomorrow? Tomorrow might be calm.

All right. I'll hide high up. I'll do that. Anyway, why speak in a wind? Didn't I wait for a wind to say: you saved my life?

> Ding dong bell,
> Pimber's down our well.

Didn't I wait until a wind could blow away my lie?

> Who never did him any harm,
> But wound his soul through a sleeve
> of arm.

Just the same I thought the way you walked through town, Henry was whispering just barely aloud, carrying your back as easy and as careless as you would a towel, newly come from swimming always, barely dry you always seemed, you were a sign. Remember that first evening when you came? You were a stranger, bare to heaven really, and your soul dwelled in your tongue when you spoke to me, as if I were a friend and not a stranger, as if I were an ear of your own. You had mud beneath your arms, mud sliding down the sides of your boots, thick stormy hair, dirty nails, a button missing. The clouds were glowing, a rich warm rose, and I watched them sail till dark when I came home. It seemed to me that you were like those clouds, as natural and beautiful. You knew the secret—how to be.

Henry cleared his throat. And had he simply been mistaken? Or had Omensetter been persuaded of his luck so thoroughly that now he guarded it like gold, and feared being thieved? Henry wrapped his arms like a kerchief round his head. Omensetter had been robbed already. Everybody but the preacher stole from him. Furber merely hated. But what I took was hope—a dream—fool's gold—quarrel—toothsome hen, Henry said. How weary he was, and sorry . . . sorry for everything. He was sorry about the rent, about the house, the damp, the open well, the river. He was sorry for Omensetter, sorry for Lucy, sorry for the children, sorry for Lucy again. He was sorry for himself. Tears pooled in his eyes.

Just the same, Henry said, I thought you measured us by your inhuman measure like the trees, and we were busy ants in hills or well-hived bees whose love was to pursue the queen and bring on death. When you put my hands in bandages and beets I thought I understood. There was no shade between us ever but the shade I'd drawn. You were the same to human or inhuman eye.

Henry slid from the log and hushed his whispering. He pushed at low shrubs until he couldn't see the sycamores. It was thick in this part of the woods. He parted the branches with his arms. Brackett Omensetter before he left had hid behind his face and made his back a wall. The man had been a miracle. He had, Henry spoke out angrily. A miracle. Not to be believed. And now he took defense against the world like everybody else. No miracle, a man, with a man's mask and a man's wall. Henry chuckled, unfastening the belt of his coat. He tugged at it. It would be strong. His pooled tears ran. If Brackett Omensetter had ever had the secret of how to live, he hadn't known it. Now the difference was—he knew. Everyone at last had managed to tell him, and now like everybody else he was wondering what it was. Like everybody else. Henry wiped his eyes. Don't look for Henry here, my dear, he's gone. He's full of foolishness, and off to kill a fox. But I'll not die as low as he did, for I could ornament a tree like the leaves of a maple. No. It should be tall. A white oak maybe, with its wide lobes. There was beauty in the pun: leave-taking. Though it wouldn't be an easy climb for a man who'd been so sick so recently. Still, the sun would reach him early there and stay the day, the wind blow pleasantly. It ought to seem like leaping to the sea. He went by cherry and by black gum trees calling their names aloud. He was the Adam who remembered them. Tears nevertheless began again. How sorry for it all he felt. How sorry for Omensetter. How sorry for Henry.

Accent, 1960
Published in *Omensetter's Luck,* 1966

The Pedersen Kid

Part One

I

Big Hans yelled, so I came out. The barn was dark, but the sun burned on the snow. Hans was carrying something from the crib. I yelled, but Big Hans didn't hear. He was in the house with what he had before I reached the steps.

It was the Pedersen kid. Hans had put the kid on the kitchen table like you would a ham and started the kettle. He wasn't saying anything. I guess he figured one yell from the crib was enough noise. Ma was fumbling with the kid's clothes, which were stiff with ice. She made a sound like whew from every breath. The kettle filled and Hans said,

Get some snow and call your pa.

Why?

Get some snow.

I took the big pail from under the sink and the shovel by the stove. I tried not to hurry and nobody said anything. There was a drift over the edge of the porch, so I spaded some out of that. When I brought the pail in, Hans said,

There's coal dust in that. Get more.

A little coal won't hurt.

Get more.

Coal's warming.

It's not enough. Shut your mouth and get your pa.

Ma had rolled out some dough on the table where Hans had dropped the Pedersen kid like a filling. Most of the kid's clothes were on the floor, where they were going to make a puddle. Hans began rubbing snow on the kid's face. Ma stopped trying to pull his things off and simply stood by the table with her hands held away from her as if they were wet, staring first at Big Hans and then at the kid.

Get.

Why?

I told you.

It's Pa I mean—

I know what you mean.   Get.

I found a cardboard box that condensed milk had come in and I shoveled it full of snow. It was too small, as I figured it would be. I found another with rags and an old sponge I threw out.   Campbell's soup.   I filled it too, using the rest of the drift. Snow would melt through the bottom of the boxes but that was all right with me. By now the kid was naked.   I was satisfied mine was bigger.

Looks like a sick shoat.

Shut up and get your pa.

He's asleep.

Yeah.

He don't like to get waked.

I know that. Don't I know that as good as you? Get him.

What good'll he be?

We're going to need his whiskey.

He can fix that need all right. He's good for fixing the crack in his face. If it ain't all gone.

The kettle was whistling.

What are we going to do with these? ma said.

Wait, Hed. Now I want you to get. I'm tired of talking. Get, you hear?

What are we going to do with them? They're all wet, she said.

I went to wake the old man. He didn't like being roused. It was too hard and far to come, the sleep he was in. He didn't give a damn about the Pedersen kid, any more than I did. Pedersen's kid was just a kid. He didn't carry any weight. Not like I did. And the old man would be mad, unable to see, coming that way from where he was asleep. I decided I hated Big Hans, though this was hardly something new for me. I hated Big Hans just then because I was thinking how Pa's eyes would blink at me—as if I were the sun off the snow and burning to blind him. His eyes were old and they'd never seen well, but shone on by whiskey they'd glare at my noise, growing red and raising up his rage. I decided I hated the Pedersen kid too, dying in our kitchen while I was away where I couldn't watch, dying just to pleasure Hans and making me go up snapping steps and down a drafty hall, Pa lumped under the covers at the end like dung covered with snow, snoring and whistling. Oh, he'd not care about the Pedersen kid. He'd not care about getting waked so he could give up some of his liquor to a slit of a kid and maybe lose one of his hiding places in the bargain. That would make him mad enough if he was sober. I tried not to hurry though it was cold and the Pedersen kid was in the kitchen.

He was all shoveled up like I thought he'd be. I shoved at his shoulder, calling his name. I think he heard his name. His name stopped the snoring, but he didn't move except to roll a little when I shoved him. The covers slid down his skinny neck so I saw his head, fuzzed like a dandelion gone to seed, but his face was turned to the wall—there was the pale shadow of his nose on the plaster—and I thought: well, you don't look much like a pig-drunk bully now. I couldn't be sure he was still asleep. He was a cagey sonofabitch. He'd heard his name. I shook him a little harder and made some noise. Pap-pap-pap-hey, I said.

I was leaning too far over. I knew better. He always slept close to the wall so you had to lean to reach him. Oh, he was smart. It put you off. I knew better but I was thinking of the Pedersen kid mother-naked in all that dough. When his arm came up I ducked away but it caught me on the side of the neck, watering my eyes, and I backed off to cough. Pa was on his side, looking at me, his eyes winking, the hand that had hit me a fist in the pillow.

Get the hell out of here.

I didn't say anything—my throat wasn't clear—but I watched him. He was like a mean horse to come at from the rear. It was better, though, he'd hit me. He was bitter when he missed.

Get the hell out of here.

Big Hans sent me. He told me to wake you.

A fat turd to Big Hans. Get out of here.

He found the Pedersen kid by the crib.

Get the hell out.

Pa pulled at the covers. He was tasting his mouth.

The kid's froze like a pump. Hans is rubbing him with snow. He's got him in the kitchen.

Pedersen?

No, Pa. It's the Pedersen kid. The kid.

Nothing to steal from the crib.

Not stealing, Pa. He was just lying there. Hans found him froze. That's where he was when Hans found him.

Pa laughed.

I ain't hid nothing in the crib.

You don't understand, Pa. The Pedersen kid. The kid—

I shittin well understand.

Pa had his head up, glaring, his teeth gnawing at the place where he'd grown a mustache once.

I shittin well understand. You know I don't want to see Pedersen. That cock. Why should I? That fairy farmer. What did he come for, hey? God dammit, get. And don't come back. Find out some shittin something. You're a fool. Both you and Hans. Pedersen. That cock. That fairy farmer. Don't come back. Out. Shit. Out. Out out.

He was shouting and breathing hard and closing his fist on the pillow. He had long black hairs on his wrist. They curled around the cuff of his nightshirt.

Big Hans made me come. Big Hans said—

A fat turd to Big Hans. He's an even bigger turd than you. Fat, too, fool, hey? I taught him, dammit, and I'll teach you. Out. You want me to drop my pot?

He was about to get up so I got out, slamming the door. He was beginning to see he was too mad to sleep. Then he threw things. Once, he went after Hans and dumped his pot over the banister. Pa'd been shit-sick in that pot. Hans got an ax. He didn't even bother to wipe himself off and he chopped part of Pa's door down before he stopped. He might not have gone that far if Pa hadn't been locked in laughing fit to shake the house. That pot put Pa in an awful good humor—whenever he thought of it. I always felt the thought was present in both of them, stirring in their chests like a laugh or a growl, as eager as an animal to be out.   I heard Pa cursing all the way downstairs.

Hans had laid steaming towels over the kid's chest and stomach. He was rubbing snow on the kid's legs and feet. Water from the snow and water from the towels had run off the kid to the table where the dough was, and the dough was turning pasty, sticking to the kid's back and behind.

Ain't he going to wake up?

What about your pa?

He was awake when I left.

What'd he say? Did you get the whiskey?

He said a fat turd to Big Hans.

Don't be smart. Did you ask him about the whiskey?

Yeah.

Well?

He said a fat turd to Big Hans.

Don't be smart. What's he going to do?

Go back to sleep most likely.

You'd best get that whiskey.

You go. Take the ax. Pa's scared to hell of axes.

Listen to me, Jorge, I've had enough of your sassing. This kid's froze bad. If I don't get some whiskey down him he might die. You want the kid to die? Do you? Well, get your pa and get that whiskey.

Pa don't care about the kid.

Jorge.

Well, he don't. He don't care at all, and I don't care to get my head busted neither. He don't care, and I don't care to have his shit flung on me. He don't care about anybody. All he cares about is his whiskey and that dry crack in his face. Get pig-drunk—that's what he wants. He don't care about nothing else at all. Nothing. Not Pedersen's kid neither. That cock. Not the kid neither.

I'll get the spirits, ma said.

I'd wound Big Hans up tight. I was ready to jump but when ma said she'd get the whiskey it surprised him like it surprised me, and he ran down. Ma never went near the old man when he was sleeping it off. Not anymore. Not for years. The first thing every morning when she washed her face she could see the scar on her chin where he'd cut her with a boot cleat, and maybe she saw him heaving it again, the dirty sock popping out as it flew. It should have been nearly as easy for her to remember that as it was for Big Hans to remember going after the ax while he was still spattered with Pa's sour yellow sick insides.

No you won't, Big Hans said.

Yes, Hans, if they're needed, ma said.

Hans shook his head but neither of us tried to stop her. If we had, then one of us would have had to go instead. Hans rubbed the kid with more snow . . . rubbed . . . rubbed.

I'll get more snow, I said.

I took the pail and shovel and went out on the porch. I don't know where ma went. I thought she'd gone upstairs and expected to hear she had. She had surprised Hans like she had surprised me when she said she'd go, and then she surprised him again when she came back so quick like she must have, because when I came in with the snow she was there with a bottle with three white feathers on its label and Hans was holding it angrily by the throat. Oh, he was being queer and careful, pawing about in the drawer and holding the bottle like a snake at the length of his arm. He was awful angry because he'd thought ma was going to do something big, something heroic even, especially for her—I know him . . . I know him . . . we felt the same sometimes—while ma wasn't thinking about that at all, not anything like that. There was no way of getting even. It wasn't like getting cheated at the fair. They were always trying, so you got to expect it. Now Hans had given ma something of his—we both had when we thought she was going straight to Pa—something valuable, a piece of better feeling; but since she didn't know we'd given it to her, there was no easy way of getting it back.

Hans cut the foil off finally and unscrewed the cap. He was put out too because there was only one way of understanding what she'd done. Ma had found one of Pa's hiding places. She'd found one and she hadn't said a word while Big Hans and I had hunted and hunted as we always did all winter, every winter since the spring that Hans had come and I had looked in the privy and found the first one. Pa had a knack for hiding. He knew we were looking and he enjoyed it. But now ma. She'd found it by luck most likely but she hadn't said anything and we didn't know how long ago it'd been or how many other ones she'd found, saying nothing. Pa was sure to find out. Sometimes he didn't seem to because he hid them so well he couldn't find them himself or because he looked and didn't find anything and figured he hadn't hid one after all or had drunk it up. But he'd find out about this one because we were using it. A fool could see what was going on. If he found out ma found it—that'd be bad. He took pride in his hiding. It was all the pride he had. I guess fooling Hans and me took doing. But he didn't figure ma for much. He didn't figure her at all. And if he found out—a woman had—then it'd be bad.

Hans poured some in a tumbler.

You going to put more towels on him?

No.

Why not? That's what he needs, something warm to his skin, don't he?

Not where he's froze good. Heat's bad for frostbite. That's why I only put towels on his chest and belly. He's got to thaw slow. You ought to know that.

Colors on the towels had run.

Ma poked her toe in the kid's clothes.

What are we going to do with these?

Big Hans began pouring whiskey in the kid's mouth but the mouth filled without any getting down his throat and in a second it was dripping from his chin.

Here, help me prop him up. I got to hold his mouth open.

I didn't want to touch him and I hoped ma would do it but she kept looking at the kid's clothes piled on the floor and the pool of water by them and didn't make any move to.

Come on, Jorge.

All right.

Lift, don't shove . . . lift.

Okay, I'm lifting.

I took him by the shoulders. His head flopped back. His mouth fell open. The skin on his neck was tight. He was cold all right.

Hold his head up. He'll choke.

His mouth is open.

His throat's shut. He'll choke.

He'll choke anyway.

Hold his head up.

I can't.

Don't hold him like that. Put your arms around him.

Well, jesus.

He was cold all right. I put my arm carefully around him. Hans had his fingers in the kid's mouth.

Now he'll choke for sure.

Shut up. Just hold him like I told you.

He was cold all right, and wet. I had my arm behind his back. He sure felt dead.

Tilt his head back a bit . . . not too much.

He felt cold and slimy. He sure was dead. We had a dead body in our kitchen. All the time he'd been dead. When Hans had brought him in, he'd been dead. I couldn't see him breathing. He was awful skinny, sunk between the ribs. We were getting him ready to bake. Hans was basting him. I had my arm around him, holding him up. He was dead and I had hold of him. I could feel my muscles jumping.

Well, jesus christ.

He *is* dead. He *is*.

You dropped him.

Dead? ma said.

He's dead. I could feel. He's dead.

Dead?

Ain't you got any sense? You let his head hit the table.

Is he dead? Is he dead? ma said.

Well christ no, not yet, not yet he's not dead. Look what you done, Jorge, there's whiskey all over.

He *is* dead. He *is*.

Right now he ain't. Not yet he ain't. Now stop yelling and hold him up.

He ain't breathing.

Yes he is, he *is* breathing. Hold him up.

I ain't. I ain't holding any dead body. You can hold it if you want. You dribble whiskey on it all you want. You can do anything you want to. I ain't. I ain't holding any dead body.

If he's dead, ma said, what are we going to do with these?

Jorge, god damn you, come back here—

I went down to the crib where Big Hans had found him. There was still a hollow in the snow and some prints the wind hadn't sifted snow over. The kid must have been out on his feet, they wobbled so. I could see where he had walked smack into a drift and then backed off and lurched up beside the crib, maybe bumping into it before he fell, then lying quiet so the snow had time to curl around him, piling up until in no time it would have covered him completely. Who knows, I thought, the way it's been snowing, we mightn't have found him till spring. Even if he was dead in our kitchen, I was glad Big Hans had found him. I could see myself coming out of the house some morning with the sun high up and strong and the eaves dripping, the snow speckled with drops and the ice on the creek slushing up; coming out and walking down by the crib on the crusts of the drift . . . coming out to play my game with the drifts . . . and I could see myself losing, breaking through the big drift that was always sleeping up against the crib and running a foot right into him, right into the Pedersen kid curled up, getting soft.

That would have been worse than holding on to his body in the kitchen. The feeling would have come on quicker, and it would have been worse, happening in the middle of a game. There wouldn't have been any warning, any way of getting ready for it to happen, to know what I'd struck before I bent down, even though Old Man Pedersen would have come over between snows looking for the kid most likely and everybody would have figured that the kid was lying buried somewhere under the snow; that maybe after a high wind someday somebody would find him lying like a black stone uncovered in a field; but probably in the spring somebody would find him in some back pasture thawing out with the mud and have to bring him in and take him over to the Pedersen place and present him to Missus Pedersen. Even so, even with everyone knowing that, and hoping one of the Pedersens would find him first so they wouldn't have to pry him up out of the mud or fetch him out from a thicket and bring him in and give him to Missus Pedersen in soggy season-old clothes—even then, who would expect to stick a foot all of a sudden through the crust, losing at the drift game, and step on Pedersen's kid lying all crouched together right beside your own crib? It was a good thing Hans had come down this morning and found him, even if he was dead in our kitchen and I had held him up.

When Pedersen came over asking for his kid, maybe hoping that the kid had got to our place all right and stayed, waiting for the blizzard to quit before going home, Pa would meet him and bring him in for a drink and tell him it was his own fault for putting up all those snow fences. If I knew Pa, he'd tell Pedersen to look under the drifts his snow fences had made, and Pedersen would get so mad he'd go for Pa and stomp out calling for the vengeance of God like he was fond of doing. Now, though, since Big Hans had found him, and he was dead in our kitchen, Pa might not say much when Pedersen came. He might just offer Pedersen a drink and keep his mouth shut about those snow fences. Pedersen might come yet this morning. That would be best, because Pa would be still asleep. If Pa was asleep when Pedersen came he wouldn't have a chance to talk about those snow fences, or offer Pedersen a drink, or call Pedersen a bent prick or a turd machine or a fairy farmer. Pedersen wouldn't have to refuse the drink then, spit his chaw in the snow, or call on God, and could take his kid and go home. I hoped Pedersen would certainly come soon. I hoped he would come and take that cold damp body out of our kitchen. The way I felt I didn't think that today I'd be able to eat. I knew every bite I'd see the Pedersen kid in the kitchen being fixed for the table.

The wind had dropped. The sun lay burning on the snow. I got cold just the same. I didn't want to go in but I could feel the cold crawling over me like it must have crawled over him while he was coming. It had slipped over him like a sheet, icy at first, especially around the feet, and he'd likely wiggled his toes in his boots and wanted to wrap his legs around each other like you do when you first come to bed. But then things would begin to warm up some, the sheet feeling warmer all the time until it felt real cozy and you went to sleep. Only, when the kid went to sleep by our crib, it wasn't like going to sleep in bed, because the sheet never really got warm and he never really got warm either. Now he was just as cold in our kitchen with the kettle whistling and ma getting ready to bake as I was out by the crib jigging my feet in our snow.   I had to go in.   I looked but I couldn't see anyone trying to come down where the road was. All I could see was a set of half-filled prints jiggling crazily away into the snow until they sank under a drift. There wasn't anything around. There wasn't anything: a tree or a stick or a rock whipped bare or a bush hugged by snow sticking up to mark the place where those prints came up out of the drift like somebody had come up from underground.

I decided to go around by the front, though I wasn't supposed to track through the parlor. The snow came to my thighs, but I was thinking of where the kid lay on the kitchen table in all that dough, pasty with whiskey and water, like spring had come all at once to our kitchen, and our all the time not knowing he was there, had thawed the top of his grave off and left him for us to find, stretched out cold and stiff and bare; and who was it that was going to have to take him to the Pedersen place and give him to Missus Pedersen, naked, and flour on his bare behind?

2

Just his back.   The green mackinaw. The black stocking cap. The yellow gloves. The gun.

Big Hans kept repeating it. He was letting the meaning have a chance to change. He'd look at me and shake his head and say it over.

"He put them down the cellar so I ran."

Hans filled the tumbler. It was spotted with whiskey and flecks of flour.

"He didn't say nothing the whole time."

He put the bottle on the table and the bottom sank unevenly in the paste, tilting heavily and queerly to one side—acting crazy, like everything else.

That's all he says he saw, Hans said, staring at the mark of the kid's behind in the dough. Just his back. The green mackinaw. The black stocking cap. The yellow gloves. The gun.

That's all?

He waited and waited.

That's all.

He tossed the whiskey off and peered at the bottom of the glass.

Now why should he remember all them colors?

He leaned over, his legs apart, his elbows on his knees, and held the glass between them with both hands, tilting it to watch the liquor that was left roll back and forth across the bottom.

How does he know?   I mean, for sure.

He thinks he knows, Hans said in a tired voice. He thinks he knows.

He picked up the bottle and a hunk of dough was stuck to it.

Christ. That's all. It's how he feels. It's enough, ain't it? Hans said.

What a mess, ma said.

He was raving, Hans said. He couldn't think of anything else. He had to talk. He had to get it out. You should have heard him grunt.

Poor poor Stevie, ma said.

He was raving?

All right, is it something you dream? Hans said.

He must have been dreaming. Look—how could he have got there? Where'd he come from? Fall from the sky?

He came through the storm.

That's just it, Hans, he'd have had to. It was blizzarding all day. It didn't let up—did it?—till late afternoon. He'd have had to. Now what chance is there of that? What?

Enough a chance it happened, Hans said.

But listen. Jesus. He's a stranger. If he's a stranger he's come a ways. He'd never make it in a blizzard, not even knowing the country.

He came through the storm. He came out of the ground like a grub. Hans shrugged. He came.

Hans poured himself a drink, not me.

He came through the storm, he said. He came through just like the kid came through. The kid had no chance neither, but he came. He's here, ain't he? He's right upstairs, right now. You got to believe that.

It wasn't blizzarding when the kid came.

It was starting.

That ain't the same.

All right. The kid had forty-five minutes, maybe an hour before it started to come on good. That isn't enough. You need the whole time, not a start. In a blizzard you got to be where you're going if you're going to get there.

That's what I mean. See, Hans? See? The kid had a chance. He knew the way. He had a head start. Besides, he was scared. He ain't going to be lazying. And he's lucky. He had a chance to be lucky. Now yellow gloves ain't got that chance. He has to come farther. He has to come through the storm all the way. But he don't know the way, and he ain't scared proper, except maybe by the storm. He hasn't got a chance to be lucky.

The kid was scared, you said. Right. Now why? You tell me that.

Hans kept his eyes on the whiskey that was shining in his glass. He was holding on hard.

And yellow gloves—he ain't scared? he said. How do you know he ain't scared, by something else besides wind and snow and cold and howling, I mean?

All right, I don't know, but it's likely, ain't it? Anyway, the kid, well maybe he ain't scared at all, starting out. Maybe his pa was just looking to tan him and he lit out. Then first thing he knows it's blizzarding again and he's lost, and when he gets to our crib he don't know where he is.

Hans slowly shook his head.

Yes yes, hell Hans, the kid's scared of having run away. He don't want to say he done a fool stunt like that. So he makes the whole thing up. He's just a little kid. He made the whole thing up.

Hans didn't like that. He didn't want to believe the kid any more than

I did, but if he didn't then the kid had fooled him sure. He didn't want to believe that either.

No, he said. Is it something you make up? Is it something you come to—raving with frostbite and fever and not knowing who's there or where you are or anything—and make up?

Yeah.

No it ain't. Green, black, yellow: you don't make up them colors neither. You don't make up putting your folks down-cellar where they'll freeze. You don't make up his not saying anything the whole time or only seeing his back or exactly what he was wearing. It's more than a make-up; it's more than a dream. It's like something you see once and it hits you so hard you never forget it even if you want to; lies, dreams, pass—this *has* you; it's like something that sticks to you like burrs, burrs you try to brush off while you're doing something else, but they never brush off, they just roll a little, and the first thing you know you ain't doing what you set out to, you're just trying to get them burrs off.   I know.   I got things stuck to me like that. Everybody has.   Pretty soon you get tired trying to pick them off. If they was just burrs, it wouldn't matter, but they ain't. They never is. The kid saw something that hit him hard like that; hit him so hard that probably all the time he was running over here he didn't see anything else but what hit him. Not really. It hit him so hard he couldn't do anything but spit it out raving when he come to. It hit him. You don't make things like that up, Jorge.   No.   He came through the storm, just like the kid. He had no business coming, but he came. I don't know how or why or when exactly, except it must have been during the blizzard yesterday. He got to the Pedersen place just before or just after it stopped snowing. He got there and he shoved them all in the fruit cellar to freeze and I'll bet he had his reasons.

You got dough stuck to the bottom of Pa's bottle.

I couldn't think of anything else to say. What Hans said sounded right. It sounded right but it couldn't be right. It just couldn't be. Whatever was right, the Pedersen kid had run off from his pa's place probably late yesterday afternoon, when the storm let up, and had turned up at our crib this morning. I knew he was here. I knew that much. I'd held him. I'd felt him dead in my hands, only I guess he wasn't dead now. Hans had put him to bed upstairs but I could still see him in the kitchen, so skinny naked, two towels steaming on him, whiskey drooling from the corners of his mouth, lines of dirt between his toes, squeezing ma's dough in the shape of his behind.

I reached for the bottle. Hans held it away.

He didn't see him do it though, I said.

Hans shrugged.

Then he ain't sure.

He's sure, I told you. Do you run out in a blizzard unless you're sure?

It wasn't blizzarding.

It was starting.

I don't run out in blizzards.

Crap.

Hans pointed the doughy end of the bottle at me.

Crap.

He shook it.

You come in from the barn—like this morning. As far as you know there ain't a gun in yellow gloves in a thousand miles. You come in from the barn not thinking anything special. You just get inside—you just get inside when you see a guy you never saw before, the guy that wasn't in a thousand miles, that wasn't in your mind even, he was so far away, and he's wearing them yellow gloves and that green mackinaw, and he's got me and your ma and pa lined up with our hands back of our necks like this—

Hans hung the bottle and the glass behind his head.

He's got me and your ma and your pa lined up with our hands here back of our necks, and he's got a rifle in between them yellow gloves and he's waving the point of it up and down in front of your ma's face real slow and quiet.

Hans got up and waved the bottle violently in ma's face. She shivered and shooed it away. Hans stopped to come to me. He stood over me, his black eyes buttons on his big face, and I tried to look like I wasn't hunching down any in my chair.

What do you do? Hans roared. You drop a little kid's cold head on the table.

Like hell—

Hans had the bottle in front of him again, smack in my face.

Hans Esbyorn, ma said, don't pester the boy.

Like hell—

Jorge.

I wouldn't run, ma.

Ma sighed. I don't know. But don't yell.

Well christ almighty, ma.

Don't swear neither. Please. You been swearing too much—you and Hans both.

But I wouldn't run.

Yes, Jorge, yes. I'm sure you wouldn't run, she said.

Hans went back and sat down and finished his drink and poured another. He could relax now he'd got me all strung up. He was a fancy bastard.

You'd run all right, he said, running his tongue across his lips. Maybe you'd be right to run. Maybe anybody would. With no gun, with nothing to stop him.

Poor child.   Wheweee.   And what are we going to do with these?

Hang them up, Hed, for Christ's sake.

Where?

Well, where do you, mostly?

Oh no, she said, I wouldn't feel right doing that.

Then jesus, Hed, I don't know. Jesus.

Please Hans, please. Those words are hard for me to bear.

She stared at the ceiling.

Dear.   The kitchen's such a mess.   I can't bear to see it.   And the baking's not done.

That's all she could think of. That's all she had to say. She didn't care about me. I didn't count. Not like her kitchen. I wouldn't have run.

Stick the baking, I said.

Shut your face.

He could look as mean as he liked, I didn't care. What was his meanness to me? A blister on my heel, another discomfort, a cold bed. Yet when he took his eyes off me to drink, I felt better. I was going to twist his balls.

All right, I said. All right. All right.

He was lost in his glass, thinking it out.

They're awful cold in that cellar, I said.

There was a little liquor burning in the bottom. I was going to twist his balls like the neck of a sack.

What are you going to do about it?

He was putting his mean look back but it lacked enthusiasm. He was seeing things in his glass.

I saved the kid, didn't I? he finally said.

Maybe you did.

You didn't.

No. I didn't.

It's time you did something, then, ain't it?

Why should I? I don't think they're freezing. You're the one who thinks that. You're the one who thinks he ran for help. You're the one. You saved him. All right. You didn't let his head hit the table. I did that. You didn't. No. It was you who rubbed him. All right. You saved him. That wasn't the kid's idea, though. He came for help. According to you, that is. He didn't come to be saved. You saved him, but what are you going to do now to help him? You've been feeling mighty, ain't you? thinking how you did it. Still feel like a savior, Hans? How's it feel?

You little bastard.

All right. Little or big. Never mind. You did it all. You found him. You raised the rumpus, ordering everybody around. He was as good as dead. I held him and I felt him. Maybe in your way he was alive, but it was a way that don't count. No—but you couldn't leave him alone. Rubbing. Well I felt him . . . cold . . . christ!   Ain't you proud? He was dead, right here, dead. And there weren't no yellow gloves. Now, though, there is. That's what comes of rubbing. Rubbing . . . ain't you proud? You can't believe the kid was lying good enough to fool you. So he was dead. But now he ain't. Not for you. He ain't for you.

He's alive for you too. You're crazy. He's alive for everybody.

No he ain't. He ain't alive for me. He never was. I never seen him except he was dead. Cold . . . I felt him . . . christ! Ain't you proud? He's in your bed. All right. You took him up there. It's your bed he's in, Hans. It was you he babbled to. You believe him too, so he's alive for you then. Not for me. Not for me he ain't.

You can't say that.

I am saying it though. Hear me saying?   Rubbing . . . You didn't know what you was bringing to, did you? Something besides the kid came through the storm, Hans. I ain't saying yellow gloves did neither. He didn't. He couldn't. But something else did. While you was rubbing you didn't think of that.

You little bastard.

Hans, Hans, please, ma said.

Never mind that. Little or big, like I said. I'm asking what you're going to do. You believe it. You made it. What are you going to do about it? It'd be funny if right now, while we're sitting here, the kid's dying upstairs.

Jorge, ma said, what an awful thing—in Hans's bed.

All right. But suppose. Suppose you didn't rub enough—not long and hard enough, Hans. And suppose he dies up there in your bed. He might. He was cold, I know. That'd be funny because that yellow gloves—he won't die. It ain't going to be so easy, killing him.

Hans didn't move or say anything.

I ain't no judge. I ain't no hand at saving, like you said. It don't make no difference to me. But why'd you start rubbing if you was going to stop? Seems like it'd be terrible if the Pedersen kid was to have come all that way through the storm, scared and freezing, and you was to have done all that rubbing and saving so he could come to and tell you his fancy tale and have you believe it, if you ain't going to do nothing now but sit and hold hands with that bottle. That ain't a burr so easy picked off.

Still he didn't say anything.

Fruit cellars get mighty cold. Of course they ain't supposed to freeze.

I leaned back easy in my chair. Hans just sat.

They ain't supposed to freeze, so it's all right.

The top of the kitchen table looked muddy where it showed. Patches of dough and pools of water were scattered all over it. There were rusty streaks through the paste and the towels had run. Everywhere there were little sandy puddles of whiskey and water. Something, it looked like whiskey, dripped slowly to the floor and with the water trickled to the puddle by the pile of clothes. The boxes sagged. There were thick black tracks around the table and the stove. I thought it was funny the boxes had gone so fast. The bottle and the glass were posts around which Big Hans had his hands.

Ma began picking up the kid's clothes. She picked them up one at a time, delicately, by their ends and corners, lifting a sleeve like you would the flat, burned, crooked leg of a frog dead of summer to toss it from the road. They didn't seem human things, the way her hands pinched together on them, but animal—dead and rotting things out of the ground. She took them away and when she came back I wanted to tell her to bury them—to hide them somehow quick under the snow—but she scared me, the way she came with her arms out, trembling, fingers coming open and closed, moving like a combine between rows.

I heard the dripping clearly, and I heard Hans swallow. I heard the water and the whiskey fall. I heard the frost on the window melt to the sill and drop into the sink. Hans poured whiskey in his glass. I looked past Hans and Pa was watching from the doorway. His nose and eyes were red, his feet in red slippers.

What's this about the Pedersen kid? he said.

Ma stood behind him with a mop.

3

Ever think of a horse? Pa said.

A horse? Where'd he get a horse?

Anywhere—on the way—anyplace.

Could he make it on a horse?

He made it on something.

Not on a horse, though.

Not on his feet.

I ain't saying he made it on anything.

Horses can't get lost.

Yes they can.

They got a sense.

That's a lot of manure about horses.

In a blizzard a horse'll go home.

That's so.

You let them go and they go home.

That's so.

If you steal a horse, and let him go, he'll take you to the barn you stole him from.

Couldn't give him his head then.

Must have really rode him then.

And known where he was going.

Yeah, and gone there.

If he had a horse.

Yeah, if he had a horse.

If he stole a horse before the storm and rode it a ways, then, when the snow came, the horse would be too far off and wouldn't know how to head for home.

They got an awful good sense.

Manure.

What difference does it make? He made it. What difference does it make how? Hans said.

I'm considering if he could have, Pa said.

And I'm telling you he did, Hans said.

And I've been telling you he didn't. The kid made the whole thing up, I said.

The horse'd stop. He'd put his head into the wind and stop.

I've seen them put their rears in.

They always put their heads in.

He could jockey him.

If he was gentle and not too scared.

A plower is gentle.

Some are.

Some don't like to be rid.

Some don't like strangers neither.

Some.

What the hell, Hans said.

Pa laughed. I'm just considering, he said. Just considering, Hans, that's all.

Pa'd seen the bottle. Right away. He'd been blinking. But he hadn't missed it. He'd seen it and the glass in Hans's hand. I'd expected him to say something. So had Hans. He'd held on to the glass long enough so no one would get the idea he was afraid to, then he'd set it down casual, like he hadn't any reason to hold it or any reason to put it down, but was putting it down anyway, without thinking. I'd grinned but he hadn't seen me, or else he made out he hadn't. Pa'd kept his mouth shut about the bottle, though he'd seen it right away. I guess we had the Pedersen kid to thank for that, though we had him to thank for the bottle too.

It's his own fault for putting out all them snow fences, Pa said. You'd think, being here the time he has, he'd know the forces better.

Pedersen just likes to be ready, Pa, that's all.

Hell he does. He likes to *get* ready, that cock. Get, get, get, get. He's always getting ready, but he ain't never *got* ready. Not yet, he ain't. Last summer, instead of minding his crops, he got ready for hoppers. Christ. Who wants hoppers? Well that's the way to get hoppers—that's the sure way—get ready for hoppers.

Bull.

Bull? You say bull, Hans, hey?

I say bull, yeah.

You're one to get ready, ain't you? Like Pedersen, ain't you? Oh what a wrinkled scrotum you got, with all that thinking. You'd put out poison for a million, hey? You know what you'd get? Two million. Wise, oh these wise men, yeah. Pedersen *asked* for hoppers. He *begged* for hoppers. He went on his knees for hoppers. So me? I got hoppers too. Now he's gone and asked for snow, gone on his knees for snow, wrung his fingers off for snow. Is he ready, tell me? Hey? Snow? For real snow? Anybody ever ready for real snow? Oh jesus, that fool. He should have kept his kid behind them fences. What business—what—what business—to send him here. By god, a man's got to keep his stock up.　　Look—Pa pointed out the window. See—see—what did I tell you—snowing . . . always snowing.

You seen a winter it didn't snow?

You were ready, I guess.

It always snows.

You were ready for the Pedersen kid too, I guess. You was just out there waiting for him, cooling your cod.

Pa laughed and Hans got red.

Pedersen's a fool. Wise men can't be taught. Oh no, not old holy Pete. He never learned all the things that can fall out the sky and happen to wheat. His neck's bent all the time too, studying clouds—hah, that shit. He don't even keep an eye on his kid in a blizzard. A man by god's got to keep his stock up. But you'll keep an eye out for him, hey, Hans? You're a bigger fool because you're fatter.

Hans's face was red and swollen like the skin around a splinter. He reached out and picked up the glass. Pa was sitting on a corner of the kitchen table, swinging a leg. The glass was near his knee. Hans reached by Pa and took it. Pa watched and swung his leg, laughing. The bottle was on the counter and Pa watched closely while Hans took it.

Ah, you plan to drink some of my whiskey, Hans?

Yeah.

It'd be polite to ask.

I ain't asking, Hans said, tilting the bottle.

I suppose I'd better make some biscuits, ma said.

Hans looked up at her, keeping the bottle tilted. He didn't pour.

Biscuits, ma? I said.

I ought to have something for Mr. Pedersen and I haven't a thing.

Hans straightened the bottle.

There's a thing to consider, he said, beginning to smile. Why ain't Pedersen here looking for his kid?

Why should he be?

Hans winked at me through his glass. No wink would make me a friend of his.

Why not? We're nearest. If the kid ain't here he can ask us to help him hunt.

Fat chance.

He ain't come through. How do you consider that?

I ain't considering it, Pa said.

Why ain't you? Seems to me like something worth real long and fancy considering.

No it ain't.

Ain't it?

Pedersen's a fool.

So you like to say. I've heard you often enough. All right, maybe he is. How long do you expect he'll wander around looking before he comes over this way?

A long time. A long time maybe.

The kid's been gone a long time.

Pa arranged his nightshirt over his knee. He had on the striped one.

How long's a long time? Hans said.

The kid's been gone.

Oh Pedersen'll be here before too long now, Pa said.

And if he don't?

What do you mean, if he don't? Then he don't. By god, he don't. It ain't no skin off my ass. If he don't he don't. I don't care what he does.

Yeah, Big Hans said. Yeah.

Pa folded his arms, looking like a judge. He swung his leg. Where'd you find the bottle?

Hans jiggled it.

You're pretty good at hiding, ain't you?

I'm asking the questions. Where'd you find it?

Hans was enjoying himself too much.

I didn't.

Jorge, hey. Pa chewed his lip. So you're the nosy bastard.

He didn't look at me and it didn't seem like he was talking to me at all. He said it like I wasn't there and he was thinking out loud. Awake, asleep—it didn't fool me.

It wasn't me, Pa, I said.

I tried to get Hans's attention so he'd shut up, but he was enjoying himself.

Little Hans ain't no fool, Big Hans said.

No.

Now Pa wasn't paying attention.

He ain't no kin to you, Pa said.

Why ain't he here then? He'd be looking too. Why ain't he here?

Gracious, I'd forgot all about Little Hans, ma said, quickly taking a bowl from the cupboard.

Hed, what are you up to? Pa said.

Oh, biscuits.

Biscuits? What in hell for? Biscuits. I don't want any biscuits. Make some coffee. All this time you been just standing around.

For Pedersen and little Hans. They'll be coming and they'll want some biscuits and coffee, and I'll put out some elderberry jelly. The coffee needed reminding, Magnus, thank you.

Who found the bottle?

She scooped some flour from the bin.

Pa'd been sitting, swinging. Now he stopped and stood up.

Who found it? Who found it? God dammit, who found it? Which one of them was it?

Ma was trying to measure the flour but her hands shook. The flour ran off the scoop and fell across the rim of the cup, and I thought, Yeah, You'd have run, Yeah, Your hands shake.

Why don't you ask Jorge? Big Hans said.

How I hated him, putting it on me, the coward. And he had thick arms.

That snivel, Pa said.

Hans laughed so his chest shook.

He couldn't find nothing I hid.

You're right there, Hans said.

I could, I said. I have.

A liar, Hans, hey? You found it.

Pa was somehow pleased and sat on the corner of the table again. Was it Hans he hated most, or me?

I never said Jorge found it.

I've got a liar working for me. A thief and a liar. Why should I keep a liar? I'm just soft on him, I guess, and he's got such a sweet face. But why should I keep a thief . . . little movey eyes like traveling specks . . . why?

I ain't like you. I don't spend every day drinking just to sleep the night and then sleep half the day too, fouling your bed and your room and half the house.

You been doing your share of lying down. Little Hans is half your size and worth twice. You—you got a small dick.

Pa's words didn't come out clear.

How about Little Hans? Little Hans ain't showed up. Folks must be getting pretty worried at the Pedersens'. They'd like some news maybe. But Pedersen don't come. Little Hans don't come. There's a thousand drifts out there. The kid might be under any one. If anybody's seen him, we have, and if we haven't, nobody's going to till spring, or maybe if the wind shifts, which ain't likely. But nobody comes to ask. That's pretty funny, I'd say.

You're an awful full-up bastard, Pa said.

I'm just considering, that's all.

Where'd you find it?

I forgot. It needed reminding. I was going to have a drink.

Where?

You're pretty good at hiding, Hans said.

I'm asking. Where?

I didn't, I told you, I didn't find it. Jorge didn't find it neither.

You bastard, Hans, I said.

It hatched, Hans said. Like the fellow, you know, who blew in. He hatched. Or maybe the kid found it—had it hid under his coat.

Who? Pa roared, standing up quick.

Oh Hed found it. You don't hide worth a damn and Hed found it easy. She knew right away where to look.

Shut up, Hans, I said.

Hans tilted the bottle.

She must have known where it was a long time now. Maybe she knows where they're all hid. You ain't very smart. Or maybe she's took it up herself, eh? And it ain't yours at all, maybe that.

Big Hans poured himself a drink. Then Pa kicked the glass out of Hans's hand. Pa's slipper flew off and sailed by Hans's head and bounced off the wall. The glass didn't break. It fell by the sink and rolled slow by ma's feet, leaving a thin line. The scoop flew a light white cloud. There was whiskey on Hans's shirt and on the wall and cupboards, and a splash on the floor where the glass had hit.

Ma had her arms wrapped around her chest. She looked faint and she was whewing and moaning.

Okay, Pa said, we'll go. We'll go right now, Hans. I hope to God you get a bullet in your belly. Jorge, go upstairs and see if the little sonofabitch is still alive.

Hans was rubbing the spots on his shirt and licking his lips when I hunched past Pa and went out.

Part Two

I

There wasn't any wind. The harness creaked, the wood creaked, the runners made a sound like a saw working easy, and everything was white about Horse Simon's feet. Pa had the reins between his knees and he and Hans and I kept ourselves close together. We bent our heads and clenched our feet and wished we could huddle both hands in one pocket. Only Hans was breathing through his nose. We didn't speak. I wished my lips could warm my teeth. The blanket we had wasn't worth a damn—it was just as cold underneath—and Pa drank from a bottle by him on the seat.

I tried to hold the feeling I'd had starting out when we'd hitched up Horse Simon, when I was warm and decided to risk the North Corn Road to the Pedersen place. It catty-cornered and came up near the grove behind his barn. We figured we could look at things from there. I tried to hold the feeling but it was warm as new bathwater and just as hard to hold. It was like I was setting out to do something special and big—like a knight setting out—worth remembering. I dreamed coming in from the barn and finding his back to me in the kitchen and wrestling with him and pulling him down and beating the stocking cap off his head with the barrel of the gun. I dreamed coming in from the barn still blinking with the light and seeing him there and picking the shovel up and taking him on. That had been then, when I was warm, when I was doing something big, heroic even, and well worth remembering. I couldn't put the feeling down in Pedersen's backyard or Pedersen's porch or barn. I couldn't see myself, or him, there. I could only see him back where I wasn't anymore—standing quiet in our kitchen with his gun going slowly up and down in ma's face and ma shooing it away and at the same time trying not to move an inch for getting shot.

When I got good and cold the feeling slipped away. I couldn't imagine him with his gun or cap or yellow gloves. I couldn't imagine me coming on to him. We weren't anyplace and I didn't care. Pa drove by staring down the sloping white road and drank from his bottle. Hans rattled his heels on the back of the seat. I just tried to keep my mouth shut and breathe and not think why in the name of the good jesus christ I had to.

It wasn't like a sleigh ride on an early-winter evening when the air is still, the earth is warm, and the stars are flakes being born that will not fall. The air was still all right, the sun straight up and cold. Behind us on the trough that marked the road I saw our runners and the holes that Simon tore. Ahead of us it melted into drifts. Pa squinted like he saw where he knew it really went. Horse Simon steamed. Ice hung from his harness. Snow caked his belly. I was afraid the crust might cut his knees and I wanted a drink out of Pa's bottle. Big Hans seemed asleep and shivered in his dreams. My rear was god almighty sore.

We reached a drift across the road and Pa eased Simon round her where he knew there wasn't any fence. Pa figured to go back to the road but after we got round the bank I could see there wasn't any point in that. There were rows of high drifts across it.

They ain't got no reason to do that, Pa said.

It was the first thing Pa'd said since he told me to go upstairs and see if the Pedersen kid was still alive. He hadn't looked alive to me but I'd said I guessed he was. Pa'd gone and got his gun first, without dressing, one foot still bare so he favored it, and took the gun upstairs cradled in his arm, broke, and pointing down. He had a dark speckled spot on the rump of his night-shirt where he'd sat on the table. Hans had his shotgun and the forty-five he'd stolen from the Navy. He made me load it and when I'd stuck it in my belt he'd said it'd likely go off and keep me from ever getting out to stud. The gun felt like a chunk of ice against my belly and the barrel dug.

Ma'd put some sandwiches and a Thermos of coffee in a sack. The coffee'd be cold. My hands would be cold when I ate mine even if I kept my gloves on. Chewing would be painful. The lip of the Thermos would be cold if I drank out of that, and I'd spill some on my chin, which would dry to ice; or if I used the cup, the tin would stick to my lip like lousy liquor you didn't want to taste by licking off, and it would burn and then tear my skin coming away.

Simon went into a hole. He couldn't pull out so he panicked, and the sleigh skidded. We'd had crust but now the front right runner broke through and we braked in the soft snow underneath. Pa made quiet impatient noises and calmed Simon down.

That was damn fool, Hans said.

He lost his footing. Jesus, I ain't the horse.

I don't know. Simon's a turd binder, Hans said.

Pa took a careful drink.

Go round and lead him out.

Jorge is on the outside.

Go round and lead him out.

You. You go round. You led him in.

Go round and lead him out.

Sometimes the snow seemed as blue as the sky. I don't know which seemed colder.

Oh god I'll go, I said. I'm on the outside.

Your old man's on the outside, Hans said.

I guess I know where I am, Pa said. I guess I know where I'm staying.

Can't you let up, for christ's sake? I'm going, I said.

I threw off the blanket and stood up but I was awful stiff. The snow dazzle struck me, and the pain of the space around us. Getting out, I rammed my ankle against the sideboard's iron brace. The pain shot up my leg and shook me like an ax handle will when you strike wrong. I cursed, taking my time jumping off. The snow looked as stiff and hard as cement and I could only think of the jar.

You've known where that brace was for ten years, Pa said.

The snow went to my crotch. The gun bit. I waded round the hole trying to keep on tiptoe and the snow away from my crotch but it wasn't any use.

You practicing to be a bird? Hans said.

I got hold of Horse Simon and tried to coax him out. Pa swore at me from his seat. Simon kicked and thrashed and lunged ahead. The front right runner dug in. The sleigh swung around on it and the left side hit Simon's back legs hard behind the knees. Simon reared and kicked a piece out of the side of the sleigh and then pulled straight ahead, tangling the reins. The sleigh swung back again and the right runner pulled loose with a jerk. Pa's bottle rolled. From where I sat in the snow I saw him grab for it. Simon went on ahead. The sleigh slid sideways into Simon's hole and the left runner went clear of the snow. Simon pulled up short, though Pa had lost the reins and was holding on and yelling about his bottle. I had snow in my eyes and down my neck.

Simon didn't have no call to do that, Hans said, mimicking Pa.

Where's my bottle? Pa said, looking over the side of the sleigh at the torn snow. Jorge, go find my bottle. It fell in the snow here somewheres.

I tried to brush the snow off without getting more in my pockets and up my sleeves and down my neck.

You get out and find it. It's your bottle.

Pa leaned way over.

If you hadn't been so goddamn dumb it wouldn't have fell out. Where'd you learn to lead a horse? You never learned that dumb trick from me. Of all the goddamn dumb tricks I never seen any dumber.

Pa waved his arm in a circle.

That bottle fell out about here. It couldn't have got far. It was corked, thank god. I won't lose none.

Snow was slipping down the hollow of my back. The forty-five had slipped through my belt. I was afraid it would go off like Big Hans said. I kept my right forearm pressed against it. I didn't want it slipping off down my pants. I didn't like it. Pa shouted directions.

You hid it, I said. You're such a hand at hiding. You find it, then. I ain't good at finding. You said so yourself.

Jorge, you know I got to have that bottle.

Then get off your ass and find it.

You know I got to have it.

Then get off.

If I get down off here, it ain't the bottle I'm coming after. I'll hold you under till you drown, you little smart-talking snot.

I started kicking around in the snow.

Hans giggled.

There's a trace broke, he said.

What's so damn funny?

I told you that trace was worn.

I kicked about. Pa followed my feet.

Hell. Not that way. He pointed. You know about everything there is, Hans, I guess, he said, still watching me. First little thing you figure out you tell somebody about. Then somebody else knows. So then they can do what needs to be done, and you don't have to—jesus, not there, *there.* Don't it, Hans? don't it always let you out?   You ain't going deep enough.   I never figured that out. How come somebody else's knowing always lets you out? You're just a pimp for jobs, I guess. You ain't going deep enough, I said.

It ain't my job to fix traces.

Hey, get your hands in it, *your hands.* It's clean. You always was that way about manure. Why ain't it your job? Too busy screwing sheep?   Try over there. You ought to have hit it. No, *there,* not there.

I never fixed traces.

Christ, they never needed fixing while you been here hardly. Jorge, will you stop nursing that fool gun with your cock and use both hands.

I'm cold, Pa.

So'm I. That's why you got to find that bottle.

If I find it do I get a drink?

Ain't you growed up—a man—since yesterday!

I've had a few, Pa.

Ha. Of what, hey? Hear that, Hans? He's had a few. For medicine maybe, like your ma says. The spirits, the spirits, Jorgen Segren . . . ha.   He's had a few, he says. He's had a few.

Pa.

He's had a few. He's had a few. He's had a few.

Pa. I'm cold, Pa.

Maybe. Only look, for god's sake, don't just thrash about like a fool chicken.

Well, we're finished anyway, Hans said.

We're finished if we don't find that bottle.

You're finished, maybe. You're the only one who needs that bottle. Jorge and I don't need it, but there you are, old man, eh? Lost in the snow.

My gloves were wet. Snow had jammed under my sleeves. It was working down into my boots. I stopped to pick some out with a finger if I could.

Maybe some of ma's coffee is still hot, I said.

Say.   Yeah.   Maybe.   But that's *my* coffee, boy. I never got none. I ain't even had breakfast. What are you stopping for? Come on. Hell, Jorge, it's cold.

I know that better than you. You're sitting there all nice and dry, bossing; but I'm doing all the work and getting the snow inside me.

Say.   Yeah.   That's right.

Pa leaned back and grinned. He clutched the blanket to him and Hans pulled it back.

It's easier to keep warm moving around, anybody knows that. Ain't that right, Hans? It's easier to keep warm moving, ain't it?

Yeah, Hans said. If you ain't got a blanket.

See there, Jorge, hey? You just keep good and warm . . . stirring. It'd be a pity if your pee should freeze. And moving around good prevents calluses on the bottom. Don't it, Hans?

Yeah.

Hans here knows. He's nothing but calluses.

You'll wear out your mouth.

I can't find it, Pa. Maybe some of ma's coffee is still warm.

You damn snivel—you ain't looking. Get tramping proper like I told you and find it. Find it fast, you hear. You ain't getting back up on this sleigh until you do.

I started jumping up and down, not too fast, and Pa blew his nose with his fingers.

Cold makes the snot run, he says, real wise.

If I found the bottle I'd kick it deep under the snow. I'd kick it and keep kicking it until it sank under a drift. Pa wouldn't know where it was. I wouldn't come back to the sleigh either. They weren't going anywhere anyway. I'd go home, though it was a long walk. Looking back, I could see our tracks in the trough of the road. They came together before I lost them. It would be warm at home and worth the walk. It was frightening—the endless white space. I'd have to keep my head down. Winded slopes and rises all around me. I'd never wanted to go to Pedersen's. That was Hans's fight, and Pa's. I was just cold . . . cold . . . and scared and sick of snow. That's what I'd do if I found it—kick it under a drift. Then, later, a lot later in the spring, one day I'd come out here and find the old bottle sticking out of the rotting snow and stuck in the mud like dough, and I'd hide it back of the barn and have a drink whenever I wanted. I'd get some real cigarettes, maybe a carton, and hide them too. Then someday I'd come in and Pa'd smell whiskey on me and think I'd found one of his hiding places. He'd be mad as hell and not know what to say. It'd be spring and he'd think he'd taken them all in like he always did, harvesting the crop, like he said.

I looked to see if there was something to mark the place by but it was all gone under snow. There was only the drifts and the deep holes of snow and the long runnered trough of the road. It might be a mudhole we was stuck in. In the spring cattails might grow up in it and the blackbirds come. Or it might be low and slimy at first and then caked dry and cracked. Pa'd never find out how I came by the bottle. Someday he'd act too big and I'd stick his head under the pump or slap his skinny rump with the backside of a fork full of manure. Hans would act smart and then someday—

Jee-suss, will you move?

I'm cold, Pa.

You're going to be a pig's size colder.

Well, we're finished anyway, Hans said. We ain't going nowhere. The trace is broke.

Pa stopped watching me thrash the snow. He frowned at Horse Simon. Simon was standing quiet with his head down.

Simon's shivering, he said. I should have remembered he'd be heated up. It's so cold I forgot.

Pa yanked the blanket off of Hans like Hans was a bed he was stripping, and jumped down. Hans yelled but Pa didn't pay attention. He threw the blanket over Simon.

We got to get Simon moving. He'll stiffen up.

Pa ran his hand tenderly down Simon's legs.

The sleigh don't seem to have hurt him none.

The trace is broke.

Then Hans stood up. He beat his arms against his body and jigged.

We'll have to walk him home, he said.

Home, hey, Pa said, giving Hans a funny sidewise look. It's a long walk.

You can ride him, then, Hans said.

Pa looked real surprised and even funnier. It wasn't like Hans to say that. It was too cold. It made Hans generous. There was some good in cold.

Why?

Pa waded, patting Simon, but he kept his eye on Hans like it was Hans might kick.

Hans let out a long impatient streamer.

Jesus—the trace.

Hans was being real cautious. Hans was awful cold. His nose was red. Pa's was white but it didn't look froze. It just looked white like it usually did—like it was part of him had died long ago. I wondered what color my nose was. Mine was bigger and sharper at the end. It was ma's nose, ma said. I was bigger all over than Pa. I was taller than Hans too. I pinched my nose but my gloves were wet so I couldn't feel anything except how my nose hurt when I pinched it. It couldn't be too cold. Hans was pointing at the ends of the trace, which were trailing in the snow.

Tie a knot in it, Pa was saying.

It won't hold, Hans said, shaking his head.

Tie a good one, it will.

It's too cold to get a good knot. Leather's too stiff.

Hell no, it ain't too stiff.

Well, it's too thick. Can't knot something like that.

You can do it.

She'll pull crooked.

Let her pull crooked.

Simon won't work well pulling her crooked.

He'll have to do the best he can. I ain't going to leave this sleigh out here. Hell, it might snow again before I got back with a new trace.   Or you got back, hey?   When I get home I'm going to stay there and I'm going to eat my breakfast if it's suppertime. I ain't coming back out here trying to beat another blizzard and wind up like the Pedersen kid.

Yeah, Hans said, nodding. Let's get this damn thing out of here and get Simon home before he stiffens. I'll tie the trace.

Hans got down and I stopped kicking. Pa watched Hans real careful from his side of Horse Simon and I could see him smiling like he'd thought of something dirty. I started to get on the sleigh but Pa shouted and made me hunt some more.

Maybe we'll find it when we move the sleigh, I said.

Pa laughed but not at what I said. He opened his mouth wide, looking at Hans, and laughed hard, though his laugh was quiet.

Yeah, maybe we will, he said, and gave Simon an extra hard pat. Maybe we will, hey, at that.

I didn't find the bottle and Big Hans tied the trace. He had to take his gloves off to do it but he did it quick and I had to admire him for it. Pa coaxed Simon while Hans, boosting, heaved. She got clear and suddenly was going—skidding out. I heard a noise like a lightbulb busting. A brown stain spread over the sleigh track. Pa peered over his shoulder at the stain, his hands on the halter, his legs wide in the snow.

Oh no, he said.   Oh no.

But Big Hans broke up. He lifted a leg clear of the snow. He hit himself. His shoulders shook. He hugged his belly. He rocked back and forth. Oh—oh—oh, he screamed, and he held his sides. Tears streamed down his cheeks. You—you—you, he howled. Hans's cheeks, his nose, his head was red. Found—found—found, he choked.

Everything about Pa was frozen. The white hair that stuck out from his hat looked hard and sharp and seemed to shine like snow. Big Hans went on laughing. I never saw him so humored. He staggered, weakening—Pa as still as a stake. Hans began to heave and gasp, running down. In a minute he'd be cold again, worn out, and then he'd wish he could drink out of that bottle. Its breaking had made him drunk. The stain had stopped spreading and was fading, the snow bubbling and sagging. We could melt and drink the snow, I thought. I wanted that bottle back bad. I hated Hans. I'd hate Hans forever—as long as there was snow.

Hans was puffing quietly when Pa told me to get in the sleigh. Then Hans climbed awkwardly on. Pa took the blanket off Horse Simon and threw it in the sleigh. Then he got Simon started. I pulled the blanket over me and tried to stop shivering. Our stove, I thought, was black . . . god . . . black . . . lovely sooty black . . . and glowed rich as cherry through its holes. I thought of the kettle steaming on it, the steam alive, hissing white and warm, not like my breath coming slow and cloudy and hanging heavy and dead in the still air.

Hans jumped.

Where we going? he said. Where we going?

Pa didn't say nothing.

This ain't the way, Hans said. Where we going?

The gun was an ache in my stomach. Pa squinted at the snow.

For christ's sake, Hans said. I'm sorry about the bottle.

But Pa drove.

2

Barberry had got in the grove and lay about the bottom of the trees and hid in snow. The mossycups went high, their branches put straight out, the trunk bark black and wrinkled. There were spots where I could see the frosted curls of dead grass frozen to the ground and high hard-driven piles of snow the barberry stuck its black barbs from. The wind had thrown some branches in the drifts. The sun made shadows of more branches on their sides and bent them over ridges. The ground rose up behind the grove. The snow rose. Pa and Hans had their shotguns. We followed along the drifts and kept down low. I could hear us breathing and the snow, earth, and our boots squeaking. We went slow and all of us was cold.

Above the snow, through the branches, I could see the peak of Pedersen's house, and nearer by, the roof of Pedersen's barn. We were making for the barn. Once in a while Pa would stop and watch for smoke but there was nothing in the sky. Big Hans bumped into a bush and got a barb through his woolen glove. Pa motioned Hans to hush. I could feel my gun through my glove—heavy and cold. Where we went the ground was driven nearly bare. Mostly I kept my eyes on Big Hans's heels, because it hurt my neck so to look up. When I did, for smoke, the faint breeze caught my cheek and drew the skin across the bone. I didn't think of much except how to follow Hans's heels and how, even underneath my cap, my ears burned, and how my lips hurt and how just moving made me ache. Pa followed where a crazy wind had got in among the oaks and blown the snow bare from the ground in flat patches against their trunks. Sometimes we had to break through a small drift or we'd have gone in circles. The roof of Pedersen's house grew above the banks as we went until, finally, we passed across one corner of it and I saw the chimney very black in the sun stick up from the steep bright pitch like a dead cigar rough-ashed with snow.

I thought: the fire's dead, they must be froze.

Pa stopped and nodded at the chimney.

You see, Hans said unhappily.

Just then I saw a cloud of snow float from the crest of a drift and felt my eyes smart. Pa looked quick at the sky but it was clear. Hans stomped his feet, hung his head, swore in a whisper.

Well, Pa said, it looks like we made this trip for nothing. Nobody's to home.

The Pedersens are all dead, Hans said, still looking down.

Shut up. I saw Pa's lips were chapped . . . a dry dry hole now. A muscle jumped along his jaw.　　Shut up, he said.

A faint ribbon of snow suddenly shot from the top of the chimney and disappeared. I stood as still as I could in the tubes of my clothes, the snow shifting strangely in my eyes, alone, frightened by the space that was bowling up inside me, a white blank glittering waste like the waste outside, coldly burning, roughed with waves, and I wanted to curl up, face to my thighs, but I knew my tears would freeze my lashes together. My stomach began to growl.

What's the matter with you, Jorge? Pa said.

Nothing. I giggled. I'm cold, Pa, I guess, I said. I belched.

Jesus, Hans said loudly.

Shut up.

I poked at the snow with the toe of my boot. I wanted to sit down and if there'd been anything to sit on I would have. All I wanted was to go home or sit down. Hans had stopped stomping and was staring back through the trees toward the way we'd come.

Anybody in that house, Pa said, would have a fire.

He sniffed and rubbed his sleeve across his nose.

Anybody—see? He began raising his voice. Anybody who was in that house now would have a fire. The Pedersens is all most likely out hunting that fool kid. They probably tore ass off without minding the furnace. Now it's out. His voice got braver. Anybody who might have come along while they was gone, and gone in, would have started a fire someplace first thing, and we'd see the smoke. It's too damn cold not to.

Pa took the shotgun he'd carried broken over his left arm and turned the barrel over, slow and deliberate. Two shells fell out and he stuffed them in his coat pocket.

That means there ain't anybody to home. There ain't no smoke, he said with emphasis, and that means there ain't *no*body.

Big Hans sighed. Okay, he muttered from a way off. Let's go home.

I wanted to sit down. Here was the sofa, here the bed—mine—white and billowy. And the stairs, cold and snapping. And I had the dry cold toothaching mouth I always had at home, and the cold storm in my belly, and my pinched eyes. There was the print of the kid's rear in the dough. I wanted to sit down. I wanted to go back where we'd tied up Horse Simon and sit numb in the sleigh.

Yes yes yes, let's, I said.

Pa smiled—oh, the bastard—the *bastard*—and he didn't know half what I knew now, numb in the heart the way I felt, and with my burned-off ears.

We could at least leave a note saying Big Hans saved their kid. Seems to me like the only neighborly thing to do. And after all the way we come. Don't it you?

What the hell do you know about what's neighborly? Hans shouted.

With a jerk he dumped his shotgun shells into the snow and kicked at them until one skidded into a drift and only the brass showed. The other sank in the snow before it broke. Black powder spilled out under his feet.

Pa laughed.

Come on, Pa, I'm cold, I said. Look, I ain't brave. I ain't. I don't care. All I am is cold.

Quit whimpering, we're all cold. Big Hans here is awful cold.

Sure, ain't you?

Hans was grinding the black grains under.

Yeah, Pa said, grinning. Some.   I'm some. He turned around. Think you can find your way back, Jorge?

I got going and he laughed again, loud and ugly, damn his soul. I hated him. Jesus, how I did. But no more like a father. Like the burning space.

I never did like that bastard Pedersen anyway, he said as we started. Pedersen's one of them that's always asking for trouble. On his knees for it all the time. Let him find out about his kid himself. He knows where we live. It ain't neighborly but I never said I wanted him a neighbor.

Yeah, Hans said. Let the old bastard find out himself.

He should have kept his kid behind them fences. What business did he have, sending his kid to us to take care of? He went and asked for snow. He went on his knees for snow. Was he ready? Hey? Was he? For *snow*? Nobody's ever ready for *snow*.

The old bastard wouldn't have come to tell you if it'd been me who'd been lost, I said, but I wasn't minding my words at all, I was just talking. Neighbor all over him, I said, he has it coming. I was feeling the sleigh moving under me.

Can't tell about holy Pete, Hans said.

I was going fast. I didn't care about keeping low. I had my eyes on the spaces between trees. I was looking for the place where we'd left Simon and the sleigh. I thought I'd see Simon first, maybe his breath above a bank or beside the trunk of a tree. I slipped on a little snow the wind hadn't blown from the path we'd took. I still had the gun in my right hand so I lost my balance. When I put out my left for support, it went into a drift to my elbow and into the barberry thorns. I jerked back and fell hard. Hans and Pa found it funny. But the legs that lay in front of me weren't mine. I'd gone out in the blazing air. It was queer. Out of the snow I'd kicked away with my foot stuck a horse's hoof and I didn't feel the least terror or surprise.

Looks like a hoof, I said.

Hans and Pa were silent. I looked up at them, far away. Nothing now. Three men in the snow. A red scarf and some mittens . . . somebody's ice and coal . . . the picture for January. But behind them on the blank hills? Then it rushed over me and I thought: this is as far as he rid him. I looked at the hoof and the shoe which didn't belong in the picture. No dead horses for January. And on the snowhills there would be wild sled tracks and green trees and falling toboggans. This is as far. Or a glazed lake and rowdy skaters. Three men. On his ass: one. Dead horse and gun. And the question came to me very clearly, as if out of the calendar a girl had shouted: are you going to get up and walk on? Maybe it was the Christmas picture. The big log and the warm orange wood I was sprawled on in my flannel pajamas. I'd just been given a pistol that shot BBs. And the question was: was I going to get up and walk on? Hans's shoes, and Pa's, were as steady as the horse's. Were they hammered on? Their bodies stolen? Who'd left them standing here? And Christmas cookies cut in the shape of the kid's dead wet behind . . . with maybe a cherry to liven the pale dough . . . a coal from the stove. But I couldn't just say that looks like a hoof or that looks like a shoe and go right on, because Hans and Pa were waiting behind me in their wool hats and pounding mittens . . . like a picture for January. Smiling. I was learning to skate.

Looks like this is as far as he rid him.

Finally Pa said in a flat voice: what are you talking about?

You said he had a horse, Pa.

What are you talking about?

This here horse.

Ain't you never seen a shoe before?

It's just a horse's hoof, Hans said. Let's get on.

What are you talking about? Pa said again.

The man who scared the Pedersen kid. The man he saw.

Manure, Pa said. It's one of Pedersen's horses. I recognize the shoe.

That's right, Big Hans said.

Pedersen only has one horse.

This here's it, Big Hans said.

This horse's brown, ain't it?

Pedersen's horse has got two brown hind feet. I remember, Big Hans said. His is black.

It's got two brown hind feet.

I started to brush away some snow. I knew Pedersen's horse was black.

What the hell, Hans said. Come on. It's too cold to stand here and argue about the color of Pedersen's goddamn horse.

Pedersen's horse is black, Pa said. He don't have any brown on him at all.

Big Hans turned angrily on Pa. You said you recognized his shoe.

I thought I did.   It ain't.

I kept scraping snow away. Hans leaned down and pushed me. The horse was white where frozen snow clung to his hide.

He's brown, Hans. Pedersen's horse is black. This one's brown.

Hans kept pushing at me. God damn you, he was saying over and over in a funny high voice.

You knew all along it wasn't Pedersen's horse.

It went on like singing. I got up carefully, taking the safety off. Later in the winter maybe somebody would stumble on his shoes sticking out of the snow. Shooting Hans seemed like something I'd done already. I knew where he kept his gun—under those magazines in his drawer—and though I'd really never thought of it before, the whole thing moved before me now so naturally it must have happened that way. Of course I shot them all—Pa in his bed, ma in her kitchen, Hans when he came in from his rounds. They wouldn't look much different dead than alive, only they wouldn't be so loud.

Jorge, now—look out with that thing, Jorge.   Jorge.

His shotgun had fallen in the snow. He was holding both hands in front of him. Afterward I stood alone in every room.

You're yellow, Hans.

He was backing slowly, fending me off—fending—fending—

Jorge . . . Jorge . . . hey, now . . . Jorge . . . Like singing.

Afterward I looked through his magazines, my hand on my pecker, hot from head to foot.

I've shot you, yellow Hans. You can't shout or push no more or goose me in the barn.

Hey now wait, Jorge—listen— What?   Jorge . . . wait . . . Like singing.

Afterward only the wind and the warm stove. Shivering, I rose on my toes. Pa came up and I moved the gun to take him in. I kept it moving back and forth . . . Hans and Pa . . . Pa and Hans. Gone. Snow piling in the window corners. In the spring I'd shit with the door open, watching the blackbirds.

Don't be a damn fool, Jorge, Pa said. I know you're cold. We'll be going home.

. . . yellow yellow yellow yellow . . . Like singing.

Now Jorge, I ain't yellow, Pa said, smiling pleasantly.

I've shot you both with bullets.

Don't be a fool.

The whole house with bullets. You too.

Funny I don't feel it.

They never does, do they? Do rabbits?

He's crazy, jesus, Mag, he's crazy—

I never did want to. I never hid it like you did, I said. I never believed him. I ain't the yellow one but you you made me made me come but you're the yellow yellow ones, you were all along the yellow ones.

You're cold is all.

Cold or crazy—jesus—it's the same.

He's cold is all.

Then Pa took the gun away, putting it in his pocket. He had his shotgun hanging easy over his left arm but he slapped me and I bit my tongue. Pa was spitting. I turned and ran down the path we'd come, putting one arm over my face to ease the stinging.

You little shit, Big Hans called after me.

3

Pa came back to the sleigh, where I was sitting hunched up under the blanket, and got a shovel out of the back.

Feeling better?

Some.

Why don't you drink some of that coffee?

It's cold by now. I don't want to anyhow.

How about them sandwiches?

I ain't hungry. I don't want anything.

Pa started back with the shovel.

What are you going to do with that? I said.

Dig a tunnel, he said, and he went around a drift out of sight, the sun flashing from the blade.

I almost called him back but I remembered the grin in his face so I didn't.

Simon stamped. I pulled the blanket closer. I didn't believe him. Just for a second, when he said it, I had. It was a joke. Well I was too cold for jokes. What did he want a shovel for? There'd be no point in digging for the horse. They could see it wasn't Pedersen's.

Poor Simon. He was better than they were. They'd left us in the cold.

Pa'd forgot about the shovel in the sleigh. I could have used it hunting for his bottle. That had been a joke too. Pa'd sat there thinking how funny Jorge is out there beating away at the snow, I'll just wait and see if he remembers about that shovel. It'd be funny if Jorge forgot, he'd thought, sitting there in the blanket and bobbing his head here and there like a chicken. I'd hear about it when we got home till I was sick. I put my head down and closed my eyes. All right. I didn't care. I'd put up with it to be warm. But that couldn't be right. Pa must have forgot the same as me. He wanted that bottle too bad. Now it was all gone. It was colder with my eyes closed. I tried to think about all that underwear and the girls in the pictures. I had a crick in my neck.

Whose horse was it then?

I decided to keep my eyes closed a while longer, to see if I could do it. Then I decided not to. There was a stream of light in my eyes. It was brighter than snow, and as white. I opened them and straightened up. Keeping my head down made me dizzy. Everything was blurry. There were a lot of blue lines that moved.

Did they know the horse even so? Maybe it was Carlson's horse, or even Schmidt's. Maybe he was Carlson in yellow gloves, or Schmidt, and the kid, because he came in sudden from the barn and didn't know Carlson had come, saw him in the kitchen holding a gun like he might of if it'd been Schmidt, and the kid got scared and run, because he didn't understand and it'd been snowing lots, and how did Schmidt get there, or Carlson get there, if it was one of them, so the kid got scared and run and came to our crib, where the snow grew around him and then, in the morning, Hans found him.

And we'd been goddamn fools. Especially Hans. I shivered. The cold had settled in my belly. The sun had bent around to the west. Near it the sky was hazy. The troughs of some of the drifts were turning blue.

He wouldn't have been that scared. Why'd Carlson or Schmidt be out in a storm like that? If somebody was sick, they were closer to town than either the Pedersens or us. It was a long way for them in this weather. They wouldn't get caught out. But if the horse was stole, who was there but Carlson and Schmidt or maybe Hansen to steal it from?

He goes to the barn before the snow, most likely in the night, and knows horses. Oats or hay lead it out. He's running away. The blizzard sets down.

He drives himself and the horse hard, bending in the wind, leaning over far to see fences, any marks, a road. He makes the grove. He might not know it. The horse runs into the barberry, rears, goes to its knees; or a low branch of a mossycup he doesn't see knocks him into a drift; or he slides off when the horse rears as the barbs go in. The horse wanders a little way, not far. Then it stops—finished. And he—he's stunned, windburned, worn like a stone in a stream. He's frozen and tired, for snow's cold water. The wind's howling. He's blind. He's hungry, frozen, and scared. The snow is stinging his face, wearing him smooth. Standing still, all alone, it blows by him. Then the snow hides him. The wind blows a crust over him. Only a shovel poking in the drifts or a warm rain will find him lying by the horse.

I threw off the blanket and jumped down and ran up the path we'd made between the drifts and trees, slipping, cutting sharply back and forth, working against my stiffness, but all the time keeping my head up, looking out carefully ahead.

They weren't by the horse. A hoof and part of the leg I'd uncovered lay by the path like nothing more went with them. Seeing them like that, like they might have blown down from one of the trees in a good wind, gave me a fright. Now there was a slight breeze and I discovered my tongue was sore. Hans's and Pa's tracks went farther on—toward Pedersen's barn. I wasn't excited anymore. I remembered I'd left the blanket on the seat instead of putting it on Simon. I thought about going back. Pa'd said a tunnel. That had to be a joke. But what were they doing with the shovel? Maybe they'd found him by the barn. What if it really was Schmidt or Carlson? I thought about which I wanted it to be. I went more slowly in Pa's tracks. Now I kept down. The roof of Pedersen's barn got bigger; the sky was hazier; here and there little clouds of snow leaped up from the top of a drift like they'd been pinched off, and sailed swiftly away.

They *were* digging a tunnel. They didn't hear me come up. They were really digging a tunnel.

Hans was digging in the great drift. It ran from the grove in a high curve against the barn. It met the roof where it went lowest and flowed onto it like there wasn't a barn underneath. It seemed like the whole snow of winter was gathered there. If the drift hadn't ended in the grove it would have been swell for sledding. You could put a ladder on the edge of the roof and go off from there. The crust looked hard enough.

Hans and Pa had put about a ten-foot hole in the bank. Hans dug and Pa put what Hans dug in small piles behind him. I figured it was near a hundred feet to the barn. If we'd been home and not so cold, it would have been fun. But it would take all day. They were great damn fools.

I been thinking, I started out, and Hans stopped in the tunnel with a shovel of snow in the air.

Pa didn't turn around or stop.

You can help dig, he said.

I been thinking, I said, and Hans dropped the shovel, spilling the snow, and came out. I been thinking, I said, that you're digging in the wrong place.

Hans pointed to the shovel. Get digging.

We need something to carry snow with, Pa said. It's getting too damn far.

Pa kicked at the snow and flailed with his arms. He was sweating and so was Hans. It was terrible foolish.

I said you was digging in the wrong place.

Tell Hans. It's his idea. He's the hot digger.

You thought it was a good idea, Hans said.

I never did.

Well, I said, it ain't likely you'll find him clear in there.

Pa chuckled. He ain't going to find us neither.

He ain't going to find anybody if he's where I think.

Oh yeah—*think*. Hans moved nearer. Where?

As far as he got. It really didn't make much difference to me what Hans did. He could come as close as he liked. In the snow near that horse.

Hans started but Pa chewed on his lip and shook his head.

Probably Schmidt or Carlson, I said.

Probably Schmidt or Carlson, shit, Pa said.

Of course, Hans shouted.

Hans scooped up the shovel, furious, and carried it by me like an ax.

Hans has been working like a thrasher, Pa said.

You'll never finish it.

No.

It's higher than it needs to be.

Sure.

Why are you digging it then?

Hans.   Hans wants to.

Why, for christ's sake?

So we can get to the barn without being seen.

Why not cross behind the drift?

Hans.   Hans says no.   Hans says that from an upstairs window he could see over the bank.

What the hell.

He's got a rifle.

But who knows he's upstairs?

Nobody. We don't know he's even there. But that horse is.

He's back where I said.

No he ain't. You only wish he was. So does Hans, hey? But he ain't. What did the kid see if he is—his ghost?

I walked into the tunnel to the end. Everything seemed blue. The air was dead and wet. It could have been fun, snow over me, hard and grainy, the excitement of a tunnel, the games. The face of a mine, everything muffled, the marks of the blade in the snow. Well, I knew how Hans felt. It would have been wonderful to burrow down, disappear under the snow, sleep out of the wind in soft sheets, safe. I backed out. We went to get Hans and go home. Pa gave me the gun with a smile.

We heard the shovel cutting the crust and Hans puffing. He was using the shovel like a fork. He'd cut up the snow in clods around the horse. He grunted when he drove the shovel in. Next he began to beat the shovel against the snow, packing it down, then ripping the crust with the side of the blade.

Hans.   It ain't no use, Pa said.

But Hans went right on pounding with the shovel, spearing and pounding, striking out here and there like he was trying to kill a snake.

You're just wasting your time. It ain't no use, Hans. Jorge was wrong. He ain't by the horse.

But Hans went right on, faster and faster.

Hans. Pa had to make his voice hard and loud.

The shovel speared through the snow. It struck a stone and rang. Hans went to his knees and pawed at the snow with his hands. When he saw the stone he stopped. On his knees in the snow he simply stared at it.

Hans.

The bastard.   I'd have killed him.

He ain't here, Hans. How could he be? The kid didn't see him here, he saw him in the kitchen.

Hans didn't seem to be listening.

Jorge was wrong. He ain't here at all. He sure ain't here. He couldn't be.

Hans grabbed up the shovel like he was going to swing it and jumped up. He looked at me so awful I forgot how indifferent I was.

We got to think of what to do, Pa said. The tunnel won't work.

Hans didn't look at Pa. He would only look at me.

We can go home, Pa said. We can go home or we can chance crossing behind the bank.

Hans slowly put the shovel down. He started dragging up the narrow track to the barn.

Let's go home, Hans, I said. Come on, let's go home.

I can't go home, he said in a low flat voice as he passed us.

Pa sighed and I felt like I was dead.

Part Three

I

Pedersen's horse was in the barn. Pa kept her quiet. He rubbed his hand along her flank. He laid his head upon her neck and whispered in her ear. She shook herself and nickered. Big Hans opened the door a crack and peeked out. He motioned to Pa to hush the horse but Pa was in the stall. I asked Hans if he saw anything and Hans shook his head. I warned Pa about the bucket. He had the horse settled down. There was something that looked like sponges in the bucket. If they was sponges, they was hard. Hans turned from the door to rub his eyes. He leaned back against the wall.

Then Pa came and looked out the crack.

Don't look like anybody's to home.

Big Hans had the hiccups. Under his breath he swore and hiccupped.

Pa grunted.

Now the horse was quiet and we were breathing careful and if the wind had picked up we couldn't hear it or any snow it drove. It was warmer in the barn and the little light there was was soft on hay and wood. We were safe from the sun and it felt good to use the eyes on quiet tools and leather. I leaned like Hans against the wall and put my gun in my belt. It felt good to have emptied that hand. My face burned and I was very drowsy.   I could dig a hole in the hay. Even if there were rats, I would sleep with them in it.   Everything was still in the barn. Tools and harness hung from the walls, and pails and bags and burlap rested on the floor. Nothing shifted in the straw or moved in the hay. The horse stood easy. And Hans and I rested up against the wall, Hans sucking in his breath and holding it, and we waited for Pa, who didn't make a sound. Only the line of sun that snuck under him and lay along the floor and came up white and dangerous to the pail seemed a living thing.

Don't look like it, Pa said finally. Never can tell.

Now who will go, I thought.   It isn't far.   Then it'll be over.   It's just across the yard.   It isn't any farther than the walk behind the drift.   There's only windows watching.   If he's been, he's gone, and nothing's there to hurt.

He's gone.

Maybe, Jorge. But if he came on that brown horse you stumbled on, why didn't he take this mare of Pedersen's when he left?

Jesus, Hans whispered. He's here.

Could be in the barn, we'd never see him.

Hans hiccupped. Pa laughed softly.

Damn you, said Big Hans.

Thought I'd rid you of them hics.

Let me look, I said.

He must be gone, I thought. It's such a little way.   He must be gone.   He never came.   It isn't far but who will go across?   I saw the house by squinting hard. The nearer part, the dining room, came toward us. The porch was on the left and farther off. You could cross to the nearer wall and under the windows edge around. He might see you from the porch window. But he'd gone. Yet I didn't want to go across that little winded space of snow to find it out.

I wished Big Hans would stop. I was counting the spaces. It was comfortable behind my back except for that. There was a long silence while he held his breath, and afterward we waited.

The wind was rising by the snowman. There were long blue shadows by the snowman now. The eastern sky was clear. Snow sifted slowly to the porch past the snowman. An icicle hung from the nose of the pump. There were no tracks anywhere. I asked did they see the snowman and I heard Pa grunt. Snow went waist-high to the snowman. The wind had blown from his face his eyes. A silent chimney was an empty house.

There ain't nobody there, I said.

Hans had hiccups again, so I ran out.

I ran to the dining room wall and put my back flat against it, pushing hard. Now I saw clouds in the western sky. The wind was rising. It was okay for Hans and Pa to come. I would walk around the corner. I would walk around the wall. The porch was there. The snowman was alone beside it.

All clear, I shouted, walking easily away.

Pa came carefully from the barn with his arms around his gun. He walked slow to be brave but I was standing in the open and I smiled.

Pa sat hugging his knees as I heard the gun, and Hans screamed. Pa's gun stood up. I backed against the house. My god, I thought, he's real.

I want a drink.

I held the house. The snow'd been driven up against it.

I want a drink. He motioned with his hand to me.

Shut up. Shut up.   I shook my head.   Shut up. Shut up and die, I thought.

I want a drink, I'm dry, Pa said.

Pa bumped when I heard the gun again. He seemed to point his hand at me. My fingers slipped along the boards. I tried to dig them in but my back slipped down. Hopelessly I closed my eyes. I knew I'd hear the gun again, though rabbits don't. Silently he'd come.   My back slipped.   Rabbits, though, are hard to hit the way they jump around. But prairie dogs, like pa, they sit.   I felt snowflakes against my face, crumbling as they struck. He'd shoot me, by god. Was pa's head tipped? Don't look.   I felt snowflakes falling softly against my face, breaking. The glare was painful, closing the slit in my eyes. That crack in pa's face must be awful dry. Don't look. Yes . . . the wind was rising . . . faster flakes.

2

When I was so cold I didn't care I crawled to the south side of the house and broke a casement window with the gun I had forgot I had and climbed down into the basement, ripping my jacket on the glass. My ankles hurt, so I huddled there in the dark corner places and in the cold moldy places by boxes. Immediately I went to sleep.

I thought it was right away I woke, though the light through the window was red. He put them down the cellar, I remembered. But I stayed where I was, so cold I seemed apart from myself, and wondered if everything had been working to get me in this cellar as a trade for the kid he'd missed. Well, he was sudden. The Pedersen kid—maybe he'd been a message of some sort. No, I liked better the idea that we'd been prisoners exchanged. I was back in my own country. No, it was more like I'd been given a country. A new blank land. More and more, while we'd been coming, I'd been slipping out of myself, pushed out by the cold maybe. Anyway, I had a queer head, sear-eyed and bleary, everywhere ribboned. Well, he was quick and quiet. The rabbit simply stumbled. Tomatoes were unfeeling when they froze. I thought of the softness of the tunnel, the mark of the blade in the snow. Suppose the snow was a hundred feet deep. Down and down. A blue-white cave, the blue darkening. Then tunnels off of it like the branches of trees. And fine rooms. Was it February by now? I remembered a movie where the months had blown from the calendar like leaves. Girls in red peekaboo BVDs were skiing out of sight. Silence of the tunnel. In and in. Stairs. Wide tall stairs. And balconies. Windows of ice and sweet green light. Ah. There would still be snow in February. Here I go off of the barn, the runners hissing. I am tilting dangerously but I coast on anyway. Now to the trough, the swift snow trough, and the

Pedersen kid floating chest-down. They were all drowned in the snow now, weren't they? Well, more or less, weren't they? The kid for killing his family.   But what about me?   Must freeze.   But I would leave ahead of that, that was the nice thing, I was already going. Yes. Funny. I was something to run my hands over, feeling for its hurts, like there were worn places in leather, rust and rot in screws and boards I had to find, and the places were hard to reach and the fingers in my gloves were stiff and their ends were sore. My nose was running. Mostly interesting. Funny. There was a cramp in my leg that must have made me wake. Distantly I felt the soft points of my shoulders in my jacket, the heavy line of my cap around my forehead, and on the hard floor my harder feet, and to my chest my hugged-tight knees. I felt them but I felt them differently . . . like the pressure of a bolt through steel or the cinch of leather harness or the squeeze of wood by wood in floors . . . like the twist and pinch, the painful yield of tender tight together wheels, and swollen bars, and in deep winter springs.

I couldn't see the furnace but it was dead. Its coals were cold, I knew. The broken window held a rainbow and put a colored pattern on the floor. Once, the wind ran through it and a snowflake turned. The stairs went into darkness. If a crack of light came down the steps, I guessed I had to shoot. I fumbled for my gun. Then I noticed the fruit cellar and the closed door where the Pedersens were.

Would they be dead already? Sure they'd be. Everybody was but me. More or less. Big Hans, of course, wasn't really, unless the fellow had caught up with him, howling and running. But Big Hans had gone away a coward. I knew that. It was almost better he was alive and the snow had him. I didn't have his magazines but I remembered how they looked, puffed in their bras.

The door was wood with a wooden bar. I slipped the bar off easily but the door itself was stuck. It shouldn't have stuck but it *was* stuck—stuck at the top. I tried to see the top by standing on tiptoe, but I couldn't bend my toes well and kept toppling to the side. Got no business sticking, I thought. There's no reason for that. I pulled again, very hard. A chip fell as it shuddered open. Wedged. Why? It had a bar.   It was even darker in the fruit cellar and the air had a musty earthen smell.

Maybe they were curled up like the kid was when he dropped. Maybe they had frost on their clothes, and stiff hair. What color would their noses be? Would I dare to tweak them? Say. If the old lady was dead I'd peek at her crotch.   I wasn't any Hans to rub them. Big Hans had run. The snow had him. There wasn't any kettle, any stove, down here.   Before you did a thing like that, you'd want to be sure. I thought of how the sponges in the bucket had got hard.

I went back behind the boxes and hid and watched the stairs. The chip was orange in the pattern of light. He'd heard me when I broke the glass or when the door shook free or when the wedge fell down. He was waiting behind the door at the top of the stairs. All I had to do was come up. He was waiting. All this time. He waited while we stood in the barn. He waited for pa with his arms full of gun to come out. He took no chances and he waited.

I knew I couldn't wait. I knew I'd have to try to get back out. There he'd be waiting too. I'd sit slowly in the snow like pa. That'd be a shame, a special shame after all I'd gone through, because I was on the edge of something wonderful, I felt it trembling in me strangely, in the part of me that flew high and calmly looked down on my stiff heap of clothing. Oh what pa'd forgot. We could have used the shovel. I'd have found the bottle with it. With it we'd have gone on home. By the stove I'd come to myself again. By it I'd be warm again. But as I thought about it, it didn't appeal to me anymore. I didn't want to come to myself that way again. No. I was glad he'd forgot the shovel. But he was . . . he was waiting.   Pa always said that he could wait; that Pedersen never could. But pa and me, we couldn't—only Hans stayed back while we came out, while all the time the real waiter waited. He knew I couldn't wait. He knew I'd freeze.

Maybe the Pedersens were just asleep.   Have to be sure the old man wasn't watching. What a thing. Pa pretended sleep. Could he pretend death too? She wasn't much. Fat. Gray. But a crotch is a crotch. The light in the window paled. The sky I could see was smoky. The bits of broken glass had glimmered out. I heard the wind. Snow by the window rose. From a beam a cobweb swung stiffly like a net of wire. Flakes followed one another in and disappeared. I counted desperately, three, eleven, twenty-five. One lit beside me.   Maybe the Pedersens *were* just asleep. I went to the door again and looked in. Little rows of lights lay on the glasses and the jars. I felt the floor with my foot. I thought suddenly of snakes. I pushed my feet along. I got to every corner but the floor was empty. Really it was a relief. I went back and hid behind the boxes. The wind was coming now, with snow, the glass glinting in unexpected places. The dead tops of roofing nails in an open keg glowed white. Oh for the love of god.   Above me in the house I heard a door slam sharply. He was finished with waiting.

The kid for killing his family must freeze.

The stair was railless and steep. It seemed to stagger in the air. Thank God the treads were tight, and didn't creak. Darkness swept under me. Terror of height. But I was only climbing with my sled under my arm. In a minute I'd shoot from the roof edge and rush down the steep drift, snow smoke behind me. I clung to the stair, stretched out. Fallen into space, I'd float around a dark star. Not the calendar for March. Maybe they would find me in the spring, hanging from this stairway like a wintering cocoon.

I crawled up slowly and pushed the door open. The kitchen wallpaper had flowerpots on it, green and very big. Out of every one a great red flower grew. I began laughing. I liked the wallpaper. I loved it; it was mine; I felt the green pots and traced the huge flower that stuck out of it, laughing. To the left of the door at the head of the stair was a window that looked out on the back porch. I saw the wind hurrying snow off toward the snowman. Down the length of it the sky and all its light was lead and all the snow was ashy. Across the porch were footprints, deep and precise.

I was on the edge of celebration but I remembered in time and scooted in a closet, hunkering down between brooms, throwing my arms across my eyes. Down a long green hill there was a line of sheep. It had been my favorite picture in a book I'd had when I was eight. There were no people in it.

I'd been mad and pa had laughed. I'd had it since my birthday in the spring. Then he'd hid it. It was when we had the privy in the back. God, it was cold in there, dark beneath. I found it in the privy torn apart and on the freezing soggy floor in leaves. And down the hole I saw floating curly sheep. There was even ice. I'd been seized, and was rolling and kicking. Pa had struck himself and laughed. I only saved a red-cheeked fat-faced boy in blue I didn't like. The cow was torn. Ma'd said I'd get another one someday. For a while, every day, even though the snow was piled and the sky dead and the winter wind was blowing, I watched for my aunt to come again and bring me a book like my ma'd said she would. She never came.

And I almost had Hans's magazines.

But he might come again. Yet he'd not chase me home, not now, no.   By god, the calendar was clean, the lines sharp and clear, the colors bright and gay, and there were eights on the ice and red mouths singing and the snow belonged to me and the high sky too, burningly handsome, fiercely blue.   But he might. He was quick.

If it was warmer I couldn't tell but it wasn't as damp as by the boxes and I could smell soap. There was light in the kitchen. It came through the crack I'd left in the closet door to comfort me. But the light was fading. Through the crack I could see the sink, now milky. Flakes began to slide out of the sky and rub their corners off on the pane before they were caught by the wind again and blown away. In the gray I couldn't see them. Then they would come—suddenly—from it, like chaff from grain, and brush the window while the wind eddied. Something black was bobbing. It was deep in the gray where the snow was. It bounced queerly and then it went. The black stocking cap, I thought.

I kicked a pail coming out and when I ran to the window my left leg gave way, banging me against the sink. The light was going. The snow was coming. It was coming almost even with the ground, my snow. Puffs were rising. Then, in a lull when the snow sank and it was light enough to see the snowbank shadows growing, I saw his back upon a horse. I saw the tail flick. And the snow came back. Great sheets flapped. He was gone.

3

Once, when dust rolled up from the road and the fields were high with heavy-handled wheat and the leaves of every tree were gray and curled up and hung head down, I went in the meadow with an old broom like a gun, where the dandelions had begun to seed and the low ground was cracked, and I flushed grasshoppers from the goldenrod in whirring clouds like quail and shot them down. I smelled wheat in the warm wind and every weed. I tasted dust in my mouth, and the house and barn and all the pails burned my eyes to look at. I rode the broom over the brown rocks. I hunted Horse Simon in the shade of a tree. I rode the broom over the brown meadow grass and with a fist like a pistol butt and trigger shot the Indian on Horse Simon down. I rode across the dry plain. I rode into the dry creek. Dust rose up behind me. I went fast and shouted. The tractor was bright orange. It shimmered. Dust rolled behind it. I hid in the creek and followed as it came. I waited as its path curved toward me. I watched and waited. My eyes were tiny. I sprang out with a whoop and rode across the dry plain. My horse had a golden tail. Dust rolled up behind me. Pa was on the tractor in a broad-brimmed hat. With a fist like a pistol butt and trigger, going fast, I shot him down.

Pa would stop the tractor and get off and we'd walk across the creek to the little tree Simon stood his bowed head under. We'd sit by the tree and pa would pull a water bottle out from between its roots and drink. He'd swish it around in his mouth good before he swallowed. He'd wipe off the top and offer it to me. I'd take a pull like it was fiery and hand it back. Pa'd take another drink and sigh and get on up. Then he'd say: you feed the chickens like I told you? and I'd say I had, and then he'd say: how's the hunting? and I'd say pretty good. He'd nod like he agreed and clap Simon on the behind and go on off, but he'd always say I'd best not play in the sun too long. I'd watch him go over the creek, waving his hat before his face before he put it on. Then I'd take a secret drink out of the bottle and wipe my lips and the lip of it. After that I'd go and let the ragweed brush against my knees, and then, sometimes, go home.

The fire had begun to feel warm. I rubbed my hands. I ate a stale biscuit.

Pa had taken the wagon to town. The sun was shining. Pa had gone to meet Big Hans at the station. There was snow around but mud was flowing and the fields had green in them again. Mud rode up on the wagon wheels. There was sweet air sometimes and the creek had water with the winter going. Through a crack in the privy door I saw him take the wagon to the train. I'd a habit, when I was twelve, of looking down. Something sparkled on the water. It was then I found the first one. The sun was shining. Mud was climbing the wagon wheels and pa was going to the train and down the tight creek snow was flowing. He had a ledge beneath the seat. You could reach right down. Already he had a knack for hiding. So I found it and poured it out in the hole. That was the last year we had the privy because when Big Hans came we tore it down.

I ate an apple I'd found. The skin was shriveled but the meat was sweet.

Big Hans was stronger than Simon, I thought. He let me help him with his chores, and we talked, and later he showed me some of the pictures in his magazines. See anything like that around here? he'd say, shaking his head. Only teats like that round here is on a cow. And he would tease, laughing while he spun the pages, giving me only a glimpse. Or he would come up and spank me on the rump. We tore the privy down together. Big Hans hated it. He said it was a dirty job fit only for soldiers. But I helped him a lot, he said. He told me that Jap girls had their slice on sideways and no hair. He promised to show me a picture of one of them, and though I badgered him, he never did. We burned the boards in a big pile back of the barn and the flames were a deep orange like the sun going down and the smoke rolled darkly. It's piss wet, Hans said. We stood by the fire and talked until it sank down and the stars were out and the coals glowed and he told me about the war in whispers and the firing of big guns.

Pa liked the summer. He wished it was summer all year long. He said once whiskey made it summer for him. But Hans liked the spring like me, though I liked summer too. Hans talked and showed me this and that. He measured his pecker once when he had a hard one. We watched how the larks ran across the weeds and winked with their tails taking off. We watched the brown spring water foam by the rocks in the creek, and heard Horse Simon blow and the pump squeak.

Then pa took a dislike to Hans and said I shouldn't go with Hans so much. And then, in the winter, Hans took a dislike to pa as he almost had to, and Hans said fierce things to ma about pa's drinking, and one day pa heard him. Pa was furious and terrible to ma all day. It was a night like this one. The wind was blowing hard and the snow was coming hard and I'd built a fire and was sitting by it, dreaming. Ma came and sat near me, and then pa came, burning inside himself, while Hans stayed in the kitchen. All I heard was the fire, and in the fire I saw ma's sad quiet face the whole evening without turning, and I heard pa drinking, and nobody not even me said anything the whole long long evening. The next morning Hans went to wake pa and pa threw the pot and Hans got the ax and pa laughed fit to shake the house. It wasn't long before Hans and I took to hating one another and hunting pa's bottles alone.

The fire was burning down. There was some blue but mostly it was orange. For all Pedersen's preparing like pa said he always did, he hadn't got much wood in the house. It was good to be warm but I didn't feel so set against the weather as I had been. I thought I'd like winter pretty well from now on. I sat as close as I could and stretched and yawned.   Even if his cock was thicker . . . I was here and he was in the snow.   I was satisfied.

He was in the wind now and in the cold now and sleepy now like me. His head was bent down low like the horse's head must be and he was rocking in the saddle very tired of holding on and only rocking sleepy with his eyes shut and with snow on his heavy lids and on his lashes and snow in his hair and up his sleeves and down inside his collar and his boots. It was good I was glad he was there it wasn't me was there sticking up bare in the wind on a horse like a stick with the horse most likely stopped by this time with his bowed head bent into the storm, and I wouldn't like lying all by myself out there in the cold white dark, dying all alone out there, being buried out there while I was still trying to breathe, knowing I'd only come slowly to the surface in the spring and would soon be soft in the new sun and worried by curious dogs.

The horse must have stopped though he made the other one go on. Maybe he'd manage to drive this one too until it dropped, or he fell off, or something broke. He might make the next place. He just might. Carlson's or Schmidt's. He had once before though he never had a right or any chance to. Still he had. He was in the thick snow now. More was coming. More was blowing down. He was in it now and he could go on and he could come through it because he had before. Maybe he belonged in the snow. Maybe he lived there, like a fish does in a lake. Spring didn't have anything like him. I surprised myself when I laughed the house was so empty and the wind so steady it didn't count for noise.

I saw him coming up beside our crib, the horse going down to its knees in the drift there. I saw him going to the kitchen and coming in unheard because of all the wind. I saw Hans sitting in the kitchen. He was drinking like pa drank—lifting the bottle. Ma was there, her hands like a trap on the table. The Pedersen kid was there too, naked in the flour, towels lapping his middle, whiskey and water steadily dripping. Hans was watching, watching the kid's dirty toes, watching him like he watched me with his pin-black eyes and his tongue sliding in his mouth. Then he'd see the cap, the mackinaw, the gloves wrapped thick around the gun, and it would be the same as when pa kicked the glass from Big Hans's hand, only the bottle this time would roll on the floor, squirting. Ma would worry about her kitchen getting tracked and get up and mix biscuits with a shaky spoon and put the coffee on.

They'd disappear like the Pedersens had. He'd put them away somewhere out of sight for at least as long as the winter. But he'd leave the kid, for we'd been exchanged, and we were both in our own new lands. Then why did he stand there so pale I could see through? Shoot. Go on. Hurry up. Shoot.

The horse had circled round in it. He hadn't known the way. He hadn't known the horse had circled round. His hands were loose upon the reins and so the horse had circled round. Everything was black and white and everything the same. There wasn't any road to go. There wasn't any track. The horse had circled round in it. He hadn't known the way. There was only snow to the horse's thighs. There was only cold to the bone and driving snow in his eyes. He hadn't known. How could he know the horse had circled round in it? How could he really ride and urge the horse with his heels when there wasn't anyplace to go and everything was black and white and all the same? Of course the horse had circled round, of course he'd come around in it. Horses have a sense. That's all manure about horses. No it ain't, pa, no it ain't. They do. Hans said. They do. Hans knows. He's right. He was right about the wheat that time. He said the rust was in it and it was. He was right about the rats, they do eat shoes, they eat anything, so the horse has circled round in it. That was a long time ago. Yes, pa, but Hans was right even though that was a long time ago, and how would you know anyway, you was always drinking . . . not in summer . . . no, pa . . . not in spring or fall either . . . no, pa, but in the winter, and it's winter now and you're in bed where you belong—don't speak to me, be quiet. The bottle made it spring for me just like that fellow's made it warm for you.   Shut up.   Shut up.   I wanted a cat or a dog awful bad since I was a little kid.   You know those pictures of Hans's, the girls with big brown nipples like bottle ends . . .   Shut up.   Shut up.   I'm not going to grieve. You're no man now. Your bottle's broken in the snow. The sled rode over it, remember? I'm not going to grieve. You were always after killing me yourself, pa, oh yes you were. I was cold in your house always, pa.   Jorge—so was I.   No. I was. I was the one wrapped in the snow. Even in the summer I'd shiver sometimes in the shade of a tree. And pa—I didn't touch you, remember—there's no point in haunting me. *He* did. He's even come round maybe.   Oh no jesus please.   Round.   He wakes. He sees the horse has stopped. He sits and rocks and thinks the horse is going on and then he sees it's not. He tries his heels but the horse has finally stopped. He gets off and leads him on smack into the barn, and there it is, the barn, the barn he took the horse from. Then in the barn he begins to see better and he makes out something solid in the yard where he knows the house is and there are certain to be little letups in the storm and through one of them he sees a flicker of something almost orange, a flicker of the fire and a sign of me by it all stretched out my head on my arm and near asleep.   If they'd given me a dog, I'd have called him Shep.

I jumped up and ran to the kitchen, only stopping and going back for the gun and then running to the closet for the pail, which I dropped with a terrible clatter. The tap gasped. The dipper in the pail beneath the sink rattled. So I ran to the fire and began to poke at it, the logs tumbling, and then I beat the logs with the poker so that sparks flew in my hair.

I crouched down behind a big chair in a corner away from the fire. Then I remembered I'd left the gun in the kitchen. My feet were sore and bare. The room was full of orange light and blackened shadows, moving. The wind whooped and the house creaked like steps do. I was alone with all that could happen. I began to wonder if the Pedersens had a dog, if the Pedersen kid had a dog or cat maybe and where it was if they did and if I'd known its name and whether it'd come if I called. I tried to think of its name as if it was something I'd forgot. I knew I was all muddled up and scared and crazy and I tried to think goddamn over and over or what the hell or jesus christ, instead, but it didn't work. All that could happen was alone with me and I was alone with it.

The wagon had a great big wheel.   Papa had a paper sack.   Mama held my hand.   High horse waved his tail.   Papa had a paper sack. We both ran to hide.   Mama held my hand.   The wagon had a great big wheel.   High horse waved his tail. We both ran to hide.   Papa had a paper sack.   The wagon had a great big wheel.   Mama held my hand.   Papa had a paper sack.   High horse waved his tail.   The wagon had a great big wheel. We both ran to hide.   High horse waved his tail.   Mama held my hand. We both ran to hide.   The wagon had a great big wheel.   Papa had a paper sack.   Mama held my hand.   High horse waved his tail.   Papa had a paper sack. We both ran to hide.   Papa had a paper sack. We both ran to hide.

The wind was still. The snow was still. The sun burned on the snow. The fireplace was cold and all the logs were ashy. I lay stiffly on the floor, my legs drawn up, my arms around me. The fire had gone steadily into gray while I slept, and the night away, and I saw the dust float and glitter and settle down.

The walls, the rug, the furniture, all that I could see from my elbow looked pale and tired and drawn up tight and cramped with cold. I felt I'd never seen these things before. I'd never seen a wasted morning, the sick drawn look of a winter dawn or how things were in a room where things were stored away and no one ever came, and how the dust came gently down.

I put my socks on. I didn't remember at all coming from behind the chair, but I must have. I got some matches from the kitchen and some paper twists out of a box beside the fireplace and I put them down, raking the ashes aside. Then I put some light kindling on top. Pieces of orange crate, I think they were. And then a log. I lit the paper and it flared up and flakes of the kindling curled and got red and black and dropped off and finally the kindling caught when I blew on it. It didn't warm my hands any, though I kept them close, so I rubbed my arms and legs and jigged, but my feet still hurt. Then the fire growled. Another log.   I found I couldn't whistle.   I warmed my back some.   Outside snow.   Steep. There were long hard shadows in the hollows of the drifts but the eastern crests were bright.   After I'd warmed up a little I walked about the house in my stocking feet, and snagged my socks on the stairs. I looked under all the beds and in all the closets and behind most of the furniture. I remembered the pipes were froze. I got the pail from under the sink and opened the door to the back porch against a drift and scooped snow in the pail with a dipper. Snow had risen to the shoulders of the snowman. The pump was banked. There were no tracks anywhere.

I started the stove and put snow in a kettle. It always took so much snow to make a little water. The stove was black as char. I went back to the fireplace and put more logs on. It was beginning to roar and the room was turning cheerful, but it always took so much fire. I wriggled into my boots. Somehow I had a hunch I'd see a horse.

The front door was unlocked. All the doors were, likely. He could have walked right in. I'd forgot about that. But now I knew he wasn't meant to. I laughed to see how a laugh would sound.   Again.   Good.

The road was gone. Fences, bushes, old machinery: what there might be in any yard was all gone under snow. All I could see was the steep snow and the long shadow lines and the hard bright crest about to break but not quite breaking and the hazy sun rising, throwing down slats of orange like a snow fence had fallen down. He'd gone off this way yet there was nothing now to show he'd gone; nothing like a bump of black in a trough or an arm or leg sticking out of the side of a bank like a branch had blown down or a horse's head uncovered like a rock; nowhere Pedersen's fences had kept bare he might be lying huddled with the horse on its haunches by him; nothing even in the shadows shrinking while I watched to take for something hard and not of snow and once alive.

I saw the window I'd broke. The door of the barn hung ajar, banked steeply with snow. The house threw a narrow shadow clear to one end of the barn, where it ran into the high drift that Hans had tunneled in. Higher now. Later I'd cut a path out to it. Make the tunnel deeper maybe. Hollow the whole bank like a hollow tree. There was time. I saw the oaks too, blown clean, their twigs about their branches stiff as quills. The path I'd taken from the barn to the house was filled and the sun was burning brightly on it. The wind had curled in and driven a steep slope of snow against the house where I'd stood. As I turned my head the sun flashed from the barrel of pa's gun. The snow had risen steeply around him. Only the top of the barrel was clear to take the sun and it flashed squarely in my eye when I turned my head just right. There was nothing to do about that till spring. Another snowman, he'd melt. I picked my way back to the front of the house, a dark spot dancing in the snow ahead of me. Today there was a fine large sky.

It was pleasant not to have to stamp the snow off my boots, and the fire was speaking pleasantly and the kettle was sounding softly. There was no need for me to grieve. I had been the brave one and now I was free. The snow would keep me. I would bury pa and the Pedersens and Hans and even ma if I wanted to bother. I hadn't wanted to come but now I didn't mind. The kid and me, we'd done brave things well worth remembering. The way that fellow had come so mysteriously through the snow and done us such a glorious turn—well, it made me think how I was told to feel in church. The wintertime had finally got them all, and I really did hope that the kid was as warm as I was now, warm inside and out, burning up, inside and out, with joy.

MSS, 1961
Published in *In the Heart of the Heart of the Country*, 1968

ORDER OF INSECTS

We certainly had no complaints about the house after all we had been through in the other place, but we hadn't lived there very long before I began to notice every morning the bodies of a large black bug spotted about the downstairs carpet; haphazardly, as earthworms must die on the street after a rain; looking when I first saw them like rolls of dark wool or pieces of mud from the children's shoes, or sometimes, if the drapes were pulled, so like ink stains or deep burns they terrified me, for I had been intimidated by that thick rug very early and the first week had walked over it wishing my bare feet would swallow my shoes. The shells were usually broken. Legs and other parts I couldn't then identify would be scattered near like flakes of rust. Occasionally I would find them on their backs, their quilted undersides showing orange, while beside them were smudges of dark-brown powder that had to be vacuumed carefully. We believed our cat had killed them. She was frequently sick during the night then—a rare thing for her—and we could think of no other reason. Overturned like that they looked pathetic even dead.

I could not imagine where the bugs had come from. I am terribly meticulous myself. The house was clean, the cupboards tight and orderly, and we never saw one alive. The other place had been infested with those flat brown fuzzy roaches, all wires and speed, and we'd seen *them* all right, frightened by the kitchen light, sifting through the baseboards and the floor's cracks; and in the pantry I had nearly closed my fingers on one before it fled, tossing its shadow across the starch like an image of the startle in my hand.

Dead, overturned, their three pairs of legs would be delicately drawn up and folded shyly over their stomachs. When they walked I suppose their forelegs were thrust out and then bent to draw the body up. I still wonder if they jumped. More than once I've seen our cat hook one of her claws under a shell and toss it in the air, crouching while the insect fell, feigning leaps—but there was daylight; the bug was dead; she was not really interested anymore; and she would walk immediately away. That image takes the place of jumping. Even if I actually saw those two black pairs of legs unhinge, as they would have to if one leaped, I think I'd find the result unreal and mechanical, a poor try measured by that sudden, high, head-over-heals flight from our cat's paw. I could look it up, I guess, but it's no study for a woman . . . bugs.

At first I reacted as I should, bending over, wondering what in the world; yet even before I recognized them I'd withdrawn my hand, shuddering. Fierce, ugly, armored things: they used their shadows to seem large. The machine sucked them up while I looked the other way. I remember the sudden thrill of horror I had hearing one rattle up the wand. I was relieved that they were dead, of course, for I could never have killed one, and if they had been popped, alive, into the dust bag of the cleaner, I believe I would have had nightmares again as I did the time my husband fought the red ants in our kitchen. All night I lay awake thinking of the ants alive in the belly of the machine, and when, toward morning, I finally slept I found myself in the dreadful elastic tunnel of the suction tube, where ahead of me I heard them: a hundred bodies rustling in the dirt.

I never think of their species as alive but as comprised entirely by the dead ones on our carpet, all the new dead manufactured by the action of some mysterious spoor—perhaps that dust they sometimes lie in—carried in the air, solidified by night, and shaped, from body into body, spontaneously, as maggots were before the age of science. I have a single book about insects, a little dated handbook in French which a good friend gave me as a joke—because of my garden, the quaintness of the plates, the fun of reading about worms in such an elegant tongue—and my bug has his picture there, climbing the stem of an orchid. Beneath the picture is his name: *Periplaneta orientalis L. Ces répugnants insectes ne sont que trop communs dans les cuisines des vielles habitations des villes, dans les magasins, entrepôts, boulangeries, brasseries, restaurants, dans la cale des navires, etc.,* the text begins. Nevertheless, they are a new experience for me and I think that I am grateful for it now.

The picture didn't need to show me there were two, adult and nymph, for by that time I'd seen the bodies of both kinds. Nymph. My God, the names we use. The one was dark, squat, ugly, sly. The other, slimmer, had hard sheathlike wings drawn over its back like another shell, and you could see delicate interwoven lines spun like fossil gauze across them. The nymph was a rich golden color deepening in its interstices to mahogany. Both had legs that looked under a glass like the canes of a rose, and the nymph's were sufficiently transparent: in a good light you thought you saw its nerves merge and run like a jagged crack to each ultimate claw.

Tipped, their legs have fallen shut, and the more I look at them the less I believe my eyes. Corruption, in these bugs, is splendid. I've a collection now I keep in typewriter ribbon tins, and though, in time, their bodies dry and the interior flesh decays, their features hold, as I suppose they held in life, an Egyptian determination, for their protective plates are strong and death must break bones to get in. Now that the heavy soul is gone, the case is light.

I suspect if we were as familiar with our bones as with our skin, we'd never bury dead but shrine them in their rooms, arranged as we might like to find them on a visit; and our enemies, if we could steal their bodies from the battle sites, would be museumed as they died, the steel still eloquent in their sides, their metal hats askew, the protective toes of their shoes unworn, and friend and enemy would be so wondrously historical that in a hundred years we'd find the jaws still hung for the same speech and all the parts we spent our life with tilted as they always were—rib cage, collar, skull—still repetitious, still defiant, angel light, still worthy of memorial and affection. After all, what does it mean to say that when our cat has bitten through the shell and put confusion in the pulp, the life goes out of them? Alas for us, I want to cry, our bones are secret, showing last, so we must love what perishes: the muscles and the waters and the fats.

Two prongs extend like daggers from the rear. I suppose I'll never know their function. That kind of knowledge doesn't take my interest. At first I had to screw my eyes down, and as I consider it now the whole change, the recent alteration in my life, was the consequence of finally coming near to something. It was a self-mortifying act, I recall, a penalty I laid upon myself for the evil-tempered words I'd shouted at my children in the middle of the night. I felt instinctively the insects were infectious and their own disease, so when I knelt I held a handkerchief over the lower half of my face . . . saw only horror . . . turned, sick, making my eyes . . . yet the worst of angers held me through the day: vague, searching, guilty, and ashamed.

After that I came near often; saw, for the first time, the gold nymph's difference; put between the mandibles a tinted nail I'd let grow long; observed the movement of the jaws, the stalks of the antennae, the skull-shaped skull, the lines banding the abdomen, and found an intensity in the posture of the shell, even when tipped, like that in the gaze of Gauguin's natives' eyes. The dark plates glisten. They are wonderfully shaped, even the buttons of the compound eyes show a geometrical precision which prevents my earlier horror. It isn't possible to feel disgust toward such an order. Nevertheless, I reminded myself, a roach . . . and you a woman.

I no longer own my own imagination. I suppose they came up the drains or out of the registers. It may have been the rug they wanted. Crickets too, I understand, will feed on wool. I used to rest by my husband . . . stiffly . . . waiting for silence to settle in the house, his sleep to come, and then the drama of their passage would take hold of me, possess me so completely that when I finally slept I merely passed from one dream to another without the slightest loss of vividness or continuity. Never alive, they came with punctures; their bodies formed from little whorls of copperish dust which in the downstairs darkness I couldn't possibly have seen; and they were dead and upside down when they materialized, for it was in that moment that our cat, herself darkly invisible, leaped and brought her paws together on the true soul of the roach; a soul so static and intense, so immortally arranged, I felt, while I lay shell-like in our bed, turned inside out, driving my mind away, it was the same as the dark soul of the world itself—and it was this beautiful and terrifying feeling that took possession of me finally, stiffened me like a rod beside my husband, played Caesar to my dreams.

The weather drove them up, I think . . . moisture in the tubes of the house. The first I came on looked put together in Japan; broken, one leg bent under like a metal cinch; unwound. It rang inside the hollow of the wand like metal too; brightly, like a stream of pins. The clatter made me shiver. Well, I always see what I fear. Anything my eyes have is transformed into a threatening object: mud or stains, or burns, or if not these, then toys in unmendable metal pieces. Not fear to be afraid of. The ordinary fears of daily life. Healthy fears. Womanly, wifely, motherly ones: the children may point at the wretch with the hunch and speak in a voice he will hear; the cat has fleas again, they will get in the sofa; one's face looks smeared, it's because of the heat; is the burner on under the beans? The washing machine's obscure disease may reoccur, it rumbles on rinse and rattles on wash; my God, it's already eleven o'clock; which one of you has lost a galosh? So it was amid the worries of our ordinary life I bent, innocent and improperly armed, over the bug that had come undone. Let me think back on the shock. . . . My hand would have fled from a burn with the same speed; anyone's death or injury would have weakened me as well; and I could have gone cold for a number of reasons, because I felt in motion in me my own murderous disease, for instance; but none could have produced the revulsion that dim recognition did, a reaction of my whole nature that flew ahead of understanding and made me withdraw like a spider.

I said I was innocent. Well, I was not. Innocent. My God, the names we use. What do we live with that's alive we haven't tamed—people like me?—even our houseplants breathe by our permission. All along I had the fear of what it was—something ugly and poisonous, deadly and terrible—the simple insect, worse and wilder than fire—and I should rather put my arms in the heart of a flame than in the darkness of a moist and webby hole. But the eye never ceases to change. When I examine my collection now, it isn't any longer roaches I observe but gracious order, wholeness, and divinity. . . . My handkerchief, that time, was useless. . . . O my husband, they are a terrible disease.

. . . the dark soul of the world . . . a phrase I should laugh at. The roach shell sickened me. And my jaw has broken open. I lie still, listening, but there is nothing to hear. Our cat is quiet. They pass through life to immortality between her paws.

Am I grateful now my terror has another object? From time to time I think so, but I feel as though I'd been entrusted with a kind of Eastern mystery, sacred to a dreadful god, and I am full of the sense of my unworthiness and the clay of my vessel. So strange. It is the sewing machine that has the fearful claw. I live in a scatter of blocks and children's voices. The chores are my clock, and time is every other moment interrupted. I had always thought that love knew nothing of order and that life itself was turmoil and confusion. Let us leap, let us shout! I have leaped, and to my shame, I have wrestled. But this bug that I hold in my hand and know to be dead is beautiful, and there is a fierce joy in its composition that beggars every other, for its joy is the joy of stone, and it lives in its tomb like a lion.

I don't know which is more surprising: to find such order in a roach, or such ideas in a woman.

I could not shake my point of view, infected as it was, and I took up their study with a manly passion. I sought out spiders and gave them sanctuary; played host to worms of every kind; was generous to katydids and lacewings, aphids, ants and various grubs; pampered several sorts of beetle; looked after crickets; sheltered bees; aimed my husband's chemicals away from the grasshoppers, mosquitoes, moths, and flies. I have devoted hours to watching caterpillars feed. You can see the leaves they've eaten passing through them; their bodies thin and swell until the useless pulp is squeezed in perfect rounds from their rectal end; for caterpillars are a simple section of intestine, a decorated stalk of yearning muscle, and their whole being is enlisted in the effort of digestion. *Le tube digestif des insectes est situé dans le grand axe de la cavité générale du corps . . . de la bouche vers l'anus. . . . Le pharynx . . . L'oesophage . . . Le jabot . . . Le ventricule chylifique . . . Le rectum et l'iléon . . .* Yet when they crawl their curves conform to graceful laws.

My children ought to be delighted with me, as my husband is, I am so diligent, it seems, on their behalf, but they have taken fright and do not care

to pry or to collect. My hobby's given me a pair of dreadful eyes, and sometimes I fancy they start from my head; yet I see, perhaps, no differently than
Galileo saw when he found in the pendulum its fixed intent. Nonetheless,
my body resists such knowledge. It wearies of its edge. And I cannot forget,
even while I watch our moon-vine blossoms opening, the simple principle of
the bug. It is a squat black cockroach after all, such a bug as frightens house-
wives, and it's only come to chew on rented wool and find its death absurdly
in the teeth of the renter's cat.

Strange. Absurd. I am the wife of the house. This point of view I tremble
in is the point of view of a god, and I feel certain, somehow, that could I
give myself entirely to it, were I not continuing a woman, I could disarm my
life, find peace and order everywhere; and I lie by my husband and I touch
his arm and consider the temptation. But I am a woman. I am not worthy.
Then I want to cry: O husband, I am ill, for I have seen what I have seen.
What should he do at that, poor man, starting up in the night from his sleep
to such nonsense, but comfort me blindly and murmur dream, small snail,
only dream, bad dream, as I do to the children. I could go away like the wise
cicada who abandons its shell to move to other mischief. I could leave and
let my bones play cards and spank the children. . . . Peace. How can I think
of such ludicrous things—beauty and peace, the dark soul of the world—for
I am the wife of the house, concerned for the rug, tidy and punctual, surrounded by blocks.

The Minnesota Review, 1961
Published in *In the Heart of the Heart of the Country,* 1968

In the Heart of the Heart of the Country

A Place

So I have sailed the seas and come . . .
to B . . .
a small town fastened to a field in Indiana. Twice there have been twelve hundred people here to answer to the census. The town is outstandingly neat and shady, and always puts its best side to the highway. On one lawn there's even a wood or plastic iron deer.

You can reach us by crossing a creek. In the spring the lawns are green, the forsythia is singing, and even the railroad that guts the town has straight bright rails which hum when the train is coming, and the train itself has a welcome horning sound.

Down the back streets the asphalt crumbles into gravel. There's Westbrook's, with the geraniums, Horsefall's, Mott's. The sidewalk shatters. Gravel dust rises like breath behind the wagons. And I am in retirement from love.

Weather

In the Midwest, around the lower Lakes, the sky in the winter is heavy and close, and it is a rare day, a day to remark on, when the sky lifts and allows the heart up. I am keeping count, and as I write this page, it is eleven days since I have seen the sun.

My House

There's a row of headless maples behind my house, cut to free the passage of electric wires. High stumps, ten feet tall, remain, and I climb these like a boy to watch the country sail away from me. They are ordinary fields, a little more uneven than they should be, since in the spring they puddle. The topsoil's thin, but only moderately stony. Corn is grown one year, soybeans another. At dusk starlings darken the single tree—a larch—which stands in the middle. When the sky moves, fields move under it. I feel, on my perch, that I've lost my years. It's as though I were living at last in my eyes, as I have always dreamed of doing, and I think then I know why I've come here: to see, and so to go out against new things—oh god how easily—like air in a breeze. It's true there are moments—foolish moments, ecstasy on a tree stump—when I'm all but gone, scattered I like to think like seed, for I'm the sort now in the fool's position of having love left over which I'd like to lose; what good is it now to me, candy ungiven after Halloween?

A Person

There are vacant lots on either side of Billy Holsclaw's house. As the weather improves, they fill with hollyhocks. From spring through fall, Billy collects coal and wood and puts the lumps and pieces in piles near his door, for keeping warm is his one work. I see him most often on mild days, sitting on his doorsill in the sun. I notice he's squinting a little, which is perhaps the reason he doesn't cackle as I pass. His house is the size of a single garage, and very old. It shed its paint with its youth, and its boards are a warped and weathered gray. So is Billy. He wears a short lumpy faded black coat when it's cold, otherwise he always goes about in the same loose, grease-spotted shirt and trousers. I suspect his galluses were yellow once, when they were new.

Wires

These wires offend me. Three trees were maimed on their account, and now these wires deface the sky. They cross like a fence in front of me, enclosing the crows with the clouds. I can't reach in, but, like a stick, I throw my feelings over. What is it that offends me? I am on my stump, I've built a platform there, and the wires prevent my going out. The cut trees, the black wires, all the beyond birds therefore anger me. When I've wormed through a fence to reach a meadow, do I ever feel the same about the field?

The Church

The church has a steeple like the hat of a witch, and five birds, all doves, perch in its gutters.

My House

Leaves move in the windows. I cannot tell you yet how beautiful it is, what it means. But they do move. They move in the glass.

Politics

. . . for all those not in love.

I've heard Batista described as a Mason. A farmer who'd seen him in Miami made this claim. He's as nice a fellow as you'd ever want to meet. Of Castro, of course, no one speaks.

For all those not in love there's law: to rule . . . to regulate . . . to rectify. I cannot write the poetry of such proposals, the poetry of politics, though sometimes—often—always now—I am in that uneasy peace of equal powers which makes a State; then I communicate by passing papers, proclamations, orders, through my bowels. Yet I was not a State with you, nor were we both together any Indiana. A squad of Pershing Rifles at the moment, I make myself Right Face! Legislation packs the screw of my intestines. Well, king of the classroom's king of the hill. You used to waddle when you walked because my sperm between your legs was draining to a towel. Teacher, poet, folded lover—like the politician, like those drunkards, ill, or those who faucet off while pissing heartily to preach upon the force and fullness of that stream, or pause from vomiting to praise the purity and passion of their puke—I chant, I beg, I orate, I command, I sing—

> Come back to Indiana—not too late!
> (Or will you be a ranger to the end?)
> Good-bye . . . Good-bye . . . oh, I shall always wait
> You, Larry, traveller—
> stranger,
> son,
> —my friend—

my little girl, my poem by heart, my self, my childhood.

But I've heard Batista described as a Mason. That dries up my pity, melts my hate. Back from the garage where I have overheard it, I slap the mended fender of my car to laugh, and listen to the metal stinging tartly in my hand.

People

Their hair in curlers and their heads wrapped in loud scarves, young mothers, fattish in trousers, lounge about in the speedwash, smoking cigarettes, eating candy, drinking pop, thumbing magazines, and screaming at their children above the whir and rumble of the machines.

At the bank a young man freshly pressed is letting himself in with a key. Along the street, delicately teetering, many grandfathers move in a dream. During the murderous heat of summer, they perch on window ledges, their feet dangling just inside the narrow shelf of shade the store has made, staring steadily into the street. Where their consciousness has gone I can't say. It's not in the eyes. Perhaps it's diffuse, all temperature and skin, like an infant's, though more mild. Near the corner there are several large overalled men employed in standing. A truck turns to be weighed on the scales at the Feed and Grain. Images drift on the drugstore window. The wind has blown the smell of cattle into town. Our eyes have been driven in like the eyes of the old men. And there's no one to have mercy on us.

Vital Data

There are two restaurants here and a tearoom. two bars. one bank, three barbers, one with a green shade with which he blinds his window. two groceries. a dealer in Fords. one drug, one hardware, and one appliance store. several that sell feed, grain, and farm equipment. an antique shop. a poolroom. a laundromat. three doctors. a dentist. a plumber. a vet. a funeral home in elegant repair the color of a buttercup. numerous beauty parlors which open and shut like night-blooming plants. a tiny dime and department store of no width but several floors. a hutch, homemade, where you can order, after lying down or squirming in, furniture that's been fashioned from bent lengths of stainless tubing, glowing plastic, metallic thread, and clear shellac. an American Legion Post and a root beer stand. little agencies for this and that: cosmetics, brushes, insurance, greeting cards and garden produce—anything—sample shoes—which do their business out of hats and satchels, over coffee cups and dissolving sugar. a factory for making paper sacks and pasteboard boxes that's lodged in an old brick building bearing the legend OPERA HOUSE, still faintly golden, on its roof. a library given by Carnegie. a post office. a school. a railroad station. fire station. lumber-yard. telephone company. welding shop. garage . . . and spotted through the town from one end to the other in a line along the highway, gas stations to the number five.

Education

In 1833, Colin Goodykoontz, an itinerant preacher with a name from a fairy tale, summed up the situation in one Indiana town this way:

> Ignorance and her squalid brood. A universal dearth of intellect. Total abstinence from literature is very generally practiced. . . . There is not a scholar in grammar or geography, or a *teacher capable* of *instructing* in them, to my knowledge. . . . Others are supplied a few months of the year with the most antiquated & unreasonable forms of teaching read-ing, writing & cyphering. . . . Need I stop to remind you of the host of loathsome reptiles such a stagnant pool is fitted to breed! Croaking jealousy; bloated bigotry; coiling suspicion; wormish blindness; croco-dile malice!

Things have changed since then, but in none of the respects mentioned.

Business

One side section of street is blocked off with sawhorses. Hard, thin, bitter men in blue jeans, cowboy boots and hats untruck a dinky carnival. The merchants are promoting themselves. There will be free rides, raucous music, parades and coneys, pop, popcorn, candy, cones, awards and drawings, with all you can endure of pinch, push, bawl, shove, shout, scream, shriek, and bellow. Children pedal past on decorated bicycles, their wheels a blur of color, streaming crinkled paper and excited dogs. A little later there's a pet show for a prize—dogs, cats, birds, sheep, ponies, goats—none of which wins. The whirlabouts whirl about. The Ferris wheel climbs dizzily into the sky as far as a tall man on tiptoe might be persuaded to reach, and the irri-tated operators measure the height and weight of every child with sour eyes to see if they are safe for the machines. An electrical megaphone repeatedly trumpets the names of the generous sponsors. The following day they do not allow the refuse to remain long in the street.

My House, This Place and Body

I have met with some mischance, wings withering, as Plato says obscurely, and across the breadth of Ohio, like heaven on a table, I've fallen as far as the poet, to the sixth sort of body, this house in B, in Indiana, with its blue and gray bewitching windows, holy magical insides. Great thick evergreens protect its entry. And I live *in.*

Lost in the corn rows, I remember feeling just another stalk, and thus this country takes me over in the way I occupy myself when I am well . . . completely—to the edge of both my house and body. No one notices, when they walk by, that I am brimming in the doorways. My house, this place and body, I've come in mourning to be born in. To anybody else it's pretty silly: love. Why should I feel a loss? How am I bereft? She was never mine; she was a fiction, always a golden tomgirl, barefoot, with an adolescent's slouch and a boy's taste for sports and fishing, a figure out of Twain, or worse, in Riley. Age cannot be kind.

There's little hand-in-hand here . . . not in B. No one touches except in rage. Occasionally girls will twine their arms about each other and lurch along, school out, toward home and play. I dreamed my lips would drift down your back like a skiff on a river. I'd follow a vein with the point of my finger, hold your bare feet in my naked hands.

The Same Person

Billy Holsclaw lives alone—how alone it is impossible to fathom. In the post office he talks greedily to me about the weather. His head bobs on a wild flood of words, and I take this violence to be a measure of his eagerness for speech. He badly needs a shave, coal dust has layered his face, he spits when he speaks, and his fingers pick at his tatters. He wobbles out in the wind when I leave him, a paper sack mashed in the fold of his arm, the leaves blowing past him, and our encounter drives me sadly home to poetry—where there's no answer. Billy closes his door and carries coal or wood to his fire and closes his eyes, and there's simply no way of knowing how lonely and empty he is or whether he's as vacant and barren and loveless as the rest of us are—here in the heart of the country.

Weather

For we're always out of luck here. That's just how it is—for instance in the winter. The sides of the buildings, the roofs, the limbs of the trees are gray. Streets, sidewalks, faces, feelings—they are gray. Speech is gray, and the grass where it shows. Every flank and front, each top is gray. Everything is gray: hair, eyes, window glass, the hawkers' bills and touters' posters, lips, teeth, poles and metal signs—they're gray, quite gray. Cars are gray. Boots, shoes, suits, hats, gloves are gray. Horses, sheep, and cows, cats killed in the road, squirrels in the same way, sparrows, doves, and pigeons, all are gray, everything is gray, and everyone is out of luck who lives here.

A similar haze turns the summer sky milky, and the air muffles your head and shoulders like a sweater you've got caught in. In the summer light, too, the sky darkens a moment when you open your eyes. The heat is pure distraction. Steeped in our fluids, miserable in the folds of our bodies, we can scarcely think of anything but our sticky parts. Hot cyclonic winds and storms of dust crisscross the country. In many places, given an indifferent push, the wind will still coast for miles, gathering resource and edge as it goes, cunning and force. According to the season, paper, leaves, field litter, seeds, snow, fill up the fences. Sometimes I think the land is flat because the winds have leveled it, they blow so constantly. In any case, a gale can grow in a field of corn that's as hot as a draft from hell, and to receive it is one of the most dismaying experiences of this life, though the smart of the same wind in winter is more humiliating, and in that sense even worse. But in the spring it rains as well, and the trees fill with ice.

Place

Many small Midwestern towns are nothing more than rural slums, and this community could easily become one. Principally during the first decade of the century, though there were many earlier instances, well-to-do farmers moved to town and built fine homes to contain them in their retirement. Others desired a more social life, and so lived in, driving to their fields like storekeepers to their businesses. These houses are now dying like the bereaved who inhabit them; they are slowly losing their senses—deafness, blindness, forgetfulness, mumbling, an insecure gait, an uncontrollable trembling has overcome them. Some kind of Northern Snopes will occupy them next: large-familied, Catholic, Democratic, scrambling, vigorous, poor; and since the parents will work in larger, nearby towns, the children will be loosed upon themselves and upon the hapless neighbors much as the fabulous Khan loosed his legendary horde. These Snopes will undertake makeshift repairs with materials that other people have thrown away; paint halfway round their house, then quit; almost certainly maintain an ugly loud cantankerous dog and underfeed a pair of cats to keep the rodents down. They will collect piles of possibly useful junk in the backyard, park their cars in the front, live largely leaning over engines, give not a hoot for the land, the old community, the hallowed ways, the established clans. Weakening widow ladies have already begun to hire large rude youths from families such as these to rake and mow and tidy the grounds they will inherit.

People

In the cinders at the station boys sit smoking steadily in darkened cars, their arms bent out the windows, white shirts glowing behind the glass. Nine o'clock is the best time. They sit in a line facing the highway—two or three or four of them—idling their engines. As you walk by, a machine may growl at you or a pair of headlights flare up briefly. In a moment one will pull out, spinning cinders behind it, to stalk impatiently up and down the dark streets or roar half a mile into the country before returning to its place in line and pulling up.

My House, My Cat, My Company

I must organize myself. I must, as they say, pull myself together, dump this cat from my lap, stir—yes, resolve, move, do. But do what? My will is like the rosy dustlike light in this room: soft, diffuse, and gently comforting. It lets me do . . . anything . . . nothing. My ears hear what they happen to; I eat what's put before me; my eyes see what blunders into them; my thoughts are not thoughts, they are dreams. I'm empty or I'm full . . . depending; and I cannot choose. I sink my claws in Tick's fur and scratch the bones of his back until his rear rises amorously. Mr. Tick, I murmur, I must organize myself. I must pull myself together. And Mr. Tick rolls over on his belly, all ooze.

I spill Mr. Tick when I've rubbed his stomach. Shoo. He steps away slowly, his long tail rhyming with his paws. How beautifully he moves, I think; how beautifully, like you, he commands his loving, how beautifully he accepts. So I rise and wander from room to room, up and down, gazing through most of my forty-one windows. How well this house receives its loving too. Let out like Mr. Tick, my eyes sink in the shrubbery. I am not here; I've passed the glass, passed second-story spaces, flown by branches, brilliant berries, to the ground, grass high in seed and leafage every season; and it is the same as when I passed above you in my aged, ardent body; it's, in short, a kind of love; and I am learning to restore myself, my house, my body, by paying court to gardens, cats, and running water, and with neighbors keeping company.

Mrs. Desmond is my right-hand friend; she's eighty-five. A thin white mist of hair, fine and tangled, manifests the climate of her mind. She is habitually suspicious, fretful, nervous. Burglars break in at noon. Children trespass. Even now they are shaking the pear tree, stealing rhubarb, denting lawn. Flies caught in the screens and numbed by frost awake in the heat to buzz and scrape the metal cloth and frighten her, though she is deaf to me, and consequently cannot hear them. Boards creak, the wind whistles across the chimney mouth, drafts cruise like fish through the hollow rooms. It is herself she hears, her own flesh failing, for only death will preserve her from those daily chores she climbs like stairs, and all that anxious waiting. Is it now, she wonders. No? Then: is it now?

We do not converse. She visits me to talk. My task to murmur. She talks about her grandsons, her daughter who lives in Delphi, her sister or her husband—both gone—obscure friends—dead—obscurer aunts and uncles—lost—ancient neighbors, members of her church or of her clubs—passed or passing on; and in this way she brings the ends of her life together with a terrifying rush: she is a girl, a wife, a mother, widow, all at once. All at once—appalling—but I believe it; I wince in expectation of the clap. Her talk's a fence—a shade drawn, window fastened, door that's locked—for no one dies taking tea in a kitchen; and as her years compress and begin to jumble, I really believe in the brevity of life; I sweat in my wonder; death is the dog down the street, the angry gander, bedroom spider, goblin who's come to get her; and it occurs to me that in my listening posture I'm the boy who suffered the winds of my grandfather with an exactly similar politeness, that I am, right now, all my ages, out in elbows, as angular as badly stacked cards. Thus was I, when I loved you, every man I could be, youth and child—far from enough—and you, so strangely ambiguous a being, met me, heart for spade, play after play, the whole run of our suits.

Mr. Tick, you do me honor. You not only lie in my lap, but you remain alive there, coiled like a fetus. Through your deep nap, I feel you hum. You are, and are not, a machine. You are alive, alive exactly, and it means nothing to you—much to me. You are a cat—you cannot understand—you are a cat so easily. Your nature is not something you must rise to. You, not I, live in: in house, in skin, in shrubbery. Yes. I think I shall hat my head with a steeple; turn church; devour people. Mr. Tick, though, has a tail he can twitch, he need not fly his Fancy. Claws, not metrical schema, poetry his paws; while smoothing . . . smoothing . . . smoothing roughly, his tongue laps its neatness. O Mr. Tick, I know you; you are an electrical penis. Go on now, shoo. Mrs. Desmond doesn't like you. She thinks you will tangle yourself in her legs and she will fall. You murder her birds, she knows, and walk upon her roof with death in your jaws. I must gather myself together for a bound. What age is it I'm at right now, I wonder. The heart, don't they always say, keeps the true time. Mrs. Desmond is knocking. Faintly, you'd think, but she pounds. She's brought me a cucumber. I believe she believes I'm a woman. Come in, Mrs. Desmond, thank you, be my company, it looks lovely, and have tea. I'll slice it, crisp, with cream, for luncheon, each slice as thin as me.

Politics

O all ye isolate and separate powers, Sing! Sing, and sing in such a way that from a distance it will seem a harmony, a Strindberg play, a friendship ring . . . so happy—happy, happy, happy—as here we go hand in handling, up and down. Our union was a singing, though we were silent in the songs we sang like single notes are silent in a symphony. In no sense sober, we barbershopped together and never heard the discords in our music or saw ourselves as dirty, cheap, or silly. Yet cats have worn out better shoes than those thrown through our love songs at us. Hush. Be patient—prudent—politic. Still, Cleveland killed you, Mr. Crane. Were you not politic enough and fond of being beaten? Like a piece of sewage, the city shat you from its stern three hundred miles from history—beyond the loving reach of sailors. Well, I'm not a poet who puts Paris to his temple in his youth to blow himself from Idaho, or—fancy that—Missouri. My god, I said, this is my country, but must my country go so far as Terre Haute or Whiting, go so far as Gary?

When the Russians first announced the launching of their satellite, many people naturally refused to believe them. Later others were outraged that they had sent a dog around the earth. I wouldn't want to take that mutt from out that metal flying thing if he's still living when he lands, our own dog catcher said; anybody knows you shut a dog up by himself to toss around, the first thing he'll be setting on to do you let him out is bite somebody.

This Midwest. A dissonance of parts and people, we are a consonance of Towns. Like a man grown fat in everything but heart, we overlabor; our outlook never really urban, never rural either, we enlarge and linger at the same time, as Alice both changed and remained in her story. You are blonde. I put my hand upon your belly; feel it tremble from my trembling. We always drive large cars in my section of the country. How could you be a comfort to me now?

More Vital Data

The town is exactly fifty houses, trailers, stores, and miscellaneous buildings long, but in places no streets deep. It takes on width as you drive south, always adding to the east. Most of the dwellings are fairly spacious farmhouses in the customary white, with wide wraparound porches and tall narrow windows, though there are many of the grander kind—fretted, scalloped, turreted, and decorated with clapboards set at angles or on end, with stained-glass windows at the stair landings and lots of wrought iron full of fancy curls—and a few of these look like castles in their rarer brick. Old stables serve as garages now, and the lots are large to contain them and the vegetable and flower gardens which, ultimately, widows plant and weed and then entirely disappear in. The shade is ample, the grass is good, the sky a glorious fall violet; the apple trees are heavy and red, the roads are calm and empty; corn has sifted from the chains of tractored wagons to speckle the streets with gold and with the russet fragments of the cob, and a man would be a fool who wanted, blessed with this, to live anywhere else in the world.

Education

Buses like great orange animals move through the early light to school. There the children will be taught to read and warned against Communism. By Miss Janet Jakes. That's not her name. Her name is Helen something—Scott or James. A teacher twenty years. She's now worn fine and smooth, and has a face, Wilfred says, like a mail-order ax. Her voice is hoarse, and she has a cough. For she screams abuse. The children stare, their faces blank. This is the thirteenth week. They are used to it. You will all, she shouts, you will all draw pictures of me. No. She is a Mrs.—someone's missus. And in silence they set to work while Miss Jakes jabs hairpins in her hair. Wilfred says an ax, but she has those rimless tinted glasses, graying hair, an almost dimpled chin. I must concentrate. I must stop making up things. I must give myself to life; let it mold me: that's what they say in *Wisdom's Monthly Digest* every day. Enough, enough—you've been at it long enough; and the children rise formally a row at a time to present their work to her desk. No, she wears rims; it's her chin that's dimpleless. Well, it will take more than a tablespoon of features to sweeten that face. So she grimly shuffles their sheets, examines her reflection crayoned on them. I would not dare . . . allow a child . . . to put a line around me. Though now and then she smiles like a nick in the blade, in the end these drawings depress her. I could not bear it—how can she ask?—that anyone . . . draw me. Her anger's lit. That's why she does it: flame. There go her eyes; the pink in her glasses brightens, dims. She is a pumpkin, and her rage is breathing like the candle in. No, she shouts, no—the cartoon trembling—no, John Mauck, John Stewart Mauck, this will not do. The picture flutters from her fingers. You've made me too muscular.

I work on my poetry. I remember my friends, associates, my students, by their names. Their names are Maypop, Dormouse, Upsydaisy. Their names are Gladiolus, Callow Bladder, Prince and Princess Oleo, Hieronymus, Cardinal Mummum, Mr. Fitchew, The Silken Howdah, Spot. Sometimes you're Tom Sawyer, Huckleberry Finn; it is perpetually summer; your buttocks are my pillow; we are adrift on a raft; your back is our river. Sometimes you are Major Barbara, sometimes a goddess who kills men in battle, sometimes you are soft like a shower of water; you are bread in my mouth.

I do not work on my poetry. I forget my friends, associates, my students, and their names: Gramophone, Blow-gun, Pickle, Serenade . . . Marge the Barge, Arena, Überhaupt . . . Doctor Dildoe, The Fog Machine. For I am now in B, in Indiana: out of job and out of patience, out of love and time and money, out of bread and out of body, in a temper, Mrs. Desmond, out of tea. So shut your fist up, bitch, you bag of death; go bang another door; go die, my dearie. Die, life-deaf old lady. Spill your breath. Fall over like a frozen board. Gray hair grows from the nose of your mind. You are a skull already—*memento mori*—the foreskin retracts from your teeth. Will your plastic gums last longer than your bones, and color their grinning? And is your twot still hazel-hairy, or are you bald as a ditch? . . . bitch . . . . . . bitch . . . . bitch. I wanted to be famous, but you bring me age—my emptiness. Was it *that* which I thought would balloon me above the rest? Love? where are you? . . . love me. I want to rise so high, I said, that when I shit I won't miss anybody.

Business

For most people, business is poor. Nearby cities have siphoned off all but a neighborhood trade. Except for feed and grain and farm supplies, you stand a chance to sell only what one runs out to buy. Chevrolet has quit, and Frigidaire. A locker plant has left its afterimage. The lumberyard has been, so far, six months about its going. Gas stations change hands clumsily, a restaurant becomes available, a grocery closes. One day they came and knocked the cornices from the watch repair and pasted campaign posters on the windows. Torn across, by now, by boys, they urge you still to vote for half an orange beblazoned man who as a whole one failed two years ago to win at his election. Everywhere, in this manner, the past speaks, and it mostly speaks of failure. The empty stores, the old signs and dusty fixtures, the debris in alleys, the flaking paint and rusty gutters, the heavy locks and sagging boards: they say the same disagreeable things. What do the sightless windows see, I wonder, when the sun throws a passerby against them? Here a stair unfolds toward the street—dark, rickety, and treacherous—and I always feel, as I pass it, that if I just went carefully up and turned the corner at the landing, I would find myself out of the world. But I've never had the courage.

That Same Person

The weeds catch up with Billy. In pursuit of the hollyhocks, they rise in coarse clumps all around the front of his house. Billy has to stamp down a circle by his door like a dog or cat does turning round to nest up, they're so thick. What particularly troubles me is that winter will find the weeds still standing stiff and tindery to take the sparks which Billy's little mortarless chimney spouts. It's true that fires are fun here. The town whistle, which otherwise only blows for noon (and there's no noon on Sunday), signals the direction of the fire by the length and number of its blasts, the volunteer firemen rush past in their cars and trucks, houses empty their owners along the street every time like an illustration in a children's book. There are many bikes too, and barking dogs, and sometimes—hallelujah—the fire's right here in town—a vacant lot of weeds and stubble flaming up. But I'd rather it weren't Billy or Billy's lot or house. Quite selfishly I want him to remain the way he is—counting his sticks and logs, sitting on his sill in the soft early sun—though I'm not sure what his presence means to me . . . or to anyone. Nevertheless, I keep wondering whether, given time, I might not someday find a figure in our language which would serve him faithfully, and furnish his poverty and loneliness richly out.

Wires

Where sparrows sit like fists. Doves fly the steeple. In mist the wires change perspective, rise and twist. If they led to you, I would know what they were. Thoughts passing often, like the starlings who flock these fields at evening to sleep in the trees beyond, would form a family of paths like this; they'd foot down the natural height of air to just about a bird's perch. But they do not lead to you.

> Of whose beauty it was sung
> She shall make the old man young.

They fasten me.

If I walked straight on, in my present mood, I would reach the Wabash. It's not a mood in which I'd choose to conjure you. Similes dangle like baubles from me. This time of year the river is slow and shallow, the clay banks crack in the sun, weeds surprise the sandbars. The air is moist and I am sweating. It's impossible to rhyme in this dust. Everything—sky, the cornfield, stump, wild daisies, my old clothes and pressless feelings—seems fabricated for installment purchase. Yes. Christ. I am suffering a summer Christmas; and I cannot walk under the wires. The sparrows scatter like handfuls of gravel. Really, wires are voices in thin strips. They are words wound in cables. Bars of connection.

Weather

I would rather it were the weather that was to blame for what I am and what my friends and neighbors are—we who live here in the heart of the country. Better the weather, the wind, the pale dying snow . . . the snow—why not the snow? There's never much really, not around the lower Lakes anyway, not enough to boast about, not enough to be useful. My father tells how the snow in the Dakotas would sweep to the roofs of the barns in the old days, and he and his friends could sled on the crust that would form because the snow was so fiercely driven. In Bemidji trees have been known to explode. That would be something—if the trees in Davenport or Francisville or Carbondale or Niles were to go blam some winter—blam! blam! blam! all the way down the gray, cindery, snow-sick streets.

A cold fall rain is blackening the trees, or the air is like lilac and full of parachuting seeds. Who cares to live in any season but his own? Still I suspect the secret's in this snow, the secret of our sickness, if we could only diagnose it, for we are all dying like the elms in Urbana. This snow—like our skin it covers the country. Later dust will do it. Right now—snow. Mud presently. But it is snow without any laughter in it, a pale-gray pudding thinly spread on stiff toast, and if that seems a strange description, it's accurate all the same. Of course soot blackens everything, but apart from that, we are never sufficiently cold here. The flakes as they come, alive and burning, we cannot retain, for if our temperatures fall, they rise promptly again, just as, in the summer, they bob about in the same feckless way. Suppose though . . . suppose they were to rise some August, climb and rise, and then hang in the hundreds like a hawk through December, what a desert we could make of ourselves—from Chicago to Cairo, from Hammond to Columbus—what beautiful Death Valleys.

Place

I would rather it were the weather. It drives us in upon ourselves—an unlucky fate. Of course there is enough to stir our wonder anywhere; there's enough to love, anywhere, if one is strong enough, if one is diligent enough, if one is perceptive, patient, kind enough—whatever it takes; and surely it's better to live in the country, to live on a prairie by a drawing of rivers, in Iowa or Illinois or Indiana, say, than in any city, in any stinking fog of human beings, in any blooming orchard of machines. It ought to be. The cities are swollen and poisonous with people. It ought to be better. Man has never been a fit environment for man—for rats, maybe, rats do nicely, or for dogs or cats and the household beetle.

And how long the street is, nowadays. These endless walls are fallen to keep back the tides of earth. Brick could be beautiful but we have covered it gradually with gray industrial vomits. Age does not make concrete genial, and asphalt is always—like America—twenty-one, until it breaks up in crumbs like stale cake. The brick, the asphalt, the concrete, the dancing signs and garish posters, the feed and excrement of the automobile, the litter of its inhabitants: they compose, they decorate, they line our streets, and there is nowhere, nowadays, our streets can't reach.

A man in the city has no natural thing by which to measure himself. His parks are potted plants. Nothing can live and remain free where he resides but the pigeon, starling, sparrow, spider, cockroach, mouse, moth, fly, and weed, and he laments the existence of even these and makes his plans to poison them. The zoo? There *is* the zoo. Through its bars the city man stares at the great cats and dully sucks his ice. Living, alas, among men and their marvels, the city man supposes that his happiness depends on establishing, somehow, a special kind of harmonious accord with others. The novelists of the city, of slums and crowds, they call it love—and break their pens.

Wordsworth feared the accumulation of men in cities. He foresaw their "degrading thirst after outrageous stimulation," and some of their hunger for love. Living in a city, among so many, dwelling in the heat and tumult of incessant movement, a man's affairs are touch and go—that's all. It's not surprising that the novelists of the slums, the cities, and the crowds should find that sex is but a scratch to ease a tickle, that we're most human when we're sitting on the john, and that the justest image of our life is in full passage through the plumbing.

> That man, immur'd in cities, still retains
> His inborn inextinguishable thirst
> Of rural scenes, compensating his loss
> By supplemental shifts, the best he may.

Come into the country, then. The air nimbly and sweetly recommends itself unto our gentle senses. Here, growling tractors tear the earth. Dust roils up behind them. Drivers sit jouncing under bright umbrellas. They wear refrigerated hats and steer by looking at the tracks they've cut behind them, their transistors blaring. Close to the land, are they? good companions to the soil? Tell me: do they live in harmony with the alternating seasons?

It's a lie of old poetry. The modern husbandman uses chemicals from cylinders and sacks, spike-ball-and-claw machines, metal sheds, and cost accounting. Nature in the old sense does not matter. It does not exist. Our farmer's only mystical attachment is to parity. And if he does not realize that cows and corn are simply different kinds of chemical engine, he cannot expect to make a go of it.

It isn't necessary to suppose our cows have feelings; our neighbor hasn't as many as he used to have either; but think of it this way a moment, you can correct for the human imputations later: how would it feel to nurse those strange tentacled calves with their rubber, glass, and metal lips, their stainless eyes?

People

Aunt Pet's still able to drive her car—a high square Ford—even though she walks with difficulty and a stout stick. She has a watery gaze, a smooth plump face despite her age, and jet-black hair in a bun. She has the slowest smile of anyone I ever saw, but she hates dogs, and not very long ago cracked the back of one she cornered in her garden. To prove her vigor she will tell you this, her smile breaking gently while she raises the knob of her stick to the level of your eyes.

House, My Breath and Window

My window is a grave, and all that lies within it's dead. No snow is falling. There's no haze. It is not still, not silent. Its images are not an animal that waits, for movement is no demonstration. I have seen the sea slack, life bubble through a body without a trace, its spheres impervious as soda's. Downwound, the whore at wagtag clicks and clacks. Leaves wiggle. Grass sways. A bird chirps, pecks the ground. An auto wheel in penning circles keeps its rigid spokes. These images are stones; they are memorials. Beneath this sea lies sea: god rest it . . . rest the world beyond my window, me in front of my reflection, above this page, my shade. Death is not so still, so silent, since silence implies a falling quiet, stillness a stopping, containing, holding in; for death is time in a clock, like Mr. Tick, electric . . . like wind through a windup poet. And my blear floats out to visible against the glass, befog its country and bespill myself. The mist lifts slowly from the fields in the morning. No one now would say: the Earth throws back its covers; it is rising from sleep. Why is the feeling foolish? The image is too Greek. I used to gaze at you so wantonly your body blushed. Imagine: wonder: that my eyes could cause such flowering. Ah, my friend, your face is pale, the weather cloudy; a street has been felled through your chin, bare trees do nothing, houses take root in their rectangles, a steeple stands up in your head. You speak of loving; then give me a kiss. The pane is cold. On icy mornings the fog rises to greet me (as you always did); the barns and other buildings, rather than ghostly, seem all the more substantial for looming, as if they grew in themselves while I watched (as you always did). Oh my approach, I suppose, was like breath in a rubber monkey. Nevertheless, on the road along the Wabash in the morning, though the trees are sometimes obscured by fog, their reflection floats serenely on the river, reasoning the banks, the sycamores in French rows. Magically, the world tips. I'm led to think that only those who grow down live (which will scarcely win me twenty-five from *Wisdom's Monthly Digest*), but I find I write that only those who live down grow; and what I write, I hold, whatever I really know. My every word's inverted, or reversed—or I am. I held you, too, that way. You were so utterly provisional, subject to my change. I could inflate your bosom with a kiss, disperse your skin with gentleness, enter your vagina from within, and make my love emerge like a fresh sex. The pane is cold. Honesty is cold, my inside lover. The sun looks, through the mist, like a plum on the tree of heaven, or a bruise on the slope of your belly. Which? The grass crawls with frost. We meet on this window, the world and I, inelegantly, swimmers of the glass; and swung wrong way round to one another, the world seems in. The world—how grand, how monumental, grave and deadly, that word is: the world, my house and poetry. All poets have their inside lovers. Wee penis does not belong to me, or any of this foggery. It is *his* property which he's thrust through what's womanly of me to set down this. These wooden houses in their squares, gray streets and fallen sidewalks, standing trees, your name I've written sentimentally across my breath into the whitening air, pale birds: they exist in me now because of him. I gazed with what intensity. . . . A bush in the excitement of its roses could not have bloomed so beautifully as you did then. It was a look I'd like to give this page. For that is poetry: to bring within about, to change.

Politics

Sports, politics, and religion are the three passions of the badly educated. They are the Midwest's open sores. Ugly to see, a source of constant discontent, they sap the body's strength. Appalling quantities of money, time, and energy are wasted on them. The rural mind is narrow, passionate, and reckless on these matters. Greed, however shortsighted and direct, will not alone account for it. I have known men, for instance, who for years have voted squarely against their interests. Nor have I ever noticed that their surly Christian views prevented them from urging forward the smithereening, say, of Russia, China, Cuba, or Korea. And they tend to back their country like they back their local team: they have a fanatical desire to win; yelling is their forte; and if things go badly, they are inclined to sack the coach. All in all, then, Birch is a good name. It stands for the bigot's stick, the wild-child tamer's cane.

Forgetfulness—is that their object?

Oh, I was new, I thought. A fresh start: new cunt, new climate, and new country—there you were, and I was pioneer, and had no history. That language hurts me too, my dear. You'll never hear it.

Final Vital Data

The Modern Homemakers' Demonstration Club. The Prairie Home Demonstration Club. The Night-outers' Home Demonstration Club. The IOOF,

FFF, VFW, WCTU, WSCS, 4-H, 40 and 8, Psi Iota Chi, and PTA. The Boy and Girl Scouts, Rainbows, Masons, Indians, and Rebekah Lodge. Also the Past Noble Grand Club of the Rebekah Lodge. As well as the Moose and the Ladies of the Moose. The Elks, the Eagles, the Jaynettes, and the Eastern Star. The Women's Literary Club, the Hobby Club, the Art Club, the Sunshine Society, the Dorcas Society, the Pythian Sisters, the Pilgrim Youth Fellowship, the American Legion, the American Legion Auxiliary, the American Legion Junior Auxiliary, the Gardez Club, the Bridge for Fun Club, the What-can-you-do? Club, the Get Together Club, the Coterie Club, the Worthwhile Club, the Let's Help Our Town Club, the No Name Club, the Forget-me-not Club, the Merry-go-round Club . . .

Education

Has a quarter disappeared from Paula Frosty's pocketbook? Imagine the landscape of that face: no crayon could engender it; soft wax is wrong; thin wire in trifling snips might do the trick. Paula Frosty and Christopher Roger accuse the pale and splotchy Cheryl Pipes. But Miss Jakes, I *saw* her. Miss Jakes is so extremely vexed she snaps her pencil. What else is missing? I appoint you a detective, John: search her desk. Gum, candy, paper, pencils, marble, round eraser—whose? A thief. I can't watch her all the time, I'm here to teach. Poor pale fossetted Cheryl, it's determined, can't return the money because she took it home and spent it. Cindy, Janice, John, and Pete—you four who sit around her—you will be detectives this whole term to watch her. A thief. In all my time. Miss Jakes turns, unfists, and turns again. I'll handle you, she cries. To think. A thief. In all my years. Then she writes on the blackboard the name of Cheryl Pipes and beneath that the figure twenty-five with a large sign for cents. Now Cheryl, she says, this won't be taken off until you bring that money out of home, out of home straight up to here, Miss Jakes says, tapping her desk.

Which is three days.

Another Person

I was raking leaves when Uncle Halley introduced himself to me. He said his name came from the comet, and that his mother had borne him prematurely in her fright of it. I thought of Hobbes, whom fear of the Spanish Armada had hurried into birth, and so I believed Uncle Halley to honor the philosopher, though Uncle Halley is a liar, and neither the one hundred twenty-nine nor the fifty-three he ought to be. That fall the leaves had burned themselves out on the trees, the leaf lobes had curled, and now they flocked noisily down the street and were broken in the wires of my rake. Uncle Halley was himself (like Mrs. Desmond and history generally) both deaf and implacable, and he shooed me down his basement stairs to a room set aside there for stacks of newspapers reaching to the ceiling, boxes of leaflets and letters and programs, racks of photo albums, scrapbooks, bundles of rolled-up posters and maps, flags and pennants and slanting piles of dusty magazines devoted mostly to motoring and the Christian ethic. I saw a birdcage, a tray of butterflies, a bugle, a stiff straw boater, and all kinds of tassels tied to a coat tree. He still possessed and had on display the steering lever from his first car, a linen duster, driving gloves and goggles, photographs along the wall of himself, his friends, and his various machines, a shell from the first war, a record of "Ramona" nailed through its hole to a post, walking sticks and fanciful umbrellas, shoes of all sorts (his baby shoes, their counters broken, were held in sorrow beneath my nose—they had not been bronzed, but he might have them done someday before he died, he said), countless boxes of medals, pins, beads, trinkets, toys, and keys (I scarcely saw—they flowed like jewels from his palms), pictures of downtown when it was only a path by the railroad station, a brightly colored globe of the world with a dent in Poland, antique guns, belt buckles, buttons, souvenir plates and cups and saucers (I can't remember all of it—I won't), but I recall how shamefully, how rudely, how abruptly, I fled, a good story in my mouth but death in my nostrils; and how afterward I busily, righteously, burned my leaves as if I were purging the world of its years. I still wonder if this town—its life, and mine now—isn't really a record like the one of "Ramona" that I used to crank around on my grandmother's mahogany Victrola through lonely rainy days as a kid.

The First Person

Billy's like the coal he's found: spilled, mislaid, discarded. The sky's no comfort. His house and his body are dying together. His windows are boarded. And now he's reduced to his hands. I suspect he has glaucoma. At any rate he can scarcely see, and weeds his yard of rubble on his hands and knees. Perhaps he's a surgeon cleansing a wound or an ardent and tactile lover. I watch, I must say, apprehensively. Like mine detectors, his hands graze in circles ahead of him. Your nipples were the color of your eyes. Pebble. Snarl of paper. Length of twine. He leans down closely, picks up something silvery, holds it near his nose. Foil? cap? coin? He has within him—what, I wonder? Does he know more now because he fingers everything and has to sniff to see? It would be romantic cruelty to think so. He bends the down on your arms like a breeze. You wrote me: something is strange when we don't understand. I write in return: I think when I loved you I fell to my death.

Billy, I could read to you from Beddoes; he's your man perhaps; he held with dying, freed his blood of its arteries; and he said that there were many wretched love-ill fools like me lying alongside the last bone of their former selves, as full of spirit and speech, nonetheless, as Mrs. Desmond, Uncle Halley and the Ferris wheel, Aunt Pet, Miss Jakes, Ramona, or the megaphone; yet I reverse him finally, Billy, on no evidence but braggadocio, and I declare that though my inner organs were devoured long ago, the worm which swallowed down my parts still throbs and glows like a crystal palace.

Yes, you were younger. I was Uncle Halley, the museum man and infrequent meteor. Here is my first piece of ass. They weren't so flat in those days, had more round, more juice. And over here's the sperm I've spilled, nicely jarred and clearly labeled. Look at this tapelike length of intestine where I've stored my spew, the endless worm of words I've written, a hundred million emissions or more: oh I was quite a man right from the start; even when unconscious in my cradle, from crotch to cranium, I was erectile tissue; though mostly, after the manner approved by Plato, I had intercourse by eye. Never mind, old Holsclaw, you are blind. We pull down darkness when we go to bed; put out like Oedipus the actually offending organ, and train our touch to lies. All cats are gray, says Mr. Tick; so under cover of glaucoma you are sack-gray too, and cannot be distinguished from a stallion.

I must pull myself together, get a grip, just as they say, but I feel spilled, bewildered, quite mislaid. I did not restore my house to its youth, but to its age. Hunting, you hitch through the hollyhocks. I'm inclined to say you aren't half the cripple I am, for there is nothing left of me but mouth. However, I resist the impulse. It is another lie of poetry. My organs are all there, though it's there where I fail—at the roots of my experience. Poet of the spiritual, Rilke, weren't you? yet that's what you said. Poetry, like love, is—in and out—a physical caress. I can't tolerate any more of my sophistries about spirit, mind, and breath. Body equals being, and if your weight goes down, you are the less.

Household Apples

I knew nothing about apples. Why should I? My country came in my childhood, and I dreamed of sitting among the blooms like the bees. I failed to spray the pear tree too. I doubled up under them at first, admiring the sturdy low branches I should have pruned, and later I acclaimed the blossoms. Shortly after the fruit formed there were falls—not many—apples the size of goodish stones which made me wobble on my ankles when I walked about the yard. Sometimes a piece crushed by a heel would cling on the shoe to track the house. I gathered a few and heaved them over the wires. A slingshot would have been splendid. Hard, an unattractive green, the worms had them. Before long I realized the worms had them all. Even as the apples reddened, lit their tree, they were being swallowed. The birds preferred the pears, which were small—sugar pears I think they're called—with thick skins of graying green that ripen on toward violet. So the fruit fell, and once I made some applesauce by quartering and paring hundreds; but mostly I did nothing, left them, until suddenly, overnight it seemed, in that ugly late September heat we often have in Indiana, my problem was upon me.

My childhood came in the country. I remember, now, the flies on our snowy luncheon table. As we cleared away they would settle, fastidiously scrub themselves and stroll to the crumbs to feed where I would kill them in crowds with a swatter. It was quite a game to catch them taking off. I struck heavily since I didn't mind a few stains; they'd wash. The swatter was a square of screen bound down in red cloth. It drove no air ahead of it to give them warning. They might have thought they'd flown headlong into a summered window. The faint pink dot where they had died did not rub out as I'd supposed, and after years of use our luncheon linen would faintly, pinkly, speckle.

The country became my childhood. Flies braided themselves on the flypaper in my grandmother's house. I can smell the bakery and the grocery and the stables and the dairy in that small Dakota town I knew as a kid; knew as I dreamed I'd know your body, as I've known nothing, before or since; knew as the flies knew, in the honest, unchaste sense: the burned house, hose-wet, which drew a mist of insects like the blue smoke of its smolder, and gangs of boys, moist-lipped, destructive as its burning. Flies have always impressed me; they are so persistently alive. Now they were coating the ground beneath my trees. Some were ordinary flies; there were the large blue-green ones; there were swarms of fruit flies too, and the red-spotted scavenger beetle; there were a few wasps, several sorts of bees and butterflies—checkers, sulphurs, monarchs, commas, question marks—and delicate dragonflies . . . but principally houseflies and horseflies and bottle flies, flies and more flies in clusters around the rotting fruit. They loved the pears. Inside, they fed. If you picked up a pear, they flew, and the pear became skin and stem. They were everywhere the fruit was: in the tree still—apples like a hive for them—or where the fruit littered the ground, squashing itself as you stepped . . . there was no help for it. The flies droned, feasting on the sweet juice. No one could go near the trees; I could not climb; so I determined at last to labor like Hercules. There were fruit baskets in the barn. Collecting them and kneeling under the branches, I began to gather remains. Deep in the strong rich smell of the fruit, I began to hum myself. The fruit caved in at the touch. Glistening red apples, my lifting disclosed, had families of beetles, flies, and bugs, devouring their rotten undersides. There were streams of flies; there were lakes and cataracts and rivers of flies, seas and oceans. The hum was heavier, higher, than the hum of the bees when they came to the blooms in the spring, though the bees were there, among the flies, ignoring me—ignoring everyone. As my work went on and juice covered my hands and arms, they would form a sleeve, black and moving, like knotty wool. No caress could have been more indifferently complete. Still I rose fearfully, ramming my head in the branches, apples bumping against me before falling, bursting with bugs. I'd snap my hand sharply but the flies would cling to the sweet. I could toss a whole cluster into a basket from several feet. As the pear or apple lit, they would explosively rise, like monads for a moment, window-less, certainly, with respect to one another, sugar their harmony. I had to admit, though, despite my distaste, that my arm had never been more alive, oftener or more gently kissed. Those hundreds of feet were light. In washing them off, I pretended the hose was a pump. What have I missed? Childhood is a lie of poetry.

The Church

Friday night. Girls in dark skirts and white blouses sit in ranks and scream in concert. They carry funnels loosely stuffed with orange and black paper which they shake wildly, and small megaphones through which, as drilled, they direct and magnify their shouting. Their leaders, barely pubescent girls, prance and shake and whirl their skirts above their bloomers. The young men, leaping, extend their arms and race through puddles of amber light, their bodies glistening. In a lull, though it rarely occurs, you can hear the squeak of tennis shoes against the floor. Then the yelling begins again, and then continues; fathers, mothers, neighbors joining in to form a single puls-ing ululation—a cry of the whole community—for in this gymnasium each body becomes the bodies beside it, pressed as they are together, thigh to thigh, and the same shudder runs through all of them, and runs toward the same release. Only the ball moves serenely through this dazzling din. Obedi-ent to law, it scarcely speaks but caroms quietly and lives at peace.

Business

It is the week of Christmas and the stores, to accommodate the rush they hope for, are remaining open in the evening. You can see snow falling in the cones of the streetlamps. The roads are filling—undisturbed. Strings of red and green lights droop over the principal highway, and the water tower wears a star. The windows of the stores have been bedizened. Shamelessly they beckon. But I am alone, leaning against a pole—no . . . there is no one in sight. They're all at home, perhaps by their instruments, tuning in on their evenings, and like Ramona, tirelessly playing and replaying themselves. There's a speaker perched in the tower, and through the boughs of falling snow and over the vacant streets, it drapes the twisted and metallic strains of a tune that can barely be distinguished—yes, I believe it's one of the jolly ones, it's "Joy to the World." There's no one to hear the music but myself, and though I'm listening, I'm no longer certain. Perhaps the record's playing something else.

New American Review, 1967
Published in *In the Heart of the Heart of the Country,* 1968

THE FIRST WINTER OF MY MARRIED LIFE

The first winter of our married life, we lived in a slum near the edge of the Wabash. The university had thrown up half a dozen prefabricated duplexes during the war and rented them out to the faculty, whom it also impoverished in other ways. The war was over. I had persuaded Martha to marry me. I carried certain glorious credentials, and we were both ready to make a start in life, as the saying was then. It proved a bitter winter in every respect. We lived side by side with a fellow from biology: his sink butted our sink; his john rubbed the rear of ours; the shower stalls were linked; and we shared laundry and storage sheds like a roll towel in a public lavatory. Our garbage went in a common can and we parked our cars nose to tail in the street like sniffing dogs. Often the mailman got our letters mixed.

In front, the property was divided in fair-minded halves the way Solomon, in his wisdom, would surely have apportioned it (around their gum tree they planted crocus bulbs, while around our Chinese elm we put in daffs); but the backyard was enclosed by a weak wire fence which any gumptious turf would have shoved aside in a single season. There our lawn lay in pale passivity while weeds pushed through its flimsy sod like the spikes of a florist's frog. We were conscientious renters, though, and by unspoken agreement, took carefully measured turns to mow the dandelions and plantain down.

The walls were thin, and soon we were sharing our quarrels too. The sounds of lovemaking passed between us like cups of borrowed sugar, and cooking odors were everywhere like the same paint. When the cold-water tap on our tub was first turned, a shudder went through the pipe to which it was attached, it seemed to me, all the way to the reservoir. A single furnace fired us, but somehow all our ducts were tangled, so that the moans and groans of the house would wander like lost souls, carried through them on the warm rising air, to emerge with a bright irrelevant clarity ("... on the sofa..." "Carrie called..." "... later... —n't the time...") in any odd place at all and abruptly as a belch—occasionally even returning to the room where they'd been made—echoes as battered as our cooking pans.

When we met on the walk outside, often hugging groceries or lugging books—just because we heard our toilets flush—we scarcely spoke, our heads hidden behind redly stenciled paper sacks; and in the laundry room, encounters were so brief and polite the gas man knew us better. Martha's ardor oddly came and went, and although I knew it was connected with the goings-on next door, it did not simply wax and wane with them; the correlation was more complicated, duplicitous, remote.

We were soon ashamed of our own sounds, as if every sign of life we made were a form of breaking wind. We were ashamed because we believed we heard the pop and creak of their floors, their stairs and settling springs, when normally we never noticed our own; because the scream of their kettle called us to our quiet kitchen; because we struggled to restore some sense to the voices which burbled and rumbled behind our common walls as one strains a pulpy juice for jelly; and we had to assume that they were curious too, had exchanged lewd grins, held fingers aside their noses like Santa Claus in that stupid poem, and had at least once listened through a wineglass to passages of passion of one kind or other. They would have been mostly about money then, for at that time we hadn't any, nor could we hear any harmony in the loose rattle of our change; so we fought like children about whether we should spend or save.

Martha kept faith in a challenging future. I lapsed like an unpaid policy. Hence Martha conserved while I consumed. She sold. I bought. She bawled me out. She wanted me to quit smoking. It was a selfish habit, she said. She claimed we couldn't afford to buy books or pay dues in my damn clubs or fees for regular checkups. Nothing's going to go wrong with a nice soft body like yours, she said, palping me like a roasting turkey. The university's library was large. There were lots of free lectures, and all the good movies would come round again like the famous comets. But who wants to watch a film as ancient as the family album? who cares about last year's lovers, or all those stabbings stale as buns, or auto chases on worn-out tires, I said, exasperation showing in my prose.

But we cut back. We inspected the dates on our pennies. I felt like a shabby freeloader, attending receptions just to snuffle up the cake and cookies, pocket mints. We kept magazines until they were old enough to be reread; converted boxes, cans, and jars, by means of découpage, a little sanding and shellac, into jaundiced baskets, pencil crocks, and letter bins—Christmas

presents for the folks which only cost us our pride. I licked her slender virginal lips like a Roman emperor. The simple pleasures are the best, she said.
I cadged returnables from our neighbor's trash; she returned the empties,
saved trading stamps, suggested an extensive use of departmental stationery,
the department phone for distant friends. Off and on I'd hunger for a steak,
a melon, or a mound of shrimp. I think the wine we drank was trampled in
Vermont.

Indiana's cold came down the river like a draft, and the deep-gray sky
grew closer every day. Chimney smoke seemed simply an extension of it, as
did one's steaming breath. I had suffered many a Midwest winter, but I had
never been married to the snow. During an embrace, I would discover my
arm clamped about my wife's waist like a frozen limb.

At first the snow helped. It kept us in. We played parcheesi to calm our
nerves. Martha would cook chicken livers again, and then, because they were
so cheap—dear god—immediately again. She recommended peanut butter and claimed beans were a good buy. They blow balloons up your ass,
I'd shout, with an embarrassed unoriginality, and then we would both look
warily up and down, ducking the outcry as if I'd just hurled a tennis ball
against the wall. In this toilet-tissue house, I'd hiss poisonously in her ear,
we can't afford to fart. Then, even when there was boot-deep snow, a cold
scarf of wind, I'd leave the place to pout, closing the front door cautiously,
violence in my silent face.

They'd designed our building like a pair of paper mittens, but the left
mitten had been limp when we moved in, otherwise we might have been
warned; and when its new tenants arrived, we found nothing amiss in the
movers' tread or the gruff reality of their voices. The clear scrape of cardboard cartons did not trouble us, or the thump of heavy chests. Besides, it
was warm, and windows were open. We simply had new neighbors. There
was a hand now stuffed in the other glove. The noise was natural. Things
would settle down. We hoped they would prove to be sympathetic types,
maybe even friends. Then a headboard bumped rhythmically against what
we'd thought was our most private wall. Their vacuum cleaner approached
and receded like a train. Waters were released which gushed and roared and
even whistled. Didn't I hear a male voice singing "Lazy Mary" one morning?
Whose life could ever be the same?

After that we tiptoed, grew footpads, became stealthy. When we heard
their closet hangers jangle like cattle on a hill far away, we shut our doors
so silently the latches snicked like a rifle. I had heard his heavy smoker's
hack (hollow, deep and wet as a well), so we took multivitamins to ward off
coughs, then syrups to stifle them when colds caught us anyway, and increasingly felt like thieves and assassins.

Our ears were soon as sensitive as a skinless arm, and we spoke in whispers, registered the furtive drip of remote taps. It was like living in front of a mike as you might pose and smirk in front of a mirror. We heard ourselves as others might hear us; we read every sound the way we read the daily paper; and we came to feel as though we were being chased, caught, charged, and humiliatingly arraigned for crimes against the public silence—for making obscene sounds at the symphony or crying out loud at the circus.

In the flush of our shame, we wanted no one to know us, so we held hats in front of our voices, coats over our sinks and grains. We treated even the crudest iron cooking pot as if it were Limoges, slowing our motions as movies had shown us we should to defuse explosives. I ceased singing in the shower. We kissed only in distant corners, and as quietly as fish. We gave up our high-spirited games. Martha no longer cried out when she came, and I grew uncertain of her love. Small incidents were absurdly enlarged the way the whine of a mosquito is magnified by an enclosing darkness: a fallen spoon sounded like a broken jar, a shattered glass was a spilled tray, a dropped book a bomb. I exaggerate now, but it's true that as our neighbors sensed our presence the way we had theirs, they sent their sounds to Coventry too, and the house was shortly filled—palpably stuffed—with silence like a stomach's ache.

I began to suffer from insomnia. The dark boneless hollow of our bedroom seemed the menacing shape of my future, and I stared into it as if the energy of my eyes would act as a light. Maybe, less than a forearm away, another husband was doing the same—one whole half of his hopes discovered to be empty as a soldier's sleeve. It was not the kind of commencement I had counted on. I thought of my career (it was the commonest cliché) as one great climb—stretches of superhuman effort spelled by brief stops for rest and acclimation. People and towns would assume their true size, dwindling like the past behind me, becoming merely part of the grand patterns of history. I knew I would have to strain every nerve (as it was uncomfortably put) to realize my ambitions. A simple inspection of the past was child's play, but the composition of history was not a young man's work; it was not an arena for the display of an ill-informed or immature mind; no inept cape, however flamboyant, could turn aside the charges of time; it was not everybody's satisfying hobby or soothing Sunday scribble; for how many great ones were there in a century? when poets were as plentiful as pilchards and paintings bloomed like fields of fall weeds. I would have to climb beyond bias, become Olympian, part the clouds: and already I have resolved to work with material so racial and rednecked and cruel and costly (the extirpation of the Jews exceeded any subject), what tools or gloves or masks or prophylactic washing up would protect me from contamination? It was not like the commitment of the poet, whose projects were likely to last as long as his latest erection—whether for elegy, ode, or little lyric—or till the clit was rubbed like an angry correction.

I suddenly realized, considering this, that perhaps I spent so readily because I felt more secure in my future, while Martha conserved because she felt she hadn't any.

Home life (ho-hum life, my colleague Culp insisted) . . . the home . . . The orphanage in my hometown was called The Home. The home was supposed to be a help; a place of rest and solace you returned to at night and went forth from refreshed like a watered plant. Despite the fact that my childhood home had been nothing like that, and although I had the satisfying cynicism of a young man who has read about more evil than he's seen, and even though I already had the deepest misgivings about every form of human relation; nevertheless, I hadn't married to be miserable, to be picked apart by fury and malice, crushed by common chores; I fully expected to inhabit such a place of peace and pleasure: a castle, a home, and Eden.

 . . . within which the body of one's wife warmed and restored, as it had the elders of Israel from the beginning. The magic of her scented flesh made you the man you need to be "out there" where the war was (didn't the magazines and movies say so? the daily papers and the pulpit?); but already it was my work which stood steady when the world rocked. I had scarcely picked up my pen when it began to replace my penis in everyone's affections. It wasn't fair. Culp, a man I at first found amusing, and brash as a bush on a hill of dung, claimed he went to work solely to summon the strength, simply to find the courage (he said), only to gain the time (he would insist) to close the clasp on his briefcase and go home. Oh, to grow the guts! It's like leaving a full glass, he would say, staring like a lover at his desk. Although (the *l*'s rolled as though he were bowling) . . . although I am naturally capable of living without children or chatter or contretemps for long periods, I deliberately dull the memory, he always said; I put my mind's eye out; I promise myself there'll be peace, there'll be plenty, at eleven twenty-two Liane Lane, my little mortgaged lean-to, my cottage at Lake Concrete; and by god such sanctimonious self-deceptions work until I see it sitting like a sick chicken in a mud yard, till I hear my driveway gravel crunch like dry cereal under my wheels, till I put my key in that stiff marital lock again.

I understood Culp's attitude. The office hound was a common enough creature. But, like cancer, I wasn't going to contract it. Like auto accidents, it was something which broke the legs of other people. At home (he sighs like a whistle) I sit in my easy and read the Wanteds. It's my pornography. I dream of all the jobs I might be doing which would take me off, out, up, and away;

I'd be Peter Pan if they paid me peanuts; and when my hunger becomes overwhelming, I assuage it by chewing on checkbooks till the bills taste paid.

It wasn't fair. Martha slept like a plant, her senses all drawn in, at rest within her like a rug; while I marched into my sleeplessness as if it were a desert I was crossing (at the head of a column of sweaty and mutinous men); but the pain I felt was neither dry nor hot, but, rather, like a winter which will not release its grip—long gray rains raining coldly into May.

Our neighbors became our single subject. Their sounds composed a text we grew rabbinical about. From the slow sizzle of fat in a frying pan we inferred not the bacon but the pig, and their various treads upon the stairs drew a map of their marital emotions like those one gets from friends to find their cottage at the lake. (Deception. Lost ways. I knew that.) As for our own life: we cared only for concealment, nor could I burble at Marty's breasts as in the old days, or let an erection chase her through the house like a toy spear; and since our quietness kept our movements hidden, we would inadvertently sneak up on one another (sometimes Marty would shriek—it was hide and seek—when I came upon her suddenly). There was a time when our startles seemed funny. Then we would glare at the offending wall and grin at each other; but eventually the tide of attention turned, and we could only smirk at some empty corner of the ceiling and sneer at ourselves instead.

We were two pairs of turtledoves—linked by leases, not by flesh, thank god!—but they were our Siamese twin, nevertheless, the mocking shadow of our sensuality; and we had scarcely reached our car in the morning when the examination of their habits began: we were outraged, amused, we giggled like girls; we had nasty arguments on points of interpretation; we considered confusing them with a barrage of false sounds, by launching attacks of heavy breathing; I suggested some interesting scenarios, but Martha would not fall in with them. We tended to take sides, Martha preferring the trail the male left, naturally spores whose righteous quality escaped me altogether. My trust twisted to suspicion. Perhaps she was already their accomplice; perhaps she heard their passion more eagerly than she felt mine. Was the other side of the wall growing greener grass, I asked her, exasperation once more showing in my prose. Without receiving a squeak for an answer, I dropped Marty off at the local historical museum, where she'd got a job minding tomahawks, propping stuffed squirrels in attitudes of life on branch-resembling sticks, and dusting flints.

The only plus was the pleasure we both took in discussing odd and often silly circumstances with the many acquaintances we were making at the university then; and we naturally lingered over the more scandalous details, describing the pressures of so public a private life on souls as newly glued by lust and law as we were. A little untoward heat (we said) might melt us down from one another like a custard from its coating; a sudden jar might shatter our fragile ties; an unexpected stress might stretch our sympathies to a point beyond elastic (so we went on, piling comparison up like fruit in a market window); we might weaken like moistened cardboard and our bottom pop. So our misery became entertainment like stories of the war, and from what had been a heap of jagged shards we shaped a graceful vase—something slightly salacious in the lush red-figured style. We guessed, and guessed again, and guessed some more, enlarging on our information like any secret service until facts were so larded with conjecture it became impossible to distinguish the marbling from the meat.

We were thought to be amusing—fresh, unique—(I *do* believe that)—and we certainly didn't hesitate to extricate whatever criticism of my powerful employer—our poor absent landlord—was implicit in our histories, but held it up for view and comment like a hair found floating in the soup, comparing the ironies of our situation to the slice of lemon which lies beside the cup of life; and these gibes provided an additional pleasure for our listeners, as it turned out, since the university was thought to be composed of three strata at that time—deans, dissidents, and dunces—with no one we met admitting to either ambition or stupidity; so we went wild; we put grotesques in every role as real as any real ones, bringing them forth as Dickens might have done—through tubas—each with traits as neatly cubed, distinct, and freshly baked as cakes on a plate of cakes.

My student days kept step as I marched away into marriage, the military, and my profession. College had been a long and boring banquet whose food I'd somehow digested yet couldn't excrete. There were those hierarchies and ordered rows around me still, like the hedges of a labyrinth; a tropical torrent of judgments, of ranks and scores, fell without fertility; the division of days into periods of improvement, hours of regulated relaxation, a few moments of pleasure paid for by pitiless stretches of melancholy which ceased only in beery sleep, went on incessantly like the little clicks of a pedometer; for what was the distance from Martha to masturbation when you put an interior tape to it? . . . yes, there was, in particular, life at close quarters.

The memory of those makeshift apartments in Urbana followed me now like a homeless animal. I could see again the room which greed had eaten out of attics like moths, coal cellars covered in oilcloth like the inside of a cheap coffin, the paneled garages smelling of grease; I reoccupied those stools under dormers which made you double up to shit, closets where the clothes rod was a water pipe; and I remembered a friend who had an entry straddled by a shower stall, another whose bed backed against a boiler, but I particularly could not drive away the image of those tiny preused Polish toilets which were as close to the living room as a lamp to its chair, so that we couldn't help hear the gush of the girls, always good for a giggle, and had to aim our stream against the quiet porcelain to be discreet ourselves, or pinch it painfully thin.

I saw that Martha suffered far more than I from our unaccustomed close-ness. Women weren't used to long lines of nakedness as soldiers are, or the sycamores in winter. Gaunt, bleached, bony, the trees seemed a cold growth of the snow itself, a solidification of melting air the way icicles were a con-gealed product of the sun.

I also recalled squatting in a cold hole once on perimeter patrol, listening with the same intensity for the enemy (and since I didn't know what the enemy would sound like, I made it up out of movies: the crunch of a boot in the snow, a frightened wheeze, the unmistakable clink of metal), my ears like those dishes they tune to the stars. The world was cemetery-still, and dark as the dead beneath the stones.

Now the silence was a great white field which Martha and I fled over like lines of running ink.

The trouble was, when I thought about it, that we were always the butts on the body of our anecdotes—the goats, the fall guys—the grotesques who were so amusing. And then it occurred to me to wonder whether they weren't telling tales too, over there in biology, among faculty members we never met; and the thought was terribly sobering somehow, as if our plight were a pro-gram like Fibber McGee's that no one would want to miss; except there were two versions, two lines of listening, the right line and the left, like lobes of the brain or parties in politics; and which one was funnier, I had to speculate, which one's butts were bigger, in which did the fall guys prat more convinc-ingly, the goats smell raunchier?

And Martha, who was always so saving, wanted to go out all the time to bars and movies, to drop in on friends where, after the customary inquiries about health and children, the rigmarole would begin again. Since we had no privacy in private, we sought it out in public. The strategy didn't succeed for either of us. Though alone in a movie with a gray screen dancing, she would throw my hand away, when it crept into hers, like a used-up Kleenex, because we were married now and had, she said, no need to grope or fondle. In bars we would back ourselves in booths and speak, when we did, like con-spirators. People will think we're married, all right, she said; married—but to other people. Isn't it getting to be that way (this was the general form of my reply); at home, don't you listen more to that other guy?

The cash we were conserving slipped away like our affections, literally through our fingers, as our touch became callous and mechanical. Martha grew testy about the money because she was the one who was spending it; and she grew testy about the loss of affection because she had stopped bringing me up and never would bother again, as if her own large beauty should henceforth be enough; and though it was enough, her attitude made me resent every erection, and dislike the effect her nakedness had on me. What if all the blood became noisy, I said. What if I whistled through them like their kettle? What if, she said. What if?

In the early fall I had already begun to go down to the river to see the face of winter in the water, the slow logs and dry shoals. Crickets and hoppers were still rising ahead of my feet like miniature quail, and the weeds which had bearded the banks during the long stand of summer were high and heavily in seed; but the water returned their image to a sky which was as quiet as the river. My own face too fell open in the middle like the habit of a book, and by looking down, I could watch myself staring up, eyes already a bit puffy, the coming winter in my face. It was a smooth look, like an oiled door.

Here it was, our first winter, and we should have been rolled around one another like rugs. We should have been able to overcome small obstacles such as walls which were too flimsy to hold up, hide, or impede anything—which were not obstacles at all—yet here we were, our love cut judiciously in two like the front yard. How thin the skin, yet how small the poor theory that gets through, I thought, a proverb showing in my prose, a pun in my proverb like a worm. This nonsense of ours was using up my life and there was nothing I could do about it. Then I wondered whether she wasn't ashamed of me, ashamed to be heard with me in public, as though I whinnied. Would she lead a frank and noisy life with a brawny stud? Would she giggle and scream and writhe when they made love; compel that other couple to wish for pleasures they were inadequately equipped for and could not achieve even through installment dreaming?

He was tall and very thin and very dark. She was petite. She skittered, but his tread was erratic as one might imagine a scarecrow's to be—with unskillful and unfeeling feet. Mine was regular as meter (I *did* believe that), and Martha's was . . . Martha's was that of a thousand-pound thistle. She put on bras and slips and blouses and sweaters, then added blazers and heavy wraps on top of that—overclothes to cover my eyes. Do you want to disappear entirely, to be snowed under layers of skirts, smocks, and mufflers? Instead, it was I who disappeared like a magician's assistant. I knew she waited until I left the house to remove her diaphragm, a smelly elastic device that no longer went in as automatically as change in a purse or keys tossed in a drawer, and would never replace the ear as an organ. I said you're making me into a stranger. Her nose peered between the tan slats of a venetian blind she opened with scissored fingers. Our neighbor's Plymouth was, or was not, parked behind us. She felt grubby, she said. I received no requests to do her back. The museum, she complained. Dusty work. Scaly scalp. She washed always behind the bathroom door with washcloths moistened with mineral oil; dusted the davenport with damp rags; did the dishes at dawn; read in a dim light. She could slither from street dress to housecoat to nightgown without allowing a fellow a peek's worth, as one always imagined the bride of a Bedouin to be able, or a girl scout under a blanket—a skill I hadn't counted on. No one phoned. The brush man did not knock. She said it's late. What you couldn't see, perhaps you couldn't hear. I could hear a fork strike an empty plate.

The first snowfall that year caught the trees with their leaves still clinging to them, and the weight of the wet snow did what the wind hadn't—pulled them free to settle on the surface of the river. There, for a few moments at least, they resembled massive, slowly moving floes. It was a vagrant similarity, but it sucked me up from Indiana the way Dorothy was inhaled out of Kansas, placing me in an airplane near the pole where I could see below me the rocking gray water and great herds of icebergs seeking their death down the roll of the globe.

This sudden switch of vision was indeed like a light, and gave me some understanding of the actual causes of our absurd situation. We were living in an image, not in a flimsy wartime throw-up. There was no longer any reality to the clatter of pans and dishes, shoefall, outburst, sigh of a cushion; there was no world around our weary ears, only meaning; we were being stifled by significance; everything was speech; and we listened as the house talked only in order to talk ourselves, to create a saving anecdote from our oppression, a Jewish character, a Jewish joke.

Walking along the edge of the river, I no longer saw those lovely pale leaves pass me like petals, as if some river flower were blooming oddly out of season (poetry appearing abruptly in my social prose); rather, I took them to be elements of a threatening metaphor, because I had suddenly seen that the world was held together only by frost and by freezing, by contraction, that its bowels contained huge compressors and ice-cold molds; so the place where I stood looking over a trivial Indiana landscape—snow freshly falling upon an otherwise turgid, uninteresting stream—was actually a point on the hazardous brink of Being. Consequently there appeared before me an emblem of all that was—all that was like a frozen fog—exhaust from the engines of entropy; and I saw in the whitened leaves floating by me an honesty normally missing from Nature's speech, because this adventitious coating threw open the heart of the Law: this scene of desolation—relieved only by the

barren purity of the trees—this wedge was all there was; and then I understood that the soft lull of August water was but a blanket on a snowbank; the
dust that a wave of wind would raise was merely the ash of a dry summer
blizzard; the daffodils which would ring our Chinese elm were blooming
spikes of ice, encased in green like a thug's gloves; there was just one season;
and when the cottonwoods released their seeds, I would see smoke from the
soul of the cold cross the river on the wind to snag in the hawthorns and
perish in their grip like every love.

Uninterpreted, our neighbor's noises were harmless, and soon would have
been as dim in our consciousness as the steady eeeeeen of an electric clock,
or the slow glow of the nightlight; as it was, the creak of a spring signified a
body on the bed; a body, a bed—that meant fornication, transports of passion as long as a line of lorries, the free use of another for the pleasure of the
self, the power to produce forgetfulness, ease, peace, sleep; it meant a disturbing measure now lay alongside our own love like a meter bar—how long?
how large? how full? how deep? how final and sufficient? how useful? wise?
how cheap?—and in virtue of such steps our minds had moved the whole
arc of the dial, from unpremeditated act to accidental sound, from accidental sound to signal, from signal to sense, from sense to system, from system
to . . . the chaos implicit in any complete account.

For a month we fell toward the ice at the center of hell (grandeur finally
showing in my prose), and I think it was the weather which convinced us
we were bored and beaten by surveillance; we were at last embarrassed by
the bloated selves our stories had made of us; close quarters had become
half-dollars, although, in this small pocket, we jangled together without real
change. But now the wind came up the river like a steamer. The windows iced
over. Would pipes freeze? I called responsible people and received assurances
which didn't assure me. We told our friends of these fresh troubles, but I felt
none of their former warm interest. We had worn the rug until I couldn't
read its welcome. The center was gone. Only "we/me" remained beneath
the shuffle of our feet. So we struggled into English sweaters and wore wool
socks; we went to movies to replace our feelings, and sat in bars to keep warm
and lose touch. With malice in my symbolism, I drank boilermakers—to
lose track, I said, without a smile to greet the pun—and on place mats which
displayed a map of the campus the color and shape of a spilled drink, I wrote
to friends about positions in the South.

Culp was the only exception. He retold our stories for us, harboring our
grudges until they seemed the flagships of his own fleet. He became another
kind of auditor, his intense interest hemming us in on what we might otherwise have thought was our free and open elbow—the out side. Perhaps it

was Culp who had worn our welcome thin, for he would show up at parties, picnics, and processions, to chortle and nudge, allude and remind, elaborating on our originals until they began to shrink within the convoluted enclosures he gave them, the way paintings dwindle inside heavy ornate frames, or turtles hide. That predatory historian, Martha fumed, has kidnapped our life, and she was right, but not for ransom, as I still believe Culp holds whole booths of convention bars enthralled with reminiscences of those difficult early years of his marriage, when he lived in a hut on the banks of the Wabash (a double hovel, he called it), encountering everywhere in his own air the image of another, as, of course, he said, like finding someone else's fart in your own pants.

How are you, I'd ask Martha with real worry. How are you feeling? Of course I was concerned for my own safety. I wanted to know if a storm was coming. It sometimes seemed to me I could see snow sliding out of the ceiling and melting on us as it melted on the river, though now the river was beginning to freeze, to disguise the flow of its feeling beneath a shell of ice. The sycamores were stoic, and there were deep crusted holes in the drifts where I'd walk. I found my tracks a comfort. Where I had been I would be again, returning to old holes, yet they were only the weather's memory. I wondered whether this winter's warfare would disappear in the spring, or would we be mired down in mud like the troops in Flanders?

We'll look for another place, I promised. What's in the fine print? Perhaps we can break our lease; maybe keep a big flea-barking dog. Martha's enthusiasm was persuasively unconvincing. Perhaps she didn't want to be alone with me again. Did she sense what was surfacing? Maybe she liked the protection. Say, I said, suppose I turned vicious, you'd be safe. One peep would be as good as calling police. Martha mimed a scream, her mouth so wide it would have swallowed a fist. Oh no, even if you were murdering me, they wouldn't murmur, she said—would we murmur? We might shout "shut up!" like they do in the big-city movies; we might bang on pipes the way you do to call the super; we might return outcries like party invitations. Martha shrugged. Her cleavage was another cunt. Well, I might do any one of those things, I suppose, she said; I think they're in my nature; but not you—oh no, not you, ever. It would be impolite and forward and beneath your blessed dignity. Then why am I staring at the floor like a schoolboy? The gods look down, don't forget, she said. Our floors were made of that hard asphalt tile which broke your feet (I had dubbed the color "abattoir brown" when we'd first moved in), and that's what I saw when I hung my head: the frozen bleeding feet of every piece of furniture which had stood there through the war, leaving their pitiful dents, as if the scars were records of wounds in the weight which made them; and of course that was it, the world was tipping toward the north, relations were in deep reverse, blooms invading their buds, snow rising like steam from the earth, as in this doubled house, where stoves seemed warmed by their pots and compliments were a curse; for now, when I entered my pale, silent, snowed-over wife, given legally to me by family, god, and social custom, it was through a cunt which lit up like an exit, and I was gone before I arrived.

The gods, I said. Marty? the gods? You speak of the gods to someone who was never a choirboy. I'm the sort of lonely little gid who looks into his shoes for a sight of the stars.

I had wanted to be put in charge of her body, not exactly as though she were a platoon, but as though my soul would wear her flesh for a change, and I would look out for her elbows as though they were my own, eat well, and not take cold; but she wouldn't play. I remembered kids like that when I was a kid. They wouldn't be the baby or the pupil or the robber or the renegade; they wouldn't lie still like the sick or the wounded; they would never fetch, seek out, or serve. They were too afraid. I'm not a train, Whiffie, and I don't need a conductor. You mean you're not a plane, and you don't need a pilot. I'm not a boat and don't need a skipper. I'm not a field that needs a tractor. I hate those images. I'm a daughter, but I *have* a father.

She could have had my body in exchange, but who wants to be the boss of a barnyard, the cock for such a nervous vane? Speaking of images, Marty, how's the one you are living in presently; the one that's made you the thunder sheet in the sound-room, a roof in a heavy rain? But it was no use. She no longer cared for what I cared for. Henceforth she'd let her body burgeon like a lima bean in a Dixie cup, though there were no kids, yet, to instruct or entertain. If she had deeded it to me; if she . . . well, both of us would be as trim now as the molding of a painted window.

Surely we haven't gone so fast in these few weeks we've passed middle age in our marriage? Is it the sound barrier we've broken, and are they the boom, now, we're supposed to hear? It makes no sense. It makes at least one, she always answered, even when we were courting, because the statement was a tic like mine, like that obnoxious nasal sniff I had, she said. As a matter of fact, Marty darling, we've grown as sluggish as a pair of snakes, and if any such barrier burst, it would have to happen from the slow side of swift, like your hymen, remember? I said, letting my prose grow unshavenly toward scratch. In this house sound certainly departs for all points like the humans of Hiroshima, she said, serene and uninsulted. Sometimes I think that's all they are over there—echoes of us—that whole half of the house is an echo, a later ring of our present life, and it's me, then, I hear, going up their stairs.

On *her* feet? that scatter of pins?

Save your jokes for the next show, Whiff. She smiled with a meanness I hadn't seen. And she had begun to braid her hair again, a bad sign, and write long letters to her mother—one a day, like pills. Oh no, Koh, not on *her pins*, on his *needles*, she said. Martha stared at our barely wrappered wall for a moment so pointedly I thought there might be a gap through which she saw a table or a teapot more substantial than the shadows of our own. What are his shoes, anyway, but the sound of my steps? You'll find my feet fastened beneath those almost negligible legs and skinny trunk next time you meet.

No such luck, Marty. Clutching groceries or garbage like a pair of paper bellies, what else do we embrace? In any case, we never see a shoe.

You've heard that small black head of his—haven't you?—like a photographer's box, go click? She laughed but I never understood the cause. The pleasure it implied seemed out of place. He's a thorough look-see sort of man—complete—including that long lank hair which shuts out the light; and there's his dark transparent face as well, like exposed film you can safely see the sun through at the noon of an eclipse.

Martha did nothing to erase the extravagance of her description. A luksi sort of man, I thought. Of the monkeys, that's not the one I would have picked; but I must admit to receiving a chill from this news—a chill, a chill—though in a perverse way it restored my weakened self to life like a dead drink that's suddenly got a plop of fresh ice.

The silences which came between us now were as regular as spaces on a page of type, and far more impervious to any message than our walls.

You called yourself a gid. That must be good. So what's a gid? She hated to ask. She knew how I loved an answer.

A gid is a small god, Marty, the human kind, with more features than powers—the difference, you might say, between poetry and prose. With my fingers I made a meager measure. Mayor Daley is a gid. And Franco. Fred Astaire. Lowell Thomas.

Then you're not a gid. Do they come in smaller sizes, like bras?

I hated her when she was smart-assing. A gid is as small as gods get. There's no volume for a vowel deeper down or deeper in.

She wondered whether it came from "giddyup" or "yid" or simply "giddy," and then scornfully concluded it wasn't a word, that I'd merely made it up. We argued wearily about whether a made-up word could be one, and whether making up words was a form of lying, though neither of us cared. Well, in any case, you're not a gid, she said. I hated her when she was hard-boiling. I hated her when she crossed her arms across her chest like a prison matron in the movies. Her cleavage was another cunt. Hey, why don't we? why don't we invite them to dinner? Perhaps we can reach an understanding. Maybe we can work something out.

I don't want to know him any better than I do already, Martha said, carrying a summer *Vogue* into the john.

I was resolutely bent on comedy. If we could trade one-liners maybe we could continue to live. I suggested we let our little throw rugs grow so we could comb them across our cold bald floors.

It may be, Martha said distantly.

I began to wish I had the wind's indifference to what it did. Shall I water them then? I tried to shout. Her first flush filled both houses like the bowl. There were always two. But she had begun to hide her habits from me. She kept the corners of the toast out of her coffee; she didn't twist her table napkin, she no longer whistled while doing crosswords, or used toilet paper to blow her nose. She started rubbing toothpaste on her gums with her right forefinger, and thrusting pencils between her braids. She didn't get dog-eared books; she kept caps firmly on her jars of cleansing cream; she stopped slapping around the house in scuffs. I was simply at a loss. She didn't stick her lips anymore, but that might have been fashion. I waited for that second flush, which didn't come. She was disguising herself. Her voice would get gruff. Soon I could expect to see a stranger's expression on her face and a mask on her muff.

With even these petty expectations taken from me, all I had left was a little inner determination, gid-greed, ambition like a stunted bud; but I silently resolved that what Ike is, and Cotton Mather was, Whiffie Koh would be.

We lit electric fires but no others. Except for them our house was a cold grate, and we were as alive as sifting ash. Peeled outside-in by Marty's transformations—bewildered, shocked—I only professed to be surprised so she would believe I always knew. But knew what? Was my blonde Martha taking on that little woman's ways? The joke became our medium of exchange.

We would drive them out like demons. I made the sign of the cross—incorrectly—and muttered Latin imprecations. Let's burn sulfur, I said. For a week I tried raising my voice and being rowdy. Martha read old *Cosmo*s and did puzzles ripped from the *Saturday Review*. It's like living in a waiting room, she said. And hearing you bawl about like someone calling trains.

That's it, I said. If I took a snapshot of our life right now, what would it look like? yeah, a drawing, a cartoon. We've bound our own feelings like feet. Our cheeks have porked. My eyes are two dots. Everything we say belongs in a balloon. Listen to your own sweet voice: stars, contorted ampersands,

and yellow lightning bolts. Marty, these last few weeks I've felt myself emptying into outline, as if beer could become its bottle, and because we're posed
here in pitchfork, arrowed tail, and red flesh, how can our misery be any
more than lines? Hey, remember how we honeyed one another? Has so much
changed we've gathered only ants and flies? Marty? listen—

Lis-sen, she said. That's all I do. My left ear is as long and flat as this wall
I've pressed it to so amorously, and I've kept the other to the ground as well,
just as hard and down and often, so the right one here is wide and tired and
dirty like the floor. My nose, Koh, in case you care, gets nothing up a nostril
now but doorbell buzz and blender whirr.

So we turned up the radio to stifle our whispers and smother our shouts,
as torturers did in the movies, but discovered that then we couldn't hear anything they were up to either, and that wouldn't do.

The entire house seemed to have shrunk. It had become a cheerless, shabby
rented room, soon to be a bureau drawer. I had been about to suggest that
we stop bugging one another, but a dreary cold light fell out of the kitchen
to confound me, and my voice lay down in my throat.

The other day I saw a fire alarm—long yellow streaks like slaps across the
face of the street. I've three bruises on my arm. It's the vicious way he turns
off taps. Notice that? They roll marbles across their kitchen floor. He leans
over her like a lens.

Marty, come on. It's our closeness in the crazy place—our closeness has
kept us apart—but the natural, decent, and sensible thing to do would be
to complain to the university together—club up, unionize, make common
cause. We *have* a common cause, you know.

She acknowledged this by gestures, each Italian and obscene. Remember
how those woppy Eytie kids would gun their Vespas through the streets? The
noise came at you as though they were hurling the cobbles. Well, they loved
it. They loved their loud cocks. They loved their ball-like wheels. They loved
to stick it up those narrow Roman ways. A vigorous finger speared the air.
She failed to strip skin from her teeth. Can't you hear them next door, then?
that continuous applause? the cheers? They love it—this noise we volley.
They wouldn't trade for Willie Mays.

I hated her when she was hard-assing. I hated her when her plump face
resembled that of some mean and pouty child, as—so often—it resembled
Charles Laughton's. But, Marty, it can't really be that only our half of the
house is cold. Noise isn't a trolley on a one-way *milano* street. It can't be that
moisture is collecting on our sills and not theirs, or that just our drafts are so
brisk the blinds rise and the drapes wave.

It may be, Martha said. What if?

You know, Whiff, sometimes, in a marriage, only one side hears the other cough.

Yeah? Well. What of it? Are we married to them, then? Is that the situation?

One side is cold, sometimes, in a marriage, she said. One eye does all the weeping.

Yeah. Right. Sure thing. But is our nose stuck in their moldy jam pot? And who is the cold carrot around here anyhow? which side of our bed has a marble mattress?

Shush, she said. They've just come in.

Shit, I shouted, on the run; but no sound could give me satisfaction, nor the silence after my slam.

The bitterness of it. I had hoped her flesh might warm my life; but my body isn't blubber for your burning, she had crudely said. Alas, one's dreams are always a cliché, yet I had hoped she would fill what I felt was an emptiness; but I'm not going to let you wear me like a padded bra so you can seem complete, she said.

The wind was an acid eating at my face, my anger another sort of acid searing my insides. Soon they would be near enough to greet. There was a hint of starlight, as there often was during the many clear nights of this pitiless winter, the thin moon a menacing sickle, and the dark artery of the river ran through closing ice toward a heart far out of sight, I imagined, like a lurking troll beneath a bridge. I couldn't drive her from her fantasies, however I tried. She was persistent as a bee. My boots went again where my boots had been, and I was aware, without pleasure, of the repetition. What was my passion for this ample woman but just that amplitude, that generous expanse of self? and now her hair was coiled, her thighs tense, her feelings like a tissue wadded in an anxious hand.

We went from apology to explanation to excuse like partners at a progressive dinner.

It bothers me to be an object in other people's obscenities, she said—the dirt in a dirty joke—a filthy thought you can't wash clean or even get a little soap near.

Even in *my* polite pornographies, I asked, with another attempt at gaiety, which would burst before blowing up like a bad balloon.

In yours, especially, now I've been his leading lady. Her head wagged toward the wall in a gesture of such furious rejection I became immediately jealous. It bothers me to be all crotch. It bothers me.

And so I thoughtlessly said I wouldn't mind being all prick, dropping my left like an amateur, exposing myself; and of course I received her swift,

professional retort. Replies rose in my throat, but they had the quality of yesterday's radish, so I did not return her pings with any pong of mine. I don't
see even a shadow to start at, let alone a reality to run from, I said; how can
you know what either of them is thinking?

I know what *I* am thinking. I know what *my* thoughts watch. I know how
he drinks his morning milk. I have the measure of his mustache, and how far
along his lip his tongue creeps. I know what he sees in his wife. I know how
he pees, and when he shits, how many squares of paper are pulled off. I hear
the rattle of the roll. I know what he wants.

My anger would never leave me. I had contracted a malarial disease. Naturally I had to hear what she imagined our neighbor saw in his wife, and
Martha answered, predictably: the same things you see in me—our sentences
two halves of the same dull bell. A hammer, I said, is what I see. A pliers.
God damn it, Marty, don't cheat on the truth so transparently. Do you want
a use? the least utility? Just what do you believe I see when I see inside you?
the peep show follies?

Hair and heat and pink toes. You see a plate of steaming meat.

I wished right then there were a god I could invoke to damn her truly, but
the thought of her skin cracking open in some supreme heat gave me only
a jack-off's relief. Of course I shouldn't have felt as if my soul had left me,
but her words—common enough, really—were like that winter wind which
rushes by so fast you can't get a bit of it for breathing.

Not quite, Marty, I said. When I look at you I see a stew congealing in
its grease.

The bitch didn't even weep.

The bitterness of it. I could remember her body in its beauty waiting for
me with the calmness of the coverlet. I too had looked at her like a lens, and
she had posed for me, opened as easily as eyes to my eyes; showed a boisterous
bust, a frank and honest hip, a candid cunt, as one might hand round snap-
shots of a trip. Then it struck me. Perhaps she believed, in those handsome
early days when our lust was in its clean beginnings and the politics of the
penis had not yet confused and corrupted everything, that I was gazing past
her smooth full cheeks and succulent lobes toward Martha the grandly scutch-
eoned Muhlenberg I'd married, or grazing quite beyond her meadowed chest
to Marty the blonde Amazonian lass, so she didn't mind my meddling senses,
my nosey fingers, my tireless tongue; whereas now she knew I was admiring
nothing but her beauty right along; and though it might be, like wealth, of
immense use, it remained an alien and external burden if you thought of
adding it to the self, because—well—she believed she possessed her looks
like one might a Pekinese or poodle, and who would want to incorporate a

cold-nose, pissy-nervous, yapping one of those? yes, wasn't that it? for hadn't I always wondered that very thing about women, who I had learned could be sensuous and passionate beyond my poor capacities; who would calculate faster than Clever Hans—cook, sing, farm, run households, wag ass and empire with equal ease and often with the same moves, betray causes, author novels, and learn French—but in whom I had never seen, for instance, what a sculptor must, namely how dirty the mind gets where it feeds like a root in the earth, or the extraordinary way the concrete is composed of numbers and relationships like sand, the fugal forms of feeling which outstrip all proof, or finally the snowy mountainous elevations, the clouded unscaled peaks, the cold remote passions of the purely physical sublime?

You don't get it, do you, Martha said. You think I'm being cranky and perverse. You think I should be locked up like a dirty line in a limerick. Koh. You dear love. You runt. You dunce. She smiled to lower the line of her malice, but there was still enough to wet my hair. I went to the bathroom a moment ago, she said. First I heard my own feet, you know? I heard the click of the light switch, the snick of the latch, the rubbered settle of the seat. It shames me to think that someone else may hear what I just heard, what I just made—the splash of my pee, that lovely shush of bubbles like soda dying in its glass—because these are my sounds, almost internal to me, Koh, the minor music of my privacy, and to hear them is to put a hand on me in a very personal place.

I heard the same snick, I said. It signals your safety, doesn't it? as if I might burst in behind you to piss between your legs myself.

Oh Koh. Please. It's not simply that my noises might be embarrassing—a rumbling stomach or some raucous break of wind—or even that to hear them one would have to be a sneak—although such factors weigh . . . they weigh . . . but neither is the painful one, the last cruel twist which wrings me out.

Slowly seeping down like egg white on a wall: my depression was that desperate. A kitchen table grainy with crumbs, an ashtray heaped with butts like the burned-out bodies of our voided thoughts, a faded cushion and a shredded towel—companions for this exercise—then a light that rattled away off plates like a falling fork. And so I said: have you heard your legs lock, Marty? No snick there, no click; rather, a sound like the settle of the seat.

Oh—

Not O, I said. No. X. Have you seen your arms cross on your chest like a sign warning Railroad?

Koh—

And when my hands fall on your bottom, I said, not to spank, because we never enjoyed that relation, but like a cornflake, a tree seed, ever so lightly, as air through an open doorway, surely you've felt those buttock muscles tighten?

Please, Whiff. Please be serious. Please.

Seriousness, I answered, has all but overcome my prose.

I remember wanting to understand, to throw my sympathy like an arm around her shoulders (at one point I thought, "gee, she's still my girl," as if we were pinned or going steady and I was selfishly rushing her responses); but I was also angry, disappointed, deeply affronted (I began to believe we wouldn't last the year out), since here she was defending her bloomers before I'd fully got her skirt up, and I was bitter as though bereft, because the cause of her present sensitivity seemed just a case of damn bad luck, like getting flashed by the cops while making out in Lovers' Lane, and had nothing to do, inherently, with us as a couple. My outrage rapidly became metaphysical. I called down on all women the character of my mother like a plague, and then cursed them with her fate.

You know that passage in *Middlemarch*—

I knew no passage in *Middlemarch,* but I can recall insisting that it was every female's favorite fiction.

—where she says about marriage that there's something awful in the nearness it brings?

I was sitting in a sugar-maple chair the sticky color of its syrup. I was uncomfortably near the knobs on metal cabinets, size of my eyes. Martha was wearing a large floral print which made her look like a trellis. To my well-fed Marty, I was a bed-and-boarding party. Wisecracks, rhymes, lay discarded like the Sunday paper. At such close quarters, our war was now down to nickels and dimes.

I've been watching us together, Koh, and I've been thinking too of our twins over there like animals in a neighboring cage, and I'm convinced now that we need to live in at least the illusion that a certain important portion of our life passes unobserved; that there are walks we take which leave no tracks; acts whose following sounds are not broadcast like the bark of dogs; events to which no one need or should respond; which have, in effect, no sensuous consequences.

I wished that this were one of them, but a metal kettle and a kitchen stool threatened immediate animation—to dance à la Disney to a tune by Dukas. The cute I couldn't handle. The spout would say something like "Toot!"

I don't want to hear all I do—every squeak in my works. I want a bit of oblivion, Koh. I want a little rest from awareness. You've made me so conscious of my chest, I'm counting breaths.

I was rolling like a spool. There's no coughless cold, kiddo; no blow without a little snot, no ding without its answering ling, no—

How I hate it when you try to crack wise. You can't break clean. You mash. Sure, sneer. Never mind. You can't ride away on the back of a joke. That's what I'd like to do myself, though: become deaf to what's dumb. Grin. Go ahead. How I hate it when you put that smile on like a dirty sock. Whiff, I'm sick of the shimmy, jounce, and rattle of staying alive. I want a world for a while without echoes and shadows and mirrors, without multiples of my presence. I could cut off my silhouette and not cry.

You're a sweet one to want a smooth ride. I thought you liked life a little hump-woof-and-rumpy.

Well, Willie, at least you offer me a model, a measure, something to go by when I wonder in what way you love me: exactly like a marksman loves his bull's-eye. All you want to do is score.

She spread the slats to check for their car, facing her sweatered back to my dismay.

On our own, she said softly. Left alone . . . in time . . . to some things we can go mercifully blind, as our ears will grow swiftly indifferent, thank god, and all our other senses . . . indifferent to ourselves and the cells we calendar our days in.

Above the sink the lamp sang, and the small chain leaked from its harsh fluorescent light in little links like melting ice.

Remember when my mother had her asshole out, Marty said (she knew how I hated her coarseness, but she was an *afficionado* of my shame); remember how she had to shit in a sack? She got used to it. She got used to it because she had to to survive. She got used to it because nobody dared to remind her. The subject was delicately *dropped*.

Like those A-bombs under their umbrellas. Marty, you can't cancel the fallout on account of rain, when it's the bloody rain itself.

What I want, Whiff—if it goes off—I want a chance to ignore the noise. Yeah, cover your ears like one of those monkeys to mock me, but I'm no longer lost in our love as I once was. I keep surfacing. I feel on film.

You don't like the lead in our little blue movies? the star part? It can't be that you're bored with the graceless grunt and huffy-puffy business?

You'll laugh at me alone this time, lover. I can't keep you company. You sprawl there with your little friend crawling down your trousers waiting for me to weep so you can take it out and put it in, because quarreling makes it uncaring, hence stiff and amorous like the little toy soldier it is. Go on. Take it off somewhere on vacation. Run away to the river. Amuse the ice. The two of you can take a leak, have a good laugh with the snow and the weeds.

I did as I was told, throwing on my coat as though I were throwing off everything else. The sky was hard and brilliant with stars like a run of the right hand in a piece by Liszt. The cold air rinsed my lungs and gave them definition. All those hidden inner organs took my walk and lived no differently than I did. Even our porous duplex didn't overstep its bounds. Beneath my weight, the cold snow crushed like crisp paper in a fist.

With Martha I loved what I'd always loved: an outline, a surface, a shape—yes—a nipple, a lip; yet I'd become an alien in her household, an unwanted presence, worse than roaches or the wind, because she thought she was more than a footfall, a weight, a slack wet mouth or sack of warm skin, when no one was other than their image, print, and circumcision—none of us—we were nothing but a few rips in the general stuff of things, like rust on a nickel blade, and we were each running down like radium into rays.

So I was the thin dark man next door now, not the fair round pudge she'd married. I was the swiveling radar dish, the probe, the lens, the receiver of all her transmissions. Still, it would have been useless to remind her that a dog could smell the absence of her clothes, so she'd be naked to it, though they were walls away, since she was contemptuous of my philosophizing, which she'd called mental masturbation more than once; yet if we conceived the world properly we would realize that the birds, ants, and insects also know us this way: as a shadow, a sound, a scent, a sudden intrusive substance, a cutting edge—never as a soul which (please god) does not exist except in a moist cold cloud like my present breath; and that, however quiet we were, however much we muffled our ears and stoppered our mouths, little could be kept from the earth and air around us, lion our lives upwind as we'd like, because it was alive as an antelope, all ear and apprehension, anticipation and alarm.

I was too much the whole of that wide world. Yes. I sniffed you out wherever you went like a hound. I would rush from another room to say: you coughed, is everything ok? but for you that was spying, not concern; so when I rubbed your rump I did so only to molest you; and when I offered to comb your hair you wondered what was up, and jeered when you saw what was. You wanted a love which would have been a lie—to lie beyond the nostril and the hip—an imaginary island like Atlantis or those happy beaches of the blessed it cost them nothing to enjoy beyond the payment of their death.

The mouth was refused first, before her back was turned like the last page. What are we, Marty, but sense and inference? and when I feel your smooth warm skin, your breasts like playful puddles; when I nuzzle your underarms or scent the ultimate *nostos* of your nest? what do I infer from what I sense? surely not the brittle stick you've thrown me. Be large, I begged. You will be less, my love, if you give me less.

The bitterness of it. But there was, as in everything, some recompense. It was true I enjoyed the way my feet distressed the snow; and I approved the sycamores who had no pretensions and wouldn't have hid their bones from me on any account, or condemned my pleasures. I did not applaud the river for its beauty, because along this stretch it had none. I loved it, rather, for its welcoming indifference, the way the cold was cold, and kept me together. What, of this world of memories, a young gent's hopes, the pale ashes of desire, could I control, or oversee, or lie in wait for like the man next door I now would always be?

It was a winter so prolonged their crocus bloomed beneath the snow, and the sun dreamed.

Out of a frozen bottle would be forced the frozen cream; and I felt my heart expand against my chest, my coat, as though squeezed, to press against the tree trunks, push against the pointed stars, spread out upon a sterile land.

We'd remain married. I would see to that. One life would not be long enough for my revenge. The coarse baritone in which I made my vows came like an errant echo from another skull, an outcry left behind on the stage like an actor's closing lines. My voice in my fist, I promised the wind, trampling underfoot my former prints, Iago now the new friend, blade, and ancient, of my prose.

Granta, 1979
Published in *The Tunnel,* 1995

Three Passages

An Invocation to the Muse

O brood O muse upon my mighty subject like a holy hen upon the nest of night.

O ponder the fascism of the heart.

Sing of disappointments more repeated than the batter of the sea, of lives embittered by resentments so ubiquitous the ocean's salt seems thinly shaken, of letdowns local as the sofa where I copped my freshman's feel, of failures as frequent as first love, first nights, last stands; do not warble of arms or adventurous deeds or shepherds playing on their private fifes, or of civil war or monarchies at swords; consider, rather, the slightly squinkered clerk, the soul which has become as shabby and soiled in its seat as worn-out underwear, a life lit like a lonely room and run like a laddered stocking.

Behold the sagging tit, the drudge-gray mopped-out cunt-corked wife, stale as yesterday's soapy water, or study the shiftless kind, seedy before any bloom, thin and mean as a weed in a walk;

Smell the grease that stands rancid in the pan like a second skin, the pan aslant on some fuel-farting stove, the stone in its corner contributing what it can to the brutal conviviality of close quarters;

Let depression like time payments weigh you down; feel desperation and despair like dust thick in the rug and the ragged curtains, or carry puppy pee and plate scrapings, wrapped in the colored pages of the Sunday paper, out to the loose and blowing, dog-jawed heap in the alley;

Spend your money on large cars, loud clothes, sofa-sized paintings, excursions to Hawaii, trinkets, knickknacks, fast food, golf clubs, call girls, slimming salons, booze;

Suffer shouting, heat rash, chilblains, beatings, betrayal, guilt, impotence, jail, jealousy, humiliation, VD, vermin, stink.

Sweat through a St. Louis summer and sing of that.

O muse, I cry, as loudly as I can, while still commanding a constricted scribble, hear me! help me! but my nasty echo answers: one muse for all the caterwauling you have called for! where none was in that low-life line of work before?

It's true. I'll need all nine for what I want to do—perhaps brand-new—all nine whom Hesiod must have frigged to get his way, for he first spoke their secret names and hauled their history by the snout into his poem. For what I want to do . . .

Which is what—exactly? to deregulate Descartes like all the rest of the romancers? to philosophize while performing some middle-age adultery? basically enjoying your anxieties like raw lickker when it's gotten to the belly? I know—you want to make the dull amazing; you want to Heidegger some wholesome thought, darken daytime for the TV, grind the world into a grain of Blake.

O, I deny it! On the contrary! I shall not abuse your gift. I pledge to you, if you should choose me, not to make a mere magician's more of less, to bottle up a case of pop from a jigger of scotch. I have no wish to wine water or hand out loaves and fishes like tickets on a turkey. It is my ambition to pull a portent—not a rabbit but a *raison d'être*—from anything—a fish pond, top hat, fortune cookie—you just name it—a prophecy in Spengler's fanciest manner, a prediction of a forlorn future for the world from—oh, the least thing, so long as it takes a Teutonic tone—a chewed-over, bubble-flat wad of baseball gum, say, now hard and sour in the street, with no suggestion of who the player's picture was, impersonal despite its season in someone's spit, like a gold tooth drawn from a Jew's jaw.

Misfits, creeps, outcasts of every class; these are my constituents—the disappointed people—and if I could bring my fist down hard on the world they would knot together like a muscle, serve me, strike as hard as any knuckle.

Hey, Kohler—hey, Koh—whistle up a wind. Alone, have I the mouth for it? the sort of wind I want? Imagine me, bold Kohler, calling out for help—and to conclude, not to commence—to end, to halt, to 30, stop, leave off, to hush a bye forever . . . to untick tock.

In My Youth

In my youth . . . my sacred youth . . . in eaves sole sparrowe sat not more alone than I . . . in my youth, my saucer-deep youth, when I possessed a mirror and both a morning and an evening comb . . . in my youth, my pimpled, shamefaced, sugared youth, when I dreamed myself a fornicator and a poet; when life seemed to be ahead somewhere like a land o' lakes vacation cottage, and I was pure tumescence, all seed, afloat like fuzz among the butterflies and bees; when I was the bursting pod of a fall weed; when I was the hum of sperm in the autumn air, the blue of it like watered silk, vellum to which I came in a soft cloud; O minstrel galleons of Carib fire, I sang then, knowing naught, clinging to the tall slim wheat weed which lay in a purple haze along the highway like a cotton star . . . in my fumbling, lubricious, my unlubricated youth, when a full bosom and a fine round line of Keats, Hart Crane, or Yeats produced in me the same effect—a moan throughout my molecules—in my limeade time, my uncorked innocence, my jelly-belly days, when I repeated OLIO DI OLIVA like a tenor; then I would touch the page in wonder as though it were a woman, as though I were blind in my bed, in the black backseat, behind the dark barn, the dim weekend tent, last dance, date's door, reaching the knee by the second feature, possibly the thigh, my finger an urgent emissary from my penis, alas as far away in its buttoned pants as Peking or Bangkok, so I took my heart in my hand, O my love, O my love, I sighed, O Christina, Italian rose; my inflated flesh yearning to press against that flesh becoming Word—a word—words which were wet and warm and responsive as a roaming tongue; and her hair was red, long, in ringlets, kiss me, love me up, she said in my anxious oral ear; I read: Milton! thou shouldst be living at this hour; for I had oodles of needs, if England didn't; I was nothing but skin, pulp, and pit, in my grapevine time, during the hard-on priesthood of the poet; because then—in my unclean, foreskinned, and prurient youth—I devoutly believed in Later Life, in Passion, in Poetry, the way I thought only fools felt about God, prayer, heaven, foreknowledge, sin; for what was a poem if not a divine petition, a holy plea, a prophecy; and in that BrassBrite Tomorrow, that FineLine time, having left my youth with a leap as Hart Crane had his life (a simile which should have taught me something, which should have been a warning), I believed I would finally be what I believed in; I would really live what I had dreamed of; I would rape and write and enrich myself; tongue a tender ear, a velutinous cunt, kiss and compose with one mouth, in the same breath, and maybe fly a plane like Raoul Lufbery and learn German so I could recite my Rilke during daring Immelmann turns, during any break between books or other coital excesses: *kannst du dir,* I'd chant, *kannst du dir denn denken dass ich jahre, so* . . . a stranger, a pelican in desert wilde, no to-fro angel, hiving verb, though poets were the bees of the invisible, Rilke said, and everybody religiously repeated it through my dubious youth—*ein Fremder unter Fremden fahre*—a stranger among strangers, myself the strangest, Kohler the kookiest, because I could never bring myself to enter adolescence, but kept it about like a bit of lunch you think you may eat later, and later come upon at the bottom of a bag, dry as dust, at the back of the refrigerator, bearded with mold, or caked like sperm in the sock you've fucked, so that gingerly, then, you throw the mess out, averting your eyes, just as Rainer complained he never had a childhood—what luck!—never to have suffered birthpang, nightfear, cradlecap, cold lake in your lung; never to have practiced scales or sat numbly before the dentist's hum or picked your mother up from the floor she's bled and wept and puked on; never to have been invaded by a tick, sucked by a leech, bitten by a spider, stung by a bee, slimed on by a slug, seared by a hot pan, or by paper or acquaintance cut, by father cuffed; never to have been lost in a crowd or store or parking lot or left by a lover without a word or arrogantly lied to or outrageously betrayed—really what luck!—never to have been a silent witness to a quarrel, to have been drenched by a spew of hate—what luck!—never to have had a nickel roll with slow deliberation down a grate, a balloon burst, toy break; never to have skinned a knee, bruised a friendship, broken trust; never to have had to conjugate, keep quiet, tidy, bathe; to have lost the chance to be hollered at, bullied, beat up, to watch your mother weep (being nothing, indeed, to have no death), and not to have had an earache, life's lessons to learn, or sums to add reluctantly right up to their bitter miscalculated end—what sublime good fortune, the Greek poet suggested—because Nature is not accustomed to life yet; it is too new, too incidental, this shiver in the stone, too novel altogether, and would just as soon cancel it; erase, strike, stamp it out—this dubbed-in youth, this gicky GroBoy time—so that I would never have been jeered at, called Bullocky Bill on account of my tiny testicles and puny weenie, had I not been available, or caused to cough in a long naked army line, to spread my rash-eaten cheeks to the amusement of a hundred eyes, or in a park in Prague gently jacked off by a boy who fondled me from behind a newspaper (or was it a magazine?), napkin neatly in his idle hand; and shame need never have lit me like a match, as I burned my slender candlesoft Being back then, in my old cold youth, until its head was black—best never to drag a breath out of the competing wind, the Greek poet advised, because Being is basically made of heartless hunks and soulless flabs; it is inert, resists flow, dislikes disturbance, distrusts goals; in fact, it is fat as a Buddha, sluggish, still as statues, and as pitilessly bronze.

A Fugue

My dad wouldn't let me have a dog. A dog? A dog we don't need. My mom made the neighbor's spitz her pal by poisoning it with the gin she sprinkled on the table scraps. Feed it somewhere else, my dad said. A dog we don't need. My dad wouldn't let me have a dog. Our neighbor's spitz—that mutt—he shits in the flower beds. Dog doo we don't need. At least feed it somewhere else, my dad said. My mom made the table scraps tasty for her pal, the neighbor's spitz—that mutt—by sprinkling them with gin. You're poisoning Pal, my dad said, but never mind, we don't need that mutt. My mom thought anything tasted better with a little gin to salt it up. That way my mom made the neighbor's spitz her pal, and maddened dad who wouldn't let me have a dog. He always said we didn't need one; they crapped on the carpet and put dirty paws on the pants leg of guests and yapped at cats or anyone who came to the door. A dog? A dog we don't need. We don't need chewed shoes and dog hairs on the sofa, fleas in the rug, dirty bowls in every corner of the kitchen, dog stink on our clothes. But my mom made the neighbor's spitz her pal anyway by poisoning it with the gin she sprinkled on the table scraps like she was baptizing bones. At least feed it somewhere else, my dad said. My dad wouldn't let me have a pal. Who will have to walk that pal, he said. I will. And it's going to be snowing or it's going to be raining and who will be waiting by the vacant lot at the corner in the cold wet wind, waiting for the damn dog to do his business? Not you, Billy boy. Christ, you can't even be counted on to bring in the garbage cans or mow the lawn. So no dog. A mutt we don't need; we don't need dog doo in the flower beds, chewed shoes, fleas; what we need is the yard raked, like I said this morning. No damn dog. No mutt for your mother, either, even if she tries to get around me by feeding it when my back is turned; when I'm away at work earning her gin money so the sick thing can shit in a stream on the flower seeds; at least she should feed it somewhere else; it's always hanging around; is it a light string in the hall or a cloth on the table to be always hanging around? No. Chewed shoes, fleas, muddy paws and yappy daddle, bowser odor: a dog we don't need. Suppose it bites the postman: do you get sued? No. I am the one waiting at the corner vacant lot in the rain, the snow, the cold wet wind, waiting for the dog to do his damn business, and I get sued. You don't. Christ, you can't even be counted on to clip the hedge. You know: snicksnack. So no dog, my dad said. Though we had a dog nevertheless. That is, my mom made the neighbor's pal her mutt, and didn't let me have him for mine, either, because it just followed her around—yip nip—wanting to lap gin and nose its grease-sogged bread. So we did have a dog in the house, even though it just visited, and it would rest its white head in my mother's lap and whimper, and my father would throw down his paper and say shit! and I would walk out of the house and neglect to mow or rake the yard, or snicksnack the hedge or bring the garbage cans around. My dad wouldn't let me have a dog. A dog? A dog we don't need, he said. So I was damned if I would fetch.

Conjunctions, 1983
Published in *The Tunnel,* 1995

AUGUST BEES

Now it is another day. Rain is speaking gently to the terrace. I speak gently, sometimes, to myself. How soft the light is, mingled with the wet. We had one shortened summer month together, Lou and I. . . . my god, even the decade's gone. Pleading the pressures of work, I excused myself from my life and settled in a second-story room in western New York. A wooden stair fell from one widened window like a slide of cards. We hung our towels there, a shirt sometimes, a slip as discreet as a leer. I remember particularly the quiet empty streets, the long walk through the shade to the beach. Well, it was scarcely a beach, though there was a pier, and even in August the water was cool in those naillike scratches the glaciers had made. My chief memory is of the heat, the silence, your pale breasts. I do not understand what makes another body so appealing. A souvenir scarf—but from where?—salmon-pink and exuberantly fringed, lay across the dresser. And there was an old commode. Amazing. Was there any remainder? was it all ash? And the walls were . . . ? the walls . . . ? Was there a rug, its design by a dime-store Indian? If you grasped the stair rail, white paint would powder your hand. Every morning we ate an orange, and you walked off to the lake to swim while I read till eleven when I met you there. We circled the lake so closely we kept our image always in the water, and we ate our lunch from the same brown sack we used to feed the ducks, the sack the grocer dropped our oranges in, half a dozen at a time. The scent of the peel would often linger on my thumbs, the zest of the rind still lodged beneath the nail near the quick. Then, in the afternoon, we would nap and sweat through the deep heat, our limbs loose as rags, and walk once more down the elm-tented street for a dip, holding hands which had held our bodies together better than our bones. In the evenings I wrote or we listened to the radio a little, and you would let your long hair dry on our single pillow. It was the simplest sort of life, empty of everything except ourselves, the contentment we were wrapped in like patriotic bunting. I wrote the section on secondary schools in *G & I** almost entirely out of my head—easily, so easily—even the songs,

> *Unsern Führer lieben wir,*
> *Unsern Führer ehren wir,*
> *Unsern Führer folgen wir,*
>   *Bis wir Männer werden . . .*

hardly taking thought. Bugs would bang against the screen during the early hours of the night, a car might cough, or very far away a truck labor up a hill, and the morning light would be gray and heavy with humidity. I would stand naked at the top of our wooden stairs while you completed your sleep, accosting a day which wasn't quite ready, and waiting for a breeze to brush the hair on my legs the way your breath would caress me in advance of your tongue.

We were happy that summer because we had no history. I know that now. Our winter room was full of the snow which had fallen between us, the cold wind my wife blew, your desire to have all of me, as though I were entirely at leisure, and had no book, no profession, no family, no commitments to the world. I only wanted to play *eine, meine, mine, mu,* and you eventually tired of being a meadow for my slow fat herds; but in that warm still heavy summer even the stars were wet, and I would wait for a wind, a faint stir in the grass tips, that movement of life in the poplars which signified a breeze, and through the screen, with its fly's-eye view, watch the light slide along your body as if that were air, too, suddenly become skin.

It sometimes seems to me, in my morbidly fanciful moments, as if old age were aimed at, not simply suffered, for I fled my youth as if it were a plague; I wanted no more of adolescence than I sought its acne. Our decrepitudes reduce our past to rows of funny photos in the family album of a stranger. We can release our early life to pop in alien trees or burst in the upper air like freed balloons. I can recall someone shouting slogans in a German street, but that loud rowdy could never have been played by the soft-voiced and suety professor I have since become; nor can I long for you any longer in the old way—that pain is also past—since the lover who lingered over you like a nurse through an illness—I see that now—is now another man, no longer a lover of any kind, just as you are, Lou, a different set of lips, another pair of breasts, some further furry tunnel.

---

* *Guilt and Innocence in Hitler's Germany,* the narrator's major historical work. He is a teacher of history in a major Midwestern university.

Who really wants to be what they have been? only those like Lou whose souls are the same as their bodies; those whose bodies have beauty and skill, grace and accomplishment. Time is an enemy of matter, not of mind, and history (as I said to Governali), history, so long as it is tied to Time like a tin can to the wedding car, can only be a recital of deaths and declines.

I'm not your second-story man anymore; another story has intervened. The beauty which I had from you is no longer mine. The pale pattern of your bra, like something which has lain too long across grass, as that scarf lay across its dresser, is one I watch a former self observe, a self which could have returned through the screen to spread himself like a brown glaze over your breasts, not this body which is all mind now—and a mind which is pure bleach.

Well, I regret the loss of the lover who loved you (hourly, I regret it), but not the loss of the slogan shouter, as if my forties had canceled my twenties out, and my fifties stamped PAID on both. Please go away now. I remember particularly our sandaled footfalls and your hand, the light way it led the swing of our arms.

Suddenly the temperature fell like a stone scuffed over a cliff, and when you woke, as surprised by the chill as the trees, I tossed you a towel to cover yourself, and you held to your breasts half a dozen honey bees which had sought shelter in its warm damp folds. Your outraged cries of violation come back to me as I write, as though you were here in my study to be stung again. Am I still that astonished self? that innocent who bit you from afar? Later, small red spots would come out on your chest when you showered, real memories of a flesh I could not scar with my kisses or, with my worship, bless. It got hot again, but our summer's month was over. For as long as we were together, you held those bees against me.

> A swarm of bees in May
> Is worth a load of hay;
> A swarm of bees in June
> Is worth a silver spoon;
> A swarm of bees in July
> Is not worth a fly.

Delta, 1979
Published in *The Tunnel,* 1995

THE SUNDAY DRIVE

This was years ago. . . . Martha, the children, and I had driven into the country to collect weeds. At that time, Martha was in what I called her "pluck and pickle" phase, and she loved to gather great heaps of weeds each autumn to tie and hang head-down in carefully sorted bunches in the basement. Placed in vases later, even the most unlikely plants displayed an intensely distilled yet vagrant beauty: dry pods like petals, petals like furled flags, the stiff twigs like an explosion of cracks in a wall. We would choose, when we could, one of those fine fall days when the sky is such a deep and cloudless blue it descends straight to earth like a curtain to the stage, and you can almost see the leaves beginning to turn, as if hastened by the light. We would take some baloney for the kids, some bread and cheese, and lunch among the leftovers, down old roads and unmowed berms, where life still went on randomly, out of the reach of sprays and scythes. The Cheshire would crumble on the bread, as suddenly out of place as pollen in this world of the ripe expended seed. The cattails stood like daydream candy on a stick, and the fields were thick with brittle stems and cream and gray grasses resilient as wire. It was difficult, sometimes impossible, to make footway through them, and of course we wore long pants and sleeves to protect ourselves from burrs, insects, poison ivy, barbed wire, nervous bees.

In this part of the country autumn is the only season one can celebrate; and it is not simply that the land becomes violet and mauve and pink and gold, as if sunsets were its new cash crop and sprang freely from the earth; or because the trees turn, overcoming the eye with color and the soul with misgivings, the way we presume the weeds do; or that the pumpkins and gourds are gathered, potatoes forked into unrinsed heaps; or even because the densely enclosing stands of corn have been cut, unshuttering space along

the roads like a sudden shout. These things count, of course, as does the limpid blue we're drenched by. This blue is what *"azur"* means to a French poet:
a palpable infinity, something in front of which one puts a rapturous "O,"
and after which a point of exclamation. This time of year rain falls through a
dry sky, while in the summer the wet air wets it, so the raindrops come down
coated like pellets of moist dust. Flamboyance and poetry aside, it's how this
season goes to its death that is finally entrancing, and one feels compelled to
"get out in it," as if the season were a process one could enter and exit like a
dance going on on a dance floor.

Provided the weather was good, I planned to be impulsive and suggest
an expedition. By keeping my counsel, and waiting until the last minute, I
would avoid the anxious anticipations of the children, their possible disappointments, their inevitable nervous nagging. The calendar plays every tune
in its time—the roll with its prefigured holes has simply to come round—and
the right weekend did, almost at once. Sunday proved blue as a burned knife.
Sighting the sky as if I were going to shoot it, I determined the precise degree
of its fidelity: the true blue of its ulterior blueness, the whiteness of its inner
wind. It would remain fine. So we packed the picnic basket; put a ground
cloth and blanket in the trunk of the car; collected two pairs of kitchen
shears and one pair of tough garden clippers, lots of paper sacks, and a can
of insect repellent beginning to rust around its rims, somewhat as I was. In
the glove compartment of the Dodge Martha stuffed a little illustrated book
of ferns and flowers, crudely colored, as if there were only four hues, each
harsh; and then we coasted backward out of the drive until the car's engine
caught, its starter being somewhat cantankerous. Carl cried out, "Here we
come, critters," and I got the gears engaged.

Martha is quiet, and the roads are so calm and empty we almost motor—as
it was once called—we almost motor along. When we reach the river road,
the Wabash will begin to loop in and out of the eye, the turgid brown stream
papered now with the sycamores' wide dry leaves. I slow down but I sense in
the kids some thrust in their limbs, some running alongside, and I realize,
too, that Martha doesn't enjoy having cars come so swiftly up behind us to
horn their way past. A pickup truck rushes up, then bleeps by, so I sort of
slip us off the road down a gravel track that only tractors take, sometimes
with their low wagons in tow, and bump a bit from rut to rut until we reach
a steep bank where the water stands below us so still and thick the leaves
have to tell us it's flowing. From the slope where I've cautiously parked the
car in order to provide for a dead-stick getaway, Carl has already picked up
two stones and a short piece of branch and thrown them through the leaves
into a water that rises sluggishly above the hit, a hole the leaves close; and his

brother has had to be grabbed by the backside of his sweater as he staggers drunkenly along the bank. It seems to me I'm still pulling the key from the ignition when Martha calls out to Carl, *"Kumm!"* and drags his brother back into the car by the scruff. There is an uninteresting patch of scurfy-leafed French grass in my face, some winter grape, a briar, a bit of thug bush. "Not here," Martha says, so I release the brake.

"At least let Carl get in before we go."

"Carl can try getting in as quick as he got out."

I consider tossing Carl into the river, where he'll make a plop like a mushroom made of mud and disappear, the leaves quilting over him: nightie-night. The engine of the old Dodge coughs, catches, the car bucks briefly as the gears go in, but we're off. Martha frowns in lieu of a public statement. She's sore because I haven't had the battery replaced. Perhaps that's what's wrong: today the battery, yesterday the yard. Carl is testy because he'd counted on playing football with a friend, had, in fact, his shoulder pads bra'd across his chest and had thrown himself into a sexy pose like an acrobat into a net when I snapped on my surprise like a morning light: it is Sunday, I said; there is sunshine; the sumacs have set fire to the woods; the weeds are high and crawling with bugs—awhisper with them; the Sunday drive, my boy, has arrived like an unexpected guest. He half suspects I'm punishing him for his little play with the pads. So we try a better spot farther on—no luck—the children complaining because they want to see a muskrat, play ball, and catch fish. Martha argues with them as if they really expected to see or capture anything of the sort. She denies even our most fanciful wishes as if they were complaints about her food, her love. How dare you dream without my permission: that's her attitude. We have periods of being used to it. "You don't want *that*," she likes to say, staring at the piece of pie we've chosen, while a white wad of Kleenex, no doubt the rejected wish itself, falls from her suddenly relaxed fist. "You can't want to chew such goo," she says, fishing a hunk of purple taffy from behind a cheek, wrapping it at once in tissue, flicking it out of existence with a swift wrist as if snapping something evil or ugly from her fingers. "You *don't*," she says to Carl with conviction, "you *don't* hate your brother; you *love* your brother," she says, lightly slapping the face he's made and gently shaking his shoulders. "We *all* love one another in this house, you hear me! *My God*, we sure do, it's *awful* how much." Her slaps are both admonitions and gestures of condolence. "Don't slouch. Sit straight. Throw back your shoulders. Breathe! In! Escalate!" And her shoulders pull partly away from her body, the straps of her bra tighten, her breasts swell like inflating balloons. Perhaps that's where Carl got his notion of how to play with the pads. "You *adore* carrots—since a baby! Don't you remember? You used to chew the spoon." The tines of the fork showing through the vegetable like a row of nails, a round is firmly thrust in the kid's pinched-open mouth. And to me she used to say, "You can't *like* doing that," in competing tones of scorn and incredulity, so that now my wishes no longer run downward in those directions.

Soon the wrangling is intense, Martha a sea in a cut-rate storm, winds whistling across the soul's mouth, angry with the children because she's mad at me, the children willing to carry on their crabbing because neither of them wanted to come. I could let the car careen into the river, leaping out at the last minute, of course—Carl has shown me how—geronimo!—momentum would carry the Dodge clear of the immediately muddy shore and drop it into the liquefied shit beyond. A splat would rise like a wild cry. I see our venerable vehicle upside down in the silt, sinking slowly out of sight, the wheels wobbling around as if all the shafts were broken: bye-bye.

I can envision it so clearly because I've been so often to the movies.

Is that a fragment of a white arm?

So we try another place farther on—no luck—and then I veer away from the river, cross the main road to go up the ridge on the other side, pass people carrying dressed-up babies out of a country church. "At this time of day?" The males made no remark. They had grown sullen. We sat in our silence as though in heavy coats.

I had lost us at last on a half-grassy track that was wandering in and out of a thin woods and following, I suppose, the path of least resistance, when we approached an artifical rise on which a spur of track had been mounted. "Just over the hill is heaven," I promised, but I couldn't raise a scoff. I proceeded slowly. These roads are not kind to large cars. Once gingerly over, we saw the barns—a line of them—and an abandoned barnyard: an overgrown fence, broken gate, high grass, of course weeds. "We have been lost and found our way." Red-hatted, white: the barns are beautiful. Even Martha looks pleased. I know not to believe looks, but she does look pleased. Four doors open simultaneously and we pile out. I am, however, not parked on a slope.

Since Martha and the kids are happy clipping stalks and stems, I walk back to the rails for a better view of the barns. They've been built, it appears from this vantage, of wood shingle, melancholy, and roofing tin. I could come upon them, from this point, like Pizarro or Cortés upon the habitation of an ancient people. The barns are separated from the road by two isolated lines of track, by a drainage ditch a little bridge skips, and by a clearing now crowded with vegetation: a rude patch of thistles and then a silver-gray swatch of immeasurably delicate grass, and finally a lot of plants quite tall and imposing, which I cannot identify. So the barns seem to rise out of a sea of fronds and pods and tiny leaves. There are three of them, steaming beam to beam like ships, each gable ridge a prow, although they vary slightly in size and certainly in design. The farthest one to the west, and so struck last by the sun when it sets, is attended by three scaling gray silos. Wrapped in loops of fine wire, they rise beside it like the gigantic stumps of some prehistoric tree, and their shapes, as well as the patterns of the stains that have descended their sides, and the lines of the vines that have climbed them, delight the eye the way good monumental sculpture does, by the force of its immediate mass and the caress of its eventual texture. There they store all that darkness that a day like this has defeated, and retain it for release at another time.

The middle barn is appropriately crowned with a fat and multi-shuttered cupola, which has a weather vane on top of it cut in the flat metal figure of a circling hawk: a conceit I find, in a farmer, also metaphysical. The eastern barn is slightly smaller, though more romantic, as though it held wisps of nostalgia instead of the absent hay it has. Nearly circumscribed by its own crippled fence, its single large upper loading door points darkly up into its own angular eave, while the building's solid presence seems to recede from my gaze into the past as though there were, in its world, a vanishing point from which it would not return. The barn windows, dark as though the holes themselves were looking out, and rimmed in red like tired eyes, seem symmetrically placed in the siloed barn, and in the hawk-shaded one as well, but irregularly in the smaller structure, which also lets its west wall lean out beyond the high hip of its roof to create a creature of singularly gawky beauty. The buildings face a large tract of bottom land, which the Wabash regularly floods to feed fresh mud. Their tin roofs, in the shape of a Dutch cap, are what you see first, for they slope toward their own feet like local hills and serve both as roof and wall, their color a melted run of rust and pale blood the sun seems to have set in motion as though a clear stream were passing through the pigment.

Well, I was right, the wind *is* white. There is a slight sliver of ice in it, the last hint of coolness in a dying drink. A calm elation has come over me, and the barns are the cause. I understand that much, although I am unable to explain why I am elated or why I am calm. Perhaps we aren't in the ordinary world anymore and these are the barns of the three bears. I watch my wife and the children move about, cutting and collecting. Carl is in a hurry, as if someone else will get everywhere first. Martha is wearing, I notice, one of my old favorites—a granny dress she's put on now because the dress is long and old and doesn't matter. I liked it because it hid her fat. But she knew that. In a moment I shall leave this little rise and look for a place to set out lunch. A piece of Brie is melting on my tongue. What good has it done me to love olives? It would be wonderful if the rails were to tremble and hum and life come down them ahead of some train. The white shingles gleam in the sunlight, and the sky whistles its way everywhere, bringing its blue tune to the deepest woods. The sumacs soften, despite their intensity, and even the clear yellow of the mulberry leaves has a gray interior. Anyway, it's not a palette that would appeal to Mondrian. Only in a painting or a poem can you find true purity . . . perhaps in a little song. Not in a woman. Not in a man. Not in me. The contrast between sky, roof, and wall is pleasing indeed, pleasing as is the difference between what is natural here and what is man-made: the wheat-weed stem, the shingle, a puddle, the rope's end.

While the barns have been neglected, they were obviously in wonderful condition once, and nothing has been trashed since. In the little bear's barn I'll discover later one rear window that has a triangular hole in it, and out of that hole will hang the frayed end of an old rope. When I cut into our bread's crisp crust, tiny bits of it will fly about, and the softness of the sawing sound will be pleasing as a creek. I notice that the siloed barn has undoored openings, and that deep within the feed passage, near where I'll find an ancient tractor parked, dangles a single bare and burning bulb, lit as if to say, "I am alive," so maybe the fallen condition of the fences—the unmowed yard and rampant weeds—is relatively recent. After lunch, beside an outbuilding of indeterminate function, I'll run into an old gas pump, its glass gone of course, the screw still up in the wire that has supported the bowl that held the fuel, dressed in rust like a fashionable statue of a pump, half a lifetime out of use. Another mark of man's presence here, the pump has become a work of art, but not one of man's making. The puddle lies in a wheel's rut and the weeds fill in a clearing. When I sliced the bread—what? Little bits of being fly up whenever I make a cut.

These barns have been abandoned, but they have been abandoned to beauty. They are no longer barns. The barns are themselves. A leftover light is burning. They have been left alone to breathe. I see I am standing in three times—mine, theirs, the weeds'—now. It is utterly awful and I don't mind. I am thinking about lunch and a mouthful of wine. Carl will not peel off the crusts of his baloney bread. Martha is waving, holding five feet of black mustard stalk above her head. I shall have the furniture carried out, heavy as it is, and the kids light as they are. My life shall become barns. In one, one light lit. Sometimes I often know what I want but I'm not allowed to have it. In an earlier part of our companionship, on a day and in a place like this, Martha and I would have made love. Sheltered each other like awnings. My seed won't dry into anything a vase can celebrate. Our history is as leafless already as these trees will be. Still, all of this was years ago now; we are waging other wars; and now none of these conditions obtains.

Esquire, 1984
Published in *The Tunnel*, 1995

EMMA ENTERS A SENTENCE
OF ELIZABETH BISHOP'S

The slow fall of ash

Emma was afraid of Elizabeth Bishop. Emma imagined Elizabeth Bishop lying naked next to a naked Marianne Moore, the tips of their noses and their nipples touching; and Emma imagined that every feeling either poet had ever had in their spare and spirited lives was present there in the two nips, just where the nips kissed. Emma herself was ethereally thin, and had been admired for the translucency of her skin. You could see her bones like shadows of trees, shadows without leaves.

Perhaps she should have been afraid of Miss Moore instead of Miss Bishop, because Emma felt threatened by resemblance—mirrors, metaphors, clouds, twins—and Miss Moore was a tight-thighed old maid like herself; wore a halo of ropy hair and those low-cut patent leather shoes with the one black strap which Emma favored, as well as a hat as cockeyed as an English captain's, though not in the house, as was Emma's habit; and wrote similitudes which Emma much admired but could not in all conscience approve: that the mind's enchantment was like Gieseking playing Scarlatti . . . what a snob Miss Moore was; that the sounds of a swiftly strummed guitar were—in effect—as if Palestrina had scored the three rows of seeds in a halved banana . . . an image as precious as a ceramic egg. Anyway, Gieseking was at his best playing a depedaled Mozart. Her ears weren't all wax, despite what her father'd said.

When you sat in the shadow of a window, and let your not-Miss-Moore's-mind move like a slow spoon through a second coffee, thoughts would float to view, carried by the current in the way Miss Bishop's river barges were, and they would sail by slowly too, so their cargoes could be inspected, as when father yelled "wax ear" at her, his mouth loud as a loud engine, revving to a roar. All you've done is grow tall, he'd say. Why didn't you grow breasts? You grew a nose, that long thin chisel chin. Why not a big pair of milkers?

Emma'd scratch her scalp until it bled and dandruff would settle in the sink or clot her comb; the scurf of cats caused asthma attacks; Elizabeth Bishop was short of breath most of the time; she cuddled cats and other people's children; she was so often suffocated by circumstance, since a kid, and so was soon on her back in bed; that's where likeness led, like the path into the woods where the witch lived.

Perhaps Emma was afraid of Elizabeth Bishop because she also bore Bishop as her old-maid name. Emma Bishop—one half of her a fiction, she felt, the other half a poet. Neither half an adulteress, let alone a lover of women. She imagined Elizabeth Bishop's head being sick in Emma's kitchen sink. Poets ought not to puke. Or injure themselves by falling off curbs. It was something which should have been forbidden any friend of Marianne Moore. Lying there, Emma dreamed of being in a drunken stupe, of wetting her eraser, promising herself she'd be sick later, after conceiving one more lean line, writing it with the eraser drawn through a small spill of whiskey like the trail . . . the trail . . .

In dawn dew, she thought, wiping the line out with an invented palm, for she knew nothing about the body of Elizabeth Bishop, except that she had been a small woman, round-faced, wide-headed, later inclined to be a bit stout, certainly not as thin as Emma—an Emma whose veins hid from the nurse's needle. So it was no specific palm which smeared the thought of the snail into indistinctness on the tabletop, and it was a vague damp too which wet Miss Bishop's skin.

Emma was afraid of Elizabeth Bishop because Emma had desperately desired to be a poet, but had been unable to make a list, did not know how to cut cloth to match a pattern, or lay out night things, clean her comb, where to plant the yet-to-be-dismantled ash, deal with geese. She looked out her window, saw a pigeon clinging to a tree limb, oddly, ill, unmoving, she. the cloud

Certain signs, certain facts, certain sorts of ordering, maybe, made her fearful, and such kinds were common in the poetry of Elizabeth Bishop; consequently most of Elizabeth Bishop's poems lay unseen, unsaid, in her volume of Bishop's collected verse. Emma's eye swerved in front of the first rhyme she reached, then hopped ahead, all nerves, fell from the page, fled. the bird

So she really couldn't claim to have understood Elizabeth Bishop, or to have read Elizabeth Bishop's poems properly, or fathomed her friend Marianne Moore either, who believed she was better than Bishop, Emma was sure, for that was the way the world went, friend overshading friend as though one woman's skin had been drawn across the other's winter trees. a cloud

Yes, it was because the lines did seem like her own bones, not lines of transit or lines of breathing, which was the way lines were in fine poems normally, lines which led the nurse to try to thump them, pink them to draw blood—no, the violet veins were only bone; so when death announces itself to birds they, as if, freeze on the branches where the wind whiffles their finer feathers, though they stay stiller there, stiffer than they will decay.

When, idly skimming (or so she would make her skimming seem), Emma's eye would light upon a phrase like "deep from raw throats," her skin would grow paler as if on a gray walk a light snow had sifted, whereupon the couplet would close on her stifled cry, stifled by a small fist she placed inside her incongruously wide, wide-open mouth. ". . . a senseless order floats . . ." Emma felt she was following each line's leafless example by clearing her skin of cloud so anyone might see the bird there on her bone like a bump, a swollen bruise. She was fearful, for she felt the hawk's eye on her. She was fearful of the weasel 'tween her knees. fearful

Emma owned an Iowa house, empty and large and cool in the fall. Otherwise inhospitable. It had thin windows with wide views, a kitchen with counters of scrubbed wood, a woodshed built of now wan boards, a weakly sagging veranda, weedy yard. At the kitchen table, crossed with cracks and scarred by knives, Emma Bishop sat in the betraying light of a bare bulb, and saw both poets, breasted and breastless, touching the tips of their outstretched fingers together, whereas really the pigeon, like a feathered stone, died in her eye.

Emma was living off her body the way some folks were once said to live off the land, and there was little of her left. Elizabeth Bishop's rivers ran across Emma's country, lay like laminate, created her geography: cape, bay, lake, strait . . . snow in no hills

She would grow thin enough, she thought, to slip into a sentence of the poet's like a spring frock. She wondered whether, when large portions of your pleasure touch, you felt anything really regional, or was it all a rush of warmth to the head or somewhere else? When Marianne Moore's blue pencil canceled a word of Elizabeth Bishop's—a word of hers hers only because of where it was, words were no one's possession, words were the matter of the mind—was the mark a motherly rebuke or a motherly gesture of love? Thou shalt not use spit in a poem, my dear, or puke in a sink.

There'd been a tin one once, long ago replaced by a basin of shallow enamel. It looked as if you could lift it out like a tray. It was blackly pitted but not by the bodies of flies. A tear ran down one side, grainy with tap drip, dried and redried.

How had she arrived here, on a drift? to sit still as pigeon on a kitchen stool and stare at the window while no thoughts came or went but one of Moore or two of Bishop and the hard buds of their breasts and what it must have meant to have been tongued by a genius.

She would grow thin enough to say, "I am no longer fastened to this world; I do not partake of it; its furniture ignores me; I eat per day a bit of plainsong and spoon of common word; I do not, consequently, shit, or relieve my lungs much, and I weigh on others little more than shade on lawn, and on memory even less." She was, in fact, some several months past faint.

Consequently, on occasion, she would swoon as softly as a toppled roll of Christmas tissue, dressed in her green chemise, to wake later, after sunset, lighter than the dark, a tad chilly, unmarked, bones beyond brittle, not knowing where

or how she had arrived at her decision to lie down in a line of verse and be buried there; that is to say, be born again as a simple set of words, "the bubble in the spirit-level." So, said she to her remaining self, which words were they to be? grave behaving words, map signs

That became Miss Emma Bishop's project: to find another body for her bones, bones she could at first scarcely see, but which now were ridgy, forming W's, Y's, and Z's, their presence more than circumstantial, their presence more than letters lying overleaf.

She would be buried in a book. Mourners would peer past its open cover. A made-up lady wipes her dark tears on a tissue. Feel the pressure of her foot at the edge of the page? see her inhale her sorrow slowly as though smelling mint? she never looked better, someone will say. heaven sent

Denial was her duty, and she did it, her duty; she denied herself; she refused numbering, refused funds, refused greeting, refused hugs, rejected cards of printed feeling; fasted till the drapes diaphanated and furniture could no longer sit a spell; said, "I shall not draw my next breath." Glass held more heaviness than she had. Not the energy of steam, nor the wet of mist, but indeed like that cloud we float against our specs when we breathe to clean them. Yet she was all care, all

Because now, because she was free of phlegm, air, spit, tears, wax, sweat, snot, blood, chewed food, the least drool of excrement—the tip of the sugar spoon had been her last bite—her whole self saw, the skin saw, the thin gray-yellow hair saw, even the deep teeth were tuned, her pores received, out came in, the light left bruises where it landed, the edge of the stool as she sat cut limb from thigh the way a wire passes the flesh of cheese, and pain passed through her too like a cry through a rented room. Because she had denied herself everything—life itself—life knew she was a friend, came near, brought all

Ask nothing. you shall receive

She was looking at the circular pull on the window's shade, her skin was drawn, her fingers felt for it, her nose knew, and it was that round hole the world used to trickle into her. With Emma down to her *E,* there was plenty of room, and then she, she would, she would slip into a sentence, her snoot full of substance, not just smell, not just of coffee she hadn't cupped in a coon's age, or fresh bread from back when, or a bit of peony from beside a broken walk, but how fingers felt when they pushed a needle through a hoop of cloth, or the roughness of unspread toast, between her toes a memory of being a kid, the summer's sunshine, hearty as a hug, flecks of red paper blown from a firecracker to petal a bush, the voices of boys, water running from a hose, laughter, taunts, fear they would show her something she didn't want to know

red rows the clapboard shells her reading eye slid swallowing solemnly as if she'd just been told of someone's love, not for her, no, for the sea nearby in Bishop's poems, a slow wash of words on a beach hissing like fat in the flame, brief flare-up before final smoke

Aunts trying hats on, paper plates in their laps—no—dog next door barking in his sleep, how about that? the flute, the knife, the shrivelled shoes I spell against my will with two *l*'s, how about that? her ear on the pull, the thread-wrapped ring, swell of sea along sunsetted shore, Maine chance, I'm now the longing that will fill that line when I lie down inside it, me, my eye, my nips, fingertips, yes, ribs and lips aligned with Moore's, whose hats, maybe, were meant in the poem, the poem, the poem about the androgynous aunts, exemplary and slim, vernal eyed, shaded by brim, caring for their cares, protecting their skin. a cloud

Now I am the ex of ist I am the am I always should have been. Now I am this hiss this thin this brisk I'm rich in vital signs, in lists I in my time could not make, the life I missed because I was afraid, the hawk's eye, owl's too, weasel's greed, the banter of boys, bang, bleeding paper blown into a bush, now I urinate like them against the world's spray-canned designs and feel relief know pride puff up for their circle jerk fellowship and spit on spiders step on ants pull apart peel back brag grope, since it is easy for me now, like sailing boats, making pies, my hair hearing through the ring the rumble of coastal water, rock torn, far from any Iowa window, now I am an ab, a dis, pre's fix, hop's line.

Out there by the bare yard the woodshed stood in a saucer of sun where she once went to practice screaming her cries and the light like two cyclists passing on a narrow road, the light coming in through cracks between the shed's warped boards, the ax she wouldn't handle, its blade buried in an ash tree's stump the shed had been built around so the stump would still be of service though its tree had had to come down, dad said, it would have a life like an anvil or a butcher's block because as long as you had a use you were alive, birds flew at the first blow, consequently not to cry that the tree'd been cut, groaning when it fell its long fall, limbs of leaves brushing limbs of leaves as though driven by a wind, with plenty of twig crackle too, like a sparky fire, the heavy trunk crashing through its own bones to groan against the ground, scattering nests of birds and squirrels, but now she was screamed out, thinned of that, or the thought of the noble the slow the patiently wrought, how the tree converted dirt into aspiration, the beautiful brought down, branches lofty now low and broken, the nests of birds and squirrels thrown as you'd throw a small cap, its dispelled shade like soil still, at toppled tiptop a worm's web resembling a scrap of cloud, it should have been allowed to die in the sky its standing death, she'd read whatever there is of love let it be obeyed, well, a fist of twigs and leaves and birdspit rolled away, the leaves of the tree shaking a bit yet, and the web

whisperating
what was left

A fat cloud, white as a pillow of steam, hung above the tree, motionless, as if drawn, as if all wind were gone, the earth still, entirely of stone, while the tree alone fell, after the last blow had been withdrawn, and the weeds which had tried and failed to be a lawn waited their bruise.

The house, like herself, was nowhere now. It was the reason why she fled facts when she came upon them, words like "Worcester, Massachusetts," dates like "February, 1918." Em had decided not to seek her fate but to await it. Still, suppose a line like that came to claim her. It was a risk.

I have lost this, lost that, am I not an expert at it? I lost more than love. I lost even its glimpse. Treefall. Branchcrash. That's all. Gave. Gave. Gave away. Watched while they took the world asunder. Now even my all is small. So I am ready. Not I hope the brown enormous odor . . . rather, a calm cloud, up the beach a slowing run of water

wait

far from the flame,

They were women. They were poets. But Miss Bishop probably knew a man or two, had him inner, while Miss Moore drew another pair of bloomers on. Hardly a match. Miss Bishop smoked, drank, wheezed, stood in the surf, barefooted about, fished. Miss Moore hunted for odd words. Exercised her fancy at the track. My father would stare at my bony body. Shake his head sadly. Nothing there to raise a dick. I'd be bare. Stand there. Bedsided. Scared. Oh yes mortified. Ashamed. All my blood in two lines below my eyes. Streaked with rose like twilit clouds. I'd stand. Before the great glass. It would be to see as he saw the then smooth skin, rose-lit, cheek to lay a cheek against, smooth to smooth I suppose, or wipe a weeping eye.

They were women. They were poets. But Miss Bishop lusted after love. Miss Moore cooled like a pie on a sill. Hardly a match. Not my wish to be Elizabeth Bishop. Not for me, either, to be Miss Moore. Yet alike as a pod houses its peas.

Unfit for fooling around. Like those Emmas before me, I read of love in the light of a half-life, and the shadow of its absent half gives depth to the page. My made-up romances are probably better, probably worse than reality. I am a fire at which my swain warms his hands. I am a fire quenched by a shower of scorn. Tenderness and longing alternate with cruelty and aversion. I study how to endure monsoons of driving snow.

Let's see how you're coming along. I'd have to slip out of my dress. Why are you wearing a bra? what's there to bra about. After he left I'd stand in the cold puddle of my clothes, step to the mirror to see for himself myself and my vaginal lips clasped like devout hands, praying to God to let me die before another day.

There was nothing to see, he said, so why did he inspect me as if I were going to receive a seal from the FDA? Elizabeth Bishop's father died of Bright's disease when she was still a child, and her mother went mad in Elizabeth's teens. My mother took her sturdy time dying. The day she died in her bed in this house, she had washed the windows of her room, though she could scarcely stand, and fluttered the curtains with arms weak with disease. Bustling about like a bee but without a buzz. Keeping out of reach, I now know. Wiping mirrors free from any image. Staying away by pretending to care and tend and tidy and clean and sweep and mend and scour and polish. Married to a gangplank of a guy. She scarcely spoke to me. I think she was ashamed of the way she let him make me live.

I learned to read on the sly. I failed my grades, though in this dinky town you were advanced so your puberty would not contaminate the kiddies. Despite the fact that I hadn't any puberty, my father said. But I read on the sly the way some kids smoked or stroked one another through their clothes. I read in fear of interruption. So I learned to read fast. I also read mostly first verses, first chapters, and careened through the rest, since my ear, when it turned to catch a distant tread, swung my eyes away with my brow toward the sound.

The ash came down but I never believed why. The shed was built around the stump to become an altar where my father chopped firewood or severed chickens from their heads. Slowly the stump was crisscrossed with cuts, darkened by layers of absorbed blood, and covered with milling crowds of tiny tiny ants. Traditionally, kids went to the woodshed for a whaling. Although once upon a time I stood still as a stick by the edge of my tot-wide bed, I now went to the shed to get undressed under my father's disappointed eye. Staring at hairs. And had he said something lewd, had he laid a hand, had he bent to breathe upon my chest, had his dick distended his pants, his point would have been disproved. I'd have elicited some interest.

He watched me grow like a gardener follows the fortunes of his plants, and what he wanted was normalcy. I dimly remember, when a child, how my father would hold me in his lap and examine my teeth. Something coming in there. He would push his finger down upon the spot. This tooth is loose, he'd say, with some semblance of pleasure, wiggling it painfully back and forth. Well, he was a farmer. And I was crop. Why not?

Getting a man was the great thing. My mother had got a man and what had that got her? Knocked up. With me. That's what. Maybe my father hoped he'd see, when I stripped, a penis lifting its shy self from the slot between my legs. Flat as I was, he may have thought there was a chance. There was no chance either way.

I might have been a boy in his balls but I was dismantled in her womb.

a residue of rain

Emma Bishop let the light on the table tell her about the weather. Sadness was the subject. Disappointment. Regret. The recipe? a bit of emptiness like that of winter fields when the fierce wind washes them; acceptance, yes, some of that, the handshake of a stranger; resignation, for what can the field do about the wind but freeze? what can the hand do but grasp the offered other? and a soupçon of apprehension, like clods of earth huddled against the frost they know will knock someday, or an envelope's vexation about the letter it will enclose; then a weariness of the slow and gentle variety, a touch of ennui, an appreciation of repetition. This sadness had the quality of a bouquet garni discreetly added to the sauce; it offered a whiff of melancholy, subtle, just enough to make the petals of plants curl at their tips. A day of drizzle in the depths of November. Not definite enough yet? All right: the quiet hour after . . . the nearly negligible remains . . . an almost echo.

The theme: leave-taking. Bidding adieu to a familiar misery. So . . . long . . . . . . The house was empty. The light was late, pale, even wan. The table lay in the light as though dampened by a rag. Emma Bishop saw her fingers fold up like a fan. Her lifelike light. So . . . long . . . . . . Nothing stays the ancients said but the cloud stood above the treetop while it toppled, still as painted, her father murdering her tree's long limbs before they had loosened their leaves. Why, then, should anything be loved if it was going to be so brutally taken away? He had seen the tree *be* in Emma Bishop's bright eyes. Beneath it, weeds where she rested and read. When she no longer had to hide her occupation.

It had been of some interest to Emma that her father had ceased his inspection of her bared body after her mother died. As if . . . As if it had been to distress her mother he undressed her, had walked around her like a car he might buy, had a list of factors to check for flight safety, to justify his then saying: see what you've given me, what you've grown, you are a patch of arid earth, your child is spindly, awkward, chestless, wedge-chinned and large-eyed, stooped too, not as though gangly but as though old.

She had been a ten-month kid, she'd been told. Maybe during that tenth month her weenie had withered.

Over time Emma began to perceive her parental world for what it was. Her father farmed by tearing at the earth, seeding soy with steel sticks, interested in neither the soil nor the beans, but only in what the beans would bring; interested in the sky for the same reason, in the wind, in rain. The creek overflowed once and flooded a meadow. He saw only a flooded field. He didn't see a sheet of bright light lying like a banner over the plowed ground. And the light darkened where the lumps neared the surface. Emma watched the wind roughen the water so that sometimes the top of a clod would emerge like new land. Crusoe in England? in Iowa. She imagined.

And her mother scrubbed their clothes to remove the dirt, not to restore the garments; and wiped up dust to displace it, not to release the reflection in the mirror or the view through the glass or the gleam from the wood. She pinned wash to its line as if she were handcuffing a criminal. Emma saw dislike run down her arms like sweat and transform the task. She didn't say to the pan, "Let me free you from this grease." She said to the grease, "Get thee away, you snot of Satan."

Emma ultimately preferred her furniture tongued and grooved, glued rather than nailed, for the nail had not only fixed Christ's hands to the cross, it had driven Eve into labor and a life of grief. Her mother wouldn't cry over spilled milk, but she would silently curse, her lips retreating from a taste. Emma learned to see the spatter as a demonstration of the laws of nature and as a whimsical arrangement of pale gray-blue splotches. When she read that infants sometimes played with their stools, she knew why.

Maybe her father stopped inspecting her when he saw her watching, simply watching him; when his naked face and naked gaze were gazed at, gazed at like urine in the pot, yellow and pearly; when his hard remarks were heard like chamber music.

He wore boots on account of the manure, he said, though they hadn't had horses or any other sort of animal in Emma's time. Except the chickens. The rooster's crude proud cry rose from the roof of the coop and from the peak of Bishop's poem. Perhaps it had a line that would do. He'd pull the boots off and leave them on the back porch, where Emma would find his handprints on their dusty sides. The handprints, thought Emma, were nice. There were prehistoric handprints placed in caves. Her father's boots were four hands high. Maybe five.

As a young girl, Emma had run around barefoot until she began to loathe any part of her that was uncovered, her face and hands first, her feet finally; and she realized her toughened undersoles had little to no sensation. Now her feet were both bony and tender and could feel the floor tremble when the train passed, three fields and one small woods away.

She herself was a residue, her life light as the light in her inherited house. Emma's mother had died in the bed she had no doubt grown to loathe, a bed full of him every night until her illness drove him out, lying there in a knot, staring up through the dark at death—who would not want it to come quick? Emma wondered whether her mother had ever had a moment of . . . exultation. Little cruelties cut her down. The rubadubdub of every day's labor, always going on as long as there was light. Same old cheap china on the table. The same old dust seeping in to shadow the mirrors and coat the sills. The same old rhubarb brought from the patch, the stored carrots and apples and sprouting potatoes. The same unrelenting sun in the summer. Then deep cold and blowing snow. The three of them in different corners of the house. Emma would sit on the floor of her room, reading, her back against a faintly warm radiator, afghan over her knees, squinting at the page through inadequate glasses. She would occasionally hear her mother sweeping or washing, or the rhythmic treadling of her sewing machine. Her father would be busy with his figures, rearranging, recalculating, hoping to improve the columns' bleak assessments, since outgo regularly threatened to overtake income. But they sewed their own sacklike dresses; they ate their cold stored root crops; they killed and plucked and cooked their own chickens, though Emma didn't eat dinner those nights, not since she'd fainted in front of a fistful of freshly withdrawn innards; they scavenged pieces of firewood out of their neighbor's woods; they picked berries and crab apples and dande-lion greens, and jarred elderberry and made apple jelly and canned beans and tomatoes, and even fed the chickens homegrown corn: so what did this outgo come to? Not much, her father allowed. But they were eating from their kitchen garden like squirrels and rabbits, out of the nut-and-berried woods like the deer. The soybeans weren't fertilized and they couldn't afford those newfangled chemicals. The only machine still working was her dad's arms and legs and cursing mouth.

on morning grass,

I've died too late into your life, her mother said to Emma, who was rocking slowly in the rocker by her bed. Emma wondered what she meant, it sounded like a summing up; but she knew an explanation wouldn't be agreeable to hear so she didn't ask for one; she didn't want to wonder either, but she was haunted by what seemed a sentence of some sort, and kept on wondering. Her rocking was not a rocking really. It was a little nervous jiggle transmitted to the chair. Emma would never have a husband to stare at her body, she had her father for that; she'd never have to do for anybody, never have to sew but-tons on a shirt or open her thighs or get him off in time to church. But her life would be like her mother's just the same. They'd endure until they died. That would be it. Over the world, as far as she could see, that was it.

The dying had enormous power. Emma wondered whether her mother knew it. Everything the dying said was said "deathbed." Everything the dying said was an accusation, a summation, a distillation, a confession. "I died too late into your life." Which was it? confession, distillation, delusion, summa-tion, provocation?

Her mother tried to get God to take her part against her disease, but churchgoing did no good; prayers went as unanswered as most mail; the days came and went and weren't appreciated. She couldn't keep anything in her stomach. She was in the bathroom longer than she was in bed. "Maybe I should be like Emma and not eat," she said. Was it a gift, to have been given a life like that? Close to no one. Never to see delight rise in another's eyes when they saw you. Dear Heavenly Father, let me suffer a little while longer. Let me linger in this vale of tears and torment. I have potatoes to fork and rinse, windows to wipe, dishes to do, rips to mend.

Her father fell over in a field. Nose down in the dirt. A dog found him.

At his funeral somebody said well, he died with his boots on, and some mourners appeared confounded by the remark, some looked puzzled, and some smiled as much as was seemly, but none of the mourners mourned.

The world was a mist and black figures slowly emerged from the mist as they had in one of the few movies she'd seen, when the townsfolk were bury-ing a family who'd been murdered by the Indians. It was a moist gray day and most people wore a dark coat against the chill. Emma in her horror held herself and stood far away from the hole so she wouldn't see them lower the man who'd brought her into the world and made her ashamed to be seen and hacked her ash to bits and cut the heads off chickens and left her a few acres of unkempt land and a dilapidated house. There was a hole in her memory now almost exactly his shape.

Emma sat on the front porch and greeted darkly dressed unaproned women while the men stood about the yard in awkward clumps waiting the decent interval. A few wives had brought casseroles of some kind. Emma never lifted the lids until she realized they'd expect their dishes to be returned. Then she dumped the spoiled contents in the meadow—smelling of mayon-naise and tuna—and wiped the bowls with grass. Forgot about them again. Only to come upon the little collection on a walk a week later. Now she couldn't remember to whom the bowls belonged. Emma huddled the crock-ery in a plastic sack and tottered the mile and a half she had to totter to reach the house of a neighbor she knew had brought something, and left the sack on the front steps. They had been trying to be helpful, she supposed, but what a trouble people were.

During the evening the air grew damper. Moonlight and mist, as Bishop wrote, were caught in the thickety woods like lamb's wool on pasture bushes. Except there was very little moonlight. It was the headlamp of the late train which allowed her to see the fog like gray hair in a comb, but only for a moment before all were gone: woods, fog, trainbeam, lamb's wool, gray hair, comb.

She sat in the same chair she'd sat in to greet grieving company, sat through an evening in which only the sky cared to snivel, and sat on after they'd left into the deep night's drizzle, hoping to catch her death; but in the morning, when the sun finally got through the fog to find her sitting in the same chair, as fixed as the leaves and flowers burned into the slats of its back, it flooded her cold wet lonely frightened immobile face impersonally, as though she were a bit of broken statue, and moved on to the pillars of the porch, knurled a bit to be fancy but picked out of a pattern book to be cheap, and then found a grimy windowpane to stain as if the grayed flush of dawn were drawn there. The sun made her open eyes close.

snow in still air,

The art of losing isn't hard to master. Emma remembered with gratitude that lesson. But she took it a step further. She lost the sense of loss. She learned to ask nothing of the world. She learned to long for nothing. She didn't require her knives to be sharp. Her knives weren't her knives anyway. She gave up property. She didn't demand dawn. When the snow came she didn't sigh at the thought of shoveling. There was no need for shoveling. Let the snow seal her inside. She'd take her totter about the house instead of the narrow path around the woods. She moved as a draft might from room to room. She ascended and descended the stairs as silently as a smell. Not to keep in trim. Not as if bored, caged, desperate. To visit things and bring them her silent regard.

Emma made her rounds among the mantises. Tending the garden in her teenage days, when she'd been put in charge of it, she would find a mantis at its deadly devotions. And she discovered that the mantis rarely ventured far from its holy place. *Mantis religiosa.* It slowly turned the color of its circumstances. There was one on the roof of the shed the shade of a shingle. Another among the squash as green as most weeds. Motionless, she watched the mantis watching, and now Emma understood the difference between its immobility and hers. The mantis was looking for a victim, her father was making his assessments, her mother was doing her chores, while Emma was watching . . . why? . . . she was letting the world in; and that could be done, she learned, anywhere, at any time, from any position, any opening—the circle of the shade's pull. She ate her fill of the full world.

No wider than a toothpick, a mantis would rest on a leaf so lightly it never stirred from the weight of the insect. The mantis rose and fell as the leaf did, a bit of leaf itself, its eye on the shiny line a little spider was lowering. Emma Bishop rose and fell as well, soft as a shadow shifting across the floor, weightless as a gaze, but as wide as a rug, as good underfoot, as trustworthy in the pot as tea.

Large snowflakes slid slowly out of a gray sky. A lot like a winged seed, they wavered as they came and lit on grass or late leaves still whole and white as doilies. They fell on her hair, clung to an eyelash, melted upon Emma's extended tongue so a thrill shivered through her and she blushed. She also tottered out in the rain when the rain was warm and fell in fat drops. Her cheeks would run and ears drip. And her hair would very slowly fill with wet, and whiten gradually the way her hair had grayed, till it became a bonnet, not her hair at all. Her outheld hands cooled until, like butterflies did a few times, the crystals lay peacefully on her palms.

Her father found out that, though Emma tended the garden, she didn't pull weeds or kill bugs. So he removed her from that duty and made her hold the guts he pulled from plucked chickens.

Elizabeth Bishop was a tougher type. She caught fish, for instance, and held their burdened-down bodies out at arm's length to study the white sea lice which infested them. She lived near water in Nova Scotia and the Keys and hung around fishhouses to note the glistening condition of the fish tubs, coated with herring scales, and the tiny iridescent flies that hover over them. Her father's slimed-on arm slid out of the cavity, his fist full of the chicken's life. He didn't look at Emma. He said: here, hold this. Could she now have enjoyed the mucus and the membranes, the chocolate and the rufous red of the liver and the . . . the white patches of fat like small snow on brick. The word was *gizzzzzzzzzardzzzs.*

Maybe not. But who had really reached sainthood in this life, and was willing to look on all things with equanimity?

Her totter took her along a lane where she'd dumped the funeral food, and there she found the cookware in an untidy pile like stones. "There's stillstuff-stuck on the sides of the Corning Ware. I don't care. Leave it there." The grass grows high at the side of the meadow. Already it's popping up between them. Let them lie. The life I missed because I was afraid. That's where we buried him. A dark day. Twilit from dawn to twilight, then, at twilight, it was night. These dishes remain to be done. His remains, his fists, are encased in a cheap box six feet in the earth, crabgrass over dirt, fog over grass, night sky over fog, blackest space. I'll take one home this time to soak in the sink. Where my thought of the poet had her sick. I alone know how glorious grime is. Go it alone. God. Go it alone.

I vowed I'd get good at it. Going alonely. Holding the bowl, with blades of grass fastened to its sides where I'd wiped it weeks past, I promised myself a betterment. They were both gone. I was free of ma's forlorn face, dad's rage. The house was mine, I reminded myself. And so it could stand nearly free of me. Stand and be. Recognized. Because I relinquished whatever had been mine. My thoughts I let go like lovebirds caged. One dish a day. I'll return them like pills. There was a nest-shaped dent in the grass where the bowl had lain. What an amazing thing! that such a shape should be at the side of a path between meadow and wood—the basin of a heatproof bowl like a footstep from the funeral.

Emma remembered, in the middle of that moment, while she was making a solemn promise to herself to do better, be better, become none, no one, the spring day she'd run into the woods to find bluebells and found instead the dogwood in bloom at the edge of a glade, each petal burned as if by a cigarette exactly as her poet, only that day discovered, had written in a poem, only that day read, in lines only that far reached and realized, before Emma's eye rose like a frightened fly from the dinner cloth.

So when the bowls were relatively rinsed she stacked them in a string sack, all six, with lids, so she tilted more than normally when she walked so many fields so many meadows to the nearest neighbor, and with a sigh and a sore arm set the sack down on the porch just so, so they'd find them soon enough, some wife and mother named not Nellie no Agatha, was that so? who would no doubt wash them all again and find good homes for them as if they were orphan kids. A tale they'd tell too to the ladies who had lent the dishes to Emma, foisted their food, their indifferent goodwill, their efforts of affection upon her. Yes, the ladies would laugh at least grin at the way they'd been returned, lumped in one sack like spuds, their pots, after so many weeks of wondering what . . . what was going on . . . and would . . . would they ever get them back.

The snow sidled out of a gray sky, and fell like ash, that slowly, that lightly, and lay on the cold grass, the limbs of trees, while the woods went hush and her quiet place grew quieter, as peaceful as dust; and soon everything was changed, black trunks became blacker, a dump of leaves disappeared, the roof of the shed was afloat in the air, the pump stuck up out of nowhere and its faint-handled shadow seemed the only thing the snow couldn't cover.

wounds we have had,

Emma Bishop had not been born on the farm but in a nearby town where five thousand people found themselves eating and sleeping and working, meeting and greeting, cooking and cleaning, going up and down, and selling and signing, licensing and opining, because it was the county seat. The farm was in the family. It belonged to Emma's great-aunt, Winnie, but when she died the farm, already run-down, fell further, and into her father's stubby unskilled mechanic's hands. Her father, when her mother met him, repaired tractors. Beneath the nail, his nails were black with green grease. Lo and behold, beyond Emma Bishop's richest imagining, her parents met, married, coupled, whereupon her mother bore, and brought a baby naked into the world, the way, it would later appear, Emma's father wanted her. Because the baby was inspected for flaws. No one found any.

Emma's mother was short slender wan, while her father was broad and flat across the front, knotty too, a pine-board kind of person. Emma, contrary to the core, was thin as a scarf and twice as tall, angular to contradict her father's bunchiness, given to swaying even when standing still, swaying like a tall stalk of corn in a field full of wind. It made her difficult to talk to, to follow her face, especially if you had to look up a little as her parents both did. Emma didn't have Marianne Moore's recessive features. Hers resembled Edith Sitwell's in being craggy.

Nevertheless, Marianne Moore saw into things, saw seeds in fruit, and saw how a tendril born of grape would wind itself like hair around a finger, cling to anything; or she would wonder what sort of sap went through the cherry stem to make the cherry red. Emma Bishop practiced by watching a worm walking, how it drew its hind end up into its middle, and then accordioned forward from the front. A rubber band could not do better. Leaving a small moist trail soon a light dry line lost on the limestone.

Her tree, where Emma went to read, was a tree of seed. It bore them in clumps, in clusters, in clouds. They were tapered like boat paddles. Her tree was very late to leaf, and every year her father would declare the ash had died, and indeed it was nothing but a flourish of sticks until, at last, fresh shoots appeared and the squirrels crept out on its branches to eat the tender stemtips. The ground around her tree would be littered with their leavings. While still small and green, seeds would begin to fall, and her father would say the ash was sick, because the seeds were so immature; but there were crowds, mobs of them left, dangling from every new twig like hands full of fingers. Moore called apple seeds the fruit within the fruit, but here the ash seeds hung in the air without the lure or protection of peel or pulp, just a thin tough husk which turned the color of straw and flew from the tree in the fall like shoutfuls of startled locusts.

The ash sucked all the water from the ground and shaded a wide round circle too where nothing much grew, a few baby ash of course, a weed or two, plantain principally, pushing up from the clay-gray earth to stand defiantly green between the roots. Its trunk was deeply furrowed, the bark itself barky, as if rain had eroded it. "This is the tree Satan's snake spoke from," Emma's father would say, his tone as certain as gospel. "It is the dirtiest tree on God's earth." The risen emblem of a fallen world.

The seeds would settle first, whirling up from the dry ground at a breath, stirred as the air stirred, and encircling the trunk with pods which curved gracefully from an oval head back to a needle-sized point, to lie in warm ocher layers like the tiniest of leaves. Her father cursed the tree as if it were littering a street against the law.

And quite a lot of little branches would break off and break a bit more when they hit the ground, causing her father still more annoyance, because the dead branches of this ash were dead in a thorough and severe way, dried as they were by the sky. Finally the five-leaflet leaves would begin to fall, the tree's seeds would come down in bunches, and everyone then knew autumn was over and that the sun always withdrew through the now bare branches, and so did the moon.

Her father said it was a moose maple and not an ash at all. Its wood is spongy, but brittle as briars. Emma protested. It was a green ash. She had made the identification. There was no moose maple in the book. That's what we call it hereabouts—a box elder, big weed, dirtiest tree. A true ash don't fall apart like that.

Despite her father's annoyance, Emma would sit upon a smooth bare root, her back against the trunk, surrounded by seeds and leaves, twigs and weeds, and read poetry books. If she'd been a boy, he might have beaten her. She could feel his eye on her, hard as a bird's. She weathered his rage as the tree weathered the wind. Then, one day, a branch, broken in a previous storm but caught by other branches, slipped out of their grasp and fell like a spear, stabbing her ankle with such a suddenness she screamed, feeling snake-bit. She saw blood ooze from the wound in astonishment, the stick lying near, stiff and dry, sharp where it had snapped. Emma bawled, not from pain or even shock, but because she'd been betrayed.

dust on the sill there,

Marianne Moore liked to use words like *apteryx* in her poems. Very mannered, her style. Edith Sitwell liked to too. Emma would suddenly say, "One fantee wave is grave and tall . . ." and suddenly sing, "The hot muscatelle siesta time fell. . . ." Her mother would hear her with astonishment, for Emma very rarely laughed, let alone sang. Even in church she just mouthed.

Now that she hadn't had to poison her mother or strike her father down in the field with the blade of a shovel, but was so alone even the chickens unfed had wandered off, she could have sung without surprising anyone, or sworn without shocking her father with unladylike language. She did sing sometimes inside herself. "In the cold, cold parlor my mother laid out Arthur. . . ." She didn't remember any more of that brutally beautiful poem. Words drifted into her eyes. When she was reading, it was always summer under the ash, and words fell softly through her pupils like ash soot pollen dust settling ever so slowly over hours over summer days a season even an entire lifetime that their accumulation was another cover. Solace for the skin.

She bore books out to the tree and made a pile. Her father glared. Why so many? Stick with one. One is plenty. But Emma couldn't stick to one. She'd begin "When night came, sounding like the growth of trees . . ." or "In the cold, cold parlor . . ." and she'd feel herself becoming tense, was it her legs folding as if up into her bottom like the worm, and her arms canting outward like the mantis that worried her? Emma had these flyaway eyes, and after a bit she'd skip to another page, or have to drop one book in order to pick up another. Edith would take Emma aback with beauty "sounding like the growth of trees." Emma'd have to stop, to repeat, to savor, to—in her head—praise, to wonder at the wonder of it, why was that Nova Scotia wake so devastating? not simply because it was being seen by a kid. "His breast was deep and white, cold and caressable." The way the boxed boy and the stuffed duck went into one another: that was making love the way she imagined it would be if it were properly done. Everyone was entered. No one was under.

A poem like the Nova Scotia poem—brief as it was—would sometimes take her weeks to read, or, rather, weeks to register all its words, and never in their printed order. That ordering would come later. One day, finally, she'd straighten the lines and march them as printed across her gaze. She could not say to her father when he glared at her, angry she knew because the books, the tree, her intense posture, the searing summer sky, were each an accusation, a reminder of another failure, that the words she read and fled from were all that kept her alive. "The mind is an enchanted thing like the glaze on a katydid-wing . . ." Words redeemed the world. Imagine! Like the glaze on a katydid-wing, sub . . . subdivided . . . sub . . . by the sun till the nettings are legion . . . the nettings are legion . . . Her father really should have kept the grease beneath his nails and never replaced it with plant smutch and field dirt. His world was mechanical, not organic. It was cause followed by effect, not higgledy followed by piggledy and the poke.

Her father's figure would appear to her, dark and distant, wading through beans. Emma tried to unresent her mother's failures too. Why hadn't her mother protested her father's cruel scrutinies? Even the browbeatings her mother received she endured in silence, though with drooping head. Why had Emma herself stood so still in his stare, less naked later with pubic hair? Skimpy. No fur there. She could have refused. Fled. Cried. She stood in the shed and screamed. She shrieked. She shrilled. But they were in the ground less likely than seeds to volunteer, to rebreed, pop up in a pot or rise from beneath bedclothes sheeted and disheveled, hearing her scream. That's all she did in the shed. And she went there less and less, needed that silly release less and less. She was even proud she could be so loud, slight and without a chest, weak and out of touch with speech.

Edith Sitwell had a lilt. She went ding dong. Did her verses breathe, Emily Dickinson wanted to know. "Safe in their Alabaster Chambers . . ." Hoo. "Untouched by Morning . . ." Emma was untouched. No man had ever laid a hand. Hardly her own, but once, curious, experimentally, secretive, ashamed, she felt herself as she supposed men did, and then withdrew in disbelief. To never again. "The meek members of the Resurrection . . ." Emma stood in the center of herself and slowly turned her attention. There were windows, sills, shades, beyond the windows a world, fields, the silhouettes of firs and oaks, a dark quick bird, and then a wall a corner crack and peel of plaster pattern of leaf and stem and flower too, counter of hardwood, wooden cabinets, one door ajar, dark as eyebrow, at the glass knob stop the little light left was captured there and the glass knob gleamed and its faint faint shadow, made light now not light's interruption, touched the soiled unpainted pine.

Mom and dad she never had await their resurrection, according to Emily. Grand go the years . . . ages . . . eons . . . empires . . . but only the words will arise, will outwear every weakness. Emma knew. That was why she waited for a line. Not an alabaster chamber or a boy's box—Arthur's coffin was a little frosted cake—but *Arthur's coffin.*

That was what the soul was, like the floor of a forest, foot of great tree, earth on which seeds leaves twiglets fell and lay a season for another season, all the eyelighted earheard words piled up there year after year from the first *no* to final *never.*

Her mother died of the chronics, her father of a fell swoop. Emma would become a certain set of words, wed, you might say, finally, and her flat chest with their warty nips placed next to Bishop's where Moore's had been. Her mother's face was closed as a nut, but you might say the same of Emma's too, who learned, as her mother doubtless had, to conceal her feelings for so long she forgot she had any.

Scream. The shed would seem to shiver with the sound. It was an awful makeshift, built of cast-off wood and some tin. Perhaps it was the tin that trembled. Hummed. Windows were unnecessary. There were parts between boards. A chicken might cluck till it was thwacked. Their bodies rocked on after. Upon her tree's stump, the tree of knowledge, blood was bled. She screamed because there was a world which contained such scenes though she also knew there was worse worse worse sorts of wickedness frequent in it.

dew, snowflake, scab:

Conversations, for instance, Emma never had. She didn't believe she could sustain one now even if the opportunity were offered, but at one time she thought she missed chatter, the sound of talk, laughter, banter, chaff. Her family exchanged grimaces sometimes; there'd be an occasional outburst of complaint; but mostly words were orders, warnings, wishes—stenographed. Emma thought her father often talked to himself. He'd sort of growl, his head would bob or wag, his lips tremble. Her mother had an impressive repertoire of sighs, a few gestures of resignation, frowns and sucked cheeks. No word of praise was ever passed, a grunt of approval perhaps, a nod, and either no shows of affection were allowed, or there was no affection to be displayed.

So Emma talked to the page. It became a kind of paper face and full of paper speech. "The conversations are simple: about food." "When my mother combs my hair it hurts." Emma, however, couldn't speak well about food. She no longer grew it. She couldn't cook it. She didn't eat it. And how could she respond to remarks about her hair. Emma unkinked her hair herself. So she at least knew what the pain of hair pulling was and how carrots felt. Wherever you are the whole world is with you. A nice motto. Emma Bishop applied herself. She worked hard, but without success at first. Her life's small space had no place for stars. A dusty boot, a mixing bowl, a backyard plot. Judge not. Another maxim. But the boot was her father's where his foot went and was shaped by how he walked; booted because of the manure, he said, though the pigeons didn't even shit on Bishop soil. The earth is dirt. That was his judgment of it, hers of him. "Illuminated, solemn." The fact was, Emma Bishop hated her mother for being weak, for giving in to her husband's minor tyrannies. Take the flat of the shovel to him when his back is turned. Instead, Emma's mother turned her own and disappeared into a chore as though on movie horseback. The spoon spun in the bowl like a captured bird.

When snow and cold kept them cooped, each of them managed most marvelously to avoid one another. If she heard her father climbing the front stairs, Emma used the back one. If her mother and father threatened to meet in the upstairs hall, one ducked into a bedroom until the other had passed. Her father would always appear to be preoccupied, his thoughts elsewhere, a posture and a look which discouraged interruption. The three of them really wanted to live alone, and Emma at last had her wish. Each of them hungered for the others' deaths. Now Emma was fed.

However, the habits of a life remained. Emma was haunted by them, and repeatedly found herself behaving as if she might any minute have to strip or encounter her mother like a rat on the cellar steps.

At more than one point, Emma pondered their acts of avoidance. And she concluded that each was afraid of the anger pent up inside like intestinal gas whose release would be an expression of noisy and embarrassingly bad manners. They also supposed that this swampy rage was equally fierce in others, and feared its public presence. With so few satisfactions, the pleasure of violence would be piercing, as if the removal of any player might redeem a dismal past, or create new and liberating opportunities, which of course it wouldn't . . . hadn't . . . couldn't. . . .

Occasionally they would have to go to town for various provisions. The tractor, their only vehicle, and very old, nevertheless purred. Emma and her mother rode in an old hay trailer, most unceremoniously, Emma with her legs dangling from the open end, which made her mother nervous. For these occasions, Emma would wear what her mother called "her frock." A piece of dirty burlap was thought to be her frock's protection from the soiled bed of the wagon, so she sat on that. And watched the dust rise languidly behind the wagon's wheels, and the countryside pass them on both sides like something on a screen. The nearby weeds were white as though floured.

For her birthday—twice—she'd been taken to a movie. The town had a small badly ventilated hall, poor sound, and a cranky projector. Actually, since they couldn't afford more than one ticket, you'd have to say Emma was sent to the movie. Both times her mother had warned her—both times to Emma's surprise—"Don't let anyone feel your knee." To Emma's nonplussed face her mother would reply: "It'll be dark, you see." Darkness and desire were, for Emma then, forever wed. The films impressed her mightily. Gaudy, exotic, splendid, they didn't at all resemble her daily life, but they were additional experience nevertheless, and showed that the strange and far away was as inexplicable as the common and nearby. Words on her pages, on the other hand, even when mysteriously conjoined, explained themselves. Moonlight and mist were mute. But a line of verse which described moonlight and mist caught in pasture bushes like lamb's wool, for instance, offered her understanding. A film might capture the fog as it crawled across the pasture, but there'd be no lamb's wool clinging to its images.

The movies weren't her world for another reason. The pictures, the figures, the scenes, the horses, the traffic passed like a parade. Highways ran into mountains, streams rattled over rocks and fell in foam. Clouds scudded across the sky, and their shadows dappled the ground. The sun set like a glowing stone. Emma's well went weeks without a lick of light, and the yard lay motionless under its dust and seeds, disturbed only by an occasional burst of breeze. The mantis waited, head kinked, hard-eyed. Her mother occupied a room as if she were household help. But Randolph Scott was out of sight in a trice. And all the sounds . . . the sounds were bright.

All the while she sat in this strange dark room with a few strange dark shapes, none of whom offered to touch her knee, and watched these grainy gaudy imaginary movements, Emma was aware that her father and her mother were out in the town's drab daylight, their shopping soon completed, waiting for the picture to be over so they could go home. They'd be stared at, their tractor and its wagon watched. As time and the film wore on, Emma became increasingly anxious. If she had any enjoyment from the show, it was soon gone. On the drive home, her mother would cover her sullenness with another coat.

Emma sat shaded from the hot summer sun by her ash–moose maple and went in her head to New Brunswick to board a bus for a brief—in the poem—trip, and view her favorite fog once again. By far her favorite fog. Yet it rendered for her her Iowa snow most perfectly. "Its cold, round crystals form and light and settle . . ." Here was at last the change: the flat close sky, the large flakes falling more softly than a whisper. Yet the snow would stay to crust and glare and deepen, to capture colors like lilac and violet because of all of the cold in those blues, and repeat them every day like her bread and breakfast oats. Settle in what? "In the white hens' feathers . . ." ". . . in gray glazed cabbages . . ." She couldn't get enough of that. ". . . in gray glazed . . . in gray glazed cabbages . . ." "on the cabbage roses . . ." The repetition enchanted her. So she repeated it.

As temporary as dew was, so they said—more meltable than oleo—the snow nevertheless stayed for months, covering the seeds which had lain for months on the hard dry monthslong ground. Then there'd be mud for months, oozy as oatmeal; whereas Randolph Scott would scoot from frame to frame like a scalded cat. Dew could be counted on to disappear by mid-morning. But you'd never sense when. What sort of change was change-less change—imperceptibly to dry the weeping world's eye—when Ann Richards rode through outfits faster than Randolph mounted his horse? And when Emma was wounded by her faithless moose maple, the scab formed so slowly it never seemed to.

By the shaded road, at the edge of a glade, in open woods, the mayapples rose, their leaves kept in tight fists until the stems reached the height of a boot and a bit, when each fist unfolded slowly to open a double umbrella a foot wide—hundreds of the round leaves soon concealing the forest floor. This was the rate of change Emma understood. Differences appeared after days of gray rain and a softening wind. As predictable as the train though. Then glossy white flowers would show up like tipped cups. Bluebells were bolder and would spread a blue haze over the muckier places. Cowslips her mother called them. But the mayapple's flower hung from a fork in the stem and well under the plant's big deep-green leaves. Finally a little jaundiced lemon-shaped fruit the size of an egg would form. At her father's insistence they'd gather a few peck-sized baskets and boil the nubbins into an insipid jellylike spread for bread.

Her father claimed the mayapple was rightly called a mandrake, but the plant didn't scream when Emma pulled a few from the ground, nor were its roots man-shaped; it grew far from the woodshed, their only gallows, and she doubted it had the power to transform men into beasts. Instead, it left some toilsome fruits to enlarge and encumber their larder.

Her father prowled the meadows and woods looking for edibles, herbs and barks he said were medicinal when turned into tea, vegetable dyes her mother would never use. Since these lands didn't belong to them, Emma felt uneasy about what she thought was a kind of theft: of nuts and berries, wild grapes and greens. Emma put no stock in her father's claim to understand nature, because he was at home and happy only around machines. His tractor was his honey.

Nor did her mind change much. It was like a little local museum. The exhibits sat in their cases year after year. Possibly the stuffed squirrel would begin to shed. The portraits continued to be stiff and grim. Until her poetry taught her to pay attention. And then she saw a small shadow—she supposed shame—pass across her father's face when he looked at her nakedness. Because she was hairing up, she supposed. And found grief beneath her mother's eye in a wrinkle. A hard blue sun-swept sky became a landscape. Even now, when they were both dead, it was still impossible to go in the shed except to scream, and, through the greater part of her growing up and getting old, from most things she still fled.

Was she screaming for the chickens or the tree?

As slowly as her scab, her father's resolution formed. The moose had wounded his daughter. It had to come down. After all, he enjoyed the solemn parental right of riddance.

light, linger, leave

Poets were supposed to know and love nature. "Nature the gentlest mother is." Purely urban or industrial poets were suspicious freaks. "Bumblebees creep inside the foxgloves, and the evening commences." She had taken the knowledge and the love for granted. "Carrots form mandrakes or a ram's-horn root sometimes." But then she learned that it was not good to be "a nature poet," and that descriptions were what girls did, while guys narrated and pondered and plumbed. Ladies looked on. Gentlemen intervened. "Nature is what we see—the hill—the afternoon—squirrel—eclipse—the bumble bee." Surely she was seeing herself as a gazer and seeking her salvation in sight. She was seeking to see with a purposeless purity, her intent always to let Being be, and become what it meant to become without worry, want, or meddlesome intervention. If anything were to alter, she must allow it to alter of itself; if anything were to freeze, even new-budded buds, she had to be grateful for that decision; if anything were to die, she'd delight in their death. For all is lawful process.

When Emma had reached such serenity, such selfless unconcern, she would be ready to disappear into her memorial dress, lie down in a sublime line of verse, a line by Elizabeth Bishop. Since she hadn't the art necessary to express the dehumanized high ground she aspired to, she would have to turn to someone who had that skill, if not such a successfully pursued impersonality. For who had? She

And the tree groaned and crashed with a noise of much paper being angrily wadded, as if God were crumpling the Contract. A cloud stood above the tree like the suggestion of a shroud to mark the spot and evidence the deed.

Miss Moore, in her silly round black hat, looking like the *Monitor*, or was it the *Merrimack*, her hands half-stuffed in a huge muff made of the fur of some poor beast, stared with consummate calm out of her jacket image at Emma. Not a mirror. Not naked but smothered in overcoat except for her pale face and pale throat. No sign of nips the size of dimes, or barely there breasts or bony hips or hair trying to hide itself in shame inside its cleft. A slight smile, calm demeanor, self-possessed. Light is speech, her poem like the camera said. "Free frank impartial sunlight, moonlight, starlight, lighthouse light, are language." But not firelight, candlelight, lamplight, flicker-given, waver-lovers. The firefly's spark, but not an ember's glow, not match flare or flashlight. Stood there. Aren't lies, deceptions, misgivings, reluctances, unforthcomings, language? Stood there. Stood there. Could one ever recover?

Chain saws her father understood. They wore like a watch a little engine.

The Bishops would dodge one another for days. Occasionally, Emma would catch a glimpse of her mother sitting in the kitchen drinking a little medicinal tea her husband had brewed to soothe her sick stomach. From her window she might see the tractor's burnt-orange figure chewing in a far field. She'd imagine cows they never had, stable a horse in their bit of barn, with a little lettuce and a carrot visit her hutch of rabbits, when a paste-white chicken would emerge from between piles of scrap wood and scrap metal as if squeezed from a tube.

Emma's eye would light; it would linger; it would leave. Life too, she was avoiding. There were days she knew the truth and was oppressed by her knowledge. These were days of discouragement, during which, almost as a penance, she would sew odd objects she had carefully collected to squares of china-white cardboard, and then inscribe in a calligrapher's hand a saying or a motto, a bit of buck-up or advice about life, which seemed to express the message inherent in her arrangement of button or bead or bright glass with a star shape of glued seeds, dry grass, or pressed petal, then, sometimes, hung from a thin chain or lace of leather, a very small brass key, with colored rice to resemble a fall tree, and a length of red silk thread like something slit.

Forget-me-not was a frequent sentiment.

These she would put in little handmade envelopes and leave in the post-box by the road for the postman to mail to the customers who answered her modest ad in *Farm Life*. Emma did not in the least enjoy this activity, which required her to look out for and gather tiny oddities of every tiny kind, to select from her lot those which would prove to be proper companions, envision their arrangement as if thrusting stems into a vase of flowers, and finally to compose a poem, a maxim, an epigram that suited their unlikely confluence. So on really down days she would do it, on days of rueful truth, which may account for the cruel turns her verses would sometimes take, veering from the saccharine path of moralizing admonitions into the wet depths of the ditch where the lilies and the cattails flourished, just to point out—because she couldn't help herself, because she had no prospects, no good looks, no pleasures herself—that the pretty was perilous, pleasure a snare, success a delusion, that beneath the bright bloom and attractive fruit grew a poisonous root.

Emma's sentiment cards were, however, a means to a greater good, for it was with the small sums her sales produced that she purchased her poetry: books by Bishop, Moore, Sitwell, and Dickinson, on-order volumes of Elinor Wylie and Louise Bogan, which, she would regularly realize, unaccountably hadn't come.

She shared grass-of-Parnassus with Elizabeth Bishop because it grew near the bluebell's sog, and in Nova Scotia too. It was a part of the inherent poetry of names: lady's slipper, sundew, jack-in-the-pulpit, forget-me-not, goldthread, buttercup, buttonbush, goldenrod, moonshine, honeysuckle, star grass, jewelweed, milkwort, butter-and-eggs, lion's heart, Solomon's seal, Venus's looking-glass, with some names based on likeness, plant character, or human attitude, such as virgin's bower, crowfoot, Queen Anne's lace, Quaker lady, wake-robin, love vine, bellwort, moneywort, richweed, moccasin flower, snakemouth, ladies' tresses, blue curls, lizard's tail, goosefoot, ragged robin, hairy beardtongue, turtlehead, Dutchman's-breeches, calico, thimbleweed, and finally bishop's cap; or because they were critter-connected much as mad-dog was, hog peanut, gopher-berry, goose tansy, butterfly weed, bee balm, moth mullen, cow-wheat, deer vine, fleabane, horseheal, goat's-rue, dogberry; or were based on location and function and friendliness like clammy ground cherry, water willow, stone clover, swamp candle, shinleaf, seedbox, eyebright, bedstraw, firewood, stonecrop, Indian physic, heal all, pitcher plant, purple boneset, agueweed, pleurisy root, toothwort, feverfew; or were simply borrowed from their fruiting season like the mayapple, or taken from root or stem or stalk or fruit or bloom or leaf, like arrowhead, spiderwort, seven-angled pipewort, foamflower, liverleaf, shrubby five-finger, bloodroot; while sometimes they gained their name principally through their growth habit, as the staggerbush did, the sidesaddle flower, prostrate tick trefoil, loosestrife, spatterdock, steeplebush, Jacob's ladder; although often the names served as warnings about a plant's hostility or shyness the way poison ivy or touch-me-not did, wild sensitive pea, lambkill, adder's tongue, poison flagroot, tearthumb, king devil, needle-grass, skunk cabbage, chokeberry, scorpion grass, viper's bugloss, bitter nightshade, and lance-leaved tickseed; or they were meant to be sarcastic and cutting like New Jersey tea, bastard toadflax, false vervain, mouse-eared chickweed, swamp lousewort, monkey flower, corpse plant, pickerelweed, Indiana poke, and the parasitic naked broom rape, or, finally, gall-of-the-earth—few of which Emma knew personally, since her father had made edibility a necessary condition for growth in the family garden, and had stepped upon her nasturtium although she'd argued for its use in salads. But peas, beans, and roots were what he wanted. Salads don't make or move a muscle, he said. So instead of cultivating or observing weeds and flowers in the field, Emma collected and admired and smelled their names and looked at their pictures in books.

"Pity should begin at home," Crusoe said, enisled as utterly as Emma was. Sometimes Emma tried to feel sorry for herself, but she scarcely had a self left or the energy available or what she thought was a good reason. Yes, she had barely made a mark on the world, her life was a waste, and she'd had little enjoyment; but on balance she had to admit she'd rather have read the word *boobs* than have them. A moose comes out of the woods and stands in the middle of the road. When the bus stops, it approaches to sniff the hot hood. "Towering, antlerless, high as a church, homely as a house . . ." Well, there were so many things she hadn't seen, a moose included, but she had envisioned that large heavy head sniffing the hot hood of the bus, there on that forest-enclosed road, at night, and understood the deep dignity in all things. "All things," she knew, embraced Emma Bishop's homely bare body standing in the middle of her room. Antlerless . . . boobless . . . with hairless pubes . . .

like a swatted fly,

Her Iowa summers were long and hot and dusty and full of flies. Ants and flies . . . In the early days, before unconcern had become endemic, her mother had insisted that the dinner table wear a white linenlike cover. Even dime-store glasses gleamed, cheap white plates shone, and tinny silverware glittered when they sat on the starchy bleached cloth amid their puddles of light-blue shadow and pale-gray curves. But through the ill-fit and punctured screens the flies came not in clouds but in whining streams. At breakfast it wasn't so bad. One or two or three had to be waved away from the oatmeal. Maybe, though, that's when Emma's aversion to food began. Flies. Raisins for the oats, her father said, waving his spoon. Sugar brings them. They love sweets, her mother said. They did seem to, and crumbs, on which they tried to stand.

These weren't manure breeders and the curse of cattle, but common blue-bottles, persistent and numerous in the peaceful sunshine. Emma would have to shake the cloth from the back porch before they'd fly. They seemed to like sugar, salt, bread crumbs, cereal, leavings of any kind, jam, and Emma learned to loathe them, their soft buzz and their small walk, their numbers and their fearless greed.

The deep dignity in all things—phoo—not in flies, not in roaches, not in fathers, not in dandelion greens.

"Nature is what we see—the hill—the afternoon—squirrel—eclipse—the bumble bee—nay—nature is heaven." Not a word about flies. There was a song about a fly, and that rhyme about the old woman who swallowed one, who knew why, but Emma could not recollect ever reading a poem about or even including a fly. Miss Moore wrote about horses, skunks, lizards, but not about flies. Emily D's little list included the bobolink, the sea, thunder, the cricket, but left out ants, mosquitoes, and of course flies. Good reason. Because she wanted to say that Nature was Heaven, was Harmony. Poetry, Emma would have to admit, later, recalling all those flies, poetry was sometimes blather. Her noble resolutions would also falter in front of the phenomenon of the fly. How could she honor anything that would lay its eggs in a wound? They carried diseases with more regularity than the postman mail, and they lived on leavings, on carrion, horse droppings, dirt. Like sparrows and pigeons. Phoo indeed.

Hadn't she lived on leavings too?

The mantis would close her forelegs like a pocketknife and eat a wasp a fly a lacewing in a trice. She'd rise up to frighten the wasp to a standstill, giving it her triangulating stare, and then strike so swiftly her claws could be scarcely seen, nails on all sides, the hug of the iron maiden.

Nature was rats and mice, briars and insect bites, cow plop and poisonous plants, chickens with severed heads and minute red ants swarming over a stump soaked in blood. It was the bodies of swatted flies collected in a paper bag.

The swatter, an efficient instrument, was made of clothes-hanger wire and window screen trimmed with a narrow band of cloth which bore the name of a hardware store. Emma became an expert, finally, at something. Sometimes she would hit them while they were still in the air and knock them into the wall, where she'd smack their slightly stunned selves into mush. Even so, they were clever little devils and could sense the swatter's approach, even though it was designed to pass without a wake or any sound through the air. They knew a blow was coming and would almost always be taking off when the screen broke their wings.

Emma killed many on the kitchen table, sliding the carcasses into a paper sack with the side of the swatter. It occurred to her that there was no word for the crushed corpse of a swatted fly. Her father liked to swing his right hand across the cloth and catch one in his closing fist, a slight smile slowly widening on his face like the circle of a pebble's plop. Where's your sack, he'd say, and when Emma held it out he'd shake the body from his palm where it was stuck. Once in a while, with that tiny smile, he'd try to hold his fist to Emma's ear so she could hear the buzz, but she would leave the room with a short cry of fear, her father's chuckle following like a fly itself.

After they'd eaten, Emma would clear the dishes away and wait a bit while the flies settled in apparent safety on the crumbed and sugared cloth. Her mother sweetened her tea with a careless spoon. Even the herbals her husband sometimes brewed for her she honeyed up one way or other. The flies would land as softly as soot. They'd walk about boldly on their sticky little feet with their proboscises extended as though requiring a cane. Her father was pleased to explain that flies softened their food with spit so they could suck it up.

Emma liked to get two at once. Each swat would bestir some of the others and they'd whiz in a bothered zigzag for a while before trying to feed again, no lesson learned, the carnage of their comrades of little concern, although a few would remain at work even when a whack fell within a yard of their grazing.

Flies seemed to flock like starlings, but the truth was they had no comrades, no sense of community. Occasionally, a crippled one would buzz and bumble without causing a stir, or a green-bottle arrive in their midst to be met by colossal indifference. Standing across from the center of the table, Emma would slap rapidly at each end in succession while uttering quiet but heartfelt *there*s each time: there and there and there.

Oh she hated the creatures, perhaps because they treated the world as she was treated. It was certainly out of character for Emma to enjoy bloodshed. However, her father approved of her zeal, and her mother didn't seem to mind, except

trace to be grieved,

for the little red dots their deaths left on the tablecloth. They'd accumulate, those spots, until their presence became quite intolerable to her mother, and she would remind Emma how hard it was to get those spots out, and about the cost of bleach, and how she hated that bag with its countless contents, she felt she heard a rustle from it now and then, it gave her the creeps. Emma wondered what, in her mother, creeps were. Later, when her mother was ill always, and vomiting a lot, Emma thought that perhaps the creeps had won out.

When the fly was flipped from the table into her sack, it would almost always leave that reminder behind, a red speck as bright as the red spider mite though larger by a little. And after the evening meal, Emma would enter a dozen specks and sometimes more into her register.

Where were they coming from? the compost heap? Her father said he saw no evidence of it. Her mother shook her head. Somewhere was there something dead? Her father hadn't encountered anything, and he walked the land pretty thoroughly. From as far away as the woods? Her mother shook her head. Well, Emma wondered, if the breeding of these flies was a miracle, God was certainly wasting his gifts. God is giving you something to do, her father said.

There was something in Emma which made her want to keep count, and other things in Emma which were horrified by the thought.

Days drew on, mostly with a monotony which mingled them, so that time seemed not slow, not fast, just not about. And she failed grades and advanced anyway, and grew like a skinny tree to be stared at, and became increasingly useless, as if uselessness were an aim. Why, her father complained, wouldn't Emma attack those bugs in the garden when she was so murderous about flies. As if he'd failed to notice that Emma had stopped swatting them many months, years, failed grades ago. Things went on in their minds, Emma imagined, out of inertia. Memory was maybe more than a lot of little red dots. The swats were still there, swatting. The paper sack still sat in a kitchen chair like a visitor. And Emma stayed on the page even when all her books were closed. The cloud

The shed got built about the ash stump. Emma could hear the hammering. Built of limbs and logs, it leaned to one side, then another. Had her father any interest in the number of nails he'd hammered while the ash shack was going up? Did he know how long the walk to the mailbox was? how many yards? Without books, Emma couldn't disappear into them. So she began to make and mail her memory cards, her versified objects, receiving for them a few dollars, and then, with this slim income, to order books of poetry by Elizabeth Bishop from an Iowa City shop. It was a great day when

POEMS

North & South

A Cold Spring

arrived, the title typed on a chartreuse ginkgolike leaf lying across the join of two fields, one white for northern snow, she supposed, the other blue for southern seas. The flap copy was typed too, and there were warm recommendations from Marianne Moore and Louise Bogan as well as the usual guys. Emma opened the book and saw a poem on a page like treasure in a chest and closed the book again and opened it and closed it many times. She held it in her two hands. Finally, it seemed to open of its own accord. She began "The Monument." Page 25. Yes, she remembered. Even the brackets [25]. "Now can you see the monument?" She could. She could see it. "It is of wood built somewhat like a box." Yes, Emma saw it. Her eyes flew flylike to the yard where the shed stood. It was a revelation.

Later on there would be others.

She turned the page and read the conclusion. "It is the beginning of a painting," the poem said, "a piece of sculpture, or poem, or monument, and all of wood." All of ash. "Watch it closely."

Emma's father probably didn't care whether she found out or not. He probably neglected to tell her he was intercepting her mail, whether going in or going out, just because he didn't care, one way or the other. He simply piled it up—the square envelopes with their cards of sewn- and glued- and inked-on sentiments and emblems, those with a few customer requests, some with simple sums inside them, a bookstore order—higgledy-piggledy on a small oak table in the room he was sleeping in now that his wife was ill and vomitous. That's where, through an open door, Emma saw her envelopes, looking otherwise innocent and unopened, and said aloud in complete surprise: that's why I never got my May Sarton.

She did not try to retrieve them. To her, they were dead as flies, leftovers from a past life. They almost puzzled her, they seemed so remote from the suspended condition she was presently in, although not that many weeks had passed, she guessed, since she'd composed her last card: four hard green pea gravels placed like buttonholes inside a wreath of mottled mahonia leaves, stained as though by iodine and flame. In a kind of waking dream, Emma tottered the hundred and more yards to where the postbox leaned from a tuft of weed at the roadside, and opened it on empty. She held on to the lid as though it might fly up, and stared hard into the empty tin, more interested in the space where the confiscation had taken place than in the so-called contraband. Empty. Its emptiness was shaped from zinc. zzzzzz . . . in . . . cckkkk. Emma knew at last something for certain: her father was poisoning her mother.

Well, it was no business of hers.

She closed the mailbox carefully so none of its emptiness would leak out.

Indeed, her mother rasped to her rest in a week's time. Her father rolled her mother in the sheets and then the blanket from her bed and laid her at length, though somewhat folded—well, knees a good ways up—in a wooden footlocker. He poured a lot of mothballs in the crannies. We won't be needing those, he said, fastening the lid with roofing nails. He slid the locker down the front stairs and lugged the box, cursing because it was heavier than he expected and awkward to carry, to the back of the wagon—lucky the wagon was small-wheeled and low—where he propped one end and lifted the other, then pushed the locker in. He never expected Emma to help. At helping she was hopeless. That's enough for one day, he said. I got to scout out a good place.

He went inside and washed all the household dishes. Grief, Emma decided, was the only explanation.

The next day she saw her father's distant figure digging in a far field. He appeared to be digging slowly because he dug for a long time.

Emma's head was as empty of thoughts as the mailbox. There was no reason to stand or sit or walk.

Got my exercise today, he said.

Marianne Moore and Elizabeth Bishop were both dead. Edith Sitwell too. Elizabeth Bishop just keeled over in her kitchen. Nobody knew. Her poems couldn't purchase her another hour.

I've got to figure how to get her in, her father said. Can't just roll her over. A fall like that might break the box open. We'll do it tomorrow.

Her father found an egg, which he had for breakfast. Emma rode in the back of the wagon with the coffin and an ironing board. The tractor dragged the wagon roughly over the plowed ground. Then reluctantly through the marshy meadow. Smoother movement steadied her horizon. Emma remembered the Randolph Scott movie. Her father had chosen a spot near the trees which appeared to have no distinction. Earth was heaped neatly on both wide sides. Emma looked in the hole. "Cold dark deep and absolutely clear."

Her father backed the wagon up to an open end of the pit. Then he pried the box up with a crowbar and forced the ironing board under it. He never expected Emma to help. He steadied the box on the board as it slid down the board from the wagon. It was, Emma realized, a mechanical problem. The board then was lowered into the grave, and the box once more sent on its skiddy way. In a cant at the bottom, her father wiggled the board out from beneath the box so at last it lay there, as settled as it was going to get. The zinc-headed nails reflected a little light.

Supposed to say a few words, her father said, so why don't you?

Poetry doesn't redeem, Emma thought. Saintliness doesn't redeem. Evening doesn't redeem the day, it just ends it.

Her father waited with a fistful of dirt ready to fling in the hole.

She was small and thin and bitter, my mother. No one could cheer her up. A dress, a drink, a roast chicken were all the same to her. She went about her house without hope, without air. Her face was closed as a nut, closed as a careful snail's. I saw her smile once but it was not nice, more like a crack in a plate. What on earth had she done to have so little done for her? She sewed my clothes but the hems were crooked.

While Emma was silent a moment, trying to remember something more to say, to recite, her father released his fistful of earth and he went for the shovel. He shoveled slowly, as if his back hurt. Dirt disappeared into dirt. The morning was cloudy but the grave was cold and dark and not so deep as it had been. The nails went out—animal eyes in a cave. Layer after layer: sheet blanket mothballs board, earth on earth on earth. Too bad we couldn't afford to do better by her, her father said, but we didn't do too bad. Emma realized he hadn't cared what her words were, probably hadn't heard. Words were one of the layers—to ward off what?

They hadn't any prayers. Emma hated hymns. Hymns weren't private enough. And you were told which one to sing. This morning, please turn to [25]. The grave filled and a little mound rose over it, the soil looking less raw, more friable. Emma rode back to the house alongside the ironing board, which was quite dirty and bedraggled. The board bounced as it hadn't bounced coming out, when it was wedged. Emma tottered to the mailbox and looked in. That was how it was inside the box, she supposed. Empty, even though

In the days, the weeks, the month which followed, Emma disappeared almost completely into her unattachments. She freed herself of food, of feeling, father. The fellow was a wraith. She was a shadow no one cast. He no longer farmed, though he often stood like a scarecrow in the field. Grief, Emma decided, was the explanation. But his grief was no concern of hers. She thought about freeing herself from verse when she realized she always had been free, for she had never respected, never followed, the form or been obedient to type.

She waited for the world, unasked, to flow into her, but she hadn't yet received its fine full flood. What if it weren't a liquid, didn't flow, but stood as if painted in its frame? What if it were like a fly indifferent to its own death? No matter. She was freeing herself of reflection. All of a sudden, she believed, the lethal line would come: "The dead birds fell, but no one had seen them fly. . . ." Perhaps it would be that one. So what if it was shot from a sonnet. The only way flies could get into a poem would be as a word. "They were black, their eyes were shut, and no one knew what kind of birds they were." Each night, night fell in huge drops like rain and ran down the eaves and sheeted across the pane. He'd move somewhere in the house. He'd move. She'd hear. "Quick as dew off leaves." The sound will be gone in the morning.

Mother beneath the earth. Others are, why not she? He waits in the soybean field for me. I must carry the shovel out to him. It is thin as I am.

Almost as worn, as hard. Mother has no marker. Many lie unknown in unsigned graves. Might we hear mother rustling under all her covers, trying to straighten her knees? To spend death with bended knee. He'll never mark her. The mound will sink like syrup into the soil. Weeds will walk. Perhaps black wood-berries will grow there as they do in Bishop's poem. My steps are soundless on the soft earth.

Emma struck her father between his shoulder blades with the flat of the spade. She hit him as hard as she could, but we can't suppose her blow would have amounted to much. She heard his lungs hoof and he fell forward on his face. Emma flung the spade away as far as she could, a few feet. What can you see now, she wondered. Or did you always see dirt?

She hadn't considered that a blow meant as a remonstrance might have monstrous consequences. She bounced floatily back to the house somewhat like a blown balloon. That's it: rage redeems. What does? evening.

And evening came. The dead birds fell. Found in the field. She hadn't missed him a minute. She hadn't for a moment worried about how angry he would be, or how he might take his anger out on her, so uppity a child as to strike her grieving father in the back. Found facedown. After a rainstorm. Heartburst. Creamed corn is a universal favorite. Dark drops fell. The field was runneled and puddlesome. Emma peered more and more through the round thread-wound shade pull. And felt the flow. The world was a fluid. Weights have been lifted off of me. I am lonely am I? as a cloud

Emma was afraid of Elizabeth Bishop. Emma imagined Elizabeth Bishop lying naked next to a naked Marianne Moore, the tips of their noses and their nipples touching; and Emma imagined that every feeling either poet had ever had in their spare and spirited lives was present there in the two nips, just where the nips kissed. Emma herself was ethereally thin, and had been admired for the translucency of her skin. You could see her bones like shadows of trees, shadows without leaves.

Some dreams they forgot. But Emma Bishop remembered them now with a happy smile. Berry picking in the woods, seeing shiny black wood-berries hanging from a bough, and thinking, don't pick these, they may be poison . . . a word thrilling to say . . . *poison* . . . us. Elizabeth Bishop used the phrase "loaded trees," as if they might like a gun go off. At last . . . at last . . . at last, she thought: "What flowers shrink to seeds like these?"

dot where it died.

The Iowa Review, 1994
Published in *Cartesian Sonata*, 1998

THE PIANO LESSON

Mr. Hirk had been found living in penury at the edge of town, his liveli-hood, as meager as it had been, taken from him by the stiffness in his fingers and the popularity of the guitar, which could apparently be played by sociopaths without any further training, its magnified twings and twangs emerging from an electrical outlet as if the little holes spoke for appliances of all kinds and for unoiled engines everywhere. Perhaps Miriam pursued the problem with more determination than she did most things because her husband had possessed some small skill with the fiddle, and as a mother she wanted to find in her son something of that talent, since she saw in Joey oth-erwise nothing of his father that she wished to see, only his ability to mimic and to mock, especially after she had to endure the fury and flounce of Joey's sister when he pretended to twirl her baton, pucker up to kiss her date, or slide about in a pair of socks to a tune she had never heard.

In any case, Miriam gossiped around until Mr. Hirk's odd name came up. To Joseph it had to seem to be a motherly whim that became a parent's punishment, because, quite apart from the lessons, which were by definition disagreeable, Mr. Hirk was a hideously misshapen man, bent and gnarly, with hands like two ill-fitting boots. He held a pencil by its unsharpened end and poked the keys with the eraser. The poking was so painful to Mr. Hirk it seemed that the sounds themselves were protests, and they were produced with rests between them marked by sighs and groans, not by signs or words of instruction: *tangk aah tongk ooh tingk oosh*. Perhaps Joey's ear-to-finger method was the only one with a chance to achieve results.

For all Joey saw, Mr. Hirk's house had just one square room whose several small windows were hidden by huge plants, a feature that Miriam found reassuring. Wide thick fleshy leaves intercepted what of the sun there was, so that greenish shadows were the ghoulish consequence when the day's light was bright. These shadows came in shades of several kinds and seemed to fall with great reluctance as if lying down on things the way Mr. Hirk had to—awkwardly, slowly, and with groans. A gooseneck lamp with a low-watt bulb hung over the playing surface, always on, always craning its brassy cord in the same curve, causing the black keys to cast in turn a small-ish almost dainty darkness of their own. Yussel Fixel saw torn wires and a violence-infested space into which he was being asked to submerge his fingers, so at first he poked them in and out at great speed.

A few pieces of furniture that Joseph Skizzen would later recognize as in the style of mission oak gloomed in those corners the piano didn't occupy, and his feet often scuffled with a rag rug. Dim walls held dimmer portraits up to failing eyes. Dust kept time, wafted as if on sound. Nothing was propi-tious. Yet when Joey lifted the lid of the piano bench as Mr. Hirk instructed him, he saw sheets of music whose character was heralded by the picture of a canoe on a moonlit lake or that of a lady in a dress with a preposterous behind, perhaps even hers, or a boy and a girl on a two-seated bike or, better, in a merry Oldsmobile. He practiced scales, of course, pursuant to the mas-tery of "Indian Love Call" or "Song of India" or "A Bicycle Built for Two."

Perhaps Joey began by protecting the broken keys from the light that played over the board itself; or maybe "Song of India" was easy to remem-ber, as was "Goodbye to Naples," a tune in Italian Caruso sang when Mr. Hirk wound his Victrola. Joey would never understand how his pounding managed to make any music at all, nor would Mr. Hirk let on that his pupil had accomplished anything harmonious either, for he was always critical, although Joey's facility must have astonished him. He taught doubled over as if in pain from what Joey and the piano played, so to be censorious he need only point to his posture. You must woo the keys, he would growl, poking them with his pencil. Here is your voice. The music must sing through your fingers. The tunes he used to tempt Joey into practicing were simple, from another age, before bombs, Joey ignorantly thought, when women wore fluffily cute clothes and lived in rose arbors or kept birds that were blue; back when the world rhymed and strummed, tapped its feet and tickled the ivories.

Mr. Hirk saw that Joey sat forward on the bench when he began to play, and this pleased him. Joey's posture did not. You are not the tower of Pisa. Do not lean, do not lurch, do not slump, do not wiggle, Mr. Hirk would admonish. Only Pisa can prosper by tilting. Arms—arms at right angles—so—straight to the keys—see—back straight. Why must boys bend!

When you give another kid the finger—you know what I speak about—

up-up-up yours, that sign? Mr. Hirk could not make the gesture. The thumb does not go up yours. The first finger does not go up yours. The middle finger—yes—because it does go up. It does. All alone it goes. So every note has a finger for it. Your hands do not reach the keys higgledy-piggledy, this way or that, but in the most efficient way to press down upon them—just right. The piano is a fancy gadget—hear that!—but you are not a gadget, and your fingers must be suitable, supple, suitable, strong yet tender, suitable, soft, as on a nipple, swift like a snake's strike. *Zzing!*

Joey had one kind of harmony with Mr. Hirk neither of them understood. When Mr. Hirk showed him a clawlike fist, Joey knew at once he was to splay his fingers. Mr. Hirk didn't think Joey's reach was wide or flexible enough. When he banged with a book, Joey softened his touch, and when Mr. Hirk was still, so still he clearly meant to be still, Joey sped. The piano was small and seemed old as its owner. Its tone was weak and hoarse, with a scratchy undercoat. Yet the sounds it made were Joey's sounds, and he adored them. They might have come from a record made before recordings had been invented.

"Daisy . . . Daisy . . . ," Joey would sing to his inner ear while his fingers felt for the equivalents. I am only pretending to play, he boasted, feeling that he was putting one over on his mom as well as Mr. Hirk. However, Mr. Hirk knew exactly what was going on, and to Joey's surprise he approved. Suppose you are playing a Beethoven sonata—as if that could ever be, Mr. Hirk said. What are you going to remember—the notes? No. The tune. In your head is the tune like a cold. Then your fingers follow. And you play the notes.

Many of Mr. Hirk's records, which sat in a dusty stack near the Victrola, had, to Joey's surprise, only one side. Yes, one side was smooth as pine. And they were heavy as plates. Empty plates. But if you got a record turning, a voice, like a faraway bird, high and light and leaping, somersaulting even, certainly atwitter, would come into the room. Amelita Galli-Curci, Mr. Hirk would say hoarsely yet in some awe, as she began. Joey had never heard the pureness of purity before. It was the soul, for sure, or the sound of angels, because weren't they birds? and didn't they dwell in a hidden sky? It was called "The Bell Song," the song she sang, though there was another aria a girl named Gilda was supposed to sing about someone whose very name had smitten her as by a stick—so suddenly—with the stunning blow of love. It was a song that would be overheard just as Joey was hearing it, yet that hearing would be followed, according to Mr. Hirk, by a consternation on the stage quite unlike the contentment that Joey felt during its blissful moments of performance.

The pedals, the pedals were a mystery. They were so far away from the keys, from the strings, from the place the music rose from; they were so hidden and other, that Joey fought them, tromped upon them, kicked them in their sides. Joey thought Mr. Hirk was cursing him at first, but he was saying, "Damp . . . damp," to no avail. Finally, he shouted, "Forget the pedals." "They wet the notes," he managed to explain. "Play to clear skies. Clear skies."

The tacky church Miriam took her children to had not a single spear of light, no rebounding shadows, no mystery, no majesty, no music of note. The congregation sang almost as badly as the choir, and cliché determined the selection of hymns. The services were in an inept Latin and the acolytes always a step late, as if they had fallen asleep. Catholics had not prospered here. The county and its seat was filled with Amish, odd Protestants, slow roads, bad organs, and poorer organists.

Mr. Hirk honeyed up to him during Joey's senior year. Joey would simply show up and play, mostly something he'd heard on the radio or a few things he'd begun by improvising, and then they would both sit in the cool gloom and listen to the Victrola that Joey had begun winding up because Mr. Hirk's fingers were presently incapable: Emma Calvé, Galli-Curci, the stentorious Caruso, and "Home Sweet Home" by Nellie Melba. Mr. Hirk no longer marked time by banging even a thin book. Now, when Joey left, with a gratitude that exceeded any he had ever felt, he would squeeze Mr. Hirk's upper arm (because he didn't dare put pressure on him anywhere else); Mr. Hirk would sigh hoarsely and watch Joey bike, it must have seemed nimbly, away, leaving Mr. Hirk alone in his room with his body's disability and his machine's recalcitrance until another Saturday came along. Joey always cranked the Victrola one more time before he left, so a few sides could be managed if Mr. Hirk could spindle a record—hard to do with his crabbed hands growing crabbier by the week. Joey rode off to an era of LPs, vinyl, and other speeds, but only Mr. Hirk had Olive Fremstad and her sound—Calvé's, Caruso's sound—sounds—hollow, odd, remote—that created a past from which ghosts could not only speak to admonish and astound, they could sing again almost as they once sang, sang as singing would never be heard sung again, songs and a singing from somewhere outside the earth where not an outstretched arm, not a single finger, could reach or beckon, request or threaten or connive.

If Joseph Skizzen later could imagine his mother, with whom he had lived so much of his life one would think he'd not want to add another sight or an additional thought of her to his consciousness; if he could clearly picture her in her culottes and gloves grubbing in her garden, literally extracting coiled white webworms from the soil and flipping them indifferently into a coffee can filled with flat cheap beer (only one moment of many he might remember), it was partly because, at the commencement of his piano lessons, he had begun envisioning Mr. Hirk, who had also unwittingly given him life, painfully bulked in a bulky chair or doubled up in a daybed he could no longer refold, waiting through the hours for Joey's bike to skid in the gravel before his door. It was a picture that prompted him not to ignore his pedals but to push hard, hurrying to arrive and kick his kickstand into place, to knock and enter Mr. Hirk's house all at once, to say "Hiyuh, Mr. Hirk, how goes it?" and slap his happy hand down on the piano bench before sitting there himself to play a new tune he'd heard that week on *Your Hit Parade,* a song already at number 7 although it was the first time for its appearance on the list. Mr. Hirk would pretend to hate the new stuff—trash and drivel and noise, he said, or treacle and slop and lies—but he would listen as if only his large ears were alive. Joey would then play the new hit from the week before, going back over his own list, making the slim recital last, turning it into his lesson, performing each of the songs on the sheets in the bench, and ending, as the order firmed itself, with "Danny Boy," as if he knew where it belonged, and without being the least embarrassed by its schmaltz, its treacle, or its prevarications.

It had to happen. One Saturday afternoon, searching for a football game, Joey tuned in the Metropolitan Opera's matinee during a moment when all its throats were rapturous. His mother stood in the doorway, somewhat dazed herself, because her intention had been to ask him to turn down the volume. The voices weren't of tin but of gold, and the orchestra was full, not a fiddle and a drum or a faint hinky-tink piano. Even Miriam sat and listened, too indifferent to her hands to fold them in her lap, until the evident sadness of events withdrew her. Neither had the slightest idea what was going on until between acts a commentator, with a voice melting over its vowels like dark chocolate, recited the plot as it was about to unfold. The tenor, it turned out, would be in a jail cell awaiting execution, and the act would open an hour before dawn at an artillery emplacement at the walls of a castle overlooking Rome. Rome! The audience will see the Vatican in the distance, the announcer says. Then, after an orchestral interlude, with the song of a shepherd boy barely audible in the distance, the tenor, told he has but an hour left to live, will be brought to the battlements, where he will write loving last words to his opera singer while sitting at a wooden desk set to one side of the stage. He writes something splendid, Joey remembered, about the shine of the stars perfuming the world. Of course the tenor would sing the words in the moment that he wrote them. Here, in this magical realm, singing words were all there were.

Joey heard everything happen as it had been foretold. The tenor's voice soared despite its despair, and Joey felt his own throat ache. It was a moment in which sorrow became sublime and his own misfortunes were, momentarily, on someone else's mind.

Now when he had a lesson, he would ask Mr. Hirk his opinion of the singers of today, not all of whom Mr. Hirk loathed; indeed, there were a few he praised. Mr. Hirk was impatient with Joey because, after all their sessions, his improvising was not improving anything but his ability to mimic. Although Mr. Hirk formed his sentences with reasonable clarity, his words emerged as if they too were rheumatic, bent a bit, their heads turned toward the ground, their rears reluctant to arrive. No . . . noth . . . nothing gained. You are copying the cat as if—that way—you could become one. Shame. You are hitting the keys a bit like my stick here, Mr. Hirk complained, when your fingers—your fingers, young shameful man—should sing; you should feel the song in their tips—on the ball where the ink stain blues it—like a tingle. Your technique—oh God—is terrible. You need to do Czernys . . . and . . . and I don't have any for you, not a page. I am a poor teacher. Naw. Nothing can be gained. I couldn't sing or whistle them. They are not for copy, the Czernys. They are for the fingers like lifting weights. Which you either do, or you don't do. Czernys. So you either get strong in the fingers or you remain weak . . . and if in the fingers, then in the head.

What Mr. Hirk hated most about Joey was his forearm. Do not move the forearm. Forget the forearm. From side to side from the wrist the fingers find their way, kneading the notes—your hands must be big slow spiders out for a walk.

Early on Mr. Hirk had grasped Joey's hands with his voice. Show me your nails! Show me! They're bitten! Look at them, poor babies. That is no way. Are you a beaver in a trap to be gnawing at yourself? Nails should never be long—short is wise—never so long they click on the keys, so they interfere with your stroke—no—but not bitten, a bad bad habit—they are not to be chewed like a straw. Nails are to be nurtured, nicened. Yes. Filed with your mother's file. Not long like a lady's but smooth, short, and smoothly rounded like the moon that is in them. That is the way. Remember. Short, round, smooth. Better if they're polished like flute keys. Hooh, he would conclude, exhausted.

Dressing Debbie was getting expensive, and Miriam felt that Joey's progress was being hampered by Mr. Hirk's physical impediments. To the point of pointlessness, she thought. Joey looked forward now to his miniconcerts, but he could not protest his mother's decision even if it was not adequately based or sincerely made. Joey was to inform Mr. Hirk on Saturday next that the present lesson was to be the final one. This, Joey had no desire to do. You hired him, you should fire him, he told his mother in the most aggrieved tone he could muster. It makes no sense for me to make a special trip just to do that, she answered in what would be her last reasonable voice. You send him his money by mail, Joey argued, why not end it the same way? That would be cold and unfeeling, she said sternly, that would be inconsiderate and impolite, even rude. Shame on you, she said. On me? Joey was unusual in his anger. Mr. Hirk is a sick old man! He has no income! He hasn't even one Czerny. He lives mostly in the dark waiting for me to come and play. I give him that relief. This was said with pride. Now you want to take his single pupil and his only pleasure away. Joey was embarrassed by his own heat. Such novel opposition was quite beyond Miriam's understanding. It made her furious. She blamed his poor upbringing on America. As someone who had been browbeaten, she could browbeat now with assurance, and she could be furious with Joey without worry because, though Joseph Skizzen was of the male sex, he was still a Joey. Ah, how you overcount yourself. How do you know what that man's pleasures are! Joey's stiff face told her that his certainties were unchanged. Then say nothing, just don't go again, you obstacle, she shouted. Whatever you do, I won't mail another fee. She ended the argument but not the issue by leaving the room in a huff that would have seemed more genuine if it hadn't had wheels.

Joey knew now that the singers on Mr. Hirk's old records were ghosts in truth, though he did not love them less for that. And Mr. Hirk had begun telling him of other singers, such as Marcella Sembrich, whom Joey had not heard, and how she had studied for years with an old piano teacher who discovered and developed her voice by taking her, willy-nilly, to the best teachers. Mr. Hirk was a bike tire turning in gravel—hard to understand—but Joey listened to his history of Marcella Sembrich as if she were a star of film, an actress of dangerous beauty. Indeed, Marcella Sembrich was her stage name, not her real name, Mr. Hirk told him. Her real name was Marcellina Kochanska—Kochanska—as a name Kochanska would not do—and she came from a part of Poland the Austrians owned. I know the place, Mr. Hirk said proudly. Lem. Berg. It runs in families like my arthritis does. The gift, I mean. I know a lot of similar histories. Her father—her father taught himself to play—from hell to hallelujah—half the instruments. So she knew notes by the time she said daddy. She was sitting up to the piano by four. Perched on a Bible. I know. It's as if I was there. And she was playing a violin her father made for her when she was six. Six! In ringlets. It's so. It's not even unusual. That same father—the father of her—taught his wife the violin. Yes. True. By seven . . . you just linger on the number, boy, linger on her age . . . by seven she was playing in the family string quartet with her brother, who was born before her, a cello's child. Then an old man who heard her, when the family minstrelized around the country to make ends meet, sponsored her for the Conservatory because he loved her as she should have been loved. In Lem. Berg. I know the building. I know the halls.

Joey had read of worms that glowed in the dark. Mr. Hirk was glowing. Like one of the plant's leaves, his face was glowing, and his voice cleaned itself up as if it were going to church.

When Marcella went to him—to Stengl, her teacher, sent by one lover to another—she was about your age—how Stengl must have adored her little fingers—with a waist that didn't require a corset. Though in later years . . . Mr. Hirk spoke of Marcella Sembrich as if she were an old friend. He spoke and he glowed. Yes, yes, Marcella stayed with him—with Stengl, stern as he was—studying—she stayed despite his sternness for eleven years. Joey heard the word "stayed" with a pang. Eleven years of piano. Mr. Hirk made a point of it. Not eleven years of voice, not five. No. Though she sang in some community choruses during that time and was thought to have a pretty soprano. Mr. Hirk always stood to talk, because, scrunched up, he was short of breath, but his voice was aimed at the floor. She married the old man, Stengl, eventually, after he'd kissed her fingers often, growing old in his role as her teacher, and after she, who had arrived as a bud, became a blossom. He had taken her to Italy to study singing, because he believed there was more to her "pretty" voice than prettiness, that inside her small light soprano there was something big and dark. Oh yes, he did hear a darkness. And that "big" voice was born there too, in sunny Italy, like a baby born to a giant. Then he swept her off to London without even telling her why. He had said to his young wife one day, We are going away to London. Why? She wanted to know of course. It was natural to want to know. You shall see, her husband said. It will be for the best. And Stengl figured out a way to get her heard there. Not just heard there . . . heard well. She sang a selection from *Lucia* with the Covent Garden Orchestra accompanying her. Imagine. The entire orchestra playing, she singing. Just imagine. You have heard of Covent Garden? On that legendary stage. She sang. There, where the great Patti had just rehearsed. She sang. Marcella Sembrich sang. Well, they rose, the violins first, to applaud her performance. They said she sang like a violin—and in fact she played that instrument, though not as well as the piano. After that the happy couple—wouldn't they have been a happy couple?—his wisdom and her fingers, her figure and her voice, his worship and his passion—traveled to Russia and Spain and America too. Where she was an astonishment. In *Lucia*. At the Met. In *I Puritani*, in *La Sonnambula*. What vocal calligraphy! You know about the Met? You should have heard her in *The Magic Flute*. Such a queen—such dark power—with her voice—she invoked it. Like a setting sun calls forth the night. For a moment Mr. Hirk was proud of his age. A piano teacher had flown the soprano to these great heights: an old man was her wings, as well as her lover, and saw her soar.

Joey knew then that he would not be able to tell Mr. Hirk he was fired, that the lessons were over—"terminated," a word Miriam had learned at work to fear—now that Mr. Hirk was finally reaching out—only figuratively, of course—to his pupil, and opening his heart's attic to him, unwrapping his enthusiasms, and—young Joey recognized—confronting the death of his hopes, the ruins of his life. Mr. Hirk, after all, lived in a small dark leaf-lit room; he was no one who had ever played or sung before the public; he had probably never even taught another who might, then, have gone on to earn acclaim. And for a pittance, for pity, he was beating book time to a boy who was only, at best, a mime, a faker who had never faked a measure of Chopin, and didn't even know what a Czerny was.

Mr. Hirk had managed to raise an admonitory finger. Marcella Sembrich, wisely counseled, he said sternly, had not strained her voice singing Wagner. Oh she was pure bel canto, pure Italian, he said with hoarse approval. Always, small Joey, she studied. Her whole career. To sing *Lucia,* to sing *Traviata.* To sing Verdi, Donizetti, Puccini. But you are playing at playing, not working at playing, you are only pleasing yourself, small Joey. Well, you must stop having fun and learn the fundamentals. Then you may be able to please someone else.

In these words small Joey heard he hadn't made Mr. Hirk happy. That's what he heard. Moreover, the name—Small Joey—was new, and not nice. These criticisms restiffened his resolve. He would hand Mr. Hirk his envelope, give him the small sum he was charging for the lessons, and say his services were no longer needed. He would do this with a dignity for which he was presently searching.

But Mr. Hirk, who had not heard what Joey was resolving, who had not felt the stiffening of anyone's will, went on without pause to another tale. This anecdote was about a true pianist. It might have been titled: "Ignace Jan Paderewski and the Spider." The story was wholly unfamiliar to Joey, who had decided not to listen. Like you, Paderewski was slow to become a student; like you he had bad teachers; like you he learned through his ears and had no technique, only instinctive fingers that went for the nearest note like kids after cake; yes, yes, like you he did not know how to work. Yet he became the greatest pianist of his time. Of his time . . . And more than that . . .

Joey let his features settle into the sullenness that Miriam found so insufferable, but Mr. Hirk's mind was in another country, an ocean and a sea away, where Joey was an eager auditor, whatever his face let on. Mr. Hirk cleared his throat of phlegm that, fortunately, never materialized.

Paderewski was studying in Vienna with Leschetizky—a name you do not know, because I have taught you nothing—and he had taken a couple of tiny rooms near the villa of this greatest of piano teachers, the author of a method named for him that had helped to eminence some of the most famous pianists of that age. Young Paderewski, as I say, had no technique; he was like you in that, small Joey, though he was, I must also say, a master of the pedal, he pedaled better than you do perched upon your bike. He did not kick the pedal, or otherwise abuse it, he caressed it—"footsie," we say, you know—he played footsie with the pedal. Never did he chew upon himself neither. He was growed up! Anyway—are you listening? This is a lesson, which is what you are here for—so—one day, in his little candlelit room as dark as this one on account of the plants, Paderewski was practicing a piece by Chopin, an exercise in thirds. You do know thirds? While he was playing, a tiny spider dropped down from the ceiling to just one side of him, a bit above the deck of the piano, on a threadlike length of web. Do you know the word "gossamer"? The spider hung there listening to the Chopin. It was no more than a dot suspended in the air—a piece of punctuation. The spider hung there while Paderewski played. Hear him? How he played, that man!

You may smile, Mr. Hirk said, although Joey hadn't softened his sullenness by a twitch. Paderewski smiled himself. He was charmed. So . . . when the exercise in thirds had been completed, he went on, as was his habit, to another one in sixths. The spider immediately scampered, as it seemed, up his silver line to the ceiling. Observing this—you see it?—Paderewski returned to the exercise in thirds and began to repeat it. Lo, believe it and behold, eh? down like a fireman his pole the spider slid. All the way to the piano deck, where he sat and once more listened. At the end of that exercise, which he had to repeat entirely because it so enchanted the spider, Paderewski went about his other business. How long must one entertain a tiny spider, no bigger than a period? Especially one who hasn't paid for its seat at the concert . . .

Joey did smile now, but he thought the story was at an end. Mr. Hirk stared vacantly into vacated space. Time in the tale . . . time in the tale was passing. That's why he stared. A stare that was to stand for elapsing hours. Then his head moved back to Joey. It was an animal's maneuver.

The next morning Paderewski returned to the piano and his practice. The thread hung there still, and down that thread came the spider again the moment the study in thirds commenced. Paderewski pursued the étude, and the spider continued to sit on the deck or hang just above it from the thread so long as the piece was played. This behavior went on, not for another day, or a few days, or a week, but for many weeks, Joey . . . many weeks. . . . Faithfully the spider appeared, quietly it listened, its brilliant tiny eyes shining like diamonds, and just as often, just as promptly, it disappeared up its rope when the étude concluded, as if annoyed, even angry, Paderewski thought, leaving beneath it the detestable sound of sixths.

I once had a small mouse that kept me company, Mr. Hirk said, though he was only foraging for food and was never an enthralled audience for my playing. No enthrallment. Not for me. So . . . where was . . . Ah . . . I am here. . . . But Paderewski . . . Well, vacation time came for Paderewski. He didn't practice in that room again for a number of weeks, and when he returned in the fall, the spider was gone, as was the spider's thread, rolled up after him perhaps, when he went searching for a more melodious space.

What is the lesson? Is that your question, Joey? Joey had heard Mr. Hirk's story despite his intended deafness and would remember it too, against every wish, but he had no curiosity about its character and therefore no question about its content. It was just an amusing oddity—this story. Like the fables of Aesop, Mr. Hirk said, rather portentously, this trifling occurrence has a moral.

The major third, my young friend, Mr. Hirk continued, changing his tone, is that upon which all that is good and warm and wholesome and joyful in nature is built. Not for it the humble, the impoverished, the sacrificial, the stoical—no—it is the ground of the garden, it signifies the real right way, as Beethoven knew when he wrote the finale for his Fifth Symphony. Mr. Hirk leaned like a broken pole against the piano. Hold out your hand, Joey, hold it out, the gnawed right hand that plays—there—that hand is pagan, it is a human hand, it is for shaking and touching and grasping and caressing; it is not made to be a fist; it is not made for praying, for gestures of disdain, for tearing one's hair or holding one's head, for stabbing, for saluting; well, now, see my hand here? this crab? this wadded clutch of knotted fingers? it is the sacred hand, the scarred and crucified claw, the toil-destroyed hand, fit only to curse its God. It has given up every good thing. Having given up every good thing, no good thing comes near. Not, certainly, the major third, the pagan chord. The foundation of nature—which is vibration. . . . Nature is nothing but vibration.

These hands—my uglies—my hands are a denial . . . they deny life. They deny you, Joey, all others' bodies; they deny me. They deny light; they keep caged the darkness clenched in their clench. They are my shame—these uglies—my pain—these uglies—my curse. It makes me sad—sorry—sad and sorry to see them. You understand? Sometimes I hide them inside of my shirt. Then I feel their heat hot on my belly.

Out of breath Mr. Hirk sat in silence for a few moments. When Monteverdi wished to say "joyful is my heart" he did so in the major third; when Handel refers to life's sweetest harmonies he does so in the major third; what is central to the "Ode to Joy" but the major third? in *La Traviata,* when they all lift their glasses and cry "Drink!"—"*Libiamo!*"—they do so to the major third; and what does Wagner use, at the opening of *The Ring,* to describe the sensuously amoral state of nature? he employs the major third; then just listen to that paean of praise in Stravinsky's *Symphony of Psalms* or the finale of Shostakovich's Fifth, and you will hear again the major third.

And the spider heard it, suspended there between floor and ceiling, felt it when the thin silver thread he hung from vibrated in sympathy with Chopin, with the étude's instructional thirds. Joey—look at the green-gray light in this room, at this secondhand light, the pallor of death . . . and what do you hear in my voice, or what would you hear if you were to hear my heart? you'd hear the minor sixth—the sixths that the spider fled from, the gold ring in *Rheingold*—the source of so much contention—Leonora's bitter tears in *Fidelio,* sorrowful Don Quixote, yes, sixths serve anguish, longing, despair, so tell me why should the spider stay when the line he clings to trembles like a tear? Only *we* wallow in bitterness, only *we* choose gray-green lives and devote ourselves to worlds, like the shadow-lean leaves of those ghost plants littering the floor—leaves, worlds—which do not exist, the traces of a light that is no longer there.

Joey made as if to go, rising from the piano bench, when Mr. Hirk's nearby presence pushed him down. Mr. Hirk hung over Joey now, supported by the piano itself, bent because of his bones. If one day you learn to play, Joey, you must play, whatever the key or the intervals are, as if *for,* as if *in,* the major third, the notes of praise. Play C. Joey struck a key. There were several C's, but Joey knew which was meant, a key that would sound a certain way. In filling our ear just now it was everywhere, Mr. Hirk said. Every. Where. Was it sitting beside that pot? No. Was it lying on the rug? Of course not. Everywhere? Ah, in the piano? No? Where it was made? Not this tone. Suppose someone shuts the door and then you, Joey, ride away on your bike. Where is the slam? eh? where is the small growl of the tire in my gravel? Why, there it is—the growl—it's in the gravel where it was made; there is the slam, too, where the door shut on the jamb! Bam! Do D. Joey did D. Hear? The note is everywhere again. Not at the end of your finger. In its own space! That's where it is, filling us up with it, making a world of its own on its own. Just one note is enough. Do E. Joey E'd. Another filling, yet the same jar! Each note makes the same space and then floods it.

Joey thought he sensed relief in Mr. Hirk's voice, like someone wound up dangerously tight might feel once they began unwinding, or the spring of a clock that was finally allowed to tell time.

Oh, a dunce might say, hey, it came from the piano. And the French horn's passage is from the middle of the rear of the orchestra, while the violins sing to the left of the conductor, violas and cellos moan on the right, the strings closing in on the winds from both sides of the fan. Like the door's slam, the dunce hears only the jamb where it was made. Because the bang, the gravel's *brrr,* means something. So he fastens them there like tied dogs. But if you insist on silence, enjoy a little shut-eye when you listen, so there's a bowl of darkness where your head was—then, in the music, where notes are made to appear through the commands of form, not by some tinkler on the triangle, Joey, not because they say something about their cause—then you can almost perceive—though squeeze-eyed—you can see what you hear, see the space, and see how one note is higher than another, farther away, or closer, closer than the heart. See, sir, the brightness of the trumpet among the constellations like a brighter star? Closer to whom, though, Joey? brighter than what? not to you or me, for we are no more than gravel or doors. Oh no. Brighter . . . closer . . . meaningful . . . to one another.

In this damn dark, Joey, when I get the phono cranked, I can follow the song exactly where it goes, and it, not Galli-Curci, it alone is real—is a rare wonder, not of this world—a wonder and a consolation.

Nor will you hear its like anywhere but in its own space. A sneeze in C? Hah. A laugh in E? A siren that runs the scale like a soprano? The notes of music live in music alone, Joey. They must be made, prepared with care. To give voice to feeling.

You will never learn anything about music that is more important than this. Mr. Hirk, with a groan, straightened somewhat. Then he used his groan for instruction. You hear it, my ache, emerge from my mouth. It has a location. Because it is in ordinary space. It is there, fastened to its cause. My grunt, I mean, not my pain. My pain is nowhere, but that's another matter. And my pain is a call like a child's for its mother. But when we listen to music we enter a singular space, Joey, a space not of this room or any road. This you must understand.

Sound them together, sound the chord, play CDE, Joey. Can you do it? Joey protested by doing it dramatically. Suppose I mix a little yellow and a little green together. What after all are my sick plants doing? Is chartreuse two colors or one? Joey naturally made no answer. One. One. One. One. The book beat on the piano seat. But in the chord I hear clearly C and D and E. They penetrate but do not disappear into one another. They are a trinity—a single sound in which I hear three. C is the Son. D is God the

Father, the sacred root, and E is the Holy Ghost. Now, Joey, can you do this? play all at once a loud C, a soft D, and an ordinary E. Which Joey did, triumphantly. Again and again to demonstrate how easily. There! You can hear them! They are everywhere yet in different places! They are one, but they are three. If theology wrote music . . . Mr. Hirk's voice trailed away. At the heart of everything, in music's space, multiple vibrations . . .

Joey was relieved to get away. Mr. Hirk was somewhat embarrassing in addition to being ugly and poor and pitiful. Needy too. His hands were beginning to look like tree roots. But Joey rode away sad himself—a small sad-infested Joey—for he had not canceled the lessons; he had been allowed no suitable occasion or merciful excuse; moreover, he had permitted shame and cowardice to dissuade him, and now he would have to mail, messageless as was his mother's habit, a few small bills in an envelope the way he understood a payoff would be made, so that next week, when the time arrived for his bike to skid in the gravel in front of Mr. Hirk's door, at the time when Joey would be expected to pop in and ask, How ya doin? there'd be nothing and no one, no bowl of silence ready to be filled with the latest tunes, only patient expectation, puzzlement, disappointment, hurt. Joey felt guilty and sorry and sad. He pedaled recklessly. He hoped his father had, at one time, felt something of the same shame.

Conjunctions, 2005
Published in *Middle C,* 2013

GARDEN

Impatiens, or Touch-Me-Not, Busy Lizzie.

Professor Skizzen was sitting sidesaddle on an orange crate he had upended in a dormer of his attic. This leftover space had become his office because he could carry on business better from any cranny that refused to accommodate a telephone. Though hidden from almost all eyes, it was lit by a single high window that provided lots of southern sun and a good view of the distant trees. If Joseph heaved up the sash, he could peer directly down upon his mother's garden, upon the tops of hedges and low shrubs, and take in the outlines of her carefully laid-out beds. In the middle stood the great vine-smothered beech, its bench, and a puddle-sized pool where Skizzen would often vainly search his reflected face for a tuneful line. Sometimes he would catch sight of his mother hunched over while wielding a hoe or, trowel in hand, sprawled upon the ground, her legs sticking out from behind a bush, her hat poking up above a forest of fronds. He had discovered to his horror (it had now become a small disturbance) that Miriam liked to sniff the earth and the low stems of her plants precisely at the point they went into the ground. Where the living and the dead intersect, Joseph had observed, but his mother would have none of it. The earth is as lively as you or I, she said. I smell it, but I also listen to it breathe.

Only a brisk walk up a rising street from where he perched, Whittlebauer sat as steady as Stonehenge, and there his students gathered. He heard the college bells divide the academic day into equal and peaceful parts, but never felt the years as they slipped away.

If Joseph's seat was not very luxurious, even precarious, rudimentary, it was appropriate, and would not encourage nodding off, which he was now inclined to do, although his customarily scrappy little lunch should have left him alert as a hunter. Two similar boxes lifted a drafting board to the level of his knees. Many years ago—oh, so many, Joseph thought now—he had come upon this castoff in a salvage shop in Urichville. On the plane of his improvisation, made interesting by ink stains, coffee spills, and the tracks of thumbtacks retreating like boxers in neutral corners, he cut out columns of fresh bad news from the daily papers, labeled them as to subject, pasted pictures with their accompanying clips into scrapbooks, and reseated a handful of raisins nearby his glass of rewarmed tea.

So much had changed since he and Miriam had moved into the Gothic "spookhouse," as he'd heard the kids call it while under the influence of Halloween. The college owned the place, as they did many of the old mansions near the campus, and let faculty members live in them rent-free, awarding the houses like prizes instead of paying their occupants a decent salary. It was also a way of keeping valued teachers from seeking more moneyed pastures. Joseph guessed that rich farmers had built these mitigations of their wealth when they retired to town. As homes, they were tall, ornate, whimsical, constructed from timber that was both local and plentiful, and band-sawn according to new techniques that made possible the extravagant filigrees of Queen Anne. Every such home was required to have at least one biblical moment pictured in art glass and positioned within a sunstruck landing window: Susanna, clothed as though she were nude and ogled by the elders, Ruth in a swath of rose-colored swath standing among the alien corn.

Miriam welcomed the large yard with cries of ancient Austrian origin. There was no doubt that she was a different woman from the mousy cottage complainer she had been during their early days in Woodbine, when she "sweated over tubs of plastic," and marched rows of unwilling flowers alongside walks and around borders, as if their modest cottage had to be outlined in petunias and forget-me-nots the way a valentine sported its scallops. Vines had climbed about like too many squirrels, shinnying downspouts and smothering lattice with wild rose and honeysuckle. Others came from the walls of the cottage—dropouts, Joseph called them—to lie in gutters like sunning snakes, causing rainwater to shower along the eaves into the sodden soil below and filling a declining number of tulips, as though they were goblets, until the petals sprang apart.

As a landlord, the college was as much an absentee as God in the deist's conception of Him, and it permitted the property to run down in a manner suitably decorous and stately. Annoying as this was, for Joseph Skizzen it had the considerable advantage of his privacy, for no one was likely to wander unwanted upon his attic masterwork or even raise an eyebrow at his and his mother's living arrangements: neither the potting table in the dining room nor his bedside scissors would cause a snook to be cocked, neither his boxes of flypaper and pots of paste, nor her piles of muddy gloves or empty packages of flower seed, already neatly sleeved over tongue depressors, waiting to mark, as though they were really graves, the place of some plant's birth.

Dicentra Spectabilis, *or Old-Fashioned Bleeding Heart, Will Self-Sow.*

Nowadays Miriam wore durable trousers that elastic closed at the ankles; she strapped on padding for her knees; fastened around her waist a carpenter's apron stuffed with tools and little sticks; drew over her coiled and braided hair a floppy broad-brimmed khaki hat; and encircled her neck with a kerchief soaked in insect repellent. Gardening was war, and like a professional soldier she also bore a firm, stern face into battle, uttering hoarse cries ("Whoa!" or "Woe to you," Joseph wasn't sure which) when, for instance, she removed an invasive violet from her carefully calibrated pools of grass. She would howl and slap her thighs whenever a stray cat came to poach, for she generally thought of the birds as her friends unless, like hawks or crows, they were predators or lazy sneaks who laid their eggs in nests not of their own contriving the way the cowardly turn-color cowbirds did. She claimed the trees needed the visits of the birds to remind them of how much they were desired.

Sometimes, momentarily defeated, she would burst into Joseph's breakfast kitchen. Ah, calamity! Where is my red-currant jelly? I shall cook *Hasenbraten . . . Hasenbraten mit Rahmsauce . . .* how would you like that? I'm sure I would love it, Mother. Well, we shall have a year's worth. Joey, I suffer from an overrun of rabbit. They are eating all my petunias; they decapitate my zinnias. It is massacre for my marigolds. Poor baby bloomers. Malignant *Hasen! Ich hasse Hasen!* They sit in the grass like city folk visiting a park, and chew my clover. They fornicate in the nighttime and give birth by dawn's break. A root of ginger, I need, and some spoonfuls of jelly. I shall *braten* them for a year—ev er so slo ly. I shall tear out their hearts and feed them to the earth. Joey, their big eyes shall become my buttons. I hope their howls shall not disturb the music in your ear.

Miriam tolerated lightning bugs, dragonflies because of their beauty, bees because of their service. She granted butterflies a pardon even though the charming worms of the swallowtail were insatiable (she'd plant extra parsley the way she once would have set a dinner plate for a visitor), but hornets received no such reprieve, because they tried to bite off frayed edges of her chicken leg when she enjoyed one for lunch.

Do not disturb the dew. Some nights the world weeps. Late-morning light, before the sun grew uncomfortable, was therefore deemed the best time for gardening, and Miriam would, as she said, work hard on behalf of her friends, moving her ministrations from shade to shade. No longer were her enemies droning noisily through the night air, or—in her husband's language of fear—were they vaguely whispered to exist behind bushes, royal beards, or in government bureaus. And she had allies: ladybugs to eat aphids, lacewings to go after white flies. Some of these good damenbugs carry parasites into the garden, she'd say—I have to watch out for that—but mostly they fatten on potato beetles and similar bad behavers. But you aren't growing potatoes, Joseph would protest, on behalf of the gorgeous black-and-gold insect as much as the welfare of the tuber (or, choosing whatever the argument seemed to require, in defense of the onion's thrips or spinach's leafminers, the squash's modestly gray bugs, cabbage's maggots, or the carrot's weevils). Ja, but our neighbors are. Better the nasty things should die here. The poor potato (or corn ear or bean pod), Joseph joshed, it's born only to be eaten by somebody. God saw to that, Miriam said with satisfaction. God made aphids, too, and . . . and . . . Joey might chant, trying to continue his indictment with a space holder—but Miriam would break in anyway—so that damenbugs would have something nice to dine on! interrupting with redoubled pleasure because she had scored a goal in her game. Joseph was then left to finish lamely. With her face, his mother brought close to him a serious smile: each of us eats, and each of us is edible. Envy eats us. The Church teaches us that. Anger, also, an eater. Miriam made her pronouncements as if they were pronouncements. This impressed Joey but irritated Joseph, who thought the tone only suitable to speakers with a certain status.

Upon her plants she loosed a vociferous stream of advice. Pointing to the bleeding heart that was prospering in its place across the yard, she would address a flower in front of her that was flimsy, and order it to do as Marlene was doing: look at that raceme of red hearts—like fat fish.

When Joseph wasn't meeting a class, he and his mother would sometimes exchange shouts about their business, pro and con and up and down. Joseph called his "reports from the ruins of reason." Miriam merely bellowed, as routinely victorious as any Caesar. She took her midday meal resting on an overturned pail and looking wan as a beaten soldier, sore-footed and weary, while Joseph munched his sandwich—lettuce and liverwurst—searching the columns for a story, and flinging bread crusts from his window. More reports from the ruins of reason. This, he would cackle, is for the birds.

Today not a single baby had been made into marmalade. Normally the Inhumanity Museum ate up agonies no one could bear to dwell on. Professor Skizzen was of two minds about the admission of such reports. An infant would be found with its neck broken. The mother had been visiting relatives who lived only so far away as the next street, and had left the child in the care of her boyfriend, a fellow of seventeen, not the father of anything yet, but formerly a backfield star. The real father had left some dim length of famishment ago, and to nowhere had reported in. The kid wouldn't stop crying and had been shaken until his lungs collapsed and his neck snapped. What to do about classifying that? Botanists always had an answer. Lucky them!

Digitalis, or Foxglove, Impossible to Duplicate.

Sometimes, when a gentle breeze made the blooms bob, and a cardinal sat at the top of their holly tree like a Christmas decoration, performing its territorial song, its tail pulsing with the effort as if it were pumping each note through some designated distance, perhaps as far as Joseph's even loftier perch, then the professor would be tempted to descend and walk about in the garden, in the cool of the shade, though Miriam thought he did so like a health inspector, his hands clasped behind his back, promising not to touch, but bending slightly to be nearer the fragrance of a flower or the wrinkled leaf that spelled fungus.

It was just that he worried over their welfare, Joseph insisted. Miriam maintained that her son didn't believe she could do anything really well except cook, and expected the garden to fall over dead of black spot, larval infestation, or webworm, at any moment. That wasn't true, Joseph felt, but he knew that it was Miriam's habit to pick black-spotted leaves off her rosebushes one by one, or routinely to rake them up from the ground around the plant if they had fallen, and then to burn her collection at a safe distance from all things as if they were the bedclothes of plague victims.

Train the beetles to munch the black spots, Joseph suggested, whet their Japanese appetites, redefine their Asian tastes, but his mother was never in the mood to humor him when the garden was involved. Let them make nice lace of the leaves, was his advice. Do you notice how they never eat the hard parts but leave the veins. Remarks of this kind would rile her, because what she got from her garden was not only reprieve and renewal, but romantic transportation to the old days—by wagon as in the old days . . . plodding horses back then . . . sing-alongs of the old songs . . . cider made of apples fallen to the ground . . . the redolent hay—when Rudi Skizzen had begun his love affair with her round wet eyes, and when, as Nita Rouse, she had barely recovered from her childhood. They eat everything but the skeleton,

Joseph said, and he was not alone in his opinions. They go clean to the bone, the way you eat a chicken's thigh. That's what, according to Mother Nature, they're supposed to do. Silent, frowning, Miriam threw up dirty hands as if to ward off his words. Am I, then, evil too? Because I chew? Professor Skizzen received a scornful look instead of an answer that might have been "maybe."

I'd rather think about the good people, not the wicked ones, Miriam could be counted on to say. Look how that primula lies on the earth like a kiss on a loved one's cheek. She would smile because she knew such sentiments embarrassed him, at the same time reaching out with her arms in tribute to the flower's intense yet tender blue, its velveteen allure. They are as pure and innocent as I was before I became a washerwoman, when we lived in the low hills on the farm, *ach,* how the day would break, as clear as birdsong. Whereupon Joey would point to the shrill green leaves the primrose possessed, almost prehistorically indented. Miriam would agree that the plant was medieval and had been sewn into tapestries in order to stay in bloom forever.

Yet it was Joey who was the tenderhearted observer of the scene, worrying about everyone's health, and suggesting remedies he had seen in old books for this or that perceived ailment. It was Miriam who ruthlessly rid herself of anyone weak, ripping the plant from the earth, not hearing, as Joey did, its pathetic outcries. It is not individuals we are growing here, but families, she insisted. I worry about the clan they come from, the kind of plant they are, not about this Hans or that Kurt or my Heinrich. Still, she named them all and lectured them all, and threatened them with failure and removal very much as the professor was forced to hector and chide his students by the system in favor with his college.

Joseph, who had cultivated snobbery as an essential professional weapon, was always surprised by Miriam's eagerness to learn the Latin names for the plants she grew, and to insist upon their use, so that when Joey spoke about the "primroses" she would correct him with "prim yew-luh," emphatically broken into its pronounceable parts. If he complimented her "Jacob's ladder," she would respond with "Po-lee-mow nee-um." When he admired her patch of lilies, she told him what he loved was called "Lil ee-um" and that they were the belles of summer. Then it was Joey's turn to complain that there were too many "um"s. It's a Latin ending, she would say with a pleased growl of disgust, because she loved to correct her professor. As they crossed the garden on a grassy lane dotted here and there with the projecting ends of quite white rocks, Miriam recited the labels she had learned, halting by the beds where the named were flourishing: Hettie Hem-er-oh-kal is, Rudy Rud-bek ee-uh, Hortense Hos tuh, Gail Gay-lar dee-uh. Connie Ko lee-us.

This new learning was both gratifying and disturbing. Everyone ought to have a proficiency, about which they could claim the honor due anyone skilled, the respect appropriate to every form of learning. For Miriam, as these proficiencies grew, the garden grew, and as the garden grew, she flourished. She became active in the Friends of Woodbine's Gardens, a group of ladies who met once a month to exchange enthusiasms, information, and neighborhood gossip—quite a lot of gossip if Joseph's ears were any measure. Nonetheless, he had to be happy his mother was finally a member of the community, had friends, as well as a familiar, much-approved, ongoing enterprise.

Yet Skizzen had no such friends, his connection with the college had become purely formal, he was close to no one, and, if anything, moved further away every day like the sun in winter. Was he improving his mind as she was? were his fingers more agile today than they had been a year ago? did he glow with pride when his students excelled, or when one of his observations was published? no and no and no the answer came. Only his madness progressed along with the museum that was its most persuasive evidence, and it was advancement that came through accumulation, not selection; repetition, not interconnection, or—he feared—any deeper understanding.

He had once thought that the many terrible deeds of men might be understood by positing some underlying evil working away in the dirt of each life like the sod webworm. Perhaps there was an unrequited urge at the center of the species, a seed or genetic quirk, an impulse, knack for destruction, a type of trichinosis, or a malignant imbecility that was forever ravenous. Maybe our wars worked to keep our numbers in check. But that hope turned out to be Heinrich Schenker's doing, who had put the idea in Skizzen's head by insisting that for every harmonic composition there ought to be such a generating center—a musical idea from which the notes that would be heard emerged, and were thereby governed, the way words issue from a mouth, and the mouth moves on account of a consciousness that is formed, at least in part, by a nature as obdurate as an underground god who hammers, at his forge, the white-hot blades of his weapons.

Nicotiana or the Tobacco Flower, Best in C+ Soil.

Joseph enjoyed the progress of the seasons, especially that period in earliest spring when the trees showed the tiniest tip of the red that was going to swell and turn into a furl of green around the end of every twig. The color was like a tentative chirp from inside an egg until you turned your head a moment, perhaps to confront invaders—cabbage whites like tossed confetti, or dandelions as orange and unacceptable as yolks where they disgraced the grass—only to find that while your attention had been withdrawn, the entire tree had burst into an applause of bloom.

Music, above all, is what drew Joseph Skizzen to the garden, particularly on those days, as crisp as radish, when the birds were establishing their territories. The air seemed to sense the seeds and the seeds to grow toward the songs of the birds, and he thought he knew the plants that had sought out the twitterers, and those that had risen for the wren, or a fern that turned, not to the sun, but to the chatter of the chickadee, so quick were the petals of its song, so sharp so plentiful so light, so showy in their symmetry, so suddenly in shade. Astilbe, a name that could be played—uh-stil bee—a plant that could be sung.

But the robins wanted worms and the white-throats wanted grain; he had read of a hunting season specifically designed for doves; the honeysuckle was rapacious, one stalk of bamboo was soon twelve, and violets choked grass while looking cute. Miriam yanked weak plants from the earth and thinned the strong as if they were Jews, but Joseph could not tease her in those terms, not an Austrian. So he suggested that perhaps a little food . . . No, not worth the bother, she'd reply while troweling a plant that had prospered in its present position for removal to a place where it would look better. I need to force these to flower, she would say while wielding a pair of snapping clippers. Deformities were dispatched without remorse, as readily as the infected or those that reverted to their prehybridized days or whose blooms surprised her by being magenta. Creams and pinks that had been together several years were ripped asunder because they were no longer thought to complement one another, and poisons were planted in otherwise wholesome specimens to kill whoever might later eat a leaf.

Miriam wanted a dog who would catch rabbits until Joseph pointed out how dogs were copiously indiscriminate poopers and dug in beds of bulbs while pretending to bury bones when it was really just for the hell of it. She then proposed acquiring a cat until he observed their tastes regarding birds and reminded her of how they yowled at night? in the afterglow of ruins? after the bombing stopped. She begged him to dispatch a garter snake that wore a streak of gold like a zipper down its back, because the snake surprised her hands when they uncovered its concealing leaves, but Joseph demurred, defending the reptile's reputation as harmless and beneficial, though she said this Eden needn't be a haven for snakes just because the first one was.

You can't improve on God, observed the professor.

He worked before hybridization, responded the faithful.

I'm not a Saint Patrick for hire either.

It's all *Scheiss* about him and the snakes. Anyway, I wasn't about to pay a saint who ain't.

Instead she released throngs of ladybugs from mail-order boxes. She also had to be persuaded about the virtues of spiders and praying mantises. Webs she abhorred, although she knew the results of their operations were desirable. These loud lemon-colored garden spiders think they own the plants they hang their webs from, and pretend to be flowers themselves, suspended from sunlight and air, feeding on gossamer.

In the alleged state of nature, Joseph would begin, it is said to be a war of all against all. I know you are teasing, Joey. No one can go against gardens. So let me be with my beauties, at peace with nature and all this world's tossing and yearning. Joseph couldn't help himself and therefore reminded his mother how unnatural gardens were, how human-handed every rose was, how thoroughly the irises were trained, how the prizes plants won in their competitions were like those awarded after a proud parade of poodles, each clipped like a hedge. She should not ignore the size of the industry whose profits depended upon fashions in flowers encouraged by the press or those ubiquitous catalogues, both of whom provoked fears of diseases, worms, and insects that could only be controlled by the poisons, hormones, and fertilizers they recommended. Nor should she make light of the myths extolling the harmless healthiness of gardening, even alleging its psychological superiority to every other avocation. She should notice how the seed companies' bankrolls grew more rapidly than their marigolds, despite extensive artificial breeding; she should also admit the plants' reputations were puffed and as pretentious as their adopted stage names—Moonglow, for instance. Had she ever laughed at the names for plants? The garden, he felt compelled to suggest, was like a fascist state: ruled like an orchestra, ordered as an army, eugenically ruthless and hateful to the handicapped, relentless in the pursuit of its enemies, jealous of its borders, favoring obedient masses in which every stem is inclined to appease its leader.

Once he had aroused his mother's ire, Joey would repent his meanness and attempt to calm her by repeating what the great Voltaire had advised . . . *Ja ja ja,* she would hurry to complete the notorious sentence, I know, I know, I should fertilize . . . cultivate . . . weed my garden. Well, widen your eyes. So I do. So you do not. What do you do? but stir me like a *gulasch* with your smarts for a spoon. Play the day till it's through with paste and snippers. As in the kinder's . . . *ja, das ist* . . . the kinder's garten. You used to play the piano in the afternoon. Day zee . . . day zee . . . the plants liked listening to her answer true. Like a cloud cooling the sun.

Sometimes her scorn, only partly assumed, stung him a bit, but he had hidden his ego so far beneath the layers of his cultivated public selves that even the hardest blow was diverted, softly absorbed, or fended off. The truth was that he was proud of his mother's garden now. She had achieved a renewed life through her interest in it, and her mind had prospered as much as her emotions had, something rarely true, he understood, of love affairs. She would literally disappear into its shrubbery, hidden on her hands and knees, planting and weeding, folding her fingers in a more fundamental form of prayer.

The garden had but one bench but there Joseph would sometimes sit to enjoy a brisk breeze because it discouraged the mosquitoes that flew in from every point on the globe, he felt, to intrude upon his peace and spoil its brief serenities. The swifts swirled about like bats, presumably stuffing themselves with pests, but there were always bugs and always would be bugs—leafminers, fire ants, flea beetles, earworms, borers—his mother had taught him that—aphids, white flies, thrips, and spider mites—the way there would always be weeds—crabgrass, foxtail, purslane, pigweed, nematodes—it was a wonder, she said, that anything worthwhile remained alive—as well as murderous diseases—leaf spot and brown patch, bean blight and root rot—*mein Gott!*—but he made these things too, to bore and spoil and chew, she would say, cursing them in her childhood German—the loopers, maggots, weevils of her flower beds and borders.

So her world and his were not so dissimilar after all.

Ilex or Winterberry, Red Sprite, Seeks Jim Dandy
for Companionship and Pollination.

From his attic window Professor Skizzen gazed down upon snowy ground. In a patch near the kitchen door, where Miriam had spread seed, numerous quarter notes swayed across a hidden score. What were the birds playing when their heads bobbed? three quick pecks, a pause, three quick pecks, a backward bound that Skizzen decided to call a stiff-legged scratch, then another pause quite brief before the series was performed again, a dance peculiar to the white-throated sparrow if his mother's identification was correct, because the oval-headed doves rattled off eighth notes like a rifle and then rested, the cardinals cocked their crests and bounded forward like balls, while grackles clacked on nearby wires. Suddenly a branch would sway, a shadow slice across the crust, or a jay caw; then the flock would flee as if blown into limbs and bushes, leaving the dove, like a lone hoot from a horn, placidly putting its beak to the ground—*tip tip tip tip*—making the most of the moment's lack of competition.

A few withered rose hips, a few bent dry fronds with enough substance for a shadow, a few brittle sticks pierced the snow's sturdy surface to lead the eye over one stretch of death to another, and encouraged the rabbits to bound across it, and the squirrels to race up a tree, snippily flashing their tails. Elsewhere, beneath the now solid sod, where there remained but little warmth from a sun a month old, moles in dark runnels rarely moved, and bulbs, that would later bloom so raucously, kept counsel to themselves as if indifferent to entreaties from their nature. Skizzen, always perverse on Tuesdays, let his thoughts offer praise to those buried blades that were so eager to push through the first wet earth offered them and flaunt their true colors. In the buried bulb. That's where growing went to winter. That was elsewhere's elsewhere.

Spring's final frost would bite those bulbs for their boasting, and bring their beauty, so fragilely composed, to a rude and cruel close, the way wily sovereigns tempt the tongues of their subjects in order to learn who might be bold enough to wag them, and thus nip oppositions, as we customarily say, in the bud. Human warmth might draw you out and leave you exposed, Skizzen concluded, and considered it a thought worth noting down for use when he spoke to his class of music's lulling little openings, childishly gleeful sometimes—"carefree" was the word . . . yes . . . sunny their disposition—strings of notes that did not pull a toy train clattering behind them as they seemed to promise, but drew open suddenly the very door of war.

Most of them used to fly away in winter—the birds—performing feats of navigation while on their varied ways that made the Magi seem novices at geography, since they, at least, had a star; but now so many simply stayed, and toughed it out, counting on the sentiments of humans who had for centuries protected those they couldn't eat, and even kept some cozy in cages most artfully fashioned for them, or prized them for their plumage, or pitted them in fights, or said they sang at night when lovers . . . well . . . so it was rumored . . . did whatever they did.

Hydrangea or Lemon Daddy, the Fickle Bush.

Joseph tried to encourage the escape of the heat that built up in the house during the summer months by keeping the attic windows open, even if he risked, through one of his rusted screens, the entry of some unfriendly flying things, especially bats, which could hang as handily upside down as his news clippings on their flypaper chains. He remembered a recent exchange with his mother, who had exclaimed: Joey, you read newspapers all day but you don't know what's happening! He had replied then that he hadn't a garden club to keep him current. Still, he paid her heed, and soon saw what he had been missing. Now his new group, strung near the opening of a dormer, featured pederasts and their victims, a bunch he had with reluctance begun collecting despite his mother's prodding because he had realized that the absence of sex crimes and criminals—rapes, bris, and other genital deformations—was possibly suspicious. Homosexuals and other aberrants, exhibitionists, porn-cones, sodomists, and other mysterious transmixups—were an absence not to be too eagerly filled, but people and practices that nevertheless belonged in any proper inhumanity museum, the nutsyfagans and other detrolleyed toonervilles—mother molesters, aliens, weirdos, those were the words—the unlike and therefore unliked, whose unnatural acts promoted inhumane behavior in the species. It gave Joseph no pleasure at all to pursue these top-ics, in fact they made him queasy, but he felt it a duty to his dream to include them. And because of his mother.

Stir reet stir reet, he thought the wrens said, and then stir reet stir reet again. Not music, he suspected. Not conversation. Only pronouncement. Cheater, the cardinals insisted. Cheater cheater cheater.

Calamint, Till Frost, Dainty of Bloom and Tart of Odor.

A stinging wind brought tears to Joey's eyes when Joseph looked down on Miriam's garden filled with captured leaves. They flew just above the mums to be caught in hedges that had lost theirs and whose briars were now eager to seize any debris the wind blew in. I still have mine, my leaves and vines, Professor Skizzen thought, fly-stuck and fluttery, though I'm not evergreen. Angered by his blurred vision, Skizzen brought his fist down on his right thigh. The blow couldn't reach through the cloth to cause a bruise.

Conjunctions, 2007
Published in *Middle C,* 2013

THE APOCALYPSE MUSEUM

The fear that the human race might not survive has been replaced by the fear that it will endure.

You cannot end an English sentence with a preposition. Skizzen had more than once read that. Or the world with "with"—leaving the whimper unwhimpered, for instance. Or with "on account of"—overpopulation, for example—unspecified. Or with "in"—omitting fire or flood or wind . . . a storm of hail the size of eyeballs. Can you imagine what it will die of? if it can actually die. There will be many endings vying for the honor. And any agent of our end will have a radiant sense of ruin. Any agent of our end will dance where the score says rest.

In the garden the cornflowers watch my small mother, Skizzen thought, watch my small mother wash her small hands in the soft loamy soil of the beds. She has dug in compost over years, compost mixed with sand, with bark, with mulching leaves, a little manure, a bit of bone meal; and with a fork she has carefully circulated the soil, turning sand and leaves and rotted peelings under one another, down where the earthworms slowly pass everything through themselves and thereby imagine shit as a city. She handles the leaves and touches the blossoms. She knows how to do it. Her grasp is vigorous, never shy or uncertain. The plants respond. Eat well. Thrive. Go to nefarious seed.

Our concern that the human race might not endure has been succeeded by the fear it will survive.

Oh . . . oh—Skizzen oh'd, in his sermons to himself—Oh, the decomposition of man will stench the sky at first but how immeasurably it will manure the soil, how thoroughly it will improve the land with all those fine bones added, while plants cover and trees stand. For the worms the climate will be tropical, they will grow longer than tunnels, and their four hearts beat for blocks. Lakes will deepen and be blue again. Clean sky will harbor happy winds. Mountainsides of aspens will be able to color and flutter without having their picture taken. Waterfalls will fall free of enterprising eyes. It will be grand.

Unless there is a universal flood and fish school in corner offices; unless there is an atomic wind and an image of our race is burned into the side of a glass cliff; unless glaciers creep down from the north almost as blue as green as winedark as the solidifying sea.

The thought that mankind might not endure has been replaced by the fear it may luck out.
Armageddon's final field was nearly measured once before. It was half a cataclysm—a clysm—maybe. Preliminary bout. A third of the world sickened during the three years of the Black Plague: 1348–1349–1350. And the plague swung its scythe four times, the last swathe reducing Europe to half what it had been the century before: in 1388–1389–1390. They believed the disease was evil advancing like an army. They said it was Satan's century. *Diabolus in musica.* That was before Passchendaele. The population of the planet diminished by a fifth.

Those who suffered the plague and survived: they suggested to Joseph Skizzen the unpleasant likelihood that Man might squeak through even a loss at Armageddon—one death per second not fast enough—and outlive the zapping of the planet, duck a fleet of meteors, hunkerbunker through a real world war with cannons going grump to salute our last breath as if horror were a ceremony, emerge to sing of bombs bursting, endure the triggers of a trillion guns amorously squeezed until every nation's ammo was quite spent, and all the private stock was fired off at the life and livestock of a neighbor, so that in battle's final silence one could hear only the crash after crash of financial houses, countless vacuum cleaners, under their own orders, sucking up official lies, contracts screaming like lettuce shredded for a salad, outcries from the crucifixion of caring borne on the wind as if in an ode, the screech of every wheel as it became uninvented, brief protests from dimming tubes, destimulated wires; though the slowing of most functions would go on in silence, shit merded up in the street to be refried by aberrant microwaves, diseases coursing about and competing for victims, slowdowns coming to standstills without a sigh, until the heavy quiet of war's cease is broken by . . . by what? might we imagine boils bursting out of each surviving eye . . . the accumulated pus of perception? a burst like what? like trumpets blowing twenty centuries of pointless noise at an already deaf-eared world . . . with what sort of sound exactly? with a roar that rattles nails already driven in their boards, so . . . so that, as the sound comes through their windows, houses will heave and sag into themselves, as unfastened as flesh from a corset; yet out of every heap of rubble, smoking ruin, ditch of consanguineous corpses, could creep a survivor—*he* was such a survivor, Joseph Skizzen, faux doctor and musician—someone born of ruin as flies are from offal; that from a cave or collection of shattered trees there might emerge a creature who could thrive on a prolonged diet of phlegm soup and his own entrails even, and in spite of every imaginable catastrophe salvage at least a remnant of his race with the strength, the interest, the spunk, to fuck on, fuck on like Christian soldiers, stiff-pricked still, with some sperm left with the ability to engender, to fuck on, so what if with a limp, fuck on, or a severed tongue, fuck on, or a blind eye, fuck on, in order to multiply, first to spread and then to gather, to confer, to wonder why, to invent, to philosophize, accumulate, connive: to wonder why this punishment? to wonder why this pain? why did we—among the we's that were—survive? what was accomplished that couldn't have been realized otherwise? why were babies born to be so cruelly belabored back into the grave? who of our race betrayed our trust? what was the cause of our bad luck? what divine plan did this disaster further? why were grandfathers tortured by the deaths they were about to sigh for? why? but weren't we special? we few, we leftovers, without a tree to climb, we must have been set aside, saved for a moment of magnificence! to be handed the trophy, awarded the prize; because the Good Book, we would—dumb and blind—still believe in, said a remnant would be saved; because the good, the great, the well-born and Internetted, the rich, the incandescent stars, will win through: that . . . that . . . that we believed, we knew, God will see to that, He will see, see to it, if He hasn't had a belly full, if the liar's, the liar's beard is not on fire like Santa Claus stuck in a chimney.

The thought that mankind might not endure has been replaced by the fear it may make it through another age of ice.
In spite of death and desolation, music, Professor Joseph Skizzen assured himself, would still be made. Toms would be tommed, the earth beaten by bones born to a rhythm if not a rhyme, a ground swept by sweet dancing feet. There would be voices raised in song to celebrate heaven, to thank the gods for the radish about to be eaten, to pray for victory in tomorrow's war, or the reinvention of the motorcar. Someone would, like Simonides, remember where everyone was sitting when the roof of the world fell in, or how the stars were configured, and would be able to identify the dead,

if anyone cared. With that feat on his résumé, Simonides could easily sell his memory-method for a lot of cabbages, many messes of pottage, thirty carloads of silver, options to buy. Because we would want everyone properly buried in their appropriately consecrated ground, sacred ground we would kill one another to acquire, to protect and fill with our grateful dead—each race decomposing, each would allege, with more dignity, more delight to those worms, more . . . more to the nth than the others.

Soon there would be family clans and prisons again. Beneath all ash, hate would still be warm enough to make tea. That's the state in which Professor Skizzen's mind would be when he left off worrying his sentence—the possibility that all of us might just check out has been overcome by the probability that some of us will never vacate our rooms or pay our bills on time or receive our just deserts—break off to imagine man's return, the triumph of the club and the broken knees of enemies, the harvesting of ferns, the refinement of war paint—each time taking a slightly different route to new triumphs and fresh renown. Upon our Second Coming, we would hate the earth and eat only air. We would live in ice like a little bit of lost light. We would grow fur and another nose. Fingernails, hard as horn, would curl like crampons. We would scuttle in and out of caves, live on insects, bats, and birds, and grow blue as a glacier. Perhaps we'd emerge in the shape of those ten-foot tropical worms, and like *Lumbricus terrestris* have many hundred species. It was so discouraging, but such thoughts had one plus: they drove him away from his obsession with words like "fear" and "concern" and "worry" and returned him to his profitable work—the study of the late piano pieces of Franz Liszt—a passion which his former colleagues found amusing, especially in an Austrian such as himself, who ought to disdain the French/Slav Musical Axis in favor of a hub that was purely German (little did they know where he'd already been!), and who had foolishly chosen one instrument when the entire Vienna Philharmonic could have been strumming and tootling his tunes.

Yes, that very orchestra where his father might have played had he chosen to imagine himself a concert violinist instead of a fleeing Jew. Joseph Skizzen's mother carried him to London like coffee in a Thermos. To grow up in a ruin, amid the blitzed, the burned, and broken, a foretaste of the soon-to-be forlorn and fallen world. Joseph preferred to think of his father's moves as resembling, when he left Vienna in the guise of a Jew, a profound departure from the tonic; and his father's sojourn in London, until he went to work in the betting parlor, as a deft modulation back to the Aryan fold; but it was difficult to account for the abandonment of his family, his departure for America, and his subsequent disappearance, in some sort of sonata form.

Changelings required impromptus, variations, bagatelles, divertimenti, to do justice to their nature. He, Joseph Skizzen, was a weathercock too.

Joseph Skizzen's surmise that mankind might not survive its own profligate and murderous nature has been supplanted by the suspicion that nonetheless it will.

The Gothic house he and his mother shared had several attic rooms, and Joseph Skizzen had decided to devote one of them to the books and clippings that comprised his other hobby: The Inhumanity Museum. He had painstakingly lettered a large white card with that name and fastened it to the door. It did not embarrass him to do this, since only he was ever audience to the announcement. Sometimes he changed the placard to one which called it The Apocalypse Museum instead. The stairs to the third floor were too many and too steep for his mother now. Daily, he would escape his sentence in order to enter yesterday's clippings into the scrapbooks that constituted the continuing record:

> Friday June 18, 1999
>
> Sri Lanka. Municipal workers dug up more bones from a site believed to contain the bodies of hundreds of Tamils murdered by the military.
>
> Same day
> Poklek, Jugoslavia. 62 Kosovars are packed into a room into which a grenade is tossed.
>
> Same day
> Pristina, Jugoslavia. It is now estimated that 10,000 people were killed in the Serbian ethnic-cleansing pogrom.

Now there was no one left in Kosovo to kill but Gypsies.
  Or

> Tuesday April 16, 2001
>
> Cotonou, Benin. The boat at the center of an international search for scores of child slaves believed to have been roaming the West African coast for more than two weeks arrived early this morning in this port.

Next day
Cotonou, Benin. Authorities boarded a ship suspected of carrying child slaves after it docked at Cotonou early today but found no sign of such children.

Next day
Cotonou, Benin. According to the manifest, there were only seven children aboard. UNICEF officials said thirty-one were placed in foster homes. The Men of the Earth charity had forty-three at their refuge. The ship's chief mate insisted that there were twenty-eight children onboard, all with their families.

The paste would have to wait on this one, which would not be a keeper unless the kids had been thrown overboard.

Skizzen clipped a few local items, but his harvest was mostly taken from *The New York Times* and the weekly newsmagazines. He ignored most crime and merely ordinary malfeasance. Occasionally he would include a shooting on the subway or the theft of donor organs, but he felt that you had to discount things done mainly from poverty or madness. Actually, human stupidity was his principal target. Stupidity was shifty. It often pretended to be smart. For instance, the other day he had saved yet another article on the preservation of small vials of smallpox—on the off chance, just in case, for scientific use, with the understanding that no species should be intentionally lost. In the same spirit, he ruled out the petty subornings popular among politicians, but he carefully saved accounts of elections in which a blatant scoundrel was voted into office by a smug, lazy, or indifferent electorate. He scissored when he spotted superstitions singing like sirens, when he caught stupidity in action, stupidity that especially embodied willful blindness or where greed or one of the other deadly sins overcame weak reason once again. Judgments could be dicey. Dust Bowl pictures were included because it was Skizzen's conclusion that human mistreatment of the soil, not Nature out of whimsical meanness and acting alone, had made the plains barren, wasted the cattle, and scoured the barns to their bare boards. Hoof and Mouth were the names of two instruments in his orchestra. Mad Cow a must. AIDS, of course, was easy, ignorance and stupidity fed and spread it, but river blindness, say, was a close call, and he ultimately rejected some very moving photographs of scar-closed eyes.

On the walls of his attic area were everywhere pinned atrocity pictures, some of them classics: the weeping baby of Nanking or the wailing Vietnamese girl running naked amid other running, wailing children on that fatal Route 1 near Trang Bang (even the name a mockery); numerous sepias of dead outlaws with their names on crude signs propped beneath their boots; clips from films that showed what struck the eyes of those who first entered the extermination camps—careless heaps of skins and bones, entirely tangled, exhibiting more knees and elbows than two-pair-to-a-death ought allow; amateurishly aimed shots of the sodden trench-corpse as well as bodies hanging over barbed battlefield wire; the bound Viet Cong officer, a pistol at the end of a long arm pointed at his head, a picture taken in the act of his execution by a so-called chief of police; then, to add class, the rape of the Sabine women, etchings of chimney sweeps, paintings of sad solitaries and painted whores, or, for the purposes of education, the consequences of car bombs, mob hits, traitors hung from lampposts—Mussolini among the many whose bodies were publicly displayed—as were niggers strung, as a lesson, from the limbs of trees; but most were images transient for readers: countless corpses from African famines, African wars, African epidemics, ditto India, ditto China but adding floods; there were big-eyed potbellied starvelings, wasted victims of disease, fields full of dead Dinka tribesmen, machine-gunned refugees on roads, misguided monks who had set fire to themselves, ghoulishly smoking up a street; and there were lots of Japanese prints that seemed to celebrate rape, paintings and pictures that glorified war or sanctified lying priests, flattered pompous kings and smugly vicious dictators, still others that celebrated serial killers and tried to put a good face on fat ward politicians or merely reported on the Klansmen, dressed like hotel napkins; the Goya etchings depicting the *Disasters of War,* in poor reproductions to be sure, were all there, as well as Bosches Xeroxed in color from an art book, a few stills from snuff films, violent propaganda posters, numerous Dorés, Grünewalds, saints suffering on grills or from flights of arrows, details from *Guernica,* examples from Grosz, close-ups of nails penetrating palms, then boards, illustrations in volumes of the Marquis de Sade, lots of photographs of the dead on battlefields or in burial grounds from *Gardner's Photographic Sketchbook of the Civil War,* many of them tampered with and staged, which created an added interest; there were drawings of medieval implements of torture, each aspect and element precisely labeled, paintings of autos-da-fé by the Spanish master, firing squads by Manet, cavalry charges and combatants at the barricades by Delacroix; the guillotine with several of its severed heads was there, as well as emasculations, circumcision ceremonies, buffalo hunts, seal cubs as they were being clubbed, executions of various kinds—by knife, by fire, by gas, by poison, by lethal injection, by trap drop, by jolt, by shot—Indians massacred, natives forced over cliffs, notable assassinations—but only if the victim wasn't deserving—as well as

wall after wall, not in Skizzen's room but out in the world, where rebel soldiers or Warsaw Jews were lined up to be gunned down and photographed
after, during, and before by the documentary-minded; close-ups of scattered
body parts, many of them less identifiable than steaks or chops, abattoirs
in operation, fine watercolors of slave ships under full sail, a clutch of Salgado gold-mine prints depicting humans toiling in holes more horrible than
Dante had imagined (and then only for the deserving), detailed photographs
of torture instruments—the iron maiden, thumbscrew, rack—from the collection kept in the Tower of London, children huddled in doorways, on
grates, coal miners in blackface, breadlines and the bloody swollen faces of
beaten boxers, women working in sweatshops or shrouded in worshipful
crowds, torchlit Nazi rallies, and the professor's prize, an original Koudelka
picturing a tipped-over tortoise, dead on a muddy Turkish road, the photograph handsomely matted and framed and hung center stage.

Mostly, though, from every place not already tacked or pasted, clippings
were loosely pinned or taped so that they would have fluttered had there ever
been a draft, as they did wave a little when Skizzen passed, dangling for quite
a ways down the wall in overlapping layers sometimes, even stuck to flypaper
Skizzen had cannily suspended from the ceiling, the whole crowd requiring
him to duck if he didn't want his head and neck tickled, and giving to the
room a cavey cachelike feeling, as if some creature, fond of collecting, lived
there, and only sallied forth like the jackdaw to find and fetch back bright
things, or, in this case, cuttings from the tree of evil, for which purpose paper
shears had been put in every room of the large house, every room including
entry, bath, and laundry, because you never knew when you might come
upon something, and Skizzen had learned not to put off the opportunity,
or delay the acquisition, since he had, early on and before this present remedy, forgotten where he had seen a particular picture or news item, and was
sadly unable to locate it again. He vividly remembered, too, how he had lost
an image on a handout by postponing its extraction when he should have
scissored it out while he was still standing on the front stoop holding in his
shocked hand a leaflet bearing a grotesque beard and a text attacking the
Amish because they were receiving special privileges, which allowed them
their own schools, when children (whose God-loving parents were faithful
members of the Church of Christ's White Messengers) were called truants
when kept from class because in school they were compelled to study—by
a sick and godforsaken society—demonically inspired opinions of Creation
and its consequences.

Next door, though the room was doorless and open to anyone who
found their way there, was the library, three of its walls lined by crude

plank-and-brick cases crammed with books bearing witness to the inhumanity of man, especially a complete set of the saints, the *Newgate Calendar*s, several on the history of the Church, the many-volumed *International Military Trials* in an ugly library binding (for sale at a very reasonable price by the superintendent of documents of the U.S. Government Printing Office), or several on the practice of slavery through the centuries, lives of the Caesars, careers of the Medicis, biographies of feminists, the fate of the Gypsies or the American Indians, and, of course, tome after tome on holocausts and pogroms, exterminations and racial cleansings from then to now, where on one page he could feed on names like Major Dr. Huhnemoerder, Oberst von Reurmont, Gruppenfuehrer Nebe, OKW Chef KGf, and General Grosch; however, the library did not merely hold works on barbaric rites and cruel customs or on spying, strikebreaking, lynching, pillaging, raping, but on counterfeiting, colluding, cheating, exploiting, blackmailing and extorting, absconding, suborning, skimming, embezzling, and other white-collar crimes as well: proof through news reports, through ideas, images, and action, of the wholly fallen and utterly depraved condition of our race—testimony that Joseph Skizzen augmented, on the few ritual occasions he allowed himself to observe and celebrate, by his reciting aloud, while standing at what he deemed was the center of his collection, alternatively from a random page of some volume chosen similarly, or from a news bulletin pulled down blindly from whatever stalactite came to hand, although he did occasionally cheat in favor of the *Newgate Calendar,* from which he would read with relish accounts of crimes like that of Catherine Hayes, who contrived, by egging on several of her many paramours, to have her husband's head cut off, in the punishment of which the righteous were seen to be even more inventively wicked than the criminal.

When the wretched woman had finished her devotions, an iron chain was put round her body, with which she was fixed to a stake near the gallows. On these occasions, when women were burnt for petty treason, it was customary to strangle them, by means of a rope passed round the neck, and pulled by the executioner, so that they were dead before the flames reached the body. But this woman was literally burnt alive; for, the executioner letting go the rope sooner than usual, in consequence of the flames reaching his hands, the fire burnt fiercely round her, and the spectators beheld her pushing the fagots from her, while she rent the air with her cries and lamentations. Other fagots were instantly thrown on her; but she survived amidst the flames for a considerable time, and her body was not perfectly reduced to ashes in less than three hours.

Joseph Skizzen put his whole heart into his voice, happy not another ear could hear him, satisfied that no one would ever see his collection either, for he was no Jonathan Edwards, although his tones were dark, round, ripe, and juicy as olives, because he had no interest in the redemption of the masses, whose moral improvement was quite fruitless in any case. He did privately admit, and thus absolve himself of it, that Joseph Skizzen was a man who enjoyed the repeated proofs that he was right.

He had acquired an impressive collection of volumes on perverse religious rituals and social practices, a few containing photographs of wives being burned by their furniture, directions concerning the cutting out of human hearts, the placement of beautifying scars and punctures, the timing of soprano-sustaining castrations, the grooming of sacrificial animals, the strategic placement of impurity huts, the designing of corsets and binding of feet, of types of dungeons, and places for the sequestration of monks, nuns, and the general run of women who weren't thought to be unclean for other reasons.

The drug trade and all it entailed, including bribery and money laundering, bored him—Joseph Skizzen had to confess to that partiality, and to the fact that the relative absence of this and similarly vulgar forms of criminal business, as well as many of the brutalities of ordinary life which rarely reached the papers, was a serious flaw in his collection, and, presumably, in his character as well. But who would know or care? That was a comfort. His work had been protected from its critics.

Movies which would pan a camera about a serial killer's poster-lined room (or a delinquent adolescent's sometimes), after the police had invaded it, in order to astonish the audience's eyes as police eyes presumably were—such scenes would cause Skizzen an unpleasant twinge on account of the situation's distant similarity, especially when the lens would dwell on newspaper clippings, lists with circled names, or photographs of Charles Manson, but he bore such surprises well, and avoided them altogether when that was possible.

So as time and life passed, Professor Joseph Skizzen took care of Miriam, the mother with whom he still lived; he played his piano, now a nice one; he prepared his classes and dealt with his students, studied Liszt, obsessively rewrote his sentence—now in its fifty-seventh version—or clipped affronts to reason, evidences of evil action, or ill feeling, from books, papers, periodicals, and elsewhere, most of them to paste in albums organized in terms of Flaws, Crimes, and Consequences, though many of the more lurid were strung up like victims on lengths of flypaper, nothing but reports of riots on one, high treasons on another, poaching, strip-mining, or deforestation on still others; and in order not to play favorites, he decorated a specially selected string with unspeakable deeds done by Jews, among them—in honor of his would-be forgotten father—the abandonment of the family.

Professor Joseph Skizzen's concern that the human race might not endure has been succeeded by his fear that it will quite comfortably survive.

Conjunctions, 2001
Published in *Middle C,* 2013

In Camera

1 The Stock

M r. Gab didn't have that gift, though his assistant, who was supposed to be stupid but only looked so, would mutter beneath his breath, when annoyed by his tasks, "he had the gift, he did, did Gab." Mr. Gab spoke seldom, and then it was to shout at the steel shutters of the shop that were always reluctant to alter their position, whatever it was, and needed to be cajoled, flattered, then threatened. Or sometimes he spoke to the steam pipes, complaining of the knocking, complaining of the excessive heat they gave off when they had to be heated and of the odor that the steam brought to the nose through layers of paint resembling aluminum. Curls the graphs, he said with as close to a curse as he came.

Mr. Gab's shop was in a part of town so drably uninteresting robbers wouldn't visit even to case its joints, something Mr. Gab fairly certainly knew, and treasured, but he had these steel shutters left over from a former, more frequented, more luxuriant time, and felt obliged to use them. One could have guessed Mr. Gab's age from these small facts: that he thought of possible intruders as "robbers," and worried about being "glommed"—terms which have no present employment. The shutters, window-wide slats of steel in Venetian style, creaked as they descended, and no longer fit firmly together or overlaid one another as they had been designed to do in some far-off factory; consequently, streetlights—lit to illuminate an empty avenue whose venerable storefronts were a menace even during the glare of sunny afternoons—would streak into the shop at night where Mr. Gab might still be sitting, long after closing, long after nodding bye-bye to his stupid assistant, staring at his prints in the darkness, prints that covered the pockmarked walls of the shop, displayed there like dead things hung from nails, as if slain while other prey were being hunted: while picking up fallen apples maybe (though he lived so far from the country), or, rather, if a brace of grouse were to fling themselves into the apple bag, or while gathering pignuts (models ago he'd sold his car) a pair of pigeons might creep into a handy box—that unlikely—while sorting buckeyes to find the feathers of a turkey, or, while pulling loganberries out of their briaries (though he wore no woolen sleeves), flushing a covey of quail instead—anyway—prizes inadvertently taken, mistakenly developed, proudly framed.

Mr. Gab certainly had his favorites. These were images he knew so intimately they were—well, not quite etched on the balls of his eyes. He needed only the least light to see them down to their last shades of gray: an Atget was frequently imagined to be the state of his street outside—Atget, the documentarian. Perhaps he'd decide on the Atget of an intersection, of *Angle de la rue Lhomond et de la rue Rataud,* its cobbles moist, in late light, sky like sour milk, taken in the *quartier du Val-de-Grâce,* where on one wall a poster was papered to say *un million, un million,* a dozen times in a voice not ever husky. "Forever," Mr. Gab would allow himself sometimes to murmur: *cours de danse givre . . .* forever . . . though the *"cours"* is gone, *"danse"* is gone, even before the War arrived in a taxi, they were gone, gone, cobbles gone too now, probably, building likely gone, the lamp most certainly gone, and the teeth of steel, like those of a large rake, that crossed the *rue* high above every head—sure, sure—that crossed the top of the image straight through the sour-milk sky and over the tree at *rue's* end—oh yes—gone, quite gone, even the tree whose feet were hid behind a low wall, deep in the shot where the road disappeared into a vee as though down a drain—ah well—cut by now, blown over, hauled off, firewooded, gone. Dear me.

"What a curb," Mr. Gab permitted himself to exclaim. At the Louvre . . . what did the advert advise and proclaim? Who could say? With the wall retreating, the posters defaced. What a glisten, though! Still . . . the curb, the glisten, the deep recession of the street remained. Right outside there, beyond that barred door, beyond the shuttered window, lay Atget's modest little street still. Still . . . made of wavering lines of glis and shales of shine. The walk protected by posts. Mr. Gab did not dare to say aloud what he succinctly thought, as he looked out through his engraved eyes: I am Atget—the world is mine.

Only during the evening following work—Mr. Gab thought that way of it, thought of it as work—shortly after he had—well—dined, but before he went slowly to bed, unbuttoning the buttons down his shirt—well, his vest first—seeing the street or some other scene all the while the buttons went as buttons do, loose from their holes, not like released birds because it was shirt that was freed, the vest that flew loose, even if it clung to his slender frame like a woman in a romance to her equally handmade lover—no—the buttons like sentries would stay sewn in their useful line perhaps for an entire shirt life, vest time. In photographs, shirts do not get much attention.

He could of course have chosen to recall the elegant details of Le Restaurant Procope's façade, the café's name like a decoration running along in front of the building's second-floor windows, each letter as bold as an escutcheon affixed to a wrought-iron balcony railing: GRAND RESTAURANT PROCOPE, and then, under the overhang, discreet as a meeting, the name again: Grand Restaurant Procope, no doubt no longer in business though one sign said *vente des vins pour la ville*—oh, the hanging lamps were like crowned heads, the walk lined with tables and paired chairs, the hour early, each empty—not the hours but the chairs—a busy day ahead of them, waiting to accommodate customers no longer alive.

Mr. Gab lived as many shopkeepers once did, both at the rear and above his establishment. He slept in a small loft a good size for bats that he reached by climbing the short stair that rose unsteadily from a corner of his kitchen, a kitchen of sorts, in whose foreshortened center Mr. Gab kept a card table and a ceramic cat. Breakfast might be an apple and an egg. Lunch—he frequently passed on lunch, though his stupid assistant ate lunch like a lion, growling over some sandwich distantly fixed. A sip of tea, a chewy biscuit maybe. Memories going back a long way. Mostly, though, he passed on lunch.

Days were dreary—oh yes—especially in a shop stuffed with gray-white gray-black photographs in cellophane sheets that had been loosely sidefiled in cardboard boxes, tag attached, maybe FRENCH XX or COUNTRYSIDE BRITISH or RAILROADS USA. He had three for trees: bare, leafed, chopped. On the walls, clipped to wire hangers that were then hung from nails, were his prizes, displayed so as to discourage buyers. Successfully. So far. For a decade.

Mr. Gab would have six or seven customers on a good day, which is what he would almost audibly say to them when they entered, making the door ring—well, it was a rattle really. His stupid assistant would answer most questions, show them the labels on the boxes, wave at the walls hung with hangers, open a filing cabinet or a case for those who fancied the pricier ones, explain the proper technique for sliding a photograph out of its sheathing, demonstrate the underhanded manner of holding it, or, with palms gently placed at edges as if it were a rare recording, explain how one could be safely examined.

The boxes were mostly of a conventional cardboard. They sat on tables or beside tables or under tables as if they'd sat there already a long time: the ink on the labels had faded; the paper of the labels had yellowed; the corners of the labels were munched. Covers were kept closed against dust and light and idle eyes by beanbags, forever in the family, inertly weighing on the boxes' cardboard flaps. The nails Mr. Gab had driven into the walls were zinc'd, which made them suitable for fastening shingles, but you couldn't have drawn one out without pulling, along with the shank, large chunks of plaster. The wire hangers themselves were in weary shape. So the pictures hung askew. As if holding on with one hand.

Mr. Gab stocked several versions of the same photograph sometimes. A round red sticker affixed to the wrap signaled a superior print, a green circle indicated one produced from the original negative, but late in its life, whereas a yellow warned the customer that the sheath enclosed a mere reproduction, however excellent it might often be. His red version of rue Rataud was as fine as the one conserved at the Carnavalet, but on the white rectangles with their softly rounded corners which Mr. Gab had pasted to the bottom of each envelope and where he identified the subject, the photographer, the method, and the negative's likely residence, he had written about the less genuine image, below a yellow ball that suggested caution, the words "*trop mauvais état,*" a little joke only scholars might understand and enjoy.

Mr. Gab's provenances were detailed and precise; however, years earlier an envious dealer had accused his rival (for Mr. Gab was then in a dinky shop across from him on another street) (and whom the envious dealer called "Grab," somehow sensing Mr. Gab's sensitivity about his name, though unaware that Mr. Gab had become silent in order to avoid being addressed by anyone as "Gabby") of accepting or otherwise acquiring (during midnight visits and stealthy trips) stolen property. How otherwise, the envious dealer complained, could one account for the presence, in prime condition, of so many rare and important photographs in such shabby shoebox circumstances? "Shoebox" was slanderous, certainly, though nothing had come of these allegations except a shady reputation, thought actually to be desirable in some circles.

A print's quality depended almost entirely upon its preservation of details, its respect for values. The fog-white sky of rue Rataud, in the version under its cautionary yellow dot, smeared the end of the street so you could not see how or where it turned, walls were muffled, and a hard light made the outlines of the cobbles disappear; while the red-tagged rue Rataud allowed the eye to count windows far away and discern a distant huddle of buildings. In the latter, the spiky rod, whose use he could not fathom, crossed the street in the guise of a determinate dark line; in the former it was dim and insubstantial, as if obscured by smoke. On red's verbose information label, Mr.

Gab had written that his photograph had come to the United States in the luggage of Berenice Abbott, from whom he had received a few prime prints of other subjects. If interested, please ask. About the history of yellow, Mr. Gab offered nothing.

The stupid assistant was not sufficiently steeped, so when, as occasionally happened, a customer wished a little history, Mr. Gab would have to hold forth, not reluctantly with regard to the information, which he believed every cultivated person should possess, but reluctantly regards speaking—making noises, choosing words, determining the line of march for a complex chronology. From the box marked DECORATIVE ELEMENTS, for instance, another Atget might be withdrawn, and Mr. Gab could inform his customer that this view of some paneling at the Hôtel Roquelaure had been purchased from Atget by Georges Hoentschel—did he know?—the designer of the Union Centrale pavilion for the 1900 World's Fair in Paris; and subsequently in an archive of great richness and variety that Hoentschel had catalogued and published in 1908 before it was sold to J. P. Morgan, who later donated the entire shebang to New York's Metropolitan Museum. Someone had dismembered a 1908 catalogue and this image—which you should please hold at its tender edges—is a limb from one of those dismemberments.

Mr. Gab did not usually remark the fact (since some found the fact disturbing) that the door was no doubt long gone, though the photograph was evidence of fine wood and careful workmanship; but because Atget had taken a portion of the decoration's portrait, the surviving image had increased in value at each exchange and become what Mr. Gab, in a rare moment of eloquence, called "a ghost worth gold." Nothing touched by this man's lens was lost, he said, each was elevated by its semblance to sublimity, even the dubious ladies of the XIXe arrondissement, three of them (two leaning, one peeking) from the traditional doorway, appetizing if you ate mud, an example of which (not the mud but the unsavory subjects) he, Mr. Gab, had in a box at the back of the shop marked NUES, even though the women were decently dressed.

The light in the store, Mr. Gab's stupid assistant persisted in judging, "was lousy." With the shutters closed, you could see how dust-covered the front windows had become, while most of the lamps were simply bulbs housed in coffee cans hung from wires punched through their bottoms. A proper tungsten lamp throwing the appropriately well-wiped light could be found at the rear of the store—"Don't call it a store," Mr. Gab always protested—where anyone who wore serious eyes could contemplate in quiet a possible purchase. The assistant believed that the entire furnishings of the store—the old oak desk where Mr. Gab presided, the swivel chair, alike in oak, the rose-colored puff upon which he sat when he was seated, the smeary windows, a door which uttered a needless warning, the faded façade from former days, which incorporated a large dim sign spelling P H O T O G R A P H Y in letters that looked as if they wanted nothing to do with one another, the scuffed and cracked linoleum floor, the pocked walls with their swaying trophies, the trestle tables upon which the cardboard boxes stood, or under which they hid, or beside which they huddled, the dumb homely handmade lamps that filled the room with the rattle of tinlight, the tall stool in a back corner where the stupid assistant perched, the rug, instead of a door, which hung over the entrance to Mr. Gab's private quarters—they were all meant to deceive detectives and most untrained and idle inspection. For the truth was—since the assistant harbored the same opinion as Mr. Gab's once-a-time rival—the stock was stupendous, of varied kind and exquisite quality, a condition which was quite unaccountable unless the prints had, at one time or other, by someone or other, been pinched.

The assistant, whose apparent stupidity was an effect of his seeming a suitable subject for Diane Arbus, knew, to cite one outré instance, that in a box at the back of the store, and in two Mr. Gab kept in a cleaning closet in his kitchen, were several beautiful pictures set in Sicily and shot in the early fifties by, of all people for Mr. Gab to have discovered, Enzo Sellerio: in particular one from Vizzini of the worn head and shoulders of a woman who had framed herself with a window that in turn was surrounded by rows and rows of descending roof tiles textured to a fare-thee-well—a woman whose gaze was one of total intensity, though her mouth expressed quizzicality, while on the sill lay an aristocracy of fingers, age infecting everything else—her fingers positioned as if she were emerging from the grave of days; then another taken through the fly chains of a Palermo doorway so that a seated man, a horse and cart, a church front, and a couple are seen as if scrimmed by a blurring rain of *o*'s; or the Chiesa Madre's quiltlike stairway viewed from above as it's being climbed by a herd of Paternò goats . . . well, where could this man who went nowhere, rarely to the edge of his neighborhood, have obtained work of this quality without hanky-panky of some kind? Without a lot of miscreation going on behind the back of every member of an honest public.

Oh . . . yes . . . Mr. Gab also had a very moving photograph—perhaps a tad mellow—of some trailer-camp kids in Richmond, California, that Ansel Adams had taken with Dorothea Lange's twin-lens Rolleiflex during the War, cropped and dodged according to his own account, and just how had that dramatic image made its way into a cello envelope and thence to a cardboard box in this silly little shop on Arsenal Avenue except if it were hiding out?

Mr. Gab was as silent about his system of supply as he was about everything else. He sold so seldom he may have been holding most of his stock for years, and in the same boxes too, long before his assistant became old enough to observe any rate of change. Nevertheless, from time to time a very big Russian-looking man in a very heavy Russian-looking coat, though not with a dead animal on his head, which would have made everyone take note, came with wild hatless hair to see, and apparently to consult with, Mr. Gab, going into his quiet private quarters for a little chat, carrying a case large, flat, and black. The Russian's big bass would soften as soon as his wide back disappeared behind the rug, which Mr. Gab held open for him as though they were entering a box at the theater. How are you this very day, my boy, the big man would thunder when the stupid assistant greeted him with a wince of recognition and a pleasant surprised smile. Annduh Missterr Gahb, my boy, is he ahbought? His accent, thick as his coat, was too eclectic to be genuine, and had been faked to cover a Russian one, the assistant thought. It was then, at the card table in the company of the ceramic cat, that the case would click open to disclose, the assistant imagined, a wondrous rarity, an August Sander maybe, filched from a German collector, a labor leader in an ill-fitting unpressed dark suit, throttled tie, intense vest, like those Mr. Gab wore, hair receding so it was now a headband, and those arms at his side ending in pugnacious little fists.

But when the assistant went later to look under Sander in the German box he found only the one which had been there through uncounted years: the hotelkeeper and his wife, Gastwirtsehepaar, around 1930, Tweedledum with Tweedledee, posed outside their vine-sided hostelry, she in her polka-dot dress and frontally folded arms, he in bow tie and white shirt and hanky, a startle of patches against the compulsory black suit, including vest—black too—tucked under the coat like a head hid in a camera's hood—uh-oh—there's one button missing, one out of four, too bad, the bottoms of the innkeeper's trousers hiked in an ungainly fashion above a pair of sturdy polished shoes, black as well, the innkeeper's arms clasped behind him so that the swell of his stomach would suggest to a hesitant guest hearty fare; well, they were both girthy full-fleshed folk as far as that goes, her eyes in a bit of a squint, his like raisins drowning in the plump of his cheeks.

What made August Sander's portraits so great—"great" was the appropriate word in the assistant's opinion—was the way his sitters made visibly manifest, like the backgrounds behind them, the lives that had shaped their pictured faces and forms, as though their daily occupations had drawn them there to be displayed for the camera with all the seriousness suitable to such a show of essential self.

If you were to look at the penetrating portrait Berenice Abbott made of

Eugène Atget when he was a wispy-haired old man with sunken cheeks, a mouth relieved of most of its teeth, assertive nose, and intense eyes, you might get a whiff of Mr. Gab too, for he was ancient early, grew up to reach old in a hurry, and then didn't change much for decades, except to solidify his opinions, much the way Atget had, both men easily angered, both men hugging their habits, each short of speech, and patient as the stones Atget alone gelatinized. Mr. Gab disavowed color with the fervor of a Puritan, and nothing in the shop had a hue you'd want to name besides the dull brown cardboard and the pillow in his chair, because the walls were once a clean cream dirtied now to nondescription, and the lino floor was like a playing board of black/white squares, a design mostly seen unmopped in public toilets, while the rug he'd hung across the door to his digs was a tweed a fade away from tan.

Mr. Gab was a stickler. His ideal was the perfect picture taken on the wing with one shot, and allowed to emerge from its development like a chick its egg, so that one saw not just the subject supremely rendered but a testimony to the unerring fineness of the photographer's eye: an eye unlike the painter's, he claimed, because the painter constructed; the painter made up his image as if the canvas were a face; while the photographer sought his composition like a hunter his prey, and took it away clean, when it was found, to present in its purity, as the result of an act of vision, the sort of seeing no one else employed, what Mr. Gab called "slingshot sight." Painting took too long, sculpture of course was worse, and encouraged thinking, permitted alterations, endured changes of mind; whereas the photographer came, saw, and shot in a Rolleiflex action, in one unified gesture like waving off a fly.

Mr. Gab knew Atget bided his time, did and redid; he knew that Edward Weston pulled images like putty into weird unnatural shapes; he knew that Walker Evans cropped like a farmer, August Sander as well, who also staged every shot with theatrical calculation; that Man Ray was like Duchamp, an incorrigible scamp; that Ansel Adams dodged and burned and renovated; that even André Kertész, who possessed, like Josef Sudek, a saintly sensibility, had more than once employed a Polaroid. . . . well, Mr. Gab didn't say very much about such lapses; he just threw up his hands, palms up/arms out, the way he did in the winter, salting his sidewalk, and said that it was beyond understanding that the same man who had taken, from an overlooking window, those pictures of Washington Square in a snow of fences—when? Nineteen seventy? well—in—anyway—a nearby year—it was dumbfounding that an artist of such supreme severity should have succumbed to Kodachromania and taken, it was said, as if he had embezzled them, two thousand Polaroids, sinking for a time as far as Cibachrome, but genius was a dark cave full of flickers; who knew what the darkness might disclose? who knew, his hands said, washing themselves in the air.

Mr. Gab forgave, and forgave again, but certain photographers had too many counts against them, like David Bailey, to mention an outstanding instance, because he bandaged the body exposing only the legendary wound with its unlikely whiskers, or did the worst sort of celebratory portrait—Yoko Ono, for god's sake—or shot up the worst sort of scene—Las Vegas, can you imagine?—consorted with cover models, and had nudes blow chewing-gum bubbles to match their bubbies or wear necklaces of barbed wire; then there was a hot lens like Irving Penn, who spent too much time in the studio, who worked for fashion magazines (advertising and news were also OUT), who photographed Marisa Berenson's perfect bosom and Rudolf Nureyev's perfect limbs because they were Berenson's boobs or Nureyev's calves, and did portraits of famous folk like Truman Capote on account of that fame, often in silly contrived poses such as Woody Allen gotten up as Groucho Marx (Mr. Gab vented exasperation), or did cutesy-pie pictures like that faucet Penn pretended was dripping diamonds, but almost worst, his malignant habit of pushing his subjects into corners where they'd be certain to feel uncomfortable and consequently conspire with the tormentor to adopt a look never before or after worn.

Nevertheless (for Mr. Gab was composed of contradictions too), Mr. Gab could show you (while complaining of its name) *Cigarette No. 69*, from a series Penn had done in '72, or a devilish distortion from the box marked NUES which Kertész had accomplished in 1933 as another revenge against women . . . well, it was admittedly beautiful, simply so, so simply blessed . . . he might mention the gracefully elongated hands pressed between the thighs, or draw attention to the dark button indenting the belly as if it were waiting to ring up a roomer on the fourth floor, the soft—oh yes—mound, also expanded into a delicious swath of . . . Mr. Gab's stupid assistant would have to say the word "pubic" . . . hair, a romantic image, really, in whose honor Mr. Gab's hands shook when he held the photo, because he'd feel himself caught for a moment in the crease of an old heartbreak (that's what an observer might presume), memories extended elastically through time until, with a snap, they flew out of thought like a pursued bird.

The customers . . . well, they were mostly not even browsers, but wanderers, or refugees from a bad patch of weather, or misinformed, even so far as to be crestfallen when they understood the Nowhere they had come to, but occasionally there'd be some otherwise oblivious fellow who would fly to a box, shove off the bag of beans, and begin to finger through the photos as you might hunt through a file, with a haste hope might have further hastened, an air of expectancy that suggested some prior prompting, only to stop and withdraw a sheet suddenly and accompany it to the light of the good lamp in the rear, where he'd begin to examine it first with a studied casualness that seemed more conspiratorial than anything, looking about like a fly about to light before indifferently glancing at the print, until at last, now as intent as a tack, he'd submit to scrutiny each inch with tight white lips, finally following Mr. Gab, who had anticipated the move, through the rug to the card table and the cat in the kitchen, where they'd have what Mr. Gab called, with a pale smile that was nearly not there, a confab.

Concerning cost. This is what his stupid assistant assumed. The meeting would usually end with a sale, a sale that put Mr. Gab in possession of an envelope fat with cash, for he accepted nothing else, nor were his true customers surprised, since they came prepared with a coat in whose inside pocket the fat envelope would be stashed. Consequently, it was a good thing the shop was so modest, the neighborhood so banal and grubby, the street, in fact, macadam to a fault, resembling Atget's avenues or stony lanes not a whit, not by a quick flip of light from a puddle or a flop of shade from an overhang, because the shop's stock was indeed valuable, and somewhere there was concealed cash with which, his stupid assistant surmised, Mr. Gab purchased further contraband, plus, if funds had been apportioned, a spot where lurked the money that tided Mr. Gab, his business, and his stupid assistant over from one week to the next (though their wants were modest) until, among the three who stepped inside at different times on an April day, a shifty third would paw through the box marked PRAGUE as if a treasure had been buried there, and then, despite nervous eyes and a tasteless cream-colored spring coat where—yes—the cash had been carried, buy a Josef Sudek that depicted Hradčany Castle circa 1915 under a glowering sky.

Mr. Gab really didn't want to let go of anything. His pleasure in a photograph, his need for it to sustain his sinking spirit, rose as the print was withdrawn and examined, and neared infatuation, approached necessity, as he and the customer, photo in front of them, haggled over the price. So Mr. Gab drove a hard bargain without trying to be greedy, though that was the impression he gave. Still, he had to let some of his prizes go if he was going to continue to protect his stock and ensure his collection's continued appreciation and applause.

Yes . . . yes . . . yes . . . the audience was small, but its appreciation was deep and vast, and its applause loud and almost everlasting.

Occasionally, as the assistant remembered, there were some close calls. A tall aristocratic-looking gentleman in expensive clothes and a light touch of gray hair chose a late afternoon to enter. Greeted by Mr. Gab in the usual way, he brusquely responded: I understand you have a photograph by Josef Sudek depicting two wet leaves. After a silence filled with surprise and apprehension, Mr. Gab replied with a question: who had informed the gentleman of that fact? He, by the way, he went on, was the owner of the shop; Mr. Gab was his name, while his visitor was . . . ? It is common knowledge in certain places, Mr. Gab, if it is indeed you, the tall man answered, and consequently has no more distinct location than a breeze. For some moments, Mr. Gab was unsure which of his two questions had been addressed. I shall, the stranger went on, show you my card directly I have seen the Sudek. *Two Wet Leaves,* he repeated. What period would that be, Mr. Gab said, somewhat lame in his delay. Though it was his stupid assistant who limped. And who did so now—limped forward in an aisle while Mr. Gab was making preparations to reply. His stupid assistant: smiling, winking one bad eye. His naturally crooked mouth turned his smile into a smirk. Later, Mr. Gab would gratefully acknowledge his assistant's attempt to Quasimodo the threatening fellow into an uneasy retreat.

But the man pushed forward on his own hook, looking sterner than a sentencing judge. You'd know, he said. You've got a print. *Two Wet Leaves.* Archival quality, I'm told. Nineteen thirty-two. You'd know. Then, casting an eye as severe as a spinster's at the layout of the shop, he added: where shall I find it? (waving a commanding hand) where is it hid? The provenance of my photographs, Mr. Gab replied with nervous yet offended heat, is clear beyond question, their genuineness is past dispute; their quality unquestioned and unthreatened.

As if Mr. Gab's ire had melted the mister's snowy glare, he made as if to communicate a smile. The assistant tried various slithery faces on and did appear to be quite stupid indeed. I should think every photograph in this place was in dire straits, sir, the man said sternly, ignoring the reassurance of his own signal. As I remember, Mr. Gab managed, *Two Wet Leaves* is quite impressive. You'd know, the man insisted, beginning a patrol of aisle one, his head bent to read the labels of the boxes. I had such a print once in my possession, obtained from Anna Fárová herself, Mr. Gab admitted. Soooo . . . the stranger straightened and turned to confront Mr. Gab. And was it taken by sly means from Anne d'Harnoncourt's exhibit at the Philadelphia? Only from Anna's hand herself, sir, Mr. Gab replied, now firm and fierce, and no other Fárová than Fárová. As if there were many, the man said frowning, you would know.

Why not an Irving Penn? This insult was not lost on their visitor, whose upper lip appeared to have recently missed a mustache. The many boxes seemed to daunt him, and it was now obvious that Mr. Gab would not be helpful. I have friends in Philadelphia, he said in a threatening tone. I understand the nearby gardens are nice, Mr. Gab rejoined. It was clear to the entire shop (and that included the china cat) that Mr. Gab had regained his courage. Was this freshly shaven man perhaps an officer of the law, the stupid assistant wondered, coughing now behind a stubby hand whose thumbnail was missing as David Smith's was in that portrait by Penn, the one in which Smith's mouth, fat-lipped and amply furred, is sucking on a pipe.

It was necessary to sidle if you wished to approach the wall, and sidle the tall man did, closing in on an image dangling there, gray in its greasy container. Is that, by god, a Koudelka, a Koudelka to be sure. His hands rose toward it. Not for sale, Mr. Gab said. Not for money. No need to remove it. But the deed was done. Slender fingers from a fine cuff parted the clip and slid the photo forth, balancing it under a blast of can light upon a delicate teeter of fingertips. Not for money? Then in trade, the man said, gazing at its darkly blanketed horse, and at the hunkered man apparently speaking to the horse's attentive head. Ah, what magical music, the man exclaimed, as if to himself. The grays . . . in the horse, the street, the wall . . . the tracks of light, the swirls and streaks of gray . . . melodious as nothing can be. Unless it was Sudek himself, said Mr. Gab. The man's lengthy head rose from the picture where it had been feeding. Yes, he said, having taken thought. Only Sudek himself.

The fingernails are especially . . . Mr. Gab began, because he couldn't help himself. Ah, and the white above that one hoof, the visitor responded, entranced. Yes, the nails, the gesture of the hand, a confused puff of tail and that wall . . . such a wall. Hoofprints, Mr. Gab prompted. Dark soft spots . . . yes . . . and so . . . would you consider a trade? the man asked smiling—fully, genuinely—as he laid the cellophane envelope carefully on top of a cardboard box and allowed the print to float down upon it. I might have in my possession—if you have too many, you would know—a Sudek myself I'd be prepared to swap. I couldn't part—Mr. Gab broke off to repeat himself. Not for trade or sale, though, if the Sudek were fine enough, he, Mr. Gab, might be prepared to purchase . . . But were you to see the Sudek, the man said, pointing toward his eyes . . .

It's a trap, Mr. Gab's assistant thought, for he only looked a bit stupid, especially with a little dab of spit moistening the open corner of his mouth. It is the immersement, the immersement of the figures in their fore- and back- and floor ground, that is so amazing, don't you agree? Mr. Gab, unsure, nodded. He's an entrapper, the assistant thought. I should show you the Sudek, the visitor said, no longer a customer but now a salesman. It sings, sir, sings. I'm willing to look at anything Sudek, Mr. Gab said, over his assistant's unvoiced series of "no"s. All right, the seller said, slipping his tall frame toward them. After reading Mr. Gab's expression, the man left abruptly, without leaving a clue to his intentions, and without closing the door behind him.

2 The Stupid Assistant

Had appeared at Mr. Gab's shop door years ago with a note from the orphanage . . . okay . . . from a welfare agency. The note was in fact in a sealed envelope, and the boy, who was at that time about ten or twelve, and wasn't yet Mr. Gab's assistant, hadn't an inkling of its contents. Nor did he care much. He was not then a very caring child. He had seen too many empty rooms filled with kids of a disownership of themselves similar to his. Mr. Gab looked at the envelope handed him and shook his head warily, as if he could read through cream. He then conferred upon the child a similar gesture, as if he saw through him too—clear to his mean streak. Here at last, hey! he said. The kid had a pudgy bloataboy body. Half of him, the right half, though undersized, seemed okay; the leftover half, however, had been severely short-changed. The head sloped more steeply than heads should, a shoulder sank, an arm was stunted, its squat hand had somewhere lost a finger, and the leg was missing most of its length. The child had consequently a kind of permanent lean which a thick wood-soled shoe did little to correct, though the fellow tried to compensate by pushing off with his short leg, and thereby tipping himself up to proper verticality. The result was that he bobbed about as though fish were biting, nibbling at bait hung deeply beneath whatever he was walking on—a sidewalk, lawn, shop floor, cindered ground.

The boy knew that he was being handed over. The lady with him had explained matters, then explained them again, and made silly claims that didn't fit what little he knew of his own cloudy history. This grouchy stranger, he was told, had been his mother's husband, but was not known to be his father. The identity of his father remained a mystery. The child's mother had not done a Dickens on him and died of childbedding, but had come down unto death with influenza when he was allegedly a month or two past the curse of his birth. Cared for by the state from then on. He went from wet nurse to children's home to foster parents back to children's home again. No one liked him. He was too ugly.

He appeared to be stupid, and most of what he did was awkward, to say the least. In close quarters he tended to carom. He learned that when you failed to understand something you were blamed for that, but that alone, thus escaping consequences. People would say: well, he didn't know any better; he's not all there. Mr. Gab called him "you stupid kid" from the very beginning, and never called him anything else, though he lived with Mr. Gab above the first shop (on the street of his envious enemy) like one of the family if there'd been a family, and in time ceased resenting the name, which was often sweetly drawled—hey-u-stew-pid—and eventually shortened to u-Stu, a result that u-Stu quite liked, though Mr. Gab pointed out that now his name was as out of kilter as u-Stu's stature and his gait.

In point of fact, there was really nothing the matter with his mind, which had somehow scuttled to the right side of his brain when his deformities were being assembled, so when his head got lopped a little on the left, his intelligence remained intact, hiding safely a bit behind and a bit above his bright right eye, and looking out of it with the force of two whole hemispheres.

For his entire life, not omitting now, Mr. Gab's assistant had watched gazes turn aside, watched notice be withdrawn, watched courses alter in order to avoid the embarrassments of his body: the bob and weave of it, its stunted members, the missing finger, the droopy eye, the little irreducible slobber that robbed his mouth of dignity, and the vacancy of a look that lacked muscle; who wanted to encounter them? face nature's mistake? pretend you were talking to a normal citizen instead of a mid-sized dope-dwarf? Kids his own age were curious, of course, and would stare holes in his shirt. Neither being ignored nor peered at were tolerable states.

U-Stu's speech had a slight slur to it on account of some crookedness at the left corner of his mouth and a bit of permanently fat lip in the same place. Simpleminded, most thought him, if they listened at all. He'd talk anyway. Ultimately he took pleasure in producing discomfiture and awkwardness, embarrassment and shame. It suited Mr. Gab to keep him around for the same reason. And he liked the name "Stu" because he felt himself to be a loose assemblage of parts that commingled in his consciousness like diced carrots and chunks of meat in juice. A few, like Boombox, the Russian furrier, would address him directly, but blarefully, so they still wouldn't see him through the dust-up of their own noise. After all, such folk had business with his master, as the assistant was sure they thought Mr. Gab was. He, on the other hand, was ugh! He was Igor. Who deals in eyes of newts. And brains of bats. Stirs into pots the kidneys of cats.

At first the silence was stifling, Mr. Gab's directions terse, his look stony; and his assistant was certain that this indifference was an act to cover revulsion; but after a while Mr. Gab began to see u-Stu's crooked mouth, saw the little bubbles of spit, heard the slur, grew accustomed to the rockabye-bounce, and accepted u-Stew's absent finger as well as the nail that was never there, not hammered off as had been, u-Stu believed, David Smith's. Then, after further familiarity was achieved, the assistant became invisible again, the way one's wife fades, or actual son recedes, seen without being seen, heard without hearing, felt without caring, even, when it was the wife, for her plump breast. This was okay in most minds because it was based upon acceptance. Like getting used to handling worms or disemboweling birds. Yet it wasn't okay to the assistant because the assistant felt he was in fact disgusting—quite—so that if you were to truly take him in you should continue to feel revulsion too: he hadn't been brought into the world merely to wobble, but to repel people by these means, and at the same time to remind them of their luck in having sailed all—not just portions—of themselves down the birth canal.

The first shop, though it had a finer front, had been much smaller, and the assistant, while yet too young to be much help, had to assist in sleeping, since Mr. Gab talked in his sleep, and snored like a roaring lion, and turned and tossed like a wave, and occasionally punched the air as if he were a boxer in training, so the boy had to shake Mr. Gab awake sometimes, or lie in the dark nearby, listen to his mumbles, and participate in the nightmares, which was one reason why the assistant said, in his own undertone, he has the gift, Gab has, the gift. The boy asked Mr. Gab if he had enemies he was defeating when he poked his pillow or flailed away at the night air, and this question helped Mr. Gab realize that their present sleeping arrangement wasn't salubrious. After some finagling, he found the space where they did their little business now, and there they established themselves, after making several trips (it was but a few blocks) to trundle cartons of prints on a handcart when it wasn't raining and if the coast was clear.

After the move, he slept in a sleeping bag at the back of the second store, at the border of Mr. Gab's quarters but not over the line, where a dog might have lain had they had one—art and dogs don't mix, Mr. Gab said (Mr. Gab squeezed his nose with a set of fingers whenever Mr. Wegman's name was mentioned), and the best kind of cat is ceramic. I shall be your guard ghoul, the assistant said, a remark which Mr. Gab didn't find funny, though he rarely laughed at anything; occasionally upon seeing a photo he would hoot; however, u-Stu wasn't sure whether his hoot was one of amusement or merely derisory, so perhaps he was never amused, though he from time to time made such a noise.

U-Stu had facial hair on half of his face, and Mr. Gab, to u-Stu's surprise, would shave him. Half a beard is not better than none, he said. Because he believed for a long time that his assistant was too stupid to shave himself, certainly too stupid to live alone, take care of himself in any ordinary way, he shaved his adolescent; initially even cut the boy's meat; carefully combed his ungainly hair; pressed his few clothes with an iron he had heated on the stove; and tried to cook things that were easy to eat. Gradually, Mr. Gab realized that although his stupid assistant chewed crookedly, his chew was nevertheless quite effective, and despite the fact that the boy was short-armed (Mr. Gab always winced at this formulation), he could manage a knife and fork (he needed to lower one shoulder to pull his short arm to the front), and with his one good eye working overtime (as Mr. Gab probably thought), he could read, shave, look at pictures, and, with a control over his body that grew better and better, he could perform his characteristic bob-and-wobble much more smoothly. U-Stu soon learned to repair fixtures, sweep the store, replace photographs in their plastic sleeves, and return them properly to their cardboard files. Oh, yes . . . and ask visitors: muh I hulp you, shur?

Mr. Gab began by speaking to the boy (he had not yet received his promotion to stupid assistant) slowly, and a little loudly, as though the boy might be a bit deaf in addition, talking to him often, contrary to his habitual silence, plainly believing that such treatment was necessary for the lad's mental health, which it no doubt was, although no number of words could make him into a lad, because lads were always strapping. This loquacity—night and day, it seemed—led the boy to believe that Mr. Gab gabbed, was a gabber by nature, so he would say to himself, almost audibly, he has the gift, he does, does Gab, as he went about his work, which was each week more and more advanced in difficulty. He could see Mr. Gab's face wrestling with the question: what shall I say today—good heavens—and on what subject? Mr. Gab's slow considered ramblings were to be the boy's schooling. Perhaps, today, he'd want to learn about bikes. I want to know about my mother, the boy asked. Mr. Gab began to answer, almost easily, taken by surprise: she resembled one of Stieglitz's portraits of O'Keeffe. She was beautiful beyond the bearing of one's eyes. Such hands. Stieglitz always photographed her hands. Her hands. As if he had awakened, Mr. Gab broke off in great embarrassment, his face flushed and its expression soon shunted to a sidetrack.

Before that blunder—I want to know about my mother—Mr. Gab had spoken to the boy of many things. He always spoke as if chewing slowly, in the greatest seriousness, early on about school and how he, Mr. Gab, had struggled through classes here after his family had come to the States, having an unpronounceable name, and not knowing the language; about his sisters and aunts, mothers and grans, never of men, because men, he said, scorned him for his interests, and broke his Brownie; he talked about the time when he had begun work in a drugstore, learning from books how to develop his prints; about, after he had gotten canned for stealing chemicals, the days he had sold door to door—brushes, pots and pans—enduring the embarrassments of repeated rejection, once even attacked, his face mopped by his own mop by an irate customer (the sunny side of things was left dark); until, eventually, having marched through many of the miseries of his life (though leaving serious gaps, even his auditor was aware of that), the subject he chose to address was more and more often the photograph, its grays and its glories.

Beneath—are u listening, u-stew-pid-u?—beneath the colored world, like the hidden workings of the body, where the bones move, where the nerves signal, where the veins send the blood flooding—where the signaling nerves especially form their net—lie all the grays, the grays that go from the pale gray of bleached linen, through all the shades of darkening, deepening graying grays that lie between, to the grays that are nearly soot-black, without light: the gray beneath blue, the gray beneath green, yes, I should also say the gray beneath gray; and these grays are held in that gray continuum between gray extremes like books between bookends. U-Stu, pay attention, this is the real world, the gray gradation world, and the camera, the way an X-ray works, reveals it to our eye, for otherwise we'd have never seen it; we'd have never known it was there, under everything, beauty's real face beneath the powders and the rouges and the crèmes. Color is cosmetic. Good for hothouse blooms. Great for cards of greeting. Listen, u-Stew, color is consternation. Color is a lure. Color is candy. It makes sensuality easy. It leads us astray. Color is oratory in the service of the wrong religion. Color makes the camera into a paintbrush. Color is camouflage. That was Mr. Gab's catechism: what color was. Color was not what we see with the mind. Like an overpowering perfume, color was vulgar. Like an overpowering perfume, color lulled and dulled the senses. Like an overpowering perfume, color was only worn by whores.

Grass cannot be captured in color. It becomes confused. Trees neither. Except for fall foliage seen from a plane. But in gray: the snowy rooftop, the winter tree, whole mountains of rock, the froth of a fast stream can be caught, spew and striation, twig and stick, footprint on a snowy walk, the wander of a wrinkle across the face . . . oh . . . and Mr. Gab would interrupt his rhapsody to go to a cabinet and take out one of Sudek's panoramic prints: see how the fence comes toward the camera, as eager as a puppy, and how the reflection of the building in the river, in doubling the image, creates a new one, born of both body and soul, and how the reflection of the dome of the central building on the other side of the water has been placed at precisely the fence's closest approach, and how, far away, the castle, in a gray made of mist, layers the space, and melts into a sky that's thirty shades of gradual. . . . see that? see how? How the upside-down world is darker, naturally more fluid . . . ah . . . and, breaking off again, Mr. Gab withdrew from a cardboard carton called PRAGUE a photograph so lovely that even the stupid not-yet assistant drew in his breath as though struck in the stomach (though he'd been poked in the eye); and Mr. Gab observed this and said ah! you do see, you do . . . well . . . bless you. The stupid not-yet assistant was at that moment so happy he trembled at the edge of a tear.

Hyde Park Corner. This picture, let's pretend, is one of the Park speakers, Mr. Gab said, pointing at a hanger. What does it tell us? Ah, the harangu- ers, they stand there, gather small crowds, and declaim about good and evil. They promise salvation to their true believers. Mr. Gab went to the wall and took down his Alvin Langdon Coburn. Held it out for u-Stu's inspection like a tray of cookies or anything not likely to remain in one place for long. There's a dark circle protecting the tree and allowing its roots to breathe. And the dark trunk too, rising to enter its leaves. In a misted distance—see?—a horse-drawn bus, looking like a stagecoach, labeled A1, with its driver and several passengers. In short: we see this part of the world immersed in this part of the world's weather. But we also see someone seeing it, someone having a feeling about the scene, not merely in a private mood, but respond- ing to just this . . . this . . . and taking in the two trees and the streetlamp's standard, the carriage, and in particular the faint diagonals of the curb, these sweet formal relations, each submerged in a gray-white realm that's at the same time someone's—Alvin Langdon Coburn's—head. And the photo tells us there are no lines in nature. Edge blends with edge until edgelessness is obtained. The spokes of the wheels are little streaks of darker air into which the white horse is about to proceed. But, my boy, Alvin Langdon Coburn's head is not now his head, not while we see what he is seeing, for he is at this moment a stand-in for God. A god who is saying: let there be this sacred light.

Mr. Gab would lower his nose as if sniffing up odors from the image. If the great gray world holds sway beneath the garish commerce of color, so the perception of its beauty hides from the ordinary eye, for what does the ordinary eye do but ignore nearly everything it sees, seeking its own weak satisfactions?

Such shadows as are here, for instance, in these photographs, are not illu- sions to be simply sniffed at. Where are the real illusions, u-Stu? They dwell in the eyes and hearts and minds of those in the carriage—yes—greedy to be going to their girl, to their bank, to their business. Do they observe the street as a gray stream? No—they are off to play Monopoly. Scorn overcame Mr. Gab, whose voice sounded hoarse. They have mayhem on their minds.

Finally, Mr. Gab had got round to the War. Mr. Gab's tour of duty—he was a corporal of supply—took him to Europe. In London he learned about the Bostonian Coburn. In Paris, he discovered Atget. In Berlin, he ran into Sander. In Prague . . . in Prague . . . Mr. Gab was mustered out in Europe and spent a vaguely substantial number of years in the Continent's major cities. More, Mr. Gab did not divulge; but he did speak at length of Italy's glories, of Spain's too, of Paris and Prague. . . . He took u-Stu on slow walks across the Charles Bridge, describing the statuary that lined it, elegizing the decaying, dusty, untouched city, mounting the endless flight of steps to the Hradčany Castle, taking in both the Černín and the Royal Gardens. They strolled the Malá Strana, the Smetana Quai, as well as those renamed for Janáček and Masaryk, had coffee in Wenceslas Square, visited St. Vitus Cathedral, and eventually crossed the Moldau bridges one word after another, each serving for two: a meaning in memory, an image in imagination.

When Mr. Gab returned to the States, he enrolled in New York's City College on the GI Bill, while working, to make ends meet, serially at several photography shops and even serving, during a difficult period, as a guard in a gallery. But now the gaps in this history of his grew ever greater, became more noticeable than before; details, which had been pointlessly plentiful about Prague buildings and Italian traffic, disappeared into vague generalities like figures in a Sudek or a Coburn fog, and most questions, when rarely asked, were curtly rebuffed.

But Mr. Gab did regale his pupil with an account of his trip in a rented truck to their present city, and u-Stu was given to understand, though the story did not dwell on cargo or luggage, that his cartons came with him, and, in Johnstown, of all places, were threatened by a downpour which forced him for a time to heave to and wait the water out, so sudden and severe it was, and how nervous he had become watching the Conemaugh River rise. The journey had all the qualities of uprootedness and flight, especially since Mr. Gab's account did suggest that he'd left New York with his college education incomplete, and a bitterness about everything academic, about study and teaching and scholarship, which only hinted at why he had abandoned his archival enterprise.

For in Europe, surrounded at first by fierce fighting, bombs made of blood and destruction, Mr. Gab had formed the intention of saving reality from its own demise by collecting and caring for the world in photographic form. There were footsteps he was following, or so he found out. Like Alvin Langdon Coburn, he had been given a camera by an uncle. Like Alvin Langdon Coburn, he had crossed the sea to London. Like Coburn, he would tour Europe, though not with his mother, who was as missing from his life, he insisted, as that of u-Stu. In the footsteps of Mr. Coburn, possibly, but not in the same shoes, for he, Mr. Gab, hadn't had a father who made shirts and died leaving his mother money. He hadn't found friends like Stieglitz and Steichen with whom he could converse, or exchange warm admirations. He sat in metal storerooms surrounded by supplies, and learned a few things about stocks and stores and shipment.

Unlike Johnstown's fabled inundation, but, rather, drip by drip, words entered Stu's ear, and filled his mind to flood stage finally; not that he needed to be instructed about the grimness of the world, or about what passed for human relations. Some of the words weren't nice ones. Mr. Gab kept his tongue clean, but now and then a word like "whore" would slip out. You will not know that word I just used, Mr. Gab said hopefully. Stu thought he meant the word "catechism," which indeed he didn't understand, but Mr. Gab meant "whore," which he proceeded to define as anyone who accepts money in return for giving pleasure . . . pleasures that were mostly illusory. There were shysters for mismanipulating the law. There were charlatans for the manufacture of falsehood. Quacks for promising health. Sharks for making illegal loans. Mountebanks to prey upon the foolishly greedy. Apparently, humanity was made of little else.

But there were, Mr. Gab assured u-Stu, the Saviors too. They bore witness. They documented. Eugène Atget had rescued Paris. Josef Sudek had done the same for Prague. August Sander had catalogued the workers of his country, as Salgado has tried to do for workers worldwide. Karl Blossfeldt, like Audubon, had preserved the wild plants. Bellocq had treated his New Orleans whores with dignity. And how about Evelyn Cameron, who had saved Montana with her single shutter? Or Russell Lee, who photographed the Great Flood of '37 as well as the Negro slums of Chicago? Or consider the work of a studio like that of Southworth & Hawes, whose images of Niagara Falls were among the more amazing ever made. He, Mr. Gab, had but one of their daguerreotypes. And Mr. Gab then disappeared into his room behind the rug to produce in a moment a group portrait taken in the Southworth & Hawes studio of the girls of Boston's Emerson School, and through the envelope, which Mr. Gab did not remove, u-Stu saw the identically and centrally parted hair of thirty-one girls and the white lace collars of twenty-eight.

Mr. Gab went on to extol the work of Martín Chambi, whom he had available only in a catalogue produced for an exhibit at the Smithsonian (so there were an unknown number of books behind the rug, perhaps in that closet, perhaps in a shelf above the boxes). Although Mr. Gab was capable of staring at a photograph uninterruptedly for many minutes, he had the annoying habit of flipping rapidly through books—dizzying u-Stu's good eye, which could only receive the briefest tantalizations of an apparently magical place, set among the most remote mountains, Mr. Gab called "Mac-choo Peechoo"—until he reached the photo he was searching for. There, there, Mr. Gab said, pointing: a young man in a most proper black suit and bow tie was standing beside a giant of a man clad in tatters, a cloth hat like an aviator's helmet in the giant's hand, a serape draped over the giant's shoulders—and—and around the small man's, a huge arm finished by fingers in the form of a great claw. The little fellow is the photographer's assistant, Mr. Gab informed his. Who, u-Stu saw, was gazing up at the face of the giant with respectful incomprehension. But one was mostly drawn to the giant's patched and tattered shirt and baggy trousers, to the barely thonged feet that had borne much, and finally to the huge stolid countenance, formed from endurance. Shots of shirts were rare.

Not all of Mr. Gab's enthusiasms were trotted out at once. They were instead produced at intervals involving months, but each was offered as if no finer effort, no better example, could be imagined. Yet u-Stu came to believe that the artist Mr. Gab called P.H. (Ralph Waldo was the other Emerson) was dearest to him, after one afternoon being shown (again from the cache in the kitchen) a simple country-and-seaside scene: a crude sailboat manned by three, and oared as well, under way upon a marshy watercourse, the row-boat's big sail, with its soft vertical curves and pale patches, in the center of the photograph, and to the left, where the reeds began, though at the distance where there had to be land, a simple farmhouse resting in a clump of low trees, a trail of chimney smoke the sole sign of occupancy.

Every photograph by its very nature is frozen in its moment, Mr. Gab said, but not every photograph portrays stillness as this one does. The sail is taut, smoke is streaming away toward the margins of the picture's world, and the postures of the oarsmen suggest they are at work; but there is little wake, the surface of the water is scarcely ruffled, not a reed is bent, the trees are without leaves, and the faint form of a small windmill shows the four blades to be unmoving. Nevertheless, it is the lucency of the low light, the line of the sail's spar, which meets on one side a shoreline, on the other a small inlet-edging fence, which holds the image still; it is the way the mast runs on into its reflection, and the long low haze stretched across the entire background at the point where earth and air blend, where the soft slightly clouded sky rises; it is the relation of all these dear tones to one another that creates a serenity which seeks the sublime, because it is so complete. Complete, u-Stu, complete.

Look. In this work, the house, the boat, the rowing men have no more weight than the boat's small shadow on the pale-white water, or the bare trees and stiff reeds, because all are simply there together. Equals added to equals yields equals. One can speak one's self insensible about the salubrious and necessary unity of humankind with nature, u-Stu-u, yet rarely enable your listener to see how the solitude, the independent being, of every actual thing is celebrated by the community created through such a composition. The light, coming from the right, illuminates the sides of the house in such a way it seems blocky and dimensional, as the boat does; however the sail, the sky, the water, and their realms, though made of a register of curves, are otherwise, and flat as a drawn shade.

At exam time, Mr. Gab would cry out: what have I been saying? What have I said? Every player is made a star when the team succeeds as a team, Stu promptly answered, whereupon Gab lost his mister and his temper at the same time, complaining of the comparison, and refusing (as he regularly did after exams) to speak to his help, who had been relegated a rank.

In this bumpy way his education proceeded, but it had an odd consequence. Stu's experience was made by someone else's words; his memory, formerly poor, was reluctant to linger on an early life that had been a bitter bit of bad business; so he adopted another person's past, and he saw what that other person said he'd seen. He kept house in another's household, and adopted points of view he never properly arrived at. Who could blame him? Would not each of us have done the same? Why not change residences when the skin that confined you was a bitter bit of bad business?

His fingers licked him through the pages of Mr. Gab's dozen or so books of photography, mostly limited to Mr. Gab's narrow enthusiasms; however, there was a recent Salgado which rendered the stupid assistant weak in one knee, though he'd been told messages were for Western Union, not for artistry. Such marvelous messages, though—these Salgados proved to be.

Stu started stepping out—a phrase to be used advisedly. He obtained a card at the local library, shoplifted a few fruits, and sat in sun-filled vacant lots, deep in the weeds, happy with the heavy air. In the library he began examining the work of the two painters Mr. Gab admitted to his pantheon: Canaletto and Vermeer. In the shops he slyly added to his meager stock by stealing small fruits: figs, limes, kiwis, cherries, berries. In the weeds, feasting on his loot, Stu would imagine he lived in an alternative world, and he'd scale everything around him down, pretend he was hunkered in a photograph, where woods were black and white and pocket-sized. In the library he was eyed with suspicion, and Stu felt certain that only the librarians' fear of a lawsuit let them lend what they did lend to him. In the open-air market, they knew he was a thief past all convicting, but they hadn't caught him yet, it was a public space, and they begged for the crowds that concealed his snitches with distracting blouses and billowy shirts. Shirts ought to receive some celebration. But he was soon run out of his weedy lot by a puritanical cop.

It was about then that Mr. Gab expelled Stu from his sleeping post, and he formally became Mr. Gab's assistant. Mr. Gab had never paid his assistant a wage, not a dime, nor had he bought him anything but secondhands; even the comb he let Stu have had been run through many an unknown head of hair. Mr. Gab was frugal, probably because he had to be, so their diet was repeatedly rice and beans. He moved his assistant into public space and a rooming house run formerly by Chinese, or so the Chinese who ran it now maintained. It had brown paper walls, a cot and a chair, a john down the hall, a window without a blind, a throw rug which—to expose a splintery floor—would wad itself into a wad while you watched. You can keep this job if you want it, Mr. Gab announced, and I'll pay you the minimum, but now you must take your meals and your sleep and your preferences out of here—out—and manage them yourself.

At first the new assistant was wholly dismayed. What had he done, he finally asked. You've grown up, was Mr. Gab's unhelpful answer. You go away, god knows where, and look at god knows what, color and comic and bosom books. Actually, it was as if Mr. Gab were clairvoyant and knew that his assistant had come on a book by Ernst Haas called *Color Photography* in the same local library where he had obtained his volume of Vermeer, and been subsequently ravished, just as Mr. Gab feared. But if Vermeer was photographic, Haas was painterly. Stu was sure Mr. Gab would say, very pretty, very nice, nevertheless not reliable. The object is lost, can you find it? torn posters and trash—that's the world? and how far into a flower can you fall without sneezing?

Reality is made of nouns, not adjectives, Gab shouted at the wall where his nouns sat in their sacred gray desuetude.

The stupid assistant suspected that Gab had listened to what was going on in his stupid assistant's head, and heard objections and reservations and hesitations and challenging questions, both personal and educational, particular and theoretic. Then said to himself: this Stu should go elsewhere with these thoughts. Ernst Haas had photographed some flowers through a screen, making romantic a symbol of romance; through an open oval in a dark room, like the inside of a camera, he had rendered a bright café scene so its reality seemed an illustration in a magazine; he'd snapped a cemetery bust at night as if the head had leached the film and raised a ghost; and Mr. Gab would certainly have denounced these startling images as mere monkey business, had he seen them: the cropped stained glass from Cluny too, glass heads looking like stone ones in a dismal darkness, a regiment of roofs in Reading, the silhouettes of fishermen fishing in a line along the Seine; but the assistant could remember now Sudek's magical garden pictures, with their multiple exposures, dramatic angles, and cannily positioned sculptures, and he found himself thinking that it wasn't fair, it wasn't fair to be so puritanical, to live with a passel of prejudices, even if each enthusiasm that was denied inspection intensified the believer's devotion.

Mr. Gab's exiled assistant came to work just before ten each morning like a clerk or a secretary, but if mum were Mr. Gab's one word, he would not utter it. Between them, throughout the day, a silence lay like a shawl on a shivering shoulder. In the flophouse where the assistant lived now there was plenty of jabbering, but he couldn't bear the cacophony, let alone find any sense to it. In his room the world had grown grossly small. The window framed an alley full of litter. The brown paper wall bore tears and peels and spots made by drops of who knew what—expectorations past. Yet in such stains lay lakes full of reeds and floating ducks and low loglike boats. Instead of the sort of wall which furnished a rich many-toned background for so many of Atget's documents; instead of the cobbled courtyard that the remainder of the photo surrounded, shadowed, or stood on; instead of gleaming disks of stone with their dark encircling lines; instead of the leaves of trees in a flutter about a field of figures; there might be—instead—a single pock, the bottom of it whitish with plaster: that's what he had to look at, descend into, dream about, not a rhyming slope of rock, its layers threaded and inked; not the veins of a single leaf like roads on a map, or a tear of paper resembling a tantrum—his rips didn't even resemble rips—or faded petals that have fallen like a scatter of gravel at the foot of a vase; not an errant flash of light centered and set like a jewel: instead he had a crack, just a crack in a window, a cob's web, or that of a spider, dewdrop clinging like an injured climber to its only rope of escape; not a clay flowerpot given the attention due a landscape; not a scratch on the hood of some vehicle, not directional signs painted on the pavement, instructions worn by the wheels of countless cars; not a black eye enlarged to resemble the purple of a blown rose. These were the images in his borrowed books, the material of his mind's eye, the Lilliputian world grown taller than that tattered Peruvian giant.

Even Mr. Gab's heroes, even Josef Koudelka, had devoted at least one frame, one moment of his art, to a slice of cheese, bite of chocolate, cut of fruit that had been strewn upon the rumpled front page of the *International Herald Tribune* to serve as a still life's prey—a spoiled fish—a party of empty bottles. That's okay, he heard Mr. Gab say, because such a shot records a lunch, a day, a time in the world. I want that, u-Stew-u, I want the world, I don't want to see through the picture to the world, the picture is not a porthole. I want the world *in*—you see—*in*—the photo. What a world it is after all! Am I a fool? Not to know what the world is; what it comes to? It is misery begetting misery, you bet; it's meanness making meanness, sure; it's calamity;

it's cruelty and greed and indifference; I know what it is, you know what it is, we know how it is, if not why—yet I want the world as it is rescued by the camera and redeemed. U-Stu-u. Paris is . . . was . . . noisy, full of Frenchmen, full of pain, full of waste, of *ordinaire;* but Atget's Paris, Sudek's Vienna, Coburn's London, even Bellocq's poor whores (I never showed you those ladies, you found out and stared at that filth yourself), Salgado's exploited, emaciated workers are lifted up and given grace when touched by such lenses; and every injustice that the world has done to the world is forgiven—*in* the photograph—in . . . in . . . where even horse-plopped cobbles come clean.

But what about, the stupid assistant began, what about Haas's *Moreno,* a photo full of steps, the dark woman walking toward a set of them, her black back to us, the red and white chickens standing on stairs . . . they'd all look better gray, he was sure Mr. Gab would say. Or the lane of leaves, that lane of trees beside the Po, or the Norwegian fjord photo, Mr. Gab, the faint central hill like a slow cloud in the water, what of them? what of them? So what, he replied on behalf of Mr. Gab, who was somewhat cross, when one can have Steichen's or Coburn's streetlamps, spend an evening full of mist and mellow glisten, bite into an avenue that's slick as freshly buttered toast.

But Mr. Gab, do you dream that Sebastião Salgado wants anyone forgiven: are the starving to be forgiven for starving? are those scenes from Dante's hell (the hell you told me about) redeemed because the miners of Serra Pelada's gold—worn, gaunt, covered with mud and rags—are, through his art, delivered from their servitude and given to Dante? am I to be forgiven for my deformities? my rocking, as if I were indeed the baby in the tree, is it okay? If cleverly clicked? o yes, Mr. Gab, you're right, I did peek at the fancy girls, and I was toasted by one in striped tights and a bonnet of hair who raised to me a shot glass of Raleigh rye, but so many of them, sad to say, had scratched-out faces, only their bare bodies were allowed to be; while Bellocq too, by the book, was said to be misshapen . . . not quite like me; but he didn't dwarf himself, I bet, and behaved himself with the girls because he understood his burden; just as it's true, I didn't do me, someone else, perhaps yourself, Mr. Gab, did, but I was not a party to the filthy act that made me, or to the horror of having insufficient room in an unsuitable womb; I didn't mangle myself, suck the nail from my own thumbs, shorten my stature, wound my mouth; yet daily I inflict them on others; I wobble along on my sidewalk and all those passerby-eyes flee the scene like shooed flies.

Should Salgado—u-Stu-u—Mr. Gab rejoins, should he then forget his skills and just picture pain picture human evil picture human greed picture desolation picture people other people have allowed to become battered trees made of nothing but barren twigs, picture many murdered, meadows murdered, hills heaved into the sea, sand on open eyes, the grim and grisly so that it approaches us the way you do on the street, so we will look away, even cross against traffic in order to avoid any encounter, because the overseers of those miners don't care a wink about them, never let their true condition sneak under a lid, form a thought, suggest an emotion—unless there is a fainter, a sluggard, a runaway—no more than the other workers, who sweat while smelting the ore, give the miners time, since no one thinks of the smelters either, the glare oiling their bare chests, no more than those who stamp some country's cruel insignia on the country's coins or dolly a load of now gold bars into a vault think of anyone else but their own beers and bad bread and breeding habits.

But Mr. Gab, sir, when I look at that huge hole in the earth, and at those innumerable heads and shoulders heavy with sacks of dirt like a long line of ants on paths encircling the pit that their own work has bit into the ground, just as you and Dante said hell's rungs do; against my will, I see something sublime, like the force of a great wind or quake or volcanic eruption.

Yes, u-Stu-u, because u have a book in hand, u aren't in the picture, u are thousands of miles from Brazil, u wear clean underclothes (I hope and suppose), but can u now reflect on your own sad condition, as molested by fate as they've been, those poor workers, because who of us at the end of the day goes home happy? do you go to your room and laugh at its luxury? You saw—it's less than the whores of New Orleans; don't you still see trash from your window, and stains on the wall, and through a pock or two if you peer into them won't you encounter again that unearthed creature covered with a silkskin of mud, a man who a moment before the photo was in a long climbing line up the laddered side of one of hell's excavations, and won't you continue to find behind him, and free of misery's place in the picture, another man, in shorts and a clean shirt studying a clipboard? and what are we to think of him, then? and what are we to think of ourselves, and the little gold rings we wear when we marry?

Starve the world to amuse a few. That's man's motto. That sums it. But now Mr. Gab's assistant didn't know—couldn't tell—who was supposed to have said it.

Alvin Langdon Coburn came up. After a day of silence, his name seemed a train of words. Alvin Langdon Coburn. As if Mr. Gab had really been talking with his assistant as his assistant had imagined. He was holding a paperback copy of Coburn's autobiography. With a finger to mark his place, Mr. Gab gave it a brief wave. I shall read u-Stu what Alvin Langdon Coburn wrote about those who do dirty tricks with their negatives. Mr. Gab's voice assumed a surprising falsetto. His assistant had never heard him read aloud out of a book before this moment—a moment that had therefore become important. "Now I must confess that I do not approve of gum prints which look like chalk drawings . . ." Mr. Gab interrupted himself. P.H. was equally fierce and unforgiving, he said. ". . . nor of drawing on negatives, nor of glycerine-restrained platinotypes in imitation of wash-drawings as produced by . . ." You won't have heard of this guy, Mr. Gab added, letting disdain into his voice like a cat into a kitchen. ". . . Joseph T. Keiley, a well-known . . ." Well known, well known—not any more known than a silent-film star. ". . . American photographer and a friend of Alfred Stieglitz." They all claimed to be that—a good, a fond friend of Stieglitz. Let's skip. ". . . I do not deny that Demachy, Eugene, Keiley and others . . ." Heard of them, have we? Are they in the history books? are they? take a look. ". . . and others produced exciting prints by these manipulated techniques. . . ." Bah bah bah-dee-bah. Here—"This I rarely did, for I am myself a devotee of pure photography, which is unapproachable in its own field." Unapproachable, you hear? Pure. That's the ticket. That's the word. Unapproachable. He snapped the book shut and sank back into a silence which said something had been proved, something once for all had been decided.

3 From the Stool of the Stupid Assistant

During the long empty hours between customers, Mr. Gab sat at his desk at the front of the shop and drowsed or thumbed through the same old stack of photographic magazines he'd had for as long as his assistant had been near enough his paging thumb to observe what the pages concerned. Most of the time Mr. Gab sat there with the immobility of a mystic. Occasionally, he'd leaf through a book, often an exhibition catalogue or a volume containing a description of the contents of a great archive, such as Rüdiger Klessmann's book on the Kaiser Friedrich Museum, over whose pages and pictures he'd slowly shake his head. Once in a while, his back still turned to his assistant, he'd raise a beckoning hand, and u-Stu would leave his stool in the rear where he was awkwardly perched while trying to read books slender enough to be steadily held by one hand, and come forward to Mr. Gab's side where he was always expected to verify, by studying the picture, Mr. Gab's poor opinion of the masterpiece.

The beckoning finger would then descend to point at a portion of a painting; whereupon Mr. Gab would say: look at that! is that a tree? that tangle of twigs? The finger would poke the plate, perhaps twice. It's an architect's tree! His voice would register three floors of disgust. It's a rendering, a sign for a tree; the man might as well have written "tree" there. Over here, by "barn," see "bush." And the fellow is said to be painting nature. (It might have been a Corot or Courbet.) See? is that a tree? is that a tree or a sign, that squiggle? I can read it's a tree, but I don't see a tree. It is not a tree anyone actually sees. Twigs don't attach to branches that way; branches don't grow from trunks that way; you call those smudges shade? To a simp they might suggest shade. To a simpleton. There's not a whiff of cooling air.

The finger would retire long enough for the assistant to make out an image and the book would snap shut like a slammed door: I am leaving forever, the slam said. A fake crack in a fake rock from which a fake weed fakes its own growth, Mr. Gab might angrily conclude: we are supposed to admire that? (then after an appropriate pause, he'd slowly, softly add, in a tone signifying his reluctant surrender to grief) that . . . ? that is artistry?

The assistant spent many hours every day like a dunce uncomfortably perched on a stool he had difficulty getting the seat of his pants settled on because it stood nearly as high as he did and furthermore because the assistant was trying to bring a book up with him held in his inadequate hand. Once up, he was reluctant to climb down if it meant he'd soon have to climb up again. So he perched, not perhaps for as long as Mr. Gab sat, but a significant interval on the morning's clock: with a view of the shop and its three rows of trestle tables topped with their load of flap-closed cardboard boxes adorned by beanbags as if they were the puffy peaks of stocking caps. The tables appeared to be nearly solid blocks since so many containers were stored underneath each one where with your foot you'd have to coax a carton to slide sufficiently far into the aisle to undo its flaps and finger through its contents. ROME I.

But Mr. Gab or his stupid assistant, whoever was closest, would rise or fall and wordlessly rush or rock to the box and lift it quickly or awkwardly up on top of the ones on the table, deflapping it smartly or ineptly and folding the four lids back before returning to chair or stool and the status quo. Mr. Weasel would occasionally come in and always want a box buried beneath a table in the most remote and awkward spot; but at least he'd pick on a container up front, where Mr. Gab would have to say good day in customary greeting and then push cartons about like some laborer in a warehouse to get at PARIS NIGHTLIFE or some similar delicacy that Mr. Weasel always favored.

Customers who came to the shop more than once got names chosen to reflect their manner of looking or the shapes they assumed while browsing, especially as they were observed from the stool of the stupid assistant. Weasel slunk. He was thin and short and had a head that was all nose. His eyes were dotted and his hair was dark and painted on. The first few times Weasel came to the store the stupid assistant watched him carefully because his moves produced only suspicion. After a number of visits, however, the Weasel simply became the Weasel, and the stupid assistant shut down his scrutiny, or rather, turned it onto his page.

Part of the stupid assistant's education was to study books which Mr. Gab assigned, not that they ever discussed them, and it would have been difficult for Mr. Gab to know, ever, if his assistant was dutiful or not, or was reading filth and other kinds of popular fiction. When he thought he had caught the Weasel, u-Stu was wading through Walter Pater. And Pater held a lot of water. U-Stu was wading waist-deep. Mr. Gab had not recommended any of what the assistant later found out were Pater's principal works, but had sent him to a collection of essays called *Appreciations* where u-Stu learned of Dryden's imperfect mastery of the relative pronoun, a failing he misunderstood as familial. All Mr. Gab asked of his assistant regarding the works he assigned (beside the implicit expectation that it would be u-Stu who would withdraw them from the library, now he had his own card) was that u-Stu was expected to select a sentence he favored from some part of the text to repeat to Mr. Gab at a suitable moment; after which Mr. Gab would grunt and nod, simultaneously signifying approval and termination.

It was not clear to u-Stu whether there were designs behind Mr. Gab's selections, but *Appreciations* contained essays on writers whose names were, to u-Stu, at best vaguely familiar, or on plays by Shakespeare like *Measure for Measure* for which slight acquaintance was also the applicable description. The first essay was called "Style" and u-Stu supposed it was Mr. Gab's target, but, once more, the piece was larded with references that, from u-Stu, drew a blank response of recognition. U-Stu resented having his ignorance so repeatedly demonstrated. To Mr. Gab he said: "this book is dedicated to the memory of my brother William Thompson Pater who quitted a useful and happy life Sunday April 24, 1887." Quite to the quoter's surprise, this sentence proved to be acceptable, and u-Stu was able to return the volume a week ahead of its due date.

This is not to say that u-Stu didn't give it a shot, and in point of fact he was in the middle of trying to understand a point about Flaubert's literary scruples (all of Mr. Pater's subjects seemed to be neurotic) when his head rose wearily from the page in time to see the Weasel slip a glassine envelope, clearly not their customary kind, into the stock of a cardboard box labeled MISCELLANEOUS INTERIORS. Skidding from his stool, he rocked toward the Weasel at full speed. Sir, he said, sir, may I help you with anything; you seem to be a bit confused. This was a formula Mr. Gab had hit upon for lowering the level of public embarrassment whenever hanky-pankies were observed.

However, as u-Stu took thought, as Mr. Gab turned to locate his assistant's voice, and as the Weasel looked up in alarm, u-Stu realized that the Weasel, so far as he had seen, was adding to, not subtracting from the contents of the container. Had u-Stu perhaps missed an extraction? Was this the latter stage of a switch?

It's all right, Mr. Stu, Mr. Gab said urgently. Mr. Grimes is just replacing a print for me. Oh, said Mr. Stu, stopping as soon as he could and calming his good eye. Mr. Grimes, the Weasel, winked in surprise and backed away from Mr. Stu in the direction of the door. Something is up, Mr. Stu thought, thinking he was now Mr. Stu, an improvement surely, a considerable promotion, a kind of bribe, but an acceptable one, coming as it did at long—he thought—last. But what was up? what? Mr. Stu retreated to his stool and Mr. Grimes slid out of the shop with never a further word. In fact, Mr. Stu couldn't remember a first word. But he'd been inattentive while tending to Walter Pater's work, and to the peevish Flaubert, who had just vowed, at the point Mr. Stu had reached in his reading, to quit writing altogether.

Mr. Gab's back was soon bent over MISCELLANEOUS INTERIORS. From his stool, where he was perched once more like some circus animal, Mr. Stu couldn't see a single interesting thing though he knew that rummaging was going on. He felt in his stomach a glob of gas, a balloon filled with rising apprehension. Mr. Gab, having done his dirty work, returned to his desk empty-handed, allowing the store to become as law-abiding as before. With his Pater closed, Mr. Stu, as he would from this morning on be called, began to fill the back of Mr. Gab's head with his own thoughts, enjoying a vacation in another body, even old Mr. Gab's, which had to be a low-rent cottage in a run-down resort, but—hey—several limps up from the ramshackle where he currently was.

Other eyes, both reasonably well off, saw through gray glass into the street where the world would scarcely pass. He imagined he was sixteen, which was perhaps his age. He had the legs of that Caravaggio cupid which had so exercised Mr. Gab when he'd come upon them the other day in Rüdiger Klessmann's catalogue of the paintings in the Berlin Museum (remember that liar's name, Mr. Gab had commanded). Naked, the kid was. Very naked. A pornpainting, Mr. Gab said in sentence. It is written here that this is the figure of a boy about twelve. Sitting on a globe. The posture is contorted, but not like Mr. Stu on his stool, Mr. Stu thought. Look, this Klessmann fellow says that every wrinkle and fold of the skin is reproduced with the utmost realism. Ut-most. Look. What do you see?

U-Stu saw a cupid with arms and thighs wide apart, as wide as full sexual reception might require, and musculated like a twenty-five-year-old wrestler, though wearing the weenie of a boy of six, one nipple showing in a swath of light which flew in conveniently from the left to dispel a general darkness; in fact to fling it aside like a parted robe and reveal a creased and belly-buttoned stomach below a strong broad chest where the nipple lay, as purple as a petal fallen from a frostbitten rose (Mr. Gab had said as if quoting). The head, however, bore a leering drunken grin as salacious as they are in Frans Hals. Those huge thighs, though, Mr. Gab fairly growled, how are they rendered? See the way they are rounded into a silk-soaked softness? (Was he quoting still?) An Amazon in the guise of a baby boy. Holding the bow of a violin! What allegorical gimcrackery! But no! another masterpaint, Mr. Gab announced, as if introducing a vaudeville act. And Klessmann dares to call this pornographic pastiche realism!

Caravaggio was simply a ruffian. His darks were merely dramatic, his colors were off, his attitudes appropriate to saloons. He was a pretender in front of reality, and reality had made him a murderer and a convict. Tenebrist indeed. Remember that word. (His assistant tried, but he understood it to mean "tenuous.") Mr. Gab could be relentless. Carrahvaggeeoh, he'd growl. For him darkness is never delicate. Carrahvaggeeoh didn't understand what a shadow was—an entire region of the world. Ah . . . we know where to go for shadows.

By now Mr. Stu was able to interpret Mr. Gab. Realism—truth—was the exclusive property of the photograph. He regularly ridiculed paintings that presented themselves as lifelike. About trompe l'oeil compositions he was particularly withering. What kind of streetcar accident has caused this rabbit, that jug, this—hah!—hunting horn, that—hah!—hat, that knife, that—hey?—horseshoe, and that key—a key!—those two dead birds?—to hop to run to fly to get carried in a carriage to see the smash, rehear the crash, and enjoy the bloody scene? What drew them to this place? These dots of detail? That's the real? reality is a stupid collection? trophies of a scavenger hunt? Whose eye would they fool?—hey?—whose?

Mr. Stu, now in the guise of Caravaggio, stretched his grand legs wide, even if he wouldn't fool anyone, and flaunted his cute little sex. Those few who might pass would never look in. Anyway. He wondered, as he had so often, what it would be like to be ordinary and have had an ordinary childhood, not one in a Home where everything had to imitate shoes in a line. And nothing had ever been his: not his bed or blanket, the table at which he drew, not a wall, not a window, not a fork or spoon, lent instead, shared, maybe his underclothes had been his, but only because they wouldn't let anyone else soil them. He'd left with the clothes on his back, as the cliché maintains, so they had to be his: his shoes, and his socks and his bulbous nose. Even now his room was rented, his books were borrowed, his stool belonged to his employer, as did the boxes of photographs, presumably they weren't all stolen. At the moment, though, he owned a violin and sat heavily on his own globe.

He'd noticed how Mr. Gab did it: how he studied a picture (this one, another Sudek, had shown up out of the blue to be held under Mr. Stu's nose) until he knew just where the darks went (had he bought it from that haughty high-hatter? that would not have been wise); dark filling almost the whole road except for the wet and glistening dirt that still defined some wagon tracks (the temptation would have been far greater than for another piece of cake), the sky too, setting with the paling sun, and walls and buildings nothing but edges, tree trunks rising into the dying light, crisp and unconfused (had it been dropped off by the Weasel? God forbid), rows of insulators perched like birds for the night on faintly wired poles, but so composed . . . made of mist . . . composed so that the bushes at one end of the panoramic rhymed with the tree limbs at the other; thus the blacks beneath held up the grays above, so the soft glow of the failing sun, which could be still seen in the darkening sky, might lie like a liquid on the muddy lane . . . and Mr. Gab would inhale very audibly, as if a sigh had been sent him from somewhere, because only once had the world realized these relations; they would never exist again; they had come and gone like a breath.

An image had been etched on an eye.

Mr. Stu had made Mister, all the same, even if he didn't have a childhood; and he had a job—a job that was his job, no one else's, as stooled to its heights as an accountant's—and he had his own room even if it was rented, even if it was paid for by his father figure; and he had a market where he could swipe fruit, a weedy field to sit in now and then, a library card for borrowing books; and a worry which was ruining his reveries. If the cops got Mr. Gab, what would become of Mr. Stu? No job then. No room. He could read in the weeds. But the authorities didn't like the appearance it gave the neighborhood when he flopped down in the empty lot and looked up at a clutter of clouds or saw inside a deeply receding blue sky a scented silent light.

With Walter Pater parked, Mr. Stu settled on his stool and set his sights on the back of Mr. Gab's head, and bore into it with his whole being until he felt he was looking out into the empty sun-blown street where now and then a figure would pass, moving more often left than right, while he wondered what was to be done, what he should do to defend them from the calamity that was coming. After closing, after, as he imagined, still wholly inhabiting Mr. Gab, he'd taken that body to bed in the Chinese flophouse where Mr. Gab's somewhat resourceful assistant had found a curtain made of mediocre lace at the market—near that stall from which, by using the crowd, he'd appropriated fruit—just a cloud of thread to tack to the wall above his window so that now when Mr. Gab's hand drew the curtain the room grew gray and a few of the city's lights spangled the frail netting where, bedclothed, u-Stu in the garb of Mr. Gab could still see, till sleep, a kind of sky, and pretend he was napping in the weeds or smelling space like a moth; so after closing, Gab gone to the flop, what was left of Mr. Stu would go through the boxes one by one and systematically, if there was a system, hunt for pictures that were likely pilfered in order to hide them . . . yes, by reswapping bodies for the task, putting Gab back in his own boots—maybe too many switcheroos to seem dreamable—and subsequently to slide the suspicious photographs into such other boxes as he'd have collected under his so far fleabagless bed, where no one would ever think to pry, thus cleansing the premises of the taint of loot and securing the safety of what was looking more and more like a possible life.

He swore that were he able to do it, he would work earnestly to improve himself during the remaining existence he'd been given, giving up both fruit and stealing; he'd pass out flyers to stimulate the store; he'd memorize a new word every day and read it—one two three four—like a regiment on the march; he'd—

What, though, could be done about the ones which perched in plain view upon the walls, yet tried to lie about their presence like the purloined letter, even though they could be seen to be what they were: Koudelka, in an instant, glorious, an icon worth worship, or an Emerson, swimming in silence through reedy weeds, or that damn Evans with the foursquareface outstaring stone, or the Abbott tucked away near the rug-hugged doorway; because Gab would feel their loss even if Mr. Stu just replaced the prints and not the hangers; put up at some risk a Harry Callahan or Marc Riboud instead, since who knew if Gab had thieved them too; he'd feel their loss like a draft through a door left ajar, the hairs on the back of his neck would whisper their names in his ears; yet the Koudelka, the Feininger had to go, guilt could not be more loudly advertised. Looking at *Lake Michigan,* Mr. Gab had muttered placement, placement, placement, three times, u-Stu supposed, to honor the three figures standing in smooth lake water, water which merged imperceptibly with a grayed-over sky, three figures perfectly decentered, and the wake of the walking bather . . . well . . . as if there'd been some calculation . . . if not by nature than by Callahan . . . alas, not a serious name. Yet Callahan, said Mr. Gab, would do.

He could not spirit these evidences from their walls. Suppose he could persuade Mr. Gab to squirrel them away in some quiet sequestership of his own where they couldn't be seen let alone seized let alone certified as

Grabbed by Gab. In so doing, in going along with Mr. Stu's suggestion, wouldn't Mr. Gab be confessing to his crimes? Then, though, if he did that, perhaps he'd be relieved of his reticence. What stories Mr. Gab could tell about each one—Cunningham's magnolia, that late Baldus, or Weston's two shells—how he had found them, stalked them, and withdrawn them from the owners' grasps (even slipped them out of their countries) as if they were already as much his as his hand was his, leaving a handclasp to wave farewell to their properties.

At first, of course, u-Stu's head, heart, conscience were all firmly set against the notion, voiced by their enemy from the earlier street, that Mr. Gab's stock contained stolen articles. His mind could not figure out how Mr. Gab might have managed. He seemed taciturn, not sly, blunt and biased, not crafty or devious, and it was difficult to envision Mr. Gab as young, vigorous, and thievish, climbing walls like a lusty vine, seeping like pulverulent air (his word to work on for the day) under door frame or window sash; yet so quick-fingered as to pry open cases in a wink, slip a photo from its frame in a trice, and then to saunter carefree and concealing from a museum or pretentious shop straight through customs declaring only a smile and a bit of a cough. Nor had he the heart to imagine Mr. Gab to be no more than a fence for those more slick and daring than he—as if Weasel were—what a laugh; yet appearances were deceiving, who knew better than he how that was, for he, Mr. Stu, no longer the Stupid Assistant, never had been, only looked so, on account of his one cross eye and leaking lip. Conscience . . . well, conscience made a coward of him. Made him fear a fall. From his stool of course. From his room, job, only relation. Because he actually would have loved to believe that Mr. Gab was a Pimpernel of prints. He knew that conscience, if it had to compete with pride, wouldn't stand a chance, and could be cowed into silence. So that to have the prince of purloiners for a pa . . . well . . . that would be okay. That would be quite all right.

He might have to get used to some such idea. Evidence was more prevalent than fingerprints. There was that envelope postmarked Montreal in which the Baldus was, contrary to custom, still kept: an absolutely perfect albumen silver print of the train station at Toulon, with the Baldus signature stamp lower right; the envelope carrying the capital letters CCA outlined in red on its front flap: rails running straight through the glass-gated shed into the everlasting; the envelope dated in a dark circle May 1, 1995: about a foot and a half wide, the sky, as almost always in Baldus, kept a clear cream, the scene so crisp as to seem seen through translucent ice; the print in heavy plastic slid between tough protective cardboard: uncluttered, freight cars parked in place, not a sight of mortal man as usually, in Édouard Baldus, was the case, a document that documented as definitely as a nailed lid; but now, so overcoated, the thing bulked in the box it was shoved in, crying out to the curious.

What a quandary. Surely Mr. Gab would see the wisdom in such a gleaning of the incriminating prints, whose very excellence made them enemies, and surely he would understand, in such circumstances, the good sense in ceasing for a time to acquire anything more that might entrap Mr. Gab against his will in the terrible toils of the law; yes, surely he would have to recognize how wise it was to heed these warnings, to back off and go double doggo; but Mr. Stu knew that Mr. Gab would bite on that Sudek if it were offered, that he could not resist Quality, which overcame him like a cold; because what he understood to be Quality was all that counted in the world, Mr. Stu had come to grasp that. Not warmth, it threatened the prints; not food, which merely smeared the fingers; not leisure, for where would an eye go on vacation but to its graphs—to bathe in their beauty as if at a beach? Not shelter, since his pictures furnished him his bricked lanes and cobbled streets, damp from rain, and all his buildings defined by shade and the white sky and the dark freshly turned fields and the veined rocks and river water frozen while falling into a steaming gorge; not a woman's love, since the photos gave up their bodies ceaselessly and were always welcoming and bare and always without cost—after, once, you had them; further than that there was the flower petal's perfection, the leaf's elemental elegance, the militancy of rail and vagrancy of river line, rows of trees, a hill, a château, a vast stretch of desert dotted with death and small mean rocks. Mr. Stu had a dim hunch about how, for Mr. Gab, they had replaced his mother's flesh. I touch you. You touch eye. That eye owns the world.

So what to do. Just broach the subject? Just say: I think, Mr. Gab, we should take these precious ones away for safer keeping. There are robbers out there looking for swag. The richness of your stock might get about, remarked here, mentioned there, whispered around until the information reaches the wrong ear. And then, in the night, when you are asleep up there, wherever it is, some thug may force his way in, easy enough even if the shutters are shut and the door is locked; these days they have pry irons and metal-cutting torches and lock picks and credit cards they cleverly put to illegal use. Mr. Gab, is that you, sir, someone said, startling Mr. Stu out of his thoughts as though they were dreams. We, sir, are the police. You have been denounced.

4 The Day of Reckoning Arrives

I've—?

You have been informed upon.

Mr. Gab gave Mr. Stu a look of such anguish and accusation his assistant's heart broke. Mr. Stu felt his blood was draining from him and put his hand to his nose. Then Mr. Stu returned Mr. Gab's anguish with his own, a pitifully twisted expression on an already twisted face. Mr. Gab immediately knew his suspicion was false and unfounded; it had followed the awful announcement as swiftly as the sting from a slap; there had been no time to take thought, show sense, conceal his feeling. He realized how horribly he had wounded his adopted kid, his loyal assistant, whom he'd helped from the Home and taught to grow up, reaching the rank of Mister. Mr. Gab understood now that he'd left a son a second time. Whose only mistake was being born. Or being in the neighborhood when Mr. Gab was nabbed.

We have a warrant.

A warrant?

To search your shop and to remove these boxes and place them in our custody while they are examined. It's been alleged you have been in receipt of stolen goods.

Mr. Gab tried to rise from his chair by pushing at its arms with his fists. I have no receipts. Long ago they each arrived, these photographs, like strangers off a boat, you understand. There are decades of desire boxed here. Though they are good photographs. I admit that. Good. It makes for envy in others. But he was not speaking to the detective, who had probably been chosen for the job because he didn't look like a detective is supposed to look, because his look, now, was deeply troubled too. And it made his figure seem puny, his hands small, his nose abruptly concluded as if it had once fallen off. Mr. Gab was not even attending to himself. He was being borne down by a lifeload of anxiety and a moment of misguided distrust.

It is said these boxes are full of stolen pictures.

They are mine. My prints. They live here.

These pictures may not belong to you.

They are prints not pictures. They are photographs not pictures. They are photographic prints.

They may not belong to you.

They do. They belong. In these, of all boxes, they belong. But Mr. Gab was not attending to the officer either. Bulky men were entering the shop, one by one, though they had begun trying to enter two by two. The detective held forward a folded sheet with an insecure hand. Out in the street, Mr. Stu saw the Russian without his hat—his hair, in the sun, shining from the effort of a thick pomade. The bulky men wore overalls with a moving-company logo on them. Here is the writ that empowers this, the detective said, beginning softly but adding a hiss by the end. He sensed he was not impressive. He shook, again, his folded paper. Mr. Gab still sat as solemn as a cat and seemed to be registering one blank after another. The warrant was placed in his lap. This gives us the right to remove (the man waved) and to search the premises. If the allegations—which I must tell you come from high up—powerful government agencies—if they are unfounded, these materials will be returned to you. You shall be receipted.

Receipted? At that, Mr. Gab gathered himself. The paper slid to the floor as he rose. For the first time, he seemed to be taking in the police and the moving men. These are my eyes, and the life of my eyes. One man bore a puzzled look but picked a box up in his arms anyway. Bring in the hand trucks, somebody said. You are using Van Lines? There will be a complete and careful inventory, the detective reassured him, looking intently about the store. Maybe you will finally learn what you have. Then he peered at Mr. Gab. You understand, sir, that later we shall want to speak to you at length. A hand trolley stacked with a box at its top marked PRAGUE rolled out. PARIS NIGHTLIFE went next.

MISCELLANEOUS LANDSCAPES followed.

There are not a lot of these prints left, Mr. Stu heard himself say.

Why don't you help us by taking those pictures on the hangers down, the detective suggested to Mr. Stu. That way, nothing will get bent or soiled. So Mr. Stu did. First finding an empty carton to keep them in. Which took time, because he was bloodless as a voodoo victim, and the bulky men and their boxes were in all the aisles. The enormity of everything took his blood's place.

One of the movers stopped for a moment to stare at a photograph Mr. Stu was about to unfasten. How dare you, Mr. Stu shouted. The burly man shrugged and went about his business. No one else cared.

Mr. Gab no longer protested. He simply stood beside his desk and chair and with an empty gaze followed the men as they pushed their trolleys past him. Mr. Stu made out a truck parked at the curb. Against its pale-gray side the Russian figure leaned. As each box was loaded into the rear of the truck, he wrote something on a clipboard. Mr. Stu suddenly thought: where are his witnesses? Every transaction took place in the back, behind the rug, between the two interested parties, and was always in cash, Mr. Stu had been given to understand. There weren't any records. What could they prove?

Mr. Stu rocked into the movers' doorway. You shit from a stuffed turkey, he shouted, though it was doubtful the Russian understood him, he hardly looked up from his list. Turkey turd, yeah! A big moving man easily hipped him out of the portal. We'll get you guys, he later feared he had u-stupidly said. Mr. Gab's position or posture hadn't altered. His eyes were unnaturally wide and seemed dry. Why was his face, then, so wet all over? One aisle of tables was vacant. How strange the shop seemed without its brown boxes. Now the entering men with their empty trolleys went down the open aisle and returned to the street through one that was solidly cased. Wire hangers lay in a tangle on the trestle tops. The big moving men were tossing the beanbags on the floor, often in fun. Mr. Stu thought of saving several of the displayed photos by concealing them under his shirt, but the detective had two public eyes on his every move. The toe of one of Mr. Gab's shoes was on a corner of the warrant. Tears were sliding from his eyes in a continuous clear stream.

Evidence, Mr. Stu feared. They had evidence aplenty. Who had owned the Julia Cameron before it had come to hide and hovel here? she who specialized in wild hair and white beards? about whom he'd read she had breathed the word "beautiful" and thereupon died, her photographs "tumbling over the tables." Was this an orphanage Mr. Gab ran, and were all these wonders children who had wandered or run away from their homes and families to find themselves in alleys and doorways and empty squares instead of warming hearthsides and huggie havens. No, they all had owners once and, Mr. Stu feared, had been—as if by fairies—stolen. Picsnapped. So they'd be traced—every trade and traduction. And then what? Mr. Gab's presence in the town nearest his lordship's estate, his lodging at the inn, his visit to the household—each would count against him; his travels to Paris at opportune times, his many friends in the army who might turn up a bit of art here and there for some of the crown's coins, complaints from shops about losses they had suffered shortly after his employ—they would surely count against him too; oh so many collaborators, filchers anonymous, partners in crime, many of whom would be still around to testify, and, for a break from the court, would see no need to lie. The prospect before Mr. Stu and Mr. Gab, Mr. Stu decided, was nothing short of calamitous. That was what he had thought to call it before: calamitous. In any case, and the awful moment came back to him like a bad meal, Mr. Stu could hardly work for a man who was so immediately ready to suspect him; who believed he might be a traitor, a child sent by society to win his trust, trip him up, and dispatch him to jail.

Mrs. Cameron was a woman of good character, and did not retouch, Mr. Gab had once confidently claimed, but she was far too social in her choice of subjects. Social might have been a good idea, Mr. Stu now wanted to say to Mr. Gab. Friends in high places might have stood Mr. Gab in good stead. Tennyson. Darwin. Could come to the rescue. Attest to Mr. Gab's character. Honest fellow, as trustworthy as a hound. His museum was being removed, his life looted. Such a painful wrench and one deceitfully turned. The Russian—and Mr. Stu now saw his blurry figure counting boxes as they were taken off to jail—might have been an Albanian in disguise. He might be wearing that goo to fool Mr. Gab and Mr. Stu into thinking him sufficiently shiny to do business with. In reality, he was probably some Fed who lived in town with wife and child.

What's back there, the detective said, as if asking permission when he wasn't, and pushing the rug aside to see. Kitchen, came his voice again. George, he shortly cried. One of the busy big men turned away from his work and went to join the detective out of all sight. They will surely find the special treasures, Mr. Stu thought. Soon enough the big man returned carrying within both arms a large box clasped against his chest. What's this, the detective asked when he reappeared. It has no label. Tell Amos to list it as "Kitchen Closet," he shouted after Shoulders as Shoulders bore his burden out.

Mr. Gab's eyes ran without relief.

It's terrible. Why do you have to take everything? Mr. Stu asked desperately. Can't you see how awful it is for Mr. Gab?

What?

Mr. Stu tried to speak more clearly—slowly and precisely, as, in the Home, he had once been taught. By switch and rule and ruler.

Order of the court, seized on suspicion, the detective finally said, leaving the place himself. The walls were bare except for the shiny zinc heads of the roofing nails. The tables sheltered nothing under them now, while the emptied tops merely supported that absence, and reflected the glare of canned bulbs through a mist made of shoe-scuffled dust. The air, though, was heavy, and Mr. Stu felt the trestles groan. Then the men with their big damp backs were gone. The truck was driven off, and the detective and his Albanian henchman vanished as though they'd become street trees.

Mr. Gab was where he'd been the entire time, still painfully silent, his face oozing away into grief, perhaps not to return. Mr. Stu, out of a need to soften the barrenness about them, slowly turned the cans off, so only the late-afternoon light, made gauzy by the dirty window it oozed through, illuminated the room. Then Mr. Gab moved to *wreeeeek* the shutters down. Here and there a streak of sun would reach deeply into the darkness of the shop. What are we going to do? Mr. Stu spoke to himself more clearly than he spoke to strangers. At least you have those photographs engraved on the balls of your eyes.

Don't accuse me, Mr. Gab finally said, smearing his face with a shirtsleeve. What evidence can they have—from that fellow, I mean, Mr. Stu ventured. I gave him the slip, Mr. Gab said slowly, separating the words with consternation. He wanted a receipt for his cash. So I gave him the slip. He'll have a— Well, maybe not, Mr. Stu said and received a bleak look for his pains.

Not the first times, but the last time. Then I gave him one. Still, Mr. Stu persisted, you couldn't have known—I knew, and he knew I knew, Mr. Gab said firmly. It was a Lange I had to have. A face of pain—pale gray—as if—a face worn wooden by a wind. I'm sorry, Mr. Gab added. They've taken away my beauties, but I've taken away your world, u-Stu, as thoroughly as they've taken away mine. Mr. Gab wavered when he walked, a pushover who now resembled the old rug he had hung for a door.

Mr. Stu sat carefully in Mr. Gab's chair. It was not all that comfortable. Slivers of sun, as though from a fire at their front door, raced through the shutters and ran up the rear wall, now wholly exposed, the faint shadow of a table against the plaster like a patch of unsunburned skin. When someone passed by on the sidewalk, the pattern palpitated. It was true that Mr. Gab didn't have much of a life. He sat in this not very comfortable chair most of every day, letting his eyes lie idle or roam randomly about like a foraging pooch, thinking who knew what thoughts, if he thought any, and if he thought any, who knew that either. Now, and even more often then, Mr. Gab would reluctantly help a customer, and once in a great while do a bit of business behind the rug, where the rug quite muffled the doing. You'd have to account it a life overflowing with empty. But that life had better prepare to be so much worse, and embrace mere absence like a lover. Nevertheless, who knew how to count these things: the quality of an existence—especially when you compared it to the meager stuff that took place in the deranged world outside—in walking these formerly narrow aisles, talking occasionally, eating meagerly, drinking rarely, sitting rudely on a board seat long hours, leafing a leaf from an out-of-date mag, arguing with an image in a catalogue, watching faint figures pass?

Mr. Stu let his eye run back and forth along the light like a squirrel on a wire. His life wasn't a winner either. Yet he had a job, a room, a library card. And he could open a book as if it were a door and disappear. He could inhale air in his weedy lot. He could look. He'd even learn. Yet he'd already found Sundays a stretch. He was supposed to stay home and pretend to be a person of substance in that slummy brown shoebox space of his. Itemize the alley. When the walls were whisked away? When the window went, what could he count? When his little box of belongings was put on the sidewalk outside, what would he manage? Mr. Gab, Mr. Gab, what were they to do? And when they took Mr. Gab downtown for questioning, and found what they would find in box after box, folder after folder, plastic pocket after pocket, how could either of them stand it? . . . endure it? . . . live through it? It was . . . awful . . . unrelievedly . . . foul. Mr. Gab reappeared with a bundle. He wore, for once, a wry smile. Quick as a cat Mr. Stu vacated the chair.

There are signs the dick went up the ladder to my loft, Mr. Gab said, but the dick missed this, wrapped in a sheet, under my cot. He held it out as you would a tray of sweets. There was a great wad of sheet to be clumsily unwound before a photogravure, rubber-banded between cardboards for its protection, was released. Mr. Gab put the print where a streak of sunlight crossed a trestle so they could see it. An Eastern moment, Mr. Gab said softly, and Mr. Stu saw the most beautiful silklike scene he'd ever, which Mr. Gab explained was a Stieglitz from 1901 called *Spring Showers*. Composed by a god, Mr. Gab whispered, as if the detective might overhear. He also spoke in awe, Mr. Stu knew. Like an Oriental hanging, Mr. Gab said, as though the mottled gray surface was that of cloth. Less than half a foot wide, a foot tall, made almost solely of shadow, Mr. Stu saw there in the dimness a street sweeper in wet hat and wet slicker pushing a wide broom along a wet gutter toward the photograph's wet left edge. Despite Mr. Stu's despair the image made him feel good for a moment, then worse. Just off-center, though on the same side as the sweeper, so that the right two-thirds of the picture was empty of everything except some soft faint shapes that represented traffic on the street, there grew a sidewalk tree with a gently forking trunk protected, perhaps from being pissed on, by a round wrought-iron fence whose pickets were thin as sticks. Surrounded by the sweetest vagueness, the tree rose from the walk on its own wet and wavy shadow as though that dripping shadow were a root, easing toward its dim thin upper limbs, which were dotted with brief new leaves and one perched bird, to faintly foliate away in indistinctness, though there were hints that tall buildings might block you if you entered the background, as well as shimmers that signified some moving vehicles, and the loom of a large ornamental urn—was it?—the viewer could not be sure.

What was certain was the photograph's depth, its purity, its delicacy. And the silken faintly hazy and amorphous gray that made up most of this small and simple streetside scene was the most beautiful, most comforting, most expressive quality of all. It was everywhere as wet, Mr. Stu realized, as Mr. Gab's face had been before his sleeve had swabbed it. Gloom began descending like a jacket hood, because his admiration could not keep misery away, not for long. Beauty eventually increased the pain. Perhaps not in better days. Mr. Stu understood incompleteness for he was plete aplenty. Mr. Gab understood loss because he was its cause as well as its victim. Pictures someone had taken, he'd taken, taken and hid. Now these prints had been wrenched from him in turn, and were nowhere where they might be gratefully seen—pictures that had been selfishly sequestered, then put like bad kids "in custody," to be examined by eyes that were mean and sharpened by the crude rough looks of criminals.

His shoulders in such a slump they ceased to be, Mr. Gab went with his treasure through the carpet again. Part of the rug had pulled from its tacks, so that now its hang was uneven. It bore a diamond design that Mr. Stu had never noticed before, cut deeply into its pelt. In better days he would have dreamed it outlined a playing field where figures the size of small ants might run about. Throughout the shop sunlight flickered for a moment. Someone was passing. In better days the store would still be open. Mr. Stu thought that when masses were made of mist and shadow, as they were in Stieglitz's painterly picture, and loomed without any consequences caused by bulk or weight, they possessed their own kind of being, and that the photograph, which had so little that was definite in it, nevertheless presented us with a whole world made of fragility and levitation. What would it mean to a man to have made such—there was no other word for it—such beauty? to have drawn it in through rainwatered eyes? to have captured it in a small now antiquated box? brought it to life almost amniotically? (another from his daily assignment of words) and sent it forth in the style of a far-off culture that he had learned about solely from photographic samples. Would it fill his life with satisfaction and achievement, or would it sadden him, since a loveliness of that kind could never be repeated, could never be realized again?

Mr. Gab had treasured his collection. However acquired. He had gathered good things together that had perhaps been stolen and dispersed once already. He had achieved an Archive, made his own museum in the midst of a maelstrom. Didn't that count? So Mr. Stu thought maybe Mr. Gab could say he hadn't known they were anyone's legitimate possessions any longer, but were the spoils of war, refugees of slavery, expropriation, and murder. Of course they could be returned to their proper homes if they had any, as long as it was their real wish to be rehung on the dour walls of grandiose old estates with their long cold halls given over to stuffily conventional family portraits and other tasteless bragging, to languish in the huge mansions or palaces they'd come from, or to sit in shame propped up on some lectern like a speech no one would give and no one would wish to hear; that would be okay, provided there'd be no further punishment for Mr. Gab, since he'd had pain enough from his loss to surpass that of most lovers. Lover: that was right, because who, Mr. Stu surmised, had looked at them as though they were gray lace, who had weighed a shadow against a substance, a dark line against a pale space, the curvature of a street's recession against the forefrontal block of a building, so as to feel the quality of judgment in every placement, the rightness of every relation, and how these subtle measures made the picture dance with the ideal gaiety of an ideal life.

We pass through frames, Mr. Gab had said. We walk about our rooms, our house, the neighborhood, and our elbow enters into a divine connection with a bus bench or bubbler in the park, a finial, a chair, or letter lying on a hall table, which is, in an instant—click—dissolved. The nose, the earlobe, the bosom, the elbow, the footfall, the torso's shadow pass in and out of awkward—in and out of awful—in and out of awesome combinations just as easily as air moves; the sublime, the suddenly supremely meaningful and redemptive moment is reached, achieved, left, dissolved into the dingy, only, in a few frames further, to connive at more communities. It is grace and disgrace constantly created and destroyed. The right click demonstrates how, in an instant, we, or our burro, or our shovel, or our eye or nose or nipple, were notes in a majestic symphony. A world of self-concerned things is suddenly singing a selfless concerned song: that was what the fine photographer, over and over, allowed to be *seen* in solemn apology for what should have been *heard*.

Nothing had been heard from Mr. Gab in quite a while, though Mr. Stu hadn't counted breaths; however, his employer's retreat should not have been surprising since he'd just lost a wife, more dear than life, to a bunch of hand trolleys. He'd been in the dark on his garret cot sobbing like a sad child, Mr. Stu bet, why not? In a room fixed to the top of a shabby ladder like a squirrel's nest in a tree; what could be sillier than where it was? and Mr. Stu had wanted to laugh when he first saw the way the ladder led up through a hole from which coal could once have dropped. Perhaps Mr. Gab could be comforted by the darkness since it might suggest an end to things—no more moving men moving his treasures out, treasures to be treated like contraband—less anxiety, fewer humiliations—dark at midday was what this day deserved—so perhaps he'd been somewhat slightly—well, not reassured—but protected from any additional pain, such as being pierced through and through by his unwarranted suspicion of his former employee, Mr. Stu, a feeling that had been turned on—click—like a light, when the strange man had said the phrase—the curdling phrase—"informed upon."

You have been given up, Mr. Gab. We gotcha. Dead to rights. We got yer goods too. Yer a looter, a despoiler, a thief, a fence, a flown-away father, an ungrateful and suspicious boss. Now you'll have to bear your loss like just deserts. Go to bed like your boy has, time upon time, to cry inside the pillow till the pillow flats. Go to bed like your boy has, countlessly, to imagine the bitter oncoming day. When you will walk about a barren store. When you will begin to miss me. When you'll be invited to "come downtown." Go to bed like your boy has, heart beaten by shame, sore and in despair he is alive. Go to bed like your boy has, angry at all, alone as a bone that has lost its dog. Head screams aren't effective. Head howls aren't effective. Headlongs aren't worth a damn. Seek some solace in the fact that you aren't being gnawed on at the moment, not being yelled at, at the moment, not being guffawed, not being always, at anything, the worst, to be the basket into which everything is eventually tossed. Seek solace, we advise . . . seek solace, don't we say? The one photograph that remains, had it been unshrouded and claimed, would nonetheless have been engraved on your weeping eyes.

Mr. Stu felt a wadded sheet at his uneven feet. He picked it up, to unwrap and refold, only to find his arms weren't long enough, so he spread it out on a trestle where bright slivers of sunshine from the shutters fell in lively white streaks. Mr. Stu drew a roll of masking tape from Mr. Gab's desk drawer, tape Mr. Gab used now and then to repair boxes, and began to block out the light, initially not easy because it bled through the thin tape, and it took several layers to make the glow even faint. By biting the tape into thin strips and making its stickum cling, Mr. Stu gradually darkened the room. Now there was only a halo to see by. It ran around the rug and apparently came from a light in the kitchen. Bring a pin, Mr. Gab, please, Mr. Stu called out. Though he thought he heard in his head the beating of a desperate heart, Mr. Stu boldly drew back the rug and entered the kitchen, where he found, after a few minutes of pawing about in drawers which otherwise yielded little in the way of contents, a roll of stout picture wire. Bring a pin, Mr. Gab, please, Mr. Stu shouted up the ladder at the hole that was even darker than the inside of a hose.

Mr. Stu was feeling his way to his idea. He realized, while groping between trestles, that he was performing the steps of his project in the wrong order. Consequently it was with difficulty that he found the nails he wanted on opposing walls, and with difficulty that he finally fastened one end of his wire to a conveniently big nail, and with difficulty that he unrolled the wire—held over his head—to the other side and found another roofer to wind his wire around, allowing the remainder of the roll to dangle. Now he had a firm line across the room to fling the sheet over, but he was unsure of what came next. Bring a pin, please, Mr. Gab, he called, suddenly weary and useless.

It took some time—and after the slow return of resolution—to hang the sheet, though he should have been more expert, having hung a lot of laundry out to dry in his day, even standing on a short stool to do his pinning when the line was beyond his reach. He stared into the dark, making nothing out. What's the idea? Mr. Gab asked. They stood in pitch now that Mr. Gab had turned the kitchen light off. I just thought we might— . Mr. Stu began. Ah, of course, you've occluded the shutters. Tape, Mr. Stu said. Something to do. You might have thought I was crying, Mr. Gab said. I was not. I was at a loss even for that. I didn't, Mr. Stu said, think. You might have thought I was huddling, Mr. Gab said. I was not. I was too tired to lie down. I didn't, Mr. Stu said. There is nothing for my eyes to adjust to, Mr. Gab said. It's as dark as the hole in a hose, said Mr. Stu.

They both stood without the whereabouts of the other. Say something more so I'll know where you are, said Mr. Gab, clearing his throat as if he were warning a boat about a shoal. I thought if we pinholed a bit of the tape, we'd get here, on this sheet you can't see, a bit of picture. Something to do, said Mr. Stu. Mr. Gab bumped gratefully into his desk. Mr. Stu heard its drawer being withdrawn. I've a hatpin here somewhere. Rats—ouch. No. I didn't stick myself, just thought I might have. Mr. Gab had to get close up, because the tape on the shutters was barely visible even close up. If I were to put a hole, say, here—what—

Suddenly there was a faint loose smear on the sheet. Needs to be closer up, was the opinion of Mr. Stu. Needs to be farther back, Mr. Gab decided. In the sheetlight it was easier to find the tightly fastened wire and unwind it from its nail, Mr. Gab doing one side, Mr. Stu the other. They moved in concert slowly toward the rear of the room, watching an image grow and slowly brighten. Now, cried Mr. Gab, and they both scrabbled for nailheads, feeling the wall gingerly as though it were flesh not their own, holding the wire as high as they could, which wasn't very in Mr. Stu's case, because the sheet dragged on his left side. Shouldn't let it get dirty, Mr. Gab said in his familiar cross voice, which was suddenly reassuring. The sheet, however, hadn't hung clear for many feet before it rolled over tables and caught on their crude edges. The image, now rather sharply focused, ran like a frieze across the top of the screen, but then the sheet tented toward the front of the shop as though there were a wind gusting from its rear and filling it out like a sail.

Without a further word needed, Mr. Gab and Mr. Stu began to shove the tables—not an easy thing to do—toward the sides of the store so there'd be a space for the sheet to hang and its image to cohere. Sawhorses don't roll; they wouldn't even skid; and beanbags were treacherously everywhere. Mr. Stu knew not to curse, but he nearly cried. It was futile. Why were they doing this? What had his idea been? Mr. Gab would go to prison. Mr. Stu imagined this might take place tomorrow. And homeless Mr. Stu, whose deforming birthmarks bespoke bad begetting, would get the heave-ho from every eye, from every back a turn, and even from those on pleasant picnics.

Quickly, quickly, your stool, Mr. Stu, you mustn't miss this. Mr. Stu dragged his perch awkwardly forward. Beanbags bore him malice. Mr. Gab had turned his chair to face the screen, and there . . . and there . . . there was their street, clear as clean water. There bloomed a building of red brick. Of a deep rich rose they had never before seen. It was . . . it was as if the entire brick had been hotly compressed the way the original clay had been, yet each brick was still so supremely each, because the mortar between them was like a living stream, and the pocking was as crisp as craters photographed from space, individual and maybe named for Greek gods. Where the brick encountered a lintel of gray stone, the contrast was more than bugle calls in a basement. The gray had a clarity one found only in the finest prints. Mr. Gab's hand rose toward the scene in involuntary tribute. Where the glass began its passage through the pane, light leaped the way water encircles the thrown stone, though now they were seeing it from below like a pair of cautiously gazing fish. Farther on, in the darker parts, were reflected shades of such subtlety that, still a fish, Mr. Gab gaped.

The sheet bore creases, of course. It would have to be ironed. The hang of the cloth over the wire could use some adjustment, perhaps a little weight attached to the bottom edge might improve the stretch, and the wire itself might be profitably tightened. Nevertheless, toiling in the dark, they'd done a good job.

We'll keep watching. Someone will be along soon. In a red sweater maybe. How would a red sweater look passing that brick, Mr. Gab wondered. Such a spectacle. Well, Mr. Gab, it *is* upside down, Mr. Stu said. I should say "thank you" to you, Mr. Stu, Mr. Gab said. You've given me quite a gift. And upside down will be all right. Like reflections from water. We shall adjust. I guess it will be, Mr. Stu said, but not even his ears knew whether he spoke in earnest agreement or out of sad acceptance of it. It . . . it's colored through. Yes, Mr. Stu, and what colors, too. Have you ever seen such? And look at the contours, so precise while staying soft and never crudely edgy. Never . . . you know . . . I never saw this building before. I never observed our street. We might wash the window—that bit in front of the pinhole, Mr. Stu suggested. Splendid idea, Mr. Stu, agreed Mr. Gab. But it *is* upside down, Mr. Stu ventured. They gave one another looks which were gifts not quite accepted. In color, Mr. Stu reminded. Sweet as rainbow ice cream, insisted Mr. Gab. A car . . . a cab . . . flashed by. The chariot of the sun, Mr. Gab exclaimed. Oh, Mr. Stu, this will indeed do. The bricks reddened to the color of rare roast beef. It will do just fine.

Conjunctions, 2000
Published in *Eyes,* 2015

ARTISTS

LA VIE TRÈSHORRIFICQUE

Rabelais Revisited

So what does our ancient author say is the shape of Socrates's nose? A nose of such importance, always well into other people's business, might be imagined to be sharp as a knife, pointed like a whittled stick, nostrilled in the style of the truffle pig so as to capture the least whiff of opinionated puffery and to disinhale when the odor proves to be misleading—in truth a *nez pointu,* the phrase our esteemed authority uses for the description of his mentor and his muse; however, Andrew Brown, the most recent translator of Rabelais's masterpiece, *Gargantua and Pantagruel,* knows that Socrates is never represented thus but was given pop eyes and a snub nose whenever his visage was set in stone, so he silently corrects the text and blunts the knife—". . . with his snub nose, his eyes like a bull's, and the face of a madman." Besides, John Cowper Powys, who Englished his favorite selections in 1948, set the precedent in nose snubbing. One wonders how many such corrections Brown has made, tacit as a Trappist.

Rabelais writes for the convivial, and consequently for those who must have poisoned their livers and contracted the pox, because syph was the New World's swap with Europe in their exchange of epidemics; it was the sixteenth century's AIDS, heedless pleasure's penance. And although the clap can now turn on lights, alcohol has never changed its ways. Thus he welcomes us to his feast on what might be Inflation Sunday during Hypocrites's Holiday in the Year of the Warmonger, two thousand four, or maybe fifteen thirty-two, it's much the same, since swilling, swiving, corruption and conniving, fanaticism, bigotry, and bloodshed haven't changed, and the sports bars are still full of opinion.

For a work that is rumored to be loose as a noodle, *Gargantua* moves immediately to make significant allusions. The first is to Plato's *Symposium* and the speech of Alcibiades in praise of his mentor, Socrates, whom he compares to an apothecary's box that is adorned with improbable figures, from harpies and satyrs to flying goats and saddled ducks, each image designed to provoke mirth, yet a box whose interior is as precious as a casket of the Magi, full of . . . well, among our several renderers there is some difference of opinion. Thomas Urquhart, the earliest and most esteemed translator (1653), offers "Balme, Ambergreese, Amamon, Musk, Civet, with several kindes of precious stones, and other things of great price," and our aforesaid Andrew Brown follows suit, overall more obedient to the text, whereas Penguin Books' J. M. Cohen replaces "precious stones" with "mineral essences," perhaps an improvement; however, Jacques Le Clercq (whose 1936 version spoke so persuasively to me when I was a tad because it was the translation in the Modern Library, the first library I knew) is expansive and explanatory, with "balsam of Mecca, ambergris from the sperm whale, amomum from the cardamon, musk from the deer and civet from the civet's arsehole—not to mention various sorts of precious stones, used for medical purposes, and other invaluable possessions."

Rabelais does that to you. He fills you with wind. You outgrow several sizes. Words multiply in your mind immediately the way ants invade a larder, soon more plentiful than the grounds that were spilled on the kitchen counter while making morning coffee. In *Gargantua's* day words were revered, despised, traded, banned, liberated, loved. At the wine-soaked tables of the inns, one exchanged views, lies, brags, and other tales; in the markets, bargaining went on in a dialect as local and delicious as their greens; in the doss houses, grunts were gratefully given and received; at church, the air was Latinated and, like the light, stained its priestly columns, brightened its aisles or occluded niches, and lengthened the grief in kneeling figures. Even though the world was everywhere widening to reveal fresh continents to be discovered and despoiled, heathen souls to be sought out and saved, ordinary life was the richest land so far claimed for any kingdom, because along with common things came their common names, and with the names came common knowledge: *mud puddle, haymow, oxen, minnow, lettuce, fart, smirk, seaport, wink.*

(François Rabelais paid homage to three tongues when he Latinized his French name to inscribe it in his books, and followed that with an accompanying phrase in Greek—"François Rabelais's Book and His Friends'"—assigning ownership to himself in Latin and borrower's rights to his close associates in Greek, a generosity necessary to the spread of knowledge when books were rare, and, since they were so rare, a generosity indeed. The elaborateness of this signature was matched by the general shape of his hand, which affected the scrolls and parasitic letters of the legal profession his father practiced, and was symbolic of a writing style, some thought, that fastened afterthoughts to every final flourish.)

Books were rare and books were revered. The opened cover compared to the opened eye, to a chest of treasure, a doorway to the divine, the cork in a bottle; however, books bore error on through time as well as truth, opinion, hypothesis, and conjecture, and they could fuddle the mind as well as wine. Mistakes, fakes, and falsehoods, in an opportune place, can become history, as the many mistranslations camped out on sacred tomes attest. Alcibiades did not compare Socrates to an apothecary's box but to those "Silenus-figures that sit in the statuaries' shops . . . when their two halves are disjoined, they are seen to possess statues of gods within." The actual reference is no less suitable to Rabelais's purposes than the mistaken one, yet about it the translators gather, honor-bound to preserve and repeat it.

And if we broke free of words to inspect the philosopher in person, as if that were possible, we would still have a book bag for a head, eyes colored by custom, commonplace, and superstition. He would not "look" wise, as if we knew what wisdom wore to appear stupid—furrowed brow or quizzical smile, bald because his head steamed. "You would not have given the peel of an Oinion for him," Urquhart says; you'd not have offered "an onion skin," declares Le Clercq; not "the top of an onion," Powys puts it; nary "a shred of an onion for him," Cohen has it; or "you wouldn't have given the shred of an onion skin," in Brown's opinion, accepting most that has come before but declining the tuffet; while Rabelais, if we want to bother with the source, wrote, "*n'en eussiez donné un coupeau d'oignon,*" not realizing that *coupeau* would become obsolete, and that his metaphor would be lost: "you would not give the hilltop of an onion for him."

This is a minor matter indeed, but it is interesting to note that Powys, who creeps closest to his quarry, has complained of Samuel Putnam, whose translation he praises and many favor, for ruthlessly updating the text, thus making it more readable for his generation while depriving Rabelais's own time of its age and voice. And, I might add, some of his art.

Who cares whether Grandgousier or Greatgullet (father of Gargantua) was a rollicking blade and a superlative toper, as one translator describes him; or—since there is no reference to anyone's gullet in the passage I'm looking at—was just a good fellow in his time and notable jester, according to another; or, as Andrew Brown describes him for us, was instead "a real barrel of laughs"? Brown also advises us to "check out" texts and knock back drinks, as we are wont now to do. He makes us feel comfortable in the Renaissance, as if it were putting on its show in our living room. Certainly Brown's version is more zippy and even more accurate than many. Picky points perhaps. But imagine these modest disagreements multiplied through five volumes and a hundred thousand times.

In his lively introduction to *Pantagruel*, Brown points out, apropos the same contrast between Socrates the Silenus and Socrates the Sage who opens the work, that interpretation, in Rabelais's day, was a dangerous undertaking, as much for what you might be thought to be learning as for what you actually learned; but because he is translating a later version of the text, one that Rabelais judged to be more prudent to publish than the original, there are bits, offensive to Church authorities, omitted.

Jean Plattard, in *The Life of François Rabelais*, thinks that Rabelais was born around 1494 on his father's farm, two gunshots from the Abbey of Seuilly, and a league from Chinon, the town where he grew beneath his father's wing until he began his studies to become a Franciscan monk. By the time he pens *Pantagruel* (of which *Gargantua* is a prequel) he is familiar with at least four professions and one art: the law from his father, the priesthood and medicine from their practice, the New Learning from ancient sages, and poetry through his epistolary exchanges in verse with the poet Jean Bouchet. What a stock of technical terms, argument forms, and higher powers Rabelais could employ, parody, and appeal to; what grammatical categories, rhetorical schemes, rimes *équivoques* and *batelées* (lines ambiguous and overloaded as a boat); what changes rung from words like those from bells might he muster: sixty-four verbs in the imperfect tense, necessary to roll a barrel out of town in a cluster of shove and sound—"*le tournoit, viroit, brouilloit, garbouilloit, hersoit, versoit, renversoit . . .*"—and so on—"*nattoit, grattoit, flattoit . . .*"— as, in English, we might group "crash, clash, mash, smash, slash, bash, trash, gnash . . ." to depict the passage of our armored vehicles through a village.

Later in his life, in his role as a physician, Rabelais often traveled to Lyon or Rome as a part of Cardinal Jean du Bellay's retinue, but as a young priest he did his rounds in the region of his birth, *la molle et douce Touraine,* and in the regal town of Chinon itself, once capital to a shrunken France (1528–29), known to tourists now for one of Joan of Arc's early exploits. Scholars have frequently remarked Rabelais's intensive knowledge of the region: its cloth, its donkeys, its windmills, the height of its hemp, its "sweet, easy, warm, wet and well-soaked soil," and how well he rendered them all: towns, towers, lanterns, rivers, walls, in properly apportioned paragraphs. "Dressed in his Benedictine's habit, he mixed with the people more than any writer of his time," Plattard writes. "He knew the art of loosening the tongues of the cattle-drover in the field, the artisan in his workshop, the merchant in the inn. He can, on occasion, make use of their dialect, their familiar metaphors, their customary swearwords." *Gargantua* and *Pantagruel* are so drenched, like the soil, in locales, that Albert Jay Nock devoted a chatty travelogue to *A Journey into Rabelais's France* (1934).

The heroes of the New Learning—beginning with Guillaume Budé, Thomas More, Desiderius Erasmus, his self-designated student, Rabelais, and flowering in the great Baroque outbursts of Michel Montaigne, Robert Burton, and, later, Sir Thomas Browne—were devoted multilingual quoters; however, in them, as often as not, the citations were offered as examples of ignorance and superstition on the part of their authors and held up as warnings to the unwary: what oft's been thought is now so little thought of.

To quote pagan authors is more than fun; it suggests that there are other authorities than have been favored by the scholastics, and to write about them in the vulgate is to invite readers to look on pages that the Church has resolutely kept from popular perusal—as if, on their own, such readers would be prone to misconstrue, taking a path that led straight to the stake. Moreover, it had been a habit through many centuries to consult books rather than inspect afresh what the books were presumed to be about; to cite authorities, to quote the Fathers of the Church, to pit one scholar's paragraphs against another's—thus to debate each issue inside the precincts of the word, and this lawyerlike practice was hard to break. For instance—ah yes, an instance!—a scholar whose work Rabelais read in his youth (a man pridefully disputatious, whose skull will grind its teeth at going nameless here) had written a brief essay on marital proprieties, the illiberal views of which had elicited a sturdy defense of women's rights from—worse yet!—his closest friend. This required a rebuttal, duly given in a second edition, where he beat his opponent about the brow and brain by citing, in confirmation of his position, "authorities as numerous as they were varied. [He] quoted pell-mell philosophers and poets, historians and orators, Livy and Cicero, Plato and Petrarch, Ezechiel and Propertius. The work became thus considerably enlarged. From the 27 pages which composed the original edition it had grown to 276," as—the whistle of my own citation can be heard—Jean Plattard reports (page 28).

Socrates's presence is pointed in other ways than that of his nose, since, at least as early as Abelard's *Dialectica* (1118), the Greek philosopher was a figure of fun for the schoolmen. Abelard does a jocose dance about the proposition—"if Socrates is asinine, some man is asinine"—though, as his biographer M. T. Clanchy reports, he later softened his moral disapproval (*Abelard: A Medieval Life* [Oxford: Blackwell], 1997, p. 275). Clanchy remarks that "logicians had traditionally and unthinkingly treated Socrates disrespectfully because they were not concerned with historical realities nor with people's feelings."

If Alcibiades can serve up Socrates as a sample of the wise fool, and Rabelais's reader can then remember how the renowned Erasmus has praised folly while wondering who the truly foolish are, then perhaps I may make my own reminder of how frequently it was felt that wild unseemly flatulated words would surely issue from a similarly grotesque and corpulent person. Gargantua, our hero here, is as fulminatious as his flesh is flabby, and only after decency has been drilled into him can he deliver an admirable speech in a restrained and balanced Ciceronian style. Shakespeare's Falstaff and Molière's Tartuffe are outstanding examples, as is the lesser-known character, Vanderhulk, of Thomas Nashe's *The Unfortunate Traveler*, a grotesque whose existence I was made aware of by Wayne Rebhorn in *The Emperor of Men's Minds* (another citation within a citation, worth double points). This fellow "had a sulphurous, big, swollen, large face like a Saracen, eyes like two Kentish oysters, a mouth that opened as wide every time he spake as one of those old knit trap doors, a beard as though it had been made of a bird's nest plucked in pieces which consisteth of straw, hair, and dirt mixed together." One must remark, by the way, that Rabelais would never mess up his line with real redundancy the way Nashe did—"big, swollen, large" indeed. No, Rabelais's redundancies redound. And what is a "knit trap door"? Is it a concealing rug? a confederate of the tea cozy? or a round sphincter-type opening that closes behind a netted fish? To meet new words is to encounter new wonders.

Nor should we be deceived, as we read—by coarseness, indulgence, logorrhea—to suppose there is nothing but mooning going on in *Gargantua* or *Pantagruel*, naught but cocking a snook at authority and other small-boy pranks, or simply exuberance fizzing from bottle end and fundament like an organized spritzelation of shaken soda. The point of the opening reference to Socrates's appearance and the reality of his payoff remains unaffected: this book will appear woolly and rough, its course haphazard, but its sense is consistent, unified, pure yet iridescent as though silk had swallowed water, and it has been set down more in weeping than in writing, more in despair than in glee, more when sober than when drunk; and though drunkenness is a frequent occupation of its actors, we should not fear for an actual stagger, because stage cups are always full of tea. Our author is besotted, but by words; he is intoxicated with learning, with his own strength; walls are atumblin' down, those of castle and cathedral, city and convent, college and library.

At the close of Plato's banquet, at daybreak, when all the evening's revelers and rhetoricians have passed out, Socrates rises from among the sleepers and goes to spend the balance of the day in his customary manner, for the philosopher feels no fuddle, and reason does not weary of its work; nor will it here, because the philosopher's distant student has also wakened early, left the priestly functions toward which his studious nature had initially inclined him, and begun his service as a physician, consequently as a scholar of Hippocrates and Galen, among the Greeks the more empirically inclined. Now to Rabelais's dislike of traditional schoolmen is added a disdain for the traditional physician: "These fellows get their experience by killing folks (as Pliny once complained); and they are a source of greater danger, even, than any that comes from disease itself."

Princes and their petty yet ruinous wars, indolent hypocritical monks and their parasitical lives, the theologians of the Sorbonne who misuse reason and disgrace intelligence, the venerators of holy relics and the pious pilgrims, purveyors of popular superstitions of every stripe—these are the objects of our author's scorn, as it should be our concern to steer clear of them today, though they may call their sects professions, and their parties by newer noble-sounding names.

Rabelais's anger at those who are tethered to their texts is evidence of his own released mind, but it is partly paradoxical, since he is as bookish as they. He, however, is eating fresh fruit from old trees instead of winter's barreled apples, and we can turn to him as he returned to Plato and Socrates. *Gargantua* and *Pantagruel,* so far in the past, as comets come, can arrive like a new age to surprise our eyes. These works seem written for today; they are as relevant, and possibly as futile. Between the brackets insert your favorite bêtes noires. "[These scholars and medics] can well enough see the lightboat of lies battered and leaking in every part; yet they insist upon retaining, by force and by violence, those works to which they have been accustomed from their youth up. If one endeavours to snatch these away from them, they feel that he is, at the same time, snatching away their very souls." Did the humanists not feel similarly violated when the Church arrested their Greek books? And burned their pages, set fire to their authors, and lit their readers too, as Brown notes. After Rabelais edits a new edition of Hippocrates he has a Latin couplet placed upon its title page that reads: "Here is the overflowing fount of healing lore. Drink here, unless the stagnant water of a ditch tastes better to you."

Scholars have noticed the metaphoric connection of science with salubrious imbibing in Rabelais, though it must be remembered that reading a book of symptoms is not the same as taking a pulse. "Drink" is what Gargantua cries as he's being born, instead of the customary "waa waa"; the third and fourth books are given over in large part to a search for the Divine Bottle as if it were the Holy Grail; and in the fifth part, whose authenticity is disputed, the oracle of the Dive Bouteille delivers wisdom's secret, which is—no surprise from the lips of a bottle—Drink! Moreover, Pantagruel makes a pre-Rabelaisian appearance in a medieval mystery play, where his role is that of an impish devil who gathers salt from the seashore to shake down the throats of snoring drunkards.

His salary at the Great Hospital of Lyon did not achieve jingle, and, deprived of the Church's free room and board or the indulgences of some courtly master, Rabelais must have often slept without covers or companion, eaten tack, and drunk from a dry glass. So straitened circumstances probably alerted him to the possibility of a windfall of his own when a small book, the illegitimate offspring of the Arthurian legends, anonymously transcribed from the oral tradition, sold more copies in two months than Bibles in nine years. It retold the story of how the magician Merlin created a family of giants, sort of medieval superheroes, out of the bones of two male whales, a sprinkle of clippings from Queen Genièvre's nails, plus a *soupçon* of blood from one of Sir Lancelot's wounds, to help out King Arthur through his many tribulations. Donald Frame tells us in his study, *François Rabelais* (1977), that the loving pair, Grant-Gosier (or the Great Gullet that Le Clercq has insisted on inserting into his translation wherever possible) and Galemelle (who, as Gargamelle, bears Gargantua for eleven months in Rabelais's version before dumping him with a thump into a nest of citations that prove why lengthy gestations are necessary for masterpieces) . . . well, the two make their way between grasping parentheses bearing their brute of a boy on the back of a city-sized mare "through France to join Arthur; but the parents"—who suffer a fever like a wound along the way—"die at Mont-Saint-Michel for lack of a purgative. Merlin transports Gargantua to Arthur on a cloud; fighting for Arthur, Gargantua conquers the Gos and Magos, the Dutch and the Irish, and a twelve-cubit giant in single combat. Finally, after two hundred years, he is translated to fairyland. . . ." On the other hand, Paul Eldridge, in his *François Rabelais: The Great Storyteller* (1971), claims that the parents died because of the purgative, not for want of one, and boasts that Gargantua forced all of the prisoners he'd taken (as if they were sweets, I suppose) into his hollow tooth in lieu of a filling. But I have heard that he also stuffed the cuffs of his sleeves, his game bag, and the toes of his hose with his victims. Tales of yore should yield such variations; the more there are the merrier they make us. Always consult many authorities; they will infect you with suspicion—a desirable service.

This anonymous author happily supplied the details necessary to tall tales, and we are familiar with them in the form of the Paul Bunyan legend or many of the stories that floated with the boatmen down the Mississippi or those that boasted of trappers who, bare-handed, fought bear and cougar in a frontier forest. How big, how strong, how hungry was the lumberjack, the boatman, the hunter? "Gargantua lunched off two shipfuls of fresh herrings and three casks of salted mackerel; . . . he dined on three hundred cattle and two hundred sheep; . . . he carried off the bells of Notre-Dame de Paris to hang them on his mare's neck; . . . his peals of laughter were heard seven and a half leagues away. . . ." Not a decibel less, not a yard more.

So Rabelais's monsters must outdo the outdoers . . . and they do. Their habits of hyperbole do not exclude their author, who swears in *Pantagruel's* prologue: "may I be carried off by a hundred thousand basketfuls of fine devils, body and soul, innards and entrails, if I lie by so much as a single word in the whole story"—a protestation exceeded only by the punishments to be inflicted upon readers who do not obediently believe. Like the pamphlet that preceded it, *Pantagruel* is packed with gross-out japes and overscale jokes, with mythological deeds that mock the social and religious figments that one must pretend to believe out of fear of just those pains Rabelais promises his own disbelievers—"sulphur, flames and the bottomless pit."

By turning everything topsy-turvy, *Pantagruel* mimics the meanings and rituals of medieval carnivals and festivals too, a fundamental aspect of Rabelais's human comedy famously described by Mikhail Bakhtin in *Rabelais and His World* (1968). The school of Russian formalists with which Bakhtin was associated had made considerable advances in the study of folktales and legends, particularly in terms of their narrative forms; so Rabelais's reliance on the life and laughter of common people made ideal material for the Russian critic's cast of mind. *Gargantua* and *Pantagruel* belonged to the culture of popular carnival humor, of which there were, Bakhtin felt, three basic manifestations: ritual spectacles, such as carnival pageants, fools'-day celebrations, and marketplace entertainments; written as well as oral parodies in both Latin and their local dialects; and various sorts of slanging matches, cursing patterns, catchphrases, and what we call "trash talk" now.

So the giants are giants because they began their lives outside of Rabelais's world as giants. Rabelais acknowledges this in his prologue to *Pantagruel.* However, they flourish as giants for further reasons, many of them naming and enumerative, and because a giant was a good visual symbol for a group, a class, an order, a faith, an army, a nation. Our author was painfully aware of the rapacity of kings, counts, cardinals, and bishops, whose entourages ate like the armies that periodically swept over the countryside, gobbling up everything that couldn't be hidden from them. His imagery anticipates Hobbes's invention of that artificial body, the "corporate giant."

In 1651, when Thomas Hobbes published his great work on our need to relinquish rights to form an absolute sovereignty and escape the chaos of a state of nature, he fronted his text with an engraving that depicted the figure of a king whose body was made of many men—a corporate leviathan—just as his treatise advised; and to ensure his own safety, during the difficult civil-war times in which he wrote, Hobbes gave the ruler Oliver Cromwell's face, while upon the Lord Protector's head he placed the crown of a Catholic, Charles the Second—a duplicity Rabelais would have understood, since, like so many others in his time, he published under a pseudonym at first (Alcofribas Nasier, a transparent anagram of his own name), and the books he wrote were regularly proscribed.

The little story of the medlars that appears on the first pages of *Pantagruel* furnishes a good context for the understanding of the preternatural swellings that afflict this text and all its occupants. When Cain kills Abel the earth becomes soaked in the blood of the victim and bears in consequence an abundance of fruit. The normally compact leathery crab apples that the medlar tree produces were in the subsequent season so large that three of them sufficed for a bushel. The text has scarcely taken a step, yet it has managed to traduce two biblical tales, pun on God's injunction to "be fruitful," and redo Eden's celebrated seduction as a menacing farce—which, come to think of it, it is. The side effects of medlar gorging were not all benevolent, nor should we have expected them to be, if we remember the blood of injustice that stimulated their growth: "All of them suffered from a really horrible swelling on their bodies, but not all of them had it in the same place." Some grew bellies so big they were called Almighties to mock the manner in which the Apostles' Creed refers to God, but they were good people "and from this race sprang St Paunch, and Pancake Day" (which is Brown's translation of its calendar name, "Shrove Tuesday," and true to its spirit). Some became hunchbacks; soon there were those who had phalluses so long they wrapped them around their waists like belts; still others had to bear bollocks the size of the medlars responsible, and so on into a parody of the generational lists of Genesis. This augmentation is best achieved grammatically by dispensing with the general term and replacing it with an organized mob of particulars, or requiring a noun to do the work of an adjective or a verb, as in this passage, which drew Albert Jay Nock's admiration:

There was then in the abbey [of Seuilly] a claustral monk called Friar John of the Funnels, young, gallant, frisk, lusty, nimble, quick, active, bold, adventurous, resolute, tall, lean, wide-mouthed, long-nosed, a rare mumbler of matins, unbridler of masses and runner-over of vigils; and to conclude summarily in a word, a right monk, if ever there were any, since the monking world monked a monkery.

Whether, as the schoolmen had debated, there were real universals, which had Being apart from that of their particulars, or only specific material things enjoyed existence, Rabelais knew that Man the Mighty was like a giant individual, and since he was a creature principally engaged in eating, excreting, killing, and begetting; one that used its brain to obtain cash and buy comfort, a friend of whoever might be of service, always seeking personal security, pleasant company, and a tapped keg, and forever in need of enemies to justify its own excesses; we might expect it to lay much waste wherever it was, if only by snoring, thus breaking windows, or by poisoning crops before they could be eaten through breaking wind from its last debauch. This special giant, Pantagruel, was already known to all as a provoker of thirst, a harbinger of drought and cracked earth, and in Rabelais's terms he creates desire as well, needs that swell like cheeks about an infected tooth.

But Rabelais is not long content with giants, and soon introduces a Ulysses of his own—Panurge—a cunning riddler, a sly boots, a devious trickster, yet a loyal friend whom Pantagruel meets upon the road in a wretchedly disheveled condition and whom he questions before deciding to offer assistance. In a brilliant bravura passage that could have been stolen from Joyce's *Ulysses,* Panurge replies first in German, then in Gibberish, Italian, Scots, Basque, Lanternlandish, Dutch, Spanish ("I am tired of talking so much"), Danish, Ancient Greek, Utopian, Latin, and finally, of course, in his native tongue, the French of Touraine. Impressed—as who wouldn't be?—Pantagruel orders Panurge to be properly fed, after which the polyglot sleeps till dinnertime the next day, when he comes to table "in a hop, skip, and a jump." Which is American for *quickly.*

I remember a similar kind of academic contest. In Germany a number of writers had passages from their books recited to them in a language they were unlikely to understand (in this case, it was Romanian). We were asked to identify the authors of each passage. Would we even recognize our own? I remember it well because I won. The secret was in the rhetorical rhythms that the translations retained. There is plenty of rhetorical rhythm in Rabelais, and it conveys a zest and energy, a boyish nose-thumbing glee, that is not equaled, to my ear, by any other writer. But it is not always used to make jokes, for there is much here that is serious on its face as well as strongly meant in its heart. Nor does the fun Rabelais has with higher education, the law, or the Church mean that he has embraced ignorance, lawlessness, and disbelief;

it is, rather, that, then as now, the stupid, the greedy, the hypocritical, the disloyal, or the tyrannical serve virtue as badly as they profit vice. Our lawyer jokes should not suggest we wish to dispense with legal services—just shysters; and neither should Erasmus's anticlericalism nor Rabelais's invectives against priests lead us to think they are not utterly devout. The fact is (and it is a sad one) that the age was a lot freer in its permissible range of blasphemy and verbal indecencies than we are now, though making the wrong enemies then could lose you more than a sect's bloc of bigot votes.

Pantagruel went through two editions with a swiftness that hurried *Gargantua* into existence, a work less dependent upon its predecessors, more inclined to realism than to whimsies about the wearers of the larger sizes or events exceeding the miraculous, and more likely to set its scenes in locales familiar to the reader instead of lands far away and never-never. Meanwhile, like a ragman, Rabelais has been collecting his material much as we might imagine Brueghel doing: insults, for instance, children's games, bum wipes, countries that were being conquered during the cake bakers' war. This war, like the disagreements between Tweedledum and Tweedledee, is over a trifling refusal of a bunch of griddlecake bakers to sell a portion of their wares to some shepherds who were passing a few otherwise idle and sheepish hours in preventing starlings from eating the grapes then ripening on the farmers' vines. The shepherds offered the going price, which was apparently less on the road than the bakers expected to collect once they were in town. They fire off a volley of insults in reply: in Rabelais twenty-eight of them, and in Cohen the same, but from Brown fly only twenty-six, while Le Clercq's twenty-seven are more sporadically delivered, and Urquhart overwhelms his victims with forty-two fancy revilements that fall as if a storm of hailstones came in attractively different shapes and sizes.

This rudeness leads to a quarrel that starts a fight that results in injuries that must be requited, and so from a contretemps set steaming by pride and stirred by greed, ignorance, fear, and suspicion—a nothing upon which are soon erected reasons like artillery positions—a battle—as always, fought with lies and lost lives—begins what will prosper as a war; a war that forbearance cannot forestall or calm, a war that consumes a list—aforecited—of conquered countries but also the spoils of an invading army; indeed, that list is the pillagers' verbal equivalent. "They made off with oxen, cows, bulls, calves, heifers, ewes, sheep, nanny-goats and billy-goats; hens, capons, chickens, goslings, ganders and geese; pigs, sows and piglets; they knocked down walnuts, harvested vines, carried off vinestocks, and shook down all the fruit from the trees." That, the King of the Offended Bakers said, "*would teach them to eat cake.*"

But what taskmasters habitually forget is how to teach others their lessons without having to learn any themselves.

In the course of this contest, Grandgousier (the king of the country attacked and the father of Gargantua) takes a notable prisoner, called "Swashbuckler" out of respect for Errol Flynn. After questioning this prisoner in order to learn what his enemy intended by the invasion, and discovering that Picrochole (for that was the warlord's name) means to conquer the entire country, Grandgousier (demonstrating his wisdom as well as his relevance to our times, as I am sure was his intention) releases Swashbuckler with the following observation about his opponent.

> It would have been better if he had stayed at home, governing it like a king—rather than insolently invading mine, pillaging it like an enemy. If he had governed his land he would have extended it, but by pillaging mine he will be destroyed. Be off with you, in the name of God. Follow the good; point out to your king the errors of his that you are aware of, and never give him advice for the sake of your own personal profit, for if the commonwealth is lost, so is the individual and his property. As for your ransom, I give it all to you, and desire that your weapons and your horse be returned to you. This is how things ought to be between neighbours and old friends. . . .

Swashbuckler does not depart without gifts. Nor did Rabelais's readers, who laughed, heartily, most of them, as if they had gotten the gist and digested its moral; yet who obeyed kings and cardinals, princes and priests nevertheless, where they believed their interests lay, or where their fears were focused. And so confusion and catastrophe continue, in plenty and in colorful variety, to this day. I notice there are apples in our shops so huge it takes only three of them to heap a bushel. Our ferociously fertile earth is that soaked, our fruit that malevolent.

Harper's Magazine, 2004
Published in *A Temple of Texts,* 2006

Robert Walser, an Introduction

They found Robert Walser's body in the middle of a snowy field. It was Christmas Day, so the timing of his death was perhaps excessively symbolic. I like to think the field he fell in was as smoothly white as writing paper. There his figure, hand held to its failed heart, could pretend to be a word—not a statement, not a query, not an exclamation—but a word, unassertive and nearly illegible, squeezed into smallness by a cramped hand. It would be a word, if it *were* a word (such doubtful hesitations were characteristic of Walser), which would bring to an end a life of observant idling, city strolling, mountain hikes, and woodland walks, a life lived on the edges of lakes, on the margins of meadows, on the verges of things, a life in slow but constant motion, at a gawker's pace: sad, removed, amused, ironic, obsessively absorbed.

At least three of Walser's seven siblings were successful. Success was something Walser studied, weighed, admired, mocked, refused. He had a grandfather who was a journalist, a father who bound books. He would write for periodicals himself, and author novels. He was born in Biel, by Bieler See, in northwestern Switzerland, but left school at fourteen, worked briefly in a bank; with the desire to be an actor went to Stuttgart, where he found employment in a publishing house, turned up in Zürich in 1896 to begin his odd-jobs life in earnest; and managed, by the time he was twenty, to get his first poems in a Berne newspaper.

He was a kind of columnist before the time of columns. So many of his pieces are brief, reflective, simple enough in their syntax and diction to be columns, deceptively ordinary in their observations, a little like those cozy nature notes that prop up editorial pages still, a little like some letters to the editor, too: the signature, HARMLESS CRANK, could be appended to quite a few without discordance or much malice. And yet, reading them, one is astonished that any were ever put in print, because Walser matches trivial thoughts to trivial subjects—as rug to drape—with relentless insistence, so that about ladies' shoes, for instance, he dares to believe that they are either brown or black in color; moreover, his transitions are abrupt as table edges; non sequiturs flock his pages like starlings to their evening trees; the pieces turn, often savagely, against themselves, or they dwindle away in apparent weariness and, unable to find a reason to cease, cease for want of a reason for going on.

Walser passes nine quiet years in Zürich, eight in Berlin, where he lives for a time in his brother's apartment and cares for the cat, eight more back in Biel, near his sister this time, twelve in Berne (eight go by there before he has himself institutionalized after several possibly suicidal episodes and his sister's insistence); then, finally, the remaining removed and silent twenty-three in the asylum at Herisau, taking his walks, busy about the idle business of being mad, waiting for the blank which would blanket his attendant blankness (such wordplay was characteristic of Walser), and finding it, we might say, when his heart failed in a field full of snow.

Throughout this time, he's been an inventor's assistant, worked in banks and insurance offices, as an archivist or the secretary of an art dealer, attended a school for servants, and become a butler for a bit, before he accepts insanity as his true profession.

Lightly attached to people, to the formalities of society, to any work which lies beneath another's will like a leg beneath a log, and more in love with localities and their regularities (like the seasons) which do not require him, Walser draws a borderline near poverty for himself and lives his increasingly frugal life in little rooms, in donated leftover spaces, in otherwise unoccupied attics, in circumstances straitened to the shape of his thin frame, shrunk to the size of his microscopic script, a miniaturization perhaps too suitable to his status (such patterned repetitions are characteristic). Walser is always the dog beneath the dogs, a ne'er-do-well and a nobody. He pens lines for which he receives small recognition and less pay. He composes novels which get lost or are so artfully mislaid, they might have been murdered. He stays out of other people's way, posting his innumerable ruminations to publications which not infrequently publish them—surprising even themselves. Most float back, leaf after leaf, to pile up eventually into books.

His is the perfect stroller's psychology. To his eye, everything is equal; to his heart, everything is fresh and astonishing; to his mind, everything presents a pleasant puzzle. Diversion is his principal direction, whim his master, the serendipitous the substance of his daily routine. I think that Walser most loved his lovely walks in the woods, and in particular that moment when a clearing came into view like sunshine between clouds, or a lake rose from its labor of duplicating mountains to drench the spaces between trees. In any case, his characters run away to the woods as often as creatures in fairy tales, and more often than not with similar results.

Walser's prose frequently reads as if it had been lifted from a tourist brochure, because his narrators almost never see things with Kafka's scrupulously realistic and coolly dispassionate gaze: they look upon a commonplace world in terms of conventional values and received opinions. Things are therefore said to be "lovely," "dear," "sweet," "charming," "little," "clever," "perfect," or "enchanting." Things are tritely characterized as beautiful and good, deliciously tempting, absolutely true to their type; they are as pleasing as can be imagined, as delightful as anywhere can be found. Things are meant to be presented to us exactly as they appear to smug, assured, accepted, and acceptable estimation. Walser paints a postcard world.

> A farmer's market is bright, lively, sumptuous, and gay. . . . Sun-splashed sausages have a splendid appearance. The meat shows off in all its glory, proud and purple, from the hooks on which it hangs. Vegetables laughing verdantly, oranges jesting in gorgeous yellow heaps, fish swimming about in wide tubs of water . . . This joyful, simple life, it's so unpretentiously attractive, it laughs at you with its homey, petit-bourgeois laugh. And then the sky with its topnotch, first-rate blue.

His narrators consequently split their point of view, merging their removed and alienated angles of vision with the way the observed believe and wish themselves to feel: at weddings, happy as all git-out; at funerals, sad as Niobe or Job; enjoying their gluttonies without anxiety or future pangs, exercising their tyrannies without guilt or fear of overthrow. His narrator's noses are pressed to the window: surely those are goodies there, beyond the fogged glass. The young servant thinks: look at the family eat—how delicious the food must be; listen to their laughter—how happy they are; how nice it must be to be beautifully dressed, to own a fine carriage, to live in this house I work so hard and helplessly to keep clean.

And the food *is* no doubt delicious. It *is* pleasant to be well got up and possess a closet of consequence. It *is* certainly lovely to look down on the soiled hats of passersby when wheeling through the park. It doesn't take a tired proverb to tell us that, between high life and low, high is higher. But it is also true that the wide sky is the property of rich and poor alike; that the broad lake will not refuse the body of any bather, even one cockeyed with care; that the massive range of mountains will stare indifferently at good and evil equally, at fortune or misfortune, at noble and knave; that each—sky, lake, peak—that surrounds and shelters us is honestly serene, and cool and blue—first-rate in every way.

If Kafka's neutrality widens our eyes with horror and surprise, Walser's depictions, always working within what is socially given, are equally revealing. The effect is complex, and almost wholly his own. No writer I know employs the adjectives and adverbs of value so repeatedly, with such real appreciation and conviction, with such relentless resentment. Standing alongside the lunching patrons of a Berlin bar, his word-making voice can genuinely claim that "it's a sincere pleasure to watch people fishing for frankfurters and Italian salad."

If his narrators sometimes seem to be ninnies, it is because they are beguiled by surface, by the comfort of commonplace persiflage. False faces frighten them, yet they entrust themselves to strangers whose smiles are matched by the ninnies' own grins and good feelings. They fall for any startling detail like those who are fated to stub their toes on the beach's single stone. Watch the "the good," "the true," and "the beautiful" dance hand in hand while a reassuring lie unfolds, a jolt gets delivered, in the following characteristically shrewd sentence: "Carefree and cheerful as only a true pauper can be, a good youth with a ridiculous nose wandered one day through the beautiful green countryside." Yet the ohs and ahs of these innocent souls cynically amuse the very mouths which make them, because the extent of the narrators' self-deprecation is at the same time a measure of the congratulations they will shower on themselves—superior in the form and fullness of their inferiority like a simple paper clip or tack or pin beside the welder's torch or the rivet gun.

The effect of such writing is complex and contradictory. It is as if, holding in one's hand a postcard picturing, let us say, a pretty Swiss scene—perhaps an inn at the edge of a snowy village with the Alps (as they ought to be) above, blue lake below—one were in the same look to sense behind the little window with its painted pot the shadow of a weeping woman, while in another room of the inn there was loneliness cold as the window glass, cruelty in the severely scraped and shoveled walk, death in the depths of the lake, a cloud of callousness about the mountain peaks; and then, with nary a word about what one had seen—about bitterness, sadness, deprivation, boredom, defeat, failure added to failure—it is as if, having seen these things, sensed these things, felt them like a cinder in the shoe, one were nevertheless to write (and Walser is the writer to do it) an apparently pleasant description of the pretty Swiss inn on its pretty site, colors as bright as printed paint, surfaces as shiny and slick as ice, smoke as fixed and frozen in its coils as on the quarter-a-copy card, with its space for any message, provided the message is trite and true, gay and brief.

So the prose strolls, and what it reports primarily qualifies the character and color of its concerns, not the character and color of things. As it strolls, observing what it wishes to observe, it dreams: so that about the figure of a young woman, who is cutting roses in her garden, it may place its usually decorous yet desirous arms; it selects: so that an overheard remark will be passed around like a snack on a plate; it ponders: and in the face of some innocuous scene, it can nevertheless hem and haw itself into revelations. If Walser is a descriptive writer, and he is surely that, what he is describing, always, is a state of mind . . . and mostly the same mind, it would seem.

To say that the prose strolls is to suggest that it follows the contours of its subject. There is no narrative because there is no thread. The text stops before this item, ruminates a bit, then it stops before that; it thinks one thing (who knows why?), then another; but there is no continuity, for the cat will not be followed in its flight up a tree, only caught with its back bowed and its fur erect. A shade is pulled, a pitcher sits upon a table, someone is met, the narrator is addressed, he gives banal advice, but each of those is a moment only in the arc of a life quite accidentally intersected. Nor is a thought, which might have been provoked by the drawn shade or the scared cat, allowed to grow others, to flower so far as theory, or to link up and chuff-chuff as a train. Nor will the narrator act on anything, however violent and effective he has been in his fantasies. If he says he has kissed, doubt it; if he says he is drunk, don't believe. Not even nothing does he do.

The formless look of many of these pieces, then, is only a look, because the prose does imitate the shape of its subject. If the narrator takes a walk, so does the tale; if the narrator is nervous, so is the prose. An early piece, "Lake Greifen," for instance, is already characteristic of Walser's art. Here, a very self-conscious description of a lake is set in the text the way the lake lies in its language. The doubling up of the language reflects the mirrored images of trees and sky on the surface of the water.

But let's give the description itself, in its traditional effusiveness, a chance to speak: a wide, white stillness it is, ringed in turn by an ethe-real, green stillness; it is lake and encircling forest; it is sky, such a light blue, half overcast sky; it is water, water so like the sky it can only be sky, and the sky only blue water; sweet, blue, warm stillness it is, and morning; a lovely, lovely morning.

The narrator, who has left a large city lake to seek out this small hidden one, swims far out with the greatest joy, but perhaps he has swum too far, for now he must struggle back to shore, where he lies panting and happy on the beach. What will such a swim be like, he wonders, when the lake is dark and the sky is full of stars? The story says no more (the story is over), but we can guess the rest, including the prose for the missing part: calm as slate, composed of starlight, water, and drowning.

Walser is no ordinary voyeur, consumed by the secrets he feels have enraptured his eye, because quite prominent in any of his observations is the observer himself, and that person, too, Walser is watching. He follows each thought, each feeling, from the time one arrives on the scene to the moment it leaves, with a fond but skeptical regard, so that it is the seeing of the thing seen, he sees; and then, since he is also an author, composing a page, in addition to everything else he must take into account, he watches the writing of the writing itself (both the walk through the woods and the corresponding walk of the words), until a person who has been simply encountered in *this* world becomes a person perceived in *his*, and until, in turn, this complex, pale, increasingly imaginary figure is further transformed by words into words; words which talk about themselves, moreover, which smile at their own quirks and frills, and wave farewell while a substantial and often painful world dwindles away into this detached, multi-phenomenal, pleasantly impotent, verbal object.

How absurdly philosophical we have become, Walser might exclaim at this point, and threaten (it would be characteristic) to drop our entire subject, lift my pen and his abruptly from the page.

The world he views should not become a view to be framed and hung in his attic room, or exposed to the morning amusement of casual people. He feels guilty when he turns a lovely woman into words; when a longed-for caress becomes a sentence perhaps shaped by that yearning. Walser's lyricism, which is intense, attempts to revivify his verbal world, often with images which burst like bullets from the text. In his extraordinary novel *Jakob von Gunten*, which exploits the author's experiences as a butler-in-training, he has his narrator remark about Fuchs, a fellow student, that he "speaks like a flopped somersault," a metaphor which would turn anybody's head. In this collection's piece called "Comedy Evening," he writes: "In the mezzanine beneath me, an elderly lady blew her nose with a ferociously lacy handkerchief. I found everything beautiful, enormously bewitching." In "Tobold," an important story, he tells us that "With both swiftness and, understandably, great ceremoniousness, I bore the beverage to the beautiful woman, who appeared constructed and constituted entirely of fresh milk." Had there been a woman whose soft pale lucent skin had given rise to this witticism, would it be fitting that all that is now anonymously remembered of her is the milk a fictional servant felt she was made of?

In this same significant story, there is a small speech which I call a "blurt," because the author's usual reticence is lifted, and Walser speaks directly about one of the contradictions which trouble him: that between the surface of the well-off world (to which he has devoted so many flattering phrases) and the interior gloom beneath—a gloom resembling the gloom of the poor and the ugly—lies a resemblance which is deeply troubling.

> Can princesses cry too? I've always thought it impossible. Such high-placed women, I always thought, would never insult and sully their pure, clear eyes, the pure and sparkling sky of their vision, with soiling, defiling tears, which disfigure the unchanging expression of their faces. Why are you crying? If even princesses cry, if wealthy, powerful people can lose their balance and their proud, imperious bearings, can be depressed and overcome by a profound weariness: then what can one say and how can one be surprised to see beggars and beggar-women bent over in suffering and misery, if one sees the poor and the humble wringing their piteous hands in despair, at a loss as to what more they can do than bathe themselves in unending, miserable signs and moans and in torrents of tears. Nothing, then, is certain in this world shaken by storms and afflictions. Everything, then, everything is weak. Well, if this is so, I'll be glad to die some day, I'll gladly take leave of this hopeless, sick, weak, troubled world to rest in my relaxing, dear, good grave from all my uncertainties and hardships.

The page is the dear, good grave where everything which lasts will finally rest. For Walser, this conclusion was never quite comforting enough.

Thomas Hobbes described the State of Nature as a state of war with every man's hand against every man's, and argued that only the mutual relinquishment of rights and their implementing means could guarantee peace. He furthermore wrote of the paradox of power, which meant that as any man obtained power, he would need still more power to protect it, because envy of him would increase along with the fear, since in the customary State it is the sovereign who is most perilously placed. If you were, however, a nobody, a nebbish; if you had nothing which could be desired; if you were dismally undistinguished; then perhaps you would be ignored and could go about the little business of your life unnoticed, invisible as a servant is supposed to be, performing small services quietly, unthreatened and serene.

To hold a priceless vase in your hands may be pleasing, but you are at the same time in danger of dropping it. If you possess any authority over others, you are in a position—through indolence, incompetence, or spitefulness—to injure them. Success survives on success; the higher you rise, the dizzier you become, obligations weigh, moment by moment, more heavily upon you, others begin to rest their limbs, their lives, upon your limbs and life, which the postures of sex not even secretly symbolize. Thus what Robert Walser fears, and flees from, is power when he feels it in his own hands. The power others possess is something that, like a great outcropping of rock, may fall upon you; but it is also a shade under which you may find shelter.

His mind pleads incompetence. Asylums *are* asylums. There he can guilt-lessly surrender his fate and pass his days at the behest of others. He will no longer need to write in such a way that its public obscurity is assured. He will no longer need to write. The daily walk will suffice.

Among Immanuel Kant's many important distinctions is the one he made between willing something to happen and wishing for it to occur. When we will an end, he said, we must also necessarily will some means which will be effective in obtaining it. If you hear me speaking of my love of boating and the sea, of my dream one day of owning my own yacht and sailing the Chesapeake as if it were my private lake, you will be quite properly disabused of your belief in my desire when you notice that I subscribe to not a single boating magazine; that I do not follow the Cup races in the papers; that I have not set aside any sums toward the purchase of so much as a jaunty cap; that, in fact, I spend my vacations with my family in the desert Southwest. In short, I may wish for such a luxury, but I have never willed it. When I wish, my means are dreams. Each evening, before sleep and in place of love, I imagine my vessel parting the waves: I cry to the sky the salty orders of a shipmaster and eat heartily without any fear of sickness from the sea that lies around me like my cool, uncohabited sheets. As a people, as a race, Kant observed, we always will war; we only wish for peace.

Walser's narrators (and we can presume, in this case, Walser himself) have become will-less wanderers, impotent observers of life, passive perceivers of action and passion. Only on the page will the Will risk the expression and exercise of its considerable means.

And when the circumstances of life—my six children and my fruitful but frigid wife, perhaps, my boringly repetitive work as an insurance adjuster, my rascally relatives and a harsh climate, the painfully pushed-forward designs of those who would exploit me—when these force me (as I think) to give up my own aims altogether, then I shall find myself in a classical state of power-less resentment, aggrieved because existence has become a broken promise;

and my head shall fill with willing woman, my yacht will always find the best breeze, I shall dream of flames while I stir my ashes, and my soul will swell like a balloon to float over the world, touching it only as a shadow.

The details of the disappointment will differ; the site of the defeat will shift; the resistance to one's fate or one's readiness to accept it will vary in their strength; but the pattern is plain enough, its commonness is common, indeed, its dangers real. Switzerland is a prison. Consequently the world is one.

If I were then to try to save myself through writing, how difficult it would be for me to maintain the posture of a realist, for I should have had little acquaintance with the real (indeed, less and less), rather more with the subjects of my wishes than the objects of my will. In order to confer the blessings of Being upon the small, hollow dreams of my soul, these harmlessly private elaborations will have to somehow achieve the heartless powers of the page; yet my characters must be inventions, and how quickly these inventions will feel my disdain. What value could they have if they remain so utterly in my power? So much for the story, too, which can be pushed and pulled this way and that, or dropped, suddenly, like a weighted sack into the lake.

Through a course of such "thinking," if I read him aright, Walser became a post-modernist well before the fashion. The painfully beautiful, brief "essay," "A Flaubert Prose Piece," deals with the way a successful fiction fictionalizes its author, so that both his invented woman, and the author's *moi* she was, eventually "glided and passed among the people gliding and passing by, like a dream vision within the vision of a dream."

As Walser's final confinement nears, his writing seems increasingly made of dissociated sentences. To turn time, like an hourglass, abruptly over, so that its many days fall the other way, his *feuilletons* resemble the work of Donald Barthelme, almost collagelike in their structural juxtapositions. Not a few, like the brutally disturbing "Salon Episode," have a genuinely surreal surface. The detached, desperate "inhumanity" of his work remains. It has been many years since a figure in one of his fictions has had a real name. And if one had a name, it would be generic, like Pierrot. But it is easier now to follow the inner flow beneath these scraps of language, to appreciate the simple clarity of the sentences he has constructed, to recognize that these meditations (for they have never been anything else) move not in the manner of events or in the manner of a river or in the manner, either, of thought, or in the "happy hour" fashion of the told tale (each brought so beautifully together in "Boat Trip," one of the triumphs of Walser's art), but in the way of an almost inarticulate metaphysical feeling; a response to the moves and meanings of both human life and nature, which is purged of every local note and self-interested particularity and which achieves, like the purest poetry, an understanding mix of longing, appreciation, and despair, as if they were the pigments composing a color to lay down upon the surface of something passing—sweetly regretful—like the fall of light upon a bit of lost water, or a brief gleam caught in a fold of twilit snow, as if it were going to remain there forever.

Foreword to *Masquerade and Other Stories* by Robert Walser, 1990
Published in *Finding a Form,* 1996

HALF A MAN, HALF A METAPHOR

The Unknown Kafka

I awoke one morning to find myself transformed. I had been a man, but a man who was treated by my parents and my sister like a bug. Perhaps I was not so much an insect at my office; perhaps I was something else there, a blotter or a trash basket. Perhaps, like a bum, I was warned not to loiter when I was out on the avenue, or, while traveling on the train, I became just another newspaper or another sample case. Perhaps, to my boss, I was a worm. At home, however, a bug was what I was, a bug in a bed, a bedbug, sperm of the kind you could find hidden in my name—Gregor Samsa—for doesn't "sam" mean seed, a descendant? And so one day I woke to find myself more than a metaphor, more than a figure of derision and indifference. I was a bug, big in my bed as my body was, with a body bigger than any ordinary bug's, bigger than a rat's, a dog's, though I was small, considering what my life meant to me. To others, however, I was huge, monstrous, horrifying, all I always wanted to be, all I always dreamed.

Of course I was so much more than they imagined, for when people treat you within the habitual range of their emotions, they leave reality out. I was a bug to them, but not with a firm shell, not with thorny legs or with furry feelers, no, I was a man, a son, a day-old-bread winner, who was, despite being poorly outfitted for it, just a bug, indeterminate as to species, and I lived an unimportant, mostly invisible life, and survived on leftovers, crumbs, windfalls, hand-me-downs, spills. I dwelt with my parents, of course, though they depended on my salary and should by rights have been the bugs. I had a small room with three doors and a view of the rain.

On the wall I had framed the photo of a dominatrix, you would say, a genital symbol, you would say, Sacher-Masoch's lady in furs, with one arm thrust suggestively into her furry muff, how much more obvious could you be, you might say, far above my station, too, I would guess from her furs, her gaze, but who would deny a lonely little man his dreams? to be what they've made me be. Yes, I've waked from one of them a bug because my bones are all on the outside like a screened porch and I squeak—my hinges are unfamiliar to me—when my legs wave. However, my transformation is not complete, because I am still complaining about my work, work I no longer have to do now that I am a bug for all intents, though I'm not used to that yet, so I have caught myself in the middle of my metamorphosis, halfway maybe on my journey to an active bug life, when I won't have to worry about my boss, my job, the fact that I've missed my train, endure the nagging of my parents and my sister, Grete—good life to her now, eh?—or long anymore for my mistress from the magazine, my paper love to whom I press my face; or fret my chores, my filial duties—that I'm late for work—or fret the rain that tells me, when I hear it falling, that I hear much as I used to hear—my mother chiding me about the lateness of the hour—yes—I feel much as I used to feel, can complain as I am accustomed to complain—yes, yes, thank you, Mother, I am getting up now—and, though there is a noticeable chitter in the rear parts of my words, I am confident that I am still somewhere a man. After all, I may be a bug but I am man-sized.

Did you know my father deals in muffs? receives muffs from a manufacturer, sells those muffs—as well as carded buttons, lingerie, handbags, gloves—to retail stores? Did you know that in addition to my work as a sample salesman, taking orders here, there, and everywhere as always, I help out late in the day at my father's shop, and toil (yes, that is the right word) in a government agency that handles workmen's compensations and injury claims? You have to have visible wounds and a showy limp to earn my notice. So if I brought a complaint, a petition, even my own case to my attention, I would not award a krone to myself for all my pains, the burns I have received from my father's glares.

Before I became a bug I wasn't the son my parents wanted, and now that I am a bug, I am more than ever a disappointment. I am somewhat surprised by my own calmness about this sudden change. I wonder now whether I shouldn't have enjoyed it more. It is a good excuse for remaining in bed, with a pillow and my plight protecting me from the noises of my daily duties. Do cockroaches cocoon? I lie here and ponder the problem, but mostly what occurs to me is to wonder how I shall make the next train. Being a bug is rather a bother—to get out of bed, to dress, to shave. What a relief to have a reason. I want to explain, but only my feelers will wave.

First, through the closed door, my mother reminds me; then, on the closed door, my father pounds and shouts and chides me; finally, despite the closed door, my sister asks me if I need anything. If I opened the door (my traveler's habit is to lock it) they would see a bug and be horrified (as they will be when it happens), but the real me is not a bug, the real me is not the me they know either, the real me is an author, though as unassuming as a bug, and out of sight the way a roach hides, with no point of view to speak of, inhuman in that way, but alert as any small creature who needs to remain unnoticed, whose life depends upon its disappearance, except when I assume the body of a snake and slither into the next room to request a little peace and quiet. Yes. True. I am often other animals. As in Aesop. As in Swift. One of my most recent biographers mentions "learned dogs and voracious jackals, psychotic moles, worldly-wise apes, and vainglorious mice."

A bug's biographer. You might imagine it the other way: a flea that observes the amorous frolics of its host. They do follow each other rather continuously—come in crowds—these dutiful recorders. This particular life of me has scarcely reached the shores of Amerika when another vast bio appears in Germany. The present one is by Reiner Stach, who subtitled it *The Decisive Years.* I understand that it has been given a wonderfully supple translation by Shelley Frisch. A later one, not yet at your shores, is by Peter-André Alt and subtitled *Der ewige Sohn* (*The Eternal Son*). Stach's is a splendid effort and will be hard to surpass. I shall have had one short life, but many and long are the works that try to transcribe me. Consider your own life and imagine how you would feel if the way you ate were an issue, if every weakened purpose you took to work were written up, every deception documented, the interrogations you mimicked and mocked carried on into your afterlife ("Was Franz Kafka a real man?"), and every letter you ever wrote, even those you never sent, were to be prominently printed in a learned book. Unless, of course, you had already cut yourself like a coroner into three enigmatic egos—the overburdened and suffering son, called Dr. Kafka at the Workers' Accident Insurance Institute on account of his law degree; the epistler and unhappy lover who signs himself "Franz" and begs for an immediate reply; the sensitive artist, diarist, and tormented perfectionist who stays awake to fashion nightmares for a sleeping world—while planning very carefully (though not all that consciously) for the immortality of each of them.

   (And if we were three, Felice was four. Franz almost immediately parceled her out. The first was the girl he met at Max Brod's place in Prague; the second, the one who wrote him letters from Berlin, where she lived and worked; the third, the woman with whom he strolled when he visited her apartment in Charlottenburg; and the fourth is the person who leads her own Berlin life, has friends he does not know, and visits places he has not been. What a surprising lot of folks for one romance.)

   In my writerly guise my pages will be as shocking as my present prehistoric carapace. I want to publish principally to prove to my father I can be a success at something. But not in my role as a writer; rather, in my role as a son. Perhaps I would prefer my scribblings to stay unseen and my bound and printed sheets to remain unread, even though I have carefully placed a copy of my first book on the nightstand next to my father's bed. I want his approval so I can scorn it. I want his approval though my need makes me ashamed. I depend upon his animosity, for it defines me, gives me edges, just as the man who cuts out your silhouette from a sheet of black paper does and, for the sum of loose change, gives you the profile of a piece of land. My movements are awkward, my body cumbersome, my desires mixed. I can debate the situation with my head, but however it goes—approval or blame—I remain a failure.

Yes, I remember writing a fragment of fiction about just such a situation. I am safely . . . my character is safely in his own bed, but it threatens to become his bride's bed, too, so my reluctant bridegroom imagines sending his properly decked-out body to the wedding while he remains at home, unable to venture beyond his blankets, because—well—because he is a "large beetle, a stag beetle or a cockchafer, I think . . . I would then act as though it was a matter of hibernation. . . ." My metaphor would marry and make love. I would not be required to attend.

Yes, I must be a different species. I dislike everything my family does. I cannot eat what they eat; I cannot abide their games; the noises of their life are like the scratch of chalk; and they move through my room to other rooms like trains through a station. I only come out at night, when the card game is conceded, the last door closed, my father's lungs cough, and the parental bedsprings sigh. I come out into the comforting emptiness of silence, where I may lead my counterclockwise life.

That is why, as a fiction, I define my room by doors: because I have so little privacy in daily life. Doors will dominate my correspondence, too. "Dear Fräulein," Franz shall write to Felice Bauer. "My wretched letter had to suffer through so much before it was written. Now that the door between us appears to be beginning to budge, or at least we have taken hold of the handle, I surely can, or even must, say it. The moods I get into, Fräulein! A torrent of nervousness is constantly raining down on me. What I want one minute, I don't want the next." How cautious Franz is, too. He says he must say . . . what? but he does not say . . . anything. The door appears . . . to be beginning . . . to op— . . . well, perhaps he has only touched the handle. . . . His caution is that of a cat who may be kicked at any moment.

My problem, if I were to put it simply, is the family, the dynamics of the family, the reach of relations, the forced feeding of custom and belief, the close embrace of the tribe, the shrinking circle that begins the words "obey" and "obligation" and concludes every "no" that issues from my father's mouth to sum me up as a zero. The family is formed by a system of functions: the father's, to rule and provide, direct and protect, beget and mold; the mother's, to cherish and succor, to bear and care; the child's, to obey and prepare, to mate and become mother or father in another such system, perpetuating the name, supplying the tribe with more tribesmen, adding to its coffers, filling with good repute each grave.

To love as one might like to love is impossible. Marriages are arranged. Sex is overseen by a rabbi (in my case) and directed by religious rules and with economic expectations. In fact, the law is what is loved. It is worshipped because it preserves the position of the father. Obey the powers that be and one day you shall be obeyed. What you suffer now, you shall cause others to suffer, so your early suffering shall not be in vain. I cannot swallow this. I cannot get it down. I cannot incorporate. When I was a man I could not eat the good red meat from the family table; now that I am a bug I cannot eat it either. I am thin, because I manage only lettuce and old air. My eyes grow as large as a starveling's, and my voice lacks the loud assurance of my father's, although its softness is often admired as one might admire soft cloth. I dress expensively, however, projecting a dark ethereality that has its own charm. I am too tall. My doctor finds me not quite well—bad digestion, underweight, and nervous as a gnat. He sends me off to a nudist camp. Well, not quite—to a sanitarium where sexually separated guests sometimes forgo all clothes on behalf of nature's benevolent breezes and enjoy a roll on the morning's damp, democratically naked, grass. Sickness has its own attractions. I can be too weak to work, and take to my sofa, behind closed doors, where I pillow my head in a dream. Or I reread my diaries. They make me despair. Then with great energy I can pursue a wild idea, a nutty project, while allowing my assigned duties to lapse, like a sentry who leaves the main gate to guard the latrine. The guilt I feel may be worth it, because this behavior drives my father beyond the edge of dither. Dr. Kafka brings undesirables home to dinner, but even that does little to improve my appetite. In addition, I Fletcherize my food: I cut my vegetables into small squares. Then I chew each bit slowly and with great deliberation. With distaste. My father hides behind his paper, through which, I know, he stares.

I hesitate to approach them. Girls, I mean, not the ladies whom one can hire like a hansom. Horses, apes, insects—any species other than the human—are my imaginary companions. Well, they all eat, they all mate. And there are always repercussions. As a son I am asked to breathe fumes at an asbestos factory, sit all day in the din of hammered tacks as secretaries type and the family yaps. No silence. No privacy. Not a hint of anything higher in life than a clerk's stool. Now my supervisor is hammering on my door. I try to make excuses but they don't come out right. Sometimes I am nothing but feelers.

I hesitate to approach the opposite sex—opposite, don't you say?—because sometimes I am smitten with a suddenness that leaves me dazed. A young woman like Felice Bauer, for instance, who shows up at Max Brod's house with her face empty as a plate, nevertheless entices me, she makes the right responses—she loves Goethe—she says satisfactory things—she says she finds nothing more repulsive than people who are constantly eating—and in minutes we are planning a trip to Palestine together as if we were geographical Zionists, as full of zeal as a jar of jelly. I like her to the point of sighing.

My biographer will prepare you for the abrupt obsessive nature of my attractions. Let us stop a moment to watch how Reiner Stach goes so skillfully about his business. It offers the reader a pleasure all its own. My friend Max Brod and I are visiting Weimar in order to pay our respects to the great God Goethe, and to visit his home where "the beech tree that darkened his study" had once been seen by a genius and was to be seen again as if we had traded eyes. My diary surprises me with what I've written: "While we were still sitting down below on the stairs, she ran past us with her little sister." Goethe. A garden. A girl. They will coalesce and later enliven the images of Felice Bauer with precisely the awkwardness that shows up in a tampered photograph.

But this figure was Margarethe Kirchner, the daughter of the caretaker, a carefree sixteen in an era when innocence and naïveté were expected of girls. Perhaps it was the bloom of her being in this garden given over to the dead that ensnared me. Encouraged by Brod, who was in a jovial mood, I advanced on this lovely with my smitten eyes, surprised by the absence of my customary shyness. She was called Grete. Despite this fortuitous link with the sister at whose hand I would be fed a few scraps of garbage when I became a bug, or the Grete Bloch who would become a go-between for Felice and me, biographers have largely ignored this passing item in my life, though some have allowed her a few lines, as Peter-André Alt does in his 2005 history. But Reiner Stach stages the encounter like a dramatist, allowing the little details to loom large by releasing them without fanfare at just the right time. I remember she was standing by a bush of roses.

I pursued her during the several days of our visit, and managed, with Brod's connivance, to get her alone long enough to arrange an assignation, but this was not easy: Brod was busy networking (as you say now); we had our tourist duties to attend to (Schiller, Liszt, Goethe's garden house); and

Grete was elusive, though I lay in wait as ardently as any Casanova near her sewing school, "holding a box of chocolates with a chain and a little heart." There is a snapshot of the two of us taken on my twenty-ninth birthday.

Finally, just as we were about to leave, she consented to see me for an hour. Later, when we met, she wore that "pink dress, my little heart." We walked through the park together and I stubbornly hung around into the evening, even though I knew we had nothing in common, that there was no real connection possible between us. Perhaps that was itself the attraction. When I said goodbye her eyes were swollen with tears, but it was because her partner for the ball that night had disappointed her. "A woman bringing roses disturbed even this little farewell." Yet those roses concluded the episode as if I had written it. As, in fact, I had. Moreover, I would employ her name as I would use other Gretes, for that of my poor bug's sister; and even though she would order my brittle carcass to be tossed into the trash, I'd allow her to complete the metamorphosis that I began, triumphantly fluttering away at the end, you may remember, a fully realized woman.

The biographer must interpret such facts as he has on hand only so far as they fit into the life that is being lived, and while he can speculate as often as his readers may also be invited to do, his history should be as clean of simple conjecture as wounds of infection. My story of anxiety and anguish I have strewn with helpful clues, and it unashamedly displays aesthetic elements of organization. I feel that Reiner Stach is not building imaginary bridges between gaps in the debris I left behind but is reconstructing events, from otherwise scattered facts, the way the broken lines of a sketch invite the eye to complete their intended course and see a complete form or finished pattern where there is mostly implication.

From the same materials as Reiner Stach has, I must construct myself as I step back and forth from fact to fiction—half a man and half a metaphor. Let me give you another instance: my suicide threat. Think back: I am sorely beset (for sins of absence and inattention) by problems at the asbestos plant, and my parents' subsequent nagging has rubbed me raw. I complain to my diary: "Day before yesterday was blamed because of the factory. Then one hour on the sofa thinking about jumping out the window." When I receive my censure I am Dr. Kafka. While I lie on the sofa I begin to see myself opening the window, leaning out. . . . I envision—don't I?—the family's consternation—don't I?—with some pleasure. This visit to a daydream passes, as the months do. The family pressure concerning the factory becomes intolerable. In a burst of fear, guile, hate, and guilt, in one night I write "The Judgment," a story in which a father accuses his son: you have betrayed your friend, your mother, and myself; consequently "I sentence you now to death by drowning." Thereupon the son, obedient as a dog, leaps over a rail of the Charles Bridge. He waits, hanging by his hands, for the passage of a bus to cover the sound of his splash. In that same way I also fall, a fiction, into tear-wet water. And what is my concluding line? "At that moment, over the bridge, there came and went a ceaseless stream of traffic." ". . . *unendlicher Verkehr.*" Another meaning would be: "unending intercourse." Shortly I am writing the following to Max Brod: "I realized clearly that there were only two options for me, either to jump out of the window after everyone had gone to bed or to go to the factory and my brother-in-law's office on a daily basis for the next fourteen days." Because I am now both a figure of speech and a notorious fact—"a dried-up well, water in unreachable depths and uncertain even there"—in the end I do not die of a killing routine nor of defenestration. Max Brod gets my mother to cover me and my absences with lies. In fact, everybody lies, and Father doesn't notice. Not noticing what has been noticed is a talent we Kafkas treasure.

I have only to consider my situation and immediately, expressed in a phrase, an image arises to excuse and explain me. I shall set this phrase loose in one of my literary lives. For instance, here Franz is writing to Felice about myself (why not, he should know me well): "My life consists, and has essentially always consisted, of attempts at writing, largely unsuccessful. But when I don't write, I wind up on the floor at once, fit for the dustbin." Of course, when I teach myself to be a bug, that is exactly where I shall end—dead in a charwoman's pan. Scooped away like the breath of a whistle. In the same letter he goes on to brag of how thin I am, but I shall be thinner when I write "A Hunger Artist." Then I shall resemble a small pile of old clothes.

But if you need any further demonstration of the way my genius works (and the occasional necessary unfriendliness of my biographer), consider the October 1912 expulsion of the Turks from the Balkans. The Turks were taking a beating and there were stories of atrocities, with photographs disgracing the pages of the papers. Max Brod's diary reports: "Took a walk with Kafka; the misery of the Turks reminds him of his own." Brod, for his part, writes a piece of poetic doggerel in which the misery of the Turks, as Stach puts it, "brings to mind the misery of everyone who ever lived." My biographer's estimation that "it is difficult to imagine a starker contrast to his friend's response to the war" is cutting, I admit, but if the misery of the Turks causes Brod to consider the misery of mankind, and myself to complain of mine, Brod's result is a verse shallow as a spoon, while I make mine into a masterpiece deep as the darkness in man that frightens us all. War, and the revitalization of death—DEATH LIVES! that's how you'd put it on a poster—was as real right then as the smoke from my father's factory chimneys.

.   .   .

As for ordinary living, we shall have our servants do that for us, Villiers de l'Isle-Adam said. It is a problem most serious writers face, because society is not prepared to pay for the poet's trip on its tram, and is equally unwilling to play a nanny in the home life of some novelist. It is not an offer of *vissi d'arte*, or *vissi d'amore*, by itself; it is marriage, family, work, recognized worth in the world, versus art, idleness, subversive thought, pointless practice, useless effort, repeated failure; and even if success is found in some solitary achievement, its fruit is seedless and dry and secret. It sometimes seems to be a brutal choice between being a fool or a philistine. The philistine lives, but shamefully; the foolish artist endures, repeatedly, semi-imaginary deaths and real neglect. For me this common problem was exacerbated by the closing cultural fist I found myself caught in: there was the provincial city, Prague, inside Prague the community of Germans, inside them the network of the Jews, among the Jews the family Kafka, within that—Dr. Franz Kafka—its son and heir, within him—me—the writer, longing to get out of my given skin, to escape my relatives, my race, my religion, my responsibilities, this entire region of the world . . . though if several of our Kafkas went, I would take along our language.

But instead of escaping into the wide world, Franz withdrew. I wrote in code stories he couldn't finish, stories he couldn't bear to publish, pages he locked away in drawers as much to keep them in as anyone out. On those sheets I set down his private fears, yearnings, angers, resentments, his guilt and his remorse, as indifferently as a range of hills. I wrote of rented rooms from which the furniture would be removed. I built castles without kings, imagined courts without judges, without jurors, without justice, presented matters of fact that made no sense, created a clarity that was obscure, inflicted torments upon my characters that had no cause no name no amelioration no resolution. In so doing I demonstrated the divinity that belongs to art. An art that belonged to me.

Here, in Reiner Stach's biography, are five years of my life—only five, from 1910 to 1915—all his pages based on all of mine; though he has promised to give me two more lifetimes in succeeding volumes. It will be a wonder that even I shall wonder at. Reiner Stach does not endeavor to pin me down but, rather, tries to follow me through my transformations; and when he is perplexed, and his data are divided in their recommendations, he discusses his dilemma with the reader. I listen in, because I don't have any answers. That is the marvelous and exasperating mystery of it. I am, like the rest of us, ultimately unknowable. Yes, I remember what Socrates told the Athenians, but the self was itself a discovery in those days, so the philosopher could scarcely have been aware of the quarreling bunch each one of us now represents. Neither the public official nor the reclusive author is the same Franz who signed "my" prodigious letters. Indeed, Franz is one of literature's supreme artists of the envelope and its hidden epistle—that private communication that is nevertheless meant to be heard by the whole world. On the other hand, I—monk and metaphor—find it difficult to finish anything, and have kept my novels and my stories short, enigmatic, impersonal. That other Franz wrote nonstop, at daunting length, to women, and kept a diary the way some Germans keep their dogs: they feed them, comb their coats, and take them for their daily walks.

Reiner Stach is convinced that Kafka, especially Franz, would have been horrified by the idea that any other eye than that addressed, much less the world's eye, might become privy to his correspondence, and Stach halts the progression of his story for a fine essay on the nature of the letter and the epistolary culture of the time. During 1912 at least one hundred letters are written to Felice Bauer in Berlin, who must have felt the burden of response grow heavier by the week. Letters work upon the mind in the absence of the body, whose only presence can be felt in a personalized penmanship or perhaps through a fragrance captured in a kink of the envelope, or absorbed by the paper, now so intimate a thing, since it has been inscribed by a mind the way skin is sometimes caressed by a lover's fingers. Letters bring news, companionship, business, affection, but also pain. They are full of gossip, mischief, lies, flattery, and similar, though softer, misconstructions. They are not always meant to please, and confessions that wound their writer may wound their reader, too. Remember the diabolically contrived machine of torture that I imagined for "In the Penal Colony"? how it inscribes the broken letter of the law upon the body of its guilty party, deeper and deeper digging its point into the transgressor until he expires? Letters routinely sent and received create still further, still more binding, expectations. "I will not suffer if no letter comes," Franz reassures his postmark lover. Yet if there is but the briefest delay he beseeches her like a baby—"Dearest, don't torment me like this!" Days or weeks can lie like lakes between send and receive. Perhaps a message has gone astray or fallen into the wrong hands. One day her ink may refuse to dry. Something like that has been expected. Perhaps her end of the correspondence has teetered to its demise. The totter will not rise.

Unlike conversations, replies are pondered and positioned as though they were chess pieces. And are read, reread, and assessed under varying circumstances, many moods. They become bundles. They can be wrapped in ribbon. They can crouch in an attic to leap upon a generation far away. But in the normal course of things, to receive one is to receive a sweet—to keep unopened in a pocket until a quiet unmolested moment is available, or to tear open with the urgency of lust opposed by buttons. Stach observes:

> This material, physical aspect of letters and their unceasing whiff of reality posed an irresistible temptation for Kafka. He began to hover over letters as never before. They became sexual fetishes. He spread them out in front of him, laid his face upon them, kissed them, inhaled their smell. On walks or short business trips, he took Felice's letters along with him, to fortify himself.

Letters may strive to seem natural, conversational, easy, off the cuff. They aren't. They are mostly contrived. The absence of another face, the foreclosure of immediate response—of interruptions, questions, objections—and the inability of smiles, frowns, gestures, exclamations, to burst in upon the quiet calm of composition: these felicitous conditions permit the letter to become more apparently candid, more duplicitous, more sincere in appearance, more hypocritical at heart; and because they are "evidence," because they are "on the record," and because they can be intercepted, stolen, snooped, leaked, they can be exceedingly guarded, especially self-serving, ardently devoted to their future in an archive. And if these letters are by Keats or Flaubert or Rilke, they become art. As art they require that postal distance the letters can then complain of. Their words make love of the kind the mind makes when the mind fears its body may not measure up. What did Franz write to Felice? "If I had saved up all the time I spent writing letters to you and used it for a trip to Berlin, I would have been with you long ago, and could now be gazing into your eyes."

When Franz's relationship with Felice was at an end, she saved his letters, he burned hers. Burning was what the insurance adjuster had in mind—sometimes—for my own letters, too, as well as my diaries and many of my manuscripts, but Dr. Kafka's scribbled intentions, meant for Max Brod yet tossed in a drawer and by no means consistent, suggested a will that was hardly undivided and resolute but, rather, one familiar with all the strategies that pride and high opinion may employ, including humility, even abasement. On his way to Berlin, where he intends to meet with Felice and settle the question of their engagement (I break it off), Franz writes to his sister Ottla (July 10, 1914): "I write differently from what I speak, I speak differently from what I think, I think differently from the way I ought to think, and so it all proceeds into deepest darkness." This sentence, however, proceeds like a parade. There is a P.S. "Regards to all. You mustn't show my letter or let it lie around. You had best tear it up and throw the shreds from the *pawlatsche* [balcony] to the hens in the courtyard from whom I have no secrets."

During the brief period this biography covers, in which I managed to write most of my major works, I am so busy being Dr. Kafka during the day, and spend so much of my time and energy every night writing Franz's letters to this poor puzzled patient victim of my waffling, that even Reiner Stach's judicious treatment of their inception, making, and appearance is quite swamped by Franz's pathological self-absorption—preoccupations that quite cripple the state of mind a writer needs to succeed at any substantial project in prose—namely, a calm and knowing control of the elements of his art, and the kind of focus common to laboratory lenses.

And how did I break it off? this pre-Internet love affair? I broke off my three engagements. I broke off my three books. They were engagements, too. What finished them, in a sense, finished me. If you listen at the break point of *Der Verschollene* . . . (called *Amerika* by Max Brod but now renamed *The Man Who Disappeared* by Reiner Stach's fine translator, Shelley Frisch, and by Michael Hofmann in his version for Penguin Classics, or, as you might also say, "The Man Who Went Missing") . . . if you listen you can hear notes struck that were struck at the conclusion of "The Judgment," for that story really contains most of my motifs and themes—the sound of water under a bridge while traffic passes over it; a two-way crossing above, a one-way fall below; marriage, finance, and fornication hidden like a gift in one fist, or death and oblivion in the empty palm of the other. In this case, my characters and, of course, myself in the guise of one of them, are traveling by train into the mountains—in Hofmann's splendid rendering, which retains the tumbling of the sentence—

> Blue-black formations of rock approached the train in sharp wedges, they leaned out of the window and tried in vain to see their peaks, narrow dark cloven valleys opened, with a finger they traced the direction in which they disappeared, broad mountain streams came rushing like great waves on their hilly courses, and, pushing thousands of little foaming wavelets ahead of them, they plunged under the bridges over which the train passed, so close that the chill breath of them made their faces shudder.

The Trial, you remember, ends with a knife in my namesake's heart, while a sense of shame so strong that it will outlive him—for he is dying, as he says, "like a dog"—is the single pain he feels. At the frayed ends of *The Castle,* one version of the text, where it slowly dies away with the indecision of a river, refers to K as a man "going to the dogs." And I—I confess, it is I—I write to Max Brod, what my diaries confirm, that I have fantasies in which "I lie stretched out on the ground, sliced up like a roast, and with my hand I am slowly pushing a piece of this meat toward a dog in the corner." Whether it is the breath of death that comes to warn me and make my face shudder or death itself that follows the blade as it twists into the heart, or the broken shell of a humiliated self that is shoveled up by the maid, I shall be already buried in the body of another creature when it dies, I am determined on it. There I shall live forever.

How did Franz break it off with Felice? He began by casting his ultimate refusal in the form of a proposal. All his letters testified to his dependency if not to his devotion. She knew he needed her. What would be the point of pressing a suit so continuously worn? So he simply listed all his shortcomings . . . again and again: "I am basically a cold, selfish, and insensitive person despite all my weakness, which tends to conceal rather than mitigate these qualities." It was an odd but calculated way of putting it, as if his weaknesses hid his strengths (that he was cold? selfish? insensitive? these were strengths?); because they *were* an artist's strengths: an artist must be ruthless, sacrificing self as well as lovers, family as well as friends, to the conditions of his calling. That is the romance we have woven about writing and the artist's life. The considerable competence of Dr. Kafka in his assessor's position (about which he has told Felice little) is a real weakness, because it keeps him in his cage. Franz's devotion to Felice is a real weakness, because it draws him into a life of bourgeois responsibilities. His obsessions, his insecurities, his vacillations are strengths, because they excuse him from duty, they dissipate his ardor, they weaken his marital resolve. He is cruel to be kind. He is sparing his beloved the burden of his love.

Reiner Stach quite shrewdly sees what Franz did not see: that Felice, who says yes to this backhanded ill-meant proposal immediately—a response as astonishing as the question that provoked it—wants a husband who would keep her safe and well while she enjoys her own freedoms, the way a young woman may protect herself with the companionship of a gay friend while traveling through macho-infested territories. Felice had her own family miseries—most everyone does, though she had not told Franz what they were: that her sister had secretly borne an illegitimate child, that her father had lived with a woman not his wife, that her brother was a chiseler and a deadbeat—and the idea of being lifted out of such confines in an acceptable way must have seemed appealing. "I will get used to you," she promised him . . . but Franz did not want to become acceptable. So he wrote to Felice's father about how unbearable he was. "I am taciturn, unsociable, glum, self-serving, a hypochondriac, and actually in poor health." Oh yes, and "I lack any sense of family life." Felice intercepted this letter and prevented her father from reading it. They continued to play out their engagement in a landscape of fantasy, but it had become a barren courtyard shat upon by filthy flocks of words.

How did Franz break it off? He began writing to another girl—Grete—a friend of Felice's. About Felice. About Felice at first. In precisely the same way that—at first—he wrote to Felice. Emboldened by his success with Grete, he proposed once more to Felice, who refused him quite firmly. But he persisted. Why did he persist? Because now he knew he would always be refused. And in a memorable moment, in a back room of a Berlin hotel, three women—Felice Bauer, her sister Erna, and friend Grete, like the Fates—sat in judgment of me—well, of Franz, for I was scarcely there, though I felt the pain of their presumption, their disapproval, their disappointment. Still, I would not waver from my wavering. I had my own wounds to heal. My father had hurled apples at me. My father had sentenced me to death by drowning. Publication of *The Metamorphosis* had been delayed. I had begun my own *Trial,* a trial that would go well because I would be judge as well as plaintiff, both court and accused, every worry expressed, every woman present, or warder doing his duty, taken straight from life. And now, in order to conclude this half-decade of my biography, a war arrives. It will seem to bring peace while we wait for volume two.

Nevertheless, there was another yes. Despite misgivings, despite reproaches, despite all that has already befallen her, Felice arranges a private meeting for us in a border town. Well, not all of us. I don't think Dr. Kafka was present. Except as a sign of stability in Felice's mind. There, in Franz's hotel room—where Fräulein Bauer might have compromised her virtue in some eyes by presenting herself—I embraced her as I was meant to. . . . No. What did I do? in my nervous apprehensions, cornered like a rat, what did I do? I read to her from *The Trial.* Franz cowered behind the measured wall of my words. They were about a man who spends his life waiting at a gate for admittance. These were meanings as cruel as any transformation. I was shy, of course, embarrassed, awkward, and I tried to explain myself by giving to Felice a sample of a masterpiece, an excuse for all I had done or would do; here is a slice of me, take it and eat; but this was no communion, no act of heresy; it was "going to the dogs."

Still, through it all, I remained literature, as I had so often said. I clung steadfastly to that. Dr. Kafka had his job. In fact, he got another raise. Franz would write more letters as if he hadn't written any. He was their bundle of energy, their silk ribbon, their stamp, their swirls of ink. I was insufferable—yes—I climbed my walls—yet I was literature. These were fragments shored against my ruin. I could not be deprived of that. Or my monstrosity.

Harper's Magazine, 2006
Published in *Life Sentences*, 2012

PAUL VALÉRY

I

The August evening in Geneva in 1892 which Paul Valéry chose to mislead us by calling his night of crisis, his "turning point," was shot like a scene from a stupid movie. In the spiritual background there was a distantly worshipful and wholly one-sided love affair with an unapproachable married woman, an affair of barely smothered sighs and secret languishments whose very disappointments were romantically necessary. There was, in addition, Valéry's deepening discouragement with his own work as a poet—after all, Mallarmé had already surpassed the possible—and in consequence, as a protection to pride, there had appeared in him an increasing tendency to disparage both poetry and the language from which it was made, just as someone who's cleaned a collar by cutting it off entirely is required to imagine that in this fashion he's better dressed. Nearly a year before, he had written this desperate la-de-da to Gide: "Please don't call me Poet anymore. . . . I am not a poet, but the gentleman who is bored."

Inevitably there was, as well, a willingness to find insufficient superiority even in the supreme. "The most original of our great men—Wagner, Mallarmé—stoop," he announced to the same correspondent in the smug tones of the youthfully aggrieved. They *imitate,* he reported, feeling the triumph and the shock of one who, for the first time, has seen the great chef sneeze into the soup. He had "analyzed, alas!" their expressive means and encountered everywhere, even among the most wonderful writers (he mentions specifically Poe, Rimbaud, and, again, Mallarmé), the loveliest illusions concerning the genesis and production of their poetry. Pledged to a profession that obliged them constantly to surpass themselves, they failed to remember who they were; they (it was such a snob's word) . . . they *stooped;* yet Valéry did not feel himself ready to fall in just that way just yet.

We know none of the details, and can only darkly guess the cause, but if the background of the scene of crisis contained the characteristic *Sturm und Drang* of an ambitious, gifted, randy youth of twenty-one, the foreground was filled with simple, bolt-upright sleeplessness and fright: in his head he heard the badly bowed music of his nerves, the familiar theme of *sic et non,* while, outside, this interior cacophony was accompanied the night through by a vulgarly obvious but appropriately violent thunderstorm.

Absurdly set and conventionally shot ("his whole fate played out in his head"), Valéry had his trial and his illumination in the desert, nonetheless, and came back a brave. Deciding, as Descartes did, to put his trust solely in himself (or, rather, in one part of himself—that part which was prepared to flee to pure awareness where it could be, he said, "an unmoved observer"), he became a stubborn student of his own mind, of his mental acts and processes, and of the structures and subtle modulations of consciousness.

For Valéry poetry had been, on principle and from inclination, an escape from the world ("By 'world' I mean the whole complex of incidents, demands, compulsions, solicitations, of every kind and degree of urgency," he wrote, "which overtake the mind without offering it any inner illumination . . ."). But now the world blew through him like a wind—poetry was no shutter to it. He felt insecure in its care. Somehow the independence of the self was threatened, and despite his "intellectualized" view of poetry, the poetry he wrote was predominately erotic.

In addition to the predictable appearance of Venus, Orpheus, Helen, and their friends, the use of films and gauze, the dreary azures, lilies, fountains, fruit hair, swans, and roses of conventional symbolist poetry, the moon and the murmurous wood, the ritual expostulations (hollow ohs and fatuous ahs), the early poems are stuffed, as though for Christmas, with images of images: tree, leaf, and sun shadows, dream and fire flicker, countless kinds of reflection. Here the footprint has more substance than the foot; the face finds its resemblance in another medium, floats in fountain water like a flower, trembles independently of its owner as if it had its own sorrows, looks back from the language of its own description like a lover or an accusation. The Narcissus theme has already been introduced: "I can love nothing now but the bewitching water."

He also writes a poem called "Caesar," and admires in the figure he portrays there ("all things beneath his foot") the same quality he finds the young Napoleon showing in his critical hour.* It is a characteristic he discusses

---

* In his translation of Rilke's "Orpheus, Eurydice and Hermes," Lowell adds the line, "The dark was heavier than Caesar's foot." That is how, as Valéry might have said, the undisciplined

with some shrewdness and more detachment in his essays on dictatorship: the burning concentration of will, mastery, the instant disposal of means. It is not Descartes's system, but Descartes's self he makes us a present of, and although his interpretation is so oddly perverse that only a psychological need can account for it, there is no question that Valéry thinks of the philosopher's famous moment of illumination, the moment in which analytic geometry is conceived, and the poet's own sheet-chewing night of crisis, as importantly alike, for in such moments, Valéry writes: ". . . a whole life is suddenly clarified, and every act will henceforth be subordinated to the task which is its goal. A straight line has been staked out." Napoleon had to conquer his dominions, but "Descartes created *his* Revolution and Empire at a single stroke." Valéry chose a world where he could be, as he repeatedly said, master in his own house: his head. It was a world of wait and watch.

Order, clarity, precision, shape: these properties seem so often an enemy of powerful feelings that, although they may usefully employ them the way steam is put to work by the piston, to invoke them is the same as calling the police. Anything—the starry heavens which so terrified Pascal (the one author for whom Valéry exhibits contempt)—can be scientifically observed, but the man of science, Valéry believed, "*switches off* the whole emotive system of his personality. He tries to turn himself into a kind of machine which, after recording observations, sets about formulating definitions and laws, finally replacing phenomena by their expression in terms of conscious, deliberate, and definite potentials."

Valéry's error here, and one he makes repeatedly, is the conflation of method with mind. He supposes that if the scientist or mathematician employs an objective method and pursues disinterested ends, the mind so engaged must become objective and disinterested, too. This is clearly not the case. One must play by the rules, but passionately by them; someone whose emotive system is switched off will hardly be able to think creatively.

Nevertheless, the strategy of withdrawal was shrewd. Let the poet continue to compose; let the man, Valéry, love if he needed to; let him entertain confused ideas—marry, work, worry; he, the other Paul, would observe carefully, allowing the value of each enterprise to detach itself from its original aim and fasten instead to the successive acts which the undertaking may have required and then, finally, to reach for something principled and abstract which, if it were mastered, would render writing unnecessary: namely, the method of composition itself. To have the power, yet withhold

---

mind *moves:* in a lurch through Valéry and Caesar to Lowell and Rilke, and, considering the curious accumulation of references, remains to touch Borges as if he were home base.

its use; to be divine, and not create, is to possess a double strength. It is to say: I could if I would, and I *can,* so I won't. It is also the ultimate in fastidious disdain.

Just as someone in training may run, not to win, to defeat time, or eventually to cool off in the sweet breeze of applause, but to improve his wind and strengthen his muscles, so the mind may come to problems interested mainly in the results on itself of the exercise (I was told this myself, by liars, about Latin, and it is frequently said of crosswords and chess). So Valéry looked for the chief rewards of his thinking and "poetizing," and found them in their effect upon himself.

The difficulty is that one may strengthen one's muscles or thicken one's head as well by losing as winning; it is hard to become intrigued by the successive acts of a hack's composition; quality dominates and determines everything; and it will not do to excuse yourself from that lonely, unromantic, even grubby struggle with the worst and weakest of yourself for the strength and excellence of the best of yourself by pretending, as Valéry invariably did, that he wasn't a poet; that he came to poetry by accident and might, just as well, have done something else with his mind; that he regarded poetry's arbitrary and useless forms as a few absurd hurdles to be leaped as gracefully as possible or altogether ignored; that, in any case, his works were merely exercises; that they were never finished; that it was the sheerest happenstance that they were published when they were and in the form they had, and that, in fact, the same was true of his plays, dialogues, and essays.

They were simply called forth by occasions, he claimed, and composed upon command; they were on any old subject and tailored always for a special audience; furthermore, they often had to meet some extremely silly requirements in order to come into existence at all—for example, the philosophical dialogue *Eupalinos,* which had to be, for the purposes of an elegant book's regimental design, exactly 115,800 letters long. Consequently nothing he did could be regarded as really polished, finished, or perfect—didn't he say so all the time? Thus it wouldn't do to be intense, serious, or terribly puffed, and Valéry seldom was. He was eloquent, graceful, jocular, always personal, easily distracted, disarmingly indirect (this amateur at everything), and he regarded the too solemnly ambitious with a certain scorn (tragic subjects? dear me, what a bore!). No, he was merely, he maintained, a modest man of mind, a student of consciousness during, particularly, its early fumbling moments; he took a few notes . . . oh, he kept his notebooks the way some people keep cows—perhaps there would be a little milk.

It would not do, except that it did do very well. These cavalier "English" attitudes soon outgrew pose and became fixed traits of character. After passing his critical night, Valéry did not give up poetry at once, nor did he leave for Aden or Abyssinia to run guns as Rimbaud had. Relieved of the burden of having to measure up to Mallarmé or, for that matter, to the very sensual, highly romantic poet in himself, and imagining that now his life was to follow a dedicated straight line as he felt Descartes's had (even though, at this distance, we can see that it was to transcribe two great curves across the axes of poetry and prose: away, then toward, then away from poetry again); and taking as his model another omnivorous mind, Leonardo, who—he conveniently believed—had the same interest in method, the same drive toward perfection that resulted in similarly unfinished and fragmentary works, Valéry began keeping notebooks in earnest, rising at dawn every day like a priest at his observances to record the onset of consciousness, and devoting several hours then to the minutest study of his own mind.

This scrutiny was as disciplined and severe, he often bragged, as the practice of poetry. It was coldly impersonal—wasn't the calculus? And it began to soak up all his energies. Soon he would be silent. But in the eight years between the night of crisis and 1900, and before ceasing to publish for about a dozen years, Valéry wrote two important prose works: *Introduction to the Method of Leonardo da Vinci,* and *An Evening with Monsieur Teste,* the first expressing the theoretical aims of his new labors, the second revealing their psychological value.

Odd, mannered, doctrinaire, yet exquisitely wrought, *Monsieur Teste,* from its famous opening line ("Stupidity is not my strong suit"), has seemed to its critics to show Valéry at his most arrogant and exasperating. Scarcely a fiction, it is scarcely anything else. Certainly it contains one of the more curious, though forthrightly named, characters in . . . in . . . what shall we say? fictosophy? "Mr. Head"? is that the right address? No, the wrong resonances. "Mr. Headstrong"? No, that's out of balance. Taken from an old French form of *tête* (shell, pot, head), *teste* also means "will/witness/testament," and thus combines, with only a little distortion, three qualities Valéry valued most at the time. In addition, *teste* refers to the *testes cerebri,* the optic lobes, which are called the testicles of the brain.

Although Valéry treats him with characteristically amused and skeptical reservations, Monsieur Teste nevertheless represents the ideal man of mind. He is a monster, and is meant to be—an awesome, wholly individualized machine—yet in a sense he is also the sort of inhuman being Valéry aimed to become himself: a Narcissus of the best kind, a scientific observer of consciousness, a man untroubled by inroads of worldly trivia (remember Villiers de L'Isle-Adam's symbolist slogan, "as for living, our servants will do that for us"?), who vacations in his head the way a Platonist finds his Florida in the realm of Forms. Like the good analytic philosopher he also resembles, Monsieur Teste complains constantly about the treacheries of words and the salad-forked tongue wagged so loosely by language (while his own name, perversely, is an excellent example of ambiguity well used). Teste has become almost pure potentiality, and a man in whom knowledge has finally made unnecessary the necessity to act.

Watching himself, then, Valéry grew as comfortable with contradiction as the best Hegelian. He noticed that in time attitudes would turn themselves inside out like gloves, go from bug to butterfly. He could deprecate his labors, but he would also increasingly insist upon their worth: the notebooks were his great work and he would be remembered, if at all, because of them. He sought absolute clarity, he said, and in those thoughts which, like Monsieur Teste, he felt no need to record, he pursued his thinking through ruthlessly to the end. It is curious that many of those which he did put down, and indeed published later, pursue nothing through to the end, but reveal, instead, when they don't read like diary entries or blotter jottings, that same love of aphorism, apothegm, and smart remark that is such a frequent failing of the French mind.

It's not that the notebooks aren't fascinating or important (they have yet to be translated in their entirety, but portions of them are printed as addenda to several volumes of the Bollingen *Collected Works*), it is simply that they do not come anywhere near making any methodological discovery. There are notes on love, life, literature, morals; on books read, people met, thoughts exchanged. In the actual notebooks, not the translated bits, there are cryptic lists, algebraic dithers and geometric doodles, maplike mental layouts, and occasionally a watercolor sketch: boats, windows, costumes, rooms.

A poet of the utmost formality, an admirer of ceremony, of the rigors and several clarities of mathematics; in fact, in the early thirties, in the political sphere, a little too impressed by order, though at one time, too, one of the few not a philosopher or logician who understood how much the architecture of a thought—its form—is really in the richest sense the thought itself (as this is wholly the case in poetry and the other arts); Valéry was nevertheless suspicious of systems.

He dismisses Descartes's philosophy with the suggestion (which he could have borrowed from Nietzsche) that a thinker's effort to make his ideas acceptable may lead him, inadvertently, to disguise his central thought and conceal from others the actual insecurities and confusions of his mind. Systems are like forms for writing letters: they ensure that any content will be harmonious, temperate, and polite. It will be "professional." It will be correct. Thus Valéry refused to regiment his thinking (which is the ego's way of saying it is unable to), and even his essays are organized, mainly, on aesthetic lines. His further reluctance to express what cannot be expressed gracefully leads him to seem to tease the reader, rather than, as Valéry desired, to be exceptionally honest with him.

Although Valéry himself regarded the poet's biography as an impertinent irrelevance to the work which was his real life, to realize that Valéry's long devotion to his "notebooks" was an elaborate Maginot, a barrier he lay quietly behind until he was ready, again, to let the enemy in, is, it seems to me, the most important thing to know about him. After such resistance, such abnegation of gifts, how surprisingly easy was the change. In 1912 Gide suggests he print his early poems. Although Valéry has already attempted this several times, he expresses reluctance. A typescript is given to him and he is, he says, appalled. A few revisions . . . then quite a few, whole new stanzas. He will go ahead. Perhaps an introductory poem might be composed, a few verses. . . . It is "La Jeune Parque," a poem which grows from forty lines to 512, which occupies four years of work—years of war—and, preceding the volume it was expected to preface by three years, makes him famous. When it is finally completed in 1917, he dedicates it to Gide. Long, dense, difficult, personal, obscure: these are the critics' words. More unsummarizable poems—masterpieces—follow to fill out *Charmes,* which appears in 1922. All exercises, of course, all experiments, all accidents, all unfinished . . .

It is now plain that when Valéry returned to poetry it was as an altogether superior man, for what he had loved during that muffled time was not himself but a true image, an inversion, an opposite: against the vague indefiniteness of the symbolist poetry he had begun by admiring, he had placed the precision and crispness of mathematics; against practice he'd put theory, exchanging the careless literary use of ideas for their cautious, responsible, scientific employment; from the forms for feeling and desire he had turned away to study the structures of thought, working—in the phrase of Huysmans, one novelist he allowed himself to admire—always *au rebours,* against the grain, and consequently correcting in himself a severe and weakening lean in the direction of the mystical and romantic.

This extraordinary straightening up produced a poet who was not only supremely skilled in practice, and sound in theory, but one who did not feel his work so beset by other subjects that he had to make a castle of himself and dragons out of everything else. Above all, it enabled him eventually to achieve poems that created in their readers strange yet richly integrated states of consciousness—the mind as the face of a Narcissus. They were indelible evaporations, works in which the shadows that words cast had more weight than the words themselves, and whose effects were—in his own wonderfully reflexive phrase—like the "*frémissements d'une feuille effacée*," the shiverings of an effaced leaf.

2

Built slowly, with a patience appropriate to the pyramid it is, and the pharaoh who lies within it, the Bollingen edition of *The Collected Works of Paul Valéry* has now reached the twelfth of its projected fifteen volumes.* More than a dozen forewords and introductions grace it (by Eliot, Auden, and Wallace Stevens, among others almost as distinguished); twelve translators, most of them gifted, have so far contributed their labors; and if, since 1956, when it was the first to appear, the most successful undertaking has been William McCausland Stewart's inspired version of the *Dialogues,* works which now seem unimprovable in English as well as French, the most difficult task has been that of David Paul, who has done the major poems, in addition to an excellent prose rendering of *Idée Fixe*—a kind of extended conversation insufficiently ceremonious and solemn to be a dialogue. Valéry's late, unfinished play, *My Faust,* is Paul's work, too, as well as the poet's relaxed and anecdotal pieces on the painters, *Degas, Manet, Morisot.* If I say that Mr. Paul has been only intermittently successful with the poems, that is praise, for Valéry's poetry, like Mallarmé's, is not translatable.

And not because Valéry was merely a mouthpiece for the gods—he despised that pretense—but precisely because, while courting chance, he left nothing to it. His muse was a domestic. What are we otherwise to think of the efficient, modest maid who comes to make the poet's bed, flit among the mirrors, find fresh water for his flowers?

"*Une esclave aux longs yeux chargés de molles chaînes.*" Long, shall we say her eyes are? slow? laden or burdened? and shall we believe her chains are slack, soft, loose—what? "A slave girl, her long eyes laden with soft chains," Mr. Paul decides to render it; yet are these words and these decisions about her eyes, her soul, her situation, or the poet's mind? How elusive the line is, wound in music like a gift in tissue, both wrapped and wrapping fragile as a bibelot, one as precious as the other. The language is so precisely used that its object cannot be exactly seen, for nothing is easier than to paint a resemblance, follow a line a leg makes, let the world do your creative work.

Every word in the poem has a dozen causes, so that when the poet suggests that this slave, maid, and muse of his can busy herself in his room, pass

* In 1972, when this was written. The edition is now complete.

in and out of his sight without disturbing its preoccupied "absence," as glass passes through sunlight ("*Comme passe le verre au travers du soleil*") without having to set in motion the machinery of the mind ("*Et de la raison pure épargne l'appareil*"), it is painful to hear Mr. Paul say instead: "As a window-pane traverses the sunshine, / Leaving intact the appliances of pure reason," because now only the bare "idea" remains, rather stricken and emaciated, too, as though it had lain sick in a cell for some time.

A maid straightening a room: all right, we can translate that. And to the extent a writer achieves his effects through the invention and manipulation of fictional things and people (a skill which is not a linguistic one), these effects can be suggested in another tongue or even in another medium.

Thus it is possible for me to tell you that in one of Valéry's poems there is a rower on a river. Rhythmically bending and straightening as he must, seeming to move the world rather than himself as he passes between the banks and beneath bridges, his eyes wander downcast in a landscape of reflection.

On the other side of the sky, philosophers—and others momentarily like them—are combining their concepts in amusing, instructive, or dazzling ways, and to the degree these concepts can free themselves of the language in which they were originally expressed, they can travel without too much wear and tear. Plato was an artist of ideas, as Valéry suggests all philosophers should be, and that the body is a prison for the soul is one piece of philosophical poetry with which you and I can fairly easily acquaint ourselves without knowing much Greek.

With regard to "The Rower," then, I can indicate how Valéry imagines objects and their reflections, like Narcissus and the puddle-picture of himself he loved, to be like the images of burning which smoked the walls of Plato's cave; I can describe how, in the poem, the boat's prow is urged to divide the world which seems painted in the water, shattering its calm so that of such a massive stillness no memory will remain. But Valéry bitterly objected to this kind of poetic play with ideas in Pascal and in other philosophers, because he suspected them, lest reason fail, of using the methods of poetry, like the welcome lies of politicians, to persuade, and in this way debasing both truth and beauty. In Pascal, because he was not only a splendid writer but a fine mathematician, this Jansenist unscrupulousness was intolerable.

Of course I don't need to translate the poem's exterior design, because I can exactly reproduce it; yet rhyme schemes, stanza forms, and even meters, not to say the sounds of words, their multiple associations and other shades, the syntax of the language, the tone of the "voice"—detached or angry—shared techniques, shared subjects and concerns, with all their risks, his very personal quirks, like the crotches of trees, as well as the traditions which the poet is a human and historic part of: all these—and many more—make their claims, often quite stubbornly and without any evident justice.

Valéry liked to think of forms as arbitrary obstacles set up simply for the sport, and he was happy to believe that the sport itself was one of resolution, harmony, wholeness; one in which the poet, by consciously calculated and successive steps, creates out of artificial and even antagonistic materials an object as mysteriously complete, continuous, and beautiful as the shell of a mollusk or a spider's snare. Yet not an object like theirs designed to trap or protect, but one simply *willed*—made to be because the soul is finally satisfied only by what resembles it in its supremest dreams, when it is invincibly principled, and consequently something so inwardly radiant that, like the contours of a resting woman's body, as he writes in one poem, it has to be, itself, alive . . . alive to return our gaze. And yet it must also be an object as theirs sometimes is, since it must seem, against the actuality of its contrivance, instinctive, seamless, easy . . . as though exuded through a tube or spun from a gland. But no words of mine can convey the loveliness of style and idea contained in his finer essays, "Poetry and Abstract Thought," for example, or "Man and the Seashell."

For the translator—alas—Valéry's verse succeeds. It's so fastened to the word, so confined to the tongue which expresses it, there's no remainder. Such was his intention, and to pretend, when all else fails, by freer, more expansive measures, to find some poetic corollary elsewhere is like hunting through the music of the Balinese for the musical equivalent of *Till Eulenspiegel's Merry Pranks*. Mr. Paul does not obviously wander away, but what is near and what far in this connection? Here is a poet so careful he seems always to be walking upright on his own life as though it were a swaying wire. To render him, then, as if he were forgetful and a bit careless about his budget: how shall we measure this departure?

"The Rower" is a poet struggling upstream against time and the temptations of a pleasurable drift. His oars part him from the repeated grip of the river:

> *Je romprai lentement mille liens glacés*
> *Et les barbes d'argent de sa puissance nue.*

Mr. Paul, who with the less famous poems has sometimes taken the first meaning to fly by, not troubling himself about the sense of the whole, construes this pair as follows:

> Piece by piece I shall break a thousand icy bonds,
> And the silvery barbs of her naked potency,

which is, first, careless (you don't break bonds "piece by piece"), and then incorrect (*barbes* refers to a *lappet,* a kind of apron, here), so that the consequence is confusion, and the central meaning of the line, the sexual exposure of the river by violation of its surface, is lost. In the final verses of the poem, too, Mr. Paul interprets the poet's critical concluding act of defiance as . . . well, it simply isn't clear. The rower is passing beneath bridges whose darkness oppresses him.

> the mind
> Lowers its sensitive suns, its ready eyelids,
> Until with a leap that clothes me with jewels
> I plunge into the disdain of all that idle azure.

You should have to have a court order to use "azure" in English. The early poem "Helen" begins "*Azur! c'est moi . . . ,*" which Mr. Paul renders, "Azure, it is I!" Lowell quite properly avoids the word. "I am the blue!" his poem cries, which isn't right either, but—never mind—the poem that follows is a brilliant one, if not by Valéry.

Then to transcribe these famous lines of "The Cemetery by the Sea":

> *Midi le juste y compose de feux*
> *La mer, la mer, toujours recommencée!*

in which Valéry describes the light of the noon sun falling with the kind of impartial light we get in certain classical paintings—everywhere in a rain of right angles—so that the quiet sea has no slopes with which it can contrive a shadow, and consequently seems composed of fire; a fire, indeed, like that which is said to consume the phoenix, death and birth proceeding so continuously that nothing appears to change—to transcribe these lines as

> Justicer Noon out there compounds with fires
> The sea, the sea perpetually renewed!

is to replace a delicate balance of ideas with simple awkwardness. And as the poet's shining wine subsides in its glass, the remainder remains sweetly sticky still, like flat pop.

Valéry always insisted that his interest in poetry lay in the *work,* not in the poem: in the successive acts of composition which were, for him, like the moves of a dancer passing gracefully from one position to another. And if poetry stood to prose as dancing did to walking, as he liked to say, then it did so because, like dancing, its motions served no master but the mind at play which designed them; because it became a continuum: there was the art! by seeking minuter and minuter modulations, by the steady overlay of straight lines, to achieve the curve first, and then the circle—a visible summation of many nearly invisible steps and decisions.

Shatter a stone and the bits you make are simply further stones, but break a seashell or a poem and every piece will continue to declare itself a fragment of some whole. Dancing supervenes upon the serious business of walking the way a child's skip-alongs and fence balancings accompany him as he makes his imperfect way to school. Unlike prose, poetry is not a kind of communication, but a construction in consciousness. Words in ordinary speech and trade . . . they disappear before their messages do, disposable as Kleenex; but the cry of fire in a crowded room, if it is eloquently framed and sweet enough, will snuff all sense of burning. The form will hold us there.

. . . and we become a light white ash.

Through long years of patient dedication Valéry advanced by means of even detours toward the outline of a powerful poetic theory, and I am convinced, as Auden remarks in one of the several excellent introductions to *The Collected Works,* that "In his general principles . . . Valéry is right past all possibility of discussion."

Permanence and repeatability were two qualities which Valéry thought essential. Sensations are usually simply used, or canceled by others, and those which we wish to prolong belong, he said, to "the esthetic infinite." He only glimpsed another possibility: that as the demand for culture grew it would be necessary to create along other lines, for poetry is presently composed as the paper in picnic plates is shaped. When the beans have been consumed, and the plates scraped, they can be ditched or burned. New ones appear in the stores every day, some with dashing designs, and so sturdily constructed they can carry a glass. Tomorrow, too, there will be further festivals, clean blankets and new friends, fresh glass.

Perhaps Valéry rather naïvely believed the novelists when they announced (as Zola, for example, did every day in the press) their plans to make to the world a present of reality . . . believed, that is, in the sincerity of their pretensions, although shocked by their performance. Perhaps his commitment to excellence was too great, and in poetry the sacred purity of vocabulary, narrowness of subject, the neatness of small forms, and the satisfaction of their palpable tightness, shut his eyes, as a cat's eyes shut, in self-centered satisfaction.

In any case he did not understand Flaubert; he took little interest in Proust;

about the great works of Mann and Joyce he was very noticeably silent, and of such exemplars of oddity as Gertrude Stein I doubt he ever heard; but there were, in the works he did examine, so many pages of "information," so many events, traits, qualities, and verbal formulations which could just as well have been otherwise—so much invented gossip, so many inexpressive details—that he failed to observe what his own attitudes had helped make possible: how the techniques of the modern novel were rapidly becoming the strategies of the long poem, and that original forms were being designed for such extended breaths—new chests were necessary, and larger lungs.

Edmund Wilson once wrote that Valéry's prose, "in spite of the extravagant respect with which it is treated by his admirers, is by no means so remarkable as his verse," but I find myself unable to agree. The curve that carried Valéry away from poetry a second time, and plunged him, as it seemed, in notoriety (he threw open doors and cut ribbons, made addresses, lectured, wrote testimonials and forewords, responded to requests, modestly discussed his own successes, and in 1925 accepted election to the French Academy), led him at the same time to create his dialogues, the *Eupalinos* among them, one of the most original and moving pieces of prose in any language.

The empirical distinction between poetry and prose is a wholly illusory one, a fact of which Valéry was at times perfectly aware, for the French have pioneered the prose poem; Valéry admired Rimbaud's, and wrote not a few himself; he also dabbled in the story, wrote *Monsieur Teste,* of course, made jots of plots, especially fancying the kind of flat, weird, metaphysically menacing situations Lettau could find stimulating, as Borges certainly did.

Valéry could never quite give himself up to prose (prose as he got in the bad habit of defining it), and this accounts, at least in part, for the flicker in his thought which one often finds in the essays. Perhaps his mind was too playful, perhaps it danced when it should have walked or harshly stomped, yet what is striking in even his most occasional pieces—let alone the famous ones like "The Crises of the Mind" or "The Outlook for Intelligence"—is his remarkable prescience, so that even brief asides ("Perhaps waste itself has become a public and permanent necessity"), made in 1940, or 1932, or 1929, fall further over and into the present than any wholesome shadow should. It's not just his style alone that sometimes causes the scalp to prickle.

I suspect that Valéry's success as a wise man was not due to his Leonardo-like ambitions, because his studies were not as universal or as thorough as he liked to let on, and the central concern of his life was a stubbornly restricted one; nor was it because he reasoned like a Teste, for his mind was essentially metaphoric in its operation (what he knew and liked most about architecture, for example, was almost wholly embodied in the very idea of "building"); and although his sovereign detachment certainly helped him and he was instinctively right about what to despise, he was particularly a master of the sidelong look, and the practice of composition over many years had taught him to attend to "little" things and small steps, for there, in scrupulosities only a spider might otherwise pain itself with, were the opportunities for genius. It is Valéry himself who writes: "Great events are perhaps so only for small minds. For more attentive minds, it is the unnoticed, continual events that count."

It was these small movements of which Valéry was such a master, if we think of them as the movements of a mind which has practiced passage to the point of total purity, compressing those steps, those postures and attitudes which were learned at the mirror so painfully, into one unwinding line of motion; and as we follow the body of his thought as we might that of an inspired dancer, leaving the source of his energy like flame, we have presented almost to our eye other qualities in addition to those normally thought vital and sufficient for the mind, though rare and prized like clarity and rigor, honesty, openness, interest, penetration and brevity, truth; that is to say, lightness, tact in particular, and above all, elegance and grace.

The New York Times Book Review, 1972
Published in *The World Within the Word,* 1978

A Forest of Bamboo

The Trouble with Nietzsche

Perhaps it is the fate of intellectuals who incautiously trust their thoughts to a wider public that those thoughts should be abducted and abused like a child of rich parents; or, because these ideas are sometimes attractive to the intellectually ambitious, they are subjected to obfuscation and misuse: defended by their friends but traduced, lied about, and maligned by their enemies as if theories were politicians campaigning for office. Maybe no thinker gets picked on more than another, Walter Kaufmann politely wondered at the beginning of the third edition of his book on Friedrich Nietzsche; nevertheless, he found it necessary to whack many a knuckle on the philosopher's behalf for just those depredations and incursions that any fertile but defenseless intellectual territory invites, especially when it displays, as its ideas develop, one threatening or inviting aspect after another.

The opinions of philosophers are not always greeted with yawns. Socrates was expected to execute himself, Bruno was burned, Spinoza's life threatened, a fearful Descartes seduced to Sweden, where he froze. David Hume's name, famously demonized by Samuel Johnson, was used by pestered parents to cow their children, and his grave on Edinburgh's Calton Hill was expected to burst open at the devil's summons some dark and stormy night so that the notorious disbeliever's soul could fly to its master. For many, Nietzsche has always been a bugaboo, though some regard him as an heroic destroyer of idols, the invigorating voice of skepticism, and a revealer of those embarrassing actualities that the pieties and protestations of the bourgeois have customarily concealed. Others have said that behind the bug there was no true boo. Nietzsche doubted, as Descartes did, only to restore an honest ethic to its radiant place; he embraced a genuine spirituality and wished for a kind of—a sort of—illuminated grace.

Whatever their persuasion, Nietzsche's devoted followers are like followers always are: they deplore their leader's revisions of mind and falls from faith; consequently they reinterpret or ignore his changes of heart, while what are felt to be weaknesses of character are concealed. Bertrand Russell regularly left his fellow aerialists grasping air and hoping for a net; Ludwig Wittgenstein made a huge U-turn in mid-career, thereby creating rival factions representing the Early or the Late; and Friedrich Nietzsche sometimes recolored his mind between tea and Tuesday. This is tiresome. A single unified system is required if one is to propagandize for it properly. At least there must be a final, definitive position for the mind, as though the writer were fighting a last-ditch action and were willing to die before surrendering a yard of argument. But in Nietzsche, if such a thing were to be found, it would have to be skeletal, submerged, in code, because the body of his work certainly dips up and down and turns around enough to bear a coaster full of riders who have paid mostly for the thrill. A tone of jubilant acrimony is perhaps its most consistent quality. My teachers saw no reason to speak of Nietzsche at all. In his early biography (1941) Crane Brinton suggested that, apart from his contribution to an evolutionary account of ethical ideals, he would have "a continued use among adolescents as at once a consolation and a stimulus" (*Nietzsche* [New York: Harper & Row, 1965]).

Gnomic utterances, poetic outcries, hectoring jibes, oracular episodes, diatribes, and rhapsodic seizures—personality and style—these are not characteristics that are usually thought to suit the philosophical temperament, and add to them the habit of attacking the profession and then reason itself, especially on behalf of primitive urges, instinct, or animal vitality, and they shall be quickly scraped from any academician's plate as if a passing bird had despoiled the serving.

Anthologies of essays allegedly representing the most recent opinions of their elusive subject seasonally appear. There is *Nietzsche: A Collection of Critical Essays* (1973), edited by Robert Solomon: "Our first encounter with Nietzsche typically offers us a caricature of the 'mad philosopher,' a distant yet myopic glare of fury, leaden eyebrows and drooping moustache, the posture of a Prussian soldier caught out of uniform by a French cartoonist of the 1870s"; *The New Nietzsche*, edited by David Allison (1985): "Nietzsche's biography is uninspiring, to say the least. Nonetheless, this subject appears to have been the principal source of inspiration for the tiresome array of books that has followed him"; *Why Nietzsche Now?* (1985) compiled by Daniel O'Hara in the same year, and the year I stopped collecting them: "Friedrich Nietzsche is not a serious writer" . . . but his playfulness is profound, O'Hara is careful to add; while there are explanations of these conflicting opinions in George Morgan's *What Nietzsche Means* (1941): "Can anything be good which attracts so many flies?," a judgment well put, I think; Arthur Danto tries to straighten the paper clip that describes the philosopher's course of thought with *Nietzsche as Philosopher* (1965), while *What Nietzsche Really Said* (2000), written by Robert Solomon and Kathleen Higgins, would keep the curves but set the record straight: "What Nietzsche really said gets lost in a maze of falsehoods, misinterpretations, and exaggerations," including, I might add on their behalf, scholarly slurs such as that of George Lichtheim in his *Europe in the Twentieth Century* (London: Weidenfeld and Nicolson, 1972): "It is not too much to say that but for Nietzsche the SS—Hitler's shock troops and the core of the whole movement—would have lacked the inspiration to carry out their programme of mass murder in Eastern Europe." It is, in fact, more than too much to say, and in a more honorable time might have provoked a duel.

David Krell, who translated the two volumes of Heidegger's *Nietzsche* (1961), and who therefore ought to know, says, at the beginning of his own slim volume, *Postponements: Woman, Sensuality, and Death in Nietzsche* (1986), that "Big books are big sins, but big books about Nietzsche are a far more pernicious affair: they are breaches of good taste." Authors with axes to grind, agendas to push, or slants to slide on are as numerous as stars—at least as many as one can see most nights. Biographies such as Ivo Frenzel's brief *Friedrich Nietzsche* (1966), Alexander Nehamas's *Nietzsche: Life as Literature* (1985), Ronald Hayman's *Nietzsche: A Critical Life* (1980), and Rüdiger Safranski's *Nietzsche: A Philosophical Biography* (2002) dutifully march by, but not in this review.

Curtis Cate tells us, in the introduction to his new life of Nietzsche (New York: Overlook Press, 2002), that he is writing it not for the professional philosopher but for the intelligent layman, for those who may not have read a word by this notorious blasphemer, in order to

> clear away some of the stereotypic prejudices that have, like barnacles, incrusted themselves around his name—like the naive notion that he was viscerally anti-religious—and because the existential problems he boldly tackled—how can Man find spiritual and intellectual solace in an increasingly godless age? How can the desire to be free, and not least of all, a "free-thinker," be reconciled with the notion and practice of Authority needed to save society from collective anarchy, how can the egalitarian virus endemic in the very nature of Democracy be prevented from degrading what remains of "culture," and ultimately of civility . . .

There is no concluding question mark, but these are carefully chosen flags of warning. Nietzsche has told us, and his own practice has offered evidence, that the conclusion of an argument—a belief as briefly put as a shout in the street—is almost as empty of meaning as the nearest social gesture, unless it is accompanied by the reasons that are supposed to support it, because leaving Vietnam, for instance, might have been a good idea if we believed it was an unjust war, but an equally sound recommendation if we thought we were not going to be allowed to bomb the place back into the Stone Age. "Collective anarchy" and "egalitarian virus" can be give-away phrases—if anyone wants to accept them.

Cate continues, a few pages farther on, to pose his questions.

It is easy to reproach Nietzsche for having, in his anathemas against pulpit preachers, contributed to the deluge by weakening the flood-gates of traditional morality. But the troubling question remains: what will happen to the Western world if the present drift cannot be halted, and to what sordid depths of pornographically publicized vulgarity will our shamelessly "transparent" culture, or what remains of it, continue to descend, while those who care about such matters look on in impotent dismay?

It is the mounting anger here that is interesting, although the idea that Nietzsche has flooded us with traditional morality has a certain perverse attraction: is Curtis Cate going to claim that Nietzsche is really a Republican?

In the literature about our subject, it is true that all the angles are argued, and the philosopher who preached of multiple perspectives must now suffer each passing point of view, as saints are supposed to have suffered their thorns, spears, arrows, and swords in the side. In this respect, writing a life of Nietzsche is far simpler and more straightforward than giving an account of his opinions, because, except for Nietzsche's worship of Wagner, there is little hyperbolic about the course of Nietzsche's friendships, studies, classes, travels, ailments, forest walks, or mountain hikes—well, perhaps the latter undergo some of awe's inflation—because he simply writes or he composes; because he's deep in a round of visits; he talks or teaches; he reads or rides from Naumburg to Basel in ice-cold railcars; he practices the piano; because, though he falls ill often, it is not from any height health at which may have held him; he's nervous, frail despite appearances, and easily discombobulated by bad news, by disappointment, and even if a series of precocious successes has marked his professional progress, Nietzsche nevertheless feels that an opposition to his person or his aims is everywhere active and nefarious; consequently, he is pestered by low enrollments and other academic issues, poor reviews, inadequate salary—routines of little drama and states of mind for which there is small public; and finally because what really matters to Nietzsche is what we started this list by citing—music, or better yet writing: they constitute the fiery center of his life, especially when paper is pierced by the pen, for in that place he may smite his enemies. . . . Yes, smiting his enemies is his profoundest pleasure; and he always sits down to do that.

Cate very capably carries us through Nietzsche's early life in Röcken, near Leipzig, although he does not dwell on the wholly feminized environment in which the boy was brought up after his father (a Protestant vicar whom Nietzsche in retrospect decided to adore) died of "softening of the brain" in 1849, when his son was four. Cate quotes Nietzsche's own response to his father's funeral—a memory made of tolling bells, organ music, and intoned words—but in a book distracted by data he does not dwell for a sentence's length upon the father's eleven-month illness and the cries of pain that penetrated to the street. Soon after, Cate says, Nietzsche dreamed that a white-shrouded figure rose from his father's grave, and, to tolling bells, after visiting a church, returned to the earth bearing something in its arms. "Soon after," however, was six months. Soon after this dream—namely, the next day—Nietzsche's previously healthy two-year-old brother suffered seizures and died of his convulsions.

Quite a few pages later he does say that Nietzsche had chosen to study classical philology "as a kind of *pis aller* in order to free himself from the coils of theology, with which his devout mother and his pious aunts and uncles had sought to trap and tame his intellectual energies." Cate insists that Nietzsche's rejection of religion was a purely intellectual matter, but it is hard to imagine any of this philosopher's views not fueled by emotion, and by feelings very individually formed. Nietzsche was a lover of life but a hater of most of us who live it because we did not—do not—live it properly, fully, with appropriate abandon, with delight and with mastery, the way a dancer may leap and spin and even look askance, exulting in her total control of eyelash and limb.

The early years of life were ones of constraint for Nietzsche, because of both the pious arms that held him and the regimen of schooling that the times and its institutions required. He found it easy to employ the effort needed to excel, so eager was he to break out into a wider world through any avenue of interest that offered itself. "It may have been a drawback," Nietzsche wrote,

that . . . my entire development was never supervised by a masculine eye, but that curiosity, perhaps even a thirst for learning, made me acquire the most diverse educational materials in such chaotic form

as to confuse a young mind barely out of the family nest, and to jeop-
ardize the foundations for solid knowledge. Thus, this whole period
from my ninth to my fifteenth year is characterized by a veritable passion for "universal knowledge," as I called it; on the other hand, childhood games were not neglected, but pursued with an almost fanatic
zeal, so that, for instance, I wrote little books about most of them and
submitted them to my friends. Roused by extraordinary chance in my
ninth year, I passionately turned to music and even immediately began
composing—if one can apply this term to the efforts of an agitated
child to set down on paper simultaneous and successive tones and to
sing Biblical texts to a fantastic accompaniment on the piano. Similarly, I wrote terrible poems, but with great diligence. Indeed, I even
drew and painted.

[Quoted by Frenzel, *Friedrich Nietzsche*.]

Although sectarian struggles were not absent from the wider world,
Nietzsche's immediate environment was one of complaisant Christian certitude. His father, who immediately became a mythological figure, had been a
Protestant preacher, and his family and friends would naturally have nudged
his behavior into a righteous neighborhood and filled his mind with their
beliefs and their values without, at first, feeling any need to indoctrinate, only
to be as they comfortably were. Moreover, the schools they chose for him
would naturally reinforce, in the normal course of instruction and discipline,
the same ideals: that is to say, the principal questions had been answered. You
did not live your life *in search of* but *according to*. Nevertheless, Nietzsche's
trapped intelligence found a way out to freedom through the classics: pagan
texts that were supposed to teach Greek, not what Greeks thought; to make
available their poetry and their theater without trying to answer Socrates's
searching questions or swallowing the sweet poison of Plato. They were certainly not expected to encourage the salacious disrespect prevalent in the
satyr plays or recommend Aristophanes's bawdy breaches of decorum. As
for Latin, it was, of course, the language of the Church but also that of the
Roman gods; it was the tongue of Catullus as well as the halo of Aquinas.
So if a profession was demanded of him when freedom was what he wanted,
Nietzsche could choose the door marked "classical philology." Beyond it, the
one God would become many gods, quite a few of them lustful, some drunk.

In this way, Nietzsche escaped the first circle of constraint: the family.
The family was at the heart of hell. But having reached the next level, this
inverted Virgil found himself inside the educational system. What would it
make of the mind? A tame mediocrity. There would be mentors, not moth-

ers, now; there would be pathways to power, obstacles one hurdled by practicing the right form and accepting the right help, but the struggle was of the sort in which the waistcoat could claim victory by undoing the vest. At the boarding school where the young scholar began to learn the ways of the ruler and the switch, there was one mentor who set such a bad example Nietzsche was compelled to admire him. His name was Ernst Ortlepp, a sixty-year-old translator of Shakespeare and Byron; someone who borrowed the robes of a priest, adopting a sermonizing tone without any sanction, and who testified to his fondness for Nietzsche, the prodigy sometimes in his care, by writing in his pupil's poetry notebook: "Never did I think that I would ever love again." Ortlepp was a figure out of Erasmus's *In Praise of Folly.* He sang blasphemous tavern songs, he recited Byron, and he drank like a medieval monk, often wandering from his saloon onto the weedy side of the road, which led to his incarceration once as a public nuisance. Ortlepp improvised improper tunes on the piano to entertain his flock, composed fiery defenses of the habitually put-upon Poles, and had met, consorted with, and favorably reviewed Richard Wagner.

"It was in this figure of Ortlepp, the bibulous poet, that Nietzsche first encountered the two-faced Dionysus, god of sensuous pleasure but also of the fear of death," notes Joachim Köhler in *Nietzsche and Wagner* (New Haven, Conn.: Yale University Press, 1998). "In 1864, the year Nietzsche graduated from Schulpforta, Ortlepp fell into a ditch in a drunken stupor and broke his neck. Nietzsche described him as 'a friend who sent bolts of lightning into the dark recesses of my youth.' But for as long as he lived he did not breathe a word about the nature of their relationship." Cate doesn't breathe a word about it either.

In academic halls, one writes for one's peers, and to satisfy their expectations—to win friends, to keep sponsors. Articles come first, small projects, research, translation—delicate nibbles at the hand that feeds. But an article is not an essay. Articles lie about the lay of their land. An article pretends to be clear about its objective and then must pretend to reach it. That objective will be minuscule though recondite. Moreover, the article does not halt at any point along the way to confess that its author is lost, or that its exposition has grown confused, or that there are attractive alternatives here and there, that its conclusions are uncertain or unimportant, that the author has lost interest; rather, the article insists on its proofs; it will hammer home even a bent nail; however, it does not end on a howl of triumph but on a note of humility, as if being right about something was a quite customary state of affairs. Polite applause will be the proper response. And a promotion.

Philosophy was the path out of philology, and Schopenhauer was a Hermes whose hand Nietzsche could hold on the way out. But philosophy was also another stage for the performance of academic follies. Competing schools demanded the loyalty of their members, blocked any advancement by their opponents, attacked one another in their journals, and attached themselves to outside interests—loyalists to this or that religious tenet, racial group, aim of state—whose attractive aspects could be used to their advantage. Of course they were also wrong, wrong about everything: even Nietzsche's intellectual hero proved to be clay to his boot tops, and, as Cate observes, Schopenhauer's disappointed devotees would blame the persuasive power of his rhetoric for misleading them.

In the meantime, though, Nietzsche would share his enthusiasm for Schopenhauer's *The World as Will and Representation* with Richard Wagner, who lived nearby in Tribschen and who extended the young professor an invitation to visit him, an invitation Nietzsche was eager to accept, since he had already examined a few of Wagner's scores and had been overwhelmed by the music, some of which he was able to play on the piano. If the gods of the Greeks were supposed to be Apollonian, those of the *Nibelungenlied* were Dionysian from drum to trumpet, and Wagner was their realization. Nietzsche became a warm admirer and witty companion with whom Wagner could share his grand plans for German music and celebrate his numerous dislikes. In addition, Nietzsche not only composed music and then played it; he dared to do so in the presence of the master, who at first tolerated his disciple's efforts but later wearied of these vanities, for, after all, he had so many of his own.

Nietzsche's response to music, not only to the Romantic masters but to his own improvisations, was often ecstatic. He became transported, intoxicated, even visionary. Consequently, he might naturally see the same storms of feelings to be customary for the Greeks. Indeed, Aristotle testifies to it, and Plato complains. Although Nietzsche is certainly aware of music's formal component—its abstract, even mathematical nature—he does not weigh it as he should. It is the primitive and, one might say vulgar, component of music, a vulgarity Wagner makes an art of, that earns it the highest accolade and the name "Dionysian." But to be swept away is just a prelude to the dustbin.

Having given his heart to Wagner, Nietzsche found it easy to add the new German state to his small list of beloveds, for Wagner had made the identification of himself with the new Germany easy. Both men had bemoaned the decline of its music, now in the hands of Jews like Mendelssohn, sentimentalists like Schumann, or that imitative newcomer Brahms, as if Wagner himself were not sufficient cause for celebration. Words such as "degenerate" and "purity" surfaced like corpses in the flow of their diatribes. "Cleansing" was invoked, but only its necessity. In 1870, Germany had attacked France, and patriotism was a party favor. Although Nietzsche was a pro forma citizen of Switzerland, where he taught, he could not resist the lure of the fife and drum. He was not of a temperament to remain neutral. Cate obviously enjoys expressing Nietzsche's distaste for what was seen then as the liberal (and neutral) point of view: "a tepid philosophy for tepid souls devoid of any deep-rooted, personal convictions, ever ready to compromise, to swim with the prevailing current, to dilute whatever remained of their beliefs in a bouillon of tasteless 'moderation.'"

In his youth, because the acceptable strength of a soldier's glasses was enlarged to increase enlistments, Nietzsche had a brief obligatory stint as conscript in the Mounted Field Artillery; and he quickly became one of his troop's best horsemen, only to be brought down so hard upon the pommel of his saddle by an unruly mount that it broke his sternum. For this second enlistment—because of his eyes, his past experience, and his present citizenship—Nietzsche was forced to join a medical unit, even though he knew nothing about tending the sick beyond the attentions he had given himself. Immediately, there was much to do. Behind the army, as it rapidly advanced, the wounded were left like dirty and divested clothing. Disease was also sweeping through the ranks. Rain fell and men fell, mud and maladies slowed the march. Nietzsche had to tend the sick and wounded in a drafty cattle car kept closed on account of the persistent rain, so the consequences of dysentery, diphtheria, and festering wounds could be fully inhaled. Nietzsche soon came down with his patients' infections, but coming down with an illness was something he had practiced until he was nearly perfect at it. Discomfort was a companion that would never leave his side, and one he would never renounce. But the glamour of war and pride in the new German state were now only mud, stench, and sickness.

He suffered from hemorrhoids and gastric spasms for much of his life, as well as prolonged spells of insomnia, but even more debilitating were the migraine attacks that appeared after stress or in the midst of travel, especially when the carriages were cold and the iron wheels noisy. In addition, there was the effect of light upon his aching eyes, which were steadily worsening despite drawn curtains, dark glasses, and soothing compresses. Nietzsche undertook numerous consultations with doctors, who unfortunately saw solutions and prescribed remedies that defied the motto "Do no harm." Leeches were encouraged to feed on the lobes of his ears. He was often under his mother's care, and he was frequently so sick he had to summon his sister to his side, although she was not at the time nearby. Ulcers were recurrent, his nerves made him nauseous, and stress came and went while his eyes were always on the blink. Too shortsighted to find one suitcase in a crowd of strangers, Nietzsche would lose a valuable traveling bag at a station. Drivers failed to find his hotel and dropped him in front of a tavern or a boarded shop. He would call his subsequent outrage "colic" and retire to bed . . . when he reached it. If Nietzsche tried traveling by boat, he became seasick, and again failed to locate his luggage when he landed. No wonder he would, like Tiresias—to compensate, and in self-defense—become a seer. Only Wagner could buck up Nietzsche's spirits with a bedside visit and his hearty manner.

The bearer of pain grows restless. Perhaps my hip, my catarrh, my fever, will feel better in another room, downtown, in the mountains, at the beach. And Nietzsche needed woodland shade to walk in, good air, quiet circumstances, abstemious quarters in expensive resorts. Thunderstorms unnerved him. Lightning made him seek his covers. Heat was the worst, unless it was the cold. He was always seeking solace somewhere else, although travel itself seemed to bring on migraines and seizures. The seizures were unexplained but serious and frequent. Sometimes, instead of a fit, he'd faint.

"During the past year," he wrote to his sister as 1879 drew to a dreary close, "I had *118 serious* nervous-attack days. Lovely statistic!"

Diets would do the trick, Nietzsche was told, and they nearly did him in. *Mann ist was er isst,* the saying goes, but a man is also his illnesses. When he vomited blood, quinine was prescribed. He had "chronic stomach catarrh," specialists decided, so his rectum was flushed every morning with cold water. He ate nothing but small helpings of meat accompanied by Carlsbad fruit salts, and at evening a glass of wine while the leeches were drinking. This folly went on until another physician altered the menu. It was impossible for Nietzsche to read for any unbroken length of time, and equally hard for him to have an extended thought. Tramping through the woods or hiking up hills was supposed to be good for you, and I imagine Nietzsche's increasingly epigrammatic style appealed to the trudging mind, while his habit of hyperbole suited the mountain views. Reading him, we have to remember his steadily worsening physical condition, and understand how longing for a life of healthy and happy exertion might furnish his philosophical notions with their favorite imagery. His style reflected the fact that he scribbled on scraps or dictated to friends. He wore optimism like a fur coat against the cold and, in his search for a satisfactory communal life, grew increasingly solitary.

Although Nietzsche's first essays and meditations were written in better health and circumstances, his later ones were done in defiance of his doctors' ultimate orders to avoid reading, writing, and "every form of extreme physical and intellectual exertion." But for this patient, writing was breathing and had to be done, no matter the pain and damage.

Nietzsche's first major work, *The Birth of Tragedy* (1872), was a shrewd mix of philology, philosophy, and literary criticism. Although it would be less obviously about its author than most of the work to follow, Nietzsche begins being Nietzsche here. German intellectuals had been infatuated with Greece since the 1760s, when Johann Winckelmann published his first adorations. This strange man's idolatry was fed by the fact that he never visited Greece himself but saw Athens only from the ruins of Rome, and it was encouraged by the profitability of his relationship with a fellow to whom history assigns the name Cavaceppi, a notorious "reconcocter" of antique statues. The art world's subsequent romance is investigated by E. M. Butler in her definitive study, *The Tyranny of Greece Over Germany* (1935). What the Germans believed they adored were chalk-white statues of ideally formed men and women who stood on their pedestals and pretended to be gods, each serene as a frozen lake, each perfected figure formed by a Greek master. What they also claimed to admire were the Greek philosophers and the classical world of reason, harmony, and proportion, as reverentially depicted by the Renaissance painters: clusters of togaed gentlemen reclining on stones or standing on white steps, conversing among pale columns in view of regimented groves, debating the nature of the right life. What they were actually admiring, however—Nietzsche included—were mostly marble Roman copies of Greek bronzes; copies, moreover, made by the imagination, since the originals had long since been smashed to bits or melted down to rescue the metal. When it was rumored that the sculptor Myron had done a discus thrower . . . lo! a discus thrower appeared.

When Nietzsche studied the Greek tragedies (for, after all, they *were* originals, even though a great number of these plays were also missing), what he saw were satyrs and bacchantes, furious women and horny men engaged in usurpation, revenge, and adultery; and what he read in those Greek texts was of a world that included drunken revels and much frenzy, pleasure taken in prowess of every kind, pain from the malicious blows of fate, constant conflicts of interest, not lives of rational detachment but lives of passionate commitment.

It hardly mattered whether Greek tragedy had grown from the antics of a goat god or not; the categories Nietzsche used to explain its origins were going to be in Nietzsche's permanent employ and shape his later, more developed, view of life. There is, in culture itself, a persistent tendency to replace the natural world with a human one, and thus to downplay the animal in man, that part of him he shares with beets, beasts, stones, and stars. The Greek soul had been traditionally divided into three parts, two of which linked men with the plant and animal kingdoms, and these parts were regarded as lower than reason, often demeaning, sordid, and troublesome. Nietzsche cherished his own myth about animals. Because they had no memories of the past or expectations for the future, they lived fully and richly in the present, connected with all that went on in and around them, fulfilled by their instinctive functions, feeding on others, yes, but without malice and basically at peace with their own species as well as all others.

Human beings have to get drunk to recapture this basic state—that's how badly off they are—or go to soccer matches, where they can lose their minds in beer and contribute to the madness of the crowd, or, perhaps preferably, listen to music so intensely they become the undulation of the notes, rising and falling, filling and diminishing with them, even moving their limbs to the flow like weeds at the bottom of a stream. "Consider the cattle, grazing as they pass you by: they do not know what is meant by yesterday or today, they leap about, eat, rest, digest, leap about again, and so from morn till night and from day to day, fettered to the moment and its pleasure or displeasure, and thus neither melancholy nor bored." "On the Uses and Disadvantages of History for Life," in *Untimely Meditations,* translated by R. J. Hollingdale (1983).

Yet only a small fraction of a napping cat is asleep, the antelope are on high alert as they graze, the buffalo stands still to listen, the horse lifts its head to catch a scent, the wildebeest remember to be cautious approaching the watering hole, or be scarce at evening, when the lions hunt; and they become a flash of fleeing limbs when smoke is smelled, or when a white hunter has sullied the air with his odor and dragged his ass, gun, and gear through the brush for a better shot. The community swimming pool is full of snakes and crocs. Every bird worries the whereabouts of its next meal, and pecks the dirt, bark, berry bush, or buggy air for protein. Alaskan flies can bite the flanks of a moose till it runs amok. Constant grooming is required to combat ticks, mites, lice, and fleas. Parasites luxuriate in the damp warm gloom of the guts. The glorious happiness of a mindless browse in the gentle sun is never to be enjoyed by these creatures; the peaceable kingdom is a world at war, at hunting and being hunted, at alarm and incursion, at lessons learned through pain and maiming, or death is else.

Nietzsche calls the immersed life of the beast Dionysian, whereas the Apollonian represents the specifically human, self-conscious, and hence detached mind of man. Apollonian self-regard separates us from the world, which becomes pure appearance. It dams our urges until they form a lake, and then releases spurts as it deems reasonable. The Apollonian likes the solitude and honor of the mountaintop, where his thought can see so far and delve so deep that those depths, when seen, see him; whereas the Dionysian prefers the passions of the crowd, the openness of alcohol, the bestirring of a martial air, the camaraderie of song.

Greek tragedies, if generalizations so vast can be made, are more obviously built on the quite real conflict between Dionysian tribal loyalties (the model on which feudalism is also based) and the more rational Apollonian communities asked for by the city-state. If civil societies were to prosper, blood kinships had to be put aside, family ties loosened, roots uprooted, and habits of revenge relinquished. Between ties of blood and rules of law, there could be no compromise. That was the tragedy. The hero was torn apart (as Orpheus, Osiris, and Dionysus literally were) because the future could no longer contain the past, because justice had been removed from private hands, because shame stained only the slapped cheek, and birth could not assign your rank. Nietzsche is a man afloat, who fears the reef but seeks the harbor. In him, our contemporary conflicts are writ large, and their intractable contradictions are our tragic destination. The Apollonian ideal has no better representative than Immanuel Kant, whose dream of reason was of a kingdom made by individuals so rational and so morally secure they legislated exclusively for themselves, but did this only after determining what could consistently serve as a rule for all: anarchy as it was meant to be, the achievement of the autonomous individual. This ideal is exactly where the pagan arrow lands after its long flight from Socrates's hand—at the feet of the ultimate self.

Nietzsche's insistence that the math of the classical world contained irrational numbers received small applause from his professional colleagues, and *The Birth of Tragedy* was bitterly attacked. Nietzsche, however, thrived on combat; he needed adversaries; it was necessary to his work that it be a way through a forest of ignorance; he was happy to let his enemies define him. Their protests energized him, proved him right. At the same time, Nietzsche reacted angrily to every caution he was asked to observe, to every mark of legitimacy he was expected to sport, to every kowtow he was required to perform. Because he had lost his father so early in his life, Nietzsche was especially vulnerable to mentors and too passionate in his choice of them, but they were never going to be around long. Hegel's world-historical individuals, Carlyle's heroes, and Emerson's self-reliant pioneers were everywhere hoped for, worshipped; yet, with relish, after a time of glorious regency, overthrown. It would be Schopenhauer's fate, and Wagner's also. Nietzsche would eventually overthrow himself.

Cate carefully details the remarkable career of Lou Salomé (a nimble, bright, strong-willed, yet surprisingly frail young woman, who was also escaping her past), naturally highlighting Nietzsche's "courtship" by omitting none of the affair's inept convolutions (an intellectual *ménage à trois*) as

Lou slips between the closing paws of Paul Rée (her positivist admirer, subsequently a suicide) and Friedrich Nietzsche (her other tutor—*le tiers*—and unhappy suitor) into the arms of a similarly futile and gifted swain (Andreas, her pathetic though scholarly husband, who threatened suicide if she didn't wed him), then briefly allowing Rainer Maria Rilke (her spoiled boy poet) to climb into her bed before bounding on to Gerhart Hauptmann (the playwright who has a character in one of his dramas kill himself and relieve the playwright of that necessity), until, finally—skipping a few beaus because she hid them better—she reaches Victor Tausk (fellow psychoanalytic student; soon, too, a suicide) and comes to rest in the company of Sigmund Freud (her teacher, colleague, and comforter), who, though ill of cancer, is charmed, wise, paternal . . . and appropriately famous.

This courtship, carried on at the level of eloquent adolescence by the principals involved—the beloved, her two suitors, fussy outraged mothers, nosey friends, a venomous sister—ends in misunderstanding, rumor, and scandal with tankards of bitterness all around, although, as a consequence, Nietzsche is set free of Rée, Salomé, sister, and a score of illusions about his life, which would henceforth be increasingly solitary and unfettered, except for the constant company of all those passive emotions that he rejected as often and as publicly as possible, though they privately clouded his every hour and darkened every memory. "My distrust is now so great," he wrote in an 1882 letter, "from everything I hear I feel a contempt for me."

With *Thus Spake Zarathustra* (1883–85) he would deny his demons. In the books of maxims and aphorisms that preceded *Zarathustra* as well as in those that would follow, Nietzsche used the same strategies in designing his attacks as you would for a war, because his was a philosophy of condemnation and exposure that defined its goals mainly by means of its oppositions. It did not tackle a problem, it assaulted solutions, and it did so principally by calling the solver's character into question. Logicians call this fallacy, appropriately, the *ad hominem*—i.e., against the man instead of the argument.

Moreover, the weakness of any idea and moral practice lay in its origins. Like Marx and Freud, Nietzsche looked to see in what hovel the bad had been born; in what expensive college the good had got its education; what were the "real"—that is, original—sources of some term's meaning, the reasons for this or that preference, this or that injunction, this or that exercise of power. As it had been, it still was. Logicians call this fallacy, appropriately, the genetic.

As if a crime had been committed (and Christian culture was a moral crime), the sleuth sought a motive: in the profits of the Church, the powers of the clergy, the persecution of heretics, the defense of dogma. If I tithed, I was buying my way into heaven. If I was charitable, I sought favor or wanted to feel good about myself. If I turned the other cheek, it was only for those above me and because I had to, while those below me I glad-handed and then struck with impunity. This maneuver is called the fallacy of the single cause. It also accompanies the fallacy of the fatal flaw as customarily as bread does butter, and not just because a flaw in the infallible dims the diamond, but because, when many considerations support a conclusion, a weakness in one may not be critical, whereas, after the reasons have been reduced to a single straw, a little kink is sufficient.

Nietzsche made an emotional machine of the syllogism. For instance, if he dislikes the consequence of some argument, he will allow his dislike to falsify the premises and make them merely an allegation. Evangelicals deal with Darwin that way. Nietzsche's use of language is almost entirely political: he sharpens his points by shouting, which inhibits a sober response, and repeats them insistently, as if he were running for office. He maligns the opposition, impugns its past, and adopts a prophetic tone as an excuse for vagueness.

To demonstrate the inhumanity of man to man, and therefore the corruptness of any human institution, I could cite data drawn from every column of the encyclopedia, but my evidence would not support the necessity of our malfeasances, just their prevalence. Similarly, cultural relativism relies on the testimony of a thousand quarreling tribes and ubiquitous differences of opinion. Yet from what generally is, one may infer only what will generally continue to be, never what ought to be. This mistake is sometimes called the naturalistic fallacy. The step from fact to value is so popular one might think it was a step that could be taken. St. Paul, whom Nietzsche despised, used several of these sophistical arguments to incriminate the whole of humanity—"in Adam's fall we sinned all"—since every disobedience earns the punishment due the first. Nor should I be inclined to welcome the bearers of the rack and screw into my company simply because, as Nietzsche suggests, bloodletting leaders are needed from time to time to stir things up, and disturb the repose of the mind (a version of the view that suffering can be a tonic), for I can imagine a hundred kinder ways to rise to an occasion, and find challenges that might need my mettle yet do not endanger freedom, limbs, or life. It is also true that a noble deed might be bad luck for an innocent bystander, and an evil undertaking bring bounty to another, but these outcomes should not dissuade us from good works, or excuse crime.

Nietzsche insisted that every philosophical position expressed a perspective—there were no absolute or especially preferable standpoints—but Nietzsche was allowed to have several, the rest of us only one; moreover, he misused the word in the usual way, emphasizing a subjectivity that is not necessarily present, since a geometrical perspective can be precise, as can a microscopic view or a measurement made by machine. Nietzsche accuses our slant on things of being narrow and skewed so that he can reduce it—as the strategy intends—to "only" and "merely" ours, whereas his is clear and wide and deep and sound as a sage's should be, standing on a mountaintop, using telescopic eyes.

Epigrams aren't arguments. A forest of hyperbole resembles a forest of bamboo: outside, one thinks only how to limit its growth; inside, how one may cut a path through. Some ideas are like steroids, and Nietzsche prefers those that make us stronger. "God is dead" did that for him, but he meant that the belief, not the deity, was done for, since what has never been can never cease to be. Nor is the belief—any belief—really dead: druids still frequent the forests, witches stir their kettles, mumbos jumbo, gourds rattle. Beliefs are running wild. Faiths fall, only to reappear as green and fresh as leaves. The Garden of Good Opinions has its weeds. What Nietzsche meant, and might have said—did say, in effect—was: a belief in God is no longer tenable to an educated mind. But what can we say to those educated minds that still exercise their right to be wrong?

Nietzsche threw up his hands. He exclaimed with disgust and despair. What else is there to do?

> A god who begets children on a mortal woman; a sage who calls upon us no longer to work, no longer to sit in judgment, but to heed the signs of the imminent end of the world; a justice which accepts an innocent man as a substitute sacrifice; someone who bids his disciples drink his blood; prayers for miraculous interventions; sin perpetrated against a god atoned for by a god; fear of a Beyond to which death is the gateway; the figure of the Cross as a symbol in an age which no longer knows the meaning and shame of the Cross—how gruesomely all this is wafted to us, as if out of the grave of a primeval past! Can one believe that things of this sort are still believed in?
>
> [*Human, All Too Human,* trans. R. J. Hollingdale,
> Cambridge University Press, 1986]

One stands in awe before the need of man to be deceived. When there are no satisfactory reasons for some heart-held conviction, and when it persists in spite of every philosophical complaint and scientific exposure—when, in short, argument is futile—one must look—as Nietzsche and Marx and Freud did—among folly's causes for the most vulgar, easily grasped, immediately profitable, and sanitized factors. Popular beliefs of every kind are held in a haven of unexamined premises and unacknowledged consequences. These beliefs are symptoms, not systems; they are ignorantly and narrowly held; they become treasured parts of the believer's sense of self; they are talismans to calm fears and promise hope; they tell believers they must be humble because their beliefs make them superior, and that all men are equal except the ones they are asked to shoot; they unite us as nothing else will and reassure the mind, because there really cannot be millions of such virtuous and faithful people identically mad and mistaken.

Up against such intractability, Nietzsche sermonizes from his own stump. And makes promises in terms his opposition will understand—from his perspective, mind you, but with certainty. Yet it is never clear, it seems to me, whether Nietzsche is angry with Christianity because it is absurd or because it preaches passivity and encourages acceptance. Any metaphysics or theology that denies life (those are his words), that prefers the status quo, will receive his censure. But why should one be optimistic when there is so little evidence for it? . . . in Nietzsche's life as well as ours. Because, brought to bed by a burning of the eyes, aching stomach, and bands of pain across your brow, in a cold, bare, rented room, disheartened further by your journey to it, depending upon people you can no longer trust, yet with your head nevertheless about to burst with announcements that need posting, you can have no other weapon against despair—forsaken by your own skepticism, seduced by visions of what might be, and betrayed by opportunity and your own soul—than one loud *ja-sagend* after another. But this is acceptance driven like a truck toward a checkpoint.

What is new in *Zarathustra* is Nietzsche's emphasis on process. Opinions are stationary. They should be no more than resting moments on a journey. So also customs, habits, values, hopes. We should continuously remake ourselves, because our species is the species that defies its definition, escapes its class, and evolves inside its own seed. Man must overcome man. This is not a recipe for our present practice of buying new beliefs like sporty cars and chic clothes when we can afford them, but resembles more precisely scientific refinements, progressive moral illumination, continuous learning. Everything can be comical. Let us frolic. Let us dance. Nothing is untouchable. Nothing is so serious it cannot provoke mirth. Nothing is sacred.

Back in the world of chronic pain, depressing news, and bad weather, Nietzsche is quarreling with former friends and future enemies, and grows closer in his own frayed mind to "the crucified one" than to his Zoroastrian namesake (he will soon sign letters *Der Gekreuzigte* or sometimes *Dionysos*); yet despite the insidious depredations of syphilis, which was probably the undiagnosed cause of many of his torments, he produces some of his most esteemed books, principally *Beyond Good and Evil* (1886) and *On the Genealogy of Morals* (1887). Nietzsche's behavior grew more and more uninhibited, as if, with an irony too bitter to be borne, the frenzied god had taken his body hostage, so it pranced and sang, with unthinking fingers played wild riffs on the piano, embraced strangers, or compelled him to turn on those closest to him in unrestrained fury, howling, sobbing while subsiding with weariness, then displaying a hunger for food that had not even an animal's limits. He was placed in an asylum. Later a patron, Meta von Salis, purchased a vacant villa above Weimar where Nietzsche and his sister (now his nurse and guardian) could live. Nietzsche was oblivious to the century's turn, now nearly a sofa'd corpse that visitors were allowed to view, a little like Lenin would be laid out later, although Lenin would be immune from the flu that slipped into Nietzsche's lungs, where, immobile as he was, it was soon a pneumonia that prospered until a heart attack ensued.

At the funeral services, they played Brahms.

Harper's Magazine, 2005
Published in *Life Sentences,* 2012

THE HIGH BRUTALITY
OF GOOD INTENTIONS

The great question as to a poet or a novelist is, How does he feel about life? what, in the last analysis, is his philosophy?

—HENRY JAMES

A rt, Yeats wrote in his essay on "The Thinking of the Body," "bids us touch and taste and hear and see the world, and shrinks from what Blake calls mathematic form, from every abstract thing, from all that is of the brain only, from all that is not a fountain jetting from the entire hopes, memories, and sensations of the body." Yet the world that we are permitted to touch and taste and hear and see in art, in Yeats's art as much as in any other, is not a world of pure Becoming, with the abstractions removed to a place safe only for philosophers; it is a world invested out of the ordinary with formal natures, with types and typicals, by abstractions and purest principles; invested to a degree which, in comparison with the real, renders it at times grotesque and always abnormal. It is charged with Being. Touching it provides a shock.

The advantage the creator of fiction has over the moral philosopher is that the writer is concerned with the exhibition of objects, thoughts, feelings, and actions where they are free from the puzzling disorders of the real and the need to come to conclusions about them. He is subject only to those calculated disorders which are the result of his refusal, in the face of the actual complexities of any well-chosen "case," to take a stand. The moral philosopher is expected to take a stand. He is expected to pronounce upon the principles of value.* The writer of fiction, insofar as he is interested in morals,

---

* Many contemporary philosophers feel that his function is to analyze meanings, not to discover or defend values. Some common defenses are discussed in "The Case of the Obliging Stranger" in *Fiction and the Figures of Life* (Alfred A. Knopf, 1970).

rather than, for instance, metaphysics, can satisfy himself and the requirements of his art by the exposure of moral principle in the act, an exposure more telling than life, because it is, although concrete, concrete in no real way—stripped of the irrelevant, the accidental, the incomplete—every bit of paste and hair and string part of the intrinsic nature of the article. However the moral philosopher comes by his conclusions, he does not generally suppose (unless he is also a theologian) that the world is ordered by them or that the coming together of feelings and intents or the issuance of acts or the flow of consequences, which constitute the moral facts, was designed simply in order to display them.*

It is the particular achievement of Henry James that he was able to transform the moral color of his personal vision into the hues of his famous figure in the carpet; that he found a form for his awareness of moral issues, an awareness that was so pervasive it invaded furniture and walls and ornamental gardens and perched upon the shoulders of his people a dove for spirit, beating its wings with the violence of all Protestant history; so that of this feeling, of the moving wing itself, he could make a *style*. This endeavor was both aided and hindered by the fact that, for James, art and morality were so closely twined, and by the fact that no theory of either art or morality has footing unless, previous to it, the terrible difficulties of vision and knowledge, of personal construction and actual fact, of, in short, the relation of reality to appearance had been thoroughly overcome.† James's style is a result of his effort to master, at the level of his craft, these difficulties, and his effort, quite apart from any measure of its actual success with these things, brought to the form of the novel in English an order of art never even, before him, envisioned by it.

Both Henry James and his brother were consumed by a form of The Moral Passion. Both struggled to find in the plural world of practice a vantage for spirit. But William was fatally enmeshed in the commercial. How well he speaks for the best in his age. He pursues the saint; he probes the spiritual disorders of the soul; he commiserates with the world-weary and encourages the strong; he investigates the nature of God, His relation to the world, His code; he defends the possible immortality of the soul and the right to believe: and does all so skillfully, with a nature so sensitive, temperate, and generous, that it is deeply disappointing to discover, as one soon must, that the lenses of his mind are monetary, his open hand is open for the coin, and that the

---

* See "Philosophy and the Form of Fiction" (page 641).

† See "In the Cage" in *Fiction and the Figures of Life*.

more he struggles to understand, appreciate, and rise, the more instead he misses, debases, and destroys.*

> In the religion of the once-born the world is a sort of rectilinear or one-storied affair, whose accounts are kept in one denomination, whose parts have just the values which naturally they appear to have, and of which a simple algebraic sum of pluses and minuses will give the total worth. Happiness and religious peace consist in living on the plus side of the account. In the religion of the twice-born, on the other hand, the world is a double-storied mystery. Peace cannot be reached by the simple addition of pluses and elimination of minuses from life. Natural good is not simply insufficient in amount and transient, there lurks a falsity in its very being. Cancelled as it all is by death if not by earlier enemies, it gives no final balance, and can never be the thing intended for our lasting worship.†

Even when William, in a passage not obviously composed with the book-keeper's pen, makes a literary allusion, as here:

> Like the single drops which sparkle in the sun as they are flung far ahead of the advancing edge of a wave-crest or a flood, they show the way and are forerunners. The world is not yet with them, so they often seem in the midst of the world's affairs to be preposterous. . . . ‡

it turns out to be a covert reference to "getting and spending."

Henry James was certainly aware that one is always on the market, but as he grew as an artist he grew as a moralist, and his use of the commercial matrix of analogy§ became markedly satirical or ironic and his investiga-

---

* See "A Spirit in Search of Itself" in *Fiction and the Figures of Life* for more on William's character and his differences with Henry.

† *The Varieties of Religious Experience* (New York: Modern Library), p. 163. God does a whole-sale, not a retail business, p. 484. The world is a banking house, p. 120. Catholic confession is a method of periodically auditing and squaring accounts, p. 126. Examples could be multiplied endlessly, not only in *The Varieties* but in all his work. In *The Varieties* alone, consult pp. 28, 38, 39, 133, 134, 135, 138, 330, 331, 333, 340, 347, 429n., 481, 482.

‡ Ibid., p. 450.

§ Mark Schorer's expression: "Fiction and the 'Matrix of Analogy,'" *Kenyon Review*, vol. 11, no. 4 (1949). The commercial metaphor pervades James's work and has been remarked so frequently that it scarcely requires documentation.

tion of the human trade more self-conscious and profound, until in nearly all the works of his maturity his theme is the evil of human manipulation, a theme best summarized by the second formulation of Kant's categorical imperative:

> So act as to treat humanity, whether in thine own person or in that of any other, in every case as an end withal, never as a means only.

Nothing further from pragmatism can be imagined, and if we first entertain the aphorism that, though William was the superior thinker, Henry had the superior thought, we may be led to consider the final effect of their rivalry,* for the novels and stories of Henry James constitute the most searching criticism available of the pragmatic ideal of the proper treatment and ultimate worth of man. That this criticism was embodied in Henry James's style, William James was one of the first to recognize. "Your methods and my ideals seem the reverse, the one of the other," he wrote to Henry in a letter complaining about the "interminable elaboration" of *The Golden Bowl*. Couldn't we have, he asks, a "book with no twilight or mustiness in the plot, with great vigour and decisiveness in the action, no fencing in the dialogue, no psychological commentaries, and absolute straightness in the style?"† Henry would rather have gone, he replies, to a dishonored grave.

The Portrait of a Lady is James's first fully exposed case of human manipulation; his first full-dress investigation, at the level of what Plato called "right opinion," of what it means to be a consumer of persons, and of what it means to be a person consumed. The population of James's fictional society is composed, as populations commonly are, of purchasers and their purchases, of the handlers and the handled, of the users and the used. Sometimes actual objects, like Mrs. Gareth's spoils, are involved in the transaction, but their involvement is symbolic of a buying and a being sold which is on the level of human worth (where the quality of the product is measured in terms of its responsiveness to the purchaser's "finest feelings," and its ability to sound the buyer's taste discreetly aloud), and it is for this reason that James never chooses to center his interest upon objects which can, by use, be visibly consumed. In nearly all of the later novels and stories, it is a human being, not an object—it is first Isabel Archer, then Pansy—who is the spoil, and it is by

---

* Leon Edel develops this theme in the first volume of his biography: *Henry James: The Untried Years, 1843–1870* (Philadelphia: Lippincott, 1953).

† Quoted by R. B. Perry, *The Thought and Character of William James*, 2 vols. (Boston, 1935), vol. 1, p. 424.

no means true that only the "villains" fall upon her and try to carry her off; nor is it easy to discover just who the villains really are.

Kant's imperative governs by its absence—as the hollow center. It is not that some characters, the "good" people, are busy being the moral legislators of mankind and that the others, the "bad" people, are committed to a crass and shallow pragmatism or a trifling aestheticism; for were that the case, *The Portrait* would be just another skillful novel of manners and James would be distinctly visible, outside the work, nodding or shaking his head at the behavior of the animals in his moral fable. He would have managed no advance in the art of English fiction. James's examination of the methods of human consumption goes too deep. He is concerned with all of the ways in which men may be reduced to the status of objects, and because James pursues his subject so diligently, satisfying himself only when he has unraveled every thread, and because he is so intent on avoiding in himself what he has revealed as evil in his characters and exemplifying, rather, what he praises in Hawthorne, who, he says, "never intermeddled,"* the moral problem of *The Portrait* becomes an aesthetic problem, a problem of form, the scope and course of the action, the nature of the characters, the content of dialogue, the shape and dress of setting, the points of view, the figures of speech, the very turn and tumble of the sentences themselves directed by the problem's looked-for solution, and there is consequently no suggestion that one should choose up sides or take to heart his criticism of a certain society, nor any invitation to discuss the moral motivations of his characters *as if* they were surrogates for the real.†

The moral problem, moreover, merges with the aesthetic. It is possible to be an artist, James sees, in more than paint and language, and in *The Portrait,* as it is so often in his other work, Isabel Archer becomes the unworked medium through which, like benevolent Svengali, the shapers and admirers of beautifully brought-out persons express their artistry and themselves. The result is very often lovely, but it is invariably sad. James has the feeling, furthermore, and it is a distinctly magical feeling, that the novelist takes possession of his subject through his words; that the artist is a puppeteer; his works are the works of a god. He constantly endeavors to shift the obligation and the blame, if there be any, to another: his reflector, his reverberator, his sensitive gong. In *The Portrait* James begins his movement toward the theory of the point of view. The phrase itself occurs incessantly. Its acceptance as a

* "Nathaniel Hawthorne," in *The American Essays of Henry James,* ed. Leon Edel (New York: Vintage, 1956), p. 23.

† See "The Concept of Character in Fiction" (page 657).

canon of method means the loss of a single, universally objective reality. He is committed, henceforth, to a standpoint philosophy, and it would seem, then, that the best world would be that observed from the most sensitive, catholic, yet discriminating standpoint. In this way, the aesthetic problem reaches out to the metaphysical. This marvelous observer: what is it he observes? Does he see the world as it really is, palpitating with delicious signs of the internal, or does he merely fling out the self-capturing net? James struggles with this question most obviously in *The Sacred Fount* but it is always before him. So many of his characters are "perceptive." They understand the value of the unmolded clay. They feel they know, as artists, what will be best for their human medium. They will *take up* the young lady (for so it usually is). They will *bring* her *out*. They will *do for* her; *make something of* her. She will be *beautiful* and *fine;* in short, she will inspire *interest, amusement,* and *wonder.* And their pursuit of the ideally refractive medium parallels perfectly Henry James's own, except he is aware that his selected lens dare not be perfect else he will have embodied a god again, and far more obnoxious must this god seem in the body of a character than he did in the nib of the author's pen; but more than this, James knows, as his creations so often do not, that this manipulation is the essence, the ultimate germ, of the evil the whole of his work condemns, and it is nowhere more brutal than when fronted by the kindest regard and backed by a benevolent will.

The Portrait of a Lady, for one who is familiar with James, opens on rich sounds. None of his major motifs is missing. The talk at tea provides us with five, the composition of the company constitutes a sixth, and his treatment of the setting satisfies the full and holy seven. The talk moves in a desultory fashion ("desultory" is a repetitive word) and in joking tones ("That's a sort of joke" is the repetitive phrase) from health and illness, and the ambiguity of its value, to boredom, considered as a kind of sickness, and the ambiguity of its production.* Wealth is suggested as a cause of boredom, then marriage is proposed as a cure. The elder Touchett warns Lord Warburton not to fall in love with his niece, a young lady recently captured by his wife to be exhibited abroad. The questions about her are: has she money? is she interesting? The jokes are: is she marriageable? is she engaged? Isabel is the fifth thing, then—the young, spirited material. Lord Warburton is English, of course, while the Touchetts are Americans. Isabel's coming will sharpen the contrast, dramatize the confrontation. Lastly, James dwells lovingly on the ancient red brick house, emphasizing its aesthetic appeal, its traditions, its status as a

---

* Illness, in James's novels, either signifies the beautiful thing (the Minny Temple theme) or provides the excuse for spectatorship and withdrawal, the opportunity to develop the aesthetic sense (the Henry James theme).

work of art. In describing the grounds he indicates, too, what an American man of money may do: fall in love with a history not his own and allow it, slowly, to civilize him, draw him into Europe. Lord Warburton is said to be bored. It is suggested that he is trying to fall in love. Ralph is described as cynical, without belief, a condition ascribed to his illness by his father. "He seems to feel as if he had never had a chance." But the best of the ladies will save us, the elder Touchett says, a remark made improbable by his own lack of success.

The structure of the talk of this astonishing first chapter foreshadows everything. All jests turn earnest, and in them, as in the aimless pattern of the jesters' leisure, lies plain the essential evil, for the evil cannot be blinked even though it may not be so immediately irritating to the eye as the evil of Madame Merle or Gilbert Osmond. There is in Isabel herself a certain willingness to be employed, a desire to be taken up and fancied, if only because that very enslavement, on other terms, makes her more free. She refuses Warburton, not because he seeks his own salvation in her, his cure by "interest," but, rather, because marriage to him would not satisfy her greed for experience, her freedom to see and feel and do. Neither Warburton nor Goodwood appeals as a person to Isabel's vanity. She is a great subject. She will make a great portrait. She knows it. Nevertheless, Isabel's ambitions are at first naïve and inarticulate. It is Ralph who sees the chance, in her, for the really fine thing; who sees in her his own chance, too, the chance at life denied him. It is Ralph, finally, who empowers her flight and in doing so draws the attention of the hunters.

Ralph and Osmond represent two types of the artist. Osmond regards Isabel as an opportunity to create a work which will flatter himself and be the best testimony to his taste. Her intelligence is a silver plate he will heap with fruits to decorate his table. Her talk will be for him "a sort of served dessert." He will rap her with his knuckle. She will ring. As Osmond's wife, Isabel recognizes that she is a piece of property; her mind is attached to his like a small garden plot to a deer park. But Ralph obeys the strictures *The Art of Fiction* was later to lay down. He works rather with the medium itself and respects the given. His desire is to exhibit it, make it whole, refulgent, round. He wants, in short, to make an image or to see one made—a portrait. He demands of the work only that it be "interesting." He effaces himself. The "case" is his concern. *The Portrait*'s crucial scene, in this regard, is that between Ralph and his dying father. Ralph cannot love Isabel. His illness prevents him. He feels it would be wrong. Nevertheless, he takes, he says, "a great interest" in his cousin, although he has no real influence over her.

"But I should like to do something for her. . . . I should like to put a little wind in her sails. . . . I should like to put it into her power to do some of the things she wants. She wants to see the world for instance. I should like to put money in her purse."

The language is unmistakable. It is the language of Iago. Ralph wants her rich.

"I call people rich when they're able to meet the requirements of their imagination. Isabel has a great deal of imagination."

With money she will not have to marry for it. Money will make her free. It is a curious faith. Mr. Touchett says, "You speak as if it were for your mere amusement," and Ralph replies, "So it is, a good deal." Mr. Touchett's objections are serenely met. Isabel will be extravagant but she will come to her senses in time. And Ralph says,

". . . it would be very painful to me to think of her coming to the consciousness of a lot of wants she should be unable to satisfy. . . ."

"Well, I don't know. . . . I don't think I enter into your spirit. It seems to me immoral."

"Immoral, dear daddy?"

"Well, I don't know that it's right to make everything so easy for a person."*

"It surely depends upon the person. When the person's good, your making things easy is all to the credit of virtue. To facilitate the execution of good impulses, what can be a nobler act? . . ."

"Isabel's a sweet young thing; but do you think she's so good as that?"

"She's as good as her best opportunities. . . ."

"Doesn't it occur to you that a young lady with sixty thousand pounds may fall a victim to the fortune-hunters?"

"She'll hardly fall victim to more than one."

"Well, one's too many."

"Decidedly. That's a risk, and it has entered into my calculation. I think it's appreciable, but I think it's small, and I'm prepared to take it. . . ."

* A remark characteristic of the self-made man. In the first chapter, Mr. Touchett attributes Warburton's "boredom" to idleness. "You wouldn't be bored if you had something to do; but all you young men are too idle. You think too much of your pleasure. You're too fastidious, and too indolent, and too rich." Caspar Goodwood is the industrious suitor.

"But I don't see what good you're to get of it. . . ."

"I shall get just the good I said a few moments ago I wished to put into Isabel's reach—that of having met the requirements of my imagination. . . ."

The differences between Gilbert Osmond and Ralph Touchett are vast, but they are also thin.

Isabel Archer is thus free to try her wings. She is thrown upon the world. She becomes the friend of Madame Merle, "the great round world herself": polished, perfect, beautiful without a fault, mysterious, exciting, treacherous, repellent, and at bottom, like Isabel, identically betrayed; like Isabel again, seeking out of her own ruin to protect Pansy, the new subject, "the blank page," from that same round world that is herself. It is irony of the profoundest sort that "good" and "evil" in their paths should pass so closely. The dark ambitions of Serena Merle are lightened by a pathetic bulb, and it is only those whose eyes are fascinated and convinced by surface who can put their confident finger on the "really good." Ralph Touchett, and we are not meant to miss the appropriateness of his name, has not only failed to respect Isabel Archer as an end, he has failed to calculate correctly the qualities of his object. Isabel is a sweet, young thing. She is not yet, at any rate, as good as her best opportunities. The sensitive eye was at the acute point blind. Ralph has unwittingly put his bird in a cage. In a later interview, Isabel tells him she has given up all desire for a general view of life. Now she prefers corners. It is a corner she's been driven to. Time after time the "better" people curse the future they wish to save with their bequests. Longdon of *The Awkward Age* and Milly Theale of *The Wings of the Dove* come immediately to mind. Time after time the better artists fail because their point of view is ultimately only *theirs,* and because they have brought the aesthetic relation too grandly, too completely into life.

In the portrait of Fleda Vetch of *The Spoils of Poynton* James has rendered an ideally considerate soul. Fleda, a person of modest means and background, possesses nevertheless the true sense of beauty. She is drawn by her friend Mrs. Gareth into the full exercise of that sense and to an appreciation of the ripe contemplative life which otherwise might have been denied her. Yet Fleda so little awards the palm to mere cleverness or sensibility that she falls in love with the slow, confused, and indecisive Owen Gareth. Fleda furthermore separates her moral and her aesthetic ideals. Not only does she refuse to manipulate others, she refuses, herself, to be manipulated. The moral lines she feels are delicate. She takes all into her hands. Everyone has absolute worth. Scruples beset and surround her and not even Mrs. Gareth's righteousness, the warmth of her remembered wrongs, can melt them through.

The impatience which James generates in the reader and expresses through Mrs. Gareth is the impatience, precisely, of his brother: for Fleda to act, to break from the net of scruple and seize the chance. It would be for the good of the good. It would save the spoils, save Owen, save Mrs. Gareth, save love for herself; but Fleda Vetch understands, as few people in Henry James ever do, the high brutality of such good intentions. She cannot accept happiness on the condition of moral compromise, for that would be to betray the ground on which, ideally, happiness ought to rest. Indeed, it would betray happiness itself, and love, and the people and their possessions that have precipitated the problem and suggested the attractive and fatal price.

It is not simply in the organization of character, dialogue, and action that Henry James reveals The Moral Passion, nor is it reflected further only in his treatment of surroundings,* but it represents itself and its ideal in the increasing scrupulosity of the style: precision of definition, respect for nuance, tone, the multiplying presence of enveloping metaphors, the winding around the tender center of ritual lines, like the approach of the devout and worshipful to the altar, these circumlocutions at once protecting the subject and slowing the advance, so that the mere utility of the core is despaired of and it is valued solely in the contemplative sight.† The value of life lies ultimately in the experienced quality of it, in the integrity of the given, not in the usefulness of the taken. Henry James does not peer through experience to the future, through his future to the future futures, endlessly down the infinite tube. He does not find in today only what is needful for tomorrow. His aim is, rather, to appreciate and to respect the things of his experience and to set them, finally, free.

Accent, 1958
Published in *Fiction and the Figures of Life,* 1970

---

* When, for instance, in *The Portrait* Gilbert Osmond proposes to Isabel, the furnishings of the room in which their talk takes place seem to Osmond himself "ugly to distress" and "the false colours, the sham splendour . . . like vulgar, bragging, lying talk"—an obvious commentary by the setting on the action.

† The ritual function of style is considered at length in "The Stylization of Desire" in *Fiction and the Figures of Life.*

HENRY JAMES'S CURRICULUM VITAE

The Intricately Constructed Phallus

As I opened the first volume of Sheldon Novick's biography of Henry James, *The Young Master* (New York: Random House, 1996), I had to stifle a cry of "Oh dear, are we going play palsy-walsy?" when I read, "Please allow me, after this brief preface, to direct your attention to Henry James, with whom I would like you to become better acquainted." My designated leader then began the tour of his author's life by drawing a curtain, like Parson Weems on a naughty Washington, to reveal that his man "is sitting comfortably at a sidewalk table on a broad crowded boulevard. Perhaps he is in Paris. . . ." How do you do, sir? . . . is that what I say? Then I rather impulsively asked myself whether I remembered Henry James being this chummy with anyone, although, after a thoughtful moment, I had to admit he must have been so with his nanny. Still, I wasn't sure I wanted to sit at a café table in a town I couldn't safely call by name, next door to a man palpably enjoying "his usual pink grenadine glacée, with two straws, on the white tablecloth beside him" while "watching the passersby with grave eyes." In less time than it takes to read a line, they would be "striking gray eyes," and the object of our scrutiny would assume a Napoleonic posture that, "despite [its] dignity . . . seemed to invite confidences." Ah. Confidences, of course. "A young man stops to talk, and then sits down with him." Oh dear. So my guide is going to take that tack. The paragraph, and the preface, conclude: "A couple in evening dress stop. Soon there is a circle of young people around him, and they remain until long after midnight, talking." So this is the Henry James we are to meet—a man-about-town and a magnet for youth? Well, midnight is a bit past my bedtime, I'm afraid.

I had heard the gossip. The gossip was that a number of industrious scholars had recently discovered a "hooray-he's-a-gay-guy" to put alongside Proust and Wittgenstein in the alternative pantheon, since countless previously unread, suppressed, or unpublished letters showed that the suspicion of gayness, before only briefly caught sight of, had to be changed to a conviction, because this new information replaced all prior hypotheses and removed their protections. These prior excuses for Henry James's apparent chastity were: (1) he had never had much of an active sex life on account of a lackluster libido; (2) there had occurred a mysterious injury to his back that had unmanned him elsewhere; (3) the women he loved tended to meet tragic ends—Minny Temple's death from TB had made him mourn, Constance Fenimore Woolson's suicide had made him angry—so he became as skittish as a wary cat; (4) his vital juices were so thoroughly absorbed by his writing and his delicate social studies that the impulses of ordinary men acted on him only indirectly, the way an initiated carom slowly reaches its culmination by nicking the one remaining ball into a corner pocket; (5) his psychology was such that physical desires were allowed to manifest themselves solely through an inordinate interest in the marriages of others, a trait odd for a confirmed bachelor, even though, in his circle, marriages were mostly matters of money and hierarchy, not love and passion; (6) or that ultimately James sought aesthetic transcendence, even saintliness, and was ascetic because heaving and grunting were simply not something a person of his excessive refinement should ever sink to, nor would he wish us to picture him doing anything that partook of common coarseness—eating kidneys ill-lodged in a publican's pie, for instance, or visiting the loo and enjoying his relief like Leopold Bloom.

Although the evidence was supposed to stare everybody in the face, it was also deemed scandalous and detrimental, so that otherwise admiring eyes were turned away, and mum was the word, or at least some form of discreet dismissal would be expected. Certainly, this has not been an uncommon reaction of biographers to bad news. They ignored Edith Wharton's adulterous affair with Morton Fullerton (gay himself Monday through Friday), and devoted followers of Wittgenstein wore zipped lips for some time with regard to Wittgenstein's homosexuality (as well as his "mysterical" leanings), to mention but two from a posse of precedent. For positivists the latter failing was by far the worse. Although Fred Kaplan's biography (William Morrow and Company, New York, 1992) had spoken of Henry James's homosexual tendencies plainly enough, Sheldon Novick, a lawyer by trade, apparently felt that there was still a case to be made, and in his first volume he argues his position as if he were before a jury.

The biography (which concludes with the second volume, called *Henry James: The Mature Master,* 2007) begins with another forward flash. The ill and aging James has had to leave his home in Rye and take up lodgings in London once again, and there we find him, entering his seventies, his typewriter on his desk and his literary secretary, Theodora Bosanquet, hard at it, transferring his voice to the page "through her strong, boyish fingers." But our guide has only begun beating his drum. "It is curious to think of James striding about the Chelsea flat evoking for her powerfully sensuous images, and at the last, when he was close to death, dictating *The Ivory Tower,* an intricately constructed phallus around which he set his characters dancing to Miss Bosanquet's music." If "boyish fingers" is sly innuendo, what must the ivory phallus be?

The Effeminate Old Donkey

What are the data that determine any person's life? Of the things we desire, do, see, think, or feel, what should be discarded like spoiled paper, and what should be retained? How shall the residue be weighed? How shall these elements be joined to one another? And why should we really bother putting the puzzle together at all, at such expense of time and cogitation, given that our own aims—our worship and our animus—certainly direct the construction—the gathering, the sorting—of even the least scraps of information? What is important to the genius of our author? Shall we watch, if we are able, while the Poet washes his hands in the lavatory basin? Or follow our subject's fingers slipping through her lingerie drawer? study her dance card? or count the clapping in his last ovation? Are we simply in need of matters of greasy fact, and desire to proceed directly to essentials as on a fast train, or are we altogether in love, and value like a sheared curl every wisp caught by a collar, every lip mark on a glass, any footprint made by our darling descending from a carriage, and regard the shriveled core of our hero's gnawed apple as a religious relic? Perhaps our prizes are to be those two straws lying on a café cloth, or are the ones we cherish peeking out the neck of an abandoned soda bottle?

Although we know she launched a thousand ships, we do not know the color of Helen's eyes. To look into Medusa's was to suffer consequences, but what of Henry James's gray gaze? Was what he saw sucked up and carried off into a narrative he was engaged in making, or has he saved a trait for use in creating a lady of quality? Was it filed with more looks like it—perhaps of apology or reproach—behind the master's imperious brow? Not long ago, biographers read Freud first, then made their subject a patient. It was an important but tiresome development, as most are. Other biographers buried their victims under mounds of data, a democracy of detail that admitted of no hierarchy and held out no hope. Still others loved backgrounds so much their portraits were like those avant-garde Turners that depict figures, castles, passes, peaks, disappearing in a smoke of color.

Novick is a novelistic biographer. By that I mean that a great deal of what he includes in his "life" is decoration. It is not necessary for the reader to know that "For a small fee, a stout red-faced woman carried off his dirty linen once each week and returned it heavily starched and pressed," but to learn these trivial daily tasks makes us feel at home. Still, unless the linen was metaphorically unclean, Lytton Strachey would not have given any notice to it. Of course, Strachey was not above pulling facts from their contexts as if they were aching teeth. Novick provides rich social and intellectual backgrounds for the actions he depicts. He is aware of his subject's psyche but he does not psychoanalyze. *Honorable Justice,* his fine book on Oliver Wendell Holmes, has prepared him for the necessity of historical and geographical surroundings, and he supplies them: hills, dales, barns, and towns; wars, riots, scandals, labor movements, acts of Parliament. But he is acutely aware that although James was an ordinary guy when nature required him to be— our bowels do more to make us equal than the revolver—it is Henry James's head that bends when he enters a taxi, and that not even a spot of tar on the street is safe from his scrutiny.

Novick is also attracted by the lonely little item that might enliven the page and brighten its story. Some are irresistible. When James's aunt Kate dies she leaves a rather hefty estate. Among the lesser spoils is a shawl to which Alice James is given a "life interest," and which, to an amusement that barely covers her annoyance, she understands must be returned to the estate when she herself is through with it—a restoration only her ghost can carry out.

The hazard for our text, however, is James's sexual orientation. It becomes an *idée fixe,* the "life" warped by this single somewhat suppressed inclination, and the reader begins to feel roughed up by its insistence, as if he were having to endure a repetitive ad whose message will follow him home like a stray, regardless of his dislike, his shouts and shoos, or his internal resistance. Sometimes loudly, sometimes in a whisper, the point is made. Often the issue in question is simply presumed. "His only indisputable love letters were written to men."

When we open volume two of this life we do not find ourselves curbside in perhaps Paris but in the upstairs study of Lamb House, Henry James's home in Rye, smothered in atmosphere, a sea-coal fire flickering in the corner grate. He is correcting the morning's dictation. One can almost see the camera approaching for a shot, say, of a manuscript page of *The Golden Bowl*. James's achievement matches his figure now: stout, massive, stately. Out of the dim, short days of winter, the persistent theme emerges like a figure in a trench coat. James is said to be traveling in "vaguely defined circles that a later generation—not entirely accurately or fairly—would call aristocratic and homosexual and that the middle-class press satirized as 'aesthetic.'" Yet even if not quite "fair," Sheldon Novick will mention it. Twice, in the next two pages, London's winters will be called "masculine," because they aren't the stylish Easter season of balls and banquets or the vacation flight of the family to a cooling seashore cottage. "Painters' studios . . . were masculine salons where artists and writers . . . formed intimate friendships." Friends, too, will receive this honor: "Arthur Benson was a slender, reserved, manly, and serious young man. . . ." A character, Hyacinth Robinson of *The Princess Casamassima*, when he decides not to commit the murder his anarchist organization has assigned to him, is said to have made a "manly choice."

The other sidelong word is "intimate," and these two are scattered like peekaboos about the text. When quizzed by his family about his London plans, James replies that he is "too good a bachelor to spoil by marriage." Novick gratuitously adds, "Of the intimate friendships that he has formed, he says nothing." As if he should confess to having taken up sodomy. A young, handsome (we must have these adjectives) Scandinavian sculptor, Hendrik Andersen, Novick's choice for leading man in this heart's play, is introduced with the warning that he will "be a most intimate friend." Is an intimacy measure available? Yes, it seems there is. Upon learning of the death from tuberculosis of Andersen's brother, James writes a letter whose babbling gush makes one cringe. Can its recipient really believe in the genuineness of the emotions so sloppily represented? Andersen is addressed with two "dear"s like a flight of stairs leading to a "dearest." James's heart is aching, bleeding, breaking. He is in torment. Having shown that he is in even greater pain than the griever, James invites Hendrik to Lamb House in Rye, where James is now living, so that he may "take consoling, soothing, infinitely close & tender & affectionately-healing possession of you . . . to put my arm around you & *make* you lean on me as on a brother & a lover, & keep you on & on, slowly comforted or at least relieved of the first bitterness of pain. . . ." Hendrick has lost a brother but he has gained a lover who will be—wow—another brother. So James's offer is not as erotic as it might immediately seem. While "panting" to see Benson, a new friend, the next day, James sends a note apologizing for not having written sooner, but says that, instead, he is looking forward to "answering you with impassioned lips." True—this is rather an exaggeration if taken for "hello, dear chap."

The evidence, such as it is, is in the letters, and somewhere in the 10,423 of those which we possess some explicit revelations may emerge, but what we have now are missives full of emotional hyperbole, effusive flattery, and infantile cajoling that become less convincing as the verbs of desire and the adjectives of adoration accumulate. "I love you" may carry some small weight, but "I love love love love love you" less.

Sometimes hostile witnesses can be useful to your case. Novick calls Frank Harris and Harold Frederic to the stand. James had finally reached such eminence as to attract attackers to him like mosquitoes drawn to CO_2, and one such was the new editor of *The Fortnightly Review,* Frank Harris, who "privately accused [James] of effeminacy, of being part of a shadowy conspiracy of homosexuals," and wrote in his autobiography that James's "well-formed, prominent, rather Jewish nose was the true index of his character." Unfortunately for this testimony, Harris's opinions were not expressed in print until 1925, when they were privately issued in Paris nearly a decade after the object of their malice had died. A better example is furnished by the novelist Harold Frederic, who was allowed to say in a letter to *The New York Times* (to my surprise) that "Henry James is an effeminate old donkey who lives with a herd of other donkeys around him and insists on being treated as if he were the Pope. . . ."

Oscar Wilde's plays aren't James's sort of thing, nor does their success improve his judgment of them, but James nominates Wilde for membership in one of his clubs, and supports him during his scandalous trial, although the scandal, for James, is often worse than the crime. James is not the kind of homosexual who feels he must always stick up for his sex. Novick, however, sometimes seems surprised. "In *The Tragic Muse* he gave what now seems an all-but-explicit and negative portrayal of an openly gay man. This latter has been particularly puzzling, because James's own loves were, so far as is known, exclusively male."

James was unquestionably attracted to young mostly gay men, and for a variety of reasons. There appears to have been enough sexual longing in him to serve a dozen, but in addition the young men flatter him, confirm his views and feelings; not only do their own effeminate ways match his, but, precisely because of the "feminine element" in their composition, they have more tact, sensitivity, cultural polish, and manners than bluff sailor sorts or other types of tough guy. James's androgynous character is one of his great strengths as an artist, and he knows that the feminine in men does not merely mean the loss of a rough edge, but is often the best, the most civilized, part of them. *Manly* is not his word of worship. *Civilization* is.

The Bachelor

If you are a bachelor who is going to be a bachelor because your career must not be compromised by more family obligations than you already bear, you will naturally seek out the company of like-minded single souls of both sexes but particularly of your own; so that to be often seen with men will not be worth a comment, nor will your frequenting of places where husbands are gratefully severed from their wives and children—of which an English private club is a perfect social instrument—be understood as anything less than necessary in order to enjoy, even if in visit-bits-and-pieces, what its members once, as bachelors, uninterruptedly took pleasure in: a quiet read, a nice port, a reposeful dinner, a good cigar, a leather-bound snooze. The club can be both your living and your dining room, or your library where you can borrow a book, peruse a periodical or the daily papers, rub the better shoulders.

To that end, Henry James became a member of the Reform Club, the Rabelais Club, the Savile Club, the Omar Khayyam Club, and the Athenaeum, whose library was especially alluring. "On the other side of the room sits Herbert Spencer, asleep in a chair (he always is, when I come here) and a little way off is the portly Archbishop of York with his nose in a little book." Later, in Rye, he joins the golf club, though he only goes there for tea after a long walk. To learn more of his chosen town he also frequents the local pub. James eventually has a bedsit at the Reform Club, and works there when beset by solitude's drearies at Lamb House. His steno, then Mary Weld, arrives discreetly through a side door to breach this manly bastion.

At the same time, as a bachelor you can attach yourself to the fluttering edges of various sorts of interesting or useful families by your availability for dinner, your help in small emergencies, your avuncular warmth, and, of course, because you are a person who may carry the cachet of significant guest and important friend from one place at table to another as if you were a slice of something from the roast. In addition to being agreeable, these relationships will be of great value to you when the materials that most stir your muse are the ins and outs of social commerce, the hypocrisies that support manners and put a roof on good behavior. Social life will not seem frivolous even when it is supremely so, and if you have cultivated the observant, ambitious, and witty, you will have anecdotes aplenty—ore worthy of being relieved of its roughness and rounded into impressive rings.

You will be a winner with brats of every kind, producing in them just enough fear and strangeness to induce attention and the relief of obedience. After all, the bachelor does not have to suffer the embarrassment of their education or the humiliations their maturation will inflict. In effect, you can play grandparent without the necessity of years. It is sometimes difficult for a father to put himself back in his own strident youth when he is the brunt of his child's complaint, but for the bachelor it is easy. He is already there; in a critical sense he has obtained every family's prized position—that of the only child.

The Busy Body

James spends an unaccountable amount of time socializing at his various clubs and otherwise dining out ("Dear Mrs. Bell, I am engaged to go to 4 different places this afternoon between 5 & 6:30, & to do, besides, 17 other different things"); when in London, which is often, he keeps rather regular attendance at the theater, often to see plays he will review; there are of course the customary weekend junkets to the sumptuously appointed country estates of the rich and titled—teas and shoots, stiff chairs and parlor pianos; as if evenings were not full enough, he has his own little dinners for six to preside over; then space in the day must be found in which to tend to the needs of his sister, the frequently bedridden Alice James, as well as other visits to the sick, and such good-Samaritan assignments as his tenderness insists on, for if you have many friends, you will have many bedsides. Sunday calls of courtesy are de rigueur, of course. One's calling card must get about even when its owner does not. More important burdens—the consequence of diligence and honesty—are overseeing the settlement of estates (Alice James's for instance) or acting as a literary executor, or arranging, over a considerable distance, the burial of Constance Fenimore Woolson in Rome after her suicide.

None of the day's drudgeries disappear just because you are busy elsewhere, so you must hunt for lodgings, hire servants, dispose of and acquire furniture, move from a pension in Paris to a room in Rome or a villa in Venice, because London is impossible in high season, Rye lonely in winter, Italy always enticing. During his frequent periods of depression, James is driven to seek a sunnier disposition in sunnier, lazier climes.

Visits to America were infrequent and irregular, but they required a major commitment. Often illness or death was the occasion for a crossing. He stayed in Cambridge when he had to, enjoyed New York when he could, and took a year off to travel the lecture circuit as far as Florida, the Midwest, and California, with intermittent halts to have some teeth pulled. At all points James was industriously absorbing scenes, gathering anecdotes, obtaining suggestions for plots and themes, learning about issues he might attach to his singular interests, and allowing his impressions to be absorbed by his ravenous artistic unconscious like a stockpot that is cooking its way toward cassoulet.

Then he must discover a moment for dashing off letters of a business sort or those required to retain his good standing in society (thanks for this socialite's party, that author's book, a weekend's pleasure). What cannot be dashed are publishing problems, theatrical issues, political causes. Naturally he must stay in postal range of his many, mostly intimate, pals. Novick writes that, while away from the city, James "kept in touch with his London friends by patiently writing letters in the evenings after dinner, often writing until the early hours of the morning." He saved his worn-out wrist and hand for these chores, and began dictating to a typist his articles and books, but his work as well as his social life were frequently hampered by various other physical ills: chronic backache and constipation, jaundice that seized him in Venice, those periodic depressions, attacks of gout that made him goose-step when he had to walk, and, as he aged, a case of shingles that sent him to bed, bouts of angina announcing the end, many of the latter accompanied by fears that he was bereft of friends and alone in his misery.

Meanwhile, James managed to compose new plays, or adapt some of his stories for the stage, and oversee their production; choose, edit, revise, and preface texts for The New York Edition; supply magazines with stories, articles, profiles, travel pieces, and reviews; furnish publishers with triple-decker novels, serialized romances, and singular masterpieces.

The Family Man

James's ties to his extended family were strong, yet he lived apart for most of his life, and his brothers fled the nest as if they had just burst from an egg. Women of James's class were slaves of their wombs and spent large portions of their adult lives pregnant, since families were commonly large, in a condition closer to an illness than a blessing, and one that often ended, not just shortened, their lives. Henry's mother managed to have five children in seven years, and although they were healthy kids, Alice, William, and Henry suffered from severe bouts of depression, William and Henry inherited their father's bad back, both lives would be threatened by a congestive heart, and, like a consumptive who catches cold, Henry would be a victim of his father's stammer. "James had twenty-one first cousins on his father's side alone. . . ." Henry's sense for the family bordered on the feudal, and that meant hierarchy, discipline, duty, property, and privilege. His immediate family had a dash of the ordinary in it, but father, daughter, and two of the four sons were extraordinary individuals. James himself remained uneasy about his roots until he acquired Lamb House, where he was finally firmly affixed to a place that would gather and hold history as he hoped it would hold him.

Full of envy for his sibling's success, William James does not come off very well in Novick's account. He is often in Europe for extended periods, alone; he issues invitations and then is absent when the guest arrives; he offers advice that is most always bad; he complains about the stipulations in his relatives' wills. William especially had to envy Henry's freedom from family routines, emotional demands, and daily tasks. At the same time he disapproves of his brother's swirling social rounds, since they cut into the time set aside for work. The family's complex relationships are handled deftly, and Novick uses amusing little details to enliven his account, which is often fuller than Leon Edel's earlier five-volume, businesslike approach.

As William begins to enjoy his own success and the brothers begin to share ailments like two old soldiers their war stories, they grow easy in each other's company and more confident about their responses. The pair share an intense trust in the senses; they are fascinated by the phenomenon of consciousness; both value the individual above all else and bring a moral passion to all they do. But how other and inherently at odds they also are: William the Scientist and a seeker of acceptable means, and Henry the Aesthete who values the intrinsic and the solemn worth of things in themselves: the Doer and the Viewer, one always going somewhere, the other always already there.

The Old Pro

Writing was once a genteel occupation, which meant it was meanly paid and casually esteemed. England, in particular, was a nation that cherished its amateurs. Philosophers did their thinking on their days off; writers wrote through the stillness of the night as their genius required and their obsessions demanded. Poets alertly awaited the call of their muse because she never rang twice. On the Continent, where rationalism flourished, scholars and philosophers had become professors, and what they professed was a discipline. They policed themselves, and standards were watchfully upheld. Professors formed organizations like guilds and enjoyed positions in universities and status in society. Professors were trained and professors were paid. Naturally they were rationalists, because it was important that their subject seem serious and appropriately strenuous. Empiricism was more easily espoused, and the English took to it as if the strain of thinking deep thoughts were simply bad manners. In America, Emerson, and later Josiah Royce, tried to elevate the level of thinking to German standards, but with little lasting success. Finally, the First World War destroyed most influence that remained. Who needed *Wahrheit* when sense impressions would serve?

Nevertheless, because the novel was such a popular form of entertainment, at no definite time, but gradually as twilight, it became a profession, too, even though writing was not taught in academies like painting or music. James becomes a hired scribe. So he writes what he needs to write to make a living, to get ahead, to please and increase his audience, and therefore to respond to demands of taste and form and subject. James is aware of the sort of compromises he is obliged to make if he wants to write for the lady mags and for the stage: "Oh, how it must not be too good & how very bad it must be." James knew his audience and had his order of battle, because a piece could appear first as a serial in a magazine ($), then in a nicely printed three-volume set as a novel of substance ($$), and finally in a cheap one-volume reprint for the arbor, the bedroom, or the train ($$$). If you are a realist, as James preferred to think of himself, you must undertake considerable research, and research always rolls the author toward the edge of journalism. To save time and increase income, a story may be puffed to the size of a novella, or modified to become a play, or taken apart to appear as vignettes. Travel has its pleasures but not their descriptions. Nonetheless, they pay the way. The loquacious master tries, but he can't write concisely (be, like Wilde, cynically witty) or baldly enough to achieve success in the theater.

James suffers the pains of haste, laboring to realize a deadline, canceling all the other occupations of life but for this one, a load of obligation that grows heavier as he waits for the moment when he can coldly push the installment out of the house ahead of its perfecting, onto a public whose indifference to perfection is not consoling. His wrist, hand, and arm begin to rebel against their years of labor. Eventually he will have to resort to dictation. It will be difficult for him to grant works like *The Spoils of Poynton* their due, because they underwent too many metamorphoses and would seem cobbled together, or because they were written in a rush only to light the flame under his dinner pot. Some of the disdain he felt for his readers was his shame at having written to their level. "If that's what the idiots want, I can give them their bellyful." More and more he resents the "monetary world" of the professional writer. Still, as he enters his major phase, he is sending out a prospectus for *The Ambassadors,* arranging for the publication of a volume of stories, setting aside *The Wings of the Dove,* whose plot has not impressed the publishers . . . in business up to the gaze of his great gray eyes.

James did not sum up the year's work each December 31 the way another pro, Arnold Bennett, did, noting in his journal that "This year (1928) I have written 304,000 words; 1 play, 2 films, 1 small book on religion, and about 80 or 82 articles"; but his year's receipts enabled him to lease his house in Rye. Bennett settled for a steam yacht. Neither of these word millers could complain about his output. As Novick says of James at the end of his late period: "In five years he had written a massive biography, a volume of short stories, and three of the greatest novels in the English language, all the while maintaining a busy social life, managing his own business affairs and a complex household."

The Great Masticator

In his own notebooks, James often talks to himself, tries to buck up his sagging spirits, encourage his muse to greater exertions, and remind himself of his duties to perfection. He is also not above threats. "I must make some great efforts during the next few years . . . if I wish not to have been on the whole a failure. I shall be a failure unless I do something *great!*" He gave public utterance to these standards in a lecture prepared for presentation during his travels in America, "The Lesson of Balzac." "The lesson [is] that there is no convincing art that is not ruinously expensive. . . . Nothing counts but the excellent; nothing exists . . . but the superlative." Of course, this is the lesson of Flaubert, not of Balzac, who bit off more than he could Fletcherize.

Overweight and feeling ill from the burdens of work, James resorted to the dietary methods of Horace Fletcher, the so-called Great Masticator, whose food fads were widely followed during the Victorian period. To recover his health, he begins to eat as he writes, cutting his food into very small bits, and then chewing those thoroughly (thirty-two times was recommended)— ruminatively, as the cow the cud—biting even liquids (good wines *are* chewable), swallowing slowly, savoring every flavor. You will write, read, eat less if this method is your model, and your bowel movements will be "no more offensive than moist clay, and have no more odor than a hot biscuit." A diet low in protein is also recommended. James's health does improve and he becomes a partisan of the procedure, even visiting Fletcher's palazzo in Venice. But James so ardently ground his food into gruel during his last years that he began to loathe food, if not his late style, and his doctors ordered him to cease.

James's novels were, after all, spoken into the ear and hence to the consciousness of a stenographer, who then repeated their character like orders to a set of ready fingers, fingers that spelled out what James had mulled over in order that they might be formed into an utterance in the first place; it was a slow process, like rekneading risen bread; so that now, as these words appeared on the typewriter's paper, they did so to their own reassuring music—the metronomic clack of the keys—and James's deliberate, clear, and careful dictation.

All fine writing should be speakable even if it is not actually spoken; it must be mouthed; for that is how we first learn language, how we make in the world our earliest contacts. Although the childish hug that James often promised his friends is more intimate, it has a compressed range of meanings, while we learn to say "love" as we learn to feel it, even if we later spell it "luv." To our earliest sounds cling our most ancient memories, and a word that is never said—such as "hendecasyllabic"—is dead. As James argued in his last American lecture, at Bryn Mawr, speech is "the medium through which we communicate with each other. . . . These relations are made possible, are registered, are verily constituted by our speech, and are successful . . . in proportion as our speech is worthy of its great human and social function: is developed, delicate, flexible, rich—an adequate accomplished fact. The more it suggests and expresses the more we live by it—the more it promotes and enhances life." James could not have envisioned the avid text messaging that now holds so many lines of vapidity open, as a window to a foul smell, or the thumb punching that has replaced the typist's skills, or the intoxicating space of ignorance and indifference that it promises to provide through its absence of voice, its lack of face to face, its refusal of touch.

His style is a kind of Fletcherizing, too, the cutting of his chosen experience into very small parts and the mashing of that until the original shape of the thought or feeling disappears and is replaced by a kind of cogitation that moves like a molten liquid through one thing, then another, until it finds its own form. Others may think that his stammer is a better metaphor, but "stammer" implies inability, whereas, when we properly digest our encounters, they dissolve into new uses and join the body of our being. The following example, which Novick more fully quotes (except that he ends the sentence early, with a period after "carriages"), may help to illustrate what James is doing. When Strether, in *The Ambassadors,* is standing on the balcony of his Paris apartment, inhaling the night air and sensing the palpable presence of his lost youth, the passage concludes (I have lightly diagrammed the sentence to show its rhetorical structure and phrasing):

It was   in the outside air
        as well
        as within;
    it was   in the   long watch,
            from   the   balcony,
                in the   summer night,
                of the   wide late
                                life
                of   Paris
            the   unceasing
                        soft quick rumble,
                            below,
                of the   little
                            lighted carriages
    that,
        in the press,
                            always suggested
                the   gamblers
        he had seen
                of   old
        at Monte-Carlo
                        pushing up
                        to the tables.

Mastication, as a metaphor, will perhaps serve the analytic side of James's style, but it leaves out the corresponding synthesis: how this sense of past possibilities left unfulfilled, and now beyond recovery, returns to Strether, as, so differently reconstructed, James returns it to us—through a waft of warm air, a few moving lights, and the sudden commonplace sound of a turning wheel on the carriages that will carry so many alternative lives away. Here, as always in his work, not only is every word naturally a sign ("soft quick rumble") but everything referred to by these signs is a part of the language of the world (carriage wheel) and the consequential understanding of the self (gambling tables). In this exquisite form, this perfect pace, in this small music, this crowd of meaning—here is our Henry: this is our man.

Harper's Magazine, 2008
Published in *Life Sentences,* 2012

GERTRUDE STEIN AND THE
GEOGRAPHY OF THE SENTENCE

I

When Gertrude Stein was a young girl, the twentieth century was approaching like a distant train whose hoot you could only just hear. A whole age was about to end. Nations would rededicate themselves, an entire generation bite into a fresh loaf, turn over a new leaf . . . tremble, pray. Despite this threat from the realm of number, though, most of the world went on as before, repeating itself over and over in every place, beginning and rebeginning, again and again and again.

Kipling had just written "The Phantom 'Rickshaw." Stevenson was about to bring out *The Master of Ballantrae*, Howells to publish *A Hazard of New Fortunes*, while recently young Miss Stein had composed a melodrama called *Snatched from Death, or The Sundered Sisters*.

Henry James had also been busy. *The Bostonians* and *The Princess Casamassima* appeared in the same year, almost moments ago, it must have seemed, and *Scribner's Magazine* was now serializing *A London Life*. Writing machines were prominently advertised in the same periodical, as well as a restorative medicine made of cocainized beef, wine, and iron, said to be invaluable for nervous prostration and brain exhaustion, among other things, cases of the opium, tobacco, alcohol, or chloral habit, gastric catarrh, and weak states of the voice or generative systems. Indeed, women were frequently in need of similar elixirs to combat depressions of the spirit: neurasthenia, sick headache, dyspepsia, and loss of appetite were the most common. Nevertheless, Adelina Patti was recommending Pears Soap. There were several new developments among stoves. Lew Wallace, Dr. Abbott, Motley's *Works*, Walter Besant's novels, Charles Dudley Warner, Rider Haggard, and a series labeled "The English Men of Letters" were being smartly puffed, as well as the stories of Constance Fenimore Woolson (grandniece of the novelist she was middle-named for and friend of Henry James, in Venice dead of self and fever) and an edifying volume by Charles Reade called *Bible Characters* (12mo, cloth, 75 cents).

At Gettysburg, on the twenty-fifth anniversary of the battle, George Parsons Lathrop read a very long commemorative ode.

> And, with a movement magnificent,
> Pickett, the golden-haired leader,
> Thousands and thousands flings onward, as if he sent
> Merely a meek interceder.

And at the great Paris Exposition, among the Americans represented, Thomas Hovenden showed his picture *The Last Moments of John Brown,* of which one critic said: "It is easy to believe that we are looking at a faithful transcript of the actual scene, and that photography itself could not have made a more accurate record." "It is the best American painting yet produced," wrote another. Holloway's reading stand was deemed particularly good for ladies, combining a book rest, dictionary holder, lamp stand, and invalid's table. It was sold where made, in Cuyahoga Falls, Ohio.

The profession of letters had been wide open to women for perhaps seventy years. Many of the best-selling novelists had been and were women, just as nearly all of any novel's readers were. If there were genders to genres, fiction would be unquestionably feminine. Swashbuckling historical romances were liked, Gothic scares, and folksy up-with-country sagas, too. Irving Bacheller's *Eben Holden,* a pale copy of that great success of two years before, *David Harum,* would still sell 250,000 copies in 1900. But above all by the turn of the century the domestic novel, in which the war on men was waged relentlessly right under their innocent noses, had become as necessary to female life as Lydia Pinkham's Vegetable Compound.

For some time Gertrude Stein had been absorbed, she claimed, in Shakespeare (of course), and in Wordsworth (the long dull late and densely moral poems particularly), Scott's wonderful *Waverley,* which made novel reading acceptable and popular in the United States, in the clean poems of Burns, Bunyan's allegories, Crabbe's country . . .

> Fled are those times, when, in harmonious strains,
> The rustic poet prais'd his native plains . . .

in Carlyle's *Frederick the Great,* Fielding, Smollett, and even Lecky's formidable *Constitutional History of England:* eminently heavy and respectable works of the sort I'd cite, too, if I were asked.

Prognostications of doom were also common, and increasing. Arks were readied, mountaintops sought out. Number for some was still number: a mark on a tube was magical . . . a circled day . . . a scratch on a tree . . . layer in a rock. The International Date Line runs like a wall through the ocean.

We can only guess whether the calendar had any influence on her, although later no one was to champion the new century more wholeheartedly, or attempt to identify America with modernity. The United States was the oldest country in the world, she said, because it had been in the twentieth century longer. In any case, Gertrude Stein, at age fifteen, thought frequently of death and change and time. Young girls can. She did not think about dying, which is disagreeable, even to young girls, but about death, which is luxurious, like a hot soak. The thought would appear as suddenly as moist grass in the morning, very gently, often after reading, on long reflective walks; and although it distressed her to think that there were civilizations which had perished altogether, she applauded the approaching turn. It was mostly a matter of making room. "I was there to begin to kill what was not dead, the nineteenth century which was so sure of evolution and prayers, and esperanto and their ideas," she said. It would be a closing, as the opening of puberty had been. A lid. Her own ending, even, did not disturb her. Dissolution did—coming apart at the seams—and she had, as many do, early fears of madness, especially after reading *The Cenci* or attending a performance of *Dr. Jekyll and Mr. Hyde.* She held little orgies of eating, liked to think and read of revolutions, imagined cruelties. She consumed anything, everything, as we have seen, and then complained that there was "nothing but myself to feed my own eager self, nothing given to me but musty books."

Scribner's Magazine was serializing *A London Life.* It contained plot, customs, characters, moral issues, insight, endless analysis, a little description, and went over its chosen ground often, like an elephant in mittens. There was another of those essays on the decline of the drama in a recent *Harper's.* This one was quite decent really, by Brander Matthews, and in it he argued that one reason for the apparent death of the drama was the life of the novel—the present art form of the public—in particular, the immense early success of Scott's *Waverley* novels. *Scribner's* July issue of 1888 catches up *A London Life* at the beginning of chapter V:

"And are you telling me the perfect truth when you say that Captain Crispin was not there?"

"The perfect truth?" Mrs. Berrington straightened herself to her height, threw back her head and measured her interlocutress up and down; this was one of the many ways in which it is to be surmised that she knew she looked very handsome indeed. Her interlocutress was her sister, and even in a discussion with a person long since under the charm she was not incapable of feeling that her beauty was a new advantage.

In "Composition as Explanation" Gertrude Stein would argue that between generations and over time, the "only thing different . . . is what is seen and what is seen depends upon how everybody is doing everything." "Everything is the same except composition."

She became, as she grew, increasingly unsure of who she was, a situation now so normal among the younger members of the middle class as to seem an inevitable part of middle-human development, like awkwardness and acne. Gertrude was a bit of a gawk already, aloof, cool, heavy, more and more alone. Her mother was an ineffectual invalid, gradually draining in her bed until, even before she died, she was emptied out of the world. Her father was a nuisance: stocky, determined, uneducated, domineering, quarrelsome, ambitious, notional, stern. When she was seventeen her father died, and "then our life without father began a very pleasant one."

Chapter V. In the old books there were chapters and verses, sections, volumes, scenes, parts, lines, divisions which had originated with the Scriptures ("chapter," for instance, a word for the head like *tête* and "title"); there were sentences, paragraphs, and numbered pages to measure the beat of each heart, the course of a life, every inference of reason, and the march, as they say, of time.

In *Four in America* she exposed the arbitrary conventionality of these often awkward cuts of meat.

I begin to see how I can quiver and not quiver at like and alike.
A great deal can be felt so.

Volume XII
HENRY JAMES one.

Volume XIII
The young James a young James was a young James a James. He might be and he might be even might be Henry James.

Volume XIV
Once upon a time there was no dog if there had been a dog nobody wept.
    Once upon a time there was no name and if any one had a name nobody could cover a name with a name. But nobody except somebody who had not that name wept.

Naturally the young James did not know, with William around, that he was or would be the Henry James, and Gertrude Stein had not yet covered her name with a name. In this same book, she imagines what kind of novelist George Washington would have made. She does not fail to observe that he was born in February.

Any autumn day is different

from any summer day or any winter day.

George Washington is pleased to come that is all who are ready are ready to rule.

Page 7

PLEASE do not let me wander.

Page 8

SHE is very sleepy. George Washington.

She is very sleepy. The autumn scenery when seen at a distance need not necessarily be tempted by wind. They may clear skies. But not a new moon. In autumn a new moon is well advanced. And a cloud can never cover it partly or be gracious rather to like red and blue all out but you. George Washington is famous as a nation.

Books contained tenses like closets full of clothes, but the present was the only place we were alive, and the present was like a painting, without before or after, spread to be sure, but not in time; and although, as William James had proved, the present was not absolutely flat, it was nevertheless not much thicker than pigment. Geography would be the study appropriate to it: mapping body space. The earth might be round but experience, in effect, was flat. Life might be long but living was as brief as each breath in breathing. Without a past, in the prolonged narrowness of any "now," wasn't everything in a constant condition of commencement? Then, too, breathing is repeating—it is beginning and rebeginning, over and over, again and again and again.

After all, what is the breath-before-last worth?

The youngest, she had been pampered as a baby, and she took care to be pampered all her life. "Little Gertie," her father once wrote, "is a little schnatterer. She talks all day long and so plainly. *She outdoes them all.* She's such a round little pudding, toddles around the whole day and repeats everything that's said or done." Yet she became, as she grew, increasingly unsure of who she was. Her eldest brother, soon off to college and career, seemed distant in his age, while the next, named Simon, she thought simple—as, indeed, he was. "My sister four years older simply existed for me because I had to sleep in the same room with her. It is natural not to care about a sister, certainly not when she is four years older and grinds her teeth at night."

She loved her brother Leo, but she had no trust of men. It becomes a central theme. "Menace" was the word they went around in. Still, she and Leo were invariably "two together two," although Leo always led, and when Leo went to Harvard, Gertrude later came to Radcliffe, and when Leo began to study biology at Johns Hopkins, a regular tag-along, Gertrude enrolled in medicine there, and when her brother went to Italy finally, she soon abandoned her studies to join him. They were together for a while in London, shared a flat in Paris, gathered paintings almost by not moving, like dust.

She shared something else with this brother, something deeply significant, something fundamental: an accidental life. When they thought about it, Gertrude said, it made them feel funny. The Steins had planned on having five children, and then, efficiently, had had them. However, two of these children died early enough they never "counted," and this made room for Leo, first, and then for Gertrude, so that when, at the beginning of *The Geographical History of America,* she writes, "If nobody had to die how would there be room enough for any of us who now live to have lived," she is not merely paraphrasing Hume's famous reply to Boswell, who, as the philosopher lay becalmed on his deathbed, injudiciously asked if it was not possible that there might be a future state: "It is also possible that a piece of coal put on the fire will not burn," Hume answered, meanly remaining in the realm of matter. "That men should exist forever is a most unreasonable fancy. . . . The trash of every age must then be preserved and new Universes must be created to contain such infinite numbers."

I do not believe she had any knowledge of Frederick Jackson Turner's frontier hypothesis, but her understanding of American history was based on something very like it: "In the United States there is more space where nobody is than where anybody is." There is no question that she, like Turner, thought human behavior was in great part a function of the amount of free land available. On the frontier, Turner believed, civilization was regularly being reborn. When westward the course of empire no longer took its way, Americans moved "in" and went east to Paris in order to go west within the mind—a land like their own without time. And Gertrude Stein believed Americans were readier than Europeans, consequently, to be the new cultural pioneers. The mind . . . The human mind went on like the prairie, on and on without limit.

It is characteristic of her method by and large that every general thought find exact expression in the language of her own life; that every general thought in fact be the outcome of a repeated consideration of solidly concrete cases—both wholly particular and thoroughly personal—and, further, that these occasions be examined, always, in the precise form of their original occurrence, in which, then, they continue to be contained as if they were parts of a sacred text that cannot be tampered with substantially, only slightly rearranged, as a musician might lengthen the vowels slightly or repeat the words of a lyric to compose a song, skip a little now and then, or call for an extensive reprise. "I was there to begin to kill what was not dead. . . ."

And what is Mrs. Berrington doing as we come to the end of this month's episode?

"Where are you going—where are you going—where are you going?" Laura broke out.

The carriages moved on, to set them down, and while the footman was getting off the box Selina said: "I don't pretend to be better than other women, but you do!" And being on the side of the house, she quickly stepped out and carried her crowned brilliancy through the long-lingering daylight and into the open portals.

(To be continued.)

Much must go, however good, for Gertrude Stein to be. A place must be made. But much of Gertrude Stein would have to be subtracted once she discovered who she was.

Born in Allegheny, Pennsylvania. It does seem unlikely, but in American letters the unlikely is not unusual: Hart Crane came from Garretsville, Ohio; Pound was born in Idaho; neither Michigan nor Mississippi has any prima facie promise; Wallace Stevens saw exquisite light in Reading; Katherine Anne Porter in Indian Creek, Texas; Edward Arlington Robinson in Head Tide, Maine; and for T. S. Eliot even St. Louis is odd. They mostly moved anyway. Who thinks of Robert Frost as a tyke in San Francisco? And the Steins left almost immediately for Vienna, where her father hoped that family connections there might help him in his wool business. He really did write back that little Gertie "toddles around the whole day and repeats everything that's said or done." After a period in Paris, the Steins returned to Baltimore, but soon they swapped houses, climates, coasts again, and crossed the country to live in Oakland, California, where Gertrude's father became successfully connected with, for god's sake, a cable railway company.

To be hoisted up a hill. And with certain exceptions modern American writing has been overwhelmed by space: rootlessness, we often say, that's our illness, and we are right; we're sick of changing house, of moving, of cutting loose, of living in vans and riding cycles, of using up and getting on (that's how we age), until sometimes one feels there's nothing but geography in this country, and certainly a geographical history is the only kind it can significantly have; so that the strange thing is that generally those years which both Freud and the Roman Catholic Church find crucial to our character are seldom connected to the trunk, except perhaps as decals: memorials of Mammoth Cave, ads for Herold's Club. Well, what's the point of being born in Oak Park if you're going to kill yourself in Ketchum? Our history simply became "the West," where time and life went. So what's the point in St. Paul if you are going to die in Hollywood of an alcoholic heart? Like Henry James we developed an enlarged sense of locale, but we were tourists. And Gertrude Stein lived in hotels, shops, trains, rented rooms, at aunts', with friends, in flats, with chums, and grew up with her books, her body, and her brother— nothing more, and no one else.

Of course, you could say that democracies have never had a history; that they cannot run in place; they must expand; they must have space. In New England, in the South, life went sometimes in another direction, and it was, naturally enough, one of the lures of Europe: to be in the presence of people who had lived for a long time alongside things and other people who had been allowed to live for a long time alongside them; consequently to observe objects and relations come into being, alter, age, fade, disappear, and to see that process rather constantly; to feel in things one's own use of them—like old clothes, maybe, streets, shops, castles, churches, mills—as one's own person felt one's self—in hills, paths, lakes, fields, creeks—since we seldom gawk at our own changes as though passing by on a bus, but learn to live them with the unconscious ease which daily life and custom gradually confer, like the wear of water and the growth of grass; still, Gertrude Stein blew "the American trumpet as though it were the whole of Sousa's band" and always spoke European brokenly; she was perhaps the last of our serious writers to, in the square sense, love her country, and she moved her writing, even through her own enthusiasms (Henry James and Richardson and Eliot), as painfully as through a thicket, straight into the present, where it became, in every sense of this she understood, "American" and "measureless."

But not in a moment was this accomplished. In a life. The resolution required would be heroic. Shortly after she began living in Paris with her brother, she completed a manuscript which was not published for nearly fifty years: a curiously wooden work of relentless and mostly tiresome psychological analysis which she called, with crushing candor, *Quod Erat Demonstrandum*. However, in this brief novel about the personal relationships between three depersonalized paper women, plotted as a triangle on which the lines are traveled like a tramway, the points incessantly intersected—in which, though much is shown, nothing's proved, and everyone is exhausted—

Gertrude Stein's sexual problem surfaces. Clearly, she has had a kind of love affair with another woman. Clearly, too, the circumstances of her life were now combining against her, compelling her to rely more and more upon a self she did not have. She lacked a locale which might help to define her and a family she could in general accept; she had grown into a hulksome female and become a bluestocking, yet she remained professionless and idle; in fact, she was a follower at present, fruit fly, gnat, silent in front of Leo while he lectured to their friends on his latest fads and finds: she was a faithless Jew, a coupon clipper, exile anyhow, and in addition, she was desperately uncertain of her own sexuality. The problem of personal identity, which is triumphantly overcome in *The Geographical History*, would occupy her henceforth, particularly in the most ambitious work of her career, *The Making of Americans*.

Furthermore, her brother was beginning to ridicule her writing.

Still she listened to Leo; she looked at Cézanne; she translated Flaubert; and this subordination of ear, eye, and mind eventually released her, because Flaubert and Cézanne taught the same lesson; and as she examined the master's portrait of his wife, she realized that the reality of the model had been superseded by the reality of the composition. Everything in the painting was related to everything else in the painting, and to everything else equally (there were no lesser marks or moments), while the relation of any line or area of color in the painting to anything outside the painting (to a person in this case) was accidental, superfluous, illusory. The picture was of Madame Cézanne. It had been painted by her husband. It was owned by the Steins. Thus the picture had an *identity*. But the painting was an *entity*. So a breast was no more important than a button, gray patch, or green line. Breasts might be more important than buttons to a vulgar observer, but in biology, where a mouse and a man were equal, in art, in our experience of how things are presented to us in any present moment, in mathematics—indeed, in any real whole or well-ordered system—there was a wonderful and democratic equality of value and function. There was, she said, no "up" in American religion either, no hierarchy, no ranking of dominions and powers.

Identities were what you needed to cash a check or pass a border guard. Identities had neighbors, relatives, husbands, and wives. Pictures were similarly authenticated. Poems were signed. Identities were the persons hired, the books and buildings bought and sold, the famous "things," the stars. She drew the distinction very early. In *The Geographical History* she would describe it as the difference between human nature and the human mind.

Gertrude Stein liked to begin things in February. Henry James has written *The Golden Bowl* and it will take a war to end the century, not the mere appearance of a pair of zeros on the mileage indicator. Never mind. Although the novel as it had been known was now complete, and Gertrude has meanwhile doubled her fifteen years without appreciable effect, still there was in what was being written (*Nostromo,* last year; *The House of Mirth,* just out; and *The Man of Property,* forthcoming), for instance, that socially elevated tone, the orotund authorial voice, the elegant drawing-room diction, that multitude of unfunctional details like flour to thicken gravy; there were those gratuitous posturings, nonsensical descriptions, empty conversations, hollow plots, both romance and Grub Street realism; and there so often remained the necessity, as Howells complained, to write with the printer at one's heels, therefore the need to employ suspense like a drunken chauffeur, chapter V's and other temporal divisions as though the author commanded an army, and all of the rest of the paraphernalia required by serialization and the monthly purchase of magazines.

She saw how the life of the model had been conferred upon the portrait. And in the central story of *Three Lives* (they were still stories), she captured the feeling she wanted in words.

> All that long day, with the warm moist young spring stirring in him, Jeff Campbell worked, and thought, and beat his breast, and wandered, and spoke aloud, and was silent, and was certain, and then in doubt and then keen to surely feel, and then all sodden in him; and he walked, and he sometimes ran fast to lose himself in his rushing, and he bit his nails to pain and bleeding, and he tore his hair so that he could be sure he was really feeling, and he never could know what it was right, he now should be doing.

The rhythms, the rhymes, the heavy monosyllabic beat, the skillful rearrangements of normal order, the carefully controlled pace, the running on, the simplicity, exactness, the passion . . . in the history of language no one had written like this before, and the result was as striking in its way, and as successful, as *Ulysses* was to be.

Neither *Three Lives* nor *The Making of Americans* eliminated the traditional novel's endless, morally motivated psychological analyses, though she would manage that eventually. "A Long Gay Book" was begun as another investigation of the relationships between people, in this case mainly pairs, but it gradually wandered from that path into pure song. "I sing," she said, "and I sing and the tunes I sing are what are tunes if they come and I sing. I sing I sing." For instance:

> Wet weather, wet pen, a black old tiger skin, a shut in shout and a negro coin and the best behind and the sun to shine.

She was readying herself for *Tender Buttons*. But what would never disappear from her work, despite her revolutionary zeal, was her natural American bent toward self-proclamation and her restless quest for truth—especially that, because it would cause her to render some aspects of reality with a ruthlessness rare in any writer, and at a greater risk to her art than most.

The household balance slowly tipped. Leo became enmeshed in an oddly passionless love affair, unsuccessfully underwent analysis, and looked more and more, in Mabel Dodge's judgment, like a suspicious old ram, while Gertrude, discovering the pleasures of "lifting belly," developed a "laugh like a beefsteak." Although the twentieth century had begun with Grant's massed attacks on Lee around Cold Harbor, the nineteenth had hung on despite Gertrude's efforts, only to expire somewhere along the Marne and in the mud of the Somme; but centuries don't end in an instant or easily, sometimes only in a lifetime. The Romantic Century took a lot of killing.

Alice Toklas came to live, to type, to correct the proof of *Three Lives*, which Gertrude was printing at her own expense, to manage, companion, cook, protect, while Leo at last left to fulfill his promise as a failure, taking the Matisses and the Renoirs with him, and allowing his sister finally her leeway, her chance to define herself, which she firmly, over decades, did: as an eccentric, dilettante, and gossip, madwoman, patron, genius, tutor, fraud, and queer—the Mother Goose of Montparnasse.

2

Buttons fasten, and because tender buttons are the buttons we unbutton and press, touch and caress to make love, we can readily see why they fasten. These extraordinary pieces of prose, which Gertrude perversely called poems, do much more than simply resemble the buttons she liked to collect and sort, though they are indeed verbal objects, and their theoretical affinity with the paintings of advanced cubism is profound. Like many of the canvases of Cézanne, Matisse, and Braque, each piece is a domestic still. They employ many of the methods of collage, too, as well as those of Dada disassociation.

Thematically, they are composed of the implements, activities, colors, and pleasures of home life, its quiet dangers, its unassertive thrills—cooking, cleaning, eating, loving, visiting, entertaining—and it is upon this base that the embossing of these buttons takes place. Plates are broken, pots and tables polished, meat sliced, food chopped, objects are repaired, arranged, contained. The highest metaphysical categories of sameness and difference, permanence and change, are invoked, as are the concerns of epistemology, of clarity and obscurity, certainty and doubt.*

Like a cafeteria tray, *Tender Buttons* has three sorting sections (Objects, Food, Rooms), but it is also built with three floors, so that its true shape is a cube. Objects are things external to us, which we perceive, manipulate, and confront. Next are the things which nourish us, which we take into ourselves: information, feeling, food. Finally, there are things which enclose us as our body does our consciousness, like a lover's arms, or as people are embraced by rooms. If the x-axis is divided as I've described, the y-axis is marked off into Work, or household chores, Love, or the complicated emotional exchanges between those who spend their daily life together, and Art, or in this case, the composition of odd, brilliant, foolish, accidental, self-conscious, beautiful, confused, or whimsical sentences.

For example, clinging to objects and dulling their glitter is *dirt:*

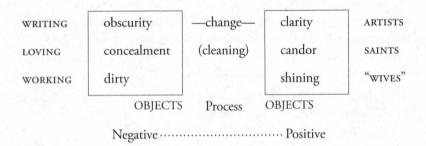

WRITING	obscurity	—change—	clarity	ARTISTS
LOVING	concealment	(cleaning)	candor	SAINTS
WORKING	dirty		shining	"WIVES"
	OBJECTS	Process	OBJECTS	

Negative ······························ Positive

That is, objects are either clean, so that they shine and glitter, gleam and dazzle, or, like the tarnish on copper pots, the grayness of dusty glass, the dinginess of soiled pillows, they are dull and dirty, as our lives become when we are left unloved and unemployed.

Throughout, the crucial word is "change." Some processes, like cleaning and mending, are basically restorative. They remove the present in order to return to and conserve the past. Others, like sewing, decorating, and cooking,

---

* Opinions about the methods, meaning, style, purpose, nature, sources, influence, or value of *Tender Buttons* vary wildly, though a consensus may be slowly emerging as time passes and tempers cool. To sample the range, for both bewilderment and profit, I suggest the reader consult: Richard Bridgman, *Gertrude Stein in Pieces* (New York: Oxford, 1970); John Malcolm Brinnin, *The Third Rose* (Boston: Atlantic Monthly Press, 1959); B. L. Reid, *Art by Subtraction* (Norman: University of Oklahoma Press, 1958); Allegra Stewart, *Gertrude Stein and the Present* (Cambridge, Mass.: Harvard University Press, 1967); Donald Sutherland, *Gertrude Stein: A Biography of Her Work* (New Haven, Conn.: Yale University Press, 1951); and Edmund Wilson, *Axel's Castle* (New York: Scribner's, 1931). Gertrude Stein talks about her intentions in *Lectures in America* (New York: Random House, 1935).

principally through operations which alter *quantity* (by shaping, enlarging, reducing, juxtaposing, mingling, and so on), create *qualities* which have not previously existed. Many times these qualities are positive, but naturally not always. In the human sphere, to which these activities are precisely proportional, similar consequences occur. Finally, both these areas are metaphorically measured against the art of writing and found to be structurally the same. Words can be moved about like furniture in their sentences; they can be diced like carrots (Stein cuts up a good number); they can be used in several different ways simultaneously, like wine; they can be brushed off, cleaned, and polished; they can be ingeniously joined, like groom and bed, anxiety and bride. Every sentence is a syntactical space (a room) in which words (things, people) act (cook, clean, eat, or excrete) in order to produce quite special and very valuable qualities of feeling. Cleaning a room can be a loving or a vengeful act, a spontaneous tidying, mere routine, or a carefully planned Spring Scrub, and one's engagement to the task can be largely mindless or intensely meant. Similarly, not a few of these buttons are as accidental as kicked stones (my typewriter writes "spoiled cushions" instead of "soiled" and I wonder whether I shouldn't leave the phrase that way), others are painfully self-conscious and referential, as planned as a political coup, while a few seem wholly momentary whims whose consequences have been self-indulgently allowed to stand.

Although the "poems" do not avoid nouns, as their author suggests she was trying to do, and have nice tasty titles ("SINGLE FISH," "SAUSAGE," "CELERY," "VEAL"), they avoid naming. Picasso's hermetic *The Clarinet Player*, for instance, painted during the same period *Tender Buttons* was being composed, offers no comment, visual or otherwise, on clarinet playing, players, or the skill of playing. After the motif has been analyzed into its plastic elements, these are modified and recombined according to entirely abstract schemes in which colors and forms predominate and respond solely to one another. The world is a source of suggestions, nothing more, and every successful work supersedes its model and renders the world superfluous to it.

Yet we are already in a tangle of terminology, because Gertrude Stein was always doing "descriptions," and she furthermore felt that naming was the special function of the poet. *Tender Buttons* is, she insists, a book of poems; poems are based, she claims, on the noun; and tender buttons are portraits, as she puts it, not of living people like Mabel Dodge and Sherwood Anderson, but of ordinary objects and common processes and simple spaces. Naming and not naming, describing and not describing, subject or sign: can we straighten this out?

In the first place, nouns are full of remembrance, since they represent collections of past experience, and although it may seem reasonable to encounter the present well padded by the past, this tends to give to every meeting of bell and clapper the same dull clonk: ah, there you are again, Socrates. We cease to listen, cease to see. So we must rid ourselves of the old titles and properties, recover a tutored innocence, and then, fresh as a new-scrubbed Adam, reword the world.

> I began to wonder at about this time just what one saw when one looked at anything really looked at anything. Did one see sound, and what was the relation between color and sound, did it make itself by description by a word that meant it or did it make itself by a word in itself. . . .
>
> I became more and more excited about how words which were the words that made whatever I looked at look like itself were not the words that had in them any quality of description. This excited me very much at that time.
>
> ["Portraits and Repetition"]

When she did her portraits, Gertrude Stein spent a great deal of her time listening, because each of her subjects was, as we all are, a talking machine, and of course what she listened to was in part a response to herself, to her talking. Now she wanted to stress seeing, because, of course, though frying pans speak and one might mutter to one's knitting, objects mainly spangled space with color and reflection.

We have bought a poodle. What shall we name it? We can, of course, confer upon it a name we idly like, and force it to conform, or we can study the beast until it says "Basket."* Yet the poet seeks the names of things because she loves the names. Al-ci-bi-a-des, we call out. Ai-e. Ai-e. Alcibiades.

> . . . you can love a name and if you love a name then saying that name any number of times only makes you love it more, more violently more persistently more tormentedly.
>
> ["Poetry and Grammar"]

To denoun and undenote, then to rename, and finally to praise the old world's raising of the new word out of the monitoring mind:

---

* Anyone interested in Gertrude Stein's attitude toward names and their relationship to the thing named should consult the Wilbur Wright and Henry James sections of *Four in America* (New Haven, Conn.: Yale University Press, 1947).

Poetry is concerned with using with abusing, with losing with wanting, with denying with avoiding with adoring with replacing the noun. It is doing that always doing that, doing that and doing nothing but that. Poetry is doing nothing but using losing refusing and pleasing and betraying and caressing nouns.

["Poetry and Grammar"]

Suppose, then, that I have a carafe of wine in front of me. My aim is to peel language from it like a label, and I shall then allow these words, put in attractive proximity, to draw other senses, sounds, and sentiments from one another. A CARAFE, THAT IS A BLIND GLASS is the name of the first Object (if these titles indeed are names),* and we observe at once (1) that, although the Object is an occasion for these words, it is the author who accounts for their singular character; and (2) that the heading possesses a maliciously ambiguous structure. The single comma is a kind of curiosity, and only one will appear in the first sentence of text which lies beneath it. Shall we read: "A carafe, that is to say, a blind glass," as if we were being given a definition; or shall we think of it as a carafe which happens to be a blind glass, in which case its blindness is not defining; or is it an exclamation, and should we come down hard as a hammer on "that": "A carafe, wow, is *that* a blind glass!"? Obviously the order runs from exclamation back through accident to necessity like a wound which leaves a scar.

The rest of the button is finished off as follows:

A kind in glass and a cousin, a spectacle and nothing strange a single hurt color and an arrangement in a system to pointing. All this and not ordinary, not unordered in not resembling. The difference is spreading.

Not every decanter is made of glass, but this is one of the glass kind. (The word "kind" will reappear.) Its opaqueness makes it a cousin to the clear. Blind people wear dark glasses because they do not desire us to see they cannot see and be disconcerted by rolling pupils or the glaze of a sightless eye. Thus this glass is not made for seeing but for being seen: it is not a pair of spectacles but a spectacle. A spectacle is normally something grand and extraordinary; however, here there is nothing unusual, nothing strange.

A bruise varies in color from purple through pale green and yellow, and as it ages, fades. I cannot say directly which of these colors the glass is, but each

---

* I have chosen this one not only because it is first, but because it has been heavily commented upon. Compare the treatment in Bridgman, *Gertrude Stein in Pieces,* and Stewart, *Gertrude Stein and the Present.*

hue is one which wine has: apple clear or straw or ruddy. The blind person's tinted glasses signify a hurt, too, and it is of course an irony when glasses are used to say that someone cannot see. Everything in a carafe flows up the neck like a pointing finger or a fountain. As we shall see. Words, as well, appear to point or fountain. Though these poems do not point, they have one. As asparagus.

Now I (the poet, the perceiver, the namer, the praiser) reflect: not upon the Object but upon the pattern I've made of my words and how they space themselves, for their space is inside them, not openly disposed upon the page as poetry normally is. I notice that my verbal combinations are, on that account, unusual (I shall brag about it), and that, although they resemble nothing else which passes for poetry, they are nevertheless not without their own system and order. . . . These sentences which form triangles, crowds, or squares go verbless as one goes naked, or which wind around Being like a fateful spindle.*

A kind	in glass	and a cousin,
a spectacle		and nothing strange
a single hurt color		and an arrangement
	in a system	
		to pointing.

GLOSS 1: These poems are like a wine-colored glass carafe. Their most common shape is that of a truncated hour-glass (an anticipatory interpretation).

GLOSS 2: The carafe is like a blind person's glasses.

So these poems are opaque containers. They have been made to fasten us through pleasure together, as indeed wine does . . . and most household objects and the acts which center on them: pots, pans, pillows, cooking, cleaning, love. The difference between these buttons and other swatches of language is going to deepen, she says, and there are going to be more and

* "I really do not know that anything has ever been more exciting than diagraming sentences. . . . I like the feeling the everlasting feeling of sentences as they diagram themselves. In that way one is completely possessing something and incidentally one's self" ("Poetry and Grammar"). These simple spatial pictures (hardly diagrams) are designed to reveal the functional rhetorical forms of her sentences.

more of them, not only because the book will pour them out on us, but because the principles of their composition will be widely imitated.*

The next button, GLAZED GLITTER, continues the theme of change with a first line which is immediately followed by a commentary:

> Nickel, what is nickel, it is originally rid of a cover.
>
> The change in that is that red weakens an hour. The change has come. There is no search. But there is, there is that hope and that interpretation and sometime, surely any is unwelcome, sometime there is breath and there will be a sinecure and charming very charming is that clean and cleansing. Certainly glittering is handsome and convincing.

Let us attempt to answer that initial question. Responses rise like hungry fish. Many household utensils are nickel-plated, because the metal they're made of may wear, rust, redden, or otherwise become unwholesome to use. Nickel is naturally shiny and easy to maintain (i.e., is a benefit without labor, a sinecure). Nickel has, in short, an impermeable surface, a glaze, which has a glitter.

But had the question been: nickels, what are nickels? we might have replied: small change.

However, if we listen intently, we shall hear inside the word two others of woeful association: "Nick," the name of the devil himself, and "hell," his hot location. Our license for following this procedure is, first, that Gertrude Stein regularly requests us to find other words within her words in exactly this way;† second, that a little research into the history of the term tells us that the original nickel was a German coin called *Kupfernickel* because, although it was a copper color, it yielded none of the metal, and for this deceit, like fool's gold, was accused of being the devil's ore; and third, that the lines which immediately follow, as well as all of the remaining poems, require it.

Snuffling at roots gives us another method for finding words in words, as well as another fundamental sense of what a tender button is: a swollen,

---

* If this is what she meant, she was of course mistaken, because the principles by which *Tender Buttons* was composed are only narrowly understood.

† In LUNCH she splits an acorn: "a corn a corn yellow and green mass is a gem." The title of the last Object, THIS IS THIS DRESS, AIDER must be read "this is distress, aid her," among other things, as we shall see. That poem contains the phrase "make a to let," in which the rent sign is missing its toy. Allegra Stewart has nice notes on these. There are innumerable others. .

underground stem or bud, a truffle.* That is, these poems are buds based on hidden roots. The fourth poem, A BOX, is explicit about this.

She often permits "this," "there," "they," and "it" to float free of any single reference, because she wants so many. These terms are like holes in buttons through which the threads pass. And in the opening line that bewildering "it" stands for all original nakedness and exposure. Stainless-steel souls, one imagines, need no cleansing, no catharsis, no cover. They are the ultimate solution to the problem of sin.

The spatial organization of this paragraph is revealing, and shows what I meant by sentences turning on the spindle of Being:

```
The change in   that                        is
                that                        red  weakens  an hour.
The change                                  has  come.
                              There is                        no search.
                        But there is,
                that hope           there is
and             that interpretation
and                  sometime
          surely      any(time)          is un wel come,
                     sometime  there  is                      breath
and                            there      will be      a sine-
     cure
and  charming
very charming                              is
                that
     clean
and  cleansing.
          Certainly    glittering        is    handsome
and  convincing.
```

* Allegra Stewart's essay on *Tender Buttons* (in *Gertrude Stein and the Present*), perhaps the most complete we have, not only sees the importance of the light imagery, and correctly names the central subject—purification—it also stresses the search for roots. Unfortunately, she frequently pushes past the operable derivations into Sanskrit. You cannot usefully explain tomorrow's murder by citing yesterday's creation of the world. The encoding, the disguising, the circular imagery, which she again locates beautifully, is soon smothered in Jungian obfuscation. The neglect of surface sense also lames her account, as well as an inexplicable reluctance to spell out the sexual references. *Tender Buttons* is an in-private, *sub-rosa*, discussion of the "marriage" of Gertrude (who, after all, is "dear spear") and Alice Toklas (probably, "child-less").

Having lost our innocence and put on knowledge with our leaf, we had to earn our keep, labor, sleep, and learn to wash. Like Alcibiades to the cloak of Socrates, cleanliness crept next to Godliness and made itself beloved by health and hospitals equally. Coverings grew grand and hid our weaknesses. We covered sculpture's plaster glands, legs of pianos, tables, too, and all our thoughts with discretions. These poems are themselves excessively discreet.

To red up is to rid oneself of whatever is extraneous and out of place (a small change, *e* for *i*), and the uppermost meaning here is how the work of tidying tires out both time and ourselves. Still, we cannot forget that "red" is the past tense of "reading," the color of blood and wine, of Jezebels, the suit of Satan, and the cent it takes five to make a nickel of. And any reader who observes Stein's sly small small-change in this passage (to mention but one of so many), must begin to be of different mind about her alleged subconscious methods of composition.

We hope of course that one day we shall be able to take it easy, draw an idle breath, purify ourselves the way we polish hardware and pots, clear tables, or better yet, cure sin, and cook without dirtying a dish. Cleaning, like confession, is a rite, and the spells it casts are effective, because a tidy house does seem for a time to be invulnerable.

There is no gratitude in mercy and in medicine. There can be breakages in Japanese. That is no programme. That is no color chosen. It was chosen yesterday, that showed spitting and perhaps washing and polishing. It certainly showed no obligation and perhaps if borrowing is not natural there is some use in giving.

The medical theme (one thread: hurt-spreading-rid-red-weakens-hope-interpretation [diagnosis]-breath-cure-clean and cleansing) is joined by the sacramental (another thread: "wine"-"Satan"-"the Fall"-hope-interpretation [hermeneutics]-breath-sinecure-cleansing) to become momentarily dominant. We do not receive mercy from God because He is grateful to us, nor does the physician feel he is discharging a debt.

"The change has come." If the change has come (unlike the coming of the Kingdom, to be sure, but love has been made with Alice for some time, and Leo has been replaced), it has come without our fumbling for it (reds, nickels, dimes, quarters, halves). One may borrow a nickel (after all, what is a nickel?) without any obligation to repay. Actually one rarely asks for the loan of such a small sum, and indeed a nickel is easy to give away. Later one learns how these little daily things add up, for a dollar contains ten dimes the way loving is made of lots of light caresses.

                        There is   no gratitude   in mercy
and   in medicine.
                        There   can be   breakages   in Japanese.
        That   is   no programme.
        That   is   no color chosen.
                             It was   chosen   yesterday,

            that showed   spitting
and   perhaps   washing
and   polishing.
                                   It

    certainly showed   no obligation
and perhaps   if
            borrowing   is   not natural
                there is   some use   in giving.

GLAZED GLITTER is a "poem" with a subject: roughly, the price of change and restoration, repairs and healing, the charm of coming clean.

A SUBSTANCE IN A CUSHION

The change of color is likely and a difference a very little difference is prepared. Sugar is not a vegetable.

Callous is something that hardening leaves behind what will be soft if there is a genuine interest in there being present as many girls as men. Does this change. It shows that dirt is clean when there is a volume.

I have quoted only two of this important section's ten paragraphs, yet these, and the two poems already so cursorily examined, make the fundamental moral and metaphysical issues apparent: the contrast between surface and depth, for example, the relation between quantity and quality, permanence and change, innocence and knowledge, giving and receiving, art and life, in and out.

Sugarcane, of course, is a vegetable, a grass, but the process of refining it transforms the juice of the stalk. Sugar is often a surface addition, as on cereal; it sweetens our coffee, for which we may be grateful; it enhances, but it does not nourish.

Again: if we multiply dust until it becomes earth, it is no longer dirt, and so long as Gertrude lived with her brother there was no suspicion, but when Alice moved in to form, in effect, a *ménage à trois,* or after Leo left, the whispering began. One must become hardened.

So sometimes work, sometimes writing, sometimes love are uppermost; sometimes one metaphorical carrier (cooking, cleaning) rises above another; key words are obsessively repeated, not only in particular paragraphs, but throughout; sometimes the sentences look over their shoulders at where they've been, and we are not always prepared for the shifts.

Although the text is, I think, overclued, the language plain, and the syntax so Spartan as to be peculiar, naked as a Dukhobor whose cause we cannot yet comprehend; nevertheless, the "total altogether of it" remains cryptic, and we are likely to feel that our interpretations are forced unless they are confirmed by readings from another direction. Some knowledge of Gertrude Stein's daily life and obsessive concerns is essential, as well as familiarity with the usual associations she makes among words, and the in-common subjects of her works. Then, not only must we fasten ourselves to Webster, as Empson chained himself to the *OED,* and avail ourselves of slang dictionaries, too, we must go to Skeat or Partridge as eagerly as a cat for cover on a cool day.

Thus this is certainly not an airtight text. It leaks. But where? and why should we care? It will not tell us what day the bridge is to be bombed, the safe rifled, or buck passed. We must set to work without reward or hope of any, and submit ourselves to the boredom of an etymological narrative.*

A BOX

Out of kindness comes redness and out of rudeness comes rapid same question, out of an eye comes research, out of selection comes painful cattle. So then the order is that a white way of being round is something suggesting a pin and is it disappointing, it is not, it is so rudimentary to be analysed and see a fine substance strangely, it is so earnest to have a green point not to red but to point again.

A box protects and conceals. It is frequently wrapped and tied. It is usually of wood or paper. Ribbons are found on it. A box contains surprises. Gifts. Pandora had one. Although a box is something one can get caught in, it is also something one can get out of. A jack is often in a box. A word is a

* To see what happens when you don't resort to etymology, compare the reading to follow with Harry Garvin's in "The Human Mind and Tender Buttons," *Widening Circle,* Fall 1973, p. 13.

box out of which we can draw other words. A woman has a box into which penises are put and from which babies are taken. To have such a box in our world, certainly in Stein's, is to be in a box (*hemmed* in). And so the passage assumes the structure of a series of Biblical begettings. Or are we listening to a recital of the pedigrees of prize stock? Etymology affirms everything at once, for the root of "box" is "tree" (the boxwood). A FAMILY TREE. THE TREE OF KNOWLEDGE.

The *manifest* text invokes two *covert,* or, in Stein's terms, covered, colored, or red, texts: a main one, the Old Testament tale of Adam and Eve, which establishes the linear order of ideas in advance of any other expression which may be placed on top of it, and whose verbal character is relatively *fixed;* and a second, subordinate one—the story of Pandora and the box of Prometheus—which is not fastened to any single formulation, and so *floats.* The *alignment* of the two covert texts is parallel, and the *relationship* between them is one of structural identity; thus the *function* of the secondary tale is to interpret and heighten and universalize the first. God makes Adam out of clay, for instance. Zeus shapes Pandora out of the same substance. Both are seen as vessels into which the breath of life is blown, and thereafter they hold that life like a liquid: wine or water. Clearly the two texts are accompanied by sets of traditional *interpretations.* For example, it is often supposed that Adam took a carnal interest in Eve only after the Fall. Both tales are antifeminist tracts. Both involve disobedience to the chief. Both are about revenge. Both explain why mankind must live in sorrow and die in delusion. And both invoke male saviors.

The principal covert text manifests itself immediately in two ways: through a *key* word or phrase—in this case, "box"—and by means of a *mirrored* rhetorical *form,* the Biblical begats. The key in the latter case, of course, is the phrase "out of." Even more darkly mirrored, with a parallel alignment and the same key, is the form of the livestock pedigree. Eventually the proportion—as men are to the Lord, so are women to men, and cattle to their owners—will control our understanding of the argument. Both forms, because of their associations, contribute substantially to the meaning of the passage. They are, that is, *significant forms.*

The manifest text contains a *coded commentary* on the covert texts. Each word must be regarded as standing for many others, the title A BOX referring to a blow as well as a container. Not only is *Tender Buttons* a *polytype* text, it is frequently *polytokenal,* too (see the formation of "kindness" in the first line). There is evidently a *metatextual metaphor* operating here. The paragraph before us is a box containing words which are also regarded as boxes. In short, the passage does not describe some object which the title designates as much as the title describes the passage. *Tender Buttons* itself is a metatextual metaphor.

The meanings we discover when we open these boxes are, like the covert texts, both floating and fixed; that is, certain associations are general: with the "red" which comes out of "kindness" we may connect a blush of pleasure, but we are not confined to exactly these words, as we shall not be to "shame" and "embarrassment" later. However, when we extract roots, such as "recircle" from "research," we are. These meanings have no serial order. They are *clustered* like grapes, and the way they are eventually fitted together depends not upon the order of words in the manifest text, but upon the way each illuminates various aspects of the covert text. At first we may want to think of "kindness" as kindness, but it is difficult to continue in that vein. Digging down, we find a few roots. We might favor "inborn" first, but "kind" seen as "nature" snaps into "-ness" understood as "state," with a satisfying certitude. We must not abandon "kindness" as kindness, though, because it is in fact the complaisance of the woman which leads to sin and kinning; but the incorporation of this surface sense into the total interpretation of the passage has to come later, after most of the ground floor has been built. Thus there is no pre-established order. We must wait until a place to fasten the meaning to the emerging sense can be found.

Except for the fact that the manifest text hides Adam and Eve like a leaf, the text is not *layered*. Certain themes or threads can be continuously followed, but sometimes one will be more obvious or dominant than another, so it is more accurate to describe the text as *woven*. Since the text often looks at itself, it is *reflexive*, and since meanings which emerge rather late in the manifest text must often be sent back to the beginning like unlucky players, the *presentation of meaning is spatial*, not temporal the way, for example, "John hit Jack" is temporal. It is temporal, that is, until we decide that "John" is Jack and "Jack" John. Then the sentence spatializes, swinging back and forth.

```
John hit Jack          Jack  hit  John          John hit Jack . . .
     |                   ↑         |                   ↑
     is                  is        is                  is
     ↓                   |         ↓                   |
John  was hit by  John          Jack  was hit by  John
```

This swing can be corralled, as Gertrude does in the case of her overly famous tag:

Civilization begins with a rose.

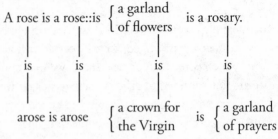

A rose is a rose::is ⎰ a garland ⎱   is a rosary.
                     ⎱ of flowers ⎰

| | | |
is   is   is   is
| | | |

arose is arose   ⎰ a crown for ⎱ is ⎰ a garland
                 ⎱ the Virgin ⎰   ⎱ of prayers

These chaplets retain the plainest syntax, but beneath the simple grammar of these buttons lie meanings which have nearly lost their syntactical value, becoming astonishingly *plastic*. Let's take a look at some of the etymological clusters.

```
              -ness = state    -ness                    -ness
Out of   kindness   comes    redness and out of    rudeness comes
         kind————————► red = kindred            rude = rubble, rubbish
         kind = nature          (dread of kin)   rud  = red
              = in-born       = blood                 = c·rude
         kin  = genus    rudd = (fish)spawn      LL. eruderare: to clear of
              = gender                           rubbish, to purify, hence
                    GENESIS                           = impurity
         (kine)
```

```
                                        -ion = state
rapid           same            question,                    out of an
rapt                    = image,    quest = judicial interrogation
rap = to snatch         likeness        = inquisition
rape
```

```
                              se = separation
                             /         \
            re = back to original        -ion = state
eye comes     research, out of      selection comes
              search = circle       lect = gather, pick (fruit)
              seek                   legere oculis: assemble letters with the eye
eye ————— see —————————► se(e) = read
```

```
painful            cattle.              So then the order is that a
pain = punishment chattel = property, esp.   ord = rank of threads in weaving
                              domesticated bovines.
```

white   some = same   sug = under
                    way of being   round   is something   suggesting
        = gleaming   wag = move   = roll   = assembly   gerere = bear
                    via = route   = role   = court   geste = tale
                            rota = public way   jest
                            rote = repetition   gestate

            dis = separate
            appoint
a pin and is it   *disappointing, it is not, it is so*   *rudimentary*
  point   pungent = prick   rud, etc.
  pen   punctuate
  penis   pugil = boxer
                     pug = fist

        ana = on, up, un-   sub = under
to be *analyzed and see a fine*   substance   *strangely,*
    lose   final   stance   externally,
    loose = free   finis = boundary =   stand = resist   from the outside
                   mark on tree
                   = end (good)
            fine = monetary settlement

it is so earnest *to have a*   *green*   *point not to red*
        = pledge   = to grow green as grass is   q.v.
        = observe closely   vide: graze
        = contest (duel)

but to point again.
    q.v. = gain-say: contradict

The entire passage is held together by underlying meanings which are greatly akin and often simply repeat one another—a familiar characteristic of Stein's manifest texts—and the passage is pushed forward as much by the progressive disclosure of these deep meanings as by ordinary linear onset. There is a cluster around what might be called the idea of an early state; there's one around gestation, blood, and pain, as well as punishment and judgment; there's still another around resistance, repetition, and property. There is finally a solution expressed in the dimmest imagery of all: the target with its black bull's-eye.

I recall particularly that Zeus, desiring to punish Prometheus for stealing fire from the gods and giving it to man, fashioned a beautiful woman out of clay, clothing her like a queen and, with the help of the Four Winds, breathing life into her according to the customary recipe. This done, he sent his glittering clay creature to the brother of Prometheus as a gift, but Epimetheus, warned not to accept any favors from Zeus (as though to "beware of gods bearing gifts"), politely refused her until Zeus frightened him by chaining his disobedient brother to a pillar high in the mountains, where a vulture ate by day the liver which grew heedlessly back by night (just as waking life was to be ruinous for us ever afterward). Pandora, of course, capricious and willful and curious, opened the box in which Prometheus had bottled all the evils which might beset man, among them delusive hope whose sting keeps us from suicide and still alive to suffer the bites of the others.

Similarly, Satan ("red"), speaking through a serpent and by tradition from a tree ("box"), tempts Eve in paradise ("kindness") to pick ("selection") and eat the apple ("box," "red"). A whole set of derivations indicates that we should interpret this act as a case of praiseworthy resistance. (No time is wasted on Adam.) *Kindness is thus reduced to rudeness.* God soon ("rapid") seeks out ("research") the impure pair ("rudeness") and holds an official investigation ("question"). He finds that their eyes ("eye") are now open; they see ("research") that they are naked, and are consequently full of shame ("red"). His judgment ("question") is that Eve shall belong to her husband like a chattel and bear her children ("kindred") henceforward in pain and labor ("painful cattle"). At the point of the first full stop, there is a definite break in the text. In order to go on, we must go back.

And who are "we" at this point? Not even Gertrude would have read this far.

Without the myths of Eve and Pandora I should have no sounding board, no principle of selection, nothing to paste my conjectures to, however remarkably I imagined them. So far what have I been made to do? I have been required to put roots and shoots and little stems and tendrils together much as their author did, to wander discouraged and confused as Hansel and Gretel through a dark wood of witches, to strike the hot right way suddenly, but just as suddenly to mire, to drag, to speed, to shout Urreek! to fall asleep, to submit to revelations, certainly to curl a lip, to doubt, unnose a disdainful snort, snick a superior snicker, curse, and then at some point not very pleasantly to realize that the game I'm playing is the game of creation itself, because *Tender Buttons* is above all a book of kits like those from which harpsichords or paper planes or model bottle-boats are fashioned, with intricacy no objection, patience a demand, unreadable plans a pleasure. So I am pulling a poem out of this BOX. The words on the page do not contain it, but their conundrum does.

Adam and Eve now beget children who, though innocent infants for a time ("rudeness") have the same inborn impulses ("kindness"), so that shortly ("rapid") they manifest the same lusts and suffer the same punishment as their parents ("rapid same question"). The cycle ("research") of generation ("kindness") is viciously continuous ("redness"), and soon ("rapid") women are being picked ("selection") as Eve once was ("eye"), and bred ("rapid") like cattle.

So God's command ("order") is that the common way ("round," "way") is a repetition ("round") of that first fornication and painful multiplication ("something suggesting a pin"). There is, in effect, a second break in the argument here, so, with a little help from the final lines, I shall loop back over these still unclear combinations. The Virgin Mother was spared both sin and pain, shame and copulation. Her child was engendered by the prick of light from a star (see the section A WAIST). While gloomily researching "point" (whose "disappoint" deprives the "pin" of its pain), I come upon the phrase *"de pointe en blanc"* (from a point in the white of a target), and everything rattles into place like iron gates. But will it rattle for you unless you labor? Something fired point-blank is fired from the outer white toward the bull's-eye—that is, from a point so close that an arrow needs no compensatory arc in its travel to the target. Its path ("way") is straight (as a pin). So the chaste way of becoming pregnant is through that gleaming straight arrow of light from a star, while the common way requires mating with a bull.

The consequences of our investigation of this basic and traditional myth, reducing it to small rubblelike bits ("rudimentary"), the paragraph goes on to say, is not disappointing, because it shows how the penis may be removed ("disappointing"), and how the woman's struggle ("substance," "earnest," and so on) to escape male domination ("analysis") can be won ("fine"). She ("a green") must turn not to her complementary, the male ("red"), but to his opposite, her own sex ("to the point again").

In sum, A BOX is an ironic argument (the jest in "suggesting") for lesbianism on the ground that such sexual practices preserve virginity, avoid God's punishment, and do not perpetuate original sin.

Now that A BOX has been broken down, we can look back at that CARAFE, THAT IS A BLIND GLASS, with eyes from which the scales have fallen. FitzGerald's Omar, among others, testifies to the commonness of the metaphor which, on Old Testament authority, pictures man as a clay vessel containing a gaseous spirit or liquidy soul.

XLIV

Why, if the Soul can fling the Dust aside,
And naked on the Air of Heaven ride,
    Wer't not a Shame—wer't not a Shame for him
In this clay carcase crippled to abide?

Mankind, before eating from the tree, was a blind glass, a carafe (an object and a word of Spanish and Arabic origin). Women were also a "kind," inborn, cousin to man, taken out of his side by caesarean; thus neither sex was a stranger to the other, and both were designed from the first for copulation. Nevertheless, as time passes and people disperse and multiply, the differences between men and women aggravate and widen.

The techniques at work here do more than allow Gertrude Stein to disguise her drift. They permit a simply astonishing condensation. The word "difference" alone contains *to carry apart, delay, disperse, to bear* (*as fruit*). And this inner economy facilitates the interweaving of contradictory strands of meaning within a single sentence.

When we try to grasp the significance of these truly peculiar pieces, it helps to remember that their composition was stimulated by a trip Gertrude and Alice made to Spain in 1912; that Robert W. Service brought out *Rhymes of a Rolling Stone* the same year; that Gertrude's household was breaking up and her affections had been rearranged; that not a line of Joyce or Eliot had appeared, though there'd been some Pound and a little of the greater Yeats; that Havelock Ellis had been arguing for the equality of women with great reasonableness and little effect, though the suffragettes were out in strength; that Rilke's thing-poems, in print, quite miraculous, quite beautiful, quite other, were in effect as invisible as the spirit of the vagina'd Spanish saints, although everywhere both writers saw sanctity's black battledress and the Southern region's austere landscape redolent with renunciation like a vine; that in fifteen years *The Well of Loneliness*, genteel, inept, and as unlibidinous as beets, will still cause a scandal; that the Dadaists haven't uttered their first da yet, let alone their second; that a play can be driven from the boards because it shows one woman giving another a bunch of violets, and that when Colette kissed Missy on the mouth in one such there was a howl of rage; that in those Andalusian towns where Jewish, Muslim, and Catholic cultures came together with a crash, their ignorant collision created buildings—rather than rubble—whose elastic functions, dubious faith, and confusing beauty were nearly proofs, even to a Jew, of a triune god; that people in the United States are really reading Rex Beach or James Oliver

Curwood; and that only Apollinaire might have preceded her in her aims, a few methods, and some effects.

Words, of course, were tender buttons, to be sorted and played with, admired and arranged, and she felt that language in English literature had become increasingly stiff and resistant, and that words had to be pried out of their formulas, freed, and allowed to regain their former Elizabethan fluidity,* but it is now evident, I think, that she had other motives—indeed, the same ones which had driven her into writing in the first place—the search for and discovery of Gertrude Stein, and the recording of her daily life, her thoughts, her passions.†

One does not need to speak in code of Adam and Eve, though if you are going to take Eve's side against the serpent, God, and Adam—all—you had better begin to dip your tongue in honey; but what about the pleasures of cunnilingus or the dildo, of what she was later, as she grew more frank, to call "lifting belly"? Even Natalie Barney was less bold in print than in the dalliance and dance and undress of her notorious salons. And Gertrude had Alice to contend with, a reader who was not as eager as she was to see their intimacies in print, and who could coldly withhold her favors if she chose.

> This must not be put in a book.
> Why not.
> Because it mustn't.
> Yes sir
>
> ["Bonne Annee," in *Geography and Plays*]

She might have to disguise it, but she was damn well going to write about it: "Suppose a collapse in rubbed purr, in rubbed purr get," for instance, a line which explodes, upon the gentlest inspection, into a dozen sexual pieces. There is "suppose," which means *to place under,* followed by the neck and lap of "collapse," which contains the French *col,* of course (the next line begins, "Little sales ladies . . ."—a phrase I construe as "little dirty girls"). "Collapse" also yields the root, *to fall* (sin) *together,* immediately after which we must deal with "rub," "purr," "get in bed," "rub her," "rubber," and Gertrude's pet name for Alice, which was Pussy.

---

* See Brinnin, *The Third Rose,* pp. 164–65.

† Bridgman's discussion of all these points is very useful. See especially chapter 7 of *Gertrude Stein in Pieces.* He says, however, that "Physical passion had been virtually absent from Gertrude Stein's work since *The Making of Americans,* or at least sufficiently disguised to be invisible." I think the latter is the case.

Here is the third-to-last button in the box labeled Objects:

PEELED PENCIL, CHOKE
  Rub her coke.

Remember those paper pencils you sharpened by peeling? Don't Jews do the same to the penis? Oral sex with such will make you choke. Certainly the writing instrument is one of Stein's household gods, as Penates are, gods of our most interior and secret parts. It's what we reach when we peel off the leaves of an artichoke: the hairy center. But isn't this a joke? The pencil has an eraser and a graphite core. A woman's core is her clitoris, which one rubs to please her. With what? a rubber cock. It *is* a joke.*
Let's push the culminating button and see what buzzes.

THIS IS THIS DRESS, AIDER
  Aider, why aider why whow, whow stop touch, aider whow, aider stop the muncher, muncher munchers.
  A jack in kill her, a jack in, makes a meadowed king, makes a to let.

This poem contrasts male and female lovemaking. There is disgust for the former, joy in the latter. The word "aider" is not only a sound shadow for *aid her* and a muffled form of "Ada," one of Gertrude's code names for Alice, it is also the original Old French root, meaning *to give pleasure to.* I have already claimed that we must read the title as THIS IS DISTRESS, AID HER, but the distress is partly explained by the twice-hidden "his," by the fact that "distress" itself gives us "strain," which immediately yields "stretch," as in the various expansions consequent to begetting. "Dress," in turn, has its roots in the Latin *directus* and the Old French *drecier,* and these extend toward "make straight," or "put in proper position," "prick up." Hence, we have (1) Ada, help me take off this dress (dis dress), and give me pleasure, for I am in sexual need, and (2) it is his doing, this stress and strain of begetting, save her from him. In short, Gertrude is to save Alice from men, while Alice is to save Gertrude from sexual want. In this passage, the square-off of male vs. female, and the balance of pleasure and pain with rescue and reward, is perfect.

Stein now imitates, perhaps too predictably, the stop/don't stop alternation of sexual excitement, but this allows her, at the same time, to render the resistance of the female and the painfulness of male penetration.

---

* William Wasserstrom has the right gloss on this in his fine essay, "Gertrude Stein: Sursy-mamericubealism," in *Twentieth Century Literature,* vol. 21, no. 1 (1975), p. 103.

1. Ada, why what are you doing? wow, how, wow, stop, oh touch, Ada, wow, Ada stop . . . and Ada, of course, is grazing, a cunnilingual metaphor.
2. Help, help, ow, ow stop ouch, help, ow, stop the muncher . . .
3. Aid her. Why aid her? how to stop the touching and help her, how?

The relation of "how" and "cow" (hence "munch" and "meadowed king") is not infrequent in Gertrude Stein. "A Sonatina" (written in 1921) is only one poem which makes the connection explicit:

> A fig an apple and some grapes makes a cow. How.
> The Caesars know how. Now.*

A similar ambivalence governs the construction of the final sentence. Shadowing "A jack in kill her" are at least three other Jacks: Jack the Giant Killer, Jack and Jill, and Jack in the Box.† Jack is normally any male, a knave, a jakes or john, and a penis, both real and artificial, while "a jack in" imitates the pump and rock of sexual stimulation. The dildo imagery, which some readers may wish to resist, becomes increasingly explicit. For instance, in "A Sonatina" again:

> Do you remember that a pump can pump other things than water . . .
> Yes tenderness grows and it grows where it grows. And do you like it.
> Yes you do. And does it fill a cow full of filling. Yes. And where does it
> come out of. It comes out of the way of the Caesars.

So: (1) if a man gets hold of her, he can kill her as a consequence of rape or pregnancy, to say nothing of the pain, the shame and humiliation. When Jack and Jill go up the hill together, Jack falls down and breaks his crown, but Jill comes tumbling after. Men merely rent the body anyway, and make the woman a toilet for their secretions; (2) when there is a dildo in her, however, she will know pleasure (die), and this jack will kill the giant one, and

---

* From *Bee Time Vine*. Gertrude is one of the Caesars. "Cows are very nice," she says. "They are between legs." See Bridgman, *Gertrude Stein in Pieces*, pp. 149–54. The connection is in any case nearly inevitable, as, for example, in Cummings's famous "anyone lived in a pretty how town."

† Allegra Stewart flails away at this passage, mentioning every Jack she can think of but missing Jill, and because she does not play her jacks on the page, misses the scatological and sexual connotations. The poem, consequently, does not come apart for her.

let in instead the meadowed king (the bull). "Let," which means both *permit* and *hinder*, perfectly represents the alternating currents here. The same toy and toying sound which seduces Ada pleasantly when she is mastered by the meadowed king, would turn her into a toilet bowl if she were jacked by a man.

Strong stuff. *Not* a joke.

In 1951 Edmund Wilson conjectured

> . . . that the vagueness that began to blur [Gertrude Stein's writing] from about 1910 on and the masking by unexplained metaphors that later made it seem opaque, though partly the result of an effort to emulate modern painting, were partly also due to a need imposed by the problem of writing about relationships between women of a kind that the standards of the era would not have allowed her to describe more explicitly. It seemed obvious that her queer little portraits and her mischievously baffling prose-poems did often deal with subjects of this sort. . . .*

but he later felt he might have overestimated the motive of sexual conceal-ment.† If the reading I have given the Object section of *Tender Buttons* is even somewhat sound, however, Wilson will have been right the first time.

Evasiveness, of course, becomes a habit, a style, a method which over-reaches its original excuse and must seek another justification, just as the

---

* Edmund Wilson, *The Shores of Light* (New York: Farrar, Straus & Young, 1952), p. 581. I also came to that conclusion in 1958. See "Gertrude Stein: Her Escape from Protective Language," in *Fiction and the Figures of Life* (New York: Alfred A. Knopf, 1970).

† Wilson couldn't find much evidence of it when he read *Two: Gertrude Stein and Her Brother*, after it had been posthumously published by Yale, so he ascribed the extremely abstract quality of that work to "an increasing remoteness in her personal relationships." The subject naturally led her already dry style into mathematical meditations ("If one is one and one is not one of the two then one is one . . .") which were transparently about the position of the self in a family of two. James Mellow points out that Wilson must have missed the portrait in that volume called "Men," which is very obviously about homosexual behavior (*The Charmed Circle: Gertrude Stein & Company* [New York: Praeger, 1974], p. 134). *Two* was written at about the same time as *Tender Buttons* (which hid its luridity under a bushel but was nevertheless lurid enough to require the basket), and was concerned about the cementing of her relationship with Miss Toklas as well as the breakup of the one with her brother. The subject was full of potentially dangerous material. Leo, who had served as a father replacement, was replaced in turn by Ger-trude herself, who, as husband to Alice, became her own father figure. If the appropriate joke about the women's movement is that it needs a good man to direct it, the attitude of Gertrude Stein was that, although the male role was the one worth playing, the only good man was a woman.

quadriplegic, who must paint with his teeth, will eventually find reasons why the bite is superior to the squeeze. Although, in a few works—the popular public ones like Alice's and Everybody's autobiographies, *Brewsie and Willie,* and *Wars I Have Seen*—Stein's style is as simple and open and even giddy as we might imagine the letters of a young girl to be, much of her work is written, like *Tender Buttons,* in a kind of code, even when, as in *How to Write,* the subject does not appear to require it; and there is no question whatever that the coding dangerously confounds the surface; for even if a passage effects a concealment, as when a body is covered by clothing, from the artistic point of view, those clothes had better dazzle us as much as the truth would, unless the concealment is only gestural and temporary, and we are expected to penetrate it at once, because the object of art is to make more beautiful that which is, and since that which is is rarely beautiful, often awkward and ugly and ill-arranged, it must be sometimes sheeted like a corpse, or dissolved into its elements and put together afresh, aright, and originally. Stein is painfully aware of the problem. Coming clean is best. "Certainly glittering is handsome and convincing."

The manifest text of *Tender Buttons* is only one segment of its total textual surface. That CHOKE is "joke" is a surface phenomenon, as is AIDER's "aid her." In a swirl of lines a horse's head may be hidden, some clouds do in fact look dragonish, and a drawing may turn itself inside out before our very eyes; thus "get in bed" lies disguised in "rubbed purr get," and an unseen *i* will fit between the words "to let." The problem is that in *Tender Buttons* the unconcealed surface usually makes no sense. AIDER, for instance, is not an active English verb, and might as well be a word in the *Wake* or in "Jabberwocky." Occasionally, instead of the word being wounded, the syntax will be: "Please a round it is ticket." Most often, however, the confusion in the surface is semantic. "This is no authority for the abuse of cheese," she will suddenly say severely, and we think we are listening to the Red Queen. "Suspect a single buttered flower," we are warned, but what is the warning?* In contrast, the other segments of the surface are usually fairly clear. "Aid her" is plainly what we are being asked to do.

Some covert texts are hidden like the purloined letter, others are concealed the way the family portrait hides the safe, still others the way the safe contains its money. That "color" is a cover, or that "cow" is cunt or that "a white way of being round" refers to immaculate conception, is nothing that can be read directly off the page. Since many of the meanings of *Tender Buttons* are etymological, the covert text can be said to be sometimes *inside* the surface

---

* Watch out for unattached flattering floozies.

text. We have only to enter the word on these occasions. However, the idea that the innocent dust which makes up Adam and Eve is a "blind glass" can be safely said to lie *beneath* its covering phrase.

We are familiar with the before and after of words and sentences because that is the way they are read and written, but now we must learn to diagram them differently.

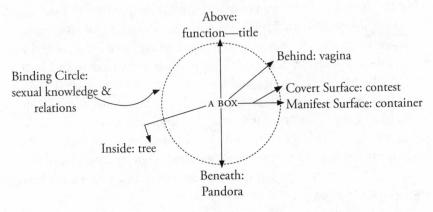

The manifest surface of A BOX is represented by the idea, container. There is a covert surface, too, that of contest or blow. Each such covert text adds to the *width* of the surface, just as its *length* is determined by the basic unity of the verbal series chosen for examination (A BOX, in this case, rather than merely BOX). In this example, we have a surface two words long and two texts wide. *Inside* A BOX is its root, "tree." *Behind* it is the slang meaning, womb or vagina. Pandora is *beneath*, while hovering *above*, though not like an angel, is its characterization as the label of a button. Because A BOX is set up as a title, it has no *immediate* before or after; there is to be imagined, before the opening of each book, an endless preceding silence, just as an equally endless one follows its close; but these are the silences of one text alone, not the quiet of all texts, for the whole of literature surrounds every work like water.

Here, then, is a notable explosion of language out of time into space. Although the button which follows A BOX makes sense, and is even funny (if the labor of reaching the punch line does not itself supply the reel which should result), it is, by and large, without the swift sensuous intake which is essential, since our response, as readers, must always run even with, if not ahead of, understanding. Basically, our knowledge of a poem serves simply to explain why we were shaken. It will never, alone, do the shaking.

In *Tender Buttons* the conflict between concealment and expression is especially intense. This kind of contest can sometimes lead to the most beautiful and powerful of consequences, so long as the victory of concealment remains incomplete, so long as the drapery leads us to dream and desire and demand the body we know it covers, so long as passion speaks through rectitude, so long as impulse laughs with the lips of duty. We can, of course, rip the clothing off anyway, as I have; but it is the promise of the nipple through the slip, the tender button, which matters to us here, and is the actual action of art; it is the hint of the hollow which holds us, and the way a stone arm encircles nothing but atmosphere so lovingly we want to believe in our being there, also surrounded, and only then as alive in our life as that stone.

"Celery tastes tastes where" (she asks) "in curled lashes and little bits and mostly in remains." It is a careful observation. "A cup is neglected by being full of size." It is a rich saying. Many of these buttons are as tender as tusks, but Gertrude Stein also wrote densely and brilliantly and beautifully and perversely and with intense contrivance and deep care and a skill which no one could recognize. In the Food section, for instance, there are passages like this one, which escapes through honkytonk and even Blake into true feeling:

Lovely snipe and tender turn, excellent vapor and slender butter, all the splinter and the trunk, all the poisonous darkening drunk, all the joy in weak success, all the joyful tenderness, all the section and the tea, all the stouter symmetry.

Or consider this extraordinary conclusion to ROASTBEEF, a passage which only she could have written, at first glance on a commonplace theme (the cycle of the seasons), yet as dense and transformational as fog, and like a chant in Latin, lovely before, during, and long after comprehension.

There is coagulation in cold and there is none in prudence. Something is preserved and the evening is long and the colder spring has sudden shadows in a sun. All the stain is tender and lilacs really lilacs are disturbed. Why is the perfect reëstablishment practiced and prized, why is it composed. The result the pure result is juice and size and baking and exhibition and nonchalance and sacrifice and volume and a section in division and the surrounding recognition and horticulture and no murmur. This is a result. There is no superposition and circumstance, there is hardness and a reason and the rest and remainder. There is no delight and no mathematics.

3

I write for myself and strangers. The strangers would go—eventually, even the self.

It took many years; she had to bring out most of her books herself; usually they appeared long after they'd been written, in silence, to indifference, incomprehension, jeers; but in time there were too many strangers: curiosity seekers, sycophants, opportunists, disciples. She hugely enjoyed her growing celebrity, but she noticed what she thought was a change in herself, and she began, vaguely, to be alarmed. In 1933 *The Autobiography of Alice B. Toklas* was published in the U.S.A. with great success, portions of it appearing in *The Atlantic Monthly.* Suddenly there was money she had earned. *Three Lives* went into the Modern Library. She was nearing sixty, 4 × her 15 yrs. It seemed like a good time to go back.

Gertrude Stein would return to the United States like a lion, she said, and word of her arrival did run in lights around the *Times* Building, reporters met her boat and filled twelve columns of the city papers with news and mostly friendly comment about her.

> ... we saw an electric sign moving around a building and it said Gertrude Stein has come and that was upsetting. . . . I like it to happen . . . but always it does give me a little shock of recognition and non-recognition. It is one of the things most worrying in the subject of identity.

She had come home but, although she was recognized in the streets of New York by strangers, she could not find again the San Francisco of her childhood.

> ... it was frightening quite frightening driving there and on top of Nob Hill where we were to stay, of course it had not been like that and yet it was like that, Alice Toklas found it natural but for me it was a trouble yes it was. . . .

Along with the face of Gracie Allen, she was caricatured by Covarrubias in *Vogue;* in Chicago she had a chance to see her own *Four Saints in Three Acts;* at Princeton police were used to hold back the crowd which came to hear her lecture. "Americans really want to make you happy." And she would plunge into traffic with a child's trusting unconcern. "All these people, including the nice taxi drivers, recognize and are careful of me."

Queerly companioned and oddly dressed, deep-voiced, direct, she loved being a celebrity and was consequently charming, her autograph was sought, and she and Alice met old friends, publishers, passersby and tradesmen, students, journalists, teachers, many who were rich and famous from all parts of a country they were both seeing from the air for the first time, the mountains subsiding like a fountain, the desert like a waterless floor of the sea, the whole land lying in lines which Masson, Braque, or Picasso might have drawn. She saw the same flatness, after so much European brick and tile, in the wooden buildings of America, but it was the map in the air which delighted her most, because it taught her what the human mind was capable of: flying without wings, seeing without eyes, knowing without evident data. Yet in East Oakland, on the shabby streets where she had played as a child, experience proved empty. What is the point of being born a little girl if you are going to grow up to be a man?

Back in France she tried to digest the lessons of her fame. A woman and artist who had been for much of her life without self or audience, she now had both; but what, after all, did it come to—this self she was famous for? In *Vogue*'s "Impossible Interview," Gracie Allen is made to say: "Now Gertie, don't you start to make sense, or people will begin to understand you, and then you won't mean anything at all." These reporters, followers, and friends—they were merely hearts that spaniel'd her at heels. . . . She'd looked back, snuffled at her roots, found, seen, felt—nothing.

The Geographical History of America is a culminating work, though not the outcome of her meditations. Those she summed up in an essay, "What Are Masterpieces?," written a year later. This book is the stylized presentation of the process of meditation itself, with many critical asides. In the manner of her earliest piece, "Q.E.D.," it demonstrates far more than it proves, and although it is in no sense a volume of philosophy (Gertrude Stein never "argues" anything), it is, philosophically, the most important of her texts. If we follow her thought as Theseus did the thread of Ariadne, I think we find at the end the justice, if not the total truth, of her boast that the most serious thinking about the nature of literature in the twentieth century has been done by a woman.

Life is repetition, and in a dozen different ways Gertrude Stein set out to render it. We have only to think how we pass our days: the doorbell rings, the telephone, sirens in the street, steps on the stairs, the recurrent sounds of buzzers, birds, and vacuum cleaners; then, as we listen, we suck our teeth; those are our feet approaching, so characteristic the tread can be identified, and that's our little mew of annoyance at the interruption, too, as well as the nervous look which penetrates the glass, the fumble with the latch, the thought: I must remember to oil this lock; whereupon we are confronted by a strange man who is nevertheless saying something totally familiar about brooms. Suppose he is truly a stranger. Still, we have seen salesmen before, men before, brooms; the accent is familiar, the tone, the tie, the crooked smile, the pity we are asked for, the submissive shoulders, yet the vague threat in the forward foot, the extended palm like the paw of a begging bear. Everything, to the last detail, is composed of elements we have already experienced a thousand and a thousand thousand times. Even those once-in-a-lifetime things—overturning a canoe in white water or being shot at, pursuing a squirrel through the attic, sexual excess—are merely unusual combinations of what has been repeatedly around. Our personal habits express it, laws of nature predict it, genes direct it, the edicts of the state encourage or require it, universals sum it up.

The range of our sensations, our thoughts, our feelings, is generally fixed, and so is our experience of relations. Make an analysis, draw up a list. Life is rearrangement, and in a dozen different ways Gertrude Stein set out to render it. We are not clocks, designed to repeat without remainder, to mean nothing by a tick, not even the coming tock, and so we must distinguish between merely mechanical repetition, in which there is no progress of idea, no advance or piling up of wealth, and that which seriously defines our nature, describes the central rhythms of our lives.

Almost at once she realized that language itself is a complete analogue of experience because it, too, is made of a large but finite number of relatively fixed terms which are then allowed to occur in a limited number of clearly specified relations, so that it is not the appearance of a word that matters but *the manner of its reappearance,* and that an unspecifiable number of absolutely unique sentences can in this way be composed, as, of course, life is also continuously refreshing itself in a similar fashion.

There are novel sentences which are novel in the same old ways, and there are novel sentences in which the novelty itself is new. In *How to Write* she discusses the reason why sentences are not emotional and paragraphs are, and offers us some sentences which she believes have the emotional balance of the paragraph.

a. It looks like a garden but he had hurt himself by accident.
b. A dog which you have never had before has sighed.
c. A bay and hills hills are surrounded by their having their distance
   very near.

Compare these with Sterne's:

d. A cow broke in tomorrow morning to my Uncle Toby's
   fortifications.

Or Hawkes's:

> e. It was a heavy rain, the sort of rain that falls in prison yards and
>   beats a little firewood smoke back down garret chimneys, that
>   leaks across floors, into forgotten prams, into the slaughterhouse
>   and pots on the stove.

Or with this by Beckett:

> f. Picturesque detail a woman with white hair still young to
>   judge by her thighs leaning against the wall with eyes closed in
>   abandonment and mechanically clasping to her breast a mite who
>   strains away in an effort to turn its head and look behind.

All right, we have answered the bell. Suppose we broke that action into parts: opening the door, coming down the stairs, mewing with annoyance, and so forth—how easily we might combine them in other ways, in new sentences of behavior, new paragraphs of life.

Mewing with annoyance reflects a state more subjective than the others. Mewing with annoyance is an event of lesser size, though it, too, is divisible. All are audible acts, unlike the secretion of saliva. Our sentence must manage them—their motion, weight, size, order, state of being must be themselves events, must pass through the space the way we pass when we skip down the stairs to the door.

Let's begin with a sentence without any special significance, selected the same way you might curiously pick up a piece of paper in the street. *In the middle of the market there's a bin of pumpkins.* Dividing this sentence as it seems natural to do, we can commence its conquest:

> a. There's a bin of pumpkins in the middle of the market.
> b. There, in the middle of the market, is a bin of pumpkins.
> c. A bin of pumpkins? There, in the middle of the market.
> d. A bin of . . . pumpkins? There? In the middle of the market?

We can make our arrangements more musical:

> e. In the middle. In the middle of the market. In the middle there's a
>   bin. There's a bin. In the middle of the market there's a bin.
> f. In the middle. In the middle of the market. In the middle of the
>   market there's a bin. A bin. In the middle of the market there's a

bin. In. A bin. In. In the market there's a bin. In the middle of the
market—pumpkin.

g. Middle of market. Middle of. Middle of. Middle of market.
Middle of bin. In the middle of market a middle of market, in the
middle of market there's a middle of bin. In the middle of market,
in the middle of bin, there's a middle of bin, there's a middle of
pumpkin, there's a middle of in.

h. Pumpkin. In in in. Pumpkin. In middle. In market. In bin.

Much of this is dreadful singsong, of course, but the play has only begun.
Besides, this is just a demonstration record. The words themselves can be
knocked apart, rhymes introduced, or conceptual possibilities pursued.

i. Middle of market. Riddle of. Middle of. Riddle of market. Middle
of bin. Not thin when in. When hollow in huddle then kindle
pumpkin.

j. Pump. Pump ump. In the middle. P p. Um, there's a bin.
Pumpkin.

And so on. And on so.

Such games soon give us an idea of the centers of conceptual energies in
any sentence, its flexibility, a feel for the feelings possible for it, all its aural
consequences; and to a child who is eagerly looking for a skull to carve some
Halloween horror on, our celebration of the sentence will seem perfectly
sensible.

The procedure is thoroughly analytical, however. It treats the elements of
the sentence as if they were people at a party, and begins a mental play with
all their possible relationships. Gertrude Stein's work rarely deals very happily with indivisible wholes.

Sometimes she treats a sentence as if it were a shopping list, and rearranges
every item in happier orders, much as we might place knickknacks on a shelf,
considering whether the spotted china dog might be seen to better advantage
in front of the jade lizard and nearer the window, or beside the tin cup borrowed from a beggar in Beirut.

Sometimes she lets us see and follow every step, but often she neglects
to give us the sentences she began with, and we find ourselves puzzled by
distant results.

Think next what might happen if we considered the sentence to be composed of various voices: in short, a play. For what else is a play? It simply cites
the separate sources of its sentences.

h. 1.	Martha.	Pumpkin.
	Mary.	In in in.
	Martha.	Pumpkin.
	Joseph.	In middle.
	John.	In market.
	M. & M.	In bin.

A musician would have no trouble in seeing how a single sentence might be treated as the consequence of a chorus, nor would a modern painter find it hard to imagine the dissolution of his plate, bread, vase, and fish into plastic elements he then rearranged in a new, more pleasing way.

Gertrude Stein did more with sentences, and understood them better, than any writer ever has. Not all her manipulations are successful, but even at their worst, most boring, most mechanical, they are wonderfully informative. And constantly she thought of them as things in space, as long and wiggling and physical as worms. Here is a description of some of them from "Poetry and Grammar":

> . . . my sentences . . . had no longer the balance of sentences because they were not the parts of a paragraph nor were they a paragraph but they had made in so far as they had come to be so long and with the balance of their own that they had they had become something that was a whole thing and in so being they had a balance which was the balance of a space completely not filled but created by something moving as moving is not as moving should be.

She understood reading, for instance. She sometimes read straight on, touching the page as lightly as a fly, but even as her mind moved there would be a halt, a turning, the eyes rising and falling in a wave, and she realized that the page itself was artificial, arbitrary with respect to the text, so she included it in the work as well, not as a thing or an action, but as an idea.

j. 1.	Page one.	Pump. Pump ump.
	Page two.	In the middle.
	Page three.	P p.
	Page four.	Um, there's a bin.
	Page five.	Pumpkin.

The understanding was, as she read, not only tormented by the physical makeup of the book, it was often troubled, too, by the content, which it had difficulty in making out. The poem does not repeat itself, but I do. I read the first four lines, and then I reread the first two. Now I am ready to go on, and I jump without a qualm to the second quatrain. Soon, however, I am back at the beginning again. There are interruptions, too. Alice asks me what I would like for dinner. Company comes. Time passes. Other texts may even intervene, many strange words from all directions. Why not, she thought, formalize all this, create something new, not only from the stops and starts and quarrels of normal thought, but from the act of attention itself, and all its snarls and tangles, leaps and stumbles.

She is not always satisfied merely to render the phenomenon. Sometimes she chooses to involve us in it. By removing punctuation, for instance. I am reading her sentence about her sentences, which I quoted above, and sliding over words as though through mud:

> . . . not filled but created by something moving as moving is not as moving . . .

I must pick myself up. Reread until I get the hang:

> . . . not filled, but created by something moving, as moving *is,* not as moving should be.

By the time I understand what she means, *I* have been composed. Thus the repetitions which mimic my own when I read make me repeat even more when I read them written down.

Listen. We converse as we live—by repeating, by combining and recombining a few elements over and over again just as nature does when of elementary particles it builds a world. Gertrude Stein had a wonderful ear and she listened as she listened to Leo—for years—not so she could simply reproduce the talk, that sort of thing was never her intention, but so she could discover the patterns in speech, the *forms* of repetition, and exploit them. At first she saw these shapes as signs of the character of the speaker, but later her aim was to confer upon the words themselves the quality she once traced to the owner of the tongue. That was Cézanne's method—the method of the human mind.

We not only repeat when we see, stand, communicate; we repeat when we think. There's no other way to hold a thought long enough to examine it except to say its words over and over, and the advance of our mind from one notion to another is similarly filled with backs and forths, erasures and crossings-out. The style of *The Geographical History of America* is often a reflection of this mental condition.

Repeating is also naming. Pumpkins have names. They are called pumpkins. But what is the word "pumpkin" called? Not Fred, not William, not Wallaby, but "pumpkin" again. And so we seem to be repeating when we are speaking in the metalanguage, or the overtongue. A division of "pumpkin" into "pump" and "kin" is not a carving of pumpkin. Nor is the finding and baking and eating of one any damage to the word. An actor's gestures name the real ones. Suppose, behind your back, I am making fun of you by imitating your hurried, impatient, heavy-shoed walk, or like an annoying child I echo your talk as you talk; then a round is being formed, a ring made of reality and its shadow, words and their referents, and of course I can dance with my image or with yours very well, mock my own methods, and suddenly discover, in the midst of my game, a meaning that's more than a vegetable's candlelit face.

The ice cream eaten is desired again, the song sung is resung, and so we often say things over simply because we love to say them over—there is no better reason.

Furthermore, Gertrude Stein knew that masterpieces were, like life itself is everywhere, perfect engines of repetition. Just as leaves multiply along a limb, and limbs alike thicket a trunk, a work of art suffers simultaneous existence in many places, and eventually is read again and again, sometimes loved by the same lips. As Borges has demonstrated so well, when that inspired madman Pierre Menard succeeded in writing a chapter or two of *Don Quixote*, word for word the same, his version was both richer and more complex than that of Cervantes. The reverse can also be the case: *Three Lives*, written by any of us now, would not be nearly so remarkable as it was then.

4

How pleasantly a doll can change its age. I do not even have to dress it differently. My eye alters and a few rags bundled about a stick assume a life, a life at any point or period I like, with any sex and any history I choose— pets, presumptions, peeves—mortal or immortal ills. Whether I imagine it's a swatchel or a queen, the stick with its scrappy sleeves remains and is like another Homer to me, focus for my fancies; yet, when I open an old album and find my photo, what tells me what the image is, since I've no faithful wad of fabric or enduring spinal tree to fix on? . . . a lingering resemblance? am I that solemn little moon-faced boy in the ribboned hat whose photographic stare is as dumbly inked upon its paper as these words are? am I that weak-eyed, pork-cheeked creature? . . . possibly; but is it a likeness which leaps out at me, one I feel, or do I have to hunt for it, piously believing that a resemblance must be there, and easily fooled by a substitute, a switch, because a dozen other boys that age may look more like me now than I do then. A sentence with such moods and tenses shows in what strange ways our lifeline's twisted, how precariously it passes from one pole of recognition to another, because, as Hume reported:

> For my part, when I enter most intimately into what I call myself, I always stumble on some particular perception or other, of heat or cold, light or shade, love or hatred, pain or pleasure. I never can catch *myself* at any time without a perception, and never can observe any thing but the perception. When my perceptions are remov'd for any time, as by sound sleep; so long am I insensible of myself, and may truly be said not to exist.

I may dress Shakespeare, like my dolly, in the costumes of other centuries, interpret him according to the latest scientific myths or social magics; nevertheless, there is something—some pale text—some basin, bowl, or bottle I am peeing my opinions in; but as I turn the album pages—black not without a reason—I only dimly remember the bow and arrow in one snapshot, the knickers in another, or the man who was my father holding me wearily in his arms at the entrance to Mammoth Cave. The little boy I was is no longer living with me. Of course, we say that some people never grow up, but the little boy I am at forty is actually the little man I am at forty, no one else.

Rilke's celebrated remark about Rodin sums up what Gertrude Stein's American trip taught her:

> Rodin was solitary before he became famous. And Fame, when it came, made him if anything still more solitary. For Fame, after all, is but the sum of all the misunderstandings which gather about a new name.

Or work of art. It is the same.

When Gertrude Stein wrote that there was little use in being born a little boy if you were going to grow up to be a man, she did not intend to deny causality or the influence of the past. She did mean to say that when we look at our own life we are looking at the history of another; we are like a little dog licking our own hand, because our sense of ourselves at any time does not depend upon such data, only our "idea" of ourselves does, and this "idea," whether it's our own or that of another, is our identity. Identities depend upon appearances and papers. Appearances can be imitated, papers forged.

She also said: "I am not I any longer when I see." Normally, as Schopenhauer first and Bergson later argued so eloquently, we see like an animal. We see prey, danger, comfort, security. Our words are tags which signify our interest: chairs, bears, sunshine, sex; each is seen in relation to our impulses, instincts, aims, in the light of our passions, and our thought about these things is governed entirely by what we consider their utility to be. Words are therefore weapons like the jaws of the crocodile or the claws of the cat. We use them to hold our thought as we hold a bone; we use them to communicate with the pack, dupe our enemies, manipulate our friends; we use them to club the living into food.

When, for instance, we give ourselves to a piece of music—not to drink, daydream, or make love, but to listen—we literally lose ourselves, and as our consciousness is captured by the music, we are in dreamless sleep, as Hume says, and are no more. We become, in becoming music, that will-less subject of knowing of which Schopenhauer spoke so convincingly.

Human nature is incapable of objectivity. It is viciously anthropocentric, whereas the human mind leaves all personal interest behind. It sees things as entities, not as identities. It is concerned, in the Kantian sense, with things-in-themselves. The human knows that men must die that others may live; one epoch go that another may take its place; that ideas, fashions, feelings pass. The human mind neither forgets nor remembers; it neither sorrows nor longs; it never experiences fear or disappointment. In the table headed Human Nature there is, therefore, time and memory, with all their beginnings, their middles, and their ends; there is habit and identity, storms and hilly country, acting, audience, speaking and adventure, dogs and other animals, politics, propaganda, war, place, practice and its guiding truths, its directing sciences, while in the table of the Human Mind there's contact rather than connection, plains, space, landscape, math, and money, not nervousness but excitement, not saying but showing, romance rather than mystery, masterpieces moreover, and, above all, Being.

Gertrude Stein was no longer merely explaining herself. She had begun to wonder what it was inside her which had written *Three Lives* rather than the novels of Lew Wallace; what it was that made masterpieces. Besant's books had sold very well and he had been admired. But he had sold to people of principally the same sort and had been read during a finger-snap of time. Masterpieces escaped both country and climate, every condition of daily life; they hurdled history; and it was not because daily life, climate, country, and history were not contents, as if in those sweetly beautiful Angelicos there were no angels. What accounted for it? in reader? writer? work? Her conclusions were not original, although their largely Kantian character is a little surprising for a student of William James and Santayana.

It was not because she was a woman or was butch—her poodles or her Fords, her vests, her friends, her sober life, her so-called curious ways, her Jewishness, none counted. Allegheny, Pennsylvania, had nothing to do with it. Her "scientific" aim in writing *The Making of Americans,* her desire to define "the bottom nature" of everyone who had or could or would be living, was mistaken and had to do with human nature, not the human mind. She had gone on repeating because she thought the world did. The world did, but what the world did, did not matter. *Tender Buttons* was pure composition, like Cézanne, or at least one could pretend it was, but the *Autobiographys* and "A Long Gay Book," *Three Lives, The Making of Americans,* many of the portraits and the plays, although they were about human nature, were fortunately written by the human mind. And it took another human mind to understand them.

There were people who were no more than their poodles. If their little dog didn't know them, who would they be? Like mirrors they reflected what fell into them, and when the room was empty, when the walls were removed and the stars pinched back in the sky, they were nothing, not even glass.

Naïvely, she thought free people formed themselves in terms of an Emersonian self-reliance; she believed in the frontier, and in the ethic of the pioneer. After all she was one. Naïvely, she thought that the average man, here in America, understood the spiritual significance of space, and was less a slave to human nature. Consequently, here the human mind should flourish, the masterpiece emerge, the animal sleep. However, *Finnegans Wake* would demonstrate best the endless roundness she had in mind, and the perfect description of her ideal had long ago appeared, in 1894: Paul Valéry's *Monsieur Teste.*

Just as the order of numbers in a sum makes no difference, just as there is no special sequence to towns on a map, the mind and the masterpiece may pass back and forth between thoughts as often and as easily as trains between Detroit, Duluth, and Denver, and chapter headings are, in fact, only the names of places. Oral literature had to be sequential (like music before tape), but type made possible a reading which began at the rear, which repeated preferred passages, which skipped. As in an atlas, the order was one of convenience, and everything was flat. A geographical history rolls time out like that. Of course, there are stories still; an evening's entertainment, that's all human nature asks for; but masterpieces have to bear repeating and repeating. There are no surprises, no suspense, no tears, no worries in them. We know what will happen to Ahab. Duncan's dead, and Anna's under her train. I can tell you the page. *The Wings of the Dove* lies spread before us now as openly as Iowa. Literature in the eyes of the human mind is like land seen from a plane. And so is Gertrude Stein when we find her. Macbeth shall murder sleep again, Tom Jones receive a beating, Heathcliff . . . ah, well . . . "Oblige me," she says, "by not beginning." Netherfield Park is let at last. Mr. Gradgrind is still proceeding on the principle that two and two are four, and nothing over. Bloom is carrying a piece of soap about. The next century is approaching like a distant train. John Barth has just written *Chimera,* Beckett has brought out *The Lost Ones,* Nabokov a book called *Transparent Things.* And they are reissuing *The Geographical History of America* almost a hundred years from the author's birthday. Oblige me, she says, "Also by not ending."

The New York Review of Books, 1973
Published in *The World Within the Word,* 1978

GO FORTH AND FALSIFY

Katherine Anne Porter and the Lies of Art

Katherine Anne Porter's reported life was made of myths, most of them planted by Porter herself, and many meant to improve her humble beginnings, refigure the course of her early years, and conceal the existence of her numerous marriages and frequent affairs. Of people fleeing their origins, some are inclined to brag about them afterward, proud of the distance they've come, while a few are so indifferent to the past they manage to recall only what is routinely demanded by official documents. That leaves those who are still ashamed or hateful of their history, desperate to deny it, and prepared to rub it out if they can. There is something feudal about this embarrassment, because it gives credence to the claim blue bloods make for their superiority. The "nobility" can not only strut and preen, they can command, since others seem driven to grovel before those of elevated status, and appear to envy any member of the upper crust who got there, whether through birth, inheritance, marriage, or by old-fashioned hook or crook.

You have to remember the past rather clearly if you are going to lie your way out of its existence, but you also have to be able to enter your new history so completely that it replaces the truth even in your own mind. Katherine Anne Porter had no actual memories of her mother or of life in tiny Indian Creek, Texas, where she had been born in 1890, so she imagined some, and then discovered them again when she searched her past, as if finding gold ore shining in the water of the stream where it's been planted.

Moreover, when you falsify your own life, you can later be open and generous in your account of it, draw upon it for any fiction you may write, confident that your real self's safety will be assured. You can even second Madame Du Barry's challenging brag, as Porter did: "My life has been incredible. I don't believe a word of it." Eventually, however, the curious, and any others who care, will grow skeptical, believe only the worst because they assume only the worst would be concealed, and—the unfortunate consequence often is—they will not mind, after so much misleading, if they mistake a truth for a lie the next time, or even every time.

Through photographs and other evidence, Joan Givner, Katherine Anne Porter's 1982 biographer, demonstrates that most of the settings for Porter's re-enactment of her life's rites of passage in "The Old Order" were actually supplied by memories of a sojourn in Bermuda when Porter was thirty-nine, despite the author's claim that they were captured from her childhood. How it ought to have been quietly overtook how it was. Thomas F. Walsh, in his essay "The Making of 'Flowering Judas,'" unweaves the many threads that have gone into this masterful story's composition, disproving Porter's claim that "my fiction is reportage, only I do something to it; I arrange it and it is fiction, but it happened." "Flowering Judas" is based on events that actually occurred, all right, but her rearrangements were so radical that even she could not remember, in her frequent accounts of the story's composition, which ones she had previously claimed to be facts and which ones were fictions. Normally, what happens in the composition of fiction is that scenes, characters, and settings for the story are lifted from different places and times in the experience of the author to create a new cast and an altered environment; but it is not, I think, customary for the writer to maintain that all of them were derived, in the order lived, from one place and one time in one life. We have to keep in mind, too, how many of the events that matter most to a young writer take place in books, those vessels of imagination that have so often rescued us from every day's disappointments, and give us pages which, never settled, sift through our unconscious still.

So, though Porter's fiction is notably lucid on the page, her life history is a biographer's nightmare, full of false connections and alleged events, and blank about substantial passages of time, as if they had happened during intermission and were never a part of the play.

After her mother's death, Porter was raised by weak men and many women in the household of her paternal grandmother, whom everyone called Cat, not because of any special grace or caution but because it shortened "Catharine" by two-thirds and cauterized its odd spelling. Cat was a dominating figure, by her granddaughter's account, and ruled her household with a Calvinist's severe self-righteous hand. In 1892 it was more than a brief toddle from Indian Creek to Cat's farm near the Texas town of Kyle, one hundred miles away, but in terms of a child's escape from the short street that a small town can seem to be, the move widened the world by at least two roads.

The five hundred people there, with their local Protestant ways, were Katherine Anne Porter's first teachers, and they supported a school where she received, from age six to twelve, the little formal education her circumstances allowed. Townsfolk went about their business in full view of her wide eyes. They also regularly read from the Good Book, in which one could be warned of serious threats to the safety of one's soul, enjoy instructive allegorical stories, and encounter great prose. School primers taught virtue and obedience, nearly every page gleamed with moral varnish, while figures like Joan of Arc and Cotton Mather provided stirring examples of the prowess possible for women, and the merciless hatred some men had for them. From her grandmother she learned manners and had the fear of God "systematically ground . . . into [her] tender bones." Loose family ties and impoverishment compelled Cat to offer free room and board, in the guise of hiring governesses, to a Miss Babb and Miss Mudd, from whom Katherine learned spanking and calisthenics.

According to Darlene Harbour Unrue's 2005 biography, *Katherine Anne Porter: The Life of an Artist,* Grandmother and her dependents provided Porter with a loving, watchful, closely guarded yet colorful environment, stocked with what would later prove to be a useful cast of characters: a former slave, Masella Daney, who remained a household helper; Daney's husband (an ironically named Squire Bunton), who lived near and rode by regularly on a mule named Aunt Fanny; as well as a couple of hired hands, one of whom was a morphine addict whereas the other (Old Man Ronk) became the model for Olaf Helton in *Noon Wine.* Cat finally completed this list with

> a long procession of dreadful old women, of a most awful gentility, who consented to act as a sort of upper house keeper and companion and general nuisance, who merely took it out by gritting their teeth at us and wishing, in low voices when no one else was by, that they could blister our skins for being such bad children.

Young ears must have been captivated by the ubiquitous voices of Southern storytellers, leaning back in stiff chairs against the hardware store's porch wall, shaded, certainly, from the sun, a length of straw caught like a savory cliché between tongue and teeth, droning on of Chancellorsville or Lee at this ford or that railhead, Jackson charging through a stand of trees, repeating the feats and foibles of relatives whose odd mien and strange ways were usually instructive and always engrossing. These figures were connected by a verbal chain of recollection that reached at least to the moment when some fabulous ancestor's feet had first hit the turf in the New World.

To sustain interest in its story, every family had to have an ancestral secret that was kept as zealously as a shrine for Mother Mary; and we should add, to all the customary local wash, the buckets of bravado and romance that kept white the Southern dream, each tale's tallness teaching how the laws that govern the truth might be repealed. Typically, these were the sort of stories that Porter's grandmother maneuvered with considerable style through occasions of former opulence and ease—gowns and balls and beaus and canapés—that made Porter "hunger for fine clothes and other comforts of wealth." In 1962, after *Ship of Fools* became a best-seller, she bought herself a "huge square-cut emerald set all around with diamonds," a ring larger than the one she had invented for La Condesa to wear in the novel and an imprudent purchase at twenty thousand bucks. It is Givner's opinion that "It was the idea of the ring, rather than the actual object, that she cherished; it became the symbol of her success and the subject of numerous anecdotes."

It has always seemed to me that the storyteller's social assignment, which furnished the origins and directed the development of narrative, was to glorify the past and its daring deeds, protect the family tree, justify male ownership of land, women, and personal property, direct and legitimize the passing of power from father to rightful heir, one generation to the next. Oral histories helped unite communities, extol their chiefs, and define the various rites and ceremonies pertaining. No wonder their tales tended to be about male gods and their heroic human counterparts. Nowadays this history is a weakening string of memories, but at one time the bard's recital was the main conduit of authority, making sense of the past, fostering acceptance, and focusing pride—whether true or false or fabled mattered only to outsiders. Old anecdotes gave present circumstances heft, scope, interest, and instruction. In so many ways you were your forebears, and the storyteller taught you whom to hate or emulate, what to aspire to, and, like the Bible, what to believe, how to behave.

Every society, every religion, every nation-state and ethnic enclave appears eager to employ such historical myths, or first fictions, in their manipulation of the masses. Certainly narratives need not take the novel's form to be effective; in fact, serious novels now seem more likely to undermine them.

For many Southern writers these romantic sagas were acceptable, and they were eager to protect the honor, habits, and basic creeds of their culture, although a lacquer of criticism contributed to the glow of objectivity. Katherine Anne Porter was sawn in two, and not by a magician. She despised the actual family system and its methods of operation: its smugly narrow, stupid views with which it infected its children; its monarchy of men, their posturing and pomposity; its stifling so-called moral grip; its hypocrisy concerning women—courting them like queens, breeding them like sows. If a man were not the ruler of a kingdom, even not the owner of all he could survey, at least he was the master of his own household, made the main decisions, chastised deviation, doled out the dough, did the deep thinking, got all the mail. Katherine Anne Porter knew this system was based on a lot of poisonous pish tosh: she had seen how weak her father was, how his mother ran the house; yet all the essential perks were still his. Daughters were to be taught householdry and how to be well married, if possible; if not, as old maids they could sew in a corner and care for the sick.

Porter passed much of her adolescent years in a series of convent schools that were so eager to snatch a young Protestant from Luther's hands they would waive tuition, a generosity that her father found irresistible. Such schooling also made her more acceptable to a nineteen-year-old suitor with wealthy parents named John Koontz, whose Catholicism could not dampen his desire for drink or lessen his pleasure in abuse. Porter's marriage to this stalwart lasted nine invisible years, most of them miserable, though it removed her from her relatives, gave her a noticeable social upgrade, and took her to a somewhat larger, mildly industrial town named Lufkin. This new location often allowed her to ride on the family's ranch nearby and feel how it was to have a mighty force between her knees.

According to Darlene Harbour Unrue, the couple's eventual divorce yielded a deposition from the husband: "Nine years after the wedding he admitted that from the beginning of their union he was frequently guilty of adultery, extreme intoxication, vile name-calling, and physical attacks that resulted in Katherine Anne's broken bones and lacerations." The charges may have been rather starved for substance, but Porter enjoyed a harvest of grievances all the same. The pair moved often but packed their problems with their pajamas. On one occasion, husband threw wife down a flight of stairs, "breaking her right ankle and severely injuring her knee." On another, he beat her unconscious with a hairbrush. The view one has of men and marriage from the foot of such a fall, or from an instrument that should only pursue fashion or caresses, tends to be as permanent as Adam's; nevertheless, Porter tried to save her marriage by converting to Catholicism, a move I find mystifying, though I was never consulted. Largely, what it meant was a redirection in her reading habits and the discovery of new authors—always a plus—while the Church's rituals encouraged her to ponder the impact of belief upon behavior and to appreciate the role of symbols in the imagination. She also learned, as she began to write, how things grow more real when they are put into words, because without storytelling the past would pale beyond even the pale of paper. The fattest, most familiar story of all is the one we tell ourselves about ourselves, repeatedly, as if before bed, as a daily comfort or admonition, throughout our lives.

When Joan Givner wrote her *Katherine Anne Porter: A Life* in 1982, her subject had four husbands (Porter customarily claimed there were three), but when the editor of this Library of America collection (*Collected Stories and Other Writings*), Darlene Harbour Unrue, published her biography of Porter in 2005, the marriage list had swollen to five, none of them Givner's early candidate, Ernest Stock, the handsome former member of the British Royal Flying Corps, with whom—it turns out—Porter had only "a relationship." I suspect that, for appearances, affairs might have been called marriages sometimes and, for convenience, marriages said to be affairs, until who knew what the situation was, and who would any longer care?

Unrue discovered that after Porter's marriage to Koontz in 1915 she wed H. Otto Taskett, a handsome Englishman who lasted the length of a sentence, though, as a fiction, he received many more in *Ship of Fools,* as did all of her husbands. Subsequently, in 1917, someone named Carl von Pless blew through Porter's life like a prairie wind. Despite what previous biographers believed, she did not marry Stock in 1926; she simply spent a summer with him in a rented house. Now and then a year would have more than one summer. After this one, Porter had gonorrhea. Then, from 1933 to 1938, following a lengthy and rocky liaison, she was married to someone as short as she was. This was Eugene Pressly, a young fellow from the Institute of Current World Affairs in Mexico City and later of American oil interests in Venezuela. He was her devoted companion on the sea voyage from Veracruz to Bremen that became the setting for *Ship of Fools,* and he would travel with her, over the next seven years, to Berlin, Paris, and New York before disappearing over the horizon en route to Venezuela.

Porter's final bet for wedded bliss was Albert Erskine, a young graduate student who had followed Robert Penn Warren from Memphis to Louisiana State University's English department. He was another "handsome young man," this time of twenty-seven, who was bewitched by her beauty, sophistication, and charm, with a background in literature that enabled him to appreciate fully the corresponding charm, sophistication, and beauty of her work. As the brief life of this marriage wore on, the charm was perhaps the first to go, Porter's sophistication was admitted to be forty-eight years of maturity instead, and her beauty quite a bad habit. To get rid of her husband, and divorce him as a favor, since he was eager to marry another woman, she established a residence in Reno.

The trouble with the men Porter married was that they were still men. She had fabulous legs suitors would insist she be proud of, the voice of a seductress, a figure that drew looks, so that men, their private part plump, would fawn and favor her and, what was more important, inadvertently make possible a fuller, freer realization of her talents and her dreams. But she often had to marry them to take the next step up, to relish the security their money and station could confer, or enjoy the acceptance society gave to such arrangements; except that when trod upon these "partners" grew sullen and unruly, wanted the pleasures of her body without giving any pleasure in exchange, so that, when refused, their passions grew petulant, their entreaties tiresome, their presence wearying.

Beauty did not make Porter proud; it made her vain; and these repeated romantic misadventures sapped her emotional energy. Perhaps they were the reason why she was a frequent procrastinator and stingy with her work. Daily life can be taxing, running around on the road can give any head and heart the dizzies, and the dizzies can cause you to sink onto strange sofas. Inconsistencies are bad assets, and Porter had her share: she was at once cold and promiscuous, romantic and calculating; she sought both solitude and society, thus the emotional space necessary for composition, and the excuses to avoid it. Although very aware of pregnancy's dangers to her health, to her way of life as well as the prospective child's, Porter longed to be a mother. In consequence, she suffered miscarriages, required abortions, and "lost children in all the ways one could."

Porter knew what it was to be poor, but she nevertheless regularly lived beyond her means. She flirted with religion but was too intelligent to commit. She deplored her humble origins, said she disliked the South, yet she longed to put down roots, and was fascinated by the myths that glorified her region. In spite of that she fled every place that offered itself in order to live like a gypsy. In her day Marxists were the most relentless of the political bores, and I feel it is to her considerable credit that no -ism or -ology could tempt her, no fashionable jargon lead her into obfuscation, or fad of intellect seduce. Porter supported liberal causes, both in print and on the street, and was vigorous in her denunciation of fascism while demonstrating a mistrust of minorities that was thoroughly Southern and deeper than a streak.

F. O. Matthiessen observed, as early as 1945, that Miss Porter (as she was then addressed) had a "high reputation among nearly all schools of critics" and was regarded as "a writer's writer," by which he meant that other authors could learn much from her consummate craftsmanship. Although Porter was thirty-two when she published her first story, "María Concepción," her signature style was in place and more assured in its use than she had come to be in her life. Her sensuous yet hard-eyed prose would never need improvement and would be flexible enough in tone (ranging from the famous impersonality of "María" to the witty sarcasm of "The Wooden Umbrella" and the revulsion of "The Leaning Tower") to accomplish whatever effect she required.

Matthiessen feared such praise might be taken to mean that her work was arty and esoteric. (I would add to those adjectives the words "fancy" and "frilly," "mannered" and "difficult.") When reviewers take the trouble to compliment a writer on her style, it is usually because she has made it easy for them to slide from one sentence to another like an otter down a slope, since they are presumably eager to find out what happens next or what fresh disclosure will yield surprise. So they are happily immersed in the account, lose all touch with mere words, and feel as if they were present when D'Arcy does this or Miranda that, or when the mangy dog chases the cat. Porter herself, who sometimes knew better, compliments Thomas Hardy on his ability to put her in his chosen place and let her *"see."* She should have said *"and let her read."*

In the same year and season that Matthiessen published his little piece in *Accent,* Gertrude Buckman wrote this about "The Leaning Tower" for the *Partisan Review:* "It has for a long time been apparent that Katherine Anne Porter consistently writes a luminous prose, of an exactness of choice and suggestiveness of phrasing, which is altogether extraordinary. Miss Porter's work has probably been subjected to the kind of scrutiny that most writers hardly dare to hope for, rarely achieve, and can almost never withstand. That Miss Porter can bear such careful reading proves her much more than simply an excellent stylist." This praise is well meant, but it is also withdrawn as quickly as it is offered. For most critics, the presence of "style" requires assurance that there is also "substance." Style is wrapping paper and ribbon, scented tag and loving inscription. If you are careful, the tissue can be reused for a birthday or another Christmas. My aunt ironed such paper as she fancied and stored it like linen napkins in folded flat stacks beneath her bed.

Style, I should like to protest, is the result of that "exactness of choice" that Porter exhibits. Whether unconsciously or by intent, the writer chooses subjects, adopts a tone, considers an order for the release of meaning, arrives at the rhythm, selects a series of appropriate sounds, determines the diction and measures the pace, turns the referents of certain words into symbols, establishes connections with companionable paragraphs, sizes up each sentence's intended significance, and, if granted good fortune because each decision might have been otherwise, achieves not just this or that bit of luminosity or suggestiveness but her own unique lines of language, lines that produce the desired restitution of the self.

You cannot miss the rhetorical beat of passages such as this one from "The Leaning Tower" of 1941 that buries the reader under shovelfuls of scorn. Charles Upton, the principal character, is taking a walk, looking for a lodging, on his sixth day as a newcomer to Berlin:

> He would wander on, and the thicker the crowd in which he found himself, the more alien he felt himself to be. He had watched a group of middle-aged men and women who were gathered in silence before two adjoining windows, gazing silently at displays of toy pigs and sugar pigs. These persons were all strangely of a kind, and strangely the most prevalent type. The streets were full of them—enormous waddling women with short legs and ill-humored faces and round-headed men with great rolls of fat across the backs of their necks, who seemed to support their swollen bellies with an effort that drew their shoulders forward.

It might seem sad enough to be so described, but the feeling is still, though dismayed, detached. The next paragraph plays rough. These depicted people are window-shopping, but the windows are both mocking and reflecting them.

> In one window there were sausages, hams, bacon, small pink chops; all pig, real pig, fresh, smoked, salted, baked, roasted, pickled, spiced, and jellied. In the other were dainty artificial pigs, almond paste pigs, pink sugar chops, chocolate sausages, tiny hams and bacons of melting cream streaked and colored to the very life. Among the tinsel and lace paper, at the back were still other kinds of pigs: plush pigs, black velvet pigs, spotted cotton pigs, metal and wooden mechanical pigs, all with frolicsome curled tails and appealing infant faces.

The expelling puffs required to cross the page over all those disgusting *p*'s, the alternation among the vowels the *p*'s accompany, the word "pig" itself, made of piss and gag, the feel of the tongue against the teeth while performing the doubled tees of "spotted cotton," the marvelous march of the metaphor as it moves from examples of the real thing through sugary still-eatable samples to reproductions in plush, then wood, and finally metal, and the mingled reflection in and through the glass of pig parts, piglike imitations, and acquired pig-resembling forms and faces: they play together to create her style in this passage and prove her worth.

Any resonance beyond rhetoric to this passage? You bet. It takes the toil of butchers, bakers, gimcrack makers to provide the fare; shopkeepers' time and money to acquire and arrange the space; an entire culture—for this is already a Nazified Germany—to collect the crowd; and Porter to imagine a lonely American looking for his lodging in this coarse and gluttonous community. The scene is a construction, as all literary descriptions are, because an actual eye would sweep the scene in one look, then send attention here and there in a flick or three. Instead, we are given a summary in the guise of a moment, a habit in an instance, and a judgment meant for forever.

The sight of fat people apparently sharpened her pen. These two sentences from *Noon Wine* are famous: "He wasn't exactly a fat man. He was more like a man who had been fat recently."

A moment ago I wrote, "to create her style . . . and prove her worth," as if I were sure that proving her worth was at least one function for perfection to perform. I suspect Porter's art had to be a form of salvation for her, but perhaps I am allowing my own attitudes to intrude the way my pack-ratty aunt scuffled into this text seven paragraphs ago. In the careful practice of the arts of prose, Porter could avoid mistakes, whereas in life she was invariably putting the wrong ring on the wrong finger. On the page she could wait until she and her skills were a match. In time she would learn her art from the kind of reading that teaches writing, and choose according to her lights, picking her mentors wisely—internationals such as Henry James and Virginia Woolf, because Southern writers were treacherous guides and might lead you to the most dangerous monster of all: Faulkner's all-swallowing world. The perfection of the work would hide the imperfections of the life. Then she could look at the past without either shame or guilt. There she would discover problems worthy of her and conquer them. Her life's journey was in the company of a load of fools as well as the freight of friends, but she would board no friends and embark the fools to Bremen from Veracruz.

Although its author might have been characterized, at one time, as a loose baseborn woman, her much-admired style bore every mark of the aristocracy and had taken her to the White House of John F. Kennedy, where she had dined more than once. That style was neither very inventive nor exploratory, but it was precise about perception, adept at dialogue and scrupulous about dialect, rich in recollection, careful with abstractions, sensuous and frank though never coarse, otherwise always high-toned, never casual or breathless as if her vowels had been running.

Porter relaxed her standards somewhat when writing essays or doing reviews (which occupy a good half of the substantial Library of America volume), but Katherine Anne in an apron is still a wonderful cook. Her pieces on Edith Sitwell, Eudora Welty, Virginia Woolf, and Katherine Mansfield are observant and generous pleasures; she roughs up a pompous T. S. Eliot in defense of Thomas Hardy, takes Lady Chatterley for a thoroughly deserved walk in the woods, and in "The Wooden Umbrella," one of three pieces on Gertrude Stein, vents her spleen with admirable wit and accuracy. Who but Gertrude and Alice wouldn't enjoy the following characterization? "Considering her tepid, sluggish nature, really sluggish like something eating its way through a leaf, Miss Stein could grow quite animated on the subject of her early family life, and some of her stories are as pretty and innocent as lizards running over tombstones on a hot day in Maryland." Porter attacks Stein with considerable understanding. The difficulty for Porter is that her being somewhat right about Stein simply doesn't matter. At the end, Gertrude sits amid the wreckage of her furniture like a Roman senator undisturbed by his city's scrumbled marble.

Porter is a discriminating and passionate critic, but she deals mostly with a work's general effects and does not venture to bore her reader with the many small strokes that, when so many are completed, create the ultimate result. Unless she is reminiscing about an experience of her own. Then the lines are drawn like bowstrings. For instance, when Eliot reads in front of Joyce (and Porter) at Shakespeare and Company: "The poet before us had a face as severe as Dante's, the eyes fiercely defensive, the mouth bitter, the nose grander and much higher bridged than his photographs then showed; the whole profile looked like a bird of prey of some sort. He might have been alone, reading to himself aloud, not once did he glance at his listeners."

Her own commentary can be eloquent—though executed with a bit of the shapelessness she is prepared to risk in an essay—when she remembers an anecdote about Tolstoy, which alleges the old man said, as mad as Lear, that he would tell the real story about women only from his coffin and only when he felt the shovelfuls falling on his face:

It's a marvelous picture. Tolstoy was merely roaring in the frenzy roused in him in face of his wife's terrible, relentless adoration; her shameless fertility, her unbearable fidelity, the shocking series of jealous revenges she took upon him for his hardness of heart and wickedness to her, the whole mystery of her oppressive femaleness. He did not know the truth about women, not even about that one who was the curse of his life. He did not know the truth about himself. This is not surprising, for no one does know the truth, either about himself or about anyone else, and all recorded human acts and words are open testimony to our endless efforts to know each other, and our failure to do so.

Our ignorance is reassuring to Porter because the self she fears she is she hopes will remain unknowable to others, while the self she wishes she were takes its public place. Yet the self she regretted and the self she desired are actually states of the populous nation that a self is: cowgirl, coquette, cook, queen, artist, the disillusioned well-used lady, and the girl with a dream—a roaring, riotous, shrewd, and foolish community of loving and quarreling equals.

During a notable moment of scrutiny as she entered her thirty-eighth year, Katherine Anne Porter confessed, "When I was quite young I decided to set my limitations moderately. Maybe this was my mistake. For by setting my bounds, I find they are real things and have a way of closing upon me without my (conscious) consent." Although O'Connor, Welty, and Porter obliged us by writing novels, it is for short stories they are generally remembered, in which more polish for small surfaces is routinely expected, whereas writers like Tolstoy, Faulkner, and Stein—well, they are moving mountains, and it doesn't matter if they leave a small mess here and there like great chefs in their kitchens. Does it?

Harper's Magazine, 2009
Published in *Life Sentences,* 2012

THREE PHOTOS OF COLETTE

First　There is a much-folded photograph reproduced in Yvonne Mitch-
Photo　ell's charming and richly illustrated biography of Colette which
　　　shows Monsieur Willy and his wife at a lonely table.* A white rail
of the sort you might find in a baroque church divides the dining room from
the rest of the apartment. This rail passes in front of us, opening only to
provide an entrance to the space, and we can easily imagine taking a rising
or descending step toward the chalk-white cloth, which, in the photograph,
advances to occupy the railing's compositional place; but whether the step
should be up or down, it is difficult, and even undesirable, to say.

Colette was always able to project an expressive image upon the photographer's plate, just as her own style gave the objects it described a lively face: the
grass snake coiled like a snail shell by her hand or the heath spiders she says
are pink and round as pearls; indeed, the quality of every quality, the rhythm
of every contour, is rendered as by a composer, so that, with the immediacy
of music and thus as suddenly as Marguerite is brought before Faust by the
magic of Mephistopheles, we are seated in a country schoolroom in company with Claudine or on the big embarrassed bed of her girlfriend, Luce,
who has fallen from the provinces to Paris like the fruit she chews, and now
serves her fat "uncle" in return for silks. The camera, too, has brought us to
a flat on the rue de Courcelles, and put us in front of this frozen tableau, the
gray domestic world of women: full of cosmetics and clutter, yet ordered
and empty, expensively utensiled, but patently futile, noisy and corseted and
fussy, deathly still.

To the right on that white rail squats a cut-glass decanter which appears
nevertheless to contain a candle, and on the left rests a large, probably brass,

* Yvonne Mitchell, *Colette: A Taste for Life* (New York: Harcourt Brace Jovanovich, 1975), pp.
68–69.

bell. Two half-full Burgundy bottles, well corked, clearly white and red, flank Willy's plate. He is eating fruit, and a basket of apples draped with grapes sits on the table in front of him. A Persian rug embarrasses the edges of the luncheon linen like a poorly fitting petticoat. When the meal is removed (. . . the bell does not look rung, though perhaps once it rang . . .), the rug remains to enliven the tabletop and disguise its scars.

It is a long way from the much-loved landscape of Colette's childhood, the woods which she described in perhaps the first pages she ever wrote:

> No small creatures in those great woods; no tall grasses; but beaten earth, now dry, and sonorous, now soft on account of the springs. Rabbits with white scuts range through them and timid deer who run so fast that you can only guess their passage. Great heavy pheasants too, red and golden, and wild boars (I've never seen one) and wolves. I heard a wolf once, at the beginning of winter, while I was picking up beech-nuts—those nice, oily little beech-nuts that tickle your throat and make you cough. Sometimes storm-showers surprise you in those woods; you huddle under an oak that is thicker than the others and listen to the rain pattering up there as if on a roof. You're so well-sheltered that when you come out of those depths you are quite lost and dazzled and feel ill at ease in the broad daylight.
>
> [*Claudine at School*]

In a mirror beyond the married pair, who sit in profile to us, the room behind our backs floats like a world on water. There is a lamp, a corner cupboard like a standing corpse, and in the distance, deeply submerged, a dark frame shorelining something that looks like a boarded-up lake. I don't see Willy's image, though over the low mantel the mirror seems well placed to perceive him. His attention is fixed on some book we cannot see, or on perhaps a bit of biscuit, crumb of cheese, or sheaf of notes. A white collar obliterates his throat. He is absorbed, composed. He wears a dark suit and a second beard behind his ears. He is distinguished and sits well forward on the caned seat of his chair.

Across from him, Colette is held firmly inside her clothes the way her napkin lies rolled and ringed beside her. A silk blouse, gray in the photograph as stone, grasps each wrist; a beaded collar closes about her neck; and a satin belt is cinched about her waist. To make room for her elbows and remove her life, she has pushed away a plate on which there remains the indistinct skin of a grape, and she is leaning forward now to rest her breasts on the table and her right cheek heavily on the peak of her clasped hands.

Her stare is nowhere, and her unnaturally pale face seems fastened to her head like a mask. Above the black velvet bow in her flattened hair there is a ghostly photo of Willy, top-hatted, hanging on the wall, while on the Oriental rug at her skirt-covered feet is a white blob like a darning egg—a toy, one supposes, a ball for Toby-Chien. The creases in the photograph appear as cracks in the plaster, as broken glass, as lines of worry on the walls, ill fortune in the furniture, as judgments, omens, anger.

Who but Willy, who adored his image and desired its presence everywhere; who had a thousand depictions of himself—including caricatures and paintings—made and printed and posted about in Paris like the herald of a social cure; who even persuaded Colette to dress herself like Polaire, the Algerian actress then playing Claudine to full loud houses, in order to enhance certain lesbian allusions; and who dared to have himself photographed standing behind his "twins" as though he were their evil Svengali, not merely their benevolent Papa; who but Willy would have posed for such a domestic picture, or permitted Colette's unhappiness or his own indifference—their total estrangement—to be so nakedly stated? Perhaps it was his own fist which folded their images together in a kiss—a curse—when he saw more than boredom in her emptied gaze, but in addition how his young wife's eyes had fallen like early apples onto a hard and distant interior earth.

It is not difficult to see ourselves what the Parisian public saw and enjoyed in these novels about Claudine which Colette had written almost accidentally, first at the suggestion and then the insistence of her greedy usurious Monsieur; but what can we find in them now but Colette? for we have read Violette Leduc since then, among others, and have played all the schoolgirl games; we have had quite enough of lewd and giggling innocence, of unaimed spite and wide-open ego, of coltish spirits, silly presumption, ignorant courage, or naïve trust. Natural wit's old hat; sweet fears, fresh hope, we've had instance after instance of; and the contrast between mistress and maid, cynicism and faith, the unripe and the spoiled, cannot strike us anymore with tragic weight or moral force. What worms we are, like Willy, to have forsaken the fruit to cannibalize its grubs!

In any case, there are no silly schoolgirls anymore, and if the public nowadays wants to know what young girls think, they are served a stronger brew than *Daisy Miller* or *What Maisie Knew.* Wedding nights are still disappointments, but scarcely surprises; the war between the sexes has never been noisier, meaner, or emptier of sense, adultery more snoozily middle-class, or homosexuality more sordid—no, and trivial commonplace lives, for Colette a specialty, have never been more blandly cream-of-wheat, more catsup leaked on steak, reaching stale middling heights; nor has the production of vapid conversation or cretinous creature comforts, shimmering baubles and other visual distractions—football, films—fallen off, on the contrary, or the use of the carnal drug; and loneliness is as large as it ever was: paper napkins snuffed in plastic glasses testify to it, the floor of every closet cries out "Love me!," wadded towels, too, windows on which the images of waiting faces have been fixed, long halls like highways, and on kitchen counters, where waxy cartons speak of it to knives smeared with crumbs and purple jelly; so that the fascination we now find in these novels about Claudine, and it is certainly there, is due solely to the ever-fresh charm—the instinctive grace— the greatness of Colette, which is certainly immense.

Colette was not the sort of natural genius whose eventual vocation appears spelled out on baby's Beethovian brow. Her intelligence, her curiosity would not allow her to remain safely at home where she really wanted to be, but let her be taken in by Willy's worldliness and sophistication, as so many were—perhaps by his masterful gaze, his sexy voice—and carried out of her little Burgundian town, where indeed hard times were another incentive, to the great city, no doubt the way captives were once brought to Rome for amusing display. She must almost immediately have felt as Rilke's hero, Malte, did: surprise that people came there to live when the place seemed best fitted to sustain physical distress, loneliness, and fear, and supplied only the facilities for dying. In any event, it was this paunchy old publicist, who picked brains better than crows clean carrion, who introduced Colette to the smoky world of men, and he did it with a thoroughness to inspire praise and discourage imitation.

The recognitions began immediately, if the wedding night is immediate enough, but only gradually did the full measure of her mistake stretch the dressmaker's tape to its tip. By and by (fine words for what it emotionally meant), her toes growing cold in the too-big bed, she was twisted by jealousy like a wet towel until she wept, and was compelled to admit that her husband did a good bit more than neglect her like a friendless pet. She was in fact left alone all day in a small cold flat with a poisonous stove, where she dined on nuts and fruit like a monkey and nibbled candy like someone kept. Then fell evening, when she was led through salons like a fox terrier on a chain, as Cocteau said, and thence to musicales which Willy might review but at which, in any case, he must be seen, and finally to cafés full of smirk and innuendo and late hours. What was there to say? to these polished and brittle homosexuals? to these softly jowled fat Don Juans? by a girl from the country? with a thick Burgundian burr? especially since they were none of them red-and-golden pheasants or even geese come down on a smooth deep lake.

Willy's jaded sexual interests were limited to her innocence, which stimulated him the way new snow invites small boys to trample it, and he had at once begun to cheat, as Colette discovered one day when, by unforgivably demeaning herself, she followed and discovered him with a foul-tongued, back-bumped dwarf, little Lotte Kinceler, whom Colette could only pity, and who later blew her mouth apart like glass, committing suicide with a symbolic substitute for what had murdered her already. Willy eventually brought his other cocottes to Colette's apartment, where they would finger her things and speak smut. He also carted his collection of pornography with them when they traveled to the country, either to visit and vacation or to escape creditors. And he clung to the skirts of bankruptcy like a bewildered boy.

This wit and bon vivant and raconteur, moreover, this powerful journalist and man-about-town, signed his name to books he hadn't written, claimed ideas he hadn't had, professed tastes he'd never formed. Willy consumed talent like a pimp, and Colette slowly realized that she'd become his latest literary whore in addition to her other duties; that the true sensitivity, intelligence, and taste, furthermore, were on her side; that grace was hers, and honest animal sensuality, the clear uncluttered eye, even good character, industry, and decent ambition, were hers rather than his; that nevertheless she had no vocation, no real role, no independence, a rudimentary education, no polish, no funds; and so she must do her stint and wait at the window and furnish his life, when he chose to share it, with slippers and prattle and pie; she must be obedient and willing and patient and pretty, cheerful and faithful on top of it, like dung decorated with whipped cream and a cherry, though now she was braidless and ill and bruised, unfresh and scrambled as crawled-over snow; still she was supposed to be grateful, and eager to unbutton his vest and remove his tie, to clasp his fat back in amorous arms, and closely regard, even admire, that thick neck swollen with blood and exertion, which rose from his trunk on those occasions like a peeled raw root, while her own body went through the sorrowful motions of love to a conclusion which had from the first time to the last to be a burning and shameful, embittering lie.

Colette could not write to her mother of her misery—not just yet— and later the *Claudines*, those ostensible fictions, gave her a chance at the truth, while her warm and optimistic letters home to Sido, by virtue of what they left out, were in effect made up. Memoirs mixed with fiction, fictions compounded of fact: these were to remain the poles of her work, and the journalism she eventually produced—made of impressionistic, on-the-spot responses—was like a switch engine shunted between these principal stops. Colette was clearly not a novelist by nature, as her beloved Balzac was. She wrote her early novels on demand; the key was turned in the lock. Her plays were also a response to pressing necessities, and she toured in them eventually, and bared her bosom, too, and struck eloquent attitudes like one of those seductive figures who advertise perfumes: in order to live, to escape being cast forever in the role of a little girl or superfluous femme; although there can be scarcely any doubt that a large part of her yearned to be fed sweets—comforted, cosseted, ruled.

Writing was furthermore a means of shading her mother's eyes. It earned Willy's parsimonious praise and shifted slowly the direction of dependency between them. As time and her success reduced these complex causes to simple considerations, Colette turned more and more openly to autobiography, to that sort of reposeful meditation which was to make her great: the evocation of nature and the celebration of the senses, the beautiful rewording and recovery of her life.

But in Paris Colette found herself strangely imprisoned in an open ruin—a marriage destroyed because of jealousy, mistrust, infidelity, a series of explosive truths—with physique and spirit weakened by her sense of the futility of everything, aching loneliness, the worn-out view from her window, her empty odd hours and odder diet. So she fell ill—what else was there to do?—sickened by fumes from a salamander stove, by the little cruelties of daily life, the slick wig of evil tongues and stupid wag of amorous pastimes, but especially by lies both large and immensely petty. She was burning—that was it—consumed by a nostalgia which became a happy characteristic of her consciousness when she was well, the way her breasts continued to gladden her body. Yet among all those innumerable disappointments which close over a soul grown small and tender as a snail to be swallowed, there was the persistent reappearance of reality like a hard shell or bitter pit. Always that. And every dream dead of the truth. The future, too—dead of it.

Sido had to be summoned at last. That resilient will which was to be the core of Claudine's charm and the center of Colette's strength during a difficult life had become as loose and limp in her body as the bedclothes on her bed, and slid away whenever she rose. Recovery was slow, but her illness won her a few more trips into the country, a little respite from the gentleman in the black hat.

Second   The second photo shows us Willy, pen in hand, forcefully facing the
Photo   photographer. He is seated at another table, also berugged, another mantel behind him, other paintings, further glass glint, smears of image and reflection, amply figured in an ample darkness.* He could well be wearing the same suit. There is a spread of papers signifying industry, a

* Mitchell, *Colette,* p. 62.

penholder, silver tray, a book or two, perhaps a magnifying glass. To his left Colette sits with her fingers holding down a passage on its page as if it could wiggle away. No doubt Willy wants this important section marked, held for him like a seat at a play. The hands are patient. They serve his needs. While Willy and the camera are tête-à-tête, Colette's gaze, as if she'd carried it between the two pictures like a brimming bowl, slips weakly over the edge of the table and disappears into the void. Her expression is one of quiet but profound sadness. The far side of her face is as white as her blouse, though barely there, and a tie covered with bursts of light falls from a high tight collar like a crack of dark sky between clouds.

To write about school in a copybook—to continue the little themes indefinitely into life—what could be more natural? but fate had to conspire almost constantly to bring it about. She and Willy stayed at her old school for a few days while on vacation one July (she writes about this "return" in *Claudine en Ménage*), and back in Paris that fall Willy suggests that she write down and spice up the best of what she remembers of those carefree girlish times. This idea, coming from Willy, was not so surprising, since Willy was used to hiring out such work, and he doubtless expected her scribblings to come to nothing. It was a therapeutic occupation, like needlepoint and tatting: perhaps it would provide some private titillation, little more, and direct her chatter from his ear to the no-longer-listening and indifferent page. Indeed, Willy found only dull trivia when he later examined the six exercise books Colette had filled. There was nothing he could use. Too bad, but no matter.

Having nibbled on the pen, Colette did not suddenly become insatiable. When Willy tossed her work deep into his black desk, she was content, as regards that, to return to her candy and her cat; yet she continued to write long letters, as she had always done, not understanding how they reflected her true and early love of language, her real vocation. Chance again put these notebooks back in Willy's hands. Two years later he happens on them while cleaning out the rear of a drawer.* He finds them interesting—useful—this time, though publishers are not easily convinced, and refuse more than once to issue Willy's saucy little novel about a pack of odd, though ordinary, kids, a pair of overly fast friends, some childish high jinks, and one long worrisome exam; and they continue to refuse even after Willy has had its actual

* Maria Le Hardouin says it was a few months (*Colette: A Biographical Study* [London: Staples, 1958]), but most biographers fix the time at two years (Mitchell, *Colette;* Margaret Crosland in her two books *Madame Colette: A Provincial in Paris* [London: Peter Owen, 1953], and *Colette: The Difficulty of Loving* [Indianapolis: Bobbs-Merrill, 1973]); Elaine Marks, *Colette* [New Brunswick, N.J.: Rutgers University Press, 1960]). Margaret Davies (*Colette* [New York: Grove Press, 1961]) suggests that it was two to three. Maurice Goudeket's memoir (*Close to Colette* [London: Secker & Warburg, 1957]) does not cover this period.

author bend a few relationships toward the piquant and perverse. *Claudine à l'École* was not published until 1900, some six years after its very circumstantial composition. Then twenty-seven, Colette had been married from her twentieth year to the Monsieur Willy who signed the volume and composed its foreword, one which put much of the truth inside a joke: that the book had been written by a schoolgirl—Claudine herself.

Sales began slowly, but with favorable reviews and word of mouth, the novel became a sensation. Willy redoubled his visits to the photographer, and set Colette to work on a second confection—a briefer, poorer book, but an even greater success. Soon hats and collars, ice creams, lotions, perfumes carried Claudine's name. Then there was the play, and more Claudines, each shorter, more ambiguous, less resolutely cheerful. Meanwhile, Colette kept herself trim in her little private gym, and began to choose her future—a future open to a woman of her present class and condition—the stage.*

Nearly unnoticed amidst the schoolgirl gush of the Claudine books, the amorous titivations, the mounting references to immediate Parisian social life—all calculated to entice—was Colette's angry exposure of the condition of young women in rural France. What was a Burgundian girl to do? In *Claudine at School*, for instance, appears this sudden paragraph of social commentary. The girls are readying themselves for a spelling test:

> There was a great hush of concentration. No wonder! Five-sixths of these little girls had their whole future at stake. And to think that all of those would become school-mistresses, that they would toil from seven in the morning till five in the afternoon and tremble before a Head-mistress who would be unkind most of the time, to earn seventy-five francs a month! Out of those sixty girls, forty-five were the daughters of peasants or manual labourers; in order not to work in the fields or at the loom, they had preferred to make their skins yellow and their chests hollow and deform their right shoulders. They were bravely preparing to spend three years at a Training College, getting up at five a.m. and going to bed at eight-thirty p.m. and having two hours recreation out of the twenty-four and ruining their digestions, since few stomachs survived three years of the college refectory. But at least they would wear hats and would not make clothes for other people or look after

---

* Nothing went to waste: this music-hall life, too, almost accidentally arrived at, would provide the background and some of the form for *Mitsou* (where a playlet is inadequately digested), as well as for *Music Hall Sidelights* (a series of vivid sketches), and *The Vagabond*, perhaps her first fully realized fiction—a novel in which the sexual dilemma of the "working woman" is beautifully defined.

animals or draw buckets from the well, and they would despise their parents.

Claudine is not in school to come to this. Nor has she been reluctantly badgered there by a mother who wishes her daughter to escape, as one of the girls who fails explains to Claudine:

> Mother sent me to boarding-school, father he didn't want it, he said I'd do best looking after the house like my sisters, and doing the washing and digging the garden. Mother, she didn't want it—it was her as they listened to. They made me ill, trying to make me learn—and you see how I come over today.

Although Colette will carry on a lifelong romance with little villages and country gardens, in her less reminiscent moods she will realize that despite her attachment to her mother, her beloved Sido, she could never have stayed put.

Come over here, little girl, and let me show you something, wheedles the dirty old world, and sweet ignorant Claudine—well—all tiptoes, she does want to be wheedled; she does want to see. Weary of innocence, she does desire to know what the sexual fuss is all about. She is a tight string eager to sound yet fearful of the music; and since she wants to take risks while retaining her safety, she will pass from one school to another, one teacher to another, one parent to another, in every case learning the unforeseen and unexpected, insecure on one leg because, mistrustful of the ground, she cannot chance having both put firmly down together.

So curiosity . . . not your window-shoppers' sort, those strollers whose eyes in muggy weather light like nervous flies on crumbs and sweets yet leave without lessening their prize or fattening themselves; but the curiosity that bites the peach to the pit and allows the mouth to fill with juice like a basin; that licks hard and listens, that fingers and sniffs and above all looks, regards—watches, stares, peers—that observes, receives, as an infant explores its world, all drool and smear, as if the world were a fistful of thumbs . . . such curiosity consumes both Colette and Claudine, and unties them from their homes, and lets them for a time believe that certain dashing older gentlemen will open the earth for them, expose life as they expect it to be exposed, and give them the only kind of experience that counts: carnal knowledge of all things.

These Claudines, then . . . they want to know because they believe they already *do* know, the way one who loves fruit knows, when offered a mango from the moon, what to expect; and they expect the loyal, tender, teasing affection of the schoolgirl crush to continue: the close and confiding companionship, the pleasure of the undemanding caress, the cuddle which consummates only closeness; yet in addition they want motherly putting right, fatherly forgiveness and almost papal indulgence; they expect that the sights and sounds, the glorious affairs of the world which their husbands will now bring before them gleaming like bolts of silk, will belong to the same happy activities as catching toads, peeling back tree bark, or powdering the cheeks with dandelions and oranging the nose; that music will ravish the ear the way the trill of the blackbird does; that literature will hold the mind in sweet suspense the way fairy tales once did; that paintings will crowd the eye with the delights of a colorful garden, and the city streets will be filled with the same cool dew-moist country morning air they fed on as children. But they shall not receive what they expect; the tongue will be about other business; one will hear in masterpieces only pride and bitter contention; buildings will have grandeur but no flowerpots or chickens; and these Claudines will exchange the flushed cheek for the swollen vein, and instead of companionship, they will get sex and absurd games composed of pinch, leer, and giggle—that's what will happen to "let's pretend."

The great male will disappear into the jungle like the back of an elusive ape, and Claudine shall see little of his strength again, his intelligence or industry, his heroics on the Bourse like Horatio at the bridge (didn't Colette see Henri de Jouvenel, editor and diplomat and duelist and hero of the war, away to work each day, and didn't he often bring his mistress home with him, as Willy had when he was husband number one?); the great affairs of the world will turn into tawdry liaisons, important meetings into assignations, deals into vulgar dealings, and the *en famille* hero will be weary and whining and weak, reminding her of all those dumb boys she knew as a child, selfish, full of fat and vanity like patrons waiting to be served and humored, admired and not observed.

Is the occasional orgasm sufficient compensation? Is it the prize of pure surrender, what's gained from all that giving up? There'll be silk stockings and velvet sofas maybe, the customary caviar, tasting at first of frog water but later of money and the secretions of sex, then divine champagne, the supreme soda, and rubber-tired rides through the Bois de Boulogne; perhaps there'll be rich ugly friends, ritzy at-homes, a few young men with whom one may flirt, a homosexual confidant with long fingers, soft skin, and a beautiful cravat, perfumes and powders of an unimaginable subtlety with which to dust and wet the body, many deep baths, bonbons filled with sweet liqueurs, a procession of mildly salacious and sentimental books by Paul de Kock and company—good heavens, what's the problem?—new uses for the limbs, a tantalizing glimpse of the abyss, the latest sins, envy certainly, a little spite, jealousy like a vaginal itch, and perfect boredom.

And the mirror, like justice, is your aid but never your friend.

Dependent as a young girl is, she has only her body to sustain her. Her body has brought her to Paris. Her body can free her from her husband if she wants to go on the stage or be a whore, but she must possess a pleasant face, a fresh complexion, good limbs, prominent breasts, a narrow waist. She will succeed only so long as she gives pleasure to men. To do that, she must know how to flatter, how to be silent, when to be weak; for women must be weak in public, strong at home, compliant in private.

The prudent woman will not accept gifts from just any body, so frigidity will be the rule. To become dependent there, to allow a male that power over you, to lose the last of your lands without a struggle, the citadel of sensation, is to surrender everything and enjoy even the humiliation of your rape.

The Claudine books do not contain the complete scenario. The independent woman goes to bed with bankers and invests her tips with wisdom on the Bourse, and the time will come when she will keep men as she was kept, requesting their erections, and requiring them to pleasure her as she was once supine and sweetly willing. A woman who has children and who remains married will someday sell her daughters off as she was sold, and by middle age the intelligent, ambitious ones will be so accomplished at managing the world through their husbands—as if soft arms were in those manly sleeves—and so skilled at beating back female competition, so sly with insinuation, clever with wigs and rouge, so unscrupulous about the truth, adept at blackmail and intrigue, hard inside as cinders, that males would fall to their knees in terrified admiration if they believed to their bones what they've hitherto only suspected, and occasionally felt: the scornful condescension which has shivered the small hairs of their skin when they turned away to sleep sometimes in bedrooms shut away from any breeze.

During wars, as it is written in *La Fin de Chéri,* when the men go off to be brave in front of one another, rump to rump and arm in arm and hand to hand (for that's *esprit de corps*), the women, as dangerous as the slaves which the Spartan soldiers left behind, take over. They discover, the way Rosie the Riveter did, that women can shape the real world as well as any man; that manipulating men has made them peculiarly fit for politics and administration; and that they become men then, improving on the species; for it never occurred to Colette (as it never did to Gertrude Stein) to question the roles, only the assignments of the players.

There is one value in this sort of life, one currency which can be cashed like grapes crushed in the mouth, spent in the released limbs, received from one's surroundings as simply as rain, and that is the quiet ease of soul called contentment, the joyful joining of the body to the world which we vaguely spell as pleasure. The realm of animals and nature, quiet open country, unassuming streams and ponds, flowering plants: these yield that pleasure up with greatest certainty and safety, and young Claudine and the mature Colette are sensualists of a greedy straightforwardness and simplicity supreme enough to put Pierre Louÿs's perversities to rout, and J.-K. Huysman's hothouse visions and rococo plans, like out-of-fashion paintings, into the museum basement.

But the body fails us and the mirror knows, and we no longer insist that the gray hush be carried off its surface by the cloth, for we have run to fat, and wrinkles encircle the eyes and notch the neck, where the skin wattles, and the flesh of the arms hangs loose like an overlarge sleeve, veins thicken like ropes and empurple the body as though they had been drawn there by a pen, freckles darken, liver spots appear, the hair . . . ah, the hair is exhausted and gray and lusterless, in weary rolls like cornered lint.

Third Photo   It is the hair we see in the final photographs, after arthritis has marooned her on that pillowed divan she calls her raft. She wears a futile sweater against the chill which swells from within now like a puff of cold breath, and a fur bedspread is draped over her former body. She is looking at us with Claudine's eyes and Colette's mouth. Her alertness is utterly unlike the hopelessness we earlier saw when she sat beside Willy. It is preternaturally intense. Her jaw juts as it always did; her nose has not lost its longish taper either; the brow has risen, lying beneath her frizzy hair like snow beneath a wintering bush; and her hands, thank god, can still form words. A table crosses her body like a bridge, running toward the window which overlooks the gardens of the Palais-Royal, and bearing, like pedestrians trooping over it, a telephone, pen and little pitcher chocked with spares, her spectacles, some papers (what's that, an address book?), a potted plant overbearingly in bloom, and plenty of bleaching sunshine. One of the immortals, she will soon die, and be given a state funeral and denied consecrated ground on the same day.

Claudine never had enough to do. She had no children, few plants, and her husband's servants. She had her husband, too, who kept her at ends as loose as carpet fringe. She gives way to her impulses and encourages her moods. She recoils from imprisonment but plays at being kept. Yet what can a plaything feel but the handling? Love is the great distraction. Romance can fill you better than pasta, and when it's digested it leaves you thin. Love gives you the sense of having been alive, but the life of love is always in the past tense, in that remembered moment when a curl touched your cheek or an amorous glance felt like a warm palm on the belly—there, where the smallest muscles tremble to the touch like an animal. Chéri, too, a male Claudine in many ways, though without her elasticity, can only hunger and fondle, fuck and sleep; find his intermittent being in his mother-mistress, Léa's arms, as Claudine finds hers in Renaud's, her equally fatherly lover. "Devoting oneself to sensual pleasure is not a career for a respectable man," Colette writes in *L'Étoile Vesper,* or for a woman who would live past fifty either, since by that time . . . time . . .

Love. Always *that* in these silly French novels. Isn't there another subject, Jouvenel had complained, beside incestuous longing, adultery, absence? Well, not really. Look at how this tiny boudoir mirror reflects all the larger relations! Because novels about love are inevitably about its failures, and the failure of love leads directly to the need for an alternative salvation which can lie nowhere else but in one's work, although most work is as impermanent as pleasure, often even hurtful, and pointless to boot; still, for a fortunate few (and if they are women they are very few and fortunate indeed), there is the chance for a redeeming relation to some creative medium—in Colette's case, as Fate finally settled it, the written word.

The better word, as she suggested her hunt was—the better word. But the better word did not fall toward her out of space like a star, nor did the untranslatable rhythms of her prose dance like urchins in the street beneath her flat. Words arose, came to her, fell in line, principally as she reflected upon her life, whether it was fiction she was writing or something else. Experience was her dictionary, and what we can observe, as we read through the *Claudine*s, is the compiling of that dictionary, and how, out of that large scrawly book of girlish words, is finally shaped an art of grave maturity, subtlety, perception, grace, one which is at once so filled with Colette's own presence and yet so open to the reader, so resolutely aimed, that it masters a mode: *le style intime,* one would be tempted to dub it, if that didn't suggest it was a naughty perfume.

The memory transcribes loops. It begins here where I am; it departs for the past, then returns to me through possibly fancy slips and spins like a yo-yo to the hand. Colette was fond of mimicking such motion, beginning a chapter with Claudine breathless from an outing or a visit, and then returning the narrative through some carriage ride or concert until Claudine is once more at home. In this way the event is bracketed by endings at both ends (and ends as it began). The immediate moment can benefit then from the play of reflection, although there is little benefit from reflection in the Claudine books, which are for the most part shallow indeed. Plunged into iniquity, Claudine emerges as clean as a washed doll.

Events are naturally related in the first person. Even *Chéri,* which is written in the third, has every quality of the quiet "I." The tone is of course girlish in these girlish books, but it is that of the confidential exchange in almost all of them: the personal letter, the intense tête-à-tête, confessions passed between chums like shared toys, or at its most innocent, it has the character of a daughter's report of what happened on her first date (one suspects the presence of Sido, listening almost in the reader's place).

Colette will copy the manner of the diary or journal, too, but also include a great deal of designedly empty and idle yet lively chatter. Opportunities will be manufactured for the exchange of confidences, though the effect is nothing like that of Henry James. Equally contrived, the result is merely artificial, and unfortunately often cheap. Verbal voyeurism is the rule. Claudine enjoys hearing how it is to be a kept woman from her former school chum Luce: "Old thing, you've got to tell me all." "He's old, my uncle, but he has impossible ideas. Sometimes he makes me get down on all-fours and run about the room like that. And he runs after me on all-fours too. . . . Then he jumps on me, bellowing: 'I'm a wild beast!'" Claudine's husband, Renaud, and Marcel, his homosexual son, are both excited by accounts of amorous encounters. "I implore you, do tell me all about Lucy. I'll be nice. . . ." "What next, Claudine, what next?" "I'll tell you everything, Claudine," Annie promises, and Claudine is soon responding: "Go on, go on, just the main facts."*

It is not the promise of dirty details which makes the style so personal and beckoning. Confessions can be as public as billboards, and our bookstores are as cluttered by beseechments and soulful outcries as our highways. It may be useful to remind ourselves how other masters of so-called female fiction sound, how done up in public prose, not plain brown paper, most conversations are. Here is an example of pure melodrama: public to its core. It has no internality. Clarissa has determined not to run off with Lovelace:

> Fear nothing, dearest creature, said he. Let us hasten away—the chariot is at hand. . . .
>
> O Mr. Lovelace, said I, I cannot go with you—*indeed* I cannot—I wrote you word so—let go my hand and you shall see my letter. . . .

* Robert Cottrell's suggestion that not all this sexual leering can be blamed on Willy is correct, I think: "Titillation resulting from an artful toying with debauchery is one of the veins Colette worked, and it crops up even in the books of her maturity" (*Colette* [New York: Frederick Ungar, 1974], p. 23). This is perhaps the best critical introduction to Colette: brief, clear, balanced, and very perceptive. Marvin Mudrick makes a similar complaint in his *Hudson Review* article, "Colette, Claudine, and Willy," vol. 16, no. 4 (1963–1964), pp. 559–72, but Mudrick's sometimes eloquent piece is also peevish, and his drearily old-fashioned conception of what counts in fiction leads him to overlook the virtues of these books while somewhat misstating their flaws.

. . . here we shall be discovered in a moment. Speed away my charmer—this is the moment of your deliverance—if you neglect this opportunity you *never* can have such another.

What is it you mean, sir? Let go my hand: for I tell you . . . that I will sooner die than go with you.

Good God! said he . . . what is it I hear!

Good God, what one hears, indeed! Well, Richardson will not greet us in his dressing gown, you can be certain of that (though in dots and dashes like something sent in Morse), nor will Jane Austen go out without her Latinated English buttoned on; but Colette is always carefully *en déshabille.* There is the unguarded expression of emotion (the all-too-frequent exclamation and oo-la-la!); there's the candid opinion dropped as casually as a grape, the glee-fully malicious judgments,

Model pupils! . . . they exasperate me so much with their good behav-ior and their pretty, neat handwriting and their silly identical flat, flabby faces and sheep's eyes full of maudlin mildness. They swot all the time; they're bursting with good marks; they're prim and underhand and their breath smells of glue. Ugh!

the broken phrases, sentences darting in different directions like fish, gentle repetitions, wholly convincing observations,

That lanky bean-pole stood and made a secret grimace, like a cat about to be sick . . .

and above all the flash of fine metaphor, sometimes one of only local gover-nance like this from *The Last of Chéri:*

He never went to the hospital again, and thereafter Edmée invited him to go only as a perfunctory gesture, such as one makes when one offers game to a vegetarian guest.

or sometimes an image which is both accurate summation and continuing symbol, as this from the same page:

He grew thoughtful now, prey to an idleness that, before the war, had been agreeable, varied, as full of meaning as the resonant note of an empty, uncracked cup.

and when we look down the length of her sentences, we see the energy which rushes up through them like the bubbler in the park—they are alive—even when otherwise they are callow and jejune, or even when they move with an almost Jamesian majesty, as they often do through the stories which make up *The Tender Shoot*, or reveal the pruned, precise lyricism, the romantic simplicity of a finely shaped head beneath a haircut:

> Few memories have remained as dear to me as the memory of those meals without plates, cutlery or cloth, of those expeditions on two wheels. The cool sky, the rain in drops, the snow in flakes, the sparse, rusty grass, the tameness of the birds.

Colette did not invent so much as modify her memory; thus her work required continual return; yet retracing well demands forgetting, too, or the early line will soon be overlaid with other lines and lose all definition. None of us now matches her skill at rendering the actual contours of experience. How far can we see out of raised eyebrows? How straight can we speak with a curled lip? Irony, ambiguity, skepticism—these aren't attitudes anymore which come and go like moods, but parts of our anatomy. However, Colette could recall a young girl's innocent offer of commitment and not dismay it with the disappointments and betrayals which she knew were sure to follow. She did not feel obliged to insist that the confusions of the loving self rise from their depths to trouble every feeling just because she knew they were there and wanted us to know she knew. Our illusions, when they shattered, spilled affection like a cheap perfume which clings to our surroundings, overscenting, so that the sick smell of ourselves is everywhere, however frantically we move. In English, how many genuine love stories have we had since Ford wrote *Some Do Not . . .* ?

Colette is being pushed to pen it; nevertheless, *Claudine in Paris* is often a sadly meretricious book. Despite its causes, and despite the fact that she herself has suffered seven years of Willy like the plague, Colette can still remember what her hopes were—how it was—and can render Claudine's feelings for this older man (handsomer than her husband to be sure, but close enough in every other way to guarantee discomfort) with a rare and convincing genuineness. In the best of these books, *Claudine Married*, there are many unreal and merely fabricated things, but the passion is real: at the sight of her beloved's breasts, she aches and fears and trembles, is full of the gentlest and most giving hunger.

Perhaps the impossibility of love should be our only subject (it was certainly one of Colette's), but living was not impossible, only difficult. There was always before her the specter, when love failed, when pleasure went out of the wet grass, and the air hung like further leaves in the quiet trees; there was always the possibility that these scents, these observations, these open mornings when the sky threw itself back out of the way like a concealing sheet; that not only would they pass as all things do, but that they'd leave no trace behind but triviality—snail slime, worm hole, bug bite, mouth with chocolate-covered corners to be buried in.

HE LIKED HIS COCOA THICK
NOT THIN

In one of her beautiful late stories, "The Photographer's Missus," she gives that missus, in explanation of her attempted suicide, the following speech:

> . . . whatever do you think came into my head one morning when I was cutting up some breast of veal? I said to myself: "I did breast of veal with green peas only last Saturday, all very nice, but one mustn't overdo it, a week goes by so fast. It's eleven already, my husband's got a christening group coming to pose at half-past one, I must get my washing-up done before the clients arrive, my husband doesn't like to hear me through the wall rattling crockery or poking the stove when clients are in the studio. . . . And after that I must go out, there's that cleaner who still hasn't finished taking the shine off my husband's black suit, I'll have to have a sharp word with her. If I get back to do my ironing before dark, I'll be lucky; never mind, I'll damp my net window-curtains down again and I'll iron them tomorrow, sooner than scorch them today. After that, I've nothing to do but the dinner to get ready and two or three odds and ends to see to and it'll be finished."

It is the beginning of an attempted end.

The late books tell us what the late photos show: in a life of love and even melodrama, a life that was lived within the skin and nerves as few have been, it was her work which won—loved her and won her love; and that finger which once held down sentences for Willy helped write others which need no help and hold themselves. The moral isn't new or arresting. Philosophers have been saying the same thing for centuries.

The New York Review of Books, 1977
Published in *The World Within the Word*, 1978

MALCOLM LOWRY

¿LE GUSTA ESTE JARDÍN

QUE ES SUYO?

¡EVITE QUE SUS HIJOS LO DESTRUYAN!

There is no o'clock in a cantina. They are dim as a church is dim, often candlelit or momentarily illuminated by sudden dusts of light from slits in dirty unscheduled walls, and there is the frequent murmur of the priests at service or the worshippers who attend, even at odd hours, the shrine of this or that outlandish saint—the Virgin for those who have nobody, for instance—sanctuaries with strange yet significant names: El Bosque or the Bella Vista Bar, the Salón Ofélia, El Petate, El Farolito (Lowry once shuffled up a book of poems called *The Lighthouse Invites the Storm*); and indeed one is drawn in, out of the Mexican light or the English or Canadian, out of Paris, from dockside or the railroad station, out of a light like a fall of hail, in Haiti, in Vancouver, at the bus depot with its day-storms, the endless sterile walkwells of airports, neon nighttimes in New York, and there is a mirror—*absolutamente necesario*—behind the bar which reflects the door, a chloro-formed square, the street beyond, and there are bottles which it multiplies, their labels, too, like the face of the drinker, names which, on the Day of the Dead in Mexico, and the day of his own demise, Malcolm Lowry's alcoholic hero reads as one reads scripture: Tenampa, perhaps, and Berreteaga, cer-tainly the beautiful Oaxaqueñan gourd of *mescal de olla* from which the same British consul's drink is measured, a flask of peppermint cordial, Tequila Añejo, Anís doble de Mallorca, a violet decanter of Henry Mallet's *delicioso*

licor, and that tall voluted column of Anís del Mono on which a devil bran-
dishes a pitchfork like a poster on a pillar, while in back of the bar there's a
barman called The Elephant, though in the Mexico of Lowry's novel *Under
the Volcano* it may be a boy with an equally absurd name like A Few Fleas,
or possibly it is a young man who is borrowing a puff of your cigarette while
you stumble aloud after the slowing train of your thought; then there will
usually be saucers of toothpicks laid about, salt, chilis, lemons, a tumbler-
ful of straws, and crossed spoons in a glass tankard on the counter, or in
the U.S.A., soggy with bottle spill and the sweat of highballs, cash-register
receipts in a smear of purple print.

Cantina means "cellar," means "cave," but it sounds like a song, and it
is Lowry's favorite playground, with its teeters, slides, and roundabouts,
its sandbox and its swings, although the Consul sits there like a bum on a
bench, the beautiful ruin of a man, now as splendidly incompetent and out
of place as a john in a junkyard. He shakes too badly to shave or to sign his
name. He misplaces his Plymouth. He neglects to pull socks on his nephritic
feet. His penis cannot stand, and he likewise falls down in the street.

The drunk returns to childhood—in this case, babyboyhood. Innocence
reclaims him. Since there is no o'clock in a cantina, he escapes his age.
Lowry, like the Consul, drank himself back through his life: from the squatter he became, the failure he was, the writer, sailor, talker, Cantabrigian,
and momentary master of the uke, the unwilling English public-schoolboy
he had been, to that rich man's fourth and quite unnecessary son where he
began; not quite to recover the past, part of which was painful as a burn,
but to go over it again and get it right, and to reach the desired condition of
helplessness. The alcoholic trance is not just a haze, as though the eyes were
also unshaven. It is not a mere buzzing in the ears, a dizziness or disturbance
of balance. One arrives in the garden again, at nursery time, when the gentle
animals are fed and in all the world there are only toys.

In such a state, like Lear's fool, he has a license to speak the truth, let
impulse loose, and not be blamed. He can lie, too, and not be blamed. He
can play, can act—playact—and not be blamed. He is excused. Unable to
fend—to eat, to dress, conduct affairs—unable to fuck: he is excused. If
pleased, he laughs; if offended, he sulks; if disappointed, he throws himself
wailing on the world like a mourner on a grave. Of course, he'll be accused
of being intoxicated, and of that charge it is absolutely necessary for him to
be guilty, but he can't be blamed for being impotent or ugly, for failing to
face up, for losing heart or job or love or money, for fecklessness, for rage:
that is the main thing, and he will happily accept this lesser charge in the
place of all the others, since it is also true that he is, in the moment of deepest

fuddle, mad, inhabited, possessed of prophetic powers, so *perfectamente borracho* that, like the most naïve children of Christ, the fools of God, he makes with his dirty lying toper's tongue the inspired speech of the Spirit, and on that ground, too, he is excused . . . excused.

Let out. Let off. Excused. Not for long, though. Not for nearly long enough. Eventually the body fails. The chemical has forced it to concoct a consciousness it cannot care for or continue; it cannot support this basin of puke or endure the ringing of these poisonous bells, the reverberations of their stink. Frequently the victim sweats his pits sore as pain passes away through the pores, and the steel shutters of the cantina come down with a crash. Later, though not enough later, not an eternity after, after only a drugged snooze, the drinker awakes with a conscience ready to be reconsumed, and to a sort of soberness so physically wretched and an awareness so vengeful and spiritually cruel that another species of hallucination takes possession of him. Kafka could not describe the transformations, or Sabbatai Zevi account for them. Thus rubbed from a bottle, the day begins again, even though it's the moon that's up, and a consciousness must reinvent the world.

For the male . . . ah . . . nightly there advances toward him the body of his presumed beloved, since it will be clock-dark eventually; it will be lovetime; and it was better when he was a baby in his bed and he was hoping not to wet it or pass blood through his nose or be frightened into screaming by shadows representing the self holding a knife or a garrote; it was better then to lie down upon dreams which would be soon shaken by the hooves of dark horses, than it was now to be in bed with a body which expected passion, and his blood to be bottled in his penis simply because there were breasts nearby or viny hair like darkness creeping across a doorway; and so daily, toward evening, it becomes desperately necessary to have a drink, to sit in the cool of a cantina, the whole of him, as if he had already penetrated the fearful crease as easily as parting strings of fly-beads and was now conversing calmly in the quieting comfort of the cunt . . . warm womb of the world . . . whatever . . . because a cantina signifies the rich enticing inwardness of all things.

The cantina is not, then, a complete calamity; it calms; it protects; it restores. It is the head itself, the container of consciousness, too, and the bar which bisects it is the bar of judgment, where cases are argued; and in the cantina everything is beautiful, even when ugly; everything is significant, even when trivial; all is orderly, even when the drinker is deranged; all is known; and even if there are headaches and the eyes fall back in their sockets like stones, even if the saloon pitches like a ship in a storm, even if every word is a groan and sickness begs the stomach for something to flush through its throat the way turds whirl in a toilet, there is always tomorrow; there is always the hope of change, the fresh resolution, and the drink to celebrate it, for didn't I just say that the container of consciousness was the brown pint, the clear quart, and haven't whole cultures worshipped the spirit in the plant, the pulque which preserves, the life in the vine? because wine winters over in the vats, it defies time; and where better to celebrate this miracle than in the cantina? although it may be a morning so awash with moonlight the sidewalks are urine-yellow, never mind, we have come round, we rebegin; let's pawn—let's drink—the typewriter, wedding ring, the clock, and have another round, a tick, another round, a tock, another round.

But you see that we really do not lose our grip, we do not really repeat as if we've forgotten already what we've said, it is just that some of our commonest connectives have come undone, we swing back and forth into our thought now like a ball on the end of a string, the body must stumble so the mind may leap, or, rather, perhaps it would be better to say that we sink down softly into things as though they were laps.

Some matters after all are magnified without alcohol, and in the ordinary course of events, for example when the sun falls asleep at midday, there is a frightful darkness like Guinness in a glass and the bar mirror smears and the bar stool turns of itself with a squeak and we are free finally to let the mind pass into the space of its speaking, mescaleening, you might say, as over water waterskiers—such is the kind of excuse we're seeking when we flip or twist or pull or pry or pop or tap the keg or cork or lid or cap or top—go like spray.

What do you have against me in your files, Lowry asks the subchief of Migración. The subchief slaps the folder facing him: "*Borracho, borracho, borracho.* Here is your life."

Nightmare and madness fly up and down like shades. Figures emerge from the walls: customs officials, pimps, bus drivers, wives, police. Fear grows the wings of evil birds. What is this semen which runs from our nose? this hot blot on the bedclothes? loaf of red bread? There's a nest of noisy ants in that canister of candy. Anxiety like light leaks—pip—from a pipe. Pip-a-dip. Pip. Flowers flattened in the wall's paper puff like adders, but they're orchid-mouthed, and at last we have someone to talk to, someone who understands the initial pronoun of our speech the way a fine sentence does the design of its writer.

It is ourselves, of course, or one member of that club, with whom we take communion in the cantina (part of us taking your part, perhaps, and playing it better, too, but remaining one of our own crowd still, leaning alone like a broom in a closet, apart from the pail and the mop as we must, because in this spiritless realm of matter, like a bar without booze, no cozy interpenetration of molecules is possible), and Lowry would hold extended conversations with empty corners and vacant chairs, but what is remarkable about that? each of us has seen street talkers deep in quarrel with invisible companions; or he would, having passed out, nevertheless remember what had been said in the presence of his absent self, so one wonders if he might sometimes have been faking, but there is a fragment of us constantly awake, alert as a lantern, microphone: why should our ear sleep when our eyes close? pip! like insects we breathe with more than our nose; it is simply that the division which occurs when we've taken a sufficiently engrossing drink is almost complete, and we meet all elements as equals: the glass that holds the hand, the hand that is a bottle to the body, the body that wickedly wobbles the world, and the mirror which imagines this immense earthquaking to be merely the sea-crossing of a cloud.

> *El espíritu*
> *Es una invención del cuerpo*
> *El cuerpo*
> *Es una invención del mundo*
> *El mundo*
> *Es una invención del espíritu*
>
> [Octavio Paz, *Blanco*]

In any case it becomes *absolutamente necesario* to have a drink. Easy for anyone whose entire intelligence and whose whole energy is bent upon it, because naturally the need has been foreseen and there is a bottle stashed under the sink or buried in the window box or hidden in the clothes hamper, and on the bad odd off chance that they have been emptied already, one mustn't lose faith, heart, or hope, because there are other opportunities, some bars open early, there are friends . . . yes, *con permiso*, just a nip to steady the nerves, calm the stomach, dispel the demons, only a drop, *amigos*, a spot, a touch, and in addition . . .

There is a cantina at every corner of the Consul's world. Sin and innocence, guilt and salvation, shape Lowry's private square of opposition, and if sanctuary and special knowledge are its gifts in one guise, and gaiety and relaxation its gifts in another, catercorner from church and gym are brothel and prison. Here men are fastened to themselves as though they were both shackle and chain, their eyes on images: above the bar to advertise Cafeaspirina a woman wearing a scarlet brassiere is depicted reclining on a scrolled divan. Outside the cantina you can see the mountain, alongside runs a deep ravine. Symbols, surely, but remote and close, steep and frightening, just the same. El Farolito, with its diminishing inner rooms, the nesting innercubes of hell, is the last cantina, sitting in the shadow of Popocatépetl as though under that volcano. There the Consul will wad himself into a slut the way we wedge with cardboard a skinny candle in its holder. There he will be mistaken for an anarchist, a Jew, a thief, a spy. There he will be murdered by backwoodsy fascists. Who has a hand upon his penis now?

Wrider? you anticrista. Sí, you anticrista prik . . .
And Juden . . .
                Chingar . . .
                        Cabrón . . .
                                You are no a de
wrider, you are de espider, and we shoota de espiders
in Méjico . . .
                You no wrider . . .
                        You Al Capón. You a
Jew chingao . . .
                You are a spider.

In the road in front of El Farolito the Consul is shot with a Colt '17. "Christ, what a dingy way to die," the Consul says, but that is merely his opinion. His body is thrown into a *barranca,* pariah dog tossed after him. Despite the fact that the scene is excessively operatic and the writing wails like an endlessly expiring soprano, there is no death in recent literature with more significance.

Las Manos de Orlac
con Peter Lorre

Several leaves from one of Lowry's little notebooks are reproduced in Douglas Day's fine biography,* and on one we can decipher:

The psychology & horror of the shakes. The real horror is in the hands. All the poison to go down into the hands, mental and physical. Burning hot. There seems almost a buzzing *inside* your hands. Fear of coming into dining room with shakes, especially with captain present.

* Douglas Day, *Malcolm Lowry: A Biography* (New York: Oxford University Press, 1973).

Eventually, he could not hold pen or pencil, not even to sign his name, and the hands which were so mysteriously stained, not like Lady Macbeth's or Orlac's were by the blood of murder, but—who knows?—by the masturbation of the bottle (the crystal phallus, in Berryman's phrase), these hands he placed on their backs on his desk, his weight standing into them as he dictated to Margerie, hours at a stretch sometimes and of course day after day, until the knuckles became callused as an ape's and the veins in his legs ballooned so badly he entered a hospital to have them stripped.* They were swollen as if he'd had babies, although by then he'd only engendered *Ultramarine,* and the *Volcano* was still in utero.

These stubby clumsy hands, which he hated and hid because they gave his condition away the way rings around the eyes, I remember, were supposed to, and which shook drunk or sober, often uncontrollably, were hands with their own mean will. While absentmindedly fondling a friend's pet rabbit, they somehow break its neck, and for two days Lowry carries the corpse of the rabbit about in a small suitcase, wondering what to do with it. "Look what happens when I try to touch something beautiful," their owner complains with a self-pity perfectly misplaced.

Yet Lowry's not a Lenny whose mice cannot survive his caresses. Yet Lowry's love is as murderous as the simpleminded. Yet . . .

And before he will agree to enter Cambridge he persuades his father to let him go, like London and O'Neill, romantically to sea, so he is driven to the dock in the family Rolls while reporters watch: RICH BOY AS DECK HAND, they headline him. He goes aboard shamed and of course finds no romance in the fo'c'sle. He sleeps in something called "men's quarters" instead. Predictably, he scrubs decks, scrapes paint, polishes brass. He observes the coolie longshoremen coupling with their women in the cargo holds. He paints a bunker black. He is despised and teased. Clumsy. Bored. He carries meals to the seamen. Is often drunk.

Perhaps life was a forest of symbols, as Baudelaire had said, but Lowry was no lumberman. He brought his shaping signs, as *a priori* as the best idealist's, to his dreams, his drunkenness, his ordinary day-to-day concerns, and his desires: sex, syph, stoker, bunker, fire . . . hand, shame, seaman. Eventually these hands refuse the vocation offered them. A poisoned brain burns there. Trapped flies buzz. Ashamed, stained, they blush, and, terrified, enraged, they shake so violently the threatened air flees through their fingers. And he would live hand to mouth all his life. A cliché. A phrase. Yet associations such as these obsess him, compel him to run in front of his own blows, to

* Dr. C. G. McNeil, "A Memory of Malcolm Lowry," *American Review,* vol. 17 (1973), pp. 35–39.

fulfill prophecies as though they were threats, and promises as though they were designs against the self, since he will die by his own hand, too . . . by bottle and by pill . . . unsteadily . . . *la petite mort.*

Lowry is a one-book author, everyone says, and the excellence of that book is accidental, because he never learned how to write; he continually started and stopped, commenced and abandoned, caught in an endless proliferation of designs, so that the more evident it became that he would never complete his great work, the grander grew his schemes: everything he wrote would enter into them, one vast voyage, long as his life, just as confusing, just as deep, with ups and downs to rival Dante; yet he was wholly absorbed in himself and consequently could not create even an alter ego able to pull on socks ahead of shoes; at the uncork of a bottle he would fall into long dull disquisitions on the powers and bewilderments of alcohol; he hammered home themes like someone angry at the nail, yet buttered his bread on both sides and every edge; then, as if determined to destroy whatever mattered most, left manuscripts about like half-eaten sandwiches, and emptied Margerie of everything except the carton she came in.

However, when one thinks of the general sort of snacky under-earnest writers whose works like wind chimes rattle in our heads now, it is easier to forgive Lowry his pretentious seriousness, his old-fashioned ambitions, his Proustian plans, his desire to pump into every sentence such significance as a Shelley or a Shakespeare had, to bring together on the page, like fingers in one fist, sense, sensation, impulse, need, and feeling, and finally to replace the reader's consciousness wholly with a lackaday magician's—drunk's—a fraud's—his own.

It was not glory or money, as a writer, Lowry wanted. He simply wanted masterpieces. He had no politics, particularly, no religion, no fastidious monkey-groomed morality, no metaphysics which would fancy up for him a world with more worth and order than a shelf of cheap sale books. It is hard to believe he believed in much, though he read Goethe and Dante, dabbled in the occult, and used the Cabbala as a symbolic scheme (even if its choreography was an afterthought), and to begin with laid down a political plot for his great book like a rug he then swept a mountain over. Attitudes he had, but attitudes aren't philosophy. Redemption through art was his real creed. He was too eager to make use of what he read to be serious about it, and, like Joyce, he carried back to his books every tin-shine thought he came across, the way jackdaws beak bright buttons off one's wash. He was not profoundly acquainted with literature either, though he was quick to name-drop: Marlowe, Maitland, or Cervantes. His work is certainly contemporary, too, in expecting the most silent creatures of its author's reading to be loud on every tongue. And, again like Joyce, like Rilke, Lowry idolized certain irrelevant Scandinavians.

The writers he really took to . . . well, he absorbed Conrad Aiken's books, unabashedly plundered his conversations, copied his life-style, both served and assaulted his person, competed for his women, occupied his home, borrowed his figure for a father. Lowry was sufficiently conscious of this habit often to deny himself any originality, and felt he had stolen from or exploited others when he had not.* Still, we must remain suspicious of these exaggerated claims of crime, inflated and misplaced to encourage our discounting or excusing them as so much talk, just as the Consul, about to be shot, hears himself accused:

Norteamericano, eh?
Inglés. You Jew.
What the hell you think you do around here?
You pelado, eh?
It's no good for your health. I shoot de twenty people.

and then, dying, gorges on the accusation as only conscience can:

Presently the word "pelado" began to fill his whole consciousness. That had been Hugh's word for the thief: now someone had flung the insult at him. And it was as if, for a moment, he had become the pelado, the thief—yes, the pilferer of meaningless muddled ideas out of which his rejection of life had grown, who had worn his two or three little bowler hats, his disguises, over these abstractions: now the realest of them all was close.

And although the account seems to be carried away by itself, as Cyrano was by his nose, it is nevertheless true that the Consul is an exploiter, because an alcoholic, in the best old sense, *depends:* depends from his wives like their drooping breasts, clings to his mistresses, his friends, as moisture trembles at a tumbler's edge; depends upon the mercy of the world . . . relies, requests, requires . . . yet in the devious way the hopeless loser hopes to win by losing big, the thorough soak employs all the brutal ruses of self-righteous helpless-

---

* If one is familiar with Aiken, one can indeed feel his presence in Lowry's books. The two authors continually intercross, because of course Lowry figures in Aiken's autofictional biography, *Ushant,* and is the model for a character called Hambo in Aiken's autofactual fiction, *A Heart for the Gods of Mexico.* They borrow each other like roommates steal shirts for an evening out, yet the bodies which wear them remain distinct and the shirts get returned after use.

ness, and by chemically keeping himself confined "in that part used to be call: soul" makes the world seem—so subversive is this stratagem—rather to depend on *him* . . . yes, and this isn't difficult, because consciousness is the thief *par excellence,* removing the appearances of things without a trace, replacing the body with the spirit.

Since the cantina is the very image of the head, the world-within which is the single subject of Malcolm Lowry's life and work, all those anxieties and adjectives, verbs of inaction, prepositions, copulations, shadowing names, and paranoid suspicions, which obsessed his creator and pursue Geoffrey Firmin—Consul, *pelado,* and *borracho*—apply perfectly to the tragedy of the *Volcano:* the progressive loss of consciousness which we call "getting on" and should call simply "passing out," instead.

To his editor, Albert Erskine:

> Dear old Albert . . .
>
> I am going steadily & even beautifully downhill: my memory misses beats at every moment, & my mornings are on all fours. Turning the whole business round in a nutshell I am only sober or merry in a whiskey bottle, & since whisky is impossible to procure you can imagine how merry I am, & lucid, & by Christ I am lucid. And merry. But Jesus. The trouble is, apart from Self, that part (which) used to be called: consciousness. I have now reached a position where every night I write 5 novels in imagination, have total recall (whatever that means too) but am unable to write a word. I cannot explain in human terms the incredible effort it has cost me to write even this silly little note, in a Breughel garden with dogs & barrels & vin kegs & chickens & sunsets & morning glory with an approaching storm & bottle of half wine.
>
> And now the rain! Let it come, seated as I am on Brueghel barrel by a dog's grave crowned with dead irises. The wind is rising too, both on the ocean & in the stomach. And I have been kind to in a way I do not deserve. . . . A night dove has started to hoot & says incessantly the word "dream, dream." A bright idea.*

The bus windows were like mirrors—looking out, one saw in—and Margerie and Malcolm were always on buses, or perhaps a plane, some mode of travel, a ship, a train, and even on foot they window-shopped, the glass

---

* Harvey Breit and Margerie Bonner Lowry, eds., *Selected Letters of Malcolm Lowry* (Philadelphia and New York: Lippincott, 1965), p. 165.

passing them, holding its images oddly upright like bottles on a tray, though they were moving, in Lowry's insistently recurring word, "downhill," since the world, for him, was always on edge, the land like his work running up and down, never nicely along, even when they found a path that had taken itself pleasantly through the woods, and every journey was mostly a descent, or, rather, descending was a spatial metaphor for "going in."

> The sense of speed, of gigantic transition, of going southward, down-ward, over three countries, the tremendous mountain ranges, the sense at once of descent, tremendous regression, and of moving, not moving, but in another way dropping straight down the world, straight down the map, as of the imminence of something great, phenomenal, and yet the moving shadow of the plane below them, the eternal moving cross, less fleeting and more substantial than the dim shadow of the significance of what they were actually doing that Sigbjørn held in his mind: and yet it was possible only to focus on that shadow, and at that only for short periods: they were enclosed by the thing itself as by the huge bouncing machine with its vast monotonous purring, pouring din, in which they sat none too comfortably, Sigbjørn with his foot up embarrassedly, for he had taken his shoe off, a moving, deafening, con-tinually renewed time-defeating destiny by which they were enclosed but of which they were able only to see the inside, for so to speak of the streamlined platinum-colored object itself they could only glimpse a wing, a propeller, through the small, foolish, narrow oblong windows.*

The paragraph encloses us like the fuselage of the plane. We progress down narrow overlapping phrases toward the bottom of the page, pushing our way through adjectives which gather like onlookers at an accident. Though feel-ings persevere, logic is lost like loose change. We suffer symbolic transforma-tions (soul: shade, window and eye, cross: plane, hellbent); endure sentences which have the qualities they were constructed to account for; our reading eye, as Sigbjørn's and the shadow of the plane, flitting over the ranges the way thought in its sphere, ourselves in our cylinders, pass like ghosts on sched-ules, wraiths with aims.

Faulkner's rhetoric also reaches for the universal as though its very pawing would create the ledge, secure the handhold. It is a style so desperate to rise, it would burst its own lungs.

* This is the first paragraph of *Dark as the Grave Wherein My Friend Is Laid* (New York: New American Library, 1968). Douglas Day and Margerie Lowry have edited this posthumous novel. There is an excellent brief introduction by Day.

And if he had not been born, mistakenly, a Leo, he would have made a perfect Pisces: swimmer, sailor, soak, souse, sponge—all that absorbent—oral, impotent, a victim of undifferentiation and the liquid element, shoreless like his writing, wallowy, encompassing, a suicide by misadventure, bottle broken, drinker, diver, prisoner of self. . . .

Thrice doubly indented, then, Lowry's books in consequence have no boundaries. They are endless wells down which in a deepening gloom that is its own perverse illumination the reader passes; therefore every effort to give them the shape and normal accelerations of the novel is as futile as flailing air; and you remember how deeply into Tartarus Uranus hurled the rebellious Cyclopes? . . . . . . an anvil and a petal: nine days.

> Clínica Dr. Vigil,
> Enfermedades Secretas de Ambos Sexos,
> Vías Urinarias, Trastornos Sexuales,
> Debilidad Sexual, Derrames Nocturnos,
> Emisiones Prematuras, Espermatorrea,
> Impotencia.

Guilty fears follow him everywhere. He is being watched. Espidered. Are those his father's eyes behind those blackened glasses? In any case, his plans are known in advance. He is awaited at the border. He will be expelled from the country. He will be evicted from his property. He will catch the VD. How? through his hands? He *has* contracted it. He believes. Long ago . . . as a sailor. It is hidden in his blood, this punishment. Any rash bespeaks its presence, since the soul contains the body. And as a child . . .

At one or two or three or four he claims to have been molested by nannies. He is five when his brother takes him to an anatomical museum in Liverpool (on Paradise Street, inevitably) where he sees bleach-pale plaster casts depicting the ravages of venereal disease. In his father's house there was no smoking. While six he suffers a fall from a bike which leaves him with a jagged scar on his knee, a wound he will later say he received when his ship was caught in a Tong war along the Chinese coast. A glass of port at Christmas was indulgence enough. When seven he complains of being bullied by the other Cub Scouts. But cold baths made men—made Englishmen—stiffened the sinews, restrung the nerves. As did tennis, rugger, swimming, shooting, golf, church, long strenuous walks. And Malcolm became good at them. Still, he is teased about the size of his penis. Away at the Caldicote School, now nine, he is struck in the eye playing ball. The injury is neglected and an infection sets in which leaves him partially blind for four years. Or so he chooses to believe. He also imagines that his mother, unable to bear the sight of her half-sighted boy, refuses to let him come home on vacations, and that everyone has left him alone.

But he is becoming a touch-me-not. In America, visiting Aiken, he meets a young woman with whom he decides he is in love. He will convince her. "His attempt at this is remarkable," Day judiciously observes, "and possibly unique in the history of erotic correspondence."

> I cannot kiss anybody else without wiping my mouth afterwards. There is only you, forever and forever you: in bars and out of bars, in fields and out of fields, in boats and out of boats . . . there is only love and tenderness of everything about you, our comings in and our goings forth, I would rather use your tooth brush than my own: I would wish, when with you on a boat, that you would be sick merely so that I could comfort you. Nor is there one ounce of criticism in this. I do not conceal in my heart the physical repulsion which, not admitted to oneself hardly, exists usually in the filthy male. I would love you the same if you had one ear, or one eye: if you were bald or dumb: if you had syphilis, I would be the same; it is the love that one stronger algebraic symbol in a bracket has for its multiple—or complement . . . it cannot live without the other.
>
> [Day, *Malcolm Lowry*, p. 109]

In short, Lowry loves her as he wants to be loved. And he wants to be loved by his mother.

Thief and exploiter: that's what we're told *pelado* means: peeled; barefoot, bald. Where in his unconscious did Lowry deposit what he knew? that *pelada* is a kind of alopecia, which means, in dictionary speech, a distempered state of the body leading to a patchy loss of hair, and arising from a venereal cause.

A resentment psychology is developing rapidly. In college a young man, presumably in love with Lowry, commits suicide, and this event, too, becomes one of the crimes which haunt his heroes. By now every crime which he conceives for himself is also another injury done him, and he is already drinking more than much.

Thus eyes, fires, follow him. Disaster. Ashes, ashes, all fall down. And it is true that he cannot competently manage his life. He *does* put himself in bad hands, the hands of exploiters (in photos his own are often in his pockets). His squatter's shack at Dollarton *does* burn; a manuscript, not the first, *is* lost; he has constantly to fear eviction; he slips from the pier he's built there, which means so much to him, and thereby injures his back; the cold drives him every winter into travel so that homelessness can continue his motto, and paradise return with the spring. He is kicked out of Mexico, in alcoholic horror held for a time in an Oaxaqueñian gaol where he decides an unsuccessful attempt to castrate him has been made. He suggests through the mail that he's been mistakenly imprisoned for spying, and that he must drink furthermore from his pisspot . . . probably.

The list winds on like a bus on a mountain road. Wounds, bruises, broken bottles, suicidal gestures, blackouts, falls, fire: attacking the self he is alone in, he cuts a ridiculous figure, and Douglas Day has difficulty depicting Lowry's redoubtable charm, for charm is evanescent and does not lend itself to anecdote. More than one friend describes Malc as puppylike, refers to his infectious disarming grin, his amazing amusing memory, his simple devotion, the bulk of his chest, his strength, the jokes told on the soul.

Yet in Grenada, his huge head shaded by a great touristy sombrero, this *borracho inglés,* trailed by mocking children and eyed by the Guardia Civil, lurches shamefully through the streets, his trousers held up by a tie. During a friendly drunken tussle shortly after arriving in America to see Conrad Aiken, he tosses his new father figure into the fireplace and fractures his skull. "Look what happens when I try to touch. . . ." Ashes, ashes, all fall . . .

And into every happening there entered, early, imagination like a liar and a thief, arranging reality as it ought and was felt to be, until sometimes it seemed to Lowry he was himself a fiction, and that the work he was writing was writing him. That enmeshment itself became a theme.

> . . . the novel is about a character who becomes enmeshed in the plot of the novel he has written, as I did in Mexico. But now I am becoming enmeshed in the plot of a novel I have scarcely begun. Idea is not new, at least so far as enmeshment with characters is concerned. Goethe, Wilhelm von Scholz, "The Race with a Shadow." Pirandello, etc. But did these people ever have it happen to *them?**

It must have begun in the most ordinary way, Malcolm Lowry's habit of making up life as he went along. It must have begun with little elabora-

---

* A quotation from "Through the Panama," *Paris Review,* no. 23 (1960). This profoundly self-reflexive novella was written in the fifties, and although its concerns are now a commonplace, the fictional techniques employed remain in advance of our time. Lowry's collection of short stories, *Hear Us O Lord from Heaven Thy Dwelling Place* (Philadelphia and New York: Lippincott, 1961), contains another masterpiece, "The Forest Path to the Spring." Margerie Lowry is apparently gathering another sheaf of shorter pieces, and Lowry's life as a dead author will soon be longer, as it is already more productive, than his life as a live one.

tions, lies as harmlessly decorative as those sugar flowers whose stony blooms enliven our birthday cakes. We all did it—added frills. We do it still: we penny-candle conversations, ice anecdotes, bake ourselves in pies. When we were maybe a boy with a ball or a worm in a can, there was no entrance easier than of fact to fancy, because we were more likely to be living on the inside of our nature then, where distant skiers safely slid the hazardous slopes of our sheeted beds, and little facts came along like sticks in a stream to be snatched up. The garage's broken window could become a bullet wound, a furtive peer-point, violent eye-crash. The step seems a small one, but the difference between an imaginary world which flows around the real one and uses it, catch as catch can, and a real world which is hung each way one turns with dreams like evergreens by bagworms, is—

And if at first our daydreams merely close and open softly on reality like a convolvulus, we find it useful later, with our little fabrications, to make life move more centrally around us. Thus do we appoint ourselves a sun, to shine and tan in turn; we compel our inner shapes and outer shadows to coalesce; we speak sternly to experience in romantic German till *der als ob ist,* pointlessness becomes plan, sheer coincidence design, and it is no longer surprising that the wages of sin should be exhibited in plaster of Paris on Paradise Street.

The wormy ubiquitousness of the sign reminds many of *Ulysses,* but the similarity is deceptive, because Lowry's feeling for the world is in no way like Joyce's, nor are his literary skills, although both pun. For Stephen Dedalus, walking along Sandymount Strand, the world is a series of words which find their final connections in the mind, but for Lowry it is not simply that some grand Master moves each piece of life into a single sentence; it is, rather, that each piece has its own lungs and legs, and a sign is, for instance, the advertising poster BOX! which follows the Consul like an urchin uttering itself. BOX! it shouts, to be sure, like one of the Furies, like a messenger of the gods. It is itself alive and menacing, as full of private mischief as any chief of Rostrums or subchief of Migración.

Lowry could not invent at the level of language, only at the level of life, so that, having lied life into a condition suitable for fiction, he would then faithfully and truthfully record it. No wonder he felt enmeshed. No wonder, too, that he had to revisit in order to revise; repeat the same difficult passage of existence in order to plunge further into it, make the necessary changes, get it right; and this meant only too often that he had to drink himself back into madness again, to resee what was to be rewritten: to fall down in a ditch, to find vultures perched on the washbasin, fold fearfully up in a corner like a pair of discarded trousers, or bruise his head between toilet and sink in some dirty anonymous john.

But he now became conscious of something more frightening yet taking place in his mind. It was a feeling that permeated the high ill-lit yellow walls of the hotel beer parlour, the long dim corridor between the two beer parlours, on which the door now seemed to be opened by an invisible hand . . . , a feeling which seemed a very part of the ugly, sad, red-and-brown tables and chairs, something that was in the very beer-smelling air, as if—the feeling perhaps someway arising, translated to this surrounding scene, from the words themselves—there were some hidden correspondence between these words and this scene, or between some ultimate unreality and meaninglessness he seemed to perceive adumbrated by them . . . , and his inner perception of this place: no, it was as if this place were suddenly the exact outward representation of his inner state of mind: so that shutting his eyes for a long moment of stillness . . . he seemed to feel himself merging into it, while equally there was a fading of it into himself: it was as though, having visualized all this with his eyes shut now he *were* it—these walls, these tables, that corridor. . . . *

Words, walls, percepts, feelings, this or that cantina, this small victory, that great defeat: all were one behind the colon, a line drawn through his writing to indicate a sum. As he merged with his environment the way numbers enter one another, disappearing entirely without losing themselves, he heard, as if in his own voice yet in a voice now no longer his, prophecies in labels, omens in emblems, spying eyes like whispers looking out of objects, threats in signs.

> La persona que destruya
> este jardín sera
> consígnada a la
> autoridad . . .

And as his guilt grew and his terrors multiplied, as his hands refused to write and his fuddled head fell farther toward his knees, he became more and more dependent on Margerie, not only for mothering and other small corrections, but for experience itself, since they went everywhere together, suffered everything together, resolved to begin a new pier, new cabin, new

* From the astonishing "Wandering Jew" chapter of *October Ferry to Gabriola* (New York: World Publishing, 1970), a work which, while now enclosed by covers, is no more than a pile of rusted and beautiful wreckage.

journey, new book, new life together, the glass which poisoned all these plans, although he often drank from it alone, held jointly; so it was Margerie's fault he was such a sot, he felt, and he saw how the powers he possessed were slowly passing to her: he needed her to punctuate his prose; he needed her to smooth out the creases in his style; he needed her guidance and her notes; he would need her to publish his posthumous works. He lived, furthermore, in the presence—literally beneath the gaze—of the person he had most injured, before whom it was no longer possible to put on a new soul like a suit for Sunday—who knew his fears, his incapacities, so many of his secrets, who knew that so many of his lies were lies. He was intolerably uncovered, and there was nowhere finally to go—both petal and anvil had arrived.

In the little English town of Ripe (place-names follow him snickering even to the grave) . . . Lowry chases his wife away with the shattered neck of a gin bottle.

It was a sort of suicide, a swallow larger and more reckless than usual, this death by misadventure, as the coroner kindly decides to call it, and dying in a scatter of food and glass was no doubt dingy enough to satisfy the Consul, though it had entelechy, like a habit which has finally completed itself. After this death, which Day describes so well, the weekly Brighton *Argus* headstoned and then columned him:

SHE BROKE

GIN BOTTLE

Found Husband Dead

Incurable

The New York Review of Books, 1973
Published in *The World Within the Word*, 1978

RILKE'S RODIN

We can pretend to know precisely. At three o'clock on the Monday afternoon of September 1, 1902, bearing the appropriate petitions of entry, although he had arranged his visit in advance, the twenty-six-year-old poet Rainer Maria Rilke appeared on the stoop of Auguste Rodin's Paris studio, and was given an uncustomarily gentle and courteous reception. Of course, Rilke had written Rodin a month before to warn of his impending arrival. It was a letter baited with the sort of fulsome praise you believe only when it is said of yourself, and it must have been an additional pleasure for Rodin to be admired by a stranger so young, as well as someone with a commission to write of the sculptor and the sculptor's work as handsomely as, in his correspondence, he already had. Rilke was enthusiasm in a shabby suit, but Rodin, who paid little mind to social appearances except when he was mixing with potential clients, was willing to set aside some time for a chat while suffering the foreigner's fledgling French without complaint. He could not have realized that he was going to be the victim of a role reversal, because it was the artist who would play the sitter for a change. Rilke had arrived with an anticipatory portrait well advanced, and his tireless pen immediately began making mental corrections. "It seemed to me that I had always known him," he wrote his wife, Clara, the following day. "I was only seeing him again; I found him smaller, and yet more powerful, more kindly, and more noble. That forehead, the relationship it bears to his nose which rides out of it like a ship out of harbor . . . that is very remarkable. Character of stone is in that forehead and that nose. And his mouth has a speech whose ring is good, intimate, and full of youth. So also is his laugh, that embarrassed and at the same time joyful laugh of a child that has been given lovely presents." (Letter to Clara Rilke, Tuesday, Sept. 2, 1902, in *Letters of Rainer Maria Rilke*, vol. 1, 1892–1910, trans. Jane Bannard Greene and M. D. Herter Norton

[New York: W. W. Norton, 1945], pp. 77–78. Hereafter, *Letters* in any given citation refers to this work.)

Released to explore the studio and its holy objects, Rilke discovers, almost immediately, a hand: *"C'est une main comme-ça,"* Rodin says, gesturing so impressively with his own broad, blunt peasant hands with their plaster-white fingers and blackened nails that Rilke fancies he sees things and creatures growing out of them. In Rilke's steamy state of mind Rodin's every word rises in the air, so that when he points to two entwined figures and says, *"c'est une création ça, une création . . ."* the poet believes, he reports to Clara, that the word *création* "had loosed itself, redeemed itself from all language . . . was alone in the world" (*Letters*, p. 78). Everything small has so much bigness in it, he exclaims to his page.

Rilke tries to take everything in as if there will not be a next day, but there is a next day, and at nine he is on the train to Meudon, a twenty-minute ride to transformation. The town clings to a hillside from whose crest the Seine can be seen snaking its way to Paris. He walks up a "steep dirty village street" to Rodin's home, Villa des Brillants, which the sculptor had bought in 1895. Rilke describes the journey to Clara with the sort of detail one saves for wonders of the world: over a bridge—no *voilà* yet—down a road—no *voilà* yet—past a modest inn—no *voilà* yet—now through a door in the villa wall that opens on a gravel path lined with chestnut trees—still no *voilà*—until he rounds a corner of the "little red-yellow house and stands"—*voilà* now!—"before a miracle—before a garden of stone and plaster figures."

Rodin had transported the pavilion from the Place de l'Alma, in which he had exhibited his work in Paris in 1900, to the small park surrounding his house, where there were already several studios set aside for cutting stone and firing clay. The pavilion was a heavily glassed light-filled hall full of plaster figures in ghostly confabulation, and it also contained huge glass cases crammed with fragments from the design of *The Gates of Hell*. "There it lies," Rilke writes, already composing his monograph,

> yard upon yard, only fragments, one beside the other. Figures the size of my hand and larger . . . but only pieces, hardly one that is whole: often only a piece of arm, a piece of leg, as they happen to go along beside each other, and the piece of body that belongs right near them. . . . Each of these bits is of such an eminent, striking unity, so possible by itself, so not at all needing completion, that one forgets they are only parts, and often parts of different bodies that cling to each other so passionately there.

> [*Letters*, p. 79]

Rilke had brought a sheaf of his poems, which Rodin dutifully fingered, although he could only admire (as Rilke imagines) their pose upon the page; otherwise he left Rilke to roam about the place, examining its treasures. The poet poured out upon these figurines and fragments a bladder-full of enthusiasm, as was his pre-Paris habit ("each a feeling, each a bit of love, devotion, kindness"); but the city's unyielding and indifferent face and the sculptor's dedicated work habits would teach the poet to see his surroundings as they were in themselves and not simply allow his glance to fall like sunshine on surfaces where it could admire its own reflection and its glitter.

Then it was lunchtime. And the first lesson, *en plein air.* They sat five at a trestle. No one was introduced. There was a tired-looking, nervous, and distracted lady who Rilke assumed was Madame Rodin. There was a Frenchman notable for a red nose, and "a very sweet little girl of about ten" who sat just across from him. Rodin, dressed for the city, is impatient for his meal. Madame replies with a torrent of apparent grievance. Rilke begins to observe—*Regarde! Regarde!* is the new command—and sees Madame giving forks, plates, glasses little pushes that disarray the table as if the meal were already over. "The scene was *not* painful, *only sad,*" he writes. The Master continues to complain as calmly as a lawyer until a rather dirty person arrives to distribute the food and insist that Rilke partake of dishes he does not desire. The poet should have been hungry—he was on his uppers—but he was also finicky to a fault, vegan of a sort, a fancied sign of his ethereal nature. Rodin rattled on agreeably. Rilke spoke of his art-colony days in Worpswede and of the painters he met there, few of whom Rodin had heard of, although that would not have surprised the poet had he realized that his acquaintances, his friends, were nobodies. And as a poet, he was invisible in this space.

Because it was full of blazing plaster casts in a pavilion that gathered light as if it were fruit. "My eyes are hurting me, my hands too," he wrote to his wife. Madame Rodin was gracious after lunch, inviting him back, as we say, "anytime you're in the neighborhood," little realizing, I imagine, that for Rilke that would be tomorrow.

And so ended the second day.

Nothing is more fragile than adoration, yet Rilke's adulation might have remained that intense, agreeably decorating a dirty pane like a window's curtain, had he not sunk into an outcast's life. Poor, alone, he sought refuge from the friendless Paris streets in the Bibliothèque Nationale, often from ten to five; or he fled by train to Meudon and its sheltering plasters, kinder to his eye, though they blinded him, than the beggars who would offer him their misfortunes for a franc; while evenings he passed in the squeeze of his room, writing letters to his wife as forlornly beautiful as letters get. The poet was, among other things, an inadequately educated youth who would play the poet even on those days he wasn't one, and who sought to unite his spirit with the spirit of his poems, so as to live several feet above the ground. Yet the great sculptor would eventually prove to be a crude, rude clown, a satyr in a smock, who was losing his strut, caught in the curves of female connivance and flattery, only to be led around eventually (in Sir Kenneth Clark's estimation) like a dancing bear (Kenneth Clark, *The Romantic Rebellion* [New York: Harper & Row, 1973], p. 353). So loyalty would demand that Rilke separate the man from his art, a split easier for a Solomon to decree than a babe to endure, and an act at odds with his inclinations.

Moreover, the fragments he so admired in Rodin's workshops, alive in every brief line that defined them, were confronted by the ugly realities of the avenues, poor creatures who every day looked more like himself.

> They were living, living on nothing, on dust, on soot, and on the filth on their surfaces, on what falls from the teeth of dogs, on any senselessly broken thing that anyone might still buy for some inexplicable purpose. Oh what kind of world is that! Pieces, pieces of people, parts of animals, leftovers of things that have been, and everything still agitated, as though driven about helter-skelter in an eerie wind, carried and carrying, falling and overtaking each other as they fall.
> [Letter to Lou Andreas-Salomé, July 18, 1903, in *Letters*, p. 109]

In these lines, written in Worpswede during the following summer, he relived for his former mistress's benefit his Paris suffering. Rilke was also rehearsing what would become the magical opening pages of his novel, *The Notebooks of Malte Laurids Brigge*. It is worth quoting a bit more in order to demonstrate the psychologically stressful difference between the euphoric celebrational style of the first Rodin monograph and its author's daily state of mind.

> There were old women who set down a heavy basket on the ledge of some wall (very little women whose eyes were drying up like puddles), and when they wanted to grasp it again, out of their sleeves shoved forth slowly and ceremoniously a long, rusty hook instead of a hand, and it went straight and surely out to the handle of the basket. And there were other old women who went about with the drawers of an old night stand in their hands, showing everyone that twenty rusty pins were rolling around inside which they must sell. And once of an

evening late in the fall, a little old woman stood next to me in the light of a store window. She stood very still, and I thought that like me she was busy looking at the objects displayed and hardly noticed her. Finally, however, her proximity made me uneasy, and I don't know why, I suddenly looked at her peculiarly clasped, worn-out hands. Very, very slowly an old, long, thin pencil rose out of those hands, it grew and grew, and it took a very long time until it was entirely visible, visible in all its wretchedness. I cannot say what produced such a terrible effect in this scene, but it seemed to me as if a whole destiny were being played out before me, a long destiny, a catastrophe that was working up frightfully to the moment when the pencil no longer grew and, slightly trembling, jutted out of the loneliness of those empty hands. I understood at last that I was supposed to buy it.

[*Letters,* pp. 109, 110]

In the novel, Malte eventually realizes with horror that he has become an Accomplice, another shabby person of the street.

When I noticed how my clothes were becoming worse and heavier from week to week, and saw how they were slit in many places, I was frightened and felt that I would belong irretrievably to the lost if some passer-by merely looked at me and half unconsciously counted me with them.

[*Letters,* p. 111]

Perhaps, when you only beg from the best families and the finest foundations, you can call yourself a development officer, but where Rilke was living now there were no banks, no fancy estates occupied by susceptible titled ladies, just *asiles de nuit,* the Hôtel Dieu, and other *hospices de la maternité.*

The path to Paris had been a circuitous one, the result of flailing more than plan. At Christmas, two years before, Rilke had returned to Prague to visit his mother, always a trying time for him, although Santa brought him a new briefcase, and on his way home he stopped in Breslau to visit an art historian, Richard Muther, who he hoped might agree to tutor him in this vast field, since Rilke was now considering a career as an art critic. Perhaps Muther might help him combine this fresh but desperate interest with a trip to Russia that Rilke was planning. It would be his second. (Ralph Freedman, *Life of a Poet: Rainer Maria Rilke* [New York: Farrar, Straus and Giroux, 1996], p. 108.) Muther was presently the editor of some pages on art for a Viennese weekly called *Zeit,* and he suggested that Rilke write something on

Russian art for its pages. Rilke promptly did so and composed another article after he had completed his trip.

When they met again, it was at the newly married couple's cottage near the art colony of Worpswede, outside Bremen. Rilke's second essay was about to appear. Muther had just completed a monograph on Lucas Cranach and sent a copy ahead of his arrival. His hosts showed him studios and introduced him to painters as a part of their mutual cultivation. A few months later, Muther would get his review and Rilke receive the Rodin commission. In that regard, he had an edge his youth and inexperience could not dull: his wife, Clara, was herself a sculptor who had studied with the Master, and for that reason they had initially planned to do the piece together. Clara's previous relationship might be expected to make entrée easier.

Rilke was eager to get out of his honeymoon house, a cute thatch that had lost a good deal of its charm after Clara had given birth. Babies often allow wives to feel they have done their sexual duty and husbands to feel they have been warned: what the house now holds will hold them. Clara was also anxious to return to work and would eventually join Rilke in his Paris penury after she had dumped little Ruth with her grandmother. (The word *join* suggests more intimacy than was sought, since they maintained separate lodgings.) The commission was urgent because the couple's funds were nearly exhausted, and, although Clara insisted on paying her own way, Rilke's sources of charity were drying up.

Rilke was learning on the run. He had no scholarly skills. Confronted by a mass of materials, he tended to freeze. "Instead of taking notes on a text with concentration and efficiency, he was forever tempted to copy the entire book" (Wolfgang Leppmann, *Rilke: A Life,* trans. Russell Stockman [New York: Fromm International, 1984], p. 174). There were many things about his subject he would have known, for they were in the air as well as the newspapers or came from Clara's recollections. But some of the things he thought he knew were wrong, and some of the things Rodin revealed about himself weren't true: that he had married *"parce qu'il faut avoir une femme,"* for instance (Letter to Clara Rilke, Sept. 5, 1902, *Letters,* p. 84), since he would not marry Rose Beuret, the woman he had lived with—unlicensed—from 1864, when she had become his model and his mistress, until their approaching deaths made such legalities matters of concern. (Rose died in February 1917, he in November of that year.)

Rodin had been born a profligate and it had apparently always been necessary to have a woman . . . or two. Waiting to pose, nude or nearly, a pair of models might lounge around the studio. When they did, they often had to assume and maintain athletically strenuous erotic positions for extended periods while he drew—comfortably wrapped—in a room Rose kept cool to save sous and suppress inclinations, although often, nearer his models and more discreet, Rodin worked at the *Dépôt des Marbres* in Paris. "Moving constantly around him as he worked were several nude models. He watched them as they moved, like Greek gymnasts, establishing a familiarity with the human body, and with muscles in movement." (Sue Roe, *Gwen John: A Painter's Life* [New York: Farrar, Straus and Giroux, 2001], p. 55.) Occasionally he would insist they caress one another. His artistic excuse for these practices was that through them women were psychologically laid bare, not merely their thighs and bosoms. Rilke, predictably, put a feminist spin on these images. Speaking of figures on *The Gates of Hell*, he says: "Here the woman is no longer an animal who submits or is overpowered. She is too awake and animated by desire, as if they had both joined forces to search for their souls." During such times that the models moved or froze in the midst of a gesture, the artist worked with great rapidity, sheets of drawings literally flying from his pad to litter the floor. At a more leisurely moment, he would apply a light wash of color to the graphite. (Albert Elsen, *Rodin* [New York: Museum of Modern Art, 1963], p. 165.) Rodin did not conceal his erotic drawings from less candid eyes but exhibited them more than once. The Musée Rodin has many thousand such sketches. Later, Picasso would exhibit a similar unremitting libidinous energy.

Without warning, the maestro would disappear for weeks from beneath Rose's eye.

These absences sometimes corresponded to brief encounters with one of his models or with one of the innumerable society women whose appetites were aroused by his reputation as a lover. But when, to excuse himself, Rodin put up a sign on the door of Studio J of the Dépôt des Marbres that read THE SCULPTOR IS IN THE CATHEDRALS, it was sometimes true he was visiting them.

> [Robert Descharnes and Jean-François Chabrun, *Auguste Rodin*,
> trans. Edita Lausanne (Secaucus, N.J.: Chartwell Books, 1967), p. 118]

Four years before Rilke's arrival, Rodin had broken off an extended affair with Camille Claudel—the gifted sister of the great poet and playwright Paul Claudel, and a splendid sculptor herself—with disastrous consequences for Camille, who had to be institutionalized, though there were doubtless other reasons for her paranoid delusions. She and Rose had passed through words to come to blows, and it is said (by those who say these things) that Camille had a habit of lurking about the grounds and that Rose had once fired a shot in the direction of some concealing plants. Camille's brother, whose Catholicism was central to his work, was not Christian enough to forgive the sculptor such a prolonged misuse of his sister, but in this case forgiveness might have been a fault.

> As for Rodin, he was nearsighted: he had the big bulging eyes of a lecher. When he worked he had his nose right on the model and on the clay. Did I say his nose? A boar's snout, rather, behind which lurked a pair of icy blue pupils. In all his sculpture, what you have is his nose working together with his hand, and sometimes you catch the face emerging from the very middle of the four fingers and the thumb. He tackles the block as a whole. With him everything is compact, massive. It is dough that gives unity. His limbs tend to get in the way.
>
> How different from my sister's light, airy hand, the sense of excitement, the perpetual presence of the spirit, the intricate and sensitive tendrils, the airiness and play of inner light!*
>
> [Descharnes and Chabrun, *Rodin,* p. 130]

While Rilke was in attendance, Rodin took up with Gwen, another sister, this time of Augustus John. She would survive the experience to become a talented painter, though she never married and the little village of Meudon held her fast her entire life. (Roe, *Gwen John,* pp. 47–81.) Through Gwen John's letters, we can follow the progress of their affair and get an idea of how many of these amours must have taken a similar path, because, if it was a unique romance for each woman, it was an established routine for the artist, who was consequently always in charge. As girls, they came to Paris to make art their career; they sought work as models in order to pay their way; sometimes they would pose for a painter who posed for Rodin and that way achieve an introduction. In Gwen's case, it was her suppleness that initially appealed to the Master, though other women doubtless had their own special qualities. Soon he would be singling her out, lending her books, asking her to make copies of certain passages he would mark for extraction, and then—*le coup de coeur*—requesting to see her work. One day, while she was in a half-naked, knee-up, head-bowed, prancing pose for the Whistler memorial statue, the kiss arrived. "I can feel, rushing across my lips, sensations of mystery and intoxication," she told him (Roe, *Gwen John,* p. 56). Gwen will dream of giving up all for him (especially her career), of becoming

---

* In *L'Oeil Écoute* (*The Eye Listens*), Claudel had written extensively about Flemish art and praised it in particular for capturing "the movement of human life toward its conclusion." In contrast, Rodin's art would have had to seem profane.

his wife, of taking his material tasks in hand and, though not a tidy, enterprising person, organizing his life. For this last task, Rodin would solicit and seduce Rainer Maria Rilke.

In his two monographs, Rilke will touch on such matters so discreetly not even he will avow his knowledge of them; but the contradiction between Rodin's life of quarrelsomeness, deceit, and sensual indulgence and his consuming artistic dedication; the difference between the studio's dusty physicality and its apparent product—abundant beauty and grace arising out of clay, marble's serene cool glisten like light in a water glass, lofty ideals caught in casts of plaster—these militant contrasts govern every line of the poet's essays, where Rilke enlists awe to ward off consternation, just as they control every surface of the artist's sculptures, including the version of the Balzac memorial that depicts the novelist with an erection. After George Bernard Shaw sat for his bust by Rodin, he wrote that "The most picturesque detail of his method was his taking a big draught of water into his mouth and spitting it onto the clay to keep it constantly pliable. Absorbed in his work, he did not always aim well and soaked my clothes."* (Quoted in Elsen, *Rodin,* p. 126.)

On Rilke's next visit Rodin held class. After a lunch which resembled the first in everything but menu, they sat on a bench that had a fine view of Paris while Rodin spoke of his work and its principles. Rilke has to run after Rodin's rapid French as though for a departing bus. The sculptor's work is manual, like that of a carpenter or mason, and produces an object unlike the memos of an office manager; consequently, to the young, the calling has lost its attraction. They don't care to get their hands dirty, but *"il faut travailler, rien que travailler,"* he likes to repeat. In fact, Rodin did little if any carving (or welding either, of course), although it is said that he liked to greet people at the door head to toe with dust and fisting a chisel. His bronzes were cast, his marbles carved, by workers he rarely saw (R. H. Wilenski. *The Meaning of Modern Sculpture* [Boston: Beacon Press, 1961], p. 25). Henri Lebossé enlarged the sculptor's plaster models to the dimensions proper for a public monument.† Rodin complains that the schools teach "the kids nowadays" to compose—to emphasize contour rather than to model and shape surfaces. *"Ce n'est pas la forme de l'object, mais: le modelé. . . ."* (Rilke, letter to Clara Rilke, Sept. 5, 1902, in *Letters,* p. 84.) Rodin's hands were his principal

* Rodin's impact on Rilke, from the French point of view, is thoroughly discussed by J. F. Angelloz in *Rainer Maria Rilke: L'Évolution Spirituelle du Poète* (Paris: Paul Hartmann, 1936), and by K. A. J. Batterby in *Rilke and France: A Study in Poetic Development* (London: Oxford University Press, 1966).

† See Albert Elsen's "Rodin's Perfect Collaborator, Henri Lebossé," in *Rodin Rediscovered,* ed. Albert Elsen (Washington, D.C.: National Gallery of Art, 1981), pp. 249–59.

tools, and with them he plopped and punched and gouged and smoothed, making both curves and straight lines wavy, allowing shoulders to flow into torsos and torsos to emerge from blocks (even when they hadn't), encouraging elbows to establish their own identity, his fingers everywhere busy at fostering the impression of life, giving strength and will to plaster, ethereality and spirit to stone.

Not to everybody's taste: Rodin's hopes for his work were revolutionary and, at first, few shared them. Lovers of the antique saw in the figure of Aphrodite the embodiment of Love. She was a god of mythology and therefore never existed, so she could only be regarded as ideal. Her thighs were to be as smooth as a peeled stick, though fleshier and amply curved. Since, as with Hamlet or Jesus for that matter, no one knew what Love looked like, her form and all her emblems eventually achieved a generic status (Jesus is tall, blond, and thin); but this stereotype was never of a particular, an instance of which you might meet on the street; instead, its entire being was devoted to the service of the universal. For fanciers of Christian figures, however, Mark and the other Testament teachers, while remaining within the type that had been cast for them, and representing the ideals of the religion as well as figures in Christian history, were nevertheless to be depicted as actual persons. Jesus may have been a scapegoat, but he must not be so idealized he becomes nothing but sacrifice. Another example: many sopranos must be able to play *La Bohème*'s Mimi; if one of them cannot make Mimi's emaciated weight, then cast, crew, and customers will pretend they are watching the role sing rather than the occupant of it. Rodin's departures from these norms were felt before they were formulated. Where would we locate the walk of *The Walking Man*? In walking itself? In this sort of stride among many? In the habitual gait of someone exercising? And particularly during his morning constitutional? This amazing figure is the expression of a specific kind of muscular movement in which the determination of the walker's will, even without the walker, is evident in them. These legs walk by themselves. Across meadows. Down streets. Through walls. The battered torso is the handle of their fork.

> *The Walking Man* as finally exhibited is the antithesis of the nineteenth century statue, for it lacks the old values of identity, assertive ego, moral message rhetorically communicated, completeness of parts and of finish, and stability. More than any other of Rodin's works, this sculpture overwhelms the viewer by the power of movement. . . . No sculptor before Rodin had made such a basic, simple event as walking the exclusive focus of his art and raised it to the level of high drama.
>
> [Elsen, *Rodin,* p. 32]

As Rodin's style developed, so did the complaints. *The Age of Bronze* was felt to be so lifelike that it must have been made from a body cast. *The Walking Man* convicted the sculptor of dismemberment. *The Man with the Broken Nose, The Crouching Woman,* and *The Old Courtesan* were attacks upon their subjects, deliberately disgusting, or perverse attempts to make the ugly attractive. *The Kiss* was too sexy or too pretty, and *The Thinker* banal—or worse, a schoolboy bathroom joke. *The Gates of Hell* had ended up an expensive hodgepodge. *The Burghers of Calais* were too sorrowful; the monument didn't depict them as behaving bravely enough. And yet his terra-cotta sketch for *The Call to Arms,* proposed to commemorate the Franco-Prussian war, was so vehement it failed consideration. The great draped *Balzac* didn't look like Balzac, while the naked *Balzac* was an affront to the writer, his art, and his public. The Balzacs, in particular, called for outrage.

> He was accused variously of having depicted his subject as a penguin, a snowman, a sack of coal, a menhir, a phantom, a colossal fetus and a shapeless larva. Other criticisms included the charge that Balzac had been reduced to the role of an actor in a gigantic Guignol, that he had just gotten out of bed to confront a creditor, or that exposing the public to such maladroit handling of proportions and physical distortion was equivalent to the dangers of a live bomb.
>
> [Elsen, *Rodin,* p. 103]

As late as 1932, R. H. Wilenski would claim, in his *The Meaning of Modern Sculpture,* that "Rodin's interest when he modeled the Balzac was concentrated in the head. Remove the head and we have nothing but a shapeless mess." Wilenski provides an illustration in which he has done the decapitation (Wilenski, p. 23, illus. Ib).

It was claimed that Rodin's Impressionistic style was better suited to painting than to sculpture, although the Impressionists weren't initially approved of either; moreover, he appeared to disobey the modernist rule that the work should reflect the nature of its materials and manufacture, yet in what but clay would his kind of modulations occur, or his mingling of limbs be easy? This much was true: Rodin's aim was to transform his materials into something ontologically alive—after all, had not God made mud into man?

Élie Faure enlists his eloquence, honed through a thousand pages of his *History of Art,* to register Rodin's errors.

> Often—too often, alas!—the gestures become contorted, the unhappy idea of going beyond plastics and of running after symbols creates groups in which the embracing figures are disjointed; the volumes fly

out of their orbit, the attitudes are impossible, and, in the whole literary disorder, the energy of the workman melts like wax in the fire. Even
in his best days, he lives and works by brief paroxysms, whose burning
sensation runs through him in flashes.

> [Élie Faure, *History of Art: Modern Art,* trans. Walter Pach
> (New York: Harper and Bros., 1924), pp. 402–3]

A good many of the misapprehensions that Rilke says constitute Rodin's
fame were fomented by social scandals, as I have tried to suggest, and the
sculptor's name continued to collect scurrilous rumors for the remainder of
his life; but at the same time his renown drew to him many who were also
famous, all bringing with them their own bounty of slander, gossip, and glorification. Isadora Duncan claims that she wants to have children of genius
by him, and Loïe Fuller would love to wind multicolored ribbons round
her body while he draws her.* Eleanora Duse will recite poetry at the Hôtel
Biron, and Wanda Landowska play Bach upon a harpsichord trucked in for
the occasion. Meanwhile, the press enjoys publishing lampoons of various
kinds, and caricatures by Sem and Belon amuse their publics. In one, Rodin
is depicted pulling the arms and legs off a female figure. I think we are to
imagine she is not alive at the time. Another, called *Terrain Rodin,* shows a
garden of disembodied heads and embracing bodies. (Descharnes and Cha-
brun, *Auguste Rodin,* p. 216.)

The Meudon days begin to pass. Rilke reads Rodin's press clippings in
the villa's little park and enjoys the garden's postcard views, or he walks up
the village slopes to a thick wood where he can brood in a solitude free of
Paris's insistent presence or Rodin's impalpable one. Among his wishes: that
he could take the forest's lofty fresh air back with him to the city, where the
heat is oppressive, the atmosphere odiferous, stale, and heavy. He presses his
face against the fence of the Luxembourg Gardens like one in jail, and even
the flowers in their beds feel constrained to be there.

On September 11, Rilke does something so transparent it almost ceases to
be devious. He writes Rodin a letter. Like a lover, he explains that his poor
French makes it difficult for him to express himself as he would like, and the
care with which he prepares his questions make them seem contrived and

---

* Lest we forget Mrs. Fuller's talent—namely, her skill with illusion—here is a juicy bit from
Cocteau: "Is it possible . . . to forget that woman who discovered the dance of her age? A fat
American, bespectacled and quite ugly, standing on a hanging platform, she manipulates waves
of floating gauze with poles, and somber, active, invisible, like a hornet in a flower, churns
about herself a protean orchid of light and material that swirls, rises, flares, roars, turns, floats,
changes shape like clay in a potter's hands, twisted in the air under the emblem of the torch and
headdress." (Jean Cocteau, *Souvenir Portraits,* trans. Jesse Browner [New York: Paragon House,
1990], p. 81.)

inappropriate for the occasion; so he is sending on a few verses in French with the hope that they will bring the two of them a little closer. After some customary fulsomeness, Rilke confesses that "It was not only to do a study that I came to be with you,—it was to ask you: how must one live?" The answer we've heard: *"il faut travailler."* However, Rilke says he has always waited for the beckon of the muse, waited for what he calls the creative hour, waited for inspiration. He has tried to form habits of diligence, but now he knows he must try again, try and succeed. Sadly . . .

> . . . last year we had rather serious financial worries, and they haven't yet been removed: but I think now that diligent work can disarm even the anxieties of poverty. My wife has to leave our little child, and yet she thinks more calmly and impartially of that necessity since I wrote her what you said: *"Travail et patience."* I am very happy that she will be near you, near your great work. . . .
>
> I want to see if I can find a living in some form here in Paris,—(I need only a little for that). If it is possible, I shall stay. And it would be a great happiness for me. Otherwise, if I cannot succeed, I beg you to help my wife as you helped me by your work and by your word and by all the eternal forces of which you are the Master.
>
> [Letter to Auguste Rodin, Sept. 11, 1902, in *Letters,* pp. 87–88]

The verses in French Rilke wrote for Rodin have a German brother, because on the same day, doubtless after the same stroll through the same park, he also penned one of the two better-known autumn poems from *The Book of Hours.* His state of mind could not be better represented.

Autumn

The leaves are falling, falling from far away,
as though a distant garden died above us;
they fall, fall with denial in their wave.

And through the night the hard earth falls
farther than the stars in solitude.

We all are falling. Here, this hand falls.
And see—there goes another. It's in us all.

And yet there's One whose gently holding hands
let this falling fall and never land.

Despite his misery, his anxiety, Rilke is greedily gathering material. These months will be among his richest. Incidents of no apparent moment will crystallize and coalesce. Here is one. At the end of September, he writes to Clara:

> Rodin has a tiny plaster cast, a tiger (antique), in his studio . . . which he values very highly. . . . And from this little plaster cast I saw what he means, what antiquity is and what links him to it. There, in this animal, is the same lively feeling in the modeling, this little thing (it is no higher than my hand is wide, and no longer than my hand) has hundreds of thousands of sides like a very big object, hundreds of thousands of sides which are all alive, animated, and different. And that in plaster! And with this the expression of the prowling stride is intensified to the highest degree, the powerful planting of the broad paws, and at the same time, that caution in which all strength is wrapped, that noiselessness . . . *

[Letter to Clara Rilke, Sept. 27, 1902, in *Letters*, p. 90]

The panther Rilke will study in the Jardin des Plantes began to find its words, I suspect, as a tiny plaster tiger with a prowling stride and broad paws; the bars of his cage were borrowed from the Luxembourg Gardens, and his gaze from the poet's own, as well as his sense of desperation. The abbreviated sonnet, J. B. Leishman suggests, was the earliest of the famous *Dinge* or "thing" poems, whose nature has been ascribed to Rilke's Rodin experience. (J. B. Leishman, ed. and trans., *Rainer Maria Rilke: Selected Works*, vol. 2, *Poetry* [New York: New Directions, 1960], p. 178. These translations are from William H. Gass, *Reading Rilke* [New York: Alfred A. Knopf, 1999].)

The Panther

His gaze has grown so worn from the passing
of the bars that it sees nothing anymore.
There seem to be a thousand bars before him
and beyond that thousand nothing of the world.

The supple motion of his panther's stride,
as he pads through a tightening circle,
is like the dance of strength around a point
on which an equal will stands stupefied.

* Rilke refers to the little tiger again in a letter to Lou Andreas-Salomé, Aug. 15, 1903, in *Letters*, p. 128.

> Only rarely is an opening in the eyes
> enabled. Then an image brims
> which slides the quiet tension of the limbs
> until the heart, wherein it dies.

Rodin's surfaces are there to suggest a reality that can only be inferred, just as fingers or a face, by gesture or expression, disclose a consciousness that would otherwise be indiscernible. Sculptures are things: they start as stuff, stuff taken from stuff like rock or clay, and they stay stuff until the artist gives them a determinate form so that, through that form, they may have life. The poet's problem is precisely the opposite. Language is our most important sign of elevated awareness, but language has weak presence. Though often on paper, it possesses no weight. A poem is like a ghost seeking substantiality, a soul in search of a body more appealing than the bare bones mere verses rattle. It is consequently not the message in a bottle that Rilke previously thought it was, nor a young man's feelings raised like a flag. All of us have emotions urgently seeking release, and many of us have opinions we think would do the world some good; however, the poet must also be a maker, as the Greeks maintained, and, like the sculptor, like every other artist, should aim at adding real beings to the world, beings fully realized, not just things like tools and haberdashery that nature has neglected to provide, or memos and laws that society produces in abundance, but *Ding an sich,* as humans often fail to be, things-in-themselves. In a strange way, Rilke's new Rodin-induced resolve will unite the poet's most primitive impulse—in this case, animism—with his most sophisticated inclination—art as an end, art that stands apart from nature and in opposition to it, since nature does not and cannot produce it.

If we look at *She Who Was the Helmet-Maker's Once-Beautiful Wife* (sometimes called *The Old Courtesan*), we shall have to pass through several necessary shifts in point of view. The woman Rodin depicts is old, bent, clinging to a rock as if the river of life were about to sweep her away, skinny and scarred, all bone and tendon, her dugs pendulous, shrunken, and flat, her belly bunchy like a wrinkled bag; whereas once, we are asked to believe, her skin was smooth, her body lithe, strong, bearing breasts that were perfect bowls and boasting hair that fell across her back like lines of music; but the body's beauty, the sculpture unoriginally says, comes to this: the condition of the prune, a figure formed from suffering and age, alive only to wonder why.

Facile feelings of pity and regret are available from this site as stamps from a post office, yet what is piercing about the piece is its beauty, a beauty that we could sentimentalize by thinking, for a moment, that even decrepit whores in this wonderful world are lovely, when, of course, they are not, abuse takes its toll, hard living, too, and the body is our first grave. It is the bronze that is glorious; it is the bronze that reminds us that age and dying, death itself, has its own life, its own stages of fulfillment, its own value and measures of success. Baudelaire's poem "A Carrion," for which Rodin and Rilke shared an admiration, is of the same genre as Villon's snows of yester-year, Rochester's dust that has closed Helen's eyes, and Yorick's dug-up skull, whose chaps are now quite fallen. It begins:

> Remember now, my Love, what piteous thing
> We saw on a summer's gracious day:
> By the roadside a hideous carrion, quivering
> On a clean bed of pebbly clay,
>
> Her legs flexed in the air like a courtesan,
> Burning and sweating venomously,
> Calmly exposed its belly, ironic and wan,
> Clamorous with foul ecstasy.

Rilke's animism is poetical, of course, but is also, in its way, religious, for it requires respect for all things equal to the respect we tend to show now for only a few, since we prize so little even in the things we prize. It gives value, as Rodin did, to every part of our anatomy, to each muscle movement—stretch, twitch, and fidget; our physical features—a silk soft earlobe, tawny limb, or crooked finger; or facial expressions—grimace, smile, or howl; as well as the very clay we come from (at least in his workshop)—wood block, slab, and plaster pot. Moreover, it endows even the accidental encounter of different parts—my hand on your shoulder—with its own dignity as a legitimate state of affairs. Gestures, expressions, postures, moods, thoughts, sudden urges merely change more rapidly than habits, attitudes, convictions, dispositions do, and can be slowed by stone to suit our scrutiny throughout a homemade eternity.

> The flies swarmed on the putrid vulva, then
> A black tumbling rout would seethe
> Of maggots, thick like a torrent in the glen,
> Over those rags that lived and seemed to breathe.*

---

* Allen Tate's wonderful translation of Charles Baudelaire, *The Flowers of Evil,* selected and edited by Marthiel and Jackson Matthews (Norfolk, Conn.: New Directions, 1955), p. 38.

It was not simply in the shop, among the fragments and the figures, that Rilke saw this willful independence and fullness of life. He encountered it on the streets of Paris. That thin pencil which rose slowly out of an old crone's fist was alive, as were the rusty pins that ran from side to side in their proffered drawer as if to escape your eye when you looked down on them. In the early morning the water from the water wagons "sprang young and light out of their pipes," the hooves of the horses struck the street "like a hundred hammers," and the cries of the vendors echoed while "the vegetables on their handcarts were stirring like a little field." But his most indelible encounter was with the man suffering from St. Vitus' dance whose gyrations and frantic coping strategies he vividly describes in a letter to Lou Salomé (another rehearsal for passages that Rilke includes in *Malte Laurids Brigge*). Rilke follows the man for several blocks as the poor fellow's shoulders twitch, his arms fly about, and his legs jig. (Letter of July 18, 1903, in *Letters,* pp. 112–15.) The man's will is at odds with his limbs, each of which has its own plans, and all four would hop off by themselves if they had their way, like the fragments in Rodin's cases.

So the surfaces of Rodin's work, which his studio light makes lively, implicitly rely upon a philosophical principle of great age and respectability—one that has been seriously entertained by Galileo, Hobbes, and Spinoza, through Freud up to the present. Since the effect in question is one of animation, it may seem odd that the principle involved is that of inertia. A body at rest will remain at rest—a body in motion will remain in motion—unless something else hectors or hinders it. When that interference occurs, the stone or the ball or the dog at the door will resist; it will attempt to restore the status quo, strive to save its situation, maintain its equilibrium, preserve its life. Spinoza called the tendency to stay the same the object's *conatus.* It is popularly thought of as the principle of self-preservation. All things would be self-sufficient, as windowless as Leibniz's monads, if they could. The condition of the fetus that is automatically fed, protected from every outside shock, surrounded by an embalming ocean, growing as it has been programmed to grow, is ideal. We are pushed out into the world; we are forced by circumstances both inside us (hunger and thirst) and outside (sensation and harm) to cope; and, as Freud argued, we are repeatedly compelled to reduce the unsettling demands of our desires to zero.

A limp that tells the world we are compensating for an injury becomes a habit hard to break even when its cause has healed and there is no longer any "reason" for it. Except that the limp wishes to remain. Our stutter wants to stay. Our fall from a ladder would be forever like a cast-out angel if we didn't fetch up in a lake of fire or at least on a floor. The fire, moreover, eats its way through every fuel it's offered only because it is eager to stay burning like that bright gem of quotation fame. As the naked models move about Rodin's studio, he observes the participating parts of their bodies until he can catch, in the middle of an action, the very will of the gesture, its own integrity and wholeness. The consciousness that inhabits us (and, as Rilke likes to imagine, inhabits even the so-called least thing) refuses to age. As we all have surely noticed, only our body gets old, and does so reluctantly, while each creak, each ache and pain, comes to stay if it can, as vigorous as a virus, youthful as our death will be, buoyant and hopeful. Dying does not want to die. Dying would make dying a career. And death has its own designs.

We can call it war if we like—Hobbes did—we can call it competition, but unities create their own momentum, complex states of affairs resist dis-enabling influence (what are bureaucrats for?), and all of the figures that make up a sculpture like *The Burghers of Calais,* each eloquent in its own way, must feel the influence of so powerful a composition. The man with St. Vitus' dance had lost control of his commonwealth. Which is what happens when parts of the body politic no longer feel safe to pursue their own plans and the grip of the state police grows weak. The group must ensure the safety of its members if it wishes to survive. Otherwise it will explode or choke itself to death. Similarly, the elements of a work of art must form a community which allows each element its own validity while pursuing the interest of the whole. A word, if it could have had a choice, must feel it would have chosen just the companions it has been given, so that when it glows with satisfaction it also makes its line shine.

Moreover, the unity of a sculptural fragment, when imagined alongside a correspondingly severed limb, insists upon its own superiority, for it can flourish quite apart from any body, whereas both amputation and amputee are damaged possibly beyond repair.

October was filled with Rilke's work on the essay, but now Clara had arrived in Paris and had her studio in the same apartment building as his, according to an arrangement he had finally worked out with his conscience. Their economic circumstances remained dire; the couple's dislike of Paris, now shared, increased; they endured their separate loneliness through the gray city's winter, living on roots and water, or so it seemed. The essay at last concluded, Rilke came down with the first of several bouts of flu and a gloom that obscured the upper half of the Eiffel Tower. By March he was ready to return to his itinerant ways, and fled for Italy, the first of many nations in which he would find refuge.

It would be three years to the month of his first meeting with Rodin before Rilke would return to Paris and Meudon, this time as an invited guest.

The Master had read Rilke's monograph by this time, since it now extolled him in French, and he welcomed the poet warmly as a trusted friend and fellow artist. The visitor was well housed, with a nice view of the valley. Rilke offered to help with some of Rodin's overwhelming paperwork and was soon hired on, as it were, full-time. Often he, Rodin, and Rose Beuret would rise early to visit the city or enjoy Versailles, and once they dared Chartres in the dead of winter, where terrible winds, because they were envious of such grandeur, Rodin said, tormented the towers. (Some details have been taken from Ruth Butler's *Rodin: The Shape of Genius* [New Haven, Conn.: Yale University Press, 1993].)

Rilke seeped into the role of Rodin's secretary, a position he wanted because it cushioned him in Meudon, because he was paid, because the work was expected to be undemanding; yet a position he did not want because it confined him to Meudon, his French might be inadequate, because it put him below stairs in Rodin's service when he had his own fish to hook and fry—the poet as ambitious as the sculptor.

Rilke planned a lecture tour on behalf of Rodin, a project that would take him to Dresden late in October, but the response to his first appearance disappointed him because, although there were "six hundred people," they were "not the right ones." Then, in Prague, he twice performed for a small crowd of mystified officials and sleepy old ladies who he imagined were more concerned with the digestion of their dinners. When Rilke asks, a few paragraphs into his text, "Are you listening?," is the question entirely rhetorical? Worse than their inattention, his take wasn't covering costs. In Berlin there were visits and readings before he repeated his Rodin lecture a final time—on this occasion with some success. (Freedman, *Life of a Poet*, pp. 233, 242.)

Spring of 1906 would find him back in Meudon, where his work, fatter than he remembered, sat upon his shoes like a heavy dog. In one of his poems he likened himself to a swan out of water, waddling his way "through things still undone." The personal epistle was an art form at which Rilke excelled, but the business letter in French was boring, intractable, foreign, and frustrating. The poet had become dilatory and the sculptor impatient. Moreover, Rilke had begun answering mail without taking the trouble to inform Rodin of the fact or the nature of the exchange, assuming an authority he did not have: once to Baron Heinrich Thyssen-Bornemisza, a wealthy German patron, once to Sir William Rothenstein, an important English art administrator and academic painter. Upon learning of these presumptions, Rodin fired Rilke with a force that expelled him from his cottage and the grounds as well as from his secretarial position. He was soon back in his little Paris room, a spent shell. (Freedman, *Life of a Poet*, p. 245.)

The poet had recovered his perilous freedom, his personal space, a space, one suspects, that was very like the space he believed Rodin's figures required, not only one which allowed you to inspect them "in the round," but a space that was theirs by right of uniqueness, that distinguished them somehow "from the other things, the ordinary things, which anyone could grasp." A small statue could, therefore, seem large. Rilke, too, required such room as respect conferred, where he might stand "solitary and luminous" with "the face of a visionary." Yet Rilke's rhetoric, when he writes about Rodin's work, is not simply a reflection of his need to enhance his own importance; it also expresses the necessity for any work of art to lay claim to the appropriate arena of its enjoyment, hence the close placement of paintings in some museums above, below, or beside one another on the same wall or the squeezing of a bust into a corner or the dumping of a figure at the end of a narrow hall that leads to the johns, the elevators, or the shops is either a sign of catastrophic overcrowding, a show of curatorial contempt, or evidence of feeble artistic force. Even a fragment should stand in its space like Napoleon, and there is ample testimony to the imperial effect of Rodin's sculptures, whatever their size. In his essay collection *Leonardo's Nephew,* James Fenton quotes Aristide Maillol—as his talk is recollected by the ubiquitous Count Kessler:

> When you view a Rodin from afar, it's small, very small. But sculpture forms part of the air all around it. Rodin has a Buddha at his place, well placed on a socle, in his garden, in front of a circle of small shrubs. Well, it's as big as that [showing it very small] and yet it's as big as the sky. It's immense. It fills everything.*

Rilke was similarly taken with this piece.

Buddha

As if he listened. Silence. Depth.
And we hold back our breath. Yet nothing yet.
And he is star. And other great stars ring him,
though we cannot see that far.

---

* James Fenton, *Leonardo's Nephew* (New York: Farrar, Straus and Giroux, 1998), p. 171. *Berlin in Lights: The Diaries of Count Harry Kessler* (New York: Grove Press, 1999) is an abridgment of the diaries and does not contain this quote, so don't hunt for it there or in the corresponding English edition.

O he is fat. Do we suppose
he'll see us? He has need of that?
Sink in any supplicating pose before him,
he'll sit deep and idle as a cat.

For that which lures us to his feet
has circled in him now a million years.
He has forgotten all we must endure,
encloses all we would escape.

Rodin's pre-eminent biographer, Ruth Butler, suggests that some additional factors were at work in Rilke's dismissal. When Rilke returned from his leisurely lecture tour, Rodin was ill with what was called the grippe. Rose Beuret was in a foul mood, which didn't improve his. So he asked George Bernard Shaw, whose bust he had been commissioned to sculpt, if he and his wife would take the train to Meudon to sit for it so that the ailing artist wouldn't have to come to his workshop in Paris. At first the Shaws came unencumbered, but when Shaw learned that Rodin didn't mind being photographed (the playwright had tried his own hand), he asked permission for his friend the American photographer Alvin Langdon Coburn to visit as well. Shaw, not easily impressed by anyone farther from himself than his beard, was aware that Rodin's thumb was a greater imprimatur than the Pope's seal, and told Coburn: "No photograph taken has touched him. . . . He is by a million chalks the biggest man you ever saw; all your other sitters are only fit to make gelatin to emulsify for his negative." (Details of this meeting are from Butler, *Rodin,* p. 390, and the quote is from *Alvin Langdom Coburn, Photographer: An Autobiography* [New York: Dover Publications, 1978], p. 22.) Even more frequently photographed were Rodin's sculptures, of course, many of the better ones the work of Eugène Druet. These Rodin sometimes stage-managed, but few of them (excepting Edward Steichen's) possess the aesthetic quality or inherent drama of Michael Eastman's contemporary images. (For Rodin's relationship to this art, see Kirk Varnedoe's article, "Rodin and Photography," in Elsen, ed., *Rodin Rediscovered,* pp. 203–48.) Rodin could not have been disappointed with Coburn's customarily lyrical view, since it shows the sculptor wearing a beard like a river and a hat we now call a "pillbox." There is a slight upward tilt to Rodin's head that resembles the heroic pose he fashioned for Balzac.

To watch Shaw pose for his immortality, he gathered a crowd, also calling the curator of the Fitzwilliam Museum, Sydney Cockerell, to his side.

Rilke joined them, almost immediately impressed with Shaw as a sitter—

the entire squad eager to write brilliantly about a glittering constellation they underestimated even while trying to exaggerate it.

In the newspaper *Gil Blas* for May 24, 1912, Shaw wrote:

Rodin worked laboriously. . . . When he was uncertain he measured me with an old iron compass and then measured the bust. If the nose was too long he cut off a section and pressed the end to close the wound with no more emotion or affectation than a glazier replacing a window. If the ear was not in its place he would cut it off and lay it on correctly, these mutilations being executed cold-bloodedly in the presence of my wife (who almost expected to see the already terribly animated clay begin to bleed) while remarking that it was quicker to do it thusly than to make a new ear.

[Quoted in Elsen, *Rodin*, p. 126]

Rilke wrote to Shaw's German publisher, Samuel Fischer:

Rodin has begun the portrait of one of your most remarkable authors; it promises to be exceptionally good. Rarely has a likeness in the making had so much help from the subject of it as this bust of Bernard Shaw's. It is not only that he is excellent at standing (putting so much energy into standing still and giving himself so unconditionally to the sculptor's hands), but he so collects and concentrates himself in that part of the body which, in the bust, will have . . . to represent the whole Shaw, that his whole personality seems to become concentrated essence.

[Quoted in Butler, *Rodin*, pp. 390–91]

They all took a break to attend the celebration for the installation of *The Thinker* in front of the Panthéon. Shaw, not to be outdone (and as excellent at sitting as standing), persuaded Coburn to photograph him the very next day, naked following his morning bath, in the pose presently before the Panthéon. The photo exists for posterity's wonder. Rilke was visibly taken with the English genius, who didn't mind adulation even from callow unknowns. Apart from that, during Rodin's week of work, and worse, during his week of triumph, Shaw had clearly been competing for attention if not glory with a sundry that included Rodin's secretary and Rodin's statue. Butler says: "It was Rilke who paid the price for the mischievous Englishman's visit" (Butler, *Rodin*, p. 191).

Although Rilke would suggest to Rodin the purchase of the Hôtel Biron, later the Rodin Museum, and for a time live in that building (as Cocteau would, who claimed to have a role in its preservation), his intimacy with Rodin was over. Two days after Shaw's departure for London, on May 10, 1906, Rilke was "dismissed like a thieving servant." We can pretend to know precisely.

The Georgia Review, 2004
Published in *A Temple of Texts,* 2006

Ezra Pound

I t is too easy—the name game—in this case.

Christened "Pound, Ezra Loomis." If used as a verb, "pound" means to beat. If used as a noun, "pound" signifies a unit of weight, a measure of money, pressure of air, or physical force. From time to time, apropos poetry, Pound wondered which should be sovereign, the verb or the noun, and concluded, if his practice may be entered as evidence, that the verb was most noticed when knocked off the sentence like a phallus from a kouros—"Spire-top alevel the well-curb"—and when effects were hammered back into their causes with naillike hyphens—"Seal sports in the spray-whited circles of cliff-wash"—hence into a compaction like a headache . . . splitting.

As location, a pound sequesters sick animals and strays. "Places of confinement for lawbreakers" is the definition that immediately precedes Pound's name in *The American Heritage Dictionary,* after which we encounter the listing for "pound of flesh" and read of "a debt harshly insisted upon." Certainly a pound is a large bite by any standard, yet it resembles, in being Shylock's payment, the *neschek* of the Jews: money for the rent of money; not a gnaw, but, in the way it feels coming due, not a nibble either. It is a tax on use, this thinning of the dime, as if money would otherwise be free of entropy; although to put the bite on someone has come to mean to beg for a loan, possibly as a return of favor, where the request is clearly not intended to invite the interest of the loan's own teeth. So one meaning of "pound" has a relative called "blood money." It suggests racial forfeiture.

On the other hand, the pound of flesh we subtract from the flank of a steer may increase our girth and relieve many a primordial anxiety. We call it "putting our money to work." Wear and repair, profit or loss, depends upon your point of view, the angle of the bank and the direction of the bounce.

Our poet depended without protest, for much of his life, upon funds supplied by the family of his wife.

Ezra Loomis Pound was born in a tidy white frame house in Hailey, Idaho. Hailey was like the little mining town of song and soapy story, salooned among mountain-sized stones; yet when Ezra's father moved back to Philadelphia, it was to work at the United States Mint, unintentionally obedient to the resonances of his name. Consequently, Pound was Amurrican right down to the potato, right down to the silver and gold in them thar hills, or, as we complained of it during the Depression, to the paper in them thar bills.

Pound had a Homer for a father, and, following his Pre-Raphaelite devotion to whatever was medieval, an almost German love for the Greeks. Appropriate to this passion was his grandmother's maiden name, Loomis. Penelope wove and unwove and rewove on one to put off her suitors, but the return of her hero was also artfully, persistently postponed, since he was usually stranded somewhere, an exile—as the poet would say—enisled.

Then there was his allegedly Egyptian initial syllable, *Ez,* which he said meant "rising," so that it could be followed by *ra,* which, of course, stood for the sun. His parents pronounced that ending, wrongly, "ray," but got the part about getting up in the morning right. It was a version he preferred for a long time. Everybody else's "Ezra" was Hebrew, a prophet's name meaning "help" and designating a scribe of the Law of the Lord. The Biblical Ezra believed in racial purity too, and castigated the Israelites for spilling their holy seed among strangers—taking strange wives and adopting their ways. Pound's alternative reading, "Rising Sun," aside from the pun on his aspirations, sounded Sioux or Cheyenne rather than Egyptian. In the end, he settled for a folk-marked "Ole Ez," a designation backwoodsy, cracker-barrel, and American, clean through from clown to crank, and admirably suited to the village explainer he had become. Suffering a village explainer, Gertrude Stein said, was all right if you were a village, but if not . . . not.

On the way to that comfortable "old shoe" locution, Pound enjoyed learning that the phonetic translation of his name into Japanese would yield a joke—"This picture of a phallus costs ten yen"—as well as the fact that James Joyce had instructed his children, because of Ezra's kind monetary assistance, to address him as "Signore Sterlina." He invented Aesopian names for T. S. Eliot and himself. He was Brer Rabbit while Eliot was Possum, both down-South aka's, and as quaint as a picture postcard of St. Louis. He spent some time as "E.P."—a memo signer's initial—and concealed himself behind various noms de plume like someone playing peekaboo: he translated a French thriller while pretending to be Hiram Janus (a two-faced American hick, we must presume), and signed the art and music reviews he wrote for *New Age* with the names B. H. Dias and William Atheling; whereas he was simply T.J.V. when he covered drama for *Atheneum,* and Marius David Adkins on the day he was fired from a similar post at *Outlook.* It was not for shame he hid himself, because he padded his slender study of George Antheil's nearly nonexistent theory of harmony with old performance notices. As Alfred Venison he wrote terrible parodies of Tennyson. Pound also recognized the cute connection of his name with Robert Browning's Rabbi Ben Ezra even before Conrad Aiken began calling him that. These nicks, dimins, and anons were but a few of his personae, since he sometimes summoned the spirits of Andreas Divus, Sextus Propertius, Bertran de Born, Arnaut Daniel, François Villon, Guido Cavalcanti, and others, including the tortured soul of the poet Ri Haku (whom misconception created when Ole Ez read the Chinese ideograms for Li Po as if they were Japanese), in each case in order to seize them for his muse.

He also liked to press his name into words like "EZthority," "EZucation," and "EZuversity," as if they were slabs of fresh cement (and in a manner now associated with the fast-food chain—"Egg McMuffin"), just as he constantly jostled the language and upset its spelling, not quite concealing his resentments and animosities behind the jocular.

Pound realized that some people thought he resembled the Saviour, an appearance he did not neglect to cultivate; nevertheless, he worried more than a little about his Semitic look and claimed, concerning his given name, that "the goddam yitts pinched it as they did everything else." Of course, it was the Quakers who pinched it (if pinching, here, is possible), and his father who attached it to a family name as plain and workmanlike and literal as Smith, Carpenter, or Wright.

What's in a name? Pound would distort the names of people he came, for whatever reason, to dislike—thus Lincoln Kirstein was dubbed "Stinkum Cherrystein," and the radio commentator H. V. Kaltenborn, called "Kaltenstein"; "-stein" was apparently his all-purpose Jewish suffix. Gertrude Stein felt that people grew to resemble the name they had been given, as if it contained an important element of their fate. In the case of Ezra Pound, whose self was so problematic, around his first name there remained an uneasy aura, while his last had a weight too relevant to his obsession.

Ezra, whose person was mostly putty and pretense and whose home address was next door to Nowhere, invented a rude and outrageous "poetic" self to perform its dance in public. Behind an American air of confidence and bumptious arrogance, he concealed uncertainties, shyness, innocence, naïveté—American as well, Yankee as all git. He also hid his massive ignorance of nearly everything, including literature, behind a few out-of-focus facts and generally impertinent judgments, becoming, in this way, a person of opinions: views he then watched at work as children watch an ant farm. He used his undoubted generosity to insinuate himself into other people's lives, appropriating, if not their efforts, at least their reputations, to himself. He behaved a lot like a manager of prizefighters who has a stable of stiffs, one of whom he might send out against the opposition at selected times, and whose failures he would excuse and defend as energetically as he would crow over their occasional success. He created movements, galloped to the sound of every trumpet, railed and hectored, bullied and petted, aided and pressured, handing out advice as if it were alms; and while in the business of doing the Lord's work and waging the good fight, actually did win some big ones, really did assist some important writers at critical times (most particularly Eliot and Joyce), and did improve the state of poetry (although, listening to the pipsqueaking that passes for poetry these days, his improvements were not to be prolonged).

Pound was a pirate, and plundered selected texts as if they were captured ships. He embraced principles he rarely if ever practiced (like the vague admonishments of "Imagism"), maneuvered both behind the scenes and in front of the lights, always in support of "modernism," a movement in his own case oddly made of pagan materials, medieval mannerisms, and Swinburnean swan song.

                                                    Between them,

        Cave of Nerea,
                she like a great shell curved,
        And the boat drawn without sound,
        Without odour of ship-work,
        Nor bird-cry, nor any noise of wave moving,
        Nor splash of porpoise, nor any noise of wave moving,
        Within her cave, Nerea,
                                she like a great shell curved
        In the suavity of the rock,
                        cliff green-gray in the far,
        In the near, the gate-cliffs of amber . . .

Eventually form went one way and content another, the meter was thumped on a tub, and the message pasted like a label to the snake oil he was selling. When his work was right, it was as pure as a line drawn by Matisse. It possessed the pleasure of a sweet, long-empty song—monotonous, incantatory, sybaritic—descriptive of what was not, or was no longer, or had been at one time written of, and sounding as if it had been overheard while being whispered through the pages of the past like an echo from Nerea's cave, as if it came from the touch of a bit of lonely beach to the lap of a spent wave.

> And the wave
> > green clear, and blue clear,
> And the cave salt-white, and glare purple,
> > cool, porphyry smooth,
> > > the rock sea-worn.
> No gull cry, no sound of porpoise,
> Sand as of malachite, and no cold there,
> > > the light not of the sun.

In *A Serious Character: The Life of Ezra Pound,* Humphrey Carpenter has measured out Pound's long, problematic life at about eleven pages per year. "Measure" is, I think, the right word. Differently than in many massive biographies, where the data sogs like the morning porridge into groddy heaps through which the author's spoon can be seen to have faintly stirred, here the disposition that has been made of what is known about Pound is always orderly and clear, with a minimum of fatuous conjecture, especially of the psychological kind, untrammeled by idiosyncrasies of style or pushy charm of manner, and with an apt sense for the proper weight to be placed on each detail of the life so as to balance it against the others, including a fine understanding of the role of the work, its quality and meaning, as it bears upon that life or is a product of it.

The course and character of Humphrey Carpenter's narrative is so subtle yet unassuming that the reader only belatedly realizes with what calm and patient control the biographer has permitted the mud of his study to settle so that a figure may emerge, and how free for his own responses he has allowed the reader to feel, although Carpenter certainly makes, and makes known, his own estimates. This book's covers do not enclose a volume of evasions and excuses, nor do they open on a courtroom or lead us to the analyst's couch. The scholar's high tone, averted eye, and carefully washed hands are not in evidence here; nor is the accusatory rant of the reactionary (with whom Ezra Pound had so much in common, in literary matters as well as political), and it is this splendid judiciousness—fair, lucid, calm, unflinching, complete—that distinguishes the biography, and quite beautifully enables *A Serious Character,* in Pound's fine phrase about the proper aim of verse, "to cut a shape in time."

As I followed Carpenter's account of Pound's career, rereading the poetry at each point where the level of the *Life* reached it, my memories of all those initial meetings with the man in his letters, and the poet in his verse, accompanied me, just as I imagine similar recollections will flavor the pages of many readers of the biography. I remembered the stunning impression that the early poems made: their lyrical intensity, odd phrasing, original line breaks, exotic qualities, the unashamed "this is poetry" feel of it, the sudden intrusion of the colloquial—invariably electric—nevertheless a contemporary way of speaking, which was then bent into strange archaic shapes. We filled our mouths with his lines, heard the word with Ezra's matchless ear, and listened to a noble, raucous, wrathful music.

> Damn it all! all this our South stinks peace.
> You whoreson dog, Papiols, come! Let's to music!
> I have no life save when the swords clash.
> But ah! when I see the standards gold, vair, purple, opposing
> And the broad fields beneath them turn crimson,
> Then howl I my heart nigh mad with rejoicing.

And in the letters I found a man my heart could hold close: exuberant, playful, dedicated, generous, and full of rage over all the right things. How he hated the philistines—oughtn't we all?—and hadn't he shaken the dust of provincial America from his feet to walk the romantic paths of the troubador poets? hadn't he shoveled the nineteenth century, that hated age with all its bourgeois ways, into the grave? and blown outmoded sentiments into smithereens, and commanded us, instead, to make it new? brash? fresh? right? true?

And hadn't Ezra Pound befriended the young and supported everything experimental? and gone out of his way to encourage quality, however various, in Frost, Eliot, Joyce, Ford, Lewis, Williams? And when T. S. Eliot had ceased to be an affront and become a façade, Ezra Pound was still rattling his chains—a ghost, perhaps, but with the power to affright. And when T. S. Eliot had thrown that simple and popular plain-style about his shoulders like a shawl, and turned into a regular pundito—despicable in his respectability— Ezra had continued to be complex, dense, and disagreeable—an irregular bandito—doing what we were all supposed to be doing: distancing ourselves from the ruck, our hand against every hand that wasn't thumbing its nose. So if you were not a friend and fan and follower of Ezra Pound, you were at the very least a simp and a lazily inactive enemy of art, and hence of all real advancement in man. It meant you were still in love with that "old bitch gone in the teeth, / For a botched civilization" we all took such easy advantage of, enjoyed, and gleefully rejected.

So when, in 1949, the first Bollingen Prize for Poetry was awarded to *The Pisan Cantos* by a divided and distracted and courageous jury, how we all rushed to the freshly drawn front lines in order to spit ink at our enemies. If we had reservations (and I had a good many), we left them behind as though they were plows, while our weapons were seized like the throat of the foe. Pound shouldn't have gotten the prize, because *The Pisan Cantos* were, on the whole and with the exception of the now famous "Pull down thy vanity" passage, a chaotic and self-indulgent mess, and certainly not superior as a work to William Carlos Williams's second *Paterson* volume, against which it chiefly contended. Yet Pound should have gotten the prize because that was the most powerful punch which could be thrown at the reactionary's nose. However, he had given aid and comfort to the enemy . . . and what an enemy! But he was now most wrongly incarcerated, plopped into a loony bin, and unable to stand trial or further embarrass anybody, since we U.S.'ers had stooped to a ruse of the Reds and called him gone in the head. If our society was going to treat literature with an indifference both casual and pro-found, it had no business punishing any poet for what that poet said. Still, should we show sympathy for this traitor and anti-Semite whose vile hatreds rise from his verse like steam from fresh dung? Nevertheless, there are lines here and there, lines like feathers fallen from angels; there are heavenly tones, and places where the words pace as only Pound could pace them, back and forth, as someone in meditation; and surely there should be a prize for that.

It is difficult to admit to a flaw in Flaubert, any lapse in late Cézanne, or to say that Schoenberg had perhaps not found the right way, or that certain magisterial albeit monotonous and soporific works of our Modern Move-ment were a mistake, a mistake worse than dreadful—merely dreary. It is difficult because the enemy is still out there, growing stronger with every so-called advance in the media, in the scoop-up profit of its enterprise and the passivity of the experience it provides, growing more philistine, more commercial, more hopelessly "pop" during every advertising break, through every sappy sitcom minute.

Humphrey Carpenter has sailed serenely between those who would now just as soon forget the Problem of Ezra Pound and those who, just as intently, would like to get the bastard. Carpenter has accomplished this not by being either mealymouthed or serpent-toothed, but by making certain that when he was confronted with an aesthetic judgment, he made one, and when he was faced with a moral judgment, he made that; and by not harping or playing prosecuting attorney; and by not shoveling loads of unpleasantness under acts of generosity or rhymes of genius; by refusing every special plea; and, above all, by keeping calm. He sees through Ezra Pound without, on that account, failing to see him. It is a feat worthy of salute.

562 THE WILLIAM H. GASS READER

In the United States, it can at present be taken for granted that a serious writer in almost every genre will be at least liberal. The "Poets for Reagan" T-shirt was a humorless joke. However, the camps of the early modernists in most of the arts (not in theater or architecture) were full of fascists, fascist sympathizers, and other lovers of on-time trains; there were many anti-Semites, sexists, denigrators of other races, upper-class apes, and royalist snobs. The list is dismayingly long, shamefully familiar, and I shall not write it down. Although they may have taken over the aesthetic left, their revolutionary fervor did not spell past the *g* in lives typically "bourgeois." Writers had not yet gotten used to the fact that in contemporary society their presence, their opinions, their work and its quality, mattered not a whit. The state would not alter its course half a smidge whatever their ravings, and the writers deeply resented this indifference. Robert Frost was adored as much for his white hair and his aw-shucks country manners as he was for his cold-comfort country pomes. Inside Pound there was a fuming Ezra, inside Eliot a droning Elder Statesman, inside Faulkner a bag of South wind.

We can follow, in Pound's career, the classic course of the disease that arises from the continued sufferance of social disdain and unconcern: how it begins in this or that specific instance of rejection; how the poet starts to glory in the fact of it, to form his very self in terms of such an image; how he augments the facts by acting within that definition and earning further and confirming slights; and, finally, how a theoretical raison d'être arrives, after the fact, indeed, but in time to justify one's hostility as a perfectly honorable and adequate response to the connivance, animosity, and stupidity of the world.

Ezra Pound called the Jews yitts. My father called them Yids or kikes, and as much as I detested his thought and its hostile tone, and refused to listen to any more bitter jokes about President Rosenfeld, I grew used to it; it did not surprise or shock. (Pound referred to the president as "Jewsfeldt" and "Stinkie Roosenstein.") Anti-Semitism was fashionable, and came in many cuts. There was the anti-Semitism of the snob, who viewed Jews with the faint distaste reserved for every nouveau riche and social climber; there was the economic anti-Semite, who associated the Jews with moneylenders and shylocks of all sorts, from simple shopkeepers to munitions czars; there was the religious Jew-hater, who still thought of them as Christ-killers; there was the political Jew-baiter, who felt they infiltrated the system secretly, seized control of it, and, in effect, went about poisoning wells; and there was the racial purist, the blood-taint anti-Semite, who feared, more than anything, the fouling of family lines and the mixing of races and was especially apprehensive about customs and qualities even faintly from the East. It was natural for these antagonisms to join and run together for a while like wild dogs, but they could separate too, and even snap at one another sometimes. Henry James's anti-Semitism appears to have been mainly social, as we might expect, and T. S. Eliot's was probably of the same kind; whereas Ezra Pound's was principally economic and political. He certainly couldn't care that they'd killed Christ.

It was felt that even the safely assimilated Jew was wont to wear black beneath his gay party gear; that he had that funny skullcap to cover his nefarious thoughts; and that behind his practiced worldly smile was concealed a cunning Talmudic look. Jews slunk through society, clannish and conniving, in league with anything you didn't like, secret emissaries of the East, supporters of Communism and revolution, and possessed of a guile gained over centuries of gulling the Gentile to get rich. Even in Hailey, Idaho, where there weren't any, they knew that.

The mind's well-being was the well that was poisoned. One doesn't own a little anti-Semitism as if it were a puppy that isn't big enough yet to poop a lot. One yap from the pooch is already too much. Nor is saying "it was only social" a successful excuse. Only social, indeed . . . only a mild case. The mild climate renders shirtsleeves acceptable, loosens ties and collars, allows extremes to seem means, makes nakedness normal, facilitates the growth of weeds. Since the true causes of anti-Semitism do not lie with the Jews themselves (for, if they did, anti-Semitism might bear some semblance of reason), they must lie elsewhere—so, if not in the hated, then in the hater, in another mode of misery.

Rationalist philosophers, from the beginning, regarded ignorance and error as the central sources of evil, and the conditions of contemporary life have certainly given their view considerable support. We are as responsible for our beliefs as for our behavior. Indeed, they are usually linked. Our brains respond, as well as our bodies do, to exercise and a good diet. One can think of hundreds of beliefs—religious, political, social—which must be as bad for the head as fat is for the heart, and whose loss would lighten and enliven the spirit; but inherently silly ones, like transubstantiation, nowadays keep their consequences in control and relatively close to home. However, anti-Semitism does not; it is an unmitigated moral catastrophe. One can easily imagine how it might contaminate other areas of one's mental system. But is it the sickness or a symptom of a different disease? Humphrey Carpenter's levelheaded tone does not countenance Pound's corruption. It simply places the problem plainly before us, permitting us our anger and our pity.

Donald Hall's luminous memoir of his meetings with Pound in *Their Ancient Glittering Eyes* reports that Pound repented of his anti-Semitism, calling it a mistake and a "suburban prejudice"; but the tone of that repentance is all wrong, suggesting that Pound had made some error in arithmetic on his tax forms which turned out to have unpleasant consequences. Anti-Semitism is not a "mistake," or even a flaw, as if it left the rest of its victim okay and in good working order. As with racism, a little does more than go a long way; it goes all the way.

Karl Shapiro, who had opposed giving the Bollingen Prize to Pound, wrote then that, in his opinion, "the poet's political and moral philosophy ultimately vitiates his poetry and lowers its standards as literary work." I think, however, that, although the poetry has certainly been vitiated by something, the evidence of Carpenter's *Life* is not that Pound's anti-Semitism was responsible, but, rather, that a virulent strain of the mistrust of one's own mind (a fear of thinking, like a fear of heights) and a habit of emotional disassociation were the chief culprits. Pound had no moral philosophy because he was incapable of the consecutive steps of thought, of the painstaking definition or systematic and orderly development of any idea. Carpenter wonderfully extracts and puts before us the faltering steps of Pound's "argument" in his *ABC of Economics,* for instance, and they are the staggers of a drunk. He dismisses *Guide to Kulchur,* with good reason, as a disjunctive mélange of rant and bile. Disjunction is Pound's principal method of design. If he saw the world in fragments, it was because he needed fragments, and because his psyche hated wholes.

In a whole, the various parts might get in touch with one another. In a whole, the grounds for their meeting might be discovered and explored; but Pound preferred spontaneously combustible juxtapositions, ignitions that would take place without the need of connection, as if powder and flint would fire without a strike, or any spark.

Pound took care never to interrogate the fragments themselves (because he might inadvertently treat them as wholes). He asked neither how they were constituted nor where they had been, just as he kept the pieces of his family in fragments: his wife, Dorothy Shakespear, in one place; his son as soon as possible in another; his mistress, Olga Rudge, in a third; their daughter in yet a fourth; and so on. He would seek out remote and relatively exotic figures to write about and translate (where he would not be so easily exposed, and where his cavalier way with data would go relatively unobserved). He perfected the snip system of quotation, and the snipe system of assault, never keeping to the field but darting about from concealment to concealment like an Indian. He created collages out of pieces of his mind, his peeves, his helter-skelter reading; and he flitted from enthusiasm to enthusiasm like an angry bee, because his enthusiasms encouraged him to sip, to fly, to sting.

He detested academics (many of whom he bamboozled just the same), and I suspect it was because they "dwelled." They hung over and on to things; they wrung them like wash sometimes, leaving them flat and dry; but they did probe and pick and piece together. Pound wanted to treat most of his opinions as beyond question or analysis, beyond explanation, as if everyone ought to know what they were, and how they were, and why (Carpenter demonstrates this repeatedly); thus he protected the emptiness of his ideas from being discovered by keeping the lights in their rooms lit but never going in.

The poet's irascibility, his bullying, his bluster, his adoption of moral outrage, his name-calling, his simplifications, his omissions—how long the list is—work to keep the wondering, thinking, quizzing world at bay. If you are confident that four and four make eight, you may be bored if asked to prove it, but hardly angry and outraged. Vilification protects the self-evident from any self for whom it won't be.

It is always dangerous to define yourself, as Pound increasingly did, in terms of your beliefs: I am Catholic; I am an anarchist; I am a fan of the flat earth. An attack on them is an attack on you, and leads to war. You can fight for a cause and make it come about, but you can never make an idea come true like a wish, for its truth is—thank heaven—out of all hands. What could Pound do, built of opinions like a shack, but hate every wind?

Pound's letter-writing style (and then his public prose and then his poetry) exhibits the same traits. Hokey spellings, jokey down-home ruralities, punny inventions undercut the seriousness of whatever's said, even when it is cantankerous. Caps give weight to words which otherwise wouldn't receive it, and offer directions to the understanding which could not be got from the sentences themselves, because neither feeling nor conviction arises from within this prose. It is all punched in from outside. Sentences often fail to complete themselves. The rattle of ideas is regularly broken by conceptual silences that open suddenly like fissures (the hiatus is more frequent than the comma), by leaps of thought that do not include the notion of a landing. Pound's wartime broadcasts from Rome on the fascist radio (which were the basis for charges of treason later brought against him) were clad in such homespun that a few thought he had to be hoodwinking his sponsors.

No. Ezra was in earnest. This was one role he would play through to the curtain. As Carpenter's account shows (and it is a genuinely moving one, even when it must move through this sort of material), Pound regretted his internment; he did indeed become "a man on whom the sun has gone down" (in a phrase from *The Cantos*); but he never really recanted; he never admitted he was wrong; he took courage from his fears to the end.

What Pound was afraid to face (I feel) was the fact that he was not, himself, a self, that he was a bundle of borrowed definitions, including that of the poet. Carpenter quotes Wyndham Lewis's accurate observation that Pound was "that curious thing, a person without a trace of originality of any sort" except the remarkable ability to wear a mask, adopt a tone. "When he can get into the skin of somebody else . . . he becomes a lion or a lynx on the spot." Leslie Fiedler has wondered whether Pound wasn't principally a parodist, so dependent was he upon texts other than his own.

I have to agree with Carpenter that the well-known "Portrait d'une Femme" is more nearly a picture of Pound himself than of its ostensible model, Olivia Shakespear. The lady is seen as a still sea crossed by trading boats and awash with shipwreck and driftgifts. The poem concludes:

> For all this sea-hoard of deciduous things,
> Strange woods half sodden, and new brighter stuff:
> In the slow float of differing light and deep,
> No! there is nothing! In the whole and all,
> Nothing that's quite your own.
>   Yet this is you.

It is true (I think) that most of Pound's best poetry is based upon the work of someone else, and stems from his ability to release another language into English. It was what made him such an excellent editor. Time and time again, in *The Cantos,* amid a barren and chaotic landscape, poetry miraculously blazes up, and at the bottom of that fire a Chinese classic like *Li Ki,* for instance, will be found fueling it, or some other distant text. With so little spring left in his own legs, he could still rebound beautifully from someone else's words, because they—not love or landscape or the pleasures and problems of life—were his muse. Like lighter fluid's flame, these phrases (where, paradoxically, Pound was at last pure Pound) consume themselves without leaving a scorch, mar, or any other trace on the page. Lines like these—flames like these—"lick."

> This month are trees in full sap
> Rain has now drenched all the earth
>   dead weeds enrich it, as if boil'd in a bouillon.

In his role as a modernist, Ezra Pound is a great disappointment. He was a minor master of collage, certainly a fundamental modernist technique, but he valued content over form, message over manner; a lot of his best language was artificial, and, as in the lines above, almost purely decorative, as if it had to be torn from time and place before it could flutter at all: a lyrical oasis amid hate's acrid heat. Pound championed many poets and novelists, but not for long, and not always with real understanding; he didn't like much modern art despite his enthusiasm for Gaudier-Brzeska; and although he had a hand in the Vivaldi revival, and was linked in love with a musician, and composed an opera with which he paralyzed all available ears, he disliked Beethoven, is said to have been tone deaf, and took no part in the serious musical movements of his time, as either a listener or an advocate. Consigned by society to the periphery, he began to take an interest in, and choose, the peripheral, and like many American writers he began to fade, concerning himself more and more, as the years went by, with the crank he was turning.

I suppose most of us want to make a difference. Pound wanted to make a real dent—not (I am afraid) because his dent would make a difference, but because it would make him. If poetry proved impotent, he would turn to prophecy, to politics, to dreams. If he could not act, he could at least assume the posture. So the dent he made was a stage dent, one which would do to advance the action of the play, but which was contained within the inconsequential frame of the stage. Poet/prophet: they were together in the old days, but they were two roles now, and neither paid.

Humphrey Carpenter concludes his exemplary biography with, appropriately, fragments: a few summary pronouncements, none of them about money. The last is a word in the margin of the *Nicomachean Ethics* at a point in the introduction where the translator is summarizing the Philosopher's views. "The life of Action," Horace Rackham writes, "has no absolute value: it is not part of, but only a means to, the End, which is the life of Thought," and Pound's marginal word is "Nuts."

What a lovely word game we could conclude these remarks by playing. It is a very American response—"Nuts!" It is what our generals say when they are surrounded by Germans and asked to surrender. It is what adolescents say when they mean "balls." It is what people called Ezra, so they wouldn't have to call him something else. It also involves just the right textual bollix, because for Aristotle pure act and pure thought are one and the same.

Times Literary Supplement (London), 1989
Published in *Finding a Form,* 1996

IMAGINARY BORGES AND HIS BOOKS

Among Paul Valéry's jottings, André Maurois observes the following: "Idea for a frightening story: it is discovered that the only remedy for cancer is living human flesh. Consequences."

One humid Sunday afternoon during the summer of 1969, in a slither of magazines on a library table, I light like a weary fly upon this, reported by Pierre Schneider: "One of Jean-Paul Riopelle's stories is about a village librarian who was too poor to buy new books; to complete his library he would, whenever he came across a favorable review in a learned journal, write the book himself, on the basis of its title."

Both of these stories are by Borges; we recognize the author at once; and their conjunction here is by Borges, too: a diverse collection of names and sources, crossing like ignorant roads: Valéry, Maurois, Riopelle, Schneider—who could have foreseen this meeting of names in *The New York Review*?

Shaken out of sleep on a swift train at night, we may unblind our compartment window to discover a dim sign making some strange allegation; and you, reader, may unfist this paper any moment and pick up a book on raising herbs instead, a travel folder, letter from a lover, novel by Colette; the eye, mind, memory which encounters them as vague about the distance traversed as any passenger, and hardly startled anymore by the abrupt change in climate or terrain you've undergone.* How calm we are about it; we pass from a kiss to a verb and never tremble; and, having performed that bound, we frolic or we moon among our symbols, those we've assigned to Henry Adams or those we say are by Heraclitus, as if there were nothing to it. Like the hours we spent mastering speech, we forget everything; nor do our logi-

---

* Unless the changes are forcibly called to our attention. See "The Leading Edge of the Trash Phenomenon" in *Fiction and the Figures of Life* (New York: Alfred A. Knopf, 1970).

cians, our philosophers of language, though they may coax us like cats do their fish, very often restore what we once might have had—a sense of wonder at the mental country we inhabit, lost till we wander lost into Borges, a man born as if between syllables in Argentina, where even he for many years believed he had been raised in a suburb of Buenos Aires, a suburb of adventurous streets and visible sunsets, when what was certain was that he was raised in a garden, behind a wrought-iron gate, and in a limitless library of English books.*

Just as Carriego, from the moment he recognized himself as a poet, became the author of verses which only later he was permitted to invent, Borges thought of himself as a writer before he ever composed a volume. A nearsighted child, he lived where he could see—in books and illustrations (Borges says "shortsighted," which will not do); he read English authors, read and read; in clumsy English wrote about the Golden Fleece and Hercules (and inevitably, the Labyrinth), publishing, by nine, a translation of *The Happy Prince* which a local teacher adopted as a text under the impression it was the father's doing, not the son's. In Switzerland, where his family settled for a time, he completed his secondary education, becoming more and more multitongued (acquiring German), yet seeing no better, reading on. He then traveled extensively in Spain, as if to meet other authors, further books, to enlarge the literary landscape he was already living in—deepening, one imagines daily, his acquaintance with the conceptual country he would eventually devote his life to. Back in Argentina, he issued his first book of poems. He was twenty. They sang of Buenos Aires and its streets, but the few lines Christ quotes give the future away:

> Perhaps that unique hour
> increased the prestige of the street,
> giving it privileges of tenderness,
> making it as real as legend or verse.

---

* Or so he asserts in the prologue to *Evaristo Carriego,* according to Ronald J. Christ (*The Narrow Act: Borges' Art of Allusion* [New York: New York University Press, 1969]), although errors are constantly creeping in—his, Christ's, mine—errors, modifications, corruptions, which, nevertheless, may take us nearer the truth. In his little note on Carriego, does he not warn us that Carriego is a creation of Carriego? and in the parable "Borges and I" does he not say, "I am quite aware of his perverse custom of falsifying and magnifying things"? does he not award all the mischievous translations of *A Thousand and One Nights* higher marks than the pure and exact one of Enna Littmann? and in his conversations with Richard Burgin (*Conversations with Jorge Luis Borges* [New York: Holt, Rinehart & Winston, 1969]) does he not represent memory as a stack of coins, each coin a recollection of the one below it, and in each repetition a tiny distortion? Still, we can imagine, over time, the distortions correcting themselves, and returning to the truth through a circle like a stroller and his dog.

Thus he was very soon to pass, as he says himself, from "the mythologies of the suburbs to the games with time and infinity," which finally made him famous—made him that imaginary being, the Borges of his books.

Becoming Borges, Borges becomes a librarian, first a minor municipal one like our poor French village author, and then, later, with the fall of Perón, after having been removed for political reasons from that lesser post, the director of the National Library itself.

Idea for a frightening story: the books written by the unknown provincial librarian ultimately replace their originals, which are declared to be frauds. Consequences.

Inside the library, inside the books, within their words: the world. Even if we feel it no longer, we can remember from our childhood the intenser reality which opened toward us when, like a casket lid, a cover rose and we were kings on clipper ships, cabin boys on camelback, Columbuses crossing swimming holes to sack the Alps and set free Lilliput, her golden hair climbing like a knight up the wall of some crimson battle tent . . . things, men, and moments more than merely lived but added to ourselves like the flesh of a fruit. In Borges's case, for instance, these included the lamp of Aladdin, the traitor invented by H. G. Wells who abandoned his friend to the moonmen, and a scene which I shall never forget either, Blind Pew tapping toward the horses which will run him down. Señor Borges confides to Burgin's tape that

> I think of reading a book as no less an experience than traveling or falling in love. I think that reading Berkeley or Shaw or Emerson, those are quite as real experiences to me as seeing London. . . . Many people are apt to think of real life on the one side, that means toothache, headache, traveling and so on, and then on the other side, you have imaginary life and fancy and that means the arts. But I don't think that distinction holds water. I think that everything is a part of life.

Emerson? Many of Borges's other enthusiasms are equally dismaying, like the Russians' for Jack London, or the symbolist poets' for Poe; on the whole they tend to be directed toward obscure or marginal figures, to stand for somewhat cranky, wayward, even decadent choices: works at once immature or exotic, thin though mannered, clever rather than profound, neat instead of daring, too often the products of learning, fancy, and contrivance to make us comfortable; they exhibit a taste that is still in its teens, one becalmed in backwater, and a mind that is seriously intrigued by certain dubious or jejune forms, forms which have to be overcome, not simply exploited: fantastic tales and wild romances, science fiction, detective stories, and other, similar modes which, with a terrible theological energy and zeal, impose upon implausible premises a rigorous gamelike reasoning; thus for this minutely careful essayist and poet it's not Aristotle, but Zeno, it's not Kant, but Schopenhauer; it's not even Hobbes, but Berkeley, not Mill or Bradley, but—may philosophy forgive him—Spencer; it's Dunne, Beckford, Bloy, the Cabbalists; it's Stevenson, Chesterton, Kipling, Wells and William Morris, Browne and De Quincey Borges turns and returns to, while admitting no such similar debt to James, Melville, Joyce, and so on, about whom, indeed, in these *Conversations,* he passes a few mildly unflattering remarks.*

Yet in the country of the word, Borges is well traveled, and has some of the habits of a seasoned, if not jaded, journeyer. What? see Mont Saint Michel again? that tourist trap? far better to sip a local wine in a small café, watch a vineyard comb its hillside. There are a thousand overlooked delights in every language, similarities and parallels to be remarked, and even the mightiest monuments have their neglected beauties, their unexplored crannies; then, too, it has been frequently observed that our childhood haunts, though possibly less spectacular, less perfect, than other, better advertised, places, can be the source of a fuller pleasure for us, because our familiarity with them is deep and early and complete, because the place is ours; while for other regions we simply have a strange affinity—they do not threaten, like Dante or the Alps, to overwhelm us—and we somehow find our interests, our designs, reflected in them. Or is it we who function as the silvered glass? Idea for a frightening story.

Thus, reading Borges, we must think of literature as a landscape, present all at once like space, and we must remember that literary events, unlike ordinary ones—drinking our coffee or shooting our chancellor—repeat themselves, although with variations, in every mind the text fills. Books don't plop into time like stones in a pond, rippling the surface for a while with steadily diminishing waves. There is only one Paris, we suppose, and one Flaubert, one *Madame Bovary,* but the novel has more than a million occurrences, often in different languages, too. Flaubert may have ridden a whore

---

* I am of course not suggesting that Borges regards Wells, say, as a better writer than Joyce, or that he pays no heed or tribute to major figures. Christ's treatment of this problem is fair and thorough. He tells us, incidentally, that in an introductory course on English literature, Borges's own interests led him to stress the importance of William Morris. Though Borges himself appears in most ways a modest man, such preferences are nevertheless personal and somewhat vain. Just as Borges becomes important by becoming Borges, Morris becomes important by becoming Borges, too. "An author may suffer from absurd prejudices," he tells us in his fine and suggestive lecture on Hawthorne, "but it will be impossible for his work to be absurd if it is genuine, if it responds to a genuine vision." As for Spencer, it might be worth noting that this philosopher tended to think of art as a form of *play.*

with his hat on, as has been reported, but such high jinks soon spend their effects (so, comparatively, does the murder of any Caesar, although its initial capital is greater), whereas one sentence, divinely composed, goes on and on like the Biblical proverbs, the couplets of Pope, or the witticisms of Wilde.

We may indeed suspect that the real power of historical events lies in their descriptions; only by virtue of their passage into language can they continue to occur, and, once recorded (even if no more than as gossip), they become peculiarly atemporal, residing in that shelved-up present which passes for time in a library, and subject to a special kind of choice, since I can choose now to read about the war on the Peloponnesus or the invasion of Normandy; change my climate more easily than my clothes; rearrange the map; while on one day I may have traveled through Jonson to reach Goldsmith, they are not villages, and can be easily switched, so that on the next I may arrive directly from De Quincey, Goethe, or Thomas Aquinas. New locations are constantly being created, like new islands rising from the sea, yet when I land I find them never so new as all that, and having appeared, it is as if they had always been.*

It is a suggestion, I think, of Schopenhauer† (to whom Borges turns as often as he does to Berkeley) that what we remember of our own past depends very largely on what of it we've put our tongue to telling and retelling. It's our words, roughly, we remember; oblivion claims the rest—forgetfulness. Historians make more history than the men they write about, and because we render our experience in universals, experience becomes repetitious (for if events do not repeat, accounts do), and time doubles back in confusion like a hound which has lost the scent.

Troy, many times, was buried in its own body, one city standing on the shoulders of another, and students of linguistic geography have observed a similar phenomenon. Not only are there many accounts, both factual and fictional, of Napoleon's invasion of Russia (so that the event becomes multiplied in the libraries), there are, of course, commentaries and critiques of these, and then again examinations of those, which lead, in turn, to reflec-

* That all our messages are in the present tense, as I have tried to suggest, is fundamental to Barthelme's method of composition. See "The Leading Edge of the Trash Phenomenon."

† Borges's good friend and collaborator, Bioy Casares, once attributed to a heresiarch of Uqbar the remark that both mirrors and copulation were abominable because they increased the number of men. Borges momentarily wondered, then, whether this undocumented country and its anonymous heresiarch weren't a fiction devised by Bioy's modesty to justify a statement, and perhaps it's the same here. It should be perfectly clear, in any case, that Schopenhauer has read Borges and reflects him, just as Borges reflects both Bioy and Borges, since the remark about mirrors and copulation appears more than once.

tions upon them, and so on, until it sometimes happens that the originals are quite buried, overcome (idea for a frightening story), and though there may be a definite logical distance between each level, there is no other; they sit side by side on our shelves. We may read the critics first, or exclusively; and is it not, in fact, true that our knowledge of most books is at least secondhand, as our knowledge of nearly everything else is?

Borges knows of the treacheries of our histories (treachery is one of his principal subjects)*—they are filled with toothache—and in his little essay called "The Modesty of History" suggests that most of its really vital dates are secret—for instance, the introduction, by Aeschylus, of the second actor.†
Still, this is but one more example of how, by practicing a resolute forgetfulness, we select, we construct, we compose our pasts, and hence make fictional characters of ourselves, as it seems we must to remain sane (Funes the Memorious remembers everything, while the Borges who receives a Zahir in his drink change following a funeral one day finds the scarred coin literally unforgettable; both suffer).

It isn't always easy to distinguish *ficciones* from *inquisiciones,* even for Borges (of the famous Pierre Menard, he says: ". . . it's not wholly a story . . . it's a kind of essay . . ."), though the latter are perhaps more unfeignedly interrogations. It is his habit to infect these brief, playful, devious, solemn, *outré* notes, which, like his fictions, are often accounts of treacheries of one sort or other, with small treacheries of his own, treasons against language and its logic, betrayals of all those distinctions between fact and fancy, real life and dreaming, memory and imagination, myth and history, word and thing, fiction and essay, which we're so fond of, and find so necessary, even though keeping them straight is a perpetual difficulty.

If, as Wittgenstein thought, "philosophy is a battle against the bewitchment of our intelligence by means of language," then Borges's prose, at least, performs a precisely similar function, for there is scarcely a story which is not built upon a sophistry, a sophistry so fanatically embraced, so pedantically developed, so soberly defended, it becomes the principal truth in the world his parables create (puzzles, paradoxes, equivocations, and obscure and idle symmetries which appear as menacing laws); and we are compelled to

---

* He published his *Universal History of Infamy* in 1935, a work which is very carefully not a universal history of infamy. See Paul de Man, "A Modern Master," *New York Review of Books,* Nov. 19, 1964.

† Professor Celerent has complained bitterly that there is scarcely a history of Western Europe which troubles itself to mention Aristotle's invention of the syllogism—one of that continent's most formative events. "Suppose," he says, "that small matter had been put off, as it was in India, to the 16th century?"

wonder again whether we are awake or asleep, whether we are a dreamer or ourselves a dream, whether art imitates nature or nature mirrors art instead; once more we are required to consider whether things exist only while they are being perceived, whether change can occur, whether time is linear and straight or manifold and curved, whether history repeats, whether space is a place of simple locations, whether words aren't more real than their referents—whether letters and syllables aren't magical and full of cabbalistic contents—whether it is universals or particulars which fundamentally exist, whether destiny isn't in the driver's seat, what the determinate, orderly consequences of pure chance come to, whether we are the serious playthings of the gods or the amusing commercial enterprises of the devil.

It is not the subject of these compulsions, however, but the manner in which they are produced that matters, and makes Borges an ally of Wittgenstein. It is not hard to feel that Borges's creatures are mostly mad. This is, in many ways, a comforting conclusion. The causes, on the other hand, remain disturbing; they resemble far too literally those worlds theologians and metaphysicians have already made for us and in which we have so often found ourselves netted and wriggling. When Schopenhauer argues that the body in all its aspects is a manifestation of the will, he is composing poetry; he is giving us an idea for a frightening story, one which derives its plausibility from facts we are quite unpoetically aware of (teeth are for biting), but the suggestion that the will grew its body as a man might make some tool to do his bidding is a fiction which, if we responded to the cry for consequences implicit in it, would advertise its absurdity with the mad metaphysical fantasy which would grow from its trunk like a second head.

Thus the effect of Borges's work is suspicion and skepticism. Clarity, scholarship, and reason: they are all here, yet each is employed to enlarge upon a muddle without disturbing it, to canonize a confusion. Ideas become plots (how beautifully ambiguous, for Borges, that word is), whereupon those knotty tangles the philosopher has been so patiently picking at can be happily reseen as triumphs of aesthetic design.* In the right sun, suspicion can fall far enough to shadow every ideology; the political schemes of men

---

* Borges has made this point repeatedly himself (in the Epilogue to *Other Inquisitions*, for example); yet his commentators persist in trying to pin on him beliefs which, for Borges, are merely materials. They want him more imaginary than he already is. Perhaps this accounts for the statement—written, we can imagine, with a smile—which Borges includes in each of the little forewords he has written to imprimatur the books about him: in Barrenechea, in Burgin (he "has helped me to know myself"), in Christ ("Some unsuspected things, many secret links and affinities, have been revealed to me by this book"), though he does not refrain, in the latter instance, from adding: ". . . I have no message. I am neither a thinker nor a moralist, but simply a man of letters who turns his own perplexities and that respected system of perplexities we call philosophy into the forms of literature."

can seem no more than myths through which they move like imaginary creatures, like fabulous animals in landscapes of pure wish; the metaphors upon which they ride toward utopia now are seldom seen (such is the price one pays for an ignorance of history) to be the same overfat or scrawny nags the old political romancers, puffing, rode at windmills in their time, and always futilely. "The illusions of patriotism are limitless." Hitler tries to turn the world into a book; he suffered from unreality, Borges claims, and collaborated in his own destruction. Under the right sun one may observe little that is novel. The world of words spins merrily around, the same painted horses rising and falling to the same tunes, and our guide delights in pointing out each reappearance. We have seen this before: in Persepolis, and also in Peking . . . in Pascal, in Plato, in Parmenides. The tone, throughout, is that of a skeptical conservative (this shows up very clearly, too, in his conversations with Burgin). Least government is best, and all are bad. They rest on myth. "Perhaps universal history is the history of a few metaphors." And we have had them all already, had them all.

As a young poet Borges pledged himself to Ultraism, a Spanish literary movement resembling Imagism in many ways, whose principles he carried back to Argentina in his luggage. It demanded condensation, the suppression of ornament, modifiers, all terms of transition; it opposed exhortation and vagueness—flourish; it praised impersonality, and regarded poetry as made of metaphors in close, suggestive combinations. It was primarily a poetry of *mention,* as Borges's prose is now, and Christ has no difficulty in showing how these early slogans, like the literary enthusiasms of his childhood, continue to affect the later work. Any metaphor which is taken with literal seriousness requires us to imagine a world in which it can be true; it contains or suggests a metaphorical principle that in turn gives form to a fable. And when the *whole* is an image, local images can be removed.

Borges makes much of the independence of the new worlds implied by his fiction; they are "contiguous realities"; the poet annexes new provinces to Being; but they remain mirror worlds for all that; it is our own world, *misthought,* reflected there. And soon we find in Wittgenstein himself this ancient idea for a frightening story: "Logic is not a body of doctrine, but a mirror-image of the world."

Mirrors are abominable. A photographer points her camera at Borges like a revolver. In his childhood he feared mirrors—mahogany—being repeated . . . and thus becoming increasingly imaginary? In the beautiful bestiary (*The Book of Imaginary Beings*) which has just been translated for us,* it is suggested that one day the imprisoned creatures in our looking glasses

* Jorge Luis Borges with Margarita Guerrero, *The Book of Imaginary Beings,* trans. Norman Thomas di Giovanni in collaboration with the author (New York: Dutton, 1969).

will cease to imitate us; fish will stir in the panes as though in clear water; and "we will hear from the depths of mirrors the clatter of weapons." How many times, already, have we been overcome by imaginary beings?

This bouquet which Borges has gathered in his travels for us consists largely of rather harmless animals from stories, myths, and legends, alphabetically arranged here in the texts which first reported them or in descriptions charmingly rebuilt by Borges. Most of these beasts are mechanically made—insufficiently imaginary to be real, insufficiently original to be wonderful or menacing. There are the jumbles, created by collage: centaurs, griffins, hydras, and so on; the mathematicals, fashioned by multiplication or division: one-eyed, half-mouthed monsters or those who are many-headed, sixteen-toed, and triple-tongued; there are those of inflated or deflated size: elves, dwarfs, brownies, leviathans, and fastitocalon; and finally those who have no special shape of their own—the proteans—and who counterfeit the forms of others. A few, more interesting, are made of metal, and one, my favorite, the A Bao A Qu, is almost wholly metaphysical, and very Borges.

There's no longer a world left for these creatures to inhabit—even our own world has expelled them—so that they seem like pieces from a game we've forgotten how to play. They are objects now of curiosity or amusement, and even the prospect of one's being alive and abroad, like the Loch Ness serpent or abominable snowman (neither of whom is registered here), does not deeply stir us. Borges's invented library of Babel is a far more compelling monster, with its mirrored hallways and hexagonal galleries, its closets where one may sleep standing up, its soaring and spiral stairways. Even those lady-faced vultures the harpies cannot frighten us, and hippogriffs are tame. It is that library we live in; it is that library we dream; our confusions alter not the parts of animals anymore, they lead on our understanding toward a culmination in illusion like a slut.

And which is Borges, which his double? which is the photograph? the face perverted by a mirror? image in the polish of a writing table? There is the Borges who compiles *A Personal Anthology,** and says he wishes to be remembered by it, and there is the Borges who admits to Burgin that he did not put all of his best things in it; there is the Borges who plays with the notion that all our works are products of the same universal Will, so that one author impersonally authors everything (thus the labors of that provincial librarian are not vain), and the Borges whose particular mark is both idiosyncratic and indelible. The political skeptic and the fierce opponent of Perón: are they one man? Can the author of *The Aleph* admire Chesterton? Wells? Croce?

* *A Personal Anthology,* ed. Anthony Kerrigan (New York: Grove Press, 1967).

Kipling? And what about those stories which snap together at the end like a cheap lock? with a gunshot? Is this impish dilettante the same man who leaves us so often uneasily amazed? Perhaps he is, as Borges wrote so wonderfully of Valéry,

> A man whose admirable texts do not exhaust, or even define, his all-embracing possibilities. A man who, in a century that adores the chaotic idols of blood, earth, and passion, always preferred the lucid pleasures of thought and the secret adventures of order.

Yet can this be a figure that same age salutes? Consequences.

The New York Review of Books, 1969
Published in *Fiction and the Figures of Life,* 1970

Invisible Cities

I talo Calvino's *Invisible Cities* is one of the purer works of the imagination. It is prose elevated to poetry without the least sign of strain. Nevertheless, it has its subjects: memory, desire, the imagination that makes art, and the elusive nature of the mind. In addition, it is a profound study of the character of the city.

Invisible Cities is also a bookended book. It borrows the shape of its content from *The Travels of Marco Polo* and the material of its structure from Dante's *Inferno*. The first is a work which happenstance brought into being; the second, with its guided descent through a series of spooling circles, is one which art, cunning, and revenge composed. Both are works of travel, both mention marvels, both were written by soldiers—contemporaries— long absent from their native cities, both stand at the beginning and ending of an era.

Marco Polo, in the company of his uncle and his father, traders who had been to the East once before, reached the country of Kublai Khan, and his court in Peking, in 1275. Polo became a favorite of the khan, who loved to listen to his remarkable tales and employed him on business trips in central and western China. Polo is even said, by his own testimony, to have ruled the city of Yangchow for three years. In 1292, after seventeen years in China and a journey home which took an additional three, he returned to his native city. His arrival was poorly timed. Venice was momentarily at war with Genoa, and Polo, who offered his services to the navy, was captured and imprisoned for a year in the enemy's city. While thus confined, he dictated his book, a history of his travels, as well as a compilation of hearsay about the East, to one Rustichello, a fellow prisoner.

Why did he entrust the setting down of his book to another? May we suppose that Polo, who came from a well-to-do family, could write Latin, the language of the scholar, but never spoke it; that he spoke Chinese, and, of course, Italian, the popular speech of his people, but never wrote it? Perhaps he wished to reach a wider audience and chose a vernacular, as Dante did, but had at his disposal during the time of his confinement only a friend who wrote a French as full of Italian as an éclair with cream.

In any case, his history is a work shaped by the mouth and meant for the ear, just as *Invisible Cities* is, and it had to be assembled and arranged from recollections. It was doubtless spoken to "pass the time," to enlarge the prisoner's sequestered world and amuse his companions. Like the stories of *The Decameron*, of *The Canterbury Tales* and *A Thousand and One Nights*, the recital of these cities is meant to amuse; they are designed to educate; above all, they carry their auditors out of reach of death, out of sight of their confinement, and drive ennui away like a cur from a broom. It is little wonder, then, that Calvino's book begins with a section titled "Cities and Memory." Polo spoke of astonishing things indeed, and was possibly as truthful as he could be when he told of the existence of paper money, of asbestos, of coal, of spices of all kinds, and particularly when he described the amazing cities of the East. Chapter after chapter of his book simply depict the character of this city, this province, or that. Surely his memory was spurred and directed by the questions of his listeners, just as the khan interrogates Polo in Calvino's account.

It was a time when cities behaved like nations and went to war with a frequency and ferocity which only the Peloponnesian War may have rivaled. Dante, traveling too, asks for aid—"Help me now; o memory that set down what I saw"—as he takes the steep and savage path to stand before the gates of hell: THROUGH ME THE WAY INTO THE SUFFERING CITY, THROUGH ME THE WAY TO THE ETERNAL PAIN. Florence for Dante. Venice for Polo. And hell for us all—the invisible city.

The Travels of Marco Polo remained one of the principal sources of our knowledge of the East for centuries. The edition which should interest us most, perhaps, is the one in the Bibliothèque Nationale (Codex 2810). It dates from the fifteenth century and contains twenty-five colored illustrations—illustrations by an artist who had never been east of the Danube, of course. This pictorial edition was reprinted by Calvino's publisher, Einaudi, during the 1950s. My own Englished version dates from 1958. There can be little doubt that Calvino consulted the aforementioned Italian edition when he was composing *Invisible Cities* in 1971. It may, in fact, have inspired him (as the Visconti pack of tarot cards did when he wrote *The Castle of Crossed Destinies*), although the small doubt one is duty-bound to entertain is decisive.

Still, the illustration one encounters when Polo's book breaks open at one of its central sewings is of "the noble and magnificent city of Kin-sai," even if its pinnacles and flags, its tin, slate, and tile roofs, its dark dormers, the water which rushes through its streets, the bridges which loop over them, depict a kind of Venice, a Venice done in Tuscan tones, a Venice where the water streams between the buildings like windblown hair.

Marco Polo's cities were certainly invisible, as any remembered city, any sought-after city, any city rendered in words will be. Even at this moment, words are violating our vision; vision is vitiating our thought. The reduction of a concept to a single instance, the replacement of an individual by some generalizing name: this is an agon as old as philosophy itself. If we were watching a native dance in New Guinea, what we said in our surprise at the appearance of a mud man, if it went beyond directions like "Look!," would interfere fatally with our perception, just as our response to the mock attack of a camel driver disgruntled by the size of his tip, if it consisted of a moral lecture, might veil his amused but businesslike eyes; and what our reporter's pencil is inclined to write about the start of the dogsled race from Anchorage to Nome depends as much on presuppositions as the contest does on snow, for the truth here is simple and painful: the words which appear to reach out and envelop that clay creature, camel driver, or team of dogs have a greater inheritance from reality than do the mud men, camels, or sled dogs innocently enjoying custom or the laws of physics. The most ordinary words, as we are aware, are more general, more repeatable, more far-reaching in every area of implication, in their harness undeterminably stronger than our momentary perception of sixteen happy animals who perhaps believe they are out for an afternoon run. Think of the word *polis*—"city"—itself: a word which will be young still when every other city is a midden or in unsieved dust. It is the wretchedness of this truth (wretched because it is the dogs and their driver most of us admire; it is the mud man who frightens or amuses us, not a newspaper account; it is an ice-cream cone, not the words "ice cream," we want to put in our mouths), it is the injustice of any one word's overweening reality, which has made this truth so invisible.

What could Marco Polo's bedazzled readers do, as they followed his description of the noble and magnificent city of Kin-sai, but think of Western towers and stone cornices and piered bridges, of Western water, when they visualized the city his words brought to life? All the cities he told about seemed exotic, magical, splendid beyond belief, cities of longing, but of their—the readers'—longing, and therefore clothed in the colors of the readers' lives. The difficulty is the same for us today when we read of the cities of desire depicted by Calvino's Polo for the khan: of Despina, for instance, the city which looks like a steamship when approached on camelback and we are weary of being swaysick on the sand; then like a camel when seen from the sea and we are anxious for the steadiness of the earth. We might imagine still another, which sails its innumerable terraces into the sea like a ship. Both Kin-sai and Despina provide us with examples of the sorry impossibility of "seeing" through words, let alone "seeing" with them, although Calvino, Polo, we, and the Great Khan try.

Imprisoned by either walls or words, it is all the more important to try: to dream beyond the bricks; beyond the outer courtyard with its watchtowers, guards, guns; beyond the words which screen us from the world; beyond our own aims, fears, normally trivial aches and pains, which we nevertheless enlarge and objectify as bruises in hillsides, as knocks in walls, as cuts through mountains, as the leveling of plains. It is necessary to leave our cell and see the city—see the city in the cell, as the painter of legend perceives some stirring shape in spit or an errant puddle—to leave for a city whose walls rise around us everywhere the same, faceless as concrete and equally cold, or as difficult to dent as glass may be and as remorseless, as resistant to experience as plastic; such surfaces refuse the past, reject the scratches which calendared by days the ten years Gesualdo lay in rags, cast in a corner for climbing a vine to glimpse a bathing lady; these will not be found here, nor the small crack we may imagine is a river, nor the wallpaper whose patterns make a map, or patches of plaster damp like sweat in the pit of an arm; the mind cannot throw itself or any image against such pitiless sameness. Avoid such cities, such cells: all places where the light falls evenly as rain on day and night alike.

Cities can be cleansed even of themselves when they do not understand the true nature of their inhabitants, as was the case with one of Calvino's "Hidden Cities," Theodora, which cleared its skies of condors only to observe the increase of serpents, and whose victory over the spiders gave the flies free rein, while the extermination of the termites granted a kingdom to the woodworm. When, at last, the rats and roaches and gnats and flies, the fruit flies and mosquitoes and every sort of vermin—all growing, flying, and creeping things—had been swept from the city, a city whose dream it seems to have been to be a hospital for the healthy, then

> the other fauna [came] back to the light from the library's basements where the incunabula were kept; it was leaping from the capitals and drainpipes, perching at the sleepers' bedside. Sphinxes, griffons, chimeras, dragons, hircocervi, harpies, hydras, unicorns, basilisks [resumed] possession of their city.*

* All quotations from Calvino's *Invisible Cities* are from the translation of William Weaver (New York: Harvest, 1974).

In one of my imaginary cities, after a long period of misrule by birds, phonographs, and people, paintings left their frames and draped different landscapes over the baseball diamonds, Sabine ladies lolled about the shady streets, alert for adventure, and all the tinted animals roamed free. Their leader said simply: when the city reckoned its inhabitants, it neglected the antique pots, the rugs which had emigrated years before from Isfahan, the Chippendales, the Ensors, the Bonheurs, the stone idols, discontented lamps.

Marco Polo's actual prison companion, one Rustichello of Pisa, is, in Calvino's recasting, the Great Khan himself, confined to his kingdom, now grown so large it feels swollen and gangrenous, so distant in its borders that its edges can't be touched, vaporous and unreal except in the sober clear recitals of his friend and sometime ambassador the Venetian adventurer, who brings him news—news not of places, not of Westport or the Bronx, of college towns or ghettos, but of "Hidden Cities," "Cities and the Dead," "Continuous Cities," "Thin Cities," of "Cities and Signs": in short, of systems, meshes, interlocks, of webs. There is, for instance, the city of Zaira, which is not made of its bastions and arcades and steps but, like a burned-over forest, consists instead

> of relationships between the measurements of its space and the events of its past: the height of a lamppost and the distance from the ground of a hanged usurper's swaying feet; the line strung from the lamppost to the railing opposite and the festoons that decorate the course of the queen's nuptial procession; the height of that railing and the leap of the adulterer who climbed over it at dawn.

If the khan has been captured by his own conquests and is now no freer in the middle of his immensities than a rowboat on the ocean, or as we are, jetting along at thirty thousand feet, Rustichello has been made a monarch by means of metaphor, because it is indeed to a king in this book that Polo speaks, to a different kind of fellow prisoner; and it is through the king's eyes that a design is discerned in the fierce smolder and aimless fire of his tales. A mind is made by the mind's eyes.

Scheherazade, staving off death with her stories, must borrow or invent, because she never leaves her husband's side; we may wonder, as we listen to Marco Polo tell the khan of the cities he has seen, whether he has ever really left his hometown or has simply turned round and round many times in one place, or unfolded from one bud an astonishing plenitude of petals, transforming a simple fountain by resemblance into a robust pot of blooming chives.

Fifty-five cities compose—invisibly, concurrently, continuously—Italo Calvino's epitomic city. Yes, it turns out to be the Venice we know so well, perhaps through a sober daily life there, or a few ecstatic visits, certainly from repeated readings and innumerable fantasies. Nevertheless, it is that same Venice which Marco Polo himself confesses he cannot imagine existing, even after Kublai Khan points out to him, with a negligent gesture which signifies some dearer purpose, the palaces whose marble steps lie immersed in water, the balconies which overhang the canals, the city's shimmering domes and silent campaniles. Venice is thus one miracle made of many, a contraction of the fabulous the way fingers form a fist, for it has preserved the evanescent marvels met with in Marco Polo's travels like fossils in its own stones and has flung over its fluid causeways such surprises as only lonely caravans encounter; yet it is also a Venice which has become plural, dispersed, ephemeral again, because it represents far more cities than those, real or imaginary, mentioned in Calvino's elegant and ruthlessly patterned text. It is not simply a symbol standing for Heidelberg, Frankfurt, Chicago, or New York, where one might actually have set foot; or those places which have perished, like Babylon beneath the weight of years; or those that exist like misery before the onset of its cause, as improbable as birdsong whistled underwater—that is, those cities not yet found or even founded or fully realized—such as survive in fancy like Atlantis or my imagined city of Yclept (with its footfall-formed steps, its undimmable flowers, its playing fields in the shape of colorful cotton yarns, its not-yet-built barns for the storage of leftover letters like the letter B, where there will be gay blades in solemn scabbards, bees' knees spread out to dry on trays, bales of bated breath) or, for that matter, the way those ubiquitous utopias persist, like flocks of wishes with one wing, they are so incessantly and inadequately dreamt.

Venice cannot be said to serve simply as a sign, then, or an exemplification, for it has also become the city inside every city, the city beneath every city, the city that contains the cities that *are,* including the ones which barely subsist on the maps, their location indicated only by the dimmest of pink dots—specks which could, like a red mite, imperceptibly shift—as well as those cities which cannot be blotted out the way the ports of the Phoenicians were: I mean the camps of catastrophe, cities of sewers and open wounds and mass graves and the still-shitting dead, cities bombed into existence like Beirut or Sarajevo; cities like Cairo, scalded by their atmosphere, whose admired autumnal sunsets are caused by clouds of fetid gas; cities where growths of garbage define the parks, and every alley is intestinal; the cities we can only forget, it seems, by repeating them like a gunshot, by reproducing . . . reinvesting, rebuilding, reinhabiting . . . by re-enacting their several and similar hells, not smoothly and professionally, but stupidly and clumsily, as if they were scenes in a high-school play.

Calvino's cities spiral toward us as if unrolled by Polo before the eyes of his host. There are nine panels, each introduced to us by a brief snatch of conversation between the traveler and the king, and each concluded by the completion of that conversation, so that these passages, italicized in the text, form wholes of their own—nine of them as we descend, as Dante did, into the IN . . . into, as Sartre said, the hell that is other people. The first group, as well as the last, contains ten accounts of fabulous cities, while each of the middle seven sets forth five. The image they form is that of a spool. If we add to the list of cities described the nine conversations which surround or variously intrude upon them, we arrive at a total of sixty-four sections, not accidentally the sum of the squares, eight on each edge, which make up the board for chess, a game beloved by the khan. It is also, of course, the grid of every great city. Each is built, like Calvino's book, upon an invisible graph. The chessboard is only incidentally a set of paths, for these paths are principally corridors of power, influence, force.

"Leaving there," the recital of the cities begins, begins with departure, a departure from an unnamed place, a city more invisible than any of the others; "leaving there," the logarithm of the cities begins, because the way Polo's descriptions are unwound resembles a spiral, the spool of fate, the pattern sidles; "leaving there and proceeding for three days toward the east," we reach the first of the memory cities, Diomira, a name which means "to look through with wonder." The words "leaving there and proceeding" inform readers that they have entered an account which has been going on who knows how long? "Leaving there and proceeding for three days toward the east, you reach Diomira, a city with sixty silver domes, bronze statues of all the gods, streets paved with lead, a crystal theater, a golden cock that crows each morning on a tower." As many domes as an hour has numbers. A city which is careful to include all the ages: gold cock, silver domes, bronze statues, lead streets, a crystal theater. If you happen to arrive during the ninth month, "when the days are growing shorter and the multicolored lamps are lighted all at once at the doors of the food stalls and from a terrace a woman's voice cries ooh!," you will experience the kinds of connections the city always offers: those rational (as dusk comes on, so do the lamps) and random (a woman's voice cries ooh!). A cat has startled her; a caress has moved her; she has seen with appreciation the multicolored lights enliven the doorways. "But the special quality of this city for the man who arrives there on a September evening . . . is that he feels envy" for those who believe they are experiencing a kind of déjà vu, another evening like this one that's in front of us, twilit, lamps just now coloring the open stalls, ooh! . . . envy because they "think they were happy, that time."

What can this envy mean? in our initial city, a city we associate with memory? Shouldn't we envy those who still believe that once, when young, they were happy, because they will have colored the past with sweet lights and made a lost ooh! seem romantic? The lead streets run back beyond the bronze gods, statued beneath those silver domes, to let us remember that, so long ago, the cock who greeted the dawn was golden, and golden was his crow. The man who, *leaving there,* arrives here knows otherwise.

The man who arrives in Diomira on a September evening is, of course, the khan, first of all, who is following Marco Polo's words as if on a camel; and then each of us, hearing the emperor hear his Venetian. The second city is a city of memory too. Isidora, or "gift of Isis," is built like Calvino's book is built; that is, of "spiral staircases encrusted with spiral seashells, where perfect telescopes and violins are made, where the foreigner hesitating between two women always encounters a third, where cockfights degenerate into bloody brawls among the bettors." The visitor arrives, weary of the wilderness where he has dreamt of a city he would like to enter. Yet the visitor cannot dream of a city he has not known, only of those he knew as a young man, and these are the cities he desires. So Isidora is a city he dreams too late, since "he arrives at Isidora in his old age. In the square there is the wall where the old men sit and watch the young go by; he is seated in a row with them. Desires are already memories."

The book of Marco Polo's actual travels told of marvels and mysteries. Its many sections were long on useful learning but rather short on moral lessons. Here, however, we have fables Aesop might have managed, not by imagining animals but by imagining cities. In Diomira we learn why we love the "good old days." In Isidora we are told that the future we desire is none other than our nostalgic longings. In Dorothea ("gift of God"), the town to which we come next, we discover that there are many paths through life, many cities in every city, many manners of description, because Dorothea can be understood (as *Invisible Cities* must be) in terms of its formal structure—four green canals divide the city into nine quarters, "each with three hundred houses and seven hundred chimneys," each with its own monopoly, for instance, on "bergamot, sturgeon roe, astrolabes, amethysts," and each with its rigorous kinship laws—or, alternatively, through metonymy, by inferring the nature of the whole from a perception of its parts: women with fine teeth and a direct gaze, fluttering banners, turning wheels . . . in short, from particular details. Polo chooses both these methods when he has his "conversations" with the khan, because it will be some time before he learns to speak the khan's tongue.

From the foot of the Great Khan's throne, a majolica pavement extended. Marco Polo, mute informant, spread out on it the samples of the wares he had brought back from his journeys to the ends of the empire: a helmet, a seashell, a coconut, a fan. Arranging the objects in a certain order on the black and white tiles, and occasionally shifting them with studied moves, the ambassador tried to depict for the monarch's eyes the vicissitudes of his travels, the condition of the empire, the prerogatives of the distant provincial seats.

From our own journeys (since each of us is Polo to another's khan), we may return with other wares, but that won't matter, for what will render them significant will be their placement on the pavement, the flights of influence they suggest, the orders they elicit from the eye, as I recently returned from a trip with the image of a painted board imprisoned on a roll of film in my valise: the painted board which served as a shutter, a metal drainpipe which fell down a yellow wall like a black stripe, a shaded lamp with a netted globe held out from that wall by a rod, a vase of dried flowers in a niche the shutter shielded when it was closed, while below this company sat an altogether Austrian stack of firewood, the log ends like stones in a country wall. I returned, not with these images alone, but with the wonder of their relationships.

What we frequently fail to understand is that a city is not an assemblage of buildings streaked by highways and streets; it is a subtle pattern of powers, like the board. Kublai Khan realizes that if he could understand the rules which direct and facilitate the movements of these objects, ignoring their specific shapes and unique natures, he would hold like a scepter in his hand the essentials of his empire and govern accordingly; so he replaces the objects Polo has been maneuvering about on the majolica pavement with pieces from his chess set, their ivory as slick as a kid's slide, and then he assigns to these, in a purely algebraic fashion, meanings appropriate to the moment: let x equal a seashell or a fan, perhaps; let the knight be, for now, an equestrian statue superbly stony in the square it stands on, for the pieces are as variable as a, b, and c; and let us permit the queen to be a lady looking down behind a fan from her balcony at a fountain, possibly at a topiaried tree into whose trunk she is quickly transmuted, into the pulp of its fruit, into a palmful of seeds.

The wise khan might imagine, then, a city made solely of movements, like some of the cities of desire which Marco Polo describes, a city composed entirely of staircases and paths, streets and thoroughfares and boulevards and alleys, elevators and playgrounds, sidewalks and tram lines and drawer slides and subways and bus stops and zippers and toilet chains and construction cranes. It is a city in which every block is a kind of smoky port.

In this scenario, young Frank Presto (or whomever we choose) is no longer the promising young lawyer, young husband and father, baseball fan, wearer of a pair of black-and-tan trousers, the young flutter in the king's eye he might be elsewhere—not in this city. In this city he is simply a commuter; he leans against doorjambs; he casters across his office from desk to window, from secretary to Xerox machine. His age is irrelevant. Age is an avenue of the demographic city. His promises rust in the wreckage that is the city of broken hopes. At this moment, Frank is only an element of circulation, a drop of blood in the body of the city whose skin we have just lifted like a shirt. And the khan plays game after game of city/chess like this, searching for secrets in the interlocking lines, in these moderate abstractions—in a white rook, black queen—through which he believes divergent avenues, or a city's radial center, might be seen.

For such a city, the khan could have calculated to a nit's pick the fall of bodies from high windows, the hubbub of behinds behind the copier, and, on their way from plate to mouth, the evasive loops of forks entangled in spaghetti. Trajectories, blinks, droplets of flu sneeze, the jitter of the pinball, brain scans, congregations of handshakes, goodbye waves, the flight of Time where the clock's hands hide its face: he might imagine all of these. Let's say he does. *"At times he thought he was on the verge of discovering a coherent, harmonious system underlying the infinite deformities and discords, but no model could stand up to the comparison with the game of chess."* So the king presses on. He no longer interprets the pieces, lets them shadow forth a figure kneeling beside the fountain; he simply makes the proper moves, ponders the rules, admires the purity of each play's endless designs, the menace inherent in their innocent configurations.

There are, of course, "Thin Cities"—here, cities which grow like galls on the trunk of a river, which fill in a valley like morning mist, which lean against the irregular side of a mountain—and none of these "cities" can be said to be standing on a grid. But in the first place, the grid goes about with us like a compass on the bridge. Rays rush out of our eyes and reach for the horizon, and if we completely lose our place, as Dante did in that dark wood, if we become disoriented as though we had been spun around, then north will seem straight ahead, south will lie behind us like history, and west and east will empty out on either hand. The jumbled streets of old trading quarters, casbahs, and ghettos, those crowds of houses so dense that the streets become pushed inside: these tangles were always marks of a village or possibly a town, but never a city; and we visit them in cities the way we visit a museum, to contemplate the past, to read our real age, to see again in the barrio's local bustle its tight life, the small seed which has grown beyond all community like a pumpkin in a pea patch and is held together now, not by eyesight and kettle smell, but by invisible wires and inaudible messages, voices on errands, words relayed like lightning, letters which seem to leap up at once in many places like armed men from the dragon's teeth. And as the village grows into a city, the grid appears like the beard on a youth, and lengthens with it toward those weakening knees.

The game proceeds, yet a reckoning arrives. As Kublai Khan stares at a square just vacated by a fleeing king, he sees that these games of chess come literally to nothing (a weedy plant commands more harmony), and in that moment Khan and his game fall from Plato's orbit, because beneath the pieces the board is bare, the stones of all his cities' buildings dissolve in the lines which bound them, and these run pointlessly—invisibly—off into space. But Marco Polo counsels the king to part the pavement. On that slick ivory surface, on the fired clay, in that open square of wood which is at once a piece of playing field and a square of the city, what can one further see? the footprint of a pavement? perhaps a taut and angry fiber? the glaze of a dreaming eye? logs lazily adrift in a slow-moving river? a woman peering from an upstairs window? Every object is itself a cell which would contain us, yet every end has its outlet as well; and as we pass through a cave's yawn to the hollow of a hollow tree, from that hollow to an open door or window, we cross one threshold to achieve yet another, even more wondrous, wider world.

When the concept of the city, with its concrete streets and concrete towers, has been replaced by that of the game, with its architectural grid and gun range, its system of implicit threats, its irregular spheres of influence; and when that game, furthermore, has been, in its interest, exhausted; then the materials of the contest, its dinky tools, the ivory itself, its fingered skin, the shape of the cross on the king's crown, are entreated for results. A pillar becomes a tree, a tree a totem. The grid gives way, the board parts like the Red Sea, and the land it lay on reappears, as warm as a baby's blanket. We are not simply back with youthful—partly promising—Frank Presto again. We have crawled up his nose. We have entered his ear. We inhabit his lust. We are the bees who buzz in his brain.

Let me recapitulate our progress. It is a pattern to be found in all the arts. We begin our pursuit of the city by examining the particular, the things that cities are made of—squares, streets, buildings, bridges, people, parks— allowing the least leaf to be engraved upon our faces as though it has been long pressed there. We endeavor to give to the shallowest saucer great depth, but we do so through the intensity of our attention, by dwelling on the small bob of its basin, the thin rule of gold around its rim, the cup which will squat there when the tea is finally ready. We collect facts. We describe things as we believe they really are. Not only our streets, but our lanes, our halls and closets, are named in this realm of reference, this freeway of denotation. The procedure will give us one sort of city: a city of idle odors and random sounds, a city of character, of what is popularly called "place." Our city will have a personality, for we shall have rendered the gestures of its spirit, the way in which it resembles a young girl, a lecherous uncle, an old maid. Our city will be a richly human body made of countless bones. Many a corner will strike us like an elbow. Many a path will wear like a hole through our shoe. Many a brick will stiffen at our touch. The light will fall irregularly throughout the city, palely in this place, brightly in another, after the manner of our understanding.

Not content with this, we soon seek—in the playing fountain, the shaded courtyard, the kneeling man, the fan, in the look that leaps like a tree through the stone pavement—a pattern of powers, of influence and agitation; and like the Great Khan we withdraw toward the game, although it is still people we see moving about like pawns, and not yet pawns we see moving about like people. This method will give us still another sort of city, a city in which system is beginning to be born, in which terms are beginning to be replaced by relations, in which roles are beginning to define their representatives, and not the reverse.

As we see, the mathematically minded monarch scarcely creates one state of thought when he calculates another—pressing on, pushing his luck—so that soon he is reaching the particular only through the Idea, and what was earlier a bit of evidence for a generalization is now only an instance of one, just as an apple is an instance of the Idea "apple," the Idea "one." The signifier has swallowed the signified, although you may still observe it as a swell in the stomach, like a bulge beneath the bedclothes of a bereaved and sleeping body.

The khan comes at last to mathematics, to the ideal, to the city as a series of abstract interactions, to complete, unabashed *invisibility;* although we must recognize, as Calvino does, that there are invisibilities of at least two distinct kinds. The first is what is before us at the moment, in our mathematical mood, an unvarnished invisibility, an invisibility, in short, which does not hide itself, which comes clean, as it were, and which is, in that sense, not invisible at all. And then there is the second sort, which is like the proverbial needle, the purloined letter, or the figure in the carpet, palpable, present, but unnoticed, like a floating ghetto, an invisible visibility, hidden from us like a flaw in our character, embraced without realization or recognition. Better a visible invisibility, Aristotle is sometimes thought to have said.

But mathematics is only a game—don't we hear that often offered as an excuse for collective ignorance? Where is the city now, at this level of quiet unstreeted Idea? However, with Marco Polo as our guide, what help do we and the Great Khan receive? We return to the particular, it's true; we shall enter the door instead of merely passing through it—doors of every design desire us. We are about to bruise our eyes upon the hard ebony inserts of the game board; nevertheless, the game board is not that simple city square we began with, that regimental crisscrossing like the streets of Manhattan; it is but a small square of ruled wood, lined cloth, blind as a boarded window, yet full of look. What has really happened to us?

We have begun to listen to the sound of our own words, not merely to their meanings; we have begun to circle their shapes like a walk around a town; we have turned to the representatives of thought for sustenance, not to the thoughts themselves, or to the things those thoughts were presumably about; for just as trees are bark and leaves and light, and the forest is trees and leaflight too, so the city is made of millions of small forms and fine textures, of the very near and the quite far, and, like the wilderness, may have its own mountains, depending on place and point of view, tiredness and timing.

A city is a wall for words, misunderstood or simply imitated in spray paint; but it is a house for houses too, and so should have its doors and sudden windows, its stairs and stories, its halls and dining rooms and dens. We have explored our chosen city through the dreams of its streets and derelict alleys, its suspension bridges and bridle paths, the way Polo has in describing his cities to the king. Now we remain with the mute sign itself. The map of the city is the city. Billboards and building declarations are the city; every sort of symbol—the Arch, the Eiffel Tower, the Rialto or the Doges' Palace, the Canalettos—is the city the way the Capitol and our heroes Washington and Lincoln organize the aspirations of the nation. Our romance with the dome, that basin of the spirit, passionately continues, despite occasional detours for an adultery.

Shortly new words will begin to be heard in the sounds which old words make, as for instance in "swoon," which I understand, now that I speak it clearly and listen with a pure ear, is not the languid faint I formerly feared, but the casual and quiet glide path of a paper airplane.

> *The quantity of things that could be read in a little piece of smooth and empty wood overwhelmed Kublai; Polo was already talking about ebony forests, about rafts laden with logs that come down the rivers, of docks, of women at the windows.*

When we live in only one city, in only one kind of city, in an invisible city, we abstract—we cut apart—ourselves; and sometimes our cities are like abattoirs, fish markets, and butcher shops where our gesticulating corpses hang from hooks and our hearts crawl about like crabs in a basket.

I recall of Cairo the little shelters I saw on rooftops; people perched like pigeons on the cooling towers; the narrow warped boards which bridged the buildings, rocking even with a child's weight; the flapping lines of clothes strung between malfunctioning antennas to be wind-washed; the buckets in which water was kept; the small smokes from cooking fires, as acrid as an outcry, otherwise lost in the larger dusts from the desert and the exhaust haze from the cars. Not a city, surely, inside a city, but places for living, if you could call them such, which were not places ever intended for that: beneath the arches of the ancient aqueduct, on stairwells, within abandoned crates and cartons, derelict cars, in the barren concrete skeletons of unfinished buildings, in archeological excavations beside the pyramids—everywhere, spaces filled with people like water welling up from the ground.

In Manila I sat on a floor of broomed dirt, in a house surrounded by a sea of mud, and stared at the gray screen of an inoperative TV—for there was no electricity in the entire community—drinking tea from a cup so rough around the rim that one finger received a cut. Again in Manila, in vacant lots Marcos had had boarded up so the squatters would be hidden from the public and the highways, mothers, children lay on mattresses open to the sky—no fencing there to conceal them from the hotel windows—and received the frequent rains as if they were a blessing, twisting their clothes into ropes to wring the water out. As in Shanghai long ago, as in Hong Kong now, one can find river and seaways paved with boats, and upon the boats life, as indifferently abundant as mist, clinging to everything, moistening the sails and the polished railings.

Venice was, like Hong Kong, particularly a trading center, its buildings so fragile they seemed to be waiting to be taken down and sold, and such is Calvino's Esmeralda: a place of varying routes, of many noble and nefarious choices. It does indeed seem, with its paths and canals, its bridges and little alleyways and steps, its courtyards and churches, to be one vast area for movement and passage and travel. "A map of Esmeralda should include, marked in different colored inks, all . . . routes, solid and liquid, evident and hidden." The surveyor's task is made difficult by the swallows that follow and fly seditious flight plans. We have already visited this city, however, where, as you may recall, we found Frank Presto, somewhat besmitten, unrolling with difficulty, in the cramped and scarcely concealed corner behind his duplicating machine, a silk stocking it will not do to snag. How coolly Doris, for that is her present name, reclines within her secretarial dreams, for she is in motion, though reclining, like her city, and intends to rename herself Evita when the right time comes.

Phyllis, the city which follows Esmeralda in the text, is also like Venice, with surprises for the eye everywhere. But habit deadens our appreciation, and soon the city becomes imperceptible: "the city fades before your eyes, the rose windows are expunged, the statues on the corbels, the domes," like torches, turn to smoke.

Not only are there cities which belong to the past, and are now invisible for that reason; but there are cities of the present whose existence is quite evident to any traveler with eyes alert and curious, but which are hidden to the inhabitants, who no longer need to experience their postboxes, their scented trees, in order to allow their dogs to piss against them on their twice-daily walks. A neighborhood may be missed entirely by a preoccupied visitor. I certainly do not notice now the soles of my feet, my weight, my restless or resentful ears, opposing opinions. Frank Presto has not observed the dust which has already gathered at the back of his new machine, much of which has been swept off by the milling movements of a sleeve. Great stretches of so many cities in our country are indistinguishable, and even when we peer at them (while searching for a fast-food joint, for instance), they are simply stretches, highways which have thrown out little asphalt lots along them like oozes of rust on a pipe. Amid so much tastelessness, it takes a pretty tasteless gesture to create a locale.

But when are cities invisible because they have no identity, and when is it because of our indifference, our bemused eye? We tolerate incongruities as we tolerate religions. Not far from one of the largest hotels in Anchorage, a pleasant little hovel nestles. Behind it one may see a sign advertising car parts. It has a front yard—odd enough for the business district—where a snowman leans wearily west. Between the melting man and the frozen house, with its mandatory evergreen, stand the bony poles of a huge tepee. Our cities are like seas, and it is not uncommon to see one building seize and swallow another like a shark. Several cities come together in this corner of Anchorage, exposing their bones like elbows out of sleeves, nudging one another in the same space. Cities of custom and history and commerce and comfort come together like a crash in the street. But we are used to crashes in the street, just as we are used to collisions beyond the curbs.

All future cities are invisible as a matter of course, including the Chicago which my train has not yet entered; or they have no substance, like the suburb which will be appended to Des Moines, and not even seen then by the people who live in Moline. In addition, there are dreamtowns, Disneylands, various Parises of pleasure. Venice is easily each of these.

Yes, says the vapid traveloguer, Venice is a magical city, a city whose light is famous, whose doges were powerful, whose churches and plazas and monuments and palaces and museums are splendid, whose riches in paintings, tapestries, statuary, armor, glass, and other fine things are immeasurable. Oh, men were men then. It is a city that has captured the imagination of people of all times and places, provided they are actually, ostensibly, or invisibly German. Yet the canals of Venice stink of garbage; the city is old and dirty and sinking into its own swill. There is pigeon shit on the pigeon shit; there is the smell of mold and rot and sour wine everywhere; the plumbing is antiquated, although the city is nothing but plumbing; slime coats boat steps; the climate is conducive to fevers; rats are so prevalent they have made the city famous as a rest home and haven for cats. Venice has known power, wealth, greatness, shame. Now it is a poorly maintained museum and tourist trap. People carry pieces of Venice away in their valises: bits of cornice, slivers of Murano glass, plates of great and complex grace, as radial as some cities. It exists in the past even now, for there are no motorcars in the city; but the present is present, nevertheless, in the noise of the vaporetti, in the din of the transistors, in the magazines from Milan and the pornographic paperbacks.

There is so much water in Venice that the city doubles itself constantly. The Ca' d'Oro glistens on the surface of the Grand Canal; orange rind clings to its mirrored filigree. Cities are sometimes called twins because they reflect each other across a river, like Minneapolis and St. Paul, and there are a number of twins among Calvino's creations. In Eudoxia, for instance, we can find a carpet which contains a complete map of the city, or perhaps the city is an image of the carpet, as the carpet may, in turn, map the sky. To illuminate the landing of a stairway, panels of stained glass foresee the development of the city. Which are the true forms and which the false? We can ask this question even when we believe we know which is the solid city and which the reflection.

Two boys of my invention are leaning over the railing of a bridge, staring down, hoping for the sight of a condom among the effluvia, or a useful box, a thrilling corpse. What floats by, scarcely noticed, is the image of the heartbreak of one lad, the eventual bankruptcy of the other.

In Calvino's Eusapia the populace has built catacombs which are a replica of the city, or have the dead built the city that stands aboveground like stones to mark their place? Ambiguities abound. Intentions are concealed. Is that canal my imaginary boys were staring at now flowing through the mirror in a Berlin palace? and is the innocent labyrinthine hedgerow which decorates the courtyard of the Hôtel Carnavalet really an incendiary plan for the restoration of the monarchy? Calvino's text gives birth to questions it does not raise. I wonder what the dead bury up there in Eusapia's broad day: grain? bulrushes perhaps? banks of cloud grass?

I live, myself, in a city of defeated expectations, a city of inept lies. One arrives at the train station in order to book a room for the night (there are no trains); lest I adapt myself to this new arrangement, another station will sell me chandeliers or office equipment. When will shopping centers become warehouses if warehouses are already gallerias, ateliers, or rifle museums? Theaters quietly unseat themselves and perform their plays outdoors. One may dine rather well in a rehabilitated church (astonishing phrase!), at a table overlooking the no-longer-sanctified altar, where they keep the register of reservations, and return home to one's apartment in the recycled synagogue. So what if the window represents, in its painted glass, the eye of God?

Schools may be anything but schools: an old folks' home, an orphanage, an antiques bazaar, a detention center. Here, a grocery store sells art supplies; there, a gas station pumps meat and milk. Firehouses are especially vulnerable. This one is a raisin-cookie company. That one sells quilts. Abandoned power stations put on a beguiling puppy face and hope their shape will suggest something. One year a section of the city is a slum, the next year it is chic and saved. Soon, in such deceptive cities, mailboxes will swallow the mailman's hand, trees will help schoolchildren cross the street safely, the red light will mean run, and no one will speak for fear of being taken seriously. As for myself, I await the day when Holly Bush Lane is a row of brothels and the tall glass towers of insurance and finance contain nothing but waxed cartons of lemonade and drifts of surplus grain.

But the falsehoods began when the first earth was moved. The train station was built to resemble the Siena city hall or a castle in the Alps, itself a fake so fulsome it implicates the mountain. Banks were reassuring Greek temples at first, or colonial mansions, before they became gift shops, while a few now specialize in Chinese cuisine, each dish exquisite like the lakefront in some cities, the menu extensive, the meal a hodgepodge. Homes were built back then (though now "back then"s have overcome us like crime) to resemble ships, as was the governor's house in Macao, funnier than most jokes; some lie becalmed in fields still, or, like some buildings in Venice, marooned in an oil slick. There are cities in which railings have been known to overleap streets and run wildly in search of a porthole, a whiff of salt air, a flying fish. Usually ruins are remaindered, but occasionally one will become a piece of art, like a broken window, shattered marriage, derelict fuel pump, or pierced façade. Not every building remarries readily. Dirigible hangars have their own climate; clouds form; it even rains; it is not possible to play golf in them at every time of day.

Calvino allows each kind of city to appear, to fill a place on the board with one of its five manifestations (rook, castle, bishop, king, queen), to enjoy its springlike "break of day." However, every such epiphany, every "showing forth," goes ahead according to rules which have been rigorously formulated and pitilessly enforced (rules which I understand but choose not in this place to disclose). Having briefly shown itself, each city disappears the way an image on a scroll winds gently out of sight, possibly to return, but not on this trip.

There are timeless cities, not because they seem eternal, but because everything about them is the same age, like the nose, ears, chin of a face. Canberra, for instance, is a stage set which springs to life when you open your curtain, but it was not there while you slept. Like Clayton, Missouri, it has no history; it is not yet a city. The elderly hide themselves, their yellowing valentines and their laces. Yet such places, like Clayton, Missouri, will set aside a few blocks to be historical, to be designated Old Town and fronted by a gate. Then the modestly middle-aged houses of Old Town will be systematically demolished so that expensive banal duplexes can be built on their semi-historic graves.

Did we speak of the devil? Here is Zora, a city as memorable as a jingle. It is a honeycomb in which we can place those things we want to remember. It is a city of labeled jars, of canisters which contain rice and recollections. Zora is not a city memorable in itself (in itself, it is self-effacing, almost invisible), but it is made of memory lanes like an old melody. We might imagine, for instance, an extensive cemetery, and then remember our friends and acquaintances, their names and most significant deeds, by carving them on tombstones carefully selected to signify the essential nature of their being. Of course, if they lack an essential nature, the tombstones may resemble nothing except one another. However that turns out, is not the organization of the spaces in the celebrated memory theater of Giulio Camillo the same? Isn't it what we mean when we say that something—the way you slipped that folded fifty into your bodice—is engraved on our memory? or the time, as kids, we jumped our bicycles over the steps in front of the cathedral in Cologne? Surely it's better than saying that your name has been writ on water. Yes, certainly, Venice is such a theater, where Marco Polo stored the cities of the East like spices brought back aboard ship, and where every bridge in every city sees its own feet and curving belly; and we have but to look round the rounded corner of the Gritti Palace to encounter Polo's memory of Olinda, the city which developed in concentric circles like a tree, the old walls and quarters expanding as it grew so that its bark could continue to encompass it, and whose newer sections, increasingly thin where they begin, press out from the inskirts of a city whose center has, by now, reached and resembled the horizon.

If we weary of the name Venice and of that *V* through which the gondo-liers paddle, carol, and collect their fees, Florence can satisfactorily replace it, because *Invisible Cities,* as I've said, is a book about still another book, Dante's *Inferno,* composed as nearby to *The Travels of Marco Polo* as George-town is to the Capitol. The nine sections of Calvino's text resemble the nine circles of hell through which Virgil escorts Dante, although Marco Polo car-ries the khan with him largely by turns of the wheel of the word. There is a definite, not to say plummetous, descent from the first part, which opens with "Cities and Memory," to the final one, which begins with "Cities and the Dead," after which we fall more precipitously toward those cities which are said to be "hidden."

In Calvino, though, we meet cities on our journey, not Dante's miserable men:

> Below that point we found a painted people,
> who moved about with lagging steps, in circles,
> weeping, with features tired and defeated.
> And they were dressed in cloaks with cowls so low
> they fell before their eyes, of that same cut
> that's used to make the clothes for Cluny's monks.
> Outside, these cloaks were gilded and they dazzled;
> but inside they were all of lead, so heavy
> that Frederick's capes were straw compared to them.
> A tiring mantle for eternity!*

The dead, like those in Dante's hell, often live more fully in that death than when they were alive. Now, finally, they have a look in their eyes. Nor do we know what rough candidate for the pit is this moment slouching toward Bethlehem to set off a bomb.

In Calvino, as in any actual urbanity, Augustine's City of God and City of Satan share the same streets and avenues, interpenetrate equally every rela-tion. As I've argued, a single city is at once a cemetery, a slaughterhouse, a lying-in hospital, and a bordello. I have no doubt that the fountain which breathes its broken hopes in that forlorn Córdoba courtyard purls merrily in a cloister in Seville. Frank Presto will present his new secretary not only with a new pair of stockings but with a garter belt in black net to match them, even hold them up, but their love is shadowed by its own remote ruins now; the kneeling figure we observed earlier—who might have been fishing a fan from a fountain—that figure may simply be waiting for the shutters of the

---

* *Inferno,* canto XXIII, lines 58–67. I am quoting from Allen Mandelbaum's splendid transla-tion (Berkeley: University of California Press, 1980), p. 198.

surrounding apartments to open to allow in the cool night air and his lecher-ous eyes.

The technique of this magical and fabulous fiction concerns the recogni-tion of the Real, which is its insistent subject. Calvino has described him-self as having a geographical neurosis, and we might imagine that here he has allowed that neurosis to rule, if not ruin, him; but Calvino remains the realistic writer he was at the start of his career: an author of social protest, of political engagement. He recognizes now (if this book can be entered as evidence) that being Real does not mean being committed to the imitation of the commonplace, the promises of parties and politicians, the trite, the ordinary, the mercilessly clichéd—and all imitation is commonplace; it is itself a cliché. On the contrary, Reality does not consist of things, their col-lections, or their shallow denominations. Chicago is not the trumpet of its towers, which herald it only as we approach. Reality is not a set of simple situations, nor is it one shade of anything, one blue color or brown shirt. It is not even a single system of relations—invisible as they all are. The experi-ence of the city exceeds our experience of Proust. A great city's life lies in the details, in the details as they fulfill a whole. Consider what a little grass does to a set of steps, and then multiply . . . multiply. . . . Consider what a crack of light does to the dungeon, and multiply for freedom and for sky. Consider the multiplication not only of niceties but of vulgarities as well: signs, poles, wires, trash, broken glass, peeling paint, rotting boards. And multiply . . . multiply. . . . A hand like a hot towel held against the head, outcries of every kind, more numerous than beans, shit from a million bowels. This book, *Invisible Cities,* mistaken as an instance of the wild and woolly, is respectable in its traditional intentions: it would tell the truth; it would point a moral, suggest a way.

Calvino brings each of his cities before us through mime, and by danc-ing, as poor Polo must do at first, since he does not know the Great Khan's language. He renders each of them by means of essential relations—possibly dwellings or thickets of dwellings of odd kinds—not simply, then, of those parts which will somehow allow themselves to stand for their whole, either routinely, as a piece of pie must, or even more routinely, as a statistical sam-ple lies its way into everybody's confidence; but, rather, more metaphorically, poetically, if you like, so that one detail resonates with the presence of the rest like the last *l* in the toll of the chapel bell.

Isn't that what happens to the elements of a successful city: they satisfy our needs, allow our lusts, remind us of our past, inhabit our future, encour-age our reveries? Hölderlin's house stands, as it should, on a stream lined with dreams. The feel for the meaning and quality of a door or a gate does not stop there, opening both out and in at the same time the way a lamp in a window excites an exchange of light. What is a text but a community of words? A poem, to be sure, may stand on a white hill all alone like a country church, but a fiction is all jostle and solicitation, like a crowded marketplace.

> The man who knows by heart how Zora is made, if he is unable to sleep at night, can imagine he is walking along the streets and he remembers the order by which the copper clock follows the barber's striped awning, then the fountain with the nine jets, the astronomer's glass tower, the melon vendor's kiosk, the statue of the hermit and the lion, the Turkish bath, the café at the corner, the alley that leads to the harbor.

For this sort of writing, in William Weaver's unmatchable translation, "exquisite" is an inadequate adjective. Can't we believe that on many a Trieste night, James Joyce lay awake walking the Dublin streets, rereading the signs, resting his cane in a comfortable and familiar crack?

We have seen cities clothed in colored tiles, courtyards composed of images and ancient scripts and antique statuary, streets lined with streams, lined with inclining tables and dissipated awnings. There are neighborhoods where, in the shelter of the trees, the houses contrive to dream the American dream. A single building can sometimes overpower an entire city and, like the Arch in St. Louis, become more than an emblem, more than a feat to be admired: a conscience to be obeyed.

It would be a serious error to imagine that each city portrayed in Calvino's urban bestiary is a part of a larger, unexperienced megalopolis the way Westwood, Chevy Chase, Society Hill, and Shaker Heights are parts, even metaphorically. They are not hairs or fingernails or skin. They constitute entire cities in themselves. Like the body's circulation system or the interaction of the glands, they are just not *complete,* for the complete city is not only a city of signs like Las Vegas, each sign signifying still another, no real referent anywhere—but a city without either edge or center, one of Calvino's "Continuous Cities," like Los Angeles. In addition, it is a concentrated, pointed city, one that sits like a cap of snow on a hill's head and melts its sewage on the fields and roads below. And it is each of the fifty-five towns the text takes us through, including those that disappeared ahead of history and before we reached the title page—governmental cities too, capitals with a capital *C,* and those which will be paraded by our absent or our sleeping eye as the text turns silently inside itself, thinking like a drill bit does, bringing more aspects to inner view . . . continuously, invisibly.

Fifty-five is not a final figure. *"The catalogue of forms is endless: until every shape has found its city, new cities will continue to be born."* Yet cities come to an end when they lose their boundaries, when neighborhoods, districts, regions flow together with the sameness of a flooding river, masses of indistinctly different men covering the country. Then we encounter cities in the shape of Kyoto-Osaka, cities without shape, cities without limits or centers.

Not the last city, but the last one in Calvino's text, is Berenice, the unjust city, a meat grinder. Yet, out of reach and between the cogs and blades, another Berenice exists, a just city, one which deserves its name—"bringer of victory." Here, hidden, the just recognize one another by their manner of speech, by their temperate habits, their unflamboyant though tasty cuisine (which includes squash blossoms and beans). Here, however, within the very virtues of the just and their secret city, lies the sense of their superiority like the celebrated canker in the rose. To realize that your righteousness deprives you of the pleasures and privileges the unjust enjoy drives you to despise justice and resent your own virtue. By means of this grim dialectic, another unjust city, hidden beneath the hidden, begins to grow, a cancer called "just cause." The evil make the good see themselves as better than it's a good idea they should.

> From my words you will have reached the conclusion that the real Berenice is a temporal succession of different cities, alternately just and unjust. But what I wanted to warn you about is something else: all the future Berenices are already present in this instant, wrapped one within the other, confined, crammed, inextricable.

In the unjust city—our cultureless world—the just—the cultured—recognize one another as citizens of the same secret city, but their very isolation and the protections of superiority they must adopt to survive encourage a bitter hubris, which costs them the esteem they had fancied was their fitting reward.

The ultimate moral of our story comes, as it ought, on the last page, when the disappointed Kublai Khan complains: "*It is all useless, if the last landing place can only be the infernal city, and it is there that, in ever-narrowing circles, the current is drawing us.*'" And Polo replies:

> "*The inferno of the living is not something that will be; if there is one, it is what is already here, the inferno where we live every day, that we form by being together. There are two ways to escape suffering it. The first is easy for many: accept the inferno and become such a part of it that you can no longer see it. The second is risky and demands constant vigilance and apprehension: seek and learn to recognize who and what, in the midst of the inferno, are not inferno, then make them endure, give them space.*"

This is not, perhaps, a startling conclusion, but neither is the news that one must cultivate one's garden. They are, however, important conclusions, simply shaped but complex in their context, and even considerably true.

And now if certain listeners, readers, travelers, should complain that they have seen the sacred city of Kin-sai before, not fifty-five towns in one town, only one in one; that they have seen the same woman lean from the same window more than once, and inferred that the flirt and the snoop were twins; that they have noticed how the same lesson lay unlearned in this city and in that, and concluded that the citizens were identical dumb students in a single slow school; that they have heard the words "gate," "square," "street," "tower," "vista," "courtyard," "steeple," "minaret" repeated like the rattle of a child's drum—noisily, pointlessly, in every wrong rhythm—heard the words and nothing more; then my, Marco Polo's, and the good khan's answer has to be, I think, that if you believe all crossings are alike because they are all called crossings, you shall shortly be at sea, for not all crossings even cross; and if you believe that, because different bricks must similarly repeat themselves to make a wall, no wall resembles any other, or conversely, that every brick wall hides the same house; if you think the beggar you gave money to on Monday is the banker who, on Tuesday, received your intimidated check, then you had better be happy to live in one thin city your lifeline long (for there will be no point in going to another), a city where everyone will have one dog, one car, one lingering cough, one husband and/or wife, the way we each have one mother; and I can only pity those who see no difference between Colette, who leaned down from her window in the Palais-Royal that ripe May day and threw her fan into the fountain, and Cecile, who, in the maddening mug of one of St. Louis's insufferable summer evenings, hurled the straw hat with which she was trying to cool her honey-blond head at the back of a prowling tom, so that it fell in a slow swoon through the wet night air, only to be crushed in the gush of water coming from the hydrant in which we kids were playing . . . well, I can only pity and avoid them. For we—wet ourselves—watched the straw hat come apart like rushes drawn away into the current of a river, and while what might have been one of the world's eyes slowly began to lift its steel lid from the street, Polo, my playmate, said he heard in the hydrant the murmur of a distant falls, saw in its cooling spillage a great lake beyond, then docks, patient donkeys, a chimneyed house, a young woman watching from her window.

VIA, 1986
Published in *Tests of Time*, 2002

ON EVIL

The Ragged Core of a Sweet Apple

I s the motorcar evil? Of course not, because it can have no intentions, no interior life, nurse no resentments, and harbor no malice. In daily life, it has become commoner than the cold. In the moral realm, the auto lacks pizzazz. It is merely an instrument of evil, crippling or killing thousands every year, consuming many of the resources of the earth, eviscerating cities as routinely as butchers their beef, poisoning the atmosphere, fostering illusions of equality and dominion, encouraging envy and macho competitions, facilitating adolescent fornication, and ravaging the countryside. Its horrid offspring are garages, interchanges, hamburger stands, and gas stations. Popular delusions, much destruction, its increasing casualties do not make the motorcar evil, because these consequences were never aimed at. The word in vogue for the damage it does is "collateral." But the most considerable obstacle to calling the car "evil" is that its effects are easily explicable. Carbon monoxide is odorless, but that is the extent of its mystery. The price we pay for our automobiles seems more onerous to us than the cost of their use. Just add air bags and buckle up. Our callous indifference to ruinous truth may be less readily formulated.

Perhaps the cigarette is Evil. Because it has within it, like Old Nick in "nicotine," habituating elements that mimic the resolutions of intention. Because it encourages cancer to attack the lips that lip it, the lungs that suck its smoke, the eyes its blown smoke stings. Suppose the hands that held a wheel too many hours too many miles so many gallons began to lose their fingers. Then how would we feel? That justice had been done? For there is something that's suitable about dying from your vices: playing the slots, wasting water, eating burgers. If sins only sickened the sinner, if cramp crippled the fingers of the forger, if every quarter fed to the toothy machine clogged the player's small intestine, there would be some satisfaction in this world. A few zealots—foolish optimists about a moral universe—believe that AIDS is God's punishment for buggery, and that just deserts are at last being generously served. What of such thoughts? Is it in their vicinity that evil really lies? What sort of heart beats at that rate?

How about vices that have their virtues (most do), or go simply unrecognized and are therefore without stigmata? Movies of the thirties, forties, and fifties were filmed through clouds of Chesterfield, Old Gold, Lucky, and Camel smoke. Cigarettes were the expressive heart of human gesture. Like lighting a lady's Lucky. Like settling the tobacco in its tube by tapping it on a fingernail. It provided important moments of delay—while thoughts were collected, composure was attained. The methods for mooching a fag were numerous and expressive, as was spelling a long, slow, lazy sigh in smoke. Such rituals were social essentials.

We have learned to mistrust appearances. Beauty was the showing forth of virtue during pagan days, when virtue meant "manly" (that is, strong and brave); that was back when ample breasts and generous hips signified plow-girl fitness and maternity skills. But the devil, we've been warned, puts on a saintly face. Or at least a salesman's pleasant smile—seductive yet friendly. Where is his profit in being scary? Gluttony and lust, both beguiling sirens, kill millions every year. Fricatrixes and fornicators waste away, go mad, and die, while wives and mistresses, who must be fornicators, too, are shamed, abandoned, and enslaved by repeated pregnancies—if they survive the new life they carry; if their new life lives and they don't pull through just to bury another baby. So the cigarette's calming qualities were a wicked deception: "All is well," our inner crier cried to the soul's sleeping city; "Keeping your kool is what counts," our innkeeper counseled. Once aware . . . no; once convinced . . . no; finally scared by its consequences and their cost, we gave up smoking to become self-righteous. Alleging that we'd been fooled, we sued.

I have for some time insisted that every virtue has seven vices, and one day I intend to prove it. I have used neatness as a showcase because it cancels, hides, and opposes history. Miss Tidy believes that everything has its place and that everything should be there. To deny the parade happened, ticker tape and flagwave must be swept and furled; to pretend the party was never thrown, its empties need to be recycled, its tin horns packed away; to be able to say some war was ever foolishly waged, its wounds needlessly suffered, accounts must be scrubbed, documents shredded, evidence dug up, and history rewritten. This starchy daughter of the regiment loves roll call, frequent inspections, and the constancy of the pyramids. Moreover, one might argue, without being simply contrary, that chastity is a vice and adultery a virtue. Which one does the sonnet favor?

Nor is any virtue, in Kant's terms, unqualifiedly virtuous, for if we were to give our allegiance exclusively to one of them (by dreaming of a society without hunger, for instance), we should have to sacrifice too much else. So that no one might starve, we might give everyone a job. To do that (and the Soviet Union and China did do that), we find ourselves asking six men to dig a hole that two might easily shovel, and demand that women we've trained as nurses sweep the street instead. People will not look for or find congenial jobs, but labor when and where they are posted. Making work for others is one such assignment. Roads are repaired with forks and spoons when the aim is full employment, and slowdowns are de rigueur. Shop stewards take frequent breaks and the featherbedding is of swan's down. Hurry up and wait is the military solution. When standing in ranks or queues, life is as level as a desert and time is too heavy to handle.

As Milton inadvertently demonstrated, goodness is confining and limits God's sphere of action, turning Him into a droning bore. Eve ate to break the monotony. Eve ate to enjoy the appetite it would give her. Without misbehavior and misfortune, there would be no news. Some philosophers like to argue that *good* and *evil* are co-relative terms, and, like *long* and *short*, are necessary to each other. To know the meaning of *evil*, you must understand the meaning of *good*, as Satan certainly does, since he is a fallen angel. I'm sure he wondered how perfection could survive change. Perfection is more immobile than a mountain. Or, if in motion, as continuous as a heavenly body or a looped tape. Nietzsche thought a grazing cow could be happy because it had no memory of the past or vision of the future, hence no regrets, no anxieties, no invidious comparisons—an eternal now was enough.

Without history, how would we remember the injuries done to us by the grandfathers of our enemies? There is no other way to hand down hate from one generation to another; prejudice is fed on the excrement from former days; the chronicle of previous misdeeds is read aloud every day in the marketplace; catechisms are recited in the presence of sacred books. Our unfortunate lapses, on the other hand . . . Maybe Miss Tidy was right. There was no last night.

In his brilliant novel *The Living End,* Stanley Elkin gave God the best possible reason for the mess and misery of His Creation: it makes a better story.

My father had a driving habit. Many do, I suspect. Such men simply like "to take a drive" the way some step outside now "to have a smoke." "What if everybody did?" is the question Immanuel Kant suggested we put to ourselves (though less crudely than I have done). One can understand why philosophers are morally inconvenient. Which is worse: sickening people the way power plants and factories do, or polluting streams by hosing hogs? In any case, repeating the offense seems essential to the elevation of the cause. And the cause, to achieve evil, must be elevated. LADIES AND GENTLE-MAN, NOW PERFORMING IN THE CENTER RING! RACIAL CLEANSING AND THE CONFISCATORS! Evil cannot be a simple sideshow—the momentary ogle of a bearded lady or a lewd peek at some hermaphrodite's minuscule appliances. Evil is a limelight hog and wouldn't mind a little wash from the hose.

Aristotle thought moral virtue was a habit. Certainly vice is. Think of rape and murder as a serial rather than a snapshot—six unrelated killings in a week versus four in a month with the same MO. The American soldier who mistakenly shot Anton Webern can say oops, but not if he's done away with the entire Vienna Philharmonic. What onetime act can be called "evil," reach that kind of high-pitched crime? The crucifixion? There have been many. Christ's? Yes, but He had to be crucified. He had to suffer: our sins required their goat; nor would we be in a position to be saved as He was without a death for Him to rise from on a ladder of hallelujahs. The Resurrection was a proof, a promise, and a preview. All rise; here comes the judge. Had Pontius Pilate known the plot, perhaps we might admire him now for handing down a sentence so hard on the shepherd, yet so humanly necessary for his flock.

If repetition is at least sometimes a significant factor, numbers—higher and higher totals—would seem to matter. A RECORD NUMBER OF CHEV-ROLETS WERE WRECKED THIS LABOR DAY WEEKEND. I have wondered how many Jews had to die before their deaths qualified as a holocaust, in contrast, say, to just another pogrom. How many Africans must starve before the UN is moved to make a motion? Which fish was it that grew too mercurial? The straw that broke the camel's back was number—what? How much does the breakage depend on the camel? If the Iraqis kill one GI a day, how many days will it be before we withdraw? What a surprise withdrawal will be, because, every day, our casualties were light. So was the straw.

It is apparently worse if the crimes committed against large numbers are not only intentional but organized as if they were actually one outcome. The Chevrolets were wrecked higgledy-piggledy, Africans die of unexpected thirst and unplanned famine, but the Armenians were the chosen targets of the Turks. The German solution to the Jewish question was a bureaucratic action: offices were opened, agents hired, papers signed, file cabinets filled.

The ancient Greeks did not trouble themselves much about evil. The malfunctions of man and nature were—to a point—easily understood: there were many gods and no dogma. The gods lusted, quarreled, were jealous of their prerogatives, and possessive about their powers. Under cover of animals, they raped young ladies, or in a fume of frustration turned the recalcitrant into trees. During wars, they chose sides and constantly interfered with the fulfillment of human intentions—bent flights of arrows, slowed swings of swords. Sacrifices were expected. If the gods demanded the slaughter of daughters, this became inconvenient. It was nonetheless like paying tithes. Evil itself was not an issue.

Bad luck could follow a family the way original sin semened its way through the womb of humanity, but, by and large, quarrels were personal, you and the god of light or wine or wheat or war had your bones to pick the way Prometheus's innards were repeatedly vultured, though his crime—the theft of fire from the hearth of the gods—was so serious, his punishment required renewal and his liver grew back overnight like a weed. When Prometheus suffered, he suffered alone; perhaps his mother might be disturbed in her sleep, but not, certainly, the boy next door or the grocer across town or some Spartan and his young companion. If, at Creation, the work went awry, it did so because the real was to mirror the ideal and could not be replicated in lowly sensuous materials without compromising its purity and falsifying its nature. Is Liberty really a torch-bearing lady? This world, Plato said, is but reflection and shadow.

Evil, as something more than routine wickedness, appears when the pagan world is swept aside by the Judaic/Christian. In its place there is dogma, with heresy as its offspring; law, hence centralized authority and clerical bureaucracy; duty, thus an even fiercer patriarchy than there had been; overwhelming authority, and the dictatorship of a deity who has triumphed over other chiefs and other tribes, banishing their gods in order to rule alone. Although He (for it is a He in deed if not in anatomy) is given powers beyond dreaming, He must nevertheless assume family or saintly disguises in order to get done all He must do, and includes Himself in His Creation (since it is now His) like a drawing done in the draftsman's blood. Consequently, pantheism's presence is assured, and polytheism is only faintly obscured, because there are acres of angels in heaven and will be scores of saints on the earth. One of those angels, fallen from favor, is henceforth blamed for everything, since he possesses weapons of mass destruction and has moles and other minions everywhere that the ferrets of the Inquisition find convenient to go.

The realm of death is where the Titans once ruled, too deeply underground to be responsible for crops, and there the Prince of Darkness was sent, like a child to his room, for disobedience. The sun, the source of light and therefore understanding, blazed from above. The Form of the Good was the sun of the spiritual world, Plato said. Even earlier than he, light (knowledge) was identified with excellence, and darkness (ignorance) with evil. That is, ethical and epistemological concepts were fundamentally intertwined. This is the organizing premise of Susan Neiman's splendid new history of modern philosophy, *Evil in Modern Thought* (Princeton, N.J.: Princeton University Press, 2002), though she gives a priority to the ethical chicken that I might reserve for the epistemological egg.

The Greeks were concerned with right and wrong, less so with law and obligation. Knowledge exercised its moral suasion from within, but when there is one God, and when, as always, that God has rules, disobedience is the source and substance of every sin. From the first, philosophers and theologians tended to differ about this, and do so to this day. With the optimism every tautology confers, Plato insisted that men would follow the Good if they knew what it was (and if they did not behave, it was because their information, like the CIA's, was faulty). In the Judaic/Christian tradition, the law was handed out, to my mind, like leftover cheese to a starving population. *What* it was, was not nearly as important as *that* it was. Survival depended on unity, unity on regulation. Nourishment of whatever kind was the necessity. That there was a rule of law was more important than what the law ruled.

There is a day in every year when the hours of light precisely equal the hours of darkness, and the position of the sun (on a sundial) graphically represents the advance and retreat of its shine. These facts become characters in a moral story and soon enjoy the untrammeled dance of metaphor. The struggle between good and evil in the roles of day and night was continuous throughout the world because neither could be destroyed, only temporarily diluted or delayed. The seasons similarly warred with one another, each victorious, each beaten or making a comeback, arriving like the marines or fleeing the scene. Manichaeanism is an attractive theory if you want to simplify the problem of evil by making sense of it.

There were two warring forces, Mani, the man from Baghdad, said. Christ, the glowing God, represented the spiritual and ethical realm, while Satan, a night rider, represented what in pop cult is called "the darkside." The tourney between them was eternal. Mani (who proclaimed his prophetic role in c. 240) borrowed from everybody, especially his Persian predecessor, Zoroaster, who had divided the region's deities into bright and dim, set them at odds, and reserved salvation for the faithful (though my language once more favors the identification of evil with ignorance). The pleasure you might take in your own good fortune was ambiguous, because someone else was paying its price, while the pain of your misfortunes was ironic, for you rarely knew who was enjoying the helping of happiness that you were being denied.

The triumph of monotheisms (odd there should be so many Almighties and no one able to put the others out of business) put a considerable intellectual strain on their attendant apologists, who were constantly personifying the moral characteristics of human action and giving them to the deity: God was vengeful, angry, loving, grateful, and forgiving, as well as attentive and merciless. They let these reified forces run loose as hounds. ". . . there is almost nothing that has a name," Hobbes complained, "that has not been esteemed amongst the Gentiles, in one place or another, a God, or Divell . . ." (*Leviathan,* pt. i, chap. 12). In an effort to restore purity to waters irretrievably contaminated, and order to thoughts irrecoverably muddled, they put polytheism back in action, as I have already suggested (God has a son and that son a surrogate mother, St. Christopher fills in for Hermes, imps hide in closets, dybbukim take possession of the innocent, and witches fly through the skies).

Between a gloriously perfect God and the human soul, imprisoned in the dirt of life and its own body, intermediaries were deemed necessary, and countless numbers of them appeared immediately if not before the need was seen. No ideology can exist without them. They literally keep it alive. Call them Popes, prophets, Mahdis, saints, bishops, mahatmas, lamas, rabbis, mullahs, merely clerics: they were as human as you and I, and as hungry—therefore as greedy; as fearful as you and I—and soon as cruel; as agile and inventive, as lusty and carelessly knockabout as you and I. They murdered their enemies and were murdered in turn, urged righteous war on infidel nations, and occasionally preached peace as if they believed in it. They pursued the evil in others the way some sought the deer and the fox, and scoured their religious institutions till they were cleansed of heresy. Like nations, leagues, and alliances, these institutions needed evil, the enemies who harbored it, and those who threatened them. Evil rarely feels so confident that it will risk appearing naked and without the tailless, unhoofed look of the good. Never mind that the world was made better because some of its members were burned alive.

You don't need a theory to explain this. You need only history.

When Susan Neiman takes up the tale of woe that is our Western intellectual enterprise, it is 1755 and Lisbon has just been shaken by an earthquake, with much loss of life, property, and confidence. Moreover, the disaster has taken place on the Day of the Dead, November 1, a calendar moment that would nowadays, like 9/11, be subject to many fanciful interpretations. Intellectuals sent twitters of pity to the ruined city, but to the side of their injured views they brought palliating judgments and soothing rationalizations. The air had been sweet with the optimism of Alexander Pope, and a light breeze bore Leibniz's phrase—"This is the best of all possible worlds"—to every attentive ear. Newton had banished chaos. "God said, let Newton be, and all was light." The argument for design had been triumphantly upheld. Every event served a noble purpose and revealed the hand of divine providence in all things. Indeed, the human hand was evidence enough. It was how cleverly it held its knife that was admired, not the thrust that lodged it in a victim's chest.

In response to the tragedy, Voltaire first wrote a poem, a copy of which he requested a friend pass on, along with another on natural law, to Jean d'Alembert, Denis Diderot, and Jean-Jacques Rousseau. Upon their receipt, Rousseau objected to the Lisbon poem because it appeared to be an attack on Providence and therefore upon God himself. He complained that by overemphasizing human wretchedness, Voltaire had caused us to be more conscious of that wretchedness. This presumably made us more miserable, instead of more informed. Then, like a schoolmaster, Rousseau summed the problem in a single sentence: "If God exists, he is perfect; if he is perfect, he is wise, powerful, and just; if he is wise and powerful, everything is for the best; if he is just and powerful my soul is immortal." This domino-arranged rhetoric made its fall-down easy for Voltaire. If the Lisbon earthquake was not for the best, then, according to Rousseau's reasoning, God did not exist. But, we might reply, as if philosophy were a game, that the quake was for the best after all. Didn't fires encourage cities to build in brick and stone? Plagues compel them to improve their sanitation systems? So who knew what good would come from a vigorous shaking up?

A poem was an insufficient response to twenty thousand deaths, so Voltaire, familiar with the satirical tradition of Erasmus, Montesquieu, and Swift, as well as the pessimistic Pope of the *Dunciad,* in the space of a few days wrote *Candide*—a better idea. The absurd could only be answered with ridicule. A few important facts did not escape Voltaire. The problem of evil was as much an invention of the human mind (and the emotions that often drove it into nonsense and contradiction) as it was the result of human nature or its environment. It frequently took catastrophes to stir us into action. Superstitions fell as well as buildings; dogmas died when all those people did. Good and evil were seen to be significantly intertwined. Good intentions did sometimes pave the road to hell, but malicious emotions and wicked ambitions often produced profitable politics, greed useful inventions, and envy many masterpieces.

Indeed, the victims of such catastrophes were all remembered as loving helpmates, breadwinners, heroic rescuers, decent citizens, devoted parents, consumers you could count on. After all, among the victims of 9/11 were bankers and brokers. Business and its commerce suffered. It was an attack on affluent America and its secretaries.

The problem of evil comes in two ontological sizes. The first is factual: Does it exist as a part of the human condition, and if it does, what is its nature? What are its causes? And how may we rid the world of them? Agents of evil are often identified with evil itself, as the members of Al Qaeda were after 9/11, making evil easier to remove, as if punishing them would fumigate Enron or allow Serbs to walk upright. The second is philosophical: How shall we define evil? Is its character human, natural, or divine? What is its justification? And what does its presence indicate? (Ordinary things signify; evil "portends.") Evil seems to be something added to simple immorality the way we put bananas in pancakes . . . or is it the way we brown a roast? Rape and theft, for instance, appear to differ the way cats and dogs or species do, whereas evils are more unified, like shades of red: the rape (of one's mother [is evil]), the theft (of donor organs [is evil]). There are numerous subsidiary questions, of course, but these are the main ones. Occasionally, an issue will wear out its welcome and, without further argument, dwindle away. Events like the Lisbon earthquake or the Holocaust may prompt intellectual inquiries, and their results, in turn, may influence how we choose to cope with evil in the world; but many cosmic moral problems are purely philosophical, because they are the result of assumptions that have been embarrassed by facts or come to grief on the shoals of events. Following the Final Solution, God's apologists had a lot of explaining to do. Humanists were equally shamefaced. A few threw up their hands. Wasn't it futile to speak of morality after such a failure of morality? Nevertheless, a thousand thumbs were thrust into the dike. Excuses were released like birthday balloons. The majority of these rationalizations continue to be theological and are not regarded with much seriousness by professional philosophers.

The history of philosophy can be roughly described as a series of proposed solutions to specific intellectual puzzles, followed by evaluations and rejoinders that lead to new solutions and fresh mysteries. That is: a thinker finds himself in a fix, thinks he has found a way out, is told he has failed dismally, valiantly, narrowly, utterly, tries to fix his fix, only to have more faults found, and so on; meanwhile, the kibitzers adopt one version of the fix as their own and begin to tinker with it. In this game of serve and volley, God has been called upon to rescue many a system from disaster, a savior indeed for principles that have been threatened with their own kind of extinction.

God certainly existed, at least as an apparently viable hypothesis, at the time Susan Neiman begins her history with the Voltaire-Rousseau quarrel, and she immediately examines Immanuel Kant's reaction to Rousseau's belief that the impulses in man that have led to the establishment of corrupt and corrupting societies are not evil in themselves but could have been (and can be) used to create social relations that do not suffer from the mistakes that have been previously made. Rousseau suggests that if children were taught, by word and example, that life punished vice and rewarded virtue, they would be able to follow their basically good impulses with confidence instead of trepidation. As it is, the virtuous are victimized, being more than usually defenseless. But Rousseau's view of history has insufficient scope, for the good are not handicapped, surely, if it is the classical virtues they possess. Wisdom, courage, temperance, justice: these are not traits of the modest and humble, but of the strong, assured, and forthright. Pagan virtues give their owners an edge, allowing them honesty, for instance, because the truth takes grit to give and guts to receive. In their lives, inordinate demands have not been made on attitudes or emotions such as "sympathy" and "love," nor has obedience become the center of their moral interests.

If you are a Kantian, and believe that virtue should be sought for its own sake (as Aristotle also did), then to wish, out of a sense of fairness, for a world where goodwill and good character might be rewarded rather than exploited would be a terrible mistake, because, in such circumstances, no one could say whether virtue or its profit had been pursued. Suppose there were a Providence and that no leaf fell without its say-so; then, Kant argues, "all our morality would break down. In his every action, man would represent God to himself as rewarder or avenger. This image would force itself on his soul, and his hope for reward and fear of punishment would take the place of moral motives." (Quoted in Neiman, *Evil in Modern Thought,* p. 68.) I think, on this point, Kant underestimated our human capacity for self-deception and forgetfulness. Many people believe in Providence and its Overseer, but when a tornado blows away the trailer park they lived in, they thank God for sparing them and congratulate themselves, neglecting to notice who the wolf was who sent the wind their way and flindered everything they treasured. We know that gambling is for losers, that unprotected sex is risky, as drinking and then driving at high speeds is murderous, but we do these things all the same, and even congratulate those who escape the consequences; so I'm sure we'd be happy to call ourselves virtuous for investing in good deeds only because they paid prolific dividends. We want our happiness to be crowned with laurel leaves, as if we deserved our prosperity, our reputation, our suburban ease. At best, we may have earned it.

As Kant points out, happiness is a legitimate human end, but it is not virtue's medal. The virtuous can only hope to be *worthy* of happiness—like Job, whose suffering instructs us how far from justice are its deserts.

People are fond of excusing the deity from theological difficulties by maintaining that we cannot know God or His intentions, but they don't really believe what they say, since they continue to attribute to Him all sorts of enterprises. Prayer similarly assumes too much. That God has intentions of any kind assumes too much. That God cares assumes too much. That God exists in any form, or does not exist in any guise, assumes too much. Most human worship is idolatrous: it is commercial, narcissistic, childish— "Watch me, Daddy, while I somersault on the lawn"—"Jesus is looking out for me"—"God made my first million, and for that reason I have given it to the church; the remaining forty mil are mine." Instead, "Whereof one cannot speak, one should keep trap shut."

Neiman follows these arguments (which I have described too tersely for their own good), as they weave like impatient drivers through her book, paying great attention to nuance and detail while employing a scholarship that's wide-ranging as well as thorough; yet she represents them in a prose that is both clear and supple, turning intellectual corners without tire screech, and keeping even her careful pace vigorous and unimpeded by jargon or faddish ideological pretensions. Readers need only be willing to think while they read, and they will have a wonderful tussle, for hers is a subject of the greatest importance, open to opinions of every kind, and she approaches it in a manner that allows you to agree with pleasure, and disagree without animosity or any loss of esteem, experiencing that kind of happiness that comes when the mind is stretched to its own benefit; because when philosophy is done well (the doing is rare and difficult), then the trip is as breathtaking on account of the turns in the tracks as in the view from the windows, and the traveler is at last reluctant to complete a journey whose purpose seemed at first defined by its destination.

God was cleared of evildoing by denying His existence. It was His only excuse, Stendhal remarked, though a good one. However, when Nature was discovered to be indifferent, not just to our fate or to the fate of salmon, buffalo, or redwood forests but to life of any kind, to Nature's own reification even—indifferent to the indifference of its minerals, to the careless flow of its streams, to the fecundity of its own mothering nature—then man became the prime suspect. The old argument from design, whose candidates for the intelligent cause were God, Nature, and Man—the latter two plainly set up to be lopped off—was turned as topsy-turvy as a lotto basket; since it now had to be acknowledged that not only was Nature the origin of all those dismaying "acts of God" insurance companies don't have to pony up for but it had allowed human societies of every stripe and character, of peculiar practices and dubious moral ideals (such as human sacrifice, public executions, racial cleansing, clitoridectomies, slavery, inquisitions, professional wrestling, scarification, and so on) to flourish the way the Aztecs and the

Mayans or the Greeks and Romans did, as well as Islam managed at one time, or China during certain dynasties, the British Empire most recently, and even the American ego. Yet when these high societies stumble, fall, or fade away, it pays no never mind. Hills and valleys do not weep for Adonais or for anybody else. Nature's built-in sanctions (men are mortal) inhibit no one, including the intellectuals, who invent new immortalities to combat the death rate, because there is always a brisk market for solace and the honey of future rewards. Maybe it is the manufacture of myth and the promotion of superstition that is evil. I rather like that idea.

Neiman follows the argument like a sleuth, and indeed her book is a kind of thriller: What is it that menaces us? Will we find what evil is, and how may we escape it? She is a superb teacher, giving each side its due, accompanying the arguments with explanations that clarify, instruct, and surprise. The path leads from a God found absent past a Nature that's indifferent till it fetches up at the house of man himself: a castle made of rock, on a rugged mountain's top, its walls surrounded by a moat and defended by crenellated towers. For man to exist in harmony with nature had come to mean that he had to eat his meat raw, behave with indifference to everyone but his buddies, be wholesomely rude and free of customary social restraints. "Spontaneous" and "instinctive" were momentarily admirable words. A popular physical culture movement aped Greek and Roman statuary. The Reich liked hikers. Gauguin said he spat when he heard the word "civilization" (I bet he didn't), and others said they drew their pistols (I bet they did).

However, by this time, love of a "native" life was hopelessly reactionary. Perhaps, perversely, evil wrapped itself in glorious animality—D. H. Lawrence's Nature Boy, Adolf Hitler's blue-eyed blond ones—now that heaven was empty and the earth cruelly unconcerned. As the poet Rainer Maria Rilke wrote, "We're not in tune. Not like migratory birds. Outmoded, late, in haste, we force ourselves on winds which let us down upon indifferent ponds." ("Fourth Elegy," *Duino Elegies*.) Without other devices, man surrounded himself with man. But was that a help? What, after all, were the moat and walls and towers for, the readied molten oil, the axes and the arrows? Not the bumblebee. Safe inside, we died of damp, infected by our own wastes, impoverished by the expense and loneliness of self-defense. Safe inside, we dozed while Judas opened the gate. When we woke to realize we were no longer safe inside, we murdered one another with a zeal that could only be described as sacerdotal. Our own bodies flung our own bodies to the dogs. We had not been created in God's image, but in that other guy's.

In the heyday of our reign, lies about man were as prevalent as those about God had been. We wore our hubris like a festival hat. The entire universe had been made for us. That's why the earth was the center of the solar system. Among the creatures of that earth, we were its hilly aim, the fairest of them all. Man was the measure. Wasn't that the ancient claim? So every human being was of intrinsic worth, equal with every other, and worthy of protection and praise; although we didn't really believe a word of the "worth and equality" cliché, since we were so callous about the welfare of our own species as to shock every other creature into kindness. But not for long were we the glory and the center. As Freud pointed out, the earth has been demoted, our kind tossed among the others like a dirty rag. Perhaps we had a rank. Perhaps we were stationed ahead of the giant lizards that might return when we melted the polar ice, but we certainly were listed behind cockroaches, which had already lived longer than we and had better prospects; nor were we even masters of our fate, but prey to drives as remorseless—and desires as insatiable—as wharf rats.

Human beings have rarely given their own lives good grades. Schopenhauer, for instance, was amply prefigured by the ancients. Only persistent thoughts of death, which most men have hated even more than life itself, made them hang around. Neiman quotes Goethe. "In all times and all countries things have been miserable. Men have always been in fear and trouble, they have pained and tortured each other; what little life they had, they made sour one to the other. . . . Thus life is; thus it always was; thus it will remain. That is the lot of man." (Neiman, *Evil in Modern Thought*, pp. 209–10.)

What has emerged for me from this wrestle of the human mind with its own inhumanity, as Neiman opens her final chapter by returning to Lisbon's quake and the fascinating doctrinal wars it stimulated, is that, while the ground of evil is mere immorality, the cause of evil is evil itself. We know that white bigotry produces black bigotry, and black bigotry confirms white. I drive by to shoot your aunt; you drive by and shoot my uncle. I drive by to do in your papa; you drive by to do in my mama—merrily merrily, life becomes obscene. This tit-for-tat forms a circle rightly named "vicious." But its beginnings lie in a muddle of ordinary misunderstanding and commonplace misfortune, in fatherly tyranny and motherly meanness. To steal Hannah Arendt's adjective, beginnings are usually banal: job losses here, status losses there, humiliations here, foreclosures there, new people moving in, ethnic irritations, chagrin, lifetime disappointment. There is nothing anyone does wrong exactly, but living habits grate, values clash, competitions occur that do not make for harmony and happiness, but, rather, encourage slander and acrimony. Put-upon, people tend to club together, and "club" is the right word. Their enemies, the agents of their economic woes, and the authors of intolerable blows to their pride, belong to another club, driven together by present prejudice and past subjugations of their own. Clubs, gangs, tribes, sects, cults, parties, movements, blocs: collections of people who have given their loyalty (hearts and minds, as it's often put) to a group whose reason for being is complaint and whose aim is redress and vengeance. Resentment is pursued like a hobby. The weak lie in wait for their opportunity to achieve justice through the infliction of reciprocal pain. They wait to be empowered.

Injustices (and fancied ones are soon added to the real) are catalogued and kept fresh for future use by politicians who lie, bureaucrats who organize, preachers who rant, historians who colorize, and schoolteachers who read and repeat every calumny they can collect, preparing their children to carry on crime. We are the pure, the chosen, the faithful, the saved, they brag— the state, the church, the schools, and finally the nation brays—while *they* are the beshat; *they* are the damned, the sinners, idolaters, and agents of evil. Soon every citizen has been trained in fear and blame and hatred like soldiers for battle. We call this being a good patriot.

The sandhog wishes to hold his jackhammer, the computer geek his keyboard. Surely that is reasonable. Everyone takes their local miseries to the schools for instruction, to court for justice, church for benediction, history for justification of their historical blames and claims, to the military for reassurance and saber rattle, the state for presumption, pride, and swagger; and there they receive indoctrination, bias, mythmaking, fabrication, bluster, and braggadocio. Evil, it seems to me, is a mosaic made of petty little pieces placed in malignant positions mostly by circumstance in company with the mediocrity of the bureaucratic mind, and empowered, of course, by a gunslinger's technology.

Auschwitz, as Neiman suggests, was our Lisbon, although we have had a number of powerful before-and-after shocks: Passchendaele, the Soviet Gulags, Hiroshima, Cambodia, Kosovo, Rwanda . . . a list too long for 9/11 to obscure, crimes greater than our monuments can justify. However, we are ingenious, and we try: (1) The Holocaust was a display of God's wrath at Europe's left-wing, atheist, assimilating Jews—an excuse as old as Eden. (2) The human race advances by means of suffering and catastrophe the way we learn to fix bridges that fall down or prevent spaceships from exploding— but historical progress, even painful, is now impossible to carry a torch for. (3) Oh dear, God does work in mysterious ways, but this "event" was unique in its mystery and horror, so much so it falls out of history altogether, and has no real forerunners, as it will have no progeny; hence only its survivors are competent to comment on it; otherwise, silence and awe is all that's appropriate (Neiman slights this one, my favorite). (4) It was the largest and best-organized pogrom in a long history of anti-Semitic persecutions, so, apart from size, there is no surprise; the Germans are demonically gifted, and this ritual of purification was German through and through; moreover, for most Germans, the killing was done at a distance and never became news; therefore, it was as easy to ignore as the mass murderer next door—a move that gets the human race off the hook at the expense of only one nation. (5) The evil that was Auschwitz is not like next year's SUV, simply bigger and more dangerous, or even a vehicle that runs on brand-new fuel, but an evil as novel as a new species, unique as number 3 claims, and therefore naturally mind-boggling—here, the theory of emergent evolution is applied to dastardliness, keeping the Holocaust historical. (6) Since God is gone and nature excused, evil is simply a moral matter, and the question now is: just how much human behavior is so "natural" that nothing can be done about it except, as against earthquakes, to build better? We are what we are and that's all we are, said Popeye the Sailor. And Michel Foucault agrees with Popeye, because he argues that the haves are permanently at war with the have-nots. Get used to it, he sternly tells us. It is no longer a matter of Manichaean good versus evil, but a contest between those who have it and those who don't, until those who don't do, and those who do don't, whereupon the combatants switch ends of the field and go at it again.

Certainly, human horrors are old hat. It is history's major burden, our principal trait. In these recent cases, the surprise is the size of the crimes, not just the sum of the victims but also the zeal and numbers of those committing them. Still, it is business as usual down at the old abattoir and carnage yard. It's simply that business is now done at the global conglomerate level. In the near future, we shall drone our enemies to death between rounds of gamblers' golf or cowboy cookouts by the corral.

Neiman leads the reader through a careful analysis of the relation of intention, act, and consequence to kinds of useful knowledge and degrees of awareness. I give my son the keys to the car, knowing he has a tendency to drive too fast, but I don't want him to drink, to speed, to hit another car, injure his girl, raise my insurance rates, bill me for repairs, contaminate the atmosphere, violate his curfew, or make his mother mad, though I know some of these things will happen and that others are likely. "Intention" as a concept is as slippery as an icy street. Moreover, degrees of awareness are mostly issued by poor schools: if I stick a finger in hot grease, I know I will be burned immediately; if I fail to visit the dentist in six months, maybe I shall pay for it, but later (on a payment plan the British call "the never-never"). How many consequences am I responsible for when I loan the car or when, obedient to orders given me, I sign a writ of execution? How far should I see through eyes my superiors will shade and vector for me?

If Nature is morally indifferent (though not neutral exactly), and mankind is a species contained within Nature, then men can be indifferent, too. Or favor their own species, their own language, their own tribe, as Nature allows peonies their love of ants, or crows the flocks they fly in or the roadkill they flock to pick over, or we, for that matter, the meat we eat, leaves we chew, or friends we make. We can call good what our pecking orders suggest, and each of us support what supports our survival. Or not: everything that happens, including the "unnatural," is natural. Tautology tells us so.

But Nature, even from the moral point of view, is not a homogeneous entity. Actually, the word is a wastebasket and probably should never be used for anything other than collecting its ambiguities. There are profound differences between rocks and trees (as the Greeks already knew), between trees and birds, and birds and men, who are ultimately conscious creatures. As conscious creatures, we are aware of what it means to be neutral or indifferent or callous or uncaring or cruel and malevolent. Consciousness may seem transcendent to some, an impotent epiphenomenon to others, and a mistake to a few; but it is with that consciousness that we give meaning to a world that we should be grateful is as meaningless as an earth's shake, because otherwise its purposes would have to be deemed whimsical and malicious. It is consciousness that allows us to devise our works of art and discover Nature's laws, but it is also consciousness where we harbor hate, and allow our reason to be crowded into a servant's corner, our perceptions to be few and skewed, our sympathies buckled about us like a belt, our beliefs burdened to breaking by superstition.

A great portion of the human race is literally homeless; mass migration is one of the darkest marks of our age, with the hunger, disease, and suffering that attend such displacements. But all of us—even in the comforts of Palm Springs or Beacon Hill—are metaphysically homeless anyway. Consciousness, as Nietzsche observed, although our fundamental means of connection with the world, has cut us off from it, because we cannot live in the moment like an animal, but rather dwell in anger at the past and anguish over our future. Home is supposed to spell ease, identity, love, and that wonderful Victorian invention, comfort. Which it can do and sometimes actually does—if one can afford it. Above all, it is our refuge from the world, where we seek protection from its heartless pains. But what a dreary illusion that is. Home is also where we commit murder, mayhem, and suicide, where we shake a crying child loose from its life, where we quarrel like squirrels toward eventual divorce, where we grow accustomed to tyranny and the utility of lies, where we cultivate ignorance and pass on bigotry like a chronic cough, where children get to disobey and disappoint their parents, and parents to abandon them, where we find to what lengths "ought" has gone to escape "is," and where the tribe that we have allowed to define us claims its prize.

Evil is as man-made as the motorcar. I suspect that, like the motorcar, evil as a prevalent state of things suits a lot of people. If nature is uneven, we can try to even it, but it is we who have made a habit of injustice, and we who must design the institutions that will discourage resentment, malice, ill will, and ignorance while fostering justice, intelligence, learning, and respect. The question is whether it is better to die of a good life or from a bad one. If we fail (and I wouldn't bet on our success), there will be one satisfaction: we shall probably be eaten by our own greed, and live on only in our ruins, middens, and the fossil record.

Harper's Magazine, 2004
Published in *A Temple of Texts,* 2006

KINDS OF KILLING

The Flourishing Evil of the Third Reich

In order to prepare private citizens for the military, a humiliating and painful bullying is generally prescribed. Its aim is to inculcate obedience and create callousness. Leaders must be resolute and heartless, prepared to send any enemy "to their deaths, pitilessly and remorselessly," as the Führer demanded. Next a campaign of denigration of the chosen opponent is undertaken. This is designed to reduce the humanity of the enemy and to prepare a social web of support for behavior that is basically cruel, immoral, and normally disapproved. It strengthens every aspect of your plans if the society that you represent brings to the project a tradition of paternal domination and abuse, reaching from the family to the Kaiser and to its final station, God. Deep feelings of injury, inferiority, and large reserves of resentment— the fresher the better—are nearly essential. Any widespread unhappiness within your country can then be directed at the selected scapegoat by every available instrument of indoctrination and propaganda. If the enemy can be enticed to return fire, that will help solidify the nation's resolve. Since a saw's cut is painful either way it moves, the soldier knows that it is safer to risk death at the front rather than execution in the rear. A general sense of uneasiness helps, as if you knew someone were watching where you walked, reading your mail, and overhearing you talk. This atmosphere of anxiety can be sustained when the agents of power are pitiless. The master craftsmen of the Third Reich, whose state-of-war posture is so painstakingly studied in this superb but disheartening history of bad behavior,* had set their sights upon Poland at the time the third and final volume of Richard Evans's masterwork begins, and had made all the necessary preparations I have just enumerated.

* Richard J. Evans, *The Third Reich at War* (New York: Penguin Press, 2009).

Although preserving the purity of the bloodline is a commandment of tribal behavior, the Germans had expanded its meaning to include concerns about inner strength as well as physical health and racial genetics. Now the blood *in* the bloodline, not just its course, could be studied, and this gave to the most primitive of superstitions a scientific appearance. Dressed in laboratory coats, euthanasia could also be embraced. The Poles, like the mad, the ill, the old, and others at the edge of death, were incapable of a full-fledged human life. They carried disease, lived in filth, were born almost too stupid to breathe; their incompetence was as catching as the lice they bore; they should be confined to the muddles they made and their ignorance encouraged. Germany's earnest efforts to rub out any influence Polish intellectuals might have on their society, by removing them from their own lives, seem odd when dealing with such a presumably dumb bunch.

The novelty of the war that was beginning with the German attack in September 1939—aside from the journalistically popular concept of Blitzkrieg—was its unusual aim: not the defeat of another army but the destruction of a population. From Germans already living in Poland the SS formed militias of men whose grievances toward the indigenous population reached murderous levels with astonishing ease, and bands of "red legs" of this sort, obeying only the orders of their hearts, began organized shooting parties. The size of the payback for alleged Polish atrocities was 4,247 on October 7; by November, in Klammer, two thousand had been added; near Mniszek, ten thousand more Poles and Jews of every age and sex were shot at the edges of the gravel pits that were to serve as their graves; in a wood near Karlshof, eight thousand more were massacred. The cleansing continued, picking up speed as efficiencies improved. Finding so many murderers among ordinary people had not proved difficult. Moreover, these unconscionable activities were not the result of a long harsh military campaign and disappointing losses but were available for use the moment the war began, with its immediate, immoderate, and overwhelming victories.

The German army, when it began to do its part, specialized in burning any village in which the least resistance was encountered. The SS, as well as the regular police, were initially disposed to carry out the murder of specific persons instead of the anonymous many, and to be singled out might be a victim's only victory. This slaughter was ameliorated (the word cannot be read without a grimace) when the authorities recognized that Germany had a serious need for workers, with so many men gone from their jobs and away for the war. Every available body was then rounded up and sent off as a labor replacement wherever one was needed in the Fatherland. The "recruitment" of foreign labor was a considerable preoccupation of German bureaucracy during the entire war and eventually included putting to work prisoners of war from both fronts. Many a Polish house was emptied or a village stripped of its population, so that looting and pillaging became a military habit, and the rape of women was implicitly encouraged by the army. The greed of many in the high command was as huge, and as frankly bragged of, as Falstaff's pride in his belly. Hitler wanted to establish a museum of stolen property in his hometown of Linz. Göring desired to display his art as he did his hunting trophies above the many sofas furnishing his numerous *Schlösser*.

This great war was not one war but many, fought in different places, under different circumstances, and at different times; but the German troops remembered to bring with them to new encounters the bad habits formed when they invaded Poland. Their behavior was still able to produce surprise. "Where is the traditional German sense of honour?" wrote one inhabitant of occupied Athens. "They empty houses of whatever meets their eye. In Pistolakis's house they took the pillow-slips and grabbed the Cretan heirlooms from the valuable collection they have. From the poor houses in the area they seized sheets and blankets. From other neighbourhoods they grab oil paintings and even the metal knobs from the doors." Of course, the pillowcases became bags for bearing off heirlooms, and the knobs, if metal, were needed back home. Looting was rarely random among the officer class.

Like a monstrous babe born from the brow of Rabelais, this war was only a few months old and already it had become a major crime against humanity. The German government, noticing that too much booty was escaping the clutches of the state, simply announced in September 1939 that it had acquired for its own use the contents of the entire store. Acquisitions then began in earnest. The army took over farms and anything else that might supply food; universities lost their scientific instruments; every iron object, length of copper, or zinc downspout, steel girder, tin saucepan, and—yes— doorknob was scooped up, melted down, and sent to work in the mills of the Reich. "Even the Warsaw Zoo's collection of stuffed animals was taken away." There appeared to be a bounty on Polish priests, who were deported, incarcerated, shot. Schools were closed and their equipment destroyed. Businesses were commandeered and landed estates requisitioned. As the winter grew harsh, the German police borrowed the Poles' sheepskin coats if they saw a serviceable one pass in the street. In town after town, the names of the avenues and alleyways were replaced. In sum, everything Polish was banned, burned, stolen, eaten, removed, imprisoned, or deported, and sooner or later entire populations were slaughtered far more carelessly than cattle.

Some senior German officers, who still believed in the traditional rules of engagement and the gallantries of military etiquette, and who were therefore increasingly disturbed by the rapacious behavior of the militias, began to protest and to make arrests, but Hitler immediately issued an amnesty for acts motivated by "bitterness against the atrocities committed by the Poles." Colonel-General Johannes Blaskowitz, who was at that time Commander in Chief East, complained in a memo to the Führer of the horrible atrocities that now shadowed the conscience of the country, and of crimes the state would see reason to regret later; but many officers were only too happy to hand whatever brutality they saw or guilt they bore over to the SS, and soon Blaskowitz had another, much less important post. Demotions were lessons to others.

The grander aim behind these persecutions was the emptying of Poland of its Jewish/Polish inhabitants in order to fill it with repatriated Germans. After all, if you are going to acquire a bigger house, its previous owners should not be still flushing the toilets. Expulsions could be rather prompt— twenty minutes in some cases—and the journey cold. One trainload delivered the bodies of forty frozen children, dead on arrival but at their proper station. Eighty-eight thousand Poles and Jews of Posen were whisked away in this fashion during early December 1939, to be sorted out. Relocation took more time, and a lot more money, since the genuine Germanness of people who had often lived for years away from the Fatherland had to be verified, fakers detected, Jews and weaklings weeded out, and some recompense made to the winners for their losses.

Page after page rolls by the reader's eye bearing these, even now, astonishing statistics—shocking, revolting, numbing, relentless—that sum up how many broken families, beaten bodies, and murdered men and women, how much loot and illicit booty, how many cruelties had, during this month or that, in simple village or chaotic battlefield, been undertaken and accomplished. The record is rich with irony. For every sincere member of the master race there were those who took bribes from the Jews as often as they took their lives. While the big—the organized—war went on, small wars everywhere flared and flowered. When food became scarce, the black markets had specials. The vast government organization had more cracks than any comedian, and up and down them thousands of busy creatures scurried, carrying baskets of fruit, tins of fish, bundles of carrots, barrels of oil, bolts of silk, as well as the traditional cigs, booze, chocolates, and lingerie. I wonder what one day's collection of screams might fetch.

With acres of their fields burned, crops requisitioned, and farmers enslaved, the population began to starve. Rations, if you were a Pole, came to no more than 669 calories a day. Jews received 184. An officer's spit might contain that much. Robbers roamed the roads and forests. Diseases spread as the body's resistance failed. In France, when Germany overran it, refugees fled one city only to fill another. Friends turned upon friends. Denunciation replaced *"bonjour."* So the campaign of extermination was going nicely. Thin women were the only ones around but nonetheless inviting, exchanging syphilis for a few hundred calories of love.

On the eastern edges of Poland, where the Russians were employing very similar methods of murder and deportation, conditions, though sometimes different, were no better, and the killing contest, at an admittedly rough count, continued to turn out a draw. Jews scarcely knew which way to run, nor dared they stay in place, since anti-Semitism was, in Poland (as it was in Hungary, Romania, Ukraine), a flourishing native plant. Evans is succinct: "The deliberate reduction of Poland to a state of nature, the boundless exploitation of its resources, the radical degradation of everyday life, the arbitrary exercise of unfettered power, the violent expulsion of Poles from their homes—all of this opened the way to the application of unbridled terror against Poland's Jews."

Is this particular mistreatment of the Jews entirely the result of years of Nazi propaganda or even of ancient misgivings? Is something more going on? Because, even if I think no better of my neighbor than I do my dog, I treat my dog rather well, and can find the time to feed her, pet her, train her, walk her around. Even if I think of my neighbor as a leper, I might be expected to wish no more for him than removal to a colony; moreover, I might be assumed to think of my leper's daughter as disgusting and far from desirable, when in fact I cannot wait to take her in my arms as roughly as necessary, her skin as intimate to me as mine, and then to enter her every aperture. Do I not care where I send my sperm?

The previous volumes of this history will help the reader confront such questions, because they chronicle the historic events that led to National Socialism's seizure of power in Germany (*The Coming of the Third Reich,* 2003), and then to its solidification (*The Third Reich in Power,* 2005). This particular period in history has given rise to a myriad of questions, some perhaps odd, others almost mysterious. For instance, only one conglomeration of events can be called "the Holocaust." To write of "a" holocaust suggests there might have been others, and damages this one's almost sacred status. Is, then, its singularity enough to deprive it of any place in a customary causal path so that history cannot account for it? Or is the Holocaust just the largest of a class of catastrophes, like eruptions, hurricanes, and landslides are? How many must die to achieve the number necessary to count as a holocaust? Fifty thousand? Four hundred thousand? Three million? Is it like deciding that among winds one is the windiest?

Perhaps it is how well organized and sponsored these massacres were that makes them so special. They were a real corporate enterprise, involving the apparatus of a nation-state. On the other hand, Croats, Hungarians, Romanians, including the Poles who were picked on, even the French and the Dutch Nazis, eagerly helped out. Many other issues are theological, such as wondering what God's purpose was in levying such punishment upon the Jews. Questions of this kind do not trouble historians much. On the other hand, the failure of nearly every element of humanistic interest and accomplishment in Germany to dissuade, slow down, or oppose the actions of the state, borders on total, and this sad futility is discouraging to those who thought that "higher culture" included a more refined morality. Is the fact that older generations of Germans were more likely to disapprove of mass murder due to the younger ones' enduring an earlier and longer period of brainwashing, or just to their higher level of testosterone?

There are several strategies one might employ for lessening the guilt of the Germans without denying the fact of their crimes. A number are currently operating in the guise of (fraudulent) memoirs or romanticizing movies. A few such were cited earlier this year by Jacob Heilbrunn in an article for *The New York Times*. Heilbrunn remarks that "the further the Holocaust recedes into the past, the more it's being exploited to create a narrative of redemption." Recently, stories of German opposition to Nazi actions have become particularly popular. There is, however, little that is exotic or daring about the occasional leaflet campaigns the Social Democrats managed to set going as late as the summer of 1934. Evans, in his second volume, points out, "By this time, almost all the other leading Social Democrats who had remained in Germany were in prison, in a concentration camp, silenced or dead." Even those who would endeavor to kill Hitler were mostly motivated by their conviction that Germany was finally losing the war, rather than by any deep-seated objections to his policies. At least, that was the opinion the London *Times* found in its review of *Germans Against Hitler* by Hans Mommsen (2008) and *Luck of the Devil* (2009) by Ian Kershaw. Although one dead fly may ruin an entire porridge, an innocent olive will not render benevolent a poisoned glass.

Richard Evans is a veteran of these revisionist wars, having earned a few medals for his testimony against one of honesty's enemies, David Irving, who had the chutzpah to sue Deborah Lipstadt (a professor at Emory University) for libeling him in her book *Denying the Holocaust: The Growing Assault on Truth and Memory* (1993)—a careful exposure of this movement's bowellike (regular, hidden, contemptible) strategies. Evans's evidence has been presented in his own *Lying About Hitler: History, Holocaust, and the David Irving Trial* (2001). Irving lost his case, but these apologists are not easy to discourage. They lurk about the edges of conflicts like this, especially now that the Internet lends its facilities to any voice that cares to attach a pseudonymous name or academic title to a site from which they can fire off innuendos, profit from ignorance, and cast suspicion. Another excellent exposure of revisionist methods can be found in Pierre Vidal-Naquet's *Assassins of Memory: Essays on the Denial of the Holocaust* (1987). If there are any purely "intellectual crimes," denying the reality of the Holocaust is surely one of them.

Still, one excuse that I rather like is the presumption that any group of people, finding themselves in the same sort of situation, their histories stocked with similar resentments, would act in a comparably vengeful fashion. Suppose that I have been a pitiful powerless person my whole life, and the victim of war, humiliation, and economic collapse. Now, suddenly, finally, I carry your life in my holster, I can act with impunity and at whim, but I must remind the world of my elevation by repeated demonstrations, the more vulgar, petty, and disgusting the better. So after I have raped this Polish–Tunisian–Greek–Gypsy girl, who certainly deserved it, I shall invent little sadistic extras to demand of her: that she clean the public latrines with her blouse. Jewish bystanders shall be required to doff their silly hats. Polish scum shall be made to lie flat in the mud and kiss dirt. While they are thus prone I shall try not to wobble when I walk upon one of them, but they are incorrigibly lumpy.

But it was the Romanian members of the Iron Guard who did the human race proud when they forced two hundred Jewish men into a slaughterhouse, flayed them from their clothes, and made them walk the line to their stockyard executions, after which their corpses were hung up on meat hooks that had been run through their throats. Those German "doctors," who looked upon the Jewish children in their hands very much as we do laboratory mice, yet wishing to erase any evidence of their experiments upon them, considerately shot the kids full of morphine and had them hung on hooks for SS men to yank as one has to tug when extricating clothes from a crowded closet.

"Croatian Ustashe units," perhaps out of friendly rivalry and to demonstrate that victims didn't have to be Jewish, "gouged out the eyes of Serbian men and cut off the women's breasts with penknives." They also carried out clever sting operations by promising amnesty to any villager who converted to Catholicism and then beating to death with spiked clubs the 250 who showed up at a Glina church for the conversion ceremony. At other times they just used ordinary hammers.

And to those making inquiries later, I shall say I did so because someone wearing the appropriate suit of authority or religious habit said it was okay. I shall say I did so because I've had a rather hard life myself. I shall say I did so because I am really scared of these flat-black-hatted machinates whose evil ways I've heard about on the radio. They are moneylenders, evil connivers, members of the Red Menace. Just look at them: dirty and diseased, bearing beards just begging to be tugged, eating grass like meadow cows. Down what dark twisted avenue of delight does this delight await me? And if I were a member of the Iron Guard that day, would I now—would anyone?—excuse myself by saying those Jews deserved the punishment of the slaughterhouse?

Well, we were preoccupied with our lives at the time, and didn't notice.

Is it somehow more or less awful if one man kills another hand to hand, or by bomb from a plane, or with a signature at the end of a page? What legitimizes murder: being a soldier in a nice tidy correctly declared war? Or a marine who is taking part in an unprovoked and pre-emptive attack? Perhaps we are considering a civilian who does in one of the enemy with a hay fork, or a member of the militia who acts in obedience to an order and delivers a merciful shot to the head of a prisoner kneeling before a pit previously prepared for his folded form. What is the degree of difference?

Contrary to common belief, monoxide fumes can be ghastly; reports about how it feels to be buried alive are slight; hanging is far too slow a method; poison is also unpromising. Is it okay to kick in a kidney because its owner is dirty, wearing the wrong clothes, clerks in a hardware store, is a disloyal Red, a moron, merely blind, walks with a limp, or should these people be sent to hospitals, psycho wards, and other capitals of euthanasia?

How should I know? I was preoccupied with my life at the time, and paid no mind.

Do we really have to fuss a lot over who deserves to die? Chance or whim does in the unlucky. Other times it is death by doctor, lawyer, Indian chief. Pre-emptive strikes against progeny, including mass sterilizations, were studied. "Senior SS officers fantasized about such methods being applied to 10 million racially inferior people, or to Jewish men needed only for labor. . . ." These were happy times for serial killers, and for those who needed to let off steam in order to seek anger relief. I wonder if the statisticians who are so devoted to numbers have calculated how many commonplace outrages were committed under cover of the general criminality. Well, you must know that the Russians are massacring millions too. And after the way I—we—they've been treated, what did you expect? The Jews took it lying down. Starvation, disease did it, whatever it was, not I. The Americans dropped that bomb, didn't they? Listen, I let the Warsaw Jews have their own mayor. Because it was winter, a load of young children froze while enjoying their train ride. Some things can't be helped. A few hearts failed from fear of being gassed, or waiting in line and being last. But, gee, there are more Jews now than ever.

More Poles too. And that proves that there were never as many killed as has been maintained. Look at what the Allies did to Dresden. What gas chambers? I don't see any gas chambers.

When are we to know we have the final solution to the Jewish question? When we shall not have to live in the world of their awareness.

Richard Evans's three volumes of disagreeable details, masterfully ordered and presented with ruthless clarity, are not centrally concerned with actual fighting, although a good account can be found there. His indictment is principally based on the political and cultural climate that created a monster out of an apparently civilized nation-state. And it does not fail to quote from countless witnesses whose eyes had to shed—like tears—their disbelief of a barbarism for which only the human species could find the evil energies. Whether one must wear a yellow star . . . excuses are inadequate; whether one is banished from the queue for daily rations . . . excuses are inadequate; whether one is murdered in an unimaginably mean way . . . excuses are inadequate; whether that wretch whom I shot from a passing window turns out to be twenty or two thousand destined to crumple into open graves . . . excuses are inadequate; and if we feel rage . . . well . . . welcome to our ambiguous skin: victor hates victim for making him victorious.

Murder machines, such as those gas-driven engines of death that the Germans designed to facilitate their task, are the sort of thing that catches the popular imagination, but the quiet, at no point wholly observable, method of starvation is the ultimate choice: profitable while being cheap, and requiring no implements, no death chambers, no immediate executioners either. Disposing of the bodies when you have shot five hundred in the woods, or at the end of a week of inhalations when you have more corpses than you know how to discreetly burn, becomes an increasingly sensitive and annoying problem; so it is comforting to contemplate how economical starvation is, beginning with the victims' feeding on themselves, thus reducing smoky fats, with a good chance they will finally fall upon those of their own who have fallen and endeavor to devour them. For sport, in a camp for captured Soviet soldiers, guards would bet on which dogs might leave upon their prisoners the most damaging tooth marks, but this was purely for entertainment and not very efficient for murder on a mass scale.

If you kill all the Jews, who will be left able to accuse you? Hardly anyone else will care and many will be quietly grateful.

The war against the Soviet Union began as felicitously as the invasion of Poland: many quick and easy victories, rapid advances, inconveniently large numbers of captive soldiers, much pillaging including the seasonal collection of winter coats, frequent rapes, pointless vandalism, random killings, and the gradual re-realization that prisoners might be better used as workers than as starvelings. Nevertheless, of the approximately 5.7 million Soviet prisoners, "3,300,000 . . . had perished by the time the war was over." As if anticipating the counterclaim (which is supposed to alter one's appalled reaction), Evans immediately continues: "By comparison 356,687 out of about 2 million German prisoners taken by the Red Army, mostly in the later stages of the war, did not survive." Moreover, many died in Soviet camps from the same straitened circumstances the general population suffered. They starved; we starved; he, she, or it starved with happy uniformity. Even curtains at windows grew thin.

As if to demonstrate who among the barbarous was Hun in Chief, the Nazis frequently attacked fine homes and furnishings as if the mirrors were shooting back. Soldiers burned some of Tolstoy's manuscripts when they arrived at Yasnaya Polyana, and in Klin drove motorcycles back and forth over sheets of Tchaikovsky's musical scores. Mostly, though, soldiers complained of the miserable conditions of life that Russian villages offered them. "Partisan resistance prompted further reprisals, leading more to join the partisans, and so the escalating cycle of violence continued." This inevitability, ironically, seems to have escaped the notice of present-day nations. What is the use of an upper hand if you can't spank someone with it?

Success has its penalties. The advance was so rapid that many Soviet troops were passed like hitchhikers on the road, and these unattached men joined the local partisans, made a nuisance of themselves behind the lines, and earned for others as well as themselves reprisals, which often meant that hostages would be executed, many by hanging from suitable trees, which often spoiled the view higher officers had from their very temporary accommodations.

Snow and cold began to kill people without regard to race or place of origin. Once more the Jews were going to lose their coats. The eyes of the troops wept in the face of the wind and it spoiled their aim. Their swollen feet had to be cut from their shoes. And Polish lice were now a third force. Like the lice, the Russians were too numerous. Killing them all was impossible, though corpses fell like falling snow into growing heaps. It did begin to look as if the enemy had better shovels.

One of the many shocks this book delivers is the reader's realization that— after following a trail of murder and usurpation through two and one-quarter volumes, during which death is more frequent than the words, cruelty and conflict more common than punctuation, murder spread equally over all their pages—the killing is now going to begin in earnest. "There is also some evidence that Ukrainian nationalists in Lemberg nailed bodies to the prison wall, crucified them or amputated breasts and genitals to give the impression that the Soviet atrocities were even worse than they actually were." I'm glad they had a good reason. Despite the fact that some Ukrainians were mighty busy beating Jews with the poor man's arsenal—clubs studded with nails— the Nazis complained that their attempts " 'to incite pogroms against Jews have not met with the success we hoped for.' "

Entire cavalry brigades were now assigned the task of destroying Jews. One such group especially distinguished itself by shooting "more than 25,000 Jews in under a month." At first, the executioners were not to waste bullets on women but simply to drive them into the Pripet Marshes, the greatest area of swampy woodland in Europe, where they might drown; the marshes were only deep enough for wading, however, so the women, like the men, had to be shot. The Germans were not to be slowed by these set- backs. They found ravines, and in the one called Babi Yar, after undressing and lying down in neat rows—victim upon the just-victimized as blanket upon sheet—the Jews were bulleted behind the neck to a total of 33,771.

Men cannot imagine such numbers. They can only perform them.

Any reluctance that was felt by members of the military was overcome by an anti-Semitism almost as old as their ages, by fears of reprisal for themselves, because of the shame they felt at being taken for sissies, and on account of the payments in plunder that fed their greed. "The great major- ity of officers and men took part willingly . . . and raised no objections." In some cases, Serbian prisoners would be used to collect from a fresh kill of Jews the contents of their pockets, and the soldiers would risk giving these people penknives to cut off ring fingers. A handy chart, of which Evans has many, shows by means of variously striped shades the numbers killed in the area stretching from Leningrad in the north to Vilna (248,468), from Minsk to Kursk (91,012), Kiev to Stalino (105,988), and Taganrog to Simferopol (91,678) during the years 1941–43. Only once more shall I give in to out- rage and cite another particularly instructive moment among thousands that might be chosen, in order to draw your attention to Hans Krüger, head of the local security police in Stanislawów, Galicia, who threw a picnic for the shooters to enjoy between shootings and oversaw the massacre "with a bottle of vodka in one hand and a hot-dog in the other. . . ." You may think this picture is simply grotesque. There is another in which we see an officer so horrified by the sordid conditions in which some Jewish children were being held that he approved of their immediate execution in order to spare them further pain. This exhibits a concern that might be expected for chickens.

By now (July and August of 1941), few soldiers were squeamish; their Aus-

trian officers were still eager; shooting Jews was a sport as habitual as bowling on weekends; and anyone handy might be murdered just to meet the
monthly quotas. The instruction that came down from Hitler was to kill
"'anyone who even looks askance.'" Evans is quite clear about the evidence
that "many people in the senior ranks of the Party and state administration
were fully informed of the massacres being carried out by the SS Task Forces
in the east."

By the time the United States entered the war, the expansion of Germany's murderous ambitions had grown from one of forcible Polish relocation to pogroms that involved the whole Eastern Front, subsequently to the
entire continent of Europe, and bore unmistakable signs, finally, of global
aspirations. This would mean that the assimilated Jews of Germany, who
had lost their homes and many possessions but otherwise had been "merely"
harassed by a lengthening list that included petty bans on buying flowers or
being forbidden to sit in deck chairs or rules denying them cats, would now
be removed to camps in the East. The boxcars began their tryouts for grainy
documentary movies. Between October 1941 and February 1942, fifty-eight
trainloads of those "useless eaters" who were declared unfit for forced labor
carried fifty-three thousand Jews to camps in the East.

Who could have imagined there were so many Jews; that just removing
them to overnight ghettos in Poland or Ukraine would put such a strain
upon every mile of track and every engine's boilers; that so many departments of government would be required, soldiers to shoot them, munitions
to make, guards to control them, shovels to dig and to cover their graves?
Better methods had to be found for both death and disposal. Perhaps those
employed with such success in the programs of euthanasia might be brought
into play—sealed chambers and car exhaust—and camps built solely for
death's purpose. So thirty gas vans were built in Berlin. They could kill sixty
at a time, an improvement of ten over previous model years. Occasionally a
child survived whose mother had so severely swaddled it the fumes could not
penetrate the cloth. It was a doubtful stroke of luck, since the guards would
smash such babies' heads against convenient trees.

Timing became important. Himmler had to bawl out one overzeal-
ous police chief in Riga who had a trainload of Berlin deportees killed too
promptly, thus possibly alarming those Jews still in Berlin and causing them
to be more difficult to handle. The range of extermination now clearly
included the whole of occupied Europe. Yet it was the twentieth of January
1942 before the infamous Wannsee meeting on the Final Solution to the Jewish question took place. No final solution seems to have been reached, but
a semifinal one was. Elderly Jews would be sent to old folks' camps. Since

the holding stations were about to take on the balance of German Jews, the Eastern Jews who presently filled them would have to be eliminated to make room. Gassing vans were amply available. Jews able to work would build roads and die on waysides. "Extermination through labor" was not a new idea, but it was an economical and effective one. There was no need to coddle these creatures, for when one perished another was available.

The propaganda machine was making its own carbon monoxide. Everything the Germans were doing to the Jews, the Jews had done to Germans, or would do if they could. They had started the war; they were eating away at the Reich's magnificent culture; they wanted to destroy Germany as it presently stood. Goebbels instructed the media to be unrelenting. "'The Jews must now be used in the German press as a political target: the Jews are to blame; the Jews wanted the war; the Jews are making the war worse; and, again and again, the Jews are to blame.'" I do think Goebbels had begun to believe his own lies, but could an entire nation be deceived by nonsense so palpable it . . . But I forget. Nazism was a secular religion. Its sacred book was *Mein Kampf.* The Red Menace embodied another form of worship, which held *Das Kapital* to its heart. Their godfathers just weren't in heaven, and could use the phone. Whether Jew or Christian, Nazi or Commie: they all had plenty of practice living in illusion and hating one another.

During the years 1941–43, Berlin Jews, who were not supposed to have their composure ruffled by hearing the worst of bad news, heard the bad news nevertheless and escaped by suicide. It was a wonder there were any trains left able to carry munitions. The idea that many people still didn't know what was going on represents another wild lie. If the Jews, who weren't supposed to know, knew, everybody did. Like the disciplined lines of white crosses at Arlington, numbers representing the sizes of the shipments march across Evans's text. Perhaps these pages more accurately resemble a schedule of departures than a cemetery, but their meanings are the same.

Jews were not the only victims of the Nazis' murderous frenzy; nor, on the Eastern Front, was the Soviet army Germany's sole enemy; because the moment the Czechs began to act up they were sorted out for deportation, sterilization, and execution, just as the Poles had been, and—as always—the Gypsies too, who were consistently preyed upon, as well as other racial odds and ends. When Czech partisans managed to assassinate their region's SS protector, Reinhold Heydrich, they hoped to provoke from the Nazis their customary kinds of retaliation, in order to reawaken a resistance movement that Heydrich's policies had managed to frighten or lull into passivity. In so doing they demonstrated how easily the same gloves of callousness that the

Germans wore could be put on, and how good the fit was. Lidice was only the notorious part of the cost.

Until November 1941, the extermination camps had not yet been built. A score of SS officers would run them; Ukrainians, taken from their own camps and given special training, would provide the raw manpower; and a few specialists recruited from the victims themselves (tailors, carpenters, cobblers, *und so weiter*) could supply the standard operational skills. All that otherwise might be needed, aside from the airtight gas chambers to create the corpses, earthen pits and crematoria to manage their disposal, were some houses for the SS and barracks for the auxiliary servants of the industry. These camps were extraordinarily efficient except that sometimes the wooden killing boxes began to leak and had to be replaced by concrete ones. At Belzec, the first of these specialized death camps, seventy-five thousand Jews were gassed and their bodies burned in its initial thirty days of operation. Eventually, the number would approach six hundred thousand.

Jews still in Poland were at full alarm, and many had to be killed in their houses and on the streets before their trains departed, they had become so obstreperous. Lest we focus our dismay too narrowly: Poles stood by and laughed at the sight—laughed then looted.

The second camp was modeled after the first except the gas chambers were housed in a brick building. Hot weather, however, caused the corpses in the burial pits to swell and rise from the ground in small hills. This putrefaction began to contaminate the local water. A horrible smell was pervasive and seemed to beckon rats and other scavengers, so the SS filled a pit with wood and set it on fire, but bodies that are already all bones burn badly, even when placed on grills and turned now and then, as you might on a company cookout. Cremations continued to make problems, and scientific studies were undertaken to discover the most efficient methods of getting air to and around mounds of corpses so that the fire could breathe. As the Jews, naked, their possessions confiscated for auction in Berlin, were driven to the gas chambers at Treblinka, the third camp, by biting dogs and men with whips and iron bars, their wails of despair and screams from pain were alarming others, so the SS recruited a small orchestra to drown the hubbub by playing local hit tunes.

When, in April 1943, Himmler ordered the camps closed and their presence erased, the job was almost done, although the task had become more difficult and on several occasions a few prisoners of war and a passel of Jews had broken out, killing several guards and embarrassing officials. The Germans covered some sites with shrubbery, trees, and flowers; this concealment remained rudimentary, but even the most inadequate erasures would give comfort later to those who denied the existence and/or operation of the gas chambers. By the summer of 1944 grave robbers had arrived, looking for the gold that might have been missed, only to turn up bones and rotting clothes.

Evans supplies very instructive details of the camps' procedures so that we may measure just how flourishing evil can become when provided with healthy circumstances. The novelty of Auschwitz was the use of a chemical pesticide called Zyklon-B, whose most active ingredient was sulfuric acid and whose lethal fumes were discovered by an accident that asphyxiated a cat. It was used in obedience to the following directions: "The men were herded into the room, the doors were sealed, then powdered Zyklon-B was shaken down through holes in the roof. The warmth generated by the bodies packed into the chamber below quickly turned it into a deadly gas." Those chosen for work detail had a serial number tattooed on their left arm that is now notorious and essential to the cinema.

Some camps were for show, like the back lots of movie studios, and were unable to make direct contributions to the killings, only to mislead chosen visitors about them. In a few ghettos (Warsaw is the best known) there were uprisings as well as scattered signs of individual resistance by the Polish underground; but what slowed the German war on humanity (besides the Soviet army) was simply the size and consequent inefficiency of it. Evans ascribes the principal cause of the monstrous behavior required of its organizers to their "visceral hatred of Jews," but the word "visceral" tends to beg the question. How was anti-Semitism, so patently false in all its ages of activity, able to lodge itself in so many minds and thereafter weaken—no, remove—their moral character? How, in general, do people become slaves of foolish ideologies, support them with treasure, allegiance, and time, and act, at their behest, so vilely, so contrary to their own interest? History is full of absurdities masquerading as absolutes. Like whooping cough, beliefs get to children early, make their symptoms chronic, hold out useless hopes, and offer vain excuses. It is reason's business to disbelieve, but the voices of reason have as much effect here as frogs in a swamp.

This book has many themes that a reader might follow instead of the bloody course I've chosen, such as the struggles for power among the many Nazi administrators when any one of them was trying to obtain status, protect his perks, or strengthen his grip, during both sweet times and sour. Hitler repeatedly replaced one medal bearer with another and blamed them for trying to save their troops when the order was to die. Meantime, in the midst of a war that was not going well, there were other wars that developed a personality of their own the way Verdun did during World War I: such as the siege of Leningrad ("the city's inhabitants were starving, eating cats, dogs, rats and even each other"); the struggle for Stalingrad ("Even those who were not hospitalized were sick, starving, frostbitten and exhausted"); or the Battle of Kursk ("the greatest land battle in history").

Setting cities on fire seemed the favored method of bringing death from the air. Evans's description of the raids and incendiary bombings of Hamburg is especially graphic. Although troops did get dug in, as they had in World War I, panzers brought fluidity to the front line that matched the maneuvers of armadas of planes.

As all the wars that made up the Second World War began to go badly, so did the temperament of the German people and their enthusiasm for it. It could be observed that Party members no longer wore their Party badges. After the bombing of Hamburg, angry citizens who observed that symbol in the street might tear the insignia from the wearer's coat. The Germans could become audibly grouchy if the government cut their ration of bread, but not so much when it killed Jews. By this time in the concluding history of the Third Reich the numbers in the text no longer refer to murdered undesirables or captured soldiers but to bushels of imported wheat, the total of factory workers building airplanes, or the limit of calories allowed each citizen; and the narrative, always heavy with statistics, is likely to sink out of the view of the eye.

In the aftermaths of heavy and repeated bombing, dazed German citizens were forced to find places among the ruins of their cities to bury bodies wrapped in paper like parcels, since the cemeteries were full and incineration was not feasible. What could burn, had. The dead were hidden in mass graves amid household furnishings—beds, jars, pots, clothing, carpets, cabinets—strewn about in a tumble of plaster, bricks, and stones. The picture Evans paints contradicts the view, frequently held, that the bombings did not have any noticeable effect on the German people's will to fight. That will was weakening rapidly, as was that of the armed forces, increasingly beset on multiple fronts, misled by Hitler's intransigence, and compelled by the Soviets' superior numbers to retreat. Such cohesiveness as remained depended upon a continuing hatred of Jewry and Soviet Communism, loyalty to their comrades in arms, and a realistic awareness of the consequences of defeat; as well as a fear of their own officers, frantic to maintain discipline, who were fond of courts-martial, and the firing squads that shot twenty-one thousand men as a result of the incredible three million trials ordered for numerous offenses. The Reich also began to lose allies—Bulgaria first, then all of Italy, whose failures Germany was required to punish by corralling 650,000 Italian soldiers for chain-gang-style labor (fifty thousand eventually died in harness) and executing six thousand others who resisted.

As the German armies fell back they enjoyed the classic revenge of burning any hospital, handy town, field, or manor they encountered, as well as employing some of the lesser forms of vandalism: feasting in occupied homes, stealing bedding, toys, clothes, shoes, and relaxing after their larger exertions by trying on the owner's hats, smashing what would readily smash, and leaving toilets aswim with their stools. Jews were required to ransom themselves with gold. This could occasionally work. Members of the partisan resistance were sometimes shot in conveniently located catacombs, an admirable economy of means. The German troops did not fail to use geography as a weapon, flooding the Pontine marshes back to pre-Mussolini levels and reintroducing malarial mosquitoes that produced at least ninety-eight thousand cases for them in two years, not all deadly, although the Germans took the local quinine with them when they fled. Straight-out germ warfare was unusual for the Nazis, who preferred more indirect methods—to overwork and starve their victims until they fell ill of disease.

Death is the repeated motif of this essay, and necessarily of Evans's monumental book, because death and the threat of death were the principal tools of Nazi rule—the noose, the gas, the gun. For citizens, a list of actions punishable by death might begin with the use of a weapon while committing a crime, hoarding food supplies, damaging military equipment, or making faulty munitions, and end with anything that hindered the war effort, including an injurious comment. Criminals serving a term greater than eight years were too costly to the state to keep swaddled in prison's comforts and were likely to be packed off "for extermination by labor." Some due for release before eight years had passed were retained until they qualified for this extinction. "So many executions were taking place in Germany's state prisons by this time that the Ministry of Justice allowed them at any time of the day instead of, as previously, only at dawn." And the prisons filled and emptied like bowls of peanuts on a bar.

So hospitals, prisons, courts, police, ordinary murderers, labor gangs, suicides, soldiers, Gestapo, the SS, partisans, local militias, enemy fire were all active agents of death, death from all sides, the way a billiard caroms: death that fell from the air, death borne by swampy water, death that opened from the earth as if every furrow were a mouth, death by whispered denunciation, death by every means imaginable including highway accidents, common fevers, cancers, strokes, and old age. Yet only one Nazi unit was called the Death's Head, indicating considerable restraint. Of course, there was little need for public boasting about the regime's death-dealing skills. The two Christian institutions (the Lutheran and the Catholic Churches) were quite aware of the killing sprees in their countries of residence but remained mum out of fear of reprisals either from the regime if the Nazis won or from the Jews if Germany lost. This also may have been the most common attitude among the general population. "From 1943 onwards, they were mentally preparing themselves to deflect this retribution as far as they were able, by denying all knowledge of the genocide once the war was lost."

That the war was lost only increased the feverish pace of the killings, which were now defended as a moral necessity, a task to be completed despite temptations to tenderness, and because the cleansing was almost complete. Himmler's message was: The world may condemn us for carrying out such an unpleasant assignment, but somebody's got to do it. The Jews who remained to be gassed lived mostly in Hungary, whose Admiral Miklós Horthy had refused so far Hitler's requests to hand them over. The German army moved in and immediately began carrying out their obligations by transporting 438,000 Jews to Auschwitz before Horthy was able to put a stop to their shipments.

Once a repressive regime begins to stumble, there will be many ready to help with a push, but in Germany every sort of opposition had been so effectively frightened into silence or rubbed out during the time National Socialism reached or solidified its power that even Hitler's most ardent enemies remained compromised, divided, and weak. The Prussian conservatives were often guilty themselves of ordering Jews into camps, or willing, as a postwar gesture, to repeal the legal rules against Jews only because "the very small number of Jewish survivors would no longer constitute a 'danger for the German race.'" For some, discrimination was legit if murder wasn't.

The plots to assassinate Hitler were often ham-handed and always unlucky, but they led to lots of death anyway, as the conspirators were executed or killed themselves—to the sum of five thousand. For those arrested, the firing squad was preferred, and for the suicides, the revolver or poison capsule were both more popular than the grenade. For the cinema fans, films were made during which numerous traitors were hanged by a thin rope to slow the strangle, and their pants pulled down for the purpose of postmortem humiliation. Hitler particularly liked these showings. Under the policy of "leave no possible enemy behind," wives, children, cousins, aunts, and uncles of the plotters were sent to Ravensbrück.

V1 and V2 rockets bore the same old bombs, only the method of delivery was new; however, nuclear weapons were unique to life and death equally. The scale of their killing could not yet be clearly imagined, but it was believed to be considerable. It would be the ultimate triumph for a death-mad world and would, again, put the German nation at the wheel. Had Hitler wished to hurry the appropriate research, there still would not have been time or materials enough to complete the project. Hitler did not have any enthusiasm for nuclear physics anyway, because it was an area of study he felt belonged too intimately to the Jews. There was at least one very promising nerve gas, but it was difficult to manufacture without killing many of its makers, and continued to have the same flaws poison gas has always had: it blows where the wind goes. As Albert Speer admitted, they also had drones on the drawing table, jet planes, and heat-seeking missiles, but these advancements would have to wait for the Americans, who would have German expertise to aid them.

In the last days, to settle old scores while pretending the enemy was within, Germans began killing one another. It was nearly as if anyone who looked gloomy should be shot. But they were still killing with dedication if not cleverness and invention. Five hundred sixty-five inmates of a women's prison were, in the middle of an icy winter, walked to another jail twenty-two miles away. They kept falling over one another until only forty remained. From households there was little to loot, but women were still available for rape. Former dignitaries, foreign and domestic, who hadn't been murdered but held hostage instead, were executed forthwith. Those in prison for whatever reason were killed simply because they were handy, just in case, and because the Jews were already dead and someone should be dying: "sick inmates were shot in their beds. . . ." Advancing enemy armies made the murder industry in the concentration camps a matter of some urgency. Yet evidence of gas chambers, shooting locales, and burial parks had to be removed too, and it was difficult to clean up and kill at the same time. Russian prisoners of war, retreating along with German troops, died of weather, deep snows, and neglect. Killing was now casual wherever you were in the combat zone. Death marches so disorganized they "meandered across the country, even doubling back on themselves," at least emptied a camp by scattering bodies over treks of sometimes 250 miles. Nothing but surrender or the arrival of Allied armies slowed and finally ended this last deadly tantrum.

The Germans had failed to drown women in the Pripet Marshes and had neglected that form of murder almost altogether, but now, as if wishing to fulfill every possibility, the regional leader for Hamburg, Karl Kaufmann, loaded ten thousand leftovers onto three ships tied up in Lübeck. These vessels were by happenstance bombed by British planes, and most of the prisoners, crowded into holds like slaves, drowned when the ships exploded, rolled over, and sank.

When the Red Army reached Auschwitz it found many corpses, but the SS had left seven thousand prisoners in some stage of life, and they had not destroyed every evidence of the camp's activity. "Russian soldiers painstakingly catalogued 837,000 women's coats and dresses, 44,000 pairs of shoes and 7.7 tons of human hair." Finally, the Germans had acquired enough coats.

The Nazis were down for the count, but the count was only at nine when Allied warplanes kicked dozens of towns nearly out of existence (Dresden, most infamously) and the Red Army arrived to repopulate the ruins by raping the women who remained. They brought with them destruction, pillage, theft, murder, and savage revenge. Death, it seems, was also an Allied deity.

Evans, after his usual sober and responsible account of how the end came for Hitler and Goebbels, writes: "The deaths in the bunker and the burned-out streets above were only the crest of a vast wave of suicides without precedent in modern history." This penultimate killing was sometimes done out of an ancestral sense of honor, or to avoid the shame and indignity of a trial that would brand them as criminals, or to avoid the mistreatment of their displayed corpses, or out of despair for Germany and the failure of their enterprises; but not often because they were wrong, not because they were guilty, not because they were moral monsters and could no longer bear the creatures of evil they had become.

Afterward, death would add still more to its roster with trials and hangings. Not just the guilty paid its price. In what was perhaps the final irony, many survivors of the camps would kill themselves because they were alive.

Harper's Magazine, 2009
Published in *Life Sentences*, 2012

THEORY

PHILOSOPHY AND THE
FORM OF FICTION

I

So much of philosophy is fiction. Dreams, doubts, fears, ambitions, ecstasies . . . if philosophy were a stream, they would stock it like fishes. Although fiction, in the manner of its making, is pure philosophy, no novelist has created a more dashing hero than the handsome Absolute, or conceived more dramatic extrications—the soul's escape from the body, for instance, or the will's from cause. And how thin and unlaced the forms of *Finnegans Wake* are beside any of the *Critiques*; how sunlit Joyce's darkness, how few his parallels, how loose his correspondences. With what emotion do we watch the flight of the Alone to the Alone, or discover that *"der Welt ist alles, was der Fall ist,"* or read that in a state of nature the life of man is "solitary, poor, nasty, brutish, and short." Which has written the greater *Of Human Bondage,* or brooded more musically upon life's miseries, or dwelled more lovingly upon the outlines of its own reflection? Is it not exhilarating to be told that the "desire and pursuit of the whole is called love"? And if we wish to become critical we can observe that Descartes's recourse to a gland in the skull to account for our intercourse with ourselves is a simple failure of the imagination, and that for the philosophers, God is always in His machine, flying about on wires like Peter Pan.

Novelist and philosopher are both obsessed with language, and make themselves up out of concepts. Both, in a way, create worlds. Worlds? But the worlds of the novelist, I hear you say, do not exist. Indeed. As for that— they exist more often than the philosophers'. Then, too—how seldom does it seem to matter. Who honestly cares? They are divine games. Both play at gods as others play at bowls; for there is frequently more reality in fairy tales than in these magical constructions of the mind, works equally of thought and energy and will, which raise up into sense and feeling, as to life, acts of pure abstraction, passes logical, and intuitions both securely empty and as fitted for passage as time.

Games—yet different games. Fiction and philosophy often make most acrimonious companions. To be so close in blood, so brotherly and like in body, can inspire a subtle hate; for their rivalry is sometimes less than open in its damage. They wound with advice. They smother with love. And they impersonate one another. Then, while in the other's guise and gait and oratory, while their brother's smiling ape and double, they do his suicide. Each expires in a welter of its own surprise.

Philosophers multiply our general nouns and verbs; they give fresh sense to stale terms; "man" and "nature" are their characters; while novelists toil at filling in the blanks in proper names and at creating other singular affairs. A novelist may pin a rose to its stem as you might paper a tail to its donkey, the rose may blush at his command, but the philosopher can elevate that reddening from an act of simple verbal predication to an angellike ingression, ennobling it among Beings. The soul, we must remember, is the philosopher's invention, as thrilling a creation as, for instance, Madame Bovary. So I really should point out, though I shall say little more about it, that fiction is far more important to philosophy than the other way round. However, the novelist can learn more from the philosopher, who has been lying longer; for novelizing is a comparatively new, unpolished thing. Though philosophers have written the deeper poetry, traditionally philosophy has drawn to it the inartistic and the inarticulate, those of too mechanical a mind to move theirs smoothly, those too serious to see, and too fanatical to feel. All about us now, the dull and dunce-eyed stool themselves to study corners.

Souls, essences, the bickering legions of immortals, the countless points of view which religion and philosophy have shaped, are seldom understood as metaphorical, as expressions of our wishes and our fears, as desperate political maneuvers, strategies of love or greed, as myths which make a sense which some men may, at moments, need; for the celebrated facts of life, whatever they are, are not very forceful, and even the most stubborn and most brutish ones (that man must eat to live, for instance) allow an indefinite number of attitudes and interpretations, including vegetarianism or solemn pronouncements in favor of fish or stern edicts against pork and beans.

If games, then sometimes dangerous ones. Let us suppose for a moment that both our Russells and our Becketts are engaged in telling us *how it is,* that the novelist and the philosopher are companions in a common enterprise, though they go about it in different ways. The objects I see and sometimes label—pencil, paper, table, penny, chair—each seems solid yet is pocked with spaces, each seems steady yet is made of moving pieces: shape, steadiness, solidity, and color . . . are these illusions? I call the penny round, but I'm reminded I see an ellipse. I say the pencil's yellow, yet perhaps the yellow's painted in by eye, the yellow is the reading of a signal maybe, although the reading does not reside within the receiver, and possibly its actual home is in the mind. The what? The mind. Who, or what, is that? A character. Like Micawber. Going on in the firm belief that something will turn up. Hasn't he made my world strange, this philosopher? I find I have a body, then a mind. I find that the world I live in, the objects I manipulate, are in great part my constructions. I shortly come to believe in many invisible beings, gods and angels, wills and powers, atoms, voids. Where I once thought an anger "out there" like a demon, a color "out there" in an object, connections "out there" holding hands with things, I now think otherwise. Loose bundles of affections and sensations pass me like so many clouds of dust in space (and, dear heaven, who am I?).

Beckett tells us that we live in garbage cans; sit at the side of empty roads, in emptiness awaiting emptiness; crawl blindly through mud. My skin is the tattered dirty clothing of a tramp, my body a broken bicycle, my living space is earth to just beneath my shoulders, my speech the twittering of an unoiled pump. Hasn't he made my world strange, this novelist? No, of course our lives are not a muddy crawl—*apparently*. But that is mere appearance. We're fooled constantly. We think our emotions fine when they are coarse; we think our ideas profound when they are empty, original when commonplace; we think at first we are living richly, deeply, when all we possess is a burlap bag, unopened tins, dirty thoughts, and webby privates.

I cannot help that my home still looks well furnished, or my body trim; I cannot help the colors which I seem to come upon, or the unflinching firmness of my chair; I cannot help I glory in my sex or feel and think and act as one and not as a divided community; for I'm incurably naïve, incurably in love with deception; still, I can be taught, I can learn suspicion, learn that things aren't really what they seem; I can learn to hate my pleasures, condemn my desires, doubt my motives, deny my eyes, put unseen creatures in the world and then treat them with greater reverence, give them greater powers than those I innocently know—to bow and bow and bow in their direction; I can replace my love for people with a love for principle,* and even pursue a life beyond the grave as a program for the proper pursuit of this one. Bravo, novelists and philosophers; good show.

Save the appearances, Plato said. Then make them all realities. No better

* This point is developed at length in "The Case of the Obliging Stranger" in *Fiction and the Figures of Life* (New York: Alfred A. Knopf, 1970).

way. Yet without that splendid distinction, the novelist as philosopher and the philosopher as novelist would both be out of business.

2

The aesthetic aim of any fiction is the creation of a verbal world, or a significant part of such a world, alive through every order of its Being. Its author may not purpose this—authors purpose many things—but the construction of some sort of object, whether too disorderly to be a world or too mechanical to be alive, cannot be avoided. The story must be told and its telling is a record of the choices, inadvertent or deliberate, the author has made from all the possibilities of language. Whether or not it was correct of Aristotle to reason, as he apparently sometimes did, from the syntax of the Greek language to the syntax of reality, the art of fiction consists of such reasoning, since its people and their destinies, the things they prize, the way they feel, the landscapes they inhabit, are indistinct from words and all their orderings.

The artist's task is therefore twofold. He must show or exhibit his world, and to do this he must actually make something, not merely describe something that might be made. This takes tremendous technical skill, and except in rare and highly favored persons, great labor.* Furthermore, he must present us with a world that is philosophically adequate, and this requires of him the utmost exercise of thought and sensibility. No one should mistake the demand. It is not for a comprehensive and correct philosophy. Truth, I am convinced, has antipathy for art. It is best when a writer has a deep and abiding indifference to it, although as a private person it may be vital to him. If the idea of truth is firmly defined and firmly held in line—if it is not, like Proteus, permitted to change its shape at every questioning—the very great difference between the theoretical formulations of the philosopher and the concrete creations of the novelist must make itself felt. The concepts of the philosopher speak, the words of the novelist are mute; the philosopher invites us to pass through his words to his subject: man, God, nature, moral law; while the novelist, if he is any good, will keep us kindly imprisoned in his language—there is literally nothing beyond.† Of course, if the phi-

---

* For more on this, see "In Terms of the Toenail: Fiction and the Figures of Life" in *Fiction and the Figures of Life*.

† This is a recurrent theme—see especially "The Concept of Character in Fiction" (page 657)—though I qualify it in "In Terms of the Toenail: Fiction and the Figures of Life" in *Fiction and the Figures of Life*.

losopher has made up his subject, as I suspect he has made up God, sin, and sense data, then he is performing for us, at least in part, as the novelist performs. Theology, it appears, is one-half fiction, one-half literary criticism.

A philosophy may be "adequate" without being true. If it answers, or shows how to answer, the questions its assumptions and its inferential laws allow, it is complete; if its conclusions follow from these assumptions as its rules dictate, it is consistent; and if the questions it permits are, in any degree, the same that everyday life puts to the ordinary man, it and its answers are to that degree significant; for the everyday questions of ordinary life are always addressed to those ultimate appearances which we remember must be saved. Any philosophy complete, consistent, and significant is, in the sense here used, adequate. It is adequate within its range, although its range may not be vast. A long and complex novel, or series of novels, however, may present us with a world complete through every principle and consequence, rivaling in its comprehensiveness the most grandiose philosophical systems; while a brief story may exhibit only an essential part from which we may infer, at our desire and leisure, much of the remainder. Finally, the artist is not asked to construct an adequate philosophy, but a philosophically adequate world, a different matter altogether. He creates an object, often as intricate and rigorous as any mathematic, often as simple and undemanding as a baby's toy, from whose nature, as from our own world, a philosophical system may be inferred; but he does not, except by inadvertence or mistaken aesthetic principle, deem it his task to philosophize. A man who makes a thing that moves utilizes the laws of motion, although he may be unaware of their existence. All he cares about is the accomplishment of his particular design. The worlds which, in like manner, the writer creates, are only imaginatively possible ones; they need not be at all like any real one, and the metaphysics which any fiction implies is likely to be meaningless or false if taken as nature's own. The man who makes machines intuitively, the laws of heat and light and motion in his fingers, is inventive. Indeed, he may invent, in the principles of its running, what science knows nothing of. The writer, similarly, thinks through the medium of which he is the master, and when his world arises, novel and complete—sometimes as arbitrary and remote from real things as the best formal game, sometimes as searchingly advanced and sharp to the fact as the gadget of the most inspired tinker—his world displays that form of embodied thought which is imagination.

Nature is more than its regulations. Galileo follows the swinging Pisa Cathedral lamps with his dreadful eyes, but it is not the spill of light and shadow, the halo or the burning, that attracts him. It is the quantity in the action, the principle in the thing. So any maker, bent on rendering concrete the dominion of number, must find the qualities of sensation which will embody them.* Nor can he merely name the qualities over, for what he makes is a world, not a diagram, and what he makes must live. Swinging has a law, but before the law of swinging come the swings.

Writers whose grasp of aesthetic principles is feeble, or whose technique is poor and unpracticed, or whose minds are shallow and perceptions dim, give us stories which are never objects for contemplation, but arguments; they give us, at best, dramatized philosophy, not philosophically significant drama; or, if they know they must exhibit or present, show us Bradleyan selves in Berkeleyan suits sitting down to Boolean tea.

The philosophy that most writers embody in their work, with those amendments and additions which any strong personality will invariably insist upon, since it can only identify itself with what it calls its own begetting, is usually taken unconsciously from the tradition with which the writer is allied. As a result, a writer whose work has little aesthetic merit may retain an historical or a philosophical interest. He may have represented, in just the confused way it existed, the world his generation saw and believed they lived in; or he may have produced a model of some philosopher's theoretical vision; and since the philosopher's vision is as often as not blind at the last to the signals of reality, it may be as near to the sight of fact his theory will ever come. On such occasions the work is commentary. Some novels are of very great philosophical importance, as it is doubtless one test of a philosophy to imagine, more simply than the cosmos itself does, what it would be like to live under its laws—whether, in other words, with its principles it is possible to build something that will run. Such imaginative construction is particularly useful for the evaluation of moral and political systems. One wants to know what people, good according to Kant or Nietzsche or William James, are like, and how it feels to house the conscience of St. Paul or guard with the eyes of Augustine the affairs of the city of God. An artist may precede the sciences in discovery, just as the inventor may, by incorporating in his work ideas which turn out true, but his success in this is not aesthetic, and depends entirely on what science decides.

An idea must first be thought before it can be tested, but a principle encased in fiction has, most likely, not been thought of at all. It has been used. This may have been what Plato had in mind when he classified his citizens according to their nearness to the Forms. Certainly it is one thing to employ an idea, another to state it in a manner suitable to thought, while yet another to carry out the tests which make it true or false. It is a sadly limited

---

* More on embodiment in "The Concept of Character in Fiction."

view of the power of mind in man to suppose that only truth employs or pleasures it. It appears that any expression suitable to science must be quantitatively abstract, and that thought itself proceeds by quantities and extensions, yet one may contemplate the most purely abstract and most purely quantitative system for the values of the system's sake, and so far as this is done, and is the end of such pure systems, they, and the opposite pole of art, have the same appreciative aim, and are in value much akin; for creative thought and creative imagination are not so much spurred on by truth in any synthetic sense as by sublimity—a vision of absolute organization. It is really a moral insistence, this insistence that truth be first, whether it is the Platonist, who requires that Ideas do the work of things, or the Pragmatist, who demands that things perform the functions of ideas.

3

For the purposes of analysis we can regard the sentences of fiction as separate acts of creation. They are the most elementary instances of what the author has constructed. Wittgenstein believed for a time that a proposition, in the disposition of its names, pictured a possibly equivalent arrangement of objects. This is a pleasant fancy, and plainly must be true . . . of fictions; though sentences in stories should do more than simply configure things. Each should contrive (through order, meaning, sound, and rhythm) a moving unity of fact and feeling.

Before us is the empty page, the deep o'er which, like God, though modestly, we brood. But that white page, what is it? Perhaps it is the ideally empty consciousness of the reader—a dry wineskin or a *tabula rasa*. And if, as authors, we think this way, then what we want is a passive mind and, as in love, an utterly receptive woman. Thus our attitudes, before the first act of creation, make a philosophical difference. What shall we sail upon it first?

All known all white bare white body fixed one yard legs joined like sewn,

Beckett's "Ping" begins. An audacious first term: all. The sentence isolates its words; they slowly fall, slowly revolve, slowly begin to group themselves. We are in the hands of an ancient atomist.

All known all white bare white body fixed one yard legs joined like sewn. Light heat white floor one square yard never seen. White walls one yard by two white ceiling one square yard never seen.

Stately monotonous strokes, like measured beats of a gong, occur within, but do not fill, this void. Though here the gong sometimes emits a ping. Truly, nothing is previous. Groups first formed form the first connections, and are repeated.

> Bare white body fixed only the eyes only just. Traces blurs light grey almost white on white. Hands hanging palms front white feet heels together right angle. Light heat white planes shining white bare white body fixed ping fixed elsewhere.

With what remarkable confidence, on the other hand, does Jane Austen reach for our responses. She does not form a chaos or create from nothing. Her pen moves through us; we part a bit and yield the paths of her design. How much we are expected to know already: manners, values, social structure. She thinks in far, far longer lengths; her silences are like the silences which occur in happy conversations; her spaces are interiors, tamed and quiet; she does not begin, she ends, in terror, and the metaphysical.

Let's descend into the sentence briefly, on a rope for our return. How amazing they can be, how strange. The shortest one can spell us back to infancy. ("A cow broke in tomorrow morning to my Uncle Toby's fortifications," for instance.) The meaning of a sentence may make a unity, comprise some whole, but inevitably its concepts are loosed one by one like the release of pigeons. We must apprehend them, then, like backward readers: here's a this, now a that, now a this. The sentence must be sounded, too; it has a rhythm, speed, a tone, a flow, a pattern, shape, length, pitch, conceptual direction. The sentence confers reality upon certain relations, but it also controls our estimation, apprehension, and response to them. Every sentence, in short, takes metaphysical dictation, and it is the sum of these dictations, involving the whole range of the work in which the sentences appear, which accounts for its philosophical quality, and the form of life in the thing that has been made.

In Beckett's sentences, quoted above, there is no subordination, but a community of equals—well, hardly a community either, though the primordial relationship of adjective to noun is not entirely suppressed. This is not the place to get lost in details, but we are all aware of the kind of influence Aristotle's subject-predicate logic had on his philosophy, and on all those which followed for quite a long time. The novelist's characteristic grammatical forms affect the building of his book at least as much, though we must be careful to notice not only his words' syntactical pasts, but their present syntactical functions. So some sentences are crowded with nouns; some contain largely connectives. Some sentences are long and tightly wound; others are as hard and blunt as a hammer. Some combine events of contrasting sizes, like a sneeze and the fall of Rome; others set dogs at bears, link the abstract and the concrete, quality and number, relation and property, act and thing. In some worlds the banjo and its music are two banjos; in others all the instruments dissolve into their music, that into a landscape or a climate, thus finally, through the weather, to an ear.

The Humean sentence will reduce objects to their qualities, maintain an equality between them by using nonsubordinating conjunctions, be careful not to confuse emotion and reflection with perception, but at the same time will allow their presence in the same onward flow. Everywhere, Hume makes his world out of lists and collections. Some novelists, like I. B. Singer, for example, drain the mental from their books as if it were pus in a wound. Thoughts are rendered as public speech; there is recourse to journals; incidents and objects are presented always as the public might see them; and even inner temptations—lusts, hates, fears—receive embodiment as visibly material demons.* Henry James's sentences are continuous qualifications, nuance is the core and not the skin;† and the average idealist, proceeding with a similar scrupulosity, treats his entire work as the progressive exploration and exposure of a single subject. It would suit him if there were no ordinary periods, no real beginning or real end, if every word were an analytic predicate of one ultimate Idea.

Imagine for a moment we are making up a man, breathing life into a clay lung.

> He stood in the mud: long, thin, brown in his doctor's gown of fur, with his black flapped cap that buttoned well under his chin and let out his brown, lean, shaven and humorous face like a woodpecker's peering out of a hole in a tree.

What is the shape of Achilles's nose? what color were his eyes? Achilles is what Achilles does; he has no secret wishes, secret dreams; he has no cautiously hidden insides. Shall we make our man on that model, out of deeds? or shall we see him through his station: prince or clown, clerk or plumber, servant or secretary, general or priest? Shall we dress him in his features as

---

* This is a central concern of my essay on Singer, "The Shut-In" in *Fiction and the Figures of Life*.

† See "The High Brutality of Good Intentions" (page 415) and "In the Cage" in *Fiction and the Figures of Life*.

Ford here puts Magister Nicholas Udal in his clothes? Whether a man has thick lips or thin, crafty ones or cruel, we can always count on Ford to tell us, though in other men's fictions many are lipless. The colon contrives to give the qualities which follow it to Udal's whole muddy standing, not to Udal and his form alone. Observe what happens if we remove it, and at the same time alter the order of our apprehension of these details:

> *He was long, thin, and brown in his doctor's gown of fur, with his black flapped cap that buttoned well under his chin and let out his brown, lean, shaven and humorous face like a woodpecker's peering out of a hole in a tree. He stood in the mud.*

The original passage is packed with possessives, the dominant relation is that of ownership, but the Magister need not own everything. Can we feel the effect of progressively loosening these ties, the clothing first, and then the features?

> *He stood in the mud: long, thin, brown in a doctor's gown of fur, with a black flapped cap that buttoned well under his chin and let out his brown, lean, shaven and humorous face like a woodpecker's peering out of a hole in a tree.*

> *He stood in the mud: long, thin, brown in a doctor's gown of fur, with a black flapped cap that buttoned well under a chin and let out a brown, lean, shaven and humorous face like a woodpecker's peering out of a hole in a tree.*

Perversely, let us let him own his clothes but not his face.

> *He stood in the mud: long, thin, brown in a doctor's gown of fur, with his black flapped cap that buttoned well under a chin and let out a brown, lean, shaven and humorous face like a woodpecker's peering out of a hole in a tree.*

It is not simply that our understanding of Udal changes; our understanding changes because Udal has become a figure in a changed world.

We might at first be inclined to think that style is a form of perception; that each sentence reveals the way the writer looks at the world—

for example, observe the differences between (1) We walked through the woods. The trees had leaves. The leaves were newly green. (2)

We walked through the woods. New leaves greened the trees. (3) We walked the greening woods. (4) It seemed the greening woods walked while we stood.

—but, strictly speaking, style cannot be, itself, a kind of vision; the notion is very misleading, for we do not have before us some real forest which we might feel ourselves free to render in any number of different ways; we have only the words which make up this one. There are no descriptions in fiction, there are only constructions,* and the principles which govern these constructions are persistently philosophical. The same, for that matter, is true of narration, dialogue, character, and the rest. Just as the painter's designs help make his object, the lines of the novelist offer no alternatives, they are not likely interpretations of anything, but are the thing itself.

4

Thus so many of the things which are false or foolish when taken to the world—in religion or philosophy—become the plainest statements of what's true when taken to fiction, for in its beginning *is* the word, and if the aesthetic aim of any fiction is the creation of a world, then the writer is creator—he is god—and the relation of the writer to his work represents in ideal form the relation of the fabled Creator to His creation.

Once, God was regarded as the cause of all, as the Great Historian with a plan for His people, the Architect, the Lawgiver, the principle of Good; so that if Mary sickened, the cause was God, and if Mary died, it was God who called her Home, and if anything happened whatever, it was ordained by Him, indeed it was counted on, by Him, from the beginning. He saw things, all things, plain—plainer surely than any novelist ever saw his story before a word of it went down. So that really, in this created world, there are no necessary beings, there are no categorical creatures, and events do not follow one another out of the past, because of the past, but everlastingly out of God, because of God. In a movie, too, where everything is predestined, the illusion of internal structure is maintained, as though one part of the film explained the occurrence of another. However, the director had the scenes shot; had them spliced as he desired; and the sensation that the villain's insult has provoked the hero's glove is an appearance often not even carefully contrived. In the story of Mary, if Mary dies, the novelist killed her, her broken heart did not. The author of any popular serial knows, as Dickens did, that

* See "The Concept of Character in Fiction."

to the degree he makes his world real to his readers, to that degree they will acknowledge his authorship; hold him responsible; and beg him to make the world good, although evil seems present in it; beg him to bring all to a moral and materially glorious close, in clouds and hallelujahs. Though such appeals may cause smiles in the sophisticated, they are appeals more rationally directed to the actual power than those, exactly parallel, delivered by the faithful in their prayers to God. The novelist is uncomfortable. He may enjoy his alleged omnipotence, his omniscience and omnipresence, but with it, spoiling it, is responsibility. What about all that perfection? Can he take upon himself this burden? Can he assure his readers that his world is good, whatever happens? He can explain evil no better than the theologian; therefore shortly the novelist who assumes the point of view of the omnipotent, omniscient, and omnipresent narrator begins to insist upon his imperfection; apologize, in a gentle way perhaps, for his cutpurses, whores, his murderers, and in general surrender his position. "I'm sorry Becky doesn't seem as sweet as she should, but what can I do about it? That's just how she is." "Well, I'm terribly sorry about all this sordidness, as sorry as you are," he may say, "but that's how the world is, and what am I, poor fellow, but a dime-store mirror held to it?" This is a sly device. And the worlds which the novelist creates are shortly deprived of their deities. At last the convention seems acceptable only if it's all in fun. God snickers and pushes parsons into ditches. And when the novelist begins to explain that, of course, omnipotence is artistically vulgar; that one must limit oneself to a point of view, he is insisting, for *his* world, upon the restriction of knowledge to the human, and often only to a few of these, and finally only to rare moments occurring in the best minds. He gives up his powers to a set of principles. He allows himself to be governed by them, not to govern, as if God stepped down in favor of moving mass and efficient causes, so to say: "This is not mine; I do not this; I am not here." Novels in which the novelist has effaced himself create worlds without gods.

Even outside books time passes. These days, often, the novelist resumes the guise of God; but he is merely one of us now, full of confusion and error, sin and cleverness. He creates as he is able; insists upon his presence and upon his wickedness and fallibility, too. He is not sure about what he knows; his powers have no great extension; he's more imperfect than otherwise; he will appeal to us, even, for sympathy. Why not? He's of his time. Are there any deities who still have size?

An author may make up his own rules, like the god of the Deists, or take them from experience where he thinks he finds them ready-made; but the control which these rules exercise is little like that exercised by the laws of nature, whatever they are. The star-crossed lovers in books and plays are doomed, not because in the real world they would be, but because, far more simply, they are star-crossed. Simple slum conditions, as we know, do not so surely produce a certain sort as in novels they are bound to, and no amassing of detail is sufficient to ensure a perfectly determinate Newtonian conclusion. Authors who believe they must, to move their fictions, hunt endlessly through circumstances for plausible causes as they might hunt for them in life, have badly misunderstood the nature of their art—an enterprise where one word and one inferring principle may be enough.

As in a dice race, when we move over the squares with our colored disks, the dice impel us and the ruled lines guide. There are no choices. The position of each disk is strictly determined. We see the track, we know the throw, we can predict the new arrangement. Such a game is the simplest kind, and forms the simplest system. There is one rule of inference. Any principle that permits the rational expectation of some situation upon the occurrence of another is a principle of inference, and such a principle is called a rule when the conclusion to be inferred awaits an inferring power—a power that must be, therefore, ordered to its task—and is called a law when the inferring power acts, as it were, from within its premises. The form of the game, however, lies in number, the winner he who rolls the highest score; but this form is imaged out upon a table; disks describe the level of addition; and these are transmogrified by fancy into Thoroughbreds, while the player, through this really peculiar evidence of the superiority of man, becomes the owner of a stable. The adding of the dice can be expressed in many ways. This simple system is the foundation of many more complicated ones. There are principles, one might call them, of embodiment, wherein the players are enjoined to treat the disks and the squared path as representing the units and the total of addition. There are yet other principles, here assumed, that call the squared-up path a track, the flat disks horses. The game may make these assumptions explicit, but if it does not, the player may imagine for himself any other suitable kind of linear contest.

When God abdicates, or at least sanctions a belief in the end of miracle, He gives over his rule to inference. For fiction, the rules can be as many as the writer wishes, and they can be of any kind he wishes. They establish the logic, the order, of his world. They permit us to expect one event will follow another, or one sentence another, or one word another. To the degree words, sentences, and, materially, things and happenings follow without rule, the world is a world of chance. Since no work can exhibit a conformity to principle so complete each word is, in its place and time, inevitable and predictable, all fictional worlds contain at least an element of chance, and some, of course, a very high degree of it. It is merely a critical prejudice that requires from fiction a rigidly determined order. Chance, too, is a kind of principle, and can be brought to the understanding of reason. In the natural realm, the principle of causality is often regarded as the inferring instrument. Causality, in general, makes out the possibility of predicting events from the evidence of others. Since the inferring power is thought to reside otherwise than in the observer, any particular expression of it is a law. When, as in the game above, it is impossible to predict the future organization of a system on the basis simply of its present state and its governing rules or laws, and when the prediction must await the unpredictable disclosure of further facts— for instance, what the dice will read—then the system is a system based on chance. It must be borne in mind that the results of the game proceed inevitably from its nature, and that a system based on chance remains as beautifully systematic as any other. If what the fates decree must come to pass, chance can lie only in the way to it. Or each affair may be seen necessarily to unfold out of its past without anyone's being able to guess the ultimate consequences. Again, certainty and doubt about both end and means may be so shrewdly mixed, the reader is delightfully tossed between cruel suspense and calm inevitability. In the dice game, the players finger disks, but if the game, by its conventions, calls them horses, they are horses. However, to a fellow who, his disk dead-even with the others, resolutely calls all disks, and only waits the adding up of his account, art must ever be a failure; for it can succeed only through the cooperating imagination and intelligence of its consumers, who fill out, for themselves, the artist's world and make it round, and whose own special genius partly determines the ultimate glory of it.

The causal relation itself may be logically necessary or psychologically customary, formal or final, mechanical or purposive. It may be divinely empowered or materially blind. Causality in fiction is usually restricted to the principle that controls the order of constructed events, considered separately from whatever rule may govern the placement of symbols, the dress of the heroine, the names of the characters, and so on, if any rule does govern them. An event, however, may be anything from the twitch of an eyebrow to the commission of adultery, and a cause, any event which leads beyond itself to another. The plot (to risk that rightly abused word) is composed of those events the novelist has troubled to freshly arrange as causes, as opposed to those he has thrown in for vividness, but which cause nothing, or those concerning which he has let nonfictitious nature have its way. Nonfictitious nature has its way about a good deal. If in a story it rains, the streets usually get wet; if a man is stabbed, he bleeds; smoke can still be a sign of fire, and screams can be sounds of damsels in distress. No novel is without its assumptions. It is important to find them out, for they are not always the same assumptions the reader is ready, unconsciously, to make. Hawthorne could count on more than Henry James, as James complained. Do we any longer dare to infer goodness from piety, for example, evil from promiscuity, culture from rank?

And has not the world become, for many novelists, a place not only vacant of gods, but also empty of a generously regular and peacefully abiding nature on which the novelist might, in large, rely, so to concentrate on cutting a fine and sculptured line through a large mass taken for granted, and has it now also seemed to him absent of that perceptive and sympathetic reader who had his own genius and would undertake the labor, rather easy, of following the gracious turns that line might take; so that, with all these forms of vacantness about him, he has felt the need to reconstitute, entire, his world; to take nothing, if he felt the spur of that conceit, for granted, and make all new, distinct, apart, and finally, even, to provide, within the framework of his vision, the ideal reader, the writer's words his mind and eyes?

5

The use of philosophical ideas in the construction of fictional works—in a very self-conscious and critical way, I mean—has been hastened by the growing conviction that not only do these ideas often represent conceptual systems of considerable complexity, they have the further advantage of being almost wholly irrelevant as accounts of the real world. They are, that is, to a great degree *fictional* already, and ripe for fun and games. Then, too, the novelist now better understands his medium; he is ceasing to pretend that his business is to render the world; he knows, more often now, that his business is to *make* one, and to make one from the only medium of which he is a master—language. And there are even more radical developments.

There are metatheorems in mathematics and logic, ethics has its linguistic oversoul, everywhere lingos to converse about lingos are being contrived, and the case is no different in the novel. I don't mean merely those drearily predictable pieces about writers who are writing about what they are writing, but those, like some of the work of Borges, Barth, and Flann O'Brien, for example, in which the forms of fiction serve as the material upon which further forms can be imposed. Indeed, many of the so-called antinovels are really metafictions.*

Still, the philosophical analysis of fiction has scarcely taken its first steps.

---

* A number of the preceding points are developed in "Mirror, Mirror," concerning Nabokov; in "Pricksongs & Descants," concerning Coover; in "The Leading Edge of the Trash Phenomenon," concerning Barthelme; and in "Imaginary Borges and His Books" (page 568). All can be found in *Fiction and the Figures of Life*.

Philosophers continue to interpret novels as if they were philosophies themselves, platforms to speak from, middens from which may be scratched important messages for mankind; they have predictably looked for content, not form; they have regarded fictions as ways of viewing reality and not as additions to it. There are many ways of refusing experience. This is one of them.*

So little is known of the power of the gods in the worlds of fiction, or of the form of cause, or of the nature of soul, or of the influence of evil, or of the essence of good. No distinction is presently made between laws and rules of inference and conventions of embodiment, or their kinds. The role of chance or of assumption, the re-creative power of the skillful reader, the mastery of the sense of internal life, the forms of space and time: how much is known of these? The ontological significance of the subordinate clause, or the short stiff sentence regularly conjoined to more, or new words, or inversion—all passed over. Writers are seldom recognized as empiricists, idealists, skeptics, or stoics, though they ought—I mean, now, in terms of the principles of their constructions, for Sartre is everywhere recognized as an existentialist leaning left, but few have noticed that the construction of his novels is utterly bourgeois. No search is made for first principles, none for rules, and in fact all capacity for thought in the face of fiction is so regularly abandoned as to reduce it to another form of passive and mechanical amusement. The novelist has, by this ineptitude, been driven out of healthy contact with his audience, and the supreme values of fiction sentimentalized. The art of the novel is now a mature art, as constantly the source of that gratification found in the purest and profoundest contemplation as any art has ever been, and the prospect of a comprehensive aesthetic that will provide for its understanding and its judgment is promising and grand. The novel is owed this. It has come, in darkness, far. But it will not stir further until the appreciation of it has become *properly* philosophical.

First published in *The Philosopher Critic,* ed. Robert Scholes, 1970
Published in *Fiction and the Figures of Life,* 1970

* Others are discussed in "Even if, by All the Oxen in the World" (page 58) and "The Artist and Society" in *Fiction and the Figures of Life.*

THE CONCEPT OF CHARACTER IN FICTION

I

I have never found a handbook on the art of fiction or the stage, nor can I imagine finding one, that did not contain a chapter on the creation of character, a skill whose mastery, the author of each manual insists, secures for one the inner secrets of these arts: not, mind you, an easy thing: rather as difficult as the whole art itself, since, in a way, it *is* the whole art: to fasten in the memory of the reader, like a living presence, some bright human image. All well and good to paint a landscape, evoke a feeling, set a tempest loose, but not quite good enough to nail an author to his immortality if scheming Clarence, fat, foul-trousered Harry, or sweetly terraced Priss do not emerge from the land they huff and rage and eat in fully furnished out by Being; enough alive, indeed, to eat and huff in ours—dear God, more alive than that!—sufficiently enlarged by genius that they threaten to eat up and huff down everything in sight.

Talk about literature, when it is truly talk about something going on in the pages, if it is not about ideas, is generally about the people in it, and ranges from those cries of wonder, horror, pleasure, or surprise, so readily drawn from the innocently minded, to the annotated stammers of the most erudite and nervous critics. But it is all the same. Great character is the most obvious single mark of great literature. The rude, the vulgar, may see in Alyosha nothing more than the image of a modest, God-loving youth; the scholar may perceive through this demeanor a symbolic form; but the Alyosha of the untutored is somehow more real and present to him than the youth on his street whom he's known since childhood, loving of his God and modest, too, equally tried, fully as patient; for in some way Alyosha's visionary figure will take lodging in him, make a model for him, so to reach, without the scholar's inflationary gifts, general form and universal height; whereas the neighbor may merely move away, take cold, and forget to write. Even the most careful student will admit that fiction's fruit survives its handling and continues growing off the tree. A great character has an endless interest; its fascination never wanes. Indeed, it is a commonplace to say so. Hamlet. Ahab. Julien Sorel. Madame Bovary. There is no end to their tragedy. Great literature is great because its characters are great, and characters are great when they are memorable. A simple formula. The Danish ghost cries to remember him, and obediently—for we are gullible and superstitious clots—we do.

It hasn't always been a commonplace. Aristotle regarded character as a servant of dramatic action, and there have been an endless succession of opinions about the value and function of characters since—all dreary—but the important thing to be noted about nearly every one of them is that whatever else profound and wonderful these theories have to say about the world and its personalities, characters are clearly conceived as living outside language. Just as the movie star deserts herself to put on some press agent's more alluring fictional persona, the hero of a story sets out from his own landscape for the same land of romance the star reached by stepping there from life. These people—Huckleberry Finn, the Snopeses, Prince Myshkin, Pickwick, Molly Bloom—seem to have come to the words of their novels like a visitor to town . . . and later they leave on the arm of the reader, bound, I suspect, for a shabbier hotel, and dubious entertainments.

However, Aristotle's remark was a recommendation. Characters ought to exist for the sake of the action, he thought, though he knew they often did not, and those who nowadays say that, given a sufficiently powerful and significant plot, the characters will be dominated by it, are simply answered by asking them to imagine the plot of *Moby-Dick* in the hands of Henry James, or that of *Sanctuary* done into Austen. And if you can persuade them to try (you will have no success), you may then ask how the heroes and the heroines come out. The same disastrous exercise can be given those who believe that traits make character like definitions do a dictionary. Take any set of traits you like and let Balzac or Joyce, Stendhal or Beckett loose in a single paragraph to use them. Give your fictional creatures qualities, psychologies, actions, manners, moods; present them from without or from within; let economics matter, breeding, custom, history; let spirit wet them like a hose: all methods work, and none do. The nature of the novel will not be understood at all until this is: *from any given body of fictional text, nothing necessarily follows, and anything plausibly may.* Authors are gods—a little tinny sometimes but omnipotent no matter what, and plausible on top of that, if they can manage it.*

Though the handbooks try to tell us how to create characters, they carefully never tell us we are making images, illusions, imitations. Gatsby is not an imitation, for there is nothing he imitates. Actually, if he were a copy, an illusion, sort of shade or shadow, he would not be called a character at all. He must be unique, entirely himself, as if he had a self to be. He is required, in fact, to act *in character*, like a cat in a sack. No, theories of character are not absurd in the way representational theories are; they are absurd in a grander way, for the belief in Hamlet (which audiences often seem to have) is like the belief in God—incomprehensible to reason—and one is inclined to seek a motive: some deep fear or emotional need.

There are too many motives. We pay heed so easily. We are so pathetically eager for this other life, for the sounds of distant cities and the sea; we long, apparently, to pit ourselves against some trying wind, to follow the fortunes of a ship hard beset, to face up to murder and fornication, and the somber results of anger and love; oh, yes, to face up—*in books*—when on our own we scarcely breathe. The tragic view of life, for instance, in Shakespeare or in Schopenhauer, Unamuno, Sartre, or Sophocles, is not one jot as pure and penetratingly tragic as a pillow stuffed with Jewish hair, and if we want to touch life where it burns, though life is what we are even now awash with— futilely, stupidly drawing in—we ought not to back off from these other artifacts (wars, pogroms, poverty: men make them, too). But of course we do, and queue up patiently instead to see Prince Hamlet moon, watch him thrust his sword through a curtain, fold it once again into Polonius, that foolish old garrulous proper noun. The so-called life one finds in novels, the worst and best of them, is nothing like actual life at all, and cannot be; it is not more real, or thrilling, or authentic; it is not truer, more complex, or pure, and its people have less spontaneity, are less intricate, less free, less full.†

It is not a single cowardice that drives us into fiction's fantasies. We often fear that literature is a game we can't afford to play—the product of idleness and immoral ease. In the grip of that feeling it isn't life we pursue, but the point and purpose of life—its facility, its use. So Sorel is either a man it

* This has already been discussed in "Philosophy and the Form of Fiction" (page 641). In "Mirror, Mirror" (in *Fiction and the Figures of Life* [New York: Alfred A. Knopf, 1970]) I complain that Nabokov's omnipotence is too intrusive.

† I treat the relation of fiction to life in more detail in *Fiction and the Figures of Life* in "In Terms of the Toenail: Fiction and the Figures of Life." The problem is handled in other ways in "The Artist and Society," "Even if, by All the Oxen in the World" (page 58), and "The Imagination of an Insurrection."

is amusing to gossip about, to see in our friends, to puppet around in our dreams, to serve as our more able and more interesting surrogate in further fanciful adventures; or Sorel is a theoretical type, scientifically profound, representing a deep human strain, and the writing of *The Red and the Black* constitutes an advance in the science of—what would you like? sociology?

Before reciting a few helpless arguments, let me suggest, in concluding this polemical section, just how absurd these views are which think of fiction as a mirror or a window onto life—as actually creative of living creatures— for really one's only weapon against Tertullians is ridicule.

There is a painting by Picasso which depicts a pitcher, candle, blue enamel pot. They are sitting, unadorned, upon the barest table. Would we wonder what was cooking in that pot? Is it beans, perhaps, or carrots, a marmite? The orange of the carrot is a perfect complement to the blue of the pot, and the genius of Picasso, neglecting nothing, has surely placed, behind that blue, invisible disks of dusky orange, which, in addition, subtly enrich the table's velvet brown. Doesn't that seem reasonable? Now I see that it must be beans, for above the pot—you can barely see them—are quaking lines of steam, just the lines we associate with boiling beans . . . or is it blanching pods? Scholarly research, supported by a great foundation, will discover that exactly such a pot was used to cook cassoulet in the kitchens of Charles the Fat . . . or was it Charles the Bald? There's a dissertation in that. And this explains the dripping candle standing by the pot. (Is it dripping? no? a pity. Let's go on.) For isn't Charles the Fat himself that candle? Oh no, some say, he's not! Blows are struck. Reputations made and ruined. Someone will see eventually that the pot is standing on a table, not a stove. But the pot has just come from the stove, it will be pointed out. Has not Picasso caught that vital moment of transition? The pot is too hot. The brown is burning. Oh, not *this* table, which has been coated with resistant plastic. Singular genius—blessed man—he thinks of everything.

Here you have half the history of our criticism in the novel. Entire books have been written about the characters in Dickens, Trollope, Tolstoy, Faulkner. But why not? Entire books have been written about God, His cohorts, and the fallen angels.

2

Descartes, examining a piece of beeswax fresh from the hive, brought it near a flame and observed all of its sensible qualities change. He wondered why he should believe that wax remained. His sensations lent him nothing he could fasten his judgment firmly to. Couldn't he give that puddle in his hand another name? He might have added that the sleights of the mountebanks did not bewilder him. Somehow he knew Milady's hanky didn't disappear in a fist to emerge as a rose. It occurred to Descartes then that perhaps his imagination was the unifying faculty. But the wax was capable of an infinite number of spills, reaching every stage of relaxation, and he was unable, he writes in what is now a brilliant phrase, "to compass this infinity by imagination." How, then? Some higher, finer capacity was required. His knowledge of the wax, soft or hard, sweet or flat, became an intuition of the mind.

Like so many philosophical arguments, this one was erected upside down, and consequently is a bit unsteady on its head. How, I'd rather ask, from the idea of wax, can we predict and picture just this sticky mess? What do we see when we peer through a glass of words?

If we ask this question of Hume, he will give us, as usual, a brilliantly reasonable, and entirely wrong answer—out of the habit empiricists have, I suppose, of never inspecting their experience. Nothing is more free than the imagination of man, he says; "it can feign a train of events, with all the appearance of reality. . . ." *With all the appearance of reality . . .* Then we might suppose that it's my imagination which allows me to descend from a writer's words, like a god through the clouds, and basket down on sweet Belinda's belly at the moment of her maximum response (or, less excitingly, to picture upon the palm in my mind a slowly sprawling blob of molten wax).

To imagine so vividly is to be either drunk, asleep, or mad. Such images are out of our control and often terrifying. If we could feign with *every* appearance of reality, we would not wish to feign *Nostromo,* or even *Pride and Prejudice.* Of course, the imagination cannot give us every appearance of reality, and just as well, but perhaps it can give us every appearance of a *faded* reality: the shadow of Belinda's body on the bed (so far has this theory fallen through the space of a sentence!), an image seen the way I see this print and paper now, though with the mind's disocular eye. Or, as Gilbert Ryle writes:

> Sometimes, when someone mentions a blacksmith's forge, I find myself instantaneously back in my childhood, visiting a local smithy. I can vividly "see" the glowing red horseshoe on the anvil, fairly vividly "hear" the hammer ringing on the shoe and less vividly "smell" the singed hoof. How should we describe this "smelling in the mind's nose"?*

* In *The Concept of Mind* (New York: Barnes & Noble, 1950).

Certainly not by explaining that there is a smell in me, a shadow of a smell, a picture of a smell, an image, and putting to my noseless spirit the task of smelling it. Not as a bruise to its blow, as Ryle says, are our imaginings related to our experience. Yet Hume sometimes supposes that imagination works like madness. If it can give to fiction all the appearance of reality, how is one to know what to believe when an author's words, stirring in us like life, managing our minds with the efficiency of reality, throw Anna Karenina under the train's wheels before our eyes?

Here is the whole thing in a single passage:

> The imagination has the command over all its ideas and can join and mix and vary them in all the ways possible. It may conceive fictitious objects with all the circumstances of place and time. It may set them in a manner before our eyes, in their true colors, just as they might have existed. But as it is impossible that this faculty of imagination can ever, of itself, reach belief, it is evident that belief consists not in the peculiar nature or order of ideas, but in the manner of their conception and in their feeling to the mind.*

The name of this feeling is belief, and I am given it by the greater intensity and steadiness with which actual impressions occupy me—a narrow difference, one only of degree. Don't mystery stories make us lock our doors?

But I should suppose that "seeing things" through novels did not involve succumbing to a drunken frenzy, finding animals in walls or naked ladies draped on desert rocks like some long-celibate St. Anthony.

We do visualize, I suppose. Where did I leave my gloves? And then I ransack a room in my mind until I find them. But the room I ransack is abstract—a simple schema. I leave out the drapes and the carpet, and I think of the room as a set of likely glove locations. The proportion of words which we can visualize is small, but quite apart from that, another barrier to the belief that vivid imagining is the secret of a character's power is the fact that when we watch the pictures which a writer's words have directed us to make, we miss their meaning, for the point is *never* the picture. It also takes concentration, visualization does—takes slowing down; and this alone is enough to rule it out of novels, which are never waiting, always flowing on.

---

* David Hume, *An Enquiry Concerning Human Understanding* (New York: Oxford University Press, 2007). There is reason to suppose that Hume thinks the imagination plays with ideas only after they have lost all vivifying power. Then, however, their arrangement could satisfy only our conceptions of things, not our perceptions of them.

Instantly Hugh's shack began to take form in her mind. But it was not a shack—it was a home! It stood, on wide-girthed strong legs of pine, between the forest of pine and high, high waving alders and tall slim birches, and the sea. There was the narrow path that wound down through the forest from the shore, with salmonberries and thimbleberries and wild blackberry bushes that on bright winter nights of frost reflected a million moons; behind the house was a dogwood tree that bloomed twice in the year with white stars. Daffodils and snowdrops grew in the little garden.*

And so forth. Do you have all that? the salmonberries and the thimbleberries? I'm afraid you'll be all day about it. One reason is that our imaginings are mostly imprecise. They are vague and general. Even when colored, they're gray.

A hare vaguely perceived is nevertheless a specific hare. But a hare which is the object of a vague image is a vague hare.†

Consequently, writing which carefully defines its object, however visual its terms, sets the visual successfully aside. It does, that is, if what we see inside us are misty visual schemata. But

Suppose that I have an image of a head that is nonspecific about baldness, is this not rather queer? For presumably this head must be neither bald nor not bald nor even a half-way house with just a few hairs.‡

Enter Mr. Cashmore, who is a character in *The Awkward Age*.

Mr. Cashmore, who would have been very redheaded if he had not been very bald, showed a single eyeglass and a long upper lip; he was large and jaunty, with little petulant movements and intense ejaculations that were not in the line of his type.

We can imagine any number of other sentences about Mr. Cashmore added to this one. Now the question is: what is Mr. Cashmore? Here is the answer I

* Malcolm Lowry, *Under the Volcano* (New York: Reynal and Hitchcock, 1947).

† Jean-Paul Sartre, *The Psychology of Imagination* (New York: Citadel, 1961).

‡ J. M. Shorter, "Imagination," in *Mind*, vol. 61 (Oct. 1952), pp. 528–42.

shall give: Mr. Cashmore is (1) a noise, (2) a proper name, (3) a complex system of ideas, (4) a controlling conception, (5) an instrument of verbal organization, (6) a pretended mode of referring, and (7) a source of verbal energy.* But Mr. Cashmore is not a person. He is not an object of perception, and nothing whatever that is appropriate to persons can be correctly said of him. There is no path from idea to sense (this is Descartes's argument in reverse), and no amount of careful elaboration of Mr. Cashmore's single eyeglass, his upper lip or jauntiness is going to enable us to *see* him. How many little petulant movements are there? Certainly as many as the shapes which may be taken by soft wax. If we follow Hume, we think we picture things through language because we substitute, on cue, particular visual memories of our own, and the more precisely language defines its object, the less likely we are to find a snapshot in our book to fit it. Our visualizations interfere with Mr. Cashmore's development, for if we think of him as someone we have met, we must give him qualities his author hasn't yet, and we may stubbornly, or through simple lack of attention, retain these later, though they've been explicitly debarred. "On your imaginary forces work," *Henry V*'s prologuer begs. "Piece out our imperfections with your thoughts. . . . Think, when we talk of horses, that you see them / Printing their proud hoofs i' th' receiving earth," and then the audience (and the similarly situated novel reader) is praised for having done so; but this is worse than the self-congratulating pap which periodically flows from the bosom of the "creative" critic, because these generous additions destroy the work as certainly as "touching up" and "painting over." The unspoken word is often eloquent.

> Well, I finally met Mr. Mulholland.
> Oh, what's he like?
> He has large thumbs.

Characters in fiction are mostly empty canvas. I have known many who have passed through their stories without noses, or heads to hold them; others have lacked bodies altogether, exercised no natural functions, possessed some thoughts, a few emotions, but no psychologies, and apparently

---

* (1) He is always a "mister," and his name functions musically much of the time. "He was an odd compound, Mr. Cashmore, and the air of personal good health, the untarnished bloom which sometimes lent a monstrous serenity to his mention of the barely mentionable, was on occasion balanced or matched by his playful application of extravagant terms to matters of much less moment." What a large mouthful, that sentence. His name (2) locates him, but since he exists nowhere but on the page (6), it simply serves to draw other words toward him (3), or actualize others, as in conversation (7), when they seem to proceed from him, or remind us of all that he is an emblem of (4), and richly interact with other, similarly formed, and similarly functioning verbal centers (5).

made love without the necessary organs. The true principle is direct enough: Mr. Cashmore has what he's been given; he also *has* what he *hasn't*, just as strongly. Mr. Cashmore, in fact, has been cruelly scalped.

Now, is there a nose to this Mr. Cashmore? Let's suppose it—but, then, of what sort? We're not told. He is an eyeglass without eyes, he has no neck or chin, his ears are unexplored. "Large"—how indefinite a word. But would it have been better to have written "sixteen stone"? Not at all, nor do we know how this weight is disposed. If it is impossible to picture Mr. Cashmore, however carefully we draw him, will it be easier to limn his soul? Or perhaps we may imagine that this sentence describes not Mr. Cashmore, out or in, but his impression—what sort of dent he makes in his surroundings. He gives the impression of a man who would have been redheaded if he hadn't been bald. Very well. What impression, exactly, is that? Will it do to think of Mr. Cashmore as a man with red eyebrows and a red fringe above his ears, but otherwise without hair? That would rephrase Mr. Cashmore, and rephrase him badly. The description of Mr. Cashmore stands as James wrote it, even if Mr. Cashmore hasn't a hair on his body. As a set of sensations Mr. Cashmore is simply impossible; as an idea he is admirably pungent and precise.

Similarly, it is not at all correct to infer that because Mr. Mulholland has thumbs, he has hands, arms, torso, self. That inference destroys the metaphor (a pure synecdoche), since his thumbs are all he seems to be. Mr. Mulholland is monumentally clumsy, but if you fill him in behind his thumbs, clumsiness will not ensue.

So sometimes, then, we are required to take away what we've been given, as in the case of Mr. Cashmore's red hair; sometimes it's important to hold fast to what we've got and resist any inclination we may have to elaborate, as in the case of Mr. Mulholland, who I said had thumbs; and sometimes we must put our minds to the stretch, bridging the distances between concepts with other concepts, as in the two examples which follow; or we may be called upon to do all these things at once, as in what I promise will be my final misuse of poor Mulholland.*

Well, I finally met Mr. Mulholland.
Oh, what's he like?
A silver thimble.

* The entire matter is far more complicated than I have indicated. Not only is there a linear order of apprehension (the reader is first told Mr. Mulholland has been seen, then that he was walking his thumbs), but also an order, in depth, of implications. Analysis, in searching out these implications, frequently upsets this order, bringing the bottom to the top. Meanings, uncovered, must be put back as they were found. It is a delicate operation.

I saw Mr. Mulholland today.
Oh, what was he doing?
Walking his thumbs.

Mr. Mulholland's face had
a watchful look. Although
its features had not yet arrived,
they were momentarily expected.

To summarize, so far:

1. Only a few of the words which a writer normally uses to create a character can be "imaged" in any sense.

2. To the extent these images are faded sensations which we've once had, they fill in, particularize, and falsify the author's account.

3. To the degree these images are as vivid and lively as reality is, they will very often be unpleasant, and certainly can't be "feigned." Then words would act like a mind-expanding drug.

4. To the degree these images are general schemata, indistinct and vague, the great reality characters are supposed to have becomes less plausible, and precise writing (so often admired) will interfere with their formation.

5. Constructing images of any kind takes time, slows the flow of the work; nor can imagining keep up, in complexity, with the incredibly intricate conceptual systems which may be spun like a spiderweb in a single sentence.

6. We tend to pay attention to our pictures, and lose sight of the meaning. The novelist's words are not notes which he is begging the reader to play, as if his novel needed something more done to it in order to leap into existence.

Words in daily life are signposts, handles, keys. They express, instruct, command, inform, exhort—in short, they serve; and it is difficult to think of our servants as kings.* But among real things words win the gold medals for Being. Ortega y Gasset asks us to imagine we are looking through a window at a garden.

The clearer the glass is, the less (of the glass) we will see. But then making an effort we may withdraw attention from the garden; and by retracting the ocular ray, we may fixate it upon the glass. Then the garden will disappear in our eyes and we will see instead only some confused masses of color which seem to stick to the glass. Consequently to see the garden and to see the glass in the windowpane are two incom-

---

* See "Gertrude Stein: Her Escape from Protective Language" in *Fiction and the Figures of Life* and "The Medium of Fiction" (page 672).

patible operations. . . . Likewise he who in the work of art aims to be moved by the fate of John and Mary, or of Tristan and Iseult, and readjusts to them his spiritual perception will not be able to see the work of art. . . . Now the majority of people are unable to adjust their attention to the glass and the transparency which is the work of art; instead they penetrate through it to passionately wallow in the human reality which the work of art refers to. If they are invited to let loose their prey and fix their attention upon the work of art itself, they will say they see nothing in it, because, indeed, they see no human realities there, but only artistic transparencies, pure essences.*

Ortega seems to believe, however, that words are windows through which something can be seen, and I have argued that words are opaque, as opaque as my garden gloves and trowel, objects which, nevertheless, may vividly remind me of spring, earth, and roses. Or Uncle Harry, Africa, the tsetse fly, and lovesick elephants.

On the other side of a novel lies the void. Think, for instance, of a striding statue; imagine the purposeful inclination of the torso, the alert and penetrating gaze of the head and its eyes, the outstretched arm and pointing finger; everything would appear to direct us toward some goal in front of it. Yet our eye travels only to the finger's end, and not beyond. Though pointing, the finger bids us stay instead, and we journey slowly back along the tension of the arm. In our hearts we know what actually surrounds the statue. The same surrounds every other work of art: empty space and silence.†

3

A character, first of all, is the noise of his name, and all the sounds and rhythms that proceed from him. We pass most things in novels as we pass things on a train. The words flew by like the scenery. All is change.‡ But there are some points in a narrative which remain relatively fixed; we may depart from them, but soon we return, as music returns to its theme. Characters are those primary substances to which everything else is attached. Hotels,

* José Ortega y Gasset, *The Dehumanization of Art* (New York: Anchor Books, 1956).

† The way in which both the reader and the world are drawn into the novel is discussed in "In Terms of the Toenail: Fiction and the Figures of Life."

‡ Of course, nothing prevents a person from feeling that life is like this. See "A Spirit in Search of Itself" in *Fiction and the Figures of Life.*

dresses, conversations, sausage, feelings, gestures, snowy evenings, faces—
each may fade as fast as we read of them. Yet the language of the novel will
eddy about a certain incident or name, as Melville's always circles back to
Ahab and his wedding with the white whale. Mountains are characters in
Malcolm Lowry's *Under the Volcano,* so is a ravine, a movie, mescal, or a
boxing poster. A symbol like the cross can be a character. An idea or a situation (the anarchist in *The Secret Agent,* bomb ready in his pocket), or a particular event, an obsessive thought, a decision (Zeno's, for instance, to quit
smoking), a passion, a memory, the weather, Gogol's overcoat—anything,
indeed, which serves as a fixed point, like a stone in a stream or that soap in
Bloom's pocket, functions as a character. Character, in this sense, is a matter of degree, for the language of the novel may loop back seldom, often, or
incessantly. But the idea that characters are like primary substances has to be
taken in a double way, because if any thing becomes a character simply to the
degree the words of the novel qualify it, it also loses some of its substance,
some of its primacy, to the extent that it, in turn, qualifies something else. In
a perfectly organized novel, every word would ultimately qualify one thing,
like the God of the metaphysician, at once the subject and the body of the
whole.* Normally, characters are fictional human beings, and thus are given
proper names. In such cases, to create a character is to give meaning to an
unknown X; it is *absolutely* to *define;* and since nothing in life corresponds to
these X's, their reality is borne by their name. They *are,* where it *is.*

Most of the words the novelist uses have their meanings already formed.
Proper names do not, except in a tangential way. It's true that Mr. Mulholland could not be Mr. Mull, and Mr. Cashmore must bear, as best he can, the
curse of his wealth forever, along with his desire for gain. Character has a special excitement for a writer (apart from its organizing value) because it offers
him a chance to give fresh meaning to new words. A proper name begins as
a blank, like a wall or a canvas, upon which one might paint a meaning, perhaps as turbulent and mysterious, as treacherous and vast, as Moby-Dick's,
perhaps as delicate, scrupulous, and sensitive as that of Fleda Vetch.

I cannot pause here over the subject of rhythm and sound, though they
are the heartbeat of writing, of prose no less than poetry.

> Their friend, Mr. Grant-Jackson, a highly preponderant pushing per-
> son, great in discussion and arrangement, abrupt in overture, unex-
> pected, if not perverse, in attitude, and almost equally acclaimed and

---

* There is no reason why every novel should be organized in this way. This method constructs
a world according to the principles of Absolute Idealism. See "Philosophy and the Form of
Fiction."

objected to in the wide midland region to which he had taught, as the phrase was, the size of his foot—their friend had launched his bolt quite out of the blue and had thereby so shaken them as to make them fear almost more than hope.*

Mr. Grant-Jackson is a preponderant pushing person because he's been made by *p*'s, and the rhythm and phrasing of James's writing here prepares and perfectly presents him to us. Certainly we cannot think of Molly Bloom apart from her music, or the gay and rapid Anna Livia apart from hers.

If one examines the texture of a fiction carefully, one will soon see that some words appear to gravitate toward their subject like flies settle on sugar, while others seem to emerge from it. In many works this logical movement is easily discernible and very strong. When a character speaks, the words seem to issue from him and to be acts of his. Description first forms a *nature,* then allows that nature to *perform.* We must be careful, however, not to judge by externals. Barkis says that Barkis is willing, but the expression *functions* descriptively to qualify Barkis, and it is Dickens's habit to treat speech as if it were an attribute of character, like tallness or honesty, and not an act. On the other hand, qualities, in the right context, can be transformed into verbs. Later in the book don't we perceive the whiteness of the whale as a design, an intention of Moby-Dick's, like a twist of his flukes or the smashing of a small boat?

Whether Mr. Cashmore was once real and sat by James at someone's dinner table, or was instead the fabrication of James's imagination,[†] as long as he came into being from the world's direction he once existed outside language. The task of getting him in I shall call the problem of rendering. But it must be stressed (it cannot be stressed too severely) that Mr. Cashmore may never have had a model, and may never have been imagined either, but may have come to be in order to serve some high conception (a Mr. Moneybags) and represent a type, not just himself, in which case he is not a reality *rendered,* but a universal *embodied.*[‡] Again, Mr. Cashmore might have had still other parents. Meanings in the stream of words before his appearance might have suggested him, dramatic requirements may have called him forth, or he may have been the spawn of music, taking his substance from rhythm and allit-

* Henry James, "The Birthplace."

† Some aspects of this imagination are dealt with in "The High Brutality of Good Intentions," and "In the Cage" in *Fiction and the Figures of Life.*

‡ See "Philosophy and the Form of Fiction."

eration. Perhaps it was all of these. In well-regulated fictions, most things are *overdetermined.*

So far I have been talking about the function of a character in the direct stream of language, but there are these two other dimensions, the rendered and the embodied, and I should like to discuss each briefly.

If we observe one of J. F. Powers's worldly priests sharpening his eye for the pin by putting it through his clerical collar, the humor, with all *its* sharpness, lives in the situation, and quite incidentally in the words.* One can indeed imagine Powers thinking it up independently of any verbal formula. Once Powers had decided that it would be funny to show a priest playing honeymoon bridge with his housekeeper, then his problem becomes the technical one of how best to accomplish it. What the writer must do, of course, is not only render the scene, but render the scene inseparable from its language, so that if the idea (the chaste priest caught in the clichés of marriage) is taken from the situation, like a heart from its body, both die. Far easier to render a real cornfield in front of you, because once that rendering has reached its page, the cornfield will no longer exist for literary purposes, no one will be able to see it by peering through your language, and consequently there will be nothing to abstract from your description. But with a "thought-up" scene or situation, this is not the case. It comes under the curse of story. The notion, however amusing, is not literary, for it might be painted, filmed, or played. If we inquire further and ask why Powers wanted such a scene in the first place, we should find, I think, that he wanted it in order to embody a controlling "idea"—at one level of abstraction, the worldliness of the Church, for instance. If he had nuns around a kitchen table counting the Sunday take and listening to the Cubs, *that* would do it. Father Burner beautifully embodies just such a controlling idea in Powers's celebrated story "The Prince of Darkness." Both rendering and embodying involve great risks, because they require working into a scientific order of words what was not originally there. Any painter knows that a contour may only more or less enclose his model, while a free line simply and completely is. Many of the model's contours may be aesthetically irrelevant, so it would be unwise to follow them. The free line is subject to no such temptations. Its relevance can be total. As Valéry wrote: "There are no details in execution."

Often novelists mimic our ordinary use of language. We report upon ourselves; we gossip. Normally, we are not lying; and our language, built to refer, actually does. When these selfsame words appear in fiction, and when they follow the forms of daily use, they create, quite readily, that dangerous

* I enlarge on this aspect of Powers's work in "The Bingo Game at the Foot of the Cross" in *Fiction and the Figures of Life.*

feeling that a real Tietjens, a real Nickleby, lives just beyond the page; that through that thin partition we can hear a world at love.* But the writer must not let the reader out; the sculptor must not let the eye fall from the end of his statue's finger; the musician must not let the listener dream. Of course, he will; but let the blame be on himself. High tricks are possible: to run the eye rapidly along that outstretched arm to the fingertip, only to draw it up before it falls away in space; to carry the reader to the very edge of every word so that it seems he must be compelled to react as though to truth as told in life, and then to return him, like a philosopher liberated from the cave, to the clear and brilliant world of concept, to the realm of order, proportion, and dazzling construction . . . to fiction, where characters, unlike ourselves, freed from existence, can shine like essence, and purely Be.

The New American Review, 1969
Published in *Fiction and Figures of Life,* 1970

* See "The Medium of Fiction."

THE MEDIUM OF FICTION

It seems a country-headed thing to say: that literature is language, that stories and the places and the people in them* are merely made of words as chairs are made of smoothed sticks and sometimes of cloth or metal tubes. Still, we cannot be too simple at the start, since the obvious is often the unobserved. Occasionally we should allow the trite to tease us into thought, for such old friends, the clichés in our life, are the only strangers we can know. It seems incredible, the ease with which we sink through books quite out of sight,† pass clamorous pages into soundless dreams. That novels should be made of words, and merely words, is shocking, really. It's as though you had discovered that your wife were made of rubber: the bliss of all those years, the fears . . . from sponge.

Like the mathematician, like the philosopher, the novelist makes things out of concepts. Concepts, consequently, must be his critical concern: not the defects of his person, the crimes on his conscience, other men's morals, or their kindness or cruelty. The painter squeezes space through his pigments. Paint stains his fingers. How can he forget the color he has loaded on his brush or that blank canvas audience before him? Yet the novelist frequently behaves as if his work were all heart, character, and story; he professes to hate abstraction, mathematics, and the pure works of mind. Of course, unlike poetry, and despite its distinguished figures, for a long time now the novel has been an amateur's affair, an open field for anybody's running, and it has

---

* For the people, see "The Concept of Character in Fiction" (page 657).

† This, as well as the comparison with mathematics, is returned to in "In Terms of the Toenail: Fiction and the Figures of Life" in my *Fiction and the Figures of Life* (New York: Alfred A. Knopf, 1970).

drawn the idle, sick, and gossipaceous, the vaguely artistic—prophets, teachers, muckrakers—all the fanatical explainers, those dreamily scientific, and those anally pedantic.

Paint stains the fingers; the sculptor's hair is white with dust; but concepts have no physical properties; they do not permit smell or reflect light; they do not fill space or contain it; they do not age. "Five" is no wider, older, or fatter than "four"; "apple" isn't sweeter than "quince," rounder than "pear," smoother than "peach." To say, then, that literature is language is to say that literature is made of meanings, concepts, ideas, forms (please yourself with the term), and that these are so static and eternal as to shame the stars.

Like the mathematician. For the novelist to be at all, in any way, like a mathematician is shocking. It's worse than discovering your privates are plastic. Because there's no narration among numbers. It is logically impossible. Time's lacking.

When David Hilbert, the great logician, heard that a student had given up mathematics to write novels, he is supposed to have said: "It was just as well; he did not have enough imagination to become a first-rate mathematician."

The yammer of thought, the constant one-after-another of sounds, the shapes of words, the terrible specter of spelling, are each due to this fact that meanings are heavenly bodies which, to our senses, must somehow announce themselves. A word is a concept made flesh, if you like—the eternal presented as noise. When I spell, then, let's say, "avoirdupois," I am forming our name for that meaning, but it might, just as well, be written down "dozzo," or still more at length, with the same lack of logic, "typary," "snoddle," or "willmullynull." "Avoirdupois." An unreasonable body. Nonetheless lovely. "Avoirdupois."

There is a fundamental contradiction in our medium.* We work with a marble of flaws. My mind is utterly unlike my body,† and unless you're an angel, so, I am certain, is yours. Poor Descartes really wrote on the problems of poets: word sense and word sound, math and mechanics, the mind and its body, can they touch? And how, pray God, can they resemble? In the act of love, as in all the arts, the soul should be felt by the tongue and the fingers, felt in the skin. So should our sounds come to color up the surface of our stories like a blush. This adventitious music is the only sensory quality our books can have. As Frost observed, even the empty sentence has a sound, or, rather—I should say—*is* a series of nervous tensions and resolves. No artist

---

* See "Gertrude Stein: Her Escape from Protective Language" in *Fiction and the Figures of Life.*

† The contrast which is meant here is not that often alleged to exist between thought and feeling, but that between consciousness and things.

dares neglect his own world's body, for *nothing else,* nothing else about his book is physical.

In the hollow of a jaw, the ear, upon the page, concepts now begin to move: they appear, accelerate, they race, they hesitate a moment, slow, turn, break, join, modify, and it becomes reasonable to speak of the problems of narration for the first time. Truly (that is to say, technically), narration is that part of the art of fiction concerned with the coming on and passing off of words—not the familiar arrangement of words in dry strings like so many shriveled worms, but their formal direction and rapidity. But this is not what's usually meant.

For most people, fiction is history; fiction is history without tables, graphs, dates, imports, edicts, evidence, laws; history without hiatus—intelligible, simple, smooth. Fiction is sociology freed of statistics, politics with no real party in the opposition; it's a world where play money buys you cardboard squares of colored country; a world where everyone is obediently psychologi-cal, economic, ethnic, geographical—framed in a keyhole and always nude, each figure fashioned from the latest thing in cello-see-through, so we may observe our hero's guts, too, if we choose: ah, they're blue, and squirming like a tickled river. For truth without effort, thought without rigor, feeling with-out form, existence without commitment: what will you give? for a wind-up world, a toy life? . . . six bits? for a book with a thicker skin? . . . six bucks? I am a man, myself, intemperately mild, and though it seems to me as much deserved as it's desired, I have no wish to steeple quires of paper passion up so many sad unelevating rears.

Nay, not *seems,* it *is* a stubborn, country-headed thing to say: that there are no events but words in fiction. Words mean things. Thus we use them every day: make love, buy bread, and blow up bridges. But the use of language in fiction only mimics its use in life. A sign like GENTS, for instance, tells me where to pee. It conveys information; it produces feelings of glad relief. I use the sign, but I dare not dawdle under it. It might have read MEN or borne a mustache. This kind of sign passes out of consciousness, is extinguished by its use. In literature, however, the sign remains; it sings; and we return to it again and again.

In contrast, the composer's medium is pure; that is, the tones he uses exist for music, and are made by instruments especially designed. Imagine his feel-ings, then, if he were forced to employ the meaningful noises of every day: bird calls, sirens, screams, alarm bells, whistles, ticks, and human chatter. He could plead all he liked that his music was pure, but we would know that he'd written down sounds from a play unseen, and we would insist that it told a story. Critics would describe the characters (one wears a goatee) and quarrel over their motives, marriages, or mothers, all their dark genes. Although no one wonders, of a painted peach, whether the tree it grew on was watered properly, we are happily witness, week after week, to further examination of Hamlet or Madame Bovary, quite as if they were real. And they are so serious, so learned, so certain—so laughable—these ladies and gentlemen. Ah well, it's merely energy which might otherwise elucidate the Trinity.

So the novelist makes his book from boards which say LADIES and GENTS. Every scrap has been worn, every item handled; most of the pieces are dented or split. The writer may choose to be heroic—poets often are—he may strive to purify his diction and achieve an exclusively literary language. He may pretend that every syllable he speaks hasn't been spit, sometimes, in someone else's mouth. Such poets scrub, they clean, they smooth, they polish, until we can scarcely recognize their words on the page. "A star glide, a single frantic sullenness, a single financial grass greediness," wrote Gertrude Stein. *"Toute Pensée émet un Coup de Dés,"* wrote Mallarmé. Most novelists, however (it is one of the things that make them one), try to turn the tattering to account—incorporate it cleverly—as the painter does when he pastes up a collage of newspaper, tinfoil, and postage stamps. He will recognize, for example, that stories are wonderful devices for controlling the speed of the mind, for resting it after hard climbs; they give a reassuring light to a dark place, and help the reader hold, like handsome handles, heavy luggage on long trips.

A dedicated storyteller, though—a true lie-minded man—will serve his history best, and guarantee its popularity, not by imitating nature, since nature's no source of verisimilitude, but by following as closely as he can our simplest, most direct and unaffected forms of daily talk, for we report real things, things which intrigue and worry us, and such resembling gossip in a book allows us to believe in figures and events we cannot see, shall never touch, with an assurance of safety which sets our passions free. He will avoid recording consciousness, since consciousness is private—we do not normally "take it down"—and because no one really believes in any other feelings than his own. However, the moment our writer concentrates on sound, the moment he formalizes his sentences, the moment he puts in a figure of speech or turns a phrase, shifts a tense or alters tone, the moment he carries description, or any account, beyond need, he begins to turn his reader's interest away from the world which lies among his words like a beautiful woman among her slaves, and directs him toward the slaves themselves. This illustrates a basic principle: if I describe my peach too perfectly, it's the poem which will make my mouth water . . . while the real peach spoils.

Sculptures take up space and gather dust. Concepts do not. They take up us. They invade us as we read, and they achieve, as our resistance and their forces vary, every conceivable degree of occupation. Imagine a worry or a pain, an obsessive thought, a jealousy or hate so strong it renders you insensible to all else. Then while it lasts, you are that fear, that ache, for consciousness is always smaller than its opportunities, and can contract around a kernel like a shell. A piece of music can drive you out and take your place. The purpose of a literary work is the capture of consciousness, and the consequent creation, in you, of an imagined sensibility, so that while you read you are that patient pool or cataract of concepts which the author has constructed; and though at first it might seem as if the richness of life had been replaced by something less so—senseless noises, abstract meanings, mere shadows of worldly employment—yet the new self with which fine fiction and good poetry should provide you is as wide as the mind is, and musicked deep with feeling. While listening to such symbols sounding, the blind perceive; thought seems to grow a body; and the will is at rest amid that moving like a gull asleep on the sea. Perhaps we'll be forgiven, then, if we fret about our words and continue country-headed. It is not a refusal to please. There's no willfulness, disdain, exile . . . no anger. Because a consciousness electrified by beauty—is that not the aim and emblem and the ending of all finely made love?

Are you afraid?

The Nation, 1966
Published in *Fiction and the Figures of Life,* 1970

The Baby or the Botticelli

We are to imagine a terrible storm like that which opens Verdi's *Otello*. The pavement of the *piazzetta* is awash. St. Mark's pigeons are flying about, looking for land. The Venetian sun has gone down like a gondola in the lagoon. As we wade along in the dying light, a baby in a basket passes. It is being swept out to sea with the rest of the city's garbage. So is a large painting, beautifully framed, which floats its grand nude by us as if she were swimming. Then the question comes, bobbing like a bit of flotsam itself: Which one should we save, the tiny tot or the Tintoretto? the kid in the crib or the Canaletto?

It may be that during two thousand or more years of monsoons, tidal waves, and high water, this choice has not once actually presented itself; yet, undismayed, it is in this form that philosophers frequently represent the conflict between art and morality—a conflict, of course, they made up in the first place. Baby or Botticelli. What'll you have?

Not only is the dilemma an unlikely one; the choice it offers is peculiar. We are being asked to decide not between two different actions but between two different objects. And how different indeed these floating objects are. The baby is a vessel of human consciousness, if its basket isn't. It is nearly pure potentiality. It must be any babe—no one babe but babe in general, babe in bulk—whose bunk is boating by. Never mind if it was born with the brain of an accountant, inflicted with a cleft palate, or given Mozartian talents: these are clearly irrelevant considerations, as are ones concerning the seaworthiness of the basket, or the prospect of more rain. One fist in this fight swings from the arm of an open future against the chest of a completed past. . . .

. . . A completed past because we have to know the pedigree of the painting or it's no contest. If it is the rosy nude who used to recline behind the bar in Harry's, or just another mislaid entrant in the latest Biennale, then the conditions of the case are fatally altered and there is no real conflict of interest, though the blank space behind the bar at Harry's will surely fill us with genuine sorrow each Scotch-and-water hour. It is not between infant and image, then, that we are being asked to choose, but between some fully realized aesthetic quality and a vaguely generalized human nature, even though it is a specific baby who could drown.

It is the moralists, of course, who like to imagine these lunatic choices. It is the moralists who want to bully and beat up on the artists, not the other way around. The error of the artists is indifference. Not since Plato's day, when the politicians in their grab for public power defeated the priests, the poets, and the philosophers, have artists, except for an occasional Bronx cheer, molested a moralist. Authors do not gather to burn good deeds in public squares; laws are not passed by poets to put lying priests behind bars, nor do they usually suggest that the pursuit of goodness will lead you away from both beauty and truth, that it is the uphill road to ruin. Musicians do not hang moralizing lackeys from lampposts as though they were stringing their fiddles; moralizing lackeys do that.

On the other hand . . . We know what the other, the righteous hand is full of: slings and arrows, slanders and censorship, prisons, scaffolds, burnings and beatings. To what stake has Savonarola's piety been bound by the painters he disgraced? Throughout history, goodness has done more harm than good, and over the years moralists have managed to give morality a thoroughly bad name. Although lots of bad names have been loaned them by the poets, if the poets roast, they roast no one on the coals, only upon their scorn, while moralists, to their reward, have dispatched who knows how many thousands of souls.

The choice, baby or Botticelli, is presented to us as an example of the conflict between Art and Ethics, but between Art and Ethics there is no conflict, nor is this an instance, for our quandary falls entirely within the ethical. The decision, if there is one to make, is moral.

The values that men prize have been variously classified. There may be said to be, crudely, five kinds. There are, first of all, those facts and theories we are inclined to call true, and which, we think, constitute our knowledge. Philosophy, history, science presumably pursue them. Second, there are the values of duty and obligation—obedience and loyalty, righteousness and virtue—qualities that the state finds particularly desirable. Appreciative values of all kinds may be listed third, including the beauties of women, art, and nature, the various sublimes, and that pleasure which comes from the pure exercise of human faculties and skills. Fourth are the values of self-realization and its attendant pleasures—growth, well-being, and the like—frequently called happiness in deference to Aristotle. Finally, there are those that have to do with real or imagined redemption, with ultimate justice and immortality. Some would prefer to separate political values like justice or freedom from more narrowly moral ones, while others would do the same for social values like comfort, stability, security, conditions often labeled simply "peace." But a complete and accurate classification, assuming it could be accomplished, is not important here. Roughly, we might call our goals, as tradition has, Truth, Goodness, Beauty, Happiness, and Salvation. (We can reach port, sometimes, even with a bad map.)

If we allow our classificatory impulse to run on a little longer, it will encourage us to list at least four customary attitudes that can be taken toward the relationship of these value areas to one another. First, one can deny the legitimacy or reality of a particular value group. Reckless pragmatists and some sophists deny the objective existence of all values except utility, while positivists prefer to elevate empirical truth (which they don't capitalize, only underscore) to that eminence. It is, of course, truth thinned to the thickness of a wire, which is fine if you want to cut cheese. The values that remain are rejected as attitudes, moods, or emotions—subjective states of various sorts like wishing, hoping, willing, which suggest external objects without being able to establish them. I happen to regard salvation values as illusory or mythological, since I deny any significance to the assumptions on which they are grounded, but other people may pick out different victims.

Second, we might accept the values of a certain sphere as real enough, but argue that some or all of them are reducible to others, even eventually to one. Reductionism is characteristic of Plato's famous argument that virtue is knowledge; of Keats's fatuous little motto, Beauty is Truth; of materialists and idealists equally. Rather than reduce moral values to those of happiness, Aristotle simply ignored them.

Third, we can try to make some values subordinate to others. This is not the same as reduction. One might argue that artistic and moral values are mutually exclusive, or unique, and yet support the superiority of one over the other. There are, however, two kinds of subordination. One asserts that X is more important than Y, so that when one has to choose between them (baby or Botticelli), one must always choose the baby. When one is designing buildings, for instance, beauty regularly runs afoul of function and economy. The other sort of subordination insists not only that X is more important, or "higher" in value, than Y, but that Y should serve or be a means to X: the baby is a model for the baby in the Botticelli. The slogan "Form follows function" is sometimes so understood. I take crude Marxism to require this kind of sacrifice from the artist.

Fourth, it is possible to argue, as I do, that these various value areas are significantly different. They are not only different; they are not reducible, but are independent of one another. Furthermore, no one value area is more important, abstractly considered, than any other. In short, these various values are different, independent, and equal.

This does not imply that in particular instances you should not choose one over the other and have good reasons for doing so; it is simply that what is chosen in any instance cannot be dictated in advance. Obviously, if you are starving, whether your food is served with grace and eaten with manners is less than essential. Should you skip dinner or lick the spilled beans from the floor? Should you choose to safeguard a painting or the well-being of its model? Should you bomb Monte Cassino?

That attachment to human life which demands that it be chosen over everything else is mostly humbug. It can be reasonably, if not decisively, argued that the world is already suffering from a surfeit of such animals; that most human beings rarely deserve the esteem some philosophers have for them; that historically humans have treated their pets better than they have treated one another; that no one is so essential he or she cannot be replaced a thousand times over; that death is inevitable anyhow; that it is our sense of community and our own identity which lead us to persist in our parochial overestimation; that it is rather a wish of philosophers than a fact that man be more important than anything else that's mortal, since nature remains mum and scarcely supports the idea, nor do the actions of man himself. Man makes a worse god than God, and when God was alive, he knew it.

Baby or Botticelli is a clear enough if artificial choice, but it places the problem entirely in the moral sphere, where the differences involved can be conveniently overlooked. What differences?

The writing of a book (the painting of a painting, the creation of a score) is generally such an exacting and total process that it is not simply okay if it has many motives; it is essential. The difference between one of Flaubert's broken amatory promises to Louise Colet and his writing of *Madame Bovary* (both considered immoral acts in some circles) is greater even than Lenin's willingness to board a train and his intended overthrow of the czar. Most promises are kept by actions each one of which falls into a simple series; that is, I meet you at the Golden Egg by getting up from my desk, putting on my coat, and getting into my car: a set of actions each one of which can be serially performed and readily seen as part of "going to lunch." I may have many reasons for keeping our date, but having promised becomes the moral one.

However, when I create a work of art, I have entered into no contract of any kind with the public, unless the work has been commissioned. In this sense, most aesthetic acts are unbidden, uncalled for, even unexpected. They are gratuitous. And unlike Lenin's intention to overthrow an empire (which can scarcely be an intention of the same kind as mine to meet you for lunch, involving, as it does, several years, thousands of folks, and millions of rubles), my writing will, all along, be mine alone, and I will not normally parcel out the adjectives to subordinates and the sex scenes to specialists, or contract out the punctuation.

I have many reasons for going to the Golden Egg, then: I am hungry; you are pretty; we have business; it is a good place to be seen; I need a change from the atmosphere of the office; you are paying, and I am broke—oh, yes . . . and I promised. All these interests are easily satisfied by our having lunch. There is no need to order them; they are not unruly or at odds.

So why am I writing this book? Why, to make money, to become famous, to earn the love of many women, to alter the world's perception of itself, to put my rivals' noses out of joint, to satisfy my narcissism, to display my talents, to justify my existence to my deceased father, to avoid cleaning the house; but if I wish to make money, I shall have to write trash, and if I wish to be famous, I had better hit home runs, and if I wish to earn the love of many women, I shall have more luck going to work in a bank. In short, these intentions do conflict; they must be ordered; none of them is particularly "good" in the goody sense; and none is aesthetic in any way.

But there is so much energy in the baser motives, and so little in the grander, that I need hate's heat to warm my art; I must have my malice to keep me going. For I must go, and go on, regardless. Because making a work of art (writing a book, being Botticelli) requires an extended kind of action, an ordered group of actions. Yet these actions are not the sort that result, like a battle, in many effects, helter-skelter: in broken bodies, fugitive glories, lasting pains, conquered territories, power, ruin, ill will; rather, as a funnel forms the sand and sends it all in the same direction, the many acts of the artist aim at one end, one result.

We are fully aware, of course, that while I am meeting you for lunch, admiring your bodice, buying office equipment, I am not doing the laundry, keeping the books, dieting, or being faithful in my heart; and when I am painting, writing, singing scales, I am not cooking, cleaning house, fixing flats. The hours, the days, the years of commitment to my work must necessarily withdraw me from other things, from my duties as a husband, a soldier, a citizen.

So the actions of the artist include both what he does and, therefore, what he doesn't do; what he does directly and on purpose, and what he does incidentally and quite by the way. In addition, there are things done, or not done, or done incidentally, that are quite essential to the completion and character of the work, but whose effects do not show themselves in the ultimate object or performance. As necessary as any other element, they disappear in the conclusion like a middle term in an argument. A deleted scene, for instance, may nonetheless lead to the final one. Every line is therefore many lines: words rubbed out, thoughts turned aside, concepts canceled. The eventual sentence lies there quietly, "Kill the king," with no one but the writer aware that it once read, "Kiss the king," and before that "Kiss the queen." For moralists, only too often, writing a book is little different from robbing a bank, but actions of the latter sort are not readily subject to revisions.

The writer forms words on a page. This defaces the page, of course, and in this sense it is like throwing a brick through a window; but it is not like throwing a brick through a window in any other way. And if writing is an immense ruckus made of many minor noises, some shutting down as soon as they are voiced, then reading is similarly a series of acts, better ordered than many, to be sure, but just as privately performed, and also open to choice, which may have many motives, too, the way the writing had. Paintings and performances (buildings even more so) are public in a fashion that reading and writing never are, although the moralist likes to make lump sums of everything and look at each art as if it were nothing but a billboard or a sound truck in the street.

If we rather tepidly observe that a building stands on its street quite differently from a book in its rack, must we not also notice how infrequently architects are jailed for committing spatial hanky-panky or putting up obscene façades? Composers may have their compositions hooted from the hall, an outraged patron may assault a nude, a church may be burned to get at the God believed to be inside, but more often than not it is the *littérateur* who is shot or sent to Siberia. Moralists are not especially sensitive to form. It is the message that turns their noses blue. It is the message they will murder you for. And messages that are passed as secretly as books pass, from privacy to privacy, make them intensely suspicious. Yet work which refuses such interpretations will not be pardoned either. Music which is twelve-toned, paintings which are abstract, writing which seems indifferent to its referents in the world—these attacks on messages themselves—they really raise the watchdog's hackles.

In life, values do not sit in separate tents like harem wives; they mix and mingle rather like sunlight in a room or pollution in the air. A dinner party, for example, will affect the diners' waists, delight or dismay their palates, put a piece of change in the grocer's pocket, bring a gleam to the vintner's eye. The guests may be entertained or stupefied by gossip, chat, debate, wit. I may lose a chance to make out, or happily see my seduction advance past hunt-and-peck. The host may get a leg up in the firm whose boss he's entertaining; serious arguments may break out; new acquaintances may be warmly made. And if I, Rabbi Ben Ezra, find myself seated next to Hermann Göring, it may put me quite off the quail—quail that the *Reichsmarschall* shot by machine gun from a plane. There should be no questions concerning the rabbi's qualms. It would be a serious misjudgment, however, if I imagined that the quail was badly cooked on account of who shot it, or believed that the field marshal's presence had soured the wine, although it may have ruined the taste in my mouth. It might be appropriate to complain of one who enjoyed the meal and laughed at the fat boy's jokes. Nevertheless, the meal will be well prepared or not, quite independently of the guests' delightful or obnoxious presence, and it would be simpleminded to think that because these values were realized in such close proximity, they therefore should be judged on other than their own terms—the terms, perhaps, of their pushier neighbors.

The detachment it is sometimes necessary to exercise in order to disentangle aesthetic qualities from others is often resented. It is frequently considered a good thing if moral outrage makes imbeciles of us. The aesthete who sees only the poppies blowing in Flanders fields is a sad joke, to be sure, but the politicized mind is too dense and too dangerous to be funny.

I have been mentioning some differences between moral acts as they are normally understood (keeping promises, saving the baby) and what might be called artistic ones (dancing the fandango, painting the Botticelli), and I have been drawing attention to the public and private qualities of the several arts lest they be treated *en bloc*. Finally, I have suggested that values have to be judged by sharply different standards sometimes, though they come to the same table. However, my dinner party differs from Petronius's banquet in another essential: it is "thrown" only once. Even if the evening is repeated down to the last guest's happy gurgle, the initial party can be only vaguely imitated, since you can't swallow the same soup twice (as a famous philosopher is supposed to have said). The events of my party were like pebbles tossed into a pond. The stones appear to shower the surface of the water with rings, which then augment or interfere with one another as they widen, although eventually they will enlarge into thin air, the pond will become calm, and the stones' effects will be felt only after eons, as they lie, slowly disintegrating, on the bottom.

Art operates at another level altogether. Petronius's story does not fling itself like a handful of stones at the public and then retire to contemplate the gradual recession of its consequences, but occurs continually as readers re-enact it. Of course these readings will not be identical (because no reading is written or automatically becomes a printed part of the text), but the text, unless it has been mutilated or re-edited, will remain the same. I shall recognize each line as the line I knew, and each word as the word that was. The letter abides and is literal, though the spirit moves and strays. In short, the mouth may have an altered taste, but not the soup.

For this reason the powers of events are known to be brief, even when loud and unsettling, and unless they can reach the higher levels of historical accounts—unless they can reach language—the events will be forgotten and their effects erased. Accounts, too, can be lost or neglected, so those texts that are truly strong are those whose qualities earn the love and loyalty of their readers, and enlist the support and stewardship of the organizations those readers are concerned with and control (schools, societies, academies, museums, archives), because the institutions encourage us to turn to these now canonical texts again and again, where their words will burn in each fresh consciousness as if they had just been lit.

Moralists are right to worry about works of art, then, because they belong to a higher level of reality than most things. Texts can be repeated; texts can be multiplied; texts can be preserved; texts beget commentaries, and their authors energize biographers; texts get quoted, praised, reviled, memorized; texts become sacred.

The effects of a text (as every failed commission on pornography has demonstrated) cannot be measured as you measure blows; the spread of a text cannot be followed like the course of an epidemic; there is no dye that can be spilled upon the ground to track the subtle seepages of its contamination. Texts are not acts of bodies but acts of minds; for the most part, then, they do not act on bodies as bodies act, but on minds as minds do.

Most religions do not gather their followers about God, as they pretend, or attract the faithful to the high ideals they claim to serve and defend: no— these believers have sold their souls to a book, and sit inside a text as though it were a temple, and warm themselves with the holy, unmistaken, and enduring Word. They protect the Word; they preach the Word; the blade of their sword is made mostly of the Word; and any other word is suspicious, likely to be an enemy bent on endangering the authority of whatever's gospel.

The position I am trying to defend is not that literature has no relation to morality, or that reading and writing, or composing, or painting, aren't also moral, or possibly immoral, acts. Of course they can be. But they are economic acts as well. They contribute to their author's health or illness, happiness or melancholy. They fill libraries, concert halls, museums. And much more. The artistic value of a book, however, is different from its economic value, and is differently determined, as is its weight in pounds, its utility as a paperweight or doorstop, its elevating or edifying or life-enhancing properties, its gallery of truths: new truths, known truths, believed truths, important truths, alleged truths, trivial truths, absolute truths, coming truths, plain unvarnished truths. Artistic quality depends upon a work's internal, formal, organic character, upon its inner system of relations, upon its structure and its style, and not upon the morality it is presumed to recommend, or upon the benevolence of its author, or its emblematic character, when it is seen as especially representative of some situation or society.

As I have already suggested, values may reinforce one another, or interfere with their realization in some thing or person. The proximity of Herr Göring may put me off my feed. Perhaps I ought to be put off. Perhaps the chef should have poisoned the quail. Perhaps each of the guests should have left in a huff. And the housemaid and the butler grin as they quaff champagne in the kitchen, grin so little bones appear between their open teeth. How's the pâté no one invited would eat? Deelish.

Wagner's works are not wicked simply because he was; nor does even the inherent vulgarity deep within the music quite destroy it. Frost's poetry seems written by a better man than we've been told he was. In fact, we are frequently surprised when an author of genius (like Chekhov) appears to be a person of some decency of spirit. The moral points of view in works of art differ as enormously as Dante's do from Sophocles's, or Shakespeare's from Milton's. Simply consider what we should have to say if the merit of these writers depended at all upon their being correct, even about anything. In any case, Balzac sees the world quite differently than Butor does; Goethe and Racine cannot both be right; so if being right mattered, we should be in a mess indeed, and most of our classics headed for the midden.

How many of us are prepared to embrace the cuckoo-clock concepts of Blake and Yeats? Or perhaps Pound? How about Kipling? D. H. Lawrence? The Marquis de Sade?

If author and art ought not to be confused, neither should art and audience. If we were to say, as I should prefer, that it is the moral world of the work which ought to matter to the moralist, not the genes of the author's grandfather, or the Jean who was a longtime lover, or a lean of the pen holder toward the political right or left, we ought also to insist that the reactions of readers aren't adequate evidence either. If Wagner's anti-Semitism doesn't fatally bleed into his operas and, like a bruise, discolor them, and if Balzac's insufferable bourgeois dreams don't irreparably damage his fictions, then why should we suppose the work itself, in so much less command of its readers than its author is of the text, will communicate its immoral implications like a virus to the innocents who open its covers?

To be sure, authors often like to think of their works as explosive, as corrupting, as evil. It is such fun to play the small boy. Lautréamont asks Heaven to "grant the reader the boldness to become ferocious, momentarily, like what he is reading, to find, without being disoriented, his abrupt and savage path through the desolate swamps of these somber and poison-filled pages." Yet this is an operatic attitude; reading is never more than reading, and requires a wakeful understanding—that is all. Certainly we should like to think that we had written some "poison-filled pages," but no luck. Even chewing them won't make you sick, not even queasy. And if you feel the least bit odd afterward, it's the ink.

If the relation of morality to art were based simply on the demand that art be concerned with values, then almost every author should satisfy it even if he wrote with his prick while asleep. (Puritans will object to the language in that sentence, and feminists to the organ, and neither will admire or even notice how it was phrased.) Henry Miller's work has been condemned, but Henry Miller is obsessed with ethical issues, and his work has a very pronounced moral point of view. *Madame Bovary* was attacked; *Ulysses* was forbidden entry into the United States; *Lady Chatterley's Lover* was brought to court, where they worried about signs of sodomy in it; *Lolita*, of course, was condemned; and, as Vonnegut has said (who also has suffered such censorship), so it goes. How long the list would be, how tiresome and dismaying and absurd its recital, if we were to cite every work that has been banned, burned, or brought into the dock.

It is simply not possible to avoid ethical concerns; they are everywhere; one is scarcely able to move without violating someone's moral law. Nor are artists free of the desire to improve and instruct and chastise and bemoan the behavior of their fellow creatures, whether they call themselves Dickens, D. H. Lawrence, or Hector Berlioz. Céline is so intensely a moral writer that it warps his work. That is the worry. "There are still a few hatreds I'm missing," he wrote. "I am sure they exist." Hate, we mustn't forget, is a thoroughly moralized feeling.

It is the management of all these impulses, attitudes, ideas, and emotions (which the artist has as much as anyone) that is the real problem, for each of us is asked by our aims, as well as by our opportunities, to overcome our past, our personal aches and pains, our beloved prejudices, and to enlist them in the service of our skills, the art we say we're loyal to and live for. If a writer is extended on the rack of love, let pain give the work purpose, and disappointment its burnished point. So the artistic temperament is called cold because its grief becomes song instead of wailing. To be a preacher is to bring your sense of sin to the front of the church, but to be an artist is to give to every mean and ardent, petty and profound feature of the soul a glorious, godlike shape.

It is actually not the absence of the ethical that is complained of when complaints are made, for the ethical is never absent. It is the absence of the *right* belief, the *right* act, that riles. Our pets have not been fed; repulsive enthusiasms have been encouraged, false gods pursued, obnoxious notions noised about; so damn these blank and wavy paintings and these hostile drums, these sentences that sound like one long scratch of chalk.

Goodness knows nothing of Beauty. They are quite disconnected. If I say "shit" in a sentence, it is irrelevant what else I say, whether it helps my sentence sing or not. What is relevant is the power of certain principles of decorum, how free to be offensive we are going to be allowed to be. When the dowager empress of China, Cixi, diverted funds intended for the navy to construct a large and beautiful marble boat, which thousands now visit at the Summer Palace in Beijing, she was guilty of expropriation. If her choice had been a free one, she would seem to have chosen to spend her money on a thing of peace rather than on things of war (a choice we might applaud); in fact, we know she simply spent the money on herself. She cannot have chosen the beauty she received, because beauty is beyond choice. The elegant workmanship which went into the boat, the pleasure and astonishment it has given to many, its rich and marvelous material, are serendipitous and do not affect the morality of the case.

When a government bans nonobjective art, it is because its very look is threatening; it is its departure from the upright, its deviationism, that is feared—a daub is a dangerous breach of decorum. Finally, when the Soviet authorities decided to loosen their restrictions on the publication of books and the holding of performances, this was not suddenly a choice of art over politics on their part; it *was* politics, and had to do with such issues as the freedom of information, the quashing of the Stalin cults, the placation of certain opponents, and so on, not with art. They knew what the novels in the drawers were about.

I do happen to feel, with Theodor Adorno, that writing a book is a very important ethical act, consuming so much of one's life; and that, in these disgusting times, a writer who does not pursue an alienating formalism (but, rather, tries to buck us up and tell us not to spit in the face of the present, instead of continuing to serve this corrupt and debauched society although it shits on every walk and befouls every free breath), is, if not a pawn of the system (a lackey, we used to say), then probably a liar and a hypocrite. (Shit cannot sing, you say? perhaps; but by the bowels, shit sells.) It is a general moral obligation to live in one's time, and to have a just and appropriate attitude toward it (to spit upon it if need be), not to live in the nineteenth century or to be heartless toward the less fortunate or to deny liberty and opportunity to others, to hold on to stupid superstitions, or fall victim to nostalgia.

But good books have been written by bad people, by people who served immoral systems, who went to bed with snakes, by people who were frauds in various ways, by schemers and panderers. And beautiful books have been written by the fat and old and ugly, the lonely, the misbegotten (it is the same in all the arts), and some of these beautiful books are, like Juan Goytisolo's, ferociously angry, and some of them are even somewhat sinister, like Baudelaire's, and some are shakingly sensuous, like those of Colette, and still others are dismayingly wise, or deal with terror tenderly, or are full of lamentable poppycock. (I am thinking most immediately of Pope's *Essay on Man*.)

I think it is one of the artist's obligations to create as perfectly as he or she can, not regardless of all other consequences, but in full awareness, nevertheless, that in pursuing other values—in championing Israel or fighting for the rights of women, or defending the faith, or exposing capitalism, supporting your sexual preferences, or speaking for your race—you may simply be putting on a saving scientific, religious, political mask to disguise your failure as an artist. Neither the world's truth nor a god's goodness will win you beauty's prize.

Finally, in a world which does not provide beauty for its own sake, but where the loveliness of flowers, landscapes, faces, trees, and sky are adventitious and accidental, it is the artist's task to add to the world's objects and ideas those delineations, carvings, tales, fables, and symphonic spells which ought to be there; to make things whose end is contemplation and appreciation; to give birth to beings whose qualities harm no one, yet reward even the most casual notice, and which therefore deserve to become the focus of a truly disinterested affection.

There is perhaps a moral in that.

Harper's Magazine, 1987
Published in *Finding a Form*, 1996

SIMPLICITIES

I

Junichiro Tanizaki wrote that we "Westerners are amazed at the simplicity of Japanese rooms, perceiving in them no more than ashen walls bereft of ornament." What he wrote is certainly true about Americans. We are amazed. Often, furthermore, we deeply approve; for simplicity—severity even—plainness—are pioneer virtues still held in high esteem by us, if rarely practiced now. Indeed, the simple, in our covered-wagon days, was directly connected, as a tool might be, to the hand and what the hand made. This simplicity implied less skill than it demanded determination, and it emerged from coarse necessity the way the vegetables we grew in the dirt near our farmhouse kitchen did: products equally of effort and rough chance, as crude as our first fence, and cultivated no farther than you would dig a well—not an inch beyond the reach of water.

The shelters we built were like the ground we broke and the implements we made—plain as their names: house, field, food, cloth, plow—simple as the simple liberties we enjoyed, though these were not freedoms from Nature, certainly, since Nature hemmed us in and made life hard; nor from thieves or Indians or illness, dangers common and recurrent as nighttime; but from society, from other people's profiteering regulations, from laws we didn't like, servitude, and our own past failures, from the exasperating complications of a civilization caught in the toils of Time, tied down by custom and privilege.

In a land whose very features were unfamiliar, where even the rules of life were strangers, where the past had been abolished so that everyone could feel they were starting life as equals from a line of opportunity which was the same for all; in such a land, with such a task, you had to learn to depend on yourself, to make a religion, as Emerson did, out of "self-reliance" and become a handyman, a "jack-of-all-trades," as it was put. But it was also true that when you did need others, you desperately needed them—to form a posse, raise a roof, to bridge a stream—nor did you have the time or training to divine obscure intentions or engage in elaborate ritual games in order to discover whether another person was a friend or an enemy, a worker or a wastrel, dependable or weak, an honest man or a rustler; so you wanted to know immediately "how the land lay," and the frank and open countenance was consequently prized, as were the looks of a man who had worked long and hard in the wind and sun, who appeared to fear God (for you were often beyond the reach of any other law), who had the confidence that came from overcoming many obstacles, who "put on no airs," "wore his heart on his sleeve," was entirely "up front," and, as the salacious saying is now, "let it all hang out"—presumably his (his wife's) wash. Nowadays, even a candid, blunt, abrasive boss can be admired because he has been "straight" with you, letting you know "where you stood."

The simple, like the straight and the plain, is relatively featureless. It reduces the number of things with which you have to cope. After all, when crossing the country by covered wagon, you took winding trails only when rivers and mountains made the circuitous the shortest way. And in the Bible, didn't God promise to make the crooked straight and the rough places plain? We liked the land we settled to be level, well drained, free of rock. We often preferred the companionship of animals, because they couldn't talk at all and could be expected to act within their species as if in a cage. It was the body which dealt with the day's difficulties. It was the body which built, which plowed, which planted, and which, on occasion, danced and sang and played. The body baked. The body begot. It was not the brain.

So our breath was supposed to be too short for long sentences. Democracy didn't encourage subordination, not in people or in any part of their speech, whether it was to fancy words or flattering phrases or complicated clauses. Honesty was suspicious of endless ramifications. Adverbs that didn't contribute to their action were needless frills. If it didn't matter to the bite of the blade what the color of the ax's handle was, you didn't write it down or say its name. Events were the chief ingredient in stories, and the main thing was not to dawdle but to offer up the verb and then get on with it. Ideas fuddled you far worse than alcohol. Theories couldn't thread a needle. You read a bit from the Good Book of an evening because, otherwise, God might blight your wheat. And you went to the Sunday Meeting for the society of it, and for the same wary reason you read. What's more, there was always another row to hoe.

How different this simplicity was from the sort praised by the subtle Tanizaki, and how misled we Westerners were when we admired an innocence we thought was our own. Those ashen walls, with their unadorned surfaces, the candles that lit them, the unpretentious wood that framed the windows, the plain mats that softened and warmed the floor, were there to receive the indefinite wavers of the flame, to grow uneven with revelation and concealment, to move, as if alive, inside their planes and provoke the profoundest contemplation.

While the walls of the American settlers existed to keep out the cold and be forgotten . . . existed to keep out the vast space of the prairie, which lay around every cabin like an endless sea . . . existed to keep out the high sky you could fall into like a pit.

The traditional Japanese room might give out onto a garden of gravel, a small raked space with one or two stones, which stood for a world or any mountain, each tame as a household bird. What of the planks whose grain will emerge only after years of timidity and suspicion, the mats that greet each footstep with a whisper which they pass among their fibers? and what of the corners in such a room, carved from darkness, where perhaps a thread of gold gleams from the flank of an otherwise invisible lacquer chest, where the dimmest hint of an ardent desire may lie wrapped in alternating layers of shadow and silk so that an additional breath bends the candle flame? These conditions, these qualities, speak to us not of simplicity, not in our sense, but of the indirect and devious, and suggest—there is the word!—they suggest that these plain surfaces and impassive features are screens on which one reality plays while another lurks behind them, and may move, when it moves, in metaphysical earnest.

One kind of simplicity is reached, then (we cannot say "achieved"), when skills and means and time and energy are minimal. It is the sort of simplicity which looks not at the causes of things but only at their effects. Who cares, it says . . . who cares what drove the nail if now its head rests in the right place? When the larder holds only a bit of ground corn, a corn cake is what we shall have. Two "I do"s shall marry a couple as well as any cathedral ceremony.

Another sort of simplicity is reached by removal and erasure, by denial and refusal. It begins with features already played upon by the artist, with surfaces into which the candle's flicker has been cut, and dark corners created with charcoal, so there need never be an actual niche or a real lantern, but only a steady, indifferent glare of light; for absences will have to be understood to be as solidly in place as any wooden headrest, waiting the head that will sleep. It begins by looking at decoration as if it were a disease, as a form of social mold, a sign of spiritual decay, another case of the showy bad taste of some nouveau riche, or the loud cosmetics of a whore. Beneath these excrescences, these layers of gilt, these scabs of fashion, is an honest beam, more richly grained and more interesting than all these distracting carvings; beneath this powder and this cream is a natural beauty who might again send the Achaeans against Troy; behind these nervous variations is a mighty theme; let us hear it. Just one time. So cleanly, so clearly, we cannot be confused, nor any flaw be disguised. We want to grasp the lines, follow the form, find the true source of our sensation. Then, when real simplicity has returned, when the essential has been restored to disclose its few rightful properties, we may let fall upon it the pale light of our mind; we may shadow it with the darkness that lives in a few of our own thoughts; we may allow to cross it the slow movements of our meditations.

Let us reconsider, for a moment, the simple objects that our ancestors made: a plain wooden bowl, for example, hollowed from a sawed round of tree trunk. A chisel bites into the heart of that wood, eats into the center of its rings of yearly growth, so that shortly a spoonful of milk could be placed in it, and then a cup's worth, although there will be bark remaining around the rim. The rind is peeled off, needless bulk is cut away, and by continued gnawing at the core, the tools of the carpenter create a basin we can begin to recognize as a bowl. Or perhaps hot coals burn the hollow in it. Its interior should be smooth enough to let liquids slosh, a spoon to scoop, a larger one to ladle, and it should rinse out easily. The wood must be hard and dense so that warm soup won't penetrate its fibers. Beyond this, little needs to be done. For the utilitarian, the means cease the moment the end is reached. A little sand will scour the bowl; a little seasoning will secure the grain. If it were a size to conveniently stack—that would be a plus. Our sentences should similarly fly to the mark, deposit their message, and disappear, as if a pigeon were to become its poop, so, when any one of us looked up to complain because our shoulder had been stained, there'd be no bird there.

Then why did we ever worry about the exact slope of the hollow our tools had chipped, the precise sheen of the wood, the slim line and smooth run of the rim? We certainly should have cared about how sturdily the dish sat, and how its sides widened so the soup could cool; but why were we concerned about the match of its rings, the quality of the grain in the base and bowl, the shape of the shadows which crept from beneath its sides?

This bowl is ceasing to be simple. Hardship forces the makeshift upon us; primitive conditions produce primitive results; urgent needs aren't choosy; indeed, the sharp teeth of need close like a trap on any victim; but when circumstances are no longer as straitened as they once were, and a bit of leisure, some small level of satisfaction, has been reached, the mind can let go of the plow's handle, can turn aside from its single thought and transform its lust into a little love.

The bowl has ceased to be simple. A word like "perfection" has us by the ear. Now we are seeking a smoothness, an evenness, an achievement in its completion that will take us days—months—beyond an efficient use of our time. We become obsessed (is it suddenly or slowly?) by geometry, by geometry's deceptive simplicities, its lucent beauty, and we see how the bowl is but a nest of circles whose circumferences are steadily shrinking and whose diameters contract.

The bowl is a celebration of complexity. We've had to set several versions aside in order to start over, trying to improve its proportions, passing before our mind's demanding eye, as though they were bathing beauties, images of other utensils whose alluring features may help us with the one we're composing. What is this resulting bowl, then, whose shaping requires the failure of so many others, which devours this base and that rim, accepts a surface, adapts a form, distorts a tendency—acquiring qualities the way an actor takes on personalities in order to realize a role? what is this object whose making is directed by memory as much as by the pots that are broken when they fail to satisfy, or the bowls that are burned as kindling when the wind turns cold, or the words that are sent away from the sentence they were to serve in and linger near it like disconsolate shades? what is this thing built so solidly of ghosts?

How reluctantly, in the United States, have we come to recognize that civilization is refinement; that it requires leisure, judgment, taste, skill, and the patient work of a solitary mind passing itself, as though it were both a cleaner and a cleansing cloth, back and forth across an idea, back and forth until the substance of it—wood or marble or music, in syllables seeking their place in some song—back and forth until the matter of it begins to gleam deeply from its buried center, deeply, where thought and thing are one, and therefore not solely from its surface, where a glitter may sometimes be glibly emitted, a glitter that comes just after a bit of light has struck, a glitter, a glit, before the beam has bounded off—a glitter, a glit—a spark, after which there will be only the light that has gone.

Apart from the simplicity associated with the pioneer spirit of America, we developed, also very early, a simplicity of a second sort, though certainly in some sympathy with the first: this was exemplified by the distilled designs, the purified life and even purer dreams, of a sect called Shakers (so named because of their custom of dancing during their religious services, and of being frequently and literally moved by their love of God). They were separatists, forming withdrawn and self-sustaining communities. They were pacifists like the Quakers (another name signifying uncontrolled movement), and believed in equality and in the actual, rather than the rhetorical, Brotherhood of Man. They were celibate and endeavored to live a life free of sexual tension and gender competition. They were undogmatic, preferring to follow their faith rather than preach it, drawing communicants not by argument and propaganda but by shining example. Since Shakers did not breed, they were never guilty of corrupting their children with their principles, and converts came to them entirely out of free choice and when in possession of a presumably mature mind.

"When a World's Fair was held several years ago in Japan," June Sprigg, a student of the Shakers, writes, "one of the most popular features was an exhibit of Shaker furniture. Chairs without carving, tables without knick-knacks, the simplicity of Shaker stoves and baskets, even the white walls and bare wood floors—all these made sense to the Japanese, who recognized and appreciated the same simplicity based on spiritual principles that characterize traditional Japanese culture."

I wonder if the visitors to the fair saw how directly the Shakers translated moral qualities into principles of craftsmanship: spare, straight, upright, plain, simple, direct, pure, square, tight, useful, orderly, unaffected, neat, clean, careful, correct. For every chair there was a peg on the wall from which it would hang while the floor was thereby more swiftly swept, and every peg was perfect. Since the chair was hung by its heels, as it were, what dust there was would settle on the bottom of the seat and not on the side where one sat. Beds folded up into the wall, and drawers drew out of anywhere. A sewing box might be fitted into a rocker, shutters slid up and down instead of swinging out into the room, and boxes were invariably nested. Every space was made of appointed places, and the tools that cleaned those hard-to-reach corners were hooked alongside a horsehair sieve sometimes, or a fluted tin mold for maple sugar.

Yet the Shakers used only the finest maple, the truest oak and clearest pine, the best slate. Grooves and pegs which were internal to a piece, and therefore never seen, were finished as finely as if they would live their whole lives out of doors. Drawers not only slid out smoothly; they said they slid, in the look of them, in the shush of their sliding; and the ingenious nesting of things, the creation of objects which did double duty, the ubiquitous ledges and holders and racks and pegs, spoke of order, and neatness, and fit—the Godliness of Utility; for though their chairs were stiff and forthright, their tables were wide and unencumbered, and their solutions to problems quite evidently inspired by necessity; there was nothing humble about their materials, pure and as prized as silver and gold. There was nothing humble about the days of careful labor that obviously went into them. There was nothing humble and spare about houses with double doors and double stairs—one for each sex. Nor is there anything humble about a building built to stand a thousand years, or in some handmade things so supremely finished they provoke us to exclaim: "Handmade, maybe, but what careful fingers, what holy hands!" There is nothing humble about perfection.

And the hidden joints, the concealed beds, the matched grains, the boxes which live their carefully concealed lives in other boxes: these are habits of the High Baroque.

Unlike pioneer simplicity, which was perforce crude and incomplete, Shaker simplicity spoke eloquently about its moral ideals. Every room was as much God's place as a church. Every object was, in its fealty to spirit, in its richness of refinement, in its strenuous demands on occupants and employers, a symbol of Divinity and Divine Law.

2

Simplicities, in short, are not all the same. When, in her masterpiece called "Melanctha," a story of black people and the problems of love, Gertrude Stein resorts to the plainness of the pioneer style, she does so to render the rhythms of black Baltimore speech, and to convey the handmade quality of such talk as it struggles to express powerful and complex feelings through the most ordinary of words and by the social patterns implicit in its echoes, rhymes, and repetitions.

> Melanctha told Rose one day how a woman whom she knew had killed herself because she was so blue. Melanctha said, sometimes, she thought this was the best thing for herself to do.
>
> Rose Johnson did not see it the least bit that way.
>
> "I don't see Melanctha why you should talk like you would kill yourself just because you're blue. I'd never kill myself Melanctha just 'cause I was blue. I'd maybe kill somebody else Melanctha 'cause I was blue, but I'd never kill myself. If I ever killed myself Melanctha it'd be by accident, and if I ever killed myself by accident Melanctha, I'd be awful sorry."

Although Ernest Hemingway's style gets some of its substance from Gertrude Stein (it is even more deeply indebted to Sherwood Anderson), its aim is less complex than hers. He borrows a bit of machismo from the pioneer, some of his ostentatious simplicity from the Shaker, and sharpens this by means of a selectivity which is severe and narrow. If Adolf Loos, architecture's enemy of ornament, felt we should sweep walls free and wipe planes clean,

Hemingway's purpose was to seize upon the basics right from the beginning and therefore be in a position to give an exact description of "the way it was." He would remove bias and cliché, our conception of how things had always been, our belief in how things ought to be, and replace them with the square-shouldered resoluteness of reality.

> Out through the front of the tent he watched the glow of the fire when the night wind blew on it. It was a quiet night. The swamp was perfectly quiet. Nick stretched under the blanket comfortably. A mosquito hummed close to his ear. Nick sat up and lit a match. The mosquito was on the canvas, over his head. Nick moved the match quickly up to it. The mosquito made a satisfactory hiss in the flame. The match went out. Nick lay down again under the blankets. He turned on his side and shut his eyes. He was sleepy. He felt sleep coming. He curled up under the blanket and went to sleep.

Brevity may serve as the soul for wit, but it is far from performing such a service for simplicity. The economy of most of Hemingway's writing is only an appearance. To shorten this passage, we could have encouraged the reader to infer more, and said: "The fire brightened when the night wind breathed upon it. The swamp was as quiet as the night." If images, implications, and connectives are allowed, a condensation can be sought which is far from simple. "A mosquito sang in his ear, so he sat and lit a match." Matches do go quickly out. No need to mention that. Moreover, Nick could be put to sleep far less redundantly. But Hemingway needs to state the obvious and avoid suggestion, to appear to be proceeding step by step. He needs the clumsy reiteration. It makes everything seem so slow and simple, plain, even artless, male.

Hemingway's search for the essential was characteristically American; that is, it was personal; he sought a correct account of his own experience, because anything less would be fraudulent and insincere. The simplifying came prior to the writing; it was to be built into the heart and the eye, into the man—hunting or fishing, running with the bulls, going to war, mastering his woman. On the whole, Hemingway's work has not held up very well, and that is perhaps because he didn't see or feel any more than he reports he felt or saw, because the way it was was really only Heming's way.

According to Democritus, the atom was so simple it could not be divided, and that simplicity, Plato thought, was the source of the soul's immortality. Only if you had parts could you come apart, and only if you came apart could you decay and die and disappear. Change itself, Parmenides argued, depended upon such minuscule divisions, but it required, in addition, the space to come apart in, for when separation occurred, something (which was a swatch of Nothing, in most cases) had to fill the breach in order to ensure that the cut would continue and not heal around the knife. So the atom remained an atom because it was a plenum and contained not even a trace of the real agent of decay: empty space.

Behind the search for the simple is a longing for the indivisible, the inde-structible, the enduring. When a noun is reified, its elements fuse. It obtains an Essence. It becomes One, Primitive, Indefinable. Or, rather: any defini-tion will be analytic. "God is good" is a version of "God is God." A rose is a rose. Business is business. And that is that.

These ultimate simples were invisible, not because they were very, very small, but because they were very, very pure. Purity is a property of simplic-ity. It is often what is sought in seeking the simple. Atoms had no qualities. Atoms had nothing to say to the senses. Atoms were geometries. They had shapes; you could count them; they weighed; they fell through the Void like drops of rain; they rebounded; they combined; and when these combina-tions came undone, they remained as unaffected by their previous unions as any professional Don Juan.

Visibility is impurity. Invisibility belongs to the gods, to the immaculate Forms, to the primeval seeds. It is not morally pure, ethereal spirits but those ghosts clotted with crime who hang about like frozen smoke in the still air. The soul, as a penance, is encumbered with flesh. Thought is brought to us in terms that can't help but demean it, as if our sincerities were written in neon. Sin and sensation together veil the truth. Simplicity serves the essential, so the simple style will stick to the plainest, most unaffected, most ordinary words; its sentences will be direct and declarative, following the basic gram-matical forms; and to the understanding, it will seem to disappear into its world of reference, more modest than most ministers' wives, and invisible as a perfect servant.

Memory, too, is a polluter. The purity of the maid lies not in an untorn hymen, which is simply a symbol, but in the fact that she brings to her husband's embrace the memory of no other arms. The purity of the maid guarantees the purity of her husband's line: that his son is his; no uncertified seed has fertilized her first, been there ahead of him to father the future with a past. A fair maid has no past. Her husband will form her, as though her breasts grew beneath his hands. So she shall wear white as a sign she is unsul-lied, suitable, and as ready as a turkey to be carved.

The ultimate simples which the early philosophers revered were near enough to numbers to make the move from Materialism to Idealism a small step. The logician, in an exactly similar fashion, seeks the supreme, unfactorable unit to begin with, and to that unit he then applies his intuition of the first fundamental logical operation—namely, addition. One, and then one more. One. And one. And one. Adam did no less. Like Roman numerals or a prisoner's day. One. And one. Bars, mars, nicks, accumulating in the direction of an unapproachable infinity. Others argue that anything either Is (like a light switch, On) or it Isn't (like a light switch, Off); that a yes or a no suffices. To build a machinelike mind. Plato's Demiurge lets the right triangle flop about like a stranded fish, and in that way it forms squares, cubes, and other polyhedrons, or it spins itself into a cone (for a cone is a triangle revolving like a door), while this shape, pivoting on its peak, will turn itself, in turn, into a sphere. With every essential figure drawn and every atom formed, the remainder of the universe is easy.

At one extreme, then, we find mathematicians, logicians, and those quantitative scientists who shave with Occam's razor; whose concepts have one (and only one) clear meaning; whose rules are unambiguous, and conclusions rigorously drawn; while, on the other hand, there are the pious craftsmen who think with their hands, reverence their materials, and build their own beds.

Simple as the simple is, and basic as butter is to French cuisine, it never seems to be nearby or abundant but has to be panned, like silver or gold, from a muddy stream. Surfaces have to be scrubbed, disguises divested, impurities refined away, truths extracted, luxuries rejected, seductions scorned, diversions refused, memories erased. Because if some things in life are simple, quite a lot is not; quite a bit is "buzzing, blooming confusion." There is, of course, deception's tangled web. There are the many mysteries of bureaucracy, the flight path of bees, the concept of the Trinity; there are the vagaries of the weather, the ins and outs of diplomacy, business, politics, adultery; there is poetry's indirection, the opacity of German metaphysics, the ornamentation of Baroque churches, and the cast of the Oriental mind.

Simplicity is not a given. It is an achievement, a human invention, a discovery, a beloved belief.

In contrast to the bubbling stew we call our consciousness (and to reprise), there are the purities of reason, which require clear rules of inference and transparent premises; there are the invisible particles of matter, those underlying elements out of which the All is made Universal by the Few; there are nascent conditions of existence, unsullied by use or age or other kinds of decay; there are definitions brief and direct as gunshots; there are modes of being that streamline the soul for its afterlife flights. Consequently, beneath simplicity itself, whenever it serves as an ideal, lie moral and metaphysical commitments of considerable density. There are Hume's simple impressions. There are Leibniz's monads. There are Lucretius's jumpy atoms. Yet we do not behold the simple simply. If our gaze is direct, its object open, our climb to the mountain's top is circuitous, the path perilous. If the foundations of Reality are simple, the grounds of Simplicity are complex.

Those who champion simplicity as a way of life are aware of the political and moral statement they are making. Gustav Stickley, who contributed so substantially to the Arts and Crafts Movement in America around the turn of the century, certainly was. For him, simplicity was not a Spartan lunch of caviar and champagne, or a lazy day sunning on the deck of the yacht. In his first collection of *Craftsman Homes,* Stickley writes:

> By simplicity here is not meant any foolish whimsical eccentricity of dress or manner or architecture, colonized and made conspicuous by useless wealth, for eccentricity is but an expression of individual egotism and as such must inevitably be short-lived. And what our formal, artificial world of today needs is not more of this sort of eccentricity and egotism, but less; not more conscious posing for picturesque reform, but greater and quieter achievement along lines of fearless honesty; not less beauty, but infinitely more of a beauty that is real and lasting because it is born out of use and taste.

For Stickley, his movement's heroic figure was an Englishman, Edward Carpenter, whose writings he much admired and frequently cites. *England's Ideal* (which is the title of one of Carpenter's books) appears to be agrarian, anticolonial, puritan, roundhead, and reformist. Our labor should not be a stranger to all that sustains us; our culture should be of our own contriving, and not something we have purchased in a shop; the true character of life ought not to be shamefully concealed; the head must have a hand, both to help it and to hold it in check. Possessions, in particular, are like unwanted immigrants—the first family to arrive is soon followed by boatloads of their relatives. Carpenter is vivid:

> It cannot be too often remembered that every additional object in a house requires additional dusting, cleaning, repairing; and lucky you are if its requirements stop there. When you abandon a wholesome tile or stone floor for a Turkey carpet, you are setting out on a voyage of which you cannot see the end. The Turkey carpet makes the old furniture look uncomfortable, and calls for stuffed couches and armchairs; the couches and armchairs demand a walnut-wood table; the

walnut-wood table requires polishing, and the polish bottles require shelves; the couches and armchairs have casters and springs, which give way and want mending; they have damask seats, which fade and must be covered; the chintz covers require washing, and when washed they call for antimacassars to keep them clean. The antimacassars require wool, and the wool requires knitting-needles, and the knitting-needles require a box, the box demands a side table to stand on and the carpet wears out and has to be supplemented by bits of drugget, or eked out with oilcloth, and beside the daily toil required to keep this mass of rubbish in order, we have every week or month, instead of the pleasant cleaning-day of old times, a terrible domestic convulsion and bouleversement of the household.

Of course, for the person who does not hear the Turkey carpet call for a stuffed couch, or rejects its demands for a walnut-wood table, or refuses to fill the table's polishing requirements, or the bottle's for a shelf, as if they were medical prescriptions; for such a person the growing snowball of belongings will never overtake and amalgamate the needs of the sagging seat or soiled cover; because the simplest thing to do with dust is never to disturb it, while wear can be watched with the same interest accorded to a sunset, and juxtapositions of hilarious quaintness or stylistic jar can often be appreciated as accurate images of the condition of life. Simplicity carries at its core a defensive neatness that despairs of bringing the wild world to heel and settles instead on taming a few things by placing them in an elemental system where the rules say they shall stay. Corners full of cupboards, nooks full of crannies, built-in shelves, seats, and drawers, deny each corresponding desire for change, for adjustment. They may begin as conveniences, but they end as impositions. It is their insistence that every function has its implement, every implement its place, every place its station, and every station its duties, as they wish the world does, and had, and did.

Labor-saving devices like the sewing machine, Carpenter argues, only provide more time for fashioning frills and flounces. Economy, like purity, like neatness, is one of simplicity's principal ingredients. We must be frugal with what we have when what we have (of premises or provisions) is so limited; but we need to be frugal whether our possessions are many or few, because frugality is inherently virtuous. In describing economy's consequences, Carpenter does not conceal the religious implications but records them, albeit with a saving smile.

For myself I confess to a great pleasure in witnessing the Economics of Life—and how seemingly nothing need be wasted; how the very stones that offend the spade in the garden become invaluable when footpaths have to be laid out or drains to be made. Hats that are past wear get cut up into strips for nailing creepers on the wall; the upper leathers of old shoes are useful for the same purpose. The under garment that is too far gone for mending is used for patching another less decrepit of its kind, then it is torn up into strips for bandages or what not; and when it has served its time thus it descends to floor washing, and is scrubbed out of life—useful to the end. When my coat has worn itself into an affectionate intimacy with my body, when it has served for Sunday best, and for week days, and got weather-stained out in the fields with the sun and rain—then faithful, it does not part from me, but getting itself cut up into shreds and patches descends to form a hearthrug for my feet. After that, when worn through, it goes into the kennel and keeps my dog warm, and so after a lapse of years, retiring to the manure-heaps and passing out on to the land, returns to me in the form of potatoes for my dinner; or being pastured by my sheep, reappears upon their backs as the material of new clothing. Thus it remains a friend to all time, grateful to me for not having despised and thrown it away when it first got behind the fashions. And seeing we have been faithful to each other, my coat and I, for one round or life-period, I do not see why we should not renew our intimacy—in other metamorphoses—or why we should ever quite lose touch of each other through the aeons.

Just suppose, though, that carelessness is the way of the world; that natural selection proceeds by means of an immense waste; that survival is hit or miss and fitness is genetic. Suppose that the deepest of energy's rhythms are random, and that nature may conserve matter but callously use up each of its particular forms. Suppose that order is only a security blanket; that there are no essences; that substance is another philosophical invention, like soul and spirit and ego and the gods, like mind and will and cause and natural law. Suppose that life will run every which way like a dispersed mob; that the words for life are "proliferation" and "opportunism," and that ends are absent and meaning, too, purposes pointless and pointlessness the rule: what will simplicity explain in such a case? what will it justify? how will its economies console? its purities protect? its neatness regulate?

So many simplicities! How is one to know where one is? what one has? We sometimes admire the naïve directness of the primitive painter, failing to notice that what is attractive is often what is not there, rather than what is; and the simplicity we associate in the United States with the Shakers can be found in the mystically inspired Piet Mondrian, as well as in other artists for whom purity of color, line, and shape represents a holiness otherwise out of reach, although what each reaches is obscured behind a different mist; then there is the meditative simplicity of someone like Tanizaki, which seems to require only a cleared space, a bare screen, a benevolent silence, into which he can cast shadows like so many heavy sacks, or project a dance of light and mind, or provoke the mosquito into speaking, or prevail on the moon to wane; perhaps nearby we can place the duplicitous simplicity of the drape or curtain behind which plots may be planned, or bring out the bland expression that lids a kettle of seething rage, or maybe we can unfold a calm screen, like a newspaper held in front of our breakfast face, behind which caresses unscheduled by any passion can continue themselves to their self-canceling conclusion; while, finally, we must find a spot beside the psychological essentialism of a writer like Hemingway, or alongside the ontological researches of a painter like Bashō, where we can put the expressive simplicities of such minimalists as Samuel Beckett and Mark Rothko, who brood upon their motifs like Cézanne on his mountain, or Flaubert on his Bovary, until any silly little thing, so intensely attended to—as words often are, as symbols are, as bodies, as beliefs—until any ugly old tatter, attended to, touched by concern, becomes as full of the possible as an egg, an embryo, a soft explosion of sperm; and we stare at the striations of a stone, for instance, as at a star, as if time itself wore every scar the stone does, as if the rock were that world of which the poet so often speaks—that world made cunningly; that world held in the palm of the hand; that flower, wooden bowl, or grain of sand, of which the poet so often speaks—speaks to another world's inattentive ear.

"Limitations of means determine style." That is the pat answer to many a talk-show question. "With one hand tied behind my back . . ." is the common boast. The simple can be a show of strength; it can place a method or a bit of material under significant stress so as to see what it is capable of, what its qualities can achieve. In the small and simple atom is a frightful force, a heat equivalent to a nation's hate, if it is unanimously released, as meaning in a lengthy sentence sometimes waits to the last syllable to explain itself, or a life of persistent disappointment bursts suddenly down the barrel of a gun, years of pent-up letdowns set loose.

Simplicity can be a boast—"See how I deprive myself"; it can be an emblem of holiness, a claim to virtues that might otherwise never be in evidence: the peasant-loving prince, the modest monarch, unspoiled star, humble savior, rich man's downcast door. But most of all it is a longing: for less beset days, for clarity of contrast and against the fuddle of grays, for certainty and security, and the deeper appreciation of things made possible by the absence of distraction, confusion, anxiety, delay. Simplicity understands completeness and closure, the full circle, something we can swing a compass round, or—to hammer out the line—get really straight.

What it does not understand so well is exuberance, abundance, excess, gusto, joy, absence of constraint, boundless aspiration, mania, indulgence, sensuality, risk, the full of the full circle, variation, elaboration, difference, lists like this, deviousness, concealment, the pleasures of decline, laughter, polyphony, digression, prolixity, pluralism, or that the devil is the hero in the schemeless scheme of things. If our North Pole is Samuel Beckett and our South Pole is Anton Webern, our equator is made by François Rabelais with Falstaff's belt.

Thinking now of how complex simplicity is, perhaps we have an answer (though I do not remember previously posing any question). Before the buzzing, blooming abundance of every day, facing the vast regions of ocean and the seemingly limitless stretch of empty space; or—instead—wincing at the news in the daily papers (you had not thought the world—as wide as earth, water, and air are—could contain so much crime, such immense confusion, this daunting amount of pain); or—instead—reading the novels of Henry James and James Joyce and Melville and Mann, or living in Proust or traveling in Tolstoy, you are again impressed by immensity, by the plethora of fact, by the static of statistics and the sheer din of data, by the interrelation of everything, by twists and turns and accumulations, as in this sentence going its endless way; yet as one proceeds in science, as one proceeds through any complex aesthetic surface, as one proceeds, the numerous subside in the direction of the few (the Gordian knot is made, it turns out, of a single string), the power of number grasps vastness as though each Milky Way were the sneeze of a cicada; so that, slowly perhaps, steadily certainly, simplicity reasserts itself. The simple sentence is achieved.

Thinking, then, of how simple complexity turns out to be, I can understand, when we began with a bowl chipped from a bit of wood, how its innocence drew suitors. Simplicity disappeared the way a placid pool is broken when a bit of bread brings a throng of greedy carp to boil, or when the mind turns plain mud or simple wood into moving molecules, those into atoms orbiting alarmingly, these into trings, trons, and quarks, until the very mind that made them gives up trying to calculate their behavior. At such times, and in such times as these, don't we desire the small garden into which we can carry our battered spirit, or perhaps a small room at the top of some tower, a hut in a forest, a minibike instead of a Toyota, a bit of smoked salmon on an impeccable leaf of lettuce, a small legacy from a relative long forgotten whose history is no burden and no embarrassment? only one servant?

Tanizaki explains to us how the high shine of lacquerware (whose surface under electric light is so harsh and vulgar) becomes softly luminous in the candlelight it was meant for; how the voluminous folds of a lady's garment may hide her body from us, only to permit her to seduce us with her wit.

He allows us to see that the simplest step is nevertheless a step in a complex series, a series whose sum is simple. Cultures are both complex and simple, the way the world is. Having reached that world, with the poet's help, from a grain of sand, and found that stretch of sand peopled with every sort of sun-bather, we must remember to disembody bather and sand again, to simplify the beach and its sighing surf, so that now we watch the water run up that sand, as full of foam as ale is, only to slow and subside and slip back into the sea again, leaving a line at each wave lap—a line as pure as a line by Matisse, a line as purely sensuous as the outline of some of those bathers, lying on a beach one grain of which we'd begun with, when we said we could see the world in a bit of grit.

The Review of Contemporary Fiction, 1991
Published in *Finding a Form,* 1996

The Music of Prose

To speak of the music of prose is to speak in metaphor. It is to speak in metaphor because prose cannot make any actual music. The music of prose has the most modest of inscriptions. Its notes, if we could imagine sounding them, do not have any preassigned place in an aural system. Hence they do not automatically find themselves pinned to the lines of a staff, or confined in a sequence of pitches. Nor is prose's music made of sounds set aside and protected from ordinary use as ancient kings conserved the virginity of their daughters. In the first place, prose often has difficulty in getting itself pronounced at all. In addition, any tongue can try out any line; any accent is apparently okay; any intonation is allowed; almost any pace is put up with. For prose, there are no violins fashioned with love and care and played by persons devoted to the artful rubbing of their strings. There are no tubes to transform the breath more magically than the loon can by calling out across a lake. The producers of prose do not play scales or improve their skills by repeating passages of De Quincey or Sir Thomas Browne, although that might be a good idea. They do not work at *Miss iss ip pi* until they get it right. The sound of a word may be arbitrary and irrelevant to its meaning, but the associations created by incessant use are strong, so that you cannot make the sound *m o o n* without seeming to mean "moon." By the time the noun has become a verb, its pronunciation will feel perfectly appropriate to the mood one is in when one moons, say, over a girl, and the "moo" in the mooning will add all its features without feeling the least discomfort. In music, however, the notes are allowed to have their own way and fill the listeners' attention with themselves and their progress. Nonmusical associations (thinking of money when you hear do-re-me played) are considered irrelevant and dispensable.

In sum, prose has no notes, no scale, no consistency or purity of sound, and only actors roll its *r*'s, prolong its vowels, or pop its *p*'s with any sense of purpose.

Yet no prose can pretend to greatness if its music is not also great; if it does not, indeed, construct a surround of sound to house its meaning the way flesh was once felt to embody the soul, at least till the dismal day of the soul's eviction and the flesh's decay.

For prose has a pace; it is dotted with stops and pauses, frequent rests; inflections rise and fall like a low range of hills; certain tones are prolonged; there are patterns of stress and harmonious measures; there is a proper method of pronunciation, even if it is rarely observed; alliteration will trouble the tongue, consonance ease its sounds out, so that any mouth making that music will feel its performance even to the back of the teeth and to the glottal's stop; mellifluousness is not impossible, and harshness is easy; drumroll and clangor can be confidently called for—lisp, slur, and growl; so there will be a syllabic beat in imitation of the heart, while rhyme will recall a word we passed perhaps too indifferently; vowels will open and consonants close like blooming plants; repetitive schemes will act as refrains, and there will be phrases—little motifs—to return to, like the tonic; clauses will be balanced by other clauses the way a waiter carries trays; parallel lines will nevertheless meet in their common subject; clots of concepts will dissolve and then recombine, so we shall find endless variations on the same theme; a central idea, along with its many modifications, like soloist and chorus, will take their turns until, suddenly, all sing at once the same sound.

Since the music of prose depends upon its performance by a voice, and since, when we read, we have been taught to maintain a library's silence, so that not even the lips are allowed to move, most of the music of the word will be that heard only by the head and, dampened by decorum, will be timorous and hesitant. That is the hall, though, the hall of the head, where, if at all, prose (and poetry, too, now) is given its little oral due. There we may say, without allowing its noise to go out of doors, a sentence of Robert South's, for instance: "This is the doom of fallen man, to labour in the fire, to seek truth in *profundo*, to exhaust his time and impair his health and perhaps to spin out his days, and himself, into one pitiful, controverted conclusion"; holding it all in the hush of our inner life, where every imagined sound we make is gray and no more material than smoke, and where the syllables are shaped so deeply in our throats nothing but a figment emerges, an *eidolon*, a shadow, the secondhand substance of speech.

Nevertheless, we can still follow the form of South's sentence as we say it to ourselves: "This is the doom of fallen man. . . ."

What is?

	. . . to labour in the fire . . .
	. . . to seek truth in *profundo* . . .
	. . . to exhaust his time . . .
and	. . . [to] impair his health . . .
and perhaps	. . . to spin out his days . . .
and	. . . [to spin out] himself . . .

"into one pitiful, controverted conclusion." That is, we return again and again to the infinitive—"to"—as well as to the pileup of "his" and "him," and if we straighten the prepositions out, all the hidden repeats become evident:

. . . to labour into one pitiful, controverted conclusion . . .
. . . to seek truth in one pitiful, controverted conclusion . . .
. . . to exhaust his time in one pitiful, controverted conclusion . . .
. . . [to] impair his health [obtaining] one pitiful, controverted
            conclusion . . .
. . . to spin out his days into one pitiful, controverted conclusion . . .
. . . [to spin out] himself into one pitiful, controverted . . .

To labour, seek, exhaust, impair, spin out . . . what? Work, truth, time, health, days, himself. Much of this tune, said *sotto voce* in any case, doesn't even get played on any instrument, but lies inside the shadow of the sentence's sound like still another shadow.

So South's prose has a shape which its enunciation allows us to perceive. That shape is an imitation of its sense, for the forepart is like the handle of a ladle, the midsections comprise the losses the ladle pours, and the ending is like a splashdown.

This is the doom of fallen man, to labour in the fire,
to seek truth in *profundo,*
to exhaust his time
and impair his health
and perhaps to spin out his days,
and himself,
into one pitiful, controverted conclusion.

In short, one wants South to say "pour out his days . . ." "in two one pit eee full, conn trow verr ted conn clue zeeunn . . ." so as to emphasize the filling of the pit. However, "spin" does anticipate the shroud which will wrap around and signify "the doom of fallen man."

In short, in this case, and in a manner that Handel, his contemporary, would approve, the sound (by revealing the spindle "to" around which the sentence turns and the action that it represents is wound) certainly enhances the sense.

However, South will not disappoint us, for he plays all the right cards, following our sample with this development: "There was then no pouring, no struggling with memory, no straining for invention. . . ." We get "pour" after all, and "straining" in addition. The pit is more than full; it runneth over.

Often a little diction and a lot of form will achieve the decided lilt and accent of a nation or a race. Joyce writes "Irish" throughout *Finnegans Wake,* and Flann O'Brien's musical arrangements also dance a jig. Here, in O'Brien's *At Swim-Two-Birds,* Mr. Shanahan is extolling the virtues of his favorite poet, that man of the pick and people, Jem Casey:

> "Yes, I've seen his pomes and read them and . . . do you know what I'm going to tell you, I have loved them. I'm not ashamed to sit here and say it, Mr. Furriskey. I've known the man and I've known his pomes and by God I have loved the two of them and loved them well, too. Do you understand what I'm saying, Mr. Lamont? You, Mr. Furriskey?
>   Oh that's right.
>   Do you know what it is, I've met the others, the whole lot of them. I've met them all and know them all. I have seen them and I have read their pomes. I have heard them recited by men that know how to use their tongues, men that couldn't be beaten at their own game. I have seen whole books filled up with their stuff, books as thick as that table there and I'm telling you no lie. But by God, at the heel of the hunt, there was only one poet for me."

Although any "Jem" has to sparkle if we're to believe in it, and even though his initials, "JC," are suspicious, I am not going to suggest that "Casey" is a pun on the Knights of Columbus.

> "No 'Sir,' no 'Mister,' no nothing. Jem Casey, Poet of the Pick, that's all. A labouring man, Mr. Lamont, but as sweet a singer in his own way as you'll find in the bloody trees there of a spring day, and that's a fact. Jem Casey, an ignorant God-fearing upstanding labouring man, a bloody navvy. Do you know what I'm going to tell you, I don't believe he ever lifted the latch of a school door. Would you believe that now?"

The first paragraph rings the changes on "known" and "loved," while the third proceeds from "know" and "met" to "seen" and "heard," in a shuffle of sentences of the simplest kind, full of doubled vowels, repeated phrases, plain talk, and far-from-subtle rhyme, characteristics that lead it to resemble the medieval preacher's rhythmic prose of persuasion. It is the speech, of course, of the barroom bore and alcoholic hyperbolist, a bit bullyish and know-it-all, even if as empty of idea as a washed glass, out of which O'Brien forms an amusing though powerful song of cultural resentment.

It is sometimes said that just as you cannot walk without stepping on wood, earth, or stone, you cannot write without symbolizing, willy-nilly, a series of clicks, trills, and moans; so there will be music wherever prose goes. This expresses an attitude both too generous and too indifferent to be appropriate. The sentence with which Dreiser begins his novel *The Financier,* "The Philadelphia into which Frank Algernon Cowperwood was born was at his very birth already a city of two hundred and fifty thousand and more," certainly makes noise enough, and, in addition to the lovely "Philadel-phia," there are "Algernon" and "Cowperwood," which most people might feel make a mouthful; but the words, here, merely stumble through their recital of facts, happy, their job done, to reach an end, however lame it is. Under different circumstances, the doubling of "was" around "born" might have promised much (as in Joyce's paradisal phrase "when all that was was fair"); however, here it is simply awkward, and followed unnecessarily by another "birth," the reason, no doubt, for Dreiser's mumpering on about the population. After another sentence distinguished only by the ineptness of its enumeration ("It was set with handsome parks, notable buildings, and crowded with historic memories"), the author adds fatuousness to his list of achievements: "Many of the things that we and he knew later were not then in existence—the telegraph, telephone, express company, ocean steamer, or city delivery of mails." "We and he" do ding-dong all right, but rather tinnily. Then Dreiser suffers a moment of expansiveness ("There were no postage-stamps or registered letters") before plunging us into a tepid bath of banality whose humor escapes even his unconscious: "The street-car had not arrived, and in its place were hosts of omnibuses, and for longer travel, the slowly developing railroad system still largely connected with canals." It makes for a surreal image, though: those stretches of track bridged by boats; an image whose contemplation we may enjoy while waiting for the streetcar to arrive.

"Bath of banality" is a bit sheepish itself, and brings to mind all the com-plaints about the artificiality of alliteration, the inappropriateness of rhyme in prose, the unpleasant result of pronounced regular rhythms in that worka-day place, the lack of high seriousness to be found in all such effects: in short, the belief that "grand" if not "good" writing undercuts its serious and sober message when it plays around with shape and the shape of its sounds; because, while poetry may be permitted to break wind and allow its leaves to waltz upon an anal breeze, prose should never suggest it had eaten beans, but retain the serious, no-nonsense demeanor of the laboring man in *At Swim-Two-Birds*.

Some tunes are rinky-dink indeed, and confined to the carnival, but I get the impression that most of these complaints about the music of prose are simply the fears of lead-eared moralists and message gatherers, who want us to believe that a man like Dreiser, who can't get through three minutes of high tea without blowing his nose on his sleeve, ought to model our manners for us, and tell us truths as blunt and insensitive, but honest and used, as worn shoes.

What they wish us to forget is another kind of truth: that language is not the lowborn, gawky servant of thought and feeling; it is need, thought, feeling, and perception itself. The shape of the sentence, the song in its syllables, the rhythm of its movement, is the movement of the imagination too; it is the allocation of the things of the world to their place in the world of the word; it is the configuration of its concepts—not to neglect them—like the stars, which are alleged to determine the fate of we poor creatures who bear their names, suffer their severities, enjoy their presence of mind and the sight of their light in our night . . . *all right . . . all right . . . okay:* the glow of their light in our darkness.

Let's remind ourselves of the moment in *Orlando* when the queen (who has, old as she is, taken Orlando up as if he were a perfumed hanky, held him close to her cleavage, and made plans to house him between the hills of her hope) sees something other than her own ancient figure in her household mirror:

Meanwhile, the long winter months drew on. Every tree in the Park was lined with frost. The river ran sluggishly. One day when the snow was on the ground and the dark panelled rooms were full of shadows and the stags were barking in the Park, she saw in the mirror, which she kept for fear of spies always by her, through the door, which she kept for fear of murderers always open, a boy—could it be Orlando?—kissing a girl—who in the Devil's name was the brazen hussy? Snatching at her golden-hilted sword she struck violently at the mirror. The glass crashed; people came running; she was lifted and set in her chair again; but she was stricken after that and groaned much, as her days wore to an end, of man's treachery.

Where shall we begin our praise of this passage, which, in *Orlando*, is merely its norm? And what shall we observe first among its beauties? perhaps, in that simple opening sentence, the way the heavy stresses which fall on "mean-," "while" (and equally on the comma's strong pause), "long," "win-," "months," "drew," and finally "on" again, make those months do just that (the three *on*'s, the many *m*'s and *n*'s don't hurt, nor does the vowel modulation: een, ile, ong, in, on, ou, on), or the way the river, whose flow was rapid enough reaching "ran," turns sluggish suddenly in the middle of the guggle in that word. Or maybe we should admire the two *and*'s which breathlessly connect a cold, snowy ground with shadowy rooms and barking stags; and then, with confidently contrasting symmetry, how the three semicolons trepidate crashing, running, lifting, while enclosing their two *and*'s in response. Or should we examine, instead, the complex central image of the figure in the glass, and the way the two clauses beginning with "which" are diabolically placed? or the consequent vibration of the sentence from the public scene of Orlando in embrace to the queen's personal shock at what she's seen out the open door, thanks to her "magic" mirror. Nor should the subtle way, through word order mainly, that Virginia Woolf salts her prose with a sense of the era—her intention quite serious but her touch kept light in order to recall the Elizabethan period without parody—be neglected by our applause.

It is precisely the queen's fear of spies and murderers which places the mirror where it can peer down the corridor to the cause of her dismay—that is the irony—but it is the placement of the reasons ("which she kept for fear of spies always by her," etc.) between the fragments of the perceptions ("through the door," "a boy," and so on) that convinces the reader of the reality of it. It is not enough to have a handful of ideas, a few perceptions, a metaphor of some originality, on your stove, the writer must also know when to release these meanings; against what they shall lean their newly arrived weight; how, in retrospect, their influence shall be felt; how the lonely trope will combine with some distant noun to create a new flavor.

What is said, what is sounded, what is put in print like a full plate in front of the reader's hungry eye, must be weighed against what is kept back, out of view, suggested, implied. The queen, in her disappointed rage, has fallen to the floor, but we are told only that she was lifted and put back in her chair again. And nothing will henceforth be the same in the last, morose moments of her life. On account of a kiss caught by a mirror through a door kept ajar out of fear of another sort of assault.

In music, sounds form phrases; in prose, phrases form sounds. The sentence fragment almost immediately above was written to demonstrate this, for it naturally breaks into units: "On account of a kiss/caught by a mirror/through a door kept ajar/out of fear of another/sort of assault." These shards, in turn, can be subdivided further: "On account / of a kiss . . ." Certain pieces of the pattern act like hinges: "kiss / caught" "door / kept," for instance, while possessives play their part, and the grammatical form that consists of an article and a noun ("a count / a kiss / a mirror / a door / a jar / a nother / a sault") stamps on the sentence its special rhythm.

Words have their own auditory character. We all know this, but the writer must revel in it. Some open and close with vowels whose prolongation can give them expressive possibilities ("Ohio," for instance); others are simply vowel-heavy (like "aeolian"); still others open wide but then close sharply ("ought"), or are as tight-lipped as "tip," as unending as "too," or as fully middled as "balloon." Some words look long but are said short (such as "rough" and "sleight"); some seem small enough but are actually huge ("otiose" and "nay"). A few words "whisper," "tintinnabulate," or "murmur," as if they were made of their meanings, while "Philadelphia" (already admired) is like a low range of hills. Some words rock, and are jokey, like "okeydokey." Or they clump, like "lump" and "hump" and "rump" and "stump," or dash noisily away in a rash of "ash / mash / bash" or "brash / crash / smash / flash" or "gnash / lash / hash / stash / cash" or "clash / trash / splash / potash / succotash." Vowel changes are equally significant, whether between "ring," "rang," and "rung," "scat" and "scoot," "pet" and "pat," "pit" and "pot," or "squish" and "squooze."

The Latinate measures of the great organist Henry James find an additional function for the music of prose. Here all it takes is a parade of the past tense ("he had") down a street paved with negations.

> He had not been a man of numerous passions, and even in all these years no sense had grown stronger with him than the sense of being bereft. He had needed no priest and no altar to make him for ever widowed. He had done many things in the world—he had done almost all but one: he had never, never forgotten. He had tried to put into his existence whatever else might take up room in it, but had failed to make it more than a house of which the mistress was eternally absent.

If some men are has-beens, poor Stransom (in James's judgment) is a had-not-been. The passage is crammed with loss—"bereft," "widowed," "failed," "absent"—in addition to the doubling of "sense," "no," "never," in succeeding sentences, and the gloomy repetition of the past tense, particularly "been" and "done." Our hero, we cannot help but hear, is a transom. He only looks on. But the music of the passage ties terms together more firmly than its syntax: "being," for instance, with "bereft," "done" with "one," "never" with "ever," and "what-" with "ever" as well. Each sentence, all clauses, commence with poor Stransom's pronoun, or imply its presence: "he had, he had, he had" trochee along like a mourning gong.

Musical form creates another syntax, which overlaps the grammatical and reinforces that set of directions sometimes, or adds another dimension by suggesting that two words, when they alliterate or rhyme, thereby modify each other, even if they are not in any normally modifying position. Everything a sentence is is made manifest by its music. As Gertrude Stein writes:

> Papa dozes mamma blows her noses.
> We cannot say this the other way.

Music makes the space it takes place in. I do not mean the Baroque chamber, where a quartet once competed against the slide of satin, the sniff of snuff, or the rustle of lace cuffs; or the long symphonic hall full of coughing, whispered asides, and program rattle; or the opera house, where the plot unfolding on the stage plays poorly against the ogling in the boxes and the distractions in the stalls; or even the family's music room, where heavy metal will one day leave its scratches like chalk screech on the windowpanes—none of these former or future pollutions of our pleasure; but again in that hall of the head (it holds so much!) where, when the first note sounds behind the lids, no late arrivals are allowed to enter, and when the first note sounds as if the piano were putting a single star down in a dark sky, and then, over there, in that darkness, another, the way, for instance, the 1926 sonata of Bartók begins, or a nocturne of Chopin's, slowly, so we can observe its creation, its establishment of relation; because we do see what we hear, and the music rises and falls or feels far away or comes from close by like from the lobe of the ear, and is bright or dim, wide or thin, or forms chains or cascades, sometimes as obvious as a cartoon of Disney's, splashy and catchy, and sometimes as continuous and broad and full as an ocean; while at other times there is only a ding here and a ping there in a dense, pitchlike lack of action, and one waits for the sounds to come back and fill the abyss with clangor, as if life were all that is.

And when we hear, *we* hear; when we see, and say, "Ah! Sport!," *we* see; our consciousness of objects is *ours,* don't philosophers love to say? and though we share a world, it is, from the point of view of consciousness, an overlapping one: I see the dog with delight, you with fear; I see its deep, moist eyes, you its cruel wet mouth; I hear its happy panting, you its threatening growl; and I remember my own loyal pooch, and you the time a pug pursued you down the street; so we say the same word, "dog," yet I to welcome and you to warn, I to greet and you to cringe; and even when we think of what our experience means and ponder the place of pets in the human scheme, thus sharing a subject, as we have our encounter, we will pursue our problem differently, organize it in dissimilar ways, and doubtless arrive at opposite ends.

But I can shape and sound a sentence in such a way my sight of things, my feeling for what I've seen, my thoughts about it all, are as fully present as the ideas and objects my words by themselves bear. D. H. Lawrence, for instance, in that great chapter of *Sea and Sardinia* called "The Spinner and the Monks," does not simply tell us he saw two monks walking in a garden.

> And then, just below me, I saw two monks walking in their garden between the naked, bony vines, walking in their wintry garden of bony vines and olive trees, their brown cassocks passing between the brown vine-stocks, their heads bare to the sunshine, sometimes a glint of light as their feet strode from under their skirts.

Anyone can put a pair of monks in a garden and even hang around to watch their no-doubt sandaled feet flash, but Lawrence is a whole person when he perceives, when he repeats, when he plans his patterns; so that, just as he himself says, it is as if he hears them speaking to each other.

> They marched with the peculiar march of monks, a long, loping stride, their heads together, their skirts swaying slowly, two brown monks with hidden hands, sliding under the bony vines and beside the cabbages, their heads always together in hidden converse. It was as if I were attending with my dark soul to their inaudible undertone. All the time I sat still in silence, I was one with them, a partaker, though I could hear no sound of their voices. I went with the long stride of their skirted feet, that slid springless and noiseless from end to end of the garden, and back again. Their hands were kept down at their sides, hidden in the long sleeves and the skirts of their robes. They did not touch each other, nor gesticulate as they walked. There was no motion save the long, furtive stride and the heads leaning together. Yet there was an eagerness in their conversation. Almost like shadow-creatures ventured out of their cold, obscure element, they went backward and forwards in their wintry garden, thinking nobody could see them.

And we go to and fro here, too, as the sentences do, passing between vowel and idea, perception and measure, moving as the syllables move in our mouths, admiring the moment, realizing how well the world has been realized through Lawrence's richly sensuous point of view.

They clothe a consciousness, these sounds and patterns do, the consciousness the words refer to, with its monks and vines, its stilled observant soul,
its sense of hearing them speak as well as seeing them striding along together,
the quality of mystery and community the passage presents by putting them
in the light of a late-winter afternoon.

And I noticed that up above the snow, frail in the bluish sky, a frail
moon had put forth, like a thin, scalloped film of ice floated out on the
slow current of the coming night. And a bell sounded.

A beautiful, precise image, translucent itself, is carried forward by an arrangement of *f*'s and *l*'s, *o*'s and *u*'s, with such security their reader has to feel he's
heard that bell even before it sounds.

Suddenly the mind and its view have a body, because such sentences
breathe, and the writer's blood runs through them, too, and they are virile
or comely, promising sweetness or cruelty, as bodies do, and they allow the
mind they contain to move, and the scene it sees to have an eye.

The soul, when it loves, has a body it must use. Consequently, neither
must neglect the other, for the hand that holds your hand must belong to a
feeling being, else you are caressing a corpse; and that loving self, unless it
can fill a few fingers with its admiration and concern, will pass no more of its
passion to another than might a dead, dry stick.

The music of prose, elementary as it is, limited as it is in its effects, is
nonetheless far from frivolous decoration; it embodies Being; consequently,
it is essential that that body be in eloquent shape: to watch the mimsy paddle
and the fat picnic, the snoozers burn and crybabies bellow . . . well, we didn't
go to the beach for that.

Antaeus, 1993
Published in *Finding a Form*, 1996

I've Got a Little List

As some day it may happen that a victim must be found,
I've got a little list—I've got a little list
Of society offenders who might well be underground,
And who never would be missed—who never would be missed!

The Lord High Executioner's list has been compiled "on the off chance," in case, because you never can tell. Students of rhetorical forms, of which the List ought to head the list, call this kind of compilation a "maybe, maybe." It belongs with the sort of wishes you would make if you had three, or the number of women you might hope to seduce if you were rich, handsome, famous, young, unafraid, and the women were still alive and lonely. Or if you were Captain Bligh, the books you would choose to be marooned with, or if you were Mr. Saturday Night, the jokes you would tell as a stand-up comic, the roles you would play if you were Sir Ralph Richardson, the renowned thespian. Since most of these "maybe"s are "never, never"s, it should be clear that some lists are actually counterfactual, like daydreams, and require the subjunctive.

However, the Lord High Executioner is dealing in possibilities which are quite real, if by real we mean "staged." "There's the pestilential nuisances who write for autographs." (The subject-verb agreement of this entry is terrible and taxes poetic license to the limit; however, the list of poetic licenses is rather a long one.) Ko-Ko's collection is also of the kind popularly called "a shit list," or variously "a hit list," "the list of Adrian Messenger," "the ten most wanted," and so on. Schindler's list is not a shit list but its contrary, a Shinola list. Otherwise, the form is the same. Ko-Ko's hit list has another quality. *The Mikado* ran for more than six hundred nights following its opening at the Savoy on March 14, 1885, and has been performed many thousands of times since. It amuses directors to revise Titipu's roll of candidates by replacing out-of-date targets with the names and characteristics of victims more suitable to changing times and places (a little local reference is always good for a laugh). (Nixon was a popular substitution until bumped by Ross Perot.) In sum, there is nothing sacred about the entries, only the list's directing principle is immortal (and the tune, of course); which is rather a good thing, for otherwise we might be reluctant to put on *The Mikado* today, because the song's second stanza begins:

> And that nigger serenader, and the others of his race,
> And the piano-organist—I've got him on the list!

We shall probably want to choose motorcyclists for summary removal from the world instead. I'm sure they'd not be missed. Or persons who chew gum and paint their toes. Or talk-show hosts and all their fans. But what about "the lady from the provinces, who dresses like a guy"? We could all happily do without the Politically Correct. By scratching the lady from the provinces off the list, thus not giving offense to transvestites, and putting an officer of the language police in her place, we can remain PC and get rid of PC at the same time: "There's the censor from the feminists, her scissors held on high, who doesn't think she castrates but would rather like to try." I think I'll keep "that singular anomaly, the lady novelist," although lady novelists are no longer singular but as plural as pokeweed, and maintain a literary lobby larger than the Plaza's Palm Court.

In its relative indifference to the nature of its members, this list of the "unmissed" resembles the yearly competitions for the Worst Dressed or what I would like to see in the Michelin guides: Destinations Worth a Detour to Avoid, daggered from one to three like the rosettes, and certainly changeable, since the number of warning icons Atlantic City may deserve will doubtless change from time to time.

Normally, lists are the purposeful coming together of names like starlings to their evening trees. They tend to confer equality on their members, also like starlings in their evening trees. The list of the ten wonders of the world does not imply that the wonder given as number one (at the front or the top) is number one. The 1,003 ladies on Don Giovanni's were each equally enjoyed, the list presumes, all equally loved. The first comestible that comes to mind, when the stomach turns its thoughts to gluttony and gluttony's groceries, generally heads the shopping list, which has normally no other order than chance associations: you just shook the last grain of salt from the shaker, the ad in the paper says that pork butts are on sale, you've had to resort to Kleenex in lieu of toilet paper.

Nowadays, despite our egalitarian and plural society (or perhaps because of it), we are obsessed by hierarchies in the form of lists. There are popular software programs known as "list servers," which manage electronic mailing lists and document their distribution over the Internet. They can make a list from a mouthful of mush. Nick Hornby's pop-cult novel *High Fidelity* describes characters whose lives are ordered by their love of lists, always superficially evaluative and always the same length: the top five Elvis Costello songs, the top five *Cheers* episodes, and, like the Lord High Executioner's list, the first five rock bands that will have to be eliminated come the Musical Revolution. The book's principal protagonist goes further: he has a list of girlfriends who caused him the greatest grief when they dumped him.

These orders, unlike one's laundry list, are imaginary. The choices set down are like the interpretations of inkblots, revelatory only of their maker. But if the comforts of mere enumeration are shallow and illusory, so are most comforts. The top six . . . (why be a slave to the five and dime?) . . . the top six illusory comforts are: a Sports Car, a Winning Team, a Savings Account, a Marriage License, a White-Collar Job, a Ranch House in the Suburbs.

Book lists are often neutrally ordered by the alphabet. Lists of things to do could suggest, by their arrangement, a succession of actions—first this, then that; find nail, shoe horse, win war—but they don't have to, and they usually don't: mow lawn, have snooze, buy beer.

The list detaches objects from their place in the world and enumerates them elsewhere. You could list the contents of your pocketbook for a Sunday-supplement article on what ladies carry in their purses. Every year, a few months after Christmas, a sprightly and amusing piece of this kind will appear in the daily paper. The jailer will make such an inventory, slipping small change, charge cards, and other incriminating items into a plastic sack along with his smirk. The seven objects most usually found are: Roll of Tums, Out-of-Date Address Book, Business Card of a Manufacturer of Glass Brick, Key to Lover's Apartment, Note to Lover from Lover's Mum Substantiating Lover's Unhappiness with Lover's Spouse, Unpaid Parking Ticket, Canadian Dime.

Sometimes a book dealer will shelve his books according to the first letter of their subject, and, within that, by author's name. This gives the ordering a hierarchy. Then the catalogue's alphabetical structure and the structure of a corresponding state of affairs in the shop will be the same. Such lists function like road maps, where cities and towns with their coordinates are enumerated on the flaps.

The organizing principles of lists, then, are

a. as encountered or found (the contents of the pocketbook),
   or as remembered (a guest list), or as needed (to reorder when
   supplies run out); or
b. as arranged by an already ordered external system, often so
   that the items on the list can be easily found (alphabetically
   or numerically, for instance), a systematizing which sometimes
   becomes hierarchical; or
c. as dictated by the order of the things themselves (library list
   and library shelves), certain inventories, or the table of contents
   of a book; or
d. as rated in terms of some principle of value or importance.

Occasionally, two or more of these organizations will be applied at the
same time. As my need for an item arises, I may put it on my list in the order
in which I shop at the supermarket: produce first, for instance, lettuce before
onions, meat before crackers, cat food before bleach, soap before shoelaces.
Notice that this is not the same as book by subject, then alphabetically by
author, because one arrangement does not logically have to precede the other.

Lists are juxtapositions, and exhibit many of the qualities of collage. The
names which appear on them lack their normal syntactical companions.
Most lists are terse, minimal, bald; they are reminders, commands, aspirations. We do not trouble to write: one medium head of nice fresh red Boston
lettuce, two large slicing tomatoes if ripe, a small bottle of Dr. Bland's salad
dressing but only if it's in that cute chef-shaped bottle, and so on. We do
not describe our New Year's resolutions or any other things to do in detail:
remember to move that Norfolk Island pine out of the sunroom, it needs a
northern exposure; or this year try not to swear so fucking much, especially
in front of the provost.

Clearly, we face complications. When I write "bleach," I usually understand myself to mean a certain brand, and when I beg myself to moderate
my passions, a terse word or two on the list (drink less, don't paw) may stand
for a thousand dreamlike meditations. Are these subjectivities mutely on the
list as well? *How do I love thee? Let me count the ways. . . .* But while the poet
is publicly boasting about the depth and breadth and height of her soul's
reach, of the purity of her feelings, and declaiming about a passion she used
to spend on saints, perhaps the *Kama Sutra* best describes her more intimate
and private impulses.

Certain words rarely appear on lists ("screw you," for instance), and here
is a list of a few of them: (a) "always," (b) "if," (c) "negation," (d) "halfheart-

edly," (e) "Lithuaneousness," (f) "partially clothed," (g) "tintinnabulation." Adjectives of a descriptive kind frequently show up on lists, however: "yellow cheese," "large eggs," "skim milk."

The punctuation most closely associated with lists is the colon, because everything that follows the colon is supposed to form a list. The colon is often an abbreviation for "namely" or "for instance," but only when there is more than one instance involved. There are thirteen ways of looking at a blackbird, namely . . .

Lists tend to suggest or supply alternatives, and these are not necessarily of things mutually exclusive: how to get spots out or ways to get to Chicago. They supply possibilities: the people who might be interested in hearing you sing, the different kinds of games you could play in a stadium, the uses for a chartreuse ceramic ashtray in the shape of a seashell.

Lists suppress the verb and tend to constantly remind us of their subject, for lists have subjects: the list *of* fruits to buy at the market, the ruck contained *in* the pocketbook, the junk *for* sale in the churchyard Friday morning, the perfumes *on* the counter, the titles of books *about* leprosy, the queens of England *before* Victoria.

Yet the verb lurks like a cur just out of reach of our kick. Most often it takes the form of a command: Buy! Remember! Invite! Do! Write! Thank! Imprison! Proposition! However, since the command itself is never set down, the list feigns passivity and politeness.

When we write the word "Kleenex" on an envelope flap, we haven't achieved a list yet, though we may have begun to make one. Two needs— "Kleenex," "cauliflower"—merely make a misfitting pair, while "Kleenex," "cauliflower," and "catnip" record an incoherent plurality. However, alliteration calls attention to the numerousness of the trio, and I think that with four we can say we have a list. Now things can be added to it, whereas before, while we could write "cauliflower" beside "Kleenex," we couldn't add "cauliflower" to a list, since we didn't have one yet. Niceties of this sort give great pleasure to the logician. As they should.

Having a list, we can properly speak of things being "on" or "off" it. "Kleenex" was not on a list until "catnip" came along. Getting off a list is no easier, certainly, than getting on one, especially if, like a train, the list is moving. Ko-Ko is perfectly willing to let us substitute appropriate victims in place of

> What d'ye call him—Thing'em-bob, and likewise . . .
> What's-his-name, and also You-know-who—
> The task of filling up the blanks I'd rather leave to you

but that's only while the list is a rough draft. People who live in trailer parks would certainly not be missed. They are on God's list, clearly, for He is always trying to upend them or knock them over with one of His Big Winds. Anyone who ever touched a gun in fun or fury could be bangedy-banged, for all I care, but others might want to be more merciful. Some of us, this very moment, unbeknownst, are being dropped from an invitation list. But when we have executed (to use the appropriate word) the command which is implicit in most lists (Do! Buy! Invite! remember that list?), plopping the bright-green bag of frozen peas on top of the spuds, and crossing out parsley too and Cheez Whiz, because they are already in our basket, we might think (having failed to consult our local logician) that the spuds and peas and parsley are no longer on the list; or, as in Ko-Ko's case, having cut off the Judicial Humorist's head, that he's there no more because he's here no more; but no, even though there is a cross across his name now, and a cross above his grave too, he's still on the list, which, without changing a line, moves its members and their status in time from "To Be Executed" to "Execute!" to "Executed." In a similar way, the grocery list becomes the register slip. So the prosecutor can ask you if you had rat poison on your shopping list the day before your wife's fatal illness, and you are not allowed to reply: "No, sir, because I crossed that item off after I bought some."

Normally, an act or object finagles its way onto a list simply by being written down in the neighborhood of the group or, better yet, finds a place in the column or the queue. It is bad manners to break into the queue or try to take over the capital of the column. Nevertheless, as we know, it happens. To the list "apples," "oranges," "lemons," "limes," "lighter fluid," where am I sensibly going to add "grapes"? Surely not after "fluid," where "AAA batteries" goes. So I squeeze it in above "limes."

There are certain lists one wants desperately to be on—the Social Register, the high-school honor roll, foursomes waiting to tee off at Pebble Beach—and these lists guard their precincts: the names of their members aren't written on napkins or the backs of envelopes. Getting on these lists is frequently expensive (bribe-style balls have to be thrown, costly caterers called in) or requires a lot of networking, ass kissing, or plain hard honest work (to make the dean's list, for instance). However, for every desirable one there is another it is essential to avoid, like the roll call way up yonder.

Thus lists have requirements for membership (or getting on), like being thought to be the right sort, and requirements for continuing to be included (or staying on), like paying your dues, and conditions which must be met if you want to be dropped (or removed), like embracing the Jewish faith. I've warned that some lists are impossible to escape. If you were ever Mabel

Dodge's fourth husband, you will always and forever be, though divorce or death overtakes you.

Could we draw up a complete list of lists? No . . . not even of the genre, let alone the species. There are all the shopping lists, just to begin with— groceries, sundries, hardware, drugs—and the Christmas cards you sent— that lot—set over against the few you received, as well as invitations for dinners, birthdays, and receptions, a column of things to do before the party—those disgusting plastic cups to purchase, three dozen paper plates the color of beef blood, candles (do we need four?), tapers (steal them from the church), oh yes, and napkins small enough to ensure that at least half a finger will be smeared with sauce. Meanwhile, there are appointments to keep, don't forget, calls to return, and the other notes necessary to jog that part of the mind which plays the role of Memory—pick up dry cleaning. More? Sure: addresses for next year's cards or the exhibition opening, the lists which fetch us catalogues, newsletters, charitable solicitations and other scams, through the mail. And those lists drawn up by scholars, cranks, and other anal-retentives so you won't have to remember: chronologies of presidents and kings, lists like the principal battles of the Civil War, or your curriculum vitae; your several spouses (but not why), your jobs, clubs-associations-committees, public works, honors, and other lies; and, closely connected, almanacs, desk-wall-pocket calendars, as well as rates and sched-ules for bus-train-boat-plane, or tides or phases of the moon, or comets and meteoric showers, or simple tables of contents: parts, sections, chapters, verse; best/worst most/least lists of every imaginable act and entity: voice throwers, horse winnings, rain amounts in August, penile dimensions, mul-tiple births, canons of excellence; next, catalogues of books or objets d'art, discographies, antiques, and inventories of household goods for insurance purposes, of the store's stock, of your wallet upon overnight confinement in the pokey (remember? I spoke of it before); notebook-type lists like a madam's clients, their preferences and prices; and then compendia of all kinds: dictionaries, encyclopedias, atlases, telephone- and cookbooks, video and Mobil guides, indexes, nearby bed-and-breakfasts; wine lists and honor rolls, restaurant and computer menus, stock and other exchanges, want ads, wish and waiting lists, shits and Shinolas (as I said); all sorts of methods and procedures, how-to's by the hundreds, for instance, Roberta Coughlin's book *The Gardener's Companion,* which contains more than 350 lists of practical and cultural information, of houseplants which will still live hung in baskets, of Shakespeare's flowers, "daisies pied and violets blue / And lady-smocks all silver-white / And cuckoo-buds of yellow hue"—but let's get on: vulgar noises that amuse children, ways to placate spouses who are irate because

723   I've Got a Little List

you've sent their delicates through the high/hot cycle, how to remove love hickeys in a hurry, persuade some young gentleman to change a tire, make bail, buy a good bagel, find a bathroom in a strange town; what's more, cook kale—or, to take a different tack, there are rule books and commandments: don't litter, foul the pathway, commit adultery, pee in the pool; profits and losses too, expenditures and sales, pages of obits, places of worship, programs of cinemas, recaps of TV serials, exhibits at museums, and rosters of teams and volunteers, which isn't the half—the fourth—the eighth of it . . . of them, I should say . . . of lists.

The libretto of *The Mikado* begins with a cast of characters, and when Gertrude Stein wrote her little play called "A List," she carefully lined her characters up in a column along the margin of the action—the action consisting mainly of a list of the phrase "a list."

MARIUS.   A list.

MABEL.   A list.

MARTHA.   A list.

MARTHA.   There is a great variety in the settlement of claims.
We claim and you claim and I claim the same.

MARTHA.   A list.

MARYAS.   And a list.

MABEL.   I have also had great pleasure from a capital letter.

MARTHA.   And forget her.

MARYAS.   And respect him.

MARIUS.   And neglect them.

MABEL.   And they collect them as lilies of the valley in this
country.

MARTHA.   A list.

["A List," in *A Stein Reader*, ed. Ulla Dydo
(Evanston, Ill.: Northwestern University Press, 1984), p. 401]

My moving van is parked outside. I need to make a list of the liftable contents of this domicile. My list will transform the relationship the house's furniture has to walls and floors from one of feet and inches, shoes and fingers, to a temporally neutral column of names (like Martha, Maryas, Mabel, and Marius). If I pretend to be Homer praising the heroes who came to make war on Troy, I am likely to arrange my song so that it shows who volunteered first, who second, and so on, giving a temporal meaning to the series which it might not ordinarily have. If I am making an action into a list, I shall have to divide it the way the flight of Zeno's arrow was divided, the way a camera would record it, because a camera is a list maker, the film nothing but a series of shots in the order of their snapping. My list might then suggest how I shall encounter dwellings on a stroll, or how I shall remember having passed them in Calvino's lovely prose.

> The man who knows by heart how [the city of] Zora is made, if he is unable to sleep at night, can imagine he is walking along the streets and he remembers the order by which the copper clock follows the barber's striped awning, then the fountain with the nine jets, the astronomer's glass tower, the melon vendor's kiosk, the statue of the hermit and the lion, the Turkish bath, the café at the corner, the alley that leads to the harbor.
>
> [*Invisible Cities,* trans. William Weaver
> (New York: Harcourt, 1974), p. 15]

I have wandered into the literary part of town before I intended to, but the list is often just such a little tour, as it is at the opening of Juan Goytisolo's extraordinary novel, a novel made of lists, *The Virtues of the Solitary Bird,* where the infamous apparition, the monster pictured by Félicien Rops as the Sower of Discord, materializes and makes its slow clogshod way through the grounds and lobby of an otherwise unnamed hotel-hospital-spa (but only, as apparitions must, subjunctively):

> . . . had it entered like everyone else through the arch of the carriage gate, crossed the little courtyard with nineteenth-century bathtubs ingeniously planted with perennials, proceeded toward the staircase and its gas lamps of outworn majesty, opened the door giving access to our ravaged and destroyed kingdom, paid sixty-five francs to the blonde cashier who gave out tickets, little individual bars of soap, shampoo, and other beauty products and aids to bodily cleanliness . . .
>
> [*The Virtues of the Solitary Bird,* trans. Helen Lane
> (London: Serpent's Tail, 1991), p. 11]

Had it entered . . . But did it? What do apparitions do?

There are philosophers who believe that our experienced reality forms a temporal list. It is a series of impressions, or complexes of impressions, which can only be recorded: this, this, this.

To sum up so far (to make a little list): When we are confronted with a list, we have to ask what the purpose of the list is, for a list is a purposeful collection. Then we have to wonder whether the list is spatially or temporally ordered or is neutral and loose in that regard. Next, we need to know whether whatever order the list has is mirrored in the things the list is a list of. Does it possess an isomorphic formality with elements outside itself? Beyond that, we have to find out where the weight of importance lies: is it in the things listed? is it in the words listed? or do both matter, and if so, to what degree? In short, is it a List of *T*'s or an *L* of Things? Finally, we must determine whether there are any other principles ordering the list apart from space-time ones, and if so, what these are. Lists of dates are obviously chronological; dictionaries are alphabetical; but when John Donne writes of death that it is a "slave to fate, chance, kings, and desperate men," sound and meter as well as meaning, structured in terms of high/low pairs, are determining the line (fate high, chance low, kings high, desperate men as low as you can get).

In addition to internal order, external relations, and aim, lists have entrance requirements (how do you get on?) and expulsion principles (getting left off, crossed off, or checked off). Lists are either open-ended (the state capitals you have visited), incomplete (birds of North America), variable (contents of a closet), or closed (books you read last year); they are finite (Aunt Millie—a beachboy—for Christmas) or infinite (even numbers, also odd), definite (three small Granny Smith apples) or vague (something for dinner). Finally, a list creates a site, something like the logician's universe of discourse, a place where everything on the list can coexist, a common space.

Jorge Luis Borges refers to a "certain Chinese encyclopedia" which says that

> animals are divided into (a) those that belong to the emperor; (b) embalmed ones; (c) those that are trained; (d) suckling pigs; (e) mermaids; (f) fabulous ones; (g) stray dogs; (h) those that are included in this classification; (i) those that tremble as if they were mad; (j) innumerable ones; (k) those drawn with a very fine camel's-hair brush; (l) etcetera; (m) those that have just broken the flower vase; (n) those that at a distance resemble flies.
>
> [*Selected Non-Fictions,* ed. Eliot Weinberger
> (New York: Viking Press, 1999), p. 231]

Michel Foucault, who makes some interesting comments on this list at the beginning of his book *The Order of Things,* says we cannot imagine the kind of place where these animals could be brought together and sorted out. There is no peaceable kingdom for them. The site is impossible to conceive.

It is certainly true that this list deliberately contains heteronomous groups of more than one sort. In the first place, its classes are not exclusive. Animals belonging to the emperor (a) might be trained (c) or embalmed (b). Redundancy is likely, as if my grocery list asked for bread as well as anything on sale. Suckling pigs and stray dogs are grouped with painted or fabulous ones in such a way as to deny the overriding importance of another distinction: that between real and imaginary, for instance, or alive and dead, as if my market list included not only milk but the nectar of the gods and three dipperfuls from the Fountain of Youth. Borges's list is so messy we cannot define its entrance requirements. It also includes categories which attack the logical structure of every list. Suppose my grocery list included "and so on" or "another of the same"? (J) "innumerable" suggests animals which in fact can't be listed, while (h) those "included in this classification" allows many to get in twice. Creatures that have (m) "just broken the flower vase" get on the list, but then must be taken off again because, as time passes, they will no longer have "just" broken it. A variation of this category might be six already eaten eggs, or half of a watermelon the moment before a fly lights on it. (K) animals "drawn with a very fine camel's-hair brush" expresses a quirk or whim—the bristles of the camel's-hair brush cannot be coarse—as if I would buy tomato soup only in a dented can. Finally, (n) those animals "that at a distance resemble flies" introduces dangerous subjective and relativistic elements. Elephants, seen from far enough away, will look like flies, while flies won't look like flies through a powerful microscope.

Yet this list has a site after all, I think, and has been cunningly put together by Borges to create one. Every entry discloses something about our principles of classification by violating several of them. And if its items violated all possible principles, we could say the list was "exhaustive." However, there are no negations on Borges's list—"animals not the totemic emblem of a football team," for instance—or, after all, any entry for "man."

Some lists list. Other lists list examples of what they wish to list. Suppose that on the surface of my shopping list there is a spot of cooking oil, a smear of jam, some bacon grease. This set of "fingerprints" is not a real list, but an inadvertent demonstration of what might be named on the real list. Foucault points out that on Borges's list only the names can be brought together, never their referents; but he fails to observe that in fact these categories belong together because by not belonging together they reveal another set of things (illogicalities), which do.

Listing is a fundamental literary strategy. It occurs constantly, and only occasionally draws attention to itself. It can be so brief as almost not to be there. "Alex went to the bank, to the casino, and to the dogs, in one day." It can be so prominent it proclaims itself as some fictional reality's single ordering device. Here is Juan Goytisolo's apparitional figure again, still slogging through the subjunctive:

> . . . then had the clogs cautiously placed themselves on the lower steps broadening the field of vision of the figure and, at the same time, that of the overawed spectators, a big loose tunic over its filiform extremities, pouches or petticoats with dozens of dolls, a floating lilac-and-rose-colored cape in which its face was enveloped as in a flag . . . its movements were viciously languid, perhaps beneath the veil or the tangled locks . . . it was now taking in the lounge, the seats to one side covered with worn red oilcloth, Second Empire gas lamps, wall paintings of Near Eastern landscapes, green hills, horsemen, silhouettes with burnooses and haiques, a spiky minaret of a mosque, a half moon white as snow, a scene full of atmosphere, nostalgically familiar to our spirited lovers for a day, composed . . . by a great artist, a discreet regular of those baths devoted to the bliss and cleanliness of the body, before, long before we, even the most intrepid veterans among us, had become initiates of the rites and ceremonies of the temple, had sought the tenderness lying in wait in the pupils of the tiger, that luminous and brutal ecstatic escape from the suffocating squalor of our lives, paradise, a flaming and fleeting paradise like all the edens of the world . . .
>
> [*The Virtues of the Solitary Bird,* p. 12]

The garb of a ghost merges with a list of things in the allegedly real world only to slip into another, of things, in a painted one, and these lists lead to a list of the painted world's qualities, and then to one which characterizes its artist as a frequent visitor to the spa, before concluding (in my selection) with a list of the pleasures of escape to be had if one accepts the embrace of the hotel, its grounds, and its steamy springs.

The list is a natural form for poems like François Villon's *Legacy,* but the lines of many of his ballads are hung like clothes from the pole of the list's purpose:

> I know flies in the milk,
> I know men by their clothes,
> I know good from bad weather,
> I know fruit by its color,
> I know trees by their sap,
> I know when all is the same,

> I know who's busy or idle,
> I know all, save myself.
>> [from "Ballad of Small Talk," trans. Anthony Bonner]

His ballads concerning the lords and ladies of bygone times are lists almost by nature, so that it hardly matters who composes them. Certainly, the fall of the high and mighty is a medieval formula. Here is John Skelton playing at it.

> Why, what cam of Alexander the greate?
> Or els of stronge Sampson, who can tell?
> Were not wormes ordeyned theyr flesh to frete?
> And of Salomon, that was of wyt the well?
> Absolon profferyd his hearte for to sell,
> Yet for al his bewte wormys ete him also;
> And I but late in honour dyd excel,
> *Et, ecce, nunc in pulvere dormio!*
>> [from "On the Death of the Noble Prince,
>> Kynge Edwarde the Forth"]

The memory of ladies lost is not confined to Villon or to such long-ago times. William Carlos Williams carries on the tradition:

> There was Margaret of the big breasts
> and daring eyes who carried
> her head, where her small brain rattled,
> as the mind might wish,
> at the best, to be carried. There was
> Lucille, gold hair and blue eyes, very
> straight, who
> to the amazement of many, married a
> saloon keeper and lost her modesty.
> There was loving Alma, who wrote a steady
> hand, whose mouth never wished for
> relief. And the cold Nancy, with small
> firm breasts
>> You remember?
>>> a high
> forehead, she who never smiled more
> than was sufficient but whose broad

mouth was icy with pleasure startling
the back and knees!

[from *Paterson*
(New York: New Directions, 1963), sect. III, p. 192]

Strolling, remembering women, bequeathing properties, determining fates, bemoaning greatness fallen once again to dust: such pastimes are so listlike the form needs no prompting to appear; but every description also creates a list, for even when the features of a face coexist (or when many impressions occur simultaneously), they cannot do so during their recital, when the nose or eyes can be placed, with the freedom of Picasso, before the chin or after an ear or in front of a topknot of disciplined hair. The qualities I might want to credit an apple—its tart juice, its crisp white flesh, its slick red skin, its tough stiff stem, and so on—proceed differently across the page than they simultaneously are in life. I can compose, then, quite a different object by arranging these properties according to some experiential order (where shape, stem, color, and skin would come first), or in terms of desire (then its flood of juice and quash of tart pulp between the teeth might lead the imagination), or by stressing symbolic factors instead (Eve, tree, worm), or by concentrating on the way the language moves, fancying a phrase like "voluminous juice" in my mouth more than the apple's taste, which can sometimes be insipid.

The list is the fundamental rhetorical form for creating a sense of abundance, overflow, excess. We find it so used in writers with an appetite for life, from Rabelais and Cervantes, or from Burton and Browne, to Barth and Elkin. Why be merely thirsty when you can brag, like Grangousier (in Jacques Le Clercq's version): "I wet, I dampen, I moisten, I humect my gullet. I drink—and all for fear of dying of aridity!" Our list, in this case, is not so much one of alternative actions as of possible words—a sequence of synonyms—the wealth of words suggesting an abundance of satisfactions. Desire is never dampened by its dampening, but only grows greater, and its object is not consumed by its consumption but is multiplied, and pleasure is not lessened by its repetition but enriched and revered. None of this is true in life, another reason why the page is to be preferred.

Our aforementioned Greatgullet loved to slake his thirst so much he sought after salted meats to increase his need.

Thus he was ordinarily well provided with hams from Mainz in Westphalia and Bayonne in Gascony; with oxtongues and chitterlings in season; with salted beef and mustard; with sausages galore—not from

Bologna, for he feared the Italian poisoner as a curer of bacon, but from Bigorre, Longaulnay, Brenne, and Rouergue, all places nearer home.

Bologna may not have gotten on the list of sources for Grangousier's meats, but it did get on the list of words. "I love Anne, not Phyllis; Margaret, not Marion; Kate, not Jane; and am indifferent to Mary, Rose, and Carolyn." The list of the beloved is three loves long; the list of names is nine.

Like the scholastics whom they are kidding, Montaigne, Burton, and Browne are fond of citation. You doubt that a child can take eleven months to come to term? Rabelais produces authorities beyond count, including Hippocrates, Pliny, Plautus, Marcus Varro, Aristotle, Aulus Gellius, Servius, Justinian, and "a thousand other fools whose number has been increased by the lawyers."

Thomas Hobbes, who thinks so little of the scholastics he'll not bother to make fun of them, nevertheless uses the list with great effect, both as a weapon of his rhetoric and in argument. Here is one of the great lists in our language, one of admirable wealth and energy, and one of overwhelming persuasive power.

And for that part of Religion, which consisteth in opinions concerning the nature of Powers Invisible, there is almost nothing that has a name, that has not been esteemed amongst the Gentiles, in one place or another, a God, or Divell; or by their Poets feigned to be inanimated, inhabited, or possessed by some Spirit or other.

The unformed matter of the World, was a God, by the name of *Chaos*.

The Heaven, the Ocean, the Planets, the Fire, the Earth, the Winds, were so many Gods.

Men, Women, a Bird, a Crocodile, a Calf, a Dogge, a Snake, an Onion, a Leeke, Deified. Besides, that they filled almost all places, with spirits called *Daemons*: the plains, with *Pan*, and *Panises*, or Satyres; the Woods, with Fawnes, and Nymphs; the Sea, with Tritons, and other Nymphs; every River, and Fountayn, with a Ghost of his name, and with Nymphs; every house, with its *Lares*, or Familiars; every man, with his *Genius*; Hell, with Ghosts, and spirituall Officers, as *Charon*, *Cerberus*, and the *Furies*; and in the night time, all places with *Larvae*, *Lemures*, Ghosts of men deceased, and a whole kingdome of Fayries, and Bugbears. They have also ascribed Divinity, and built Temples to meer Accidents, and Qualities; such as are Time, Night, Day, Peace, Concord, Love, Contention, Vertue, Honour, Health, Rust, Fever, and the like; which when they prayed for, or against, they prayed to, as if there were Ghosts of those names hanging over their heads, and letting fall, or withholding that Good, or Evill, for, or against which they prayed. They invoked also their own Wit, by the name of *Muses;* their own Ignorance, by the name of *Fortune;* their own Lust, by the name of *Cupid;* their own Rage, by the name *Furies;* their own privy members by the name of *Priapus;* and attributed their pollutions, to *Incubi,* and *Succubae:* insomuch as there was nothing, which a Poet could introduce as a person in his Poem, which they did not make either a *God,* or a *Divel.*

[*Leviathan,* pt. 1, chap. 12]

Among the more admirable kinds of lists is the menu, and among the many memorable moments in Robert Coover's novel *Pinocchio in Venice* is the meal which Professor Pinocchio nibbles at on the first evening of his arrival in Venice. He has been led to the Gambero Rosso by his hotel proprietor, who, though protesting that he is a bit off his feed, nevertheless manages to devour a nice long list of goodies, and by the hotel's porter, whose appetite has been whetted by work and a liberal tip. This roll call is interrupted by commentary, as long ones often need to be.

[The porter] proceeded to devour monumental quantities of tortellini and cannelloni, penne all'arrabbiata, rich and tangy, spaghetti with salt pork and peppers, heaps of thick chewy gnocchi made from cornmeal, tender pasticcio layered with baked radicchio from Treviso, pickled spleen and cooked tendons (or nervetti, as they call them here, "little nerves," slick and translucent as hospital tubing), bowls of risi e bisi and sliced stuffed esophagus (the professor skipped this one), fennel rolled in cured beef, and breaded meatballs with eggplant alla parmigiana. His doctor unfortunately having put him on a strict regimen . . . he was denied the pleasures of the fish course, but he was able, in all good conscience, to round off his evening's repast with a dish of calf's liver alla veneziana, wild hare in wine sauce with a homely garnishing of baby cocks, beef brains, pheasants, and veal marrow, a small suckling lamb smothered in kiwi fruit, sage, and toasted almonds, and a kind of fricassee of partridges, rabbits, frogs, lizards, and dried paradise grapes, said to be another famous specialty of the house and particularly recommended for persons on stringent diets.

[*Pinocchio in Venice*
(New York: Simon and Schuster, 1991), p. 34]

If we put all these rich words in our mouth, we shall dine well indeed, and conclude by exclaiming, as the porter does, "I'm as full as an egg."

No list of lists can pretend to be complete that hasn't one of Whitman's on it; however, just as the poet's frequent commands are pointless and unnecessary—"Flow on, river! flow with the flood-tide, and ebb with the ebb-tide!"—and followed by exclamation points as if something wondrous were being urged, his lists aren't always like the incantatory opening of "Out of the Cradle Endlessly Rocking," but are often only stubbornly grandiose. "A Song for Occupations" has a list that begins

> House-building, measuring, sawing the boards,
>   Blacksmithing, glass-blowing, nail-making, coopering,
>   tin-roofing, shingle-dressing,
> Ship-joining, dock-building, fish-curing, flagging of
>   sidewalks by flaggers . . .

and continues with a diligence that never flags:

> The cotton-bale, the stevedore's hook, the saw and buck of
>   the sawyer, the mould of the moulder, the working-
>   knife of the butcher, the ice-saw, and all the work with
>   ice . . .

line after—altogether—thirty very long lines, each lamer than the one before:

> The men and the work of the men on ferries, railroads,
>   coasters, fish-boats, canals . . .

until it concludes (the list but not the poem) with unintended humor (in addition to its leaden echo):

> I do not affirm that what you see beyond is futile, I do not
>   advise you to stop,
> I do not say leadings you thought great are not great,
> But I say that none lead to greater than these lead to.
>
>   ["A Song for Occupations," in *Poetry and Prose*
>   (New York: Library of America, 1982), pp. 360–62]

As for rodomontade, what else is the braggart but a list maker (unless he does dances in the end zone, his fine opinion of himself nothing beyond muscle), just as slanging matches are a measure of strength and endurance: you this, you that, each more awful than the other, until invention flags, the name-calling becomes mechanical, vocal exhaustion ensues, and it's over. In *The Sot-Weed Factor,* when the whores go at it, 229 nasty names are traded—English answered by French in increasingly hoarse howls.

When it comes to bluster, no one can blow wind better than Carlyle, whose work moves through its lists like a train through a tunnel—in the dark, surrounded by cinders, smoke, boiler steam, and whistle hoot. Apostrophes too are one of his specialties, and he continues to love colons, exclamation points, and compound nouns, and to knight his nouns with capital letters in the German manner.

> Frightful to all men is Death; from of old named King of Terrors. Our little compact home of an Existence, where we dwelt complaining, yet as in a home, is passing, in dark agonies, into an Unknown of Separation, Foreignness, unconditioned Possibility. The Heathen Emperor asks of his soul: Into what places art thou now departing? The Catholic King must answer: To the Judgment-bar of the Most High God! Yes, it is a summing-up of Life; a final settling, and giving-in the "account of the deeds done in the body": they are done now; and lie there unalterable, and do bear their fruits, long as Eternity shall last.
>
> [*The French Revolution,* bk. 1, chap. 4]

Is it stretching our example to claim this is a list? As most things are in Carlyle, the structure of the list is obscure, yet there with a vengeance. It is a list of Death's names or properties.

> King of Terrors
> Unknown of Separation
>   Foreignness
>   Unconditioned Possibility
> the Judgment-bar
> a summing-up of Life
> a final settling
> the "account of the deeds done in the body"
> (as long as) Eternity (shall last)

But only on the right list, where all things, when they pass away, pass to—the *Book of the Dead;* since to leave the list is to leave life, and not because life is one damn thing after another, as has been claimed, but because day after day arrives like another item to be catalogued: Saturday, September 9, I rose in a damp dawn to hear the paper delivered, dropped my poor head one more plop upon a callous pillow, listened to the cat lick her fur, followed the ambulance down a distant street, wondered what lunch would be like, if it would do me any good to smile at the morning mirror; and—because once these moments have been named, they can be rearranged, find their freedom from factuality in rhythm, sound, placement, subtleties of association, fresh conceptual systems—then I can wonder what lunch will be like, listen to fur being licked, plop my poor head upon an indifferent pillow, rise at dewy dawn to crack a smile at my morning's mirror, and leave the ambulance absolutely off, to die away in an unrecorded distance, the way I too would leave life if I didn't have my list.

Ko-Ko's claim to the contrary notwithstanding, it really doesn't matter whom you put upon the list—on the list they're *never* missed.

Salmagundi, 1996
Published in *Tests of Time,* 2002

The Test of Time

I

What must a work do to prepare to pass the Test of Time? Is it a written test, this test? and does it appear at a certain period in a work's life the way final exams do, or tenure reviews, or professional boards?

In perhaps an odd way, the answer to these questions is "yes."

Is it related to "the survival of the fittest" and the idea that the last one standing is the winner?

Sure, somewhat.

Is the test graded, and if so, by whom?

There can be no doubt that some works are felt to have stood the Test of Time better than others. The Test of Time is not simply pass/fail. One of the severest examiners is Time itself.

Is it therefore possible to receive a C-minus on the Test of Time?

Well, the equivalent.

Or is the test more like an ordeal which cars and trucks and airplanes are put through, to see if they are safe and well made?

Certainly—that too—for a work must sustain a lot of hard knocks, neglect, and rejection before it can say it has passed.

Is the Test of Time an exam which must be periodically repeated, like those for a driver's license?

More than that. The test is continuous.

Is there a theological component, like damnation, redemption, and salvation?

Alas, yes.

What happens to works which fail to pass the Test of Time?

Nobody cares.

Is the Test of Time something the state administers, or a professional board, or a training school, or is it a private kind of thing like a questionnaire in a magazine which will tell you, say, if you are sufficiently outgoing?

The state and its cultural agents administer part of it, but professions contribute, and schools share. It is also very much a private, nearly internal test, which works employ in the process of their creation.

So works which pass the Test of Time are never again ignored, misunderstood, or neglected?

No. Works which fail find oblivion. Those which pass stay around to be ignored, misunderstood, exploited, and neglected.

But they bring their authors honor, their creators praise?

Those responsible are all dead.

So what is the personal gain from making immortal works if the maker isn't immediately rewarded?

None whatever.

Is the Test of Time a rescuing argument?

Frequently.

When is it most commonly employed? In a rescue?

Yes.

Is the Test of Time, then, a good test, with a reasonable record of success?

The Test of Time is not a test at all. It is an announcement of temporary victory: "I am still alive." The dead do not report. As such, it is only old news.

So what happens, finally, to works which have withstood the Test of Time?

They become timeless.

2

We also frequently say "Time will tell" when actually it is we who read the expression on the clock, because Time's voice is simple and singular like the rattle of an alarm or the rouse of a rooster. And generally it means that we intend to postpone judgment; that we shall have to wait to find out if a marriage will be happy or a business successful, or whether some evaluation or prediction will be verified. Will the wine improve? Time will tell.

My last example was somewhat misleading. In time, Time may collect its toll, but taste will tell.

There is no more popular appeal, when considering the merit of works of art, than the one to Time, and when I say "popular" I mean across the board and up and down the scale. It is assumed that there is no better reason for granting greatness to an artist than the fact that his or her works, after several centuries, are still being seen and admired, heard or performed, or read and written of. The quality of being constantly contemporary—or of stubbornly surviving the vicissitudes of history, taste, and the whimsicalities of fashion—is the single quality most commonly found among major works of art, when all their other characteristics—medium, subject, attitude, length, complexity, profundity, range of feeling—differ considerably.

Conversely, there is no sign of future failure that's more reliable than the popularity of the moment, and by "popularity" I mean across the board in the noisy markets of popular culture, as well as up and down the scale from the cribs of country music and the pillows of sentimental romance through mid-cult's porn-corn bloodletting or foreign-film idolatry to the most recent academic trend and intellectual fawning, with its high-fashion fields of influence and its pompous lockjaw jargons.

The Test of Time is a stretch of Time conceived as a gauntlet to be run. And any long stretch will do, as if Time battered its principals equally through every section. We don't say: the period from 1750 to 1912 was particularly benign, and almost everything written then survived until they hit the bit between 1913 and 1938, which we now regard as a quarter-century of catastrophe, a typhoon of a time when most works of art were lost without remainder.

Another way of envisioning the test is spatial. Our creative acts fill the creative sky like stars. There are dim ones and bright ones. The constellation Rhetoric, which contains Cicero and Quintilian, is more distant from our system than the brilliant nova of the Greeks. Vico shines but not as brightly as Plotinus.

We must remember too (so we can discount them) that there are works which so adorn their era and wrinkle their age that you can't study the period without studying their role in it, although outside their beloved period they languish as immediately as a wildflower taken from its meadow.

Since we live in a society concerned mainly with money and amusement, it might be appropriate to examine an early use of the Test of Time: when it was employed to defend utilitarianism from the charge that the Principle of Utility was an instrument of the philistine—one of those rare cases in which the defendant defends himself, since utilitarianism and philistinism are identical twins. Jeremy Bentham asserted that pushpin was as good as poetry as far as the hedonistic calculus was concerned, if pushpin did indeed give as much pleasure to as many people as poetry did. We might replace pushpin with some mechanical amusements like arcade or video games. How would we determine the differing amounts, since a subjective inventory is impractical? Just as the level of pain for a person might be measured by the degree to which the entire organism is affected by it and mobilizes to respond, so we might estimate the expected pleasure of a particular activity indirectly by assessing the amounts of time, energy, interest, and money that are spent to achieve it—like packing a picnic lunch and driving six kids and two dogs to the beach—as well as considering the actual pleasure received through the frequency of the activity's repetition. Six kids and two dogs? that thin stony beach? never again.

On this basis, video games would appear to be far more important than poetry if we consider society as a whole. Mass culture is what it is because the masses prefer it. And they prefer it because it is easy to obtain (it does not require training or an advanced education or even an IQ). It amuses; it consoles; it allows people to vent their feelings in a relatively innocuous manner; it permits easy identification and promotes illusions of control; it establishes communities of common experience and provides the middle class and middle-class intellectuals with something they can talk about as if they had taste, brains, and breeding. Although the middle class would like to disavow any membership in the masses, the middle class is now far too large to be anything else. Besides, its taste is in no way more refined than that of the lower, only better packaged and more hypocritical. A taste for Bach partitas is not middle-class. Academics, who one might expect would be willing to support at least some examples of cultural quality, keep a hamper of towels handy to throw in the ring if any blows are actually struck. As Harold Bloom remarks in *The Western Canon* ([New York: Harcourt Brace, 1994], p. 520): "The morality of scholarship, as currently practiced, is to encourage everyone to replace difficult pleasures by pleasures universally accessible precisely because they are easier." And why not? Why play the wild bird in a world full of feeders? Whereupon, the tough-minded Benthamite might rest his case.

And shrug when accused of cultural leveling.

John Stuart Mill had a softer head (and poorer logic). Shakespeare might lose out to Mighty Morph in the short run (he, in effect, said), but if we consider the long haul, well, these lowlife entertainments disappear like morning mist, other amusements replace them, whereas great poetry, theater, fiction, art endure, and in so doing pile up pleasure points. In the long run, Proust will outplease pushpin, pinball, pachinko, and indoor soccer. To the Greatest Happiness for the Greatest Number (to which Mill had to tack on the stipulation that each person was to count as one, and no one for more than one) must be added the phrase "In the Long Run," with the long run no twenty-six-mile marathon but, rather, a race millennial in length. How long? The suspicion is: for as long as it takes to restore the canon to its eminence.

To the quantitative sum of pleasure and pain we could insist upon adding a judgment of quality as well, which might require the employment of competent observers: those able to experience the pleasures of video games and Bach chorales equally, and be in a position, then, to judge the qualitative superiority of one pleasure over another. So modified, the principle of utility is: the Greatest Happiness of the Highest Kind for the Greatest Number capable of experiencing the Highest Kind; otherwise, watch football, drink beer, and eat ice cream, you happy slobs.

Although there may be a few persons capable of enjoying honky-tonk and high mass, pork rinds and puff pastry, cello concerti and retch rock, and therefore be in a position to pronounce upon the quality of each of these endeavors as well as the cultural level of other pleasures, it should be clear that a life of idiocy and a life of civility are rarely joined, and that we have probably stretched our standard beyond its useful limit; for how do we know when the pleasures of the Bobbsey Twins have been thoroughly felt, so that, if they appear to be losing out on the qualitative side to Samuel Beckett's tramps, it may be because only the most devoted fans of each have enjoyed their favors fully, and no one can manage to be equally crazy about both?

There are at least two other problems. It may be true that *Hamlet* will outlast *NYPD Blue* and therefore amass more pleasure credits; however, this will require *Hamlet* to survive on its merits in order, eventually, to please so many more; it won't be its pleasure-giving qualities at any moment which keep it alive but, rather, its aliveness which makes its pleasure-giving possible; moreover, the proper contest is not between the latest bad play about AIDS and a distant boom from the canon, since The Nonce is meant to be consumed and discarded in order to make way for more Nonce of the same ninnified kind. Why recite Rilke or stage Racine one more time when rap will release one's venom better than most snakes, and when the visual jokes and verbal snickers which make up sleazy sitcoms will restore deserved dignity to big boobs and deep cleavage where Matisse and his odalisques flatly fail? Any popular pastime is soon replaced by another of the same sort, so that the competition we are contemplating should be between similar kinds of empty amusement or consoling kitsch in one corner, and the pot of paint lately flung in the public's face in the other—between crap as a class and the classy as a class—and this contest is no contest; it is a mismatch of monumental proportions: the balance continues to favor whatever is compliant, cheap, and easy.

Occasionally, those who confuse an egalitarianism which is politically desirable with a cultural equality which is cowardly, damaging, and reprehensible remind us of the good old days when the masses (how many?)

flocked to the pit of the Globe and laughed their lungs out (at what?) at the bad puns and tomfoolery of Shakespeare's clowns, or of the crowds who filled the Athenian theater to be cautioned by Sophocles, or of the thousands who read Dickens devotedly and wept at the death of Little Nell, or of the many comrades who filled Communist arenas to hear their Russian poets rant and brought flowers to heap at their feet as if they were prima donnas. In short, some poetry has beaten pushpin in the past, and we ought to take a peek at why instead of whining about popular taste. Cultural levelers hope the upshot of such an examination will support their view that "higher" culture no longer appeals to the people because it has forgotten the people (who are its roots, its audience, its aim), becoming elitist, hopelessly avant-garde, and out of touch with real life and real life's real problems.

However, the evidence is that whenever people have a choice (under Communism citizens had none), they will select schlock with a greed and certainty of conviction which leaves no doubt where their preferences lie; that, furthermore, they have always done so: in churches they kneel in hundreds at the gaudiest shrines; they troop in thousands to the loudest and least talented rock 'n' rollers and their spectacles; they take pasteboard passions and paper mysteries onto planes; they purchase period furniture and prechewed food; they crowd into movies which glorify stupidity; their idols are personalities, their dreams sentimental, their realities dubious gossip.

And why not? what has hoity-toity culture ever done for them? If they go to the cinema to watch Abel Gance's *Napoléon* instead of flocking to the flicks to snicker at Steve Martin, they will still be robbed on the way home; their hearts will remain in the same chest; their eyes will stay fixed on the main chance; it will take aspirin to hide their aches and pains; and not a single simpleminded belief will be changed. Levelers can find some comfort in the fact that the cultivated (society dames, academics, intellectuals, professional people), although they may not murder their spouses or rob banks as regularly as the poor and ignorant, manage to envy, conspire, cheat, abuse positions of power, begrudge or resent the success of others, lie and otherwise control events, embezzle, defraud, betray, with an eagerness equal to any, and in numbers sufficient to suggest that no major moral differences between the classes exist.

The Russian novel, English poetry, German music, Italian and Spanish painting, French food, American movies, Italian opera, the English stage, Flemish tapestries, French wine, Viennese operettas, Czech toys, Chicago architecture, Parisian style, Dutch diligence have enabled their nations and cities to act with piety, circumspection, and respect for others—haven't they? to be sensitive to needs and fears far from their own—haven't they? to avoid

aggression, aggrandizement, and exploitation, in order to act always to produce the greatest happiness for the greatest number—everyone counting,
but no one counting for more than one. Thank heaven for these higher cultures, which have brought peace and security, certainly prosperity and comfort, to the world.

A derisive noise is appropriate here. As the moral educators of mankind,
masterpieces have been one big floppola.

That is why the Test of Time has to be invoked, because the Test of Time
puts people at some distance from their selfish selves, allows them to correct
more immediate mistakes, permits missing manuscripts to be found, contexts
of interest to be enlarged, local prejudices to be overcome. The visionary and
the vulgar, the discriminating and the sentimental, the precise and the vague,
are so frequently, and against all rational expectation, found together in the
same bed that the finer qualities present are compromised and besmirched
in the eyes of those otherwise fit to see them. The crude laugh out loud or
easily weep at the scandalous scene set before them, the way Dickens's readers giggled and gasped at the doings portrayed in his lively but sentimental
cartoons. However, Dickens's language, his rhetoric, which rises sometimes
to Shakespeare's level (as well as so much else which rises with it), is ignored
by those bent on melodrama, while it is discounted by the snobbishly fastidious who see it as servicing only soap opera and special pleading. The Test of
Time sieves inhuman failings like silt through a prospector's pan, leaving a
residue which is clearly either gold or gravel.

So conceived and supported, the Test of Time is nevertheless made inef-
fective by the intractable naïveté of its assumptions. For isn't it naïve to suppose that history will allow only the best to survive? Is it that considerate?
Does history spare cultural icons when it does not hesitate to defeat virtue,
or when it permits the truth to be trampled under the feet of ignorant fanatics? Does it cry out "Halt!" when a fine building is about to be destroyed?
Does it reroute bombs? Does it encourage care and stewardship for the Fine
while forgetting the False? Haven't we been told that the human race made
progress when it replaced the great Greek gods with a bewhiskered tyrannical
granddad whose mean spirit is as big as his beard?

In what world do we live if we think only the good guys win and virtue is
always rewarded? In a free market, the vulgar, we have learned, will grab all
the meat and potatoes and elbow the refined, empty-handed, out the door.
People are wicked because wickedness gives them an advantage. When the
Romans overran Greece, they took bare-assed marble boys and busty girlies
home to decorate their villas, and melted bronzes down to make pitiless the
points of their spears. Pagans, Christians, Muslims took turns burning the

books of Alexandria's library. Invaders loot, sack, pillage, rape, and burn. Whoever they are. Whatever it is. They steal to sell. They steal to display, to vaunt, to collect. Indian mounds are leveled like harvested fields, and gold and slaves are sent back to the capital. Those who rise up against criminal divinities stupidly burn down the temples of the superstitious (which may be glorious and beautiful) instead of the superstitions of the superstitious (which are ignorant, ugly, and obscene).

Of course, we should not blame "history." History is not an agent who goes about trampling traditions into dust, ending lives, stifling others, despoiling the land, and poisoning the sea. History is humanity on its rampage. Considering the frequency of natural calamities, our treatment of warfare as a seasonal sport, and the insatiable squirrelliness of human greed, it should be an occasion for surprise when anything excellent survives.

3

How indeed does it? In the same way that Elvis Presley does. So far. It has fans. The devoted gather, often slowly at first, each fan feeling alone with her enthusiasm and despised for it—odd-eyed because El Greco or Modigliani or Picasso pleases; odd-eared because Schoenberg or Burl Ives or Bartók is thrilling; conceptually queer because Celan makes instant sense, or Hopkins thrives, or Musil musiks the mind. Or because WOW, man.

When the work which is worshipped has been roundly reviled, it becomes even more precious. It shows society up. It verifies the fan's feeling of being isolated and unappreciated, in a foreign land, surrounded by indifference or hostility. The "new" architecture is attacked because it is felt to be opposed to present preferences; the "new" music undermines an entire tradition; the "new" painting accuses reality of appearance; the "new" writing is incomprehensible, obscene, blasphemous, politically incorrect; thus each art finds its "new" adherents among those similarly disaffected.

"Fan" is a shortened form of "fanatic," and it is true that the fan's faith is often half-sighted if not entirely blind, often fueled as much by the dislike its object provokes in others as by the love its object inspires in him; so that the fan often falls for a message which isn't there, is moved by emotions which aren't expressed, by strategies which haven't been employed.

Fans form clubs or find other ways in which to share their enthusiasms. The fan's love does not resemble romantic passion in every way, because it is rarely possessive; it is more like chauvinism, in the sense that the fan's feelings make him the member of a defining cult or tribe. He's prepared to love anybody Irish, anyone French. A fan is prepared to devote far more time to the pursuit and glorification of his idol than most people are, even those who find the composer's music or the author's works intriguing or uncommonly fine. Eventually, fans will found a holy shrine. These shrines, in their turn, will employ professional "keepers of the flame"; they'll put out bulletins and publish magazines; they'll manufacture relics, peddle icons, sponsor gatherings; and before you can say "Mickey Mouse" or "Bobbie Burns" there'll be a group in place whose livelihood, not just their enthusiasm or donated time, will depend upon the continued idolization of the idol—and by the enlistment of greater and greater numbers. Economic interests are generally more reliable and enduring than love. Social status hangs upon money like a fob from a watch, and power from both. The keepers of the flame, like the clergy, will have many more reasons than adoration to carry out their duties. Not infrequently, the fan's devotion is no more than displaced patriotism, as when a poet is loved because he is Welsh or Scots, and the natives are gleeful that someone of their race with genius has been found. In any case, any adoration which isn't drama, spectacle, and public relations—which is simply rich understanding and deep appreciation—can come last.

In short, the work of art, the performer, the beneficial idea have become "the treasures of" an institution—the *Mona Lisa* in the Louvre. It is the institution and its interests which carry their symbol before them like a flag, a chalice, a trophy, across the treacherous bournes of Time. If you think it is hard to find true virtue hidden somewhere in this story, you are right. The institutions, in their turn, become tools for larger ones: if a young nation, a new movement, needs heroes and poets, some Longfellow will be chosen and brought to the schools like a captive in chains, or some hero like Nathan Hale will be installed in the national story like a bishop in the Church; this painted pop-up history will then be taught to helpless kiddies to confirm the prejudices of their parents so that the myth of a magically united and superior society can be passed on to its prospective citizens in order that they may each equally enjoy the pleasures of chauvinistic self-satisfaction, while, at the same time, conserving their oh-so-common cultural values, preserving the legitimacy of the status quo, and guaranteeing, consequently, the continued power of the state and its teams of pickpockets.

If there is someone sane you wish to drive mad, merely institutionalize him; if there is some Good you wish to besmirch, some Truth you wish to undermine, organize it; if there is some noble and glorious career you wish to destroy, parade its accomplishments past a committee.

The canon—Shakespeare, Dante, Chaucer, Cervantes, and so on—blessed by Harold Bloom—are alas not there because greatness is both steed and shield to carry them on through the indifference of history, past its nervous overseers and their obedient serfs. Leaders—political, religious, economic—care nothing for merit; they value only use. And they succeed because the led are no differently inclined. The poor may not be poor because they are poor of mind and heart (as some suggest), but their minds and hearts are certainly not a bit better for it. Their sort of simple life is simpleminded; a life close to the soil is lived near the grave; the workman's pride in the work of his hands was long ago mechanized; the rhythms of Have and Want and Get never change. Those who are "out" are not better for being there; otherwise, why would they seek a change?

But they—those who fancy they are not making out very well, like other folks are supposed to be making out in the wonderful world of those other folks—will be quick to see in what direction the canon fires, and will have the rhetoric I have just rehearsed as handy as spit in their mouths. They will memorize the ways they have been cheated; they will have care baskets of truth on their side; they can point to a campaign of discrimination, injury, neglect; they can quite rightly complain of unfairness and bigotry and misuse. They will advance their own art, their own neglected texts, their own critical methods, their own mythologies in opposition to the cultural icons in place. Nothing could be more natural, nothing more righteous than their indignation. It will seem that they alone love literature, let it act importantly, help it to shape their communities; and to a degree—lacking money, power, and other forms of glue—they will be right; but make no mistake: like the Puritans, they'll love liberty only when facing their enemies, who don't want them to have it. It will turn out, moreover, that the struggle against their common adversary will not permit internal divisions. For a time, freedom of thought and action will have to be sacrificed to the goals of the group, and so on—how often have we heard it? Not bold new behavior, not innovative notions, but conformity and compaction are the consequences.

Since minorities have no armies and few fields to fight on, their members bicker like faculties over the most minor matters, bitterly opposing this or ardently espousing that, as if a schedule change would alter the course of the Gulf Stream, a staff appointment in the history of igloo design revolutionize the building code. But these quibbles screen the truth from outsider eyes. Disciplines have been derailed, departments destroyed, careers ruined, so that "right thinking" might prevail. Tweedledum and Tweedledee are fighting with nothing over nothing because they haven't guns yet. Then it will be life and death.

Groups squabble about literature because they have other than literary uses for the literary. The schools, which are busy finding ways to get the answers to the Test of Time smuggled to their chosen favorites, as coaches slip the answers to their players so they may pass the latest examination, will now and then speak of Art and claim a disinterested purity. And there are an unorganized few (the unhappy few whom I should like to represent, "the immense minority," as Juan Ramón Jiménez so significantly puts it) who sincerely love the arts. There are those for whom reading, for example, can be an act of love, and lead to a revelation, not of truth, moral or otherwise, but of lucidity, order, rightness of relation, the experience of a world fully felt and furnished and worked out in the head, the head where the heart is also to be found, and all the other vital organs.

I have the good luck not to live in an English department, so I have not had to observe directly or suffer intimately the sophistical poses of pluralism and the opportunistic fads of fashion which the courtiers of our culture have paraded on its runways, but my feeling is "it has been ever thus." Philosophy departments, where my presence has been more frequent, have, during my brief sojourn in their narrow halls, practiced the prejudices of Idealism, Pragmatism, Positivism, Existentialism, and Phenomenology, and served the interests of special groups (a practice they once despised) by offering biomedical or business ethics, game theory, philosophical psychology, and feminist studies.

Inside the Academy, at the Symphony, within Museum walls, each warring faction will boast that God is on their side, and claim transcendence for their values and opinions. This is done by trying to ensure that only their ideas, and works correctly expressing them, get put before the public in the future, and by reanalyzing the past for as far back as the catalogue has cards (a deliberately out-of-date metaphor) in order to show, as I previously characterized their internecine struggles, that "it has been ever thus," whatever it is they say it is now.

Outside, in the vendors' streets, there are nothing but temporary tents. The lasting, the universal are despised (except by those who are still peddling the classics to old fogies). But who really wants reruns of already winded warhorses? Well, only those arrogant and rapacious revivalists who set *Rigoletto* in the Bronx and who want Dido and Aeneas to sing about their love while costumed as colonials. Their pitiful originalities would have once brought them to the gibbet or the stake.

The ideal cultural product comes powerfully packaged, creates a mighty stir, can be devoured with both delight and a sense of life-shaking revelation, provides an easy topic for talk, is guaranteed to be without real salt or any actual fat—contains no substance of any substantial kind—so that, after you have eaten it, for days you will shit only air.

So are all these works, which appear to have persisted, the way postmen once did, through dark nights and bad weather (the past's periodic eclipses of reason, and other ages of ice), here now only through evil machination or by odd accident? The poet may duck, escape his time, as Quevedo writes:

> Retired to the peace of this desert,
> with a collection of books that are few but wise,
> I live in conversation with the departed
> and listen to the dead with my eyes.
>
> [Quoted by Octavio Paz in *The Other Voice*
> (New York: Harcourt Brace, 1991), p. 111]

But the work cannot choose its companions or by itself steer a favorable course. Yet, oddly, something like that happens. Minds find minds. The intelligent heart beats in more than one head, and a wise book contains a consciousness which has at last made something wonderful of the world.

For, when I follow Thoreau's prose, I am in no ordinary footsteps. *Walden* has been read and reread; it is hallowed; it is an American classic; it sells because generations of students at all sorts of grade levels are asked to answer questions about it; and it is still seen to support this group, that cause, have relevance. How full of these tourists the woods are, how trampled the paths, how bored or nervous or put upon the picnickers feel, forced to spread their blankets over these placid pages.

Have they felt a sentence start like a rabbit from beneath their eye? Or watched a meadow made small by the sky, or studied a simple street, or felt the wind flutter a row of wash like flags hung from a window? And been taught by such a sentence what it is to be alive? Rilke wondered:

> Are we, perhaps, *here* just to utter: house,
> bridge, fountain, gate, jug, fruit tree, window—
> at most: column, tower . . . but to *utter* them, remember,
> to speak in a way which the named never dreamed they could *be*.

Gertrude Stein wondered more than once what went into a masterpiece: what set some works aside to be treasured while others were abandoned without a thought, as we leave seats after a performance; what there was about a text we'd read which provoked us to repeat its pages; what made us want to remain by its side, rereading and remembering, even line by line; what led us to defend its integrity, as though our honor were at stake, and to lead it safely through the perils that lie in wait for excellence in a world where only mediocrity seems prized. She concluded that masterpieces were addressed, not to the self whose accomplishments might appear on some dossier, the self whose passport is examined at the border, the self whose concerns are those of the Self (I and My and Me and Mine); but to the human mind, a faculty which is everywhere the same and whose business is with universals. Masterpieces teach that human differences are superficial; that intelligence counts, not approved conclusions; that richly received and precisely appreciated sensations matter, not titillation or dolled-up data; that foreplay, not payoff, is to be preferred; that imagination and conceptual solutions, not ad hoc problem solving, are what such esteemed works have in common. And we, who read and write and bear witness and wail with grief, who make music and massacres, who paint in oils and swim in blood—we are one: everywhere as awful, and as possibly noble, as our natures push us or permit us to be.

Say a sort of "amen" to that. But the trouble with transcendence is that the transcendent must rise, and to make that possible it must lighten its load, dump detail as worse than unwanted, toss aside everything that thickens life and leads us to lick it like gravy. Overboard go all gross things, as if the crude and hollow and impermanent weren't recurrent. Transcendence is not what masterworks teach me: they teach me immersion. They teach me that the trivial is as important as the important when looked at importantly. They tell me that evil is lasting and complex and significant and profoundly alluring, and that it requires our appreciative and steadfast gaze more than grace and goodness do, who receive it like starlets—only too often ready to giggle in reply.

And we, who must be transcendent too, if universals are to take any notice of us, lose ourselves in the course of this diet: our little habits, simple pleasures, traits which set us aside as a certain someone—perhaps a lovely leg we shave and sand and wax as if it held up period furniture, or a voice we exercise as we would a show horse, or the way we cheat at parcheesi or treat the sweet tooth we suffer and adore with weekend sundaes, or try to defeat the line a strategic elastic has left on our body by undressing in the dark and relying on the skin's resilience to erase the statement by morning.

Even ideas (and certainly their abstractness recommends them), when they are thought, are drenched in the particularities of time and place and mood and purpose, because minds, it turns out, are as particular as toenails, and are always like a working part of a tired foot too, companion to the other toes; so that your belief in God and my belief in the divinity of the dance aren't just notions we've put mustaches on to differentiate them, but are as peculiar to us as our visage is, our fingerprint, our taste in clothes, our loyalty, our laugh.

As Ernst Cassirer said of the aim of Kant's critical philosophy: "To step into the infinite it suffices to penetrate the finite in all its aspects."

We are in cahoots with art. We want everything to survive, even flies. And there they are, on that slope of Rilke's lines: the gate, the house, the fruit tree, window—awaiting our look to be realized, not as house or tree or window but as a smeared gray pane, a pane as gray as the walk is where it proceeds through that skimpy sick grass there past a leafless tree up to the weathered front door, ajar as if to welcome our entry, but actually left open by the whole of Yesterday when that Time went, with its features and its friends, never to return. When we entered, if we took note of the weathered top of the kitchen table when we entered, and how a dim gray light puddled in some of its scars and leaked the length of its cracks; if we saw, when we entered, how the blue pitcher stood amid crumbs of bread like a bird that's just been fed, and how a dish towel hung for an hour over the ladderback of a kitchen chair, drying its sweat-shaped patches of damp before being taken up to be dampened again; had we found the paint or prose or pipe for them; had we rhymed a skillet's sear with a knife's scratch, then we'd have them still, still as Walden's water was when Thoreau skiffed at night across it and cast a line:

> Sometimes, after staying in a village parlor till the family had all retired,
> I have returned to the woods, and, partly with a view to the next day's
> dinner, spent the hours of midnight fishing from a boat by moonlight,
> serenaded by owls and foxes, and hearing, from time to time, the creak-
> ing note of some unknown bird close at hand. These experiences were
> very memorable and valuable to me,—anchored in forty feet of water,
> and twenty or thirty rods from the shore, surrounded sometimes by
> thousands of small perch and shiners, dimpling the surface with their
> tails in the moonlight, and communicating by a long flaxen line with
> mysterious nocturnal fishes which had their dwelling forty feet below,
> or sometimes dragging sixty feet of line about the pond as I drifted in
> the gentle night breeze, now and then feeling a slight vibration along
> it, indicative of some life prowling about its extremity, of dull uncertain
> blundering purpose there, and slow to make up its mind.
>
> [*Walden,* chap. 9, "The Ponds"]

We cannot say with certainty what will live, and survival, by itself, is no guarantee of quality; but I think we can say something about what is deserv-ing. Thoreau's two unsimple sentences put me out on that pond, in prose as clear as its water is. Now I can mourn its present turbid state, and fashion a fine romance from my memory of a time when kids could stay out late to fish, and feel the distant friendship of the stars like the lights of Atlantis in the water. But the magical stillness in the prose, its easy motion, depends upon its calm and measured breathing, its quiet but ever-present music, its unhurried and appreciative perceptions, like a slow swallow of wine.

All those numbers would paralyze most paragraphs. However, here, as I move my mind along the line, holding its hush in my ear, of course I do not see the dimpling surface of the lake—the lake is miles from me, the time is out of reach, the categories of existence clash—but my consciousness *conceives* the seeing, *conceives* the thirty rods of distance to the shore, *conceives* the twitch a nibble makes, how the pole's handle tickles the angler's palm, and consequently understands the decision slowly forming down there from the nudge of the fish's nose.

There's no moment too trivial, too sad, too vulgar, too rinky-dink to be unworthy of such recollection, for even a wasted bit of life is priceless when composed properly or hymned aright, even that poor plate of peaches slowly spoiling while its portrait is being painted—not, however, the peaches themselves, which must rot to realize their nature, and not a sore tooth's twinge, and not a battle's loss or love's loss, or the cutest darling dimple, or a bite of pie the peaches could have been better put to use in; no, rather, their rendering—that's priceless: the Cézanne which gives to the mountain more than it merits, the juice which runs from alongside that aching tooth when the topmost peach is bitten, but only when a sentence performs the biting, and the juice is wiped off by the word "sleeve," and the smile of satisfaction can be read as it spreads across the face of the page.

When Hopkins wondered "how to keep," whether there was "any any,"

> none such, nowhere known some, bow or brooch or braid or brace,
>   lace, latch or catch or key to keep
> Back beauty, keep it, beauty, beauty, beauty, . . . from vanishing
>   away

he knew, of course, the answer; which was yes, "there is one," there is a place where

> the thing we freely forfeit is kept with fonder a care,
> Fonder a care kept than we could have kept it, kept
> Far with fonder a care

but he said it was "yonder," in effect, up in the air, as "high as that," when all the while he knew where it was: it was there under his forming fingers; it was in his writing, where the real god, the god he could not avow—dared not worship—worked, wrote, writing his rhetorical regrets, putting his question so perfectly the proof was in the putting.

Hopkins, in one mood, writes,

> Nothing is so beautiful as Spring—
> When weeds, in wheels, shoot long and lovely and lush;

while in a wintertime time, when his faith nears icy cinder, he complains,

> No worst, there is none. Pitched past pitch of grief,
> More pangs will, schooled at forepangs, wilder wring

but there's no contradiction here; it's not that one of them is right, that he should buck up and be brave or leave off sentimentalizing about one more season. And the fact that for a moment, in his heart, his faith is renewed or shaken, while in mine, his reader, belief being absent, faith has no place to stand or snow in which to shiver—that difference makes no difference; it is as irrelevant as yesterday's air, because opinions, principles, philosophies, systems of belief are also a part of the passing world, beauties themselves, some of them, rich in invention, as full of our longing as legs in long pants; and our longings are real, if what they long for isn't; they also need their celebration, since each of them is like a baited line sunk into a Deep beyond our seeing—searching—waiting for the nose of something there to twitch it, waiting for a nibble.

Celebrate sorrow—why not? celebrate pain, invent a Iago, bring on the awfuls, Bosch's brush awaits to do its best by the worsts. Christ hangs from the cross like an ill-hung suit, yet the meaning of His suffering is our redemption. My heresy is: redemption is on the canvas, in the image and its pigments, in the skill and attitudes that brought paint to this pass.

4

How best to ace the Test of Time? in a world where everything good happens later than you'd have liked, and everything bad breaks out before you expected it? Good times do pass, and bad ones, dear heart, for all your poetizing, are bad; the good is quick as a bird, the bad is slow as ooze, and, dearie, for all your whistling Dixie, evils are not nice. If Hopkins is down in the dumps, he is miserable down there, and no fine lines will redeem the dumps, or save him from his doubts, or relieve him of the truth: God's not going to pluck him out of the earth where he will surely lie and surely rot; not as if he were a parsnip pulled clear and shaken clean. Anyway, rinsed of the grave, he'd only be headed for the soup.

Thoreau went boating as a boy, and dropped his line, and never did it happen in prose of any kind, including his own: the line's great curve behind him as he trolled was drawn in cold pond water, crystalline. Now Walden is threatened by developers every year, and the water has been soiled by decades of rancid runoff. What has been saved, then, what has been preserved, what has withstood time? . . . and the sawyer's saws? The Binsey poplars were suddenly felled, as if in front of Hopkins's saddened eye, blunt stumps lining the bank where he passed as faithfully as the river, their short life shortened by someone who could cut, and could cancel his care before it came up into consciousness . . . who could ax one and watch it fall and then another.

> My aspens dear, whose airy cages quelled,
> Quelled or quenched in leaves the leaping sun,
> All felled, felled, are all felled.

"Wake and feel the fell of dark, not day." This is how; this is why. The paragraphs of *Walden* form in words what never happened. I agree: events encouraged those words, events surprised them into existence; but Thoreau made his memory, created water that never was. . . . Oh yes, they tossed the brands they burned to lure the fish up out of nighttime as if the sun had risen, they tossed the brands like fireworks and listened to them return to enter the water with a kiss; but they did so by swinging their arms then, and not in so many, not in any, words: "And when we had done, far in the night, threw the burning brands high into the air like skyrockets, which, coming down into the pond, were quenched with a loud hissing, and we were suddenly groping in total darkness." Thoreau was not Thoreau then, just a boy, playing a flute to charm the perch, catching pouts with threaded worms, and not a word, I'm sure, disturbed the serenity of that life.

So had it not happened—and where is that Walden now?—it would have happened anyway, but not in Time, who allows the ax to swing like a second hand, but in the prose or in the poem where, down in the dumps, a pun appears to point out to us that life, that misery, does not pun and does not rhyme and has no rhythm, sprung or otherwise, so inadequate is it; and why not let life pass, then, get along; life, thank god, happens only once, and its pains are merely painful, hurtfully plain, while in the poem pain is wrung from the poet as if he were wet wash, but since he's been pitched past pitch of grief, the ringing has a pealing sound: the pangs of pain, the procession of those *p*'s.

Didn't the poplars cage—quell—the sunlight themselves, so how can they complain? and weren't those burning brands quenched as well? One light went while rising; the other fell. Time holds occasions open like opportunities, but the poet's poem never was in time like the trees or his grief or Walden's water was mid-night. They, those things, the terrible sonnets, every one, were composed, brought by Hopkins into being, not when he was down in the dumps, not while he was Hopkins, but when he was a Poet, truly on top of the world, the muse his mother; and the poems supplant their cause, are sturdier than trees, and will strip the teeth of any saw that tries to down them.

Because when the poplars went they went without the poet's passion for them as present as their leaves. And we, as readers, are not brought to Walden Pond in some poetic time machine. We experience Walden as it passed through Thoreau's head, his whole heart there for us to pass through too, his wide bright eyes the better to see with, the patient putting together of his prose to appreciate. Of the pond, the trees, the pain, the poet may retain—through the indelibilities of his medium—moments which, in reality, went as swiftly as a whistle away; but he will also give them what was never there in the first place: much afterthought, correction, suggestion, verbal movement, emotion, meaning, music. The result is the combination of occasion, consciousness, and artful composition which we now—oh so fortunately—have. Thus the night was not as it was described, neither the fishing nor the pain; events, actions, objects, didn't repeat; the feelings were never felt, the wringing and the quelling, they were as baked as biscuits; and the thoughts were never thought that way—what thoughts there were are as long gone as the row of trees—they were composed; in sum, the pond we know, the trees, the pain, the poet's passion for each actual thing, the philosopher's concerns, mourning the fallen trees, they never were anywhere but in Hopkins's words:

> When we hew or delve:
> After-comers cannot guess the beauty been.
> Ten or twelve, only ten or twelve
> Strokes of havoc unselve
> The sweet especial scene,
> Rural scene, a rural scene,
> Sweet especial rural scene.

That is half our answer. It was lovely to be on Walden Pond at midnight, fluting the fish, but lovelier and more lasting in the verbal than in the fishing lines. It is painful to lose faith even for a moment or see a row of crudely hewn trunks where your favorite rustic scene once was, but mutilation's sorrow is inspiring in the reading, although we realize the poem does not soften the blows felt by the trees.

Here is the other half. Don't take the test. Poetry makes nothing happen, because it refuses to be a happenstance. Poems are not events. They are realities remarkably invested with value. They are a woman, a man, a mind made of words, and have no body, and hence no needs.

So be advised. For works of art, the rule reads: never enter Time, and you will never be required to exit.

Alaska Quarterly Review, 1997
Published in *Tests of Time,* 2002

"And"

is used 3,381 times in James Joyce's *A Portrait of the Artist as a Young Man,* and occurs on 7,170 occasions in that same author's *Ulysses,* from which we can conclude that the latter is a much longer book. It appears oftener than 'a' and oftener than 'an'—although its frequency lags far behind 'the' (as regards ubiquity always the winner)—and it easily outdoes 'or,' 'of,' 'it,' 'oh!,' as well as every other little word which might be presumed to be its rival, even 'is,' even 'I.'* Some snoop† has reported that of the number of words we use in ordinary correspondence, nine words ('I,' 'the,' 'and,' 'you,' 'to,' 'your,' 'of,' 'for,' and 'in'), at one time at least, comprised a fourth of the total, whereas in telephone conversations 'and' barely makes the top ten in frequency of use.

Words that get heavy, one might say almost continuous employment are invariably short. Suppose 'and' were as long as 'moreover'? It would soon *mean* "moreover," and drop to an ignominious rate of three in *A Portrait,* to a sad two in *Ulysses,* a frequency which will scarcely seed a satisfying life. And if 'and' were spelled, say, like 'Mesopotamia,' would it receive any use at all? And what would happen to the ideas it represents if we were too busy to think them, or to all the various ands in the world we could no longer trouble ourselves to designate? That ceaselessly constant conjunction of which Hume spoke would now be noted only rarely: when we were forced to

---

* Leslie Hancock, compiler, *Word Index to James Joyce's Portrait of the Artist* (Carbondale: Southern Illinois University Press, 1967), and Miles L. Hanley, compiler, *Word Index to James Joyce's Ulysses* (Madison, Wisc.: privately printed, 1937).

† The Bell System, of course (H. L. Mencken, *The American Language, Supplement Two* [New York: Alfred A. Knopf, 1948], p. 352).

remind ourselves of the connection between Punch moreover Judy, or Mutt mesopotamia Jeff.

Such is not its plight, or ours, however. On word lists, the occurrences of 'and' are merely numbered, never cited. The dictionary contains it only as a courtesy, and out of a traditional conceit of completeness. No one is going to look up 'and.' We do not "look up" manhole covers when we visit the city. So it is a squeak we are used to. It passes through the ear, the eye, the mind, unheard, unseen, and unremarked. It can copulate as openly as birds do, the way park ducks wanton on their ponds. Indeed, pigeons are more heatedly complained of, for 'and' leaves no poop on public shoulders. As a word, 'and' is an amiable nothing. It hasn't even a substantiating, an ennobling function like 'the,' which has caused many a philosopher's hackles to rise.

Joyce singled out 'the' and gave it pride of final place in *Finnegans Wake,* although one might argue that while 'the' has the last word in the body of the text, it acts only to buckle the belly of the book together, and that the pride of penultimate places is actually given to 'a,' ordinarily a halt word, a rhyme chime, a mere space maker, the shallowest exhalation: "A way a lone a last a loved a long the . . ." where it interrupts the ells as they likker across the tongue: "lone last loved long riverrun, past Eve and Adam's, from swerve of shore to bend of bay . . . a . . . a . . . a . . ." Just a few lines earlier, 'and' had been allowed to perform an equally rocking rhythmical function: "And it's old and old it's sad and old it's sad and weary I go back to you, my cold father, my cold mad father, my cold mad feary father . . ." It is worth noticing how 'old' slips into an 'O' like a woman into a wrapper: "And it's old and O it's sad and O it's sad and weary . . ." just as the *C* sound it picks up later will reinstruct our ears so that we hear, in retrospect, "And it's cold and cold it's sad and cold it's sad and weary. . . ." Of these musical methods, of course, Joyce was a master.

The anonymity of 'and,' its very invisibility, recommends the word to the student of language, for when we really look at it, study it, listen to it, 'and' no longer appears to be 'and' at all, because 'and' is, as we said, invisible, one of the threads that hold our clothes together: what business has it being a pants leg or the frilly panel of a blouse? The unwatched word is meaningless—a noise in the nose—it falls on the page as it pleases, while the writer is worrying about nouns and verbs, welfare checks or a love affair; whereas the watched word has many meanings, some of them profound; it has a wide range of functions, some of them essential; it has many lessons to teach us about language, some of them surprising; and it has metaphysical significance of an even salutary sort.

'And'

is produced initially with an open mouth, the breath flowing out, but then that breath is driven up against the roof, toward the nose, even invading it before the sound is stoppered by the tongue against the teeth. The article 'a' can be pronounced "aw," "A," "uh," "aah," or nearly forgotten, while 'the' is "thuh" or "thee," depending on position and status; but 'and' is only and always "and," although its length, like that of many such words which contain the outrush of a vowel, is relatively indeterminate: "aah-nn-duh"—where the "duh" is like a lariat lassoing the next word, filling the voice stream, allowing one's thought to continue, inhibiting interruptions: "pahst Eeev anduhAah-dummz . . ." In Middle English, and often among the vulgar since, the word has appeared in reduced circumstances, either as a conditional: an' it please your lordship, I'll drop me drawers; or as a common conjunction: an' here an' there the bullets went an' never touched me nearly. Hollywood nosh nooks, back in the thirties, bobbed it even further: "Dunk 'n Dine," their signs said, "Sit 'n Eat." There was also the nautical "spit 'n polish," and that enigmatic putdown "shit 'n Shinola."* Nothing rivals the erosion which 'and' in Spanish has had to suffer. My sources affirm that it was *Yolanda* in its early, great, romantic days, whereas now it goes about as the vulgar, hardly heard *y.'* We live in evil times.

Although the sound "and" and the word 'and' may appear and reappear in sentence after sentence, both in spoken and in written form, there is no single meaning (AND) which remains tethered to the token. The word is, perhaps, no sneakier than most words, but it is sneaky enough, hiding itself inside other sounds, pulling syllables up over its head. It is, of course, the principal element in 'randy,' 'saraband,' and 'island,' a not inconsiderable segment of 'Andorra,' 'Anderson,' 'antediluvian,' 'Spandau,' and 'ampersand,' whose elegantly twisted symbol [&—&] (the so-called short or alphabetical 'and' made by intertwining the *e* and *t* of "et") also contains it. 'Ampersand' has been reported to be a slovenly corruption of 'and per se and,' which would suggest, when the symbol is used, that it wishes to upset any implied balance or equality in favor of the leadoff term: *Dombey and Son* would mean "Dombey and equally his son," while *Dombey & Son* would mean "Dombey in himself and, in addition, his son." 'And' also lurks about in words like 'spanned,' and in apparently innocent commands like 'please put the pan down, Anne,' as well as in many allegations or simple statements of fact, for instance, that 'panders and pimps and pushers, panhandlers and prostitutes, stand like so many lamps on the streetcorners.'

* "He don't know shit from Shinola" and "He don't know the difference between shit 'n Shinola" both refer, I take it, to the condition of one's footwear, since Shinola is a shoe polish.

Not only are there more 'and's about than immediately meets the eye, the word by itself in the open is manifold in its meanings, and not in the way that most words are ambiguous either: 'bank' variously signifying a calculated bounce or guarded vault or sloping river edge; 'rank' signifying something overripe or of military station; 'tank' referring to an armored vehicle, a cylinder for gas or certain fluids, an approximate measure. 'And' is ambiguous the way prepositions are, not straightforwardly but curvaceously, almost metaphysically, multiple. Think of the differences designated by the same, seemingly simple, 'on' in (1) 'the poorhouse is on fire,' (2) 'the seafood is on the table,' (3) 'her panties were hanging on the line,' (4) 'their lacy patterns turned him on,' (5) 'now his mind was mainly on Mary.'* Such words are constantly in transit between meanings, their very indeterminacy an invitation to their contexts to seize and to shape them; and if 'bank' were like that, we should sense how we might slide down some weedy slope into the till, or how we might count on a good bounce from our rubber check.

Initially a preposition itself, and derived from 'end,' the idea of fronting or facing a boundary, the word suggested an opposition, a standing of something next to but over against something else, such as 'up' with 'down,' 'high' next to 'low,' 'peace' over against 'war.' Later, as various words collapsed into and became 'and' ('ond,' 'ant,' 'enti,' 'anda,' 'undi,' 'und,' 'unt,' 'et,' et cetera), its function as a relatively neutral conjunction increased. Now not even Proteus can match the magicality of its many metamorphoses.

A single example from Gertrude Stein's "Melanctha" should be sufficient to show our small word's true and larger nature.

She tended Rose, and[1] she was patient, submissive, soothing, and[2] untiring, while the sullen, childish, cowardly, black Rosie grumbled and[3] fussed and[4] howled and[5] made herself to be an abomination and[6] like a simple beast.

['And' #1] "She tended Rose, and she was patient, submissive, soothing . . ." This is the adverbial use of 'and.' The expression is to be read: "She tended Rose, and [in doing so] she was patient, submissive, soothing . . ." It is not so much that 'and' is an adverb here; rather, it determines the nature of application to the verb 'tended' of what follows it. We have no grammatical category for this operation.

['And' #2] ". . . she was patient, submissive, soothing, and untiring . . ."

---

* I discuss the ambiguous character of the preposition 'of,' citing fourteen different uses without presuming to have mentioned all of them, in "The Ontology of the Sentence, or How to Make a World of Words," *The World Within the Word* (New York: Alfred A. Knopf, 1978), pp. 308–38.

This 'and' begins as the 'and' of balance and coordination. That is, we have 'soothing' on the one hand balanced logically and grammatically with 'untiring' like two weights on a scale. Both words belong to the same part of speech; both are about the same length; both designate qualities of the same logical order, although soothed is something the patient is supposed to feel, while untiring is something the nurse is, and, more important, looks. But when 'soothing,' as a word, is not alone; when it is joined, on its side, by two others; then the balance goes out of whack, and the nature of our 'and' begins to alter.

$$\underline{patient,\ submissive,\ soothing} \underset{\Delta}{} \underline{untiring}$$

The 'and' we now confront means "finally." It may even mean "and in particular" or "above all." Death, Donne tells us, is "a slave to fate, chance, kings, and [finally] desperate men." This 'and,' then, moves from one meaning to another like a pointer on that imaginary scale it has suggested. It begins by intimating equality and balance, but both its position in the series (last) and its separation from the rest ('and' acts as a barrier) increase its importance, as if it were significant enough by itself to weigh as much as the other three. Principally, however, this second 'and' indicates the approaching conclusion of a list the way certain symphonic gestures ready us for the culmination of the music. "I love your lips, nose, eyes, hair, chin, and hollow cheeks, your big bank account and bust, my dear." Balances are delicate and easily tipped. The social status of a word, its force, its length, its history of use: anything can do it. Syntax sets up the scale, but semantics puts the weights in the pans. The following are out of balance: (1) "The bandit shot my son, stabbed me in the arm, and called me names," (2) "What bitter things both life and aspirin are!," (3) "I've boated everywhere—on the Po and on Pawtucket Creek," (4) "You say your marriage suffers from coital insufficiency and greasy fries?," (5) "Yeah, my wife kisses her customers and brings their bad breath to bed."

Between the words 'patient' and 'submissive' in the Stein sentence, only a comma intervenes, but that comma stands for an 'and' whose presence is purely conceptual. It is 'and' become ghostly and bodiless. It is that famously fatuous gleam in Father's eye. Indeed, one could easily write another essay on the germinal, the spermatic character of this seedy wormlike bit of punctuation. The comma resembles the law, and can command our conscience without a policeman. The absence of the officer is essential to its effect, however, for "she was patient and submissive and soothing and untiring" is another sentence entirely, and not a very forceful one.

To the logician, who is at least patient and untiring, if not soothing and submissive, a connective like 'and' or its sometime substitute, the comma, asserts the joint dependency of every element in the pursuit of truth. The logician is outspoken and prefers everything laid out on the bed like clothes for a trip. She (Melanctha) was patient; and she (Melanctha) was submissive; and she (Melanctha) was soothing; and she (Melanctha) was untiring, too—at once and altogether. One can hear what a wearisome way to go at things this is; and for some of the same reason we like our workaday words short and preferably snappy, we fold our ideas over whenever we can—wad them up—and indicate the folds with commas. The logician's assertion of mutual dependency of parts where truth is concerned is paradoxical, and tells us a good deal about 'and,' because 'and,' whenever it interposes its body, separates each quality from the others and insists that we examine them one at a time, as if they might display themselves on different days or places (as if we were saying that Melanctha was patient on Tuesday, when she wore her bright-blue dress, and untiring on Wednesday in her red riding habit, and submissive on Sunday, when she put on her smart pink smock); as if being patient and untiring were conditions which never interpenetrate or affect one another.

The logician's 'and' is indifferent to grouping and order. It is all the same to it whether (1) "Bill has a boil on his nose and water in the pot," or (2) "water in the pot and a boil on his nose," or whether (3) "Bill has a boil on his nose, water in the pot, and a plant on the sill," or (4) "a boil on his nose and water in the pot, a plant on the sill with its window on the world." To our logician, if Melanctha was soothing, then she was soothing, and while we know that she was soothing, we also know she failed to soothe, for Rose Johnson behaved like a simple beast. She was, in good Biblical fashion, an abomination. Soothing that is not soothing is not exactly the same as soothing that succeeds and soothes. It is much more likely, in fact, to be infuriating. Who, after all, enjoys being placated? there . . . there . . .

'And'

plays a major role in the meaning of many words familiar to the logician, like 'yet,' 'but,' and 'although,' although 'and' is not all of any. "Bill has a boil on his nose, but a window on the world" suggests that "Bill has a boil on his nose, and nevertheless throws open a window on the world." 'But' is often an 'although,' and 'although' is frequently an "and despite." "Bill has water in the pot, although his plant is on the sill."

In short, in addition to its full appearance as a word, 'and' can make itself felt simply as a sound, as in the expression 'canned ham,' or it can constitute the underlying meaning of another connective, such as 'but,' or it can exert itself invisibly, as a recurrent idea, a rule of organization. Counting the commas which are stand-ins for it, there are eleven 'and's in Gertrude Stein's sentence.

['And' #3] ". . . while the sullen, childish, cowardly, black Rosie grumbled and fussed . . ." Our second 'and' drew a list to a close. This third 'and' occurs immediately after the commencement of such a series. Certainly 'and,' here, suggests that 'grumbled' and 'fussed' are in balance, but 'fussed' will soon be paired with 'howled,' and momentarily find itself in a tray belonging to two different scales. As we pass along the list, accumulating the 'and's of 'grumbled and fussed and howled and made herself an abomination . . .' we must constantly shift our weight, first grouping 'grumbled' with 'fussed,' then 'fussed' with 'howled,' and finally, with four characteristics at last in place, comparing the first pair of bad behaviors with the second set.

$$\text{grumbled} \underset{\Delta}{\quad\text{fussed}\quad} \text{howled} \underset{\Delta}{\quad\text{made herself to be an abomination}}$$

The specific thing that 'fussed' does is to add itself to 'grumbled,' and the idea of addition, like those of balance, equality, difference, and coordination, is basic to our word, which is often a + sign. "Rosie grumbled and [in addition] fussed." Additions, of course, can be of many kinds. Sometimes they merely lengthen a list: (1) "Darling: remember to buy Kleenex and coffee and new strings for your mop." Sometimes, however, they alter its character, change its direction, either mildly, as (2) "I love your lips, nose, eyes, hair, chin, and fallen bosom" does, or more radically, like (3) "Duckie, don't forget catsup, kohlrabi, and some conniption, a large can, you know, the kind in sugar syrup."

Every addition implies that somewhere there's a sum. You can't add one number to another—8 to 4, for instance—if the 8 has disappeared by the time the 4 has come round to be counted. However, ordinary actions are like that. I must stop hopping if I'm to skip, and halt all skipping if I'm to jump. My present footstep cannot find the others I have made; even their sound on the sidewalk is gone. So 'fussed' adds itself to 'grumbled' only in the mind of some observer for whom the sum is one of aggravation. To Melanctha, Rose Johnson grumbled, and (in addition) fussed, and (to top it off) howled. Since Rose did not fuss because she had grumbled, her actions, as external events, merely follow one another in time, and replace one another in space, the way Hume indicates our impressions do; and this notion of a simple "Next!" is another which is fundamental to the meaning of 'and.'

Certain things cannot be added to others because they are already there by implication. To lamb stew you cannot *add* lamb. Nor is there any sense in saying that, "In addition to being triangular, their love affair had three sides." Thus, because it is a defining list, in "sullen, childish, cowardly, black Rosie," the commas do not replace a plus.

When, however, we try to add salt to sensation or affection to a mitered joint, either we exhibit a woeful lack of knowledge about English and the English-Speaking World, or we are marvelous makers of metaphor: (1) "his stew absolutely sparkled with salt and sensation"; or (2) "they made an affectionate and mitered joint"—cases where it is probably the 'and' itself which is metaphorical, pretending that it can conjoin "right and life," "he and whee," "solicitude and shrimp." These cases are rare, because most writers ignore 'of,' 'and,' 'but,' 'because,' 'why,' 'not' as possible transformers of reality, but that does not mean they are unimportant. Boundaries, outer edges, extreme cases, define.

Generally, 'and' designates only external and unnecessary relations; it deals with incidentals, separables, shoes that slip on and off; but not when it means something like "equally true." "A triangle has three sides and [it is equally true that] the sum of its interior angles is 180 degrees." To return to the metaphorical 'and' for just one more moment: "A triangle has three sides and [it is equally true that] each one of its sides is after an angle."

['And' #4] ". . . Rosie grumbled and fussed *and* howled . . ." This is the 'and' of increasing emphasis. "Rosie grumbled and [in addition] fussed and [what's more] howled." It has not lost its coordinate qualities (indeed, it is now operating as a pivot between two pairs), and it remains an additive 'and' too, but it is now in a place of weight as well. This usually requires that it occupy the last place in any series of conjunctions, and that the items of the set (in this case, names of actions) show a corresponding rise, swell, or increase in scope and importance. You might get away with "Rosie fussed and grumbled and howled," because it is difficult to regard fussing as any more serious or annoying than grumbling, but you would never find much sanction for "Rosie howled and grumbled and fussed," unless, of course, you had a special use for that kind of comedown.

Malory's celebrated lament for Lancelot uses 'and' to create a brilliant anaphoric series:

> Sir Launcelot . . . thou wert never matched of earthly knight's hand; and thou wert the courteoust knight that ever bare shield; and thou wert the truest friend to thy lover that ever bestrad horse; and thou wert the truest lover of sinful man that ever loved woman; and thou wert the

kindest man that ever struck with sword; and thou wert the goodliest person that ever came among press of knights; and thou wert the meekest man and the gentlest that ever ate in hall among ladies; and thou wert the sternest knight to thy mortal foe that ever put spear in the rest.

Omit the 'and' in "knight's hand" and the eight other 'and's which follow it, and you will lose, among other things, the sense of contrast between qualities which the conjunction heightens: the sense, throughout, of characteristics coexisting despite one another: "fire and ice," "snow and sand," "'and' and 'but.'"

['And' #5] "... and made herself to be an abomination ..." Our fifth 'and,' since it appears in series with 'and's #3 and #4, begins by signaling that it is another addition with emphasis. Indeed, it starts to withdraw some of #4's culminating force, for it is seen, now, not quite to culminate. However, the expression which follows the fifth 'and' is not a single verb, which its normal coordinating function would lead us to expect anyway, but an entire clause. Furthermore, while 'howling,' 'fussing,' and 'grumbling' are intransitive verbs, 'making' is not. I said a moment ago that addition implies a sum, and here it is: the summarizing, totalizing 'and.' "Rosie grumbled and fussed and howled and [altogether] made herself to be an abomination ..."

['And' #6] "... and like a simple beast." Our final explicit 'and' does not occur in a balancing position. Although it is in series, that series, as we have moved through it, has been undergoing transformations. 'Fussed' is added to 'grumbled,' then 'howled' is emphatically attached, and these add up to 'abomination.' Now this sum is interpreted and explained by resorting to the 'and' of equivalence, to the 'and' of "that is to say." "She made herself to be an abomination and [that is to say] like a simple beast."

We can summarize the six different functions of the spelled-out 'and's in Gertrude Stein's admirably instructive sentence this way: "She tended Rose, and [in doing so] she was patient, submissive, soothing, and [finally] untiring, while the sullen, childish, cowardly, black Rosie grumbled and [in addition] fussed and [what's more] howled and [taken altogether] made herself to be an abomination and [what is the same thing] like a simple beast."

So far, we have considered these 'and's as if they existed in relative isolation, in terms of their local impact upon one another, and not in terms of the total effect of their use. But six 'and's have surfaced in this sentence. Each one comes between its companions like a referee. Within most prepositional phrases, for instance, the sense of things follows the reading eye from left to right as seems proper. "Look → at the little dog → in its cute pink angora sweater." Because, in such formations, the so-called minor and undominant connectors come first, meaning moves toward 'dog,' then 'sweater' like a drain, although, with all those adjectives piled up in the second phrase, the drain begins to clog. But our 'and's part their elements while retaining them. They divvy, weigh, and order. They spread their objects out like dishes on a table. "And look at the little dog, and at its cute and pink and fuzzy angora sweater." Innocence is thick as custard here, because 'and' is an enemy of ordinary subordination. It appears (although this, as we saw, is somewhat illusory) . . . it appears to be unspecific and sloppy, to replace definitely understood connections with vaguely indistinct ones; hence it is frequently found in unstudied and childlike speech, or in regressive and harried circumstances. "I saw a snake and it was long and black and slithery and fork-tongued and pepper-eyed and slimy and evil and a cliché in the grass." Although such a sentence generates plenty of forward motion, most of it is due to the breathlessness implied by the repeated use of the conjunction, and not by its separative and spatializing function.

Gertrude Stein's sentence achieves its slightly breathless quality this way, but its innocent simplicity is only apparent. If one wants the child to grow up to be a man, the 'and's may be ruthlessly removed. "I saw a snake. It was long. It was black, slithery, fork-tongued and pepper-eyed. It was slimy, evil. It was a cliché in the grass." More often than not, minimalism is mere mindlessness.

In the following example, Ernest Hemingway, Gertrude Stein's anderstudy, is working for a kind of fuddled bewilderment and frightened energy by a deliberate misuse of the word. The narrator in the story "After the Storm" has just knifed a man in a bar.

Well, I went out of there and there were plenty of them with him and some came out after me and I made a turn and was down by the docks and I met a fellow and he said somebody killed a man up the street. I said "Who killed him?" and he said "I don't know who killed him but he's dead all right," and it was dark and there was water standing in the street and no lights and windows broke and boats all up in the town and trees blown down and everything all blown and I got a skiff and went out and found my boat where I had her inside of Mango Key and she was all right only she was full of water. So I bailed her out and pumped her out and there was a moon but plenty of clouds and still plenty rough and I took it down along; and when it was daylight I was off Eastern Harbor.

These 'and's do not establish parallels or connections; they suggest chasms. Between one act and another—between turning a corner and meeting a man—there is nothing. These 'and's condense or skip. They insist upon the suddenness of everything, the disappearance of time, the collision of distant spaces. Of course, these are the 'and's of nervousness, too, of worry and sleeplessness, of sheep leaping fences one after another. They cause events to ricochet.*

'And's

are almost essential for excess. They are perfect if you want to make big piles or imply an endless addition. One 'and' may make a tidy pair, closing a couple like a lock: *War and Peace,* ham and eggs, *Pride and Prejudice.* Add another, however, and the third 'and' will begin to alter the earlier ones the same miraculous way the squashed and flattened condition designated by 'mashed' is lent the fully contrasting sense of 'heaped' simply by putting it near the word 'potato.' No one is any better at this energetic mounding than the Dickens of *Dombey.* Here is part of a long passage describing the ruination of a neighborhood by some new-laid railroad tracks. It implies he is not telling us the half of it:

> There were frowzy fields, and cow-houses, and dunghills, and dust-heaps, and ditches, and gardens, and summerhouses, and carpet-beating grounds, at the very door of the railway. Little tumuli of oyster shells in the oyster season, and of lobster shells in the lobster season, and of broken crockery and faded cabbage leaves in all seasons, encroached upon its high places. Posts, and rails, and old cautions to trespassers, and backs of mean houses, and patches of wretched vegetation, stared it out of countenance.

There is the 'and' that enumerates things and conditions, as here, and helps to fork them into heaps; and there is the 'and' which multiplies names and descriptions, creating a verbal heap instead, as we frequently find in Rabelais, master of all middens, and of every excess the celebrant, and extoller, and rhapsodist.

If we momentarily return, now, to the first 'and' of Gertrude Stein's set of six, we can see that it attaches the entire remainder of our sentence to the initial "She tended Rose . . ." This 'and' is adverbial, as we saw, informing

---

* Frederick Busch discusses a part of this passage and makes some similar points in "Icebergs, Islands, Ships Beneath the Sea," in *Insights 1: Working Papers in Contemporary Criticism, a John Hawkes Symposium* (New York: New Directions, 1977), pp. 51–52.

us how well and kindly Melanctha took care of Rose, but it is adversarial in addition, setting Melanctha's conduct sharply over against that of Rose (who becomes "Rosie" when we learn of her low-class ways). So our specimen is made of that opening clause ("She tended Rose . . .") and a closing phrase (". . . like a simple beast") that precisely balances it, while between these two segments three four-term series are sung, one that belongs to Melanctha, and two that belong to Rose and describe first her character and then her behavior. At this point we encounter an 'and' (also active in the sample from Dickens) that has its home within the rhetorical structure itself, for it is as if the sentence's shape said that Melanctha was patient and Rose was sullen; Melanctha was submissive and Rose was childish, and so on, employing the 'and' of simultaneity, of "while." "Gricks may rise and Troysirs fall . . ." Joyce writes, using the same connective. Sullen Rosie grumbled, the rhetorical form also says; childish Rosie fussed; cowardly black Rosie howled and made herself to be an abomination and like a simple beast—a structure that invokes the 'and' of consequence and cause. "I bought some stock in IBM and the bottom of the market parted like a wet sack."

Dickens, by repeating "oyster shells in the oyster season" and "lobster shells in the lobster season," not only collects these two kinds of shells in the same place, his 'and' identifies two rhetorical formulas in which these four little tumuli of shells and crockery and cabbage leaves are given to us. So there are 'and's that vary in their meanings, and 'and's that differ in terms of the kinds of objects they connect: things, inscriptions, concepts, or syntactical shapes and rhetorical patterns.

In the single sentence I took from Gertrude Stein, we have now found six overt 'and's, each with a different dominant meaning, five covert 'and's, which hid themselves unsuccessfully under commas, and two 'and's that were implied by the form. Nor does this list (itself an 'and'-producing format) even remotely exhaust the various senses, sometimes several at the same time, these thirteen 'and's possess, nor did my account even minimally describe the interaction between different meanings which any one written or spoken token might represent, or do more than suggest something of the dynamics of switching and sliding sentences, as readings were anticipated, accepted, revised, rejected, retained. And we have only to glance again at the passage from Hemingway to find meanings for the word we haven't yet examined. You may recall the peculiar formation: "Well, I went out of there and there were plenty of them with him . . ." This is the 'and' of consequence, in this case inverted so that it becomes an 'and' of tardy explanation, the 'and' of belated "because." The narrator got out of there because the man he knifed had plenty of friends with him.

'And'

sometimes means "in company" or "together with," as "the passengers and all their luggage were hurled from the plane."

'And'

sometimes means "we may call these things by the same name, but the differences among them are often important and profound," as "there are doctors and doctors." This use may be regarded as a particularly pronounced example of the differentiating, or "over against," 'and.'

'And'

sometimes means "remember all the incidents, events, ideas that came before, or just before, this," as in the famous opening of Pound's *Cantos*.

> And then went down to the ship,
> Set keel to breakers, forth on the godly sea, and
> We set up mast and sail on that swart ship,
> Bore sheep aboard her, and our bodies also
> Heavy with weeping, and winds from sternward
> Bore us out onward with bellying canvas,
> Circe's this craft, the trim-coifed goddess.

'And'

is sometimes used in the spirit of "you might not believe it, but . . ." and as if in answer to an unspoken question. (1) "And yes, we did set up mast and sail on that swart ship." Or (2) "at the half we had a ten-point lead, and we still lost by two touchdowns." Or (3) "and we ate human flesh!"

Often the dangled or uncoupled or shaved 'and' expresses surprise or indignation. It is an emphatic form of the remember-what-came-before 'and.' "And you talk to me this way, after all I've done for you?" Here the 'and' of consequence has suffered a familiar disappointment. Or, "so Peking; and do you now go to Moscow?"

There are several rather antique 'and's: the 'and' of "four score and seven," the 'and' of "I'll love you forever and ever," or "we'll get together by and by." More ancient is the 'and' that sometimes substitutes for "times," as "they crowded aboard the ark two and two," or "the room was only ten and ten," now rarely resorted to, and replaced by 'by.'

There is the 'and' that turns the initial member of a coordinate pair into an adverb. In "the fire kept them nice and warm," "nicely warm" is meant. But 'nicely warm' is not a synonym, because the 'and' allows the fire to keep them nice, as if at any moment they might dry out and get tough, or evil, or mean. There is also the 'and' which replaces the infinitive: "Why don't you come up and see me sometime?" Again, this is not simply a mindless replacement for the apparently more precise "Why don't you come up *to* see me?" because 'and' equalizes "coming" and "seeing" and removes the rather insistent statement of purpose—especially important here, where seeing is probably only the first—shoeless—step.

Around some expressions there hover an astonishing number of ghostly forms, whiffs, sibilant suggestions, vague intimations, and these, as well as the more overt relationships which the reader is expected to grasp as a matter of course, help give them a feeling of classic correctness. Mae West's notorious invitation, "Why don't you come up and see me sometime?," with its careful softening of a command into a question, alters the cliché—"You folks come back and see me soon, you hear?"—basically by only one word— 'up'—and that change suggests "bedroom" to my bad ear, while 'come up' suggests "erection," 'come' suggests "climax," 'see me' "seize me" and "seed me," and so on, so that the 'and' it contains hums like a tuning fork between all these fainter and further thoughts and their terms. Mae West's seductive delivery, of course, lets us know how we are to hear her invitation, but 'up' is the verbal pointer that prepares us to flush these remaining meanings within range of our gun.

Logical and grammatical form—the fact that 'and' is a connective, and not an article, an adjective, or a noun—limits somewhat the meanings that our word may assume, but only somewhat, and there is little in these formal dispositions that can tell us in advance of experience what 'and' means. We can't even know whether we are going to be dealing with a preposition, a conjunction, or a strange kind of adverb; yet the ordinary reader is able to distinguish one use of 'and' from another with an ease that never causes us any astonishment: the syntax takes shape simultaneously with the meanings it shapes.

For we know what it is to take care of someone. We know what it is to be patient. We have seen patient caring, and the irritable, impatient kind (we can even imagine impatient patience, as if one were in a hurry to get this period of placid absorbency and affable putting-up-with over with), so that when the words call our experiences together in a sentence, the ensuing arrangement, and completed meaning, are the result of our memories of life and our understanding of language. Patience has a history as a human condition that I've encountered before and occasionally enjoyed; and the word 'patience' has a career as a concept and a mark that I have, myself, seen and heard and written down and uttered. It is the same, to a degree, with all words. That is, I remember their meanings; I remember my encounters with their referents; and I remember the company of other words that the ones in question have commonly kept. However, when I remember these things, I do not do so serially, one fact or feeling, one usage, at a time, as if I were thumbing through an index or flipping through a file. These memories have been compacted and their effects summed, although I may recollect my mother's patience during one trying time with particular distinctness, or recall the famous "now patience" passage in *Finnegans Wake* more readily than others. My mind remembers the way trained muscles do, so when I speak and read as well as I walk and bike, then we can say that I have incorporated my language; it has become another nature, an organlike facility; and *that* language, at least, will have been invested with meaning, not merely assigned it. I may have just learned that *"ne plus ultra"* signifies an ultimate or utmost point; nevertheless, the phrase will still stand aside from its referent like politeness at a doorway; but when, for me, idea and object fuse with their sign, then the sign is valuable like the coin it resembles; it is alive, a unity of mind and body that can be taught to sing, to dance.

The suggestion that we use the language of ordinary men normally is a good one, not simply because we shall reach the ear and understanding of ordinary men that way (which remains unlikely), but because such words are rich with history, both in our life and in theirs, and shine throughout with smoothness like stones that have, for vast ages, been tossed back and forth in the surf of some ancient shore, becoming eloquent, as pebbles made the mouth of Demosthenes hiss and seethe and roar. 'And' is such a polished orb. Think of the places it has been, the shoulders it has rubbed, the connections it has had, the meanings it has absorbed, the almost limitless future which yet awaits!

And

if we were suddenly to speak of the "andness" of things, we would be rather readily understood to refer to that aspect of life which consists of just one damned 'and' after another. 'And' is a truly desperate part of speech because it separates and joins at the same time. It equalizes. Neither ham nor eggs are more or less. In a phrase like "donkeys and dragons" the donkey brings the dragon down, while in the combination "sweet cream and a kiss" the thick milk begins to resemble champagne.

And

so what? The inner order of the 'and' is the list, to which we must now turn—that field where all its objects at least implicitly rest. Here is a brief list of lists: (1) the list which is made up of reminders, shorthand commands—get X, do Y, ✓ Z—such as the grocery or shopping list, the list of things to get done before leaving for Europe, before ignition and liftoff, before embarking upon a prolonged affair; and (2) there are want lists, Christmas lists, and so on, much the same; then (3) there is the inventory, and (4) the catalogue, (5) the bests and the worsts, restaurants deserving two stars and three forks, (6) statistical tables and other compilations, (7) directories, (8) almanacs, (9) hit lists, (10) dictionaries, (11) deportation orders, and (12) delightfully sheer enumerations. Some lists are as disorderly as laundry—that is, only somewhat—or as chaotic as one made for marketing, ordered only as items pop into the mind, or as supplies run out, and having no real first, middle, most, or honest end. Sometimes particular items will be underscored or starred. Certain 'and's (the 'and' for emphasis, for instance) often operate like an asterisk. Other arrangements are neutral and simply for convenience, as book lists are often alphabetical. The factors of '8' could be listed in any order without real prejudice, although I prefer '1 + 2 + 4 + 8' to other, more slipshod renditions. Occasionally, a book dealer will shelve his books according to author only, instead of by title or subject matter, and then the catalogue's alphabetical simplicity and the structure of the corresponding state of affairs in his shop will be the same.

Among the organizing principles of lists, then, are (1) things simply come upon, either the way they are remembered, as a guest list may be composed, or as found, for instance, when the police inventory your pockets before putting you away; (2) items listed in accordance with some external principle, often so that things can be easily located—for instance, numerically, alphabetically, astrologically, regimentally, cartologically, hermeneutically; and (3) as dictated by the order of things themselves, like a book's table of contents, or vice versa, as when the library's catalogue shelves the books, and commands their connections. We must suppose that God's list of things to do (on the First Day—Light, on the Second Day—Land, on the Third Day—Life, and so on) possessed a hidden internal principle, and there may be other self-generating lists of this kind.

Lists are juxtapositions, and often employ some of the techniques of collage. The collage, of course, brings strangers together, uses its 'and's to suggest an affinity without specifying what it is, and produces, thereby, a low-level but general nervousness. It is one of the essential elements of a truly contemporary style. Lists—full of 'and's as they are—remove things from their normal place, not as an artist might, by picking up a piece of paper from the street to paste upon a canvas (as the Romance maintains), but by substituting for such found objects their names, and then rearranging those. As a consequence, lists are dominated by nouns. Here is a little list of words of the sort that rarely appear on lists: 'always' is never there, or 'nevermore,' or 'if' (although there is the expression "don't give me any 'ifs,' 'ands,' or 'buts'"), less than occasionally 'subjugation,' 'halfheartedly,' 'oh yeah?,' or 'Lithuaneousness.' Even some nouns, like 'junta,' manage to stay quite away. However, adjectives of a usefully descriptive kind, those quiet, unassuming servants of nouns, frequently appear: 'yellow cheese,' 'large eggs,' 'fresh milk,' 'bitten nails.'

'And'

also always has one or two or more nouns hanging around. There are two basic configurations, although there are many variations. The first consists of two balloons held in one fist: . "A long and succulent squash." The second is the simple scale I remarked on earlier: ——— ———. "My ear is full of water and wax like a new car in the rain."

That part of punctuation most associated with lists is therefore the colon, for presumably everything that follows *it* is a list. As we know, the colon is frequently an abbreviation for "namely," or "for instance." "There are thirteen ways of looking at a blackbird: [namely] on Sunday, in the yellowing woods, with a faithless friend, following a thin fall rain, and so forth."

Lists sometimes suggest or supply alternatives, not necessarily exclusive— for example, ways of getting spots off tea trays, or means of travel which avoid Cleveland. They supply possibilities: the people who could ride on the cow catcher, the games you could play in a stadium: roller skating up and down the ramps, playing checkers on an empty seat, hide-and-seek. If I am drawing up a list of physical attitudes or comportments surprisingly suitable for modeling clothes or for sex, although there is an implicit 'and' standing between each (while leaning wearily against your partner like the man with the hoe, as though sitting slowly down upon a hassock), it is not expected that you will put all of these to use one after another as though loading groceries in a cart. These 'and's resemble 'or' more than they resemble themselves.

Lists have subjects. They are possessive. Lists are lists of. There is the list of foodstuffs needed for the ascent of Everest; there is the ruck one finds in a rucksack, items up for auction in an auction barn, wines and prices; while the little leaflet, the roster sheet, the penciled-in dance card, the back of an old envelope on which a list has been made: each of these symbolizes the tabletop or field or sorting tray, rucksack or room, where we may imagine these items have been assembled. This is sometimes called "the site."

Since a list has a subject to which its items are constantly referred (as every explicit 'and' has: 'ear' for 'water' and 'wax,' 'squash' for 'long' and 'green' and 'succulent' and 'bottle-nosed'), it suppresses its verb (to buy R, to remind one of S, to count T, to store U), and tends to retard the forward movement of the mind. We remain on the site. While the early 'and's of a series propel us onward, the later ones run breathlessly in place; thus the list is a fundamental device for creating a sense of overflow, abundance, excess. We find it almost invariably so used in Rabelais, and often in Cervantes. Why name one thing when you can invoke many? Why be merely thirsty, why simply drink, when you can cry out with Grangousier: "I wet, I dampen, I moisten, I humect my gullet. I drink—and all for fear of dying of aridity!" Here, however, our list is not one of alternative actions, but of additional *words*. I could say "moisten my gullet"; or I could say "dampen my gullet"; but, by the swollen tongues of all the sophists, I shall say both, and more, in order to suggest the greedy great gulp of life I am presently consuming. Who, indeed, could be satisfied to say, of the breasts of their beloved, simply that they are as white and soft as a hillock of junket? *Rühmen, dass ist!*

Rabelais is also full of lists of rapid talk, dialogue which does not advance the subject at all, but, rather, fills it, as drink does the bladder. Topers sail away in a wind of words, they do not hitchhike the highroads. Then there are the slanging matches, bouts of bad-mouthing: you, sir, are a sickly snerd; and you, sir, are a vulgar gurp; and you, snerd, are a suckalini; and you, gurp, are a loony goofballoof! One remembers, with fondness, the two whores and their name-calling contest in *The Sot-Weed Factor*. But the entire world is on a diet. Those whose tongues are not dry and starving are recommending a puritanical prose, small bites of life, small spoons of dehydrated water.

Lists, then, are for those who savor, who revel and wallow, who embrace, not only the whole of things, but all of its accounts, histories, descriptions, justifications. They are for those who like, in every circumstance, to Thomas Wolfe things down, to whoop it, Whitmanly, up. 'And's spew out of Wolfe as if he were a faucet for them.

And before and after that, and in between, and in and out, and during it and later on, and now and then, and here and there, and at home and abroad, and on the seven seas, and across the length and breadth of the five continents, and yesterday and tomorrow and forever—could it be said of her that she had been promiscuous?

Even the jeremiad is a list, and full of joy, for damnations are delightful. Lists are, finally, for those who love language, the vowel-swollen cheek, the lilting, dancing tongue, because lists are fields full of words, and roving bands of 'and.' Think of the many American masters of this conjunction: Faulkner, Hemingway, Stein, Melville:

Now when these poor sun-burnt mariners, bare-footed, and with their trowsers rolled high up on their eely legs, had wearily hauled their fat fish high and dry, promising themselves a good £150 from the precious oil and bone; and in fantasy sipping rare tea with their wives, and good ale with their cronies, upon the strength of their respective shares; up steps a very learned and most Christian and charitable gentleman, with a copy of Blackstone under his arm; and laying it upon the whale's head, he says—"Hands off! this fish, my masters, is a Fast-Fish. I seize it as the Lord Warden's."

Perhaps 'AND' should be sewn on the flag. Life itself can only be compiled and thereby captured on a list, if it can be laid out anywhere at all, especially if you are a nominalist.

List making is a form of collecting, of course, conservative in that sense, and dictionaries are the noblest lists of all; but lists are ubiquitous in literature. It is not merely Walt Whitman who is made of them. They are as frequent a rhetorical element as 'and' is a grammatical one. We could scarcely write much without either.

When do we have a list, however, and when not? There is no limit, presumably, to the length of lists so long as they have one, for the idea of a list implies the possibility of a complete enumeration. I may not have completed my list of all the cars with Delaware license plates which have stopped at my gas station, but an end is in sight, for my cancer is incurable and the station will soon close. I cannot make a list of all the odd numbers, only the ones, say, I like. There are an infinite number of numbers which no one will ever name. My mentioning five trillion and seven, now, will not make a dent in it. A daunting thought. It is sometimes naïvely supposed that those unnamed numbers will be either unimaginably huge (galaxies of googolplexes) or terrifyingly tiny (pi, pied), but there are almost certainly neglected numbers of no particular distinction hidden in the shadows of others, which chance has simply skipped. Another daunting thought. Or what of those lists of numbers which only spell out a name (of an insurance policy, for instance) and which aren't really functioning as a number at all? To exist so inexactly: another daunting thought.

So lists must be *of a length.* When Rabelais tells us what little Gargantua did between the ages of three and five, the entire chapter becomes an enumeration of the characteristics and qualities, the deeds, of this Herculean tyke.

> Fat? another ounce of wind and he would have exploded. Appreciative? He would piss, full-bladdered, at the sun. Cautious? He used to hide under water for fear of the rain.

However, when we write nothing but "Kleenex" on the flap of our envelope, we haven't a list yet, though we may have begun to make one; it awaits the 'and.' "Kleenex, cauliflower" is only a pair, and pairs are opposed to lists, and close upon themselves like clapping hands (though I wonder what sound this pair would make when they came together?), while "Kleenex, cauliflower, catnip" is simply a skimpy plurality. Alliteration actually makes the three items seem more numerous than they are, so I think that with four such we can say our list has truly begun. When I wrote down 'catnip,' I did not add it to a list, for there wasn't a list yet (I was, however, *making* a list); but now that we have one, various things can be said to be *on* or *off* it, or eligible for inclusion or summarily blackballed. The phrase "fate, chance, kings, and desperate men" forms a list. Notice, however, that until there was a list, 'fate,' like 'catnip' previously, was not on it; but that, once the list was made, 'fate,' we see, was always on.

There may be lists which exist mainly in an ideal realm, and which are consequently rarely realized. Maybe I've made a list of what I need to get at the grocer's: "Kleenex, chicken wings, Twinkies, thick-skinned fruit"; when actually what I really need are lemons, vitamins, and thighs. I've forgotten Chuckie's cat food, too, so my list isn't even a list of what *I* want. I really need rye crisp and secretly bottled water. When I initially collect the qualities which create a character, don't I often discard some and add others, as if, all along, I am searching for the *right set*? "Fate, chance, kings, and desperate men" is certainly a correct collection, and therefore it is a complete list. There are no more openings. My complete grocery list may include items which I cannot afford or which are unavailable anywhere in the Northern Hemisphere. So it may contain needfuls I know nothing of.

There are some lists one wants rather desperately to be on: the Honor

Roll, or the Not Nasty But Nice, for instance; but some should be shunned, like the Lord High Executioner's little list of people who surely won't be missed, or that other roll call way up yonder for which one does not wish to be eligible just yet.

Although the list by itself is a small democracy, and usually lacks hierarchies (the 1,003 women on Don Giovanni's are, presumably, all loved equally by the list, if not by the Don), when the list occurs in a literary work these conditions change, and the order of items becomes especially important. "Ah hah!" Holmes exclaims. "Our suspect has put down 'catnip' just ahead of 'Kleenex'—did you notice that, Watson?" Of course, like Holmes's cases, works of literature suffer from an excess of the essential.

The normal democracy of lists is connected with the coordinating and balancing functions of 'and,' as well as its additive and merely enumerative character—"How do I love thee, let me count the ways . . ."—yet even though the 'and's of emphasis, or of "finally," or "in sum," introduce certain small subordinations, the importance of every 'and,' and the elements it connects, even its pecking orders, remains substantially the same.

I've pointed out that listing things, or inserting an 'and' between them, can be done only by replacing the things in question with their names, and thereby transforming their relations. If you are moving, and have made a list of your belongings so that the insurance company can repay you when the wagons are lost crossing the mountains, the spatial relation between these objects (between hairbrush and table, table and footstool, footstool and rug) will be replaced (as it just was) with a simple serial relation between indifferent nouns which find their rest, now, only on a yellow sheet. The rug on which I lay as a baby to have my naked picture taken will be listed in the same way as yours—"one woolly rug/worn spot in center"—though it was there you lost your virginity, and he laid one tan hand beneath the frillies of your tennis dress, and—. Nothing but a list can restore such moments to us. A list can calmly take apart a chair and reduce its simultaneous assemblage to a song: "back, leg, cushion, square feet, embroidery, grease spot, saggy spring, slight scratch, small tear, lost tack." If I cut up an action for inclusion on a list, I shall have to divide it the way the flight of Zeno's arrow was divided, and a continuum will become an enumeration. "He ran rapidly forward, leaped, and comfortably cleared the first hurdle" makes three acts out of what was once one, and these segments can be moved about like beans. "Landing awkwardly on his left leg, already sore from last night's impromptus, he knew his run had been rapid enough for his leap at least to clear the hurdle." What has been divided, here, is no longer an action, but a memory. Indeed, I can cut up the action in a lot of ways, slicing "He ran rapidly forward" into a stride with the right foot, a stride with the left, and so on, even becoming microscopic: "shove off right, lift, swing, extend, plant, pull," etc., and in this way never reaching, any more than Achilles does, the hurdle. The camera is such a list maker, because a film is essentially a series of stills, temporally arranged and uniformly flashed so as to restore continuity at the price of illusion.

Jorge Luis Borges, who has made some of our more memorable lists, refers at one point to a "certain Chinese encyclopedia" in which it is written that

> animals are divided into (a) belonging to the Emperor, (b) embalmed, (c) tame, (d) suckling pigs, (e) sirens, (f) fabulous, (g) stray dogs, (h) included in the present classification, (i) frenzied, (j) innumerable, (k) drawn with a very fine camelhair brush, (l) *et cetera*, (m) having just broken the water pitcher, (n) that from a long way off look like flies . . .

and Michel Foucault, who claims this passage and the laughter it provoked were the initial stimulus for his book *The Order of Things*, says we cannot imagine the kind of place where these creatures could be brought together and sorted out. The site is impossible to conceive. He says that the encyclopedia, "and the taxonomy it proposes, lead to a kind of thought without space, to words and categories that lack all life and place, but are rooted in a ceremonial space, overburdened with complex figures, with tangled paths, strange places, secret passages, and unexpected communications." We read the congregation of these riddling words, but is there anywhere a sack which will sometime fill with such groceries?

'And'

always raises this issue as if it were a flag for waving. 'Bread' and 'honey' meet at the breakfast table as easily as husband and wife; they are both with us in our world, and cause scarcely a blink; but what keeps 'carrot' and 'cruelty' together besides 'c'? Every list has a length, a purpose, an order, its own entrance requirements, its own principles of exclusion, its site. Foucault has not felt the point of the Chinese encyclopedia's list, so he cannot conceive of its site, but Borges does not mean merely to confound and delight us with this crazy classification; for, at another level, it represents a well-chosen series of logical mistakes. It is a collection of examples, and is not to be taken any more literally than, let's say, remarks about the cross and the crown should be thought to be simply about crowns and crosses.

The Chinese world, we traditionally think, is upside down? Very well. So is this list. The classes it names aren't workably exclusive, but badly overlap: birds belonging to the emperor might be tamed or embalmed, and if so, they are certainly "included in the present classification." Live dogs, stuffed deer, mythological monsters are grouped so aggressively they challenge the presumably overriding importance of other distinctions—that between the real and the imaginary, for instance, or the alive and dead. Still, as widely as its net is thrown, there are too many holes in it: most wild animals will easily elude its cast, and it omits mention of those animals whose names have never been used to characterize football teams. The groups are too specific in some cases, too general in others. It offers us categories which cannot be applied, others which are vague, wholly subjective, or disastrously self-referential. In short, each example attacks some part of the logical structure of the list, and this is what, wonderlandlike, it is a list of. It may seem to suggest that there are more things in heaven and earth than are dreamt of in our taxonomies, but Borges provides us with a possible reality behind that appearance. The site of this list is in an introductory text in logic—somewhere in the chapter on classification.

One can sense what 'and' is up to also by examining writers and passages which use it sparingly, or exclude it altogether, as Beckett characteristically does, especially in later works like *How It Is,* because it is precisely the dissolution and denial of identities he wishes to stress. When, very rarely, the word appears, either it stands between terms only verbally different ("with me someone there with me still and me there still") or 'and' is used to equalize life and death ("the voice stops for one or the other reason and life along with it above in the light and we along with it that is what becomes of us"). On the other hand, you find little use of the word in writing which states subordinations clearly and precisely, as often is the case in the hierarchical prose of Henry James.

Can one word make a world? Of course not. God said: *"Es werde Licht,"* not *"Licht"* alone.* But when an 'and' appears between any two terms, as we have seen, a place where these two "things" belong together has been implied. Furthermore, the homogeneity of chaos, *"ohne Form und leer,"* has been sundered, for we must think of chaos, *'Tiefe,'* not as a helterskelter of worn-out and broken or halfheartedly realized things like a junkyard or potter's midden, but as a fluid mishmash of thinglessness in every lack of direction, as if a blender had run amok.

'And'

is that sunderer; it divides into new accords; it stands between *"Himmel und Erde";* it divides light from darkness.

---

* It is my suspicious conviction that God speaks only German.

'And'

again moves between sea and sky and their several waters, so that a new relationship arises between them, one that is external and unencumbering, although intimate as later Eve and Adam will be. Dividing earth from ocean, grass from earth, summer from winter, and night from day is again: 'and.'

'And'

those that crawl are otherwise than those that fly because of it. Finally, of course, between Himself and Himself there came a glass, a gleaming image: God and man, then. And among man, the male and the female; and within man, the soul and life and mind and body, were sorted and set, as though in left and right hands, beside but separate from one another.

'And'

then God went away to other delights, *"an Reiz und Kraft,"* leaving us with our days and nights and other downfalls, our sites and lists and querulous designs and petty plans, our sentiments and insatiables and dreamlands, with the problem of other minds, with the spirit's unhappy household in the body, with all those divisions among things which 'and' has bridged and rivered, with essences and accidents and linear implications, with all those bilious and libelous tongues, pissing angels, withheld rewards, broken promises, all those opportunities for good and evil, sex, marriage, world wars, work, and worship—and with 'and' itself—'and': a sword which cleaves things as it cleaves them.

'And'
then some.

Harper's Magazine, 1984
Published in *Habitations of the Word,* 1984

The Book as a Container
of Consciousness

"So! You've written a book! What's in it?"

When Hamlet was asked what he was reading, he replied, "Words, words, words." That's what's in it.

Imagine words being "in" anything other than the making mouth, the intervening air, the receiving ear. For formerly they were no more substantial than the rainbow, an arch of tones between you and me. "What is the matter, my lord?" Polonius asks, to which Hamlet answers, "Between who?"—twisting the meaning in a lawyerlike fashion, although he might have answered more symmetrically: Pages, pages, pages . . . that is the matter . . . paper and sewing thread and ink . . . the word made wood.

Early words were carved on a board of beech, put on thin leaves of a fiber that might be obtained from bamboo, and then bound by cords, or possibly etched in ivory, or scratched on tablets made of moist clay. Signs were chiseled in stone, inked on unsplit animal skin stretched very thin and rolled, or painted on the pith of the papyrus plant. A lot later, words were typed on paper, microfilmed, floppy-disked, Xeroxed, faxed. As we say about dying, the methods vary. Carving required considerable skill, copying a lengthy education, printing a mastery of casting—in every case, great cost—and hence words were not to be taken lightly (they might have been, indeed, on lead). They were originally so rare in their appearance that texts were sought out, signs were visited like points of interest, the words themselves were worshipped; therefore the effort and expense of writing them was mostly devoted to celebrating the laws of the land, recording community histories, and keeping business accounts.

These marks, each and every one, required a material which would receive them, and a space where they might spread out, since they were becoming visible for the first time, made formerly from air and as momentary as music. They were displacing themselves from their familiar source: the lips, teeth, tongue, the mouth, from which they normally emerged on their journey to an ear; for words were once formed nearly as easily as breathing, heard without effort, taken in automatically, along with their normal surroundings, which were also essential to their understanding—the tone and timbre of the speaker's voice, a scowl or smile crossing the face like a fox across a clearing, inflections accompanied by gestures as well as confirmed or contradicted by the posture of the body—and shaped into sentences made, as Socrates suggested, by the soul who felt them first, thought them, brought them forth like symptoms of an inner state, and was responsible for them, too, accountable because the psyche itself was their author and knew well the consequences of the word when accurately aimed, when deployed like a phalanx, armored and speared.

Before there was writing and paper and printing, before words remained in the trail left by their maker like the ashes of a fire or the spoor of a deer, another sort of stability had to be achieved, since it would scarcely do the speaking soul much good or the listener any harm if words were no more felt than a breeze briefly touching the cheek, or no more remembered than the distant ding of cattle bells, or no more noticed than the sounds of breathing, those soft sighs that are with us always, next our ear like a pillow. As we know, many of language's earliest formations have a mnemonic purpose. They made play with the materialities of speech, breaking into the stream of air that bore their sounds—displaying speed and vehemence, creating succession—and working with the sounds, the ohs and ahs themselves, possibly because, like the baby's babbling, it was fun, and a fresh feat for a new life, but more practically because when the sense of a sentence or a saying was overdetermined and the words connected by relations other than the ideas they represented by themselves, then they were more firmly posted up in memory and might like a jest be repeated and, like a jingle, acted on, leading to the casting of a vote or the purchase of bread, to the support of the very cause that the sentence, wound like that snake around one of Eve's limbs to beguile her, had slyly suggested.

When cast in lead, carved in bark, billboarded by a highway, up in lights, words had a palpability they had never had before; nor did they need all the machinery of rhyme and rhythm and phrasing, of rhetoric's schemes or poetry's alliterations, since they could be consulted again and again; they could be pored over; they could be studied, annotated, lauded, denied. For Plato, though, the written word had lost its loyalty to the psyche, which had been its source, and Phaedrus could hold beneath his cloak a roll on which another's words were written, words which Phaedrus thought he might soon pronounce, allowing them to seem his, performing passions and stating beliefs not necessarily held or felt by him, handing his conscience over to a ghost, practicing to be a president.

Although the written word made possible compilations of data, subtleties of analysis, persistence of examination, and complexities of thought which had hitherto seemed impossible, it contributed to the atrophy of memory, and, eventually, by dispelling the aura of the oral around words, to the absence of weight, consequence, and conviction as well.

Except that poets and prophets and canny politicians continued to write as if they spoke for the soul, and to this end their sentences sometimes still sang in a recognizable voice. However, the displayed word was almost immediately given fancier and fancier dress; calligraphic sopranos soon bewitched the eye; creatures, personalities, events, and other referents were pictured alongside language to amplify it, dignify it, illuminate it, give it the precious position it deserved. In fact, so unchecked and exuberant was this development of the visual that writing was often reduced to making headlines or composing captions.

Add radio to print and the word became ubiquitous. It overhung the head like smoke and had to be ignored as one ignores most noise. It was by loose use corrupted, by misuse debased, by overuse destroyed. It flew in any eye that opened, in any ear hands didn't hide, and became, instead of the lord of truth, the servant of the lie.

Readers were encouraged to race like a motorcar across the page, taking turns on two wheels, the head as silent as an empty house, eager for the general gist, anxious to get on. Rarely did a reader read in the old-fashioned, hesitant, lip-moving way—by listening rather than by looking, allowing the language fastened on the page its own performance; for then it would speak as though souled, and fly freely away into the space of the mind as it once had in the rarer atmospheres of the purely spoken world.

New notations confound old orders and create essential changes. They are not simply, as Hobbes mistakenly thought, "poor unhandsome though necessary scaffolds of demonstration." They become a part of the process they describe, the relations they denote. Zero came into being when we learned to circumnavigate its absence. Now we know Nothing is this convincing hole in "O." Given a new and supple symbol system, mathematicians make astonishing strides. Descartes's discovery of analytic geometry is based upon a new way of representing points, lines, and figures in a matrix of numbers. The alphabet helps make the mind, and language becomes not only the very vehicle of thought but much of its cargo. Music bursts forth into its modern form when signs that facilitate sight-reading emerge from neumes, and when the voice learns it must do more than merely rise and fall to please. As a consequence of the miracle of the modern scale, the composer could take down imagined music. Similarly, more than memory is served when objects are reduced to reproducible, transmissible, dots. The image is now as triumphant as money, as obnoxious as the politician's spiel, as ignored as other people's pain, as common as the cold.

In sum: there is the observed word, watched as you might an ant or an interesting bird; and there is, of course, the spoken word as well, since we still make conversation, go to plays, and look on in a contrived night while movie stars enunciate clichés as if such commonplaces were the only language; but, in addition, there are the silent sounds we make within the hall of our head when we talk to ourselves, or take any prose or poetry seriously enough to perform it, to listen with our brains, whether to a writing written when singing it was standard, as here, in this wonderful bit of early Middle English, dealing with one of the seven sins:

> The greedy glutton is the fiend's manciple. For he sticketh ever in the cellar or in the kitchen. His heart is in the dishes; his thought is all on the cloth; his life in the tun; his soul in the crock. Cometh forth before his Lord besmutted and besmeared, a dish in his one hand, a bowl in his other. Babbleth with words, and wiggleth as a drunken man that mindeth to fall, beholds his great belly; and the fiend laugheth that he bursteth.

or in this delicious bit from Jeremy Taylor, one of English prose's greatest masters, about the difficulty of dying:

> Take away but the pomps of death, the disguises and solemn bugbears, the tinsel, and the actings by candlelight, and proper and fantastic ceremonies, the minstrels and the noisemakers, the women and the weepers, the swoonings and the shriekings, the nurses and the physicians, the dark room and the ministers, the kindred and the watchers; and then to die is easy, ready, and quitted from its troublesome circumstances.

These are lines composed for the pulpit and delivered to the ear as honesty ought. Nearer to our time, there is now and then prose whose performance is only hoped for, bidden but rarely achieved, like any of Proust or James or Joyce.

> I call her Sosy because she's sosiety for me and she says sossy while I say sassy and she says will you have some more scorns while I say won't you

take a few more schools and she talks about ithel dear while I simply never talk about athel darling she's but nice for enticing my friends and she loves your style considering she breaksin me shoes for me when I've arch trouble and she would kiss my white arms for me so gratefully but apart from that she's terribly nice really, my sister . . .

Beginning with the breath, first broken into audible elements, then made visual as a hawk is admirable, soaring on similar air, and concluding in the inhibited movements of the inner voice, each of our three languages is made of more or less extended strips of signs, ribbons of words like the spool which makes up Krapp's last tape, and, geometrically speaking, is reducible to lines of variable lengths. It might be prudent simply to remind ourselves that the spaces which poetry requires to distance verses and lines from one another are operative elements in the verbal path, which, in that sense, remains equally unbroken whether prose or poetry is in question.

It is natural to suppose that the splitting up of the printed line (composed of alphabet blocks and blocklike spaces), as well as the arrangement of these lengths in rows on the plane of the page and the subsequent piling of pages one upon another to form the material volume of the text, which the book's case will then retain and protect, are all the most normal and modest of conventions, as, of course, the sounds and letters are (indeed, it constitutes a perfectly Euclidean lesson in spatial construction, beginning with points, assembling their numbers into lines, combining the lines to form planes, and, by stacking these, eventually achieving volume); and that there is nothing about the book as a material entity, neither in its pages, nor in its lines, nor in its principles of manufacture, that is essential to the meaning and nature of its text, no more than the shelf that holds the spices is a spice itself or adds to their piquancy or savor.

Even if sounds once wonderfully mimicked the various kinds of things and creatures that populated nature, and even if ancient hieroglyphs depicted their referents as faithfully as the most vulgar bourgeois painter, by now these resemblances have been forgotten and are no longer relevant, because it is the sheerest accident, as far as sense goes, that "book" and "look," "hook" and "crook," "brook" and "spook," "nook" and "cook," share twin *o*'s, like Halloween eyes, and terminate in *k* as do "kook" and "rook." Moreover, the relation between "hoot" and the owl's, "toot" and the train's, "soot" and smudge, "loot" and L.A., is perfectly arbitrary, could be anything at all, except that frequently used words tend to be short, and coarse words Anglo-Saxon.

So one is inclined by common sense and local practice to consider the book as a simple vehicle for the transportation of texts, and no more does the meaning of a text change when clapped between unaccustomed covers than milk curdles when carried by a strange maid.

However, as Whitehead suggested, common sense should find a wall on which to hang itself. That the size of type, the quality of paper, the weight of what the hands hold, the presence and placement of illustrations, the volume's age, evidence of wear and tear, previous ownership and markings, sheer expense, have no effect upon the reader and do not alter the experience of the text is as absurd as supposing that *Aïda* sounds the same to box or gallery, or that ice cream licks identically from cone or spoon or dish or dirty finger.

But, Mr. Obvious objects, the meaning of the text cannot change unless the text changes. Any reaction to that meaning is certainly dependent upon external factors, including one reader's indigestion and another reader's mood; however, the text remains the text, regardless of print, paper, and purse strings, unless you alter the words and their procession.

Three basic errors must be made before Mr. Obvious's view can begin to sustain itself. First, the nature of the word must be misunderstood; next, the concept of "text" will require an overly narrow definition; and third, the metaphysical problems every book embodies will have to be resolutely ignored. Only in this way, for Mr. Obvious, can a book remain . . . well . . . a book, what else? Furthermore, for Mr. Obvious again, the future of the book will have to seem doubtful, since new technologies have surpassed it in density of data, convenience of use, ease of reference, immediacy of communication, complexity of relation. Computers, with their keys, screens, codes, and disks, their facile methods of manipulation, their memories and hyperspaces, will do it in.

Let us consider the word, first, in terms of the ontology of its composition. This will be the same, in a way, as considering any larger units, whether they be phrases, paragraphs, pages, volumes, or sets.

The words that I am reading now, for instance, in order that I may speak them in your presence are not words in the full sense; they are, first of all, marks on an otherwise unmarked page, then sounds undulating in a relatively quiet space; however, these marks and these sounds are but emissaries and idols themselves, what logicians call tokens, of the real English words—namely "now," namely "reading," namely "am," namely "I," namely "that," namely "words," namely "the"—or what logicians refer to as the Language Type. If this were not so, then, if I were to erase the word "word" from this paragraph's opening clause—"the words that I am reading now"—or if I were to fall firmly silent in front of the *w* and refuse to go on, then there'd be no more "word" for word, written or spoken, like that momentarily notorious expression "dibbit ulla rafiné snerx," which was said once—just now—written hardly at all, given this temporary body only to disappear without ever gaining a soul, that is to say, a significance.

To be precise, we do not write words or speak them either. We use their tokens, or stand-ins. Each hand, each voice, is unique; each stamp, each line of print, is somewhat less so, though they form the same message, ACCOUNT OVERDRAWN, on the checks of hundreds of congressmen, in the headlines of the papers, in the accusations of impropriety by their constituents. But the Language Type is the same whatever the ink, the cut of the stamp, the font, the accent, tone of voice. At this level a word is more than its meanings; it is also a group of rules for its spelling and pronunciation, as well as a set of specifications which state its grammatical class and determine its proper placement and use in the normal sentence. That is, if my recent paragraph's opening had been: "I that am words reading the," we should recognize the tokens—"the" is still "the" there, as far as its marks mean and its sounds sign, but we should have trouble assigning them their Language Types, for "the" is not where "the" belongs, articling up to something.

Precisely the same distinction—that between type and token—can be made concerning sentential forms, since an assertion's shape is only embodied by a proposition and is not so enamored of its momentary location and job description that it can't serve somewhere else, even at the same time, or find that its fate is fastened to the tokens in whose sentence it is, for the nonce, displayed. Rhetorical schemata are equally abstract and repeatable. The difference is that forms are displayed while meanings are signified.

So let us journey into Plato's country for a moment, and speak of the Pure Type, not merely a linguistic one, and of a Pure Rhetorical Schema, a Sentential Form. Although *"mot"* means "word" and *"Wort"* means "word" and *"parole"* means "word" and "word," to be fair, means *"logos"* means *"verbo,"* and so on, from tongue to tongue, the pure Word they each depend on, which constitutes their common core, has no rules for its formation, since it escapes all specific materiality, has, in fact, never been written, never spoken, never thought, only dreamed during our extrapolations, envisioned solely by great Gee'd Geist, large *R*'d Reason, or the high-sided *M* of Mind.

This progression—from verbal token to Language Type and from that Type to unspoken Idea—has always seemed to some philosophers to be eminently reasonable, while it appears to others as an example of Reason capitalized, another case of reification, and, like Common Sense before, leading us astray. But imagine for a moment that all the tokens of a particular Language Type have been removed from past or present use, as the Führer wished to do with Jewish names. Even so, we would be able to generate tokens once again, since we should still have a definition, know the word's part of speech, and understand its spelling. Indeed, only intellectually is it possible to separate the spelling of a word from the word itself. To show how a word is spelled, one writes the word. However, if the Language Type were also removed, the word would at once disappear, and disappear for good, because the Pure Type has no material instantiation. It is a limit. Which means that words have a special kind of nonspecific or floating residence, because our belief even in a Pure Type depends on there being at least one material instance (or the rules for making such an instance) in existence. Which is as true of the book as of the word, for, in a way, the book itself isn't "in" any one example of its edition either, although at least one copy has to be about, or the printer's plates, along with the outline for its manufacture.

In any case, something interesting happens when we examine an extended text from the point of view of these distinctions. *Madame Bovary*, for instance, has been translated into many languages, but does this feat mean there is a Pure, un-French *Madame B,* one beyond any ordinary verbal exactness or lyrical invention? Clearly, *Madame Bovary* is confined to its language, and that language is not merely French in some broad, undifferentiated sense, but is Flaubert's so particularly that no other hand could have handled the studied pen of its composition. In short, as we rose, somewhat dubiously, from the token to the Pure Type, we now, more securely, mark the descent from a general language like French to the specific style of an artist like Flaubert or Proust. With their native tongue they speak a personal language, and may even, as in the case of Henry James, have a late as well as an early phase.

They achieve this individuality of style, as we shall see, by being intensely concerned with the materiality of the token, whether of word or sentence form or larger rhetorical scheme, although a text may be notable for its ideas or particular subject matter as well. In doing so, they defy the idea that the relation between token and type is purely arbitrary. By implication, they deny that a book only hauls its passengers.

Words really haven't an independent life. They occupy no single location. They are foci for relations. Imagine an asterisk made by innumerable but inexactly crisscrossing lines: that's one image of the word. Tokens take on meanings as well as contribute their own by the way they enter, then operate in and exit from, contexts. The Pure Type may sit like a sage on its mountaintop, pretending it is a Holy Thing, but the Language Type is dependent in great part upon the history of use that all its tokens have, for the oddity is that, if the word is not the token, it is nevertheless the token that does the word's work; that suffers age and becomes archaic; that undergoes changes, usually vulgar, in its meaning and even grammatical condition; that finds itself, if highborn, among hoi polloi or other ruck; if an immigrant, suddenly surrounded by the finest families, or rudely plopped into metaphors, hot as pots of wash, there to be stained by the dyes of strangers.

If the word is an accretion formed from its history of use, then when it scrapes against another word it begins to shave the consequences of past times and frequent occasions from its companion, as well as being shorn itself. We can imagine contexts which aim to reduce the ambiguous and rich vagueness of language and make each employed term mean and do one and only one thing (Gertrude Stein says she aimed at this effect for a time, and insisted that when words were so primly used they became nearly unrecognizable); and there are certainly others whose hope is to employ the entire range of any word's possibilities, omitting not even its often forgotten roots (as Joyce does in *Finnegans Wake*). The same token can indeed serve many words, so that, while the word "steep," set down alongside the word "bank," will withdraw a few meanings from use, it may take an adjective like "muddy" to force the other "bank"s to fail. Differentiation and determination are the goals of great writing: words so cemented in their sentential place they have no synonyms, terms so reduced to single tokens they lose their generality— they survive only where they are, the same size as their space, buried words like buried men:

> Though grave-diggers' toil is long,
> Sharp their spades, their muscle strong,
> They but thrust their buried men
> Back in the human mind again.

All our lines of language are like the rope in a tug of war: their referential character pulls them one way, in the direction of things and the material world, where "buried men" are covered corpses, no otherwise than fossil bones; while the conceptual side of our sentences drags them toward a realm of abstraction and considers them in their relation to other ideas: those, first of all, that define terms and tell us most matter-of-factly what it is to be buried, but only word for word; secondly, associations that have been picked up over time and use, like dust on travel clothes, and which shadow each essential sense to suggest, in this case, that death in one life is life in another; and, thirdly, those connections our own memories make—for instance, if these lines remind us of a few of Edwin Muir's, and link us suddenly with a land frozen into flooring, a place whose planks are crossed, let's say, by a miller's daughter one cold winter's day, in another country and in another poem, and where the implications for the buried are quite otherwise than those suggested by Yeats.

But they, the powerless dead,
Listening can hear no more
Than a hard tapping on the sounding floor
A little overhead
Of common heels that do not know
Whence they come or where they go
And are content
With their poor frozen life and shallow banishment.

Our own awareness, too, is always being drawn toward its objects, as if it were being sung to by sirens, at the same time that it's withdrawing, in the company of the cautious self-regarding self, into the safe citadel of the head; unless, of course, desire is doing the driving, for then the same sensation that is sharply focused on the being of another (an exposed chest, a piece of moist cake) will find itself inside of hunger's stomach.

These brief considerations should be sufficient to suggest that the word may be troubled by the same ontological problems which plagued Descartes (and all of us who inherited his hobbies): there are two poles to the person which are pulling the person apart, namely mind—meaning and mathematics—inside the circle of the self, and body—spatial location and mechanics—within the determined realm of things. A book is such a bodied mind. Descartes described these spheres (in the way, it seemed to him, accuracy required) as so separate, so alien from each other (for consciousness is no-thing, is no-where, and its reasoning powers, if we confine ourselves to those, are correctly exercised in free souls like ourselves in precisely the same way, just as mathematical proofs proceed, not in consequence of coercion, but from rational rule; whereas matter is unfree, fixed, almost entirely engaged in occupancy, and a tribute to cause and effect)—indeed, as so opposed in every character and quality—that we might naturally wonder how self and world could combine, meet, or merely hail each other if they are at such ontological odds; and we have seen, as I have said, how bodylike the book is, how mindlike the text, and if Descartes's critics complained that he had made of us a ghost in a machine, we might now understand the text as thought slipped warmly between cold sheets, elusive as a spirit, since its message cannot be injured by ripping up its pages or destroyed by burning its book. Dog-earing can do no damage to the significance of the sign, according to the Cartesian division; nor can the cruel reader's highlight pen clarify obscurity, a check mark change a stress, or an underline italicize a rhyme. This bifurcation of reality can be made persuasive, yet does our experience allow us to believe it?

Of course, we continue to call them copies, as if there were an exemplar still and every book were but a vassal of its Lord, an Adam to its Maker. This medieval scheme is gone; nor are books copied piecemeal anymore, the way translators seize on a huge work of Herman Wouk's, turning it, chapter by chapter, into several forms of Japanese; rather, the book is an object of mass production like a car (there is no first Ford), and both language and printing confer upon it a redoubtable generality to accompany its spiritual sameness. Like citizens in our country, all copies are truly equal, although this one, signed by the author, is somewhat more valuable; and this one, from the original edition, is to be preferred to all subsequent impressions; and this one, bound beautifully and illustrated by Picasso, is priceless (see, it's wrapped in tissue); and this one, dressed in vulgar colors and pretending to be a bosom, not a book, like a whore flaunting its contents while ashamed of its center, asks to be received as nothing but an object, a commodity for learning or for leisure use, certainly not as a holy vessel, a container of consciousness, but instead as a disposable duplicate, a carbonless copy, another dollar bill, and not as a repository for moments of awareness, for passages of thought—states which, we prefer to believe, make us most distinctly us.

Descartes endeavored (it was a futile try) to find a meeting point for mind and matter, a place where they might transact some business, but consciousness could not be moored to a material mast like some dirigible, and his famous gland could not reside in both realms at once, or be a third thing, neither one nor tuther, not with realities so completely contrary. Yet if he had looked inside his *Cogito* instead of pursuing its *ergo* to its *sum,* he would have found the simple, unassuming token, made of meaningless ink as its page is of flattened fibers, to which, in a formal yet relaxed way, were related both a referent in the world and a meaning in the mind. It was not that world; it was not that mind. Both had to happen along and find their union in the awareness of the reader.

Normally, we are supposed to say farewell to the page even as we look, to see past the cut of the type, hear beyond the shape of the sound, feel more than the heft of the book, to hear the bird sing whose name has been invoked, and think of love being made through the length of the night if the bird's name is the nightingale; but when the book itself has the beauty of the bird, and the words do their own singing; when the token is treated as if it, not some divine intention, was holy and had power; when the bird itself is figured in the margins as though that whiteness were a moon-bleached bough and the nearby type the leaves it trembles; and when indigo turbans or vermilion feathers are, with jasmines, pictured so perfectly that touch falls in love with the finger, eyes light, and nostrils flare; when illustrations refuse to illustrate but instead suggest the inside of the reader's head, where a consciousness is being constructed; then the nature of the simple sign is being vigorously denied, and the scene or line or brief rendition is being treated like a thing itself, returning the attention again and again to its qualities and its composition.

> If it's ever spring again,
>   Spring again,
> I shall go where went I when
> Down the moor-cock splashed, and hen,
> Seeing me not, amid their flounder,
> Standing with my arm around her;
> If it's ever spring again,
>   Spring again,
> I shall go where went I then.

What is this as-if "if"? It is as if the tokens were rebelling against their simple dispensable utilitarian status; it is as if they were appealing to the meanings they ostensibly bear by saying, "Listen, hear how all of me helps you, for I won't let you merely declare your intention to return to a place and a time when you saw the moor-cock amorous with his hen and held your own love fast in tribute to him, but I shall insist that my very special music become meaning, too, so that none of me, not a syllable of my substance, shall be left behind like an insignificant servant, because, as you can hear and see and feel, I am universal, too, I am mind, and have ideal connections."

Yet it is only a long-standing philosophical prejudice to insist on the superiority of what are called the "higher" abstract general things, for they feel truly ghostly, orphaned, without even a heaven to make a shining mark on, and beseech the material world to give them a worthy home, a residence they may animate and make worthwhile; they long to be some-thing, to be some-place, to know the solidity and slow change of primal stuff, so they—these ideas, these designs—will rush into the arms of Thomas Hardy's lines and, instead of passing away into one realm or other, will remain and be repeated by us, revisited as the poet revisits that meadow full of springtime: "I shall go where went I when." Like a kite, the poem rises on the wind and longs to be off, yet the line holds, held by the page—though pulling to be away, required to remain.

> Wandering through cold streets tangled like
>   old string,
> Coming on fountains rigid in the frost,
> Its formula escapes you; it has lost
> The certainty that constitutes a thing.

This stanza of Auden's describing "Brussels in Winter" discloses what rhymes do: they mate; they mate meanings on the basis of a common matter. On the basis of an accidental resemblance argue common blood. Through this absurd connection, they then claim equivalent eloquence for the mute as for the vocal.

> Only the old, the hungry and the humbled
> Keep at this temperature a sense of place,
> And in their misery are all assembled;
> The winter holds them like an Opera-House.

Rows of words become the frozen scene, while the scene is but the sounds the syllables align.

> Ridges of rich apartments loom to-night
> Where isolated windows glow like farms,
> A phrase goes packed with meaning like a van,
> A look contains the history of man,
> And fifty francs will earn a stranger right
> To take the shuddering city in his arms.

Rhymes ball their signs like snow, then throw for fun the hard-packed contents of the fist at the unwary backside of a friend, who will nonetheless laugh when he receives the blow.

It was Emerson who wrote:

> He builded better than he knew;—
> The conscious stone to beauty grew.

The stone is carved by the consciousness of the carver. That way consciousness achieves the dignity of place, and the stone overcomes its cold materiality and touches spirit.

The oscillation of interest between "thing" and "thought" inside the sign is complemented by a similar vibration in consciousness, inasmuch as we are eager to lose ourselves in our experience, enjoy what Nietzsche called a Dionysian drunkenness, and become one with what we know; but we are also anxious to withdraw, observe ourselves observing, and dwell in what Nietzsche said was a dream state but I prefer to imagine is made of the play of the mind, an Apollonian detachment, the cool of the critical as it collects its thoughts within the theater of the head.

The book contains a text. A text is words, words, more words. But some books want to be otherwise than cup to coffee at the diner's anonymous counter. That's what I've so far said. They want to be persons, companions, old friends. And part of their personality naturally comes from use. The collector's copy, slipcased and virginal, touched with gloves, may be an object of cupidity but not of love. I remember still a jelly stain upon the corner of an early page of *Treasure Island*. It became the feared black spot itself, and every time I reread that wonderful tale, I relived my first experience when, my morning toast in a negligent tilt, I saw Blind Pew approaching, tapping down the road, and Billy Bones, in terror of what he might receive, holding out a transfixed hand. I licked the dab of jelly from the spotted page.

I scribbled many a youthfully assured "shit!" in my earliest books, questioning Pater's perspicacity, Spengler's personality, or Schopenhauer's gloom (even if marginally), but such silly defacements keep these volumes young, keep them paper playthings still, in their cheap series bindings and pocketbook-colored covers, so that now they are treasures from a reading time when books were, like a prisoner's filched tin spoon, utensils of escape, enlargements of life, wonders of the world—more than companions; also healers, friends. One is built of such books, such hours of reading, adventures undertaken in the mind, lives held in reverential hands.

In a book bin at the back of a Goodwill store in St. Louis, I come upon a copy of *The Sense of Beauty*. By what route did Santayana's first work reach this place? We scarcely wonder what wallet has previously enclosed the dollar bill we're on the brink of spending, but I at least get romantic about the vicissitudes of such voyages, about hurt spines, dust, thumbprints on certain sheets, wear and tear, about top edges that have faded, and feel that some texts age like fine wine in their pages, waiting for the taste of the right eye, the best time. Pure texts have no such life. Only their tokens, and the books that keep them safe, wallow in the world.

Decorations did not always dirty the word by disgracing its depth and subtlety with lazy loops, silly leaves and flowers, poorly imagined scenes, or with characters as crudely drawn as most comics. Nor were banal texts invariably embarrassed by leather bindings, complex enclosing borders, and initial letters as elaborately tacky as a Christmas tree. The better matches were reminders of the Book's ideal: to realize within its covers a unity of type and token, the physical field supplying to its pastured words the nutrients they need to flourish, and actually making the text serve the design of a beautiful thing, while that object itself becomes something of a symbol, enlarging on the significance of the text and reminding the reader where his imagination belongs—on that page where "a phrase goes packed with meaning like a van."

If, then, the miseries of metaphysics are to be found in author, book, and reader, as well as in the whole unheeding world, and if, as its geometry suggests, a book is built to be, like a building, a body for the mind, we might usefully peer into that head where the text will sometime sound and see what elements need to be combined to complete its creation and its containment of a consciousness.

Clearly, the epistemological passage begins with the kind of awareness of the world and its regulations which the writer of our text achieves. When a thing is seen, it says its name and begs to be perceived as fully and richly as possible, because sensing of any kind transforms its innocent object, as Rilke so often wrote, into an item in consciousness: that stone jug, standing on a trestle table, gray as the wood, its lip white with dried milk; or the old mill whose long stilled wheel showers every thought about it with the tossed fall of its working water; or the worn broom, dark with oil and dust, leaning now like a shadow in a corner, quietly concerned about who will take hold of it next; and birdcall, of course, and the smell of anciently empty dresser drawers, the coarse, comforting feel of dark bread between the teeth—would any of these qualities be realized: rage in a face, print on a page, valley filled with fog, would these? the dissolve of cheese into its toast and the tongue's thoughtful retrieval of it, would that? or a cricket's click, your tentatively touched thigh, slow coast of skin, calm water, or the cat's contented sigh, would they? without the valiantly alert observer, dedicated to the metamorphosis of matter into mind, with the obligation to let nothing escape his life, never to let slip some character of things: the way wood wears at corners, or rust grows rich, lamps stand on carpets, and whistles trail away at the end of an expelled breath, a little like the affection they sometimes invite; it would all be missed, our own speech, too, the complexity of an animal's posture or a sock's sag, that wrinkle beneath the eye which wasn't there last Saturday, each gone, along with the momentary and ineffable softness of cloth a fat bus driver has all day sat on, the lost expression of faces surprised in a mirror, surprised to see they are not themselves, and—my god—all those clouds . . . if they were not first brought, as treasures are, into some sensory fulfillment.

Our ideal writer will naturally understand that experience is everywhere toned by our mood, soothed or inflamed by immediate feeling, and that these emotions are modified by what we see or think or imagine, so that sometimes new ones will emerge. I take an emotion to be a perception of the relation of the self to other things: fear or hate when they threaten me or mine, jealousy when I am faced with loss, envy when I wish I had someone else's talent, luck, or favor, love when I identify my own well-being with another's, then more generally, loneliness as a recognition that I am not sought or valued by my environment, alienation when I believe I have no real relation to the world, happiness when sufficiently deluded, melancholy when I see no possibility of improvement in my affairs, and so on. About these judgments a person may be correct or mistaken. And our ideal writer will be right about hers, able to empathize with those of others, and be adept at measuring how feeling deforms things or how cannily it makes most of its assessments.

Thought is another essential character in consciousness, going on sometimes at a tangent to perception or in indifference to emotion (as philosophers like to brag it ought), though, if I am right about one of the functions of awareness, each and every element is cognitive; and it is a fortunate person, indeed, who has feelings the head trusts, and perceptions his other faculties can count on. I can feel persecuted and be deceived; I can see snakes and be DT'd; I can believe in my project of squaring the circle and be deluded; and we do know people who can't get anything right, who marry wrong, who embrace a superstition and call it faith, whose perceptions lack clarity, color, and depth, and who have never once heard the horn in the forest. Such a person might very well wish to possess the character of a good sentence.

For the most part, our formal thought goes on in words: in what we say to ourselves, in the *sotto voce* language I have already spoken of. Plainly, a meditative person will need the data his perception furnishes and the support which sound emotions lend; but he will, in addition to the disciplines of logic, mathematics, and the scientific method, need to possess a rich vocabulary, considerable command of it, and the fruit (in facts and their relations, in words and theirs) of much skilled and careful reading, because reading is the main way we discover what is going on in others; it is the knothole in the fence, your sight of my secrets, my look at what has been hidden behind your eyes, since our organs are never shared, cannot be lent or borrowed. In order to be known, we speak. Even to ourselves.

We must notice our drives, our desires, our needs, next, although they are always calling attention to themselves. They put purpose in our behavior, position the body in the surf, urge us to overcome obstacles or make hay while the sun shines. And whatever we desire, Hobbes says, we call good, and whatever we are fearful of and loathe, we insist is bad, avoiding it even if at cost. These are cognitions, too, and we discover, when we realize our aims, whether we were right to want to go home again or were once more disappointed in the pie, the place, the conversation, and the trip.

Finally, in addition to our passions, purposes, and perceptions, the skills and deftness of our brains, there is what Coleridge called the esemplastic power—that of the creative imagination. As I am defining it, the imagi-nation is comparative, a model maker, bringing this and that together to see how different they are or how much the same. The imagination prefers interpenetration. That's its sex. It likes to look through one word at another, to see streets as tangled string, strings as sounding wires, wires as historically urgent words, urgent words as passing now along telephone lines, both brisk and intimate, strings which draw, on even an everyday sky, music's welcome staves.

Having read the classics closely, the inner self with honesty, and the world well—for they will be her principal referents—the writer must perform the second of our transformations: that of replacing her own complex aware-ness with its equivalence in words. That is, the sentence that gets set most rightly down will embody, in its languid turns and slow unfolding, or in its pell-mell pace and pulsing stresses, the imperatives of desire or the inertia of a need now replete; it will seize its subject as though it were its prey, or outline it like a lover, combining desire with devotion, in order to sense it superbly, neglecting nothing its nature needs; it will ponder it profoundly, not concealing its connections with thought and theory, in order to exhibit the play, the performance, of mind; and it will be gentle and contemplative, if that is called for, or passionate and rousing, if that's appropriate, always by managing the music, filling each syllable with significance like chocolates with cream, so that every sentence is a bit of mindsong and a fully animated body made of muscle movement, ink, and breath.

Lastly, as if we had asked Santa for nothing yet, the adequate sentence should be resonant with relations, raise itself like Lazarus though it lies still upon the page, as if—always "as if"—it rose from "frozen life and shallow banishment" to that place where Yeats's spade has put it "back in the human mind again."

How otherwise than action each is, for even if—always "even"—always "if"—I preferred to pick the parsley from my potatoes with a knife and eat my peas before all else, I should have to remember that the right words must nevertheless be placed in their proper order: i.e., parsley, potatoes, and peas . . . parsley, potatoes, and peas . . . parsley, potatoes, and peas.

That is to say, the consciousness contained in any text is not an actual functioning consciousness; it is a constructed one, improved, pared, paced, enriched by endless retrospection, irrelevancies removed, so that into the ideal awareness which I imagined for the poet, who possesses passion, per-ception, thought, imagination, and desire and has them present in amounts appropriate to the circumstances—just as, in the lab, we need more obser-vation than fervor, more imagination than lust—there are introduced patterns of disclosure, hierarchies of value, chains of inference, orders of images, natures of things.

When Auden, to return to him, "Lullaby"s this way:

> Lay your sleeping head, my love,
> Human on my faithless arm;

he puts a most important pause—"my love"—between "head" and "human," allowing the latter to become a verb, and then, by means of an artfully odd arrangement, resting the *m*'s and *a*'s and *n*'s softly on the *a*'s and *m*'s and *r*'s.

Of course, we can imagine the poet with a young man's head asleep on an arm which the poet knows has cushioned other lovers equally well, and will again; and we can think of him, too, as considering how beautiful this youth is, and pondering the fleeting nature of his boyish beauty, its endangerment now calmly ignored:

> Time and fevers burn away
> Individual beauty from
> Thoughtful children, and the grave
> Proves the child ephemeral:
> But in my arms till break of day
> Let the living creature lie,
> Mortal, guilty, but to me
> The entirely beautiful.

Yet it is scarcely likely that Auden's contemplating mind ran on just this way, making in that very moment the pun on "lie," or creating that delicious doubled interior rhyme "but to me / The entirely," which so perfectly confirms the sentiment. It's probable that the poet, passion spent, looked down on his lover in a simple sog of sympathy. Later, he recalled his countless climbs into bed, in sadness at their passing, perhaps, but with a memory already resigned, recollecting, too, certain banal routines, in order, on some small notebook's handy page, to cause a consciousness to come to be that's more exquisite, more—yes—entire, and worthy of esteem, than any he actually ever had, or you, or me.

What the poem says is not exceptional. This midnight moment will pass, this relationship will die, this boy's beauty will decay, the poet himself will betray his love and lie; but none of that fatal future should be permitted to spoil the purity of the poet's eye as it watches now, filled with "every human love." Nor can we compliment Auden's art by repeating Pope, that what it says has been "ne'er so well express'd," because that formula misses what has so beautifully been given us: a character and quality of apprehension.

Sentences, I've said, are but little shimmied lengths of words endeavoring to be similar stretches of human awareness: they are there to say I know this or that, feel thus and so, want what wants me, see the sea sweep swiftly up the sand and seep away out of sight as simply as these sibilants fade from the ear; but such sentences present themselves in ranks, in paginated quires, in signatures of strength; they bulk up in the very box that Cartesian geometry has contrived for it, to stand for the body that has such thoughts, such lines that illuminate a world, a world that is no longer their author's either, for the best of writing writes itself, as though the avalanche, in falling from the side of its mountain, were to cover the earth like paint from a roller rather than sweeping it clean or crushing objects like old sweethearts in its path.

How wrong it is to put a placid, pretty face upon a calm and tragic countenance. How awful also to ignore the essential character, the profounder functions, of the container of consciousness—to think of it even as a box from which words might be taken in or out—for I believe it is a crime against the mind to disgrace the nature of the book with ill-writ words or to compromise well-wrought ones by building for them tawdry spaces in a tacky house. "The book form," Theodor Adorno writes,

> signifies detachment, concentration, continuity: anthropological characteristics that are dying out. The composition of a book as a volume is incompatible with its transformation into momentary presentations of stimuli. When, through its appearance, the book casts off the last reminder of the idea of a text in which truth manifests itself, and instead yields to the primacy of ephemeral responses, the appearance turns against the book's essence, that which it announces prior to any specific context. . . . The newest books [have] become questionable, as though they have already passed away. They no longer have any self-confidence; they do not wish themselves well; they act as though no good could come of them. . . . The autonomy of the work, to which the writer must devote all his energies, is disavowed by the physical form of the work. If the book no longer has the courage of its own form, then the power that could justify that form is attacked within the book itself as well.
>
> ["Bibliographical Musings," trans. S. W. Nicholson,
> *Grand Street*, vol. 39 (1965), pp. 136–37]

It remains for the reader to realize the text, not only by reachieving the consciousness some works create (since not all books are bent on that result), but by appreciating the unity of book/body and book/mind that the best books bring about; by singing to themselves the large, round lines they find, at the same time as they applaud their placement on the page, their rich surroundings, and everywhere the show of taste and care and good custom—what a cultivated life is supposed to provide; for if my meal is mistakenly scraped into the garbage, it becomes garbage, and if garbage is served to me on a platter of gold by hands in gloves, it merely results in a sardonic reminder of how little gold can do to rescue ruck when ruck can ruin whatever it rubs against; but if candlelight and glass go well together, and the linens please the eye as though it were a palate, and one's wit does not water the wine, if one's dinner companions are pleasing, if the centerpiece does not block the view and its flowers are discreet about their scent, then whatever fine food is placed before us, on an equally completed plate, will be enhanced, will be, in such a context, only another successful element in the making of a satisfactory whole; inasmuch as there is nothing in life better able to justify its follies, its inequities, and its pains (though there may be many its equal) than getting, at once, a number of fine things right; and when we read, too, with our temper entirely tuned to the text, we become—our heads—we become the best book of all, where the words are now played, and we are the page where they rest, and we are the hall where they are heard, and we are, by god, Blake, and our mind is moving in that moment as Sir Thomas Browne's about an urn, or Yeats's spaded grave; and death can't be so wrong, to be feared or sent away, the loss of love wept over, or our tragic acts continuously regretted, not when they prompt such lines, not when our rendering of them brings us together in a rare community of joy.

The Wilson Quarterly, 1995
Published in *Finding a Form,* 1996

THE ARCHITECTURE OF THE SENTENCE

Essay and Drawings

"What is the goal of the world?" said Silaka Salavatya.

"Space," said Pravahana; "for all these contingent beings originate from space, and to space do they return. For space is greater (and more ancient) than they: space is the final goal."

—CHANDOGYA UPANISHAD

One: Introduction

Let me begin by trying to state the point of this project as succinctly as possible.

Two sorts of spaces concern us here. First, there are the spaces we live and work and build in, the space which the physicist studies and the space we fly through to reach Salt Lake City or Chicago from St. Louis. But there are also all the spaces of representation, those places in the head or on paper where we imagine relations and try to express them: the cartographer's projections, the painter's perspectives, society's hierarchies, the musician's scale and score, the architect's plans, the electrician's diagrams, management's flow charts, tables of tides and organization, every display of information, statistical or otherwise, and, in particular, writing itself. Here, in such spaces, we think, we plan and we design.

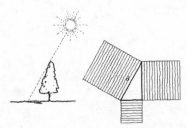

What is the relation between these two sorts of space? the real and the represented? between an engraver's perspective and an actual street? between the Social Register and a cardboard house beneath a bridge? between a note and a noise? Our investigation, merely begun here, and in the most provisional way, wonders whether it is possible to think or plan or design at all without a representational space in which to do it, and without an adequate notation through which such plans or ideas can be expressed; and whether there may not be a commonality between these arenas, a basic similarity between the relations involved, which might make possible the discovery of what it means to say of something that it is "architectural." For architecture, as we conceive it, may be the general method of constituting relations in representational spaces in order that they may be materially constructed in phenomenological spaces—in spaces as lived in.

If the consequence of human culture is basically that it surrounds man with man; that it replaces nature with convention; that it tries to tame the wilderness, intervening in everything; then architecture is the art which underlies all such construction, and its ultimate aim is to surround man, not merely with more man, but with the best—the most human—in what is human of us. If our bodies contain our consciousness, it is the business of our buildings, our cities, our culture to contain us.

A book is a building for what a brain has spun. Literature, the other pole of this enterprise—like music, like logic and mathematics—is designed to fill that consciousness from within, to contrive, inside the mind, arrangements of sound, and structures of sense, which will find their best accommodation in the public places, in the edifices, which will—in their principled depths—resemble them.

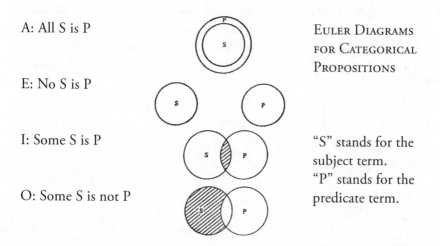

A: All S is P

E: No S is P

I: Some S is P

O: Some S is not P

EULER DIAGRAMS FOR CATEGORICAL PROPOSITIONS

"S" stands for the subject term.
"P" stands for the predicate term.

Two

1. a. Our first stop is at Aristotle and the concept of "same form." Aristotle discovered that all propositions in Greek could be reduced to four kinds: All S is P, Some S is P, No S is P, and Some S is not P. All methods of representation are based on a belief that formal relations can be reproduced in different media without significant falsification; that not only are apparently different sentences nevertheless of the same form—for instance, "The cat ate the rat" and "The professor seduced his student"—but that the music "in" the score, the music as markings on a CD, the music as vibrations in the air, music as heard sound, etc., all have the "same form." Thus a Palladian symmetry—two squares on either side of a circle—exhibits the same form as the sonata, namely, A B A, or Home-Departure-Return, which is the same as the course of the *Iliad* and the *Odyssey.*

b. Aristotle also discovered that the validity of an argument depended solely on its form, but this could not be clearly understood until the concepts which stood for S and P in any proposition were first: spatialized, and regarded as representing classes, and second: the copula (is) was given what is called an extensional interpretation. "Is" (under extensional interpretation) means either identity, class inclusion, or class membership.

c. Later Venn diagrams allowed us to "see" what made a valid argument valid.

d. The invention of a proper musical notation also enabled music to become what it is. A new musical space came into being, made of the higher and lower notes on the scale, of musical dynamics (fast, slow, loud, soft), of instrumental placement, the color and texture and length of tones, etc. And words and music sought common meanings in imitative form. The world of musical space lies behind the closed eyes, in the dark hollow of the head.

When, in our time, the scale became chromatic; when propellers and air cylinders and sirens were added to the orchestra; when electronics enlarged the realm of possible sounds; then composers had to modify the old notation or invent a new one for their new needs.

e. Early on, the Greeks, who had a predominately oral culture, and could not handily consult books, formulated elaborate methods for remembering. These methods continued well through the Renaissance and they were almost invariably architectural. One of the most famous is the memory theater of Giulio Camillo. Early in life one began picturing to oneself an imagined building, furnishing it over time with icons which stood for subjects and moods. In Camillo's theater the basic images are taken from the planetary gods, expressing, for example, the tranquillity of Jupiter, the anger of Mars, the melancholy of Saturn, the ardor of Venus, and so on. Beneath these images were drawers in which manuscripts of Cicero's speeches, appropriate to the topic symbolized, were kept. Such theaters were actually built. They anticipate the computer's hyperspace.

f. Grammarians began to try to symbolize the form of the sentence with various kinds of diagrams, all of them spatial, mostly treehouse forms which show up very early and have genealogical uses, and naturally adapt themselves to the depiction of syntactical structures, though some look more like river deltas, or even mobiles, before returning to a soberer sort of Tinkertoy geometry. These scholars recognized that the right motivation not only was the clearest or least complicated one, but actually created the ground for understanding.

g. Chomsky added deep structure to the grammarian's surface structure. The term "deep" is itself spatial. The term "deep" is also talismanic. Anything deep is veiled. Anything deep is deeply important. I have reservations about deep structure and its workability. It remains, nevertheless, basically a spatial notation project.

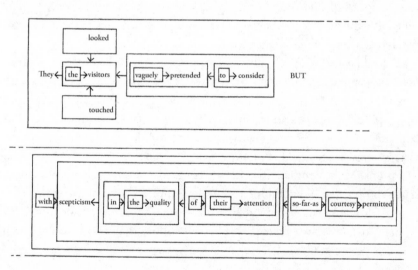

h. The most useful of these schemes is what I call the box diagram, whose function is to show how each meaning is subsumed by another until all the words of the sentence are in a single space. When we box-diagram the syntax of a sentence we are drawing the sentence's floor plan. For example: "They looked, the visitors, they touched, they vaguely pretended to consider, but with skepticism, in the quality of their attention so far as courtesy permitted." We shall encounter this sentence by Henry James again.

i. But sentences are well formed in more than logical and syntactical ways.

They are also formed with aesthetic and rhetorical intentions. Rhetoric is, in a sense, the study of the forms of the paragraph, and how phrases and clauses are arranged, not only in sentences, but in the linkage of sentence to sentence. Prosody attempts to do something with the rhythm of language. And many theorists have tried to deal with vowel music and other elements, including the actual "look" of letters.

j. When one writes, one is constructing not only a set of sentences, but a complex set of spaces (logical, grammatical, rhetorical, referential, musical, social, and so on) in which and through which the feelings, ideas, and energies of the sentences can express themselves. This is the architecture of the sentence. And sometimes architecture itself resembles a sentence. Perhaps these spaces can help us define "the architectural."

Three

1. There is a distinction to be drawn between sentences spatially formed from the outside, and those formed from the inside, as well as spaces determined at least in part by the various meanings of the sentence, rather than by the structure of the sentence alone.

a. The first sort is nicely illustrated by what is called "concrete poetry." External shaping occurs when the context of the poem or paragraph suggests an object in the world whose shape is then used to format the poem or paragraph on the page. Apollinaire's calligrams usually assume the shape of their subject. Not only does George Herbert's well-known poem imitate the Easter wings it speaks of, but those wings symbolize the poem's spiritual aspirations. More significantly, Herbert planned an entire volume of verse so that each poem would combine to form a Temple. The most extreme case is that of Morganstern's Fish, which is formed entirely from the symbols for strongly and weakly stressed syllables—symbols that form very natural scales.

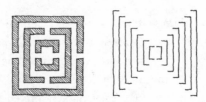

b. Above are two schematic pictures of the Frame Tale, one like a maze, the other like an accordion or nest of boxes. The general form resembles that of indirect address, of "Helen said that you told her that in the middle of the movie Melanie suddenly shouted: 'I've got to have a perm!'" Boc-caccio's *Decameron, A Thousand and One Nights,* Chaucer's *Canterbury Tales,* and Flann O'Brien's *At Swim-Two-Birds* are similarly framed. This particular diagram pictures John Barth's "Mene-laiad." Helen of Troy, having been rescued from the Trojans by her husband, is busy giving him excuses for her long stay in Paris's company, and is endeavoring to postpone what is likely to hap-pen to her: to be ravished by her long-denied husband or murdered by him out of jealousy. So each excuse is interrupted by another like a stutter, and continued to the number seven. The conclusion of story seven permits six to conclude, and so on. This means that at certain points in the work some of the words will be occurring in more than one section at a time. We can literally look through one narrative to see parts of others passing in a previous time.

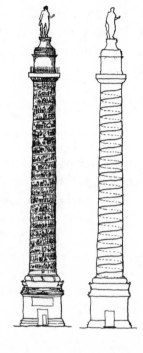

John Barth has been very inventive in other ways. A story called the "Perseid" is a retelling of the myth of Perseus as if the hero's exploits were carved on a triumphal col-umn like Hadrian's pillar, so that some parts of the piece have to be read as if they were above and to the left of the others. The story inscribes a logarith-mic spiral. Italo Calvino's *Invisible Cities* similarly unwinds, turning through Dante's descending circles.

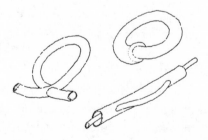

c. We are dealing with the phenomenon which logicians (traditionally lovers of erotic terminology) call embedding and which is frequently repre-sented by Klein worms. When a sentence finds itself inside another sentence, as Melanie's shout, "I've got to have a perm," does, it is said to be embedded.

Klein worms are geometric shapes which in various ways include or swallow or emerge from themselves. The sentence "David could have kissed Goliath" is engulfed by "Saul told Bathsheba that David could have kissed Goliath, but she wouldn't believe him."

d. Sentences also create space by layering their meaning, and suggesting both surface and depth. Gregor Samsa wakes to find himself a bug in a bed—that is, a bedbug—and, since the root of "Samsa" is "sam" or "seed," he is also a soiled source of DNA. The metrics of "Sam sa" resemble those of "Kaf ka," telling us who else is in this buggy bed.

e. Every sentence contains spaces where logically more words could be placed. Each word is therefore like a picket in a fence. As these spaces are filled, the fence becomes solid. The minimalist style tends to leave these spaces open. The baroque style tends to fill them.

Henry said goodbye to Larry.

Good old Henry said a short goodbye to Larry, his friend of twenty years.

The guy people called "good old Henry" said a short but fond goodbye to a sour and sullen, pale-faced Larry, his off-and-on friend of these tumultuous last twenty or so years. Etc.

Or: Goodbye, Larry, Henry said.

Goodbye.

Bye.

By.

Four

1. Sentences and paragraphs first of all function as bearers of meaning, and the basic unit of their organization is the syntax of the sentence.

2. Sentences and paragraphs, secondly, function musically, in terms of rhythm and meter, and in terms of the intonation, dynamics, and quality of sound.

3. Sentences and paragraphs operate, thirdly, at the rhetorical level, in terms of patterns, repetitions, balances, inversions, and so on.

4. Sentences and paragraphs function, in addition, kinetically, in terms of how the mouth makes them: gutturally, dentally, trippingly, etc. "The Pit and the Pendulum" is well named. Often overlooked, every mode of their manufacture is important.

5. Central to understanding the syntactical structure of the sentence is the box diagram, whose purpose is to depict the order and nature of meaning modification in the sentence by means of adjoining and inclusive spaces.

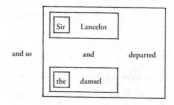

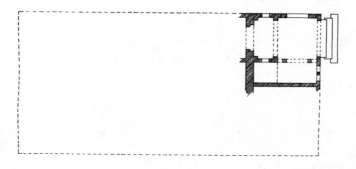

First Model Sentence: The Floor Plan

Sir Thomas Malory

And so Sir Lancelot and the damsel departed.

a. The conjunction signifies that the sentence to follow will be connected to another structure; the "so" suggests that the sentence is a consequence of that other structure. Although the syntax places Lancelot and the damsel in equal positions, as agents of the action, it is clear that Lancelot creates a much more superior space than that designated by "the damsel," who is not even given a name. Moreover, damsels are young. The socially superior space in which "Sir" puts Lancelot, his prior place in the word order, his having a name, all indicate a dominant function. "Lancelot," as a name, closes up with a stress at both ends. Compare "Arthur and the damsel departed." Even the sound of damsel echoes the so-sir-cel which precedes it, and the "am" we find there resembles the "an" of "Lancelot."

b. The rhythm of the sentence suggests a rearward movement right after Lancelot closes strongly with its "ot," since "and the damsel departed" has only two strong stresses. The verb "depart" is like a sidewalk away from the sentence's two subordinate rooms.

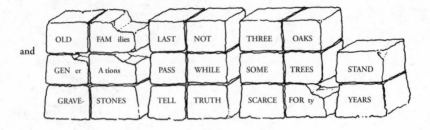

Second Model Sentence: The Wall

Sir Thomas Browne

Grave-stones tell truth scarce forty years. Generations pass while some trees stand, and old families last not three oaks.

Taking a clue from the content of the two sentences, and following the evidence of the strong beat in the paired and stressed syllables, it is easy to see, I think, that part of the success of these sentences depends upon the wall

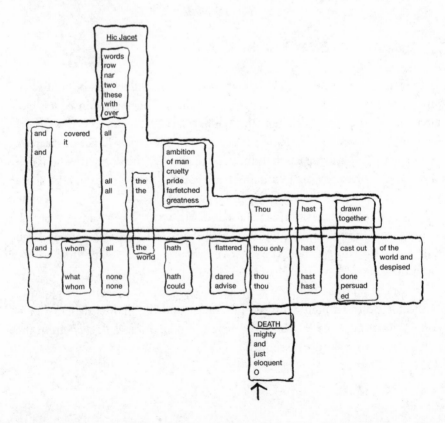

which they erect, almost as if they were gravestones themselves. The first sentence sets the pattern to the second, whose two clauses follow its sound, its beat, and its meaning. Here we have more than parallel courses. We have pile-upon structures.

Third Model Sentence: The Façade

Sir Walter Raleigh

O eloquent, just, and mighty death! Whom none could advise, thou hast persuaded; what none hath dared, thou hast done; and whom all the world has flattered, thou only hast cast out of the world and despised. Thou hast drawn together all the far-stretched greatness, all the pride, cruelty, and ambition of man, and covered it all over with these two narrow words, *hic jacet.*

We actually enter the "O" (as one is expected to do at the beginning of this kind of apostrophe, and we pass through several other *O*'s, either actual or implied, on our way to the dreaded subject: death. O elOquent, we begin, but must remember that syntactically the sentence runs: O eloquent, O just and O mighty Death! We have climbed to the threshold of this mausoleum. Parallel and antithetical clauses are ranged on either side of Death, whose name is repeatedly invoked through "thou" and "whom." As we did to form

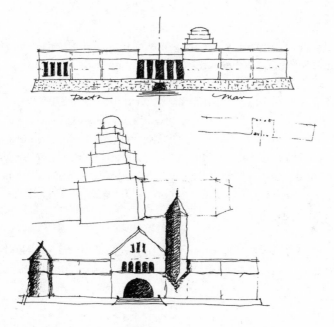

our wall, we place the parallels one above the other, being careful to match word order, sense, beat, and sound in each clause.

The antitheses completed, the passage goes straight up the catalogue of "greatness," "pride," "cruelty," and "ambition" to its bleak covering conclusion, ringing "all" and "none" like bells: this passes, all goes.

It is more than metaphorical, to arrange Raleigh's prose this way. At the same level at which we can say that score and recorded groove have the "same form," this diagram has much the same form as its verbal generator. And implies an appropriate façade.

SPACE OF THE OBSERVER: the Shopman, Prince, Charlotte.
SPACE OF THE HAND: briefly, nervously, tenderly.

Ancientries	Ornaments	Pendants	Lockets	Brooches	Buckles *326*	Brilliants	Rubies
Pearls	Miniatures	Snuffboxes	Cups *102*	Trays	Taper-stands		

SPACE OF THE TABLE: a list.
SPACE OF SOCIAL MEANING.

Fourth Model Sentence: Multiple Space

Henry James

Early in the development of Henry James's late novel, *The Golden Bowl,* we accompany an impoverished and clownishly named Italian prince, Prince Amerigo, on a shopping expedition with the lovely Charlotte Stant, an Italian-born American who is infatuated with him. The meeting is clandestine, and its purpose is the purchase of a gift for Maggie Verver, the woman whom the Prince plans to marry. At last they arrive in the antique shop where they will be eventually shown a goblet cut from a single crystal and covered skillfully in gold, a gilding which not only enhances the beauty of the bowl, but also hides a flaw in the quartz. However, first the dealer sets out a few smaller items in this singular sentence:

Of decent old gold, old silver, old bronze, of old chased and jeweled artistry, were the objects that, successively produced, had ended by numerously dotting the counter, where the shopman's slim, light fingers, with neat nails, touched them at moments, briefly, nervously, tenderly, as those of a chessplayer rest, a few seconds, over the board, on a figure he thinks he may move and then may not: small florid ancientries, ornaments, pendants, lockets, brooches, buckles, pretexts for dim brilliants, bloodless rubies, pearls either too large or too opaque for value; miniatures mounted with diamonds that had ceased to dazzle; snuffboxes presented to—or by—the too-questionable great; cups, trays, taper-stands, suggestive of pawn-tickets, archaic and brown, that would themselves, if preserved, have been prized curiosities.

As we enter the sentence, we observe first of all that the sounds of the words, normally rather arbitrary and accidental properties of what we want to convey, are the object of the greatest care, and that patterns are produced quite different from the ones which syntax requires, and these organize and direct its course. The letters *o* and *l* predominate, as they do in the phrase "the golden bowl." The word "old" is reiterated, as it ought to be in a shop full of antiques, and the metals are announced which have always named the legendary ages of man: "old gold, old silver, old bronze."

They take us down, these sounds, these patterns, these metals, the opening pun on the word "decent," they take us down steps into the shop itself, for observe how the reader's attention is constantly returned to "old," as if it were a riser. The shop, on the other hand, is created by the fiction itself, not the shape of the sentence; the sentence is interested in the shop's objects, and in the shopman himself.

The shopman is playing a game with the Prince and his companion, exactly as James is with us. He is making his moves, and each object he displays is defective in some slight way. He shows them "dim brilliants, bloodless rubies," "diamonds that had ceased to dazzle." The expression "small florid ancientries" is itself, and aptly, a bit ancient, just a little florid. The pauses, the hesitations in the passage, mimic the movement of the tradesman's hand, which touches the various brooches and pendants and pearls "briefly, nervously, tenderly." The action of the language and the action of the hand lie on parallel and resembling planes. The shopkeeper lovingly offers Charlotte and the Prince a counter-full of things. James lovingly gives us a list of words: "cups, trays, taper-stands." As readers we are placed in the position of the Prince. He sees these bibelots. We read these words. The one *is* the other. The Prince's instructed eye, and James's immaculate judgment, wittily remark the vulgar limitations of the stock, as the rich list continues, wrapped in the elegant warmth of its own sound, the delightful shimmer of its irony:

A few commemorative medals, of neat outline but dull reference; a classic monument or two, things of the first years of the century; things consular, Napoleonic, temples, obelisks, arches, tinily re-embodied, completed the discreet cluster; in which, however, even after tentative reinforcement from several quaint rings, intaglios, amethysts, carbuncles, each of which had found a home in the ancient sallow satin of some weakly-snapping little box, there was, in spite of the due proportion of faint poetry, no great force of persuasion. They looked, the visitors, they touched, they vaguely pretended to consider, but with scepticism, so far as courtesy permitted, in the quality of their attention.

In the ancient sallow satin of some weakly-snapping little box
In the ancient sallow satin of some weakly-snapping little box
In the ancient sallow satin of some weakly-snapping little box
In the ancient sallow satin of some weakly-snapping little box
In the ancient sallow satin of some weakly-snapping little box

In the ancient sallow satin of some weakly-snapping little box

James returns to his brilliantly reflective form as one still hungry goes back to the buffet, but now the concern of the sentence is the nature of the Prince's and Charlotte's attention:

They looked, the visitors, they touched, they vaguely pretended to consider, but with scepticism, so far as courtesy permitted, in the quality of their attention.

A style could scarcely be more a mirror of its own effects. The nervous nicety of word, the salesman's hesitant manipulations, the shift of both our attention as readers and that of the characters and finally the quality of their sensitivity and ours, of course, as we follow and affirm it, not to omit the author's deeper discriminations as he composes the entire scene, are combined to provide us with an almost daunting example of what a culture crystallized within a style can do.

How many spaces are there here? There is the stairspace through which we moved to reach the shop. There is the space of the observers, the Prince and Charlotte, the salesman. There is the space made by the shopkeeper's nervous, duplicitous hand. There is the table which bears these trophies, marked like a chessboard with its positivist grid. There is the social space each object suggests and belongs in, as well as the social level of the space we inhabit while we think of what to buy.

Should the architect omit any of these spaces when the total space he or she is insisting on rises into the world of sense from the pale lines of the drafting page?

Finally, let me try just once to work the other way. Here is McKim, Mead & White's plan for the Brooklyn Museum, which, as you know, was only partly realized. What sort of sentence might have its form? Since I have only partly coped with the spatial hierarchy here, this, too, will be only partly realized—however:

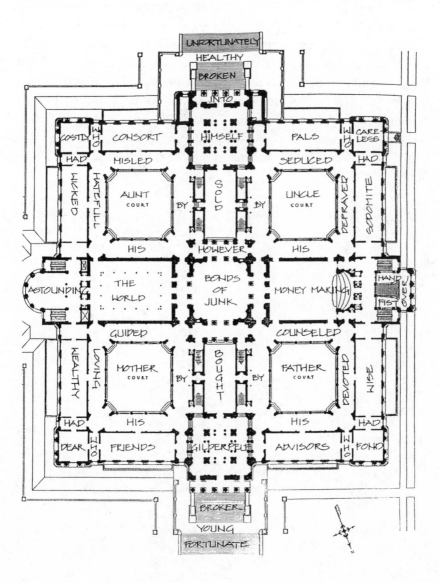

Fortunate young broker, Gilderpelf, guided by his loving mother, who had wealthy dear friends, and counseled by his devoted father, who had wise and fond advisors, bought bonds of junk, astounding the world, and making money hand over fist; however, misled by his hateful aunt, who had a wicked and costly consort, and by his depraved uncle, who had careless sodomite pals, sold himself into broken health, unfortunately.

Many sentences of this form might be imagined, but the important thing is: they would have this form.

At one end of the scale of the management of relations, there stands the mathematician, who has facilities ordinary people can scarcely imagine, but the mathematician cannot touch flesh or even rattle bones. On the other end is the architect, who works with relations realized in some material, in the connections of objects, in the concretions necessary to sense. He should remember, when he is placing stone by stone, that he is shaping a type of sentence; he should remember, when he is drawing this or that line, that he is also outlining a pattern of sounds; for the architect is the master of represented space of every kind, and that means he is the master of the making mind.

Conjunctions, 1999

Carrots, Noses, Snow, Rose, Roses

I

Marcel Proust has once again taken his vacation at Trouville. While there he contemplates adding to his monumental work a section on sea urchins and salt spray, having seen several handsome urchins worthy of his merciless and immortal memory. Meantime, in inclement weather, fogbound in the hotel lobby or by the sniffles kerchiefed to his chamber, he undertakes a novel by Monsieur André Gide and considers composing, in his best Ruskinese, a critical note on its author's use of the hyperbolic past. This he will place, naturally, in one of the more elegant reviews. And he must pen some flattery to his friends, some bitter gossip too, some biting wit. There is always so much to do. Lady Transome, a tiny but petiteless grande dame of comical Englishness, has provided a few phrases of superlative stupidity which Proust has overheard in the garden despite the dense muffling fog but thanks to a penetrating French which is like that horn that's always staring at the dog. But in whose mouth shall he put them, these squalid epiphanies? Madame Verdurin?

For anything you like, Proust is always a good case. For instance, he often did not appear to know the difference between his many occupations: his writing, his social climbing, his frequently sordid sexual career. Indeed, was there one? Writing A, B, C—all the same. Words, words, words, as Hamlet sneered. No—no difference between life and language, itch and urchin; no difference between conversation and news, a letter or an anecdote, history of advice, psychology or travel; no difference between A (writing fiction), B (composing criticism), or C (constructing a theory). Let us read at random in *Le Temps Retrouvé:*

1. a little pimpish conversation—
   "Ah! that is extremely interesting," said the Baron with a smile.
   "But I'll tell you whom I have here: the killer of oxen, the man
   of the slaughterhouses, who is so like this boy: he happened to be
   passing. Would you care to try him?"

2. some summary narrative, occasionally called history—
   Saint-Loup's death was received by Françoise with more
   compassion than that of Albertine.

3. a piece of psychological analysis—
   . . . the lover, too impatient from the very excess of his love, does
   not know how to wait with a sufficient show of indifference for
   the moment when he will obtain what he desires.

4. a letter inserted through a slot in the story—
   My dear friend, the ways of Providence are inscrutable. Sometimes
   a fault in a very ordinary man is made to serve its purposes by
   helping one of the just not to slip from his lofty eminence . . . and
   so on.

5. critical theory—
   . . . the kind of literature which contents itself with "describing
   things," with giving of them merely a miserable abstract of lines
   and surfaces, is in fact, though it calls itself realist, the furthest
   removed from reality and has more than any other the effect of
   saddening and impoverishing us . . .

Et cetera. To serve as (6), let me cite without quotation the extensive pastiche
of the Goncourts' *Journals* which Proust places beside the sand urn and the
ficus in the foyer of the volume, in a manner later to be that of Borges, in
which the Goncourts comment on characters in *À la Recherche du Temps
Perdu* as if they were in Paris and not in Proust.

Nor was the master without company in these confusions, nor is he now
alone. Half of the novels we encounter are made from diaries and journals,
leftover lifetimes and stale aperçus. A theory of fiction looms large in *The
Counterfeiters;* every third hop in *Hopscotch* finds your shoe coming down in
a pile of it; Orlando lives through three centuries of English literature and
one sex shift like a careless change of clothes; Mann packed his works with
ratiocination of every description; Rilke threw into *Malte* huge hunks of his
Paris letters—what the hell—and *Finnegans Wake* contains all its explanations. Let nothing be lost. Waste not even waste. Thus collage is the blessed
method: never cut when you can paste. No question it works. It works won-

ders, because in collage logical levels rise and fall like waves. Only an occasional philosopher is stricken with *mal de la métalangue.* In the example I just mentioned, the imaginary pages of a counterfeited work are said to describe Swann, Brichot, Cottard, and others, so much more vividly than Proust's narrator has that he despairs of having any real vocation as a writer; yet, ironically, the details of dress and jewelry, cough and stutter, so characteristic of the Goncourts, do not reveal the luminous essences behind their eyes, regardless of iris and color. This redounding of reference, which I have incompletely rendered, like a Klein worm turning to re-enter itself, is positively vertiginous. Such sea journeys, however, are otherwise soothing and strengthen the constitution. It's the salt in the salt spray, the wind up your nose.

If Proust had kept to his room to write in a letter to a friend, let's say, a scathing criticism of a performance of the 1812 Overture by the town band, there would be no possibility of confusing the artillery which went off too loudly and too late, flackering the pigeons into a shower of poop, with Marcel's amused description of the cannons' thunderously tardy entrance. It's the fog again, which has dampened the fuses. Hector Berlioz, likewise, would never have been tempted to dump a few chapters of his *Evenings with the Orchestra* into the score of *Les Troyens.*

Despite appearances—always scribble, scribble, scribble, eh, Mr. Gibbon?—the words on checks and bills of lading, in guides and invoices, the words which magnify themselves on billboards, broadsides, walls and hoardings, which nuzzle together in *billets-doux* and heart-to-hearts, words which smell a lot like stools in presidential proclamations, army orders, and political orations, whose heaps create each of our encyclopedias of information, our textbooks, articles of confederation, rules and regulations, charts and tables, catalogues and lists; the words whose ranks form our photo captions, chronicles, and soberest memorials, fill cartoon balloons with lies as bold as produce labels, constitute the warnings uttered by black skulls and red-crossed bones, make up harangues and exhortations, news, recipes and menus, computations, criticism, columns, obituaries, living bios, book reviews—so many signs from every culture and accreditation—legal briefs, subtitles, shopping lists and memos, minutes, notes, reports, summations, lectures, theories, general laws, universal truths—every other mark whatever, whether sky-writ, in the sand, or on a wall or water—these words are not in any central or essential sense the same as the passionately useless rigamarole that makes up literary language, because the words in poems, to cite the signal instance, have undergone a radical, though scarcely surprising, ontological transformation.

Gautier cried the truth out well enough to make it once for all, although for most of us an excellent outcry isn't economically a sound, therefore is actually *sotto voce,* not impressive to the market or the masses, thus not well, not true . . . still, well enough or not, he said:

> No, fools, no, goitrous cretins that you are, a book does not make gelatine soup; a novel is not a pair of seamless boots; a sonnet, a syringe with a continuous jet; or a drama, a railway . . . etc.
>
> By the guts of all the popes past, present, and future, no, and two hundred thousand times no! *u.s.w.*
>
> We cannot make a cotton cap out of a metonymy, or put on a comparison like a slipper; we cannot use an antithesis as an umbrella, and we cannot, unfortunately, lay a medley of rhymes on our body after the fashion of a waistcoat . . . and so on.

It may be scribble, scribble, scribble, Mr. Gibbon, but scribbles differ, not only in their several aims, the nature and value of the objects these activities make, or their appropriate effects, but also in the character and quality of the mind and hand that make them, and, most important, in the medium that hand shapes or mind employs: once more merely words, words, words.

The scribbles of the poet and the clerk, the novelist or biographer: they are not different the way eating soup and eating steak are, or even as two activities necessary to life, like moving one's bowels or fucking one's spouse. It isn't simply that they can't be done at the same time, like swallowing and sneezing, nor are they in conflict the way two wishes can be, such as eating cake and having it. Rather, they are opposed like people playing chess and checkers on the same board.

My concern at the moment is with the medium—sounds, shapes, concepts, designations, and connections—and I began by mentioning the novel because the novel, like a city with its apparently heterogeneous residents, has done more than any art form to mess up our understanding of the vast difference between the literary use of language and any other. A rose is a rose, Miss Stein, isn't it? we are likely to say; and a word is a word.

Paul Valéry understood the issue as few have, yet the concern of Valéry and Mallarmé for the purity of their medium, and their ardent measure of the problem as it touched poetry, led them to set the differences between poetry and fiction on the wrong stove; for they did indeed see the poet as the master of the *haute cuisine,* and the novelist at best as a *bonne femme,* a fabricator of bouillabaisse and cassoulet, of immense, rich though economical, coarse but nourishing peasant fare, a kind of kitsch and kitchen *bricoleur,* one who skillfully made do with *pot au feu, marmites,* chowders, stews: fat books, fat bellies, and heavy beer. In a way they were right, of course, but the peculiar literary function of fiction, from at least Boccaccio, and certainly to the present, has been first of all the transformation of life into language, and then the further metamorphosis of that language into literature . . . still another, much remoter, squarer sphere.

And of course now fiction is the advanced, the hard and formal form, since poets have embraced carelessness like a cocotte.

Although I've given it a name as distinguished as any duke's, ontological transformation is such an unassuming process it often passes unnoticed, as indeed does osmosis and, much of the time, digestion. Its action is often abrupt, simple, miraculous. A succulent center-cut pork chop, for instance, which has slid from its plate into a sack of garbage becomes swill in a twinkling. I don't know how we should describe a toilet bowl impastoed with raw ground beef (if not an old Oppenheim or a new Duchamp), but the hamburger has, in this case, been digested without the trouble of taking the usual tubes. And what about the transformation of the bowl? Conversely, anything thrown into Proust becomes Proustian, because this great novel, like so many others, is a veritable engine of alteration, a vast vat of cleansing acid—rendering, refining, purifying—polishing its particular mode of Being to the point of total wordshine the way a Bugatti body spells out speed.

Yet what is this purity which Mallarmé strove so prodigiously to achieve and sustain if it is not simply snobbery, a kind of paper aristocracy set up for the word, a misplaced fastidiousness, an excuse for weak, even unmanly, hyperattenuated poetic effects? I believe, quite to the contrary, however, that Mallarmé's aim is so central to the artist's enterprise that our definition of the medium, our understanding of the activity, and our appreciation of the results is conditioned by it; for the fact is that the language of the poet or novelist is not the language of everyday, nor is the grammar of his sentences, if he chooses to write such things, nor are the general forms of his compositions, even if the words of gutter and grade school appear in them, or they seem to mimic the flattened formats of history, or to be tainted by psychology, or to wear ennobling morals on the ends of their sleeves like paper cuffs.

Sometimes we sense the dissimilarities at once. What happens when we stray into Kafka, *Three Trapped Tigers, Pale Fire,* Hermann Broch, Beckett, Barth, or Borges? It's as if we'd stepped into a two-pound puddle of mirror glass and come out as wet as Alice.

So one says, but simple saying, unlike simple syrup, will not soothe. Poetry, I shall nevertheless insist, is concerned with a certain purity, fiction with purification, while prose, in essays such as this one, experiments with the interplay of genres, attempting both demonstration and display, skids of tone and decorum associated formerly with silent films, jazz bands, and the slide trombone.

Ontological transformation, purity, and form: these three notions must now be knotted together—tangled too—for what is a knot but a tangle made on purpose? Suppose we take up transformation first.

2

Let me make a snowman and see what comes of it.

I begin by gathering snow around a tightly fisted core the way a leaper on a ledge collects a crowd, pressing it together from above, enlarging it with repeated rolls until it can't be budged. For this work I certainly don't want leaves, bare earth, or bumpy ground.

The roll appears to stand well where it is. Good.

As it happens, I can barely lift the next lump above my knees, which leads me to consider whether God was ever stupid or clever enough to grow a lemon so sour He couldn't suck it, as I seem nearly to have done. Gertrude Stein, I remember, wondered whether God could make a two-year-old mule in a minute. Impossibilities of every kind confront us. Anyway, the last hunk is the size of a soccer ball and elevates easily. I don't care at all for that hole in my mitten. Curse the cold.

Now that I've stacked these three chunks like cups, into the head I'm prepared to press two pieces of coal, a carrot, and a long mop string. A pipe helps hold the string, which is rather limp, to this freshly Adam'd face. There is a semblance of a smile somewhere on this cold waste, but I wanted something enigmatic . . . a fierce expression . . . or a sad one . . . anyhow holy . . . at least wise. . . . Curse chance. Curse fate.

Large coals button down the belly. Three of them, like sweet dark cherries. I decide against a belt. Around what is now the throat I wrap my muffler with the filthy fringe. Then through what might be arms I thrust the handle of a broken broom, and at the snowman's shapeless feet I place a pair of sullen overshoes whose buckles will no longer snap. It's been rather messy, making this metaphysical miracle, but great fun, and certainly simple enough if you don't mind chapped hands. So. *Voilà!* It's done, and it will do.

No. Not quite. The head wants a hat.

Now, I have not made this snowman to amuse my children. Did God create the world to amuse His? The snowman stands there, smiling into the wind, a lesson in ontology, an incredible confluence of contexts, a paradigm for poetry and the pure world of the word.

I am able to make the snowman because the snow on the ground is of the right wetness and because I have learned how such snow packs. Furthermore, I am able to make the snowman, not because I know how to reproduce the shape of a man in snow (I don't), but because I know how to reproduce the traditional form: three heaps, five coals, one carrot, and assorted props as they prove available and are desired: muffler, broom, shoes, pipe, and hat. The mop string is my own improvement. The creative impulse tires but never sleeps.

Now, if some discornered dunce were persistently to wonder what a carrot was doing in this mound of snow—pointing at it, laughing, and then growing suspicious when we told him he was looking at a nose (not a snownose, naturally, yet the nose of a snowman)—we should have to conclude that he hadn't grasped the set of crossed contexts which establishes the figure, and therefore that he couldn't understand the carrot's ontological transformation; just as we wouldn't be able to grasp it either if the carrot were simply stuck in a small ball of snow or left lying on a drift, for we would surely ask, what is that carrot doing there? and imagine that somewhere nearby a snowman had been both created and destroyed, and that this was the root that was his nose, and these were the coals that were his eyes.

The snow that makes up the snowman remains snow, though it has also become body—snowbody, one must hesitate to say—but the coals alter absolutely. They are buttons or eyes. Because of its natural shape and the new relations it has entered, the carrot does not simply stand for or resemble a nose, *it literally is a nose now*—the nose of a specific snowman. Several characteristics, which were central to its definition as a carrot, carry on. Its slim funnular form is certainly suitable, and we can pretend that orange is red in order to imagine that the nose is cold . . . uncomfortable and runny. Coals are excellent eyes because, although they themselves cannot see, they are easily seen, whereas a gray mop string may only faintly make its smirk.

Already it's plain that there are degrees and distances of ontological transformation. We can also begin to formulate some canons of correctness or competency or completeness, since a carrot will clearly work better as a nose than a jelly spoon or toilet-paper tube; coals are better eyes than gravel, and better buttons than buttons, if the buttons are small or pale or pearl or gold. If an expensive meerschaum were placed in the snowman's mouth, a silk Parisian scarf wrapped around his neck, a fine shiny top hat pushed down on his head, and winter shoes by Gucci fitted to his feet, we should still know what these things were supposed to be—the snowman's scarf, hat, shoes— but they would be Guccis still, a hat, a pipe, to be rescued, wiped, restored to a context more protective of it. My god, the cry would quickly come, that's my Yves Saint Laurent you've wrapped round the neck of that frozen spook. So, again, if emeralds were his eyes, we should wonder, and resist the intended transformation; but if a Buddha or a great statue of Zeus were bejeweled, if the rings on the fingers of Siva were rich beyond estimate, we should not be in the least surprised. We know that the halo of the Madonna may quite properly be gold. Expense is appropriate to the priceless.

To be sure we understand what's going on, let's run down the figure of the snowman like a melt of ice and evaluate what's happened.

Hat: it is clearly still a hat, and it is exactly where a hat should be (on a head or on a rack), but since the head's a snow head, the hat can't function in a hatty manner, hiding the hair. The transformation has scarcely taken a quarter-turn, since the relation of brim to crown remains the same, as does that of hat to head. It's not, however, the head of a walrus or an ape. It's not, in short, a simple shift of species. Rather, the move is mimetic, because if we had sculpted an ape in the snow we might well have hatted him.

Head of small snow: snow in the head and body of the snowman has gained definition. Snow has been removed from snow and fastened to other snows so that the ordinary idle relation of flake to flake has been irremediably altered. There are no longer any bits to the ball (the crystalline stars have been mashed like boiled potatoes), but the relation of snow to snow is now significant, not haphazard as before. Of course, we know that nowadays a snowman needn't be made of snow. It can be made of Styrofoam, for instance. Pink snowmen are possible, and I once saw a snowwoman in the front yard of a frat house, with big boobs, naturally, and a crowd of soapless Brillo pads for pubic hair. Incidentally, this illustrates another kind of resistance: the drag of commentary and the tow of wit, since we are forced to smile, albeit wanly, at the symbolic appropriateness of the rough mesh, and return again and again to Brillo's humble abrasive function in the world.

One might argue, of course, that a Styrofoam snowman is an imitation of a snowman the way the snowman is an imitation; but is a man with a wooden leg a man, and would we continue to say yes if his eyes, nose, brain, and tongue were too, so long as he saw and smelled and spoke, even in wooden tones? and reasoned, and paid his bills, begot with a clothespin, and died of gunshot wounds? One might as well deny that soybean steak is steak. But I shall leave such gentle questions to the metaphysicians, who in future may be formed of Styrofoam too, that splendid insulation against opposites: the wet and dry, the heat and cold, the love and strife of Reality.

Eyes of coal: changes of the kind we've been considering consist of the rearrangement of defining characteristics. Deepest darkness is quite ho-hum and by-the-way to carbon, but to the snowman, sooty eyes are traditional and basic. Coal could be pink or green (who would care?), but snowmen are compositions in black and white. Obviously, we are dealing in valueless chips, because pieces of coal a snowman's eye-size are but fallen crumbs to a hungry flame. Some substitutes can be tolerated: licorice drops, for instance.

Nose of carrot: one might use a white radish or a turnip or a beet for variety, but the nose must be a winter root and, like the coal, a customary winter object. Eatability is not a virtue.

Smile of limp mop string: here is something out of character. Originality's sole opportunity, the string is, by itself, the most expressive element, not merely because it forms a mouth, but for the same reason that a fifteenth line in a sonnet, or a triple rhyme, becomes the verbal focus of the whole.

Pipe: a cheap corncob, of course, not only to cut down our resistance to these rearrangements, but also because the fellow we are creating is invariably a tramp like the scarecrow, or, as the hat has already suggested (and the broom will reiterate), a chimney sweep composed ironically from a contrapositive print.

Muffler: hat, pipe, and muffler are all giveaways (the Goodwill will get them otherwise), and their insertion into this reality will only modify them somewhat. Any man made of snow is a kind of icon, but the letters of a word are not signs in the same sense that the word is. Similarly, the parts of a snowman are not normally themselves signs. They are simply parts. Replacing a part with a sign for that part is a little like having run out of *A*'s during anagrams or scrabble and pressing a few spare *Z*'s into service to stand for them.

Torso of middle-sized snow: the human body has been divided into three pieces, but the section that is most massive in the human being is reduced in his imitation, because the stability of the snowman requires the larger roll at the bottom. Part of the art of any art consists in persuading reality to give up its mimetic demands. Did not Plato tell us, in the *Timaeus,* that Reason had, often, to persuade Necessity? Soon enough, indeed, genres become themselves tyrannical. Snowballs hurled with force into the chest may change the sex of the statue without appreciably enlarging its center, but a snowman with sculptured scarf and hat and pair of boots would be more purely *snow,* but less traditionally *man.*

Buttons of coal: notice how easily the same piece may be a button or an eye, and the same mark may be a rose • rose or an arise • rose depending upon its placement. So a coat-button may suggest the button of the belly, *Tender Buttons,* other buttons. Sly.

Broom: we have already spoken of the sweep. Unaccountably, as though covered by a cold unconsciousness which protects it from a deeper, harder freeze, the distant origins of the image remain alive to push through the slush like a crocus.

Legs of large and pedimental snow: in its role as the bottom of the body, our initial lump lies largely neglected unless some effort is made to tent the base or force the footless trunk into leaky boots or a floppy galosh. Otherwise, this primal mass mainly elevates the buttons and the eyes, the hat, the secret smile, above the vast layer of impersonal snow which surrounds and blankets everything, till each of them reaches an area of visual prominence. It had better be the first thing we shape, because not only is it an Atlas to the rest, its diameter determines the dimensions of the torso and the head, and its place becomes our snowman's station in the world. As a matter of simple priorities, even a dog knows to get a leg up before he wets the post. Snowmen are not meant to locomote, but to stand stiffly where the first roll rests, and later to decay in the advancing sun, *memento mori* for the winter, waterclocks to count the coming of the spring.

So the snowman is a poet after all. May he melt languidly down the fair cheeks of our subject. When H and O make water, we can turn our heads away, but it won't matter, because the transformation takes place quite invisibly and without any noticeable fuss. The ingredients in cooking do the same. Seurat's dotty color mixes, likewise all of Mondrian's jittery squares, do their work without our conscious aid. Op Art counts, like rhetoric, on this underhanded handling. There is also a large class of ontological transformations based upon the mysteries of term change: the mash of crystals in the pack of snow, for instance. There is another in which one term is permitted to retreat in the direction of the sign (or to advance, as your prejudice requires), which is what the broom, pipe, boots, and muffler did. Hat too. Language slips from mode to mode with scarcely a hiss, as in "Johns love Mary," where the *s* has simply slid back a syllable in a standard demonstrational sentence. Or the relation itself may change, as the carrot's did, the string's, the coals', or as in "John is transplanting Mary." What we are looking for is a fundamental alteration in the way a thing is, and that's why I played a little game with oxymoronic combinations earlier. String beans big as bombs are just big beans. "Robert robs Phyllis" clearly doesn't do it either. The difference doesn't have to be dramatic, though the consequences often are. John can believe Mary, but what happens if he asserts her? He gets slapped.

Stendhal put it perfectly:

> The young woman leaned over the counter, which gave her an opportunity to display a superb figure. Julien observed this; all his ideas altered.

If we travel the axis from raw to cooked, in the phrase of Lévi-Strauss, we carry our carrot out of nature into culture, out of the cave and into the sun, which, like becoming a lawyer in order to be a judge, a candidate and then a mayor, requires a change of status which can be expressed only in big bills. We have appropriated the wild plant, selected the seed, cultivated the root, pulled it from the earth in a moist moment, scraped it clean, chopped it into rounds like the rings of trees, and cooked it slowly with thick chunks of beef; but the carrots we find flavoring our stew are still carrots, however educated the chef has made them. We eat the raw carrot as readily as any other kind, and call both by the same name even when there has been a considerable alteration in appearance. The cold unscraped carrot we planted above the snowman's mouth, on the other hand, resembles its former self perfectly, rooty all the way, just as the words of poems do; for poetry is not a process of acculturation, but a process of ontological transformation, and essences, not appearances, mere accidents and qualities, are involved. For the cooked carrot there's a different taste—we can see what's happened to it—while the bland face of the word remains unruffled regardless of what it's been forced to say: thus the change (so secret, so internal) needs another signal.

Fiction has never enjoyed the grand proscenium or gilded frame or pneumatic breasts which plays, painting, women, and poetry possess to announce their nature—poems scattering their words on the page like a burst packet of seed. Fiction has no undermound to raise its sentences into the wind or to shadow the page with a written shout, and this has meant that the number of dunderheads reading Balzac the way they would skim *Business Week* is considerably larger. Language needs these signals. In most cases, the writer doesn't respell his words, though Joyce does, and the flavor of Locke and Hobbes depends in part on punctuation. Significantly, the major changes take place through the intervention of that rare reader who perceives the shift, as we do when we contemplate the carrot's nosy, phallic, icicular shape, and that shift is, again, primarily relational.

Meanwhile, imagine that John is translating Mary into Japanese.

And all the elements that make up the figure leave at least some of the relationships that previously defined them, abandon at least some of the functions they formerly had, to create together a novel context from scraps and shards of old ones, to face one another like the coal or carrot in the snowman's face. As eyes and nose, they need each other; as carrot or coal, they couldn't care. And this figure we heaved up and patted round and tricked out—it will do nothing from now on but suffer; and we shall photograph our children standing beside it to show how large or small it is / they were.

Picasso's snowman we encase in a glass-faced freezer. Why couldn't he have molded his of Styrofoam like a good fellow? The flux is such a pain.

3

We could try to start clean. Suppose, as composers, we had to work with hydraulic sighs and door squeaks, warning whistles, temple bells, and war whoops. We should have, first of all, to snip these unruly noises from their sources (we hear a stealthy footfall in the floor's creak), and then remove them from any meanings they might have been assigned (fire, four o'clock, beep beep, watch out!); otherwise, we wouldn't be composing music but creating sound effects. Instead of the *Boléro,* we'd hear a chorus of heavy breathing. There would be, inevitably, *plot.*

There are notes, and there are noises. Notes never occur naturally. God, during His half-dozen days in the sun, did not command a single violin to sing. He made light, land, growing things, fish, animals, man; but nary a painting or a playlet. Let there be tympani. He never ordered it . . . the insufferable bourgeois.

When he considers the composer, envy covers Valéry like the skin of a drum. The ultimate in craftsmanship is devoted to fashioning the instruments that resonate the strings; endless hours of practice perfect their playing, and skills are discovered which Nature for centuries let go to waste (the Greeks produced not a single gifted pianist, and for want of a Wurlitzer who knows what Bach lost or we were spared?). In contrast, what must the poem suffer? Everything. Shakespeare, that fortunate man, did not live to hear Hamlet say "words, words, words" with a Southern slur, and what of all those pupils in the Bronx reciting "O my Luve's like a red, red rose"? or the bacchantes who have lately torn Rimbaud limb from lovely limb?

Then, too, like that signal I asked for, ceremony surrounds every musical performance. The conductor lifts his baton. A hush falls. Our ears are finely tuned. We are ready to listen . . . and it isn't for burglars in the basement. But a book falls open to "An Ordinary Evening in New Haven," and it is: it is quite ordinary; there is the bustle of the bus station, perhaps, the raucous rattle-tattle of children, the slam of pans—we're here, we're there, at home or out of doors—and when the book falls open there is no trumpet blast, no one flashes a painting in front of the startled air, nothing whatever happens. We see the words of Wallace Stevens as the poem begins:

> The eye's plain version is a thing apart,
> the vulgate of experience . . .

but we do not begin. We see the words but do we dare perform them? Let them lie there, pepper on the page. Besides, the bus is late.

> Words, lines, not meanings, not communications,
> Dark things without a double, after all . . .

and we stumble down the stanzas like unlit stairs—was that our call? why are the people queuing? where's our case?—until we topple into the blankness of the ended page:

> A great bosom, beard and being, alive with age.

A word is a wanderer. Except in the most general syntactical sense, it has no home. "Rose" is a name, a noun, an action: where does that put us? somewhere between Utah and the invention of the Ferris wheel. Sounds, however—the notes of music—they are as relational as numbers; they appear in a thoroughly organized auditory space. Even when nothing is playing, even during the dead of night when the clock ticks with trepidation, the great grid is there, measure after measure marked with rests.

Such is the purity of music, not the purity of poetry, and certainly not the purity of prose (there, where the rose is, blooming beautifully behind its protective, nitrogenic consonant), because fiction is in ever worse shape, contaminated beyond redemption by anyone but a god. The poet struggles to keep his words from saying something, although, like the carrot, they want to go to seed.

If the composer's material has already been transformed for the purposes of his art, so that if we woke up to the oboe it would be *that* (A on the oboe) we'd wake up to, think what the maker of our snowman (I believe, indeed, that it was I) must do to achieve the same results. So, if I succeeded in impressing my work with inner worth the way Yeats did his symbol system, you would have to be reminded that it was not snownoses that were being served for dinner alongside the roast; while Picasso, or while Joyce or Proust, to continue the parallel, if they shaped that frat-house joke, would cause us all to wonder why we were scouring our pots with pubic hair. Meaning depends upon what context is the master, Humpty Dumpty sort of said, and Humpty Dumpty was, as usual, right when revised.

Here is a summary of the kinds of changes which progressively take place as language is ontologically transformed in the direction of poetry. Everybody knows about them already. It is the consequences that are ignored or denied.

1. Adventitious, accidental, and arbitrary properties of words, such as their sound, spelling, visual configuration, length, dentition, social status, etc., become essential; other properties, normally even more problematic

and tangential (whether the word is of Anglo-Saxon origin or has Romance roots, and so on; or even whether "sore" is an anagram or "rose" rhymes with "squoze"), make themselves available. I furnish the following example of an anagrammatic rhyme:

> I once went to bed with a Rose
> whose petals I hardly let close.
> Then I said to my florist:
> never mind what the cost is,
> send me a dozen of those.

The way ordinary ink becomes a sign by coiling about correctly until the insensible suddenly says "Salamander!" and enters the spirit the way that lizard is alleged to do—safely as moist fingers through flame—that way, the way of the ink, is almost the best example of ontological transformation we have; and it is ironic that poetry works to retransform the word into its ink again, make it neither pure meaning nor matter, but that fabled "third thing" of which poets, alchemists, and Hegel speak.

2. Logically necessary connections between concepts are loosened or untied altogether, and meanings which are characteristically associational become strictly implied. In Blake's poem

> O Rose thou art sick.
> The invisible worm,
> That flies in the night
> In the howling storm:
>
> Has found out thy bed
> Of crimson joy:
> And his dark secret love
> Does thy life destroy.

it is still true that the rose is a flower, but we cannot go much further in that direction, the genus is scarcely implicated. *In this poem,* the rose is a maidenhead (by no means accidentally), and its enemy, the worm that flies in the night, is invoked as much by the implicit rhyme with "sperm" as by the idea of the phallus. The maiden, the flower, and the maiden's flower, are being addressed simultaneously, and they're being told that time flies, beauty and youth are fragile, life feeds on life, good attracts evil, and so on . . . clichés of an unconquerable dullness.

3. Grammatical categories are no longer secure. Here is Joyce's gloss on the inheritance of the meek, the emancipation of the slaves, the freeing of the serfs, and the liberation of women—a passage which, like Proust, illustrates everything . . . almost *proves.*

> Hightimes is ups be it down into outs according! When there shall be foods for vermin as full as feeds for the fett, eat on earth as there's hot in oven. When every Klitty of a scolderymeid shall hold every yard-scullion's right to stimm her uprecht for whimsoever, whether on privates, whather in publics. And when all us romance catholeens shall have ones for all amanseprated. And the world is maidfree. Methanks.

In some contexts, not only are the words put out of their customary place like cats out of doors, the standard syntax of the language is scarcely operating even as an implicit grid. Mallarmé's famous *Un Coup de Dés* is an example.

4. The language no longer denotes or names, in the ordinary sense. The carrot does not name a nose. It is one. The word "Rose," in the following little jingle of Gertrude Stein's, does not name a girl, it is the girl . . . a verbal girl, to be sure, the best kind.

> My name is Rose.
> My eyes are blue.
> My name is Rose,
> and who are you?
> My name is Rose,
> and when I sing,
> I am Rose
> like anything.

When a rose has been picked, popped in a vase, peered at, rearranged, and watched, the flower has left its function, family, future far behind; but language, conceived as the servant of our needs, is denied that possibility. I can hold a stone to the light, set it in silver, let it decorate my finger, even permit it to reveal my marital intentions, but I'm not supposed to walk through Kant as through a cathedral, admiring the beauties of the nave, transept, and choir, curious about the catacombs, dubious about the dome, and positively frightened by the spire. What an affront to the serious purposes of the great man! Isn't that the conventional opinion? Only the writer who writes to provide such careless strolls is worse, they say. This villain, who puts words together with no intention of stating, hoping, praying, or persuading . . .

only imagining, only creating . . . is to many immoral, certainly frivolous, a trivial person in a time of trouble (and what time is not?), a parasite upon whatever scrofulous body the body politic possesses at that moment. And roses are intolerably frivolous too, and those who grow them, snowmen and those who raise them up, and drinking songs and drinking, and every activity performed for its own inherent worth.

5. Verse forms, rhyme schemes, metrical devices, and so on are as peculiar to poetry as the scale is to music. No doubt, in early oral cultures, they had an important mnemonic function. Now, though of course they do help to make poetry memorable, they have become almost as arbitrary and remote from life, meaning, and any useful exercise of mind as the sounds of words themselves. I cannot see any significant connection between the sonnet and its favorite subject, love (have you noticed anything fourteen-line-ish about it?), whereas the tabular structure of a tide table immediately furnishes its sufficient reason. These poem patterns are like hurdles. Low or high, they do define the race; but there might easily be others: a leapfrog relay, or the hundred-meter cartwheel. In any case, the limerick, the villanelle, respetto do not suffer transformation. They are already where they need to be, but the patterns they insist on require many of the changes I've suggested occur.

6. The language of literature does not disappear like steaming breath or memos in the shredder, nor is it preserved for patriotic purposes ("Give me liberty, or give me death!"), out of religious awe, like Deuteronomy, or historical reverence, like Washington's Farewell Address. "Come live with me and be my love" is not an invitation. Nor is Raleigh's reply a real one. The text is surely not sacred, and, though utopian, is unpolitical. Its mode is that of blandishment and seduction, but it is addressed to no one, all sexes are equally charmed. The poem is not bent on getting anyone to bed. It certainly contains no truths, pretends to none, and will in no way ennoble its reader. And how much wisdom you expect to find as you move along from Marlowe to Shakespeare ("Where the bee sucks, there suck I"), and thence to Donne and Milton, will depend on how foolish, unreflective, or unread you are.

It was this quality of maintaining itself in consciousness, of requiring continued repetition, of returning attention over and over again to itself like a mirror that will not allow reflections to escape its surface, that Valéry found most significant and valued most in every art. All the transformations I've talked about have this ultimate integrity in mind; for against what do the great lines of poetry reverberate, if not the resoundings of other lines?

7. I said that the poet struggles to keep his words from saying something, and as artists we all struggle to be poets. Yet what does this come to? Does it really mean that poems can't speak? that they are gagged or threatened? Both

the snowman and the daffodil can measure spring; my ring says I'm engaged or a graduate of the class of '43, and we all know about the last rose of summer. The true muteness of any expression can be measured by the degree to which the justification of the symbol combinations comes to rest within the expression itself, just as the reason for putting a coffin in the ground is that there's a body in it. If I cry "Fire!" we look around and sniff for smoke. If I make a promise or hold a belief or adopt a faith, where is the profit? If I make an assertion, what is the truth? If I draw a conclusion, where are the premises, what is their ordering, how goes the proof? One could continue this catechism for all the conditions that bring any speech or piece of writing into existence, graffiti included, common prayers a specialty of the house. So what justifies the snowman? symbolism? photos of the children? its service as a slush clock? Fun. Building a bigger snowman than my neighbor might explain my exertions, but it wouldn't vindicate them, and of course most of our actions have little clearance from the gods. Like light under a door, we do them for the thickest of causes and the thinnest of reasons.

We must not be misled by the ubiquitous presence of causes like bugs at a picnic. A hundred thousand factors, including evidence, may lead a man to his beliefs; however, for their scientific adequacy, only the evidence matters. Similarly, the causes of the composition of *Finnegans Wake* might mount into the millions, matching the misprints, but only its own inner constitution (its radiance, wholeness, clarity) will guarantee its right to be read, to be repeated, praised, and pondered; without further service or apology to confront our consciousness with an overwhelming completeness, an *utterness* a god would bite its lip to see, and which, as those same gods once were, totally entitles it to be.

The responsibility of any science, any pure pursuit, is ultimately to itself, and on this point physics, philosophy, and poetry unite with Satan in their determination not to serve. Any end is higher than utility, when ends are up.

We can approach the problem from yet another direction. We are tiresomely familiar in philosophy with the distinction between analytic and synthetic propositions, and one way of describing the difference between them depends upon the kind of things one would do to justify forming the propositions in the first place. The presence of the predicate, in an analytic proposition, is justified (1) by grammatical form, and (2) by the appearance of that predicate in the definition of the subject term. Such expressions ("A bird is an English chick"; "A chick is an American doll"; "A doll is a man-made plaything") can be said to be equivalences or exfoliations of meaning rather than statements of fact (as "The price of a proper plaything is a hundred bucks a night"). In the latter case we justify the presence of the money in the predicate by going to the unseemly world outside the judgment and finding the corresponding relation. Actually, as Plato argued, analytic judgments refer to an organized system of concepts, and analytic judgments are true when they reflect that system correctly.

In any case, literary language, rather than empty as analytic formulations are sometimes said to be, is so full, so overdetermined, so inevitable in its order, that to look elsewhere for reasons why Hopkins's physically and contextually responsive lines run on as they do:

> Summer ends now; now, barbarous in beauty, the stooks arise
> Around; up above, what wind-walks! what lovely behaviour
> Of silk-sack clouds! has wilder, wilful-wavier
> Meal-drift moulded ever and melted across skies?

is to want reductive causes, as if to explain Homer, Milton, Joyce, or Euler by their blindness.

To sum up, before saying a final word about the function of fiction: as language moves toward poetry, it becomes increasingly concrete, denying the distinction between type and token, the sign and its significance, name and thing. It does not escape conventional syntax altogether, but the words may shift grammatical functions, some structures may be jettisoned, others employed in uncustomary ways, or wrenched out of their usual alignment. Terms redefine themselves, relegating what was once central to the periphery, making fresh essence out of ancient accidents, apples out of pies. Language furthermore abandons its traditional semantic capacities in favor of increasingly contextual interaction. The words respond to one another as actors, dancers do, and thus their so-called object is not rendered or described but constructed. Consequently, such language refuses all translation, becomes frozen in its formulas, and invites, not use, not action, not consumption, but appreciation, contemplation, conservation, repetition, praise. If we are prepared to grant that a class is different from a thing, a hymen other than a flower; that an adverb never was a noun, validity a various aim than truth, snowmen not mere assemblages of old clothes, coals and carrots, yesterday's leftover snows; then it becomes impossible to imagine that the language of literature is not ontologically of another order than that of ordinary life, its chronology, concerns, and accounts.

In terms of the ordinary meanings of meaning, poems, made of words, contain none.

Yet I hear, undaunted, undisturbed, the voice of Tolstoy chiding me: why are you wasting your time with snowmen when the basement needs cleaning? some starving ghetto baby would appreciate that carrot; that muffler might keep many a cold neck warm; and these boots, despite their holes, would do wonders for a wino.

True . . . true . . . all true—these echoes from *What Is Art?*, that masterpiece of the missed point.

When fiction turns its back on the world and walks into wonderland, it seems an even greater betrayal, because fiction has been such a repository of data, dense as the population of Calcutta and long as the Eastern Seaboard, and because fiction has so plainly explored social, economic, and political issues, manners and masturbation, rabble and rouser, religion and race. Furthermore, fiction has always followed prose forms developed for other than artistic reasons, composing imaginary letters, newsy lying gossip, and made-up lives; but the history of the novel tells another story too. Except for those original, narrowly mnemonic patterns which prose eschews, and the tight rhymes and regular rhythms these sometimes require, fiction now unabashedly employs every other resource of poetry, inventing new modes and methods, but at the same time reaching back for the rhetorical schemes of the great stylists like Sir Thomas Browne, Hobbes, Burton, and Taylor, straight through Schopenhauer, De Quincey, and Cardinal Newman to Nietzsche, Santayana, and the limpid yet palpable intelligence of Valéry himself. There are few poets today who can equal, in their aesthetic exploitation of language, in their depth of commitment to their medium, in their range of conceptual understanding, in the purity of their closed forms, the work of Nabokov, Borges, Beckett, Barth, Broch, Gaddis, or Calvino, or any of half a dozen extraordinarily gifted South Americans.

Joyce did data in, Mann ideas, Proust all the rest. With language still guidebook-right about the region, and thus with language which is reluctant, like the Brillo pads or Gucci boots, to leave its world of fruitful description and honest use, Joyce transforms an actual Dublin—even Dublin, think of that—into an idle centerpiece of gleaming conception, yet, for all its idleness and gleaming, an object with more realized human value, and a greater chance for immortality, than the city itself; because when, like Bloom, we enter a bar, what do we see there, what do we hear? words humming like a craftsman deep in his work; words folding in on one another like beaten eggs, like lovers mingling in the middle of their sleep; words sliding away into sentences never before imagined or discovered . . . words.

An illgirt server gathered sticky clattering plates. Rock, the bailiff, standing at the bar blew the foamy crown from his tankard. Well up: it splashed yellow near his boot. A diner, knife and fork upright, elbows on table, ready for a second helping stared towards the foodlift across his stained square of news-paper. Other chap telling him something with his mouth full. Sympathetic listener. Table talk. I munched hum un thu Unchster Bunk un Munchday. Ha? Did you, faith?

When Joyce describes Dublin his lines literally rub it out, the city disappears beneath them, as Plato says Atlantis did, on account of ambition, to leave no word in writing.

Think of a whole world rubbed out and rearranged in music, voice, and meaning. A dangerous game. Can the novelist find a form which will accept it all—a Moloch—a way to the underworld, through the mouth of a demon, for the world? The novel, we used to think, was an instrument of secular love; it brooded upon the universe of people's passions and their things; both landscape and social scene were happily alike to it, and the brooding too was brought in democratically, like the nurse with the child. Now, with some alarm, we notice that right along the love was sacred, for the saint who shows his saintliness by kissing lepers loves not lepers but saintliness, and life has once again been betrayed by form.

In the slag of time, numbers were forced to shed like snakes their dizzy altitudes and deeps, their splendid curvatures, their shapes which were like snowy fields dotted with stones; or if the triangle of four, like a flying wedge, or if nine, like the disposition of a marching band, although Pythagoras would have seen a different image. And rectangles, circles, hollow squares, the blessed spheres themselves, were eventually compelled to deflate like the lake's last inner tube, one dimension collapsing upon another until even points disappeared like midges in a wind, and the vast empty regions of space were left to the merely regionous, not even round dwelled there; and physical bodies, which formerly had slid down inclined planes with all the dignity of elephants, crossed the street like fickle customers to become the cash concern of massage parlors and sun lamps, not physicists as before, who suddenly ceased stitching cannonballs across the countryside and took up equations like drink, so that the substance of their studies became far too subtle and refined by our time to sweat.

Why should we be surprised to see the same development in literature? Connections in the world, the rule of thumb, the sun, the lever in the leg and arm, the yearly thaw, as we begin to understand them, are ultimately replaced by those ambitious understudies, the ideas themselves, and once where hinges were, and without oil, were squeaks, concepts oillessly swing in winds from nowhere. It's not that our studies have lost their relevance to the spit and cough and curse of daily life. It is, rather, that they seek their rules, and find their justifications, elsewhere. Never fear. We can still break a leg with a logarithm.

The ambitions of fiction are greater, if not purer, than poetry's. But the function of both is the detachment of language from the fort. From, that is, the main body. One ought to hear the bones snap. It is as if our idea were to empty out the whole house onto a snowy figure so great and multifaceted and polymath that it could incorporate a grand piano, that string of fish which Uncle Schuyler caught, the portrait of Great-Grandfather Gass, in chalk, by several hands, an antique chamber pot, including a puddle of ancient pee, now like paint, and a needle-pointed divan, a glass of ale, a diaphragm; and at no time during the accumulation would we say: my god, you're getting snow between the black keys of our Steinway, but always, rather: ah! a snow-man so inclusive as to be by Master François Rabelais himself, including the bathroom and eight rolls of saffron-flowered paper.

What a shame it will be when the monster melts, and returns all our goods to the world and themselves, the way props are sometimes returned from the stage to those less real rooms in our homes.

What a pity, indeed. What a shame. What a loss.

The Journal of Philosophy, 1976
Published in *The World Within the Word*, 1978

THE SOUL INSIDE THE SENTENCE

I

Since we should listen with our eyes when we read, it is not rough justice if we see with our ears when we hear, but a scale so finely balanced we can set all difference down to dust; therefore, let us begin in what seems the best way possible by facing our adversary squarely and providing ourselves with a few sounds put together as beautifully as English prose permits.

Certain funeral urns of pagan origin were once unearthed near Norwich, and Sir Thomas Browne, not then of course a knight, confided to a neighboring friend the earnest lessons, as he perceived them, of these tombs. The roundly orchestrated paragraphs of *Urn-Burial* remind us how short life is, how certain death, how deep and incorruptible oblivion, and how always futile it has been to commemorate the soft body's brevities by means of its somewhat sterner bones.

> Circles and right lines limit and close all bodies, and the mortall right-lined circle must conclude and shut up all. There is no antidote against the Opium of time, which temporally considereth all things; Our Fathers finde their graves in our short memories, and sadly tell us how we may be buried in our Survivors. Gravestones tell truth scarce fourty years: Generations passe while some trees stand, and old Families last not three Oaks. To be read by bare Inscriptions like many in *Gruter,* to hope for Eternity by AEnigmatical Epithetes, or first letters of our names, to be studied by Antiquaries, who we were, and have new Names given us like many of the Mummies, are cold consolations unto the Students of perpetuity, even by everlasting Languages.

These sentences have a psychology because they have a soul; and how anything like a soul, even as ethereal as it is by reputation, can contrive to squeeze itself among so many sickly if not lifeless syllables; how any series of ordinary words containing, in this case, Christian commonplaces and the pulpit's platitudes, can rise up from its page, not merely like a snake from its basket, but into immaterial lengths of song, as though the serpent had become the music which entranced it: that rare bit of magic, and its unmasking, is the elusive object of this enterprise.

It is not unfair to make our initial selection from the greatest age of English prose, for that is precisely what we need to confront: greatness; and wonder at it, and in wondering wonder further at the will—the will to create such greatness—like a wondrous wind behind it.

Words are with us everywhere. In our erotic secrecies, in our sleep. We're often no more aware of them than our own spit, although we use them oftener than legs. So of course, in the customary shallow unconscious sense, we comprehend the curse, the prayer, and the whoop. We've heard roars of rage as raw as grubbed-up roots, and hunger's whimper from at least the dog. We've digested suave excuses like iced cake, and gotten sick on slander, drunk on lies. With words we follow the metaled links of honest argument and hearken with the same ear to the huckster's pitch and the king's command. Because of words, deep designs can be licked from a shallow dish, although not a few false promises, grandly served, are soon flat as a warm drink. Yet they lift our spirits—these poor weak words. They guide and they coerce. They settle fights, initiate disputes, compound errors, elicit truth. How long have we known it? They gather dust, too, and spoil in jokes which draw our laughter like the flies.

Yet how are we to understand an activity which seems as natural as making water; and on the surface so much like the hoot and holler of the crowd as to be quite indistinct from churchy verses, accepted sentiment, songstuff, speeches, gossip, news; when in fact it is rare as eclipses, unnatural as the gait of a classical dancer, and otherwise so far from any point of contact with ordinary rhyme and verbal rattle that we might more acceptably compare Columbus to a requiem or iodine with Indiana? Among the thousands of words and the millions of their combinations, even among the serious meditations of devoted and intelligent women and men, in a life of principled and practiced writing, only occasionally can we observe Beauty on the verge of coming into being—unobtrusively, almost in shame—shall we say the way Aphrodite slipped ashore on the calcified splash of her father's balls?

And what of the desire, then, to manufacture sentences which will persist past all utility, live outrageously beyond their means like exiled aristocracy or reckless nouveau riche, outlasting fashion and every novelty of thought or fad in phrasing? sentences in language like a vaulter's limber pole to leap times, to transcend the initial circumstances of their making as well as each succeeding situation which might reasonably require them, as if one set of Last Words might be properly the first learned, and so to welcome, as if summoned, as if always appropriately dressed, every moment after?

I am speaking of sentences, for instance, like this one:

What a deale of cold busines doth a man mis-spend the better part of life in! in scattering *complements,* tendring *visits,* gathering and venting *newes,* following *Feasts* and *Playes,* making a little winter-love in a darke corner.

Or even more simply:

Gardens were before gardeners, and but some hours after the earth.

Soon the hand which shaped them, and the mouth, too, which spoke what the fingers first formed, are left entirely behind, so that these sentences of Ben Jonson and Sir Thomas Browne are as much ours now as theirs. Only their quality continues to give them a right to be. Displaced to study hall or bus station, uttered under the heart as beneath the breath, they act like anxious tics; repressed, they return: and we protect and repeat them as though they were charms against our insecurities.

In general, work of the highest quality does not come about in a moment, nor has it a single source called genius, talent, or inspiration. The muses were invented as a cover for our ignorance. The factors involved are alarmingly complex, and disturbingly variable. Only in the arts would a man expect to paint on weekends with any prospect of success, or indite verses on the cuffs of his account books. Physics would not be taken up so lightly, or mathematics either. The wider course and spread of events which mold men and women and make for their achievement is like a life of weather in which only a few bolts are likely to startle the blue sky, or snow cool the Sahara; and we know perfectly well that fine work is usually the result of a long process of preparation, plus an intense concentration of skill and knowledge on some special and specific problem. Without the burning glass, a genial sunshine sets not even tinder to smoking.

Since it is not difficult to distinguish a lifetime of athletic activity from one spring spent in training, or that, in turn, from a single contest, it should not be hard to mark the differences between conception and gestation, practice and performance, trigger and load, or measure the small but rarely sparkable gap between what's simply acceptable work and what's rare and accomplished; yet we regularly make a mess of the matter, confusing the perfect poet the poseur is concerned to project with the real artist's ordinary boring imperfections, and refusing to observe the qualitative change of mind which comes between composition and revision, writing and erasing, changing and retaining, or dreaming and doing, the way second thoughts come down between lovers like a drawn shade; as if we did not want to know what it is to think and see and form and feel in writing, to repeat, redo, revise, get on, excuse, backtrack, straighten, set aside; as if it were all one to misjudge, invent, accept, construe, steal, ponder, cut, approve, give up, knuckle under—possibly because they all very often occur in the same time, place, person, and creative gesture; as if writing were one skill, and not twenty; as if it took one kind of mind, and not many.

It should not be terribly difficult, either, to recognize that the kind of character an artist needs in order to get any sort of work done in our world will not greatly explain the character that work has when—in relief, or in pain and disappointment—it does get done at last. The obstacles overcome, the fences taken at a stride or slowly and awkwardly climbed, are left behind. They are the wake of writing, not the hull of the craft.

> For fourteen years I have not had a day's real health; I have wakened sick and gone to bed weary; and I have done my work unflinchingly. I have written in bed, and written out of it, written in hemorrhages, written in sickness, written torn by coughing, written when my head swam for weakness; and for so long, it seems to me I have won my wager and recovered my glove. . . . I was made for a contest, and the Powers have so willed that my battlefield should be this dingy, inglorious one of the bed and the physic bottle.

This passage tells us, of course, of Robert Louis Stevenson's illnesses and his courage ("Character is what he has," James said), and particularly of his pride, which it hoists like a flag; but in the quotation itself there is a quality which neither the author's personality nor his environment will explain—its doubled-up *w*'s, its cadence, its *energy,* its shape—for Stevenson was writing here to Meredith, and he was not going to appear unshaven in such a presence ("Before all things, he is a writer with a style," James said).

When a real inspirational storm strikes, as it did Rilke, it strikes not John Jerk but a genius; it is as prepared for as a blitzkrieg; and it is the summation of a lifetime of commitment and calculation. If we think it odd the gods should always choose a voice so full and gloriously throated, when they could presumably toot through any instrument, we should remember that it is their choice of such a golden throat, each time, that makes them gods.

The miseries of adolescence—loneliness; lack of recognition, status, self-hood; sexual need—prompt many to seek relief in writing, and even in those instances where skills are easily acquired and talent seems plentiful, the passion for the beautiful is soon as dry as paint, and the writer (now in the breastfallen middle of her age) sits silent as a hill, or is content to repeat what previously pleased, or (rich now, famous, sexually successful) allows his former cool and skeptical regard to be as warm and generous as his fatuous admirers' misty eyes, so that, fattened by her own vain estimation, yet Orlando no longer, the writer's weaknesses spread like the flesh, and the odor of the alleged "late manner" (unlike the redolent flowering of pure James) is that of a rancid youth or aged maid; therefore, the psychological disabilities which propelled the writer into prose in the first place must remain unresolved, the relief obtained paltry and wretched indeed; the pain which preceded the pain of the present must painfully continue to the last; the mad raw youth must be the old man mad; for what is fame—don't we pretend to believe?—but a distracting noise, and sexual pleasure a promise which draws itself away with a toot like a departing train? what is the strength of a steel pen when the soul's grasp on itself is loosening? what pride of prick or cunt's conceit can disguise from the spirit the spirit's repeated humiliations? where can money go to buy more genius—don't we say?—in the wet earth, as Browne warns, will wealth keep away the common rot, improve our prose, purchase a plot on Parnassus, when our modest dot of immortality faints like a distant star in a bright and boundless sky?

Then they should cherish their afflictions, one supposes; but, otherwise, writers as persons are surely as various as books themselves; although, again in general, we can expect to find them ambitious, almost by definition, persistent, stubborn, single-minded and selfish, diligent and devoted, fierce and determined—we might say, "obsessed"—for there will be few to encourage and fewer to reward; thus we are likely to find them incorruptible and patient, too, with a passion for perfection—as far as their work is concerned—vain as flowers; yet, away from their desks and papers and their plots, they may be lazy cheats and careless liars, inconstant and insecure and simpleminded and vulgar and dense, or vague and evenly agreeable, softly spousy, uncritical and undemanding, kind, sweet, modest (ah, do go on), scheming, mean, tyrannical, plain. They smoke, pop pills, and drink a lot. They commit industriously gray adulteries, complain of editors, the laziness of agents, the foolishness of critics, the fickleness of the public, their own lack of fame, of love, their deplorable lack of money, their conveniently bad health. Envy is as common as the fly. So are bad posture, fat, eyeglasses, genital deficiency. But we could find similar constellations of qualities around every occupation. These collections twinkle but light little, and they come out for the hack as often as the artist.

Alcohol, like illness, may momentarily reduce a writer's level of repression, cigarettes may give the nerves something to do, sex may strengthen a weakened ego, drugs may dull the sense of failure, coffee may produce an illusion of alertness, seasons may supply subjects or encourage moods, energies may ebb and flow through times of day like sunlight among clouds, little rituals may give comfort, anal ordering some security, sensory cues, like those apples whose odor as they spoiled gave Schiller a lift, may stimulate the flow of that saliva which moistens the pen in poets who work like dogs. Creative rites are rites of magic, and, like magic, cannot explain success. Concentration, of course, is necessary. Fears, petty worries must be put aside. And as one's relation to one's work deepens, the level of tension rises, anxiety accompanies accomplishment, skepticism, like a skull, grins at one's approval, and the fear, when things are going well, that the thread will be lost, the onward rush cease, the next word fail to appear, becomes nearly intolerable, as is the thought that it may go on, winding one tight and toward a resolution which will never come; for climaxes in writing are rare, and mostly it is plod, mostly it is routine—the same cold flesh on the same old spouse—mostly it is dull and tense and hard, and rarely does it seem creative.

"Creativity" has become a healthy, even a holy word. Its popularity is recent; its followers alarmingly American. The command has gone out from gurus of every persuasion—Be creative!—an injunction which is followed by the assurance that it's actually better for you than bowling; and millions have eagerly, anxiously responded. The pursuit and practice of something labeled creativity is now as epidemic as tennis or jogging, and apparently will be as difficult to discourage, now it's here, as trailer parks, poverty, or moviegoing.

These merely social phenomena would be unimportant to our theme if they did not conveniently illustrate a confusion which has crippled most psychological studies of the creative process from the beginning. One common assumption has been that ambition, aim, or intention is psychologically sufficient: that if I regularly stumble over a stick held three feet in the air, I am as much of a vaulter's mind as a vaulter; that if I am in agony over the smudges on my canvas, my agony is as Rothko's or Cézanne's; that if I am struggling to compose a be-my-valentine, I am as angry and frustrated as Hart Crane was when he hurled his Underwood out a window because it refused to write in Spanish; but if I'm displacing the bar at three feet, it's clear that I haven't encountered the vaulter's peculiar difficulties yet, and if I am fudging my tax returns, I haven't suddenly entered the world of mathematical invention like a Dorothy dropped in Oz. Poker for peanuts or pennies is not the same game as one with limitless stakes, and there are certain driving skills which come into play only at high speeds; so that even if there's a resemblance between walking a fallen log and crossing a piece of structural steel amidst the worries of work, wind, and altitude, the achievements are in no way the same, although, again, exhortations like "careful to keep your balance" are in both cases appropriate and certainly appreciated.

People call themselves poets and painters, and seek help for their failures, as I might come to a psychiatrist to discover the causes of my vaulter's block or to find out why I can't get anywhere in nuclear physics. Indeed, regularly people push through the turnstiles of the critic's day who feel very strongly the need to pass as poets, to be called "creative," to fit themselves into a certain social niche, acquire an identity the way one acquires plants there's no time to tend or goldfish that can't be kept alive, and their problems are important and interesting and genuine enough; but they are not the problems of poets as poets, any more than the child who tiptoes to school on the tops of fences has the steelworker's nerves or nervousness or rightly deserves his wage.

Oftener than ever, artists are inventing their own forms, and when there is no model or master; when there is, in effect, nothing to copy; when a loose scatter of words on a page nicely impersonates a poem; counterfeiting becomes easy, since it is no longer itself an art. Mannikins aren't ugly or inadequate people, though they may be ugly or inadequate mannikins, and most of the verses we encounter we do not encounter in poems—neither in good ones nor in bad. Consequently, many studies of creative people are not studies of creative people; they are not even studies of people who mimic or imitate creative people; for if I, being as noteless and unmusical as a stone, sat down to compose a symphony, the sounds I made on the piano, the blots I put on my staffy paper, would be child's play, not imitation, and only another child, as ignorant of everything as I am, would be taken in.

If mastering an art were like learning to walk or drive a car, if it were merely a matter of fitting our psyches into the world like a key; or even if it involved cleansing ourselves of unconscious contaminations until we were released to do what was always well within our power—to swim underwater, kill the king, maintain an erection—then we could treat creativity as a craft the way Aristotle does, and shelve it alongside the other intellectual virtues;

but there are no manuals for the imagination; it does not make love in a well-lighted room; its failures are as hard to understand as its successes are, for if most verse is not yet poetry of any kind, most poetry of every kind is poor from birth, and this poverty is oddly as difficult to achieve by rule, advice, or aim as inherited wealth. When the Duchess of Newcastle writes

Life scums the cream of beauty with Time's spoon . . .

she becomes one of the sour immortals, or when, according to legend, Alfred Austin, perhaps without peer among impoverished poets, composed this couplet:

> They went across the veldt
> As hard as they could pelt . . .

he deserved his laureate. To write as badly as Wordsworth is not easy. Even for Wordsworth it was as difficult as when Wordsworth was writing well.

So, even when the writer is undeniably great, or at least large, as in the case of Dostoevsky, the creative element is seldom the real concern of the student. The author's works are treated as though they were longitudinal reveries, pipe dreams, couch speech, through which, like a clouded window, the psychophile hopes to catch sight of his beloved, much as medieval theologians peered through the word and works of God toward what was presumably the crystalline source of His Being; except that the manner of these investigations leaves us in some doubt about why they were undertaken, since the genius is soon gone from Goethe, the artist left out of Proust, the poet omitted from Hölderlin, the prophet erased from Blake. Freud was certainly frank enough when he wrote at the beginning of his essay on Dostoevsky that "before the problem of the creative artist, analysis must, alas, lay down its arms."

Among such abandoned arms, do I dare to pick up even a pouch of damp power?

2

At the conclusion of Freud's 1915 paper on the unconscious, while considering with his customary unempirical daring the passage of such material into our awareness, Freud extended the views he had earlier expressed in *Die Traumdeutung* by suggesting that before any idea could become conscious it had first to find a sign, and that consequently the content of the preconscious must consist of thoughts which had found verbal formulation. It is one of the mind's more marvelous moments, and made at least this heart leap up. By pulling at the one end offered us, how many silken scarves, like the tail of a kite so far away we cannot see it, can be drawn from the sleeve of this incredible magician?

Initially, and from the psychoanalytic point of view, we might imagine that, just as dreams use the scraps of a previous sleeplessness to piece themselves into being, so our ideas of objects, too, might float up to present view on the backs of our past perceptions of them, but Freud believed instead that

> thought proceeds in systems that are so remote from the original residues of perception that they have no longer retained anything of the qualities of these residues, so that in order to become conscious the content of the thought-systems needs to be reinforced by new qualities.*

Our earliest communications may have taken place in silence, through the cozy inferences and the warm smells of touch; all the same, cooing continues to accompany it. The sounds we make as babes, unlike the things we touch when we kick, or smell when we root, or taste when we suck, are among the first sensations we fashion for ourselves like our own pee or poop, or the sense of movement in our muscles. Even now I cannot cry out color and thereby create it, or flavor my saliva with a wine-dark savory, or saddle my nose with leather like a horse; but I can sing, I can chant, I can talk; so I think we can set it down as our first general principle that the satisfactions of babbling are particularly intense in our budding poet, because we soon sense that our noises do not simply leak from us like a washerless tap, but that these sounds, which are such dramatically effective parts of the external world, are securely fastened to our will. *They are something we produce.* Surrounded by our own scent, slowly aware of our limbs, we soon swaddle ourselves in our own sounds, as we shall live later with the dearest companion of our life: the voice of consciousness, the words which become the self.

We should never forget, then, that from that very beginning, when the word made the world, the word has been one of the most important "objects" in human experience. We were born into language as into perception, pain, and pleasure. We shortly associated it with heads, eyes, lips, tongues, and eventually with the hidden internality of things. In turn, we manufactured

* Sigmund Freud, "The Unconscious," in *Collected Papers,* vol. 4 (New York: Basic Books, 1959), pp. 134–35.

our own noise, and long before we knew the meaning words bore, we knew the meanings which bore them, the emotional contexts of revenge and reward in which they were formed.

It is of course the dynamics of speech which allows us to communicate ahead of any understanding: the whisper, mutter, and war cry, the drone, drawl, slur, bark, stutter, scream, or otherwise the various precisions of articulation appropriate to the actor, pedant, or priest, every intonation and inflection, too, the rhythm and the pace, every overtone, projection, inner energy, the recognizable return of the same sounds, the total up and down of the verbal path, stress and pause and peace, the facial surround—the smiling and the shouting mouth—these give to the talk they contain an almost gestural expressiveness, symptomatic as a blush on the cheek or blood in the penis, just as the configurations of the parental face and body underlie the emotional life of most lines and shapes.

Language without rhythm, without physicality, without the undertow of that sea which once covered everything and from which the land first arose like a cautious toe—levelless language, in short, voiceless type, pissless prose—can never be artistically complete. Sentences which run on without a body have no soul. They will be felt, however conceptually well connected, however well designed by the higher bureaus of the mind, to go through our understanding like the sharp cold blade of a skate over ice.

Upon the crucifixion of Christ, "cold care and cumbrance has come to us all," the *Piers Plowman* poet writes, and the passion of that simple and immortal line lies as deep inside us as our bones.

The language of science should serve the reality principle; the language of art serves the soul. When Flaubert wrote to George Sand that "It is hardly necessary that words express ideas. So long as one assembles them in harmonious sequence, the object of art is served," he undoubtedly went too far. Meeting this condition is clearly necessary, but Tennyson, Poe, and Swinburne, among others, have shown that it is not sufficient.

Though he may never understand what he's been taught, a child soon learns that it's not his wants which his parents so persistently oppose, but his method of expressing them—his imperious haste, his tactless greed—and that if he finds the right way, not only will his needs be met, the meeting will be eager. It's not permissible to say you want sexual pleasure from your mom, but you can say you want to be like dad when you grow up, and even dad will pat his little rival proudly on the head.

If we think of ourselves, for a moment, purely in verbal terms, as a function and source of words (appropriate enough for a writer, and nothing less than the truth in the case of fictional characters), our unconscious becomes a voiceless darkness, dark because it's mute, and "the force that through the green fuse drives the flower" is simply undifferentiated instinct, and its trials are those of any leaf reaching for light, or root searching for moisture.

Society civilizes us by stylizing our desires, and it is not, as Gertrude Stein has said, the various facts of life which separate one generation or one culture from another, but the manner of their composition. The suggestion which Freud makes (one that is central to the account of creativity I am in the fuddled process of proposing) is that when thoughts are kept from consciousness by being denied their signs, it is not the thought itself the door is slammed on, but certain expressions of it, so that the ego is required to write and rewrite until its unfriendly editor is satisfied.

If every original desire can be thought of as a secret sentence of the self, then every modification can be regarded as a method of rewriting, initially so that the desire can be allowed expression, and eventually so that the desire can be satisfied.* There are six basic elements in such sentences, and it is these which are altered as revision proceeds: (1) the wish itself, originally an undifferentiated lust, a roar of wind through the loins, the belly, and the bowels; (2) the alleged owner of the wish (an "I" which is fronting for an "it"); (3) the strength of the wish measured in terms of the mobilization of the resources of the psyche in its service; (4) the valence of the wish, its active or passive character; (5) the object in the world associated through experience with the reduction of the drive; and, finally, (6) the organ of the body through which satisfaction is to be achieved.

Instincts are transformed in accordance with certain quasi-logical operations until acceptable versions are found. These are compromises, sometimes, of an oddly ambivalent character, like "yes, we have no bananas, especially if you like pears" (and, of course, what will be found acceptable will vary with age as well as other circumstances). The following exchange between the id and its editors may illustrate, though crudely and incompletely, a part of the process.

Original Wish: [Diffusion]	I want the pleasure of touching myself.	Infantile Narcissism: Enjoyment of Self in Self.
Original Wish: [Localization]	I want the pleasure of playing with my genitals.	
Denial:	THAT'S MASTURBATION!	

* I have discussed many of these points at greater length in "Anatomy of Mind," in *The World Within the Word,* pp. 208–52.

Original Wish: [Relocation]	I want the pleasure of playing with my toes . . . sucking my thumb . . . picking my nose . . .	
Denial:	WHAT HORRIBLE HABITS!	
Introjection: [Same Sex]	I want the pleasure of touching your genitals.	Adolescent Narcissism: Enjoyment of Self in another self of the same sex. Bonding.
Denial:	THAT'S HOMOSEXUALITY!	
Introjection: [Opposite Sex]	I want the pleasure of touching your genitals.	Adult Narcissism: Enjoyment of Self in another self of the opposite sex. Marriage.
Denial:	ONLY IF YOU ARE OLD ENOUGH! ONLY IF YOU ARE MARRIED! ONLY TO BEGET CHILDREN! ONLY IF X IS OF THE RIGHT CLASS, RACE, RELIGION, ETC.!	
Projection:	You want the pleasure of touching my genitals.	Exhibitionism or Prudery, depending on psychological use.
Denial:	YOU MATA HARI! YOU VAMP!	
Partial Reversal: [Change of Voice or Role]	I want the pleasure of being touched.	Passivity.
Denial:	TROLLOP! SLUT!	
Full Reversal: [Change of Voice and Valence]	I want the shame of being molested, raped, beaten, etc.	Masochism.
Denial:	BE A MAN! DON'T BE A PATSY! WOMEN REALLY ASK FOR IT. OK, TAKE THAT!	

Sublimation: [Object/Organ Substitution]	I really enjoy working with clay.	Narcissism of Art: Enjoyment of Self in things.
Denial:	THAT'S CHILD'S PLAY! TAKE UP ACCOUNTING!	
Repression:	I want the pleasure of touching you with what I most want touched.	Mutual Masturbation or Sexual Intercourse.
Denial:	I WOULDN'T LET YOU TOUCH ME WITH CLARK GABLE'S PHALLUS!	
Repression:	I love you.	Romantic Love, or Mutual Masturbation of both Mind and Body.
	That was a very touching thing to say. Say it again, and again, and again.	
Art:	All right. "How do I love thee, let me count the ways. . . ."	

We lose a great deal when we civilize our requests. Style alters its object. The tantrum displays the urgency, the dismay, the anger, the bodily involvement, both the power and the impotence—the drama—of the demand. But we learn to ask politely, discreetly, deviously, indirectly. We learn the art of acceptable disguise. Nonetheless, although we may secretly express our voyeurism by exhibiting ourselves, hide our envy behind excessive admiration, our fear of rejection behind a generalized contempt, front our masochism with aggression; still, satisfying one desire by indulging in its opposite makes for a slender settlement. Whatever the public result, sweet Narcissus is the one we care for, whose features we love, whose genitals we want to be in bliss. Writing, I shall outrageously say, is blissing. But at what remove? And these days, with what sort of amorous engine?

So my guess is that the superego says no, not to the wishes of the id, but to certain formulations of them. Art is an elaborate euphemism for what the soul says is dirt. And the censor may say no so often, with such ancestral severity, that we think the desire itself is being denied. Certainly the primal crime is not the deed, the satisfaction of some disallowed wish, it is the very possession of the desire in the first place, for our psyche believes as Jesus did that if a man looks at a woman with adultery in his loins, he has committed adultery with her in his heart; and if he has committed adultery with her in his heart, he might just as well have committed adultery with his loins . . . never mind the contradiction of his continuing ache. Nonetheless, we will allow ourselves to express any wish we can find a suitable code for. Mother minds if Sally wants to play with her stools (so unladylike and messy), but finger paints are perfectly all right, and so are rolls of clay and lumps of wet sand which look like whatever the cat's made. Mother not only forbids certain acts; in addition, she teaches the child in what form her wishes will be found acceptable.

A dream is also in code, but the secrets which the dreamwork tries to hide merely have to be hidden. So long as the superego recognizes the meaning of the message, the message will be sent back like a bad bottle. The preconscious contains thoughts which have passed our severest, although least sophisticated, censor, but our disguises aren't costumes we can doff, they become us. A prince we may be, but the prince is a frog.

Although, in practice, it has been the psychoanalyst's special vice to push aside composition in search of content, the unity of style and meaning is a profound social and psychological truth. There may be, in principle, many ways to cook a goose, but the method we choose and fix on, by becoming our only one, defines us, as we define it. The way we keep the Sabbath *is* the Sabbath. Means join their ends and become ends enlarged—coated with custom. Ego and superego are not enemies in this enterprise. If we watch, in fact, how our wants are rewritten, we shall see soon enough that they sit at adjoining desks in the editorial office, and teach the same lessons.

3

In the following little drama, we can witness, distantly within our hero—Frank—a desire struggling weakly for expression.

I WANT MY MOMMY!

The superego will blue-pencil this desire at once if its meaning is indecent, but even if all that is wished for is a little comfort and assurance, the ego will cross it out if the superego doesn't: you are thirty-three, a big boy now, in fact a little fat, and besides, what will people think? What people think, how they reward or punish us, is a reality every bit as compelling as a bee sting or a painful burn. By and large, it is not inhuman nature which causes us psychological distress, but that ever-present hell (as Sartre said) made up of other people.

First Desk: *The Superego and Its Wastebasket, the Unconscious.*

The desk of the first censor is occupied by Ma, Pa, several Step-Uncles, Foster Parents, God, the Orphanage, and Immanuel Kant. Its nays are categorical. The remaining desks (and I shall count six more) are staffed by real officials. Some are salesmen; some have managerial ambitions; some are good at PR; and each is alert to the responses of the world; each is skilled at procrastination, pass-the-buck, and runaround, as efficient bureaucrats must be: full of facts, suggestions, cautions, and precautions; on the lookout, naturally, for Number One; each the internalization of means and standards; serving the pleasure principle but governed by reality—a reality which shifts from desk to desk almost kaleidoscopically, at one moment crassly material, vulgar, local, and grasping, and at another moment devoted, sacrificial, universal, and ideal.

Of course, if Frank wanted his mother's body the way he enjoyed it when he was a baby, then the superego will have already said: you mustn't say that, even to yourself. We will notice that when the ego denies something it always tries to be "reasonable," and reminds Frank that his mother is seventy-five or that she is not now nursing or wouldn't in company open her dress; whereas the superego, a notorious dogmatist and fanatic, simply says: no. In any case, the censor must have something to go on: a text. The desire must be recognized as a forbidden one before its employment can be terminated. With his id at his elbow, Frank tries again. He has noticed that his hostess, Carol Cozycott, has a gently rolling chest like the hills of Ohio and his dear mother of memory. Her hair is similarly long and dark, and her nose has a crease across it like a dog-eared page. She'd be a suitable substitute.

I WANT CAROL!

Second Desk: *The Ego and Its Wastebasket, the Preconscious.*

The first curious thing about the process of revision is that not only do we remain unaware of our initial version, we are also ignorant of the character of the writer who holds the pen (Frank doesn't know he has a fixation on this kind of contour; he believes it to be a fact that some breasts are sexier than others). Carol is your best friend's babysitter, the official at the second desk reminds Frank; you better not think about her now; perhaps another time in a quiet daydream, preferably in the tub or on the john. So the thought ("I want Carol") is thrust into the preconscious like a dirty postcard in a pants pocket.

Third Desk: *The Ego and its Second Wastebasket, Discretion.*

But Frank still wants his mommy and Carol still has her cleavage. Her pie, Frank can't help noticing, is treacly. No matter. His mother's molasses pies were always treacly, too. He'd better try to choke down another piece. The truth is, he probably doesn't remember his mother's molasses pie, and the identification of the two women remains obscure, but Frank has been well trained, and the censor at the third desk hardly has to raise his eyebrows, because Frank isn't any more likely to say "choke" aloud than he'll let out his canary. Instead, Frank says:

"Carol dear, may I have a little more of your lovely pie, please?"

The soul of discretion, Frank does not even use the word "piece," and, as one, all the editors cry:

"Good boy! It's a print!"

This example is wrongly simple, not to say squalid; nevertheless, it may enable us to discern and describe the several stages through which Frank's wish for a little maternal comfort has passed on its way to his reward: a few more calories and perhaps a little heartburn . . . also, of course, Carol's good regard.

During the first stage, deep in the unconscious like a man in the dark, the wish bumps about searching for signs. If it finds none, it cannot become conscious. It follows, since the wish may be sent back again and again, that the larger the number of employable signs, and the greater the range of trans-formational types, the better the chances are that the wish will find a for-mula. A lifetime of reading will stock the unconscious with a lifetime of signs and expressive possibilities.

I should like to suggest that all subbasement sentences of this sort contain, first of all, an id without an identity (the id does not call itself Frank); that they invariably refer to primary processes; that they are always put in the passive voice, and involve a narcissistic unity of world and body. In short: it wants (to receive) pleasure from, let's say, the body's maternal breast through the body's mouth. I want to stress this now because I believe that one aim of writing well is a narcissistic satisfaction which depends upon taking in, disarming, and reconstituting a world by means of language. This activity is largely oral and involves, most deeply, the fusion of the ability to make one's own sensory environment with the passive gratifications of the breast, though, of course, one aggressively sucks while being passively fed, and passively listens to one's own active babbling.

We enter the second stage when the initial formulation is refused and the wish cannot penetrate the preconscious. It may be that the regular occupants of the preconscious must at one time have lived in the light, if only briefly, like flying fish, so that the way to the preconscious is through consciousness, as we reach Monaco through France, but at present this is one problem whose solution we can, with pleasure, refuse to consider.

These initial revisions are crude and drastic. Passive attitudes may become active as an itch, or our desires may suffer full reversal, pain replacing the requested pleasure, or all sorts of substitutions may be made in our orders so that we come home with pot roast instead of ham, or the soul may resort to euphemisms as enthusiastically as an undertaker.

It is not a calm colloquy: the id demanding, the parent saying no. It is push against shove. Suppression is prolonged, tense, angry, often violent, and at any time later in life it will be as it was in the beginning—the sufferance of this so-called superego, who acts and orders only for our Good, as Papa Doc once did in Haiti, benevolent and brutal—because our supervisor will often be sly, devious, frequently dishonest, occasionally desperate, certainly inconsistent, divided (as Mother and Father issue different orders or are split to be conquered or strike one another with the sweet fat of an infant like the hard flat of a hand), and in this allegedly safe and soft and sweet environment attitudes will grow hopelessly ambivalent at the same time the emotional gain goes up, as if two stations were coming in at once, and these broadcasts will become insistent, obsessive, incessant, until static covers everything like dust. Increasingly, heads will ache, eyes burn, stomachs sour, hearts fail, backs break, bodies faint, while wants turn perversely grandiose in the face of every objection, annoyance following nuisance to hotels of irritation like bees back to the hive; and squalling meets suggestion, and resistance meets rebuke, and pout answers pleading, until the child draws another child out of the parent's heart (the real sibling rival at last) to confront it, total war is declared, the crib is grasped and shaken like a sieve by terrified angered hands, and then it will be wee bawling baby against big brawling bully, with odds favoring the baby by two to one.

The censor snaps his pencil, promises pain, outrages the omnipotent aspirations of the id: say please, say thank you, say uncle. Forbidden to refuse food, the child may throw up (and what can you do about that, mommy, but buy a new bucket and mop?); punished, its nose bleeds (so there, daddy-o, you brute!); it develops allergies (especially to milk), becomes asthmatic, pees in drawers filled with silks, on platters, in planters like a cat, poops in its pants or on the vinyl, has earaches, dawdles, talks too much or absolutely not, stutters to remind you how you've terrified it, or mumbles to make you ask, what?, destroys its toys or picks its nose or fights, or rubs its crotch or whines and wheedles, or cries at the sight of strangers, dogs, or beetles, makes lewd suggestions as if in all innocence, at bedtime needs lights and unsettles your sleep with its dreaming, throws up in cars or at birthday parties, becomes overexcited, plays with matches, develops a cry like a shaken saw, swears precociously, spits, has a permanently runny nose, scabs on knees and elbows, dirt like a clown's comical cosmetic around its mouth, holds tantrums in shops the way some hold public meetings, darts into the street and pushes over bicycles, filches pennies, is a victim of inexplicable frights, fads, and manias, is peevish, pouts, enjoys meaningless disobedience or extended sulks, or pesters the grown-ups like bees at a picnic, but disappears when called and hides when sought, can be sugary and solicitous, docile and loving, yet when no one is watching, scratches, pinches, hits, kicks, and bites.

We must make no mistake: childhood is a civil war, a state of nurture, if I dare to say it, where every child is the enemy of every child, including pets and plants and father, father's job and father's car, family hobbies, habits, little tics, mother's migraines and her playing cards, everybody's dreams and everybody's love affairs, not excluding meter readers and other intruders, a rabble of relatives, well-meaning friends, frets and parental worries as numerous as starlings raisining their evening trees. There are crimes committed, wounds inflicted, guilts as frequently felt and multitudinous as fleas, misunderstandings, too, misconceptions, masturbation, false success, reliefless ease.

This war has no victors, no peace table, no medals, no quarter. It must be fought to a draw or everyone loses. And it is the sword swung then, usually so useless against the swift sandal and the quicker sling, which sharpens that pen which one day shall be mightier. Nor does the struggle cease with death, for when we fall we are buried in the bodies of our children, as Sir Thomas Browne suggests, where we shall shortly be forgotten, yet where we—unforgiving as the Furies, unrelenting—in that deep forgetting find our final victory; since, like a tumor, we make our presence felt where we can walk about unrecognized, unlike the ghosts which haunt the conscience of the guilty and need belief to be. Well . . . not final victory. There's nothing final in it, really. Nature knows nothing of ends like these. Its patterns contain few figures of closure or purposive designs. Its course proceeds as randomly as crowds of cars upon a freeway—a thousand shots and not a single aim, countless plots and not one point. We are merely conduits of culture, of half- or quarter-truths, elusive meanings and iron measures: that hammer which fell so often angrily from my father's shaping fist struck my sons more severely than the soft white metal I was mistakenly believed to be.

During the third stage, which we now reach once more like a wave, a number of reformulations are made until an acceptable one is found and the thought reaches consciousness. It is possible at this point that the psyche develops a partiality for certain forms of revision, habitually sublimation, for example (blanket for body, bottle for breast), or reversal, or introjection, or the euphemisms of repression; for we notice that some writers throw bits away and begin again, some patch and piece, some pare but some accrete, so that if a sentence is wrong, a setting, or a scene, getting it right means making it longer, or scrubbing it clean, or starting over; just as when we have blundered socially, saying or doing the wrong thing, some of us must follow the foot in our mouth with its ankle, others blush furiously and fall silent, others deny having uttered the offending sentences, as if misquoted by their own ears, and produce new ones, more fashionable, more politic, amusing, or more daring.

Fourth Desk: *The Class Historian.*

A thought which reaches consciousness may not be allowed to stay: it may strike us as unimportant, or as unpleasant, or as distracting and inappropriate to the present moment. Later, we say . . . later; and during its wait the memory (for it is now that) undergoes alterations. We know how anecdotes are removed from storage like old clothes, spotted, brushed, and pressed, let out or taken in, and we carefully lace the sleeve of our personal history with lies, which really are revisions, until, eventually, a formula for the past is settled on which (flattering or not) somehow suits us by concealing our nature. We can bear to remember the war, our childhood, first love. Misery has become amusing. As students of Freud, we know that these fictions are often more revealing than the facts, just as the coat which is cut to conceal our belly may display our taste and pretentions nakedly to every eye. Such reinterpretations of the past, which Proust performed so consciously, constitute stage four.

Fifth Desk: *The Town Crier.*

During stage five, the wish, acceptable to consciousness, is inspected, and usually rewritten once more to satisfy the demands of public utterance. There are those who, it's said, say the first thing that pops into their pretty heads (like rattlebrained incompetence, it is a trait assigned, by the common consent of men, to women). They appear to hide nothing, and to be charmingly frank and direct. The child is often like this and will winningly ask the fat ugly woman why she is, or want to know of the cripple what's cracked, or of a leg how it came unstuffed.

Sixth Desk: *The Teacher's.*

What we say when we speak in public won't bear much writing down. We hem and haw, backtrack, repeat, use preformed phrases which have fallen out of the mouths of radios or slid off screens, piece our speech together out of sentence fragments, and instead of punctuating pop our cheeks or suck our teeth or wiggle our eyebrows and sometimes fingers. The moment one begins to write words down instead of sailing them into invisible dissolution in the air, one feels the censor's presence, now a new one: a grammarian, conscious of spelling, parsing, construing, phrasing, all proper forms. Do I indent three spaces? How do you address a bishop or spell "yours truly"?

All previous stages, which this argument has dragged us through, were ones in which the word was made by the mouth (even if unspoken), and if our parents have, by this time, trained us to express our savage lusts like cowed adults, both in speech and in behavior, they have had no control over our writing. Puppies still, we go to school to be paper-trained. We leave our box. This was not always the case, of course, but now it is a generally accomplished fact, and a terribly important one. We take our first formed sentences home as we do our first scrawly drawings or an injured bird we've found in the street. There our parents help or hinder, encourage or frighten us, but that step into the written, reading world is the first free one. There were once scarcely any adolescents with hair upon their genitals and a head upon their shoulders who didn't realize, reading away in their door-covered rooms, that escape lay over and through the word, just as, in the books they were devouring, liberty was always just beyond some bordering mountains, across a river, through a few trees. Nowadays, television and movies have tried to replace those walls with their tinted images, but they have so far had the kind of success we associate with billboards plugging the sun in Florida.

The average person, taught to write, writes little in a lifetime, and, with the possible exception of a few letters of love, apology, or sorrow, would never consider the composition of sentences which should transform his soul into syllables to possess the slightest interest. But what of the million fledgling writers who remain? What, when they scratch away, pen poems to one another, push stories into print the way a shy son or daughter is pushed by the parent into a room of strangers . . . what, when they establish periodicals whose life is so brief their period comes promptly after *The* . . . what do they want?

Seventh Desk: *Editors, Publishers, the Public.*

There are many pressures to publish, most of which ruffle the surface of our psychology like wind, but the principal one, I've been suggesting, is the desire to have one's wants (that is to say, the deep self itself) not merely accepted—oh no—applauded, deliriously praised: how marvelous of you to have thought that! how searching! how sensitive! how wise! how expressive! The soul where desires of such a sweet and eloquent nature dwell must be likened to a land flowing with silk, thighs, and money . . . and so on through every rich adverb and glowing et cetera. Yet how battered the instincts are by this time; what tedious vicissitudes they have gone through to reach ink; how altered, as Bottom was . . . translated into an ass!

To hurdle the barriers briefly once again: at the first desk sits accident, blind as justice but weighing nothing, grasping piggishly at whatever comes, exercising censorship only through eagerness, as the worser apple is eaten if it's nearer the mouth. At the second is the categorical THOU SHALT NOT of the Mosaic Law, while at the third we hear the incessant yes of the ego—*yes, yes, yes, but*—a devious Uriah Heep and treacherous sycophant who always counsels the id to work within the system. Then at the fourth is perched, as on a stool, a lying, smiling historian in the pay of the Home Office, who hopes for a knighthood or annually expects election to the Royal Academy. The fifth editorial advisor wheels and deals, Frenching the phone, a sophist trained in the spirit of Dale Carnegie, wrapping remarks to look like Cuban cigars or Belgian candy, and selling the staler ones—a real steal—at two for a doll. Wielding a ruler, her hair in the requisite bun, the English teacher is next, guarding the grammatical proprieties like a treasure. At last we reach the general public, which may not be so general after all: one's class at school, a small community or neighborhood, a few science-fiction fans, subscribers to the Masterpieces of the Month Club, the no longer quite so vast audience for poems, plays, and tales. As we proceed, the presence of our editors is more openly felt, their demands become better known, but their hold is also relatively weaker, the standards spongier and sometimes vacillating, inconsistently applied, increasingly unclear. Except through chance and circumstance, the approval of the crowd is hard to obtain, harder to hold, and requires, like drink, progressively larger amounts for its effect, since its plaudits are cheap and fickle, uneducated and anonymous for the most part, or neurotically loyal as fans sometimes are, local and circumscribed to the point of being pinched.

Obviously, our editors are internalized representatives, arranged roughly in rings, of all those agencies which, during our formative years, inflicted pain or permitted pleasure because of our way with words.

Of course, men and women want money, power, glory, and the love of other men and women. But why try to obtain it by writing? It's a mug's game, and only a few are driven to lengthen the line of desks. For most, it is enough that they get their piece of pie or piece of Carol. Dreiser chose to achieve his aims by writing, but not by writing well; John Locke by expressing rather carelessly a lot of liberal sentiments and dull truths; De Sade through shock; Heidegger by pedantry and obfuscation; Mill by specializing in superficiality like a decorator of cakes; but who but a lardhead would want to seek renown through the placement of eyebrows and noses, the manufacture of metaphors, the management of rhyme? Not promising. Foolish on the face of it. Foolish deeper down and foolish deeper in.

Yet psychologically the art of fine writing is very close to the art of becoming civilized, even human. It parallels, if it doesn't ape, the transformations of the instincts into acceptable acts of expression. And the final stage—the grandeurs and intimidations of style ("Gravestones tell truth scarce fourty years")—signals, like psychoanalysis itself, a return to early urges and their effects. This return is not nostalgic and nothing like regression, because it is a return armed, a conscious and controlled effort to rewrite the instincts in accord with another kind of standard, which requires the withdrawal and capture within the self of what has been excellent in the writing of the past; the digestion, over decades of feasting and fasting, of the efforts of others bent on the same improbable errand. It is, as in the case of Stephen Dedalus, the search for a verbal parent, an authority made of authors, a leviathan which when constituted will prove as unremittingly hostile, implacably severe, impossible to please, equal, or even emulate, as any other God the Father, and who will henceforth receive, like mash notes written with a poisoned pen, all our scribbler's inner ambivalences: his love and fear and jealousy, her hope and hate and hallelujah.

As far as writing itself goes, although that section of the soul which makes the money, makes the love, or makes the garden grow may remain relatively unaffected, a fine writer must accomplish five fundamental psychological tasks: (1) he must replace his present editorial staff, as far as possible, with a single, rich yet precise, wide though discriminating sense of taste, drawn from all his reading but preferably from the most inclusive tradition of excellence he can assimilate; a sense to which he gives the power of a parent; (2)

yet he must not give up in the face of the parrot who will now speak to his muse: "Not good enough, not good enough, awk! not good enough"; but gain its eventual approval for his own individual transformations; (3) he must displace, in so doing, the reality principle from world to word, so that with words and their formal structures he can (4) overcome the intense destructive urges which are the basis for his desperate creative activities; for superlative writing is love lavished on the word in order to repair a world which revengeful fantasy has destroyed, as well as to persuade its agreeable aspects to remain unchanged, because if they indicate a desire to depart, they will be savagely attacked, too, bombed into oblivion; and (5) he must compose his work in such a way that the full features of infantile life are brought up to date without the sacrifices of expression demanded by his former bosses: the complete child must come forth in the whole man or woman who invests and shapes a successful style, in a manner exactly contrary to the situation I described earlier in which an angry, teasing child reduces the adult to another angry, teasing, threatening child, and this use of the earliest urges by the most sophisticated can be achieved only if the powers that be can be persuaded to pull back, approve and praise, because only then can forgiveness be received in the peace and blessing of the great lines; only then will the psyche believe that its impulses aren't satanic, that all is not lost, that the self has not been left alone amid the debris of its own demolishment, the ashes of its anger.

I want to devote my remaining pages to a brief description of these tasks.

4

One of the fundamental facts of psychic life is that we want to wound and heal, eat and have, condemn and save, preserve and destroy, at the same time. Nothing would suit us better than the blow whose bruise blooms, or the bite whose indentations decorate, and this ambivalence only weakly names the state, since we recognize the love in those who love us by the degree of damage they are willing to sustain without causing us grief to have done so. Guiltless, we savage the peach to its pit, for what sweeter compliment can we pay anything to surpass swallowing it? May I have another piece of your lovely pie, please? The primal and still-ultimate rejection is the retch. And would we not fall in love with a vengeance, if it wreaked vengeance? and wouldn't revenge be richer if it led to love, for hate is finest when it elevates and saves. I love peaches, yet the snake I fear and flee from prospers. Strange. Suppose each time we broke our favorite plate it grew more beautiful and complete; then to smash, again to smash: what a total pleasure!

At least one important theory of art has concluded that, though the world be without purpose, or justice, or meaning (as far as reason can confidently ascertain), the unified objects which art makes of these spoiling fragments render things finally as they ought to be, for even if every actor suffered and then died during an Elizabethan tragedy (and sometimes that nearly happened), and the motives of men were mercilessly laid open like an ox that's been flayed so we might see the blood they had their baths in, the effect is not one of gloom or dismay, but of energy, wholeness, perfection, joy.

Remember Baudelaire's description of the carrion—flies at picnic upon a decaying vulva—Hamlet's little speech to Yorick's skull, or Rilke's rhetorical wonderment about his mother: did I come out of that hole in the wallpaper? or, if I may be forgiven a moment of bad manners, this brief passage from a story of my own, in which the narrator (only in thought, of course) excoriates a harmless old neighbor woman who often comes to visit him, the outburst leading to an unexpected and involuntary epiphany:

> For I am now in B, in Indiana: out of job and out of patience, out of love and time and money, out of bread and out of body, in a temper, Mrs. Desmond, out of tea. So shut your fist up, bitch, you bag of death; go bang another door; go die, my dearie. Die, life-deaf old lady. Spill your breath. Fall over like a frozen board. Gray hair grows from the nose of your mind. You are a skull already—*memento mori*—the foreskin retracts from your teeth. Will your plastic gums last longer than your bones, and color their grinning? And is your twot still hazel-hairy, or are you bald as a ditch? . . . bitch . . . . . . bitch . . . . bitch. I wanted to be famous, but you bring me age—my emptiness. Was it *that* which I thought would balloon me above the rest? Love? where are you? . . . love me. I want to rise so high, I said, that when I shit I won't miss anybody.

The emptiness which Beckett describes for us, for instance, is full. His plays are what the world would be, absurd as it is, if it were yet well spoken; but we must imagine that when God said, let there be light, He had a bad cough (look if you can at the light as it falls on Beckett's stage, pitiless and blank and even as a shroud), and when He saw what He'd made was good, His voice failed, and other words both made and judged it. Every work of art is such a judgment, such a justification of the Great World's Ways. What else did Dante do but settle scores and square accounts and make awards and set things straight? As Kafka says, the writer does not copy the world, or explain it, but declares his dissatisfaction with it, and suffers.

Some of the cases I've cited will seem extreme. After all, praise, as Rilke maintained, is the thing; but only some things in this life can be unambiguously, unironically, celebrated. The poet wanders among the animals and flowers, in landscapes finds his freedom, amid luminous skies lets his soul soar like a kestrel; for what *is* the way I want the world? wholly in my power; and the more powerless I may have found myself, as in growing up we all find ourselves, the more completely, as a writer, will I rest within the word, because as difficult as its management is: listen! I speak and these friendly syllables surround me; they have never done me any harm, for even when I ascribe them to my enemies, make up villains in a tale to torment victims I have also fabricated, the words they speak are mine, the sentiments indeed are mine, coming from every corner, the villainies as well . . . ah, yes, those *especially.*

I am present in every disguise, every twist and transformation (Proteus, in changing, cannot escape his nature as a changeling); and if I write well enough and dispose my voices artfully, *I can say anything;* only then can one dare to speak the truth about one's self, off the couch and out of an office, onto an engraving. I can, in those conditions, lay my heart bare, as Baudelaire hoped to do, not merely because unburdening is a blessing, but because I want to be blessed as the Son was by the Father, blessed first by those books which are my friends and gave me my values and taught me how I ought to live, and then, perversely, by the world, precisely because I am the sort of total sinner who wants not just the tree but the tree toad, not just the rainbow or the pot of gold, but the whole kit, the entire kaboodle. Then, after every plaything—the choir of heaven and the furniture of the earth—has been grabbed up and stuffed in my toy box, and while I sit securely on its lid with that insufferable smile of possession, rattling my heels, I expect the pleasure and praise of an emptied universe to approach me like applause.

No. That's inexact. I don't want the world to be mine (my motorcar, my wife, my house, my gloves, my dog), I want it to be *me,* the way my mother's body was before her treachery, and the nipple came away in my mouth like a handle in a surprised hand breaks from its satchel, or a button spits out its cloth.

Well, we all settle our claims out of court, for there is no judge; and we settle for less, much less . . . much . . . much . . . much less, until we settle for smidgens, seconds, leftovers, culls: the writer settles for words he can't own (suppose I owned "and" and it cost you to use it?); accepts a grammar he can't claim (and half of it hidden anyway, only Chomsky knows where); approaches traditional forms which merely shrug at his existence and he has to run to catch like a late commuter; takes on themes as fucked over as a two-buck whore would be in the days when haircuts were two bits; and looks out on a world of *les autres* who have as little claim to the language they mispronounce as he has.

Moreover, the psychological satisfactions of writing: the payment of reparations, the release from guilt, the pleasures of attack and destruction, the implicit approval of the masters, the consequent acceptance of the self, and so on—these results are often felt no farther than the borders of the artist, and as she rises from her worktable to placate her baby-husband or her baby-baby, she is merely another frazzled mum, more than generally resentful, not simply because she must leave her work, but because she must leave herself.

Among the maladies which character and circumstance combine to guarantee we shall surely suffer is the clamorous confusion of overmany and mixed motives. Remember all those interfering editors? They all want to have the last word about our words. None cares to be bypassed, and even though the writer may have discovered that the most direct way to the self is through a style as convoluted as that of Joyce or Lyly or De Quincey or Proust, or through one so Shaker-like and pure it's suddenly as though the page were awash with clear creek water and the reader could measure plainly every resting fish and count every rounding pebble; nevertheless, we are a multiple; we want the approval of both Plato and the public, the ghost of our father and the ghost of Henry James, and the ghost of Miss Tish, too, who wouldn't let us punctuate with dashes, and Carol, whose pie we really don't want another treacly piece of; so that the writer struggles with more than words, he competes with his obsessions, his screens, his weaknesses, with family lies, with strange expectations, with tastes twisted by neurosis, beliefs he wears like loud neckties, with alcohol, anxieties, with impotence, with menopausal flushes, hysterical pregnancies, manic states, sexual rage.

Everywhere, then, we encounter an overestimation of the word—those knuckles of our knowing. And what, then, is a sentence but a fist?

It is not simply that the writer thinks of his daily life largely as an excuse for speech and a source of language (that birds are blessed because they suggest their names); or that he has put lines about love and suffering, composed of sounds and thoughts responsive to him, in place of the body of his beloved, since she turns her back and will not warm; it is not simply because he can chastise his enemies in secret and safety, or spill his guts and sell them in a store; it is basically because he has himself become the word: he is its source; his id is now its energy; his ego is a mediator between the words which want to leap like salmon out of his soul and the words already there on the page, the project already begun, the life being formed out of leftover alphabets, exhausted genres, unspared parts from the remaining whole of literature, a presence which shadows that page like a long cloud across the sun; his creative superego is meanwhile seeking sanction—yea or nay—in the qualities of the great texts, searching above all for that quality most prized, most rare, most praised: that they shall not quickly pass away.

We should not leave the table without one last taste of our topic, this time Jeremy Taylor. Full of faults—forced conceits, unregulated repetitions, occasionally confused imagery and a little local awkwardness of gait—this passage pushes its problems roughly aside to become sublime. The qualities it possesses, the soul inside this sentence, all the finest writing strives for: energy, perception, passion, thought, music, movement, and imagination; yet what will it tell us: that life is hard; that we are fragile; that time is short? goodbye.

> We are as water; weak, and of no consistence, always descending, abiding in no certain place, unless where we are detained with violence; and every little breath of wind makes us rough and tempestuous, and troubles our faces; every trifling accident discomposes us; and, as the face of the waters wafting in a storm, so wrinkles itself that it makes upon its forehead furrows deep and hollow, like a grave; so do our great and little cares and trifles first make the wrinkles of old age, and then they dig a grave for us: and there is in nature nothing so contemptible, but it may meet us in such circumstances, that it may be too hard for us in our weaknesses; and the sting of a bee is a weapon sharp enough to pierce the finger of a child or the lip of a man; and those creatures which nature hath left without weapons, yet they are armed sufficiently to vex those parts of man which are left defenceless and obnoxious to a sunbeam, to the roughness of a sour grape, to the unevenness of a gravel-stone, to the dust of a wheel, or the unwholesome breath of a star looking awry upon a sinner.

Nearly everyone writes about the brevity of life: in elegies, odes, meditations like Browne's, in treatises, in anatomy texts, in stories, plays, and preachments like Taylor's—life would be long indeed if we were to listen to a millionth part. Then how shall one man or woman, among so many, say the same thing so originally, so forcefully, so beautifully, we'd recognize their pen print anywhere? ". . . the unwholesome breath of a star looking awry upon a sinner."

The sentence, then, if it is to have a soul, rather than merely be a sign of the existence somewhere of one, must be composed by our innermost being, finding in its drive and rhythm, if not in its subject, the verbal equivalent of instinct; in its sound and repetitions, too, its equivalent feeling; and then perceive its thought as Eliot said Donne did, as immediately as the odor of a rose—fully, the way we see ships at anchor rise and fall as though they lay on a breathing chest.

In Sir Thomas Browne's day death came early, often in the morning of a life, before the hair was combed; then the image in the shaving mirror often grinned like a skull, though its owner wasn't grinning; and the spirit which only one day past had moved the body so vigorously through its braggado-cios, its fucking, its sighs and singing, its drunkenness and piggery, might suddenly seem lost and wan in the new sun, so that the world which might be clean of mist by noon might also be free of both this pale glass shadow and its affrighted soul; consequently, the Elizabethan interest in death, or rather, their concern about the fragility of life, is scarcely surprising; and yet while Sir Thomas Browne tells us how futile it is to preserve our bodies, bones, or ashes, how brief and inarticulate the speech of those stones which like jaw-less teeth irrupt the lawns of our cemeteries, what is he quietly doing but fashioning a monument for his psyche which heaven will not have matter for or space or skill to build? because, in so saying what he's said, he becomes as immortal as may be, and comes as near to realizing the one real wish of us all as other wills and wishes will allow—no more is permitted; and which one of us would be unwilling to lie down among such sentences as though they were boughs for our burning? because Browne, and all those like him, did not merely bring these books of his, these eloquent passages, their memo-rable lines, into being; he brought himself into existence on the page, as it were through a hole in the word; although, as he would require us to observe, what are these urns which have lasted a thousand years when we measure them up the leg of eternity? do they extend so far as the knee, the cuff? do they reach the lace of the shoe, the tongue? possibly as far as that?—no—but if we cannot have an ever-long life, perhaps we can create a soul, within some substance elsewhere and other than ourselves, which it would be a crime on the world's part to let die.

Harper's Magazine, 1982
Published in *Habitations of the Word*, 1984

The Habitations of the Word

Plato's *Phaedrus* has seemed to some critics to have too many subjects; to be drawn first in this direction and then that, as if those uncooperative horses that it has created, flown, and thereby caused to be celebrated, were pulling apart its pages. Is it about love, or about oratory, the scholars ask; is it a vision or a recitation, an allegory or an exercise? It is at least all of these, but I should like to believe that this extraordinary dialogue is fundamentally concerned with the local habitation of the name, and with the nature of honest eloquence—the speech which is just, the speech which can be believed—and that it goes about its business by providing us with a classification, by means of model and example, of the various residences of the word, at all times seeking the best address.

When we ask ourselves what a word is we may be wondering whether it is a complex set of sounds or a more or less regular march of marks which have come to have a special significance because of all the contexts they've been used in, each one shaving its sense more closely as if polishing the skin, or we may be inquiring about the word's relations or roots, or puzzling ourselves concerning the unenviable middle place it takes between thing and thought, object and idea; but I wish to ask the word a few questions about its native state instead: *I want to know where it is from.*

The *Phaedrus* opens with a curious exchange between Socrates and Phaedrus concerning a new composition by the noted rhetorician Lysias that Phaedrus has heard only that morning. Obviously intended as a display piece to demonstrate the orator's art by taking a difficult, if not perverse, point of view, Lysias's speech argues that an impersonal lust presents, in principle, a better suit of the favor of a beautiful boy's body than love can; that selfish pleasure is a more reliable motive and provides a more secure environment for its object than passion does. Socrates shows an immediate and ironic interest in this subject, wishing only that Lysias had proved a similar superiority for poverty and age, not excluding Socrates's other debilities.* The immediate implications of Socrates's little joke are certainly serious ones: namely, that Lysias's composition has a use; that it might be employed by anyone who had the orator's leave or had paid his fee, and had a nice young man in mind; for it was out of just such an expectation of payment that Lysias had written his brief for the defense in the case of two men who had loved the same boy and come to blows over him; and again for a similar quarrel over the purchase of a slave girl; and yet another time for the prosecution of a guardian, guilty of embezzlement; or when money had tempted his pen to the defense of a farmer accused of cutting down a sacred olive grove. In one case only, as far as we know, did Lysias himself speak what he had written. On that occasion he prosecuted Eratosthenes for the execution, without trial, of Lysias's own brother, Polemarchus.[†]

When Socrates asks Phaedrus to repeat the oration for him, Phaedrus protests, calling himself an amateur (presumably with respect to the feat of memory it would require to fulfill Socrates's request), and complaining that he should not be expected to reproduce in a moment what it had taken such a wonderful writer weeks, in the inspired labor of his leisure, to create.

---

* Socrates is certainly familiar with the sort of paradoxical twist involved here, because he has already argued in the *Lysis* (205d–6a) that it is unwise to praise the youthful object of your affections: first, because encomia which are any good get noised about, and you will be more deeply and publicly shamed if you are rejected; and second, because beautiful boys are vain, and difficult to snare, so that singing their praises will only increase their inherent conceit and the difficulty of their capture. There is, of course, a good deal of hard-boiled truth in this, just as there is in Lysias's similar bit of persuasion—calculations distinguished especially by their cynicism, general correctness, and lack of customary hypocrisy.

† See *The Murder of Herodes and Other Trials from the Athenian Law-Courts,* compiled, edited, and translated, with an introduction, by Kathleen Freeman (London: MacDonald, 1946). Lysias and Polemarchus are the sons of Cephalus, a wealthy shield maker, whose business and estate are despoiled by the Thirty Tyrants. It is at the house of Cephalus, before these tragic events, that the discussion described in the *Republic* is presumably held. Lysias inherits nothing but these crimes, and must make his living by his pen. It is typical of Plato to set the time frame of his dialogues very artfully, so that his readers will be able to place the fate of the speakers, as it were, above their heads as they talk. The *Symposium* (which resembles the *Phaedrus* very closely in several elements of structure, as well as in subject, not least in its devious "Conradian" opening) is particularly poignant in this respect, for most of the participants in Agathon's victory celebration will end in political exile, disgrace, and death. The *Phaedrus* takes place at a moment when the debate between Alcidamus and Isocrates concerning the superiority of the spoken over the written word was especially intense. See the excellent account by Paul Friedländer in *Platon: Seinswahrheit und Lebenswirklichkeit,* pt. 1, chap. 5, translated, with, one suspects, as far as the title goes, an intention to mislead, as *Plato: An Introduction,* trans. Hans Meyerhoff (New York: Pantheon, 1958).

Socrates then pretends to believe his friend can do just that. He suggests that Phaedrus has already badgered Lysias into repeating his speech; more than this, that he has begged the loan of the manuscript in order to study it closely, commit it to memory even; and that Phaedrus has made his way just now beyond the city's walls in order to rehearse what he has memorized—to release into the indifferently receptive country air the winged words which he has so earnestly and carefully caged.

As it turns out, Phaedrus *has* borrowed the manuscript, and has it, held in his left hand, hidden under his cloak. He has it held in his left hand because this speech, these words, one will later realize, belong to the black horse of desire, the left-handed horse whom the charioteer must check if the soul is to rise.

Socrates insists on hearing the entire work—respoken, not silently reread—rather than the summary Phaedrus was hoping to give him, and by that gift to demonstrate, if not his command of the art of verbal memory, at least his ability to recall in the right order the principal points of an oration, an art which, much later, Cicero and Quintilian would call a memory for *res* (things: i.e., objects, subjects, important points in a discourse), instead of the more strenuous and particular one for *verba* (words got by heart). It was the memory for "things" which was so important to the sophists, jurors, politicians, and those parts of the public who felt it necessary to be able to return to mind, whenever they wished, the shape and substance of what had been said on some previous occasion; whereas it was the memory of the word, precisely as it stood among others, that largely concerned the poets and the rhapsodes and certain of the rhetoricians.*

In order to perform Lysias's allegedly eloquent composition, Socrates and Phaedrus seek out some shady spot and settle on one near the banks of the Illissus.† Their conversation is rich in allusion and reference; no god's name is taken in vain;‡ no uttered word lies idle; yet Plato's artistry, never greater

---

* See particularly the first two chapters of Frances A. Yates's *The Art of Memory* (Chicago: University of Chicago Press, 1966). If, according to Plato's Egyptian story, Theuth invented the art of writing, ancient tradition says that it was Simonides of Ceos, a poet frequently cited by Plato, who invented mnemonics. It is, of course, this art which is most immediately threatened by the hieroglyph.

† The river which Paul Valéry has turned into the incessant stream of Time in his own dialogue between Socrates and Phaedrus, the *Eupalinos*.

‡ On their way to the river they pass a place where, as Phaedrus incorrectly surmises, Boreas is said to have made off with the lovely Oreithyia, one of the daughters of the then King of Athens. Boreas had been in love with the tempestuous Oreithyia for some time, but her father kept putting Boreas off with false promises and postponements. Angry at having wasted so much

than in this dialogue, and equaled only by the philosophical poetry of the *Phaedo* and the *Symposium,* provokes the paradox of his prose; for this dialogue is to be a defense of the word which simply flies sincerely forth from an open and unencumbered heart, whereas the language which so eloquently states that case possesses qualities which are possible only to words which are not merely written, but *composed.* My shopping lists, my address book, my checks, my sick child's school excuses, are written; my lies, my love letters, my legal briefs, my limericks, my *longueurs,* are composed.

We have scarcely begun the dialogue; we have yet to hear Lysias's speech (to read the hearing of it, that is); and already various forms of the word have begun to proliferate. We encountered, first of all and quite naturally enough, the *written* words of Plato, which comprise and create the occasion and conditions of the dialogue; then we meet the *spoken* ones which Plato says were uttered by Socrates and Phaedrus; next there are those *composed* by Lysias, *borrowed* by Phaedrus, and *read aloud,* possibly *performed* by him rather than

---

of his time on mere words, Boreas became his impatient nature again, and one day swept the maiden away in a coil of air while she was dancing on the banks of the Illissus, wafting her to a rock near another stream, where, hidden behind a dark cloud—as Robert Graves describes it in *The Greek Myths,* 2 vols. (Baltimore: Penguin Books, 1955), vol. 1, pp. 170–72—he took the pleasure of his lust. Eventually, Boreas made Oreithyia an honest woman, not merely a wronged one, and she bore the god twin sons, the Argonauts Calais and Zetes, who, when they reached manhood, suddenly grew wings. The Athenians had built a temple to Boreas, and revived his worship in the city, because his winds, at their request, had scattered the Persian fleet. Oreithyia is to be identified with Eurynome, the goddess who in a whirling dance created the world, and who caught the North Wind, and formed from it with her fricative hands a phallic coil of air, the serpent Ophion, who promptly wound himself around her with the predictably pregnant result. In addition, Oreithyia is probably another name for Athene the Filly, goddess of the local horse cult, as Graves suggests. Certainly, the other stories in which Boreas is featured involve horses, for he lives in the stable of Ares on Mount Haemus, and once, disguised as a stallion, covered twelve of Erichtonius's mares (presumably not all at the same time), although, on Homer's authority, it was once widely believed that mares could conceive by turning their rears to the wind; and, indeed, it was the wind again which was capable of entering a woman's womb in a gust that bore one of her ancestors toward another life. It was perhaps such an egg of air—an abortive flatulence—which Socrates fears might be the sole result of his midwifery in the *Theaetetus.*

It is, of course, Phaedrus who wonders whether the story might be true, while Socrates, though aware of the prevailing skepticism concerning the myths, finds it hardly feasible to pooh-pooh every fantastic tale that comes along, and reduce each one to a commonplace (although he jocularly does just that), because there are so very many of them. It would be like spanking ants. So he would not send away the harmless ones to be debunked, but would prefer to accept them as they innocently present themselves, and worry, rather, about the myths dwelling in himself which he feels he must discover and expel. It is no doubt true that Plato wishes to dissuade us in advance from any desire we might have either to deride or to overallegorize the tales that Socrates himself will shortly be telling; but any pretty story would have sufficed for that maneuver. The Boreas story is chosen because of the kind of myth it is, and because of the rich connections it makes with the material soon to be brought before us.

memorized and taken to heart. Lysias's speech, although given life and spoken by Phaedrus, although approved by his breath, has not been made his; it has not been given residence in his head, which is, doubtless, a wise thing; for what is it to take a guest of this kind into the interior of the soul, whence words rise like a sudden spring; what is it to offer your hospitality to the opinions and passions, the rhythms and rhetoric, of another, perhaps far from perfect, character and mind?

Socrates declares that he can make up a better speech than Lysias's,* accepting even the rules of the game and the assumption of the debate: namely, that it is better for a youth to yield his body to one who desires but does not love him, than to one who does both (especially when the love in question is a blind and selfish passion); but Socrates is reluctant to make good on his boast, and one reason surely is, although several are evident, that the words will not be his: he must pretend to be a vessel which is filled by another, possibly by the muses whom he invokes, though even this is doubtful, for would the muses be inclined to sing on such a subject, insincerely and to a false point? Not only that, but Socrates will have to match his wholly *improvised* and *unwritten* speech against Lysias's cleverly contrived and carefully composed one. Socrates's oration is masterfully made up on the spot by a character whose very figure, as well as every known word, has been artfully imagined by Plato over years of passionate dedication. It is a so-called *unwritten* work which has been written and rewritten, we can be sure, more than once; its alleged lack of composition has been composed and recomposed; its off-the-cuff character has been indelibly inked on the page.

Socrates further guards himself against the anger of the gods (for his words cannot help but blaspheme the real Eros, who is said here to be one of them) by inventing a lover who, while pretending to be free of love's passion the better to satisfy it, will simply pronounce the words which Socrates makes up for him. Neither Socrates nor the mask that Socrates holds out in front of him believes the words being mouthed. Whose words, then, are they? Literally, they belong to no one. The first two speeches of the *Phaedrus* are exemplary orations, models, specimens, or types. Without any actual occasion to

---

* Which ought to be easy to do if Lysias's speech, as R. Hackforth thinks, is poorly put together (see *Plato's Phaedrus* [Cambridge: Cambridge University Press, 1952], p. 31). But only if we are unsure of Plato's artistry can we make this complaint, or wonder whether it is really by Lysias, as Taylor and Wilamowitz believe, or was made up by Plato, as Shorey and Hackforth think. Plato never does—and never would—give that much space to worthless writing. Just as Agathon's speech in the *Symposium* is an instance of bombast brilliantly brought off, so Lysias's speech is a superb example of rhetorical opportunism. Coleridge warned Wordsworth not to imitate a dull and garrulous discourser by being dull and garrulous, and Plato has triumphed over time to take his advice.

bring them into being, representing no actual mind, they belong to the art of eloquence, to rhetoric in the abstract; they are words quite free of responsibility to anyone. It is no wonder that Socrates feels uneasy in their presence.

In normal discourse, and especially in societies which depend principally upon the spoken word to establish and maintain community, the real origin of one's words is a serious, even critical matter. We are always forced to ask of any politician what his words mean; whether he stands behind those promises his mouth so glibly made; whether his stated intentions are really his; whether his promises weren't broken in the moment of their manufacture, as if a large crack were a part of the mold. Our presidents rarely write even their own lies, so in what sense are the lies theirs? The reader or listener must return the word to its proper habitation; the word must be sent on the same pursuit as the soul, in search of *its* truth: the sincerity of its source.

It has long been our habit to quote the words, and hence to adopt, or temporarily to borrow, the views of others. In debate I may attribute to historical figures convictions which they might have expressed on some famous occasion, although I was not present to hear them, as Thucydides did in his history, or Plato did when he composed the *Phaedo.* Again, I may cite Homer or Hesiod to give the weight of their authority to my otherwise airy opinions. I implicitly say, by so doing, that I assent, not only to the sense of their sentences, but also to their style. The breath of my lungs unites us in a common course or cause. But where do these words have their home now? Where do they reside? Are they part of my soul's very flesh and blood? Have they been the words that have nourished me from the first and formed my self and established my character, been the bone of my bones, as the very diction and verbal rhythms of the King James Bible shaped the souls of the early settlers of this country—its meanings, sounds, and meters reinforced by every family reading?

Suppose I could repeat every line of a poem as well as a recording; it nevertheless might be no more important a piece of my past than an anecdote might be, only a folly I recall for the amusement of my friends. As a child I had to *commit* to memory (please note the word, which suggests that memory is a lunatic asylum), and learn to recite in a way deemed impressive, "The shades of night were falling fast, / As through an Alpine village passed / A youth who bore 'mid snow and ice / A banner with a strange device, / Excelsior!" and I have since then simply happened to retain in some back room of my mind Auden's immortally awful couplet, "This is the night train crossing the Border, / Bringing the cheque and the postal order"; but these words have never taken up residence, as we say, in my heart, nor have they fathered or nurtured other lines, sentences, further feelings, or thoughts of any significance. Our hellos and goodbyes, our concerns for one another's health, our hope that all and sundry will have a nice day: these utterances, too, do not proceed from us any more than the dullest actor's lines do; they are as social as the dress suit, and are rarely homemade. It is Plato's point, of course, that almost the entire meaning of "I love you" depends upon what organ or area of the body is energizing the production of the words.

That dull actor, indeed, may perform his greatest service simply by saying his piece and setting free its words instead of draping some interpretation like a coat over its shoulders, because it is likely that the language has more meaning than his inflection can convey, his gestures circumscribe.

Then what of those passages that do follow us home: the sentiments and sentences which we adopt? What is the fate of some of my favorite lines of Rilke, *"Kannst Du Dir denn denken, dass ich Jahre/so: ein Fremder unter Fremden fahre?/Und nun endlich nimmst Du mich nach Haus,"* sunk like a ship inside me for so long, concealed now by what sort of sea-growth, or preserved by the salt and thus not a day older, or worn by being repeatedly given tongue? And I murmur to myself, "a stranger in a world of strangers," taking warmth and comfort from this cold conception. Then, when Rilke is remembering, at the behest of Busoni, the enchanting lines of his poem "Song of the Sea," for instance, and fervently reciting them, they are words which have gone from his soul long since to return to another region of being, for surely the place they were when he wrote them is not the place they are when he remembers and recites them. Nor are they the words that Busoni hears.

I can also recall the expressions of others as though to confront them in court; not in their own persons, of course, but by means of their immortal residues. Yet only lovers memorize the flattery they have spoken to one another; only spouses allow their sharp outcries of complaint to inscribe themselves upon their souls in an unerasable state. Generally, the word must be written down, set adrift from the self, before it can be returned to another starting point in the loins, the lungs, the larynx, or the lips of a stranger.

And when some lines of yours have set another's mouth to moving, making that sense with those sounds: is that not better than a kiss?

However, when a noble thought is implanted on a page, it can be harvested by rascals. What are the words of the Lord doing coming from that foul infidel's face? And when I quote some immortal lines as if I were in inner harmony with them,

> We do not prove the existence of the poem.
> It is something seen and known in lesser poems.

It is the huge, high harmony that sounds
A little and a little, suddenly,
By means of a separate sense. It is and it
Is not and, therefore, is . . .

whence does my conceit and confidence come, since I could never have created its controlling notion, set that sort of thought afire, let that kind of song
escape from the dirty shaded cage I call myself? How can I ever make divine
lines mine?

Wittgenstein surely must have felt that the understanding he sought with
such intensity was being carried away by his auditors in little bags and sacks
as though they had purchased it; that what was a process for him had become
a product for others; and what could Socrates do to remind his disciples that
the *logos* they loved was the *logos of his life,* and altered as he did, and grew, as
he hoped, toward the light; that wisdom was not something which could be
handed round like the mashed potatoes, but was found by means of a vocal-
ized internal investigation, a search of the soul? for the soul would move the
body wisely only if its words were wise, since it is solely through these dubious but essential diagrams of sound that the rational spirit speaks.

It is the journey to the truth which convinces the traveler that he has
arrived. To be dropped on the top of Mount Everest by helicopter is not to
gain the glory of the peak.

Often, of course, the words of others, which I have dragged squalling
into my oration like someone else's children, have little substance of their
own, but take their authority from the famous, and often imposing, figure
of their father. God's word frequently walks lamely enough for the ordinary
man to claim it. Because I say so, Zeus thunders. The orders come from me,
the Führer screams. It is not the meaning and weight and arrangement—the
argument—of the words themselves which persuades. The Sibyl's riddles, the
Oracles' ambiguities, say: Believe me, because I am in touch with divinity.
The highly organized harangues of the politicians say: Believe me, because I
can give you what you want, and tell you what you want to hear; my tongue
shall lick your ear. The carefully measured considerations of the philosopher
say: Believe me, because I am wise; but can the philosopher be wise before his
words are? and worse, where in those words can we find the Forms? where is
the deep resemblance in these syllables which will spur us to recall and spell
out the unspellable Ideas? The well-wrought verses of the poet, too—the
periods of the orator, the sophist's sleights of speech—each says: Believe me
because I am clever, resonant, beautiful; but the beauty of any such display
of talent, and exercise of skill, for Plato, rests on whether its eloquence stirs

others to theirs; and because the beauty of the truly Beautiful depends on whether it manages to be an adequate manifestation of the ultimate Good at which Truth aims.

The great value of the Platonic myths has never been, it seems to me, the support they give to certain tenets of Plato's philosophy, or their ability to float us over difficulties like benign clouds; but the conviction they create of being true *somewhere,* as if the truth were a bee in a black bag: you can hear it; you know that it's there; but it certainly isn't easy to find; furthermore, it may sting if you succeed.

We are fallen angels, Plato tells us; we were once winged, and now we live in the sty of our bodies, and move these bodies to and fro, restless as caged bears, aimless and confined. We must regrow those wings, harness our two horses, and climb the heavens in a path trod flat by the chariots of the gods: turn, as the soul of the world itself turns, until we can see beyond the bounds and body of the earth, with its neighboring stars and local sky, into that space which holds the unextended formulas of Being. Then, drawn there by its winged steeds, its base nature in harness with its best, the soul sees the unseeable. These horses are the emblems of our organs of regeneration. The sight of Beauty feeds them. Certainly, the image of winged phalli is not uncommon in Greek iconography.* In the *Theaetetus,* "seeing" is described as a kind of intercourse in which emanations from the eye and the object intermingle to give birth to twins: the object becomes white, for example, while the eye is filled with "seeing." The imagery of the cave in the *Republic* is explicitly sexual, as is the nearly pornographic account of the union of the soul with the idea of beauty embodied in a boy which we receive in the *Phaedrus.* The soul, to fulfill the functions which Plato's metaphors have imagined for it, must be hermaphroditic. It is phallic in its responses to beauty, becoming engorged, rising, pursuing its object; and in its failures, too, flaccidly falling. But it is female at that point when the Forms fertilize the soul. What is brought to birth in Meno or in Theaetetus, later, is the Ideas which have been laid there by their earlier intercourse with a beauty beyond the stars. The black horse—the dark unruly phallus—desires, if we may so speak, to unite with the body, to enter it and there to realize its seedful dreams; whereas the pale phallus seeks to reproduce creatively, by bringing the Forms into their full fruition in the mind.

In any case, the favored sense is sight. The ear does not replace the eye

* K. J. Dover, in *Greek Homosexuality* (Cambridge, Mass.: Harvard University Press, 1978), reproduces a vase (R 414) on which a woman is shown carrying a penis in the form of a bird, and a pitcher (R 259) depicts a horse whose head becomes penile. Dover discusses them on p. 133. Many of the penises on these vases have eyes (R 414, B 370, for instance).

at any point or passage. We do not sniff eternity or touch the Forms as if they were megaliths, and if they nourish us, it is with the lover's eye that we devour them. So that when our wings wither like Icarus's, close to the sun, and we fall to earth again; and when grass grows over everything we know as though it were now in a grave; the soul retains the mark, the scar, the image of what it has seen: not in a set of sentences, not in sounds sent like a message from outer space; but somehow in something like a perception. . . . Oh, mental, to be sure, not colored in, not an outline either, yet *visual:* a memory of the mind's eye.

Before we suppose that Plato has simply fallen prey to a figure of speech, and is here in no better shape than the poets to fight his way past appearance, we must recall two important points. First, as we moved through that famous classification of realities called "the divided line" in the *Republic,* we systematically rubbed out materiality, not in the direction of images, shadows, reflections, and illusions, which is the downward turning point of Things, but in the direction of the abstracted outline of objects, arriving finally at the drawings which engross the geometer: triangles, circles, squares; that is, we took away from the visual everything we dared to, and left only those minimal qualities behind which were yet necessary to keep the thing *in sight.* The taste and sound and touch and smell and inner warmth and secret kinesis of things have no representations at all in mathematics. We see the fingers we count on, the pebbles we count with, the rebus we arrange, the drawings we place upon the ground or upon the page. Second, however, and on the other side, we must remember that when we "see" the Forms, we simply grasp systems of internal relations, and nowhere in the world of actual sight do we see those either.

It is not with the eye that we speak what we have seen, and if our chief receptive action is the mind's gaze, our chief transmitting organ is the silent tongue of thought. Seeing in this sense / saying in this sense: both blind, both mute, for when in my favorite daydream I am recollecting how you looked that sunny afternoon, your body like a streak of light across the bed, what am I seeing? what is the image I have thrown upon that blackboard on the back of the lid? and when I attempt to describe the reflections of the flower stems, the way the water became green when they were thrust in the vases, what gets uttered so it can be heard outside the hall of the head?

The ladder we are called upon to climb in the *Symposium* is composed of aggressively heteronomous rungs, so that, again, we shall be able to see what all lovely things have in common, whether we are considering a body or a body of laws, a theorem or a theory; whether we are casting our eyes upon a noble youth, or have paused—thunderstruck—on the threshold of perfect Beauty; because we shall have seen a common unity through a lens of difference, inasmuch as it is precisely the differences between philosophical systems of thought, for instance, and the poets' hymns and songs, between a pair of well-appointed breasts or youthful buttocks and the Palladian design of a pantheon, which pull the concealing flesh away to leave the bones. And the adaptation of parts to a purpose, the harmony of elements which properly proportion a whole, the idea of order as it disposes itself in the Idea of Order itself—none of these things, while visible, can ever be directly seen. Beauty is not present *to* sight, but it is always available *in* it. The natural world is beautiful in this sense because, as the *Timaeus* tells us, it is the purest, most perfect and complete, *qualitative expression of quantitative law.*

When Ideas and things separate, the word is torn in two. The Platonist drives the referent of any term—the water jug, the wagon, the motorcycle—away from its meaning, its narrow definition as well as all its additional and more elusive senses. And that wicked black horse, like materialists, realists, sophists everywhere (as Plato would suppose), wants only the sweet grass in the meadow, the lively frolic, the nuzzle, the mare in heat, and would make the word swerve to serve them, conjure them up, combine; whereas the idealist, who rides the white horse if he does not wear the white hat, moves into the world of meaning like a tramp into a rich flat; there is nothing for the beggar here; here is calm connection, clean towels, fresh sheets, and wholesome sense.

Consider the task of the Demiurge, the shaping principle which Plato calls on to create the world in his dialogue the *Timaeus.* The Demiurge must mold a referent to resemble an Idea; he must implement laws with instances; he must make a form which expresses a formula—a midge, a monster, a mother-in-law, inconsolable motion—which mimics its meaning, the principle of its being; but he must do so by *working around the word;* the word is the absent guest; it is hiding out somewhere (in the soul, as I'll suggest), and there does not at first appear, on the *Phaedrus*'s extensive list of words spoken, borrowed, recited, or remembered, or among those composed, purchased, or performed, anywhere any one resembling the word of God, whose elemental utterance stilled chaos and brought light.

In Genesis we are nowhere told whether God shouted as the King will in *Hamlet,* whether he pleaded, whispered, hissed, or calmly commanded, or whether he created the word "light" by his act of uttering it; whether there was already a divine language for God to draw upon, although Adam appears to have made up the names he confers upon the animals. In any case, in this myth at least, the word preceded the world. It is clear in this case, too, that the creative power of the word lay not in itself, but in the authority of the voice which gave it life, for you or I might have said the same thing, and deep night and chaos would have gone on calmly troubling the void; unless—and here is a thought—unless it was that any creature (you or I or the snake itself) who said the first word would, by that drawing of an imprisoned sword from its tree, its stone, like a sound drawn out of silence, have become King, Creator, Overlord.

Plato's Demiurge translated the eternal Forms into colorful, scented, and sounding things; he spun a triangle to create a cone, and spun a cone to shape a sphere; however, the Demiurge did not render Reality in words. He was a sculptor, a builder, an architect, if you like, but not a poet, not a philosopher. And his task was not less than impossible if the relation between Reality and the image he was to make of it was supposed to be one of resemblance. How could he model the world of Becoming and base it on Being that way? How could he picture permanence in change, drag an Idea down into the dirt and retain anything of its pristine features, its former splendor, its generality? The Demiurge could only represent with exactitude the numbers of things, because the three members of a lovers' triangle, the Three Bears, the three persons of the Trinity, the three coins in the fountain, all embody the Idea of the number three quite perfectly. Three turtledoves do not roughly approximate or simply imitate three, they *are* three and therefore one more than a pair. But the doves multiply in a bird's way; they cannot be factored; they cannot be calmly subtracted from five gold rings in order to reach two French hens as a remainder.

Suppose, though, that we wanted to use three items of anything to represent, not three, but perhaps plurality in general; that we wanted to move from One and Two to Many. How soon would we recognize that ⚱⚱⚱ is Egyptian for "flood"; that is, heaven + <u>three</u> water jugs? or that 〰〰〰 is water, or one wave × three? or that ʃʃʃ is hair; or one hair in triplicate? Finally, how readily will we figure out that / / / (three slanted strokes) is the sign of any plurality?* And if we follow a Pythagorean pattern, how much more rapidly do our resemblances disappear to leave us puzzled:

| ● ● (four pebbles) | ⣿ (a square) | (the no. 4) = | (the idea) |
| ● ● | = ⣿ | = 4 | **JUSTICE** |

So, as the soul passes on its journey between the rude world below and the polished Forms above, it has to take a peek in both directions, as Plato suggests: "[Our] understanding is a recollection of those things which our

* Karl Menninger, *Number Words and Number Symbols: A Cultural History of Numbers* (Cambridge, Mass.: MIT Press, 1969), p. 17.

soul beheld aforetime as they journeyed with their god, looking down upon the things which now we suppose to be, and gazing up to that which truly is" (*Phaedrus*, 249c, Hackforth's translation). With the left eye the charioteer must look where the black beast is pulling it, and see, for instance, injustice down there like jaundice in a pale face; then, with his right eye, he must look past the powerful shoulders of the white horse to where the Idea of Injustice lies like a gleaming shadow among Harmony, Wholeness, Order, and their Negation. He should not be surprised at seeing that shadow there either, because the knowledge of any evil is a necessary thing, and an important good. The charioteer must match heaven's own bedstead with the bed he will shortly lie in, because only in that way can his sagging canvas cot recall to his mind the true notions of Rest and Recumbency which go some distance to define it. And if that is the case with the Demiurge's impeccable designs—that they cannot resemble the truth sufficiently to lead us alone from portrait to model; that, as fine and well intentioned as he is, the Demiurge cannot paint, say, Woman well enough so we would know her without a name affixed to her fig leaf—then in what worse case do we find ourselves when we describe the fair sex in words—ah, always so inadequately, so unfairly!—for in what way does "Woman" resemble women? Even if Plato's metaphor is ultimately inexplicable—that we "see" both Being and Becoming at the same time—he knew words well enough not to choose *them*. Plato never suggests that we read Reality in the bright light of the Good. He always insists that we *see* it; perhaps as I say I see some computations. I ask my accountant, "Let's see your results," or "Would you look over these figures?" Yet if the Forms are formulas made of figures (and therefore easy to "see"), where is the facilitating resemblance between H_2O and water, or 5,280 and a mile? How do I get, on any mimetic basis, from one to the other?

Plato has apparently provided us with three methods for gaining knowledge of the Forms. The first requires that we separate the influence of the body and lower parts of the soul upon reason, for by concentrating upon the least sensuously contaminated subjects, like geometry and mathematics, we shall be able to reason clearly, free from the prejudices of perception and the biases of desire. The second suggests that we use the visual world to remind us about what we saw on our journey to the invisible one; that we match phenomenon and Form as we once—walleyed—beheld them—together like ill-assorted twins. Finally, we should attempt to achieve accurate definitions of things (and this is the method which seems to require words) by careful collection and the formation of genres, along with the division of each collection by means of specific differences into enduring species. As we do so, we must arrive, we might suppose, at those combinations of words which lie nearest the signs made in the soul by the Forms. These three methods are not exclusive, of course, and they could be combined, or be otherwise necessary or helpful to one another.

One and the same vocabulary, as far as its sounds and marks are concerned, will conceal this double reference to Being and Becoming. On the one hand, the word "woman" will refer to Franny and Helen and Olga and Ruth, whose forms merely imitate the divine, and, on the other, it will designate an Idea whose embrace is even more to be desired; so, if I dare to add a line or two to the majestic myth that Plato has given us in the *Phaedrus,* I should simply say that as we rode higher and higher behind our horses in the van of the gods, and saw to one side of us, as though resting at the base of a great cliff, the upturned face of the world—perfumed, rouged, and screaming—while on the other side, in a relentless glare of clarity which is the look of the Good, appeared the timelessly tiered figures of the Forms; and again, as we advanced as it were along this Pythagorean fold between meaning and things, substantial shadow and insubstantial substance, we drew a line in language from one to the other: "horse," "cloud," "cavern," "firmament," "justice," "desire," we sang as we rode: "peace," "perimeter," "cabbage," "cube." From that time on our words, as if drawn by those harsh or handsome horses, sink down in the direction of things and their disconnections, to pornograph among the passions, or they rise as if winged toward meanings, ideas, regions of pure relation. (See diagram.)

Is it not for this reason that the orations of the sophists, apparently employing terms like "youth" and "love" and "desire" and "pleasure" just as Socrates would have to if he spoke on the same subject (for no one has a lien on a word), are speeches which lie as low as valleys and slowly fill with fog? They intend to speak the same lubricious lingo as their listeners, for their

The Pythagorean Double Triangle of Ten.
One triangle is the false reflection of the other.

listeners have damp souls, damp as drains, and they long to be turned in the direction of denotation, as if the word were a wind directed at the world, and they were a vane.

Throughout the dialogue, Plato has distinguished words from words, though their shells seem the same: "love" in the speech of Lysias, "love" again in Socrates's mock argument on the same theme, "love" once more in his mighty oration, and so on. Words about love are quoted, improvised, read, analyzed, scorned. Socrates speaks the word sometimes as though inspired, as though he were lending his breath to another spirit. He also uses it, and his discourse about it, to reach the ultimately wordless and wholly unutterable.

"Love," as it rests on the bright side of the soul, signifies the upward displacement of desire toward a longing for knowledge, for a reunion with the Forms. In this condition, we are like a youth or a young woman in search of our heavenly bride or bridegroom. Such an elevated word must be spoken, for who could imagine that, on the soul's journey, holding those reins, controlling those contrary horses, we have taken along a gooseneck lamp, a desk, and an ink horn? Of course, the soul has no one to speak to but itself, in the beginning. The flight of the Alone, as Plotinus represents it, is of the Alone to the Alone. Correspondingly unpicturable is the reflection of the Ideas within the silent mirror of the self.

So at the center of the spirit is the unvoiced word, the living word of reason perhaps, if you are a Platonist, but it is the rooted word, in any case, the early word, the first word, the word as worm. These original words come from, and have their home in, the realm of Forms, for they were sounded in sight of them, as though by a trumpet; yet we must not forget that their early roots (as Plato himself rather wildly suggests) grow in both directions. Although the image of the charioteer divides our task in three, it is not an entirely accurate picture of the Platonic soul (that great conception which I have turned into a metaphor for the word and its true home), because, of its three faculties, two draw us in the direction of the world, and the one representing reason must then enlist the energies and perceptions of both the other two to do its business. In the lower depths are the instincts, the hungers, the mouth, the gut, the penetrating penis; at the middle level lies sensation—sight, smell, and so on—pleasure, pain, passion, and whatever credit the Greeks gave to the idea of the will. Neither can be called white.

Nor would any of the soul's faculties recognize, in the word "love" alone, as a sound, any resemblance to either its idea or its condition, but only to "glove" and "shove" and other sounds, equally senseless and arbitrary; nor will *"lieben"* bring us any closer to its object. Love has no phonemes, no spelling, no pronunciation, only stages, disappointments, and degrees. Love is the transformation of a reproductive energy, and that notion, now that it has found a word like "love" (although its English body is a short one and without any special distinction—suppose the word for this mostly misguided exhilaration were "ululation" instead, or "cornucopia," or "Ohio"?), can be seduced into other occupations, stolen, put in compromising contexts, made to say the opposite of what it was meant to mean.

When lust uses the language, or when our passions speak urgently and plainly, the meaning of "love" is first phallic and engorged, then moody and romantic. Thus there are at least three root meanings of "love" (and three for almost every word and every discourse), one for each division of the soul. At least that is one kind of cut through things, one kind of classification. Two of these "loves," as I've said, look down at the world the way the dark horse does, at objects of sense, at acts of consummation; they celebrate the referent; the one remaining looks up at the bodiless copulations of the verb "to be"—toward the abstract, the purely inferential, the eternal. Two of these "loves" aim at reproducing their likeness in their partners: the first father sees his image reflected in his son; the second sees himself reflected in the objects his infatuation has created; while the third brings Beauty to birth in Beauty, in theory realizes yet another theory. One copulates, one courts and caresses, one contemplates. That is yet another cut, another kind of classification.

In any case, all three sources of the word are ours, and reflect our specific condition, because it is upon that curtained internal stage that the great debate between reason and the passions, the body and the mind, between things and their meanings, begins. Here, no one can make a speech in your place. Here, no words have been hired for the season. The speakers refuse to give up their rights. And there are more than a few of us, I suspect, who have been repeatedly dismayed by our spirit's petty divisions, the crossness of our purposes, the shameful politics played by all the parties in the kingdom of the ego. What shall the "I" who represents us mean when it makes its noises, when it whispers "I love you"? Will we have a clue we can regard with confidence if the object of our endearments is an enterprise? a doctrine? a bible? a boy? No wonder Socrates is fearful that we shall freeze our meaning, end the distressing debate with a blow that breaks the argument. At one moment we believe our beloved must be good and true because we desire her so (and there are some philosophers, like Hobbes, who think that all our tunes are played in this key); at another moment, however, our desires languish behind our controlling passion like a courtly lover, our penis all poem, as we look longingly up at the pedestal where our fair one stands, as cold and polished on her stone as though carved by Canova, and as worthy of worship. In Lysias's speech, which Phaedrus recites for us, desire enlists reason to gain its ends and pushes passion aside like dirt beneath a broom. In Socrates's mocking rejoinder, passion hides itself behind desire in order to make convincing a similar case; but in the famous final oration of Socrates (and it is fully an "oration"), energy and feeling are joined to order and idea to produce a metaphysical climax not entirely lacking its own passionate outcry and genital spasm. Here, the mind cares; the mind comes.

The word is like the soul itself, that intermediary thing which moves between the realms of Being and Becoming; and if my additions to the myth are not altogether unseemly, then it will be the lower parts of the *logos* as well as the *psyche* that remember the world, and the upper one which gazes on or connects itself to the Forms; and unless these separate aspects of ourselves and our language speak to one another, respond to one another, there will be no match of "thing" to the Form it is said to resemble, no string will stretch from significance to subject, for I argued that such resemblance could not be read from the thing itself, nor predicted from the Form in its featureless silence.

Lust, romantic attachment, and intellectual dedication have traveled together in that company of the gods, and that is how they come to know the nature of their rivalry. Moreover, only they can speak to one another with any chance of success, since it is indeed true that, although they use the same marks, they do not use the same meanings. There are at least three languages in any language, as I've said. And only when reason leads do the words have energy, passion, and profundity in the right proportion. Only when, we might say, paraphrasing Plato, each tongue does its own job well, and the word is borne along equally, but in good order, by all of them, has the philosopher become a proper poet; one whom, alone, we will allow to sing of the immortal Forms as Plato has.

Words which I speak to you, if you are to remember them, must be taken more deeply into the self than those which I write down, and which you can keep about your person like your tobacco, ticket stubs, or pipe. The spoken word can be questioned, because behind it there is a speaker. The spoken word is alive in a context of life: the breath, the pause, the intonation, the look of the mouth, the eye, the posture of the body, gestures of arm and tilt of head—all contribute to its meaning, confirm its ownership. The written word emasculates memory—Plato's worries on this score have proved to be correct—and the written word which is no longer a surrogate for the real one—first voiced to the self and then to the world—is a murderer of meaning. Technical terms, jargon, diagrams, the Latin names of plants, Germanic obfuscation: none of these belongs to the discourse of the soul.

Furthermore, the written word comes forward as the completion of a process, not as the process itself. It quietly omits the context of composition, of discovery. It admits no doubts, no alterations, no unmeant obscurities. A field of rejected alternatives lies invisibly about the chosen word or phrase like dead around the boy who still holds the standard, but we don't realize a battle has taken place; that blood has been shed, ideas denied, feelings changed, accidents allowed to stand; no, the completed sentence stretches itself out in the sun with ease and assurance: its figure is full, even fulsome; it already has a tan. And when many completed sentences lie together to form a treatise or a novel whose composition took many years, and went on in spite of illness, through love affairs, bankruptcy, and divorce, *they*—these sentences—will still pretend that the same author authored all of them; that they came, as they are printed, simultaneously into being; that their source was as ceaselessly constant and continuous as π. The completed text cannot be questioned and makes no reply, yet it invites overthrow; it calls for interpretation the way a stalled motorist might innocently call on a mugger or a rapist for help; and here comes the critic, eager to replace whatever words he finds in front of him with his own, and the mind that made them with his own mind, too, concealing every evidence of creativity with his own conceit. Perhaps, grown bolder, greedier, more desperate, he will try to take the work away from its feckless writer by insisting that a text is actually a pastiche of quotation, a piece of systematic plagiarism, and the writer merely a sluice through which language streams.* He will argue that the text's only home and true destination is the reader, which is a little like asserting that the true home of the bathwater is the drain, when one means only that "down the drain" is what will become of it.

Indeed, the spoken word is addressed to someone. I can see my words touch the thought, the feelings, of another. These words were made for *you,* shaped on this occasion for *your* sake, never again to be used; whereas the printed word is like a shoe which is supposed to fit every foot in society like an elastic sock. The written word repeats itself as woodenly as any signboard; it addresses itself to "whomever," and even when it finds itself in a private letter, the word can be worse than overheard: it can be stolen, reproduced, counterfeited, defaced, defamed.

The expression "to write something down" suggests a descent of thought into the fingers whose movements immediately falsify it. Consider what happens when the Form for the Triangle is displayed in a diagram: $\triangle$. This triangle receives an extension it didn't have before, because the Form Triangle is not triangular; it is not spread out in space like a piece of breakfast toast: yet

---

* For more on this point, see the final essay in this volume, "The Death of the Author."

how many schoolchildren still think that these figures are triangles through and through, and calculate each hypotenuse as if they were measuring the length of a giraffe's neck. Yet further off from any element of imitation is the word itself. Similarly, the factors of a number like 8, when written out $(2 \times 2 \times 2 \,\&\, 8 \times 1)$, must stand in line like customers at a ticket window, and an idea—complex and total and together—finds its elements laid out like the parts list for a bicycle.

Plato clearly foresaw what would happen when doctrines of depth, subtlety, and importance went abroad as innocent print. I once heard a drunk in a college tavern recite a simple and beautiful poem of Blake's. It had no home in that slack, wet mouth. And the subtleties of subtle texts are immediately ignored; the complexities are erased by reviewers who regard them irascibly, and importance is equated with popularity.*

Of course, when I have to tell you orally what I think and mean, I cannot think, perhaps, as profoundly, or simultaneously mean as much; but I shall have to be clearer if not clear; I shall never be able to say, "let x," or utter an arrogant *"aufgehoben,"* or commit an act of narratology.

What Plato did not foresee, quite, was the degree to which the written word might become as anonymous as an assassin; how it might establish a vast industry; how words would appear along roadways and on walls and the sides of buildings, not written, but *posted,* and addressed to whoever chanced to be passing. Words are stuck on bumpers, stenciled across chests so they can bounce with the breasts. He could not have imagined the multiplication of the written word, the printed word, the printout word, the painted word, the filmed and photographed word, the Day-Glo, lit-up word, the sky-written word, the repealed, and stricken, and canceled, and censored, and snipped-up, crossworded word either, and its consequent devaluation, or the total trivialization of speech and conversation in addition.

Roland Barthes celebrates the death of the author—another little god gone—by quoting a passage from *Sarrasine* to support his claim, and it bears repeating because it also supports mine.[†] Balzac is commenting on the appearance of a castrato disguised as a woman: "This was woman herself, with her sudden fears, her irrational whims, her instinctive worries,

---

* "Beware," Plato tells Dionysios in the *Second Letter,* "lest these doctrines fall among the ignorant. For there is hardly anything, I believe, that sounds more absurd to the vulgar or, on the other hand, more admirable and inspired to men of fine disposition" (314a). Paul Friedländer is excellent on this entire issue, especially in chapter 5, "The Written Work," of *Plato: An Introduction,* pp. 108–25.

† I discuss Barthes, Balzac, and *Sarrasine* at greater length in the essay which follows this one, "The Death of the Author."

her impetuous boldness, her fussings, and her delicious sensibility." Barthes asserts that this sentence has no particular source or origin, no voice, and he is surely right. The castrato, of course, must exhibit these commonplaces in his own person, otherwise he will not appear to be the "real" thing—woman herself—for the real real thing in such a society is seldom seen. Certainly, a sentence of such blatantly platitudinous blather has no "author" behind it, unless, as Barthes seems to think, cliché can hold a Bic. But he is not dismayed by this anonymity; rather, for him "writing is the destruction of every voice, of every point of origin." Such a possibility worried Plato, whose practice in prose shows us the way to avoid it, but it did not worry many of the sophists, who encouraged the sale of words like alligator shirts, nor does it bother many of them now, who embrace the individual, and the individuated sentence, only to crush its pretense to humanity, its singular style, and return it in anonymous pieces to the collectivity—itself a word almost too ugly to utter. An edict can be signed by some "authority" who thereby stands behind it and takes responsibility for it, but a style stands within every syllable and says: I have imagined this; believed this; thought this; and so I have put myself and my mark on it.

This voice, these authors, the idea of the individual, the distinct value of consciousness are all creatures of capitalism, according to Barthes, which strikes me as an odd thought, even for a falsehood, since it was the Greeks who created the soul, discovered the self, ennobled men, and sought a distinctly human good. But facts are the pets of the positivists, those descendants of the evil Enlightenment (who themselves are descendants of the Greeks). Facts bark but will not bite—not to worry—though facts will shed on the sofa, sometimes piss elsewhere than their pan. It seems that facts have foregone the French for the time being, gone out of style along with Reason. Truth with an enlarged initial, Truth (the systematic side of the sentence, if facts are stamped on the other), Truth to the ancient Idealists (who are Capitalists to the core, one must suppose), to them Truth was merely a god to be sought out and reverenced, and not, as it was for the sophists, an annoying inconvenience.

In the small myth in which Plato expresses his reservations about writing, the disadvantages he cites are certainly real and correct, as far as they go; but writing, as I've mentioned, has freed the mind (as it did Plato's) to consider far more complex matters than it ever could while operating orally, and if it has hastened the atrophy of our memory, it has saved us the trouble of holding in our head much that was not worth holding there.

Although the written and the printed word greatly impersonalize—indeed, standardize—our verbal tokens, they also objectify language, and

882 THE WILLIAM H. GASS READER

hence the thoughts and feelings it contains, in an important way. Because what is written is always "out there"; because it is public and comparatively permanent and can be examined by many at relatively the same level of access and privilege; it is far easier to hold people to what they have said, and to expect a higher standard of care to be set, because, although the author is not present in the moment to produce the text, he is not dead (unless he is a committee, a bureau, an anonymous source, a corporate "spokesperson," an advertising agency). Print is a medium which encourages a greater scrupulosity of expression, and permits more refinement of idea, than the purely spoken (unless it is employed by a committee, a bureau, an anonymous source, a corporate "spokesperson," an advertising agency, a member of Congress). Of necessity, style becomes increasingly individual as the medium becomes a largely inexpressive and neutral one (unless it is employed by a committee, a bureau, an anonymous source, a corporate "spokesperson," an advertising agency, a member of Congress, a general of the army; then the medium's inexpressive and neutral qualities are exploited). It is the oral tradition which had to employ a shortened vocabulary, standardized epithets, and other mnemonic devices which encouraged its own kind of anonymity. The writer must make up for the loss of the spoken context, of the meaningful emotional environment of the uttered word, by emphasizing, and bringing under control, the few physical elements left. Above all, the written word must be so set down that it rises up immediately in its readers to the level of the ear, and becomes a vital presence in their consciousness. It asks, that is, to be performed; to be returned to the world of orality it came from; it asks to be said, to be sung.

Imagine that I was drawn to your body as a lover is drawn; then you would see that when I touch you I want it to carry my love to your heart; but that means that my feelings must be allowed to flow into my fingers; and that means that you must allow my finger to move along your nerves like a voice within a wire; then the sound of your heart will be, as well, the sound of my voice, and the sound of my voice—not as simple sound, not because it's mine, and not because my accent is so wondrously unique, but because it contains the touch of the true word—will circulate as one blood between us. This is what honest oratory, this is what poetry, is all about.

Even if our doubts about the existence of the Forms were multiple and enormous (as mine are), there is, unquestionably, an inner speech, a speech which represents our consciousness as it goes babbling on, and this internal talk cannot be replaced by writing. We may not be able to find our way past the last word to reach a wordless realm, as Plato desires us to do, but if we fail, we shall very likely find ourselves left with the spoken word as the only medium of real thought, although a few diagrams or mental pictures may sometimes supplement it, and machines make easy many wearisome computations. However rapidly our fingers move as we type our thoughts immediately into some machine, they were in unwritten form first, and will always be so.

Finally, the language we learn is a spoken one. It is speech which contains all our childhood fantasies, all our primitive and original impulses, our horror shows, our "mother-meanings," and whatever trips past the Forms we may have taken. And it is the sound of these early words, in the total context of their production, which gives them their emotional power, and connects them so closely with our basic desires.* The dark horse is stabled in the child. So the poet, the rhetorician, the philosopher, who thinks of a page as merely a page, and not as a field for the voice; who considers print to be simply print, and does not notice the notes it forms; whose style is disheveled and overcharged with energy or overrun with feeling, or whose frigid and compulsive orderings make the mouth dry; the author who is satisfied to *see* his words, as though at a distance like sheep on a hillside, and not as concepts coasting like clouds across his consciousness—such a writer will never enter, touch, or move the soul; never fill us with the feeling that he's seen the Forms, whether or not there are any; never give us that ride up the hill of heaven as Plato has, or the sense that in accepting his words we are accepting a vision.

The Kenyon Review, 1984
Published in *Habitations of the Word,* 1984

* I have argued this point in the preceding essay in this volume, "The Soul Inside the Sentence." Other aspects of this question, which sometimes seems the single subject of the volume, are examined in "On Talking to Oneself" in *Habitations of the Word* (New York: Alfred A. Knopf, 1984) and "On Reading to Oneself" (page 46).

The Death of the Author

Popular wisdom warns us that we frequently substitute the wish for the deed, and when, in 1968, Roland Barthes announced the death of the author, he was actually calling for it.* Nor did Roland Barthes himself sign up for suicide, but wrote his way into the College of France, where he performed volte-faces for an admiring audience.†

Many of the observations that Barthes makes in his celebrated essay are suggestive, opportune, and even correct; but none of them quite drives home the stake. The reasons for this are complex. The idea of the death of the author does not match the idea of the death of god as perfectly as the current members of this faith may suppose, because we know—as they know—that there *are* authors; and we know—as they know—there *are no* gods. The death of the author is not an ordinary demise, nor is it simply the departure of belief, like an exotic visitor from the East, from the minds of the masses. The two expressions are metaphors which are the reverse of one another. The death of god represents not only the realization that gods have never existed, but the contention that such a belief is no longer even irrationally possible: that neither reason nor the taste and temper of the times can condone it. The belief lingers on, of course, but it does so like astrology or a faith in a flat earth—in worse case than a neurotic symptom, no longer even *à la mode*. The death of the author, on the other hand, signifies a decline in authority, in theological power, as if Zeus were stripped of his thunderbolts and swans, perhaps residing on Olympus still, but now living in a camper and cooking with propane. He *is,* but he is no longer a god.

* "The Death of the Author," in *Image, Music, Text,* essays selected, edited, and translated by Stephen Heath (New York: Hill and Wang, 1977), pp. 142–48.

† Jonathan Culler, *Roland Barthes* (New York: Oxford University Press, 1983), p. 119.

Barthes is careful to point out the theological overtones of his announcement.* Deities are in the business of design; they order oftener than generals; the robes the painters put them in are juridical. God handed down the tablets of the law to Moses; and Jane Austen or Harriet Beecher Stowe hands down texts to us. While it is by no means necessary to put the author's powers and responsibilities in religious terms, Beckett's schoolboy copybooks are treated like tablets, too, and attract the scribes and the pharisees as though they'd been brought from a mountain. When John Crowe Ransom, in clearly secular language, praises Milton's "Lycidas" as "a poem nearly anonymous," he means to applaud the degree to which Milton has freed the poem from its poet, and consequently from the danger of certain legal difficulties.

> Anonymity, of some real if not literal sort, is a condition of poetry. A good poem, even if it is signed with a full and well-known name, intends as a work of art to lose the identity of the author; that is, it means to represent him not actualized, like an eye-witness testifying in court and held strictly by zealous counsel to the point at issue, but freed from his juridical or prose self and taking an ideal or fictitious personality; otherwise his evidence amounts the less to poetry.†

In this case, the disappearance of the author coincides with his arrogance, his overbearing presence. Joyce has Stephen Dedalus state the aim exactly:

> The personality of the artist, at first a cry or a cadence or a mood and then a fluid and lambent narrative, finally refines itself out of existence, impersonalizes itself, so to speak. The esthetic image in the dramatic form is life purified in and reprojected from the human imagination. The mystery of esthetic, like that of material creation, is accomplished. The artist, like the God of creation, remains within or behind or beyond or above his handiwork, invisible, refined out of existence, indifferent, paring his fingernails.‡

---

* "The Death of the Author," p. 149.

† "A Poem Nearly Anonymous," by John Crowe Ransom, in his collection of essays, *The World's Body* (New York: Charles Scribner's Sons, 1938), p. 2.

‡ Stephen says this during a one-sided conversation with Lynch in the middle of the final chapter of *A Portrait of the Artist as a Young Man.* Lynch shortly follows this with the wry joke that God must have hidden Himself after perpetrating Ireland.

The dramatist's curtained disappearance is not complete enough for Barthes. He knows that *"Madame Bovary—c'est moi!"* remains true despite Flaubert's celebrated detachment. He knows how the deity of tradition took delight in concealing Himself. Hunt as hard as you cared to, he could easily elude you if he wished. Still, such difficulties did not dampen the desire of the faithful to find him, or weaken in any way their belief that he was there. Zeus may have hidden his passion in the shape of a swan, but we are not obliged to believe that Leda felt simply some feathers. Circumstances have kept Shakespeare's life a secret from us, yet he has been hunted like a criminal. In volume after volume, his unknown character is cleverly constructed like a ship in a bottle. So Roland Barthes wishes to slay a spirit, dispel an aura. It is the demise of just that confident, coldly overbearing creator—that so palpably erased and disdainfully imperial person of the artist—that he longs for.

It is apparent in the quotation from Joyce that when the work of writing has been done, the essential artistic task is over. The freedom from himself which the artist has given to his composition is the indifferent freedom of the Rilkean *Dinge,* an object which exists like a tree, a hat, or a stream, and like the stream scarcely needs canoes or campers to complete it; yet it is a thing whose modulated surfaces betray the consciousness it contains, and which we read, as we read words, to find the hand, the arm, the head, the voice, the self which is shaping them, which is arranging those surfaces—this second skin—to reflect an inside sun, and reveal the climate of an inner life. In the old theological mode, we thought to find God either through His revelations in sacred Scripture or by studying what was thought to be His other great work of symbolization—the world; we applied ourselves, that is, to natural or to revealed religion. Nowadays, when the artist deliberately disappears, he may wish it to be thought that his work "just came about" naturally; grew the way crystals collect to create a flake of snow, perhaps, or more slowly, as deltas silt, or suddenly, the way islands rise up calamitously out of the sea; or, more ideally, in the manner in which a mollusk exudes a chamber about itself, quietly from within, brooding as the old gods did upon a basin of dark cloud and wind perhaps, or with a cluck now and then like a errant clock, intuitively shaping a shell. In this case, when the artist hides, it is in order to represent skill as instinct, intellect as reflex, choice as necessity, labor as slumberous ease.

Valéry writes:

Perhaps what we call *perfection* in art (which all do not strive for and some disdain) is only a sense of desiring or finding in a human work the sureness of execution, the inner necessity, the indissoluble bond between form and material that are revealed to us by the humblest of shells.*

For Joyce, of course, this writing from which its designer—the deity—disappears seems authorless because there is no book to weigh in one's hands, no print, no page, no poet's voice: it is *performed;* the theater buries the text inside the bodies of its actors, where their organs are. But we are also aware of the similarly scenic art of Henry James, of his effaced narrators and substitute selves, of various Ishmaels and many Marlowes, or of those poems which appear on parchmented pages as though scratched there by creatures long extinct.

Calm covers the peaks.
Among the treetops
a breath hangs like a leaf.
In the deep woods
birdsong sleeps.
At the foot of hills
slopes find their peace.
Be patient. Wait.
Soon, you, too, will cease.†

Richardson slips onto the title page of *Clarissa Harlowe* disguised as S. Richardson, the simple printer who has collected and edited the letters which constitute her unhappy history; Defoe suggests that Moll Flanders is the pseudonym of a well-known lady who tells her somewhat unwholesome story in his book; *Gulliver's Travels* is introduced by one Richard Sympson, an "ancient and intimate friend" of the author, and the man into whose economizing hands these papers have fallen (he tells us he's cut out dull stretches of seafaring stuff); while *The History of Henry Esmond* is brought before us by that late Virginia gentleman's daughter, Rachel Esmond Warrington, now, alas, a widow. These novels have very ostensible authors, to be sure, but they are artificial ones, surrogate pens or "dildos." Still, no one will imagine that Defoe or Swift or Thackeray felt that by placing these fictions in front of himself he was risking anonymity. A dildo is the discarded part of a dream.

Actually, a volume of letters, however modestly brought before the public,

---

* Paul Valéry, "Man and the Seashell," trans. Ralph Manheim, in vol. 13, *Aesthetics,* of *The Collected Works in English* (New York: Pantheon, 1962), p. 27.

† Adapted from Goethe.

inordinately multiplies "authors," whose names appear, we suppose, at the end of every communication. These artful dodges (and it would be absurdly awful if they fooled anyone) strengthen the concepts of source and voice and purpose, control and occasion, which are central to the notion of a commanding creator, precisely because they call them into playful question. Thackeray pretends not to be responsible for *The History of Henry Esmond,* neither for writing it nor for bringing it to public notice, but Thackeray intends to accept all praise and moneys due.

A few writers like us to believe that they are simply telling a story they have heard elsewhere; that they are therefore just "passing on," somewhat as any gossip might, some juicy bits, and cannot be held accountable for the sad and sordid facts involved; but many authors accept their responsibilities calmly enough and make no effort to conceal themselves or minimize the extent of their powers. Trollope, for instance, is a comfortable theist who appears on page after page in order to sustain and continue and comfort his creation. He is invariably concerned and polite. "We must beg to be allowed to draw a curtain over the sorrows of the archdeacon as he sat, sombre and sad at heart, in the study of his parsonage at Plumstead Episcopi." Furthermore, he will try to talk the reader out of what might be, perhaps, a too hasty judgment of character and motive. "He was avaricious, my readers will say. No—it was for no love of lucre that he wished to be Bishop of Barchester."

The appearance of the author by our fireside; his chatty confidential tone; his certainty that he knows what we think and how we feel; his slightly admonitory manner; the frequent comparisons he draws between our condition and that of his characters; the comfortable clichés he draws around us like a shawl: these devices more readily make his world and his people real; whereas deists like Flaubert, like Henry James, like Joyce, who are satisfied to kick their creations out of the house when they've come of age; who wind their works up and then let them run as they may, and who cannot be recalled to rejoin or revise or reconsider anything by any plea or spell of magic or sacrifice or prayer; who leave it up to us to calculate and judge: their world is far less friendly, far less homey, far less "real." When Trollope comments: "Our archdeacon was worldly—who among us is not so?" he deftly implicates us in his activities.* We are all together in this, he suggests; I am speaking of the world each of us lives and loves and suffers in—no other, he implies; whereas the brilliant opening of *The Fifth Queen* is so immediately vivid and pictorial we must be somewhere outside it, viewing it as we might a painting or a movie screen. Trollope's relaxed and slippered style is just as skillful in its way as Ford's, but Ford's world is unmediated and set adrift; we

---

* These quotations are, of course, from the opening chapter of *Barchester Towers.*

shall never find a path through its cold and passionate landscapes on which our feet can be safely set; we shall only be able to observe these historical figures connive and betray and ruin, and the light fall unsteadily on walls wet with the cold sweat of another age.

Pantheism is not out of the question as a possibility either. *The Notebooks of Malte Laurids Brigge* invent "another self" whose very name is a rhythmic echo of Rainer Maria Rilke; yet this other self, its almost unendurably beautiful and squalid encounters, these records of lonely reading and empty rooms and lovely yet lost objects, this static parade of exquisite perceptions that constitute the frozen friezelike flow of the book, are so infused with the poet's presence, the poet's particular sensibilities, that Malte, his surrogate, cannot avoid surrendering his self to his author's *style,* even when the outcome of his life appears to be different from his creator's. We might permit Malte to possess the thought that *"Denn Verse sind nicht, wie die Leute meinen, Gefühle (die hat man früh genug),—es sind Erfahrungen,"* but the movement of the mind (from cities, people, and things to animals, birds, and blooms), the music of the words (*"Um eines Verses willen muss man viele Städte sehen, Menschen und Dinge, man muss die Tiere kennen, man muss fühlen, wie die Vögel fliegen, und die Gebärde wissen, mit welcher die kleinen Blumen sich auftun am Morgen"**), the romantic innocence of the idea, are unmistakably Rilkean. As we read along, Trollope's manner discreetly retires from sight and Mrs. Proudie and Mr. Slope are shortly there before us as plainly as two dogs in the yard. Malte feels, to be sure, yet what Malte feels can only have been informed and inhabited and carried to him by his ceaselessly zealous creator.

When authorship is denied, it is often in order to extol certain sources or origins instead. It is easier for poets to pretend that they are merely an ear trumpet for the muse, that they have been so smitten with inspiration they scarcely recognize their own rhymes; because the creative pain of the poet can sometimes be measured in moments, especially if she scribbles; but the novelist cannot persuasively invent a spirit whose relief requires several years of sluiced transcendence, as if somewhere a spigot had been left on. Our author, in this unlikely case, is simply a conduit, or a place where the collective unconscious has risen up to refresh us like a bubbler in the park.

The *Geist* has been known to gather up unwary authors somewhat as Zeus used to do with fleeing maidens, and plump them with proper thoughts and attitudes. If writers were not the instruments of history, as princes and

---

* "For poems are not, as people think, simply emotions (one has emotions early enough)— they are experiences. For the sake of a single poem, you must see many cities, many people and Things, you must understand animals, must feel how birds fly, and know the gesture which small flowers make when they open in the morning." From bk. 1, sect. 14: "I think I should begin to do some work . . . ," trans. Stephen Mitchell (New York: Random House, 1983).

politicians often were, they were at least a showcase, a display of the spirit, like a museum's costumed effigies, if not among its principal actors. Historical forces of this sort are as crudely imaginary as deities have always been, although probably not nearly as harmful, since they cannot capture the imagination of millions the way divinities do, especially the dime-store kind. But of course the *Geist* can go behind a curtain and come back out as the *Volk* or the *Reich* instead of the *Zeit*. Taine's version of this recipe would certainly have been familiar to Barthes, whose notion combines the concept of the author as conduit with that of the author as focal point: that hot spot where many causal rays have been concentrated.

Taine wished to understand his subjects (whether Spenser, Lyly, or Milton), in the first place by re-creating the so-called external image of the man; by setting him out in the kind of clear hindsight which is the common sense and direction of history; and then to penetrate that picture to the moral condition which lay behind those features and animated them. Finally, he sought in race, epoch, and environment the conditions which came together to create the local climate of his case. He fashions, in other words, a chain of authors: the public figure, the inner man, the milieu. It is the right pull upon that chain which brings the gush.

There is clearly considerable satisfaction to be had in the removal of the poet from his or her position in the center of public adulation. Taine maliciously writes about

> A modern poet, a man like De Musset, Victor Hugo, Lamartine, or Heine, graduated from college and travelled, wearing a dress-coat and gloves, favored by ladies, bowing fifty times and uttering a dozen witticisms in an evening, reading daily newspapers, generally occupying an apartment on the second story, not over-cheerful on account of his nerves, and especially because, in this dense democracy in which we stifle each other, the discredit of official rank exaggerates his pretensions by raising his importance, and, owing to the delicacy of his personal sensations, leading him to regard himself as a Deity.*

Indeed, it is no longer the painter or the poet whom the public looks for, talking or scribbling away in some café's most prominent corner, but (after Cocteau, who taught everyone the trade) a Sartre or a Barthes whom we hope to catch a glimpse of—a Lacan or Foucault, or some other impresario of ideas.

* Hippolyte Adolphe Taine, *History of English Literature*, trans. Henry Van Laun, 3 vols. (New York: Colonial Press, 1900), vol. 1, p. 2.

Parlor games, in which a poem is composed one line at a time by inebriated guests, cancel authorship by allowing too many cooks to stir the broth. Occasionally, for sport and in despair, fiction writers will alternate the writing of a novel's chapters, and, equally rarely, talents like Ford's and Conrad's will collaborate with a modest sort of success. In most cases, the schoolboy botches which result are so far from creating "a sense of a world" that no one would think to wonder about that world's authorship anyway.

The *renga*, a chain poem which made its first appearance in Japan in the eighth century, is a more serious collaboration; it is more serious simply because the participants generally are. When contemporary poets turn to it, their feelings are not dissimilar to Barthes's:

> In contrast with the conception of a literary work as the imitation of antique models, the modern age has exalted the values of originality and novelty: the excellence of a text does not depend on its resemblance to those of the past, but on its unique character. Beginning with romanticism, tradition no longer signifies continuity by repetition and by variations within repetition; continuity takes the form of a leap, and tradition becomes a synonym for history: a succession of changes and breaks. The romantic fallacy: the literary work as an odd number, the reflection of the exceptional ego. I believe that, today, this idea has reached its end.*

When, however, the *renga* turns out to be a chain forged in four different languages, we can justifiably suspect that oddness, and difference, will be its most striking distinction, and that the four authors will neither hide themselves behind one another nor disappear into the collective anonymity of the text, but will sign their names to the poem, and write of the feelings they had while composing it in reports which remind one of the ecstatic early accounts of group sex.†

---

* Octavio Paz, from his introduction to Octavio Paz, Jacques Roubaud, Edoardo Sanguineti, and Charles Tomlinson, *Renga: A Chain of Poems* (New York: George Braziller, 1971).

† See Paz's introduction. He speaks first of a "feeling of abandonment," then a "sensation of oppression," followed by a "feeling of shame," a "feeling of voyeurism," a "feeling of returning." It is all very operatic. They are only writing a poem, after all, these poets; but they must pretend they are having a religious experience. The fiction is that the poem is all-important, when only the fact that they are writing it together really is.

Anonymity can be chosen by the poet because it is a humbling or self-mortifying condition. One wishes to give up the selfish self and become a selfless self. Selflessness is the highest form of selfishness there is because of the demands "it" makes upon others.

It is not that "authorless" work in any of the senses I have so far suggested can never be excellent, or that novels with a great degree of authorial visibility must always be romantic, bourgeois, and decadent, because fine work of both kinds exists; rather, it should be recognized that the elevation or removal of the author is a social and political and psychological gesture, and not an aesthetic one. We can characterize art as anonymous or not, but this characterization will tell us nothing, in advance of our direct experience of the building, the canvas, the score, or the text, about its artistic *quality*. Furthermore, this "anonymity," as we've seen, may mean many things, but one thing which it cannot mean is that *no one did it*.

Unless one imagines a computer which has been fed every rule of language, the principles of every literary genre, the stylistic tics of all the masters and their schools, and so on. Then poem and story might emerge from this machine, to the astonishment, boredom, or ruin of readers, like race or market results; and it could say—if asked, as Polyphemus was—that no man did it.

So art can seem authorless to me because *I don't know who did it;* or because *I can't tell who did it;* because *I don't care who did it;* or because *it simply doesn't matter who did it;* or because *it just happened and nobody did it.* That is: one is the piece of sea wrack I pick up from the beach; another is like "Ding, dong, bell, / Pussy's in the well"; still another resembles your average TV serial segment; and then there is that tune I know from somewhere, but can't remember, and can't guess; and that enigmatic couplet carved on an ancient rock whose author has vanished forever into the hard lilt of its cruel vowels.

It may at first seem that the effacement of the author was an act of modesty, and the familiar fatherly storyteller's style of Trollope, and other writers like him, was authoritarian and manipulative, inasmuch as they gave nothing away to the reader, and took on the point of view of a tower; but the opposite is clearly the case. Trollope knows everything necessary to tell the tale, to be sure, and presents himself comfortably in that cloth; but Flaubert is not telling a tale, he is constructing a world; he is putting it together atom by atom, word by word. Trollope is merely inserting his characters into the well-known world of his readers, readers who take their daily life enough for granted that long ago they stopped looking at it; they scarcely any longer even live it, but use all their inner tubes to float on top; so that when Trollope looks and lives, his readers are surprised at what they see and feel. Flaubert, however, cannot count on the comfortable collusion of his readers to solidify his world through their inattention and neglect; it is not the reader's funny bone he wishes to tickle, but the text he wishes to shape so securely a reader will not be necessary. Flaubert wants to expose his "readers" to their world of papered-over problems and foully bloated hopes by unupholstering their souls, lowering their ceilings to the true level of their aspirations; he wants to demonstrate to them that they are only devouring the world and making shit out of their lives; he can hardly count on their help; their "help" would subvert his enterprise. Flaubert cannot ask for, cannot count on, readers in the old sense, then, for each is only too likely to be another *hypocrite lecteur,* however much each also is *mon semblable, mon frère.* Thus the author becomes a god, instead of someone's garrulous uncle, because the author now disdains those lower and local relations, and has left home sweet home in disgust. *Madame Bovary* is not a chair for a fat burgher's Sunday snooze; it *is* the fat burgher himself, breaded and greasy and mostly buns. His home is a White Castle.

When the author detaches himself from the text, he detaches the reader at the same time, then, and it is this unpleasant consequence which Barthes is responding to. Trollope is telling his story to someone, and even when, as in the case of the epistolary novel, the messages are not addressed to the reader directly, they are addressed to someone; they remain communications; and the three-term relation of writer-letter-recipient is maintained. But if no one has written or posted the word, then no one is addressed by the word. The letter is no longer a letter. A does not equal A. What would the sign 𝔅𝔲𝔶 𝔅𝔢𝔲𝔤𝔢'𝔰 𝔅𝔢𝔢𝔯 mean or be if it were carefully posted at one of the poles?

The author becomes a god at the moment he no longer believes in gods, and just because the gods are dead; yet not because, as Taine implies, he suddenly sees a vacancy (although socially that might very well describe his motives), but because a world without God must be a world without true believers, too. Yet this writerless, readerless world must be made by someone, a deity of the undivine kind, a god in lower case.

The moment God goes, the text becomes sacred (unalterable, revered, studied, paraphrased, guarded, handed on). Consider the deist's contention. If God is on permanent vacation elsewhere, then this world is all there is; it is the entire text; only from it can truths be learned; and if this world is to run, and run successfully, it must run on by itself, on its own four wheels; while, finally, if God gave us a message when He made this world, He did not wait around for our understanding or reply, both of which become, if not irrelevant to us, certainly irrelevant to Him (since He is out of hearing), as well as to the world itself (which is blind and dumb and deaf and thoroughly uncaring). It is not clear that it is a text in the traditional sense. Suppose that, idling down an alley as is my wont, I pick up a scrap of paper which has blown from some pile of trash. Examining it, I read:

WILL'S WHEEL ALINEMENT SERVICE
sugar   nappies
strong clock for Aunt Helen
33 BAD CLIMATE ROAD

Like the sign that said **Buy Beuge's Beer**, these words have wandered away, even from one another. A reminder without mind, purpose, or point, like works of modern art, they merely appear. Made of words, they are not now a message. What is there here to take to heart, to puzzle over, to believe?

The basic folly of Bouvard and Pécuchet (those two aforetime Beckettean clowns) is that, in a world like WILL'S WHEEL ALINEMENT SERVICE, they do, nevertheless, believe things; they believe them right into the ground; they sincere systems to death; they accept explanations like a crematorium its corpses. In *Finnegans Wake* a hen scratches a meaningless message out of a midden. Both world and work are simply *here*. No one asked for either. John Barth's Todd Andrews has enormous difficulties making up his mind what is what or which or whether.* The world we're in is one of authorless accident, comical suffering, and tragic confusion; it is the world of WILL'S WHEEL ALINEMENT SERVICE, while the *Wake* is entirely internal, its "nothing" signifying sound and fury. The *Wake* is a replacement for the world. Unlike the world, it is overmade of meanings. Like the world, it does not mean.

If the author goes, taking the reader with him, into some justifiable oblivion, he does not omit to leave his signature behind, just the same. Indeed, he not only signs every sheet, he signs every word. Erased, Flaubert's careful concern cries out, "Me me me." Removing himself, Henry James in his late manner maître d's everything. The *Wake* culminates, just before it doesn't conclude: "mememormee! Till thousendsthee." Here is a further example of pure signature prose:

> . . . I felt acutely unhappy about my dutiful little student as during one
> hundred and fifty minutes my gaze kept reverting to her, so childishly
> slight in close-fitting gray, and kept observing that carefully waved dark
> hair, that small, small-flowered hat with a little hyaline veil as worn
> that season and under it her small face broken into a cubist pattern by

---

* In *The Floating Opera* (New York: Doubleday, 1956). Barth is not to be seen. Andrews is writing his own story, but he immediately points out how limited his powers are: he cannot imagine, he is stuck with the truth. "I look like what I think Gregory Peck, the movie actor, will look like when he's fifty-four. . . ." (The comparison to Mr. Peck isn't intended as self-praise, only as description. Were I God, creating the face of either Todd Andrews or Gregory Peck, I'd change it just a trifle here and there.) When a fictional figure speaks to the reader the way Trollope spoke to him, and as Todd Andrews not infrequently does, he intends the reader to become a fiction. How else will they hold a conversation?

scars due to a skin disease, pathetically masked by a sunlamp tan that hardened her features, whose charm was further impaired by her having painted everything that could be painted, so that the pale gums of her teeth between cherry-red chapped lips and the diluted blue ink of her eyes under darkened lids were the only visible openings into her beauty.

The "I" of this brief instructional tale* is not that of the great Vladimir, Napoleon of Prose, but the style is certainly his. We are meant to be dazzled, humbled, tossed into awe as though it were a ditch alongside the road.

The "I" is not Nabokov—no—yet this "I" teaches literature (French, not Russian) at a girls' college (not a women's college, not Cornell) in an Ithaca, New York, climate (no mistaking that upper New York snow and ice, icicles carefully described), so that we are led roundabout to wonder if. Again, this sort of teasing is deliberate.

Whether the scholar sees the genial Trollope seated comfortably in the text, or the irascible Flaubert skulking angrily behind his, critics continue to "tyrannically center," as Barthes puts it, "the image of literature on . . . the author, his person, his life, his tastes, his passions . . ."[†] but they have reached their quarry by different routes: content in the first case, style in the second. Of course, Trollope's tone tells a tale as well as Nabokov's does, but Nabokov's arrogance is formal, relational, and his control is not that of a fatherly czar but that of the secret police. The performative "I declare," "I sing," "I write," does not, in fact, cut the text off at the point of the pen, as Barthes seems to think. Nabokov's passage *is* a performance . . . and a good one. In this sense, Trollope's touch could only dull the master's quill.

The problem is not, I think, whether the author is present in the work in one way or another, or whether the text will ever interest us in her, her circle, her temper and times; but whether the text can take care of itself, can stand on its own, or whether it needs whatever outside help it can get; whether it leads us out and away from itself or regularly returns us to its touch the way we return to a lovely stretch of skin. Certainly, some readers are anxious to be distracted, and arrive in a work like a nervous traveler at a depot. There are four winds, and four cardinal points of the compass; there are seven precious

---

* Vladimir Nabokov, "The Vane Sisters," in *Tyrants Destroyed and Other Stories* (New York: McGraw-Hill, 1975). The balance of "between . . . lips" and "under . . . lids" is particularly artful, as is the repeated use of "small," and the music of passages like "the diluted blue ink of her eyes . . ."

† "The Death of the Author," p. 143.

metals, seven days of the week, and ten wonders of the world; but there are six regularly scheduled trains out of the text:

Hermeneutical Heaven: Replacement of the Text with Its Interpretation

Construction of the
Text: How to Write

Literary Tradition
Influences

Historical Context/
Bio of the Writer

World as Referent
"Truth about Life"

1 2 3 4 5 6

Reader as Interpreting Subject or Rhetorical Object

When Nabokov halts his "I" on its walk in order to render an icicle in full formation, there is no question that the world, with its notions about the proper procedures for freezing and thawing, is partly directing his pen. Is it, then, the artful author of this passage?

> . . . I had stopped to watch a family of brilliant icicles drip-dripping from the eaves of a frame house. So clear-cut were their pointed shadows on the white boards behind them that I was sure the shadows of the falling drops should be visible too. But they were not. The roof jutted out too far, perhaps, or the angle of vision was faulty, or, again, I did not chance to be watching the right icicle when the right drop fell. There was a rhythm, an alternation in the dripping that I found as teasing as a coin trick.

And are the laws of light and shadow determining this?

> And as I looked up at the eaves of the adjacent garage with its full display of transparent stalactites backed by their blue silhouettes, I was rewarded at last, upon choosing one, by the sight of what might be described as the dot of an exclamation mark leaving its ordinary position to glide down very fast—a lot faster than the thaw-drop it raced.

And is the world of melting snow and forming ice our readerly destination? Do we want to stand in the snow, too, with this "I" which is soon then to be ourselves? But this "I" cannot be ourselves, for its observations are both beyond us and beyond the world.

> This twinned twinkle was delightful but not completely satisfying; or rather it only sharpened my appetite for other tidbits of light and shade, and I walked on in a state of raw awareness that seemed to trans-

form the whole of my being into one big eyeball rolling in the world's socket.*

Physical phenomena clearly have a finger if not a hand in the composition of these passages, but the choice of event, selection of details, arrangement of elements, turns of phrase, and pace of words, all the higher functions of relevance and association, imagery and implication: these are controlled by Nabokov and increasingly by the character of the little device he is creating; that is, a short story about two sisters, Cynthia and Sybil Vane (Sybil will be a suicide, Cynthia a victim of heart disease), and Cynthia's belief in haunting shades and interfering spirits. As the text grows, its demands grow; but the text can make these demands only in terms of certain principles of composition which the author accepts: coherence, for instance, fulfillment of expectation, sufficient reason, and so on.

Imagine, for a moment, that our text were a chair. We might say our six kinds of things about it, and each remark might be relevant to some interest or other we might have; but what is important to notice, here, is what gets left out, goes unsaid.

1. This chair has clearly been built in accordance with patterns first displayed in Clarence Chipfall's design book (1837). Certainly not early, probably not late, I should say it was a mid-Chipfall chair. Festooning the legs with shredded velvet, however, suggests an Ottoman influence, probably added later.

2. If you tip the chair over you can see that it is fashioned of interlocking pieces of cherry and lime wood, grooved so as to pass the seater's energy along a transfiguring path into the large fat oak legs.

3. The stern right-angularity of this steel-stiffened chair signifies the puritanical ideal in one of its revengeful modes. This is an electric chair, if you like, before electricity.

4. Anyone who sits in this chair will be reminded of two things principally: their onerous duties and their extraordinary powers, for its harshness is regal, its squareness that of the pew in a country church.

5. Chipfall's mother had carried little Chipper in a wooden tube upon her back until well past twelve, whereupon he erupted from the tube with a terrible cry; that cry is probably the pain behind the painful sidearms this chair presses against us.

* "The Vane Sisters"; these three passages are from pp. 119, 120.

6. We would expect chairs of this sort to come from the kind of hung-up and repressed capitalist lackey which Chipfall represented so perfectly.

Although there are many references, here, to how this chair must feel when sat in, they are used only as evidence for other elements and aspects, and whether the chair is handsome or not; whether it is lovely to look at, to touch, to loll in, to place in positions of interest in a room: these qualities are ignored. Yet in fiction, quality ought to author everything.

Actually, Roland Barthes, while appearing to free the text from such externals, is going to tie it rather firmly to two of them: the literary tradition and social usage on the one hand, and the reader's caprices on the other. He sees the writer as a kind of whirling drain, sucking texts into its ambiguous body and then concentrating their fall upon the page. The text, Barthes argues, is

a multidimensional space in which a variety of writings, none of them original, blend and clash. The text is a tissue of quotations drawn from innumerable centres of culture. Similar to Bouvard and Pécuchet, those eternal copyists, at once sublime and comic and whose profound ridiculousness indicates precisely the truth of writing, the writer can only imitate a gesture that is always anterior, never original. His only power is to mix writings, to counter the ones with the others, in such a way as never to rest on any one of them.*

Let us shape a situation which will really fit Barthes's conditions. The lanky young man who bags our groceries has just dropped the flour on top of the broccoli. He hoists the sack into the cart, and says, with a vacant smile he points vaguely in our direction:

HAVE A NICE DAY

* "The Death of the Author," p. 146. These views are the consequence of Barthes's work on *S/Z,* and his disclosure of all the "codes" which come together in *Sarrasine,* the Balzac short story which he has taken as his specimen text, and quotes again in his essay on the death of the author.

Our young man is scarcely the author of this unmeant hope we have just now been commanded to realize. The English language provides its grammar and vocabulary; our present sales and marketing customs furnish the expression itself; the manager of the store supplies the impulse and determines its timing (so that the bagger does not utter his platitudes and *then* bruise the broccoli). The carry-out boy (whose jacket says, "I'm Fred," although this is a bit misleading since he's borrowed the coat from a friend, having forgotten, in his habitual a.m. haste, to wear his own) is a willing automaton. Still, we can see his lips move inside that smile like a little wrinkle in a wrinkle, and we hear the words issue from him. Suppose they were written on his jacket? that jacket whose name is Fred. In that case, there wouldn't even be a cartoon balloon around the words, with a string depending from it toward his mouth. The expression would resemble our odd scrap on which WILL's WHEEL ALINEMENT SERVICE was found—"alignment" spelled, we would have to observe, in a typically lower-class way, obedient to the social code. As Barthes argues, writing removes the writer from the words.

Our author thinks, "Orlando—Orlando was," and then writes "He" (to stand for Orlando, for there could be no doubt about his sex, though the fashion of the time did something to disguise it); writes that Orlando was in the act of slicing—swinging—cutting—slicing—using words which are transcribed by her secretary's typing machine (losing the effect of that lovely swirling hand, so especially graceful at crossing *T*'s), and subsequently mailed to an editor who will peevishly mark it up (wondering if our author oughtn't to write "blackamoor" instead of simply "moor" and a whole lot else in the same vein), only to pass the ms on to a printer who, in due course, will produce new and original errors in the galleys. When the galleys are finally corrected, everyone within reach of both a pencil and the words will have had a hand in them. During this process it even might look for a time as if Orlando were going to be replaced by Rudolph at a pretty copy editor's suggestion, but, to the relief of literature, at the last moment a *stet* is put beside his name, allowing Orlando to remain. So now he can be seen (for there can be no doubt about her sex) at the top of the book's first page, slicing at the head of a moor which is swinging from the rafters.

Office memos, guidelines, brochures, official handouts, architectural programs, presidential speeches, screenplays are oftener in worse case because they are customarily constructed on assembly lines, by gangs and other committees, by itinerant troupes of clerical assistants. The Surgeon General warns us that smoking is hazardous to our health. Does *he*? Does *he* indeed?

Every step I have described has taken us away from the vocal source (if there was one, for perhaps she never said aloud or to herself, "Orlando," since it is a name people are often embarrassed to utter), and removed its original maker from significant existence the way Will's scrap of paper, which we fetched from the wind and took to the pole, was removed; yet this is hardly surprising, because no one *authors* their speech, they simply speak it. It is necessary to say we author what we write precisely because what we write is disconnected from any mouth we might actually observe rounding itself for the *O*'s required to produce "Or lan dO"; so that the question imperatively arises: who, indeed, has made these marks? whose is the responsible pen?

"Suddenly a burst of applause which shook the house greeted the prima donna's entrance," Balzac writes,* after carefully collecting the correct clichés, for applause always bursts; when it does so it always shakes the house; it invariably greets an entrance, which, of course, is what actors and actresses *make.* No wonder Barthes uses *Sarrasine* as an example of the dead hand of the author, for it would be hard to compose a more dismally anonymous sentence, except that Balzac has had practice, and this one is succeeded and preceded by hundreds of others its equal. "The Marquis went out at five," Paul Valéry's *bête noire* (it was certainly not his *bête bleue*), is, by comparison, inimitable. Balzac creates strangeness out of phrases which his readers will be *completely used to and entirely comfortable with.* As his readers sail along through the story, they will not have to think or realize or re-create or come to grips with anything. Nothing can trouble this salvelike surface. *Sarrasine* is a story whose merit is to seem not to be there, and one can imagine Balzac removing originality from it like unwanted hair.†

Virginia Woolf no doubt changed many things while she wrote, adding images, crossing out details, removing words, transposing paragraphs, perhaps pages, reconceiving the entire enterprise, falling into foul moods, later climbing out of them, altering herself when she mooned over Vita Sackville-West and remembered Knole, somewhat as her hero progresses from one sex to another. Was Joyce the selfsame man who began *Finnegans Wake* when, fifteen years later, he woke from it? Certainly Malcolm Lowry's bout with *Under the Volcano* (begun when he was a much younger and certainly less well-informed writer than Joyce was when he began the *Wake*) involved more than one personality and bears witness to different levels of skill and conception. *Malte Laurids Brigge* is many things, and one of them was to be a course of therapy for a deeply troubled Rilke so that he would not become

---

* Roland Barthes, "(216) ★ ACT.: Theater: 6; entrance of the star," in *S/Z,* trans. Richard Miller (New York: Hill and Wang), 1974, p. III.

† Every attempt at something striking, such as the features of a beautiful woman—"each pore has a special brilliance"—is catastrophic (Barthes, *S/Z,* p. 34).

"his other self." It is unlikely that one inflexible self wrote *Orlando,* nor did it spring into being all at once, as it does when we open its covers now. We know how all the other Orlandos influenced her; how she researched the Great Frost before she composed that amazing description of it; how faithfully she frequented the British Museum, and how much she loved memoirs, biography, and other historical texts.

A poet's life, like Chatterton's, may be no longer than a midge's, and yet many poems may be appended to his name, because poems can occasionally be blurted; but works of prose, as I've pointed out, involve time in an essential way, and can have a single author only in the traditional metaphysical sense that they possess (as even the saddest of ordinary mortals does) an enduring, central, stubbornly unchanging self, that "me" that is the permanent object of the "I," perhaps within the child as a state of lucent potentiality, and translucent to the point of invisibility when past its prime, but an unshakable unity nevertheless.

Even quite integrated normal persons, as we know, have many capabilities and moods and temperaments, so that simple "evenness" is not the answer, although it is commonly felt that a unified work of literature should seem to have a single author (unless, like the style of much of *Sarrasine,* the work is so undistinctive, bland, and featureless—so anonymous, so nerdsome—as to suggest a corporate, collective self); so that what any actual author must do, divided as she often is into whore and housewife and shrew and mum and cook and clotheshorse and Girl Scout, nanny and nursemaid, choirgirl and choregirl and list maker, cheerleader and hash slinger and Model C, Gentle Annie and Madame La Morte and La Belle Dame Sans Merci, into left breast—ummm!—then right, and eardrum off which the brags of men bounce with a sissboom, boomsiss we all enjoy, and eye in whose loving gaze great men grow up from little lads and finks and fat louts into troubadours and totem designers and business thieves and all that . . . while contriving to preserve as many faces as the moon . . . to vary and interest and entice . . . and all that . . . is to construct the ideal abstract author of her text, and then try to accommodate, corset if necessary—constrict—her multifarious nature to that less variable but often more reliable and attractive, though entirely artificial, being: the real fiction of the fiction. From the poem the reader projects the poet, too—not a person but the poet of the poem.

Hume has warned us that if we wish to infer a creator solely from the evidence of a creation, we cannot attribute to it any other character, qualities, or power than would be strictly necessary to produce the thing, the song, or world in question. Nor can we forget (when we are busy imagining the author of *Waverley* or *Lady Chatterley's Lover* or *The World as Will and Repre-*

sentation or *The Life of Reason*) the silly, incompetent, or wicked things the work accomplishes as well—the insane mix of planning and chance, absurdity and design, incompetence and skill, which is the rule in most cases— just because we wish to bring "good ole glory" to a name, for the name will no longer designate the necessary author or the less necessary personality behind the art, but still another kind of slippery fiction.

The intention of the author is only occasionally relevant, but if we believe at all in the Unconscious, or in the impossibility of literally nothing escaping the author's clear awareness and control, then the artificial author (the author which the text creates, not the author who creates the text) will be importantly different from the one of flesh and blood, envy and animosity, who holds the pen, and whose picture enlivens the gray pages of history. Strictly speaking, Scott is both more and less than *the* author of *Waverley.**

Insofar as an expression such as "the author of *Waverley*" is a definite description of Scott and is, like his various names and nicknames, substitutable for him in any sentence, then it is possible to write: "The author of *Waverley* was born last night during a rainstorm." This suggests considerable foreknowledge, or it suggests, as it did to Leibniz, that one's future is indeed a seed inside the self. But the death of Scott did not coincide with the death of the author of *Waverley.* The author of *Waverley* is still alive.

In certain cases, further complications arise. When an author devotes a great portion of a writing life to one work, as Dante did, or Spenser did, or Proust, then the likelihood that the work itself will begin to overwhelm and almost entirely occupy the arena of ordinary life grows great, because the writer will surely have imagined marriages more interesting than her own, deaths more dismaying than that of Uncle Charley, or invented characters with more quality than her children, who simply sniffle, skin knees, and fail in school; she will not carry on her fictional affairs like boring conversations; she will have fallen in love with a rake of her own devising. Proust's book became a second cork-lined room around him; Flaubert's letters reflect the fact that his writing desk is both board and bed; the nighttime life of the *Wake* compensates for a failing sight. That is, works not only imply an artificial author, they profoundly alter, sometimes, the nature of the historical one. God Himself, I suspect, has been made worse by the world.

That characters get out of control, that the uncompleted text takes over its completion, was a commonplace long before E. M. Forster complained

---

* For example, consult the little parable "Borges and I," in *Labyrinths,* ed. Donald A. Yates and James E. Irby (New York: New Directions, 1964), pp. 246–47. Borges writes: "I live, let myself go on living, so that Borges may contrive his literature, and this literature justifies me."

of it,* or Flann O'Brien made it a compositional directive.† And Vladimir Nabokov's little story about the Vane sisters doubles the dialectical interference of text with intention, intention with text. Cynthia's death provokes in the narrator the expectation of her ghostly appearance. His sleep is soon troubled by a dream about her, but this is hardly the apparition he hopes for and fears. Though the narrator puzzles himself about it, the dream yields him nothing. He and the story conclude:

> I could isolate, consciously, little. Everything seemed blurred, yellow-clouded, yielding nothing tangible. Her inept acrostics, maudlin evasions, theopathies—every recollection formed ripples of mysterious meaning. Everything seemed yellowly blurred, illusive, lost.‡

Nabokov, however, has not concluded *his* fun, for the first letters of the words which make up that final paragraph provide a message: 'IciclEsbycyntHiameterfrommesybil'; that is: "Icicles by Cynthia, meter from me, Sybil."

If the author had not waited until the twentieth century to pass on, but had gone off more quickly, rather like fish, Galileo wouldn't have had to publish his work anonymously and in another country far from his own place of residence; nor would all those amiable works of erotica have had to hide their heads—they could have ridden out happily headless, written simply by a raunchy *Weltgeist;* Charlotte Brontë wouldn't have had to give birth to Currer Bell or die as C. B. Nicholls while trying to recover from her pregnancy; nor should we have seen originate a distinct species of posthumous writing, a genre practiced to perfection by Kafka, and one to which some work of Descartes, and the *Dialogues* of Hume, belong. The pseudonyminal pranks of Saki, Kierkegaard, and Brian Ó Nualláin (a.k.a Brian O'Nolan, Myles na gCopaleen, John James Doe, George Knowall, Brother Barnabas, the Great Count O'Blather, and Flann O'Brien) would not have been necessary.

The author of *At Swim-Two-Birds* may have been born during a rainstorm, but Flann O'Brien, which is the name of the author of *At Swim-Two-Birds,* was not. Many and sharp are the philosophical rocks in this apparently calm, cool pool.

If Roland Barthes had been interested in radically simplifying the Final

* In *Aspects of the Novel* (New York: Harcourt Brace, 1927), p. 102.

† In *At Swim-Two-Birds* (London: Longmans Green, 1939). O'Brien is a text weaver, his novel is a "book web," and he even uses a pseudonym, yet few novels belong more completely to their makers.

‡ "The Vane Sisters," p. 238.

904 THE WILLIAM H. GASS READER

Solution to the Author Question (and I've tried to indicate and describe, here, some of the members of this rather heteronomous race) by removing those authors who come to claim every fresh text like red ants to a wound, he could have adopted the "single author" theory first, either as it is alluded to by Borges or proposed by Gertrude Stein or implied by Hegel. Then, with this plurality of persons—real, inhuman, artificial, and imaginary—reduced to manageable proportions, a single stroke across the top of the word would have been enough. An ~~author~~ can't author anything.

Stein distinguishes (to consider her version for only a moment)* between what she calls human nature, on the one hand (a physical existence which establishes for the writer a notable identity in time and a visitable locale in space; the person whose likeness is taken up to put on postage stamps, who cashes the checks, and whose character can be counterfeited if one gets hold of the appropriate documents and facts; the "I" of "I am I because my little dog knows me," the border guard's identity), and the human mind, on the other (a universal level of creativity and thought which moves evenly between Kant-like entities, between *Ding*s and *Sich*s; that elevation we refer to when we speak of the way a work may transcend its Oxford, Mississippi, milieu, for instance, its Colombian quaintness, the author's alcoholism or mushy obsession with mom, to achieve a readily understandable meaning and an immediately shareable emotion, the "I" of "I am not I any longer when I see," because I have allowed myself to become the object).

Every author has an identity, but masterpieces are written by the human mind, not by human nature, which only lends them their common smell and color, their day-to-day dust. The implication is that readers differ as dogs do, though all have a nose and a tail. Readers dislike works which seem superior to them, indifferent to them, proud. It is sometimes pedagogically profitable to pretend that *Mansfield Park,* for instance, was written by Thomas Mann, just to see what such an assumption does to our ordinary expectations, and normal ways of reading. A masterpiece is often read (without any classroom coaxing) as if it were by James Michener or Harold Robbins (it is the principal way Proust suffers from his society-swallowing and gossipacious fans); but the works of the human mind are really addressed to other human minds. The ineffable persona which a poem implies will be "the human mind" if the poem achieves greatness in someone's otherwise empty head, may flatter its eager reader into a feeling of self-transcendence, but that will be as temporary as any flatulence; meanwhile, the fatuous little *New Yorker* story that has caused an additional foot to fall along the avenues will fasten its agreeable

* Gertrude Stein, *The Geographical History of America,* with an introduction by W. H. Gass (New York: Vintage, 1973). This book develops, perhaps at unnecessary length, ideas contained in her somewhat earlier essay "What Are Masterpieces, and Why Are There So Few of Them?"

reader to a nice white rock in Westchester or to a club in O'Hara country, and leave him to be consumed by what consumes him: hungry trademarks and vicious localisms and greedy proper names. It will stimulate his determinate and causal—his purely chemical—self. The anonymity which the superb poem or fiction presumably possesses, according to some theories, may consequently depend on a kind of spiritual consanguinity.

The ordinary author, then, may indeed be no more than a blender of texts, and hence may have no "life" left when times change, fads fail; but Roland Barthes is not hailing the death of these authors—inevitable anyway—but the death of the *real* ones, so that their texts may survive in the hearts of their readers. Why must they be orphaned, if not to find new homes? The death of God, the death of the author—aren't we really calling for the death of the father?

Because we borrow, beg, buy, steal, or copy texts; because texts enter our eyes but remain in the blood; because we are, as authors, plagiarists and paraphrasers and brain pickers and mockingbirds; because of these and other like habits we are, in effect, translating texts from one time to another and one context to another and one language to another. If, instead of repeating, "Have a nice day," we suggested to strangers that they "lead a good life," we have simply rearranged a slightly different little cluster of clichés. But all that any author works with, in the beginning, is given her by one corrupted magus after another: the language, the life she leads, the literary tradition, schools she attends, the books she reads, the studies she has undertaken; so she cannot lay claim to some syntax or vocabulary, climate of ideas or custom of entertaining, as hers, and hers alone, and therefore as special as she is. Nor is that inadequacy she is supposed to feel at the close of her office hours the feeling of a freak. Of course, a great deal of what we all do and think and feel and write is no more uniquely had or imagined than the balloon I drew to represent the voice cloud of the bagger; the stream of life is rarely more than a pisser's trickle; and literally millions of sentences are penned or typed or spoken every day which have only one source—a spigot or a signboard, and not an author;* they have never been near a self which is so certain of its spirit and so insistent on its presence that it puts itself in its syllables like Mr. Gorgeous in his shimmering gown. "When all that was was fair," Joyce writes, describing paradise, and in that simple rearrangement of the given

---

* "(439) *This was woman herself, with her sudden fears, her Irrational whims, her instinctive worries, her impetuous boldness, her fussings, and her delicious sensibility,* ★ SEM: Femininity. The source of the sentence cannot be discerned. Who is speaking? Is it Sarrasine? the narrator? the author? Balzac-the-author? Balzac-the-man? romanticism? bourgeoisie? universal wisdom? The intersecting of all these origins creates the writing." (Barthes, *S/Z*, pp. 172–73.) In Barthes's "The Death of the Author," p. 142, this condition is suggested as the norm for *all* writing.

and the inevitable and the previous, he triumphs, making something new, in Pound's sense, and in that way *breaking through the circle of society.* With one's pittance, one can make another pittance or a palace.

The Goethe poem which I quoted earlier with deceitful intent is scarcely his anymore (nor would he claim it).* None of the formalities match. The idea may still be there, like an ancient tree in a neglected park. But that's what we do: for good or ill we incessantly transmute. What I am emptying my bladder of, behind that tree in that neglected park, was once a nice hot cup of green tea.

Balzac never betrays the bourgeois, never breaks through the circle of society, because he employs forms which they understand and use themselves (for instance, the ladderlike structure of life in school—first grade, second grade, third grade, and so on; the ladderlike structure of life in the family—birth, bawl, crawl, walk, talk, read, write, disobey; the ladderlike structure of life in the church—birth, baptism, confirmation . . . in business, in society, the same sort of ladder; each rung of which points the way and evaluates all progress, not just from cradle to grave, but from birth to bequest); Balzac relishes their stereotypes and pat phrases and vulgar elegancies; his taste is that of the turtle which has found itself in a robust soup; he, too, would flatter the reader, the public, the world which receives him until it receives him well and warmly; and Roland Barthes, for all his fripperies like lace on a sleeve, for all his textual pleasures, which imply a more courtly era, is no better, accepting a pseudoradical role as if it were the last one left in the basket.

Balzac's revelations, however critical and "daring" and suggestive, pet the bourgeois to the purr point because they are revelations which remain in their world and in their language like dummies in a window. Though more perceptive than most, more sensitive, even more moral and upright (let us grant), and undoubtedly a genius, Balzac is more moral the way more money is more money; his is the ultimate hosanna of utility; however hard his eye, his look will land light.

Sarrasine is corrupt in both its art and its attitudes, and this is the one thing Roland Barthes's extensive commentary neglects to point out. Rodin's statue of a nude and arrogant Balzac is a bother to us, but not to Balzac, whose arrogance is the arrogance of the best men of business, and who deserves to be wearing at least a hat. That is why we need authors: they refuse. Readers, on the other hand . . . readers . . . readers simply comprise the public.

Salmagundi, 1984

Published in *Habitations of the Word,* 1984

---

* "Uber allen Gipfeln / ist Ruh / in allen Wipfein / spürest du / kaum einen Hauch. / Die Vöglein schweigen im Walde. / Warte nur: balde / ruhest du auch."

APPRECIATIONS

Most of these essays and fictions appeared, though always in a somewhat different form, in the following books or periodicals:

Eyes (Alfred A. Knopf, 2015): "In Camera" first appeared in *Conjunctions,* no. 34, 2000.

Middle C (Alfred A. Knopf, 2013): *Conjunctions* first published "The Apocalypse Museum" (no. 37, 2001), "The Piano Lesson" (no. 44, 2005), and "Garden" (no. 49, 2007).

Life Sentences (Alfred A. Knopf, 2012): "Retrospection" first appeared in this book. *Harper's Magazine* first published "A Forest of Bamboo: The Trouble with Nietzsche" (2005), "Half a Man, Half a Metaphor" (2006), "Henry James's Curriculum Vitae" (2008), "Go Forth and Falsify: Katherine Anne Porter and the Lies of Art" (2009), and "Kinds of Killing: The Flourishing Evil of the Third Reich" (2009).

A Temple of Texts (Alfred A. Knopf, 2006): "Fifty Literary Pillars" first appeared in Special Collections, Olin Library, Washington University, 1991. *Harper's Magazine* first published "La Vie Trèshorrificque: Rabelais Revisited" (2004) and "On Evil: The Ragged Core of a Sweet Apple (2004). "Rilke's Rodin" first appeared in *The Georgia Review,* 2004.

Tests of Time (Alfred A. Knopf, 2002): "*Invisible Cities*" first appeared in *VIA,* 1986. "I've Got a Little List" first appeared in *Salmagundi,* no. 109–10, 1996. "The Test of Time" first appeared in *Alaska Quarterly Review,* 1997.

Cartesian Sonata (Alfred A. Knopf, 1998): "Emma Enters a Sentence of Elizabeth Bishop's" first appeared in *The Iowa Review,* vol. 24, no. 2, 1994.

Finding a Form (Alfred A. Knopf, 1996): "The Baby or the Botticelli" first appeared in *Harper's Magazine,* 1987. "Ezra Pound" first appeared in the *Times Literary Supplement* (London), 1989. "Robert Walser, an Introduction" first appeared as the foreword to *Masquerade and Other Stories* by Robert Walser, The Johns Hopkins University Press, 1990. "Simplicities" first appeared in *The Review of Contemporary Fiction,* vol. 11, no. 3, 1991. "The Music of Prose" first appeared in *Antaeus,* 1993. "The Book as a Container of Consciousness" first appeared in *The Wilson Quarterly,* 1995.

The Tunnel (Alfred A. Knopf, 1995): "The First Winter of my Married Life" first appeared in *Granta,* vol. 1, Sept. 1979. "August Bees" first appeared in *Delta,* no. 8, 1979. "Three Passages" first appeared in *Conjunctions,* no. 4, 1983. "The Sunday Drive" first appeared in *Esquire,* Aug. 1984.

Habitations of the Word (Alfred A. Knopf, 1984): "On Reading to Oneself" was originally given as a university commencement speech in 1979. *Harper's Magazine* first published "The Soul Inside the Sentence" (1982) and " 'And' " (1984). "The Habitations of the Word" first appeared in *The Kenyon Review,* vol. 6, no. 4, 1984. "The Death of the Author" first appeared in *Salmagundi,* 1984.

The World Within the Word (Alfred A. Knopf, 1978): "Paul Valéry" first appeared in *The New York Times Book Review,* 1972. *The New York Review of Books* first published "The Doomed in Their Sinking" (1972), "Gertrude Stein and the Geography of the Sentence" (1973), "Malcolm Lowry" (1973), and "Three Photos of Colette" (1977). "Carrots, Noses, Snow, Rose, Roses" first appeared in *The Journal of Philosophy,* vol. 17, no. 19, 1976.

Fiction and the Figures of Life (Alfred A. Knopf, 1970): "The High Brutality of Good Intentions" first appeared in *Accent,* vol. 18, no. 1, 1958. "Even if, by All the Oxen in the World" first appeared in *Frontiers of American Culture,* ed. Ray B. Browne et al., Purdue University Press, 1968. "Imaginary Borges and His Books" first appeared in *The New York Review of Books,* 1969. "The Concept of Character in Fiction" first appeared in *The New American Review,* no. 7, 1969. "Philosophy and the Form of Fiction" first appeared in *The Philosopher Critic,* ed. Robert Scholes, 1970. "The Medium of Fiction" first appeared in *The Nation,* 1966.

In the Heart of the Heart of the Country (Harper & Row, 1968): "The Pedersen Kid" first appeared in *MSS,* 1961. "Order of Insects" first appeared in *The Minnesota Review,* vol. 1, no. 3, 1961. "In the Heart of the Heart of the Country" first appeared in *New American Review,* 1967.

Omensetter's Luck (The New American Library, Inc., 1966): "The Love and Sorrow of Henry Pimber" first appeared in *Accent,* vol. 20, no. 2, 1960.

"The Architecture of the Sentence" first appeared in *Conjunctions,* no. 32, 1999.

A NOTE ON THE TYPE

This book was set in Adobe Garamond. Designed for the Adobe Corporation by Robert Slimbach, the fonts are based on types first cut by Claude Garamond (c. 1480–1561). Garamond was a pupil of Geoffroy Tory and is believed to have followed the Venetian models, although he introduced a number of important differences, and it is to him that we owe the letter we now know as "old style." He gave to his letters a certain elegance and feeling of movement that won their creator an immediate reputation and the patronage of Francis I of France.

Composed by North Market Street Graphics, Lancaster, Pennsylvania
Printed and bound by Berryville Graphics, Berryville, Virginia
Designed by Maggie Hinders